OFFICIAL HISTORIES
of the
Great War 1914-1918

OFFICIAL HISTORIES
of the
Great War 1914-1918

Neil J. Wells

The Naval & Military Press

Published by

The Naval and Military Press Ltd
Unit 10 Ridgewood Industrial Park,
Uckfield, East Sussex,
TN22 5QE England

Tel: +44 (0) 1825 749494
Fax: +44 (0) 1825 765701

www.naval-military-press.com
www.military-genealogy.com
www.militarymaproom.com

This bibliography is dedicated to my grandfather
71955 Sergeant Harty James Wells, R.A.M.C.
137th Field Ambulance, 40th Division,
who served his country with distinction throughout some of the
bloodiest battles of the Great War, 1915-1919.

Preface

Origins:

The origins of this book lay in my collection of Great War official histories. Originally I did not intend to create a bibliography; instead I began by cataloguing my collection of official histories mainly for my own reference. The next stage was when I tried to create a list of histories that I did not own with the aim to hunt them down and purchase them. This proved much harder than I first imagined and, as time passed, realised that the field of official histories for the 1914-1918 war was enormous. With all this information gathered, it then dawned on me that this information would be useful to other people, not only collectors like myself seeking volumes, but also book dealers and historians alike, and this is how this bibliography came into being.

Therefore simply by merging my catalogue with my 'wants list', I have arrived at this bibliography. My original catalogue has thus been greatly expanded to incorporate many other titles and it is intended that this bibliography of official histories is to be as complete as possible[1]. However, I am sure that there will still be gaps! Even now official histories are still being produced.

There have been many bibliographies of official histories over the years, the best being Robin Higham's bibliography *Official Histories*[2], published forty years ago, but these bibliographies, including Higham's, are now dated; they are incomplete and with errors occurring in them all.

Most publishers, if they still exist, have incomplete records of what they actually published, with the result that in the past, information about the histories was often sketchy. This has resulted in that the bibliographers have had to draw information from sources other than the publishers'[3], sometimes with rather strange results. By necessity, the compilers of these earlier bibliographies made use of academic libraries and governmental institutions, mainly those of military colleges and military archives to supply the required details which, although generally correct, had a number of errors and omissions, ranging from simple typing or translational errors from the reviewers to incomplete sets from within the reviewed libraries, causing volumes to be left out from the listings. These incomplete sets at the time of review were probably caused by volumes being out on loan, misplaced, stolen[4] or destroyed[5] and, in some cases, due to the time span taken to write and publish the sets, volumes that had not been purchased or, in other cases, had yet to be written and published. In Higham's bibliography for instance, two volumes were listed as one - the French Official Histories were published in paperback format to be bound as the purchaser wished[6]. In the set that was reviewed, two of the thinner volumes had been bound as one, presumably to save on binding costs, and hence were listed as one within Higham's study!

Definitions:

In his book, Higham asked a number of historians and bibliographers to define their definitions of official histories. For the purpose of this study, I define official histories as:

---

[1] Official publishers catalogues, private collectors, historical associations, national archives, national libraries, book dealers catalogues and the World Wide Web official sites.

[2] *Official Histories*, by Robin Higham, published by Kansas State University Library, 1970. This study covers all periods of official histories not just that of the Great War.

[3] Even the British Government's publisher H.M.S.O. did not keep complete records as shown by their *Histories of the First and Second World Wars Sectional List* published in 1965, which is far from being complete.

[4] In the case of an American university, a complete set of German naval official histories went missing, presumed stolen (as noted in Paul G. Halpern's *A Naval History of World War 1*).

[5] A number of academic libraries in Europe were damaged by fire especially during the Second World War period with the result that their copies of official histories had sadly been destroyed.

[6] Publishing paperbacks for later binding was quite a common practice in France up to the nineteen-sixties. There were other countries that adopted the same practice to various degrees – for example, Germany published some of their officials histories in three types of binding:

i) Deluxe - bound in leather

ii) Standard - bound in cloth

iii)Cheap - paperback with the potential for rebinding.

An 'Official History', which could be works on military, political or diplomatic subjects, is a study that was authorised, then written or compiled[7] for official use by or on behalf of an official organisation using official (often internal and restricted) source information.

The term 'Official use' varied from country to country and from period to period, but can be broken down into the following categories:

1. General Histories
2. Detailed Educational Histories
3. Propaganda

'Official use' could be for internal use within the organisation or for external use such as for the general public or for foreign governments. This will be discussed in greater detail below in the Notes on Official Histories.

An 'official organisation' could be a specially formed governmental historical department or a special armed service's historical section, which was normally associated with the related General Staff. It could also be a smaller sub department within an organisation that wished to write more detailed history.

The special government departments were set up to plan; research and write the official histories, for example Britain's "Historical Section of the Committee of Imperial Defence" [8]. These organisations would employ individuals recruited internally from within or recruit external experts and academics to partake in the writing of the histories. Where a specialist government department was not created, then the historical sections from within the different General Staffs often wrote the histories. It was common practice for the organisation to plan a conceptual framework for its official history, which was to be written around. This was especially true of the multi volume histories or where each individual volume was to be written by a team of historians.

There were a number of smaller sub departments such as the various General Staffs' training sections that wished to record their own special aspect of the war's history for their own internal use, where the coverage in the more formal histories was found to be lacking. These internal official histories were quite often restricted to internal use only and were not for sale to the general public.

Therefore, included within this overall grouping of official histories, there are not only the sets that were written as part of the original authorised official histories as per the concept laid down by the assigned bodies, but also a number of "reports", "staff papers" and "Educational Text Books" that covered aspects of the war history, but were still written with official approval (for example The Royal Air Force Staff College text book *A Short History of the Royal Air Force*).

To differentiate between the more formal general official histories and these less formal internal educational studies, I have split them into 'Primary Official Histories' covering the former group and 'Secondary Official Histories' covering the latter.

Based upon my definition above, it could be argued that regimentals and divisional histories should be regarded as official histories. However, I have not included them within this listing, since they cover purely unit histories with limited coverage of the war, as opposed to war histories that have a much more general coverage of the war.

It is therefore hoped that within the scope of this bibliography, this new listing will be almost complete. However, again as noted within the text, there are still thought to be gaps especially in the secondary official histories.

Notes on Official Histories:

The following questions are often raised: Who wrote the official histories? Did every nation involved in the Great War produce one? Why were they written? What was the point of them? Who were they written for? How accurate are they? Are they to be trusted? Were all the sets completed? Did they take on a standard appearance? Is the writing of official histories complete? Are there any more histories to be written? And finally how useful are they today?

---

[7] A number of the histories consisted of compilations of base information – for example, documents, maps and photographs.

[8] Other examples of these historical offices were Austria's "Österreichischen Bundesministerium für Heereswesen und vom Kriegsarchiv", France's "Ministère de la Guerre, État de l'Armée - Service Historique", Germany's "Reichsarchiv" and Italy's "Ministero della Guerra, Maggiore Esercito: Ufficio Storico."

A surprisingly large number of nations produced official histories in some form or another, however there were a small number of states that did not.

Apart from the warring states, there have been official histories written by countries that came into being in the aftermath of the Great War, namely Czechoslovakia and Finland and, in the case of Poland, was recreated with the collapse of the three central European Empires. In other cases, by countries that at the time of writing had ceased to exist as independent states, namely Montenegro and Serbia which had become Yugoslavian republics. Éire (The Republic of Ireland) was at the time of the Great War under the control of H.M. (British) Government. The actions of Irish servicemen serving within the British Army have been recorded in the British official history. However, the Easter Uprising and the actions of the Irish republicans were covered by a report commissioned by H.M. (British) Government in 1916 and, similar to H.M. (British) Government's South African report on the Boer rebellion, this report is regarded as an Irish official history. Even neutral countries during the war - Norway and Sweden - have written official histories covering the impact of that war on their neutrality, especially the naval war and the effect of the British and German blockades upon their citizens and their seaborne trade.

Finally, there are a number of countries that have not written an official coverage of their part or that of their citizens in the Great War, for example I have found no trace of official histories having been written or published in Albania or Bosnia and Herzegovina who were involved militarily in the war, nor Spain and the Nederlands (Holland) who were not involved.

***

One of the best descriptions of official histories is to be found in Peter Edwards' essay *Continuity and Change in the Australian Official History Tradition*:

> "All the official histories series have aimed to provide a comprehensive account of the nation's involvement in war, to be read by a general audience. Although official histories started as part of the professional education of military staffs in the late nineteenth century, they became in the twentieth century part of the era of mass armies and total war. The underlying concept is that if every member of the population is liable to be involved in a war, then everyone should be able to read about it."[9]

However in the words of Antony Beevor describing history generally, but could equally be applied to official histories:

> "...selective and manipulative view of history." [10]

Official histories dated back to Roman times but, in the modern sense date from about the middle of the nineteenth century. Historically there are a number of reasons for writing the official histories. Initially, well before the Great War, Official Histories were written by and for the use of the military. They tended to be written in the "report" format, recording what had actually happened, so that future military experts and professionals could make their own judgements and conclusions from the full descriptions of the facts stated within. Those works did not make for easy reading – certainly not for the general public, hence they tended not to be read outside of military circles.

It was the New Zealand government in the aftermath of the Great War who took the steps to develop the concept that with total war involving the whole population, the official histories should be aimed at the people who had fought, had worked for the cause, or had given so much sacrifice for the nation.

From the Second World War another concept has evolved. Based on the fact that, as a general rule, military professionals at that time were not educated to a very high academic standard, especially in the art of analysing history, academics had been asked to write the official histories using the techniques that they had learnt in higher education and to make conclusions from the facts that they presented. Those academics had been required through compulsory service to serve during the course of a war, giving them a first hand knowledge allowing them to write about the said war.

---

[9] *Continuity and Change in the Australian Official History Tradition* by Peter Edwards in 'The Last Word? Essays on Official History in the United States and British Commonwealth', edited by Jeffrey Grey published by Praeger Publishers in 2003 - pp 71.
[10] Antony Beevor: "The Battle for Spain" pp 240, Weidenfeld & Nicolson 2006.

Today's view therefore is that, in essence, official histories should be a combination of all three of the above concepts. The works should be foremost for military use, recording the events as they happened in detail. They should also be for the public at large, since it is they who have given so much both personally and financially. Finally they should show how the earlier generation of leaders tried to resolve the problems facing them giving the lessons to be learnt from their successes as well as their mistakes.

There are problems with all of the above concepts.

i. The purely military history written by the military specialist can be subject to a deliberate editing of the truth for personal or political reasons giving a bias view of the events.
ii. The populist histories can be watered down for ease of reading by the non specialist with the result that they become almost unusable to the military professional.
iii. That of non military academics reaching the wrong conclusion or, at worst, developing a preconceived conclusion based on their own personal ideals and ideologies by fitting a limited, censored number of facts to suit their jaundiced concepts!

In the case of the diplomatic histories, they were written as governmental justifications for going to war, showing the reasons and actions that led to the outbreak of the war, with the view of laying the liability elsewhere. Often these diplomatic histories were composed simply of statements, letters, minutes of meetings, memorandums and other forms of communications, which were found mainly in the closed state archives. However, the authors, with the intention that any incriminating evidence would be deliberately suppressed leaving their government in a favourable light, often censored these histories. They were written as propaganda tools in the battle for world opinion, especially amongst the neutral governments whose favourable judgement they sought and to apportion the guilt away from their own government.

In theory, the armed services' histories were to be written more honestly - as history textbooks to show the successes and failures of prosecuting the war. This concept is based on the idea that lessons could be learnt in the event of any future conflict. Indeed a fine example of this concept was that of the British Kirke Committee. This committee was set up under the chairmanship of Lieutenant General Walter Kirke in about 1930 to study the events of the 1914-1918 war. The committee's report, written by Major General A.E. McNamara, was largely based on the earlier volumes of the British official histories, namely the ones completed up to the drafting of the report, which included the *Military Operations, France and Belgium 1916 volume 2* along with the volumes for the *Military Operations, Egypt and Palestine*; the "*Military Operations, Gallipoli* and the *Campaign in Mesopotamia*. Based on the committee's findings, the British Army's Field Regulations were changed, incorporating the lessons learnt. For the same reason, the need for a textbook in case of future campaigns in Iraq and Iran, the writing of the British official history, *Operations in Persia 1915-1919*, was accepted against the objections of H.M. Government's Foreign Office on legal grounds.

Of course the armed services' official histories were and still are written with a nationalistic perspective. This bias is due to the authors being concerned mainly with how their national armed services had performed and not how other nations had performed. Because of this viewpoint, the official histories became incomplete pictures of the world war in general. References were made of the enemy, and sometimes of an ally during a joint operation, or when that ally had a direct impact upon the national armed services, but as a general rule limiting themselves to just reporting on the national unit.

An extreme case of this nationalistic bias with regard to armed services' official histories writing was that of the Australian official history *Official History of Australia in the War of 1914-1918*, especially the part devoted to the military operations. The general editor of this history and author of the military operations volumes, *Doctor* Charles E.W. Bean, wrote these histories at the time when Australia was defining its nationhood. He therefore quite naturally built up the significance of the Australian 'army corps' and that of the Australian soldier's fighting prowess to the detriment of the soldiers from other allied nations, notably those from Britain. He placed an inordinate amount of blame for Australian failings and losses upon the British High Command, even though some of the blame should have been laid at Australians within the British High Command structure.

There were cases where the reasons for writing the military and naval histories were not based on the original concept, but followed the more political line of the diplomatic histories concepts.

The authors of the British aviation history *The War in the Air* deliberately highlighted the role of British strategic bombing, which was out of all proportion to the other functions performed by the British air services during the war. Walter Raleigh, followed by Henry Jones, was faced with writing the history during the immediate post war period when the newly formed Royal Air Force was under threat of disbandment. Against the background of political maneuverings to save funds by amalgamating the air service with the other services, it was important for the R.A.F. to find a function that would help to keep its independence. To this end the authors, especially Jones, emphasized the importance of the strategic bombing campaign during the war. Whilst the object of this political campaigning proved successful, it did unbalance the final work overall.

Even though the writing was to be faithful to the events that were being recorded, there was a fair bit of corruption that slipped into a number of the histories.

A high proportion of the historians, editors and endorsers producing the arm services' histories were ex-senior officers of the various services. This has had various advantages and disadvantages. The main advantage was that often these individuals had first hand experiences of the events during the war and, in many cases, having overseen the actions under review and therefore could accurately record them. They also had an in depth understanding of the military subject matters. However on the negative side, there were always the possibilities that there would be perversions of the truth, especially in the protection of themselves or of former colleagues, notably senior commanders. It has even been known that the blame for major failings was shifted onto others, often outside parties.

The authors of the Austro-Hungarian official military history (*Österreich-Ungarns Letzter Krieg 1914-1918*) under the editorship of *Doktor* Edmund Glaise-Horstenau (a former Austrian staff officer) followed a policy of protecting their former army commander *Feldmarschall* Franz *Graf* Conrad von Hötzendorf.

The German official naval history (*Der Krieg zur See 1914-1918*) was written by a team of historians in the *Marine-Archiv* under the watchful eye of the *Präsident des Marine-Archiv* (the President of the Naval Archives). There were three presidents during the course of writing. The staff of the *Marine-Archiv* was made up of mainly ex-naval officers who had served in the navy during the war. Unfortunately, these ex-officers, with deep loyalties to the navy, tended to produce rather biased and apologetic works. To correct those corruptions, the present day *Militärgeschichtlichen Forschungsamt* (The Military History Research Office) has started to rework the volumes of *Der Krieg zur See 1914-1918, Der Krieg in der Nordsee*, the first being the final volume of the set, *Siebenter Band, Von Sommer 1917 bis zum Kriegsende 1918*.

Similarly, the German official military history (*Der Weltkrieg 1914-1918*) was written in the *Reichsarchivs* (State Archives) and, as such, was commonly known as the *Reichsarchivwerk* (the work of the State Archives). Like the naval official history, the various volumes were written by a team of historians, most of who had served as army staff officers during the war and had passed into the army reserve. They worked under the general editorship of the *Präsident des Reichsarchivs* (the President of the State Archives). Like the naval archives, there were three presidents during the course of writing. It came therefore as no surprise that the three presidents over the period of writing had an editorial policy of protecting the army and its reputation. Initially the earlier volumes defended the conceptual and detail planning of the former *Großer Generalstab* (the Great General Staff) and especially that of *Generalfeldmarschall* Alfred *Graf* von Schlieffen who, although retired in 1905, had left as his legacy the concepts that formed the basis for most of the pre war planning. In the mid nineteen-thirties, with the advent of the Nazi Party forming the German Government, the writing of the *Der Weltkrieg* took a more sinister turn for the worse. The editors and authors within the *Reichsarchivs* took a more party line towards German military history of the Great War with regard to the "stab in the back" reason for Germany's failings and ultimate defeat.

In some cases the authors were required to revise their work based on comments from reviewers who had been involved in the events described in the narration under consideration. A fine example of this was the British official history, *Naval Operations, Volume III* (which covered the Battle of Jutland.) This volume was completed within five years of the end of the war and seven years from the end of the battle in question; there were a number of the senior British commanders who had been involved in this battle still serving in the Royal Navy at the Admiralty. These officers were given the opportunity to review the draft of this history, and had various disparaging remarks about themselves removed from the text. Later, when the original objectors had retired from the Admiralty (most of them were by then deceased), this volume was republished with its text updated. There was no attempt to revert to the original draft text.

Since it was written, the British official military history has often been accused by historians of being deceitful by suppressing and misrepresenting the facts; in particular for not laying the responsibility for the huge number of British and commonwealth casualties onto the British High Command, especially the Commander of the British Expeditionary Force, France and Belgium from 1915 to the end of the war, Sir Douglas Haig. However it was not the intention of the British official historian and general editor of the military operations set, Sir James Edmonds (an ex-member of Haig's staff), to draw conclusions and therefore apportion blame, but to report on what actually happened. It is arguable that, by so doing, he did indeed protect Haig and a number of the other senior officers. Equally it can be argued that the reader can make his own judgements and conclusions. For very constructive studies on this argument, see Andrew Green's *Writing the Great War: Sir James Edmonds and the Official Histories 1915-1948* and Jay Luvass' essay *The First British Official Historians*.[10]

Unpalatable facts were sometimes reduced in significance by under narration. The coverage of the rather significant French Army's 1917 mutinies (according to Guy Pedroncini, the mutinies affected 43% of the French front line infantry[11]) was covered by only a few paragraphs in the French official military history (*Les Armées Françaises dans la Grande Guerre*.)

***

From the reader's point of view, there appears to be incomplete sets of official histories, with whole campaigns seemingly missing.

A number of the sets that were started were indeed left incomplete. Generally this was because the missing volumes were either not written due to the lack of funds, or a change in the political situation that changed the whole governmental concept behind the official reporting of an event that was deemed to be of no interest. There were three sets that were not completed. They were the Bulgarian, the Canadian and the Hungarian official histories. In the case of the former and the latter, the projects were stopped due to the advent of the Second World War, followed by the change in the political orientation of their post war governments. In the case of the original Canadian official history set, the project was stopped on economical grounds; a compact single volume history of the Great War was written in 1962 in line with the Canadian Second World War official histories that had just been completed.

In general, except for the three unfinished sets noted above, the official histories sets that were intended to be written were indeed completed; the volumes that seemed to be missing were written but, due to the sensitive nature of them, not published for general consumption. There is one notable exception the British official history, *Military Operations, East Africa, Volume II: October 1916-November 1918*. Lieutenant Colonel Charles Norden was to write it as one volume but during the course of writing it was decided to split it into two parts. Norden completed the first volume and in fact had started work upon the first drafts of the second, but unfortunately died before he could complete it. With his death, the work on this second volume was stopped and it was never resumed, leaving the British official history series missing a volume.

In some cases, the sets that appeared to have been left incomplete, with volumes missing, were in fact completed with all the volumes being written, where the 'missing' volumes were not issued for general readership nor had a delayed publishing. These volumes, often of a sensitive nature to the national government at the time of writing, were issued as confidential with small print runs and limited circulation. Examples being the above mentioned British official history, *Operations in Persia 1915-1919*; the British official history, *The Blockade of the Central Empires 1914 - 1918* and the two final volumes of the German official history, *Der Weltkrieg* volumes 13 and 14.

The coverage of German colonial campaigns is sketchy with China and East Africa being covered by only one naval history, leaving the coverage of the other German colonies within Africa and the Pacific incomplete. It is assumed that the *Reichsarchiv* did not feel that it was necessary or worth the expense to write the histories covering these campaigns.

Finally, in another case, the British official history, *The Occupation of Constantinople 1918-1923* was written but not published at all. It was deemed to be irrelevant at the time of completion and therefore a waste of the limited funding available to publish it.

***

A note for the book dealers or collectors: As is to be expected, there has been no standardisation in the production of the official histories between the various countries. There is, however, a degree of standardisation within the sets of histories produced in each country. The Australians produced identical volumes dimensionally in their 15 volume official history *Official History of Australia in the War of 1914-1918* and *Official History of the Australian Army Medical Services in the War of 1914-1918*: all the volumes measuring 21cm x 13.5cm x 5.8cm even though the number of pages within the volumes varied from just over 400 to well over 1000. As can be seen in the descriptions of the volumes listed below there were, even within a set of a standard sized and formatted, the occasional

[10] ***Writing the Great War: Sir James Ednonds and the Official Histories 1915-1948***, by Andrew Green published by Frank Cass Publishers in 2003. The First British Official Historians, by Jay Luvass can be found in the introduction of the British section within **'Official Histories'**, by Robin Higham, ibid.

[11] ***Les mutineries de 1917***, by Guy Pedroncini published by Presses universitaires de France, in 1967.

differences. An example being the British official histories where the *Statistics of the Military Effort of the British Empire during the Great War* is a large (33cm x 21cm) paper soft back compared with the majority of the series which were smaller (22.5cm x 16cm) cloth covered hardbacks.

Obviously the condition of the volumes today varies considerably based on how well they have been kept. Hardback volumes have generally survived quite well, with volumes in mint condition occasionally coming on to the market. Much more scarce is to find volumes which were issued with dust jackets where the dust jackets have survived. Most dust jackets, if they have survived, show the signs of their age, but it is still possible, although quite rare, to find jackets in mint condition. It is also rare to find a soft back volume in it original condition, most having been bound. Of the bound soft back volumes, it is common to find them in a reasonable state. Those that are to be found that were not bound tend to be rather tatty.

***

Is the writing of official histories worldwide complete? Are there any more histories to be written?

Most of the formal sets by the different nations regarding the Great War have now been completed, with the exceptions already noted. However a number of governmental historical offices are still very active and are still producing works related to the Great War, as well as works on other wars.

It has been stated that the Russian government is sponsoring a new Russian official history, to be published on the centenary of the start of the Great War in 2014. The Italians and Turks completed their main sets relatively late to those of other nations in 1988 and 2002 respectively.

The Czech and Slovakian, Finnish, French, German, Italian, Greek, Polish and Turkish historical offices have all been working on various Great War projects in recent years. The Czech and Slovakian, Finnish, French, Italians and Polish offices are producing a number of new works covering various aspects that were not covered before. Subjects covered range from aerial warfare through to propaganda.

With the problems associated with their histories noted above, the Germans have started to revise and reissue their naval volumes.

As more research has revealed new information, the Greeks and Turks have also decided to revise and reissue volumes from within their main sets, taking the opportunity to correct earlier printing errors in the first editions. They are also producing more populist summaries of their sets or sub sets - in the case of the Greeks, a summary of their two volume set, and with the Turks the sub sets of the Gallipoli battles and the European campaigns. Both the Greeks and the Turks have taken this one step further by translating those summaries into English, thereby catering for the English speaking community.

***

For further details see the notes relating to each individual volume.

Conclusion:

Edward J. Drea made the comment in his essay '*Change Becomes Continuity: The Start of the U.S. Army's 'Green Book' Series*':

"...'official history' conjured up visions of court historians dutifully scribbling an uncritical account of events to support or enhance the prestige of their civilian or military masters."[13]

This sums up the opinion of a lot of people concerning official histories. Drea then continues to discredit this statement using the American official history series for the Second World War as an example.

In truth the official histories were written for different reasons over the course of time conveying what was required of them, but based on a framework of detailed facts. The official historians in the 1920's and 1930's were allowed access to the confidential archive data that was

---

[13] *Change Becomes Continuity: The Start of the U.S. Army's 'Green Book' Series*, by Edward J. Drea, in '*The Last Word? Essays on Official History in the United States and British Commonwealth*', edited by Jeffrey Grey published by Praeger Publishers in 2003 - pp 83.

closed to other historians – material which has in some cases since been destroyed. When viewed with all the above limitations, the official histories are still one of the best sources of base information which, when used collectively and selectively, probably cannot be bettered without major study work within the world's surviving governmental or institutional archives, which in some cases, are now impossible.

Introduction

Breakdown of this Bibliography:

Since my main interest is of armed conflict, the main purpose of this bibliography is to cover official histories of the armed services.

I have divided this study into two sections. The first section is a bibliography of Primary Official Histories covering military, naval and aviation histories. The second section is a chronology of events cross-referenced to the related Primary Official Histories. Finally I have listed the secondary official histories and diplomatic official histories in the appendices.

How to use this Bibliography:

With each book I have tried to give the full title, along with their volume numbers. There are cases where the title on the cover or spine differed from that shown on the title page. In these cases I have used the title as given on the title page and noted any differences on the cover or spines in the volume notes. Numbering the volume sometimes became confused or disjointed. It was decided initially that the British series of *Military Operations, France and Belgium* should be numbered sequentially as well as by individual year. However after Volume V (*Military Operations, France and Belgium 1916 Volume I*) this practice was stopped so that the sixth volume in the series (*Military Operations, France and Belgium 1916 volume II*) was not given a sequential number. This may have been due to the fact that this was the first volume to be written out of chronological sequence.

A number of nations officially translated official histories from other nations and, on occasion, officially translated non-official books again from other nations. Examples of these officially translated books are as follows:

    i.   Britain's Historical Section of the Committee for Imperial Defence translated General A. von Kluck's non-official autobiographical account of the opening campaigns *Der Marsch auf Paris und die Marneschlacht 1914* as *The March on Paris and The Battle of the Marne 1914*.

    ii.   Germany translated the first part of A.C. Bell's British Naval Official History *The Blockade of the Central Empires 1914 - 1918* as *Die Englisch Hungerblockade im Weltkrieg 1914 – 1915*[14].

    iii.   The United States Navy's Naval War College Department translated a number of the German Naval Official Histories – *Der Krieg zur See 1914 – 1918*.

    iv.   The Italian 'Ufficio Storico' (Historical Office) translated a great number of official and non-official histories. These including official ones from Austria – *Österreich-Ungarns Letzter Krieg 1914-1918*, Britain – *Military Operations: Egypt and Palestine* - and Germany – *Der Weltkrieg: Die Militarischen Operationen zu Lande* – as well as a number of non-official works mainly autobiographies by leading wartime figures.

No translations have been listed, since I have listed the official histories within the original country's list.

The peace treaties were published in a number of countries that were involved in the Great War and in their respective languages; however I have only listed the British ones to save repetition.

In Part One I have listed the books first by Country, then by service, then by sets in alpha-numerical order, and finally chronologically.

I have tried to show all of the titles of the official histories listed as near as possible as they appear on the title page, in terms of the type of case (uppercase or title case), the language and the type of script (font). The majority of the titles were printed in capital letters, but in a small number of cases they were printed using title case, namely with capital letters at the start of the main words. It did not follow that a nation's official histories were consistent in the type of case, for example New Zealand's general set *Official History of New Zealand's Effort in the Great War* used title case whilst their

---

[14] Interestingly, Bell's **The Blockade of the Central Empires 1914 - 1918** which was originally published in 1937, was immediately placed on the British Government's Confidential list of publications and was not removed from that list and released to the British public until 1961, yet the German translation was published in 1943 and went on general sale to the German public at the same date of publication.

medical history used uppercase *NEW ZEALAND MEDICAL SERVICES IN THE GREAT WAR - 1914-1919*. The titles have been shown in the original language of publication, with non-English titles having an English translation. The type of script of the original book has been used. This applies to the following: most of the German histories were published in Fraktur script (sometimes referred to as *Alte Deutsche schriften* – Old German script); the Greek histories were published in modern Greek script; the Japanese histories were published in the Japanese syllabic scripts (hiragana, katakana, kanji and romaji); the earlier Turkish histories were published in Ottoman Turkish script (a variant of the Perso-Arabic script) and those of Russia and some of the Balkan states' histories were published in Cyrillic script. Since most Western Academic libraries catalogue using Latin script, I have transliterated the Greek, Ottoman and Cyrillic scripts into Latin script, using the following standards: ISO 9:1995 for Cyrillic (with allowances for local Balkan variations) and ISO 843:1997 for the Greek script. For ease of reading I have repeated those German titles in Fraktur script using modern Latin script.

I have included a block of information under each individual book title. This data is principally for dealers and collectors, giving an idea of the structure of the volume. The information given covers the physical details of the book, such as dimensional size, binding, number of pages, illustrations etc. The data is arranged in the following way and order:

> Author(s). | Height in centimetres x width in centimetres. | Colour and type of covers. | Gilt titles on the covers and spine. | Colour of dust jacket. | Number of introductory pages + number of text pages. | Page edging finish – if untrimmed. | Number of appendices. | Number of maps. | Number of photographs. | Number of sketches and diagrams. | Number of tables. | Number of sections. | Publisher. | Publication date /copyright date. | Language the volume was written in. | Type of script used where it is not standard modern script.

All of the above data applies only to a few volumes. In cases where data is not applicable to a volume, it has been left out, i.e. the type of script detail is only relevant to German, Greek, Japanese and Russian/Balkan histories – since the other countries used standard Latin script. This detail has not been included for the Latin scripted volumes. Equally I have in some cases not been able to track down the relevant information to complete the data for individual volumes. In such cases I have either placed a question mark (?) in the relevant data field where the information is known to be missing (such as the number of pages), or where it is not known if the information applies or not (if the book had maps or photographs for example); I have left the field out all together. I have shown the name of the author(s) as it appears on the title page or covers of the volume. If the author's name(s) was abbreviated with initials, I have added, where known, his full name(s) in brackets. Where a volume has not an author's name(s) shown, then I have stated that the author was anonymous and then added the authors name(s) if known in brackets.

Concerning parenthesis within the text, I have used round brackets to show:

i. Where round brackets were used in the original title.
ii. The English translation of non-English titles for example La Belgique et la Guerre (*Belgium and the War.*). The translations are also shown in italics. The German Official Histories, where the titles have been shown in Fraktur script, and repeated in modern script as well as the English translation, have been shown thus: Der Weltkrieg. (Der Weltkrieg. - *The World War.*)
iii. The date of the publication of the revised edition or of the first public edition where the first edition was published for restricted circulation. For example 1944 (1956). Note I have not given the reprinting date with the data block unless the text was revised. I have, however, given the reprint date in the individual volume's notes.
iv. Canadian volumes that were published in both English and French as separate volumes – the French volumes are shown below the English ones as a separate entity complete with their own data block. It is then cross referenced back to the English version within brackets. For example: in the case of The Official History of the Royal Canadian Air Force, the French version is listed as Histoire officielle de l'Aviation royale du Canada. (French version of the above)
v. Where the volume was written by a team under an editor, then the editor is noted. For example Edmund Glaise-Horstenau (editor); Eduard Czegka, ….et al.

However I have used square brackets to define:

i. The full name(s) of an author where his or her first name(s) appear(s) on the title page abbreviated as initials, for example C.F. Aspinall-Oglander has been shown as C.F. [Cecil Faber] Aspinall-Oglander.

ii. Title or awards of the authors that were not shown on the title page, again using Aspinall-Oglander for an example, his rank has been added as [*Brigadier General*] C.F. [Cecil Faber] Aspinall-Oglander.

iii. The names of authors or contributors to volumes whose names are not credited and are not shown on the title page. For example using the first volume of *Gallipoli,* the non-named contributors have been listed after the named author whose name appears on the title page; [*Brigadier General*] C.F. [Cecil Faber] Aspinall-Oglander [*Captain* G.S. Gordon, and *Lieutenant General Sir* Gerald Ellison]

iv. Defining the continents of a part of a set other than the narration where the continents are not shown within the title i.e. [map box].

I have added notes below the data block giving additional information were applicable. These notes cover such aspects as to clarify the original title or to give a more detailed description of the subject matter related within the individual history, where the title is felt to be misleading or incomplete. For example, where a volume has only a sequence number and no description, the dates of the period or the related actions covered have been given such as the title of the British *Naval Operations.* Where a volume had a complex writing or publishing history, I have given a brief outline, for example *Der Weltkrieg Band 13.* Finally, the republishing date or dates have been stated, if a volume has been reprinted along with the publisher if different from the original publishing house. This covers the reprinting of the American, Australian and British official histories.

A number of organizations (official and non-official) have started to reproduce the official histories in an electronic format. These electronic format volumes are therefore noted as well as the type of electronic format used – pre recorded Compact Disc Read-Only-Media's (CD ROM's) or on the World Wide Web ('www' - the Internet). The information from the Internet has been displayed using either Hyper Text Markup Language ('html') or in an Adobe Acrobat Portable Document Format ('pdf') file. For example, some of the American histories have now been published on CD ROM's and all the Australian histories have been made available on the Internet as a 'pdf' files.

The intention of Part Two is to aid researchers in relating the relevant official history to a particular event. The chronological listing covers armed services' histories only. The list is based on the two official British works: the Historical Section of the Committee of Imperial Defence's *Official History of the War - Principal Events 1914-1918* and the Ministry of Information's *Chronology of the War* in three volumes complied by *Major General Lord* Edward Gleichen. I have added a small number of other events that were omitted from the above sources in an attempt to give a more complete list. I have crossed-referenced the events with the "Primary" Official Histories only.

The chronological list gives the date, the event (the battle or action) and finally a list of relevant histories.

All the titles in this section have been shown in their original language; however I have used Latin script for all titles, including those that were originally in Cyrillic, Fraktur, Greek or Ottoman script, as is the standard practice of western academic libraries.

To help the researchers, I have also stated the country of origin of the official history. In order to save space I have used the following abbreviations:

AmOH .... American Official History
AuOH .... Australian Official History
AHOH .... Austro-Hungarian Official History
BgOH .... Belgian Official History
BrOH .... British Official History
BuOH .... Bulgarian Official History
CdOH .... Canadian Official History
CzOH .... Czechoslovakian Official History
EOH .... Éire (The Republic of Ireland) Official History
FnOH .... Finnish Official History
FrOH .... French Official History
GmOH .... German Official History
GrOH .... Greek Official History
HOH .... Hungarian Official History
IOH .... Italian Official History
JOH .... Japanese Official History
MOH .... Montenegrin Official History

```
NZOH................ New Zealand Official History
NwOH .............. Norwegian Official History
PlOH ................. Polish Official Histories
PgOH................ Portuguese Official Histories
RoOH ............... Romanian Official History
RuOH ............... Russian Official History
SeOH................. Serbian Official History
SAOH............... South African Official History
SwOH............... Swedish Official History
TOH ................. Turkish Official Histories.
```

The cross referencing section is a guide only and is based on the dates that the volumes cover. In some cases only a passing comment and in others no mention of the event is made at all. However the reference will give the reader an idea of the background in which the event took place. Note that I have not included the Finnish or Polish Official Histories in Part Two since these two histories are diplomatic-political-military histories and do not give coverage to military actions.

Note on the Illustration:

I have illustrated the cover of this study with a photograph of original official history volumes in their original format, albeit aged. All the volumes featured are first editions with the result that the conditions of them vary considerably from almost mint to poor. The condition of an individual volume is based on two things: its age, for some are close to ninety years old, and the quality of the original printing/binding, which in some cases was quite poor.

Most of the hardback books were issued with dust jackets. However it is now rare to find an official history with its original dust jacket. This is because the original purpose of dust jackets was to protect the books during shipment. Being seen as part of the packaging, most were therefore discarded on receipt of the book.

A lot of the official histories were bound and sold as paperbacks for rebinding to the purchaser's requirements; with their pages left uncut ready for the binder. Hence it is rare that they have survived in their original format - as paperbacks - normally they are found bound. If a paperback volume is found unbound, then it is normally in quite poor condition, especially the paper covers, and it is even less likely to find one with its page edges left untrimmed.

Acknowledgements

Although much of this work is based on my own library, I have had to find missing information from other sources, mainly from within academic libraries. Also with my limited knowledge of the languages used in the writing of the various official histories, I have had to have help in the translation of a number of titles. I therefore owe a great deal of thanks to a large group of people whose help has been invaluable to me. Their names follow:

Cesar Alfonso and Raquel Blanco for their help in locating the Spanish Diplomatic Official History title.

Антоний Ангелов (Antoniy Angelov) for his help in the translation of the Bulgarian Official Histories titles.

The librarian and staff of the Bayerische Staats Bibliothek, München, especially Theodor Bauer, Christina Belmahi, Tobias Fendt, Annemarie Kaindl, and Andrea Maier-Sall for all their help using the library's electronic cataloguing system, the complexity of which totally confused this rather technophobe compiler.

Johannes Bayer, librarian of the Bayerische Armeebibliothek, Bayerisches Armeemuseum, Ingolstadt, for his help with tracking down some of the more difficult histories to find, especially of the volumes of the French Official History, Military Operations.

Margaret Clifton, Research Specialist of the Science Reference Services, Library of Congress, Washington, D.C., for her help on the US Official Histories.

Lieutenant-Colonel Edward J. Erickson U.S. Army (Retired) for a lot of the information and help that he supplied on the Turkish Official Histories.

Doktor Achim Füch, archivist of the Bayerisches Hauptstaatsarchiv - Abteilung IV Kriegsarchiv, München, who gave me access to the German Official History, Military Operations, volumes 13 and 14.

Siri Granum, the librarian of Nasjonalbiblioteket, Oslo (The National Library of Norway) and Mette Guderud, the head librarian of Forsvarsmuseets bibliotek, Oslo (The [Norwegian] Defence Museum's Library) for their help with the Norwegian Official History as well as Magnus Try for his help in the translation of the Norwegian Official History title.

Patrick Hawe of the Leabharlann Náisiúnta na hÉireann (The National Library of Ireland) for his help in identifying the Éire (The Republic of Ireland) official history.

Michi Katayama and Yoshihiko Katayama their help in the translations of the Japanese Official Histories titles.

Ευάγγελος Κουντούρης (Evangelos Kountouris) for his help in the translation of the Greek Official Histories titles.

Hein Maassen of the Koninklijke Bibliotheek, The Hague (The Dutch Royal Library) for confirming that the Dutch did not write any official histories covering the Great War.

Matti Munnukka of FENNICA, (National Bibliography of Finland), for his help in tracking down the Finnish Official Histories.

Isabelle Remy, Documentaliste of the Mémorial de Verdun, for her help with tracking down some of the more difficult histories to find, especially of the volumes of the French Official History, Military Operations.

Marianne Schreiner and Isabella Schreiner for their help in translating the Serbian Official Histories titles.

Andrei Stefan for his help in the translation of the Romanian Official Histories titles.

Annica Thorell of the Kungliga biblioteket, Stockholm (The National Library of Sweden), Suzanne Wallinder of the Riksdagbiblioteket and esecially Johan Andersson of the Anna Lindh-biblioteket, Stockholm for tracking down the Swedish Official History.

Kristoffer Vestereng o f the Kongelige Bibliotek, Copenhagen (The Danish Royal Library) and Jes Andersen of the Biblioteksstyrelse, Copenhagen (The Danish National Library Authority) for confirming that the Danes did not write any official histories covering the Great War.

Oleg Zukhov and Cristina Bianchi for their help in the translations of the Russian Official Histories titles.

The librarian and staff of the University of Chicago Library for their help on the Hungarian Official Histories.

The curator and staff of the Greek Ministry of National Defence War Museum, Athens, for their help in locating the Greek Official Histories.

As with electronic cataloguing, I am equally inept at photography. Therefore I owe my old friend, Thomas H. Bull, who kindly took the cover photograph that illustrates this study, a large amount of gratitude.

If I have inadvertently forgotten anybody, please forgive me.

In a work of this nature, there are bound to be errors! I have tried to keep these errors to a minimum. However any errors that may have slipped through are of course mine and I apologise for them most whole-heartedly, especially if I cause any inconvenience in researches or book hunting.

Finally there are three people to whom I owe a great deal of thanks. The first two are old friends of mine; both are book dealers, Glenn Mitchell of Peter Harrington Books and Tim Harper of World War Books, for all their help and suggestions throughout this project. The last is my long-suffering wife, Barbara, who has had a great deal of tolerance with my obsession and yet has still managed to help and encouraged me on my long track to complete this study. She even found time to proofread the draft manuscript and correct the introduction and the notes that accompany the main bibliography.

Contents

Section 1 – List of the Official Histories

Section 2 – Chronology of Events related to the Official Histories

Appendices

Post Script

Photograph:

The cover illustration shows original Great War official histories from different countries. They are from left to right the British *History of the War based on Official Documents by Direction of the Historical Section of the Committee of Imperial Defence - Military Operations Togoland and the Cameroons* (in original dust jacket); the German *Der Weltkrieg - Die Militarischen Operationen zu Lande Dreizehnter Band* (deluxe binding); the Canadian military *Official History of the Canadian Forces in the Great War 1914 – 1919. Volume I. General Series.* (in original dust jacket); the Italian military *L'Esercito italiano nella Grande Guerra 1915-18 Volume IV Tomo 3 Bis – Documenti* ; the Austro-Hungarian military *Österreich-Ungarns Letzter Krieg 1914-1918 Band IV*; the German naval *Der Krieg zur See 1914-1918, Der Krieg in den türkischen Gewässern, Zweiter Band, Der Kampf un die Meerengen* (deluxe binding) and the New Zealand military *Official History of New Zealand's Effort in the Great War: Volume II The New Zealanders in France* (in original dust jacket).

Part One

Primary Official Histories Bibliography

American Primary Official Histories

The United States of America's official histories were written mainly within the historical departments of the services to which the histories related. The following departments were involved in the production of the histories: The Naval History Division, The Navy Medical Department, The Army Historical Division Department, The Army War College Historical Section, The Office of Air Force History, Bureau of Medicine and Surgery, U. S. Navy, The Army Medical Department – The Surgeon General's Office, Air Service Medical Department and The U.S. Army Military Board of Allied Supply. The American Battle Monuments Commission also produced a guide complete with an historical background.

The American official histories' bodies are still active limiting themselves to producing works on recent conflicts. They do however from time to time re-release older works on the Great War.

General;

THE OFFICIAL RECORD OF THE UNITED STATES PART IN THE GREAT WAR.

Colonel Leonard P. [Porter] Ayres | 23cm x 16cm | Khaki Cloth Hardback | Gilt with seal on front cover | 310pp | 12 maps | 13 sketches + 60 diagrams | Government Printing Office | 1919 | English Text.

This volume "**The Official Record of the United States' Part in the Great War**" was an enlarged version of Colonel Ayres' earlier work "War with Germany: Statistical Summary", which was published earlier in 1919.

This volume can be viewed on the Internet Archive world wide web (it can be viewed either in 'html' or as a 'pdf file'):

http://www.history.ncdcr.gov/twc/twc.aspx?appId=1001andfile=data/records.xmlandstyle=styles/recordDetail.xslandstyleParams=recordId=808

This is a product of the North Carolina Exploring Cultural Heritage Online project's world wide web page (a consortium of the North Carolina State Archives, the State Library of North Carolina, and the North Carolina Museum of History which goes under the general heading "Wildcats Never Quit").

AMERICAN ARMIES AND BATTLEFIELDS IN EUROPE.

Anonymous (American Battle Monuments Commission) | 25cm x 19.5cm | Black Cloth Hardback | Gilt with seal on front cover | xii + 547pp | ? photographs | 10 maps + 3 separate large folding maps | 6 colour plates | Government Printing Office | 1938 | English Text.

This volume "**American Armies and Battlefields in Europe**" was a revision of the book "**A Guide to the American Battlefields in Europe**" which was published by the American Battle Monuments Commission in 1927. Although originally designed as a battlefield guide to the American War monuments it was revised to include quite detailed descriptions of the United States Army's military operations.

It was republished in 1992. In 2001 it was revised and enlarged then reissued as part of the CD-ROM as mentioned below with the "**Order of Battle of the United States Land Forces in the World War - American Expeditionary Forces**".

Naval Operations[1];

U.S. OFFICE OF NAVAL RECORDS AND LIBRARY – MONOGRAPHS: PUBLICATION NO. 1 - GERMAN SUBMARINE ACTIVITIES ON THE ATLANTIC COAST OF THE UNITED STATES AND CANADA.

Anonymous (*Captain* C.C. Marsh *U.S.N.* et al – Historical Section, Navy Department) | 24.8cm x 19.7cm | Beige Paper Softback | 163pp | 2 folding maps in rear pocket | 39 photographs | Government Printing Office | 1920 | English Text.

This volume "**German Submarine Activities on the Atlantic Coast of the United States and Canada**" can be viewed on the Internet Archive world wide web:

---

[1] According to Higham the Naval History Division planned to publish in 1970 a monograph entitled "**German Submarine Operations off the Eastern Seaboard of the United States during World War I**". However I have failed to find any evidence to confirm actual publication of this book.

http://www.archive.org/details/germansubmarinea00unitrich

U.S. OFFICE OF NAVAL RECORDS AND LIBRARY – MONOGRAPHS: PUBLICATION NO. 2 - THE NORTHERN BARRAGE AND OTHER MINING ACTIVITIES.

Anonymous (*Commander* Simon P. [Peter] Fullinwider *U.S.N.* – Historical Section, Navy Department) | 24.8cm x 19.7cm | Beige Paper Softback | 146pp | 2 maps | 34 photographs | Government Printing Office | 1920 | English Text.

This volume "**The Northern Barrage and other Mining Activities**" can be viewed on the Internet Archive world wide web:

http://www.archive.org/details/northernbarrageo00unitrich

U.S. OFFICE OF NAVAL RECORDS AND LIBRARY – MONOGRAPHS: PUBLICATION NO. 3 - DIGEST CATALOGUE OF LAWS AND JOINT RESOLUTIONS, THE NAVY AND THE WORLD WAR.

Anonymous (Compiled by *Ensign* Sargeant Prentiss Knut *U.S.N.* – Historical Section, Navy Department) | 24.8cm x 19.7cm | Beige Paper Softback | 64pp | 14 tables | Government Printing Office | 1920 | English Text.

This volume "**Digest Catalogue of Laws and Joint Resolutions, The Navy and The World War**" can be viewed on the Internet Archive world wide web:

http://www.archive.org/details/digestcatalogueo00unitrich

U.S. OFFICE OF NAVAL RECORDS AND LIBRARY – MONOGRAPHS: PUBLICATION NO. 4 – "THE NORTHERN BARRAGE" (TAKING UP THE MINES).

Anonymous (Prepared by *Commander* Noel Davis *U.S.N.* and *Lieutenant Commander* William K. Harrill *U.S.N.* – Historical Section, Navy Department) | 24.8cm x 19.7cm | Beige Paper Softback | 79pp | 1 map | 32 photographs | Government Printing Office | 1920 | English Text.

This volume ""**The Northern Barrage**" (Taking up the Mines)" can be viewed on the Internet Archive world wide web:

http://www.archive.org/details/northernbarrage00harrgoog

U.S. OFFICE OF NAVAL RECORDS AND LIBRARY – MONOGRAPHS: PUBLICATION NO. 5 - HISTORY OF THE BUREAU OF ENGINEERING.

Anonymous (*Rear Admiral* Robert Stanislaus Griffin *U.S.N.* – Historical Section, Navy Department) | 24.8cm x 19.7cm | Beige Paper Softback | v + 176pp | 97 photographs | 11 sketches | 7 tables | 1 flow chart | Government Printing Office | 1922 | English Text.

This volume "**History of the Bureau of Engineering**" can be viewed on the Internet Archive world wide web:

http://www.archive.org/details/historyofbureauo00unitrich

U.S. OFFICE OF NAVAL RECORDS AND LIBRARY – MONOGRAPHS: PUBLICATION NO. 6 - THE UNITED STATES NAVAL RAILWAY BATTERIES IN FRANCE.

Anonymous (*Lieutenant Commander* Edward Breck *U.S.N.* – Historical Section, Navy Department) | 24.8cm x 19.7cm | Beige Paper Softback | v + 97pp | 2 maps | 34 photographs | 2 tables | Government Printing Office | 1922 | English Text.

This volume "**The United States Naval Railway Batteries in France**" was reprinted 1988 by the Naval Historical Center. A new introduction has been added increasing the number of pages to xiv + 97pp.

It can be viewed on the Internet Archive world wide web:

http://www.archive.org/details/unitedstatesnava00unitrich

U.S. OFFICE OF NAVAL RECORDS AND LIBRARY – MONOGRAPHS: PUBLICATION NO. 7 - THE AMERICAN NAVAL PLANNING SECTION, LONDON.

Anonymous (*Captain* D.W. [Dudley Wright] Knox *U.S.N. Retired* et al – Historical Section, Navy Department) | 24.8cm x 19.7cm | Beige Paper Softback | 537pp | 9 maps | Government Printing Office | 1923 | English Text.

The 'U.S. Office of Naval Records and Library – Monographs' are listed as such on the Department Of The Navy - Naval Historical Center's (Washington) publication list which is found on their website. Of note is that the individual monographs were titled as 'Publications' and not as 'Monographs', however the loose charts found in the map pockets at the end of the first two volumes have the description 'Monographs' printed upon them.

U.S. NAVAL PORT OFFICERS IN THE BORDEAUX REGION, 1917-1919, ADMINISTRATIVE REFERENCE SERVICE REPORT NO. 3.

[*Doctor*] Henry P. [Putney] Beers (under the supervision of *Doctor* R.G.[Robert Greenhalgh] Albion and *Lieutenant Commander* E. [Emmett] J. Leahy - Office of Records Administration, Administrative Office, [U.S.] Navy Department) I 23cm x 15cm I Paper Softback I 59pp I 2 folding maps in rear pocket I Office of Records Administration, Administrative Office, Navy Department, Government Printing Office I 1943 I English Text.

U.S. NAVAL FORCES IN NORTH RUSSIA (ARCHANGEL AND MURMANSK), 1918-1919, ADMINISTRATIVE REFERENCE SERVICE REPORT NO. 5.

[*Doctor*] Henry P. [Putney] Beers (under the supervision of *Doctor* R.G.[Robert Greenhalgh] Albion and *Lieutenant Commander* E. [Emmett] J. Leahy - Office of Records Administration, Administrative Office, [U.S.] Navy Department) I 23cm x 15cm I Paper Softback I 56pp I 1 folding maps in rear pocket I Office of Records Administration, Administrative Office, Navy Department, Government Printing Office I 1943 I English Text.

DEMOBILIZATION OF CIVILIAN PERSONNEL BY THE U.S. NAVY AFTER THE FIRST WORLD WAR, ADMINISTRATIVE REFERENCE SERVICE REPORT NO. 8.

Bess Glenn (under the supervision of *Doctor* R.G. [Robert Greenhalgh] Albion and *Lieutenant Commander* E. [Emmett] J. Leahy - Office of Records Administration, Administrative Office, [U.S.] Navy Department) I 23cm x 15cm I Paper Softback I 43pp I Office of Records Administration, Administrative Office, Navy Department, Government Printing Office I 1945 I English Text.

Naval Aviation in World War 1.

Adrian O. Van Wyen (Chief of [U.S.] Naval Operations) I 26cm x 20.3cm I Paper Softback I 90pp I 128 photographs I 1 sketch I 1 table I Government Printing Office I 1969 I English Text.

This volume "**Naval Aviation in World War 1**" was reprinted in 1976.

HISTORY OF THE NAVAL OVERSEAS TRANSPORTATION SERVICE IN WORLD WAR I.

Lewis P. [Painter] Clephane I 26cm x 20.3cm I Paper Softback I xxi + 283pp I Government Printing Office I 1969 I English Text.

This volume "**History of the Naval Overseas Transportation Service in World War I**" can be viewed on the HyperWar Foundation world wide web:
http://ibiblio.org/hyperwar/AMH/XX/WWI/USN/NOTS/index.html

NAVY ORDNANCE ACTIVITIES, WORLD WAR 1917-1918.

Rear Admiral Ralph Earl *U.S.N.* (U.S. Navy Department. Bureau of Ordnance) I 22.9cm x 20.3cm I Burgundy Cloth Hardback I Gilt I iv + 323pp I 204 photographs I Government Printing Office I 1920 I English Text

This volume "**Navy Ordnance Activities, World War 1917-1918**" can be viewed on the Internet Archive world wide web:
http://www.archive.org/details/navyordnanceact00ordngoog

ACTIVITIES OF THE BUREAU OF YARDS AND DOCKS, NAVY DEPARTMENT, WORLD WAR, 1917 – 1918.

Anonymous (*Rear Admiral* C. [Charles] W. Parks *U.S.N.* et al - U.S. Bureau of Yards and Docks) I 22.9cm x 20.3cm I Green Cloth Hardback I Gilt I 522pp I 32 illustrations I Government Printing Office I 1921 I English Text

This volume "**Activities of the Bureau of Yards and Docks, Navy Department, World War, 1917 – 1918**" can be viewed on the Internet Archive world wide web:
http://www.archive.org/details/activitiesburea00dockgoog

Occupation;

U.S. NAVAL DETACHMENT IN TURKISH WATERS, 1919-1924, ADMINISTRATIVE REFERENCE SERVICE REPORT NO. 2.

[*Doctor*] Henry P. [Putney] Beers (under the supervision of *Doctor* R.G.[Robert Greenhalgh] Albion, *Doctor* R.[Robert] H. Bahmer and *Lieutenant Commander* E.[Emmett] J. Leahy - Office of Records Administration, Administrative Office, [U.S.] Navy Department) I 23cm x

15cm | Paper Softback | 29pp | Office of Records Administration, Administrative Office, Navy Department, Government Printing Office | 1943 | English Text.

Marine Operations;

THE UNITED STATES MARINES CORPS IN THE WORLD WAR.
> Major Edwin N. [North] McClellan U.S.M.C. (Historical Branch, G-3 Division, Headquarters, U.S. Marine Corps) | 23cm x 15cm | Paper Softback | Gilt | 108pp | 37 tables | Government Printing Office | 1920 | English Text.
> This volume "**The United States Marines Corps in the World War**" was reprinted 1968 with an additional appendix increasing the number of pages to 109. The Appendix gives revised casualty statistics based on research carried out after the original publication of the monograph.
> The reprint volume can be viewed on the world wide web by the Air University, Maxwell-Gunter Air Force Base, Montgomery, Alabama:
> *http://www.au.af.mil/au/awc/awcgate/usmchist/war.txt*

Military Operations;

Chief Editor: Brigadier General Harry J. Malony, Chief of the U.S. Army Historical Division Department.

UNITED STATES ARMY IN THE WORLD WAR 1917 – 1919. VOLUME 1, ORGANIZATION OF THE AMERICAN EXPEDITIONARY FORCES.
> Anonymous (Robert S. Thomas [Editor]) | 26cm x 20cm | Black Cloth Hardback | Gilt | vii + 426pp | 2 maps | 1 photograph | Government Printing Office | 1948 | English Text.
> This volume "**United States Army in the World War 1917 – 1919. Volume 1**" was reprinted 1988.

UNITED STATES ARMY IN THE WORLD WAR 1917 – 1919. VOLUME 2, POLICY-FORMING DOCUMENTS OF THE AMERICAN EXPEDITIONARY FORCES.
> Anonymous (Robert S. Thomas [Editor]) | 26cm x 20cm | Black Cloth Hardback | Gilt | ii + 651pp | 1 photograph | Government Printing Office | 1948 | English Text.
> This volume "**United States Army in the World War 1917 – 1919. Volume 2**" was reprinted 1989.

UNITED STATES ARMY IN THE WORLD WAR 1917 – 1919. VOLUME 3, TRAINING AND USE OF AMERICAN UNITS WITH THE BRITISH AND FRENCH.
> Anonymous (Robert S. Thomas [Editor]) | 26cm x 20cm | Black Cloth Hardback | Gilt | i + 743pp | 2 maps | 4 photograph | Government Printing Office | 1948 | English Text.
> This volume "**United States Army in the World War 1917 – 1919. Volume 3**" was reprinted 1988.

UNITED STATES ARMY IN THE WORLD WAR 1917 – 1919. VOLUME 4, EARLY MILITARY OPERATIONS OF AMERICAN EXPEDITIONARY FORCES: CAMBRAI, SOMME, LYS, CHATEAU THIERRY.
> Anonymous (Robert S. Thomas [Editor]) | 26cm x 20cm | Black Cloth Hardback | Gilt | iv + 806pp | 54 maps | 7 photograph | Government Printing Office | 1948 | English Text.
> This volume "**United States Army in the World War 1917 – 1919. Volume 4**" was reprinted 1989.

UNITED STATES ARMY IN THE WORLD WAR 1917 – 1919. VOLUME 5, MILITARY OPERATIONS OF THE AMERICAN EXPEDITIONARY FORCES: CHAMPAGNE-MARNE AND AISNE-MARNE.
> Anonymous (Robert S. Thomas [Editor]) | 26cm x 20cm | Black Cloth Hardback | Gilt | iv + 693pp | 18 maps | 23 photograph | Government Printing Office | 1948 | English Text.
> This volume "**United States Army in the World War 1917 – 1919. Volume 5**" was reprinted 1989.

UNITED STATES ARMY IN THE WORLD WAR 1917 – 1919. VOLUME 6, MILITARY OPERATIONS OF THE AMERICAN EXPEDITIONARY FORCES: OISE-AISNE, YPRES-LYS, VITTORIO VENETO.
> Anonymous (Robert S. Thomas [Editor]) | 26cm x 20cm | Black Cloth Hardback | Gilt | iii + 563pp | 14 maps | 14 photograph | Government Printing Office | 1948 | English Text.

This volume "**United States Army in the World War 1917 – 1919. Volume 6**" was reprinted 1990.

UNITED STATES ARMY IN THE WORLD WAR 1917 – 1919. VOLUME 7, MILITARY OPERATIONS OF THE AMERICAN EXPEDITIONARY FORCES: SOMME OFFENSIVE.

Anonymous (Robert S. Thomas [Editor]) I 26cm x 20cm I Black Cloth Hardback I Gilt I ii + 921pp I 23 maps I 5 photograph I Government Printing Office I 1948 I English Text.

This volume "**United States Army in the World War 1917 – 1919. Volume 7**" was reprinted 1990.

UNITED STATES ARMY IN THE WORLD WAR 1917 – 1919. VOLUME 8, MILITARY OPERATIONS OF THE AMERICAN EXPEDITIONARY FORCES: ST. MIHIEL.

Anonymous (Robert S. Thomas [Editor]) I 26cm x 20cm I Black Cloth Hardback I Gilt I iv + 324pp I 4 maps I 22 photograph I Government Printing Office I 1948 I English Text.

This volume "**United States Army in the World War 1917 – 1919. Volume 8**" was reprinted 1990.

UNITED STATES ARMY IN THE WORLD WAR 1917 – 1919. VOLUME 9, MEUSE-ARGONNE OPERATIONS OF THE AMERICAN EXPEDITIONARY FORCES.

Anonymous (Robert S. Thomas [Editor]) I 26cm x 20cm I Black Cloth Hardback I Gilt I v + 598pp I 17 maps I 80 photograph I Government Printing Office I 1948 I English Text.

This volume "**United States Army in the World War 1917 – 1919. Volume 9**" was reprinted 1990.

UNITED STATES ARMY IN THE WORLD WAR 1917 – 1919. VOLUME 10, THE ARMISTICE AGREEMENT AND RELATED DOCUMENTS.

Anonymous (Robert S. Thomas [Editor]) I 26cm x 20cm I Black Cloth Hardback I Gilt I v + 1240pp I 1 map I Government Printing Office I 1948 I English Text.

This volume "**United States Army in the World War 1917 – 1919. Volume 10**" was reprinted in two parts 1991 and 1992.

UNITED STATES ARMY IN THE WORLD WAR 1917 – 1919. VOLUME 11, THE AMERICAN OCCUPATION OF GERMANY.

Anonymous (Robert S. Thomas [Editor]) I 26cm x 20cm I Black Cloth Hardback I Gilt I iii + 475pp I 2 maps I 1 photograph I Government Printing Office I 1948 I English Text.

This volume "**United States Army in the World War 1917 – 1919. Volume 11**" was reprinted in 1991 by the Government Printing Office and in 2005 by the University Press of the Pacific on behalf of the Center of Military History; United States Army in Softback format. The 2005 edition ISBN: 1410224759 has 488pp.

UNITED STATES ARMY IN THE WORLD WAR 1917 – 1919. VOLUME 12, REPORTS OF THE COMMANDER-IN-CHIEF, STAFF SECTIONS AND SERVICES, PART I.

Anonymous (Robert S. Thomas [Editor]) I 26cm x 20cm I Black Cloth Hardback I Gilt I i + 355pp I Government Printing Office I 1948 I English Text.

This volume "**United States Army in the World War 1917 – 1919. Volume 12**" was reprinted 1991.

UNITED STATES ARMY IN THE WORLD WAR 1917 – 1919. VOLUME 13, REPORTS OF THE COMMANDER-IN-CHIEF, STAFF SECTIONS AND SERVICES, PART II.

Anonymous (Robert S. Thomas [Editor]) I 26cm x 20cm I Black Cloth Hardback I Gilt I i + 388pp I Government Printing Office I 1948 I English Text.

This volume "**United States Army in the World War 1917 – 1919. Volume 13**" was reprinted 1990.

UNITED STATES ARMY IN THE WORLD WAR 1917 – 1919. VOLUME 14, REPORTS OF THE COMMANDER-IN-CHIEF, STAFF SECTIONS AND SERVICES, PART III.

Anonymous (Robert S. Thomas [Editor]) I 26cm x 20cm I Black Cloth Hardback I Gilt I i + 442pp I 1 map I Government Printing Office I 1948 I English Text.

This volume "**United States Army in the World War 1917 – 1919. Volume 14**" was reprinted 1991.

UNITED STATES ARMY IN THE WORLD WAR 1917 – 1919. VOLUME 15, REPORTS OF THE COMMANDER-IN-CHIEF, STAFF SECTIONS AND SERVICES, PART IV.

Anonymous (Robert S. Thomas [Editor]) I 26cm x 20cm I Black Cloth Hardback I Gilt I i + 502pp I 1 map I 1 photograph I Government Printing Office I 1948 I English Text.

This volume "**United States Army in the World War 1917 – 1919. Volume 15**" was reprinted 1991.

UNITED STATES ARMY IN THE WORLD WAR 1917 – 1919. VOLUME 16, GENERAL ORDERS G.H.Q., AMERICAN EXPEDITIONARY FORCES.

Anonymous (Robert S. Thomas [Editor]) I 26cm x 20cm I Black Cloth Hardback I Gilt I i + 775pp I 2 maps I 1 photograph I Government Printing Office I 1948 I English Text.

This volume "**United States Army in the World War 1917 – 1919. Volume 16**" was reprinted 1992.

UNITED STATES ARMY IN THE WORLD WAR 1917 – 1919. VOLUME 17, BULLETINS G.H.Q., AMERICAN EXPEDITIONARY FORCES.

Anonymous (Robert S. Thomas [Editor]) I 26cm x 20cm I Black Cloth Hardback I Gilt I i + 267pp I Government Printing Office I 1948 I English Text.

This volume "**United States Army in the World War 1917 – 1919. Volume 17**" was reprinted 1992.

When the idea of an Official History for the United States Army in the First World War was first put forward in 1919, it was turned down on the basis that "no one would believe it anyway!" although the main reason was eccnomic. Instead the booklet "**War with Germany: Statistical Summary**" (154pp) that Colonel Ayres had written and published in 1919 was enlarged to 310 pages with appendices and republished later the same year under the title "**The Official Record of the United States Part in the Great War**".

At the end of World War Two, the U.S. Army Historical Division Department decided to write an Official History for the Second World War, but it was then realised that the first war had likewise not been covered in a full official history of any real depth. Therefore Robert S. Thomas of the Historical Department put together the "**United States Army in the World War 1917 – 1919**". Published in seventeen volumes in 1948, it consisted of a collection of orders, memorandums, minutes of meetings, etc., and was illustrated with photographs and maps.

In the late 1980s the Government Printing Office decided to reprint the entire set which they duly did over the period 1989-1992.

In 2001 the Government Printing Office reproduced the "**United States Army in the World War 1917 – 1919 Volumes 1 – 17**" on CD-ROM (Compact Disc Read Only Memory) which also included the "**Order of Battle of the United States Land Forces in the World War - American Expeditionary Forces**" (ISBN 0-16-067116-7). This collection also included "**American Armies and Battlefields in Europe**" and a set of sixteen prints of Great War scenes painted by US Army Official War Artists along with a guide to the prints.

Finally in 2005 the University Press of the Pacific republished the "**United States Army in the World War 1917–1919 Volume 11**" calling it "**United States Army in the World War, 1917-1919: American Occupation of Germany**" with no reference to the volume sequence number. ISBN: 1410224759.

Order of Battle;

ORDER OF BATTLE OF THE UNITED STATES LAND FORCES IN THE WORLD WAR - AMERICAN EXPEDITIONARY FORCES. VOLUME 1 GENERAL HEADQUARTERS, ARMIES, ARMY CORPS, SERVICES OF SUPPLY AND SEPARATE FORCES. [2]

---

[2] This set, "**Order of Battle of the United States Land Forces in the World War - American Expeditionary Forces**" was republished in 1988 with volume 1 and 2 as originally published. However Volume 3 was republished in three parts instead of the original two parts. Volume 3 Part 1 becoming Part 1 and Part 2 and Volume 3 Part 2 becoming Part 3. The republished Volume 3 Part 2 had a new introduction and the republished Volume 3 Part 3 (originally Part 2) had a new appendix added. The changes are as follows:

Order of Battle of the United States Land Forces in the World War - American Expeditionary Forces Volume 3 Zone of the Interior Part 1 Organizations and Activities of the War Department.

x + 547pp. I 6 maps. I 54 tables. I Government Printing Office I 1988.

Order of Battle of the United States Land Forces in the World War - American Expeditionary Forces Volume 3 Zone of the Interior Part 2 Territorial Departments, Tactical Divisions Organized in 1918, and Posts, Camps, and Stations.

xiii + 453pp. I 42 maps. I 1 table. I Government Printing Office I 1988.

Anonymous (U.S. Army War College Historical Section) | 23cm x 14.5cm | Black Cloth Hardback | Gilt | xi + 412pp | Government Printing Office | 1937 | English Text.
This volume was republished in 1988.

ORDER OF BATTLE OF THE UNITED STATES LAND FORCES IN THE WORLD WAR - AMERICAN EXPEDITIONARY FORCES. VOLUME 2 DIVISIONS.

Anonymous (U.S. Army War College Historical Section) | 23cm x 14.5cm | Red Cloth Hardback | Gilt | vii + 451pp |Government Printing Office | 1932 | English Text.
This volume was republished in 1988.

ORDER OF BATTLE OF THE UNITED STATES LAND FORCES IN THE WORLD WAR - AMERICAN EXPEDITIONARY FORCES. VOLUME 3 ZONE OF THE INTERIOR PART 1 ORGANIZATIONS AND ACTIVITIES OF THE WAR.

Anonymous (U.S. Army War College Historical Section) | 23cm x 14.5cm | Blue Cloth Hardback | Gilt | ix + 993pp | 48 maps. | 55 tables. | Government Printing Office | 1949 | English Text.
This volume was republished in 1988. It was split into two volumes becoming Volume 3 Part 1 and Volume 3 Part 2.

ORDER OF BATTLE OF THE UNITED STATES LAND FORCES IN THE WORLD WAR - AMERICAN EXPEDITIONARY FORCES. VOLUME 3 ZONE OF THE INTERIOR PART 2 DIRECTORY OF TROOPS.

Anonymous (U.S. Army War College Historical Section) | 23cm x 14.5cm | Blue Cloth Hardback | Gilt | v + 600pp | 41 maps | 1 table. | Government Printing Office | 1949 | English Text.
This volume was republished in 1988 but due to the splitting of Part 1 into two parts this volume become Volume 3 Part 3.
As mentioned above the Government Printing Office reproduced the "Order of Battle" in CD-ROM format in 2001.

Aviation Activities;

The United States Air Service in World War I. Volume 1: The Final Report and A Tactical History.

Colonel Edgar S. [Staley] Gorrell, U.S.A.A.F. and Maurer Maurer (Editor - The Office of Air Force History) | 23cm x 14.5cm | Brown Cloth Hardback | Gilt | xiv + 448pp | 29 diagrams and sketches | Government Printing Office | 1921 (1978) | English Text.

The United States Air Service in World War I. Volume 2: Early Concepts of Military Aviation.

Colonel Edgar S. [Staley] Gorrell, U.S.A.A.F. and Maurer Maurer (Editor - The Office of Air Force History) | 23cm x 14.5cm | Brown Cloth Hardback | Gilt | xv + 460pp | 97 illustrations | Government Printing Office | 1921 (1978) | English Text.

The United States Air Service in World War I. Volume 3: The Battle of St. Mihiel.

Colonel Edgar S. [Staley] Gorrell, U.S.A.A.F. and Maurer Maurer (Editor - The Office of Air Force History) | 23cm x 14.5cm | Brown Cloth Hardback | Gilt | xi + 794pp | Government Printing Office | 1921 (1978) | English Text.

The United States Air Service in World War I. Volume 4: Postwar Review.

Colonel Edgar S. [Staley] Gorrell, U.S.A.A.F. and Maurer Maurer (Editor - The Office of Air Force History) | 23cm x 14.5cm | Brown Cloth Hardback | Gilt | xiv + 617pp | 145 photographs | 43 ttables | Government Printing Office | 1921 (1978) | English Text.
"The United States Air Service in World War I" was written by order of Major General Mason M. Patrick U.S.A.A.F. in December 1918 by Colonel Gorrell and his staff. It was published internally within the Air Force as "Information Circulars" during 1921, and it was finally republished for the general public by The Office of Air Force History in 1978.[3]

Order of Battle of the United States Land Forces in the World War - American Expeditionary Forces Volume 3 Zone of the Interior Part 3 Directory of Troops.
    v + 600pp | 41 maps | 1 Appendix | 1 table. | Government Printing Office | 1988.
[3] It has been noted by David J. Fitzpatrick in **"Researching World War I: A Handbook"** (Greenwood Press, 2003) edited by Robin Higham and Dennis E. Showalter that a second set titled **"The United States Air Service in World War I"** of five volumes was published in 1978 (page 259

Medicals Activities;

THE MEDICAL DEPARTMENT OF THE UNITED STATES NAVY WITH THE ARMY and MARINE CORPS IN FRANCE IN WORLD WAR I.

> [*Lieutenant*] G.G. [George George] Strott | 22.9cm x 15.2cm | Navy Blue Cloth Hardback | Gilt | x + 322pp | 4 maps | 35 photograph | Bureau of Medicine and Surgery, U. S. Navy Department, Government Printing Office | 1947 | English Text.
> Republished by Battery Press in 2005 as Navy Medics with the Marines 1917-1919.

THE MEDICAL DEPARTMENT OF THE UNITED STATES ARMY IN THE WORLD WAR; VOLUME I THE SURGEON GENERAL'S OFFICE.

> *Major General* Merritte W. [Weber] Ireland (Editor), *Colonel* Charles Lynch, *Lieutenant Colonel* Frank W. [Watkins] Weed and Loy McAfee | 30.5cm x 24.8cm | Burgundy Red Cloth Hardback | Gilt | 1389pp | 3 appendices | 24 charts | 9 plates | Government Printing Office | 1923 | English Text.
> This volume can be viewed on the Internet Archive world wide web as a 'pdf file':
> *http://www.archive.org/details/WW1ArmyMedDeptHistV1*

THE MEDICAL DEPARTMENT OF THE UNITED STATES ARMY IN THE WORLD WAR; VOLUME II ADMINISTRATION OF THE AMERICAN EXPEDITIONARY FORCES.

> *Major General* Merritte W. [Weber] Ireland (Editor), *Colonel* Joseph H. [Herbert] Ford | 30.5cm x 24.8cm| Burgundy Red Cloth Hardback | Gilt | 1123pp | 3 appendices | 4 charts | 3 plates | 165 figures | Government Printing Office | 1927 | English Text.
> This volume can be viewed on the Internet Archive world wide web as a 'pdf file':
> *http://www.archive.org/details/WW1ArmyMedDeptHistV2*

THE MEDICAL DEPARTMENT OF THE UNITED STATES ARMY IN THE WORLD WAR; VOLUME III FINANCE AND SUPPLY.

> *Major General* Merritte W. [Weber] Ireland (Editor), *Colonel* Edwin P. [Philip] Wolfe | 30.5cm x 24.8cm| Burgundy Red Cloth Hardback | Gilt | 935pp | 1 appendix | 50 figures | Government Printing Office | 1928 | English Text.
> This volume can be viewed on the Internet Archive world wide web as a 'pdf file':
> *http://www.archive.org/details/WW1ArmyMedDeptHistV3*

THE MEDICAL DEPARTMENT OF THE UNITED STATES ARMY IN THE WORLD WAR; VOLUME IV ACTIVITIES CONCERNING MOBILISATION CAMPS AND PORTS OF EMBARKATION.

> *Major General* Merritte W. [Weber] Ireland (Editor), *Major* Albert S. [Sidney] Bowen | 30.5cm x 24.8cm| Burgundy Red Cloth Hardback | Gilt | vii + 491pp | 67 tables | Government Printing Office | 1928 | English Text.
> This volume can be viewed on the Internet Archive world wide web as a 'pdf file':
> *http://www.archive.org/details/WW1ArmyMedDeptHistV4*

THE MEDICAL DEPARTMENT OF THE UNITED STATES ARMY IN THE WORLD WAR; VOLUME V MILITARY HOSPITALS IN THE UNITED STATES.

> *Major General* Merritte W. [Weber] Ireland (Editor), *Lieutenant Colonel* Frank W. [Watkins] Weed | 30.5cm x 24.8cm | Burgundy Red Cloth Hardback | Gilt | 857pp | 204 figures | 22 tables | Government Printing Office | 1923 | English Text.
> This volume can be viewed on the Internet Archive world wide web as a 'pdf file':
> *http://www.archive.org/details/WW1ArmyMedDeptHistV5*

THE MEDICAL DEPARTMENT OF THE UNITED STATES ARMY IN THE WORLD WAR; VOLUME VI SANITATION.

> *Major General* Merritte W. [Weber] Ireland (Editor), *Colonel* Weston P. [Percival] Chamberlain and *Lieutenant Colonel* Frank W. [Watkins] Weed | 30.5cm x 24.8cm| Burgundy Red Cloth Hardback | Gilt | 1141pp | 14 charts | 242 figures | 100 tables | Government Printing Office | 1926 | English Text.
> This volume can be viewed on the Internet Archive world wide web as a 'pdf file':
> *http://www.archive.org/details/WW1ArmyMedDeptHistV6*

---

book entry 138 and page 263 book entry 235). However, I have not been able to confirm that this second set was actually produced.

THE MEDICAL DEPARTMENT OF THE UNITED STATES ARMY IN THE WORLD WAR; VOLUME VII TRAINING.

Major General Merritte W. [Weber] Ireland (Editor), *Colonel* William N. [Newbold] Bispham | 30.5cm x 24.8cm| Burgundy Red Cloth Hardback | Gilt | viii + 1211pp | 1 appendix | 2 photograph | 33 figures | Government Printing Office | 1927 | English Text. This volume can be viewed on the Internet Archive world wide web as a 'pdf file': *http://www.archive.org/details/W1ArmyMedDeptHistV7*

THE MEDICAL DEPARTMENT OF THE UNITED STATES ARMY IN THE WORLD WAR; VOLUME VIII FIELD OPERATIONS.

Major General Merritte W. [Weber] Ireland (Editor), *Colonel* Charles Lynch, [*Colonel*] Joseph H. Ford and *Lieutenant Colonel* Frank W. [Watkins] Weed | 30.5cm x 24.8cm | Burgundy Red Cloth Hardback | Gilt | 1097pp | 5 appendices | 55 photograph | 4 charts | 23 tables | 99 figures | Government Printing Office | 1925 | English Text. This volume can be viewed on the Internet Archive world wide web as a 'pdf file': *http://www.archive.org/details/WW1ArmyMedDeptHistV8*

THE MEDICAL DEPARTMENT OF THE UNITED STATES ARMY IN THE WORLD WAR; VOLUME IX COMMUNICABLE AND OTHER DISEASES.

Major General Merritte W. [Weber] Ireland (Editor), *Lieutenant Colonel* Joseph F. Siler | 30.5cm x 24.8cm | Burgundy Red Cloth Hardback | Gilt | 628pp | 53 charts | 97 tables | Government Printing Office | 1928 | English Text. This volume can be viewed on the Internet Archive world wide web as a 'pdf file': *http://www.archive.org/details/WW1ArmyMedDeptHistV9*

THE MEDICAL DEPARTMENT OF THE UNITED STATES ARMY IN THE WORLD WAR; VOLUME X NEUROPSYCHIATRY.

Major General Merritte W. [Weber] Ireland (Editor), *Colonel* Thomas Pearce Bailey, [*Lieutenant Colonel*] Frankwood E. [Earl] Williams and *Sergeant* Paul O. Komora[4], *Colonel* Thomas W. [William] Salmon and *Sergeant* Norman Fenton | 30.5cm x 24.8cm| Burgundy Red Cloth Hardback | Gilt | xiii + 543pp | 88 tables | 20 figures | Government Printing Office | 1929 | English Text. This volume can be viewed on the Internet Archive world wide web as a 'pdf file': *http://www.archive.org/details/WW1ArmyMedDeptHistV10*

THE MEDICAL DEPARTMENT OF THE UNITED STATES ARMY IN THE WORLD WAR; VOLUME XI PART I SURGERY. ORTHOPEDIC SURGERY AND NEUROSURGERY

Major General Merritte W. [Weber] Ireland (Editor), *Lieutenant Colonel* Edward K. Dunham | 30.5cm x 24.8cm| Burgundy Red Cloth Hardback | Gilt | xxxiv + 1324pp | 5 photograph | 92 tables | 615 figures | Government Printing Office | 1924 | English Text. This volume can be viewed on the Internet Archive world wide web as a 'pdf file': *http://www.archive.org/details/WW1ArmyMedDeptHistV11-1*

THE MEDICAL DEPARTMENT OF THE UNITED STATES ARMY IN THE WORLD WAR; VOLUME XI PART II SURGERY. EMPYEMA, MAXILLOFACIAL SURGERY, OPHTHALMOLOGY, OTOLARYNGOLOGY.

Major General Merritte W.[Weber] Ireland (Editor), *Lieutenant Colonel* Edward K. Dunham, Robert H. [Henry] Ivy and Joseph D. [Davis] Eby, [*Lieutenant Colonel*] George E. [Edmund] de Schweinitz, Allan Greenwood, [*Colonel*] S.J. [Samuel] Morris and [*Colonel*] James F. McKernon | 30.5cm x 24.8cm| Burgundy Red Cloth Hardback | Gilt | 827pp | 34 photograph | 71 charts | 80 tables | 756 figures | Government Printing Office | 1924 | English Text. This volume included 24 colour plates. This volume can be viewed on the Internet Archive world wide web as a 'pdf file': *http://www.archive.org/details/WW1ArmyMedDeptHistV11-2*

THE MEDICAL DEPARTMENT OF THE UNITED STATES ARMY IN THE WORLD WAR; VOLUME XII PATHOLOGY OF THE ACUTE RESPIRATORY DISEASES and GAS GANGRENE.

Major General Merritte W. [Weber] Ireland (Editor), *Major* George R. [Russell] Callender and *Major* James F. [Francis] Coupel | 30.5cm x 24.8cm| Burgundy Red Cloth Hardback |

---

[4] This author's name has been shown as both Paul O. Komora and Piul O. Komora in various documents. Paul was possibly an Anglicisation of his original name or Piul could just possibly be a typing error. His name was shown on the title page as Paul O. Komora.

Gilt | xiv + 583pp | 14 appendices | 24 photograph | 312 figures | 14 charts | Government Printing Office | 1929 | English Text.

This volume can be viewed on the Internet Archive world wide web as a 'pdf file':
http://www.archive.org/details/WW1ArmyMedDeptHistV12

THE MEDICAL DEPARTMENT OF THE UNITED STATES ARMY IN THE WORLD WAR; VOLUME XIII PART I PHYSICAL RECONSTRUCTION AND VOCATIONAL EDUCATION. PART II ARMY NURSE CORPS.

Major General Merritte W. [Weber] Ireland (Editor), [*Major*] A.G. [Arthur Griswold] Crane (Part 1) and Julia C. [Catherine] Stimson (Part 2) | 30.5cm x 24.8cm| Burgundy Red Cloth Hardback | Gilt | xi + 998pp | 14 charts | 107 figures | Government Printing Office | 1927 | English Text.

This volume can be viewed on the Internet Archive world wide web as a 'pdf file':
http://www.archive.org/details/WW1ArmyMedDeptHistV13

THE MEDICAL DEPARTMENT OF THE UNITED STATES ARMY IN THE WORLD WAR; VOLUME XIV MEDICAL ASPECTS OF GAS WARFARE.

Major General Merritte W. [Weber] Ireland (Editor), Wilder D. [Dwight] Bancroft and H.C. [Harold] Bradley | 30.5cm x 24.8cm| Burgundy Red Cloth Hardback | Gilt | 876pp | 12 appendices | 37 charts | 15 plates | 97 tables | 242 figures | Government Printing Office | 1926 | English Text.

This volume can be viewed on the Internet Archive world wide web as a 'pdf file':
http://www.archive.org/details/WW1ArmyMedDeptHist_V14

THE MEDICAL DEPARTMENT OF THE UNITED STATES ARMY IN THE WORLD WAR; VOLUME XV PART I STATISTICS – ARMY ANTHROPOLOGY.

Major General Merritte W. [Weber] Ireland (Editor), Charles B. [Benedict] Davenport and *Major* Albert G. [Gallatin] Love | 30.5cm x 24.8cm| Burgundy Red Cloth Hardback | Gilt | ii + 636pp | 147 appendices | 42 plates | 258 tables | Government Printing Office | 1921 | English Text.

It is to be noted that all the appendices are given as tables and as such there are 211 tables in the main narration and 147 tables in the appendices making a total of 258 tables.

This volume can be viewed on the Internet Archive world wide web as a 'pdf file':
http://www.archive.org/details/WW1ArmyMedDeptHistV15-1

THE MEDICAL DEPARTMENT OF THE UNITED STATES ARMY IN THE WORLD WAR; VOLUME XV PART II STATISTICS – MEDICAL AND CASUALTY STATISTICS.

Major General Merritte W. [Weber] Ireland (Editor), *Major* Albert G. [Gallatin] Love | 30.5cm x 24.8cm| Burgundy Red Cloth Hardback | Gilt | xiv + 1368pp | 3 appendices | 54 plates | 122 tables | Government Printing Office | 1925 | English Text.

This volume can be viewed on the Internet Archive world wide web as a 'pdf file':
http://www.archive.org/details/WW1ArmyMedDeptHistV15-2

AIR SERVICE MEDICAL MANUAL.

Anonymous (U.S. War Department, Air Service, Division of Military Aeronautics.) | 26.7cm x 19cm | Grey paper softback | 38pp | 13 photograph | 3 sketches | Government Printing Office | 1918 | English Text.

This volume can be viewed on the Internet Archive world wide web as a 'pdf file':
http://www.archive.org/details/airservicemedica00unitrich

AIR SERVICE MEDICAL.

Anonymous (U.S. War Department, Air Service, Division of Military Aeronautics.) | 26.7cm x 19cm | Grey paper softback | 446pp | 166 photograph | 42 sketches | 79 tables | 51 graphs | 2 flow charts | Government Printing Office | 1919 | English Text.

This volume "**U.S. War Department, Air Service, Division of Military Aeronautics. Air Service Medical.**" consisted of two parts of which Part I was a reproduction of the previous volume "**U.S. War Department, Air Service, Division of Military Aeronautics. Air Service Medical Manual.**"

This volume can be viewed on the Internet Archive world wide web as a 'pdf file':
http://www.archive.org/details/servicemedica00unitairrich

AVIATION MEDICINE IN THE A.E.F.

Colonel William Holland Wilmer (U.S. War Department, Air Service, Division of Military Aeronautics.) | 26.7cm x 19cm | Grey paper softback | 322pp | 1 appendix | 20 figures | 60 tables | 25 graphs | 5 sketches | Government Printing Office | 1920 | English Text.

This volume can be viewed on the Internet Archive world wide web as a 'pdf file':
http://www.archive.org/details/aviationmedicin00wilmgoog

Munitions and Supply Activities;

AMERICA'S MUNITIONS 1917-1918.

Benedict Crowell | 24.7cm x 19.6cm | Dark Blue Cloth Hardback | Gilt | 592pp | 410 photograph | 2 sketches | 195 tables and graphs | Government Printing Office | 1919 | English Text.

REPORT OF THE MILITARY BOARD OF ALLIED SUPPLY; VOLUME 1.

Anonymous | 24.7cm x 19.6cm | Light Blue Cloth Hardback | Gilt | 577pp | 1 map | 17 photograph | Government Printing Office | 1924 | English Text.

REPORT OF THE MILITARY BOARD OF ALLIED SUPPLY; VOLUME 1. [Maps].

Anonymous | 24.7cm x 19.6cm | Light Blue Cloth Hardback | Gilt | 235 maps | Government Printing Office | 1924 | English Text.

REPORT OF THE MILITARY BOARD OF ALLIED SUPPLY; VOLUME 2.

Anonymous | 24.7cm x 19.6cm | Light Blue Cloth Hardback | Gilt | viii + 1173pp | 10 photograph | Government Printing Office | 1925 | English Text.

Australian Official Histories

The Australian official histories were written by members of the Australian War Memorial office.

The origin of the Australian War Memorial was an idea to create an Australian war museum which led to the setting up of the Australian War Records Section. It was based on a suggestion by C.E.W. Bean (one of the Australian war correspondents who later became the Australian official historian), but along the lines of the Canadian War Records Office, which had been formed at the beginning of 1916. The Australian War Records Section was formed in London on 16 May 1917 under the command of Captain John L. Treloar.

The Australian War Records Section had the brief to collect and store all kinds of material ranging from paperwork and photographs through to objects and artefacts pertaining to the Australian Imperial Force for the future museum. In 1919, the Australian War Records Section's collection was transferred from London to Australia to become the archive of the Australian War Museum. The museum and its archives were later renamed the Australian War Memorial under the directorship of Treloar.

It was from this time that the work of the Australian official history started under the general editorship of Bean based on the information compiled by Treloar.

The Australian War Memorial is still active and has produced three major official history sets over the years since the completion of the Great War official history set. It also covers a lot of other activities including an active world wide web site *http://www.awm.gov.au*.

General [including Military Operations, Naval Operations and Aviation Activities];

OFFICIAL HISTORY OF AUSTRALIA IN THE WAR OF 1914-1918. VOLUME I THE STORY OF ANZAC PART I.

C.E.W. [Charles Edwin Woodrow] Bean | 21cm x 13.5cm | Burgundy Red Cloth Hardback | Gilt | plain paper dust jacket + card mailing box[5] | xlviii + 662pp | 24 maps | 56 photographs | 86 diagrams and sketches | Angus and Robertson Ltd | 1921 | English Text.

Covers the Gallipoli campaign during April 1915 only.

The University of Queensland Press republished this volume in 1981. All of the reprints of the various volumes were produced in both hardback and softback. Each of the hardback volumes came with an illustrated dust jacket – the same illustration being used on the front cover of the softback volumes.

This volume can be viewed as a 'pdf file' on the Australian War Memorial world wide web site:

http://www.awm.gov.au/histories/first_world_war/volume.asp?levelID=67887

OFFICIAL HISTORY OF AUSTRALIA IN THE WAR OF 1914-1918. VOLUME II THE STORY OF ANZAC PART II.

C.E.W. [Charles Edwin Woodrow] Bean | 21cm x 13.5cm | Burgundy Red Cloth Hardback | Gilt | plain paper dust jacket + card mailing box | xviii + 975pp | 28 maps | 99 photographs | Angus and Robertson Ltd | 1924 | English Text.

Covers the Gallipoli campaign during the period May 1915 – January 1916.

The University of Queensland Press republished this volume in 1981.

This volume can be viewed as a 'pdf file' on the Australian War Memorial world wide web site:

http://www.awm.gov.au/histories/first_world_war/volume.asp?levelID=67888

OFFICIAL HISTORY OF AUSTRALIA IN THE WAR OF 1914-1918. VOLUME III FRANCE 1916.

C.E.W. [Charles Edwin Woodrow] Bean | 21cm x 13.5cm | Burgundy Red Cloth Hardback | Gilt | plain paper dust jacket + card mailing box | xviii + 1036pp | 2 appendices | 9 maps | 78 photographs | 1 diagrams and sketches | Angus and Robertson Ltd | 1929 | English Text.

---

[5] All of the "**Official History of Australia in the War of 1914-1918**" volumes including "**The Australian Army Medical Services in the War of 1914-1918**" were produced with a dust jacket. The original use of the dust jackets was to protect the books during shipment and generally the dust jackets were disgarded once the books had arrived at their destinations. However, as well as the dust jacket, the Australian War Memorial supplied a card mailing box for these sets.

The University of Queensland Press republished this volume in 1982.

This volume can be viewed as a 'pdf file' on the Australian War Memorial world wide web site:

http://www.awm.gov.au/histories/first_world_war/volume.asp?levelID=67889

OFFICIAL HISTORY OF AUSTRALIA IN THE WAR OF 1914-1918. VOLUME IV FRANCE 1917.

C.E.W. [Charles Edwin Woodrow] Bean | 21cm x 13.5cm | Burgundy Red Cloth Hardback | Gilt | plain paper dust jacket + card mailing box | xi + 1030pp | 3 appendices | 4 maps | 54 photographs | Angus and Robertson Ltd | 1933 | English Text.

The University of Queensland Press republished this volume in 1982.

This volume can be viewed as a 'pdf file' on the Australian War Memorial world wide web site:

http://www.awm.gov.au/histories/first_world_war/volume.asp?levelID=67890

OFFICIAL HISTORY OF AUSTRALIA IN THE WAR OF 1914-1918. VOLUME V FRANCE 1918 PART I.

C.E.W. [Charles Edwin Woodrow] Bean | 21cm x 13.5cm | Burgundy Red Cloth Hardback | Gilt | plain paper dust jacket + card mailing box | xii + 825pp | 5 appendices | 4 maps | 60 photographs | Angus and Robertson Ltd | 1937 | English Text.

The University of Queensland Press republished this volume in 1983.

This volume can be viewed as a 'pdf file' on the Australian War Memorial world wide web site:

http://www.awm.gov.au/histories/first_world_war/volume.asp?levelID=67891

OFFICIAL HISTORY OF AUSTRALIA IN THE WAR OF 1914-1918. VOLUME VI FRANCE 1918 PART II.

C.E.W. [Charles Edwin Woodrow] Bean | 21cm x 13.5cm | Burgundy Red Cloth Hardback | Gilt | plain paper dust jacket + card mailing box | lxxvi + 1099pp | 1 appendix | 2 maps | 59 photographs | Angus and Robertson Ltd | 1942 | English Text.

The University of Queensland Press republished this volume in 1983.

This volume can be viewed as a 'pdf file' on the Australian War Memorial world wide web site:

http://www.awm.gov.au/histories/first_world_war/volume.asp?levelID=67892

OFFICIAL HISTORY OF AUSTRALIA IN THE WAR OF 1914-1918. VOLUME VII SINAI AND PALESTINE.

H.S. [Henry Somer] Gullett | 21cm x 13.5cm | Burgundy Red Cloth Hardback | Gilt | plain paper dust jacket + card mailing box | xviii + 844pp | 1 appendix | 49 maps | 83 photographs | 28 diagrams and sketches | Angus and Robertson Ltd | 1923 | English Text.

The University of Queensland Press republished this volume in 1984.

This volume can be viewed as a 'pdf file' on the Australian War Memorial world wide web site:

http://www.awm.gov.au/histories/first_world_war/volume.asp?levelID=67893

OFFICIAL HISTORY OF AUSTRALIA IN THE WAR OF 1914-1918. VOLUME VIII AUSTRALIAN FLYING CORP.

F.M. [Fred] Cutlack | 21cm x 13.5cm | Burgundy Red Cloth Hardback | Gilt | plain paper dust jacket + card mailing box | xiv + 493pp | 9 appendices | 19 maps | 53 photographs | 10 diagrams and sketches | Angus and Robertson Ltd | 1923 | English Text.

The University of Queensland Press republished this volume in 1984.

This volume can be viewed as a 'pdf file' on the Australian War Memorial world wide web site:

http://www.awm.gov.au/histories/first_world_war/volume.asp?levelID=67894

OFFICIAL HISTORY OF AUSTRALIA IN THE WAR OF 1914-1918. VOLUME IX ROYAL AUSTRALIAN NAVY.

A.W. [Arthur] Jose | 21cm x 13.5cm | Burgundy Red Cloth Hardback | Gilt | plain paper dust jacket + card mailing box | xli + 649pp | 33 appendices | 28 maps | 90 photographs | 2 diagrams and sketches | Angus and Robertson Ltd | 1928 | English Text.

The University of Queensland Press republished this volume in 1987 and again in 1993.

This volume can be viewed as a 'pdf file' on the Australian War Memorial world wide web site:

http://www.awm.gov.au/histories/first_world_war/volume.asp?levelID=67895

OFFICIAL HISTORY OF AUSTRALIA IN THE WAR OF 1914-1918. VOLUME X SOUTHERN PACIFIC.

> S.S. [Seaforth] MacKenzie | 21cm x 13.5cm | Burgundy Red Cloth Hardback | Gilt | plain paper dust jacket + card mailing box | xviii + 412pp | 5 appendices | 8 maps | 87 photographs | Angus and Robertson Ltd | 1927 | English Text.
>
> The University of Queensland Press republished this volume in 1987.
>
> This volume can be viewed as a 'pdf file' on the Australian War Memorial world wide web site:
>
> *http://www.awm.gov.au/histories/first_world_war/volume.asp?levelID=67896*

OFFICIAL HISTORY OF AUSTRALIA IN THE WAR OF 1914-1918. VOLUME XI AUSTRALIA DURING THE WAR.

> Ernest Scott | 21cm x 13.5cm | Burgundy Red Cloth Hardback | Gilt | plain paper dust jacket + card mailing box | xxx + 922pp | 13 appendices | 1 map | 67 photographs | Angus and Robertson Ltd | 1936 | English Text.
>
> The University of Queensland Press republished this volume in 1989.
>
> This volume can be viewed as a 'pdf file' on the Australian War Memorial world wide web site:
>
> *http://www.awm.gov.au/histories/first_world_war/volume.asp?levelID=67897*

OFFICIAL HISTORY OF AUSTRALIA IN THE WAR OF 1914-1918. VOLUME XII PHOTOGRAPHIC RECORD.

> *Captain* G. H. Wilkins M.C., *Captain* J. F. Hurley, *Lieutenant* H. F. Baldwin and *Lieutenant* J. P. Campbell. | 21cm x 13.5cm | Burgundy Red Cloth Hardback | Gilt | plain paper dust jacket + card mailing box | xi + 672pp | 753 photographs | Angus and Robertson Ltd | 1923 | English Text.
>
> Note: This volume has not been republished by the University of Queensland Press nor has the the Australian War Memorial reproduced it on their web site.
>
> All of the "**Official History of Australia in the War of 1914-1918**" volumes including "**Official History of the Australian Army Medical Services in the War of 1914-1918**" were produced with exactly the same volume width (5.8cm) even though the number of pages varied from just over 400 to well over 1000. The method to achieve this consistency in volume width was to use different paper weights (thicknesses) - namely thicker paper for the volumes with the least number of pages, then reducing the paper weight as the number of pages increased in the larger volumes.

Medicals Activities;

OFFICIAL HISTORY OF THE AUSTRALIAN ARMY MEDICAL SERVICES IN THE WAR OF 1914-1918, VOLUME I; PARTS I, II and III NON WESTERN FRONT.

> *Colonel* A.G. [Arthur Graham] Butler [*MD*] | 21cm x 13.5cm | Dark Blue Cloth Hardback | Gilt | plain paper dust jacket + card mailing box | xxvi + 873pp | 5 appendices | 24 maps | 117 photographs | 8 diagrams and sketches | Australian War Memorial | 1930 | English Text.
>
> The three parts were published in one volume.
>
> This volume can be viewed as a 'pdf file' on the Australian War Memorial world wide web site:
>
> *http://www.awm.gov.au/histories/first_world_war/volume.asp?levelID=67898*

OFFICIAL HISTORY OF THE AUSTRALIAN ARMY MEDICAL SERVICES IN THE WAR OF 1914-1918, VOLUME II WESTERN FRONT.

> *Colonel* A.G. [Arthur Graham] Butler [*MD*] and *Colonel* R.M. [Rupert Major] Downes [*MD*] | 21cm x 13.5cm | Dark Blue Cloth Hardback | Gilt | plain paper dust jacket + card mailing box | xvi + 1010pp | 14 appendices | 13 maps | 92 photographs | 37 diagrams and sketches | Australian War Memorial | 1940 | English Text.
>
> This volume can be viewed as a 'pdf file' on the Australian War Memorial world wide web site:
>
> *http://www.awm.gov.au/histories/first_world_war/volume.asp?levelID=67899*

OFFICIAL HISTORY OF THE AUSTRALIAN ARMY MEDICAL SERVICES IN THE WAR OF 1914-1918, VOLUME III SPECIAL PROBLEMS.

> *Colonel* A.G. [Arthur Graham] Butler [*MD*], *Colonel* F.A. [Frederick Arthur] Maguire [*MD*] and *Captain* R.W. [Raphael West] Cilento [*MD*] | 21cm x 13.5cm | Dark Blue Cloth

Hardback | Gilt | plain paper dust jacket + card mailing box | xxvi + 1103pp | 69 photographs | Australian War Memorial | 1943 | English Text.

This volume can be viewed as a 'pdf file' on the Australian War Memorial world wide web site:

http://www.awm.gov.au/histories/first_world_war/volume.asp?levelID=67900

Austro-Hungarian Official Histories

The Austria-Hungary official histories were written by the authority of the various historical departments as follows: the navy's, Anregung des Marine-Verbandes vom Kriegsarchiv [Marinearchiv] (*Naval Federation of the War Archives [Naval Archives]*) and the army's, Österreichischen Bundesministerium für Heereswesen und vom Kriegsarchiv (*Austrian Federal Ministry for Army Affairs and of the War Archives*).

In the case of the Marinearchiv *Linienschiffleutnant außer Dienst* H. H. Sokol was employed to write the naval history.

The Österreichischen Bundesministerium für Heereswesen und vom Kriegsarchiv employed mainly ex-members of the Austrian General Staff to write the Österreich-Ungarns Letzter Krieg 1914-1918 under the general editorship of *General der Infantrie Doktor* Edmund von Glaise-Horstenau (also an ex-member of the Austrian General Staff and the director of the Bundesministerium.[6]) Each volume was written by a team of historians, each specialising in various aspects of the individual history (mobilisation, eastern front, southern front, Balkan front etc.). With so many ex-members of the General Staff writing the histories there was to some degree a corruption of the histories to show the Austrian General Staff, or individuals (in some cases the author himself) in a more favourable light. Certainly the former Chief of the General Staff of the Austro-Hungarian Army in 1914, Feldmarschall Franz Graf Conrad von Hötzendorf's reputation was defended to the utmost by the official historians.

Naval Operations;

Österreich-Ungarns Seekrieg 1914-1918 Lieferung I. (*Austro-Hungary's Sea War 1914-1918 Part I.*)

> *Linienschiffleutnant außer Dienst* H. H. [Hans Hugo] Sokol I 25cm x 17.5cm I Grey Paper Soft Back I 184pp I 4 photograph I 4 maps I Amalthea-Verlag I 1930 I German Text.

Österreich-Ungarns Seekrieg 1914-1918 Lieferung I Beilagen. (*Austro-Hungary's Sea War 1914-1918 Part I Supplements.* [Appendices/Loose Maps])

> *Linienschiffleutnant außer Dienst* H. H. [Hans Hugo] Sokol (cartographer Theodor Braun) I 25cm x 17.5cm I White Paper Soft Back I 60pp I 3 appendices I 3 maps I Amalthea-Verlag I 1930 I German Text.
> Pre May 1915 - Pre war planing and development for war either with Italy as an ally or Italy as an enemy.

Österreich-Ungarns Seekrieg 1914-1918 Lieferung II. (*Austro-Hungary's Sea War 1914-1918 Part II.*)

> *Linienschiffleutnant außer Dienst* H. H. [Hans Hugo] Sokol I 25cm x 17.5cm I Grey Paper Soft Back I 146pp I 2 maps I 8 photograph I Amalthea-Verlag I 1930 I German Text.

Österreich-Ungarns Seekrieg 1914-1918 Lieferung II Beilagen. (*Austro-Hungary's Sea War 1914-1918 Part II Supplements.* [Appendices/Loose Maps])

> *Linienschiffleutnant außer Dienst* H. H. Sokol (cartographer Theodor Braun) I 25cm x 17.5cm I White Paper Soft Back I 10pp I 3 appendices I 4 maps I Amalthea-Verlag I 1930 I German Text.
> Naval operations during the period May 1915 – May 1917 and submarine Operations before March 1916.

Österreich-Ungarns Seekrieg 1914-1918 Lieferung III. (*Austro-Hungary's Sea War 1914-1918 Part III.*)

> *Linienschiffleutnant außer Dienst* H. H. [Hans Hugo] Sokol I 25cm x 17.5cm I Grey Paper Soft Back I 148pp I 4 photograph I Amalthea-Verlag I 1931 I German Text.

Österreich-Ungarns Seekrieg 1914-1918 Lieferung III Beilagen. (*Austro-Hungary's Sea War 1914-1918 Part III Supplements.* [Appendices/Loose Maps])

---

[6] Edumnd von Glaise-Horstenau become one of the first Austrian Nazis well before the Anschluß. He became the second in command of the Austrian Nazi Party and a Austrain government minister without portfolio. After the Anschluß he joined the Wehrmacht and during the Second World War took a leading military-administrative role in the occupation of Yugoslavia. He was arrested and sent for trial at Nürnberg (Nuremburg) and in 1946 whilst being held at Langwasser Military Camp, Nürnberg he commited suicide.

Linienschiffleutnant außer Dienst H. H. [Hans Hugo] Sokol (cartographer Theodor Braun) | 25cm x 17.5cm | White Paper Soft Back | 8pp | 2 appendices | 2 maps | Amalthea-Verlag | 1931 | German Text.

Naval operations during the period May 1917 – November 1917 and submarine Operations March 1916 – May 1917.

Österreich-Ungarns Seekrieg 1914-1918 Lieferung IV. (*Austro-Hungary's Sea War 1914-1918 Part IV.*)

Linienschiffleutnant außer Dienst H. H. [Hans Hugo] Sokol | 25cm x 17.5cm | Grey Paper Soft Back | c156pp | c1 map | c4 photographs | Amalthea-Verlag | 1932 | German Text.

Österreich-Ungarns Seekrieg 1914-1918 Lieferung IV Beilagen. (*Austro-Hungary's Sea War 1914-1918 Part IV Supplements.* [Appendices/Loose Maps])

Linienschiffleutnant außer Dienst H. H. [Hans Hugo] Sokol (cartographer Theodor Braun) | 25cm x 17.5cm | White Paper Soft Back | c13pp | 3 appendices | c3 maps | Amalthea-Verlag | 1932 | German Text.

Submarine Operations May 1917 – November 1918.

Österreich-Ungarns Seekrieg 1914-1918 Lieferung V. (*Austro-Hungary's Sea War 1914-1918 Part V.*)

Linienschiffleutnant außer Dienst H. H. [Hans Hugo] Sokol | 25cm x 17.5cm | Grey Paper Soft Back | c157pp | c1 map | c4 photographs | Amalthea-Verlag | 1933 | German Text.

Österreich-Ungarns Seekrieg 1914-1918 Lieferung V Titelseite/Inhatsverzeichnis/ Verzeichnis der Abkürzungen/Vorwort/ Beilagen. (*Austro-Hungary's Sea War 1914-1918 Part V Title-Page/Contents/Abbreviations/Foreword/Supplements.*)

Linienschiffleutnant außer Dienst H. H. [Hans Hugo] Sokol (cartographer Theodor Braun) | 25cm x 17.5cm | White Paper Soft Back | xvi + c13pp | c1 map | Amalthea-Verlag | 1933 | German Text.

Naval Air Operations and Operations on the River Danube.

The "Österreich-Ungarns Seekrieg 1914-1918" was published in instalments, each part consisting of a text section and a separate supplement. Judging by the size of each of the first three parts compared with the overall size of the history, it is believed that it was published in five parts, each of approximately 200 pages. The supplements consisted of Appendices and loose Maps, except for the last part which consisted of the final Appendices and the 'book's preamble' as listed above. The text sections were produced in paperback format for later binding. Since this amounted to just under 800 pages in all, they were often bound in multiple volumes, even though the page numbering for all the parts were consecutive. A reprint was published in 1967 as two hardback volumes and a map folder, and so based on this confusion, it has often been stated incorrectly that when originally published, this set consisted of two volumes and that it was published in 1933, the date shown on the title page. Note that when complete the "**Österreich-Ungarns Seekrieg 1914-1918**" consists of the following:

xvi + 791pp of text + 104pp of appendices | 11 appendices | 12 maps | 24 photographs

The complete volume was translated into French by R. Jouan with a preface by the French official naval historian *capitaine de frégate* Adolphe Laurens. It was abridged and published by Éditions Payot under the title "**La marine Austro-Hongroise dans la guerre mondiale, 1914-1918**"

Military Operations;

ÖSTERREICH-UNGARNS LETZTER KRIEG 1914-1918 BAND I. (*Austro-Hungary's Last War 1914-1918 Volume I.*)

Doktor Edmund Glaise-Horstenau (editor); Eduard Czegka, Maximilan Hoen, Rudolf Kiszling, Viktor Meduna-Riedburg, Eduard Steinz, Ernst Wisshaupt and Georg Zöbl. | 23.5cm x 17 5cm | Light Blue Cloth Hard Back | Gilt | xx + 834pp | Verlag der Militarwissenschaftlichen Mitteillingen | 1929 [1930/31] | German Text.

There was a print run of 6000 copies. A revised second edition published in 1931 had a print run of 2000 copies.

This volume can be viewed on the Internet Archive world wide web as a 'pdf file': *http://www.archive.org/details/sterreichungar01austuoft*

The first volume of the "**Österreich-Ungarns Letzter Krieg 1914-1918**" covers the pre war military planing against Russia and Serbia, and the posibility of war against Italy. Followed by the opening military campaigns of 1914. It also includes an Order of Battle of the Austro-Hungarian Army in August 1914.

According to Graydon A. Tunstall in his "**Planning for War Against Russia and Serbia**" (Columbia Universty Press, 1993), the "**Österreich-Ungarns Letzter Krieg 1914-1918 Band I**" was published in 1929, but had to be withdrawn, and had to have some of its sections rewritten. This volume deals in part with the pre-war planning and the Austro-Hungarian mobilization at the start of the War. The latter part being written by *Major* Emil Ratzenhofer although his name does not appear in the list of authors. As Ratzenhofer was an ex-leading member of the Austro-Hungarian Army's General Staff's Railway Bureau, he covered the work of the Railway Bureau with "scanty, insufficient, and faulty" information and was required to rewrite this section. It was republished in 1931 although the copyright date is shown as 1930.

ÖSTERREICH-UNGARNS LETZTER KRIEG 1914-1918 BAND I BEILAGEN. (*Austro-Hungary's Last War 1914-1918 Volume I Supplements.* [Maps])

Doktor Edmund Glaise-Horstenau (editor) | 23.5cm x 17 5cm | Light Blue Cloth Hard Back | Gilt | 27 maps | 56 diagrams/sketches | Verlag der Militarwissenschaftlichen Mitteilingen | 1929 [1930/31] | German Text.

ÖSTERREICH-UNGARNS LETZTER KRIEG 1914-1918 BAND II. (*Austro-Hungary's Last War 1914-1918 Volume II.*)

Doktor Edmund Glaise-Horstenau (editor); Josef Brauner, Eduard Czegka, Jaromir Diakow, Friedrich Franek, Rudolf Kiszling, Eduard Steinz and Ernst Wisshaupt. | 23.5cm x 17 5cm | Light Blue Cloth Hard Back | Gilt | xvi + 814pp | Verlag der Militarwissenschaftlichen Mitteilingen | 1931 | German Text.

There was a print run of 7400 copies.

This volume can be viewed on the Internet Archive world wide web as a 'pdf file':

http://www.archive.org/details/sterreichungar02austuoft

The second volume of this set covers the military campaigns in the first half of 1915.

ÖSTERREICH-UNGARNS LETZTER KRIEG 1914-1918 BAND II BEILAGEN. (*Austro-Hungary's Last War 1914-1918 Supplements.* [Maps])

Doktor Edmund Glaise-Horstenau (editor) | 23.5cm x 17 5cm | Light Blue Cloth Hard Back | Gilt | 40 maps | 36 diagrams/sketches | Verlag der Militarwissenschaftlichen Mitteilingen | 1931 | German Text.

ÖSTERREICH-UNGARNS LETZTER KRIEG 1914-1918 BAND III. (*Austro-Hungary's Last War 1914-1918 Volume III.*)

Doktor Edmund Glaise-Horstenau (editor); Josef Brauner, Rudolf Kiszling, Franz Mühlhofer, Ernst Wisshaupt and Georg Zöbl. | 23.5cm x 17 5cm | Light Blue Cloth Hard Back | Gilt | xviii + 624pp | Verlag der Militarwissenschaftlichen Mitteilingen | 1932 | German Text.

There was a print run of 6000 copies.

This volume can be viewed on the Internet Archive world wide web as a 'pdf file':

http://www.archive.org/details/sterreichungar03austuoft

The Third volume of this set covers the military campaigns of in the second half 1915.

ÖSTERREICH-UNGARNS LETZTER KRIEG 1914-1918 BAND III BEILAGEN. (*Austro-Hungary's Last War 1914-1918 Volume III Supplements.* [Maps])

Doktor Edmund Glaise-Horstenau (editor) | 23.5cm x 17 5cm | Light Blue Cloth Hard Back | Gilt | 32 maps | 20 diagrams/sketches | Verlag der Militarwissenschaftlichen Mitteilingen | 1932 | German Text.

ÖSTERREICH-UNGARNS LETZTER KRIEG 1914-1918 BAND IV. (*Austro-Hungary's Last War 1914-1918 Volume IV.*)

Doktor Edmund Glaise-Horstenau (editor); Josef Brauner, Eduard Czegka, Jaromir Diakow, Friedrich Franek, Walther Heydendorff, Rudolf Kiszling, Franz Mühlhofer, Ernst Wisshaupt and Georg Zöbl. | 23.5cm x 17 5cm | Light Blue Cloth Hard Back | Gilt | xviii + 747pp | Verlag der Militarwissenschaftlichen Mitteilingen | 1933 | German Text.

There was a print run of 5200 copies.

This volume can be viewed on the Internet Archive world wide web as a 'pdf file':

http://www.archive.org/details/sterreichungar04austuoft

The fourth volume of this set covers the military campaigns in the first half of 1916.

ÖSTERREICH-UNGARNS LETZTER KRIEG 1914-1918 BAND IV BEILAGEN. (*Austro-Hungary's Last War 1914-1918 Volume IV Supplements.* [Maps])

> *Doktor* Edmund Glaise-Horstenau (editor); | 23.5cm x 17 5cm | Light Blue Cloth Hard Back | Gilt | 68 maps | 5 diagrams/sketches | Verlag der Militarwissenschaftlichen Mitteillingen | 1933 | German Text.

ÖSTERREICH-UNGARNS LETZTER KRIEG 1914-1918 BAND V. (*Austro-Hungary's Last War 1914-1918 Volume V.*)

> *Doktor* Edmund Glaise-Horstenau (editor); Josef Brauner, Eduard Czegka, Walther Heydendorff, Rudolf Kiszling, Carl Klumpner and Ernst Wisshaupt. | 23.5cm x 17 5cm | Light Blue Cloth Hard Back | Gilt | xviii + 792pp | Verlag der Militarwissenschaftlichen Mitteillingen | 1934 | German Text.
>
> There was a print run of 5000 copies.
>
> This volume can be viewed on the Internet Archive world wide web as a 'pdf file':
> *http://www.archive.org/details/sterreichungar05austuoft*
> The fifth volume of this set covers the military campaigns in the second half of 1916.

ÖSTERREICH-UNGARNS LETZTER KRIEG 1914-1918 BAND V BEILAGEN. (*Austro-Hungary's Last War 1914-1918 Volume V Supplements.* [Maps])

> *Doktor* Edmund Glaise-Horstenau (editor) | 23.5cm x 17 5cm | Light Blue Cloth Hard Back | Gilt | 67 maps | Verlag der Militarwissenschaftlichen Mitteillingen | 1934 | German Text.

ÖSTERREICH-UNGARNS LETZTER KRIEG 1914-1918 BAND VI. (*Austro-Hungary's Last War 1914-1918 Volume VI.*)

> *Doktor* Edmund Glaise-Horstenau (editor); Eduard Czegka, Friedrick Franek, Walther Heydendorff, Rudolf Kiszling, Carl Klumpner, Ernst Wisshaupt and Georg Zöbl. | 23.5cm x 17 5cm | Light Blue Cloth Hard Back | Gilt | xvi + 792pp | Verlag der Militarwissenschaftlichen Mitteillingen | 1936 | German Text.
>
> There was a print run of 4800 copies.
>
> This volume can be viewed on the Internet Archive world wide web as a 'pdf file':
> *http://www.archive.org/details/sterreichungar06austuoft*
> The sixth volume of this set covers the military campaigns of 1917

ÖSTERREICH-UNGARNS LETZTER KRIEG 1914-1918 BAND VI BEILAGEN. (*Austro-Hungary's Last War 1914-1918 Volume VI Supplements.* [Maps])

> *Doktor* Edmund Glaise-Horstenau (editor) | 23.5cm x 17 5cm | Light Blue Cloth Hard Back | Gilt | 78 maps | Verlag der Militarwissenschaftlichen Mitteillingen | 1934 | German Text.

ÖSTERREICH-UNGARNS LETZTER KRIEG 1914-1918 BAND VII. (*Austro-Hungary's Last War 1914-1918 Volume VII.*)

> *Doktor* Edmund Glaise von Horstenau and Rudolf Kiszling (editors), Eduard Czegka, Jaromir Diakow, Maximilan Ehnl, Friedrick Franek, Walther Heydendorff, Franz Mühlhofer, Rudolf Prochaska, Ernst Wisshaupt and Georg Zöbl. | 23.5cm x 17 5cm | Light Blue Cloth Hard Back | Gilt | xix + 856pp | Verlag der Militarwissenschaftlichen Mitteillingen | 1938 | German Text.
>
> There was a print run of 4600 copies.
>
> This volume cannot be viewed on the Internet Archive world wide web as a 'pdf file':
> The seventh volume of this set covers the military campaigns of 1918

ÖSTERREICH-UNGARNS LETZTER KRIEG 1914-1918 BAND VII BEILAGEN. (*Austro-Hungary's Last War 1914-1918 Volume VII Supplements.* [Maps])

> *Doktor* Edmund Glaise von Horstenau (editor) | 23.5cm x 17 5cm | Light Blue Cloth Hard Back | Gilt | 67 maps | Verlag der Militarwissenschaftlichen Mitteillingen | 1938 | German Text.

ÖSTERREICH-UNGARNS LETZTER KRIEG 1914-1918 REGISTER-BAND. (*Austro-Hungary's Last War 1914-1918 Index.*)

> *Doktor* Edmund Glaise von Horstenau (editor) | 23.5cm x 17 5cm | Light Blue Cloth Hard Back | Gilt | xiii + 330pp | Verlag der Militarwissenschaftlichen Mitteillingen | 1938 | German Text.
>
> There was a print run of 4000 copies.
>
> *Doktor* Edmund Glaise von Horstenau, the director of the Österreichischen Bundesministerium für Heereswesen und vom Kriegsarchiv and general editor of the "**Österreich-Ungarns Letzter Krieg 1914-1918**", had the "von" removed from his name on the title pages of the earlier volumes, but had it re-inserted for the 1938 Band VII and the Register-Band.

There were ten Supplements published in addition to the "**Österreich-Ungarns Letzter Krieg 1914-1918**" between 1930 and 1937 as follows:

Erganzungsheft 1 zum Werke "Österreich-Ungarns Letzter Krieg". (*Supplemental booklet 1 to the Work "Austro-Hungary's Last War".*)..1930
Erganzungsheft 2 zum Werke "Österreich-Ungarns Letzter Krieg". (*Supplemental booklet 2 to the Work "Austro-Hungary's Last War".*)..1931
Erganzungsheft 3 zum Werke "Österreich-Ungarns Letzter Krieg". (*Supplemental booklet 3 to the Work "Austro-Hungary's Last War".*)..1932
Erganzungsheft 4 zum Werke "Österreich-Ungarns Letzter Krieg". (*Supplemental booklet 4 to the Work "Austro-Hungary's Last War".*)....................................... c1932
Erganzungsheft 5 zum Werke "Österreich-Ungarns Letzter Krieg". (*Supplemental booklet 5 to the Work "Austro-Hungary's Last War".*)..1933
Erganzungsheft 6 zum Werke "Österreich-Ungarns Letzter Krieg". (*Supplemental booklet 6 to the Work "Austro-Hungary's Last War".*)....................................... c1933
Erganzungsheft 7 zum Werke "Österreich-Ungarns Letzter Krieg". (*Supplemental booklet 7 to the Work "Austro-Hungary's Last War".*)....................................... c1933
Erganzungsheft 8 zum Werke "Österreich-Ungarns Letzter Krieg". (*Supplemental booklet 8 to the Work "Austro-Hungary's Last War".*)..1933
Erganzungsheft 9 zum Werke "Österreich-Ungarns Letzter Krieg". (*Supplemental booklet 9 to the Work "Austro-Hungary's Last War".*)..1934
Erganzungsheft 10 zum Werke "Österreich-Ungarns Letzter Krieg". (*Supplemental booklet 10 to the Work "Austro-Hungary's Last War".*)..1937

Belgian Official Histories

All the Belgian official histories were written by members of the Service Historique des Forces Armée (*Belgian Army Historical Service*), except for the naval history, which was authorized by the Ministère de la Défense nationale (*Ministry of National Defence*).

General [including Diplomatic and Military];

LA BELGIQUE ET LA GUERRE TOME I: LA VIE MATÉRIELLE DE LA BELGIQUE DURANT LA GUERRE MONDIALE. (*Belgium and the War, Book I: Belgium's Material Life during the World War.*)
> Georges Rency [pseud. van Albert Stassart] | 25cm x 32cm | Bordeaux Red Hardback | Paper Dust Jacket | iv + 390pp | 279 photographs | 3 colour illustrations | Henri Bertels | 1920 | French Text.

LA BELGIQUE ET LA GUERRE TOME II: L'INVASION ALLEMANDE. (*Belgium and the War, Book II: The German Invasion.*).
> Joseph Cuvelier | 25cm x 32cm | Bordeaux Red Hardback | Paper Dust Jacket | ii + 405pp | 9 maps | 299 photographs | Henri Bertels | 1921 | French Text.

LA BELGIQUE ET LA GUERRE TOME III: LES OPERATIONS MILITAIRES. (*Belgium and the War, Book III: Military Operations.*)
> *Staff Lieutenant Colonel* [Maurice Albert Émile] Tasnier and *Staff Major* [Raoul François Casimir] van Overstraeten | 25cm x 32cm | Bordeaux Red Hardback | Paper Dust Jacket | iv + 403 pp | 24 maps | 1 plan | 2 colour illustrations | 338 photographs | Henri Bertels | 1923 | French Text.

LA BELGIQUE ET LA GUERRE TOME IV: HISTOIRE DIPLOMATIQUE. (*Belgium and the War, Book IV: Diplomantic History.*)
> Alfred de Ridder | 25cm x 32cm | Bordeaux Red Hardback | Paper Dust Jacket | iv + 386 pp | 7 maps | 315 photographs | 2 colour illustrations | Henri Bertels | 1923 | French Text.

Naval Operations;

LES ANCETRES DE NOTRE FORCE NAVALE. (*The Origins of Our Naval Force.*)
> Louis Leconte (Ministère de la Défense Nationale) | 24cm x 16cm | Grey cloth Hardback | i + 664p | Ministère de la défense nationale | 1952

Military Operations;

DÉFENSE DE LA POSITION FORTIFIÉE DE NAMUR EN AOÛT 1914. (*Defence of the Namur Fortified Position in August 1914.*)
> Anonymous | 26cm x 16cm | paper softback | xviii + 756 pp | Imprimerie Typo de l'institut Cartographique Militaire | 1930 | French Text.
> This set is also listed as "**La défense des fortifiée de Namur, 1914**" and "**La défense des fortifiée de Namur, en août 1914**". It was authorised by the Royaume de Belgique, Ministère de la Défence Nationale. Etat-major général de l'armée. Section de l'historique.

DÉFENSE DE LA POSITION FORTIFIÉE DE NAMUR EN AOÛT 1914. (*Defence of the Namur Fortified Position in August 1914.*) [Map and photograph box]
> Anonymous | 26cm x 16cm | card folder | 22 maps | 73 photograph | Imprimerie Typo de l'institut Cartographique Militaire | 1930 | French Text.

LES CAMPAGNES COLONIALES BELGES 1914-1918. VOLUME I. INTRODUCTION, LES OPERATIONS AU CAMEROUN, LES OPERATIONS EN RHODÉSIE, LA PÉRIODE DÉFENSIVE A LA FRONTIÈRE ORIENTALE. (*The Belgian Colonial Campaigns, 1914-1918. Volume I. Introduction; The Operations in the Cameroons; The Operations in the Rhodesia; The Defensive Period on the Oriental Frontier.*)
> Anonymous (Service Historique des Forces Armée) | 23.5cm x 16cm | Beige Paper Softback | 406pp | 37 maps | 21 photographs | Imprimerie Typographique de l'Institut Cartographique Militaire | 1927 | French Text.

LES CAMPAGNES COLONIALES BELGES 1914-1918. VOLUME II. LA CAMPAGNE DE TABORA 1916. (*The Belgian Colonial Campaigns, 1914-1918. Volume II. The Tabora Campaign 1916.*)

> Anonymous (Service Historique des Forces Armée) | 23.5cm x 16cm | Beige Paper Softback | 252pp | 62 maps | 55 photographs | Imprimerie Typographique de l'Institut Cartographique Militaire | 1929 | French Text.

LES CAMPAGNES COLONIALES BELGES 1914-1918. VOLUME III. LA CAMPAGNE DE MAHENGE 1917. (*The Belgian Colonial Campaigns, 1914-1918. Volume III. The Mahenge Campaign 1917.*)

> Anonymous (Service Historique des Forces Armée) | 23.5cm x 16cm | Beige Paper Softback | 458pp | 20 maps | 16 photographs | Imprimerie Typographique de l'Institut Cartographique Militaire | 1932 | French Text.

British Official Histories

The main British official histories were written by members of the Historical Section of the Committee of Imperial Defence under the committee secretary *Lieutenant Colonel* E.Y. Daniel and the directorship of *Brigadier General Sir* James Edmonds. Edmonds also acted as the general editor for the military volumes.

A second committee known as the Committee for Control was set up to interact between the Historical Section and the various interested government departments including the Treasury, the Foreign Office, the India Office, the Admiralty, the General Staff of the British Army, the War Office and the Air Ministry. Apart from committee members, individuals were occasionally asked to attend the committee meetings, one such being [*Sir*] Winston S. Churchill who attended the meetings covering the Gallipoli volumes.

The volumes were normally the cooperation between a researcher-compiler and an author who wrote the narration of the volumes. *Captain* C.T. Atkinson did much of the compiling for the military volumes starting work on collecting material as early as 1915, whilst Edmonds himself wrote a large number of the military volumes.

The military volumes were in the main written by ex-army staff officers whilst the Naval and Air Force histories were written by civilian academics. The Munitions volumes were written by civil servants who were working for or had worked for the Ministry of Munitions.

History of the Great War, Based on Official Documents - By direction of the Historical Section of the Committee of Imperial Defence. [7]:

Chronology;

HISTORY OF THE WAR BASED ON OFFICIAL DOCUMENTS BY DIRECTION OF THE HISTORICAL SECTION OF THE COMMITTEE OF IMPERIAL DEFENCE - PRINCIPAL EVENTS 1914-1918.
> Anonymous [*Major* Henry Terence Skinner, *Captain* Harry Fitz Maurice Stacke et al.] | 33cm x 21cm | Light Blue Cloth Hardback | Gilt | 421pp | His Majesty's Stationery Office. | 1922 | English Text.
> There was a print run of 1000 copies.
> Referred to on the spine as 'List of Principal Events 1914-1918'
> This volume was republished as a softback (grey paper wraps) by The London Stamp Exchange Ltd, in 1987. The Naval and Military Press Ltd republished it as a softback (illustrated wraps) edition in 1995 and again in 2001.

Naval Operations;

HISTORY OF THE WAR BASED ON OFFICIAL DOCUMENTS BY DIRECTION OF THE HISTORICAL SECTION OF THE COMMITTEE OF IMPERIAL DEFENCE - NAVAL OPERATIONS, VOLUME I, TO THE BATTLE OF THE FALKLANDS DECEMBER 1914.
> *Sir* Julian S. [Stafford] Corbett | 22.5cm x 16cm | Midnight Blue Hardback | Gilt | White Paper Dust Jacket | xiv + 470pp | 4 appendices | 13maps | 5 sketches (including 4 ship silhouettes) | Longmans, Green and Co. | 1920 (1938)[8] | English Text.

---

[7] The titles of the British Official History are shown on the front of the dust jackets and on the title pages, generally as 'History of the Great War, Based on Official Documents - By direction of the Historical Section of the Committee of Imperial Defence' followed by the detailed description of the particular book (for example; 'Military Operations – France and Belgium, 1917 – The German Retreat to the Hindenburg Line and the Battles of Arras.') However the titles are shown on the spines in a simplified form as 'Official History of the War' followed by a simplified description (for example on the above case it is shown as - 'Military Operations – France and Belgium 1917 *', where the * represents the volume number of the period covered; in this case Part 1). I have used the full title for this listing.

[8] The date of the publication of the "revised" editions of Naval Operations volumes I and III are shown in parenthesis.

This volume "**Naval Operations Volume I**" was up-dated and corrected to information gained from new sources (mainly from the German official history) published since the original publication date and was republished in 1938 as the second edition. It had an increase in the number of pages in the introduction to xix which included a Preface to Revised Edition. The revisions mainly related to the Heligoland Bight Action in Chapter VII and the cruise of the German raider S.M.S. Berlin in Chapter XVII. The revised edition of this text volume was issued with a light blue paper dust jacket.

The Imperial War Museum Department of Printed Books in association with the Battery Press republished the 'revised' edition of this volume in 1997, without a dust jacket. The Imperial War Museum Department of Printed Books in association with the Naval and Military Press Ltd republished it again in 2003 as a soft back.

This volume includes the escape of the German ships - S.M.S. Goeben and S.M.S. Breslau; the Heligoland Blight Action; The sinkings of the British ships - H.M.S. Cressy, H.M.S. Hogue, H.M.S. Aboukir, H.M.S. Hawke and H.M.S. Audacious; The defence of Antwerp; the hunt for the German cruisers – S.M.S. Karlsruhe, S.M.S. Emden and S.M.S. Königsberg; the battles of Coronel and the Falklands; and the initial mopping up of the German Colonies in Africa and in the Far East.

HISTORY OF THE WAR BASED ON OFFICIAL DOCUMENTS BY DIRECTION OF THE HISTORICAL SECTION OF THE COMMITTEE OF IMPERIAL DEFENCE - NAVAL OPERATIONS, VOLUME I. [Map Box.]

Sir Julian S. [Stafford] Corbett | 22.5cm x 16cm | Midnight Blue Hardback | Gilt | White Paper Dust Jacket | 18 maps | Longmans, Green and Co. | 1920 (1938) | English Text.

Based on the information used in the text volume, maps 9 and 10 were replaced by a single map showing the cruise of the German raider S.M.S. Berlin, thereby reducing the number of maps in this map case to 17. This new map was given both number 9 and the number 10 thereby allowing the references within the text volume to remain unaltered. This map case was issued with a light blue paper dust jacket.

HISTORY OF THE WAR BASED ON OFFICIAL DOCUMENTS BY DIRECTION OF THE HISTORICAL SECTION OF THE COMMITTEE OF IMPERIAL DEFENCE - NAVAL OPERATIONS, VOLUME II. [Text and Maps.]

Sir Julian S. [Stafford] Corbett | 22.5cm x 16cm | Midnight Blue Hardback | Gilt | White Paper Dust Jacket | xi + 448pp | 3 appendices | 17 maps | Longmans, Green and Co. | 1921 (1939) | English Text.

Like **Volume I** a revised edition of "**Naval Operations Volume II**" was republished in 1939 to include fresh information from new sources (mainly from the German official history and the British official history "**Military Operations, Gallipoli**"). The second edition was issued with a light blue paper dust jacket. In 1997 the Imperial War Museum Department of Printed Books in association with the Battery Press republished this volume without a dust jacket. The Imperial War Museum Department of Printed Books in association with the Naval and Military Press Ltd republished it again in 2003 as a soft back.

This volume covers the period January to May 1915 and includes the German raids on the East Coast of Britian, the Battle of the Dogger Bank; the destruction of the Dresden; the failed attempt at forcing the Dardanelles, and the loss of the Lusitania. It includes large folded maps in a fodder attached to the front and rear covers.

HISTORY OF THE WAR BASED ON OFFICIAL DOCUMENTS BY DIRECTION OF THE HISTORICAL SECTION OF THE COMMITTEE OF IMPERIAL DEFENCE - NAVAL OPERATIONS, VOLUME III.

Sir Julian S. [Stafford] Corbett | 22.5cm x 16cm | Midnight Blue Hardback | Gilt | White Paper Dust Jacket | xiv + 470pp | 9 appendices | 7 maps | Longmans, Green and Co. | 1923 (1940) | English Text.

This volume "**Naval Operations Volume III**" was revised and republished in 1940. Before it was first published, as was normal practice, the original draft was issued to the Admiralty and key personages (including *Admiral of the Fleet, the Right Honourable, the Earl* Beatty (David Beatty), who at that time was the First Sea Lord of the Admiralty, and *Admiral of the Fleet the Viscount* Jellicoe (John Jellicoe), the former commander of the Grand Fleet at the time of Jutland), for review and comment. During this period there was still an ongoing acrimonious debate over the failures of the Royal Navy during the Battle of Jutland between Beatty's supporters and Jellicoe's supporters within the Admiralty. According to *Captain* J.E.T. Harper, changes were then made to the text based on the comments received to the original draft and imply that these changes were at the request of Beatty. Some of those changes were directly related to the performance of Beatty during the Battle of Jutland.[9]

The 1923 text was then in 1940 up-dated and corrected to information gained from new sources published mainly from the German official history. There was no attempt to revert the revised first edition back to the original proof draft, thereby removing Beatty's alterations. When republished this volume had an increase in the number of pages in the introduction to xvi, and two additional pages were inserted into the narration between pages 326 and 327. The page numbers in the new edition were not changed with the two new pages being given numbers 326a and 326b, allowing the page numbers that followed to remain the same as in the original edition. However the number of maps was reduced to 6. The revised edition of this text volume was issued with a light blue paper dust jacket.

The Imperial War Museum Department of Printed Books in association with the Battery Press republished the 1940 revised volume in 1995 as a hard back without a dust jacket.

The Imperial War Museum Department of Printed Books in association with the Naval and Military Press Ltd republished it again in 2003 as a soft back.

This volume covers the period May 1915 to June 1916 and includes the continuation of the Dardanelles Campaign up to its conclusion with the evacuation of the British forces from the Gallipoli Peninsula; the destruction of the Königsberg; the Arabic and Baralong incidents; the Irish Rebellion; the air raid on the Scheswig Air Base and the Battle of Jutland.

HISTORY OF THE WAR BASED ON OFFICIAL DOCUMENTS BY DIRECTION OF THE HISTORICAL SECTION OF THE COMMITTEE OF IMPERIAL DEFENCE - NAVAL OPERATIONS, VOLUME III. [Map. Box.]

Sir Julian S. [Stafford] Corbett | 22.5cm x 16cm | Midnight Blue Hardback | Gilt | White Paper Dust Jacket | 46 maps | Longmans, Green and Co. | 1920 (1940) | English Text.

This map case was issued with a light blue paper dust jacket.

HISTORY OF THE WAR BASED ON OFFICIAL DOCUMENTS BY DIRECTION OF THE HISTORICAL SECTION OF THE COMMITTEE OF IMPERIAL DEFENCE - NAVAL OPERATIONS, VOLUME IV.

Sir Henry [John] Newbolt | 22.5cm x 16cm | Midnight Blue Hardback | Gilt | White Paper Dust Jacket | xiii + 412pp | 2 appendices | 11 maps | Longmans, Green and Co. | 1928 | English Text.

This volume "**Naval Operations Volume IV**" covers the period June 1916 to April 1917 and includes mainly the German submarine campaign and the German surface raiders' campaigns. It includes the sinking of H.M.S. Hampshire and the death of Lord Kitchener; the cruises of S.M.S. Moewe, S.M.S. Leopard, S.M.S. Seeadler and S.M.S. Wolf; the naval war in Africa, the Middle East and the Mediterranean; the evacuation of the Serbian Army and the impact of the war on Greece.

Unfortunately Sir Julian S. Corbett died before he could complete the Naval Operations set. Sir Henry Newbolt was therefore enlisted to complete volumes IV and V.

The Imperial War Museum Department of Printed Books in association with the Battery Press republished this volume in 1996 without a dust jacket. The Imperial War Museum

---

[9] J.E.T. Harper R.N. was one of the original proof readers who high-lighted in his copy of the first edition the changes between the proof copy and the published edition. All of his annotations are related to the Battle of Jutland chapters only – Chapters XVI through to XXI. He stated on the opening page of Chapter XVI (page 313) the following:

> "Very few of the alterations were made by Admiralty request, but were made because facts could not always be as deductions. As the account now stands it is greatly impaired, the original was not worthy of Corbett as it shows some bias. The altered wording however puts Beatty's actions in a better light than Corbett considered justified."

Assuming Harper's annotation are true, then there were a number of what appear to be minor additions, deletions and alterations in wording that when added together certainly put Beatty into a much more favourable light, for example: the sentence in the proof copy (page 365) "Thus the passage across the battle front to which Admiral Beatty was committed in his keenness to keep a grip on his own particular adversary spoilt a promising opening to the action." was replaced in the published edition by "Thus the enforced passage of Admiral Beatty across the battle front, due to the sudden appearance at the moment of contact of the enemy battle fleet on an unexpected bearing, which necessitated deployment on the port wing, spoiled a promising opening to the action.".

Department of Printed Books in association with the Naval and Military Press Ltd republished it again in 2003 as a soft back.

HISTORY OF THE WAR BASED ON OFFICIAL DOCUMENTS BY DIRECTION OF THE HISTORICAL SECTION OF THE COMMITTEE OF IMPERIAL DEFENCE - NAVAL OPERATIONS, VOLUME IV. [Map. Box.]

Sir Henry [John] Newbolt I 22.5cm x 16cm I Midnight Blue Hardback I Gilt I White Paper Dust Jacket I 12 maps I Longmans, Green and Co. I 1928 I English Text.

In the Map Case of "**Naval Operations Volume IV**" maps 12 and 13 were not included with the note "will be included in the next volumes" placed next to the map numbers in the map index. The maps were not given any description and it is therefore not known if they were included in the following volume. However on reviewing the dates of the maps in the later volume against the periods covered by the two volumes concerned (volumes IV and V), it appears that they were indeed not included. Therefore, assuming that the maps were not included with the later volume, it is not known what they were to be about.

HISTORY OF THE WAR BASED ON OFFICIAL DOCUMENTS BY DIRECTION OF THE HISTORICAL SECTION OF THE COMMITTEE OF IMPERIAL DEFENCE - NAVAL OPERATIONS, VOLUME V.

Sir Henry [John] Newbolt I 22.5cm x 16cm I Midnight Blue Hardback I Gilt I Light Blue Paper Dust Jacket I xx + 452pp I 11 appendices I 11 maps I Longmans, Green and Co. I 1931 I English Text.

This volume "**Naval Operations Volume V**" covers the period April 1917 to November 1918 and includes the continuation of the war against the German submarine campaign including: the introduction of the Convoy System; the laying of the Northern barrage and the blocking expeditions against Zeebrugge and Ostend.

The Imperial War Museum Department of Printed Books in association with the Battery Press republished this volume in 1996 without a dust jacket. The Imperial War Museum Department of Printed Books in association with the Naval and Military Press Ltd republished it again in 2003 as a soft back.

HISTORY OF THE WAR BASED ON OFFICIAL DOCUMENTS BY DIRECTION OF THE HISTORICAL SECTION OF THE COMMITTEE OF IMPERIAL DEFENCE - NAVAL OPERATIONS, VOLUME V. [Map Box.]

Sir Henry [John] Newbolt I 22.5cm x 16cm I Midnight Blue Hardback I Gilt I Light Blue Paper Dust Jacket I 31 maps I Longmans, Green and Co. I 1931 I English Text.

Seaborne Trade Activities;

HISTORY OF THE WAR BASED ON OFFICIAL DOCUMENTS BY DIRECTION OF THE HISTORICAL SECTION OF THE COMMITTEE OF IMPERIAL DEFENCE - SEABORNE TRADE, VOLUME I, CRUISER PERIOD.

C. [Charles] Ernest Fayle I 22.5cm x 16cm I Midnight Blue Hardback I Gilt I White Paper Dust Jacket I xvii + 442pp I 11 maps I John Murray I 1920 I English Text.

This volume covers the following as per the index: Pre-war and Outbreak of War; Legal; Control of the Atlantic; Mining of the North Sea; Trade in the Far East; Trade in the Pacific; The Crusies of SMS Emden and SMS Karlsruhe; The Battles of Coronel and the Falklands; The German Change in Strategy to Submarines; Auxiliary Cruisers

The Imperial War Museum Department of Printed Books in association with the Battery Press republished this volume in 1997.

This volume can be viewed on the Internet Archive world wide web:

http://www.archive.org/details/seabornetrade01fayluoft

HISTORY OF THE WAR BASED ON OFFICIAL DOCUMENTS BY DIRECTION OF THE HISTORICAL SECTION OF THE COMMITTEE OF IMPERIAL DEFENCE - SEABORNE TRADE, VOLUME I, [Map Case]

C. [Charles] Ernest Fayle I 22.5cm x 16cm I Midnight Blue Hardback I Gilt I White Paper Dust Jacket I 9 maps I John Murray I 1920 I English Text.

The collaboration between the Imperial War Museum Department of Printed Books and the Battery Press reproduced the map case in 1997.

HISTORY OF THE WAR BASED ON OFFICIAL DOCUMENTS BY DIRECTION OF THE HISTORICAL SECTION OF THE COMMITTEE OF IMPERIAL DEFENCE - SEABORNE TRADE, VOLUME II, SUBMARINE CAMPAIGN PART I.

C. [Charles] Ernest Fayle | 22.5cm x 16cm | Midnight Blue Hardback | Gilt | White Paper Dust Jacket | xvii + 409pp | 2 maps | John Murray | 1923 | English Text.

This volume covers the following as per the index: Submarine Operations February 1915 – December 1916.

The Imperial War Museum Department of Printed Books in association with the Battery Press republished this volume in 1998.

HISTORY OF THE WAR BASED ON OFFICIAL DOCUMENTS BY DIRECTION OF THE HISTORICAL SECTION OF THE COMMITTEE OF IMPERIAL DEFENCE - SEABORNE TRADE, VOLUME III, SUBMARINE CAMPAIGN PART II.

C. [Charles] Ernest Fayle | 22.5cm x 16cm | Midnight Blue Hardback | Gilt | White Paper Dust Jacket | xx + 501pp | 3 appendices | 14 maps | John Murray | 1924 | English Text.

This volume covers the following as per the index: Submarine Operations December 1916 – November 1918 and after.

The Imperial War Museum Department of Printed Books in association with the Battery Press republished this volume in 1998.

Blockade Activities;

HISTORY OF THE WAR BASED ON OFFICIAL DOCUMENTS BY DIRECTION OF THE HISTORICAL SECTION OF THE COMMITTEE OF IMPERIAL DEFENCE - THE BLOCKADE OF THE CENTRAL EMPIRES 1914-1918.

A.C. [Archibald Colquhoun] Bell | 27.5cm x 19.5cm | Midnight Blue Hardback | Gilt | xvi + 845pp | 4 appendices | 84 tables | His Majesty's Stationery Office. | 1937 (1961) | English Text.

There was a print run of 750 copies.

At the planning stage of the British official history it was decided to include a volume covering the British naval blockades of the central powers. Work on this volume entitled **"The Blockade of the Central Empires 1914-1918"** was completed in 1921, but due to H.M. Government's (The Foreign office) concerns over the international legalities of the blockades it was decided not to published it. However in 1937 with another European war looming, the decision was reversed and it was published, but as 'confidential' with a very restricted circulation. It was finally released for public circulation in 1961.

Merchant Navy Activities;

HISTORY OF THE WAR BASED ON OFFICIAL DOCUMENTS BY DIRECTION OF THE HISTORICAL SECTION OF THE COMMITTEE OF IMPERIAL DEFENCE - THE MERCHANT NAVY, VOLUME I.

[*Sir*] Archibald [Spicer] Hurd | 22.5cm x 16cm | Midnight Blue Hardback | Gilt | White Paper Dust Jacket | xiv + 473pp | 12 maps | 3 photographs | John Murray | 1921 | English Text.

This volume covers the following as per the index: Pre-war and Legal; Cruiser Warfare; The Crusies of SMS Emden; protection against Cruisers; Auxiliary Patrols; Submarines Warfare; the Sinking of RMS Lusitania.

The Imperial War Museum Department of Printed Books in association with the Naval and Military Press Ltd republished it again in 2003.

This volume can be viewed on the Internet Archive world wide web:

http://www.archive.org/stream/merchantnavy01hurduoft

HISTORY OF THE WAR BASED ON OFFICIAL DOCUMENTS BY DIRECTION OF THE HISTORICAL SECTION OF THE COMMITTEE OF IMPERIAL DEFENCE - THE MERCHANT NAVY, VOLUME II.

[*Sir*] Archibald [Spicer] Hurd | 22.5cm x 16cm | Midnight Blue Hardback | Gilt | White Paper Dust Jacket | xvii + 464pp | 3 appendices | 12 maps | 4 photographs | John Murray | 1923 | English Text.

This volume covers the following as per the index: Submarines in British Home Waters; Auxiliary Craft; Fishermen; Fishing Boats in War Service; Troop Transports; Blockade of Germany; Shipping in the Mediterranean; ss Persia; the Capture and Execution of Captain Fryatt.

The Imperial War Museum Department of Printed Books in association with the Naval and Military Press Ltd republished it in 2003.

This volume can be viewed on the Internet Archive world wide web:
http://www.archive.org/details/merchantnavy02hurduoft

HISTORY OF THE WAR BASED ON OFFICIAL DOCUMENTS BY DIRECTION OF THE HISTORICAL SECTION OF THE COMMITTEE OF IMPERIAL DEFENCE - THE MERCHANT NAVY, VOLUME III.

[*Sir*] Archibald [Spicer] Hurd I 22.5cm x 16cm I Midnight Blue Hardback I Gilt I White Paper Dust Jacket I xix + 400pp I 3 appendices I 15 maps I 2 photographs I John Murray I 1924 I English Text.

This volume covers the following as per the index: Patrol Work February 1917 – November 1918; 10th Cruiser Squadron March-December 1917; Submarines Campaign; Dazzle Painting; Auxiliary Patrols; the Sinking of Hospital Ships; Merchant Seamen Prisoners.

The Imperial War Museum Department of Printed Books in association with the Naval and Military Press Ltd republished it in 2003.

Military Operations;

Brigadier General Sir James E. [Edward] Edmonds [Editor][10]

HISTORY OF THE WAR BASED ON OFFICIAL DOCUMENTS BY DIRECTION OF THE HISTORICAL SECTION OF THE COMMITTEE OF IMPERIAL DEFENCE - MILITARY OPERATIONS, EAST AFRICA, VOLUME I: AUGUST 1914-SEPTEMBER 1916.

Lieutenant Colonel Charles Norden [*Captain* Henry FitzMaurice Stacke] I 22.5cm x 16cm I Bright Red Hardback I Gilt I Brown Paper Dust Jacket I xl + 603pp I 6 appendices I 28 maps I 5 photographs I 2 diagramsI His Majesty's Stationery Office. I 1941 I English Text.

There was a print run of 1500 copies.

The Imperial War Museum Department of Printed Books in association with the Battery Press republished this volume in 1992 without a dust jacket.

The following note was added below the author's name on the title page: "Founded on a draft by the late Major H. FitzM. Stacke, M.C., P.S.C. The Worcestershire Regiment." The research and draft for a single volume "Military Operations, East Africa" was completed by Major Stacke who died just after he had sent out the draft for review in 1935. Lieutenant Colonel Norden was therefore recruited to complete this work. Using Stacke's researches and the correspondence that arose from the proof read copies, Norden started to rewrite the original draft, intending to expand it into two volumes. Having completed the first volume, unfortunately Norden also died before he could start work on the second volume. The second volume was therefore neither written nor published; however eight of the original Stacke draft chapters have survived and can be viewed in the National Archives at Kew (London). The remaining draft chapters are as follows:

Chapter XII; the German breakthrough from the West, 1916 Oct.-Nov.
Chapter XIII; operations from the coast, 1916 Oct.-Dec.
Chapter XIV; advance to the Rufiji, 1916 Dec.-1917 Feb.
Chapter XV; operations in the West 1916 Dec.-1917 Mar.
Chapter XVI; pursuit of Wintgens and Naumann, 1917 Mar.-Oct.
Chapter XVII; the campaign of 1917: preliminary.
Chapter XVIII; Kilwa, Nyangou and Tandamuti (with extract from military despatch dated 1918 Apr.5.
Chapter XIX: Nhamacurra Battle: Actions at Namirrue and Nhamacurra.

Chapters XVI and XVIII were filed in the National Archives in 1937 and it can be assumed that the other chapters were also filed around this date. From the dates given in the chapter

---

[10] The official historian Sir James E. Edmonds planned the original structure of the British Military Operations set. He wrote the majority of the histories, however he enlisted the help of *Brigadier General* C.F. Aspinall-Oglander, *Major* A.F. Becke, *Captain* Cyril Falls, *Lieutenant General Sir* George MacMunn, *Captain* W. Miles, *Lieutenant General* Charles Norden, *Major* H. FitzM. Stacke and *Captain* G.C. Wynne to write the remaining histories within the series, however they were all edited by Edmonds. *Brigadier General* F. Moberly, a retired Indian Army officer, was recruited by the Indian Army Historical office to write the histories where the Indian Army played an important role – see note below. *Major* A.F. Becke was commission by Edmonds to draw up the maps.

titles, it would appear that these chapters are a straight forward continuation from those in the published volume. This implies that the chapter numbering system was based on the original single volume concept for this history, suggesting that Norden increased the number of chapters during his rewriting. Hence the reason for splitting the original volume into two.

The chapters are contained in the National Archives' files CAB 44/4 through to CAB 44/10 and CAB 45/69 – each file containing one chapter. For further information concerning the remaining draft chapters see The National Archives world wide web site: *http://www.nationalarchives.gov.uk/catalogue/browser.asp*

HISTORY OF THE WAR BASED ON OFFICIAL DOCUMENTS BY DIRECTION OF THE HISTORICAL SECTION OF THE COMMITTEE OF IMPERIAL DEFENCE - MILITARY OPERATIONS, EGYPT AND PALESTINE VOLUME I: FROM THE OUTBREAK OF WAR WITH GERMANY TO JUNE 1917.

Lieutenant General Sir George [Fletcher] MacMunn and *Captain* Cyril [Bentham] Falls | 22.5cm x 16cm | Bright Red Hardback | Gilt | Brown Paper Dust Jacket | xviii + 445pp | 15 appendices | 18 maps | 6 photographs | 2 diagrams| His Majesty's Stationery Office. | 1928 | English Text.

There was a print run of 1500 copies.

The Imperial War Museum Department of Printed Books in association with the Battery Press republished this volume in 1996 without a dust jacket.

This volume covers the operations of the Egyptian Expeditionary Force (E.E.F.) and includes the beginnings of the Arab Revolt in Arabia masterminded by *Captain* (later promoted to *Lieutenant-Colonel*) T.E. [Terrence Edward] Lawence. The revolt being part of the British-Arab campaigns to protect the southern flank of the E.E.F., with operations leading to the capture of Mecca, Wejh and Aqaba. Lawence drafted the two chapters on the revolt.

HISTORY OF THE WAR BASED ON OFFICIAL DOCUMENTS BY DIRECTION OF THE HISTORICAL SECTION OF THE COMMITTEE OF IMPERIAL DEFENCE - MILITARY OPERATIONS, EGYPT AND PALESTINE VOLUME I: FROM THE OUTBREAK OF WAR WITH GERMANY TO JUNE 1917. [Map Case.]

Major A.F. [Archibald Frank] Becke | 22.5cm x 16cm | Bright Red Hardback | Gilt | Brown Paper Dust Jacket | 15 maps | His Majesty's Stationery Office. | 1928 | English Text.

HISTORY OF THE WAR BASED ON OFFICIAL DOCUMENTS BY DIRECTION OF THE HISTORICAL SECTION OF THE COMMITTEE OF IMPERIAL DEFENCE - MILITARY OPERATIONS, EGYPT AND PALESTINE VOLUME II: PART I FROM JUNE 1917 TO THE END OF THE WAR.

Lieutenant General Sir George [Fletcher] MacMunn and *Captain* Cyril [Bentham] Falls | 22.5cm x 16cm | Bright Red Hardback | Gilt | Brown Paper Dust Jacket | xxviii + 394pp + xiv | 28 maps | 5 photographs | 2 diagrams| His Majesty's Stationery Office. | 1930 | English Text.

There was a print run of 3000 copies.

The Imperial War Museum Department of Printed Books in association with the Battery Press republished this volume in 1996 without a dust jacket.

HISTORY OF THE WAR BASED ON OFFICIAL DOCUMENTS BY DIRECTION OF THE HISTORICAL SECTION OF THE COMMITTEE OF IMPERIAL DEFENCE - MILITARY OPERATIONS, EGYPT AND PALESTINE VOLUME II: PART II FROM JUNE 1917 TO THE END OF THE WAR.

Lieutenant General Sir George [Fletcher] MacMunn and *Captain* Cyril [Bentham] Falls | 22.5cm x 16cm | Bright Red Hardback | Gilt | Brown Paper Dust Jacket | 353pp (numbered 395-748) | 27 appendices | 16 maps | 5 photographs | His Majesty's Stationery Office. | 1930 | English Text.

There was a print run of 3000 copies.

The Imperial War Museum Department of Printed Books in association with the Battery Press republished this volume in 1996 without a dust jacket.

This volume covers the campaigns of the E.E.F. as it advanced through Palestine and Jordan climaxing at the Battle of Megiddo, which led to the rout of the Turkish forces into Lebanon and Syria. The capture of Jerusalem in Palestine (Israel) and Damascus in Syria are included. Also included is the continuation of the Arab Revolt in Arabia, as it then spread northwards, linking up with the E.E.F. and partaking in their campaigns. It includes details of the Arab Gorilla raids against the Hejaz railway and makes mention of the capture of Medina.

HISTORY OF THE WAR BASED ON OFFICIAL DOCUMENTS BY DIRECTION OF THE HISTORICAL SECTION OF THE COMMITTEE OF IMPERIAL DEFENCE - MILITARY OPERATIONS, EGYPT AND PALESTINE VOLUME II: PART I FROM JUNE 1917 TO THE END OF THE WAR. [Map Case.]

Major A.F. [Archibald Frank] Becke I 22.5cm x 16cm I Bright Red Hardback I Gilt I Brown Paper Dust Jacket I 24 maps I His Majesty's Stationery Office. I 1930 I English Text.

HISTORY OF THE WAR BASED ON OFFICIAL DOCUMENTS BY DIRECTION OF THE HISTORICAL SECTION OF THE COMMITTEE OF IMPERIAL DEFENCE - MILITARY OPERATIONS, FRANCE AND BELGIUM 1914 VOLUME I: MONS, THE RETREAT TO THE SEINE, THE MARNE AND THE AISNE: AUGUST-OCTOBER 1914.[11]

Brigadier General J.E. [James Edward] Edmonds I 22.5cm x 16cm I Bright Red Hardback I Gilt I Brown Paper Dust Jacket I xxvi + 543pp I 54 appendices I 15 maps I 5 photographs I 2 diagramsI Macmillan and Co Ltd. I 1922 (1933) I English Text.

Two Addenda and Corrigenda sheets for this volume were issued with France and Belgium 1914 Volume II and France and Belgium 1915 Volume I.

This volume was reprinted in 1925 and was called the second edition. It was then revised and republished in 1933 to become the third edition. Shearer Publications reprinted this third edition in 1984 (only the text volume was reprinted by Shearer who did not produce its associated map case). It was issued with a red paper dust jacket with a reproduction of a painting on the front. The Imperial War Museum Department of Printed Books, in collaboration with the Battery Press, republished the third edition in 1996. To reduce the cost, the Imperial War Museum Department of Printed Books and the Battery Press reproduced all the coloured maps in black and white and for the same reason did not issue it with a dust jacket. This applied to all of the Imperial War Museum Department of Printed Books and the Battery Press reproductions - both text volumes and map cases.

Finally the Imperial War Museum Department of Printed Books in collaboration with the Naval and Military Press republished the third edition in paperback format in 2009. With this edition all of the original coloured maps have been reproduced in colour. The Naval and Military Press has republished all of the large format maps from the France and Belgium set on a CD ROM.

This volume can be viewed on the Internet Archive world wide web:

http://www.archive.org/details/militaryoperatio01edmouoft

The map case has not been reproduced in internet format.

Based on the first footnote of the preface in the subsequent volume "**Military Operations, France and Belgium 1914 Volume II**", Edmonds' conceptual planning for the Western Front operations set was to be two volumes covering 1914; one for 1915; two for 1916; two for 1917 and three for 1918, totalling ten volumes in all. Although official approval was given for ten volumes, the number of volumes were increased during the writing stage to fourteen.

The third edition was edited for errors, then up-dated and corrected to information gained from new sources published since the original publication date, mainly from the French and German official histories, as well as British, French and German regimental histories. There was also a wider coverage of the work of the Royal Flying Corps during the war of manoeuvre during the period not covered by the first volume of the '**The War in the Air**". It was the only volume of the Military Operations so treated; the errors found in the proceeding volumes were corrected by the issue of errata notifications, which were distributed in later volumes. When republished, this third volume had an increase in the number of pages in the introduction and the text to xxix + 592pp, as well as an increase in the number of maps to 24. An Addenda and Corrigenda for the third edition was issued with France and Belgium 1918 Volume II. Both the second and third edition was issued with a brown paper dust jacket. Since *Brigadier General* J.E. Edmonds became a Knight Bachelor in the New Year's

---

[11] The first five volumes of the Military Operations - France and Belguim sub set were given sequential volume numbers that were shown on the front and spine of the dust jackets only. As an example **Military Operations Volume III, France and Belgium 1915 Volume I: Winter 1914-15, Neuve Chappelle, Ypres: December 1914-May**. However the title pages and spines of the five volumes were shown without sequential volume numbers as per the rest of the set. This may have been deliberate or possibly a mistake by the dust jacket printers.

honours of 1928, the third edition had his name on the title page revised to *Brigadier General Sir* James E. Edmonds.

HISTORY OF THE WAR BASED ON OFFICIAL DOCUMENTS BY DIRECTION OF THE HISTORICAL SECTION OF THE COMMITTEE OF IMPERIAL DEFENCE - MILITARY OPERATIONS, FRANCE AND BELGIUM 1914 VOLUME I: MONS, THE RETREAT TO THE SEINE, THE MARNE AND THE AISNE: AUGUST-OCTOBER 1914. [Map Case.]

Major A.F. [Archibald Frank] Becke I 22.5cm x 16cm I Bright Red Hardback I Gilt I Brown Paper Dust Jacket I 34 maps I Macmillan and Co Ltd. I 1922 I English Text.

Like its associated text volume, it was reproduced in 1925 and again a revised version with an extra two maps, making 36 maps in total, was produced in 1933. Both had the brown paper dust jacket.

The collaboration between the Imperial War Museum Department of Printed Books and the Battery Press produced the third edition map case with the maps in black and white.

HISTORY OF THE WAR BASED ON OFFICIAL DOCUMENTS BY DIRECTION OF THE HISTORICAL SECTION OF THE COMMITTEE OF IMPERIAL DEFENCE - MILITARY OPERATIONS, FRANCE AND BELGIUM 1914 VOLUME II: ANTWERP, LA BASSEE, ARMENTIERES, MESSINES AND YPRES: OCTOBER-NOVEMBER 1914.

Brigadier General J.E. [James Edward] Edmonds I 22.5cm x 16cm I Bright Red Hardback I Gilt I Brown Paper Dust Jacket I xxvii + 548pp I 45 appendices I 18 maps I Macmillan and Co Ltd. I 1925 I English Text.

This volume "**Military Operations, France and Belgium 1914 Volume II**" includes a summary of the expansion of the British Army from a peacetime to a wartime footing. It also includes a cursory description of the British expeditions against the German Colonies. Both accounts are to be found in the Introduction.

Six Addenda and Corrigenda sheets were issued with the following volumes: France and Belgium 1915 Volume I; France and Belgium 1915 Volume II; France and Belgium 1916 Volume I; France and Belgium 1916 Volume II; France and Belgium 1918 Volume I and France and Belgium 1918 Volume III.

The Imperial War Museum Department of Printed Books in association with the Battery Press republished this volume in 1995.

Finally the Imperial War Museum Department of Printed Books in collaboration with the Naval and Military Press republished this volume in paperback format in 2009. With this edition all of the original coloured maps have been reproduced in colour.

The Internet Archive has reproduced this volume "**Military Operations, France and Belgium 1914 Volume II**" on their world wide web page:

http://www.archive.org/details/3edmilitaryopera02edmouoft.

The map case has not been reproduced in internet format.

HISTORY OF THE WAR BASED ON OFFICIAL DOCUMENTS BY DIRECTION OF THE HISTORICAL SECTION OF THE COMMITTEE OF IMPERIAL DEFENCE - MILITARY OPERATIONS, FRANCE AND BELGIUM 1914 VOLUME II: ANTWERP, LA BASSEE, ARMENTIERES, MESSINES AND YPRES: OCTOBER-NOVEMBER 1914. [Map Case.]

Major A.F. [Archibald Frank] Becke I 22.5cm x 16cm I Bright Red Hardback I Gilt I Brown Paper Dust Jacket I 40 maps I Macmillan and Co Ltd. I 1925 I English Text.

The Imperial War Museum Department of Printed Books in association with the Battery Press republished this map case in 1995 with the maps in black and white.

HISTORY OF THE WAR BASED ON OFFICIAL DOCUMENTS BY DIRECTION OF THE HISTORICAL SECTION OF THE COMMITTEE OF IMPERIAL DEFENCE - MILITARY OPERATIONS, FRANCE AND BELGIUM 1915 VOLUME I: WINTER 1914-15, NEUVE CHAPPELLE, YPRES: DECEMBER 1914-MAY.

Brigadier General J.E. [James Edward] Edmonds and Captain G.C. [Graeme Chamley] Wynne I 22.5cm x 16cm I Bright Red Hardback I Gilt I Brown Paper Dust Jacket I xliii + 433pp I 36 appendices I 21 maps I Macmillan and Co Ltd. I 1927 I English Text.

Five Addenda and Corrigenda sheets were issued with the following volumes: France and Belgium 1915 Volume II; France and Belgium 1916 Volume I; France and Belgium 1918 Volume I; France and Belgium 1918 Volume II and the Italy volume.

The Imperial War Museum Department of Printed Books in association with the Battery Press republished this volume in 1992.

Finally the Imperial War Museum Department of Printed Books in collaboration with the Naval and Military Press republished this volume in paperback format in 2009. With this edition all of the original coloured maps have been reproduced in colour.

HISTORY OF THE WAR BASED ON OFFICIAL DOCUMENTS BY DIRECTION OF THE HISTORICAL SECTION OF THE COMMITTEE OF IMPERIAL DEFENCE - MILITARY OPERATIONS, FRANCE AND BELGIUM 1915 VOLUME I: WINTER 1914-15, NEUVE CHAPPELLE, YPRES: DECEMBER 1914-MAY. [Map Case.]

Major A.F. [Archibald Frank] Becke | 22.5cm x 16cm | Bright Red Hardback | Gilt | Brown Paper Dust Jacket | 13 maps | Macmillan and Co Ltd. | 1927 | English Text.

The collaboration between the Imperial War Museum Department of Printed Books and the Battery Press reproduced the map case with the maps in black and white.

HISTORY OF THE WAR BASED ON OFFICIAL DOCUMENTS BY DIRECTION OF THE HISTORICAL SECTION OF THE COMMITTEE OF IMPERIAL DEFENCE - MILITARY OPERATIONS, FRANCE AND BELGIUM 1915 VOLUME II: BATTLES OF AUBERS RIDGE, FESTUBERT AND LOOS [JUNE-DECEMBER].

Brigadier General Sir James E. [Edward] Edmonds | 22.5cm x 16cm | Bright Red Hardback | Gilt | Brown Paper Dust Jacket | lii + 488pp | 21 appendices | 44 maps | Macmillan and Co Ltd. | 1928 | English Text.

James Edmonds became a Knight Bachelor in the New Year Honours of 1928 and hence his name on the title page of his official histories was revised to *Brigadier General Sir* James E. Edmonds.

Three Addenda and Corrigenda sheets were issued with the following volumes: France and Belgium 1916 Volume I; France and Belgium 1916 Volume II and France and Belgium 1918 Volume III.

The Imperial War Museum Department of Printed Books in association with the Battery Press republished this volume in 1995.

Finally the Imperial War Museum Department of Printed Books in collaboration with the Naval and Military Press republished this volume in paperback format in 2009. With this edition all of the original coloured maps have been reproduced in colour.

HISTORY OF THE WAR BASED ON OFFICIAL DOCUMENTS BY DIRECTION OF THE HISTORICAL SECTION OF THE COMMITTEE OF IMPERIAL DEFENCE - MILITARY OPERATIONS, FRANCE AND BELGIUM 1915 VOLUME II: BATTLES OF AUBERS RIDGE, FESTUBERT AND LOOS [JUNE-DECEMBER]. [Map Case.]

Major A.F. [Archibald Frank] Becke | 22.5cm x 16cm | Bright Red Hardback | Gilt | Brown Paper Dust Jacket | 11 maps | 1 Diagram/Sketch | Macmillan and Co Ltd. | 1928 | English Text.

The collaboration between the Imperial War Museum Department of Printed Books and the Battery Press reproduced the map case in 1995 with the maps in black and white.

HISTORY OF THE WAR BASED ON OFFICIAL DOCUMENTS BY DIRECTION OF THE HISTORICAL SECTION OF THE COMMITTEE OF IMPERIAL DEFENCE - MILITARY OPERATIONS, FRANCE AND BELGIUM 1916 VOLUME I: SIR DOUGLAS HAIG'S COMMAND TO THE 1ST JULY: BATTLE OF THE SOMME.

Brigadier General Sir James E. [Edward] Edmonds | 22.5cm x 16cm | Bright Red Hardback | Gilt | Brown Paper Dust Jacket | xxxvi + 523pp | 27 maps | Macmillan and Co Ltd. | 1932 | English Text.

An Addenda and Corrigenda sheet was issued with France and Belgium 1918 Volume I.

This volume includes the build up to and the first day of the Battle of the Somme.

The Imperial War Museum Department of Printed Books in association with the Battery Press republished this volume in 1993.

Finally the Imperial War Museum Department of Printed Books in collaboration with the Naval and Military Press republished the third edition in paperback format in 2009. With this edition all of the original coloured maps have been reproduced in colour.

HISTORY OF THE WAR BASED ON OFFICIAL DOCUMENTS BY DIRECTION OF THE HISTORICAL SECTION OF THE COMMITTEE OF IMPERIAL DEFENCE - MILITARY OPERATIONS, FRANCE AND BELGIUM 1916 VOLUME I: SIR DOUGLAS HAIG'S COMMAND TO THE 1ST JULY:BATTLE OF THE SOMME. [Appendices]

Brigadier General Sir James E. [Edward] Edmonds | 22.5cm x 16cm | Bright Red Hardback | Gilt | Brown Paper Dust Jacket | viii + 232pp | 26 appendices | Macmillan and Co Ltd. | 1932 | English Text.

The Imperial War Museum Department of Printed Books in collaboration with the Naval and Military Press republished this volume in paperback format in 2009.

HISTORY OF THE WAR BASED ON OFFICIAL DOCUMENTS BY DIRECTION OF THE HISTORICAL SECTION OF THE COMMITTEE OF IMPERIAL DEFENCE - MILITARY OPERATIONS, FRANCE AND BELGIUM 1916 VOLUME I: SIR DOUGLAS HAIG'S COMMAND TO THE 1ST JULY: BATTLE OF THE SOMME. [Map Case.]

Major A.F. [Archibald Frank] Becke | 22.5cm x 16cm | Bright Red Hardback | Gilt | Brown Paper Dust Jacket | 11 maps | 1 Diagram/Sketch | Macmillan and Co Ltd. | 1932 | English Text.

The collaboration between the Imperial War Museum Department of Printed Books and the Battery Press reproduced the map case with the maps in black and white.

HISTORY OF THE WAR BASED ON OFFICIAL DOCUMENTS BY DIRECTION OF THE HISTORICAL SECTION OF THE COMMITTEE OF IMPERIAL DEFENCE - MILITARY OPERATIONS, FRANCE AND BELGIUM 1916 VOLUME II: 2ND JULY 1916 TO THE END OF THE BATTLES OF THE SOMME.

Brigadier General Sir James E. [Edward] Edmonds | 22.5cm x 16cm | Bright Red Hardback | Gilt | Brown Paper Dust Jacket | xxxvii + 601pp | 51 maps | 1 photograph | Macmillan and Co Ltd. | 1938 | English Text.

Two Addenda and Corrigenda sheets were issued with the following volumes: France and Belgium 1917 Volume I and France and Belgium 1918 Volume III.

Shearer Publications reprinted this edition in 1986 (again like their first reprint of 1914 Volume I only the text volume was reprinted by Shearer who did not produce its associated map case). It was issued with a red paper dust jacket with a photograph on the front. The Imperial War Museum Department of Printed Books in association with the Battery Press republished this volume in 1992.

Finally the Imperial War Museum Department of Printed Books in collaboration with the Naval and Military Press republished this volume in paperback format in 2009. With this edition all of the original coloured maps have been reproduced in colour.

HISTORY OF THE WAR BASED ON OFFICIAL DOCUMENTS BY DIRECTION OF THE HISTORICAL SECTION OF THE COMMITTEE OF IMPERIAL DEFENCE - MILITARY OPERATIONS, FRANCE AND BELGIUM 1916 VOLUME II: 2ND JULY 1916 TO THE END OF THE BATTLES OF THE SOMME. [Appendices and Map Case.]

Brigadier General Sir James E. [Edward] Edmonds and *Major* A.F. [Archibald Frank] Becke | 22.5cm x 16cm | Bright Red Hardback | Gilt | Brown Paper Dust Jacket | x + 119pp | 33 appendices | 6 maps | Macmillan and Co Ltd. | 1938 | English Text.

The large format maps are carried in a folder attached to the inside rear cover.

The collaboration between the Imperial War Museum Department of Printed Books and the Battery Press reproduced this combined appendices and map case in 1994.

The Imperial War Museum Department of Printed Books in collaboration with the Naval and Military Press republished this volume in paperback format in 2009. The large format maps have not been reproduced.

HISTORY OF THE WAR BASED ON OFFICIAL DOCUMENTS BY DIRECTION OF THE HISTORICAL SECTION OF THE COMMITTEE OF IMPERIAL DEFENCE - MILITARY OPERATIONS, FRANCE AND BELGIUM 1917 VOLUME I: THE GERMAN RETREAT TO THE HINDENBURG LINE AND THE BATTLES OF ARRAS [JANUARY - 6TH JUNE].

Captain Cyril [Bentham] Falls | 22.5cm x 16cm | Bright Red Hardback | Gilt | Brown Paper Dust Jacket | xxxvii + 586pp | 25 maps | Macmillan and Co Ltd. | 1940 | English Text.

An Addenda and Corrigenda sheet was issued with the Italy volume.

The Imperial War Museum Department of Printed Books in association with the Battery Press republished this volume in 1992 with the maps in black and white.

Finally the Imperial War Museum Department of Printed Books in collaboration with the Naval and Military Press republished this volume in paperback format in 2009. With this edition all of the original coloured maps have been reproduced in colour.

HISTORY OF THE WAR BASED ON OFFICIAL DOCUMENTS BY DIRECTION OF THE HISTORICAL SECTION OF THE COMMITTEE OF IMPERIAL DEFENCE - MILITARY OPERATIONS, FRANCE AND BELGIUM 1917 VOLUME I: THE GERMAN RETREAT TO THE HINDENBURG LINE AND THE BATTLES OF ARRAS [JANUARY - 6TH JUNE]. [Appendices]

Captain Cyril [Bentham] Falls | 22.5cm x 16cm | Bright Red Hardback | Gilt | Brown Paper Dust Jacket | xi + 158pp | 52 appendices | 25 maps | Macmillan and Co Ltd. | 1940 | English Text.

The Imperial War Museum Department of Printed Books in association with the Battery Press republished this volume in 1994.

The Imperial War Museum Department of Printed Books in collaboration with the Naval and Military Press republished this volume in paperback format in 2009.

HISTORY OF THE WAR BASED ON OFFICIAL DOCUMENTS BY DIRECTION OF THE HISTORICAL SECTION OF THE COMMITTEE OF IMPERIAL DEFENCE - MILITARY OPERATIONS, FRANCE AND BELGIUM 1917 VOLUME I: THE GERMAN RETREAT TO THE HINDENBURG LINE AND THE BATTLES OF ARRAS [JANUARY - 6TH JUNE]. [Map Case.]

Major A.F. [Archibald Frank] Becke | 22.5cm x 16cm | Bright Red Hardback | Gilt | Brown Paper Dust Jacket | 12 maps | Macmillan and Co Ltd. | 1932 | English Text.

The collaboration between the Imperial War Museum Department of Printed Books and the Battery Press reproduced the map case with the maps in black and white.

HISTORY OF THE WAR BASED ON OFFICIAL DOCUMENTS BY DIRECTION OF THE HISTORICAL SECTION OF THE COMMITTEE OF IMPERIAL DEFENCE - MILITARY OPERATIONS, FRANCE AND BELGIUM 1917 VOLUME II: 7TH JUNE - 10TH NOVEMBER: MESSINES AND THIRD YPRES (PASSCHENDAELE).

Brigadier General Sir James E. [Edward] Edmonds [*Captain* Cyril [Bentham] Falls and *Captain* G.C. [Graeme Chamley] Wynne] | 22.5cm x 16cm | Bright Red Hardback | Gilt | Brown Paper Dust Jacket | xl + 489pp | 26 appendices | 29 maps | 8 photographs | His Majesty's Stationery Office. | 1949 | English Text.

An Addenda and Corrigenda sheet was issued with the Italy volume.

The Imperial War Museum Department of Printed Books in association with the Battery Press republished this volume in 1991.

Finally the Imperial War Museum Department of Printed Books in collaboration with the Naval and Military Press republished this volume in paperback format in 2009. With this edition all of the original coloured maps have been reproduced in colour.

Captain Cyril Falls was assigned in 1939 by *Brigadier General Sir* James Edmonds to write "**Military Operations, France and Belgium 1917 Volume II**" and he proceeded to start work immediately. However Falls resigned from the Historical Section of the Committee of Imperial Defence after only a month of work upon the history, when he accepted an appointment with the Times Newspaper of London.

Falls was replaced by *Captain* G.C. Wynne. Wynne had already written jointly with Edmonds one of the series namely "**Military Operations, France and Belgium 1915 Volume I**". Edmonds, as was his normal practice with all the official histories, sent draft copies of the chapters as they were completed out for review to a wide number of interested parties. One of the reviewers *General Sir* Hubert Gough who had been the commander of the 5th Army during the Battle of Third Ypres (Passchendaele) took exception to what he perceived to be references that put all the blame for the mishandling of this battle upon himself. He wrote to Edmonds pointing out that *General* (later *Field Marshal*) *Sir* Douglas Haig as commander of the British Expeditionary Force (the B.E.F.) and his staff at that time had had a large input in the planning of this offensive and, as such, they should take part of the blame. Edmonds passed this information on to Wynne so that it could be incorporated into the history. Wynne duly rewrote some of the offending sections adding some but not all of Gough's comments. This was the start of a long dialogue between the three men with Wynne being asked to make more changes to the history over the course of completion.

Wynne finally finished writing the history in 1946, however he did not removed all of the objectionable comments. Therefore Edmonds took the step to rewrite those parts of the history correcting what he saw as the mistakes. Edmonds' rewritten history became the final draft and as such it was sent to His Majesty's Stationery Office (H.M.S.O. - the publishers) for publishing. In the bitter argument that followed between Wynne and Edmonds, Wynne insisted that his name be removed from the title page in protest, even though he wrote the greater portion of this volume. This resulted in that Edmonds' name only appears on the title page. This volume therefore had numerous draft versions written by three authors between 1939 and 1948.

The volume was published after the Second World War using His Majesty's Stationery Office instead of Macmillan and Co Ltd. It did not have a companion map case, instead it had a map folder for the large format maps mounted on the inside back cover. It was for economic reasons that both these changes occurred. This applied to all of the post Second World War productions.

HISTORY OF THE WAR BASED ON OFFICIAL DOCUMENTS BY DIRECTION OF THE HISTORICAL SECTION OF THE COMMITTEE OF IMPERIAL DEFENCE - MILITARY OPERATIONS, FRANCE AND BELGIUM 1917 VOLUME III: THE BATTLE OF CAMBRAI [11TH NOVEMBER -DECEMBER].

Captain Wilfrid Miles | 22.5cm x 16cm | Bright Red Hardback | Gilt | Brown Paper Dust Jacket | xvi + 399pp | 25 appendices | 24 maps | His Majesty's Stationery Office. | 1949 | English Text.

This volume was published after the Second World War using His Majesty's Stationery Office instead of Macmillan and Co Ltd It did not have a companion map case, instead it had a map folder for the large maps mounted on the inside back cover.

An Addenda and Corrigenda sheet was issued with the Italy volume.

The Imperial War Museum Department of Printed Books in association with the Battery Press republished this volume in 1991.

Finally the Imperial War Museum Department of Printed Books in collaboration with the Naval and Military Press republished this volume in paperback format in 2009. With this edition all of the original coloured maps have been reproduced in colour.

HISTORY OF THE WAR BASED ON OFFICIAL DOCUMENTS BY DIRECTION OF THE HISTORICAL SECTION OF THE COMMITTEE OF IMPERIAL DEFENCE - MILITARY OPERATIONS, FRANCE AND BELGIUM 1918 VOLUME I: THE GERMAN MARCH OFFENSIVE AND ITS PRELIMINARIES [JANUARY - 21ST MARCH].

Brigadier General Sir James E. [Edward] Edmonds [*Lieutenant General Sir* Launcelot Kiggell] | 22.5cm x 16cm | Bright Red Hardback | Gilt | Brown Paper Dust Jacket | xxx + 569pp | 22 maps | Macmillan and Co Ltd. | 1935 | English Text.

The Imperial War Museum Department of Printed Books in association with the Battery Press republished this volume in 1995.

Finally the Imperial War Museum Department of Printed Books in collaboration with the Naval and Military Press republished this volume in paperback format in 2009. With this edition all of the original coloured maps have been reproduced in colour.

Brigadier General Sir James Edmonds decided that the France and Belgium series was to be written in chronological order with the exception of this volume, which covered the German March Offensive of 1918. Due to the speed of the German advance during the opening days of the offensive, which caused great confusion within the British Army units involved, the unit dairies were not kept up to date. This led to individuals who had quite often not been involved in the battle to bring these unit records up to date at a later date. This made the normal source of base data for the official history unreliable. Since Edmonds at this time was committed to writing the earlier 1914 volumes, he was not available to write this history. For this reason Edmonds in 1924 recruited *Lieutenant General Sir* Launcelot Kiggell (General Sir Douglas Haig's former Chief of Staff during the period covered) to write this history with the intention that key figures could be interrogated to make up for the lack of source information. However, like the intentionally fast track Gallipoli volumes, work progressed slowly and by 1926 very little had been done and the small amount that had been written was regarded as "colourless." Kiggell was therefore asked to resign.

Edmonds first choice of a replacement for Kiggell was *Brigadier General* C.F. Aspinall-Oglander but unfortunately he was still engaged in writing the Gallipoli volumes. It soon became apparent that the Gallipoli set would take much longer than originally intended and that Aspinall-Oglander would not be available for some time.

Therefore Edmonds decided to take over the work and write it himself once his "**France and Belgium 1916 Volume I**" had been completed. This then cause a delay in publication until to 1935.

HISTORY OF THE WAR BASED ON OFFICIAL DOCUMENTS BY DIRECTION OF THE HISTORICAL SECTION OF THE COMMITTEE OF IMPERIAL DEFENCE - MILITARY OPERATIONS, FRANCE AND BELGIUM 1918 VOLUME I: THE GERMAN MARCH OFFENSIVE AND ITS PRELIMINARIES [JANUARY - 21ST MARCH]. [Appendices]

Brigadier General Sir James E. [Edward] Edmonds I 22.5cm x 16cm I Bright Red Hardback I Gilt I Brown Paper Dust Jacket I viii + 148pp I 32 appendices I 27 maps I Macmillan and Co Ltd. I 1935 I English Text.

The Imperial War Museum Department of Printed Books in association with the Battery Press republished this volume.

Finally the Imperial War Museum Department of Printed Books in collaboration with the Naval and Military Press republished this volume in paperback format in 2009. With this edition all of the original coloured maps have been reproduced in colour.

HISTORY OF THE WAR BASED ON OFFICIAL DOCUMENTS BY DIRECTION OF THE HISTORICAL SECTION OF THE COMMITTEE OF IMPERIAL DEFENCE - MILITARY OPERATIONS, FRANCE AND BELGIUM 1918 VOLUME I: THE GERMAN MARCH OFFENSIVE AND ITS PRELIMINARIES [JANUARY - 21ST MARCH]. [Map Case.]

Major A.F. [Archibald Frank] Becke I 22.5cm x 16cm I Bright Red Hardback I Gilt I Brown Paper Dust Jacket I 13 maps I Macmillan and Co Ltd. I 1935 I English Text.

The collaboration between the Imperial War Museum Department of Printed Books and the Battery Press reproduced the map case with the maps in black and white.

HISTORY OF THE WAR BASED ON OFFICIAL DOCUMENTS BY DIRECTION OF THE HISTORICAL SECTION OF THE COMMITTEE OF IMPERIAL DEFENCE - MILITARY OPERATIONS, FRANCE AND BELGIUM 1918 VOLUME II: MARCH - APRIL: CONTINUATION OF THE GERMAN OFFENSIVE.

Brigadier General Sir James E. [Edward] Edmonds I 22.5cm x 16cm I Bright Red Hardback I Gilt I Brown Paper Dust Jacket I xxviii + 550pp I 17 appendices I 32 maps I Macmillan and Co Ltd. I 1937 I English Text.

An Addenda and Corrigenda for this volume was issued with France and Belgium 1917 Volume I and France and Belgium 1918 Volume III.

The Imperial War Museum Department of Printed Books in association with the Battery Press republished this volume in 1995.

Finally the Imperial War Museum Department of Printed Books in collaboration with the Naval and Military Press republished this volume in paperback format in 2009. With this edition all of the original coloured maps have been reproduced in colour.

HISTORY OF THE WAR BASED ON OFFICIAL DOCUMENTS BY DIRECTION OF THE HISTORICAL SECTION OF THE COMMITTEE OF IMPERIAL DEFENCE - MILITARY OPERATIONS, FRANCE AND BELGIUM 1918 VOLUME II: MARCH - APRIL: CONTINUATION OF THE GERMAN OFFENSIVE. [Map Case.]

Major A.F. [Archibald Frank] Becke I 22.5cm x 16cm I Bright Red Hardback I Gilt I Brown Paper Dust Jacket I 26 maps I Macmillan and Co Ltd. I 1937 I English Text.

An Addenda and Corrigenda sheet was issued with the "**France and Belgium 1917 Volume I.**"

The collaboration between the Imperial War Museum Department of Printed Books and the Battery Press reproduced the map case with the maps in black and white.

HISTORY OF THE WAR BASED ON OFFICIAL DOCUMENTS BY DIRECTION OF THE HISTORICAL SECTION OF THE COMMITTEE OF IMPERIAL DEFENCE - MILITARY OPERATIONS, FRANCE AND BELGIUM 1918 VOLUME III: MAY-JULY: THE GERMAN DIVERSION OFFENSIVES AND THE FIRST ALLIED COUNTER-OFFENSIVE.

Brigadier General Sir James E. [Edward] Edmonds I 22.5cm x 16cm I Bright Red Hardback I Gilt I Brown Paper Dust Jacket I xxxii + 385pp I 3 appendices I 3 maps I 20 diagramsI Macmillan and Co Ltd. I 1939 I English Text.

This volume was published without a companion map case, instead it had a map folder for the larger map mounted on the inside back cover. It is assumed that this was due to economic reasons.

The Imperial War Museum Department of Printed Books in association with the Battery Press republished this volume in 1994.

Finally the Imperial War Museum Department of Printed Books in collaboration with the Naval and Military Press republished this volume in paperback format in 2009. With this edition all of the original coloured maps have been reproduced in colour.

HISTORY OF THE WAR BASED ON OFFICIAL DOCUMENTS BY DIRECTION OF THE HISTORICAL SECTION OF THE COMMITTEE OF IMPERIAL DEFENCE - MILITARY OPERATIONS, FRANCE AND BELGIUM 1918 VOLUME IV: 8TH AUGUST - 26TH SEPTEMBER: THE FRANCO - BRITISH OFFENSIVE.

Brigadier General Sir James E. [Edward] Edmonds | 22.5cm x 16cm | Bright Red Hardback | Gilt | Brown Paper Dust Jacket | xxv + 623pp | 23 appendices | 35 maps | His Majesty's Stationery Office. | 1947 | English Text.

This volume was published after the Second World War using His Majesty's Stationery Office instead of Macmillan and Co Ltd. It did not have a companion map case, instead it had a map folder for the large maps mounted on the inside back cover.

The Imperial War Museum Department of Printed Books in association with the Battery Press republished this volume in 1993.

Finally the Imperial War Museum Department of Printed Books in collaboration with the Naval and Military Press republished this volume in paperback format in 2009. With this edition all of the original coloured maps have been reproduced in colour.

HISTORY OF THE WAR BASED ON OFFICIAL DOCUMENTS BY DIRECTION OF THE HISTORICAL SECTION OF THE COMMITTEE OF IMPERIAL DEFENCE - MILITARY OPERATIONS, FRANCE AND BELGIUM 1918 VOLUME V: 26ᵀᴴ SEPTEMBER - 11ᵀᴴ NOVEMBER: THE ADVANCE TO VICTORY.

Brigadier General Sir James E. [Edward] Edmonds and *Lieutenant-Colonel* R. [Robert] Maxwell-Hyslop | 22.5cm x 16cm | Bright Red Hardback | Gilt | Brown Paper Dust Jacket | xxix + 675pp | 7 appendices | 43 maps | His Majesty's Stationery Office. | 1949 | English Text.

This volume was published after the Second World War using His Majesty's Stationery Office instead of Macmillan and Co Ltd It did not have a companion map case, instead it had a map folder for the large maps mounted on the inside back cover.

An Addenda and Corrigenda sheet was issued with the Italy volume.

The Imperial War Museum Department of Printed Books in association with the Battery Press republished this volume in 1993.

Finally the Imperial War Museum Department of Printed Books in collaboration with the Naval and Military Press republished this volume in paperback format in 2009. With this edition all of the original coloured maps have been reproduced in colour.

HISTORY OF THE WAR BASED ON OFFICIAL DOCUMENTS BY DIRECTION OF THE HISTORICAL SECTION OF THE COMMITTEE OF IMPERIAL DEFENCE - MILITARY OPERATIONS, GALLIPOLI VOLUME I: INCEPTION OF THE CAMPAIGN TO MAY 1915.

[*Brigadier General*] C.F. [Cecil Faber] Aspinall-Oglander [*Captain* G.S. Gordon, and *Lieutenant General Sir* Gerald Ellison] | 22.5cm x 16cm | Bright Red Hardback | Gilt | Brown Paper Dust Jacket | xxxii + 385pp | 3 maps | 20 diagrams| William Heinemann Ltd. | 1929 | English Text.

The Imperial War Museum Department of Printed Books in association with the Battery Press republished this volume in 1992.

HISTORY OF THE WAR BASED ON OFFICIAL DOCUMENTS BY DIRECTION OF THE HISTORICAL SECTION OF THE COMMITTEE OF IMPERIAL DEFENCE - MILITARY OPERATIONS, GALLIPOLI VOLUME I: INCEPTION OF THE CAMPAIGN TO MAY 1915. [Appendices and Maps.]

[*Brigadier General*] C.F. [Cecil Faber] Aspinall-Oglander and *Major* A.F. [Archibald Frank] Becke | 22.5cm x 16cm | Bright Red Hardback | Gilt | Brown Paper Dust Jacket | vii + 77pp | 29 appendices | 4 maps | William Heinemann Ltd. | 1929 | English Text.

The large format maps are carried in a folder attached to the inside rear cover.

HISTORY OF THE WAR BASED ON OFFICIAL DOCUMENTS BY DIRECTION OF THE HISTORICAL SECTION OF THE COMMITTEE OF IMPERIAL DEFENCE - MILITARY OPERATIONS, GALLIPOLI VOLUME II: MAY 1915 TO THE EVACUATION.

[*Brigadier General*] C.F. [Cecil Faber] Aspinall-Oglander | 22.5cm x 16cm | Bright Red Hardback | Gilt | Brown Paper Dust Jacket | xxxii + 517pp | 35 maps | 19 diagrams| William Heinemann Ltd. | 1932 | English Text.

In 1932 this volume was serialised in an edited form by the British newspaper the Daily Telegraph. The Imperial War Museum Department of Printed Books in association with the Battery Press republished this volume in 1992.

HISTORY OF THE WAR BASED ON OFFICIAL DOCUMENTS BY DIRECTION OF THE HISTORICAL SECTION OF THE COMMITTEE OF IMPERIAL DEFENCE - MILITARY

OPERATIONS, GALLIPOLI VOLUME II: MAY 1915 TO THE EVACUATION. [Appendices and Maps.]

> [*Brigadier General*] C.F. [Cecil Faber] Aspinall-Oglander and *Major* A.F. [Archibald Frank] Becke | 22.5cm x 16cm | Bright Red Hardback | Gilt | Brown Paper Dust Jacket | vii + 85pp | 20 appendices | 6 maps | William Heinemann Ltd. | 1932 | English Text.
> The large format maps are carried in a folder attached to the inside rear cover.
> The Gallipoli volumes had a turbulent writing history, similar to that of the second volume of France and Belgium 1917 and the first volume of France and Belgium 1918. Due to the nature of the Gallipoli campaign, the Historical Section of the Committee of Imperial Defence wanted this history to be written and published as soon as possible to counter the many incriminations being levelled at various individuals involved in the campaign within the un-official histories then being produced. With this in mind, a civilian academic *Captain* G.S. Gordon was commissioned to write this history early in January 1919. However after four years and a costly visit to the Gallipoli peninsula both in expense and time, Gordon had only written three chapters. Due to the slowness of the writing there were moves afoot to dismiss Gordon. However before this could be enacted, he resigned from the Historical Section so that he could concentrate on his academic career at Leeds University.
> As a result of Gordon's resignation, *Lieutenant General Sir* Gerald Ellison was brought in to replace him in 1923. Ellison, an ex-staff officer who had served at Gallipoli, had very strong views on who was to blame for the poor planning and mishandling of the Gallipoli campaign. He was especially aggrieved at what he regarded as the amateur strategy by *Mr.* W.S. Churchill M.P. (later *Sir* Winston Churchill - The First Lord of the Admiralty at the time of the campaign conception) and proceded to air his views in his writing. Ellison utilised some of the work already completed by Gordon and expanded the first volume to nine chapters. The Committee for Control reviewed the draft chapters in early December 1924 with the result that Ellison was asked to redraft them removing the political references of blame. The committee told Ellison that the Official Military History was to cover Military Operations and that he should remove any non-military, especially political references. When he refused the committee asked Ellison for his resignation.
> Therefore in late January 1925 *Brigadier General* C.F. Aspinall-Oglander became the third historian to work upon the Gallipoli history. Like Ellison before him, Aspinall-Oglander had served at Gallipoli as a senior staff officer and had strong views concerning aspects of the planning and running of the campaign, as well as where the blame for the failures of the campaign lay – some of which were of a political nature. Quickly he started work on the first volume retaining a lot of Ellison earlier comments and came into conflict with both Edmonds and the committee. However he managed to complete the two volumes by skilful use of language acceptable to the committee, but keeping his and Ellison's views in place. In some cases he simply transferred the objectionable comments from one chapter to another and in others from the first to the second volume, which seems to have satisfied the committee, although Edmonds was never quite happy with this history.

HISTORY OF THE WAR BASED ON OFFICIAL DOCUMENTS BY DIRECTION OF THE HISTORICAL SECTION OF THE COMMITTEE OF IMPERIAL DEFENCE - MILITARY OPERATIONS, ITALY, 1915-1919.

> *Brigadier General Sir* James E. [Edward] Edmonds and *Major-General* H.R. [Henry Rodolph] Davis | 22.5cm x 16cm | Bright Red Hardback | Gilt | Brown Paper Dust Jacket | xxix + 450pp | 11 appendices | 2 maps | 19 diagrams| His Majesty's Stationery Office. | 1949 | English Text.
> The large format maps are carried in a folder attached to the inside rear cover.
> The Imperial War Museum Department of Printed Books in association with the Battery Press republished this volume in 1992.

HISTORY OF THE WAR BASED ON OFFICIAL DOCUMENTS BY DIRECTION OF THE HISTORICAL SECTION OF THE COMMITTEE OF IMPERIAL DEFENCE - MILITARY OPERATIONS, MACEDONIA, VOLUME I: FROM THE OUTBREAK OF WAR TO THE SPRING OF 1917.

> *Captain* Cyril [Bentham] Falls | 22.5cm x 16cm | Bright Red Hardback | Gilt | Brown Paper Dust Jacket | xvi + 409pp | 8 appendices | 5 maps | 16 diagrams| His Majesty's Stationery Office. | 1933 | English Text.

There was a print run of 2000 copies.

The Imperial War Museum Department of Printed Books in association with the Battery Press republished this volume in 1996.

HISTORY OF THE WAR BASED ON OFFICIAL DOCUMENTS BY DIRECTION OF THE HISTORICAL SECTION OF THE COMMITTEE OF IMPERIAL DEFENCE - MILITARY OPERATIONS, MACEDONIA, VOLUME I: FROM THE OUTBREAK OF WAR TO THE SPRING OF 1917. [Map Case.]

Major A.F. [Archibald Frank] Becke I 22.5cm x 16cm I Bright Red Hardback I Gilt I Brown Paper Dust Jacket I 12 maps I His Majesty's Stationery Office. I 1933 I English Text.

The collaboration between the Imperial War Museum Department of Printed Books and the Battery Press has reproduced the map case.

HISTORY OF THE WAR BASED ON OFFICIAL DOCUMENTS BY DIRECTION OF THE HISTORICAL SECTION OF THE COMMITTEE OF IMPERIAL DEFENCE - MILITARY OPERATIONS, MACEDONIA, VOLUME II: FROM THE SPRING OF 1917 TO THE END OF THE WAR.

Captain Cyril [Bentham] Falls I 22.5cm x 16cm I Bright Red Hardback I Gilt I Brown Paper Dust Jacket I xvi + 365pp I 21 appendices I 6 maps I 11 diagramsI His Majesty's Stationery Office. I 1935 I English Text.

There was a print run of 2000 copies.

The Imperial War Museum Department of Printed Books in association with the Battery Press republished this volume in 1996.

HISTORY OF THE WAR BASED ON OFFICIAL DOCUMENTS BY DIRECTION OF THE HISTORICAL SECTION OF THE COMMITTEE OF IMPERIAL DEFENCE - MILITARY OPERATIONS, MACEDONIA, VOLUME II: FROM THE SPRING OF 1917 TO THE END OF THE WAR. [Map Case.]

Major A.F. [Archibald Frank] Becke I 22.5cm x 16cm I Bright Red Hardback I Gilt I Brown Paper Dust Jacket I 11 maps I His Majesty's Stationery Office. I 1935 I English Text.

The collaboration between the Imperial War Museum Department of Printed Books and the Battery Press has reproduced the map case.

Macedonia is often referred to as Salonika – the supply port and base camp. The town of Salonika is now known as Thessaloniki.

HISTORY OF THE WAR BASED ON OFFICIAL DOCUMENTS BY DIRECTION OF THE HISTORICAL SECTION OF THE COMMITTEE OF IMPERIAL DEFENCE - CAMPAIGN IN MESOPOTAMIA VOLUME I.

Brigadier General F. [Frederick James] Moberly. I 22.5cm x 16cm I Bright Red Hardback I Gilt I Brown Paper Dust Jacket I ix + 402pp I 7 appendices I 9 maps I 3 photographs I His Majesty's Stationery Office. I 1923 I English Text.

There was a print run of 1500 copies.

This volume was reprinted in 1927. The Imperial War Museum Department of Printed Books in association with the Battery Press republished this volume in 1997.

This volume covered the period from August 1914 to April 1916.

Mesopotamia is the area covered by present day Iraq and eastern Syria.

This set the "**Campaign in Mesopotamia**" had the following note added to each of the volumes title page just below the title: "Compiled, at the request of the Government of India, under the direction of the Historical Section of the Committee of Imperial Defence." H.M. Government of India (H.M. Indian Office) considered writing an official history of the war covering the part played by the Indian Army. However it was soon realized that since the Indian Army always acted in unison with the British Army and that the British actions would be covered by the British official history, the Indian actions would also be covered by the British history. They decided that it would be a pointless exercise duplicating what was going to be in the British official history. Accordingly the decision was taken to help with the British production and an offer of financial help was made to the Historical Section of the Committee of Imperial Defence, which was duly taken up. The Historical Section therefore commissioned a retired Indian Army officer, *Brigadier General* F. Moberly; to write the histories relating to the area where Indian troops took an active part – namely the Mesopotamia and Persia volumes – at the H.M. Government of India expense.

HISTORY OF THE WAR BASED ON OFFICIAL DOCUMENTS BY DIRECTION OF THE HISTORICAL SECTION OF THE COMMITTEE OF IMPERIAL DEFENCE - CAMPAIGN IN MESOPOTAMIA VOLUME II.

Brigadier General F. [Frederick James] Moberly. | 22.5cm x 16cm | Bright Red Hardback | Gilt | Brown Paper Dust Jacket | xiv + 581pp | 23 appendices | 15 maps | 9 photographs | His Majesty's Stationery Office. | 1924 | English Text.

There was a print run of 1500 copies.

The Imperial War Museum Department of Printed Books in association with the Battery Press republished this volume in 1997.

This volume covered the period from April 1916 to March 1917: The Attempt on Baghdad, The Siege and Fall of Kut-al-Amara.

HISTORY OF THE WAR BASED ON OFFICIAL DOCUMENTS BY DIRECTION OF THE HISTORICAL SECTION OF THE COMMITTEE OF IMPERIAL DEFENCE - CAMPAIGN IN MESOPOTAMIA VOLUME III.

Brigadier General F. [Frederick James] Moberly. | 22.5cm x 16cm | Bright Red Hardback | Gilt | Brown Paper Dust Jacket | xii + 460pp | 9 appendices | 15 maps | 10 photographs | His Majesty's Stationery Office. | 1926 | English Text.

There was a print run of 1500 copies.

The Imperial War Museum Department of Printed Books in association with the Battery Press republished this volume in 1997.

This volume covered the period April 1917: The Capture and Consolidation of Baghdad.

HISTORY OF THE WAR BASED ON OFFICIAL DOCUMENTS BY DIRECTION OF THE HISTORICAL SECTION OF THE COMMITTEE OF IMPERIAL DEFENCE - CAMPAIGN IN MESOPOTAMIA VOLUME IV.

Brigadier General F. [Frederick James] Moberly. | 22.5cm x 16cm | Bright Red Hardback | Gilt | Brown Paper Dust Jacket | xvi + 447pp | 9 appendices | 14 maps | 17 photographs | His Majesty's Stationery Office. | 1927 | English Text.

There was a print run of 1500 copies.

The Imperial War Museum Department of Printed Books in association with the Battery Press republished this volume in 1997.

This volume covered the period from May 1917 to November 1918: The Campaign in Upper Mesopotamia to the Armistice.

HISTORY OF THE WAR BASED ON OFFICIAL DOCUMENTS BY DIRECTION OF THE HISTORICAL SECTION OF THE COMMITTEE OF IMPERIAL DEFENCE - OPERATIONS IN PERSIA 1915-1919.

Brigadier General F. [Frederick James] Moberly. | 22.5cm x 16cm | Bright Red Hardback | Gilt | Brown Paper Dust Jacket | xxii + 490pp | 5 appendices | 14 maps | 9 photographs | His Majesty's Stationery Office. | 1929 (1987) | English Text.

The Imperial War Museum Department of Printed Books in association with the His Majesty's Stationery Office republished this volume in 1987 in a red paper dust jacket.

There was a print run of 500 copies.

Persia is now modern day Iran.

Like the "**Campaign in Mesopotamia**" set, this volume the "**Operations in Persia**" had the following note added on the title page just below the title: "Compiled, at the request of the Government of India, under the direction of the Historical Section of the Committee of Imperial Defence." After he wrote the Campaign in Mesopotamia *Brigadier General* F. Moberly suggested that he should write a history that covered the operations in Persia during the period 1915 to 1919. His Majesty's Government - The Indian Office agreed with his suggestion and sanctioned the history, which Moberly duly wrote during 1928. His Majesty's Government's Foreign Office was then informed about the new history and become quite anxious about its contents, because they had made a number of agreements with the former Imperial Russian Government concerning Persia. The Foreign Office feared that the new Soviet Russian Government would find the old treaties within the Russian government's archives and that some of the British actions in Persia could be deemed to be unlawful against the terms of the treaties and hence put His Majesty's Government in an unfavourable light internationally. The Foreign Office therefore asked for the history to be suppressed, but Moberly argued that it was an important history, especially if the lessons were to be learnt for future campaigns in the area. Because of this argument it was agreed between the Indian

Office, Historical Section of the Committee of Imperial Defence and the Foreign Office to go ahead but the history would be published with a restricted issue.

The history was then published in 1929 with a limited print run of only 500 copies and with a very restrictive circulation. Since His Majesty's Government - The Indian Office, funded it, 150 copies were sent to India and were marked 'Secret', whilst the remaining 350 remained in Britain marked 'Confidential'[9]. Not all of the 'British' and 'Indian' copies were released, those that were, were to a small number of named reciprocates – mainly institutions. Of the 350 'British' copies only about fifty were released mainly to libraries in 1929 and a few more were released in 1932. They were produced as 'paperbacks' and only bound in the standard bright red 'hardback' covers when issued. The remainder that had not been issued were then pulped. It is not clear how many of the 'Indian' copies were issued and how many were destroyed.

In 1987, fifty-eight years after the original restricted release, the Imperial War Museum republished the history for public circulation in association with Her Majesty's Stationery Office.

HISTORY OF THE WAR BASED ON OFFICIAL DOCUMENTS BY DIRECTION OF THE HISTORICAL SECTION OF THE COMMITTEE OF IMPERIAL DEFENCE - MILITARY OPERATIONS, TOGOLAND AND THE CAMEROONS.

Brigadier General F. [Frederick James] Moberly. | 22.5cm x 16cm | Bright Red Hardback | Gilt | Brown Paper Dust Jacket | xxv + 469pp | 8 appendices | 15 maps | 43 photographs | His Majesty's Stationery Office. | 1931 | English Text.

There was a print run of 2000 copies.

The Imperial War Museum Department of Printed Books in association with the Battery Press republished this volume in 1995.

This volume the "**Military Operations, Togoland and the Cameroons**" had the following note added on the title page just below the title: "Compiled, by arrangement with the Colonial Office, under the direction of the Historical Section of the Committee of Imperial Defence."

Occupations;

HISTORY OF THE WAR BASED ON OFFICIAL DOCUMENTS BY DIRECTION OF THE HISTORICAL SECTION OF THE COMMITTEE OF IMPERIAL DEFENCE - THE OCCUPATION OF THE RHINELAND 1918 - 1929.

Brigadier General Sir James E. [Edward] Edmonds. | 22.5cm x 16cm | Bright Red Hardback | Gilt | Brown Paper Dust Jacket | xxv + 444pp | 26 appendices | 7 maps | His Majesty's Stationery Office. | 1944 (1987) | English Text.

The Imperial War Museum Department of Printed Books in association with Her Majesty's Stationery Office republished this volume in 1987 in a green paper dust jacket.

Finally the Imperial War Museum Department of Printed Books in collaboration with the Naval and Military Press republished this volume in paperback format in 2009. With this edition all of the original coloured maps have been reproduced in colour.

Originally, there were two volumes planned as part of the 'Official History of the War' series covering the post war occupations of former enemy states, namely Germany and Turkey. Due to Foreign Office objections relating to possible unlawful actions by the British occupation forces, the writing of them was cancelled. However even when the writing was cancelled, research for these volumes was conducted in the 1930s. Interest in the occupation of Germany was revived in 1942 with what was then seen as the turning point of the Second World War and an invasion of mainland Europe seemed possible in the future. Therefore the decision was taken to authorize the 'occupation' book. *Brigadier General Sir* James Edmonds took it upon himself to write both 'occupation' volumes in 1943 even though it was only intended that the German volume was to be sanctioned. This resulted that only the

---

[9] The category 'Secret' was the highest form of H.M. Government restriction that covered documents. It was intended that the document categorised 'Secret' was to be lent out only on short term loans to a very select number of named senior officers. 'Confidential' the second highest category that H.M. Government's could impose on a document allowed for a larger number of officers down to lower grades to view the document. In both cases the document had to be returned.

German volume, which was titled 'The Occupation of the Rhineland 1918-1929', being published. With the Foreign Office objections still in mind, as well as some of Edmonds' remarks about the Germans, it was decided to published it internally with a 'confidential' restriction and a limited print run of only 100 copies. It was published in 1944 in time for the post war occupation of Germany.

HISTORY OF THE WAR BASED ON OFFICIAL DOCUMENTS BY DIRECTION OF THE HISTORICAL SECTION OF THE COMMITTEE OF IMPERIAL DEFENCE - THE OCCUPATION OF CONSTANTINOPLE 1918 - 1923.

Brigadier General Sir James E. [Edward] Edmonds. (transcribed by Neil Wells) | 22.5cm x 16cm | illustrated card softback | xiv + 60pp | 7 appendices | 12 photographs | 2 maps. | Naval and Military Press Ltd. | 2010 | English Text.

This history 'The Occupation of Constantinople 1918-1923' as related above was planned in the early outlining stage of the Military Operations series and research for it was carried out even though the writing of it had been cancelled. When *Brigadier General Sir* J. Edmonds was given the go ahead for its companion volume ('The Occupation of the Rhineland 1918-1929'), he also wrote this one, finishing it in 1944. Since it had not been sanctioned during 1944 it was not published. This was probably due to a lack of financial support. A copy of his draft manuscript has survived in the National Archives at Kew. Based on this original draft, the Naval and Military Press published this volume.

Constantinople is present day Istanbul, Turkey.

Order of Battle;

HISTORY OF THE WAR BASED ON OFFICIAL DOCUMENTS – ORDER OF BATTLE OF DIVISIONS PART 1 - THE REGULAR BRITISH DIVISIONS.

Major A.F. [Archibald Frank] Becke. | 27cm x 19cm | Grey Paper Hardback Red Cloth Spine | ix + 130pp | His Majesty's Stationery Office. | 1935 | English Text.

There was a print run of 770 copies.

Two Addenda and Corrigenda sheets were issued with the following volumes: Order of Battle of Divisions Part 3A and Order of Battle of Divisions Part 3B.

Ray Westlake Books republished this volume in 1989. The Imperial War Museum Department of Printed Books in association with the Naval and Military Press Ltd republished it again in 2009.

HISTORY OF THE WAR BASED ON OFFICIAL DOCUMENTS – ORDER OF BATTLE OF DIVISIONS PART 2A - THE TERRITORIAL FORCE, MOUNTED DIVISIONS AND THE 1ST LINE TERRITORIAL FORCE DIVISIONS (42ND-56TH).

Major A.F. [Archibald Frank] Becke. | 27cm x 19cm | Grey Paper Hardback Red Cloth Spine | ix + 157pp | His Majesty's Stationery Office. | 1936 | English Text.

There was a print run of 550 copies.

Three Addenda and Corrigenda sheets were issued for this volume with the following volumes: Order of Battle of Divisions Part 3A; Order of Battle of Divisions Part 3B and Order of Battle of Divisions Part 4.

Ray Westlake Books republished this volume in 1989. The Imperial War Museum Department of Printed Books in association with the Naval and Military Press Ltd republished it again in 2009.

HISTORY OF THE WAR BASED ON OFFICIAL DOCUMENTS – ORDER OF BATTLE OF DIVISIONS PART 2B - THE 2ND LINE TERRITORIAL FORCE DIVISIONS (57TH-69TH) WITH THE HOME SERVICE DIVISIONS (71ST-73RD) AND 74TH AND 75TH DIVISIONS.

Major A.F. [Archibald Frank] Becke. | 27cm x 19cm | Grey Paper Hardback Red Cloth Spine | ix + 147pp | His Majesty's Stationery Office. | 1937 | English Text.

There was a print run of 520 copies.

Three Addenda and Corrigenda sheets were issued for this volume with the following volumes: Order of Battle of Divisions Part 3A; Order of Battle of Divisions Part 3B and Order of Battle of Divisions Part 4.

Ray Westlake Books republished this volume in 1988. The Imperial War Museum Department of Printed Books in association with the Naval and Military Press Ltd republished it again in 2009.

HISTORY OF THE WAR BASED ON OFFICIAL DOCUMENTS – ORDER OF BATTLE OF DIVISIONS PART 3A - NEW ARMY DIVISIONS (9TH-26TH).

Major A.F. [Archibald Frank] Becke. | 27cm x 19cm | Grey Paper Hardback Red Cloth Spine | xi + 162pp | His Majesty's Stationery Office. | 1939 | English Text.

Three Addenda and Corrigenda sheets were issued for this volume with the following volumes: Order of Battle of Divisions Part 3A; Order of Battle of Divisions Part 3B and Order of Battle of Divisions Part 4.

Ray Westlake Books republished this volume and volume Part 3B as one volume – nd c.1989. The Imperial War Museum Department of Printed Books in association with the Naval and Military Press Ltd republished it again in 2009.

HISTORY OF THE WAR BASED ON OFFICIAL DOCUMENTS – ORDER OF BATTLE OF DIVISIONS PART 3B - NEW ARMY DIVISIONS (30TH-41ST) AND 63RD (RN) DIVISION.

Major A.F. [Archibald Frank] Becke. | 27cm x 19cm | Grey Paper Hardback Red Cloth Spine | viii + 155pp | His Majesty's Stationery Office. | 1946 | English Text.

An Addenda and Corrigenda sheet was issued with this volume.

Ray Westlake Books republished this volume and volume Part 3A as one volume – nd c.1989. The Imperial War Museum Department of Printed Books in association with the Naval and Military Press Ltd republished it again in 2009.

HISTORY OF THE WAR BASED ON OFFICIAL DOCUMENTS – ORDER OF BATTLE OF DIVISIONS PART 4 - THE ARMY COUNCIL, G.H.Q., ARMIES AND CORPS, 1914-1918.

Major A.F. [Archibald Frank] Becke. | 27cm x 19cm | Grey Paper Hardback Red Cloth Spine | x + 302pp | His Majesty's Stationery Office. | 1946 | English Text.

There was a print run of 500 copies.

An Addenda and Corrigenda sheet was issued with this volume and with the Military Operations, Italy volume.

Ray Westlake Books republished this volume in 1990. The Imperial War Museum Department of Printed Books in association with the Naval and Military Press Ltd republished it again in 2009.

HISTORY OF THE WAR BASED ON OFFICIAL DOCUMENTS – ORDER OF BATTLE OF DIVISIONS PART 5

Non-Official see footnote [13].

Aviation Activities;

---

[13] **Non-Official Histories - Order of Battle;**

The Order of Battle of Divisions, Part 5 was originally planned as part of the above Official History of the War – Order of Battle of Divisions set, but for unknown reasons, possibly financial, it was not written at the time when Parts 1 through to 4 by *Major* Becke. Therefore, F.W. Perry, a non official historian, compiled Part 5 splitting it into two parts - Parts 5A and 5B - in the early 1990's to complete this official set albeit un-officially. Although they are not "Official Histories" per se, I have listed them here under the sub heading "Order of Battle - Non-Official Histories" to complete the set. Ray Westlake in 2008 created a more complete index for this set than the index within the individual Order of Battles.

HISTORY OF THE WAR BASED ON OFFICIAL DOCUMENTS – ORDER OF BATTLE OF DIVISIONS PART 5A - THE DIVISIONS OF AUSTRALIA, CANADA AND NEW ZEALAND.

F.W. Perry. | 30cm x 21.5cm | Red Cloth Hardback | 104pp | Ray Westlake Books. | 1992 | English Text.

HISTORY OF THE WAR BASED ON OFFICIAL DOCUMENTS – ORDER OF BATTLE OF DIVISIONS PART 5B - THE INDIAN ARMY DIVISIONS.

F.W. Perry. | 30cm x 21.5cm | Red Cloth Hardback | 180pp | Ray Westlake Books. | 1993 | English Text.

HISTORY OF THE WAR BASED ON OFFICIAL DOCUMENTS – ORDER OF BATTLE OF DIVISIONS INDEX.

Ray Westlake | 27cm x 19cm | Illustrated Hardback | 75pp + 33pp left blank for notes | The Naval and Military Press Ltd. | 2009 | English Text.
ISBN:1-847349-25-0

HISTORY OF THE WAR BASED ON OFFICIAL DOCUMENTS BY DIRECTION OF THE HISTORICAL SECTION OF THE COMMITTEE OF IMPERIAL DEFENCE – THE WAR IN THE AIR, Being the Story of The part played in the Great War by the Royal Air Force. VOL. I.[14]

[*Sir*] Walter [Alexander] Raleigh. | 22.5cm x 16cm | Air Force Blue Hardback | Gilt | White Paper Dust Jacket | xix + 489pp | 8 maps | 1 diagram| Oxford Clarendon Press. | 1922 | English Text.

Unlike the previous volumes in the British official history series where there were only one title page per volume, this sub set the '**War in the Air**' had two title pages. The first page had the general set title '**History of the War Based on Official Documents by Direction of the Historical Section of the Committee of Imperial Defence**' and on the second page had the volume title '**The War in the Air. Being the Story of The part played in the Great War by the Royal Air Force.**' followed by the volume number. The titles for this sub set are a combination of the two title pages.

This volume '**War in the Air, Volume I**' was republished by Oxford Clarendon in 1939.

Hamish Hamilton republished this volume in 1969. The Imperial War Museum Department of Printed Books in association with the Battery Press republished this volume in 1998. Naval and Military Press in association with The Imperial War Museum Department of Printed Books produced a softback with colour illustrated covers in 2002.

Unfortunately Walter Raleigh died after he completed this the first volume of the 'War in the Air' set. H.A. Jones was therefore enlisted to complete the set.

This volume covers the period from pre-war to the winter 1914. It includes British flying operation during the Mons and First Yypres campaigns as well as the Royal Naval Air Service air raids on Friedrichshafen and Cuxhaven.

This volume can be viewed on the Internet Archive world wide web:

http://www.archive.org/stream/warinairbeingsto01raleuoft

HISTORY OF THE WAR BASED ON OFFICIAL DOCUMENTS BY DIRECTION OF THE HISTORICAL SECTION OF THE COMMITTEE OF IMPERIAL DEFENCE – THE WAR IN THE AIR, Being the Story of The part played in the Great War by the Royal Air Force. VOL. II.

H.A. [Henry Albert] Jones. | 22.5cm x 16cm | Air Force Blue Hardback | Gilt | White Paper Dust Jacket | xix + 508pp | 13 maps | Oxford Clarendon Press. | 1928 | English Text.

Hamish Hamilton republished this volume in 1969. The Imperial War Museum Department of Printed Books in association with the Battery Press republished this volume in 1999. Naval and Military Press in association with The Imperial War Museum Department of Printed Books produced a softback with colour illustrated covers in 2002

This volume covers Air Operations in the Dardanelles; Air Operations on the Western Front Spring 1915 – Autumn 1916; Naval Air Operations 1915.

HISTORY OF THE WAR BASED ON OFFICIAL DOCUMENTS BY DIRECTION OF THE HISTORICAL SECTION OF THE COMMITTEE OF IMPERIAL DEFENCE – THE WAR IN THE AIR, Being the Story of The part played in the Great War by the Royal Air Force. VOL. III.

H.A. [Henry Albert] Jones. | 22.5cm x 16cm | Air Force Blue Hardback | Gilt | White Paper Dust Jacket | xxii + 443pp | 6 maps | Oxford Clarendon Press. | 1931 | English Text.

The Imperial War Museum Department of Printed Books in association with the Battery Press republished this volume in 1998. Naval and Military Press in association with The Imperial War Museum Department of Printed Books produced a softback with colour illustrated covers in 2002

This volume covers Air Operations in East Africa (including operations against SMS Königsberg); Air Operations in South West Africa; German Bombing Operations on targets in Great Britain 1914 - 1916; Air Operations on the Western Front Winter 1916 – Spring 1917 (including the Battle of Arras).

---

[14] All the volumes of the "**War in the Air**" set have two title pages. The first page gives the set title "History of the War based on Official Documents by Direction of The Historical Section of The Committee of Imperial Defence" and the second page gives the sub set title and the volume number - "War in the Air…Volume I".

HISTORY OF THE WAR BASED ON OFFICIAL DOCUMENTS BY DIRECTION OF THE HISTORICAL SECTION OF THE COMMITTEE OF IMPERIAL DEFENCE – THE WAR IN THE AIR, Being the Story of The part played in the Great War by the Royal Air Force. VOL. III. [Map Case.].

H.A. [Henry Albert] Jones. | 22.5cm x 16cm | Air Force Blue Hardback | Gilt | White Paper Dust Jacket | 42 maps | Oxford Clarendon Press. | 1931 | English Text.

HISTORY OF THE WAR BASED ON OFFICIAL DOCUMENTS BY DIRECTION OF THE HISTORICAL SECTION OF THE COMMITTEE OF IMPERIAL DEFENCE – THE WAR IN THE AIR, Being the Story of The part played in the Great War by the Royal Air Force. VOL. IV.

H.A. [Henry Albert] Jones. | 22.5cm x 16cm | Air Force Blue Hardback | Gilt | White Paper Dust Jacket | xxii + 484pp | 21 maps | Oxford Clarendon Press. | 1934 | English Text.

The Imperial War Museum Department of Printed Books in association with the Battery Press republished this volume in 1998. Naval and Military Press in association with The Imperial War Museum Department of Printed Books produced a softback with colour illustrated covers in 2002

This volume covers Air Operations on the Western Front Summer 1917 – Summer 1918 (including the Battle of Messines).

HISTORY OF THE WAR BASED ON OFFICIAL DOCUMENTS BY DIRECTION OF THE HISTORICAL SECTION OF THE COMMITTEE OF IMPERIAL DEFENCE – THE WAR IN THE AIR, Being the Story of The part played in the Great War by the Royal Air Force. VOL. V.

H.A. [Henry Albert] Jones. | 22.5cm x 16cm | Air Force Blue Hardback | Gilt | White Paper Dust Jacket | xxiv + 537pp | 21 maps | Oxford Clarendon Press. | 1935 | English Text.

The Imperial War Museum Department of Printed Books in association with the Battery Press republished this volume in 1998. The Naval and Military Press in association with The Imperial War Museum Department of Printed Books produced a softback with colour illustrated covers in 2002

This volume covers German Bombing Operations on targets in Great Britain 1917 - 1918; Air Operations in Egpyt, Darfur, Palestine 1914 - 1917; Air Operations in Mesopotamia 1916 – march 1918; Naval Air Operations in the Mediterranean 1916 – March 1918.

HISTORY OF THE WAR BASED ON OFFICIAL DOCUMENTS BY DIRECTION OF THE HISTORICAL SECTION OF THE COMMITTEE OF IMPERIAL DEFENCE – THE WAR IN THE AIR, Being the Story of The part played in the Great War by the Royal Air Force. VOL. V. [Map Case.].

H.A. [Henry Albert] Jones. | 22.5cm x 16cm | Air Force Blue Hardback | Gilt | White Paper Dust Jacket | 28 maps | Oxford Clarendon Press. | 1935 | English Text.

HISTORY OF THE WAR BASED ON OFFICIAL DOCUMENTS BY DIRECTION OF THE HISTORICAL SECTION OF THE COMMITTEE OF IMPERIAL DEFENCE – THE WAR IN THE AIR, Being the Story of The part played in the Great War by the Royal Air Force. VOL. VI.

H.A. [Henry Albert] Jones. | 22.5cm x 16cm | Air Force Blue Hardback | Gilt | White Paper Dust Jacket | xxvii + 583pp | Oxford Clarendon Press. | 1937 | English Text.

The Naval and Military Press in association with The Imperial War Museum Department of Printed Books produced a softback with colour illustrated covers in 2002. The Imperial War Museum Department of Printed Books in association with the Battery Press republished this volume in 2003.

This volume covers R.A.F. Independent Bombing Air Operations; Air Operations in Mesopotamia, Persia, India, Macedonia, the Italian Front 1914 - 1917; Naval Air Operations in the Mediterranean Summer and Autumn 1918; Naval Air Operations over British Home Water; Air Operations on the Western Front Autumn 1918 (including the Battles of Amiens and Bapaume).

HISTORY OF THE WAR BASED ON OFFICIAL DOCUMENTS BY DIRECTION OF THE HISTORICAL SECTION OF THE COMMITTEE OF IMPERIAL DEFENCE – THE WAR IN THE AIR, Being the Story of The part played in the Great War by the Royal Air Force. APPENDICES

H.A. [Henry Albert] Jones. | 22.5cm x 16cm | Air Force Blue Hardback | Gilt | White Paper Dust Jacket | vii + 173pp | 46 appendices | 2 charts | 41 tables | Oxford Clarendon Press. | 1937 | English Text.

The Naval and Military Press in association with The Imperial War Museum Department of Printed Books produced a softback with colour illustrated covers in 2002 The Imperial War Museum Department of Printed Books in association with the Battery Press republished this volume in 2003.

Transportation Activities;

HISTORY OF THE WAR OFFICIAL DOCUMENTS BY DIRECTION OF THE HISTORICAL SECTION OF THE COMMITTEE OF IMPERIAL DEFENCE - TRANSPORTATION ON THE WESTERN FRONT 1914-1918.

Colonel A.M. [Alan Major] Henniker | 22.5cm x 16cm | Bright Red Hardback | Gilt | Brown Paper Dust Jacket | xxxiv + 531pp | 7 appendices | 17 maps | His Majesty's Stationery Office. | 1937 | English Text.

There was a print run of 1000 copies.

The Imperial War Museum Department of Printed Books in association with the Battery Press republished this volume in 1992.

Finally the Imperial War Museum Department of Printed Books in collaboration with the Naval and Military Press republished this volume in paperback format in 2009. With this edition all of the original coloured maps have been reproduced in colour.

HISTORY OF THE WAR OFFICIAL DOCUMENTS BY DIRECTION OF THE HISTORICAL SECTION OF THE COMMITTEE OF IMPERIAL DEFENCE - TRANSPORTATION ON THE WESTERN FRONT 1914-1918. [Map Case.].

Major A.F. [Archibald Frank] Becke. | 22.5cm x 16cm | Bright Red Hardback | Gilt | Brown Paper Dust Jacket | 14 maps | His Majesty's Stationery Office. | 1937 | English Text.

The Imperial War Museum Department of Printed Books in association with the Battery Press republished this map case in 1992 with the maps in black and white.

Medical Activities;

(*Major General* W.G.[William Grant] Macpherson [Editor])
HISTORY OF THE WAR BASED ON OFFICIAL DOCUMENTS – MEDICAL SERVICES: GENERAL HISTORY VOLUME I. MEDICAL SERVICES IN THE UNITED KINGDON; IN BRITISH GARRISONS OVERSEAS; AND DURING OPERATIONS AGAINST TSINGTAU, IN TOGOLAND, THE CAMEROONS, AND SOUTH-WEST AFRICA.

Major General Sir W.G. [William Grant] Macpherson. | 23cm x 14.5cm | Green Hardback | Gilt | xv + 463pp | untrimmed pages | 7 appendices | 7 maps | 15 photographs | 9 diagrams| His Majesty's Stationery Office. | 1921 | English Text.

There was a print run of 1500 copies.

This volume has been republished by The Naval and Military Press in 2009.

This volume can be viewed on the Internet Archive world wide web:

http://www.archive.org/stream/medicalservicesg01macpuoft

HISTORY OF THE WAR BASED ON OFFICIAL DOCUMENTS – MEDICAL SERVICES: GENERAL HISTORY VOLUME II. THE MEDICAL SERVICES ON THE WESTERN FRONT, AND DURING THE OPERATIONS IN FRANCE AND BELGIUM IN 1914 AND 1915.

Major General Sir W.G. [William Grant] Macpherson. | 23cm x 14.5cm | Green Hardback | Gilt | xi + 510pp | untrimmed pages | 3 appendices | 33 maps | 20 diagrams| His Majesty's Stationery Office. | 1923 | English Text.

There was a print run of 1500 copies.

This volume has been republished by The Naval and Military Press in 2009.

HISTORY OF THE WAR BASED ON OFFICIAL DOCUMENTS – MEDICAL SERVICES: GENERAL HISTORY VOLUME III. MEDICAL SERVICES DURING THE OPERATIONS ON THE WESTERN FRONT IN 1916, 1917 AND 1918; IN ITALY; AND IN EGYPT AND PALESTINE.

Major General Sir W.G. [William Grant] Macpherson. | 23cm x 14.5cm | Green Hardback | Gilt | vii + 556pp | untrimmed pages | 3 appendices | 28 maps | 79 photographs | 14 diagrams| His Majesty's Stationery Office. | 1924 | English Text.

There was a print run of 1500 copies.

This volume has been republished by The Naval and Military Press in 2009.

HISTORY OF THE WAR BASED ON OFFICIAL DOCUMENTS – MEDICAL SERVICES: GENERAL HISTORY VOLUME IV. MEDICAL SERVICES DURING THE OPERATIONS ON THE GALLIPOLI PENINSULA; IN MACEDONIA; IN MESOPOTAMIA AND NORTH-WEST PERSIA; IN EAST AFRICA; IN THE ADEN PROTECTORATE AND IN NORTH RUSSIA. AMBULANCE TRANSPORT DURING THE WAR.

Major General Sir W.G. [William Grant] Macpherson. I 23cm x 14.5cm I Green Hardback I Gilt I xvi + 711pp I 3 appendices I 52 maps I 178 photographs I 7 diagrams I His Majesty's Stationery Office. I 1924 I English Text.

There was a print run of 1500 copies.

This volume has been republished by The Naval and Military Press in 2009.

HISTORY OF THE WAR BASED ON OFFICIAL DOCUMENTS – MEDICAL SERVICES: HYGIENE OF THE WAR VOLUME I.

Major General Sir W.G. [William Grant] Macpherson, *Colonel Sir* W.H. [William Heaton] Horrocks and *Major General* W.W.O. [Wilfred William Ogilvy] Beveridge. I 23cm x 14.5cm I untrimmed pages I 4 appendices in 14 parts I Green Hardback I Gilt I xii + 400pp I His Majesty's Stationery Office. I 1923 I English Text.

HISTORY OF THE WAR BASED ON OFFICIAL DOCUMENTS – MEDICAL SERVICES: HYGIENE OF THE WAR VOLUME II.

Major General Sir W.G. [William Grant] Macpherson, *Colonel Sir* W.H. [William Heaton] Horrocks and *Major General* W.W.O. [Wilfred William Ogilvy] Beveridge. I 23cm x 14.5cm I untrimmed pages I 4 appendices in 9 parts I Green Hardback I Gilt I vii + 506pp I His Majesty's Stationery Office. I 1923 I English Text.

There was a print run of 1500 copies.

The Marmite Food Extract Co. Ltd reprinted nine pages from this volume in 1923 as a promotion for yeast. The pages were chapter 3 pages 83-86 and chapter 5 pages 150-152.

HISTORY OF THE WAR BASED ON OFFICIAL DOCUMENTS – MEDICAL SERVICES: PATHOLOGY.

Major General Sir W.G. [William Grant] Macpherson, *Major General Sir* W.B. [William Boog] Leishman and *Colonel* S.L. [Stevenson Lyle] Cummins. I 23cm x 14.5cm I Green Hardback I Gilt I vii + 600pp I untrimmed pages I 2 colour illustration on 2 plates I 2 photographs I His Majesty's Stationery Office. I 1923 I English Text.

It is believed that there was a print run of 1500 copies.

This volume can be viewed on the Internet Archive world wide web:

http://www.archive.org/stream/191418medicalserv00macpuoft

HISTORY OF THE WAR BASED ON OFFICIAL DOCUMENTS – MEDICAL SERVICES: SURGERY OF THE WAR VOLUME I.

Major General Sir W.G. [William Grant] Macpherson, *Major General Sir* A.A. [Anthony A.] Bowlby, *Major General Sir* Cuthbert [Sidney] Wallace and *Colonel* [Thomas] *Sir* Crisp English. I 23cm x 14.5cm I Green Hardback I Gilt I vii + 618pp I untrimmed pages I 5 appendices I 24 colour illustration on 16 plates I His Majesty's Stationery Office. I 1922 I English Text.

There was a print run of 1000 copies.

It is not known why this volume had a print run of 1000 instead of 1500 in line with the rest of the Medical Services series.

HISTORY OF THE WAR BASED ON OFFICIAL DOCUMENTS – MEDICAL SERVICES: SURGERY OF THE WAR VOLUME II.

Major General Sir W.G. [William Grant] Macpherson, *Major General Sir* A.A. [Anthony A.] Bowlby, *Major General Sir* Cuthbert [Sidney] Wallace and *Colonel* [Thomas] *Sir* Crisp English. I 23cm x 14.5cm I Green Hardback I Gilt I vii + 604pp I untrimmed pages I 12 colour illustration on 7 plates I 17 diagrams I His Majesty's Stationery Office. I 1922 I English Text.

There was a print run of 1500 copies.

HISTORY OF THE WAR BASED ON OFFICIAL DOCUMENTS – MEDICAL SERVICES: DISEASES OF THE WAR VOLUME I.

Major General Sir W.G. [William Grant] Macpherson, *Major General Sir* W.P. [Wilmot Parker] Herringham, *Colonel* T.R. [Thomas Renton] Elliott and *Lieutenant Colonel* A. [*Sir* Andrew] Balfour. I 23cm x 14.5cm I Green Hardback I Gilt I viii + 550pp I untrimmed pages I 3 maps I 71 charts I 99 tables I 8 colour illustration on 7 plates I 25 diagrams I His Majesty's Stationery Office. I 1922 I English Text.

There was a print run of 1500 copies.

This volume can be viewed on the Internet Archive world wide web:

http://www.archive.org/stream/medicalservicesd01macpuoft

HISTORY OF THE WAR BASED ON OFFICIAL DOCUMENTS – MEDICAL SERVICES: DISEASES OF THE WAR VOLUME II.

Major General Sir W.G. [William Grant] Macpherson, *Major General Sir* W.P. [Wilmot Parker] Herringham, *Colonel* T.R. [Thomas Renton] Elliott English and *Lieutenant Colonel* A. [*Sir* Andrew] Balfour. I 23cm x 14.5cm I Green Hardback I Gilt I viii + 621pp I untrimmed pages I 14 charts I 91 tables I 35 photographs I 7 colour illustration on 7 plates I 30 diagramsI His Majesty's Stationery Office. I 1923 I English Text.

There was a print run of 1500 copies.

This volume can be viewed on the Internet Archive world wide web:

http://www.archive.org/details/medicalservicess02macpiala

HISTORY OF THE WAR BASED ON OFFICIAL DOCUMENTS – MEDICAL SERVICES: CASUALTIES AND MEDICALS STATISTICS OF THE GREAT WAR.

Major T.J. [Thomas John] Mitchell [*DSO, MD, RAMC*] and *Miss* G.M. Smith [*MBE*]. I 23cm x 14.5cm I Green Hardback I Gilt I xx + 382pp I 21 sections I His Majesty's Stationery Office. I 1931 I English Text.

There was a print run of 1500 copies.

The Imperial War Museum Department of Printed Books in association with the Battery Press republished this volume in 1997.

HISTORY OF THE WAR BASED ON OFFICIAL DOCUMENTS – VETERINARY SERVICES.

Major General Sir L.J. [Layton John] Blenkinsop and *Lieutenant Colonel* J.W. [John Wakefield] Rainey. I 25cm x 15.5cm I Maroon Cloth Hardback I Gilt I ix + 782pp I 5 appendices in 19 parts I His Majesty's Stationery Office. I 1925 I English Text.

There was a print run of 1500 copies.

Statistics;

STATISTICS OF THE MILITARY EFFORT OF THE BRITISH EMPIRE DURING THE GREAT WAR.[15]

Anonymous I 33cm x 21cm I White Paper Softback I 880pp I 4 appendices I 390 tables I His Majesty's Stationery Office. I 1922 I English Text.

There was a print run of 1000 copies.

This volume was republished as a hardback (maroon cloth with a white dust jacket) by The London Stamp Exchange Ltd, in 1987. The Naval and Military Press Ltd republished it in softback format in 1995 and again in 2001.

Munitions Activities[16];

THE HISTORY OF THE MINISTRY OF MUNITIONS: VOLUME I INDUSTRIAL MOBILISATION 1914-15. PART I MUNITIONS SUPPLY 1914-15.

Anonymous I 21cm x 13.5cm I Blue Grey Paper Softback I 150pp I 4 appendices I 26 tables I His Majesty's Stationery Office. I 1920 I English Text.

There was a print run of 250 copies.

THE HISTORY OF THE MINISTRY OF MUNITIONS: VOLUME I INDUSTRIAL MOBILISATION 1914-15. PART II THE TREASURY AGREEMENT.

Anonymous I 21cm x 13.5cm I Blue Grey Paper Softback I v + 118pp I 9 appendices I 8 tables I His Majesty's Stationery Office. I 1920 I English Text.

There was a print run of 250 copies.

THE HISTORY OF THE MINISTRY OF MUNITIONS: VOLUME I INDUSTRIAL MOBILISATION 1914-15. PART III THE ARMAMENTS OUTPUT COMMITTEE.

---

[15] This volume makes no reference to the set title "History of the War" nor to "The Historical Section of the Committee of Imperial Defence".

[16] "**The History of the Ministry of Munitions**" was published as a series of paperback booklets, which were grouped together to form volumes. The booklets were often bound together as twelve volumes. The Naval and Military Press has republished these this set bound as volumes.

Anonymous | 21cm x 13.5cm | Blue Grey Paper Softback | vii + 153pp | 15 appendices | 3 tables | His Majesty's Stationery Office. | 1920 | English Text.

There was a print run of 250 copies.

THE HISTORY OF THE MINISTRY OF MUNITIONS: VOLUME I INDUSTRIAL MOBILISATION 1914-15. PART IV THE MUNITIONS OF WAR ACT 1915.

Anonymous | 21cm x 13.5cm | Blue Grey Paper Softback | iii + 71pp | 2 appendices | His Majesty's Stationery Office. | 1920 | English Text.

There was a print run of 250 copies.

THE HISTORY OF THE MINISTRY OF MUNITIONS: VOLUME II GENERAL ORGANISATION OF MUNITIONS SUPPLY. PART I – CHAPTER IV MR CHURCHILL'S ADMINISTRATION – CO-ORDINATED EFFORT.

Anonymous | 21cm x 13.5cm | Blue Grey Paper Softback | iv + 32pp | His Majesty's Stationery Office. | 1920 | English Text.

There was a print run of 250 copies.

THE HISTORY OF THE MINISTRY OF MUNITIONS: VOLUME II GENERAL ORGANISATION OF MUNITIONS SUPPLY. PART I ADMINISTRATIVE POLICY AND ORGANISATION.

Anonymous | 21cm x 13.5cm | Blue Grey Paper Softback | vii + 307pp | 16 appendices | 3 tables | 5 charts | His Majesty's Stationery Office. | 1921 | English Text.

There was a print run of 250 copies.

THE HISTORY OF THE MINISTRY OF MUNITIONS: VOLUME II GENERAL ORGANISATION OF MUNITIONS SUPPLY. PART I – SUPPLEMENT: LIQUIDATION OF THE HISTORY OF THE MINISTRY OF MUNITIONS.

Anonymous | 21cm x 13.5cm | Blue Grey Paper Softback | iv + 45pp | 1 appendix | 1 table | His Majesty's Stationery Office. | 1922 | English Text.

There was a print run of 250 copies.

Note that Volume II Part I was issued in three sections: '**Part I – Chapter IV Mr Churchill's Administration**' was the first to be issued in 1920. '**Part I Administrative Policy and Organisation**' was issued next in 1921 and included the chapter 4 which had already been published. Finally in 1922 '**Part I – Supplement**' was issued. No reason has been found why chapter 4 was published first and independently of the other chapters in this part.

THE HISTORY OF THE MINISTRY OF MUNITIONS: VOLUME II GENERAL ORGANISATION OF MUNITIONS SUPPLY. PART II – CHAPTER II THE PROBLEM OF CENTRAL CONTROL.

Anonymous | 21cm x 13.5cm | Blue Grey Paper Softback | iv + 41pp | 1 appendix | His Majesty's Stationery Office. | 1920 | English Text.

There was a print run of 250 copies.

THE HISTORY OF THE MINISTRY OF MUNITIONS: VOLUME II GENERAL ORGANISATION OF MUNITIONS SUPPLY. PART II LOCAL ORGANISATION IN THE UNITED KINGDOM UNDER THE DEPARTMENT OF AREA ORGANISATION.

Anonymous | 21cm x 13.5cm | Blue Grey Paper Softback | x + 172pp | 5 appendices | 7 tables | His Majesty's Stationery Office. | 1921 | English Text.

There was a print run of 250 copies.

Note that Volume Part II was issued in two sections: '**Part II – Chapter II The Problem of Central Control**' in 1920 and '**Part II Local Organisation in the United Kingdom under the Department of Area Organisation**' in 1921. Chapter II was totally rewritten when it reappeared in the completed 1921 Part II.

THE HISTORY OF THE MINISTRY OF MUNITIONS: VOLUME II GENERAL ORGANISATION OF MUNITIONS SUPPLY. PART III MUNITIONS ORGANISATION IN THE UNITED STATES OF AMERICA.

Anonymous | 21cm x 13.5cm | Blue Grey Paper Softback | vi + 129pp | 10 appendices | 7 tables | 1 chart | His Majesty's Stationery Office. | 1921 | English Text.

There was a print run of 250 copies.

THE HISTORY OF THE MINISTRY OF MUNITIONS: VOLUME II GENERAL ORGANISATION OF MUNITIONS SUPPLY. PART IV MUNITIONS ORGANISATION IN CANADA.

Anonymous | 21cm x 13.5cm | Blue Grey Paper Softback | vi + 81pp | 3 appendices | 3 tables | His Majesty's Stationery Office. | 1922 | English Text.

There was a print run of 250 copies.

THE HISTORY OF THE MINISTRY OF MUNITIONS: VOLUME II GENERAL ORGANISATION OF MUNITIONS SUPPLY. PART V INDIA.

Anonymous | 21cm x 13.5cm | Blue Grey Paper Softback | ii + 25pp | 1 appendix | 1 table | His Majesty's Stationery Office. | 1920 | English Text.

There was a print run of 250 copies.

THE HISTORY OF THE MINISTRY OF MUNITIONS: VOLUME II GENERAL ORGANISATION OF MUNITIONS SUPPLY. PART VI AUSTRALIA.

Anonymous | 21cm x 13.5cm | Blue Grey Paper Softback | ii + 18pp | His Majesty's Stationery Office. | 1920 | English Text.

THE HISTORY OF THE MINISTRY OF MUNITIONS: VOLUME II GENERAL ORGANISATION OF MUNITIONS SUPPLY. PART VII CONTINENTAL ORGANISATION.

Anonymous | 21cm x 13.5cm | Blue Grey Paper Softback | ii + 22pp | 1 appendix in 2 parts | His Majesty's Stationery Office. | 1920 | English Text.

There was a print run of 250 copies.

THE HISTORY OF THE MINISTRY OF MUNITIONS: VOLUME II GENERAL ORGANISATION OF MUNITIONS SUPPLY. PART VIII INTER-ALLIED ORGANISATION.

Anonymous | 21cm x 13.5cm | Blue Grey Paper Softback | iv + 99pp | 5 appendices | 6 tables | 1 chart | His Majesty's Stationery Office. | 1921 | English Text.

There was a print run of 250 copies.

THE HISTORY OF THE MINISTRY OF MUNITIONS: VOLUME III FINANCIAL AND CONTRACTS. PART I FINANCIAL ADMINISTRATION.

Anonymous | 21cm x 13.5cm | Blue Grey Paper Softback | iv + 167pp | 1 appendix | 2 tables | 1 diagram | His Majesty's Stationery Office. | 1920 | English Text.

There was a print run of 250 copies.

THE HISTORY OF THE MINISTRY OF MUNITIONS: VOLUME III FINANCIAL AND CONTRACTS. PART II CONTRACTS.

Anonymous | 21cm x 13.5cm | Blue Grey Paper Softback | v + 200pp | 17 appendices | 16 tables | His Majesty's Stationery Office. | 1920 | English Text.

There was a print run of 250 copies.

THE HISTORY OF THE MINISTRY OF MUNITIONS: VOLUME III FINANCIAL AND CONTRACTS. PART III FINANCING OF PRODUCTION.

Anonymous | 21cm x 13.5cm | Blue Grey Paper Softback | v + 121pp | 3 appendices | 3 tables | His Majesty's Stationery Office. | 1922 | English Text.

There was a print run of 250 copies.

THE HISTORY OF THE MINISTRY OF MUNITIONS: VOLUME IV THE SUPPLY AND CONTROL OF LABOUR 1915-1916. PART I LABOUR SUPPLY JULY-DECEMBER 1915.

Anonymous | 21cm x 13.5cm | Blue Grey Paper Softback | vi + 114pp | 6 appendices | 1 table | His Majesty's Stationery Office. | 1918 | English Text.

There was a print run of 250 copies.

THE HISTORY OF THE MINISTRY OF MUNITIONS: VOLUME IV THE SUPPLY AND CONTROL OF LABOUR 1915-1916. PART II LABOUR REGULATION AND THE MINISTRY OF MUNITIONS (AMENDMENT) ACT, 1916.

Anonymous | 21cm x 13.5cm | Blue Grey Paper Softback | iv + 128pp | 5 appendices | 7 tables | His Majesty's Stationery Office. | 1918 | English Text.

There was a print run of 250 copies.

THE HISTORY OF THE MINISTRY OF MUNITIONS: VOLUME IV THE SUPPLY AND CONTROL OF LABOUR 1915-1916. PART III THE LIMITATION OF RECRUITING.

Anonymous | 21cm x 13.5cm | Blue Grey Paper Softback | viii + 109pp | 12 appendices | 9 tables | His Majesty's Stationery Office. | 1919 | English Text.

There was a print run of 250 copies.

THE HISTORY OF THE MINISTRY OF MUNITIONS: VOLUME IV THE SUPPLY AND CONTROL OF LABOUR 1915-1916. PART IV THE PROGRESS OF DILUTION.

Anonymous | 21cm x 13.5cm | Blue Grey Paper Softback | viii + 183pp | 19 appendices | 22 tables | 3 charts | His Majesty's Stationery Office. | 1920 | English Text.

There was a print run of 250 copies.

THE HISTORY OF THE MINISTRY OF MUNITIONS: VOLUME V WAGES AND WELFARE. PART I THE CONTROL OF MEN'S WAGES.

Anonymous | 21cm x 13.5cm | Blue Grey Paper Softback | vii + 264pp | 7 appendices in 13 parts | 7 tables | His Majesty's Stationery Office. | 1922 | English Text.
There was a print run of 250 copies.

THE HISTORY OF THE MINISTRY OF MUNITIONS: VOLUME V WAGES AND WELFARE. PART II THE CONTROL OF WOMEN'S WAGES.

Anonymous | 21cm x 13.5cm | Blue Grey Paper Softback | vi + 201pp | 6 appendices in 11 parts | 9 tables | His Majesty's Stationery Office. | 1922 | English Text.
There was a print run of 250 copies.

THE HISTORY OF THE MINISTRY OF MUNITIONS: VOLUME V WAGES AND WELFARE. PART III WELFARE: THE CONTROL OF WORKING CONDITIONS.

Anonymous | 21cm x 13.5cm | Blue Grey Paper Softback | vii + 202pp | 4 appendices | 8 tables | His Majesty's Stationery Office. | 1922 | English Text.
There was a print run of 250 copies.

THE HISTORY OF THE MINISTRY OF MUNITIONS: VOLUME V WAGES AND WELFARE. PART IV THE PROVISION OF CANTEENS IN MUNITIONS FACTORIES.

Anonymous | 21cm x 13.5cm | Blue Grey Paper Softback | iii + 28pp | 2 appendices | His Majesty's Stationery Office. | 1922 | English Text.
There was a print run of 250 copies.

THE HISTORY OF THE MINISTRY OF MUNITIONS: VOLUME V WAGES AND WELFARE. PART V PROVISION OF THE HOUSING OF MUNITIONS WORKERS.

Anonymous | 21cm x 13.5cm | Blue Grey Paper Softback | iv + 92pp | 2 appendices in 4 parts | 6 tables | His Majesty's Stationery Office. | 1922 | English Text.
There was a print run of 250 copies.

THE HISTORY OF THE MINISTRY OF MUNITIONS: VOLUME VI MAN POWER AND DILUTION. PART I RELEASE OF MUNITIONS WORKERS FOR MILITARY SERVICE.

Anonymous | 21cm x 13.5cm | Blue Grey Paper Softback | vi + 130pp | 6 appendices | 2 tables | His Majesty's Stationery Office. | 1922 | English Text.
There was a print run of 250 copies.

THE HISTORY OF THE MINISTRY OF MUNITIONS: VOLUME VI MAN POWER AND DILUTION. PART II THE CONTROL OF INDUSTRIAL MAN POWER, 1917-18.

Anonymous | 21cm x 13.5cm | Blue Grey Paper Softback | vi + 103pp | 5 appendices | 3 tables | His Majesty's Stationery Office. | 1922 | English Text.
There was a print run of 250 copies.
Note that Part II and Part III as originally planned were "by force of circumstances" condensed into an enlarged Part II with extra appendices. No Part III was published.

THE HISTORY OF THE MINISTRY OF MUNITIONS: VOLUME VI MAN POWER AND DILUTION. PART IV STATISTICAL REVIEW OF MAN POWER.

Anonymous | 21cm x 13.5cm | Blue Grey Paper Softback | vi + 76pp | 28 tables | His Majesty's Stationery Office. | 1918 | English Text.
There was a print run of 250 copies.
Note Part IV was misprinted as Part I on the title page. It was correctly printed on the front cover.

THE HISTORY OF THE MINISTRY OF MUNITIONS: VOLUME VII THE CONTROL OF MATERIALS. PART I REVIEW OF COMMERCIAL CONTROL.

Anonymous | 21cm x 13.5cm | Blue Grey Paper Softback | v + 150pp | 4 appendices | 5 supplements in 19 parts | 2 tables | His Majesty's Stationery Office. | 1922 | English Text.
There was a print run of 250 copies.

THE HISTORY OF THE MINISTRY OF MUNITIONS: VOLUME VII THE CONTROL OF MATERIALS. PART II IRON AND STEEL.

Anonymous | 21cm x 13.5cm | Blue Grey Paper Softback | vi + 161pp | 8 appendices in 10 parts | 28 tables | His Majesty's Stationery Office. | 1922 | English Text.
There was a print run of 250 copies.

THE HISTORY OF THE MINISTRY OF MUNITIONS: VOLUME VII THE CONTROL OF MATERIALS. PART III NON-FERROUS METALS.

Anonymous | 21cm x 13.5cm | Blue Grey Paper Softback | vii + 197pp | 8 appendices | 24 tables | His Majesty's Stationery Office. | 1922 | English Text.
There was a print run of 250 copies.

THE HISTORY OF THE MINISTRY OF MUNITIONS: VOLUME VII THE CONTROL OF MATERIALS. PART IV MATERIALS FOR EXPLOSIVE MANUFACTURE.

Anonymous | 21cm x 13.5cm | Blue Grey Paper Softback | vi + 103pp | 18 appendices | 6 tables | His Majesty's Stationery Office. | 1921 | English Text.

There was a print run of 250 copies.

THE HISTORY OF THE MINISTRY OF MUNITIONS: VOLUME VII THE CONTROL OF MATERIALS. PART V TRANSPORT, STORAGE AND SALVAGE.

Anonymous | 21cm x 13.5cm | Blue Grey Paper Softback | v + 64pp | 1 appendix | 4 tables | His Majesty's Stationery Office. | 1922 | English Text.

There was a print run of 250 copies.

THE HISTORY OF THE MINISTRY OF MUNITIONS: VOLUME VIII CONTROL OF INDUSTRIAL CAPACITY AND EQUIPMENT. PART I REVIEW OF STATE MANUFACTURE.

Anonymous | 21cm x 13.5cm | Blue Grey Paper Softback | iv + 91pp | 2 tables | His Majesty's Stationery Office. | 1922 | English Text.

There was a print run of 250 copies.

THE HISTORY OF THE MINISTRY OF MUNITIONS: VOLUME VIII CONTROL OF INDUSTRIAL CAPACITY AND EQUIPMENT. PART II THE NATIONAL FACTORIES.

Anonymous | 21cm x 13.5cm | Blue Grey Paper Softback | vii + 259pp | 4 appendices | 23 tables | His Majesty's Stationery Office. | 1922 | English Text.

There was a print run of 250 copies.

THE HISTORY OF THE MINISTRY OF MUNITIONS: VOLUME VIII CONTROL OF INDUSTRIAL CAPACITY AND EQUIPMENT. PART III ENGINEERING SUPPLIES.

Anonymous | 21cm x 13.5cm | Blue Grey Paper Softback | vii + 138pp | 19 appendices | 10 tables | His Majesty's Stationery Office. | 1920 | English Text.

There was a print run of 250 copies.

THE HISTORY OF THE MINISTRY OF MUNITIONS: VOLUME VIII CONTROL OF INDUSTRIAL CAPACITY AND EQUIPMENT. PART IV CONTROL OF ENGINEERING CAPACITY: ADMINISTRATIVE MACHINERY.

Anonymous | 21cm x 13.5cm | Blue Grey Paper Softback | iii + 18pp | His Majesty's Stationery Office. | 1921 | English Text.

There was a print run of 250 copies.

THE HISTORY OF THE MINISTRY OF MUNITIONS: VOLUME IX REVIEW OF MUNITIONS SUPPLY. PART I MUNITIONS PROGRAMMES.

Anonymous | 21cm x 13.5cm | Blue Grey Paper Softback | v + 61pp | 6 appendices | 5 tables | His Majesty's Stationery Office. | 1922 | English Text.

There was a print run of 250 copies.

THE HISTORY OF THE MINISTRY OF MUNITIONS: VOLUME IX REVIEW OF MUNITIONS SUPPLY. PART II DESIGN AND INSPECTION.

Anonymous | 21cm x 13.5cm | Blue Grey Paper Softback | vi + 117pp | 6 appendices | 3 tables | His Majesty's Stationery Office. | 1922 | English Text.

There was a print run of 250 copies.

It was planned that Volume IX Review of Munitions Supply was to have a third part with a title '**Part III Statistical Review of Output**' however this part was not issued.

THE HISTORY OF THE MINISTRY OF MUNITIONS: VOLUME X THE SUPPLY OF MUNITIONS. PART I GUNS.

Anonymous | 21cm x 13.5cm | Blue Grey Paper Softback | v + 97pp | 1 appendix in 2 parts | 2 tables | His Majesty's Stationery Office. | 1922 | English Text.

There was a print run of 250 copies.

THE HISTORY OF THE MINISTRY OF MUNITIONS: VOLUME X THE SUPPLY OF MUNITIONS. PART II GUNS AMMUNITION: GENERAL.

Anonymous | 21cm x 13.5cm | Blue Grey Paper Softback | iv + 69pp | 1 appendix | 1 table | His Majesty's Stationery Office. | 1921 | English Text.

There was a print run of 250 copies.

THE HISTORY OF THE MINISTRY OF MUNITIONS: VOLUME X THE SUPPLY OF MUNITIONS. PART III GUNS AMMUNITION: SHELL MANUFACTURE.

Anonymous | 21cm x 13.5cm | Blue Grey Paper Softback | vi + 122pp | 5 appendices | 5 tables | His Majesty's Stationery Office. | 1922 | English Text.

There was a print run of 250 copies.

THE HISTORY OF THE MINISTRY OF MUNITIONS: VOLUME X THE SUPPLY OF MUNITIONS. PART IV GUNS AMMUNITION: EXPLOSIVES.

Anonymous | 21cm x 13.5cm | Blue Grey Paper Softback | vii + 146pp | 1 table | His Majesty's Stationery Office. | 1921 | English Text.

There was a print run of 250 copies.

An erarata sheet was issued with this volume.

THE HISTORY OF THE MINISTRY OF MUNITIONS: VOLUME X THE SUPPLY OF MUNITIONS. PART V GUNS AMMUNITION: FILLING AND COMPLETING.

Anonymous | 21cm x 13.5cm | Blue Grey Paper Softback | v + 89pp | 4 tables | His Majesty's Stationery Office. | 1921 | English Text.

There was a print run of 250 copies.

THE HISTORY OF THE MINISTRY OF MUNITIONS: VOLUME X THE SUPPLY OF MUNITIONS. PART VI ANTI-AIRCRAFT SUPPLIES.

Anonymous | 21cm x 13.5cm | Blue Grey Paper Softback | iv + 59pp | 1 appendix | 1 table | His Majesty's Stationery Office. | 1920 | English Text.

There was a print run of 250 copies.

THE HISTORY OF THE MINISTRY OF MUNITIONS: VOLUME XI THE SUPPLY OF MUNITIONS. PART I TRENCH WARFARE SUPPLIES.

Anonymous | 21cm x 13.5cm | Blue Grey Paper Softback | vi + 139pp | 13 appendices | 6 tables | His Majesty's Stationery Office. | 1920 | English Text.

There was a print run of 250 copies.

THE HISTORY OF THE MINISTRY OF MUNITIONS: VOLUME XI THE SUPPLY OF MUNITIONS. PART II CHEMICAL WARFARE SUPPLIES.

Anonymous | 21cm x 13.5cm | Blue Grey Paper Softback | vi + 113pp | 6 tables | His Majesty's Stationery Office. | 1921 | English Text.

There was a print run of 250 copies.

THE HISTORY OF THE MINISTRY OF MUNITIONS: VOLUME XI THE SUPPLY OF MUNITIONS. PART III OPTICAL MUNITIONS AND GLASSWARE.

Anonymous | 21cm x 13.5cm | Blue Grey Paper Softback | iv + 152pp | 7 appendices in 14 parts | 3 tables | His Majesty's Stationery Office. | 1920 | English Text.

There was a print run of 250 copies.

THE HISTORY OF THE MINISTRY OF MUNITIONS: VOLUME XI THE SUPPLY OF MUNITIONS. PART IV RIFLES.

Anonymous | 21cm x 13.5cm | Blue Grey Paper Softback | iv + 68pp | 1 table | His Majesty's Stationery Office. | 1921 | English Text.

There was a print run of 250 copies.

THE HISTORY OF THE MINISTRY OF MUNITIONS: VOLUME XI THE SUPPLY OF MUNITIONS. PART V MACHINE GUNS.

Anonymous | 21cm x 13.5cm | Blue Grey Paper Softback | iv + 27pp | 1 table | His Majesty's Stationery Office. | 1922 | English Text.

There was a print run of 250 copies.

THE HISTORY OF THE MINISTRY OF MUNITIONS: VOLUME XI THE SUPPLY OF MUNITIONS. PART VI SMALL ARMS AMMUNITION.

Anonymous | 21cm x 13.5cm | Blue Grey Paper Softback | iv + 106pp | 3 appendices in 5 parts | 3 tables | His Majesty's Stationery Office. | 1920 | English Text.

There was a print run of 250 copies.

THE HISTORY OF THE MINISTRY OF MUNITIONS: VOLUME XII THE SUPPLY OF MUNITIONS. PART I AIRCRAFT.

Anonymous | 21cm x 13.5cm | Blue Grey Paper Softback | vi + 200pp | 6 appendices | 1 table | His Majesty's Stationery Office. | 1921 | English Text.

There was a print run of 250 copies.

THE HISTORY OF THE MINISTRY OF MUNITIONS: VOLUME XII THE SUPPLY OF MUNITIONS. PART II AERIAL BOMBS.

Anonymous | 21cm x 13.5cm | Blue Grey Paper Softback | iv + 32pp | 5 tables | His Majesty's Stationery Office. | 1920 | English Text.

There was a print run of 250 copies.

THE HISTORY OF THE MINISTRY OF MUNITIONS: VOLUME XII THE SUPPLY OF MUNITIONS. PART III - CHAPTER I THE EVOLUTION OF THE FIRST TANKS.

Anonymous | 21cm x 13.5cm | Blue Grey Paper Softback | iv + 48pp | 5 appendices | 1 table | His Majesty's Stationery Office. | 1919 | English Text.

There was a print run of 250 copies.

THE HISTORY OF THE MINISTRY OF MUNITIONS: VOLUME XII THE SUPPLY OF MUNITIONS. PART III TANKS.

Anonymous | 21cm x 13.5cm | Blue Grey Paper Softback | iv + 99pp | 4 appendices | 3 tables | His Majesty's Stationery Office. | 1920 | English Text.

There was a print run of 250 copies.

Note that there were two Part III's – Titled '**Part III - Chapter I The Evolution of the First Tanks** and **Part III Tanks.**' The first part consisted of one chapter and the second part of six chapters including a Chapter I. It appears that the original plan of splitting Part III into two sections was not followed through when two years later the second part was produced.

THE HISTORY OF THE MINISTRY OF MUNITIONS: VOLUME XII THE SUPPLY OF MUNITIONS. PART IV MECHANICAL TRANSPORT VEHICLES.

Anonymous | 21cm x 13.5cm | Blue Grey Paper Softback | iv + 63pp | 1 appendix | 6 tables | His Majesty's Stationery Office. | 1921 | English Text.

There was a print run of 250 copies.

THE HISTORY OF THE MINISTRY OF MUNITIONS: VOLUME XII THE SUPPLY OF MUNITIONS. PART V RAILWAY MATERIALS AND ROPEWAYS.

Anonymous | 21cm x 13.5cm | Blue Grey Paper Softback | iv + 53pp | 2 appendices | 3 tables | His Majesty's Stationery Office. | 1921 | English Text.

There was a print run of 250 copies.

THE HISTORY OF THE MINISTRY OF MUNITIONS: VOLUME XII THE SUPPLY OF MUNITIONS. PART VI AGRICULTURAL MACHINERY.

Anonymous | 21cm x 13.5cm | Blue Grey Paper Softback | iv + 36pp | 4 appendices | 3 tables | 1 chart | His Majesty's Stationery Office. | 1919 | English Text.

There was a print run of 250 copies.

The complete set of '**The History of the Ministry of Munitions**' was republished as twelve volumes (containing all of the above parts) in microfiche format by Harvester Press in 1976.

The Naval and Military Press republished '**The History of the Ministry of Munitions**' set again as 12 volumes in 2009. This set has been bound in 13 parts with the 1022 pages of Volume II being split into two parts; Volume II/1 being the three publications that make up Part I and Volume II/2 being the publications that make up Parts II through VIII. All the Naval and Military Press produced volumes being produced in both hardback and softback.

Bulgarian Official Histories

The Bulgarian official history was written by members of the Министерство на войната. Щаб на армията. Военно-историческа (Ministerstvo na vojnata. Štab na armijata. Voenno-istoričeska - *Ministry of Defense. Army Staff History Section*). Unfortunately all work on this history was stopped towards the end of the Second World War leaving it uncompleted.

Military Operations;

БЪЛГАРСКАТА АРМИЯ ВЪ СВѢТОВНАТА ВОЙНА 1915-1918 Г. ТОМЪ I. (Bŭlgarskata armija vŭ svĕtovnata vojna 1915-1918 g. Томй I - *The Bulgarian Army in The Great War 1915 – 18 Volume I).*

> Anonymous - Щаб на армията. Военно-историческа (Štab na armijata. Voenno-istoričeska) | 26.5cm x 19cm | Green card Softback. | ? + ?pp | Državna Peuatnica | 1936 | Bulgarian Text. | Bulgarian Cyrillic.

БЪЛГАРСКАТА АРМИЯ ВЪ СВѢТОВНАТА ВОЙНА 1915-1918 Г. ТОМЪ II. ВОЙНАТА СРЕЩУ СЪРБИЯ ПРЕЗ 1915 ГОДИНА. НАСТѪПЛЕНИЕТО НА I АРМИЯ ПРЕЗЪ ГРАНИЦАТА ОТЪ 1-И ДО 14-И ОКТОМВРИЙ. (Bŭlgarskata armija vŭ svĕtovnata vojna 1915-1918 g. Томй II Voinata creštu Srbija prez 1915 godina. Nastžplenieto na I Armiâ Prezъ Granicata otъ 1-i do 14-i Oktomvrij. - *The Bulgarian Army in The Great War 1915 –18 Volume II War against Serbia in 1915. Advance of the I Army Across the Frontier from 1 to 14 October.)*

> Anonymous - Щаб на армията. Военно-историческа (Štab na armijata. Voenno-istoričeska) | 26.5cm x 19cm | Green card Softback. | xvi + 930pp + i | 7 appendices | 9 tables | Državna Peuatnica | 1936 | Bulgarian Text. | Bulgarian Cyrillic.

БЪЛГАРСКАТА АРМИЯ ВЪ СВѢТОВНАТА ВОЙНА 1915-1918 Г. ТОМЪ II. ВОЙНАТА СРЕЩУ СЪРБИЯ ПРЕЗ 1915 ГОДИНА. НАСТѪПЛЕНИЕТО НА I АРМИЯ ПРЕЗЪ ГРАНИЦАТА ОТЪ 1-И ДО 14-И ОКТОМВРИЙ. КАРТОГРАФ (Bŭlgarskata armija vŭ svĕtovnata vojna 1915-1918 g. Томй II Voinata creštu Srbija prez 1915 godina. Nastžplenieto na I Armiâ Prezъ Granicata otъ 1-i do 14-i Oktomvrij. Kartograf. - *The Bulgarian Army in The Great War 1915 –18 Volume II War against Serbia in 1915. Advance of the I Army Across the Frontier from 1 to 14 October. Maps)*

> Anonymous - Щаб на армията. Военно-историческа (Štab na armijata. Voenno-istoričeska) | 26.5cm x 19cm | Green card Softback. | 54 maps | Državna Peuatnica | 1936 | Bulgarian Text. | Bulgarian Cyrillic.

БЪЛГАРСКАТА АРМИЯ ВЪ СВѢТОВНАТА ВОЙНА 1915-1918 Г. ТОМЪ III. ВОЙНАТА СРЕЩУ СЪРБИЯ ПРЕЗ 1915 ГОДИНА. НАСТѪПЛЕНИЕТО НА II АРМИЯ ВЪ МАКЕДОНИЯ. (Bŭlgarskata armija vŭ svĕtovnata vojna 1915-1918 g. Томй III Voinata creštu Srbija prez 1915 godina. Nastžplenieto na II Armiâ vъ Makedoniâ. - *The Bulgarian Army in The Great War 1915 –18 Volume III War against Serbia in 1915. Advance of the II Army into Macedonia).*

> Anonymous - Щаб на армията. Военно-историческа (Štab na armijata. Voenno-istoričeska) | 26.5cm x 19cm | Green card Softback. | xii + 1160pp + iii | 4 appendices | 4 tables | Državna Peuatnica | 1938 | Bulgarian Text. | Bulgarian Cyrillic.

БЪЛГАРСКАТА АРМИЯ ВЪ СВѢТОВНАТА ВОЙНА 1915-1918 Г. ТОМЪ III. ВОЙНАТА СРЕЩУ СЪРБИЯ ПРЕЗ 1915 ГОДИНА. НАСТѪПЛЕНИЕТО НА II АРМИЯ ВЪ МАКЕДОНИЯ. КАРТОГРАФ. (Bŭlgarskata armija vŭ svĕtovnata vojna 1915-1918 g. Томй III Voinata creštu Srbija prez 1915 godina. Nastžplenieto na II Armiâ vъ Makedoniâ. Kartograf. - *The Bulgarian Army in The Great War 1915 –18 Volume III War against Serbia in 1915. Advance of the II Army into Macedonia. Maps.)*

> Anonymous - Щаб на армията. Военно-историческа (Štab na armijata. Voenno-istoričeska) | 26.5cm x 19cm | Green card Softback. | 25 maps | Državna Peuatnica | 1938 | Bulgarian Text. | Bulgarian Cyrillic.

БЪЛГАРСКАТА АРМИЯ ВЪ СВѢТОВНАТА ВОЙНА 1915-1918 Г. ТОМЪ IV. ВОЙНАТА СРЕЩУ СЪРБИЯ ПРЕЗ 1915 ГОДИНА. НАСТѪПЛЕНИЕТО НА I АРМИЯ КЪ ДОЛИНАТА НА Р. МОРАВА И ТОВА НА СЕВЕРНАТА ГРУПА ОЉ II АРМИЯ КЪМЪ ЛѢСКРОВЕЦЪ И ПРИЩИНА ОЉ 22-И ДО 31-И ОКТОМВРИЙ. (Bŭlgarskata armija vŭ svĕtovnata vojna 1915-1918 g. Томй IV. Voinata creštu Srbija prez 1915 godina. Nastžplenieto

na I Armiâ Къ Dolinata na R. Morava i Tova na Severnata Grupa olj II Armiâ Къмъ Lžskrovecъ I Priština olj 22-i do 31-i Oktomvrij. - *The Bulgarian Army in The Great War 1915 – 18 Volume IV. War against Serbia in 1915. The Advance of the I Army along the River Morava Valley whilst the Northern Group of the II Army Advance into Leskovac and Prisina 22 - 31 October.*)

Anonymous - Щаб на армията. Военно-историческа (Štab na armijata. Voenno-istoričeska) | 26.5cm x 19cm | Green card Softback. | xvii + 1029pp + ii | 1 appendix | 8 tables | Duržavna Peuatnica | 1940 | Bulgarian Text. | Bulgarian Cyrillic.

БЪЛГАРСКАТА АРМИЯ ВЪ СВѢТОВНАТА ВОЙНА 1915-1918 Г. ТОМЪ IV. ВОЙНАТА СРЕЩУ СЪРБИЯ ПРЕЗ 1915 ГОДИНА. НАСТѪПЛЕНИЕТО НА I АРМИЯ КЪ ДОЛИНАТА НА Р. МОРАВА И ТОВА НА СЕВЕРНАТА ГРУПА ОЉ II АРМИЯ КЪМЪ ЛѢСКРОВЕЦЪ И ПРИЩИНА ОЉ 22-И ДО 31-И ОКТОМВРИЙ. КАРТОГРАФ. (Bǔlgarskata armija vǔ světovnata vojna 1915-1918 g. Tomǔ IV. Voinata creštu Srbija prez 1915 godina. Nastžplenieto na I Armiâ Къ Dolinata na R. Morava i Tova na Severnata Grupa olj II Armiâ Къмъ Lžskrovecъ I Priština olj 22-i do 31-i Oktomvrij. Kartograf. - *The Bulgarian Army in The Great War 1915 –18 Volume IV. War against Serbia in 1915. The Advance of the I Army along the River Morava Valley whilst the Northern Group of the II Army Advance into Leskovac and Prisina 22 - 31 October. Maps.*)

Anonymous - Щаб на армията. Военно-историческа (Štab na armijata. Voenno-istoričeska) | 26.5cm x 19cm | Green card Softback. | 50 maps | Duržavna Peuatnica | 1940 | Bulgarian Text. | Bulgarian Cyrillic.

БЪЛГАРСКАТА АРМИЯ ВЪ СВѢТОВНАТА ВОЙНА 1915-1918 Г. ТОМЪ V. КОСОВСКА ОПЕРАЦИЯ. (Bǔlgarskata armija vǔ světovnata vojna 1915-1918 g. Tomǔ V Kosovcka operatsiya. - *The Bulgarian Army in The Great War 1915 –18 Volume V. The Kosovo Operation.*)

Anonymous - Щаб на армията. Военно-историческа (Štab na armijata. Voenno-istoričeska) | 26.5cm x 19cm | Green card Softback. | ? + ?pp | Duržavna Peuatnica | 1946 | Bulgarian Text. | Bulgarian Cyrillic.

БЪЛГАРСКАТА АРМИЯ ВЪ СВѢТОВНАТА ВОЙНА 1915-1918 Г. ТОМЪ V. КОСОВСКА ОПЕРАЦИЯ. КАРТОГРАФ. (Bǔlgarskata armija vǔ světovnata vojna 1915-1918 g. Tomǔ V Kosovcka operatsiya. Kartograf. - *The Bulgarian Army in The Great War 1915 – 18 Volume V. The Kosovo Operation. Maps.*)

Anonymous - Щаб на армията. Военно-историческа (Štab na armijata. Voenno-istoričeska) | 26.5cm x 19cm | Green card Softback. | ? maps | Duržavna Peuatnica | 1946 | Bulgarian Text. | Bulgarian Cyrillic.

БЪЛГАРСКАТА АРМИЯ ВЪ СВѢТОВНАТА ВОЙНА 1915-1918 Г. ТОМЪ VI. ?.[17] (Bǔlgarskata armija vǔ světovnata vojna 1915-1918 g. Tomǔ VI. ?. - *The Bulgarian Army in The Great War 1915 –18 Volume VI. ?.*).

Anonymous - Щаб на армията. Военно-историческа (Štab na armijata. Voenno-istoričeska) | 26.5cm x 19cm | Green card Softback. | ? + ?pp | Duržavna Peuatnica | ? | Bulgarian Text. | Bulgarian Cyrillic.

БЪЛГАРСКАТА АРМИЯ ВЪ СВѢТОВНАТА ВОЙНА 1915-1918 Г. ТОМЪ VI. ?. КАРТОГРАФ. (Bǔlgarskata armija vǔ světovnata vojna 1915-1918 g. Tomǔ VI. ?. Kartograf. - *The The Bulgarian Army in The Great War 1915 –18 Volume VI. ?. Maps.*)

Anonymous - Щаб на армията. Военно-историческа (Štab na armijata. Voenno-istoričeska) | 26.5cm x 19cm | Green card Softback. | ? maps | Duržavna Peuatnica | ? | Bulgarian Text. | Bulgarian Cyrillic.

БЪЛГАРСКАТА АРМИЯ ВЪ СВѢТОВНАТА ВОЙНА 1915-1918 Г. ТОМЪ VII. ?. (Bǔlgarskata armija vǔ světovnata vojna 1915-1918 g. Tomǔ VII. ?. - *The Bulgarian Army in The Great War 1915 –18 Volume VII. ?.*)

---

[17] I have found no examples of volume VI and VII of this set "**Българската Армия Въ Свѣтовната Война 1915-1918 Г**". It is assumed that they were both written and published. However, it is possible that, like other international sets that were published out of sequence, these two volumes were to be completed out of sequence, but due to other factors were then not published.

Anonymous - Щаб на армията. Военно-историческа (Štab na armijata. Voenno-istoričeska) | 26.5cm x 19cm | Green card Softback. | ? + ?pp | Državna Peuatnica | ? | Bulgarian Text. | Bulgarian Cyrillic.

БЪЛГАРСКАТА АРМИЯ ВЪ СВѢТОВНАТА ВОЙНА 1915-1918 Г. ТОМЪ VII. ?. КАРТОГРАФ. (Bŭlgarskata armija vŭ světovnata vojna 1915-1918 g. Tomŭ VII. ?. Kartograf. - *The Bulgarian Army in The Great War 1915 –18 Volume VII. ?. Maps.*)

Anonymous - Щаб на армията. Военно-историческа (Štab na armijata. Voenno-istoričeska) | 26.5cm x 19cm | Green card Softback. | ? maps | Državna Peuatnica | ? | Bulgarian Text. | Bulgarian Cyrillic.

БЪЛГАСКАТА АРМИЯ ВЪ СВѢТОВНАТА ВОЙНА 1915-1918 Г. ТОМЪ VIII. ВОЙНАТА СРЕЩУ РУМЪНИЯ ПРЕЗ 1916 ГОДИНА. ПОДГОТОВКА НА ВОЙНАТА И ТУТРАКАНСКАТА ОПЕРАЦИЯ. (Bŭlgarskata armija vŭ světovnata vojna 1915-1918 g. Tomŭ VIII Voinata creštu Rumŭniya prez 1916. Podgotovka na Vojnata i Tutrakanskata Operaciâ. - *The Bulgarian Army in The Great War 1915 –18 Volume VIII The War against Romania during 1916. Preparation for War and the Tutrakanskata Operation.*)

Anonymous - Щаб на армията. Военно-историческа (Štab na armijata. Voenno-istoričeska) | 26.5cm x 19cm | Green card Softback. | xii + 795pp + iii | 6 maps | 4 appendices | 7 tables | Državna Peuatnica | 1939 | Bulgarian Text. | Bulgarian Cyrillic.

БЪЛГАСКАТА АРМИЯ ВЪ СВѢТОВНАТА ВОЙНА 1915-1918 Г. ТОМЪ VIII. ВОЙНАТА СРЕЩУ РУМЪНИЯ ПРЕЗ 1916 ГОДИНА. ПОДГОТОВКА НА ВОЙНАТА И ТУТРАКАНСКАТА ОПЕРАЦИЯ. КАРТОГРАФ. (Bŭlgarskata armija vŭ světovnata vojna 1915-1918 g. Tomŭ VIII Voinata creštu Rumŭniya prez 1916. Podgotovka na Vojnata i Tutrakanskata Operaciâ. Kartograf. - *The Bulgarian Army in The Great War 1915 –18 Volume VIII The War against Romania during 1916. Preparation for War and the Tutrakanskata Operation. Maps.*)

Anonymous - Щаб на армията. Военно-историческа (Štab na armijata. Voenno-istoričeska) | 26.5cm x 19cm | Green card Softback. | 15 maps | Državna Peuatnica | 1939 | Bulgarian Text. | Bulgarian Cyrillic.

БЪЛГАРСКАТА АРМИЯ ВЪ СВѢТОВНАТА ВОЙНА 1915-1918 Г. ТОМЪ IX. НАСТѪПЛЕНИЕТО НА III АРМИЯ ВЪ ДОБРУДЖА. (Bŭlgarskata armija vŭ světovnata vojna 1915-1918 g. Tomŭ IX Nastžplenieto na III armija v Dobrudzha - *The Bulgarian Army in The Great War 1915 –18 Volume IX Advance of the III Army into Dobruja.*)

Anonymous - Щаб на армията. Военно-историческа (Štab na armijata. Voenno-istoričeska) | 26.5cm x 19cm | Green card Softback. | x + 896pp | 4 maps | 1 cart | 5 tables | Državna Peuatnica | 1943 | Bulgarian Text. | Bulgarian Cyrillic.

БЪЛГАРСКАТА АРМИЯ ВЪ СВѢТОВНАТА ВОЙНА 1915-1918 Г. ТОМЪ IX. НАСТѪПЛЕНИЕТО НА III АРМИЯ ВЪ ДОБРУДЖА. КАРТОГРАФ. (Bŭlgarskata armija vŭ světovnata vojna 1915-1918 g. Tomŭ IX Nastžplenieto na III armija v Dobrudzha. Kartograf. - *The Bulgarian Army in The Great War 1915 –18 Volume IX Advance of the III Army into Dobruja. Maps.*)

Anonymous - Щаб на армията. Военно-историческа (Štab na armijata. Voenno-istoričeska) | 26.5cm x 19cm | Green card Softback. | 15 maps | Državna Peuatnica | 1943 | Bulgarian Text. | Bulgarian Cyrillic.

Canadian Official Histories

The Canadian official histories were written by members of the Historical Section of the General Staff of the various services, Department of National Defence, under the authority of The Minister of National Defence. (*Ministère de la défense nationale. Direction-Histoire et patrimoine.*) [18]

In January 1916 the Canadian War Records Office was established in London by Sir Max Aitken (later Lord Beaverbrook) under authorization of Sir Robert Borden, the then Prime Minister of Canada. It was intended that the Canadian War Records Office (not to be confused with the Canadian Records Office which was mainly concerned with collecting statistics) would collect Canadian Army documents such as unit war dairies with the aim of writing an official history of the Canadian Expeditionary Force. The records in the Canadian War Records Office were shipped to Ottawa in the autumn of 1919 and formed the archive within the Army Historical Section of the General Staff. It is from these records that the official histories were based.

Brigadier-General A. E. Cruikshank was appointed Canadian official historian in January 1917 with the instruction to write "the history of the present war". Cruikshank decided to write an official prequel history relating to the Canadian military up to 1914. On his recommendation a Historical Section of the General Staff was created and in November 1918 he became its first Director. Before Cruikshank retired in May 1921, he completed the five volume series of his early Canadian history and had written the first of his Great War volumes; however it was felt that it was far too brief with only twenty-eight pages of text and, although printed, it was not issued.

Cruikshank's place as director of the Historical Section of the General Staff was taken by *Major* A. Fortescue Duguid. Duguid initially worked out a framework for the official history consisting of seven military operation volumes along with four special volumes focusing on medical services, military engineering, the nursing services and the chaplains' services. Duguid then set to work on the first volume, but progress was slow, delayed first by the need to sort and then to check all the documents that had been returned by the Canadian War Records Office. In the meantime Duguid commissioned Sir Andrew Macphail (the Professor of the History of Medicine at McGill University,) to research and write the first of the special histories, namely the medical volume. Macphail's finished work exceeded the scope of the history, including criticism of prominent figures including Sir Sam Hughes, the Canadian Minister of Militia. Although published, the volume caused much anger leading to the other three special volumes to be cancelled. It took Duguid over seventeen years to complete the first volume of the military operation and although he continued work on the second volume throughout the Second World War, the Great War project was abandoned due to post-war economies.

In 1940, a new historical team was created to cover the Second World War with *Colonel* Charles Perry Stacey appointed as Historical Officer in the Canadian Military Headquarters, London. When the war finished in 1945, Stacey was appointed the Official Historian and Director of the Historical Section. Stacey and his team were commissioned to write the official history of Canadian Second World War. With the completion in 1960 of the first three volumes of the Canadian Second World War official history[19], Stacey retired from his historical posts. His place was taken by *Colonel* Gerald William Lingen Nicholson, who then wrote in 1961 a Great War equivalent to the Second World War volumes to fill in the gaps left by the uncompleted Duguid set.

Just after Stacey was appointed, in May 1941, Gilbert Norman Tucker, was commissioned to research and write a complete naval official history covering the entire history of the Royal Canadian Navy from its beginning to date namely the Second World War. Therefore Tucker planned a three-volume history; however due to defence cuts, only the first two were volumes were actually written and were both published in 1952. Only the first volume covers the Great War, the other covered the Second World War.

There was a long delay before the official history of the Royal Canadian Air Force was given ministerial approval. Stacey's campaign for an official aviation history, with approval finally given in

---

[18] Most of the Canadian Official Histories have been published both as English and French editions. The French editions are listed under the English editions.

[19] Official History of the Canadian Army in the Second World War. Volume I: Six Years of War: The Army in Canada, Britain and the Pacific [Colonel C. P. Stacey, 1955]. Volume II: The Canadians in Italy 1943-1945. [Lieutenant Colonel G. W. L. Nicholson, 1956]. Volume III: The Victory Campaign. The Operations in North-West Europe 1944-1945 [Colonel C. P. Stacey, 1960]. Volume IV: Arms, Men and Governments: The War Policies of Canada 1939-1945 [Colonel C. P. Stacey, 1970]

1960. Although Stacey did a lot of the preliminary research work, it was Sydney F. Wise in 1966 that was commissioned to continued the research and to write it. Like the naval history, the aviation history was to cover the entire history of the Royal Canadian Air Force with it being foreseen to consist of a three-volume set. Only the first volume covers the Great War which was published in 1980. There were a number of problems with the Great War volume. It was initially thought that the British official history "The War in the Air" covered the Canadian imput on the airwar and it took a long time to convince the authorities that there was a need for such a history. Once the approval had been received, the next task was to build an archive of records since none had been set up during the war. It took from 1967 to 1973 to scour the Public Record Office, London and Canadian repositories for documents, along with personal papers and reminiscences from former airmen. This brought to the surface new unknown batches of Canadian documents. It was not until 1980 before the writing and publishing for this volume could be completed.

General;

REPORT OF THE MINISTRY: OVERSEAS MILITARY FORCES OF CANADA, 1918.
> Anonymous - Overseas Military Forces of Canada. | 30.5cm x 24.8cm | Grey Green Cloth Hardback | xv + 533pp | 16 maps | 31 photographs | 13 diagrams| His Majesty's Stationary Office. | 1919 | English Text.
> It appears that a French language version of this volume was not published.
> This volume can be viewed on the Canadian Forces' world wide web as a 'pdf file':
> *http://www.cmp-cpm.forces.gc.ca/dhh-dhp/his/docs/OVERSEAS_report1918_E.pdf*

Naval Operations;

THE NAVAL SERVICE OF CANADA: IT'S OFFICIAL HISTORY. VOLUME I ORIGINS AND EARLY YEARS.
> Gilbert Norman Tucker *Ph.D* | 25.5cm x 17cm | Blue Grey Cloth Hardback | gilt | blue and white dust jacket | xii + 436pp | 10 maps | 19 photographs | 1 sketche | King's Printer. | 1952 | English Text.
> It appears that a French language version of this volume was not published.
> This volume can be viewed on the Canadian Forces' world wide web as a 'pdf file':
> *http://www.cmp-cpm.forces.gc.ca/dhh-dhp/his/docs/Naval_Svc_vol1_e.pdf*
> or Internet Archive world wide web also as a 'pdf files':
> *http://www.archive.org/details/navalserviceofca01tuckuoft*

Military Operations;

THE CANADIAN FORCES IN THE GREAT WAR 1914 – 1919.
OFFICIAL HISTORY OF THE CANADIAN FORCES IN THE GREAT WAR, 1914-1919. GENERAL SERIES. VOLUME I. FROM THE OUTBREAK OF WAR TO THE FORMATION OF THE CANADIAN CORPS, AUGUST 1914-SEPTEMBER 1915.
> *Colonel* A. [Archer] Fortescue Duguid | 25.5cm x 17.8cm | Dark Red Cloth Hardback | Gilt | Brown Paper Dust Jacket | xxv + 596pp | 9 maps | King's Printer. | 1938 | English Text.

THE CANADIAN FORCES IN THE GREAT WAR 1914 – 1919.
OFFICIAL HISTORY OF THE CANADIAN FORCES IN THE GREAT WAR, 1914-1919. GENERAL SERIES. VOLUME I. FROM THE OUTBREAK OF WAR TO THE FORMATION OF THE CANADIAN CORPS, AUGUST 1914-SEPTEMBER 1915.
[Chronology, Appendices, Maps.]
> *Colonel* A. [Archer] Fortescue Duguid and *Captain* J.I.P. Neal [Cartographer] | 25.5cm x 17.8cm | Dark Red Cloth Hardback | Gilt | Brown Paper Dust Jacket | liii+460pp | 14 maps | King's Printer. | 1938 | English Text.

L'ARMÉE CANADIENNE DANS LA GRANDE GUERRE 1914-1919.
HISTOIRE OFFICIELLE DE L'ARMÉE CANADIENNE DANS LA GRANDE GUERRE 1914-1919. SÉRIE GÉNÉRALE. VOLUME I. DEPUIS LE DÉBUT DES HOSTILITÉS JUSQU'À LA FORMATION DU CORPS EXPÉDITIONNAIRE CANADIEN AOÛT 1914 À SEPTEMBRE 1915. (version in French of the above.)

Colonel A. [Archer] Fortescue Duguid | 25.5cm x 17.8cm | Dark Red Cloth Hardback | Gilt | Brown Paper Dust Jacket | xxv + 596pp | 9 maps | Imprimeur du Roi. | 1947 | French Text.

L'ARMÉE CANADIENNE DANS LA GRANDE GUERRE 1914-1919.

HISTOIRE OFFICIELLE DE L'ARMÉE CANADIENNE DANS LA GRANDE GUERRE 1914-1919. SÉRIE GÉNÉRALE. VOLUME I. DEPUIS LE DÉBUT DES HOSTILITÉS JUSQU'À LA FORMATION DU CORPS EXPÉDITIONNAIRE CANADIEN AOÛT 1914 À SEPTEMBRE 1915. [Chronology, Appendices, Maps.] (version in French of the above.)

> *Colonel* A. [Archer] Fortescue Duguid and Captain J.I.P. Neal [Cartographer] | 25.5cm x 17.8cm | Dark Red Cloth Hardback | Gilt | Brown Paper Dust Jacket | liii+460pp | 14 maps | Imprimeur du Roi. | 1947 | French Text.
>
> These books had two title pages with the series title on the first and the description of the volume on the second. As noted above only Volume I of a planned series of seven military operation volumes was completed and published.

Canadian Expeditionary Force 1914 - 1919. The Official History of the Canadian Army in the First World War.

> *Colonel* G.W.L. [Gerald William Lingen] Nicholson | 30.5cm x 24.8cm | Red Cloth Hardback | Gilt | White and red Paper Dust Jacket | xiv + 621pp | 17 maps | 49 photographs | 55 sketches | Queen's Printer/Imprimeur de la Reine. | 1962 | English Text.

Le Corps expéditionaire canadien, 1914-1919. Histoire de la participation de l'Armée canadienne à la Première Guerre mondiale. (version in French of the above.)

> *Colonel* G.W.L. [Gerald William Lingen] Nicholson | 30.5cm x 24.8cm | Red Cloth Hardback | Gilt | White and red Paper Dust Jacket | xiv + 621pp | 17 maps | 49 photographs | 55 sketches | Queen's Printer/Imprimeur de la Reine. | 1963 | French Text.
>
> This volume has been republished on a CD-ROM.

Aviation Activities;

The Official History of the Royal Canadian Air Force. Volume 1. Canadian Airmen and the First World War.

> S.F. [Sydney] Wise | 30.5cm x 24.8cm | Grey Cloth Hardback | Gilt | Grey Paper Dust Jacket | xx + 771pp | 27 maps | 213 photographs | 5 diagrams| University of Toronto Press (Department of National Defence). | 1980 | English Text.

Histoire officielle de l'Aviation royale du Canada. Volume 1 Les aviateurs canadiens dans la Première Guerre mondiale. (version in French of the above.)

> S.F. [Sydney] Wise | 30.5cm x 24.8cm | Grey Cloth Hardback | Gilt | Grey Paper Dust Jacket | xx + 835pp | 27 maps | 213 photographs | 5 diagrams| University of Toronto Press (Department of National Defence). | 1982 | French Text.
>
> Only the first volume covers the Great War.

Medical Activities;

OFFICIAL HISTORY OF THE CANADIAN FORCES IN THE GREAT WAR 1914 – 19. THE MEDICAL SERVICES.

> *Sir* Andrew MacPhail | 25.5cm x 17.8cm | Dark Red Cloth Hardback | Gilt | Brown Paper Dust Jacket | viii + 428pp | 1 map | His Majesty's Stationery Office. | 1925 | English Text.
>
> This volume can be viewed on the Internet Archive world wide web as a 'pdf file':
> *http://www.archive.org/details/medicalservices00macpuoft*

Czechoslovakian Official Histories

The Czechoslovakian official histories were written under the authority of the former Czechoslovakian Government by academics.

Czechoslovakia during the 1914-1918 period was part of the Hapsburg Empire and, as such, did not exist as an independent state until the break up of that empire in the dying stages of the Great War - Czechoslovakia proclaimed its independence on 28 October 1918, becoming the Czechoslovak Republic.[20] However during the war its peoples, especially the Czechs, fought not only for their Austro-Hungarian masters, but a large number of them deserted and fought for their independence with the enemies of the Hapsburgs. Although the Austro-Hungarian official history "**Österreich-Ungarns Letzter Krieg 1914-1918**" covers the service of the loyal Czechoslovakians during the war, the two works listed below cover the Czechs who fought against the Hapsburgs for their independence.

Military Operations;

První československý odboj. Československé legie 1914-1920. (*The First Czechoslovak Resistance. Czech Legions 1914-1920.*)
> *Ph. Dr.* Miroslav Gregorovič *C.Sc.* | 20.5cm x 15cm | Light blue plastic covered card Softback | 64pp | Vydalo Vydavatelství a nakladelství H and H. | 1992 | Czech Text. ISBN: 80-85467-54-2
>
> This volume is part of the "Panorama dějin. Nové pohledy" series. It covers the Czech Legion in France, Russia and Italy.

O samostatny československý stát 1914-1918. (*Founding an Independent Czechoslovak State 1914-1918.*)
> Jan Galandauer. | 21cm x ?cm | 117pp | Státní pedagogické nakl. | 1992 | Czech Text. ISBN: 80-04-26140-X

---

[20] Czechoslovakia has since split into the Czech Republic and the Slovak Republic (Slovakia) on 1 January 1993.

Éire (The Republic of Ireland) Official History

The Éire (The Republic of Ireland) official history was written under the authority of H.M. Government of Britain (the ruling body, both during the period covered and at the time of writing) by a Royal Commission.[21]

Military Operations;

Irish Rebellion, 1916: Royal Commission on the Rebellion in Ireland. Report, Minutes of Evidence and Appendix of Documents.

Charles Hardinge, 1st Baron Hardinge of Penshurst. | 33cm x 21cm | White Paper Softback | 126pp | His Majesty's Stationery Office. | 1916 | English Text.

The Irish Rebellion of 1916 is now commonly known as the 1916 Easter Uprising. It was funded in part by the Imperial Government of Germany in an attempt to distract Britain, especially the British army, from engaging the German Army in Europe and as such is regarded as part of the Great War. The Royal Commission was set up to review and then report the events leading up to the uprising, the uprising itself and then its suppression.

---

[21] The government of Ireland at the time of the 1916 Easter Uprising was H.M. Government of the United Kingdom. Ireland became a British Dominion state know as the Irish Free State on 6 December 1922, and in 1948 it became truly independent becoming the republican state of Éire (The Republic of Ireland).

Finnish Official Histories

The Finnish official histories were written by members of the Venäläissurmat Suomessa (*Prime Minister's Cabinet Office*) as part of their War Victims 1914-22 Project. In recent years the Finnish Government has started to officially sanction a number of academic works covering Finnish involvement in military operations mainly relating to actions in the Finnish Civil War and the Second World War. The War Victims 1914-22 Project is part of the overall work being conducted by the Venäläissurmat Suomessa.

Although Finland did not exist as a nation between 1914 and 1917, it declared its independence from Imperial Russia just after the Russian October Revolution of 6 December 1917, a number of Finns were involved in the Great War serving as individuals with the warring nations on both sides. Therefore the Venäläissurmat Suomessa has produced the two volumes below covering the activities of those individuals during the Great War period.

Military Activities;

VENÄLÄISSURMAT SUOMESSA VUOSINA 1914-22. Osa 1. Sotatapahtumat 1914-22. Krigsdöda ryssar I Finland 1914-22. Del 1. Krigshändelser 1914-17. (*Russian Deaths in Finland during 1914-22. Volume 1:. War Events 1914-22. Russian War Victims in Finland, 1914-1922. Part 1: Hostilities from 1914 to 1917.*)

Lars Westerlund (editor) Harry Halen, Kristina Kalleinen, Jyrki Loima, Åke Söderlund, Kenneth Gustavsson and Elena Dubroskaja. l 25 cm x ?cm l card softback l 283pp + i l 25 photographs l 8 sketches l Valtioneuvoston kanslia julkaisusarja. l 2004 l Finnish Text.
ISSN 0782-6028, ISBN 952-5354-43-1

This volume is available on the Venäläissurmat Suomessa world wide web site as a 'pdf files':

www.vnk.fi/julkaisukansio/2004/j01-venalaissurmat-suomessa-1914-22-osa-1/pdf/fi.pdf

There is a difference in the title of this volume between the cover page and the title page. On the cover the title is shown as "**Venäläissurmat Suomessa 1914-22. Osa 1. Sotatapahtumat 1914-22**". However on the title page the title is shown as "**Venäläissurmat Suomessa vuosina 1914-22. Osa 1**".

This is part of a series with only Volume 1 Part 1 being related to the Great War. The other parts of this series being related to the Finnish Civil War 1918, Aunus Expedition 1919 and the Russo-Finnish conflicts during the Russian Civil War 1918 - 1922.

SUOMALAISET ENSIMMÄISESSÄ MAAILMANSODASSA: Venäjän, Saksan, Ison-Britannian, Ranskan, Australian, Uuden Seelannin, Etelä-Afrikan, Yhdysvaltain, Kanadan ja Neuvosto-Venäjän armeijoissa vuosina 1914-22 menehtyneet suomalaiset sekä sotaoloissa surmansa saaneet merimiehet. (*Finns in the First War World: Finns who perished during 1914-22 while serving in the armies of Russia, Germany, the Untied Kingdom, the United States, Canada, France, Australia, New Zealand,South Africa and Soviet Russia and including Finnish Seamen Killed in War-Related Incidents.*)

Lars Westerlund (editor) Tuomas Hoppu, Matti Lackman, Krister Björklund, Olavi Koivukangas and Carl-Fredrik Geust. l 25 cm x ?cm l Black and blue card softback with photograph l 231pp l 7 maps l 49 photographs l 5 sketches l 38 tables l Valtioneuvoston kanslia julkaisusarja. l 2004 l Finnish Text.
ISSN 0782-6028, ISBN 952-5354-48-2

This volume is available on the Venäläissurmat Suomessa world wide web site as a 'pdf files':

www.vnk.fi/julkaisukansio/2004/j06-suomalaiset-I-maailmansodassa/pdf/fi.pdf

French Official Histories

The French official histories were written by members of the various historical departments as follows: For the navy, the Service Historique de l'État-Major de la Marine (*Naval General Staff Historical Service*); for the army, the Ministère de la Guerre, État de l'Armée - Service Historique (*Ministry of War, Army Staff's Historical Service*) and for the French Air Force the Service Historique de l'Armée de l'Air (*Air Force Historical Service* – S.H.A.A.) [22]

The Service Historique de la Marine tended to publish their historical studies as articles within their magazine La Revue Martine. However, where studies were too long to be published as articles, then books were produced.

The Ministère de la Guerre, État de l'Armée - Service Historique completed the military operation volumes in 1937 before the start of the Second World War; however it has been stated by James Davilla and Arthur Soltan in their "French Aircraft of the First World War" (Flying Machine Press, 1997) that the Ministère de la Guerre, État de l'Armée - Service Historique were planning to add a twelfth volume to the series covering the Army Air Service. This volume was delayed because of the Second World War and was then cancelled after that war, probably due to financial reasons.

The Service Historique de l'Armée de l'Air was formed in 1934 after the creation of the independent French Air Force and since the Second World War has produced a number of publications.

The Service Historique de la Marine and the Service Historique de l'Armée de l'Air have produced only case studies and not a more comprehensive history covering all aspects of the service during the Great War.

Naval Operations;

INTRODUCTION À L'ÉTUDE DE LA GUERRE SOUS-MARINE. (*Introduction to the Study of Submarine Warfare.*)
> *Captaine de frégate* Adolphe Laurens (chef de la Service Historique de l'État-Major de la Marine) | 26cm x 20cm | yellow paper softback. | 233pp | 13 photographes | 6 maps | 7 tables. | Augustin Challamel. | 1921 | French Text.

HISTOIRE DE LA GUERRE SOUS-MARINE ALLEMANDE 1914 - 1918. (*History of German Submarine Warfare 1914 - 1918.*)
> *Captaine de frégate* Adolphe Laurens (chef de la Service Historique de l'État-Major de la Marine) | 25cm x 16cm | white paper softback. | 461pp | 20 photographs | 16 silhouettes | Société d'éditions géographiques, maritimes et coloniales, ancienne maison Challamel. | 1930 | French Text.

PRÉCIS D'HISTOIRE DE LA GUERRE NAVALE, 1914 - 1918. (*Historical Summary of the Naval War, 1914 - 1918.*)
> *capitaine de frégate* Adolphe Laurens (chef de la Service Historique de l'État-Major de la Marine) | 26cm x 20cm | yellow paper softback. | 300pp | ? photograph | ? maps | ? tables. | Éditions Payot. | 1929 | French Text.
> Collections of documents, studies and memoirs from the naval archives.

LA GUERRE DES CROISEURS DU 4 AOÛT 1914 À LA BATAILLE DES FALKLAND. TOME 1. (*The Cruiser Warfare.*)
> *Capitaine de frégate* [Louis] Paul [André] Chack[23] | 26cm x 20cm | white paper softback | 374pp | 1 tables | Augustin Challamel. | 1922 | French Text.

---

[22] The Ministère de la Guerre, État de l'Armée - Service Historique was the forerunner of the present day Service Historique de l'Armée de Terre (S.H.A.T. - *Historical Service of the Army*). The Service Historique de la Marine became the Service Historique de l'Armée de la Marine (S.H.A.M. - *Historical Service of the Navy*). The Service Historique de l'Armée de Terre, the Service Historique de l'Armée de la Marine and the Service Historique de l'Armée de l'Air, along with the Service Historique de l'Armée de la Gendarmerie now form the Service Historique de la Défense (S.H.D. – *Defence Historical Service*) which is part of the Ministère de la Défense (*French Ministry of Defense*).
[23] During Paul Chack's employment with the Service Historique de la Marine between 1921 and 1934 he wrote and had published a number of naval histories without official authorisation namely 'On se bat sur mer', 'Sur les Bancs de Flandre', 'Ceux du Blocus' and 'Pavillons Haut'. In 1934 Chack became a leading member of the Parti Populaire Français (an anti-Communist party with fascist

This volume covers from August 4th to October 1st 1914.

LA GUERRE DES CROISEURS DU 4 AOÛT 1914 À LA BATAILLE DES FALKLAND. TOME 1. [CARTE] (*The Cruiser Warfare.* [*maps*].)

> *Capitaine de frégate* [Louis] Paul [André] Chack | 26cm x 20cm | white paper box | 9 large format maps | Augustin Challamel. | 1923 | French Text.

LA GUERRE DES CROISEURS DU 4 AOÛT 1914 À LA BATAILLE DES FALKLAND. TOME 2. (*The Cruiser Warfare.*)

> *Capitaine de frégate* [Louis] Paul [André] Chack | 26cm x 20cm | white paper softback | 508pp | 6 maps | 4 maps | 10 appendices | Société d'éditions géographiques, maritimes et coloniales, ancienne maison Challamel. | 1923 | French Text.
>
> This volume covers from October 1st 1914 to the battle of the Falklands.

LA GUERRE DES CROISEURS DU 4 AOÛT 1914 À LA BATAILLE DES FALKLAND. TOME 2. [CARTE] (*The Cruiser Warfare.* [*maps*].)

> *Capitaine de frégate* [Louis] Paul [André] Chack | 26cm x 20cm | white paper box | 11 large format maps | Société d'éditions géographiques, maritimes et coloniales, ancienne maison Challamel. | 1923 | French Text.

COMBATS ET BATAILLE SUR MER. SEPTEMBRE 1914 - DÉCEMBRE 1914. (*Naval Battles and Combats. September 1914 – December 1918.*)

> *Capitaine de corvette* Claude Farrère and *Capitaine de frégate* [Louis] Paul [André] Chack | 19cm x ?cm | white paper softback | 283pp |? photograph | ? maps | Ernest Flammarion. | 1925 | French Text.
>
> This volume covers the actions at Tahiti and Penang, the sinking of S.M.S. Emden, the battle of Coronel and the battle of the Falklands.

LA DÉFENSE DES FRONTIÈRES MARITIMES. (*The Defence of the Coastal Frontiers.*)

> *Capitaine de Corvette* J[Jacques] Avice | ?cm x ?cm | white paper softback | 185pp | untrimmed pages | ? photograph | ? maps | Augustin Challamel. | 1922 | French Text.

Blockade Activities;

HISTOIRE DU BLOCUS NAVAL (1914 - 1918.) (*The Story of the Naval Blockade (1914 -1918.)*)

> *Lieutenant de Vaisseau* Louis Guichard | 23cm x 14cm | yellow paper softback? | 239pp | ? photograph | ? maps | Éditions Payot. | 1929 | French Text.
>
> This book 'Le Blocus Naval' was translated into English by Christopher R. Turner under the title 'The Naval Blockade', published by Philip Allan and Co in 1930.

Military Operations;

LES ARMÉES FRANÇAISES DANS LA GRANDE GUERRE: PREMIER TOME LA GUERRE DE MOUVEMENT - OPERATIONS ANTÉRIEURS AU 14 NOVEMBRE 1914. PREMIER VOLUME LES PRÉLIMINARIES - LA BATAILLE DES FRONTIÈRES.[24] (*The French Army in the Great War: First Book The War of Movement – Operations prior to 14th November 1914. First Volume The Preliminaries – The Battle of the Frontiers.*)

> *Lieutenant-Colonel d'Infanterie Breventé* Lambert-Daverdoing, *Commandant d'Infanterie* Henri Carré, *Capitaine d'Infanterie* Besson, *Capitaine d'Infanterie* Denolle and *Capitaine de Cavalière* du Boys de Riocour | 27cm x 22cm | Light Grey Paper Softback | xv + 484pp | Imprimerie Nationale. | 1922 | French Text.

LES ARMÉES FRANÇAISES DANS LA GRANDE GUERRE: TOME I - 1[ER] VOLUME ANNEXE VOLUME. (*The French Army in the Great War: Book I – 1st Volume. Appendices Volume.*)

---

tendency) and during the Second World War he worked for the Vichy government. He was arrested on 23 August 1944 and tried as a traitor. Having been found guilty on 18 December 1944 he was condemned to death and was duly executed by firing squad on 9 January 1945.

[24] The main narration volumes of the French official military operations series have two title pages. On the first page, only the title in full is shown. On the second page, the title is abbreviated (in this case to **LES ARMÉES FRANÇAISES DANS LA GRANDE GUERRE: TOME PREMIER - PREMIER VOLUME**); however, other publishing details (authority, publisher, place and date of publication) are shown. The titles for the appendices volumes and the map boxes are shown in abbreviated format.

Anonymous | 27cm x 22cm | Light Grey Paper Softback | 1026pp | untrimmed pages | 1281 appendices | 1 table | Imprimerie Nationale. | 1922 | French Text.

LES ARMÉES FRANÇAISES DANS LA GRANDE GUERRE: TOME I - 1ER VOLUME. CARTES Nos 1 à 38. (*The French Army in the Great War: Book I – 1st Volume. Maps No's 1 to 38.*)

Anonymous | 27cm x 22cm | Light Grey Card Box | 38 maps | Imprimerie Nationale. | 1922 | French Text.

LES ARMÉES FRANÇAISES DANS LA GRANDE GUERRE: PREMIER TOME LA GUERRE DE MOUVEMENT - OPERATIONS ANTÉRIEURS AU 14 NOVEMBRE 1914. DEUXIÈME VOLUME LA MANOEUVRE EN RETRAITE ET LES PRÉLIMINARIES DE LA BATAILLE DE LA MARNE. (*The French Army in the Great War: First Book The War of Movement – Operations prior to 14th November 1914. Second Volume The Retreat to and the Preliminaries of the Battle of the Marne.*)

Chef de Bataillon d'Infanterie Henri Carré, *Capitaine d'Artillerie* Besson, *Capitaine d'Infanterie* de Geuser, *Capitaine d'Infanterie* Chatinières, *Capitaine d'Infanterie* Denolle, *Capitaine de Cavalière* du Boys de Riocour, *Capitaine d'Infanterie* Boutaud de Lavilleon and *Capitaine d'Infanterie* Labouche | 27cm x 22cm | Light Grey Paper Softback | viii + 842pp | Imprimerie Nationale. | 1925 | French Text.

LES ARMÉES FRANÇAISES DANS LA GRANDE GUERRE: TOME I - 2E VOLUME. ANNEXE 1RE VOLUME. (*The French Army in the Great War: Book I - 2nd Volume. Appendices 1st Volume.*)

Anonymous | 27cm x 22cm | Light Grey Paper Softback | 1043pp | untrimmed pages | 1388 appendices | 1 table | Imprimerie Nationale. | 1925 | French Text.

LES ARMÉES FRANÇAISES DANS LA GRANDE GUERRE: TOME I – 2E VOLUME. 2E ANNEXE. (*The French Army in the Great War: Book I – 2nd Volume. Appendices 2nd Volume*)

Anonymous | 27cm x 22cm | Light Grey Paper Softback | 1040pp | untrimmed pages | 1278 appendices | 1 table | Imprimerie Nationale. | 1925 | French Text.

LES ARMÉES FRANÇAISES DANS LA GRANDE GUERRE: TOME I - 2E VOLUME. CARTES Nos 1 à 34. (*The French Army in the Great War: Book I - 2nd Volume. Maps No's 1 to 34.*)

Anonymous | 27cm x 22cm | Light Grey Card Box | 34 maps | Imprimerie Nationale. | 1925 | French Text.

LES ARMÉES FRANÇAISES DANS LA GRANDE GUERRE: TOME I – 2E VOLUME. CARTES Nos 35 à 77. (*The French Army in the Great War: Book I – 2nd Volume. Maps No's 35 to 77.*)

Anonymous | 27cm x 22cm | Light Grey Card Box | 43 maps | Imprimerie Nationale. | 1925 | French Text.

LES ARMÉES FRANÇAISES DANS LA GRANDE GUERRE: PREMIER TOME LA GUERRE DE MOUVEMENT - OPERATIONS ANTÉRIEURS AU 14 NOVEMBRE 1914. TROISIÈME VOLUME [*] LA BATAILLE DE LA MARNE.[25] (*The French Army in the Great War: First Book The War of Movement – Operations prior to 14th November 1914. Third Volume [*] The Battle of the Marne.*)

Chef d'Escadron d'Artillerie Besson, *Chef de Bataillon d'Infanterie* Lambert, *Chef de Bataillon d'Infanterie* Chatinières, *Chef de Bataillon d'Infanterie* Lefranc, *Chef de Bataillon d'Infanterie* Denolle, *Capitaine d'Artillerie* Lefèvre and *Capitaine d'Infanterie* Brochet | 27cm x 22cm | Light Grey Paper Softback | xii + 676pp | untrimmed pages | 12 maps | Imprimerie Nationale. | 1931 | French Text.

LES ARMÉES FRANÇAISES DANS LA GRANDE GUERRE: PREMIER TOME LA GUERRE DE MOUVEMENT - OPERATIONS ANTÉRIEURS AU 14 NOVEMBRE 1914. TROISIÈME VOLUME [**] LA BATAILLE DE LA MARNE. (*The French Army in the Great War: First Book The War of Movement – Operations prior to 14th November 1914. Third Volume [**] The Battle of the Marne.*)

Chef d'Escadron d'Artillerie Besson, *Chef de Bataillon d'Infanterie* Lambert, *Chef de Bataillon d'Infanterie* Chatinières, *Chef de Bataillon d'Infanterie* Lefranc, *Chef de Bataillon*

---

[25] Like a number of books in this series, **Les Armées Françaises dans la Grande Guerre**, volumes with large number of pages (in this case 1412 pages), were published in two parts. The second parts having only one title page. It is common practice for the two parts to be distinguished by adding asterics [*] to the the titles, although this was not included in the original title pages.

d'Infanterie Denolle, *Capitaine d'Artillerie* Lefèvre and *Capitaine d'Infanterie* Brochet | 27cm x 22cm | Light Grey Paper Softback | 736pp | untrimmed pages | 3 appendices | Imprimerie Nationale. | 1931 | French Text.

LES ARMÉES FRANÇAISES DANS LA GRANDE GUERRE: TOME I – 3^E VOLUME. ANNEXES 1RE VOLUME. (*The French Army in the Great War: Book I – 3rd Volume. Appendices 1st Volume.*)

Anonymous | 27cm x 22cm | Light Grey Paper Softback | 1056pp | untrimmed pages | 1358 appendices | 1 table | 2 maps | 1 diagram| Imprimerie Nationale. | 1932 | French Text.

LES ARMÉES FRANÇAISES DANS LA GRANDE GUERRE: TOME I – 3^E VOLUME. ANNEXES 2^E VOLUME. (*The French Army in the Great War: Book I – 3rd Volume. Appendices 2nd Volume.*)

Anonymous | 27cm x 22cm | Light Grey Paper Softback | 966pp | untrimmed pages | 1259 appendices | 1 table | 1 diagram | Imprimerie Nationale. | 1932 | French Text.

LES ARMÉES FRANÇAISES DANS LA GRANDE GUERRE: TOME I – 3^E VOLUME. ANNEXES 3^E VOLUME. (*The French Army in the Great War: Book I – 3rd Volume. Appendices 3rd Volume.*)

Anonymous | 27cm x 22cm | Light Grey Paper Softback | 1302pp | untrimmed pages | 1584 appendices | 1 table | 1 diagram | Imprimerie Nationale. | 1932 | French Text.

LES ARMÉES FRANÇAISES DANS LA GRANDE GUERRE: TOME I – 3^E VOLUME. ANNEXES 4^E VOLUME. (*The French Army in the Great War: Book I – 3rd Volume. Appendices 4th Volume.*)

Anonymous | 27cm x 22cm | Light Grey Paper Softback | 955pp | untrimmed pages | 1094 appendices | 1 table | 1 diagram | Imprimerie Nationale. | 1932 | French Text.

LES ARMÉES FRANÇAISES DANS LA GRANDE GUERRE: TOME I – 3^E VOLUME. CARTES Nos 1 à 33. (*The French Army in the Great War: Book I – 3rd Volume. Maps No's 1 to 33.*)

Anonymous | 27cm x 22cm | Light Grey Card Box | 33 maps | Imprimerie Nationale. | 1931 | French Text.

LES ARMÉES FRANÇAISES DANS LA GRANDE GUERRE: TOME I – 3^E VOLUME. CARTES Nos 34 à 75. (*Book I – 3rd Volume. Maps No's 34 to 75.*)

Anonymous | 27cm x 22cm | Light Grey Card Box | 42 maps | Imprimerie Nationale. | 1931 | French Text.

LES ARMÉES FRANÇAISES DANS LA GRANDE GUERRE: PREMIER TOME LA GUERRE DE MOUVEMENT - OPERATIONS ANTÉRIEURS AU 14 NOVEMBRE 1914. QUATRIÈME VOLUME LA BATAILLE DE L'AISNE, LA COURSE À LA MER, LA BATAILLE DES FLANDRE, LES OPERATIONS SUR LE FRONT STABILISE. 14 SEPTEMBRE - 14 NOVEMBRE 1914. (*The French Army in the Great War: First Book The War of Movement – Operations prior to 14th November 1914. Fourth Volume The Battle of the Aisne, the Race to the Sea, Battle of the Flanders, the Operations to Stabilise the Front. 14th September - 14th November 1914*)

Chef de Bataillon d'Infanterie Breventé Moreigne, *Chef de Bataillon d'Infanterie Breventé* de Mascureau, *Capitaine d'Artillerie* Lefèvre, *Capitaine d'Infanterie* Laugery and *Capitaine d'Infanterie* Brochet | 27cm x 22cm | Light Grey Paper Softback | vi + 568pp | untrimmed pages | 6 appendices | 1 map | 5 diagrams| Imprimerie Nationale. | 1933 | French Text.

LES ARMÉES FRANÇAISES DANS LA GRANDE GUERRE: TOME I – 4^E VOLUME. ANNEXES 1RE VOLUME. (*The French Army in the Great War: Book I – 4th Volume. Appendices 1st Volume.*)

Anonymous | 27cm x 22cm | Light Grey Paper Softback | 1054pp | untrimmed pages | 1070 appendices | 1 table | 1 diagram| Imprimerie Nationale. | 1933 | French Text.

LES ARMÉES FRANÇAISES DANS LA GRANDE GUERRE: TOME I – 4^E VOLUME. ANNEXES 2^E VOLUME. (*The French Army in the Great War: Book I – 4th Volume. Appendices 2nd Volume.*)

Anonymous | 27cm x 22cm | Light Grey Paper Softback | 841pp | untrimmed pages | 1034 appendices | 1 table | 1 diagram| Imprimerie Nationale. | 1934 | French Text.

LES ARMÉES FRANÇAISES DANS LA GRANDE GUERRE: TOME I - 4^E VOLUME. ANNEXES 3^E VOLUME. (*The French Army in the Great War: Book I – 4th Volume. Appendices 3rd Volume.*)

Anonymous | 27cm x 22cm | Light Grey Paper Softback | 948pp | untrimmed pages | 1075 appendices | 1 table | 1 diagram| Imprimerie Nationale. | 1934 | French Text.

LES ARMÉES FRANÇAISES DANS LA GRANDE GUERRE: TOME I – 4^E VOLUME. 4^E ANNEXES. (*The French Army in the Great War: Book I - 4th Volume. Appendices 4th Volume.*)

Anonymous | 27cm x 22cm | Light Grey Paper Softback | 1036pp | untrimmed pages | 1101 appendices | 1 table | 5 diagrams| Imprimerie Nationale. | 1934 | French Text.

LES ARMÉES FRANÇAISES DANS LA GRANDE GUERRE: TOME I – 4^E VOLUME. CARTES Nos 1 à 28. (*The French Army in the Great War: Book I – 4th Volume. Maps No's 1 to 28.*)

Anonymous | 27cm x 22cm | Light Grey Card Box | 28 maps | Imprimerie Nationale. | 1933 | French Text.

LES ARMÉES FRANÇAISES DANS LA GRANDE GUERRE: TOME I – 4^E VOLUME. CARTES Nos 29 à 59. (*The French Army in the Great War: Book I – 4th Volume. Maps No's 29 to 59.*)

Anonymous | 27cm x 22cm | Light Grey Card Box | 31 maps | Imprimerie Nationale. | 1933 | French Text.

LES ARMÉES FRANÇAISES DANS LA GRANDE GUERRE: DEUXIÈME TOME LA STABILISATION AU FRONT - LES ATTAQUES LOCALES - 14 NOVEMBRE 1914 – 1 MAI 1915. (*The French Army in the Great War: Second Book The Stabilisation of the Front – Local Attacks - 14th November 1914 – 1st May 1915.*)

Chef de Bataillon d'Infanterie Herlaut, *Capitaine d'Infanterie* de Geuser, *Capitaine d'Infanterie* Chatinières and *Capitaine d'Infanterie* Villate | 27cm x 22cm | Light Grey Paper Softback | viii + 734pp | Imprimerie Nationale. | 1931 | French Text.

LES ARMÉES FRANÇAISES DANS LA GRANDE GUERRE: TOME II. 1RE ANNEXES VOLUME. (*The French Army in the Great War: Book II. Appendices 1st Volume.*)

Anonymous | 27cm x 22cm | Light Grey Paper Softback | 1240pp | untrimmed pages | 778 appendices | 1 table | 3 diagrams| Imprimerie Nationale. | 1931 | French Text.

LES ARMÉES FRANÇAISES DANS LA GRANDE GUERRE: TOME II. 2^E ANNEXES VOLUME. (*The French Army in the Great War: Book II. Appendices 2nd Volume.*)

Anonymous | 27cm x 22cm | Light Grey Paper Softback | 1182pp | untrimmed pages | 726 appendices | 1 table | 4 diagrams| Imprimerie Nationale. | 1931 | French Text.

LES ARMÉES FRANÇAISES DANS LA GRANDE GUERRE: TOME II. CARTES Nos 1 à 30. (*The French Army in the Great War: Book II. Maps No's 1 to 30.*)

Anonymous | 27cm x 22cm | Light Grey Paper Softback | 30 maps | Imprimerie Nationale. | 1931 | French Text.

LES ARMÉES FRANÇAISES DANS LA GRANDE GUERRE: TROISIÈME TOME III LES OFFENSIVES DE 1915 - L'HIVER DE 1915–1916 - 1 MAI 1915–21 FÉVRIER 1916. (*The French Army in the Great War: Book III The Offensives of 1915 – The Winter 1915/1916 - 1st May 1915–21st February 1916.*)

Chef d'Escadron de Cavalière Breventé Janet, *Capitaine d'Infanterie* Chatinières, *Capitaine d'Infanterie* Lefranc and *L'Officier d'Administration de 1re Classe du Service d'Etat-Major* Landousie | 27cm x 22cm | Light Grey Paper Softback | ix + 720pp | untrimmed pages | 8 diagrams| Imprimerie Nationale. | 1923 | French Text.

LES ARMÉES FRANÇAISES DANS LA GRANDE GUERRE: TOME III. ANNEXES 1RE VOLUME. (*The French Army in the Great War: Book III. Appendices 1st Volume.*)

Anonymous | 27cm x 22cm | Light Grey Paper Softback | 1141pp | untrimmed pages | 812 appendices | 1 table | 4 diagrams| Imprimerie Nationale. | 1924 | French Text.

LES ARMÉES FRANÇAISES DANS LA GRANDE GUERRE: TOME III. ANNEXES 2^E VOLUME. (*The French Army in the Great War: Book III. Appendices 2nd Volume.*)

Anonymous | 27cm x 22cm | Light Grey Paper Softback | 1244pp | untrimmed pages | 756 appendices | 1 table | 11 diagrams| Imprimerie Nationale. | 1925 | French Text.

LES ARMÉES FRANÇAISES DANS LA GRANDE GUERRE: TOME III. ANNEXES 3^E VOLUME. (*The French Army in the Great War: Book III. Appendices 3rd Volume.*)

Anonymous | 27cm x 22cm | Light Grey Paper Softback | 1395pp | untrimmed pages | 1396 appendices | 1 table | 1 map | 1 diagram| Imprimerie Nationale. | 1926 | French Text.

LES ARMÉES FRANÇAISES DANS LA GRANDE GUERRE: TOME III. ANNEXES 4^E VOLUME. (*The French Army in the Great War: Book III. Appendices 4th Volume.*)

Anonymous | 27cm x 22cm | Light Grey Paper Softback | 932pp | untrimmed pages | 470 appendices | 1 table | 4 maps | 20 diagrams| Imprimerie Nationale. | 1926 | French Text.

LES ARMÉES FRANÇAISES DANS LA GRANDE GUERRE: TOME III. CARTES Nos 1 à 60. (*The French Army in the Great War: Book III. Maps No's 1 to 60.*)

Anonymous | 27cm x 22cm | Light Grey Paper Softback | 60 maps | Imprimerie Nationale. | 1924 | French Text.

LES ARMÉES FRANÇAISES DANS LA GRANDE GUERRE: TOME IV VERDUN ET LA SOMME. PREMIER VOLUME LES PROJETS OFFENSIFS POUR 1916 ET LA BATAILLE DE VERDUN - 21 FÉVRIER–1 MAI 1916. (*The French Army in the Great War: Book IV Verdun and the Somme. First Volume Plans for 1916 Offensives and the Battle of Verdun - 21st February–1st May 1916.*)

Lieutenant-Colonel d'Infanterie Breventé Appert, *Capitaine d'Infanterie Breventé* Besse, *Capitaine d'Infanterie* Laxague and *Capitaine d'Infanterie* Maubert | 27cm x 22cm | Light Grey Paper Softback | viii + 666pp | untrimmed pages | 6 appendices | Imprimerie Nationale. | 1926 | French Text.

LES ARMÉES FRANÇAISES DANS LA GRANDE GUERRE: TOME IV – 1RE VOLUME. ANNEXES 1RE VOLUME. (*The French Army in the Great War: Book IV- 1st Volume. Appendices 1st Volume.*)

Anonymous | 27cm x 22cm | Light Grey Paper Softback | 1044pp | untrimmed pages | 904 appendices | 1 table | 9 diagrams| Imprimerie Nationale. | 1926 | French Text.

LES ARMÉES FRANÇAISES DANS LA GRANDE GUERRE: TOME IV – 1RE VOLUME. ANNEXES 2E VOLUME. (*The French Army in the Great War: Book IV- 1st Volume. Appendices 2nd Volume.*)

Anonymous | 27cm x 22cm | Light Grey Paper Softback | 971pp | untrimmed pages | 744 appendices | 1 table | 2 maps | 5 diagrams| Imprimerie Nationale. | 1931 | French Text.

LES ARMÉES FRANÇAISES DANS LA GRANDE GUERRE: TOME IV – 1RE VOLUME. ANNEXES 3E VOLUME. (*The French Army in the Great War: Book IV – 1st Volume. Appendices 3rd Volume.*)

Anonymous | 27cm x 22cm | Light Grey Paper Softback | 954pp | untrimmed pages | 667 appendices | 1 table | 15 maps | 21 diagrams| Imprimerie Nationale. | 1931 | French Text.

LES ARMÉES FRANÇAISES DANS LA GRANDE GUERRE: TOME IV – 1RE VOLUME. CARTES Nos 1 à 38. (*The French Army in the Great War: Book IV – 1st Volume. Maps No's 1 to 38.*)

Anonymous | 27cm x 22cm | Light Grey Paper Softback | 38 maps | Imprimerie Nationale. | 1926 | French Text.

LES ARMÉES FRANÇAISES DANS LA GRANDE GUERRE: TOME IV VERDUN ET LA SOMME. DEUXIÈME VOLUME LA BATAILLE DE VERDUN ET LES OFFENSIFS DES ALLIES - 1 MAI–3 SEPTEMBRE 1916. (*The French Army in the Great War: Book IV Verdun and the Somme. Second Volume The Battle of Verdun and the Allied Offensive – 1st May–3rd September 1916.*)

Lieutenant-Colonel d'Infanterie Breventé Acacie, *Commandant d'Infanterie* Altairac, *Chef d'Escadron de Cavalière Breventé* Gallini, *Commandant d'Infanterie Breventé* Denolle, *Capitaine d'Infanterie* Laxague and *Capitaine d'Artillerie Breventé* Courbis | 27cm x 22cm | Light Grey Paper Softback | viii + 445pp | untrimmed pages | 14 maps | 24 diagrams| Imprimerie Nationale. | 1933 | French Text.

LES ARMÉES FRANÇAISES DANS LA GRANDE GUERRE: TOME IV – 2E VOLUME. ANNEXES 1RE VOLUME [*]. (*The French Army in the Great War: Book IV – 2nd Volume. Appendices 1st Volume [*].*)

Anonymous | 27cm x 22cm | Light Grey Paper Softback | 784pp | untrimmed pages | 560 appendices | 3 maps | 14 diagrams| Imprimerie Nationale. | 1933 | French Text.

LES ARMÉES FRANÇAISES DANS LA GRANDE GUERRE: TOME IV – 2E VOLUME. ANNEXES 1RE VOLUME [**]. (*The French Army in the Great War: Book IV – 2nd Volume. Appendices 1st Volume [**].*)

Anonymous | 27cm x 22cm | Light Grey Paper Softback | 814pp | untrimmed pages | 581 appendices | 1 table | 1 map | 7 diagrams| Imprimerie Nationale. | 1933 | French Text.

LES ARMÉES FRANÇAISES DANS LA GRANDE GUERRE: TOME IV – 2E VOLUME. ANNEXES 2E VOLUME [*]. (*The French Army in the Great War: Book IV – 2nd Volume. Appendices 2nd Volume [*].*)

Anonymous | 27cm x 22cm | Light Grey Paper Softback | 770pp | untrimmed pages | 671 appendices | 1 map | 8 diagrams| Imprimerie Nationale. | 1933 | French Text.

LES ARMÉES FRANÇAISES DANS LA GRANDE GUERRE: TOME IV – 2E VOLUME. ANNEXES 2E VOLUME [**]. (*The French Army in the Great War: Book IV – 2nd Volume. Appendices 2nd Volume [**].*)

Anonymous | 27cm x 22cm | Light Grey Paper Softback | 778pp | untrimmed pages | 586 appendices | 1 table | 5 maps | 7 diagrams| Imprimerie Nationale. | 1933 | French Text.

LES ARMÉES FRANÇAISES DANS LA GRANDE GUERRE: TOME IV – 2ᴱ VOLUME. ANNEXES 3ᴱ VOLUME. (*The French Army in the Great War: Book IV - 2ⁿᵈ Volume. Appendices 3ʳᵈ Volume.*)

Anonymous | 27cm x 22cm | Light Grey Paper Softback | 1170pp | untrimmed pages | 784 appendices | 1 table | 2 maps | 21 diagrams| Imprimerie Nationale. | 1933 | French Text.

LES ARMÉES FRANÇAISES DANS LA GRANDE GUERRE: TOME IV - 2ᴱ VOLUME. CARTES Nos 1 à 26. (*The French Army in the Great War: Book IV – 2ⁿᵈ Volume. Maps No's 1 to 26.*)

Anonymous | 27cm x 22cm | Light Grey Paper Softback | 26 maps | Imprimerie Nationale. | 1933 | French Text.

LES ARMÉES FRANÇAISES DANS LA GRANDE GUERRE: TOME IV VERDUN ET LA SOMME. TROISIÈME VOLUME BATAILLE DE LA SOMME (FIN) - OFFENSIVES FRANÇAISES À VERDUN – 3 SEPTEMBRE - FIN DÉCEMBRE 1916. (*The French Army in the Great War: Book IV Verdun and the Somme. Third Volume The Final Part of the Battle of Somme – The French Offensive at Verdun - 3ʳᵈ September - End of December 1916.*)

Lieutenant-Colonel d'Infanterie Breventé Acacie, *Commandant d'Infanterie* Altairac and *Chef d'Escadron de Cavalière Breventé* Gallini | 27cm x 22cm | Light Grey Paper Softback | x + 540pp | untrimmed pages | 2 appendices | 1 map | 7 diagrams| Imprimerie Nationale. | 1935 | French Text.

LES ARMÉES FRANÇAISES DANS LA GRANDE GUERRE: TOME IV – 3ᴱ VOLUME. ANNEXES 1ᴱ VOLUME [*]. (*The French Army in the Great War: Book IV – 3ʳᵈ Volume. Appendices 1ˢᵗ Volume [*].*)

Anonymous | 27cm x 22cm | Light Grey Paper Softback | 864pp | untrimmed pages | 620 appendices | 1 table | 11 maps | 18 diagrams| Imprimerie Nationale. | 1935 | French Text.

LES ARMÉES FRANÇAISES DANS LA GRANDE GUERRE: TOME IV 3ᴱ VOLUME. ANNEXES 1ᴱ VOLUME [**]. (*The French Army in the Great War: Book IV – 3ʳᵈ Volume. Appendices 1ˢᵗ Volume [**].*)

Anonymous | 27cm x 22cm | Light Grey Paper Softback | 875pp | untrimmed pages | 472 appendices | 1 table | 6 diagrams| Imprimerie Nationale. | 1935 | French Text.

LES ARMÉES FRANÇAISES DANS LA GRANDE GUERRE: TOME IV – 3ᴱ VOLUME. ANNEXES 2ᴱ VOLUME [*]. (*The French Army in the Great War: Book IV – 3ʳᵈ Volume. Appendices 2ⁿᵈ Volume [*].*)

Anonymous | 27cm x 22cm | Light Grey Paper Softback | 912pp | untrimmed pages | 549 appendices | 1 table | 5 maps | 16 diagrams| Imprimerie Nationale. | 1935 | French Text.

LES ARMÉES FRANÇAISES DANS LA GRANDE GUERRE: TOME IV – 3ᴱ VOLUME. ANNEXES 2ᴱ VOLUME [**]. (*The French Army in the Great War: Book IV – 3ʳᵈ Volume. Appendices 2ⁿᵈ Volume [**].*)

Anonymous | 27cm x 22cm | Light Grey Paper Softback | 856pp | untrimmed pages | 368 appendices | 1 table | 15 maps | 51 diagrams| Imprimerie Nationale. | 1935 | French Text.

LES ARMÉES FRANÇAISES DANS LA GRANDE GUERRE: TOME IV – 3ᴱ VOLUME. CARTES Nos 1 à 22. (*The French Army in the Great War: Book IV – 3ʳᵈ Volume. Maps No's 1 to 22.*)

Anonymous | 27cm x 22cm | Light Grey Paper Softback | 22 maps | Imprimerie Nationale. | 1935 | French Text.

LES ARMÉES FRANÇAISES DANS LA GRANDE GUERRE: TOME V L'OFFENSIVES D'AVRIL 1917, LES OPERATIONS À OBJECTIFS LIMITES – 1 NOVEMBRE 1916-1 NOVEMBRE 1917. PREMIER VOLUME L'OFFENSIVES D'AVRIL 1917. (*The French Army in the Great War: Book V The April 1917 Offensive and the Limited Objectives Operations - 1ˢᵗ November 1916-1ˢᵗ November 1917. First Volume The April 1917 Offensive.*)

Lieutenant-Colonel d'Infanterie Beaugier, *Lieutenant-Colonel d'Infanterie Breventé* Labordère, *Chef de Bataillon d'Infanterie* Cardot, *Chef de Bataillon d'Infanterie Breventé* Jullien, *Chef d'Escadron de Cavalière* Lecoq, *Chef de Bataillon d'Infanterie* Rouquette, *Capitaine d'Infanterie* Libermann and *Capitaine d'Infanterie* Ory. | 27cm x 22cm | Light Grey Paper Softback | xv + 823pp | Imprimerie Nationale. | 1931 | French Text.
This volume covers Neiville's Spring Offensive.

LES ARMÉES FRANÇAISES DANS LA GRANDE GUERRE: TOME V – 1RE VOLUME. ANNEXES 1^E VOLUME. (*The French Army in the Great War: Book V – 1st Volume. Appendices 1st Volume.*)

> Anonymous | 27cm x 22cm | Light Grey Paper Softback | 1674pp | untrimmed pages | 860 appendices | 1 table | 26 diagrams| Imprimerie Nationale. | 1932 | French Text.

LES ARMÉES FRANÇAISES DANS LA GRANDE GUERRE: TOME V – 1RE VOLUME. ANNEXES 2^E VOLUME. (*The French Army in the Great War: Book V – 1st Volume. Appendices 2nd Volume.*)

> Anonymous | 27cm x 22cm | Light Grey Paper Softback | 1709pp | untrimmed pages | 1090 appendices | 1 table | 24 diagrams| Imprimerie Nationale. | 1932 | French Text.

LES ARMÉES FRANÇAISES DANS LA GRANDE GUERRE: TOME V – 1RE VOLUME. CARTES Nos 1 à 29. (*The French Army in the Great War: Book V – 1st Volume. Maps No's 1 to 29.*)

> Anonymous | 27cm x 22cm | Light Grey Card Box | 29 maps | Imprimerie Nationale. | 1931 | French Text.

LES ARMÉES FRANÇAISES DANS LA GRANDE GUERRE: TOME V – 1RE VOLUME. CARTES Nos 30 à 61. (*The French Army in the Great War: Book V – 1st Volume. Maps No's 30 to 61.*)

> Anonymous | 27cm x 22cm | Light Grey Card Box | 31 maps | Imprimerie Nationale. | 1931 | French Text.

LES ARMÉES FRANÇAISES DANS LA GRANDE GUERRE: TOME V L'OFFENSIVES D'AVRIL 1917, LES OPERATIONS À OBJECTIFS LIMITES – 1 NOVEMBRE 1916-1 NOVEMBRE 1917. DEUXIÈME VOLUME LES OPERATIONS À OBJECTIFS LIMITES. (*The French Army in the Great War: Book V The April 1917 Offensive and the Limited Objectives Operations - 1st November 1916-1st November 1917. Second Volume The Limited Offensive Operations.*)

> Lieutenant-Colonel d'Infanterie Beaugier, Chef de Bataillon d'Infanterie Cardot, Chef d'Escadron de Cavalière Maistre, Chef d'Escadron de Cavalière Desrousseaux de Médrano and Capitaine d'Infanterie Breventé Lyet. | 27cm x 22cm | Light Grey Paper Softback | xiv + 1366pp | untrimmed pages | 9 appendices in 15 parts | 14 diagrams| Imprimerie Nationale. | 1936 | French Text.
> This volumes covers Petain's Limited Offensive Operations.

LES ARMÉES FRANÇAISES DANS LA GRANDE GUERRE: TOME V – 2^E VOLUME. ANNEXES 1^E VOLUME. (*The French Army in the Great War: Book V – 2nd Volume. Appendices 1st Volume.*)

> Anonymous | 27cm x 22cm | Light Grey Paper Softback | 1143pp | untrimmed pages | 639 appendices | 1 table | 4 diagrams| Imprimerie Nationale. | 1937 | French Text.

LES ARMÉES FRANÇAISES DANS LA GRANDE GUERRE: TOME V – 2^E VOLUME. ANNEXES 2^E VOLUME. (*The French Army in the Great War: Book V – 2nd Volume. Appendices 2nd Volume.*)

> Anonymous | 27cm x 22cm | Light Grey Paper Softback | 1212pp | untrimmed pages | 700 appendices | 1 table | 2 diagrams| Imprimerie Nationale. | 1937 | French Text.

LES ARMÉES FRANÇAISES DANS LA GRANDE GUERRE: TOME V – 2^E VOLUME. CARTES Nos 1 à 36. (*The French Army in the Great War: Book V – 2nd Volume. Maps No's 1 to 36.*)

> Anonymous | 27cm x 22cm | Light Grey Paper Softback | 36 maps | 5 diagrams| Imprimerie Nationale. | 1936 | French Text.

LES ARMÉES FRANÇAISES DANS LA GRANDE GUERRE: TOME VI L'HIVER 1917–1918 - L'OFFENSIVES ALLEMANDE - 1 NOVEMBRE 1917–18 JULLIET 1918. PREMIER VOLUME LA PRÉPARATION DE LA CAMPAGNE DE 1918, L'OFFENSIVES ALLEMANDE DE L'OISE À LA MER DU NORD. (*The French Army in the Great War: Book VI Winter 1917–1918 - The German Offensive - 1st November 1917–18th July 1918. First Volume The Preparation of the Campaign of 1918, The German Offensives between the Oise and the North Sea.*)

> *Lieutenant-Colonel d'Infanterie Breventé* Tournés, *Capitaine de Cavalière* Berthemet and *Capitaine d'Artillerie* Lefèvre. | 27cm x 22cm | Light Grey Paper Softback | xii + 532pp | Imprimerie Nationale. | 1931 | French Text.

LES ARMÉES FRANÇAISES DANS LA GRANDE GUERRE: TOME VI – 1RE VOLUME. ANNEXES 1RE VOLUME. (*The French Army in the Great War: Book VI – 1st Volume. Appendices 1st Volume.*)

Anonymous | 27cm x 22cm | Light Grey Paper Softback | 1204pp | untrimmed pages | 484 appendices | 1 table | 14 diagrams| Imprimerie Nationale. | 1932 | French Text.

LES ARMÉES FRANÇAISES DANS LA GRANDE GUERRE: TOME VI – 1RE VOLUME. ANNEXES 2^E VOLUME. (*The French Army in the Great War: Book VI – 1st Volume. Appendices 2nd Volume.*)

Anonymous | 27cm x 22cm | Light Grey Paper Softback | 898pp | untrimmed pages | 821 appendices | 1 table | 5 diagrams| Imprimerie Nationale. | 1932 | French Text.

LES ARMÉES FRANÇAISES DANS LA GRANDE GUERRE: TOME VI – 1RE VOLUME. ANNEXES 3^E VOLUME. (*The French Army in the Great War: Book VI – 1st Volume. Appendices 3rd Volume.*)

Anonymous | 27cm x 22cm | Light Grey Paper Softback | 1052pp | untrimmed pages | 804 appendices | 1 table | 21 diagrams| Imprimerie Nationale. | 1932 | French Text.

LES ARMÉES FRANÇAISES DANS LA GRANDE GUERRE: TOME VI – 1RE VOLUME. CARTES Nos 1 à 36. (*The French Army in the Great War: Book VI – 1st Volume. Maps No's 1 to 36.*)

Anonymous | 27cm x 22cm | Light Grey Paper Softback | 36 maps | Imprimerie Nationale. | 1931 | French Text.

LES ARMÉES FRANÇAISES DANS LA GRANDE GUERRE: TOME VI L'HIVER 1917–1918 - L'OFFENSIVES ALLEMANDE - 1 NOVEMBRE 1917–18 JUILET 1918. DEUXIÈME VOLUME L'OFFENSIVES ALLEMANDE CONTRE LES ARMÉE FRANÇAISES. (*The French Army in the Great War: Book VI Winter 1917–1918 - The German Offensive - 1st November 1917–18th July 1918. Second Volume The German Offensives against the French Army.*)

Chef d'Escadron d'Artillerie Lefèvre and *Capitaine de Cavalière* Berthemet. | 27cm x 22cm | Light Grey Paper Softback | x + 567pp | untrimmed pages | 8 appendices | 11 diagrams| Imprimerie Nationale. | 1935 | French Text.

LES ARMÉES FRANÇAISES DANS LA GRANDE GUERRE: TOME VI – 2^E VOLUME. ANNEXES 1RE VOLUME. (*The French Army in the Great War: Book VI – 2nd Volume. Appendices 1st Volume.*)

Anonymous | 27cm x 22cm | Light Grey Paper Softback | 1062pp | untrimmed pages | 857 appendices | 1 table | 19 diagrams| Imprimerie Nationale. | 1935 | French Text.

LES ARMÉES FRANÇAISES DANS LA GRANDE GUERRE: TOME VI – 2^E VOLUME. ANNEXES 2^E VOLUME. (*The French Army in the Great War: Book VI – 2nd Volume. Appendices 2nd Volume.*)

Anonymous | 27cm x 22cm | Light Grey Paper Softback | 886pp | untrimmed pages | 720 appendices | 1 table | 12 diagrams| Imprimerie Nationale. | 1934 | French Text.

LES ARMÉES FRANÇAISES DANS LA GRANDE GUERRE: TOME VI – 2^E VOLUME. ANNEXES 3^E VOLUME. (*The French Army in the Great War: Book VI – 2nd Volume. Appendices 3rd Volume.*)

Anonymous | 27cm x 22cm | Light Grey Paper Softback | 892pp | untrimmed pages | 764 appendices | 1 table | 4 diagrams| Imprimerie Nationale. | 1934 | French Text.

LES ARMÉES FRANÇAISES DANS LA GRANDE GUERRE: TOME VI – 2^E VOLUME. CARTES Nos 1 à 32. (*The French Army in the Great War: Book VI – 2nd Volume. Maps No's 1 to 32.*)

Anonymous | 27cm x 22cm | Light Grey Paper Softback | 32 maps | Imprimerie Nationale. | 1935 | French Text.

LES ARMÉES FRANÇAISES DANS LA GRANDE GUERRE: TOME VII LA CAMPAGNE OFFENSIVES DE 1918 ET LA MARCHE AU RHIN - 18 JUILET 1918-28 JUIN 1919. PREMIER VOLUME 18 JUILET 1918-25 SEPTEMBRE 1918. (*The French Army in the Great War: Book VII The 1918 Offensive Campaign and the March to the Rhine – 18th July 1918-28th June 1919. First Volume 18th July 1918 – 25th September 1918.*)

Lieutenant-Colonel d'Infanterie Breventé Laure, *Capitaine d'Infanterie* Andriot and *Capitaine d'Infanterie* Labouche. | 27cm x 22cm | Light Grey Paper Softback | viii + 407pp | untrimmed pages | 13 appendices | 36 diagrams| Imprimerie Nationale. | 1923 | French Text.

LES ARMÉES FRANÇAISES DANS LA GRANDE GUERRE: TOME VII – 1RE VOLUME. ANNEXES 1RE VOLUME. (*The French Army in the Great War: Book VII – 1st Volume. Appendices 1st Volume.***)**

Anonymous | 27cm x 22cm | Light Grey Paper Softback | 711pp | untrimmed pages | 670 appendices | 1 table | 29 diagrams| Imprimerie Nationale. | 1923 | French Text.

LES ARMÉES FRANÇAISES DANS LA GRANDE GUERRE: TOME VII – 1RE VOLUME. ANNEXES 2^E VOLUME. (*The French Army in the Great War: Book VII - 1st Volume. Appendices 2nd Volume.***)**

Anonymous | 27cm x 22cm | Light Grey Paper Softback | 735pp | untrimmed pages | 623 appendices | 1 table | 24 diagrams| Imprimerie Nationale. | 1923 | French Text.

LES ARMÉES FRANÇAISES DANS LA GRANDE GUERRE: TOME VII – 1RE VOLUME. CARTES Nos 1 à 37. (*The French Army in the Great War: Book VII – 1st Volume. Maps No's 1 to 37.***)**

Anonymous | 27cm x 22cm | Light Grey Paper Softback | 37 maps | Imprimerie Nationale. | 1923 | French Text.

LES ARMÉES FRANÇAISES DANS LA GRANDE GUERRE: TOME VII LA CAMPAGNE OFFENSIVES DE 1918 ET LA MARCHE AU RHIN - 18 JULIET 1918-28 JUIN 1919. DEUXIÈME VOLUME 26 SEPTEMBRE 1918-28 JUIN 1919. (*The French Army in the Great War: Book VII The 1918 Offensive Campaign and the March to the Rhine – 18th July 1918-28th June 1919. Second Volume 25th September 1918-28th June 1919.***)**

Capitaine d'Infanterie de Feriet, *Capitaine d'Infanterie* Joubert, *Capitaine d'Infanterie* Testu de Balincourt and *Capitaine d'Artillerie Breventé* Roux. | 27cm x 22cm | Light Grey Paper Softback | viii + 446pp | untrimmed pages | 4 appendices in 20 parts | 26 diagrams| Imprimerie Nationale. | 1938 | French Text.

LES ARMÉES FRANÇAISES DANS LA GRANDE GUERRE: TOME VII – 2^E VOLUME. ANNEXE VOLUME. (*The French Army in the Great War: Book VII – 2nd Volume. Appendices Volume***)**

Anonymous | 27cm x 22cm | Light Grey Paper Softback | 992pp | untrimmed pages | 591 appendices | 1 table | 5 diagrams| Imprimerie Nationale. | 1938 | French Text.

LES ARMÉES FRANÇAISES DANS LA GRANDE GUERRE: TOME VII – 2^E VOLUME. CARTES Nos 1 à 21. (*The French Army in the Great War: Book VII – 2nd Volume. Maps No's 1 to 21.***)**

Anonymous | 27cm x 22cm | Light Grey Paper Softback | 21 maps | Imprimerie Nationale. | 1938 | French Text.

LES ARMÉES FRANÇAISES DANS LA GRANDE GUERRE: TOME VIII LA CAMPAGNE D'ORIENT (DARDANELLES ET SALONIQUE). PREMIER VOLUME LA CAMPAGNE D'ORIENT JUSQU'A L'INTERVENTION DE LA ROUMANIE - FÉVRIER 1915 - AOÛT 1916. (*The French Army in the Great War: Book VIII The Eastern Campaigns. [The Dardenelles and Macedonia]. Volume 1 The Eastern Campaigns before the Intervention of Romania - February 1915-August 1916.***)**

Colonel d'Infanterie Breventé Lepetit, *Lieutenant-Colonel d'Infanterie Breventé* Tournyol du Clos, *Capitaine d'Infanterie* Riniéri and *Lieutenant d'Artillerie* Gallard de Dananche. | 27cm x 22cm | Light Grey Paper Softback | vii + 575pp | untrimmed pages | 14 appendices | 16 diagrams| Imprimerie Nationale. | 1923 | French Text.

Macedonia is often refered to as Salonika – the supply port and base camp. The town of Salonika is now known as Thessaloniki.

LES ARMÉES FRANÇAISES DANS LA GRANDE GUERRE: TOME VIII – 1RE VOLUME. ANNEXES 1RE VOLUME. (*The French Army in the Great War: Book VIII - 1st Volume. Appendices 1st Volume.***)**

Anonymous | 27cm x 22cm | Light Grey Paper Softback | viii + 798pp | untrimmed pages | 438 appendices | 1 table | 2 diagrams| Imprimerie Nationale. | 1924 | French Text.

LES ARMÉES FRANÇAISES DANS LA GRANDE GUERRE: TOME VIII – 1RE VOLUME. ANNEXES 2^E VOLUME. (*The French Army in the Great War: Book VIII - 1st Volume. Appendices 2nd Volume.***)**

Anonymous | 27cm x 22cm | Light Grey Paper Softback | 832pp | untrimmed pages | 750 appendices | 1 table | 1 diagram| Imprimerie Nationale. | 1927 | French Text.

LES ARMÉES FRANÇAISES DANS LA GRANDE GUERRE: TOME VIII – 1RE VOLUME. ANNEXES 3^E VOLUME. (*The French Army in the Great War: Book VIII - 1st Volume. Appendices 3rd Volume.***)**

Anonymous | 27cm x 22cm | Light Grey Paper Softback | 943pp | untrimmed pages | 732 appendices | 1 table | 1 diagram| Imprimerie Nationale. | 1927 | French Text.

LES ARMÉES FRANÇAISES DANS LA GRANDE GUERRE: TOME VIII – 1^(RE) VOLUME. CARTES Nos 1 à 64. (*The French Army in the Great War: Book VIII - 1^(st) Volume. Maps No's 1 to 64.*)

Anonymous | 27cm x 22cm | Light Grey Paper Softback | 64 maps | 1 photoraph | 5 diagrams | Imprimerie Nationale. | 1923 | French Text.

LES ARMÉES FRANÇAISES DANS LA GRANDE GUERRE: TOME VIII LA CAMPAGNE D'ORIENT (DARDANELLES ET SALONIQUE). DEUXIÈME VOLUME LA CAMPAGNE D'ORIENT DEPUIS L'INTERVENTION DE LA ROUMANIE EN AOÛT 1916 JUSQU'EN AVRIL 1918. (*The French Army in the Great War: Book VIII The Eastern Campaigns [The Dardenelles and Macedonia]. Second Volume The Eastern Campaigns after the Intervention of Romania from August 1916 to April 1918.*)

Colonel d'Infanterie Breventé Lepetit, *Lieutenant-Colonel d'Infanterie Breventé* Tournyol du Clos, *Chef de Bataillon d'Infanterie* Riniéri, *Chef de Bataillon d'Infanterie* Cardot and *Capitaine d'Artillerie* Druène. | 27cm x 22cm | Light Grey Paper Softback | iv + 643pp | untrimmed pages | 2 appendices | 24 diagrams| Imprimerie Nationale. | 1933 | French Text.

LES ARMÉES FRANÇAISES DANS LA GRANDE GUERRE: TOME VIII – 2^(E) VOLUME. ANNEXES 1^(RE) VOLUME. (*The French Army in the Great War: Book VIII - 2^(nd) Volume. Appendices 1^(st) Volume.*)

Anonymous | 27cm x 22cm | Light Grey Paper Softback | 828pp | untrimmed pages | 786 appendices | 1 table | 2 diagrams| Imprimerie Nationale. | 1934 | French Text.

LES ARMÉES FRANÇAISES DANS LA GRANDE GUERRE: TOME VIII – 2^(E) VOLUME. ANNEXES 2^(E) VOLUME. (*The French Army in the Great War: Book VIII - 2^(nd) Volume. Appendices 2^(nd) Volume.*)

Anonymous | 27cm x 22cm | Light Grey Paper Softback | 702pp | untrimmed pages | 636 appendices | 1 table | 5 diagrams| Imprimerie Nationale. | 1934 | French Text.

LES ARMÉES FRANÇAISES DANS LA GRANDE GUERRE: TOME VIII – 2^(E) VOLUME. ANNEXES 3^(E) VOLUME. (*The French Army in the Great War: Book VIII - 2^(nd) Volume. Appendices 3^(rd) Volume.*)

Anonymous | 27cm x 22cm | Light Grey Paper Softback | 1000pp | untrimmed pages | 596 appendices | 1 table | 11 diagrams| Imprimerie Nationale. | 1934 | French Text.

LES ARMÉES FRANÇAISES DANS LA GRANDE GUERRE: TOME VIII – 2^(E) VOLUME. ANNEXES 4^(E) VOLUME. (*The French Army in the Great War: Book VIII - 2^(nd) Volume. Appendices 4^(th) Volume.*)

Anonymous | 27cm x 22cm | Light Grey Paper Softback | 794pp | untrimmed pages | 472 appendices | 1 table | 11 diagrams| Imprimerie Nationale. | 1934 | French Text.

LES ARMÉES FRANÇAISES DANS LA GRANDE GUERRE: TOME VIII – 2^(E) VOLUME. CARTES Nos 1 à 24. (*The French Army in the Great War: Book VIII - 2^(nd) Volume. Maps No's 1 to 24.*)

Anonymous | 27cm x 22cm | Light Grey Card Box | 23 maps | Imprimerie Nationale. | 1934 | French Text.

LES ARMÉES FRANÇAISES DANS LA GRANDE GUERRE: TOME VIII – 2^(E) VOLUME. CARTES Nos 25 à 48. (*The French Army in the Great War: Book VIII - 2^(nd) Volume. Maps No's 25 to 48.*)

Anonymous | 27cm x 22cm | Light Grey Card Box | 24 maps | 7 diagrams| Imprimerie Nationale. | 1934 | French Text.

LES ARMÉES FRANÇAISES DANS LA GRANDE GUERRE: TOME VIII LA CAMPAGNE D'ORIENT (DARDANELLES ET SALONIQUE). TROISIÈME VOLUME LA CAMPAGNE D'ORIENT D'AVRIL 1918 À DÉCEMBRE 1918. (*The French Army in the Great War: Book VIII The Eastern Campaigns [The Dardenelles and Macedonia]. Third Volume The Eastern Campaigns from April 1918 to December 1918.*)

Lieutenant-Colonel d'Infanterie Breventé Tournyol du Clos, *Chef de Bataillon d'Infanterie* Riniéri, *Chef de Bataillon d'Infanterie* Cardot and *Capitaine d'Artillerie* Druène. | 27cm x 22cm | Light Grey Paper Softback | vii + 554pp | untrimmed pages | 3 appendices in 21 parts | 22 diagrams| Imprimerie Nationale. | 1934 | French Text.

LES ARMÉES FRANÇAISES DANS LA GRANDE GUERRE: TOME VIII – 3^(E) VOLUME. ANNEXES 1^(RE) VOLUME. (*The French Army in the Great War: Book VIII – 3^(rd) Volume. Appendices 1^(st) Volume.*)

Anonymous | 27cm x 22cm | Light Grey Paper Softback | 960pp | untrimmed pages | 552 appendices | 1 table | 2 maps | 12 diagrams| Imprimerie Nationale. | 1934 | French Text.

LES ARMÉES FRANÇAISES DANS LA GRANDE GUERRE: TOME VIII – 3^E VOLUME. ANNEXES 2^E VOLUME. (*The French Army in the Great War: Book VIII - 3rd Volume. Appendices 2nd Volume.*)

Anonymous | 27cm x 22cm | Light Grey Paper Softback | 1032pp | untrimmed pages | 714 appendices | 1 table | 2 maps | 4 diagrams| Imprimerie Nationale. | 1934 | French Text.

LES ARMÉES FRANÇAISES DANS LA GRANDE GUERRE: TOME VIII – 3^E VOLUME. ANNEXES 3^E VOLUME. (*The French Army in the Great War: Book VIII – 3rd Volume. Appendices 3rd Volume.*)

Anonymous | 27cm x 22cm | Light Grey Paper Softback | 692pp | untrimmed pages | 616 appendices | 1 table | 1 diagram| Imprimerie Nationale. | 1934 | French Text.

LES ARMÉES FRANÇAISES DANS LA GRANDE GUERRE: TOME VIII – 3^E VOLUME. CARTES Nos 1 à 22. (*The French Army in the Great War: Book VIII - 3rd Volume. Maps No's 1 to 22.*)

Anonymous | 27cm x 22cm | Light Grey Card Box | 22 maps | Imprimerie Nationale. | 1934 | French Text.

LES ARMÉES FRANÇAISES DANS LA GRANDE GUERRE: TOME IX LES FRONTS SECONDAIRES. PREMIER VOLUME THÉÂTRE D'OPÉRATIONS DE LEVANT (ÉGYPTE – PALESTINE -SYRIA – HODJAZ) – LA PROPAGANDE ALLEMANDE AU MAROC. (*The French Army in the Great War: Book IX The Secondary Fronts. First Volume The Middle Eastern Theatre of Operations [Egypt - Palestine – Syria – Hodjaz] – The German Propaganda in Morocco.*)

Lieutenant-Colonel d'Infanterie Breveté Tournyol Du Clos, *Lieutenant-Colonel d'Infanterie Breveté* Naért, *Lieutenant-Colonel d'Artillerie* Bernache-Assolant, *Chef de Bataillon d'Infanterie* Cardot and *Capitaine d'Infanterie Coloniale* Chalmel. | 27cm x 22cm | Light Grey Paper Softback | xi + 240pp | Imprimerie Nationale. | 1934 | French Text.

LES ARMÉES FRANÇAISES DANS LA GRANDE GUERRE: TOME IX – 1RE VOLUME. ANNEXES VOLUME. (*The French Army in the Great War: Book IX – 1st Volume. Appendices Volume*)

Anonymous | 27cm x 22cm | Light Grey Paper Softback | 1036pp | untrimmed pages | 833 appendices | 1 table | 1 diagram| Imprimerie Nationale. | 1935 | French Text.

LES ARMÉES FRANÇAISES DANS LA GRANDE GUERRE: TOME IX – 1RE VOLUME. CARTES Nos 1 à 17. (*The French Army in the Great War: Book IX – 1st Volume. Maps No's 1 to 17.*)

Anonymous | 27cm x 22cm | Light Grey Card Box | 17 maps | Imprimerie Nationale. | 1936 | French Text.

LES ARMÉES FRANÇAISES DANS LA GRANDE GUERRE: TOME IX LES FRONTS SECONDAIRES. DEUXIÈME VOLUME LES CAMPAGNES COLONIALES: CAMEROUN – TOGOLAND. – OPÉRATIONS CONTRE LES SENOUSSIS. (*The French Army in the Great War: Book IX The Secondary Fronts. Second Volume The Colonial Campaigns: Cameroon – Togoland – Operations against the Senoussis.*)

Lieutenant-Colonel d'Infanterie Coloniale Weithas and *Lieutenant-Colonel d'Infanterie Coloniale* Rémy. | 27cm x 22cm | Light Grey Paper Softback | xii + 877pp | Imprimerie Nationale. | 1929 | French Text.

LES ARMÉES FRANÇAISES DANS LA GRANDE GUERRE: TOME IX – 2^E VOLUME. ANNEXES 1RE VOLUME. (*The French Army in the Great War: Book IX – 2nd Volume. Appendices 1st Volume.*)

Anonymous | 27cm x 22cm | Light Grey Paper Softback | 1402pp | untrimmed pages | 1206 appendices | 1 table | 13 maps | 10 diagrams| Imprimerie Nationale. | 1931 | French Text.

LES ARMÉES FRANÇAISES DANS LA GRANDE GUERRE: TOME IX – 2^E VOLUME. ANNEXES 2E VOLUME. (*The French Army in the Great War: Book IX – 2nd Volume. Appendices 2nd Volume.*)

Anonymous | 27cm x 22cm | Light Grey Paper Softback | 1220pp | untrimmed pages | 900 appendices | 1 table | 13 maps | 4 diagrams| Imprimerie Nationale. | 1931 | French Text.

LES ARMÉES FRANÇAISES DANS LA GRANDE GUERRE: TOME IX – 2^E VOLUME. ANNEXES 3^E VOLUME. (*The French Army in the Great War: Book IX – 2nd Volume. Appendices 3rd Volume.*)

Anonymous | 27cm x 22cm | Light Grey Paper Softback | 1489pp | untrimmed pages | 1226 appendices | 1 table | 2 maps | 9 diagrams| Imprimerie Nationale. | 1931 | French Text.

LES ARMÉES FRANÇAISES DANS LA GRANDE GUERRE: TOME IX – 2^E VOLUME. ANNEXES 4^E VOLUME. (*The French Army in the Great War: Book IX – 2nd Volume. Appendices 4th Volume.*)

Anonymous | 27cm x 22cm | Light Grey Paper Softback | 1112pp | untrimmed pages | 945 appendices | 1 table | 19 maps | 2 diagrams| Imprimerie Nationale. | 1931 | French Text.

LES ARMÉES FRANÇAISES DANS LA GRANDE GUERRE: TOME IX – 2^E VOLUME. CARTES Nos 1 à 26. (*The French Army in the Great War: Book IX The Secondary Fronts. Volume 2. Maps No's 1 to 26.*)

Anonymous | 27cm x 22cm | Light Grey Card Box | 26 maps | Imprimerie Nationale. | 1929 | French Text.

LES ARMÉES FRANÇAISES DANS LA GRANDE GUERRE: TOME IX LES FRONTS SECONDAIRES. TROISIÈME VOLUME LES OPÉRATIONS AU MAROC. (*The French Army in the Great War: Book IX The Secondary Fronts. Third Volume The Operations in Morocco.*)[26]

Lieutenant-Colonel d'Infanterie Laxague, *Chef d'Escadron de Cavalière* Billot, *Chef d'Escadron de Cavalière* de la Sudrie de Calvayrac, *Capitaine de Cavalière* Archambault de Beaune and *Capitaine de Cavalière* d'Ussel. | 27cm x 22cm | Light Grey Paper Softback | xi + 211pp | untrimmed pages | 10 appendices | 1 table | 9 diagrams| Imprimerie Nationale. | 1934 | French Text.

LES ARMÉES FRANÇAISES DANS LA GRANDE GUERRE: TOME IX – 3^E VOLUME. CARTES Nos 1 à 26. (*The French Army in the Great War: Book IX – 3rd Volume. Maps No's 1 to 26.*)

Anonymous | 27cm x 22cm | Light Grey Card Box | 26 maps | Imprimerie Nationale. | 1934 | French Text.

LES ARMÉES FRANÇAISES DANS LA GRANDE GUERRE: TOME X ORDRES DE BATAILLE DES GRANDES UNITÉS. PREMIER VOLUME AVANT-PROPOS, INDEX GÉOGRAPHIQUE, ABBRÉVIATIONS, GRANDS QUARTIERS GÉNÉRAUX, GROUPES D'ARMÉES, ARMÉES, CORPS D'ARMÉES. (*The French Army in the Great War: Book X Order of Battle of the Major Units. First Volume Forewords, Geographical Index, Abbreviations, Headquarters, Army Groups, Armies and Army Corps.*)

Lieutenant-Colonel d'Infanterie Breventé Pompé, *Chef de Bataillon d'Infanterie Breventé* Porsh, *Chef de Bataillon à T.T. d'Infanterie* Fargé, *Capitaine d'Infanterie* du Paty de Clam, Capitaine d'Infanterie Huillard, *Capitaine d'Infanterie* de la Charie, *Chef d'Escadron de Cavalière* Fauche, *Chef d'Escadron d'Artillerie* Pingeon, *Lieutenant-Colonel du Génie* Pacton and *Capitaine du Génie* Kont. | 27cm x 22cm | Light Grey Paper Softback | ciii + 966pp | Imprimerie Nationale. | 1923 | French Text.

LES ARMÉES FRANÇAISES DANS LA GRANDE GUERRE: TOME X ORDRES DE BATAILLE DES GRANDES UNITÉS. DEUXIÈME VOLUME DIVISIONS D'INFANTERIE, DIVISIONS DE CAVALERIE. (*The French Army in the Great War: Book X Order of Battle of the Major Units. Second Volume Infantry Divisions, Cavalry Divisions.*)

Lieutenant-Colonel d'Infanterie Breventé Pompé, *Chef de Bataillon d'Infanterie Breventé* Porsh, *Chef de Bataillon à T.T. d'Infanterie* Fargé, *Capitaine d'Infanterie* du Paty de Clam, *Capitaine d'Infanterie* Huillard, *Capitaine d'Infanterie* de la Charie, *Chef d'Escadron de Cavalière* Fauche, *Chef d'Escadron d'Artillerie* Pingeon, *Lieutenant-Colonel du Génie* Pacton and *Capitaine du Génie* Kont. | 27cm x 22cm | Light Grey Paper Softback | vi + 1092pp | Imprimerie Nationale. | 1924 | French Text.

LES ARMÉES FRANÇAISES DANS LA GRANDE GUERRE: TOME XI LA DIRECTION DE L'ARRIÈRE. (*The French Army in the Great War: Book X The Management of the Rear.*)

Général de Division Ragueneau, *Lieutenant-Colonel d'Infanterie Breventé* Sisteron and *Lieutenant-Colonel d'Infanterie Breventé* Maugin. | 27cm x 22cm | Light Grey Paper Softback | xx + 1209pp | untrimmed pages | 90 appendices | 146 diagrams| Imprimerie Nationale. | 1937 | French Text.

This volume covers the Western Front Zone of the Interior.

---

[26] I have not been able to find a copy of any annexes to this book (Tome IX Volume 3). However it is possible that this book had one or more annexes.

LES ARMÉES FRANÇAISES DANS LA GRANDE GUERRE: TOME XI. CARTES Nos 1 à 27. (*The French Army in the Great War: Book XI The Management of the Rear. Maps No's 1 to 27.*)

Anonymous | 27cm x 22cm | Light Grey Card Box | 27 maps | Imprimerie Nationale. | 1937 | French Text.

Occupations Activities;

Ministère des Armées, Etat-Major de l'Armée de Terre Service Historique - Les Armées Françaises en Orient après l'Armistice de 1918 * L'Armée Française d'Orient. L'Armée de Hongrie (11 Novembre 1918 - 10 Septembre 1919). (*French Armies in the East after the Armistice of 1918 * The French Army of the East - the Army of Hungary (November 11, 1918 - September 10, 1919).*)

Général Jean Bernachot - Ministère des Armées, Etat-Major de l'Armée de Terre Service Historique | 24cm x 15.5cm | Burgundy Red Hardcover | 355pp | 11 appendices | 11 maps | 2 tables | Imprimerie Nationale. | 1970 | French Text.

Ministère des Armées, Etat-Major de l'Armée de Terre Service Historique - Les Armées Françaises en Orient après l'Armistice de 1918 ** L'Armée du Danube. L'Armée Française d'Orient (28 Octobre 1918 - 25 Janvier 1920). (*French Armies in the East after the Armistice of 1918: French Armies in the East after the Armistice of 1918 ** The Army of the Danube - the French Army of the East (October 28, 1918 - January 25, 1920).*)

Général Jean Bernachot - Ministère des Armées, Etat-Major de l'Armée de Terre Service Historique | 24cm x 15.5cm | Burgundy Red Hardcover | 455pp | 34 appendices | 10 maps | Imprimerie Nationale. | 1970 | French Text

Ministère des Armées, Etat-Major de l'Armée de Terre Service Historique - Les Armées Françaises en Orient après l'Armistice de 1918 * Le Corps d'Occupation de Constantinople (6 Novembre 1920 - 2 Octobre 1923).** (*French Armies in the East after the Armistice of 1918 *** The Occupation Corps of Constantinople (November 6, 1920 - October 2, 1923).*)

Général Jean Bernachot - Ministère des Armées, Etat-Major de l'Armée de Terre Service Historique | 24cm x 15.5cm | Burgundy Red Hardcover | 524pp | 24 appendices | 12 maps | 9 tables | Imprimerie Nationale. | 1972 | French Text

Addendum - Army Miscellaneous;

Les Mutineries de 1917. (*The 1917 Mutinies*)

Professor Guy Pedroncini | 24cm x 15.5cm | Yellow Paper Softback | 328pp | 20 appendices | 27 table | 9 maps | 19 photographs | 4 graphs | Presse Universitaires de France. | 1967 | French Text.

The French Army mutinies of 1917 were not (for political reasons at the time of writing) recorded in any great depth or detail in the official "**Les Armées Françaises dans la Grande Guerre**". The files relating to the mutinies were closed to the French general public within the French Army archives (the Ministère de la Guerre, État de l'Armée - Service Historique followed by the Service Historique de l'Armée de Terre) for a period of one hundred years. However *Professor* Pedroncini was given official access to the files in 1967 (fifty years before the official release date) and asked to write a history covering them. Therefore, as such, this book should be regarded as an Official History.

Aviation Activities;

L'Aéronautique pendant la Guerre Mondiale. (*Aviation during the World War.*)

Anonymous | 35.5cm x 28cm | softback | viii + 735pp | ? photographs | ? tables | Maurice de Brunoff. | 1919 | French Text.

Les "as" Français de la Grande Guerre tome I. (*French "aces" of the Great War 1914-1918 Book 1.*)

Daniel Porret | 24cm x 16cm | softback | xv + 342pp | 172 photographs | 85 tables | Service historique de l'armée de l'air. | 1983 | French Text.

Les "as" Français de la Grande Guerre tome II. (*French "aces" of the Great War 1914-1918 Book 2.*)

Daniel Porret | 24cm x 16cm | softback | 376pp | 210 photographs | 106 tables | Service historique de l'armée de l'air. | 1983| French Text.

L'effort de guerre française dans le domaine aéronautique en 1914-1918. (*The French war effort in aviation, 1914-1918.*)

Général C. [Charles] Christienne and S. [Simone] Pesquiès-Courbier | ?cm x ?cm | ? Card Hardback | ?pp | ? photographs | ? diagrams| Service historique de l'armée de l'air. | 1984 | French Text.

Recrutement et formation des pilotes, 1917-1918. (*Recruitment and training of pilots, 1917-1918.*)

M. [Marcelin] Hodeir | ?cm x ?cm | ? Card Hardback | ?pp | ? photographs | ? diagrams| Service historique de l'armée de l'air. | c1980 | French Text.

Les bombardements aériens des usines sidérurgiques de l'est en 1914-1918: l'enjeu économique, militaire et politique. (*The bombing of ironworks in the east, 1914-1918: The economic, military and political game.*)

Anonymous | ?cm x ?cm | ? Card Hardback | ?pp | ? photographs | ? diagrams| Service historique de l'armée de l'air. | c1980 | French Text.

Aperçus sur la doctrine d'emploi de l'aéronautique militaire française: 1914-18. (*Observations on the doctrine employed by French Military Aviation, 1914-18.*)

P. [Patrick] Facon | ?cm x ?cm | ? Card Hardback | ?pp | ? photographs | ? diagrams| Service historique de l'armée de l'air. | c1984 | French Text.

Les escadrilles de l'aéronautique militaire française. Symbolique et histoire, 1912-1920. (*The Markings and Histories of French Mititary Aviation Squadrons 1912-1920.*)

Capitaine David Jean, *Adjudant-Chef* Bernard Palmieri, and *Sergent-Chef* Georges-Didier Rohrbacher. | 30cm x 21.5cm | Light Brown Plastic Card Hardback | 607pp | 1 colour photographs | 447 black and white photographs | 463 colour diagrams | 51 black and white diagrams | Service historique de l'armée de l'air. | 2004 | French Text.

Medical Activities;

Le Service de Santé Pendant la Guerre, 1914-1918: Tome I, Années 1914-1915. (*Medical Service during the War 1914-1918: Book I, The Years 1914-1915.*)

Médecin Inspecteur Général A. [Alfred Henri Alexandre] Mignon | 24cm x 16cm | cream card softback | 703pp | untrimmed pages | 17 maps | c58 tables | 13 diagrams| Masson and Cie. Editeurs | 1926 | French Text.

The title differed on the cover to that shown on the title page of this volume as follows "....**Tome Premières opérations militaires et stabilisation.**" (....*First Book Military Operations and Stabilisation.*)"

Le Service de Santé Pendant la Guerre, 1914-1918: Tome II, Le Service de santé à Verdun. (*Medical Service during the War 1914-1918: Book II, Medical Service at Verdun.*)

Médecin Inspecteur Général A. [Alfred Henri Alexandre] Mignon | 24cm x 16cm | cream card softback | 693pp | untrimmed pages | 18 maps | c64 tables | 7 diagrams| Masson and Cie. Editeurs | 1926 | French Text.

The title differed on the cover to that shown on the title page of this volume as follows "....**Tome II La bataille de Verdun.**" (....*Book II The Battle of Verdun.*)"

Le Service de Santé Pendant la Guerre, 1914-1918: Tome III, Le Service de santé dans le grandes offensives, juillet 1916-novembre 1918. (*Medical Service during the War 1914-1918: Book III, The Medical Service in the Great Offensives July 1916 – November 1918.*)

Médecin Inspecteur Général A. [Alfred Henri Alexandre] Mignon | 24cm x 16cm | cream card softback | 709pp | untrimmed pages | 30 maps | c51 tables | 15 diagrams| Masson and Cie. Editeurs | 1926 | French Text.

The title differed on the cover to that shown on the title page of this volume as follows "....**Tome III, Les grandes batailles offensives et défensives 1916-1917-1918.** (....*Book III, The Great Offensives and Defensive Battles 1916–1917-1918.*)"

Le Service de Santé Pendant la Guerre, 1914-1918: Tome IV, L'évolution du Service de santé pendant la guerre 1914-1918. (*Medical Service during the War 1914-1918: Book IV, The Evolution of the Medical Service during the War 1914-1918.*)

Médecin Inspecteur Général A. [Alfred Henri Alexandre] Mignon | 24cm x 16cm | cream card softback | 833pp | untrimmed pages | 2 photographs | c17 tables | 30 diagrams| Masson and Cie. Editeurs | 1927 | French Text.

The title differed on the cover to that shown on the title page of this volume as follows
"....**Tome IV, L'évolution du Service de santé pendant la guerre. (**....*Book IV, The Evolution of the Medical Service during the War.***)**"

Appareils de fractures. Appareil de pouliquen, description, application. (*Fractures Apparatus. Supporting Splint, Description, Application.***)**

> Anonymous - Ministére de la Guerre Direction du Service de Santé. | 31cm x ?cm | ? Paper Softback | 9pp | untrimmed pages | ? diagrams| Imprimerie Nationale. | 1922 | French Text.

Notice clinique et thérapeutique des lésions causées par les gaz de combat. (*Clinical Records and Treatment of Lesions caused by Gas Warfare.***)**

> Anonymous - Ministére de la Guerre Direction du Service de Santé. | 19cm x ?cm | ? Paper Softback | 54pp | untrimmed pages | ? diagrams| Imprimerie Nationale. | 1937 | French Text.

Étude de statistique chirurgicale, guerre de 1914-1918. Les blessés hospitalisés à l'intérieur du territoire; l'évolution de leurs blessures. Tome I. (*Study of Surgical Statistics, of the 1914-1918 War. The Hospitalisation of the Wounded in the Country's Interior; the Evolution of Healing the Wounds. Book I.***)**

> Anonymous - Ministére de la Guerre Direction du Service de Santé. | 31cm x ?cm | ? Paper Softback | lxxv + 451pp | untrimmed pages | ? diagrams | Imprimerie Nationale. | 1924 | French Text.

Étude de statistique chirurgicale, guerre de 1914-1918. Les blessés hospitalisés à l'intérieur du territoire; l'évolution de leurs blessures. Tome II. (*Study of Surgical Statistics, of the 1914-1918 War. The Hospitalisation of the Wounded in the Country's Interior; the Evolution of Healing the Wounds. Book II.***)**

> Anonymous - Ministére de la Guerre Direction du Service de Santé. | 31cm x ?cm | ? Paper Softback | 413pp | untrimmed pages | ? diagrams | Imprimerie Nationale. | 1924 | French Text.

Étude statistique des pertes subies par les français pendant la guerre 1914-1918: progrès accomplis dans le fonctionnement du Service de santé pendant la guerre. (*Statistical Study of the Losses Suffered by the French during the 1914-1918 War: Progress made in the Medical Service Operations during the War*)**

> *Médecin général inspecteur* Joseph-Henri-Raymond Toubert - Ministére de la Guerre Direction du Service de Santé. | 31cm x ?cm | ? Paper Softback | 39pp | untrimmed pages | ? tables | ? graphs | Charles-Lavauzelle. | c1921 | French Text.

Aviation Medicines;

Les avions sanitaires: leur évolution, leur emploi. (*Aviation Medicine: Its Development, and Employment.***)**

> *Médecin-major* Vincent - Ministére de la Guerre Direction du Service de Santé. | 27cm x ?cm | ? Paper Softback | 12pp | untrimmed pages | ? diagrams| G. Roche d'Estrez. | 1923 | French Text.

German Official Histories

The German naval official histories and monographs were written by members of the Marine-Archiv (*Naval Archives*). The Marine-Archiv employed mainly ex-naval officers to do the research and writing.

Before the end of the Great War, German military official histories were written by the historical section within the Großer Generalstab (*Great General Staff*). During the Great War an archive section was created within the historical section to collect important documents that would be useful for writing the histories. However by the terms of the Treaty of Versailles, the Großer Generalstab was disbanded and by default its historical section along with its archive sub section. As a reaction to this disbandment, the German army created the Reichsarchiv (*State Archives*), for the dual propose of writing the history of the Great War and to give employment to ex-members of the General Staff, thus keeping a nucleus of staff officers on hand ready to be remobilised in future to recreate the Großer Generalstab.

Apart from the collection and storage of military documents, the Reichsarchiv had the responsibility of writing both the military and diplomatic histories, much to the objections of the Auswärtigen Amte (*Foreign Office*) who view diplomatic histories as being within their domain.

Therefore the German military official histories for the Great War were usually written by ex-staff officers. Generally the individual official history volumes were written by teams of historians, each specialising in various aspects of the particular history such as mobilisation, the western front and the eastern front. However the battle monographs were written by individual specialists with particular knowledge of the battles concerned. With so many ex-members of the Großer Generalstab writing the histories, there was to some degree a corruption of the histories putting the Großer Generalstab as a whole or individual members of the Großer Generalstab (in some cases the author himself) into a far more favourable light.

In 1935, once the Nazi Government had come to power, the Reichsarchiv started to come under political influence. The military section, the Kriegsgeschichtliche Forschungsanstalt des Heeres (*Military War History Research Institute*) however continued the work of producing the official histories relating to the Great War which continued up to and thoughout the Second World War. At the end of the Second World War, in 1945, all the West German state archives, including the civilian ones, were grouped together and became the Bundesarchiv (in the case of the military archives, the Bundesarchiv-Militärarchiv –*Federal Archives-Military Archives*)[27]. With this expansion there was a switch to employing civilian historians within the military section of the archive.

The writing of the Great War histories had been completed by the end of the Second World War, however the last two histories, which had been completed during the war years, were not published for general readership. This was probably due to economic reasons. The Bundesarchiv in 1955 therefore published the outstanding volumes albeit with a limited print run.

In Bavaria, the Bavarian official histories were written by members of the bayerisches hauptstaatsarchiv - Kriegsarchiv (*Bavarian Main State Archive - War Archives*) again using mainly ex-Bavarian staff officers from the Großer Generalstab to do the research and writting. Likewise the Saxon and Württemberg Official Histories were produced by members, mainly ex-staff officers, of the Sächsisches Staatsarchiv - Kriegsarchiv (*Saxon State Archive - War Archives*) and the Württemberg Landsarchiv – Kriegsarchiv (*Wurttemburg National Archive - War Archives*).

---

[27] The Reichsarchiv was housed in premises in the Berlin satellite town of Potsdam. On 14 April 1945 the Royal Air Force bombed the Potsdam area destroying by fire the Reichsarchiv building. It was initially assumed that most if not all of the archives had been destroyed and lost for ever. However it has since been found over the years that a surprisingly large amount of the archive has survived. A number of the documents had been issued before and during the Great War by the German Army to the various state armies within Germany and their Austrian ally with the result that those documents have in the main survived as duplicates in these other state archives – namely the Bavarian, Saxon, Wurtemburg and Austrian state archives. Some of the archives had been removed from Potsdam before the bombing, either on loan to individuals or for safekeeping and these have since been returned. Finally it has been discovered that the Russian Red Army at the end of the Second World War found and took to Russia a very large amount of the German archive. The Russians have recently started to return the archive back to the Germans. It is at the present time unclear what and how much of the German archive were captured by and are still in the possession of the Russians.

The main official coverage of German air operations was written by the Reichsarchiv and was included in their Der Weltkrieg 1914 bis 1918: Die Militarischen Operationen zu Lande. However once the Reichsluftfahrtministerium (State Aviation Ministry) was created they produced a number of Kriegsgeschichtliche Einzelschriften der Luftwaffe (*Individual Historical War Studies of the Air Force.*)

General;

Der Große Krieg 1914 bis 1918. Kurzgefaßte Darstellung auf Grund der amtlichen Quellen des Reichsarchivs. **(Der Große Krieg 1914 bis 1918. Kurzgefaßte Darstellung auf Grund der amtlichen Quellen des Reichsarchivs. - The Great War 1914 to 1918. Abridged History from Official Sources of the State Archives.)**

> *Major außer Dienst* Erich Otto Volkmann | 24cm x 17cm | yellow paper hardback | illustrated cover | 244pp | 5 appendices | 18 maps on 3 loose sheets | Verlag von Neimar Hobbing. | 1922 | German Text. | Fraktur Script.

Chronology;

Gefechtskalender des Deutschen Heeres im Weltkriege 1914-1918. **(Gefechtskalender des Deutschen Heeres im Weltkriege 1914-1918. -** *The Battle Calendar of the German Army in the World War 1914-1918.***)**

> Anonymous (Reichskriegsministerium) | ?cm x 22cm | ? | ? + 24pp | ? tables | E.S. Mittler und Sohn. | 1935 | Greman Text. | Fraktur Script.

Die Schlachten und Gefechte des Großen Krieges 1914-1918. Quellenwerk nack den amtlichen Bezeichnungen zusammengestellt vom Großen Generalstab. **(Die Schlachten und Gefechte des Großen Krieges 1914-1918. Quellenwerk nack den amtlichen Bezeichnungen zusammengestellt vom Großen Generalstab. -** *The Battles and Encounters of the Great War 1914-1918. The Source Work of Official Names compiled by the Great General Staff.***)**[28]

> Anonymous (Großer Generalstab) | 23cm x 15.5cm | dark blue hard back | gilt | xi + 560pp | 4 appendices | 1 tables | Verlag von Hermann Sack. | 1919 | Greman Text. | Fraktur Script.
> This volume gives the name of the engagement along with the names of the German units involved.

Naval Activities;

Der Krieg zur See 1914-1918.[29]

---

[28] It was the German publishing practice during this period to have two title pages normally facing each other, the first title page had the name of set, for example "**Der Krieg zur See 1914-1918**" and the second title page the book title, namely "**Der Krieg in der Nordsee. Erster Band, Von Kriegbeginn bis Anfang September 1914**". The titles given above are a combination of both title pages thereby giving a full title. This is typical of all the German official histories.

[29] The German naval official history set "**Der Krieg zur See 1914-1918**" was broken down into seven sub sets and although each sub set was given a title, they were not given a numerical sequence number. However it has become common practice to abreviate the titles by giving the sets sequence numbers as follows:

Der Krieg in der Nordsee	= 1
Der Krieg in der Ostsee	= 2
Der Kreuzerkrieg in den ausländischen Gewässern	= 3
Der Handelskrieg Mit U-Booten	= 4
Der Krieg in den türkischen Gewässern	= 5
Die Kämpfe der Kaiserlichen Marine in den deutschen Kolonien	= 6
Die Uberwasserstreitkrafte und ihre Tecknik	= 7

Präsidenten des Marine-Archiv (the *presidents of the Naval Archives*) and general editors were as follows: *Vizeadmiral Doktor* Eberhard von Mantey (15 February 1916 to 31 March 1933), *Kontreadmiral* Kurt Aßmann (1 April 1933 to 28 June 1943) and finally *Admiral* Karl Georg Schuster (1 July 1943 to 8 April 1945).

𝔇𝔢𝔯 𝔎𝔯𝔦𝔢𝔤 𝔷𝔲𝔯 𝔖𝔢𝔢 1914–1918, 𝔇𝔢𝔯 𝔎𝔯𝔦𝔢𝔤 𝔦𝔫 𝔡𝔢𝔯 𝔑𝔬𝔯𝔡𝔰𝔢𝔢, 𝔈𝔯𝔰𝔱𝔢𝔯 𝔅𝔞𝔫𝔡, 𝔙𝔬𝔫 𝔎𝔯𝔦𝔢𝔤𝔟𝔢𝔤𝔦𝔫𝔫 𝔟𝔦𝔰 𝔄𝔫𝔣𝔞𝔫𝔤 𝔖𝔢𝔭𝔱𝔢𝔪𝔟𝔢𝔯 1914. **(Der Krieg zur See 1914-1918, Der Krieg in der Nordsee, Erster Band, Von Kriegbeginn bis Anfang September 1914. - *The War at Sea 1914-1918, The War in the North Sea, Volume One, From the beginning of the War till the beginning of September 1914*.)**

> *Korvettenkäpitan* Otto Groos | 24cm x 17cm | see note below | xv + 293pp | 21 appendices in 25 parts | 35 maps | E.S. Mittler und Sohn. | 1920 | German Text. | Fraktur Script.
> This volume covers the First Battle of the Heligoland Bight.
> This set "**Der Krieg zur See 1914-1918**" was produced with four types of bindings: a standard hardback; a more expensive deluxe hardback; a superior de luxe hardback and a cheaper paper softback for later rebinding as per the purchaser's requirements. The standard binding had hard card slate grey paper covers and a plasticized cloth spine with black text and decorations on both covers and spine. The deluxe binding was in royal blue plasticized cloth with gilt text and decorations. The superior de luxe hardback had leather spines and corners and colour patterned paper covered covers along with gilt text and decorations. The softback editions had slate grey paper wraps with black text. Although intended for later rebinding, the cheaper softback editions were often purchased by people who could not afford the more expensive hard bound editions. In order to save space, the volume numbers were shown on the spine as numerals, thereby abbreviating the title.

𝔇𝔢𝔯 𝔎𝔯𝔦𝔢𝔤 𝔷𝔲𝔯 𝔖𝔢𝔢 1914–1918, 𝔇𝔢𝔯 𝔎𝔯𝔦𝔢𝔤 𝔦𝔫 𝔡𝔢𝔯 𝔑𝔬𝔯𝔡𝔰𝔢𝔢, 𝔝𝔴𝔢𝔦𝔱𝔢𝔯 𝔅𝔞𝔫𝔡, 𝔙𝔬𝔫 𝔄𝔫𝔣𝔞𝔫𝔤 𝔖𝔢𝔭𝔱𝔢𝔪𝔟𝔢𝔯 𝔟𝔦𝔰 𝔑𝔬𝔳𝔢𝔪𝔟𝔢𝔯 1914. **(Der Krieg zur See 1914-1918, Der Krieg in der Nordsee, Zweiter Band, Von Anfang September bis November 1914. - *The War at Sea 1914-1918, The War in the North Sea, Volume Two, From the beginning of September till November 1914*.)**

> *Korvettenkäpitan* Otto Groos | 24cm x 17cm | see note for Der Krieg in der Nordsee Band 1 | xiv + 340pp | 18 appendices | 20 maps | E.S. Mittler und Sohn. | 1922 | German Text. | Fraktur Script.
> This volume covers the sinking of H.M.S. Hogue, H.M.S. Cressy and H.M.S. Aboukir.

𝔇𝔢𝔯 𝔎𝔯𝔦𝔢𝔤 𝔷𝔲𝔯 𝔖𝔢𝔢 1914–1918, 𝔇𝔢𝔯 𝔎𝔯𝔦𝔢𝔤 𝔦𝔫 𝔡𝔢𝔯 𝔑𝔬𝔯𝔡𝔰𝔢𝔢, 𝔇𝔯𝔦𝔱𝔱𝔢𝔯 𝔅𝔞𝔫𝔡 𝔙𝔬𝔫 𝔄𝔫𝔣𝔞𝔫𝔤 𝔑𝔬𝔳𝔢𝔪𝔟𝔢𝔯 1914 𝔟𝔦𝔰 𝔄𝔫𝔣𝔞𝔫𝔤 𝔉𝔢𝔟𝔯𝔲𝔞𝔯 1915. **(Der Krieg zur See 1914-1918, Der Krieg in der Nordsee, Dritter Band, Von Anfang November 1914 bis Anfang Februar 1915. - *The War at Sea 1914-1918, The War in the North Sea, Volume Three, From the beginning of November 1914 till February 1915*.)**

> *Korvettenkäpitan* Otto Groos | 24cm x 17cm | see note for Der Krieg in der Nordsee Band 1 | xiii + 300pp | 9 appendices | 21 maps | E.S. Mittler und Sohn. | 1923 | German Text. | Fraktur Script.
> This volume covers the Battle of the Dogger Bank.

𝔇𝔢𝔯 𝔎𝔯𝔦𝔢𝔤 𝔷𝔲𝔯 𝔖𝔢𝔢 1914–1918, 𝔇𝔢𝔯 𝔎𝔯𝔦𝔢𝔤 𝔦𝔫 𝔡𝔢𝔯 𝔑𝔬𝔯𝔡𝔰𝔢𝔢, 𝔙𝔦𝔢𝔯𝔱𝔢𝔯 𝔅𝔞𝔫𝔡, 𝔙𝔬𝔫 𝔄𝔫𝔣𝔞𝔫𝔤 𝔉𝔢𝔟𝔯𝔲𝔞𝔯 𝔟𝔦𝔰 𝔈𝔫𝔡𝔢 𝔇𝔢𝔷𝔢𝔪𝔟𝔢𝔯 1915. **(Der Krieg zur See 1914-1918, Der Krieg in der Nordsee, Vierter Band, Von Anfang Februar bis Ende Dezember 1915. - *The War at Sea 1914-1918, The War in the North Sea, Volume Four, From the beginning of February till December 1915*.)**

> *Korvettenkäpitan* Otto Groos | 24cm x 17cm | see note for Der Krieg in der Nordsee Band 1 | xv + 442pp | 12 appendices | 30 maps | E.S. Mittler und Sohn. | 1924 | German Text. | Fraktur Script.

𝔇𝔢𝔯 𝔎𝔯𝔦𝔢𝔤 𝔷𝔲𝔯 𝔖𝔢𝔢 1914–1918, 𝔇𝔢𝔯 𝔎𝔯𝔦𝔢𝔤 𝔦𝔫 𝔡𝔢𝔯 𝔑𝔬𝔯𝔡𝔰𝔢𝔢, 𝔉ü𝔫𝔣𝔱𝔢𝔯 𝔅𝔞𝔫𝔡 𝔙𝔬𝔫 𝔍𝔞𝔫𝔲𝔞𝔯 𝔟𝔦𝔰 𝔍𝔲𝔫𝔦 1916. **(Der Krieg zur See 1914-1918, Der Krieg in der Nordsee,**

Sometimes the sequence number and the volume number are combined for example, "**Der Krieg zur See 1914-1918, Der Handelskrieg Mit U-Booten, Vierter Band, Februar bis Dezember 1917**" becomes "**Der Krieg zur See 1914-1918, 4.4**".

Fünfter Band, Von Januar bis Juni 1916. - *The War at Sea 1914-1918, The War in the North Sea, Volume Five, From January till June 1916.*)

> *Fregattenkäpitan* Otto Groos | 24cm x 17cm | see note for Der Krieg in der Nordsee Band 1 | xx + 568pp | 17 appendices | 7 maps | Verlag Ernst Siegfried Mittler und Sohn. | 1925 | German Text. | Fraktur Script.
>
> The charts of this volume '**Der Krieg in der Nordsee, Fünfter Band, Von Januar bis Juni 1916**' were issued in a folder attached to the inside of the rear cover of the deluxe edition; however they were issued in a separate map case for the cheaper standard and paperback editions.
>
> This volume covers the Battle of Jutland.

Der Krieg zur See 1914–1918, Der Krieg in der Nordsee, Fünfter Band Von Januar bis Juni 1916. (Der Krieg zur See 1914-1918, Der Krieg in der Nordsee, Fünfter Band, Von Januar bis Juni 1916. - *The War at Sea 1914-1918, The War in the North Sea, Volume Five, From January till June 1916.*) [Map Case]

> *Fregattenkäpitan* Otto Groos | 24cm x 17cm | see note for Der Krieg in der Nordsee Band 1 | 36 maps | Verlag Ernst Siegfried Mittler und Sohn. | 1925 | German Text. | Fraktur / Latin Script.
>
> It has been stated in the 1940 'revised' British official history '**Naval Operations, Volume III**' that the charts for this volume were in fact copies of the British ones with the text translated into German, which caused a number of contradictions between the text within the narration volume and the charts.
>
> A special single volume deluxe edition of '**Der Krieg in der Nordsee, Fünfter Band, Von Januar bis Juni 1916**' was issued where the large format charts were placed in a folder attached to the inside of the rear cover instead of a separate map case.

Der Krieg zur See 1914–1918, Der Krieg in der Nordsee, Sechster Band, Von Juni 1916 bis Frühjahr 1917. (Der Krieg zur See 1914-1918, Der Krieg in der Nordsee, Sechster Band, Von Juni 1916 bis Frühjahr 1917. - *The War at Sea 1914-1918, The War in the North Sea, Volume Six, From June 1916 till Spring 1917.*)

> *Admiral außer Dienst* Walter Gladisch | 24cm x 17cm | see note for Der Krieg in der Nordsee Band 1 | xiii + 352pp | 37 maps | Verlag Ernst Siegfried Mittler und Sohn. | 1937 | German Text. | Fraktur Script.

Der Krieg zur See 1914–1918, Der Krieg in der Nordsee, Siebenter Band, Von Sommer 1917 bis zum Kriegsende 1918. (Der Krieg zur See 1914-1918, Der Krieg in der Nordsee, Siebenter Band, Von Sommer 1917 bis zum Kriegsende 1918. - *The War at Sea 1914-1918, The War in the North Sea, Volume Seven, From Summer 1917 till the end of the War 1918.*)

> *Admiral außer Dienst* Walter Gladisch | 24cm x 17cm | see note below | xiv + 368pp | 5 folding maps in pockets | 9 tables | Verlag Ernst Siegfried Mittler und Sohn. | 1965 | German Text. | Fraktur Script.
>
> This volume covers the Second Battle of the Heligoland Bight, the First Ostend Raid, the Zeebrugge Raid and the Second Ostend Raid.
>
> Towards the end of the Second World War the German Naval Archives were transfered out of the Admirality in Berlin to Schloss Tambach near Coburg for safe keeping from allied bombing. They were captured intact by the British army in April 1945 and were then handed over to the Royal Navy for review. At that time in 1945 there were still three outstanding volumes of '**Der Krieg zur See**' to be completed, although work had been started on all of them. The work on these three volumes ceased until the archives were returned to the German Federal Navy in the early 1960's. The three volumes were then completed and published - the volumes were '**Der Krieg in der Ostsee, Dritter Band**' published in 1964, '**Der Krieg in der Nordsee, Siebenter Band**' published in 1965 and '**Der Handelskrieg Mit U-Booten, Fünfter Band**' published in 1966. The standard binding had hard card slate grey paper covers and a plasticized cloth spine with black text and decorations on both covers and spine.
>
> After the Second World War, the German publishing industry ceased to use the old Fraktur Script and adopted modern fonts in its place. However in the case of the 1960's editions the older Fraktur Script was kept to keep the volumes in line with the rest of the set.
>
> This volume '**Der Krieg in der Nordsee, Siebenter Band**' was revised and enlarged in 2006 by Gerhard P. Groß. There were a number of proposed amendments by the original editors and proof readers of the 1941 Gladisch draft manuscript that were not incorporated into the 1965 edition. This was coupled with the biased representation and apologetic nature found in this final volume, where the events of October and November 1918 were deliberately under narrated. This has caused much criticism amongst academics of this

volume ever since. Therefore, Groß corrected the editorial inconsistencies as well as adding current research concepts, such as added explanatory comments and noting sources. To differentiate from the 1965 edition, this 2006 edition has been given the subtitle '**Kritische Edition**' (*Critical Edition*). A Kartenschuber (*map case*) has been added to this new edition. It is to be noted that the original 1965 text is located in the '**Kritische Edition**' between pages 33 and 420. A new 30 page introductory chapter covering the history of the volumes of the complete series has been added. The editorial differences, comments and sources have been shown in foot notes. The appendices consist of a number of statements and comments about this volume from various ex-naval officials and naval official historians written during the period that the volume was being researched and finalised. There has also been added a list of abbreviations, a section giving biographies on leading naval personalities and a bibliography. Only two of the original 1965 issued maps have been incorporated in the revised 2006 edition; however a number of missing but believed original maps have been added in the Kartenschuber. It has been republished by the same publishers Mittler und Sohns, using modern Latin script and not Fraktur script as per the 1965 original. The '**Kritische Edition**' has had a decrease in the number of introductory pages, but an increase in the number of narration pages, an increase in the number of maps and the addition of appendices to give the following breakdown:

[*Oberstleutnant Doktor*] Gerhard P[aul] Groß (*Admiral außer Dienst* Walter Gladisch) I 24cm x 17cm I plasticised hard red card covers I vii + 486pp I 10 appendices I 14 maps printed on 4 sheets I Verlag Ernst Siegfried Mittler und Sohn. I 2006 I German Text.

It is proposed that the other volumes in '**Der Krieg zur See 1914-1918**' series will be treated in a similar fashion updating the text to remove the earlier inconsistencies starting with '**Der Krieg in der Nordsee, Erster Band**'.

𝔇𝔢𝔯 𝔎𝔯𝔦𝔢𝔤 𝔷𝔲𝔯 𝔖𝔢𝔢 1914–1918, 𝔇𝔢𝔯 𝔎𝔯𝔦𝔢𝔤 𝔦𝔫 𝔡𝔢𝔯 𝔒𝔰𝔱𝔰𝔢𝔢, 𝔈𝔯𝔰𝔱𝔢𝔯 𝔅𝔞𝔫𝔡, 𝔙𝔬𝔫 𝔎𝔯𝔦𝔢𝔤𝔟𝔢𝔤𝔦𝔫𝔫 𝔟𝔦𝔰 𝔐𝔦𝔱𝔱𝔢 𝔐ä𝔯𝔷 1915. (Der Krieg zur See 1914-1918, Der Krieg in der Ostsee, Erster Band ,Von Kriegbeginn bis Mitte März 1915. - *The War at Sea 1914-1918, The War in the East Sea [The Baltic], Volume One, From the beginning of the War till Mid March 1915*.)

Korvettenkäpitan Rudolph Firle I 24cm x 17cm I see note for Der Krieg in der Nordsee Band 1 I x + 290pp I 12 maps I Verlag Ernst Siegfried Mittler und Sohn. I 1922 I German Text. I Fraktur Script.

𝔇𝔢𝔯 𝔎𝔯𝔦𝔢𝔤 𝔷𝔲𝔯 𝔖𝔢𝔢 1914–1918, 𝔇𝔢𝔯 𝔎𝔯𝔦𝔢𝔤 𝔦𝔫 𝔡𝔢𝔯 𝔒𝔰𝔱𝔰𝔢𝔢, 𝔝𝔴𝔢𝔦𝔱𝔢𝔯 𝔅𝔞𝔫𝔡, 𝔇𝔞𝔰 𝔎𝔯𝔦𝔢𝔤𝔰𝔧𝔞𝔥𝔯 1915. (Der Krieg zur See 1914-1918, Der Krieg in der Ostsee, Zweiter Band, Das Kriegsjahr 1915. - *The War at Sea 1914-1918, The War in the East Sea [The Baltic], Volume Two, The War Year 1915*.)

Käpitanleutnant Heinrich Rollmann I 24cm x 17cm I see note for Der Krieg in der Nordsee Band 1 I xvi + 385pp I 2 appendices I 34 maps I 12 photographs I 14 diagramsI Verlag Ernst Siegfried Mittler und Sohn. I 1929 I German Text. I Fraktur Script.

𝔇𝔢𝔯 𝔎𝔯𝔦𝔢𝔤 𝔷𝔲𝔯 𝔖𝔢𝔢 1914–1918, 𝔇𝔢𝔯 𝔎𝔯𝔦𝔢𝔤 𝔦𝔫 𝔡𝔢𝔯 𝔒𝔰𝔱𝔰𝔢𝔢. 𝔇𝔯𝔦𝔱𝔱𝔢𝔯 𝔅𝔞𝔫𝔡, 𝔙𝔬𝔫 𝔄𝔫𝔣𝔞𝔫𝔤 1916 𝔟𝔦𝔰 𝔷𝔲𝔪 𝔎𝔯𝔦𝔢𝔤𝔰𝔢𝔫𝔡𝔢. (Der Krieg zur See 1914-1918, Der Krieg in der Ostsee, Dritter Band, Von Anfang 1916 bis zum Kriegsende. - *The War at Sea 1914-1918, The War in the East Sea [The Baltic], Volume Three, From beginning of 1916 till the end of the War*.)

Admiral außer Dienst Ernst *Friherr* von Gagern I 24cm x 17cm I see note for Der Krieg in der Nordsee Band 1 I xv + 462pp I 14 appendices I 7 maps I 16 diagramsI Verlag Ernst Siegfried Mittler und Sohn. I 1964 I German Text. I Fraktur Script.

𝔇𝔢𝔯 𝔎𝔯𝔦𝔢𝔤 𝔷𝔲𝔯 𝔖𝔢𝔢 1914–1918, 𝔇𝔢𝔯 𝔎𝔯𝔢𝔲𝔷𝔢𝔯𝔨𝔯𝔦𝔢𝔤 𝔦𝔫 𝔡𝔢𝔫 𝔞𝔲𝔰𝔩ä𝔫𝔡𝔦𝔰𝔠𝔥𝔢𝔫 𝔊𝔢𝔴ä𝔰𝔰𝔢𝔯𝔫, 𝔈𝔯𝔰𝔱𝔢𝔯 𝔅𝔞𝔫𝔡, 𝔇𝔞𝔰 𝔎𝔯𝔢𝔲𝔷𝔢𝔯𝔤𝔢𝔰𝔠𝔥𝔴𝔞𝔡𝔢𝔯. (Der Krieg zur See 1914-1918, Der Kreuzerkrieg in den ausländischen Gewässern, Erster Band, Das Kreuzergeschwader. - *The War at Sea 1914-1918, The Cruiser War in Foreign Waters, Volume One, The Cruiser Squadron*.)

Vizeadmiral [*Dokter*] Erich Raeder I 24cm x 17cm I see note for Der Krieg in der Nordsee Band 1 I xvii + 459pp I 4 appendices I 7 maps I 15 diagramsI Verlag Ernst Siegfried Mittler und Sohn. I 1922 I German Text. I Fraktur Script.

𝔇𝔢𝔯 𝔎𝔯𝔦𝔢𝔤 𝔷𝔲𝔯 𝔖𝔢𝔢 1914–1918, 𝔇𝔢𝔯 𝔎𝔯𝔢𝔲𝔷𝔢𝔯𝔨𝔯𝔦𝔢𝔤 𝔦𝔫 𝔡𝔢𝔫 𝔞𝔲𝔰𝔩ä𝔫𝔡𝔦𝔰𝔠𝔥𝔢𝔫 𝔊𝔢𝔴ä𝔰𝔰𝔢𝔯𝔫, 𝔝𝔴𝔢𝔦𝔱𝔢𝔯 𝔅𝔞𝔫𝔡, 𝔇𝔦𝔢 𝔗ä𝔱𝔦𝔤𝔨𝔢𝔦𝔱 𝔡𝔢𝔯 𝔎𝔩𝔢𝔦𝔫𝔢𝔫 𝔎𝔯𝔢𝔲𝔷𝔢𝔯 "𝔈𝔪𝔡𝔢𝔫", "𝔎ö𝔫𝔦𝔤𝔟𝔢𝔯𝔤" 𝔲𝔫𝔡 "𝔎𝔞𝔯𝔩𝔰𝔯𝔲𝔥𝔢" 𝔐𝔦𝔱 𝔢 𝔄𝔫𝔥𝔞𝔫𝔤: "𝔇𝔦𝔢 𝔎𝔯𝔦𝔢𝔤𝔰𝔣𝔞𝔥𝔯𝔱 𝔡𝔢𝔰 𝔎𝔩𝔢𝔦𝔫𝔢𝔫 𝔎𝔯𝔢𝔲𝔷𝔢𝔯𝔰 𝔊𝔢𝔦𝔢𝔯". (Der Krieg zur See 1914-1918, Der Kreuzerkrieg in den ausländischen Gewässern, Zweiter Band, Die Tätigkeit der Kleinen Kreuzer "Emden", "Königberg" und

"Karlsruhe" Mit e Anhang: "Die Kriegsfahrt des Kleinen Kreuzers Geier". - *The War at Sea 1914-1918, The Cruiser War in Foreign Waters,Volume Two, The Actions of the Light Cruisers "Emden","Königberg" and "Karlsruhe" with an Appendix The War Cruise Actions of the Light Cruiser Geier".)*

Kontreadmiral [Dokter] Erich Raeder | 24cm x 17cm | see note for Der Krieg in der Nordsee Band 1 | xvi + 374pp | 1 appendix | 15 maps | Verlag Ernst Siegfried Mittler und Sohn. | 1923 | German Text. | Fraktur Script.

Note that the variation of the spelling of Raeder's rank - Konteradmiral.

Der Krieg zur See 1914-1918, Der Kreuzerkrieg in den ausländischen Gewässern, Dritter Band, Die deutschen Hilfskreuzer. **(Der Krieg zur See 1914-1918, Der Kreuzerkrieg in den ausländischen Gewässern, Dritter Band, Die deutschen Hilfskreuzer. -** *The War at Sea 1914-1918, The Cruiser War in Foreign Waters, Volume Three, The German Auxiliary Cruisers.)*

Vizeadmiral außer Dienst Dokter Eberhard von Mantey | 24cm x 17cm | see note for Der Krieg in der Nordsee Band 1 | vii + 374pp | 50 maps | 10 diagrams| Verlag Ernst Siegfried Mittler und Sohn. | 1937 | German Text. | Fraktur Script.

Der Krieg zur See 1914-1918, Der Handelskrieg Mit U-Booten, Erster Band, Vorgeschichte. **(Der Krieg zur See 1914-1918, Der Handelskrieg Mit U-Booten, Erster Band, Vorgeschichte. -** *The War at Sea 1914-1918, The Commerce Warfare with Submarines, Volume One, Pre-history.)*

Konteradmiral außer Dienst Arno Spindler | 24cm x 17cm | see note for Der Krieg in der Nordsee Band 1 | xiii + 271pp | 34 appendices | 34 maps | 6 diagrams| Verlag Ernst Siegfried Mittler und Sohn. | 1932 | German Text. | Fraktur Script.

Der Krieg zur See 1914-1918, Der Handelskrieg Mit U-Booten, Zweiter Band, Februar bis September 1915. **(Der Krieg zur See 1914-1918, Der Handelskrieg Mit U-Booten, Zweiter Band, Februar bis September 1915. -** *The War at Sea 1914-1918, The Commerce Warfare with Submarines, Volume Two, February till September 1915.)*

Konteradmiral außer Dienst Arno Spindler | 24cm x 17cm | see note for Der Krieg in der Nordsee Band 1 | xi + 300pp | 4 appendices | 18 maps | Verlag Ernst Siegfried Mittler und Sohn. | 1933 | German Text. | Fraktur Script.

Der Krieg zur See 1914-1918, Der Handelskrieg Mit U-Booten, Dritter Band, Oktober 1915 bis Januar 1917. **(Der Krieg zur See 1914-1918, Der Handelskrieg Mit U-Booten, Dritter Band, Oktober 1915 bis Januar 1917. -** *The War at Sea 1914-1918, The Commerce Warfare with Submarines, Volume Three, October 1915 till January 1917.)*

Konteradmiral außer Dienst Arno Spindler | 24cm x 17cm | see note for Der Krieg in der Nordsee Band 1 | xiii + 400pp | 4 appendices | 16 maps | 12 diagrams| Verlag Ernst Siegfried Mittler und Sohn. | 1934 | German Text. | Fraktur Script.

Der Krieg zur See 1914-1918, Der Handelskrieg Mit U-Booten. Vierter Band, Februar bis Dezember 1917. **(Der Krieg zur See 1914-1918, Der Handelskrieg Mit U-Booten, Vierter Band, Februar bis Dezember 1917. -** *The War at Sea 1914-1918, The Commerce Warfare with Submarines, Volume Four, February till December 1917.)*

Konteradmiral außer Dienst Arno Spindler | 24cm x 17cm (page size 21cm x 15cm) | see note for Der Krieg in der Nordsee Band 1 | vii + 560pp | 1 appendix | 15 maps | 8 tables | 51 sketches | Verlag Ernst Siegfried Mittler und Sohn. | 1941 | German Text. | Fraktur Script.

It was republished in 1966.

The page dimensions of this volume "**Der Handelskrieg Mit U-Booten. Band 4**" are of a much reduced size compared with the other volumes in this series. However the cover dimension have been kept the same as the rest so as to keep a uniform external appearance to the set.

Der Krieg zur See 1914-1918, Der Handelskrieg Mit U-Booten, Fünfter Band, Januar bis November 1918. **(Der Krieg zur See 1914-1918, Der Handelskrieg Mit U-Booten, Fünfter Band, Januar bis November 1918. -** *The War at Sea 1914-1918, The Commerce Warfare with Submarines, Volume Five, January till November 1918.)*

Konteradmiral außer Dienst Arno Spindler | 24cm x 17cm | see note for Der Krieg in der Nordsee Band 1 | vii + 447pp | 8 appendices | 3 maps | Verlag Ernst Siegfried Mittler und Sohn. | 1966 | German Text. | Fraktur Script.

𝕯𝖊𝖗 𝕶𝖗𝖎𝖊𝖌 𝖟𝖚𝖗 𝕾𝖊𝖊 1914-1918, 𝕯𝖊𝖗 𝕶𝖗𝖎𝖊𝖌 𝖎𝖓 𝖉𝖊𝖓 𝖙ü𝖗𝖐𝖎𝖘𝖈𝖍𝖊𝖓 𝕲𝖊𝖜ä𝖘𝖘𝖊𝖗𝖓, 𝕰𝖗𝖘𝖙𝖊𝖗 𝕭𝖆𝖓𝖉, 𝕯𝖎𝖊 𝕸𝖎𝖙𝖙𝖊𝖑𝖒𝖊𝖊𝖗-𝕯𝖎𝖛𝖎𝖘𝖎𝖔𝖓. **(Der Krieg zur See 1914-1918, Der Krieg in den türkischen Gewässern, Erster Band, Die Mittelmeer-Division. -** *The War at Sea 1914-1918, The War in the Turkish Waters, Volume One, The Mediterranean Division.***)**

Kontreadmiral außer Dienst Hermann Lorey | 24cm x 17cm | see note for Der Krieg in der Nordsee Band 1 | xii + 314pp | 5 appendices | 41 diagrams| Verlag Ernst Siegfried Mittler und Sohn. | 1928 | German Text. | Fraktur Script.

Note that the variation of the spelling of Lorey's rank - Konteradmiral.

𝕯𝖊𝖗 𝕶𝖗𝖎𝖊𝖌 𝖟𝖚𝖗 𝕾𝖊𝖊 1914-1918, 𝕯𝖊𝖗 𝕶𝖗𝖎𝖊𝖌 𝖎𝖓 𝖉𝖊𝖓 𝖙ü𝖗𝖐𝖎𝖘𝖈𝖍𝖊𝖓 𝕲𝖊𝖜ä𝖘𝖘𝖊𝖗𝖓, 𝖅𝖜𝖊𝖎𝖙𝖊𝖗 𝕭𝖆𝖓𝖉, 𝕯𝖊𝖗 𝕶𝖆𝖒𝖕𝖋 𝖚𝖓 𝖉𝖎𝖊 𝕸𝖊𝖊𝖗𝖊𝖓𝖌𝖊𝖓. **(Der Krieg zur See 1914-1918, Der Krieg in den türkischen Gewässern, Zweiter Band, Der Kampf un die Meerengen. -** *The War at Sea 1914-1918, The War in the Turkish Waters, Volume Two, The Fight for the Straits.***)**

Konteradmiral außer Dienst Hermann Lorey | 24cm x 17cm | see note for Der Krieg in der Nordsee Band 1 | xvi + 430pp | 55 maps | Verlag Ernst Siegfried Mittler und Sohn. | 1938 | German Text. | Fraktur Script.

𝕯𝖊𝖗 𝕶𝖗𝖎𝖊𝖌 𝖟𝖚𝖗 𝕾𝖊𝖊 1914-1918, 𝕯𝖎𝖊 𝕶ä𝖒𝖕𝖋𝖊 𝖉𝖊𝖗 𝕶𝖆𝖎𝖘𝖊𝖗𝖑𝖎𝖈𝖍𝖊𝖓 𝕸𝖆𝖗𝖎𝖓𝖊 𝖎𝖓 𝖉𝖊𝖓 𝖉𝖊𝖚𝖙𝖘𝖈𝖍𝖊𝖓 𝕶𝖔𝖑𝖔𝖓𝖎𝖊𝖓. 𝕰𝖗𝖘𝖙𝖊𝖗 𝕿𝖊𝖎𝖑: 𝕿𝖘𝖎𝖓𝖌𝖙𝖆𝖚. 𝖅𝖜𝖊𝖎𝖙𝖊𝖗 𝕿𝖊𝖎𝖑: 𝕯𝖊𝖚𝖙𝖘𝖈𝖍=𝕺𝖘𝖙𝖆𝖋𝖗𝖎𝖐𝖆. **(Der Krieg zur See 1914-1918, Die Kämpfe der Kaiserlichen Marine in den deutschen Kolonien. Erster Teil: Tsingtau. Zweiter Teil: Deutsch=Ostafrika. -** *The War at Sea 1914-1918, The War of the Imperial Navy in the German Colonies. Part One: Tsingtao. Part Two: German East Africa.***)**

Vizeadmiral außer Dienst Kurt Aßmann | 24cm x 17cm | see note for Der Krieg in der Nordsee Band 1 | xvi + 330pp | 8 appendices (4 appendices in part 1 and 4 appendices in part 2) | 11 maps | Verlag Ernst Siegfried Mittler und Sohn. | 1935 | German Text. | Fraktur Script.

The title on the spine was abbreviated to '**Der Krieg zur See 1914-1918, Die Kämpfe der Kaiserlichen Marine in den deutschen Kolonien.**'

𝕯𝖊𝖗 𝕶𝖗𝖎𝖊𝖌 𝖟𝖚𝖗 𝕾𝖊𝖊 1914-1918, 𝕯𝖎𝖊 𝖀𝖇𝖊𝖗𝖜𝖆𝖘𝖘𝖊𝖗𝖘𝖙𝖗𝖊𝖎𝖙𝖐𝖗𝖆𝖋𝖙𝖊 𝖚𝖓𝖉 𝖎𝖍𝖗𝖊 𝕿𝖊𝖈𝖐𝖓𝖎𝖐. **(Der Krieg zur See 1914-1918, Die Uberwasserstreitkrafte und ihre Tecknik. -** *The War at Sea 1914-1918, The Surface Forces and Their Techniques.***)**

Kapitän zur See (Ingenieur) außer Dienst Paul Köppen | 24cm x 17cm | see note for Der Krieg in der Nordsee Band 1 | xii + 221pp | 7 appendices | 24 maps | Verlag Ernst Siegfried Mittler und Sohn. | 1930 | German Text. | Fraktur Script.

Naval Monographs;

𝕰𝖎𝖓𝖟𝖊𝖑𝖉𝖆𝖗𝖘𝖙𝖊𝖑𝖑𝖚𝖓𝖌𝖊𝖓 𝖉𝖊𝖘 𝕾𝖊𝖊𝖐𝖗𝖎𝖊𝖌𝖊𝖘 1914-1918 𝕭𝖆𝖓𝖉 1 𝕹𝖔𝖗𝖉𝖘𝖊𝖊𝖐𝖗𝖎𝖊𝖌. **(Einzeldarstellungen des Seekrieges 1914-1918 Band 1 Nordseekrieg. -** *Naval Warfare Monographs 1914-1918Volume 1 The War in the North Sea.***)**

Vizeadmiral außer Dienst [Friedrich] Lützow | 24cm x 17cm | Sea Grey Card Hardback | 202pp | 5 appendices | 8 maps | 9 photographs | Verlag Ernst Siegfried Mittler und Sohn. | 1931 | German Text. | Fraktur Script.

𝕰𝖎𝖓𝖟𝖊𝖑𝖉𝖆𝖗𝖘𝖙𝖊𝖑𝖑𝖚𝖓𝖌𝖊𝖓 𝖉𝖊𝖘 𝕾𝖊𝖊𝖐𝖗𝖎𝖊𝖌𝖊𝖘 1914-1918 𝕭𝖆𝖓𝖉 2 𝕯𝖊𝖗 𝕶𝖗𝖊𝖚𝖟𝖊𝖗𝖐𝖗𝖎𝖊𝖌 1914-1918. **(Einzeldarstellungen des Seekrieges 1914-1918 Band 2 Der Kreuzerkrieg 1914-1918. -** *Naval Warfare Monographs 1914-1918Volume 2 The Cruiser War 1914-1918.***)**

Kapitän zur See außer Dienst Hugo von Waldeyer-Hartz | 24cm x 17cm | Sea Grey Card Hardback | 211pp | 7 maps | 9 photographs | 1 diagram| Verlag Ernst Siegfried Mittler und Sohn. | 1931 | German Text. | Fraktur Script.

Military Operations;

Der Weltkrieg 1914 bis 1918: Die Militarischen Operationen zu Lande[30]:

Präsidenten des Reichsarchivs (the *presidents of the State Archives*) were as follows: *Generalmajor außer Dienst* Hermann *Ritter* Mertz von Quirnheim (1920 to 1931), *Generalmajor außer Dienst* Hans von Häften (1931 to 1937) and finally Ernst Zipfel (1937 to 1945). Quirnheim and Häften also became the general editors of **Der Weltkrieg 1914 bis 1918: Die Militarischen Operationen zu Lande**. However Zipfel who was a relative senior member of the NSDAP (*The Nazi Party*) was more concerned with the history of "New Germany" based on the Nazi Party requirements than of military history. Therefore, the editorship of the later volumes of **Der Weltkrieg 1914 bis 1918: Die Militarischen Operationen zu Lande** was left to *Oberstleutnant außer Dienst* Wolfgang Foerster who was the Direktor der Kriegsgeschichtliche Forschungsanstalt des Heeres (*Director of the Military War History Research Institute* - the military archives of the Reichsarchivs) between 1937 to 1945.

Der Weltkrieg 1914 bis 1918: Die Militarischen Operationen zu Lande Erster Band, Die Grenzschlachten im Westen.[31] (Der Weltkrieg 1914 bis 1918: Die Militarischen Operationen zu Lande Erster Band, Die Grenzschlachten im Westen. - *The World War 1914 to 1918: Military Land Operations Volume One, The Border Battles in the West.*)

> *Generalmajor außer Dienst* Hermann *Ritter* Mertz von Quirnheim (Editor) - Reichsarchiv I 24cm x 17cm I see note I xvi + 719pp I 3 appendices I 9 maps I 7 large format maps I 8 diagrams I Verlag Ernst Siegfried Mittler und Sohn. I 1925 I German Text. I Fraktur Script. The large format maps are carried in a folder attached to the inside rear cover, whilst the smaller maps are located within the text of the volume.
>
> The first twelve volumes of this set **"Der Weltkrieg 1914 bis 1918: Die Militarischen Operationen zu Lande Band 1"** to **"Band 12"** were produced with three types of bindings: a standard hardback, a more expensive de luxe hardback and a superior de luxe hardback. The standard binding had maroon cloth hardcovers with gilt text. The de luxe binding was in royal blue cloth with gilt text and decorations. The superior de luxe hardback had leather spines and corners and colour patterned paper covered covers along with gilt text.

Der Weltkrieg 1914 bis 1918: Die Militarischen Operationen zu Lande Zweiter Band, Die Befreiung Ostpreussens. (Der Weltkrieg 1914 bis 1918: Die Militarischen Operationen zu Lande Zweiter Band, Die Befreiung Ostpreussens. - *The World War 1914 to 1918: Military Land Operations Volume Two, The Liberation of East Prussia.*)

> *Generalmajor außer Dienst* Hermann *Ritter* Mertz von Quirnheim (Editor) - Reichsarchiv I 24cm x 17cm I see note for Band 1 I xv + 390pp I 3 appendices I 25 maps I 13 large format maps I 7 diagrams I Verlag Ernst Siegfried Mittler und Sohn. I 1925 I German Text. I Fraktur Script.
>
> The large format maps and two sheets of diagrams/sketches are carried in a folder attached to the inside rear cover, whilst the smaller maps are located within the text of the volume.

Der Weltkrieg 1914 bis 1918: Die Militarischen Operationen zu Lande Dritter Band, Der Marne – Feldzug. Von der Sambre zur Marne. (Der Weltkrieg 1914 bis 1918: Die Militarischen Operationen zu Lande Dritter Band, Der Marne – Feldzug. Von der Sambre zur Marne. - *The World War 1914 to 1918: Military Land Operations Volume Three, The Marne Campaign. From the Sambre to the Marne.*)

> *Generalmajor außer Dienst* Hermann *Ritter* Mertz von Quirnheim (Editor) - Reichsarchiv I 24cm x 17cm I see note for Band 1 I xi + 427pp I 18 maps I 7 large format maps I Verlag Ernst Siegfried Mittler und Sohn. I 1926 I German Text. I Fraktur Script.

---

[30] In "**The Dogma of the Battle of Annihilation**" (Greenwood Press, 1986), Jehuda L. Wallach states that "**Der Weltkrieg: Die Militarischen Operationen zu Lande**" was written as a semi official history, however since no official history was ever produced in Germany, this series has become regarded as the German official history worldwide, even within Germany.

[31] The volume numbers of "**Der Weltkrieg 1914 bis 1918: Die Militarischen Operationen zu Lande**" were written out in full on the title page i.e. "Fünfter Band", however they were shown just as numerals on the spine i.e. "5". I have given the title as shown on the title page.

The large format maps and four sheets of diagrams/sketches are carried in a folder attached to the inside rear cover, whilst the smaller maps are located within the text of the volume.

Der Weltkrieg 1914 bis 1918: Die Militarischen Operationen zu Lande Vierter Band, Der Marne – Feldzug. Die Schlacht Marne. (Der Weltkrieg 1914 bis 1918: Die Militarischen Operationen zu Lande Vierter Band, Der Marne – Feldzug. Die Schlacht Marne. - *The World War 1914 to 1918: Military Land Operations Volume Four, The Marne Campaign. The Battle of the Marne.*)

> *Generalmajor außer Dienst* Hermann *Ritter* Mertz von Quirnheim (Editor) - Reichsarchiv I 24cm x 17cm I see note for Band 1 I xii + 576pp I 3 appendices I 16 maps I 9 large format maps I Verlag Ernst Siegfried Mittler und Sohn. I 1926 I German Text. I Fraktur Script.
>
> The large format maps and two sheets of diagrams/sketches are carried in a folder attached to the inside rear cover, whilst the smaller maps are located within the text of the volume.

Der Weltkrieg 1914 bis 1918: Die Militarischen Operationen zu Lande Fünfter Band Der Herbst – Feldzug im Osten bis zum Rückzug im Westem bis zum Stellumgskrieg. (Der Weltkrieg 1914 bis 1918: Die Militarischen Operationen zu Lande Fünfter Band Der Herbst - Feldzug im Osten bis zum Rückzug im Westem bis zum Stellumgskrieg. - *The World War 1914 to 1918: Military Land Operations Volume Five The Autumn Campaign in the East and in the West until the Withdrawal to the Positional War.*)

> *Generalmajor außer Dienst* Hermann *Ritter* Mertz von Quirnheim (Editor) - Reichsarchiv I 24cm x 17cm I see note for Band 1 I xiv + 643pp I 3 appendices I 18 maps I 13 large format maps I Verlag Ernst Siegfried Mittler und Sohn. I 1929 I German Text. I Fraktur Script.
>
> The large format maps and five sheets of diagrams/sketches are carried in a folder attached to the inside rear cover, whilst the smaller maps are located within the text of the volume.

Der Weltkrieg 1914 bis 1918: Die Militarischen Operationen zu Lande Sechster Band, Der Herbst – Feldzug der Abschluß der Operationen im Westem und Osten. (Der Weltkrieg 1914 bis 1918: Die Militarischen Operationen zu Lande Sechster Band, Der Herbst - Feldzug der Abschluß der Operationen im Westem und Osten. - *The World War 1914 to 1918: Military Land Operations Volume Six, The Autumn Campaign until the Closing of the Operations in the West and the East.*)

> *Generalmajor außer Dienst* Hermann Ritter Mertz von Quirnheim (Editor) - Reichsarchiv I 24cm x 17cm I see note for Band 1 I xiv + 500pp I 4 appendices I 21 maps I Verlag Ernst Siegfried Mittler und Sohn. I 1929 I German Text. I Fraktur Script.
>
> There are 15 of the diagrams/sketches sheets carried in a folder attached to the inside rear cover.

Der Weltkrieg 1914 bis 1918: Die Militarischen Operationen zu Lande Siebenter Band, Die Operationen des Jahres 1915. Die Ereignisse Winter und Frühjahr. (Der Weltkrieg 1914 bis 1918: Die Militarischen Operationen zu Lande Siebenter Band, Die Operationen des Jahres 1915. Die Ereignisse Winter und Frühjahr. - *The World War 1914 to 1918: Military Land Operations Volume Seven, The Operation in the Year 1915. The Events of the Winter and Spring.*)

> *Generalmajor außer Dienst* Hermann *Ritter* Mertz von Quirnheim (Editor) - Reichsarchiv I 24cm x 17cm I see note for Band 1 I xiii + 493pp I 2 appendices I 21 maps I 18 large format maps I Verlag Ernst Siegfried Mittler und Sohn. I 1931 I German Text. I Fraktur Script.
>
> The large format maps and 11 sheets of diagrams/sketches are carried in a folder attached to the inside rear cover, whilst the smaller maps are located within the text of the volume.

Der Weltkrieg 1914 bis 1918: Die Militarischen Operationen zu Lande Achter Band, Die Operationen des Jahres 1915 – Die Ereignisse im Westen im Frühjahr im Sommer und Osten vom Frühjahr bis zum Jahresschluß. (Der Weltkrieg 1914 bis 1918: Die Militarischen Operationen zu Lande Achter Band, Die Operationen des Jahres 1915 - Die Ereignisse im Westen im Frühjahr im Sommer und Osten vom Frühjahr bis zum Jahresschluß. - *The World War 1914 to 1918: Military Land Operations Volume Eight, The Operation in the Year 1915 - The Events in the West from the Spring into the Summer and in the East from the Summer to the Year's End*.)

Generalmajor außer Dienst Hans von Häften (Editor) - Reichsarchiv | 24cm x 17cm | see note for Band 1 | xiv + 666pp | 4 appendices | 32 maps | 7 large format maps | Verlag Ernst Siegfried Mittler und Sohn. | 1932 | German Text. | Fraktur Script.

The large format maps/diagrams and 12 sheets of diagrams/sketches are carried in a folder attached to the inside rear cover, whilst the smaller maps are located within the text of the volume.

Der Weltkrieg 1914 bis 1918: Die Militarischen Operationen zu Lande Neunter Band, Die Operationen des Jahres 1915 – Die Der Weltkrieg 1914 bis 1918: Die Militarischen Operationen zu Lande Ereignisse im Westen und auf dem Balkan vom Sommer bis Jahresschluß. (Der Weltkrieg 1914 bis 1918: Die Militarischen Operationen zu Lande Neunter Band, Die Operationen des Jahres 1915 – Die Ereignisse im Westen und auf dem Balkan vom Sommer bis Jahresschluß. - *The World War 1914 to 1918: Military Land Operations Volume Nine, The Operation in the Year 1915 – The Events in the West and in the Balkan Peninsula from the Summer to the Year's End*.)

Generalmajor außer Dienst Hans von Häften (Editor) - Reichsarchiv | 24cm x 17cm | see note for Band 1 | xiv + 519pp | 7 appendices | 29 maps | 5 large format maps | 1 photograph | Verlag Ernst Siegfried Mittler und Sohn. | 1933 | German Text. | Fraktur Script.

The large format maps, 18 sheets of diagrams/sketches and the photograph are carried in a folder attached to the inside rear cover, whilst the smaller maps are located within the text of the volume.

Der Weltkrieg 1914 bis 1918: Die Militarischen Operationen zu Lande Zehnter Band, Die Operationen des Jahres 1916 bis zum Wechsel in der Obersten Heeresleitung. (Der Weltkrieg 1914 bis 1918: Die Militarischen Operationen zu Lande Zehnter Band, Die Operationen des Jahres 1916 bis zum Wechsel in der Obersten Heeresleitung. - *The World War 1914 to 1918: Military Land Operations Volume Ten, The Operation in the Year 1916 until the Change in the High Command*.)

Generalmajor außer Dienst Hans von Häften (Editor) - Oberkommando Des Herres | 24cm x 17cm | see note for Band 1 | xvi + 706pp | 4 appendices | 37 maps | 7 large format maps | Verlag Ernst Siegfried Mittler und Sohn. | 1936 | German Text. | Fraktur Script.

The large format maps and 35 sheets of diagrams/sketches are carried in a folder attached to the inside rear cover, whilst the smaller maps are located within the text of the volume.

Der Weltkrieg 1914 bis 1918: Die Militarischen Operationen zu Lande Elfter Band, Die Kriegführung im Herbst 1916 und im Winter 1916/17. (Der Weltkrieg 1914 bis 1918: Die Militarischen Operationen zu Lande Elfter Band, Die Kriegführung im Herbst 1916 und im Winter 1916/17. - *The World War 1914 to 1918: Military Land Operations Volume Eleven, The Warfare in the Autumn of 1916 and in the Winter of 1916/17*.)

Oberstleutnant außer Dienst Wolfgang Foerster (Editor) - Oberkommando Des Herres | 24cm x 17cm | see note for Band 1 | xvi + 545pp | 8 appendices | 37 maps | Verlag Ernst Siegfried Mittler und Sohn. | 1938 | German Text. | Fraktur Script.

There are 31 of the diagrams/sketches sheets carried in a folder attached to the inside rear cover.

Der Weltkrieg 1914 bis 1918: Die Militarischen Operationen zu Lande Zwölfter Band, Die Kriegführung im Frühjahr 1917. (Der Weltkrieg 1914 bis 1918: Die Militarischen Operationen zu Lande Zwölfter Band, Die Kriegführung im Frühjahr 1917. - *The World War 1914 to 1918: Military Land Operations Volume Twelve, The Warfare in the Spring of 1917*.)

Oberstleutnant außer Dienst Wolfgang Foerster (Editor) - Oberkommando Des Herres | 24cm x 17cm | see note for Band 1 | xvi + 606pp | 31 maps | 7 large format maps | Verlag Ernst Siegfried Mittler und Sohn. | 1939 | German Text. | Fraktur Script.

The large format maps and 25 sheets of diagrams/sketches are are carried in a folder attached to the inside rear cover, whilst the smaller maps are located within the text of the volume.

Der Weltkrieg 1914 bis 1918: Die Militärischen Operationen zu Lande Dreizehnter Band, Die Kriegführung im Sommer und Herbst 1917. (Der Weltkrieg 1914 bis 1918: Die Militärischen Operationen zu Lande Dreizehnter Band, Die Kriegführung im Sommer und Herbst 1917. - *The World War 1914 to 1918: Military Land Operations Volume Thriteen, The Warfare in the Summer and Autumn of 1917.*)

> *Oberstleutnant außer Dienst* Wolfgang Foerster (Editor) - Oberkommando Des Herres / Bundesarchiv see note | 24cm x 17cm | maroon cloth hardcovers see note | gilt see note | xvi + 483pp | 26 maps | Verlag Ernst Siegfried Mittler und Sohn. | 1942 (1956) | German Text. | Fraktur Script.

> There are 33 sheets of the diagrams/sketches carried in a folder attached to the inside rear cover.

> During the Second World War, '**Der Weltkrieg: Die Militärischen Operationen zu Lande' 'Band 13'** and '**Band 14'** were pre-published with a limited print run of 1,500 copies of each. A very restricted number of them were issued for proof reading and were marked "Nur zum Dienstgebrauch" (*For Official Use Only*). The publishing of these two volumes were put on hold presumably because of more important publishing work required for the German war effort during that period. The remaining non-issued copies of the two volumes were put into storage in the Kriegsgeschichtliche Forschungsanstalt des Heeres (*Military War History Research Institute*), Potsdam where they were destroyed during the air raid by the Royal Air Force on 14 April 1945. Luckily, some of the proof read copies of both volumes survived since they had not been returned to the archives at the time of the bombing raid. This allowed the Bundesarchiv (*Federal Archives*), Koblenz to publish them in 1956 using the original publishing house of Verlag Ernst Siegfried Mittler und Sohn, but again with a limited print run.

> After the Second World War the Germans press ceased to use Fraktur script in their publications having adopted modern Latin fonts in its place. However in the case of '**Band 13'** and '**Band 14'**, the Fraktur script was used to keep the final volumes in line with the others of the set. Nevertheless these two volumes had a new 1956 introduction printed using Latin font. The 1956 volumes were produced with maroon cloth hardcovers with gilt text only.

Der Weltkrieg 1914 bis 1918: Die Militärischen Operationen zu Lande Vierzehnter Band, Die Kriegführung an der Westfront im Jahre 1918. (Der Weltkrieg 1914 bis 1918: Die Militärischen Operationen zu Lande Vierzehnter Band, Die Kriegführung an der Westfront im Jahre 1918. - *The World War 1914 to 1918: Military Land Operations Volume Fourteen, The Warfare on the Western Front in the Year of 1918.*)

> *Oberstleutnant außer Dienst* Wolfgang Foerster (Editor) - Oberkommando Des Herres / Bundesarchiv see note above | 24cm x 17cm | maroon cloth hardcovers see note above | gilt see note above | xvi + 793pp | Verlag Ernst Siegfried Mittler und Sohn. | 1944 (1956) | German Text. | Fraktur Script.

> Unlike the preceding volumes of Der Weltkrieg series, '**Der Weltkrieg: Die Militärischen Operationen zu Lande Band 14'** did not have a map folder for the large maps attached to the inside rear cover, instead a separated map case was provided - see below.

Der Weltkrieg 1914 bis 1918: Die Militärischen Operationen zu Lande Vierzehnter Band, Die Kriegführung an der Westfront im Jahre 1918. (Der Weltkrieg 1914 bis 1918: Die Militärischen Operationen zu Lande Vierzehnter Band 14 Die Kriegführung an der Westfront im Jahre 1918. - *The World War 1914 to 1918: Military Land Operations Volume Fourteen, The Warfare on the Western Front in the Year of 1918*) [Map Case]

> *Oberstleutnant außer Dienst* Wolfgang Foerster (Editor) - Oberkommando Des Herres / Bundesarchiv see note above | 24cm x 17cm | maroon cloth hardcovers see note above | gilt see note above | 41 maps | Verlag Ernst Siegfried Mittler und Sohn. | 1944 (1956) | German Text. | Fraktur Script.

Der Weltkrieg 1914 bis 1918: Die Militärischen Operationen zu Lande Bildermappe. (Der Weltkrieg 1914 bis 1918: Die Militärischen Operationen zu Lande Bildermappe. - *The World War 1914 to 1918: Military Land Operations Pictures Folder.*)

Generalmajor außer Dienst Hermann Ritter Mertz von Quirnheim (Editor) - Reichsarchiv | 24cm x 17cm | see note | 36 photographs | Verlag Ernst Siegfried Mittler und Sohn. | c1920 | German Text. | Fraktur Script.

The '**Bildermappe**' of '**Der Weltkrieg: Die Militarischen Operationen zu Lande**' set is a special picture folder containing 36 photographs printed on 34 plates loosely inserted. It was not given a 'Band' number, and the date of publication or copyright was not shown upon the folder or any of the plates.

Transportation Activities;

Der Weltkrieg 1914 bis 1918: Das Deutsche Feldeisenbahnwesen. Erster Band. Die Eisenbahnen zu Kriegsbeginn. (**Der Weltkrieg 1914 bis 1918: Das Deutsche Feldeisenbahnwesen. Erster Band. Die Eisenbahnen zu Kriegsbeginn.** - *The World War 1914 to 1918: The German Field Railway. First Volume. The Railways at the Beginning of the War.*)

Oberstleutnant außer Dienst Wolfgang Foerster (Editor) - Reichsarchiv | 24cm x 17cm | see note | xiv + 248pp | 17 appendices | 21 photographs | 6 large format maps | 8 large format sheets consisting of 35 sketch maps, 2 railway time table plans, 2 tables and 1 graph | 35 sketch maps | 2 railway time table plans | 16 tables | 33 sketches | Verlag Ernst Siegfried Mittler und Sohn. | 1928 | German Text. | Fraktur Script.

The first volume of '**Der Weltkrieg 1914 bis 1918: Das Deutsche Feldeisenbahnwesen**' covers the first three months of the war - August to September 1914.

Like the rest of "Der Weltkrieg 1914 bis 1918: Die Militarischen Operationen zu Lande" set this volume was produced with the three types of bindings.

Der Weltkrieg 1914 bis 1918: Das Deutsche Feldeisenbahnwesen. Zweiter Band. Die Eisenbahnen von Oktober 1914 bis zum Kriegsende. (*The World War 1914 to 1918: The German Field Railway. Second Volume. The Railways from October 1914 to the War's End.*)

Horst Rohde (Editor) - Bundesarchiv | 27.5cm x 19.5cm | Maroon Cloth Hardback | Gilt | viii + 446pp | 73 photographs | 28 tables | Verlag Ernst Siegfried Mittler und Sohn. | 2010 | German Text.

Der Weltkrieg 1914 bis 1918: Das Deutsche Feldeisenbahnwesen. Karten. (*The World War 1914 to 1918: The German Field Railway. Maps.*)

Horst Rohde (Editor) - Bundesarchiv | 26.3cm x 19.5cm | Maroon Paper Wrap | Gilt | 12 large format maps | 8 sheets of sketch maps, railway time table plans, tables and graphs | Verlag Ernst Siegfried Mittler und Sohn. | 2010 | German Text.

This sub set '**Der Weltkrieg 1914 bis 1918: Das Deutsche Feldeisenbahnwesen**' was completed in 2010 with the publication of the second volume and a map case. The sub set was produced complete with a reprint of the first volume in a slip case (26.3cm x 19.3cm x 10.3cm). The two text volumes of the 2010 produced sub set are hardbacks covered in maroon cloth, whilst the maps have a maroon coloured paper wrap; all having gilt Latin font on their spines to give the same outward appearance. However the narration of the first volume retains the Fraktur font of the original, whilst the second volume has been printed using Latin font. The maps that were found at the back of the original first volume have been placed into the map folder along with the new maps that have been produced that relate to the second volume. The two sets of maps are separated into two bundles within the case.

The sub sets has the ISBN-10: 3813208842/ ISBN-13: 9783813208849.

Regional Histories - Bavarian Military;

Die Bayern im Großen Kriege 1914-1918. (**Die Bayern im Großen Kriege 1914-1918.** - *Bavaria in the Great War 1914-1918.*)

Anonymous - Bayerischen Kriegsarchiv | 23cm x 16cm | see note | viii + 600pp | Verlag Bayerischen Kriegsarchivs. | 1923 | German Text. | Fraktur Script.

This volume was published either as a white paper hardback or as a white paper softback.

Die Bayern im Großen Kriege 1914-1918 - Kartes. (**Die Bayern im Großen Kriege 1914-1918- Kartes.** - *Bavaria in the Great War 1914-1918 - Maps.*)

Anonymous - Bayerischen Kriegsarchiv | 23cm x 16cm | White Paper Hardback | 38 maps | Verlag Bayerischen Kriegsarchivs. | 1923 | German Text. | Fraktur Script.

Regional Histories - Würtenburg Military;

𝕾𝖈𝖍𝖜𝖆𝖇𝖎𝖘𝖈𝖍𝖊 𝕶𝖚𝖓𝖉𝖊 𝖆𝖚𝖋 𝖉𝖊𝖒 𝖌𝖗𝖔𝖘𝖊𝖓 𝕶𝖗𝖎𝖊𝖌 1. 𝕭𝖚𝖈𝖍 (Schwabische Kunde aus dem großen Krieg 1. Buch - *Schwaben Accounts from the Great War Book 1.*)
> *Leutnant der Reserve* Silbereisen - Würtenburger Kriegsministeriums | 22cm x 16cm | Beige Paper Hardback | 127pp | 4 maps | 22 photographs | Im Kommissions Verlags. | 1918 | German Text. | Fraktur Script.

𝕾𝖈𝖍𝖜𝖆𝖇𝖎𝖘𝖈𝖍𝖊 𝕶𝖚𝖓𝖉𝖊 𝖆𝖚𝖋 𝖉𝖊𝖒 𝖌𝖗𝖔𝖘𝖊𝖓 𝕶𝖗𝖎𝖊𝖌 2. 𝕭𝖚𝖈𝖍 (Schwabische Kunde aus dem großen Krieg 2. Buch - *Schwaben Accounts from the Great War Book 2.*)
> *Hauptmann der Reserve* Schmückle - Würtenburger Kriegsministeriums | 22cm x 16cm | Beige Paper Hardback | 243pp | 8 maps | 28 photographs | Im Kommissions Verlags. | 1918 | German Text. | Fraktur Script.

𝕾𝖈𝖍𝖜𝖆𝖇𝖎𝖘𝖈𝖍𝖊 𝕶𝖚𝖓𝖉𝖊 𝖆𝖚𝖋 𝖉𝖊𝖒 𝖌𝖗𝖔𝖘𝖊𝖓 𝕶𝖗𝖎𝖊𝖌 3. 𝕭𝖚𝖈𝖍 (Schwabische Kunde aus dem großen Krieg 3. Buch - *Schwaben Accounts from the Great War Book 3.*)
> *Hauptmann der Reserve* Schmückle - Würtenburger Kriegsministeriums | 22cm x 16cm | Beige Paper Hardback | ?pp | ? maps | ? photographs | Im Kommissions Verlags. | 1918 | German Text. | Fraktur Script.

Military Monographs;

𝕾𝖈𝖍𝖑𝖆𝖈𝖍𝖙𝖊𝖓 𝖉𝖊𝖘 𝖂𝖊𝖑𝖙𝖐𝖗𝖎𝖊𝖌𝖊𝖘 𝕭𝖆𝖓𝖉 1 𝕯𝖔𝖚𝖆𝖚𝖒𝖔𝖓𝖙. (Schlachten des Weltkrieges Band 1 Douaumont. - *Battles of the World War Volume 1 Douaumont.*)
> Werner Beumelburg | 22cm x 15cm | see note | 2 + 189pp | 3 maps | 13 photographs | Verlagsbuchhandlung Gerhard Stalling. | 1928 | German Text. | Fraktur Script.
> This set **"Schlachten des Weltkrieges"** was produced with two types of bindings: a standard hardback, and a more expensive de luxe hardback. The standard binding had green hard card covers and green cloth spines with gilt text. The de luxe hardback had leather spines and corners and paper covered covers along with gilt text.

𝕾𝖈𝖍𝖑𝖆𝖈𝖍𝖙𝖊𝖓 𝖉𝖊𝖘 𝖂𝖊𝖑𝖙𝖐𝖗𝖎𝖊𝖌𝖊𝖘 𝕭𝖆𝖓𝖉 2 𝕶𝖆𝖗𝖕𝖆𝖙𝖍𝖊𝖓 𝖚𝖓𝖉 𝕯𝖓𝖎𝖊𝖘𝖙𝖊𝖗 𝕾𝖈𝖍𝖑𝖆𝖈𝖍𝖙 1915. (Schlachten des Weltkrieges Band 2 Karpathen und Dniester Schlacht 1915. - *Battles of the World War Volume 2 The Battles in the Carpathians and on the River Dniester, 1915.*)
> *Generalleutnant außer Dienst Freherr* von Friedeburg | 22cm x 15cm | see note for band 1 | 160pp | 9 maps | 20 photographs | Verlagsbuchhandlung Gerhard Stalling. | 1927 | German Text. | Fraktur Script.

𝕾𝖈𝖍𝖑𝖆𝖈𝖍𝖙𝖊𝖓 𝖉𝖊𝖘 𝖂𝖊𝖑𝖙𝖐𝖗𝖎𝖊𝖌𝖊𝖘 𝕭𝖆𝖓𝖉 3 𝕬𝖓𝖙𝖜𝖊𝖗𝖕𝖊𝖓 1914. (Schlachten des Weltkrieges Band 3 Antwerpen 1914. - *Battles of the World War Volume 3 Antwerp, 1914.*)
> *Generalleutnant* Erich von Tschischwitz | 22cm x 15cm | see note for band 1 | 108pp | 10 maps | 16 photographs | 3 diagrams| Verlagsbuchhandlung Gerhard Stalling. | 1927 | German Text. | Fraktur Script.

𝕾𝖈𝖍𝖑𝖆𝖈𝖍𝖙𝖊𝖓 𝖉𝖊𝖘 𝖂𝖊𝖑𝖙𝖐𝖗𝖎𝖊𝖌𝖊𝖘 𝕭𝖆𝖓𝖉 4 "𝕵𝖎𝖑𝖉𝖎𝖗𝖎𝖒" 𝕯𝖊𝖚𝖙𝖘𝖈𝖍𝖊 𝕾𝖙𝖗𝖊𝖎𝖙𝖊𝖗 𝖆𝖚𝖋 𝕳𝖊𝖎𝖑𝖎𝖌𝖊𝖒 𝕭𝖔𝖉𝖊𝖓. (Schlachten des Weltkrieges Band 4 "Jildirim" Deutsche Streiter auf Heiligem Boden. - *Battles of the World War Volume 4 "Jildirim" German Soldiers in the Holy lands.*)
> *Obergeneralarzt außer Dienst Doktor* Werner Steuber | 22cm x 15cm | see note for band 1 | 174pp | 4 maps | 32 photographs | 1 diagram| Verlagsbuchhandlung Gerhard Stalling. | 1928 | German Text. | Fraktur Script.
> Note: A Jildirim was the khaki tropical tunic worn by the German Asian Corps during the Great War.

𝕾𝖈𝖍𝖑𝖆𝖈𝖍𝖙𝖊𝖓 𝖉𝖊𝖘 𝖂𝖊𝖑𝖙𝖐𝖗𝖎𝖊𝖌𝖊𝖘 𝕭𝖆𝖓𝖉 5 𝕳𝖊𝖗𝖇𝖘𝖙𝖘𝖈𝖍𝖑𝖆𝖈𝖍𝖙 𝖎𝖓 𝕸𝖆𝖈𝖊𝖉𝖔𝖓𝖎𝖊𝖓 𝕮𝖊𝖗𝖓𝖆𝖇𝖔𝖌𝖊𝖓 1916. (Schlachten des Weltkrieges Band 5 Herbstschlacht in Macedonien Cernabogen 1916. - *Battles of the World War Volume 5 The Autumn Battle in Cernabogen, Macedonia 1916.*)
> *Hauptmann außer Dienst Doktor* Georg Strutz | 22cm x 15cm | see note for band 1 | 2 + 117pp | 8 maps | 11 photographs | 2 diagrams| Verlagsbuchhandlung Gerhard Stalling. | 1925 | German Text. | Fraktur Script.

𝕾𝖈𝖍𝖑𝖆𝖈𝖍𝖙𝖊𝖓 𝖉𝖊𝖋 𝖂𝖊𝖑𝖙𝖐𝖗𝖎𝖊𝖌𝖊𝖋 𝕭𝖆𝖓𝖉 𝟨 𝕹𝖆𝖓𝖈𝖞 𝖇𝖎𝖋 𝖟𝖚𝖒 𝕮𝖆𝖒𝖕 𝖉𝖊𝖋 𝕽𝖔𝖒𝖆𝖎𝖓𝖋 𝟣𝟫𝟣𝟦. (Schlachten des Weltkrieges Band 6 Nancy bis zum Camp des Romains 1914. - *Battles of the World War Volume 6 Nancy to the Camp des Romans in 1914.*)

> *General* Ludwig *Freiherr* von Gebsattel | 22cm x 15cm | see note for band 1 | 159pp | 10 maps | 18 photographs | 1 diagram| Verlagsbuchhandlung Gerhard Stalling. | 1926 | German Text. | Fraktur Script.

𝕾𝖈𝖍𝖑𝖆𝖈𝖍𝖙𝖊𝖓 𝖉𝖊𝖋 𝖂𝖊𝖑𝖙𝖐𝖗𝖎𝖊𝖌𝖊𝖋 𝕭𝖆𝖓𝖉 𝟩𝖆 𝕯𝖎𝖊 𝕾𝖈𝖍𝖑𝖆𝖈𝖍𝖙 𝖇𝖊𝖎 𝕾𝖙. 𝕼𝖚𝖊𝖓𝖙𝖎𝖓 𝟣𝟫𝟣𝟦 𝕿𝖊𝖎𝖑 𝟣. (Schlachten des Weltkrieges Band 7a Die Schlacht bei St. Quentin 1914 Teil 1. - *Battles of the World War Volume 7a The Battle of St. Quentin 1914 Part 1.*)

> *Major außer Dienst* Kurt Heydemann | 22cm x 15cm | see note for band 1 | 213pp | 10 maps | 27 photographs | 3 diagrams| Verlagsbuchhandlung Gerhard Stalling. | 1924 | German Text. | Fraktur Script.

𝕾𝖈𝖍𝖑𝖆𝖈𝖍𝖙𝖊𝖓 𝖉𝖊𝖋 𝖂𝖊𝖑𝖙𝖐𝖗𝖎𝖊𝖌𝖊𝖋 𝕭𝖆𝖓𝖉 𝟩𝖇 𝕯𝖎𝖊 𝕾𝖈𝖍𝖑𝖆𝖈𝖍𝖙 𝖇𝖊𝖎 𝕾𝖙. 𝕼𝖚𝖊𝖓𝖙𝖎𝖓 𝟣𝟫𝟣𝟦 𝕿𝖊𝖎𝖑 𝟤. (Schlachten des Weltkrieges Band 7b Die Schlacht bei St. Quentin 1914 Teil 2. - *Battles of the World War Volume 7b The Battle of St. Quentin 1914 Part 2.*)

> *Major außer Dienst* Kurt Heydemann | 22cm x 15cm | see note for band 1 | 251pp | 9 maps | 47 photographs | 3 diagrams| Verlagsbuchhandlung Gerhard Stalling. | 1928 | German Text. | Fraktur Script.

𝕾𝖈𝖍𝖑𝖆𝖈𝖍𝖙𝖊𝖓 𝖉𝖊𝖋 𝖂𝖊𝖑𝖙𝖐𝖗𝖎𝖊𝖌𝖊𝖋 𝕭𝖆𝖓𝖉 𝟪 𝕯𝖎𝖊 𝕰𝖗𝖔𝖇𝖊𝖗𝖚𝖓𝖌 𝖛𝖔𝖓 𝕹𝖔𝖛𝖔 𝕲𝖊𝖔𝖗𝖌𝖎𝖊𝖜𝖋𝖐. (Schlachten des Weltkrieges Band 8 Die Eroberung von Novo Georgiewsk. - *Battles of the World War Volume 8 The Conquest of Novogeorgievsk.*)

> *Hauptmann außer Dienst* Franz Bettag | 22cm x 15cm | see note for band 1 | 127pp | 9 maps | 17 photographs | 2 diagrams| Verlagsbuchhandlung Gerhard Stalling. | 1928 | German Text. | Fraktur Script.

𝕾𝖈𝖍𝖑𝖆𝖈𝖍𝖙𝖊𝖓 𝖉𝖊𝖋 𝖂𝖊𝖑𝖙𝖐𝖗𝖎𝖊𝖌𝖊𝖋 𝕭𝖆𝖓𝖉 𝟫 𝕯𝖎𝖊 𝕶𝖆𝖒𝖕𝖋𝖊 𝖚𝖒 𝕭𝖆𝖗𝖆𝖓𝖔𝖜𝖎𝖙𝖋𝖍𝖎 𝕾𝖔𝖒𝖒𝖊𝖗 𝟣𝟫𝟣𝟨 – 𝕯𝖎𝖊 𝕰𝖗𝖋𝖙ü𝖗𝖒𝖚𝖓𝖌 𝖉𝖊𝖋 𝕭𝖗ü𝖐𝖊𝖓𝖐𝖔𝖕𝖋𝖊𝖋 𝖛𝖔𝖓 𝕵𝖆𝖐𝖔𝖇𝖋𝖙𝖆𝖉𝖙 𝟤𝟣–𝟤𝟤 𝕾𝖊𝖕𝖙𝖊𝖒𝖇𝖊𝖗 𝟣𝟫𝟣𝟩. (Schlachten des Weltkrieges Band 9 Die Kampfe um Baranowitshi Sommer 1916 – Die Erstürmung des Brükenkopfes von Jakobstadt 21-22 September 1917. - *Battles of the World War Volume 9 The Fighting for Baranovitchi during the Summer 1916 – The Conquest of the Bridgeheads of Jakobstadt 21st–22nd September 1917.*)

> *Major* Walther Vogel | 22cm x 15cm | see note for band 1 | 2 + 76pp | 12 maps | 6 photographs | 2 diagrams| Verlagsbuchhandlung Gerhard Stalling. | 1928 | German Text. | Fraktur Script.

The town of Jakobstadt is now called Jekabpils in Latvia.

𝕾𝖈𝖍𝖑𝖆𝖈𝖍𝖙𝖊𝖓 𝖉𝖊𝖋 𝖂𝖊𝖑𝖙𝖐𝖗𝖎𝖊𝖌𝖊𝖋 𝕭𝖆𝖓𝖉 𝟣𝟢 𝖄𝖕𝖊𝖗𝖓 𝟣𝟫𝟣𝟦. (Schlachten des Weltkrieges Band 10 Ypern 1914. - *Battles of the World War Volume 10 Ypres 1914.*)

> Werner Beumelburg | 22cm x 15cm | see note for band 1 | 223pp | 1 appendix | 6 maps | 20 photographs | 1 diagram| Verlagsbuchhandlung Gerhard Stalling. | 1928 | German Text. | Fraktur Script.

𝕾𝖈𝖍𝖑𝖆𝖈𝖍𝖙𝖊𝖓 𝖉𝖊𝖋 𝖂𝖊𝖑𝖙𝖐𝖗𝖎𝖊𝖌𝖊𝖋 𝕭𝖆𝖓𝖉 𝟣𝟣 𝖂𝖊𝖑𝖙𝖐𝖗𝖎𝖊𝖌𝖋𝖊𝖓𝖉𝖊 𝖆𝖓 𝖉𝖊𝖗 𝕸𝖆𝖈𝖊𝖉𝖔𝖓𝖎𝖋𝖈𝖍𝖊𝖓 𝕱𝖗𝖔𝖓𝖙. (Schlachten des Weltkrieges Band 11 Weltkriegsende an der Macedonischen Front. - *Battles of the World War Volume 11 The End of the World War on the Macedonian Front.*)

> *Generalleutnant außer Dienst* Dieterich | 22cm x 15cm | see note for band 1 | 187pp | 1 appendix | 8 maps | 22 photographs | Verlagsbuchhandlung Gerhard Stalling. | 1928 | German Text. | Fraktur Script.

𝕾𝖈𝖍𝖑𝖆𝖈𝖍𝖙𝖊𝖓 𝖉𝖊𝖋 𝖂𝖊𝖑𝖙𝖐𝖗𝖎𝖊𝖌𝖊𝖋 𝕭𝖆𝖓𝖉 𝟣𝟤𝖆 𝕯𝖊𝖗 𝕯𝖚𝖗𝖈𝖍𝖇𝖗𝖚𝖈𝖍 𝖆𝖒 𝕴𝖋𝖔𝖓𝖟𝖔 𝕿𝖊𝖎𝖑 𝟣 𝕯𝖎𝖊 𝕾𝖈𝖍𝖑𝖆𝖈𝖍𝖙 𝖛𝖔𝖓 𝕿𝖔𝖑𝖒𝖊𝖎𝖓 𝖚𝖓𝖉 𝕱𝖑𝖎𝖙𝖋𝖈𝖍 – 𝟤𝟦 𝖇𝖎𝖋 𝟤𝟩 𝕺𝖐𝖙𝖔𝖇𝖊𝖗 𝟣𝟫𝟣𝟩. (Schlachten des Weltkrieges Band 12a Der Durchbruch am Isonzo Tiel 1 Die Schlacht von Tolmein und Flitsch – 24 bis 27 Oktober 1917. - *Battles of the World War Volume 12a The Breakthrough on the Isonzo Part 1 The Battles of Tolmino and Plezzo - 24th- 27th October 1917.*)

> *General der Artillerie außer Dienst* Krafft von Dellmensingen | 22cm x 15cm | see note for band 1 | 210pp | 4 maps | 25 photographs | 1 diagram| Verlagsbuchhandlung Gerhard Stalling. | 1928 | German Text. | Fraktur Script.

The towns of Tolmein and Flitsch (the German names) are located in present day Slovenia and now use the Slovenian names of Tolmin and Bolvic respectively – the Italian names have been given in the title translation as reference to the Italian Official Histories. The

Slovenian name for the River Isonzo is the Soča, however the Austrian, German and Italian Official Histories all refer to it as the Isonzo.

Schlachten des Weltkrieges Band 12b Der Durchbruch am Isonzo Tiel 2 Die Verfolgung über den Tagliamento bis zum Piave. (Schlachten des Weltkrieges Band 12b Der Durchbruch am Isonzo Tiel 2 Die Verfolgung über den Tagliamento bis zum Piave. - *Battles of the World War Volume 12b The Breakthrough on the Isonzo Part 2 The Pursuit across the Tagliamento to the Piave.*)

General der Artillerie außer Dienst Krafft von Dellmensingen | 22cm x 15cm | see note for band 1 | 296pp | 1 appendix | 3 maps | 29 photographs | Verlagsbuchhandlung Gerhard Stalling. | 1928 | German Text. | Fraktur Script.

Schlachten des Weltkrieges Band 13 Die Tragödie von Verdun 1916 Tiel I Die Deutsche Offensivschlacht. (Schlachten des Weltkrieges Band 13 Die Tragödie von Verdun 1916 Tiel I Die Deutsche Offensivschlacht. - *Battles of the World War Volume 13 The Tragedy of Verdun 1916 Part I The German Offensive Battle.*)

Studienart Ludwig Gold | 22cm x 15cm | see note for band 1 | 272pp | 54 appendices | 4 maps | 16 photographs | 13 diagrams| Verlagsbuchhandlung Gerhard Stalling. | 1926 | German Text. | Fraktur Script.

Schlachten des Weltkrieges Band 14 Die Tragödie von Verdun 1916 Tiel II Das Ringen um Fort Vaux. (Schlachten des Weltkrieges Band 14 Die Tragödie von Verdun 1916 Tiel II Das Ringen um Fort Vaux. - *Battles of the World War Volume 14 The Tragedy of Verdun 1916 Part II The Struggle for Fort de Vaux.*)

Oberstleutnant außer Dienst Alex. Schwencke | 22cm x 15cm | see note for band 1 | 226pp | 1 appendix | 4 maps | 16 photographs | 12 diagrams| Verlagsbuchhandlung Gerhard Stalling. | 1928 | German Text. | Fraktur Script.

Schlachten des Weltkrieges Band 15 Die Tragödie von Verdun 1916 III und IV Teil: Die Zermürbungsschlacht Tiel III Toter Mann – Höhe 304 und Tiel IV Thiaumont – Fleury. (Schlachten des Weltkrieges Band 15 Die Tragödie von Verdun 1916 III und IV Teil: Die Zermürbungsschlacht Tiel III Toter Mann – Höhe 304 und Tiel IV Thiaumont – Fleury. - *Battles of the World War Volume 15 The Tragedy of Verdun 1916 Parts III and IV: The Battle of Attrition Part III La Mort Homme – Côte 304 and Part IV Thiaumont – Fleury.*)

Studienart Ludwig Gold | 22cm x 15cm | see note for band 1 | 1 + 206pp | 19 maps | 1 diagram| Verlagsbuchhandlung Gerhard Stalling. | 1929 | German Text. | Fraktur Script.

Schlachten des Weltkrieges Band 16 Die Kampf um die Dardanellen 1915. (Schlachten des Weltkrieges Band 16 Die Kampf um die Dardanellen 1915. - *Battles of the World War Volume 16 The Fight for the Dardanelles in 1915.*)

Major außer Dienst Doktor Carl Mühlmann | 22cm x 15cm | see note for band 1 | 195pp | 4 maps | 62 photographs | Verlagsbuchhandlung Gerhard Stalling. | 1927 | German Text. | Fraktur Script.

Schlachten des Weltkrieges Band 17 Loretto. (Schlachten des Weltkrieges Band 17 Loretto. - *Battles of the World War Volume 17 Notre Dame de Lorette.*)

Werner Beumelburg | 22cm x 15cm | see note for band 1 | 1 + 221pp | 3 appendices | 6 maps | 17 photographs | Verlagsbuchhandlung Gerhard Stalling. | 1928 | German Text. | Fraktur Script.

Schlachten des Weltkrieges Band 18 Argonnen. (Schlachten des Weltkrieges Band 18 Argonnen. - *Battles of the World War Volume 18 The Argonne.*)

Major außer Dienst Ernst Schmidt | 22cm x 15cm | see note for band 1 | 224pp | 1 appendix | 3 maps | 22 photographs | 1 diagram| Verlagsbuchhandlung Gerhard Stalling. | 1928 | German Text. | Fraktur Script.

Schlachten des Weltkrieges Band 19 Tannenberg. (Schlachten des Weltkrieges Band 19 Tannenberg. - *Battles of the World War Volume 19 Tannenberg.*)

Oberstleutnant außer Dienst Theobald von Schäfer | 22cm x 15cm | see note for band 1 | 272pp | 3 appendices | 15 maps | 30 photographs | 3 diagrams| Verlagsbuchhandlung Gerhard Stalling. | 1928 | German Text. | Fraktur Script.

Schlachten des Weltkrieges Band 20 Somme Nord Teil 1: Die Brennpunkte der Schlacht im Juli 1916. (Schlachten des Weltkrieges Band 20 Somme Nord Teil 1: Die Brennpunkte der Schlacht im Juli 1916. - *Battles of the World War Volume 20 North of the Somme Part 1: The Focal Points of the Battle in July 1916.*)

Oberstleutnant außer Dienst Albrecht von Stosch | 22cm x 15cm | see note for band 1 | 280pp | 2 appendices | 30 maps | 16 photographs | Verlagsbuchhandlung Gerhard Stalling. | 1927 | German Text. | Fraktur Script.

Schlachten des Weltkrieges Band 21 Somme Nord Teil 2: Die Brennpunkte der Schlacht im Juli 1916. (Schlachten des Weltkrieges Band 21 Somme Nord Teil 2: Die Brennpunkte der Schlacht im Juli 1916. − *Battles of the World War Volume 21 North of the Somme Part 2: The Focal Points of the Battle in July 1916.*)

Oberstleutnant außer Dienst Albrecht von Stosch | 22cm x 15cm | see note for band 1 | 2 + 260pp | 2 appendices | 20 maps | 13 photographs | Verlagsbuchhandlung Gerhard Stalling. | 1927 | German Text. | Fraktur Script.

Schlachten des Weltkrieges Band 22 Marnedrama 1914 Teil 1. (Schlachten des Weltkrieges Band 22 Marnedrama 1914 Teil 1. - *Battles of the World War Volume 22 The Drama on the Marne Part 1.*)

Major außer Dienst Thilo von Bose | 22cm x 15cm | see note for band 1 | 202pp | 12 maps | 2 diagrams| Verlagsbuchhandlung Gerhard Stalling. | 1928 | German Text. | Fraktur Script.

Schlachten des Weltkrieges Band 23 Marnedrama 1914 Teil 2. (Schlachten des Weltkrieges Band 23 Marnedrama 1914 Teil 2. - *Battles of the World War Volume 23 The Drama on the Marne Part 2.*)

Major außer Dienst Thilo von Bose | 22cm x 15cm | see note for band 1 | 3 + 178pp | 1 appendix | 7 maps | 4 photographs | 1 diagram| Verlagsbuchhandlung Gerhard Stalling. | 1928 | German Text. | Fraktur Script.

Schlachten des Weltkrieges Band 24 Marnedrama 1914 Teil 3-1 Abschnitt: Die Kämpfe des Gardkorps und des rechten Flügels der 3 Armee vom 5 bis 8 September. (Schlachten des Weltkrieges Band 24 Marnedrama 1914 Teil 3-1 Abschnitt: Die Kämpfe des Gardkorps und des rechten Flügels der 3 Armee vom 5 bis 8 September. - *Battles of the World War Volume 24 The Drama on the Marne Part 3-1st Section; The Battles of the Guard Corps on the Right Wing of the 3rd Army from the 5th to 8th September.*)

Major außer Dienst Thilo von Bose | 22cm x 15cm | see note for band 1 | 3 + 266pp | 10 maps | 11 photographs | 1 diagram| Verlagsbuchhandlung Gerhard Stalling. | 1928 | German Text. | Fraktur Script.

Schlachten des Weltkrieges Band 25 Marnedrama 1914 Teil 3-2 Abschnitt: Der Aufgang der Schlacht. (Schlachten des Weltkrieges Band 25 Marnedrama 1914 Teil 3-2 Abschnitt: Der Ausgang der Schlacht. - *Battles of the World War Volume 25 The Drama on the Marne Part 3-2nd Section; The Exist from the Battle.*)

Major außer Dienst Thilo von Bose | 22cm x 15cm | see note for band 1 | 3 + 236pp | 1 appendix | 6 maps | 3 photographs | 1 diagram| Verlagsbuchhandlung Gerhard Stalling. | 1928 | German Text. | Fraktur Script.

Schlachten des Weltkrieges Band 26 Marnedrama 1914 Teil 4: Die Schlacht von Paris. (Schlachten des Weltkrieges Band 26 Marnedrama 1914 Teil 4: Die Schlacht von Paris. - *Battles of the World War Volume 26 The Drama on the Marne Part 4; The Battle for Paris.*)

Hauptmann außer Dienst R. Dahlmann | 22cm x 15cm | see note for band 1 | 352pp | 1 appendix | 5 maps | 2 diagrams| Verlagsbuchhandlung Gerhard Stalling. | 1928 | German Text. | Fraktur Script.

Schlachten des Weltkrieges Band 27 Flandern 1917. (Schlachten des Weltkrieges Band 27 Flandern 1917. - *Battles of the World War Volume 27 Flanders 1917.*)

Werner Beumelburg | 22cm x 15cm | see note for band 1 | 169pp | 1 map | 14 photographs | Verlagsbuchhandlung Gerhard Stalling. | 1928 | German Text. | Fraktur Script.

Schlachten des Weltkrieges Band 28 Osterschlacht bei Arras 1917 Teil 1: Zwischen Lens und Scarpe. (Schlachten des Weltkrieges Band 28 Osterschlacht bei Arras

1917 Teil 1: Zwischen Lens und Scrape. - *Battles of the World War Volume 28 The Battle East of Arras 1917 Part 1: Between Lens and the Scrape.*)

Franz Behrmann | 22cm x 15cm | see note for band 1 | 183pp | 2 maps | 12 photographs | Verlagsbuchhandlung Gerhard Stalling. | 1929 | German Text. | Fraktur Script.

Schlachten des Weltkrieges Band 29 Osterschlacht bei Arras 1917 Teil 2: Zwischen Scrape und Bullecourt. (Schlachten des Weltkrieges Band 29 Osterschlacht bei Arras 1917 Teil 2: Zwischen Scrape und Bullecourt. - *Battles of the World War Volume 29 The Battle East of Arras 1917 Part 2: Between the Scrape and Bullecourt.*)

Franz Behrmann | 22cm x 15cm | see note for band 1 | 208pp | 1 map | 12 photographs | Verlagsbuchhandlung Gerhard Stalling. | 1929 | German Text. | Fraktur Script.

Schlachten des Weltkrieges Band 30 Grolice. (Schlachten des Weltkrieges Band 30 Grolice. - *Battles of the World War Volume 30 Grolice.*)

Oberstleutnant außer Dienst Thilo von Kalm | 22cm x 15cm | see note for band 1 | 202pp | 3 appendices | 3 maps | 6 photographs | Verlagsbuchhandlung Gerhard Stalling. | 1930 | German Text. | Fraktur Script.

Schlachten des Weltkrieges Band 31 Die Tankschlacht bei Cambrai 20-29 November 1917. (Schlachten des Weltkrieges Band 31 Die Tankschlacht bei Cambrai 20-29 November 1917. - *Battles of the World War Volume 31 The Tank Battle of Cambrai 20th to 29th November 1917.*)

Hauptmann außer Dienst Doktor Georg Strutz | 22cm x 15cm | see note for band 1 | 192 | 1 appendix | 3 maps | 1 diagram| Verlagsbuchhandlung Gerhard Stalling. | 1929 | German Text. | Fraktur Script.

Schlachten des Weltkrieges Band 32 Deutsche Siege 1918. Das Vordringen der 7 Armee über Ailette, Aisne, Vesle und Ourcq bis zur Marne – 27 Mai bis 13 Juni. (Schlachten des Weltkrieges Band 32 Deutsche Siege 1918. Das Vordringen der 7 Armee über Ailette, Aisne, Vesle und Ourcq bis zur Marne - 27 Mai bis 13 Juni. - *Battles of the World War Volume 32 The German Victories 1918. The Advance of the 7th Army the Rivers Ailette, Aisne, Vesle and Ourcq to the Marne - 27th May until 13th June.*)

Major außer Dienst Thilo von Bose | 22cm x 15cm | see note for band 1 | 198pp | 4 maps | 8 photographs | 7 diagrams| Verlagsbuchhandlung Gerhard Stalling. | 1929 | German Text. | Fraktur Script.

Schlachten des Weltkrieges Band 33 Wachsende Schwierigkeiten. Vergebliches Ringen von Compiègne, Villers-Cotterêts und Reims. (Schlachten des Weltkrieges Band 33 Wachsende Schwierigkeiten. Vergebliches Ringen von Compiègne, Villers-Cotterêts und Reims. - *Battles of the World War Volume 33 Growing Difficulties. Vain Struggles at Compiègne, Villers-Cotterêts and Reims.*)

Major außer Dienst Thilo von Bose | 22cm x 15cm | see note for band 1 | 192pp | 4 maps | 6 photographs | 1 diagram| Verlagsbuchhandlung Gerhard Stalling. | 1930 | German Text. | Fraktur Script.

Schlachten des Weltkrieges Band 34 Der Letzte Deutsche Angriff Reims 1918. (Schlachten des Weltkrieges Schlachten des Weltkrieges Band 34 Der Letzte Deutsche Angriff Reims 1918. - *Battles of the World War Volume 34 The Last German Attack, Reims 1918.*)

Archivrat Alfred Stenger | 22cm x 15cm | see note for band 1 | 208pp | 1 appendix | 3 maps | 9 diagrams| Verlagsbuchhandlung Gerhard Stalling. | 1930 | German Text. | Fraktur Script.

Schlachten des Weltkrieges Band 35 Schicksalswende. Von der Marne bis zur Vesle 1918. (Schlachten des Weltkrieges Band 35 Schicksalswende. Von der Marne bis zur Vesle 1918. - *Battles of the World War Volume 35 Change of Fortune. From the Marne to the Vesle.*)

Archivrat Alfred Stenger | 22cm x 15cm | see note for band 1 | 226pp | 3 maps | 2 diagrams| Verlagsbuchhandlung Gerhard Stalling. | 1930 | German Text. | Fraktur Script.

Schlachten des Weltkrieges Band 36 Die Katastrophe des 8 August 1918. (Schlachten des Weltkrieges Band 36 Die Katastrophe des 8 August 1918. - *Battles of the World War Volume 36 The Catastrophe of the 8th August 1918.*)

Major außer Dienst Thilo von Bose | 22cm x 15cm | see note for band 1 | 201pp | 2 appendices | 5 maps | 1 photograph | 3 diagrams| Verlagsbuchhandlung Gerhard Stalling. | 1930 | German Text. | Fraktur Script.

Die Stahlernen Jahre. (Die Stahlernen Jahre. - *The Steel Years*.)

> Werner Beumelburg l 25cm x 18.5cm l leather bound hardback l Gilt l 17 + 552pp l 5 maps l 76 photographs l 152 diagrams l Verlagsbuchhandlung Gerhard Stalling. l 1929 l German Text. l Fraktur Script.

Bavarian Military Monographs;

Die Schlacht in Lothringen und in den Vogesen 1914 – Die Feuertaufe der Bayerischen Armee. Herausgegeben vom Bayerischen Kriegsarchiv. Erster Band: Friedensgestalt der Armee – Mobilmachung – Ereignisse bis 22 August. (Die Schlacht in Lothringen und in den Vogesen 1914 - Die Feuertaufe der Bayerischen Armee. Herausgegeben vom Bayerischen Kriegsarchiv. - Erster Band: Friedensgestalt der Armee - Mobilmachung - Ereignisse bis 22 August. - *The Battle in Lorraine and in the Vosges 1914 The Bavarian Army's Baptism of Fire. Published from the Bavarian War Archive First Volume: Shape of the Army in Peacetime - Mobilization - Events until 22 August.*)

> Karl Deuringer - Bayerischen Kriegsarchiv l 25cm x 18cm l Blue Cloth Hardback l 18 + 369pp l 37 maps l 46 photographs l 5 diagrams l Max Schidt. l 1929 l German Text. l Fraktur Script.

Die Schlacht in Lothringen und in den Vogesen 1914 – Die Feuertaufe der Bayerischen Armee. Herausgegeben vom Bayerischen Kriegsarchiv. Zweiter Band: Ereignisse nach dem 22 August. (Die Schlacht in Lothringen und in den Vogesen 1914 - Die Feuertaufe der Bayerischen Armee. Herausgegeben vom Bayerischen Kriegsarchiv. - *The Battle in Lorraine and in the Vosges 1914* Zweiter Band: Ereignisse nach dem 22 August. - *The Bavarian Army's Baptism of Fire. Published from the Bavarian War Archive Second Volume: Events after the 22 August.*)

> Karl Deuringer - Bayerischen Kriegsarchiv l 25cm x 18cm l Blue Cloth Hardback l 8 + 522pp l 4 appendices l 27 maps l 38 photographs l 9 diagrams l Max Schidt. l 1929 l German Text. l Fraktur Script.
>
> The titles on the covers and the spines of both Bavarian Official Monographs; "**Die Schlacht in Lothringen und in den Vogesen 1914**" and "**Der Wettlauf um die Flanke in Nordfrankreich 1914**", were printed in modern script whilst the text within the books were printed in Fraktur script. These monographs cover the Battle of Lorraine (part of Battle of the Frontiers).

Der Wettlauf um die Flanke in Nordfrankreich 1914. Herausgegeben vom Bayerischen Kriegsarchiv. Erster Band. (Der Wettlauf um die Flanke in Nordfrankreich 1914. Herausgegeben vom Bayerischen Kriegsarchiv Erster Band - *The Race Around the Flank in Northern France, 1914. Published from the Bavarian War Archive.* ["The Race to the Sea"] *First Volume.*)

> Karl Deuringer - Bayerischen Kriegsarchiv l 25cm x 18cm l Blue Cloth Hardback l xv + 468pp l 16 large format maps l 35 maps l 36 photographs l 9 diagrams l Max Schidt. l 1936 l German Text. l Fraktur Script.
>
> The title of this Bavarian Official Monographs is shown on the title page as "**Der Wettlauf um die Flanke in Nordfrankreich 1914**", however it is shown on the cover and spine in an abbreviated form as "**Der Wettlauf um die Flanke**".

Der Wettlauf um die Flanke in Nordfrankreich 1914. Herausgegeben vom Bayerischen Kriegsarchiv Zweiter Band. (Der Wettlauf um die Flanke in Nordfrankreich 1914. Herausgegeben vom Bayerischen Kriegsarchiv Zweiter Band - *The Race Around the Flank in Northern France, 1914. Published from the Bavarian War Archive.* ["The Race to the Sea"] *Second Volume.*)

> Karl Deuringer - Bayerischen Kriegsarchiv l 25cm x 18cm l Blue Cloth Hardback l 494pp l 5 appendices l 17 large format maps l 23 maps l 36 photographs l 2 tables l Max Schidt. l 1936 l German Text. l Fraktur Script.
>
> These monographs cover the Race to the Sea and the Battle of the Flanders (Ypres).

Aviation Activities[32];

Die deutſchen Luftſtreitkräfte im Weltkriege. (Die deutschen Luftstreitkräfte im Weltkriege. - *The German Air Forces in the World War.*)

> *Major* Georg Paul Neumann (Reichsluftfahrtministerium) | 25.5cm x 17.5cm | see note | x + 600pp | 9 appendices | 296 photographs | 3 maps | 18 tables | 3 sketches | 2 tables | Verlag Ernst Siegfried Mittler und Sohn. | 1920 | German text. | Fraktur script.
>
> This volume was republished as **Die gesamten deutschen Luftstreitkräfte im 1. Weltkrieg** in softback format by Europäischer Hochschulverlag, in 2011. ISBN 10: 3867416729 ISBN 13: 9783867416726.
>
> It was translated into English by J.E. Gurdon and published by Hodder and Stoughton Limited in 1921 under the title "**The German Air Force in the Great War**".
>
> Like the German naval and military histories, this volume was issued with two types of bindings; standard and deluxe. Both types were hardbacks. The standard binding was coloured light brown with paper covered end boards and a cloth covered spine.The title was printed in black and green and illustrated with a propeller also coloured black and green. The deluxe version was bound in half leather hardback with gilt titles.
>
> This volume has inscribed the following statement "Die deutschen Luftstreitkräfte im Weltkriege Unter Mitwirkung von 29 Offizieren und Beamten dee Heeres- und Marine-Luftfahrt nach amtlichen Quellen herausgegeben." (*Compiled from the Records and with the Assistance of 29 Officers and Officials of the Naval and Military Air Services.*)
>
> **Die deutschen Luftstreitkräfte im Weltkriege** is a comprehensive history of the German Air Forces during the Great War, covering all aspects of both the naval and military air services. It included such subjects as the material used (aircraft, aero engines and armaments), individual service personnel details and the various operations undertaken by the air services.

Die Deutſchen Luftſtreitkräfte von ihrer Entſtehung bis zum Ende des Weltkrieges 1918. Kriegsgeſchichtliche Einzelſchriften der Luftwaffe. Erſter Band: Die Militärluftfahrt bis zum Beginn des Weltkrieges 1914. Textband: Die Entwicklung der Heeres— und Marineflugzeuge (Die Deutschen Luftstreitkräfte von ihrer Entstehung bis zum Ende des Weltkrieges 1918. Kriegsgeschichtliche Einzelschriften der Luftwaffe Erster Band: Die Militärluftfahrt bis zum Beginn des Weltkrieges 1914. Textband: Die Entwicklung der Heeres- und Marineflugzeuge - *The German Air Forces from their Creation till the End of the World War 1918. Individual Historical War Studies of the Air Force First Volume: Military Aviation up to the Beginning of the World War 1914. Text Volume: The Development of Army and Naval Aircraft.*)

> *Dr. Ing.* Johannes Schwengler (Reichsluftfahrtministerium) | 25cm x 19cm | blue cloth hardback | Gilt | xi + 358pp | ? maps | 36 photographs | ? drawings | Verlag Ernst Siegfried Mittler und Sohn. | 1942 [1965] | German text. | Fraktur script.
>
> This volume covers pre-war aviations including: The development of German army ballooning; the development of German army airships; army aviation; naval aviation; the development of aviation in the colonies; military and naval air defense.

---

[32] The main official coverage of German air operations is included within the German Official Military History – "**Der Weltkrieg 1914 bis 1918: Die Militarischen Operationen zu Lande**". The air operations sections within Der Weltkrieg are as follows:

  i)   Band 9, Die Operationen des Jahres 1915 – Die Ereignisse im Westen und auf dem Balkan vom Sommer bis Jahresschluß ; Die Entwicklung der Luftstreitkrafte bis Ende 1915 (*The Development of the Air Force to the End of 1915.*)

  ii) Band 10, Die Operationen des Jahres 1916 bis zum Wechsel in der Obersten Heeresleitung; Der Krieg zur Air (*The War by Air.*) [Beginning of 1916 to the Summer 1916]

  iii) Band 11, Die Kriegführung im Herbst 1916 und im Winter 1916/17; Der Krieg zur Air. (*The War by Air.*) [Autumn 1916 to the Winter 1917]

  iv) Band 12, Die Kriegführung im Frühjahr 1917; Der Krieg zur Air. (*The War by Air.*) [Spring 1917]

  v)   Band 13, Die Kriegführung im Sommer und Herbst 1917; Der Krieg zur Air. (*The War by Air.*) [Summer to the Autumn 1917]

  vi) Band 14, Die Kriegführung an der Westfront im Jahre 1918; Der Krieg zur Air. (*The War by Air.*) [Winter 1917 to the end of the War]

Die Deutschen Luftstreitkräfte von ihrer Entstehung bis zum Ende des Weltkrieges 1918. Kriegsgeschichtliche Einzelschriften der Luftwaffe. Erster Band: Die Militärluftfahrt bis zum Beginn des Weltkrieges 1914. Technischer Band: Die Entwicklung der Heeres- und Marineflugzeuge. (Die Deutschen Luftstreitkräfte von ihrer Entstehung bis zum Ende des Weltkrieges 1918. Kriegsgeschichtliche Einzelschriften der Luftwaffe Erster Band: Die Militärluftfahrt bis zum Beginn des Weltkrieges 1914. Technischer Band: Die Entwicklung der Heeres- und Marineflugzeuge. - *The German Air Forces from their Creation till the End of the World War 1918. Individual Historical War Studies of the Air Force First Volume: Military Aviation Up To The Beginning Of The World War 1914. Technical Volume: The Development of the Army and Naval Aircraft.*)

Anonymous (Reichsluftfahrtministerium) I 25cm x 19cm I blue cloth hardback I Gilt I 343pp I 36 tables I Verlag Ernst Siegfried Mittler und Sohn. I 1966 I German text. I Fraktur script.

This volume covers pre-war aviations including: Development of the army airplanes; the developments in the years 1909 and 1910; increases in output and military demands 1911; airplane tests and competitions in 1912; military-technical development in 1913; development in 1914 up to the outbreak of war; technical development; development of naval aircraft 1913, 1914 up to the outbreak of war and the development of the foreign naval aircraft.

Die Deutschen Luftstreitkräfte von ihrer Entstehung bis zum Ende des Weltkrieges 1918. Kriegsgeschichtliche Einzelschriften der Luftwaffe. Erster Band: Die Militärluftfahrt bis zum Beginn des Weltkrieges 1914. Anlageband: Die Entwicklung der Heeres- und Marineflugzeuge (Die Deutschen Luftstreitkräfte von ihrer Entstehung bis zum Ende des Weltkrieges 1918. Kriegsgeschichtliche Einzelschriften der Luftwaffe Erster Band: Die Militärluftfahrt bis zum Beginn des Weltkrieges 1914. Anlageband: Die Entwicklung der Heeres- und Marineflugzeuge. - *The German Air Forces from their Creation till the End of the World War 1918. Individual Historical War Studies of the Air Force First Volume: Military Aviation up to the Beginning of the World War 1914. Appendix Volume: The Development of the Army and Naval Aircraft.*)

Anonymous (Reichsluftfahrtministerium) I 25cm x 19cm I blue cloth hardback I Gilt I 281pp I ? maps I ? photographs I ? drawings I Verlag Ernst Siegfried Mittler und Sohn. I 1966 I German text. I Fraktur script.

This volume covers the same topics of pre-war aviations as mentioned above in the Technical volume.

Die Deutschen Luftstreitkräfte von ihrer Entstehung bis zum Ende des Weltkrieges 1918. Kriegsgeschichtliche Einzelschriften der Luftwaffe. Band Zweiter: Die Militärluftfahrt bis zum Beginn des Weltkrieges 1914. Sonderband: Militärluftfahrt im Völkerrecht und deutschen Recht der Vorkriegszeit. (Die Deutschen Luftstreitkräfte von ihrer Entstehung bis zum Ende des Weltkrieges 1918. Kriegsgeschichtliche Einzelschriften der Luftwaffe Band Zweiter: Die Militärluftfahrt bis zum Beginn des Weltkrieges 1914. Sonderband: Militärluftfahrt im Völkerrecht und deutschen Recht der Vorkriegszeit. - *The German Air Forces from their Creation till the End of the World War 1918. Individual Historical War Studies of the Air Force Second Volume: Military Aviation up to the Beginning of the World War 1914. Special Volume: Military Aviation with Regards to International Law and German Rights before the Outbreak of the War.*)

Anonymous (Reichsluftfahrtministerium) I 25cm x 19cm I blue cloth hardback I vii + 106pp I 1 map I Verlag Ernst Siegfried Mittler und Sohn. I 1938 I German text. I Fraktur script.

Die Deutschen Luftstreitkräfte von ihrer Entstehung bis zum Ende des Weltkrieges 1918. Kriegsgeschichtliche Einzelschriften der Luftwaffe. Dritter Bnab: Die deutschen Luftstreitkräfte von ihrer Entstehung bis zum Ende des Weltkrieges 1918. Sonderband: Mobilmachung, Aufmarsch, und ein erster Einsatz der deutschen Luftstreitkräfte im August 1914.(Die Deutschen Luftstreitkräfte von ihrer Entstehung bis zum Ende des Weltkrieges 1918. Kriegsgeschichtliche Einzelschriften der Luftwaffe Dritter Band: Die deutschen Luftstreitkräfte von ihrer

Entstehung bis zum Ende des Weltkrieges 1918. Sonderband: Mobilmachung, Aufmarsch, und ein erster Einsatz der deutschen Luftstreitkräfte im August 1914. - *Third Volume: German Air Force from its Beginning to the End of the World War 1918. Special Volume: Mobilization, Deployment and Initial Employment of the German Air Force in August 1914.*)

    Elard Freiherr von Loewenstern and Freidrich Bertkau [maps drawn by Oberlt a. D. Rummelspacher] (Reichsluftfahrtministerium) I 25cm x 19cm I blue cloth hardback I Gilt I 120pp I 15 appendices I 14 maps I 5 photographs I Verlag Ernst Siegfried Mittler und Sohn. I 1939 I German text. I Fraktur script.

Die Deutſchen Luftſtreitkräfte von ihrer Entſtehung bis zum Ende des Weltkrieges 1918. Kriegsgeſchichtliche Einzelſchriften der Luftwaffe. Vierter Band: Die deutſchen Luftſtreitkräfte von ihrer Entſtehung bis zum Ende des Weltkrieges 1918. Techniſcher Sonderband J: Die Entwicklung der Heeres und Marineflugzeuge bis zum Aufbruch des Weltkrieges 1914. Dazu: Wie komme ich zur Kriegsmarine. (Die Deutschen Luftstreitkräfte von ihrer Entstehung bis zum Ende des Weltkrieges 1918. Kriegsgeschichtliche Einzelschriften der Luftwaffe Vierter Band: Die deutschen Luftstreitkräfte von ihrer Entstehung bis zum Ende des Weltkrieges 1918. Technischer Sonderband I: Die Entwicklung der Heeres und Marineflugzeuge bis zum Ausbruch des Weltkrieges 1914. Dazu: Wie komme ich zur Kriegsmarine. - *The German Air Forces from their Creation till the End of the World War 1918. Individual Historical War Studies of the Air Force Fourth Volume: German Air Force from its Beginning to the End of the World War 1918. Special Technical Volume 1: The Development of Army and Naval aircraft up to the Outbreak of the World War 1914. In addition: The Navy's War Preparations.*)

    Dr. Ing. Johannes Schwengler (Reichsluftfahrtministerium) I 25cm x 19cm I blue cloth hardback I Gilt I xi + 416pp I 72 appendices I 36 photographs I 9 tables I Verlag Ernst Siegfried Mittler und Sohn. I 1941 I German text. I Fraktur script.

Die Deutſchen Luftſtreitkräfte von ihrer Entſtehung bis zum Ende des Weltkrieges 1918. Kriegsgeſchichtliche Einzelſchriften der Luftwaffe. Fünfter Band: Die deutſchen Luftſtreitkräfte von ihrer Entſtehung bis zum Ende des Weltkrieges 1918. Techniſcher Sonderband JJ: Die techniſche Entwicklung der Flakwaffe bis zum Ende des Weltkrieges. (Die Deutschen Luftstreitkräfte von ihrer Entstehung bis zum Ende des Weltkrieges 1918. Kriegsgeschichtliche Einzelschriften der Luftwaffe Fünfter Band: Die deutschen Luftstreitkräfte von ihrer Entstehung bis zum Ende des Weltkrieges 1918. Technischer Sonderband II: Die technische Entwicklung der Flakwaffe bis zum Ende des Weltkrieges. - *The German Air Forces from their Creation till the End of the World War 1918. Individual Historical War Studies of the Air Force Fifth Volume: The German Air Force from its Beginning to the End of the World War 1918. Special Technical Volume II: The Technical Development of the Flak Weapons up to the End of the World War.*)

    Reinhold Hammer (Reichsluftfahrtministerium) I 25cm x 19cm I blue cloth hardback I Gilt I xv + 268pp I 62 appendices I 95 photographs I Verlag Ernst Siegfried Mittler und Sohn. I 1942 I German text. I Fraktur script.

Die Deutſchen Luftſtreitkräfte von ihrer Entſtehung bis zum Ende des Weltkrieges 1918. Kriegsgeſchichtliche Einzelſchriften der Luftwaffe. Sechſter Band: Die Deutſchen Luftſtreitkräfte von ihrer Entſtehung bis zum Ende des Weltkrieges 1918. Sonderband: Die Luftſtreitkräfte in der Abwehreſchlacht zwiſchen Somme und Oiſe vom 8 bis 12 Auguſt 1918. (Die Deutschen Luftstreitkräfte von ihrer Entstehung bis zum Ende des Weltkrieges 1918. Kriegsgeschichtliche Einzelschriften der Luftwaffe Sechster Band: Die Deutschen Luftstreitkräfte von ihrer Entstehung bis zum Ende des Weltkrieges 1918. Sonderband: Die Luftstreitkräfte in der Abwehreschlacht zwischen Somme und Oise vom 8 bis 12 August 1918. - *The German Air Forces from their Creation till the End of the World War 1918. Individual Historical War Studies of the Air Force Sixth Volume: The German Air Forces from its Beginning to the End of the World War 1918. Special Volume: Air Forces in the Repelling Battle between the Somme and the Oise between 8 to 12 August 1918.*)

Baur de Betaz (Reichsluftfahrtministerium) | 25cm x 19cm | blue cloth hardback | Gilt | 306pp | 19 appendices | 12 maps | 3 sketches | Verlag Ernst Siegfried Mittler und Sohn. | 1942 | German text. | Fraktur script.

𝕯𝖎𝖊 𝕯𝖊𝖚𝖙𝖘𝖈𝖍𝖊𝖓 𝕷𝖚𝖋𝖙𝖘𝖙𝖗𝖊𝖎𝖙𝖐𝖗𝖆̈𝖋𝖙𝖊 𝖛𝖔𝖓 𝖎𝖍𝖗𝖊𝖗 𝕰𝖓𝖙𝖘𝖙𝖊𝖍𝖚𝖓𝖌 𝖇𝖎𝖋 𝖟𝖚𝖒 𝕰𝖓𝖉𝖊 𝖉𝖊𝖋 𝖂𝖊𝖑𝖙𝖐𝖗𝖎𝖊𝖌𝖊𝖋 1918. 𝕶𝖗𝖎𝖊𝖌𝖘𝖌𝖊𝖘𝖈𝖍𝖎𝖈𝖍𝖙𝖑𝖎𝖈𝖍𝖊 𝕰𝖎𝖓𝖟𝖊𝖑𝖘𝖈𝖍𝖗𝖎𝖋𝖙𝖊𝖓 𝖉𝖊𝖗 𝕷𝖚𝖋𝖙𝖜𝖆𝖋𝖋𝖊. 𝕾𝖎𝖊𝖇𝖊𝖓𝖙𝖊𝖗 𝕭𝖆𝖓𝖉: 𝕯𝖎𝖊 𝕯𝖊𝖚𝖙𝖘𝖈𝖍𝖊𝖓 𝕷𝖚𝖋𝖙𝖘𝖙𝖗𝖊𝖎𝖙𝖐𝖗𝖆̈𝖋𝖙𝖊 𝖛𝖔𝖓 𝖎𝖍𝖗𝖊𝖗 𝕰𝖓𝖙𝖘𝖙𝖊𝖍𝖚𝖓𝖌 𝖇𝖎𝖋 𝖟𝖚𝖒 𝕰𝖓𝖉𝖊 𝖉𝖊𝖋 𝖂𝖊𝖑𝖙𝖐𝖗𝖎𝖊𝖌𝖊𝖋 1918. 𝕾𝖔𝖓𝖉𝖊𝖗𝖇𝖆𝖓𝖉: 𝕯𝖊𝖗 𝕸𝖎𝖑𝖎𝖙𝖆̈𝖗𝖎𝖘𝖈𝖍𝖊 𝕳𝖊𝖎𝖒𝖆𝖙𝖑𝖚𝖙𝖘𝖈𝖍𝖚𝖙𝖟 𝖎𝖒 𝖂𝖊𝖑𝖙𝖐𝖗𝖎𝖊𝖌𝖊 1914 𝖇𝖎𝖋 1918. (Die Deutschen Luftstreitkräfte von ihrer Entstehung bis zum Ende des Weltkrieges 1918. Kriegsgeschichtliche Einzelschriften der Luftwaffe Siebenter Band: Die Deutschen Luftstreitkräfte von ihrer Entstehung bis zum Ende des Weltkrieges 1918. Sonderband: Der Militärische Heimatlutschutz im Weltkriege 1914 bis 1918. - *The German Air Forces from their Creation till the End of the World War 1918. Individual Historical War Studies of the Air Force Seventh Volume: The German Air Force from its Beginning to the End of the World War 1918. Special Volume: The Military Homeland Defence in the World War 1914 to 1918.*)

Reinhold Hammer (Reichsluftfahrtministerium) | 25cm x 19cm | blue cloth hardback | Gilt | x + 168pp | 4 appendices | Verlag Ernst Siegfried Mittler und Sohn. | 1943 | German text. | Fraktur script.

𝕭𝖆𝖞𝖊𝖗𝖎𝖘𝖈𝖍𝖊 𝕱𝖑𝖎𝖊𝖌𝖊𝖗 𝖎𝖒 𝖂𝖊𝖑𝖙𝖐𝖗𝖎𝖊𝖌 (Bayerische Flieger im Weltkrieg – *Bavarian Airmen in the World War.*)

Anonymous | 23cm x 17cm | black cloth hardback | vi + 308pp | 20 appendices | 199 photographs | 2 maps | 1 sketch | Verlag der Inspektion des Bayerischen Luftfahrwesens | 1919 | German text. | Fraktur script.

Medical Activities;

Kriegssanitätsbericht über die Deutsche Marine 1914-1918 Band 1 Der Marinesanitätsdienst im Kriege: Überblick über den gesamten Kriegssanitätsdienst auf den einzelnen Seekriegsschauplätzen der deutschen Marine. (*War Report on the Medical Services of German Navy 1914-1918 Volume 1 The Navy's Medical Service in the War: Overview in Detail of the Entire Wartime Medical Service of the German Navy.*)

Anonymous (Marinemedizinalamt des Oberkommandos der Kriegsmarine.) | 27.8cm x 21.5cm | naval blue cloth hardback | gilt | xv + 352pp | 1 appendix | 19 photographs | 2 sketches | 8 tables | Verlag Ernst Siegfried Mittler und Sohn. | 1939 | German Text.

Kriegssanitätsbericht über die Deutsche Marine 1914-1918 Band 2 Statistik über die Erkrankungen, Verwundungen durch Kriegswaffen, Unfälle und ihre Ausgänge im Kriege 1914-1918. (*War Report on the Medical Services of German Navy 1914-1918 Volume 2 Statistics Covering Illnesses, Battle Wounds, Casualties and Invalides in the Wars 1914-1918.*)

Anonymous (Marinemedizinalamt des Oberkommandos der Kriegsmarine.) | | 27.8cm x 21.5cm | naval blue cloth hardback | gilt | vi + 309pp | 227 tables | 5 graphs | Verlag Ernst Siegfried Mittler und Sohn. | 1934 | German Text.

Kriegssanitätsbericht über die Deutsche Marine 1914-1918 Band 3 Medizinischer Teil. (*War Report on the Medical Services of German Navy 1914-1918 Volume 3 Medical Part.*)

Marinegeneralarz außer Dienst Doktor Hanns Gleitsmann (Marinemedizinalamt des Oberkommandos der Kriegsmarine.) | 27.8cm x 21.5cm | naval blue cloth hardback | gilt | ix + 450pp | 1 map | 1 sketch | c330 tables | 22 graphs | Verlag Ernst Siegfried Mittler und Sohn. | 1935 | German Text.

Note that this set Kriegssanitätsbericht über die Deutsche Marine 1914-1918 was printed using modern Latin script and not Fraktur script.

𝕳𝖆𝖓𝖉𝖇𝖚𝖈𝖍 𝖉𝖊𝖗 𝕬𝖗𝖙𝖟𝖑𝖎𝖈𝖍𝖊𝖓 𝕰𝖗𝖋𝖆𝖍𝖗𝖚𝖓𝖌𝖊𝖓 𝖎𝖓 𝖂𝖊𝖑𝖙𝖐𝖗𝖎𝖊𝖌𝖊 1914−1918 𝕭𝖆𝖓𝖉 1 (Handbuch der Artzlichen Erfahrungen in Weltkriege 1914-1918 Band 1 – *Manual of Medical Experiences in the World War 1914-1918 Volume 1*)

Otto von Schjerning | ?cm x ?cm | ? | ? + ?pp | ? maps | Verlag Ernst Siegfried Mittler und Sohn. | 1921 | German Text. | Fraktur Script.

𝕳𝖆𝖓𝖉𝖇𝖚𝖈𝖍 𝖉𝖊𝖗 𝕬𝖗𝖙𝖟𝖑𝖎𝖈𝖍𝖊𝖓 𝕰𝖗𝖋𝖆𝖍𝖗𝖚𝖓𝖌𝖊𝖓 𝖎𝖓 𝕾𝖊𝖑𝖙𝖐𝖗𝖎𝖊𝖌𝖊 1914−1918 𝕭𝖆𝖓𝖉 1 𝕭𝖆𝖓𝖉 2 (Handbuch der Artzlichen Erfahrungen in Weltkriege 1914-1918 Band 2 – *Manual of Medical Experiences in the World War 1914-1918 Volume 2*)

Otto von Schjerning | ?cm x ?cm | ? | ? + ?pp | ? maps | Verlag Ernst Siegfried Mittler und Sohn. | ? | German Text. | Fraktur Script.

𝕳𝖆𝖓𝖉𝖇𝖚𝖈𝖍 𝖉𝖊𝖗 𝕬𝖗𝖙𝖟𝖑𝖎𝖈𝖍𝖊𝖓 𝕰𝖗𝖋𝖆𝖍𝖗𝖚𝖓𝖌𝖊𝖓 𝖎𝖓 𝕾𝖊𝖑𝖙𝖐𝖗𝖎𝖊𝖌𝖊 1914−1918 𝕭𝖆𝖓𝖉 1 𝕭𝖆𝖓𝖉 3 (Handbuch der Artzlichen Erfahrungen in Weltkriege 1914-1918 Band 3 – *Manual of Medical Experiences in the World War 1914-1918 Volume 3*)

Otto von Schjerning | ?cm x ?cm | ? | ? + ?pp | ? maps | Verlag Ernst Siegfried Mittler und Sohn. | ? | German Text. | Fraktur Script.

𝕳𝖆𝖓𝖉𝖇𝖚𝖈𝖍 𝖉𝖊𝖗 𝕬𝖗𝖙𝖟𝖑𝖎𝖈𝖍𝖊𝖓 𝕰𝖗𝖋𝖆𝖍𝖗𝖚𝖓𝖌𝖊𝖓 𝖎𝖓 𝕾𝖊𝖑𝖙𝖐𝖗𝖎𝖊𝖌𝖊 1914−1918 𝕭𝖆𝖓𝖉 1 𝕭𝖆𝖓𝖉 4 (Handbuch der Artzlichen Erfahrungen in Weltkriege 1914-1918 Band 4 – *Manual of Medical Experiences in the World War 1914-1918 Volume 4*)

Otto von Schjerning | ?cm x ?cm | ? | ? + ?pp | ? maps | Verlag Ernst Siegfried Mittler und Sohn. | ? | German Text. | Fraktur Script.

𝕳𝖆𝖓𝖉𝖇𝖚𝖈𝖍 𝖉𝖊𝖗 𝕬𝖗𝖙𝖟𝖑𝖎𝖈𝖍𝖊𝖓 𝕰𝖗𝖋𝖆𝖍𝖗𝖚𝖓𝖌𝖊𝖓 𝖎𝖓 𝕾𝖊𝖑𝖙𝖐𝖗𝖎𝖊𝖌𝖊 1914−1918 𝕭𝖆𝖓𝖉 1 𝕭𝖆𝖓𝖉 5 (Handbuch der Artzlichen Erfahrungen in Weltkriege 1914-1918 Band 5 – *Manual of Medical Experiences in the World War 1914-1918 Volume 5*)

Otto von Schjerning | ?cm x ?cm | ? | ? + ?pp | ? maps | Verlag Ernst Siegfried Mittler und Sohn. | ? | German Text. | Fraktur Script.

𝕳𝖆𝖓𝖉𝖇𝖚𝖈𝖍 𝖉𝖊𝖗 𝕬𝖗𝖙𝖟𝖑𝖎𝖈𝖍𝖊𝖓 𝕰𝖗𝖋𝖆𝖍𝖗𝖚𝖓𝖌𝖊𝖓 𝖎𝖓 𝕾𝖊𝖑𝖙𝖐𝖗𝖎𝖊𝖌𝖊 1914−1918 𝕭𝖆𝖓𝖉 1 𝕭𝖆𝖓𝖉 6 (Handbuch der Artzlichen Erfahrungen in Weltkriege 1914-1918 Band 6 – *Manual of Medical Experiences in the World War 1914-1918 Volume 6*)

Otto von Schjerning | ?cm x ?cm | ? | ? + ?pp | ? maps | Verlag Ernst Siegfried Mittler und Sohn. | ? | German Text. | Fraktur Script.

𝕳𝖆𝖓𝖉𝖇𝖚𝖈𝖍 𝖉𝖊𝖗 𝕬𝖗𝖙𝖟𝖑𝖎𝖈𝖍𝖊𝖓 𝕰𝖗𝖋𝖆𝖍𝖗𝖚𝖓𝖌𝖊𝖓 𝖎𝖓 𝕾𝖊𝖑𝖙𝖐𝖗𝖎𝖊𝖌𝖊 1914−1918 𝕭𝖆𝖓𝖉 1 𝕭𝖆𝖓𝖉 7 (Handbuch der Artzlichen Erfahrungen in Weltkriege 1914-1918 Band 7 – *Manual of Medical Experiences in the World War 1914-1918 Volume 7*)

Otto von Schjerning | ?cm x ?cm | ? | ? + ?pp | ? maps | Verlag Ernst Siegfried Mittler und Sohn. | ? | German Text. | Fraktur Script.

𝕳𝖆𝖓𝖉𝖇𝖚𝖈𝖍 𝖉𝖊𝖗 𝕬𝖗𝖙𝖟𝖑𝖎𝖈𝖍𝖊𝖓 𝕰𝖗𝖋𝖆𝖍𝖗𝖚𝖓𝖌𝖊𝖓 𝖎𝖓 𝕾𝖊𝖑𝖙𝖐𝖗𝖎𝖊𝖌𝖊 1914−1918 𝕭𝖆𝖓𝖉 1 𝕭𝖆𝖓𝖉 8 (Handbuch der Artzlichen Erfahrungen in Weltkriege 1914-1918 Band 8 – *Manual of Medical Experiences in the World War 1914-1918 Volume 8*)

Otto von Schjerning | ?cm x ?cm | ? | ? + ?pp | ? maps | Verlag Ernst Siegfried Mittler und Sohn. | ? | German Text. | Fraktur Script.

𝕳𝖆𝖓𝖉𝖇𝖚𝖈𝖍 𝖉𝖊𝖗 𝕬𝖗𝖙𝖟𝖑𝖎𝖈𝖍𝖊𝖓 𝕰𝖗𝖋𝖆𝖍𝖗𝖚𝖓𝖌𝖊𝖓 𝖎𝖓 𝕾𝖊𝖑𝖙𝖐𝖗𝖎𝖊𝖌𝖊 1914−1918 𝕭𝖆𝖓𝖉 1 𝕭𝖆𝖓𝖉 9 (Handbuch der Artzlichen Erfahrungen in Weltkriege 1914-1918 Band 9 – *Manual of Medical Experiences in the World War 1914-1918 Volume 9*)

Otto von Schjerning | ?cm x ?cm | ? | ? + ?pp | ? maps | Verlag Ernst Siegfried Mittler und Sohn. | 1934 | German Text. | Fraktur Script.

𝕾𝖆𝖓𝖎𝖙𝖆̈𝖙𝖘𝖇𝖊𝖗𝖎𝖈𝖍𝖙 𝖚̈𝖇𝖊𝖗 𝖉𝖆𝖘 𝕯𝖊𝖚𝖙𝖘𝖈𝖍𝖊𝖓 𝕳𝖊𝖊𝖗𝖊𝖘 𝖎𝖒 𝕾𝖊𝖑𝖙𝖐𝖗𝖎𝖊𝖌𝖊 1914−1918 𝕭𝖆𝖓𝖉 1 𝕲𝖑𝖎𝖊𝖉𝖊𝖗𝖚𝖓𝖌 𝖉𝖊𝖘 𝕳𝖊𝖊𝖗𝖊𝖘𝖘𝖆𝖓𝖎𝖙𝖆𝖙𝖘𝖜𝖊𝖘𝖘𝖊𝖓𝖘 𝖎𝖒 𝕾𝖊𝖑𝖙𝖐𝖗𝖎𝖊𝖌𝖊 1914 − 1918. (Sanitätsbericht über das Deutschen Heeres im Weltkrieg 1914-1918 Band 1 Gliederung des Heeressanitatswessens im Weltkriege 1914 – 1918. - *Medical Services of the German Army during the World War 1914-1918 Volume 1 Army Arrangements for First Aid in the World War.*)

Anonymous | 31cm x 21cm | maron cloth hardback | gilt | viii + 333pp | 302 illustrations | 46 tables | Verlag Ernst Siegfried Mittler und Sohn. | 1935 | German Text. | Fraktur Script.
Like the rest of "Der Weltkrieg 1914 bis 1918: Die Militarischen Operationen zu Lande" set this volume was produced with the three types of bindings.

𝕾𝖆𝖓𝖎𝖙𝖆̈𝖙𝖘𝖇𝖊𝖗𝖎𝖈𝖍𝖙 𝖚̈𝖇𝖊𝖗 𝖉𝖆𝖘 𝕯𝖊𝖚𝖙𝖘𝖈𝖍𝖊𝖓 𝕳𝖊𝖊𝖗𝖊𝖘 𝖎𝖒 𝕾𝖊𝖑𝖙𝖐𝖗𝖎𝖊𝖌𝖊 1914−1918 𝕭𝖆𝖓𝖉 2 𝕯𝖊𝖗 𝕾𝖆𝖓𝖎𝖙𝖆̈𝖙𝖘𝖉𝖎𝖊𝖓𝖘𝖙 𝖎𝖒 𝕲𝖊𝖋𝖊𝖈𝖍𝖙𝖘− 𝖚𝖓𝖉 𝕾𝖈𝖍𝖑𝖆𝖈𝖍𝖙𝖊𝖓𝖛𝖊𝖗𝖑𝖆𝖚𝖋. (Sanitätsbericht über das Deutschen Heeres im Weltkrieg 1914-1918 Band 2 Der Sanitätsdienst im Gefechts- und

Schlachtenverlauf. - Medical Services of the German Army during the World War 1914-1918 Volume 2 Issues Relating to the Medical Services during the Fighting and Battles Processes.*)

Anonymous | 31cm x 21cm | maron cloth hardback | gilt | xiv + 822pp | 1 map | 1 sketch | 9 coloured graphs | 120 tables | Verlag Ernst Siegfried Mittler und Sohn. | 1937 | German Text. | Fraktur Script.

𝕾anitätſbericht über baſ Deutſchen 𝕳eereſ im 𝖂eltkriege 1914−1918 𝕭and 2 Der 𝕾anitätſbienſt im 𝕲efechtſ− und 𝕾chlachtenverlauf − 𝕶arte. **(Sanitätsbericht über das Deutschen Heeres im Weltkrieg 1914-1918 Band 2 Der Sanitätsdienst im Gefechts- und Schlachtenverlauf - Karte. -** *Medical Services of the German Army during the World War 1914-1918 Volume 2 Issues Relating to the Medical Services during the Fighting and Battles Processes - Maps.*)

Anonymous | 31cm x 21cm | maron cloth hardback | gilt | 92 maps | Verlag Ernst Siegfried Mittler und Sohn. | 1937 | German Text. | Fraktur Script.

𝕾anitätſbericht über baſ Deutſchen 𝕳eereſ im 𝖂eltkriege 1914−1918 𝕭and 3 Die 𝕶rankenbewegung bei bem Deutſchen 𝕱elb und 𝕭eſatzungſheer. **(Sanitätsbericht über das Deutschen Heeres im Weltkrieg 1914-1918 Band 3 Die Krankenbewegung bei dem Deutschen Feld- und Besatzungsheer. -** *Medical Services of the German Army during the World War 1914-1918 Volume 3 Transportation of Casualties about the German Field and Garrison Armies.*)

Anonymous | 31cm x 21cm | maron cloth hardback | gilt | vii + 145pp | 4 appendices | 165 overviews | 152 tables | Verlag Ernst Siegfried Mittler und Sohn. | 1934 | German Text. | Fraktur Script.

Miscellaneous;

This group of official histories were written by the archivists of the regional military archives and were intended as popular histories for the general public. Although the histories cover the period from the Napoleonic Wars through to the Great War, the majority of the narrations covered the Great War. The history produced by the main Germany military archive in Potsdam covered the entire German Army. However in the case of the other regional archives the histories were limited to that of the locally raised army. They provided thumbnail sketches of the engagements fought by the regional army and of the key personalities and local individuals that had been involved in heroic deeds. They also included a detailed breakdown of the structure of the region's military force that had been raised, along with a chronology of events.

Daſ 𝕭ayernbuch vom 𝖂eltkriege 1914 − 1918. 𝕰in 𝖁olkſbuch. 𝕴 𝕭and. **(Das Bayernbuch vom Weltkriege 1914 - 1918. Ein Volksbuch. I Band. –** *The Bavarian Book of the World War 1914-1918. The People's Book. Volume I.*)

Generalleutnant der Artillerie außer Dienst Konrad *Freiherr* Krafft von Dellmensingen and *Generalmajor außer Dienst* Friedrichfranz Feeser | 30cm x 23cm | see note below | XXVIII + 240pp | ? maps | 148 photographs | 4 colored drawings | 225 sketches | Verlag Chr. Belser. | 1930 | German Text. | Fraktur Script.

Daſ 𝕭ayernbuch vom 𝖂eltkriege 1914 − 1918. 𝕰in 𝖁olkſbuch. 𝕴𝕴 𝕭and. **(Das Bayernbuch vom Weltkriege 1914 - 1918. Ein Volksbuch. II Band. –** *The Bavarian Book of the World War 1914-1918. The People's Book. Volume II.*)

Generalleutnant der Artillerie außer Dienst Konrad *Freiherr* Krafft von Dellmensingen and *Generalmajor außer Dienst* Friedrichfranz Feeser | 30cm x 23cm | see note below | XVII + 658pp | ? maps | 964 photographs | 26 colored drawings | 243 sketches | Verlag Chr. Belser. | 1930 | German Text. | Fraktur Script.

This volume "**Das Bayernbuch vom Weltkriege 1914 - 1918. Ein Volksbuch**" was published with two types of cover – an ordinary and a deluxe. The ordinary version had a brown cloth hardback cover whilst the deluxe had a blue leather hardback with Gilt text.

𝕽ühmeſhalle Unſerer 𝕬lten 𝕬rmee. **(Rühmeshalle Unserer Alten Armee. -** *Reminiscences of Army Veterans.*)

Major außer Dienst Erich Otto Volkmann | 29cm x 22cm | Black Cloth Hardback | gilt | ii + 497pp | 5 maps | Militar-Verlag. | 1927 | German Text. | Fraktur Script.

𝕽ü𝖍𝖒𝖊𝖘𝖍𝖆𝖑𝖑𝖊 𝖀𝖓𝖘𝖊𝖗𝖊𝖗 𝕬𝖑𝖙𝖊𝖓 𝕬𝖗𝖒𝖊𝖊 𝕭𝖆𝖓𝖉 𝕵𝕵. 𝕯𝖎𝖊 𝕱𝖗𝖔𝖓𝖙𝖊𝖓 𝖉𝖊𝖘 𝖂𝖊𝖑𝖙𝖐𝖗𝖎𝖊𝖌𝖘 𝖎𝖒 𝕭𝖎𝖑𝖉𝖊. **(Rühmeshalle Unserer Alten Armee Band II. Die Fronten des Weltkriegs im Bilde. -** *Reminiscences of Army Veterans Volume II. The Fronts of the World War in Pictures.***)**

Major außer Dienst Erich Otto Volkmann | 29cm x 22cm | Black Cloth Hardback | gilt | xvii + 514pp | 5 maps | Militar-Verlag. | 1932 | German Text. | Fraktur Script.

𝕯𝖎𝖊 𝖂ü𝖗𝖙𝖙𝖊𝖒𝖇𝖊𝖗𝖌𝖊𝖗 𝖎𝖒 𝖂𝖊𝖑𝖙𝖐𝖗𝖎𝖊𝖌𝖊. **(Württemberger im Weltkriege. -** *Württemberg in the World War.***)**

Generalleutnant Otto von Moser | 30cm x 23cm | Green Cloth Hardback | XVI + 767pp | 5 maps | 860 photographs | 70 leader drawings | 24 colored drawings | 260 sketches | Verlag Chr. Belser. | 1927 | German Text. | Fraktur Script.

Prisoners of War;

𝕯𝖎𝖊 𝕭𝖊𝖍𝖆𝖓𝖉𝖑𝖚𝖓𝖌 𝖉𝖊𝖗 𝕶𝖗𝖎𝖊𝖌𝖘𝖌𝖊𝖋𝖆𝖓𝖌𝖊𝖓𝖊𝖓: 𝖆𝖒𝖙𝖑𝖎𝖈𝖍𝖊𝖗 𝕭𝖊𝖗𝖎𝖈𝖍𝖙 𝖉𝖊𝖗 𝕶𝖔𝖒𝖒𝖎𝖘𝖘𝖎𝖔𝖓 𝖟𝖚𝖗 𝖀𝖓𝖙𝖊𝖗𝖘𝖚𝖈𝖍𝖚𝖓𝖌 𝖉𝖊𝖗 𝕬𝖓𝖐𝖑𝖆𝖌𝖊𝖓 𝖜𝖊𝖌𝖊𝖓 𝖛ö𝖑𝖐𝖊𝖗𝖗𝖊𝖈𝖍𝖙𝖘𝖜𝖎𝖉𝖗𝖎𝖌𝖊𝖗 𝕭𝖊𝖍𝖆𝖓𝖉𝖑𝖚𝖓𝖌 𝖉𝖊𝖗 𝕶𝖗𝖎𝖊𝖌𝖘𝖌𝖊𝖋𝖆𝖓𝖌𝖊𝖓𝖊𝖓 𝖎𝖓 𝕯𝖊𝖚𝖙𝖘𝖈𝖍𝖑𝖆𝖓𝖉. **(Die Behandlung der Kriegsgefangenen: amtlicher Bericht der Kommission zur Untersuchung der Anklagen wegen völkerrechtswidriger Behandlung der Kriegsgefangenen in Deutschland. -***The Treatment of Hostile Prisoners of War: Official Report of the Commission to Examine the Accusations of the Nation's Illegal Treatment of Prisoners of War in Germany.***)**

Anonymous | 24cm x 17cm | see note | ? + 104pp | ? maps | Hobbing. | 1920 | German Text. | Fraktur Script.

Statistics;

𝕯𝖊𝖗 𝖂𝖊𝖑𝖙𝖐𝖗𝖎𝖊𝖌 1914 𝖇𝖎𝖘 1918: 𝕶𝖗𝖎𝖊𝖌𝖘𝖗ü𝖘𝖙𝖚𝖓𝖌 𝖚𝖓𝖉 𝕶𝖗𝖎𝖊𝖌𝖘𝖜𝖎𝖗𝖙𝖘𝖈𝖍𝖆𝖋𝖙 𝕰𝖗𝖘𝖙𝖊𝖗 𝕭𝖆𝖓𝖉, 𝕯𝖎𝖊 𝖒𝖎𝖑𝖎𝖙ä𝖗𝖎𝖘𝖈𝖍𝖊, 𝖜𝖎𝖗𝖙𝖘𝖈𝖍𝖆𝖋𝖙𝖑𝖎𝖈𝖍𝖊 𝖚𝖓𝖉 𝖋𝖎𝖓𝖆𝖓𝖟𝖎𝖊𝖑𝖑𝖊 𝕽ü𝖘𝖙𝖚𝖓𝖌 𝕯𝖊𝖚𝖙𝖘𝖈𝖍𝖑𝖆𝖓𝖉𝖘 𝖛𝖔𝖓 𝖉𝖊𝖗 𝕽𝖊𝖎𝖈𝖍𝖘𝖌𝖗ü𝖓𝖉𝖚𝖓𝖌 𝖇𝖎𝖘 𝖟𝖚𝖒 𝕬𝖚𝖋𝖇𝖗𝖚𝖈𝖍 𝖉𝖊𝖘 𝖂𝖊𝖑𝖙𝖐𝖗𝖎𝖊𝖌. **(Der Weltkrieg 1914 bis 1918: Kriegsrüstung und Kriegswirtschaft Erster Band, Die militärische, wirtschaftliche und finanzielle Rüstung Deutschlands von der Reichsgründung bis zum Ausbruch des Weltkrieg. –** *The World War 1914 to 1918: Armament and War Production First Volume, The Military, Economic and Financial Armament of Germany from the Establishment of the Realm to the Outbreak of World War.***)**

Oberstleutnant außer Dienst Wolfgang Foerster (Editor) - Reichsarchiv | 24cm x 17cm | see note | xii + 496pp | 2 tables | Verlag Ernst Siegfried Mittler und Sohn. | 1930 | German Text. | Fraktur Script.

Like the rest of "**Der Weltkrieg 1914 bis 1918: Die Militarischen Operationen zu Lande**" set this volume was produced with the three types of bindings.

The volume number of "**Der Weltkrieg 1914 bis 1918: Kriegsrüstung und Kriegswirtschaft.**" was written out in full on the title page i.e. "Erster Band" however it was shown just as a numeral on the spine i.e. "1". I have given the title as shown on the title page.

Only one volume of "**Der Weltkrieg 1914 bis 1918: Kriegsrüstung and Kriegswirtschaft, Erster Band, Die militärische, wirschaftliche und finanzielle Rüstung Deutschlands von der Reichsgründung bis zum Ausbruch des Weltkrieg**" was produced along with its supplement volume.

𝕯𝖊𝖗 𝖂𝖊𝖑𝖙𝖐𝖗𝖎𝖊𝖌 1914 𝖇𝖎𝖘 1918: 𝕶𝖗𝖎𝖊𝖌𝖘𝖗ü𝖘𝖙𝖚𝖓𝖌 𝖚𝖓𝖉 𝕶𝖗𝖎𝖊𝖌𝖘𝖜𝖎𝖗𝖙𝖘𝖈𝖍𝖆𝖋𝖙 𝕾𝖔𝖓𝖉𝖊𝖗𝖇𝖆𝖓𝖉 𝕬𝖓𝖑𝖆𝖌𝖊𝖓 𝖟𝖚𝖒 𝕰𝖗𝖘𝖙𝖊𝖓 𝕭𝖆𝖓𝖉. **(Der Weltkrieg 1914 bis 1918: Kriegsrüstung und Kriegswirtschaft Sonderband Anlagen zum Ersten Band. –** *The World War 1914 to 1918: Armament and War Production Special Supplement Volume to the First Volume***)**

Oberstleutnant außer Dienst Wolfgang Foerster (Editor) - Reichsarchiv | 24cm x 17cm | see note | ix + 534pp | 101 appendices | 21 tables | 4 maps | Verlag Ernst Siegfried Mittler und Sohn. | 1930 | German Text. | Fraktur Script.

The volume number of "**Der Weltkrieg 1914 bis 1918: Kriegsrüstung und Kriegswirtschaft.**" was written out in full on the title page i.e. "Erster Band", however it was shown just as a numeral on the spine i.e. "1". I have given the title as shown on the title page.

Photographs;

Der Weltkrieg im Bild Bund 1 Originalaufnahmen des Krieg Bild und Filmamtes. (**Der Weltkrieg im Bild Bund 1 Originalaufnabmen des Krieg Bild und Filmamtes. –** *The World War in Pictures Volume 1 Original War Photographs from the Film Office.*)

> Anonymous – (Reichsarchiv) | 24cm x 17cm | leather bound hardback | Gilt | 350pp | c400 photographs | Verlag "Der Weltkrieg im Bild" - Alleinge Vertriebsftelle. | 1926 | German Text. | Fraktur Script.

Der Weltkrieg im Bild Bund 2 Frontaufnahmen auf den Archiven der Entente. (**Der Weltkrieg im Bild Bund 2 Frontaufnahmen aus den Archiven der Entente. -** *Front photographs from the Entente Archives.*)

> Anonymous (Reichsarchiv) | 24cm x 17cm | leather bound hardback | Gilt | 350pp | c400 photographs | Verlag "Der Weltkrieg im Bild" - Alleinge Vertriebsftelle. | 1936 | German Text. | Fraktur Script.

Greek Official Histories

The Greek army's official history was written by members of the Γενικό Επιτελείο Στρατού Διεύθυνσης Ιστορίας Στρατού (*Army General Staff Historical Directorite.*) It consists of a complete history of the modern Greek army from its beginnings during the early part of the nineteenth century through to the present day. Only the volumes listed below cover the period of the Great War.

Military Operations;

Ο ΕΛΛΗΝΙΚΟΣ ΣΤΡΑΤΟΣ ΚΑΤΑ ΤΟΝ ΠΡΩΤΟ ΠΑΓΚΟΣΜΙΟΝ ΠΟΛΕΜΟΝ 1914-1918 ΤΟΜΟΣ ΠΡΩΤΟΣ - Η ΕΛΛΑΣ ΚΑΙ Ο ΠΟΛΕΜΟΣ ΕΙΣ ΤΑ ΒΑΛΚΑΝΙΑ. **(Ho Hellenikos Stratos kata ton Proton Pankosmion Polemon 1914-1918 Tomos 1 - H Hellas kai ho Polemos eis ta Balkania.** - *The Greek Army during the First World War 1914 – 1918 Volume One – Greece and the War in the Balkans.*)

Αντισυνταγματάρχης (*Lieutenant Colonel*) Αριστείδης Ομηρίδης Σκυλίτσης [Editor] Γενικό Επιτελείο Στρατού Διεύθυνσης Ιστορίας Στρατού (*Army General Staff Historical Directorite.*) I 24.5cm x 16.5cm I see note I xix + 375pp I 37 appendices I 1 + 31 maps I 22 photographs I 3 tables I Εκδοση Διευθύνεως Ιστορίας Στρατού (*Army History Directorate Publications.*) I 1958 [1970] I Greek text. I modern Greek script.
A revised edition of this volume was produced in 1970.
A single large format map is carried in a sheaf attached to the inside rear covered.

Ο ΕΛΛΗΝΙΚΟΣ ΣΤΡΑΤΟΣ ΚΑΤΑ ΤΟΝ ΠΡΩΤΟ ΠΑΓΚΟΣΜΙΟΝ ΠΟΛΕΜΟΝ 1914-1918 ΤΟΜΟΣ ΔΕΥΤΕΡΟΣ - Η ΣΥΜΜΕΤΟΧΗ ΤΗΣ ΕΛΛΑΔΟΣ ΕΙΣ ΤΟΝ ΠΟΛΕΜΟΝ 1918. **(Ho Hellenikos Stratos kata ton Proton Pankosmion Polemon 1914-1918 Tomos 2 H Summetochh ths Hellados eis ton Polemon 1918.** - *The Greek Army during the First World War 1914 – 1918 Volume Two – Greece's Participation in the War 1918.*)

Αντισυνταγματάρχης (*Lieutenant Colonel*) Αριστείδης Ομηρίδης Σκυλίτσης [Editor] Γενικό Επιτελείο Στρατού Διεύθυνσης Ιστορίας Στρατού (*Army General Staff Historical Directorite.*) I 24.5cm x 16.5cm I see note I xix + 304pp I 46 appendices I 1 + 26 maps I 17 photographs I 3 tables I Εκδοση Διευθύνεως Ιστορίας Στρατού (*Army History Directorate Publications.*) I 1961 I Greek text. I modern Greek script.
A single large format map is carried in a sheaf attached to the inside rear covered.
This two volume set "Ο Ελληνικός Στρατός Κατά Τον Πρώτο Παγκόσμιον Πόλεμον 1914-1918", was produced with two types of bindings: a pre bound hardback and a paper softback with cream paper wraps and untrimmed pages for future binding. The hardback version had green cloth with gilt text on the spine and Greek army's emblem embosed on the front cover. The original edition of the softback version had black text whilst the revised edition had the black text and additionally the Greek army's emblem coloured in yellow printed on the front cover.

ΕΠΙΤΟΜΗ ΙΣΤΟΡΙΑ ΤΗΣ ΣΥΜΜΕΤΟΧΗΣ ΤΟΥ ΕΛΛΗΝΙΚΟΥ ΣΤΡΑΤΟΥ ΣΤΟΝ ΠΡΩΤΟ ΠΑΓΚΟΣΜΙΟ ΠΟΛΕΜΟ 1914-1918. **(Epitomh Istopia Ths Eummetochhs Tou Ellhnikou Stratou Ston Prpsto Pagkosmio Polemo 1914-1918.** - *A Concise History of the Participation of the Greek Army in The First World War 1914-1918.*)

Υποστράτηγος (*Major General*) Μιχαήλ Δούβας [Editor] Γενικό Επιτελείο Στρατού Διεύθυνσης Ιστορίας Στρατού (*Army General Staff Historical Directorite.*) I 24.5cm x 16.5cm I Green Cloth Hardback I Gilt I xxv + 362pp I 40 maps I 59 photographs I 5 tables I Εκδοση Διευθύνεως Ιστορίας Στρατού (*Army History Directorate Publications.*) I 1993 I Greek text. I modern Greek script.

A Concise History of the Participation of the Hellenic Army in The First World War 1914-1918.
Major General Michael Douvas [Μιχαήλ Δούβας - Editor] Hellenic Army General Staff. I 24.5cm x 16.5cm I Green Cloth Hardback I Gilt I Green Illustrated Paper Dust Jacket I xxvi + 320pp I 40 maps I 59 photographs I 5 tables I Aristide D. Caratzas Publisher/Melissa International Ltd in association with the Army History Directorate Publications. I 1999 I English text.
ISBN: 960-7897-37-4
The original version of "**Επίτομη Ιστορία Της Συμμετοχής Του Ελληνικού Στρατού Στον Πρώτο Παγκόσμιο Πόλεμο 1914-1918**" published in 1993 was written and published in Greek using modern Greek script. However as with a number of other volumes from the

entire Greek army official history series especially the World War Two volumes, it was translated into English and republished six years later, the English title being "**A Concise History of the Participation of the Hellenic Army in The First World War 1914-1918**".

Hungarian Official Histories

The Hungarian army official histories were written by members of the Magyar Királyi Hadtőrténelmi levéltár (*the Hungarian State Archives.*) Unfortunately all work on this history was stopped towards the end of the Second World War leaving it uncompleted.

Military Operations;

A VILÁGHÁBORÚ 1914-1918. KŰLŐNŐS TEKINTETTEL MAGYARORSZÁGRA ÉS A MAGYAR CSAPATOK SZEREPLÉSÉRE SZERKESZTI ÉS KIADJA A M. KIR. HADTŐRTÉNELMI LEVÉLTÁR. I KŐTET. KŰLPOLITIKAI VISSZAPILLANTÁS. A VILÁGHÁBORÚ KITŐRÉSE. ESEMÉNYEK AZ OROSZ HARCTÉREN 1914 ÉVI AUGUSZTUS HÓ 20-IG.[33] (*The World War 1914-1918. In Particular to the Role of Hungary and the Hungarian Army. Volume I. Review of Foreign Policy. The Outbreak of the World War. The Events of the Russian Campaign up to 20th August 1914.*)

    Anonymous (Kamil Aggházy and Valér Stefán [Magyar Királyi Hadtőrténelmi Levéltár]). | 24.8cm x 17.5cm | see note below | 239pp | 6 appendices | 4 maps | 5 tables | 12 organisation charts | Stadium Sajtóvállalat Részvénytarsasag. | 1928 | Hungarian Text.

    This set "**A világháború 1914-1918**" was published with two types of binding, a deluxe hardback binding in green leather with gilt titles and logo and a cheaper softback in light green card. The map cases likewise were published in the same type of bindings.

    Note that the publishers name was abrevated from the late volumes of theis series, eg. "Stadium Sajtóvállalat Részvénytarsasag" instead of "A Stadium Sajtóvállalat Részvénytarsasag Nyomasa".

A VILÁGHÁBORÚ 1914-1918. KŰLŐNŐS TEKINTETTEL MAGYARORSZÁGRA ÉS A MAGYAR CSAPATOK SZEREPLÉSÉRE SZERKESZTI ÉS KIADJA A M. KIR. HADTŐRTÉNELMI LEVÉLTÁR. I KŐTET. KŰLPOLITIKAI VISSZAPILLANTÁS. A VILÁGHÁBORÚ KITŐRÉSE. ESEMÉNYEK AZ OROSZ HARCTÉREN 1914. ÉVI AUGUSZTUS HÓ 20-IG. (*The World War 1914-1918. In Particular to the Role of Hungary and the Hungarian Army Volume I. Review of Foreign Policy. The Outbreak of the World War. The Events of the Russian Campaign up to 20th August 1914.*) [Map Case]

    Anonymous (Magyar Királyi Hadtőrténelmi Levéltár) | 24.8cm x 17.5cm | see note for A világháború 1914-1918. I Kőtet. | 6 large format maps | Stadium Sajtóvállalat Részvénytarsasag. | 1928 | Hungarian Text.

A VILÁGHÁBORÚ 1914-1918. KŰLŐNŐS TEKINTETTEL MAGYARORSZÁGRA ÉS A MAGYAR CSAPATOK SZEREPLÉSÉRE SZERKESZTI ÉS KIADJA A M. KIR. HADTŐRTÉNELMI LEVÉLTÁR. II KŐTET. AZ OROSZ HARCTÉREN LEFOLYT ESEMÉNYEK 1914 AUGUSZTUS 30-IG. (*The World War 1914-1918. In Particular to the Role of Hungary and the Hungarian Army. Volume II. The Conduct of the Russian campaign 30 August 1914.*)

    Anonymous (Kamil Aggházy and Valér Stefán [Magyar Királyi Hadtőrténelmi levéltár]). | 24.8cm x 17.5cm | see note for A világháború 1914-1918. I Kőtet. | Gilt | 562pp | 2 sketches | A Stadium Sajtóvállalat Részvénytarsasag Nyomasa. | 1930 | Hungarian Text.

A VILÁGHÁBORÚ 1914-1918. KŰLŐNŐS TEKINTETTEL MAGYARORSZÁGRA ÉS A MAGYAR CSAPATOK SZEREPLÉSÉRE SZERKESZTI ÉS KIADJA A M. KIR. HADTŐRTÉNELMI LEVÉLTÁR. II KŐTET. AZ OROSZ HARCTÉREN LEFOLYT ESEMÉNYEK 1914 AUGUSZTUS 30-IG. (*The World War 1914-1918. In Particular to the Role of Hungary and the Hungarian Army. Volume II. The Conduct of the Russian campaign 30 August 1914.*) [Map Case]

---

[33] This set "**A világháború 1914-1918**", similar to the German practice, had two title pages, however unlike the German volumes, the title pages were both on the first right hand pages (ie page 2 and page 4). The first title page had the set name "**A világháború 1914-1918**" and the second the volume title or description. In the earlier volumes an abridged set name also appeared on the second (volume) title page, but this practice was stopped after volume 5. The titles given above for this set are a combination of both title pages thereby giving the full title.

Anonymous (Magyar Királyi Hadtörténelmi Levéltár) | 24.8cm x 17.5cm | see note for A világháború 1914-1918. I Kőtet. | 19 large format maps | 45 sketch maps | A Stadium Sajtóvállalat Részvénytarsasag Nyomasa. | 1930 | Hungarian Text.

A VILÁGHÁBORÚ 1914-1918. KŰLŐNŐS TEKINTETTEL MAGYARORSZÁGRA ÉS A MAGYAR CSAPATOK SZEREPLÉSÉRE SZERKESZTI ÉS KIADJA A M. KIR. HADTŐRTÉNELMI LEVÉLTÁR. III KŐTET. AZ 1914. EVI GALÍCIAI BEVEZETŐ NYÁRI HADJÁRAT ESEMÉNYEK 1914 AUGUSSZTUS 31-ITŐL SZEPTEMBER 16-ÁIG. A KELETPOROSZORSZÁGI HADMŰVELETEK 1914 SZEPTEMBER. ÉLSŐ FELÉNEN ESEMÉNYEK A NYUGATI HADSZÍNTÉREN A HÁBORÚ KITŐRÉSÉTŐL 1914 SZEPTEMBER KŐZEPÉIG. (*The World War 1914-1918. In Particular to the Role of Hungary and the Hungarian Army. Volume III. The 1914 Preliminary Galician Military Summer Expedition 31 August – 16 September 1914. The Keletporoszországi Operations September 1914. Also on the Kitőrésétől Affair in the Occidental Theatre of War Middle September 1914.*)

Anonymous (Kamil Aggházy and Valér Stefán [Magyar Királyi Hadtörténelmi Levéltár]). | 24.8cm x 17.5cm | See note for A világháború 1914-1918. I Kőtet. | Gilt | 666pp | A Stadium Sajtóvállalat Részvénytarsasag Nyomasa. | 1933 | Hungarian Text.

This volume covers the opening campaigns of the great powers during the period of September 1914 (the Austrian-German-Russian-French fronts.)

A VILÁGHÁBORÚ 1914-1918. KŰLŐNŐS TEKINTETTEL MAGYARORSZÁGRA ÉS A MAGYAR CSAPATOK SZEREPLÉSÉRE SZERKESZTI ÉS KIADJA A M. KIR. HADTŐRTÉNELMI LEVÉLTÁR. AZ 1914. ÉVI GALÍCIAI BEVEZETŐ NYÁRI HADJÁRAT. ESEMÉNYEK 1914 AUGUSSZTUS 31-ITŐL SZEPTEMBER 16-ÁIG. A KELETPOROSZORSZÁGI HADMŰVELETEK 1914 SZEPTEMBER. ÉLSŐ FELÉNEN ESEMÉNYEK A NYUGATI HADSZÍNTÉREN A HÁBORÚ KITŐRÉSÉTŐL 1914 SZEPTEMBER KŐZEPÉIG. (*The World War 1914-1918. In Particular to the Role of Hungary and the Hungarian Army. Volume III. The 1914 Preliminary Galician Military Summer Expedition 31 August – 16 September 1914. The Keletporoszországi Operations September 1914. Also on the Kitőrésétől Affair in the Occidental Theatre of War Middle September 1914.*) [Map Case]

Anonymous (Magyar Királyi Hadtörténelmi Levéltár) | 24.8cm x 17.5cm | see note for A világháború 1914-1918. I Kőtet. | 8 large format maps | 45 sketch maps | A Stadium Sajtóvállalat Részvénytarsasag Nyomasa. | 1933 | Hungarian Text.

A VILÁGHÁBORÚ 1914-1918. KŰLŐNŐS TEKINTETTEL MAGYARORSZÁGRA ÉS A MAGYAR CSAPATOK SZEREPLÉSÉRE SZERKESZTI ÉS KIADJA A M. KIR. HADTŐRTÉNELMI LEVÉLTÁR. IV KŐTET. AZ OSZTRÁK-MAGYAR MONARCHIA 1914. ÉVI AUGUSZTUSI SZERBIA ÉS MONTENEGRÓ ELLENI HADJÁRATA. (*The World War 1914-1918. In Particular to the Role of Hungary and the Hungarian Army. Volume IV. The Serbian and Montenegrin Counter Campaign against the Austro-Hungarian Monarchy, August 1914.*)

Anonymous (Kamil Aggházy and Valér Stefán [Magyar Királyi Hadtörténelmi levéltár]). | 24.8cm x 17.5cm | See note for A világháború 1914-1918. I Kőtet. | Gilt | 413pp | A Stadium Sajtóvállalat Részvénytarsasag Nyomasa. | 1929 | Hungarian Text.

This volume covers the period of August 1914 relating to the Hungarian campaigns only.

A VILÁGHÁBORÚ 1914-1918. KŰLŐNŐS TEKINTETTEL MAGYARORSZÁGRA ÉS A MAGYAR CSAPATOK SZEREPLÉSÉRE SZERKESZTI ÉS KIADJA A M. KIR. HADTŐRTÉNELMI LEVÉLTÁR. IV KŐTET. AZ OSZTRÁK-MAGYAR MONARCHIA 1914. ÉVI AUGUSZTUSI SZERBIA ÉS MONTENEGRÓ ELLENI HADJÁRATA. (*The World War 1914-1918. In Particular to the Role of Hungary and the Hungarian Army. Volume IV. The Serbian and Montenegrin Counter Campaign against the Austro-Hungarian Monarchy, August 1914.*) [Map Case]

Anonymous (Magyar Királyi Hadtörténelmi Levéltár) | 24.8cm x 17.5cm | see note for A világháború 1914-1918. I Kőtet. | 6 large format maps | 4 sketch maps | 3 organisation charts | A Stadium Sajtóvállalat Részvénytarsasag Nyomasa. | 1929 | Hungarian Text.

A VILÁGHÁBORÚ 1914-1918. KŰLŐNŐS TEKINTETTEL MAGYARORSZÁGRA ÉS A MAGYAR CSAPATOK SZEREPLÉSÉRE SZERKESZTI ÉS KIADJA A M. KIR. HADTŐRTÉNELMI LEVÉLTÁR. V KŐTET. AZ OSZTRÁK-MAGYAR MONARCHIA 1914. ÉVI SZEPTEMBER-DECEMBERI SZERBIA ÉS MONTENEGRÓ ELLENI HADJÁRATA. (*The World War 1914-1918. In Particular to the Role of Hungary and the*

Hungarian Army. Volume V. The Serbian and Montenegrin Counter Campaign against the Austro-Hungarian Monarchy, September - December 1914.)

Anonymous (Kamil Aggházy and Valér Stefán [Magyar Királyi Hadtőrténelmi Levéltár]). | 24.8cm x 17.5cm | See note for A világháború 1914-1918. I Kőtet. | Gilt | 712pp | 4 appendices | A Stadium Sajtóvállalat Részvénytarsasag Nyomasa. | 1932 | Hungarian Text.

This volume covers the period of September 1914 relating to the Hungarian campaigns only.

A VILÁGHÁBORÚ 1914-1918. KŰLŐNŐS TEKINTETTEL MAGYARORSZÁGRA ÉS A MAGYAR CSAPATOK SZEREPLÉSÉRE SZERKESZTI ÉS KIADJA A M. KIR. HADTŐRTÉNELMI LEVÉLTÁR. V KŐTET. AZ OSZTRÁK-MAGYAR MONARCHIA 1914. ÉVI SZEPTEMBER-DECEMBERI SZERBIA ÉS MONTENEGRÓ ELLENI HADJÁRATA. (*The World War 1914-1918. In Particular to the Role of Hungary and the Hungarian Army. Volume V. The Serbian and Montenegrin Counter Campaign against the Austro-Hungarian Monarchy, September - December 1914.*) [Map Case]

Anonymous (Magyar Királyi Hadtőrténelmi Levéltár) | 24.8cm x 17.5cm | see note for A világháború 1914-1918. I Kőtet. | 9 large format maps | 64 sketch maps | 2 organisation charts | 4 orders of battle | A Stadium Sajtóvállalat Részvénytarsasag Nyomasa. | 1932 | Hungarian Text.

A VILÁGHÁBORÚ 1914-1918. KŰLŐNŐS TEKINTETTEL MAGYARORSZÁGRA ÉS A MAGYAR CSAPATOK SZEREPLÉSÉRE SZERKESZTI ÉS KIADJA A M. KIR. HADTŐRTÉNELMI LEVÉLTÁR. VI KŐTET. 1914. SZEPTEMBER MÁSODIK FELÉNEK ÉS OKTÓBER HAVÁNAK ESEMÉNYEI A KELETI (OROSZ) ÉS A NYUGATI (FRANCIA) HADSZÍNTÉREN. (*The World War 1914-1918. In Particular to the Role of Hungary and the Hungarian Army. Volume VI. The Pursuit against Us in September 1914 and the October's Events on the Oriental (Russian) and the Occidental (French) Fronts.*)

Anonymous (Kamil Aggházy and Valér Stefán [Magyar Királyi Hadtőrténelmi Levéltár]). | 24.8cm x 17.5cm | See note for A világháború 1914-1918. I Kőtet. | Gilt | 453pp | A Stadium Sajtóvállalat Részvénytarsasag Nyomasa. | 1934 | Hungarian Text.

This volume covers the period of October 1914 relating to the Hungarian campaigns only.

A VILÁGHÁBORÚ 1914-1918. KŰLŐNŐS TEKINTETTEL MAGYARORSZÁGRA ÉS A MAGYAR CSAPATOK SZEREPLÉSÉRE SZERKESZTI ÉS KIADJA A M. KIR. HADTŐRTÉNELMI LEVÉLTÁR. VI KŐTET. 1914. SZEPTEMBER MÁSODIK FELÉNEK ÉS OKTÓBER HAVÁNAK ESEMÉNYEI A KELETI (OROSZ) ÉS A NYUGATI (FRANCIA) HADSZÍNTÉREN. (*The World War 1914-1918. In Particular to the Role of Hungary and the Hungarian Army. Volume VI. The Pursuit against Us in September 1914 and the October's Events on the Oriental (Russian) and the Occidental (French) Fronts.*) [Map Case]

Anonymous (Magyar Királyi Hadtőrténelmi Levéltár) | 24.8cm x 17.5cm | see note for A világháború 1914-1918. I Kőtet. | 16 large format maps | 1 sketch map on a small sheet | 20 sketch maps on 6 large sheets | 3 organisation charts | 4 orders of battle | A Stadium Sajtóvállalat Részvénytarsasag Nyomasa. | 1934 | Hungarian Text.

A VILÁGHÁBORÚ 1914-1918. KŰLŐNŐS TEKINTETTEL MAGYARORSZÁGRA ÉS A MAGYAR CSAPATOK SZEREPLÉSÉRE SZERKESZTI ÉS KIADJA A M. KIR. HADTŐRTÉNELMI LEVÉLTÁR. VII KŐTET. 1914. NOVEMBER ÉS DECEMBER HAVÁNAK ESEMÉNYEI. (*The World War 1914-1918. In Particular to the Role of Hungary and the Hungarian Army. Volume VII. November and December's Havának Affairs in 1914.*)

Anonymous (Kamil Aggházy and Valér Stefán [Magyar Királyi Hadtőrténelmi Levéltár]). | 24.8cm x 17.5cm | See note for A világháború 1914-1918. I Kőtet. | Gilt | 700pp | 4 tables | A Stadium Sajtóvállalat Részvénytarsasag Nyomasa. | 1937 | Hungarian Text.

This volume covers the period October-November 1914 relating to the Hungarian campaigns only.

A VILÁGHÁBORÚ 1914-1918. KŰLŐNŐS TEKINTETTEL MAGYARORSZÁGRA ÉS A MAGYAR CSAPATOK SZEREPLÉSÉRE SZERKESZTI ÉS KIADJA A M. KIR. HADTŐRTÉNELMI LEVÉLTÁR. VII KŐTET. 1914. NOVEMBER ÉS DECEMBER HAVÁNAK ESEMÉNYEI. (*The World War 1914-1918. In Particular to the Role of Hungary and the Hungarian Army. Volume VII. November and December's Havának Affairs in 1914.*) [Map Case]

Anonymous (Magyar Királyi Hadtőrténelmi Levéltár) | 24.8cm x 17.5cm | see note for A világháború 1914-1918. I Kőtet. | 29 large format maps | 1 time line table | 1 order of battle | A Stadium Sajtóvállalat Részvénytarsasag Nyomasa. | 1937 | Hungarian Text.

A VILÁGHÁBORÚ 1914-1918. KŰLŐNŐS TEKINTETTEL MAGYARORSZÁGRA ÉS A MAGYAR CSAPATOK SZEREPLÉSÉRE SZERKESZTI ÉS KIADJA A M. KIR. HADTŐRTÉNELMI LEVÉLTÁR. VIII KŐTET. 1915. ELSŐ NÉGY HAVÁNAK ESEMÉNYEI. (*The World War 1914-1918. In Particular to the Role of Hungary and the Hungarian Army. Volume VIII. First Four Havának Affairs in 1915.*)

Anonymous (Kamil Aggházy and Valér Stefán [Magyar Királyi Hadtőrténelmi Levéltár]). | 24.8cm x 17.5cm | See note for A világháború 1914-1918. I Kőtet. | Gilt | 919pp | A Stadium Sajtóvállalat Részvénytarsasag Nyomasa. | 1939 | Hungarian Text.

This volume covers the period April 1915 relating to the Hungarian campaigns only.

A VILÁGHÁBORÚ 1914-1918. KŰLŐNŐS TEKINTETTEL MAGYARORSZÁGRA ÉS A MAGYAR CSAPATOK SZEREPLÉSÉRE SZERKESZTI ÉS KIADJA A M. KIR. HADTŐRTÉNELMI LEVÉLTÁR. VIII KŐTET. 1915. ELSŐ NÉGY HAVÁNAK ESEMÉNYEI. (*The World War 1914-1918. In Particular to the Role of Hungary and the Hungarian Army. Volume VIII. First Four Havának Affairs in 1915.*) [Map Case]

Anonymous (Magyar Királyi Hadtőrténelmi Levéltár) | 24.8cm x 17.5cm | see note for A világháború 1914-1918. I Kőtet. | 26 large format maps | 1 order of battle | A Stadium Sajtóvállalat Részvénytarsasag Nyomasa. | 1939 | Hungarian Text.

A VILÁGHÁBORÚ 1914-1918. KŰLŐNŐS TEKINTETTEL MAGYARORSZÁGRA ÉS A MAGYAR CSAPATOK SZEREPLÉSÉRE SZERKESZTI ÉS KIADJA A M. KIR. HADTŐRTÉNELMI LEVÉLTÁR. IX KŐTET. 1915. MÁJUS ÉS JÚNIUS HAVÁNAK ESEMÉNYEI. (*The World War 1914-1918. In Particular to the Role of Hungary and the Hungarian Army. Volume IX. May and June Havának Affairs in 1915.*)

Anonymous (Kamil Aggházy and Valér Stefán [Magyar Királyi Hadtőrténelmi Levéltár]). | 24.8cm x 17.5cm | See note for A világháború 1914-1918. I Kőtet. | Gilt | 825pp | A Stadium Sajtóvállalat Részvénytarsasag Nyomasa. | 1940 | Hungarian Text.

This volume covers the period May-July 1915 relating to the Hungarian campaigns only.

A VILÁGHÁBORÚ 1914-1918. KŰLŐNŐS TEKINTETTEL MAGYARORSZÁGRA ÉS A MAGYAR CSAPATOK SZEREPLÉSÉRE SZERKESZTI ÉS KIADJA A M. KIR. HADTŐRTÉNELMI LEVÉLTÁR. IX KŐTET. 1915. MÁJUS ÉS JÚNIUS HAVÁNAK ESEMÉNYEI. (*The World War 1914-1918. In Particular to the Role of Hungary and the Hungarian Army. Volume IX. May and June Havának Affairs in 1915.*) [Map Case]

Anonymous (Magyar Királyi Hadtőrténelmi Levéltár) | 24.8cm x 17.5cm | see note for A világháború 1914-1918. I Kőtet. | 75 large format maps | A Stadium Sajtóvállalat Részvénytarsasag Nyomasa. | 1940 | Hungarian Text.

A VILÁGHÁBORÚ 1914-1918. KŰLŐNŐS TEKINTETTEL MAGYARORSZÁGRA ÉS A MAGYAR CSAPATOK SZEREPLÉSÉRE SZERKESZTI ÉS KIADJA A M. KIR. HADTŐRTÉNELMI LEVÉLTÁR. X KŐTET. AZ 1915. ÉVI NYÁRI ESEMÉNYEK. (*The World War 1914-1918. In Particular to the Role of Hungary and the Hungarian Army. Volume X. The 1915 Summer Affairs.*)

Anonymous (Kamil Aggházy and Valér Stefán [Magyar Királyi Hadtőrténelmi Levéltár]). | 24.8cm x 17.5cm | See note for A világháború 1914-1918. I Kőtet. | Gilt | 949pp | A Stadium Sajtóvállalat Részvénytarsasag Nyomasa. | 1942 | Hungarian Text.

This volume covers the period July-August 1915 relating to the Hungarian campaigns only.

A VILÁGHÁBORÚ 1914-1918. KŰLŐNŐS TEKINTETTEL MAGYARORSZÁGRA ÉS A MAGYAR CSAPATOK SZEREPLÉSÉRE SZERKESZTI ÉS KIADJA A M. KIR. HADTŐRTÉNELMI LEVÉLTÁR. X KŐTET. AZ 1915. ÉVI NYÁRI ESEMÉNYEK. (*The World War 1914-1918. In Particular to the Role of Hungary and the Hungarian Army. Volume X. The 1915 Summer Affairs.*) [Map Case]

Anonymous (Magyar Királyi Hadtőrténelmi Levéltár) | 24.8cm x 17.5cm | see note for A világháború 1914-1918. I Kőtet. | 57 large format maps | A Stadium Sajtóvállalat Részvénytarsasag Nyomasa. | 1942 | Hungarian Text.

Italian Official Histories

The primary Italian official histories written before the end of the Second World War were by the members of the historical departments of the then two armed services. For the navy this was done by the Ufficio Storico della Regia Marina (*[Italian] Royal Navy Historical Office*), and for the army, the Ministero della Guerra, Maggiore Esercito: Ufficio Storico (*Ministry of War, Army Staff's Historical Office*). Since an independent Italian Air Force did not exist before the end of the Second World War the histories of the naval and military air services during this period were written by the respective service historical departments.

Since the Second World War and with the formation of the Italian Republic, the Italian armed services have been combined into the Ministro della Difesa (*[Italian] Ministry of Defence*), which included their historical departments along with their archives. The historical departments have been renamed the Ufficio Storico della Marina Militare (*Navy Military Historical Office*), and the Ufficio Storico Stato Maggiore dell'Esercito (*Army General Staff's Historical Office*) respectivily. With the Italian Navy and Army under the one government department, the Italian Air Force has become an independent service and as such now has its own historical department and archives – it being the Ufficio Storico Stato Maggiore dell'Aeronautica (*Air Force General Staff's Historical Office*).

All of the Italian historical offices are still very active producing various histories covering different periods and including secondary histories covering aspects of the Great War.

Pre War Military Planning;

STATO MAGGIORE DELL'ESERCITO - UFFICIO STORICO - L'ITALIA NELLA TRIPLICE ALLEANZA. I PIANI OPERATIVE DEL STATO MAGGIORE VERSO L'AUSTRIA-UNGHERIA DAL 1885 AL 1915. (*The Army's General Staff - Historical Office – Italy in the Triple Alliance. The Operation Plans of the General Staff against Austria-Hungary from 1885 to 1915.*)
> Maurizio Ruffo | 24cm x 17.5cm | white paper covered hardback | 311pp | 33 colour photographs | 22 black and white photographs | 13 images | Ministero della Guerra. | 1998 | Italian Text.

Naval Operations;

UFFICIO STORICO DELLA REGIA MARINA - LA MARINA ITALIANA NELLA GRANDE GUERRA VOLUME I VIGILIA D'ARMI SUL MARE. (*The Royal Navy's Historical Office – The Italian Navy in the Great War Volume I On the Eve of the War at Sea.*)
> G. [Guido] Almagià and A. Zoli | 20cm x 14cm | Light Grey Paper Softback | 469pp | 2 appendices | Vallecchi Editore. | 1935 | Italian Text.

UFFICIO STORICO DELLA REGIA MARINA - LA MARINA ITALIANA NELLA GRANDE GUERRA VOLUME II L'ITERVENTO DELL'ITALIA A FIANCO DELL'INTESA E LA LOTTA IN ADRIATICO. (*The Royal Navy's Historical Office – The Italian Navy in the Great War Volume II The Intervention of Italy on the Side of The Allies and the Struggle in the Adriatic.*)
> F. [Fausto] Leva | 20cm x 14cm | Light Grey Paper Softback | 631pp | 9 appendices | 4 diagrams | Vallecchi Editore. | 1936 | Italian Text.

UFFICIO STORICO DELLA REGIA MARINA - LA MARINA ITALIANA NELLA GRANDE GUERRA VOLUME III SVILUPPI DELLA GUERRA ADRIATICO DAL SALVATAGGIO DELL'ESERCITO SERBO SINO ALLA FINE DELL'ANNO 1916. (*The Royal Navy's Historical Office – The Italian Navy in the Great War Volume III The Adriatic War from the Rescue Of The Serbian Armed Forces until the End of the Year 1916.*)
> L. [Luigi] Castagna | 20cm x 14cm | Light Grey Paper Softback | 550pp | Vallecchi Editore. | 1938 | Italian Text.

UFFICIO STORICO DELLA REGIA MARINA - LA MARINA ITALIANA NELLA GRANDE GUERRA VOLUME IV LA GUERRA AL TRAFFICO MARITTIMO LE OPERAZIONI IN ADRIATICO FINO ALLA BATTAGLIA NAVALE DEL 15 MAGGIO 1917. (*The Royal Navy's Historical Office – The Italian Navy in the Great War Volume IV The War against Maritime Traffic and the Operations in the Adriatic until the Naval Battle of May 15 1917.*)
> L. [Luigi] Castagna | 20cm x 14cm | Light Grey Paper Softback | 605pp | 3 appendices | Vallecchi Editore. | 1938 | Italian Text.

UFFICIO STORICO DELLA REGIA MARINA - LA MARINA ITALIANA NELLA GRANDE GUERRA VOLUME V LA LOTTA CONTRO IL SOMMERGIBILE - MAGGIO-OTTOBRE 1917. (*The Royal Navy's Historical Office – The Italian Navy in the Great War Volume V The Struggle Against the Submarine - May-October 1917.*)

S. [Silvio] Salza | 20cm x 14cm | Light Grey Paper Softback | 493pp | 1 diagram | Vallecchi Editore. | 1939 | Italian Text.

UFFICIO STORICO DELLA REGIA MARINA - LA MARINA ITALIANA NELLA GRANDE GUERRA VOLUME VI LA LOTTA CONTRO IL SOMMERGIBILE - OTTOBRE 1917-GENNAIO 1918. (*The Royal Navy's Historical Office – The Italian Navy in the Great War Volume VI The Struggle Against the Submarine - October 1917- January 1918.*)

S. [Silvio] Salza | 20cm x 14cm | Light Grey Paper Softback | 581pp | 3 diagrams | Vallecchi Editore. | 1939 | Italian Text.

UFFICIO STORICO DELLA REGIA MARINA - LA MARINA ITALIANA NELLA GRANDE GUERRA VOLUME VII VERSO LA VITTORIA CONTRO IL SOMMERGIBILE - GENNAIO-LUGLIO 1918. (*The Royal Navy's Historical Office – The Italian Navy in the Great War Volume VII Towards the Victory Against The Submarine - January-July 1918.*)

S. [Silvio] Salza | 20cm x 14cm | Light Grey Paper Softback | 809pp | 2 maps | 4 diagrams | Vallecchi Editore. | 1940 | Italian Text.

UFFICIO STORICO DELLA REGIA MARINA - LA MARINA ITALIANA NELLA GRANDE GUERRA VOLUME VIII LA VITTORIA MUTILATA IN ADRIATICO. (*The Royal Navy's Historical Office – The Italian Navy in the Great War Volume VIII The Mutilated Victory in the Adriatic.*)

S. [Silvio] Salza | 20cm x 14cm | Light Grey Paper Softback | 846pp | 3 appendices | 3 maps | 7 diagrams| Vallecchi Editore. | 1942 | Italian Text.

Blockade Activities;

UFFICIO DEL CAPO DI STATO MAGGIORE DELLA R. MARINA, UFFICIO STORICO: CRONISTORIA DELLA GUERRA MARITTIMA - GLI AVVENIMENTI DELLA GUERRA NEI RIFLESSI DELLA LEGISLAZIONE MARITTIMA VOLUME 1° - PERIODO DELLA NEUTRALITA AGOSTO 1914-MAGGIO 1915. (*Office of the Chief of the General Staff of the Royal Nav, Historical Office: Naval War Chronicle - The Events of the War in Light of Marine Legislation Volume 1 - The Neutrality Period August 1914 -May 1915.*)

Generale/Professore G. [Gennaro] Laghezza (Regia Marina) | 28.8cm x 20cm | Brown Paper Softback | vii + 216pp | 5 photographs | 4 charts | 4 diagrams | 2 tables | Tip. dell'Ufficio del Capo di Stato Maggiore della Regia Marina. | 1930 | Italian Text.

UFFICIO DEL CAPO DI STATO MAGGIORE DELLA R. MARINA, UFFICIO STORICO. CRONISTORIA DELLA GUERRA MARITTIMA - GLI AVVENIMENTI DELLA GUERRA NEI RIFLESSI DELLA LEGISLAZIONE MARITTIMA VOLUME 2° PERIODO DAL 24 MAGGIO 1915 AL 31 DICEMBRE 1915. (*Office of the Chief of the General Staff of the Royal Navy, Historical Office: Naval War Chronicle - The Events of the War in Light of Marine Legislation Volume 2 – The Period of 24 May to 31 December 1915.*)

Generale/Professore G. [Gennaro] Laghezza (Regia Marina) | 28.8cm x 20cm | Brown Paper Softback | ?pp | ? | Tip. dell'Ufficio del Capo di Stato Maggiore della Regia Marina. | 1935 | Italian Text.

Naval Statistics;

UFFICIO DEL CAPO DI STATO MAGGIORE DELLA R. MARINA, UFFICIO STORICO. LA MARINA ITALIANA NELLA GUERRA MONDIALE 1915-18. DATI STATISTICIE SINTESI. (*Office of the Chief of the General Staff of the Royal [Italian] Navy, Historical Office: The Italian Navy in the World War, 1915-18 Statistical Data and Systhesis.*)

Anonymous (Ministero della Marina - Ufficio Storico) | 30cm x 21cm | Light Brown Hardback | 70pp | 3 appendices | 6 charts | 45 tables | 30 photographs | 12 graphs | Vallecchi Editore. | 1926 | Italian Text.

This volume was translated into English and published in 1927 under the title "**Office of the Cheif of the Royal Italian Navy. Historical Section. The Italian Navy in the World War, 1915-18. Facts and Figures.**"

Military Operations;

MAGGIORE ESERCITO: UFFICIO STORICO – L'ESERCITO ITALIANO NELLA GRANDE GUERRA 1915-18 VOLUME I LE FORZE BELLIGERANTI – NARRAZIONE. (*The General Army's Historical Office - The Italian Army in the Great War 1915-1918 Volume I Introduction – Narration.*)
    Anonymous (Ministero della Guerra, Comando del Corpo di Stato Maggiore, Ufficio Storico) | 24cm x 17.5cm | light blue paper covered hardback with cloth hinges with cloth hinges | xxiv + 317pp | 14 maps | 1 photograph | Istituto Poligrafico Dello Stato. | 1927 | Italian Text.
    This volume was revised and republished in 1974.

MAGGIORE ESERCITO: UFFICIO STORICO – L'ESERCITO ITALIANO NELLA GRANDE GUERRA 1915-18 VOLUME I BIS LE FORZE BELLIGERANTI - ALLEGATI. (*The General Army's Historical Office - The Italian Army in the Great War 1915-1918 Volume I Second Part Introduction - Appendices*)
    Anonymous (Ministero della Guerra, Comando del Corpo di Stato Maggiore, Ufficio Storico) | 24cm x 17.5cm | light blue paper covered hardback | 120pp | 71 appendices in 75 parts | Istituto Poligrafico Dello Stato. | 1927 | Italian Text.
    This volume was revised and republished in 1974.

MAGGIORE ESERCITO: UFFICIO STORICO – L'ESERCITO ITALIANO NELLA GRANDE GUERRA 1915-18 VOLUME II LE OPERAZIONI DEL 1915 – NARRAZIONE. (*The General Army's Historical Office - The Italian Army in the Great War 1915-1918 Volume II Operations in 1915 – Narration.*)
    Anonymous (Ministero della Guerra, Comando del Corpo di Stato Maggiore, Ufficio Storico) | 24cm x 17.5cm | light blue paper covered hardback with cloth hinges | xxiv + 614pp | 12 maps | Istituto Poligrafico Dello Stato. | 1929 | Italian Text.
    This volume covers the Italian front and includes the First, Second, Thrid and Fourth Battles of the Isonzo.

MAGGIORE ESERCITO: UFFICIO STORICO – L'ESERCITO ITALIANO NELLA GRANDE GUERRA 1915-18 VOLUME II BIS LE OPERAZIONI DEL 1915 – DOCUMENTI. (*The General Army's Historical Office - The Italian Army in the Great War 1915-1918 Volume II Second Part Operations in 1915 - Documents.*)
    Anonymous (Ministero della Guerra, Comando del Corpo di Stato Maggiore, Ufficio Storico) | 24cm x 17.5cm | light blue paper covered hardback with cloth hinges | xxxii + 503pp | Istituto Poligrafico Dello Stato. | 1929 | Italian Text.

MAGGIORE ESERCITO: UFFICIO STORICO – L'ESERCITO ITALIANO NELLA GRANDE GUERRA 1915-18 VOLUME II TER LE OPERAZIONI DEL 1915 - TAVOLE, CARTE, PANORAMI E SCHIZZI. (*The General Army's Historical Office - The Italian Army in the Great War 1915-1918 Volume II Thrid Part Operations in 1915 - Tables, Maps, Panoramas and Sketches.*)
    Anonymous (Ministero della Guerra, Comando del Corpo di Stato Maggiore, Ufficio Storico) | 24cm x 17.5cm | light blue paper covered hardback with cloth hinges | c39 maps and photographs | Istituto Poligrafico Dello Stato. | 1929 | Italian Text.

MAGGIORE ESERCITO: UFFICIO STORICO – L'ESERCITO ITALIANO NELLA GRANDE GUERRA 1915-18 VOLUME III TOMO 1 LE OPERAZIONI DEL 1916 - GLI AVVENIMENTI – NARRAZIONE. (*The General Army's Historical Office - The Italian Army in the Great War 1915-1918 Volume III Book 1 Operations in 1916 The Events – Narration.*)
    Anonymous (Ministero della Guerra, Comando del Corpo di Stato Maggiore, Ufficio Storico) | 24cm x 17.5cm | light blue paper covered hardback with cloth hinges | xxiii + 432pp | 30 maps (18 coloured) | 12 large format coloured maps | 3 tables | Istituto Poligrafico Dello Stato. | 1931 | Italian Text.
    The large format maps are carried in a folder attached to the inside rear cover.
    This volume covers the Italian front during the period January to April 1916 and includes the Fifth Battle of the Isonzo. Unlike the later volumes of this series which include the period covered within the title, this one does not; however its title is often referred to as "**L'esercito Italiano nella Grande Guerra 1915-18 Volume III Tomo 1 Le Operazioni del 1916 - Gli Avvenimenti dal Gennaio al Aprile.**" (*The Italian Army in the Great War 1915-1918 Volume III Book 1 Operations in 1916 The Events from January to April.*)

MAGGIORE ESERCITO: UFFICIO STORICO – L'ESERCITO ITALIANO NELLA GRANDE GUERRA 1915-18 VOLUME III TOMO 1 BIS LE OPERAZIONI DEL 1916 - GLI

AVVENIMENTI– DOCUMENTI. (*The General Army's Historical Office - The Italian Army in the Great War 1915-1918 Volume III Book 1 Second Part Operations in 1916 - The Events - Documents.*)

Anonymous (Ministero della Marina - Ufficio Storico) | 24cm x 17.5cm | light blue paper covered hardback with cloth hinges | xx + 455pp | Istituto Poligrafico Dello Stato. | 1931 | Italian Text.

MAGGIORE ESERCITO: UFFICIO STORICO – L'ESERCITO ITALIANO NELLA GRANDE GUERRA 1915-18 VOLUME III TOMO 2 LE OPERAZIONI DEL 1916 - GLI AVVENIMENTI DAL MAGGIO AL LUGLIO – NARRAZIONE. (*The General Army's Historical Office - The Italian Army in the Great War 1915-1918 Volume III Book 2 Operations in 1916 - The Events from May to July– Narration.*)

Anonymous (Ministero della Guerra, Comando del Corpo di Stato Maggiore, Ufficio Storico) | 24cm x 17.5cm | light blue paper covered hardback with cloth hinges | xvi + 334pp | Istituto Poligrafico Dello Stato. | 1936 | Italian Text.

This volume covers the Italian front and includes the Austrian Trentino Offensive, the Italian local attacks on the Trentino Front and the Italian Trentino Counter-Offensive.

MAGGIORE ESERCITO: UFFICIO STORICO – L'ESERCITO ITALIANO NELLA GRANDE GUERRA 1915-18 VOLUME III TOMO 2 BIS OPERAZIONI DEL 1916 - GLI AVVENIMENTI DAL MAGGIO AL LUGLIO – DOCUMENTI. (*The General Army's Historical Office - The Italian Army in the Great War 1915-1918 Volume III Book 2 Second Part Operations in 1916 - The Events from May to July - Documents.*)

Anonymous (Ministero della Guerra, Comando del Corpo di Stato Maggiore, Ufficio Storico) | 24cm x 17.5cm | light blue paper covered hardback with cloth hinges | xii + 217pp | 115 appendices | 1 map | 44 tables | Istituto Poligrafico Dello Stato. | 1936 | Italian Text.

MAGGIORE ESERCITO: UFFICIO STORICO – L'ESERCITO ITALIANO NELLA GRANDE GUERRA 1915-18 VOLUME III TOMO 2 TER OPERAZIONI DEL 1916 - GLI AVVENIMENTI DAL MAGGIO AL LUGLIO - TAVOLE, CARTE, PANORAMI E SCHIZZI. (*The General Army's Historical Office - The Italian Army in the Great War 1915-1918 Volume III Book 2 Thrid Part Operations in 1916 - The Events from May to July - Tables, Maps, Panoramas and Sketches.*)

Anonymous (Ministero della Guerra, Comando del Corpo di Stato Maggiore, Ufficio Storico) | 24cm x 17.5cm | light blue paper covered hardback with cloth hinges | 51 maps | 7 panorama photographs | Istituto Poligrafico Dello Stato. | 1936 | Italian Text.

MAGGIORE ESERCITO: UFFICIO STORICO – L'ESERCITO ITALIANO NELLA GRANDE GUERRA 1915-18 VOLUME III TOMO 3 LE OPERAZIONI DEL 1916 - GLI AVVENIMENTI DAL AGUSTO AL DICEMBRE – NARRAZIONE. (*The General Army's Historical Office - The Italian Army in the Great War 1915-1918 Volume III Book 3 Operations in 1916 – The Events from August to December – Narration.*)

Anonymous (Ministero della Guerra, Comando del Corpo di Stato Maggiore, Ufficio Storico) | 24cm x 17.5cm | light blue paper covered hardback with cloth hinges | xv + 318pp | 1 appendix | Istituto Poligrafico Dello Stato. | 1937 | Italian Text.

This volume covers the Italian front and includes the Sixth, Seventh, Eighth and Ninth Battle of the Isonzo.

MAGGIORE ESERCITO: UFFICIO STORICO – L'ESERCITO ITALIANO NELLA GRANDE GUERRA 1915-18 VOLUME III TOMO 3 BIS – DOCUMENTI. (*The General Army's Historical Office - The Italian Army in the Great War 1915-1918 Volume III Book 3 Second Part Operations in 1916 – The Events from August to December - Documents.*)

Anonymous (Ministero della Guerra, Comando del Corpo di Stato Maggiore, Ufficio Storico) | 24cm x 17.5cm | light blue paper covered hardback with cloth hinges | xv + 471pp | 249 appendices | 2 diagrams | Istituto Poligrafico Dello Stato. | 1937 | Italian Text.

MAGGIORE ESERCITO: UFFICIO STORICO – L'ESERCITO ITALIANO NELLA GRANDE GUERRA 1915-18 VOLUME III TOMO 3 TER - TAVOLE, CARTE, PANORAMI E SCHIZZI. (*The General Army's Historical Office - The Italian Army in the Great War 1915-1918 Volume III Book 3 Thrid Part Operations in 1916 – The Events from August to December - Tables, Maps, Panoramas and Sketches.*)

Anonymous (Ministero della Guerra, Comando del Corpo di Stato Maggiore, Ufficio Storico) | 24cm x 17.5cm | light blue paper covered hardback with cloth hinges | 42 maps | 7 panorama photographs | 7 diagrams | Istituto Poligrafico Dello Stato. | 1937 | Italian Text.

MAGGIORE ESERCITO: UFFICIO STORICO – L'ESERCITO ITALIANO NELLA GRANDE GUERRA 1915-18 VOLUME IV TOMO 1 LE OPERAZIONI DEL 1917 - GLI AVVENIMENTI DAL GENNAIO AL LUGLIO – NARRAZIONE. (*The General Army's Historical Office - The Italian Army in the Great War 1915-1918 Volume IV Book 1 Operations in 1917 –The Events from January to May – Narration.*)

Anonymous (Ministero della Guerra, Comando del Corpo di Stato Maggiore, Ufficio Storico) l 24cm x 17.5cm l light blue paper covered hardback with cloth hinges l xxviii + 324pp l 22 diagrams l Istituto Poligrafico Dello Stato. l 1940 l Italian Text.
This volume covers the Italian front and includes the Tenth Battle of the Isonzo.

MAGGIORE ESERCITO: UFFICIO STORICO – L'ESERCITO ITALIANO NELLA GRANDE GUERRA 1915-18 VOLUME IV TOMO 2 BIS – DOCUMENTI. (*The General Army's Historical Office - The Italian Army in the Great War 1915-1918 Volume IV Book 1 Second Part Operations in 1917 –The Events from January to May - Documents.*)

Anonymous (Ministero della Guerra, Comando del Corpo di Stato Maggiore, Ufficio Storico) l 24cm x 17.5cm l light blue paper covered hardback with cloth hinges l xx + 685pp l 344 appendices l Istituto Poligrafico Dello Stato. l 1940 l Italian Text.

MAGGIORE ESERCITO: UFFICIO STORICO – L'ESERCITO ITALIANO NELLA GRANDE GUERRA 1915-18 VOLUME IV TOMO 1 TER - TAVOLE, CARTE, PANORAMI E SCHIZZI. (*The General Army's Historical Office - The Italian Army in the Great War 1915-1918 Volume IV Book 1 Thrid Part Operations in 1917 –The Events from January to May - Tables, Maps, Panoramas and Sketches.*)

Anonymous (Ministero della Guerra, Comando del Corpo di Stato Maggiore, Ufficio Storico) l 24cm x 17.5cm l light blue paper covered hardback with cloth hinges l 18 maps l 5 panorama photographs l 17 diagrams l Istituto Poligrafico Dello Stato. l 1940 l Italian Text.

MAGGIORE ESERCITO: UFFICIO STORICO – L'ESERCITO ITALIANO NELLA GRANDE GUERRA 1915-18 VOLUME IV TOMO 2 LE OPERAZIONI DEL 1917 - GLI AVVENIMENTI DAL GIUGNO AL SETTEMBRE – NARRAZIONE. (*The General Army's Historical Office - The Italian Army in the Great War 1915-1918 Volume IV Book 2 Operations in 1917 – The Events from June to September – Narration.*)

Anonymous (Ministero della Difesa, Stato Maggiore dell'Esercito, Ufficio Storico) l 24cm x 17.5cm l light blue paper covered hardback with cloth hinges l xx + 460pp l 44 maps l Istituto Poligrafico Dello Stato. l 1954 l Italian Text.
This volume covers the Italian front covering the Eleventh Battle of the Isonzo.

MAGGIORE ESERCITO: UFFICIO STORICO – L'ESERCITO ITALIANO NELLA GRANDE GUERRA 1915-18 VOLUME IV TOMO 2 BIS – DOCUMENTI. (*The General Army's Historical Office - The Italian Army in the Great War 1915-1918 Volume IV Book 2 Second Part Operations in 1917 – The Events from June to September - Documents.*)

Anonymous (Ministero della Difesa, Stato Maggiore dell'Esercito, Ufficio Storico) l 24cm x 17.5cm l light blue paper covered hardback with cloth hinges l xxviii + 855pp l 366 appendices l 12 diagrams l Istituto Poligrafico Dello Stato. l 1954 l Italian Text.

MAGGIORE ESERCITO: UFFICIO STORICO – L'ESERCITO ITALIANO NELLA GRANDE GUERRA 1915-18 VOLUME IV TOMO 2 TER - TAVOLE, CARTE, PANORAMI E SCHIZZI. (*The General Army's Historical Office - The Italian Army in the Great War 1915-1918 Volume IV Book 2 Thrid Part Operations in 1917 – The Events from June to September - Tables, Maps, Panoramas and Sketches.*)

Anonymous (Ministero della Difesa, Stato Maggiore dell'Esercito, Ufficio Storico) l 24cm x 17.5cm l light blue paper covered hardback with cloth hinges l 24 maps l 13 panorama photographs l Istituto Poligrafico Dello Stato. l 1954 l Italian Text.

MAGGIORE ESERCITO: UFFICIO STORICO – L'ESERCITO ITALIANO NELLA GRANDE GUERRA 1915-18 VOLUME IV TOMO 3 LE OPERAZIONI DEL 1917 - GLI AVVENIMENTI DAL OTTOBRE AL DICEMBRE – NARRAZIONE. (*The General Army's Historical Office - The Italian Army in the Great War 1915-1918 Volume IV Book 3 Operations in 1917 –The Events from October to December – Narration.*)

Anonymous (Ministero della Difesa, Stato Maggiore dell'Esercito, Ufficio Storico) l 24cm x 17.5cm l see note below l 748pp l 15 appendices l 12 maps l 1 photograph l Istituto Poligrafico Dello Stato. l 1967 l Italian Text.
This volume was issued with the standard light blue paper covered hardback with cloth hinges covers. A special deluxe edition was also published with a binding of royal blue leatherette with silver titles. Although the date of this edition (1967) was the fiftieth anniversary of the Battle of Caporetto, there was no connection, since other non Great War volumes were treated similary by the Ufficio Storico.

This volume covers the Italian front and includes the Austro-German Offensive in the Julian Alps - the Twelfth Battle of the Isonzo (The Battle of Caporetto).

MAGGIORE ESERCITO: UFFICIO STORICO – L'ESERCITO ITALIANO NELLA GRANDE GUERRA 1915-18 VOLUME IV TOMO 3 BIS – DOCUMENTI. (*The General Army's Historical Office - The Italian Army in the Great War 1915-1918 Volume IV Book 3 Second Part Operations in 1917 –The Events from October to December - Documents.*)

Anonymous (Ministero della Difesa, Stato Maggiore dell'Esercito, Ufficio Storico) l 24cm x 17.5cm l see note above l xvii + 501pp l 248 appendices l 12 diagrams l Istituto Poligrafico Dello Stato. l 1967 l Italian Text.

MAGGIORE ESERCITO: UFFICIO STORICO – L'ESERCITO ITALIANO NELLA GRANDE GUERRA 1915-18 VOLUME IV TOMO 3 TER - TAVOLE, CARTE, PANORAMI E SCHIZZI. (*The General Army's Historical Office - The Italian Army in the Great War 1915-1918 Volume IV Book 3 Thrid Part Operations in 1917 –The Events from October to December - Tables, Maps, Panoramas and Sketches.*)

Anonymous (Ministero della Difesa, Stato Maggiore dell'Esercito, Ufficio Storico) l 24cm x 17.5cm l see note above l 21 maps l 11 panorama photographs l Istituto Poligrafico Dello Stato. l 1967 l Italian Text.

MAGGIORE ESERCITO: UFFICIO STORICO – L'ESERCITO ITALIANO NELLA GRANDE GUERRA 1915-18 VOLUME V TOMO 1 LE OPERAZIONI DEL 1918 - GLI AVVENIMENTI DAL GENNAIO AL MAGGIO – NARRAZIONE. (*The General Army's Historical Office - The Italian Army in the Great War 1915-1918 Volume V Book 1 Operations in 1918 – The Events from January to June – Narration.*)

Anonymous (Ministero della Difesa, Stato Maggiore dell'Esercito, Ufficio Storico) l 24cm x 17.5cm l light blue paper covered hardback with cloth hinges l 793pp l 3 diagrams l Istituto Poligrafico Dello Stato. l 1980 l Italian Text.

This volume covers the Italian front and includes the Austrian Summer Offensive, 1918 - the Battle of the Piave.

MAGGIORE ESERCITO: UFFICIO STORICO – L'ESERCITO ITALIANO NELLA GRANDE GUERRA 1915-18 VOLUME V TOMO 1 BIS – DOCUMENTI. (*The General Army's Historical Office - The Italian Army in the Great War 1915-1918 Volume V Book 1 Second Part Operations in 1918 – The Events from January to June - Documents.*)

Anonymous (Ministero della Difesa, Stato Maggiore dell'Esercito, Ufficio Storico) l 24cm x 17.5cm l light blue paper covered hardback with cloth hinges l xiii + 480pp l 212 appendices l 8 maps l Istituto Poligrafico Dello Stato. l 1980 l Italian Text.

MAGGIORE ESERCITO: UFFICIO STORICO – L'ESERCITO ITALIANO NELLA GRANDE GUERRA 1915-18 VOLUME V TOMO 1 TER - TAVOLE, CARTE, PANORAMI E SCHIZZI. (*The General Army's Historical Office - The Italian Army in the Great War 1915-1918 Volume V Book 1 Thrid Part Operations in 1918 – The Events from January to June - Tables, Maps, Panoramas and Sketches.*)

Anonymous (Ministero della Difesa, Stato Maggiore dell'Esercito, Ufficio Storico) l 24cm x 17.5cm l light blue paper covered hardback with cloth hinges l 41 maps l Istituto Poligrafico Dello Stato. l 1980 l Italian Text.

MAGGIORE ESERCITO: UFFICIO STORICO – L'ESERCITO ITALIANO NELLA GRANDE GUERRA 1915-18 VOLUME V TOMO 2 LE OPERAZIONI DEL 1918 - GLI AVVENIMENTI DAL GIUGNO AL NOVEMBRE – NARRAZIONE. (*The General Army's Historical Office - The Italian Army in the Great War 1915-1918 Volume V Book 2 Operations in 1918 – The Events from July to November – Narration.*)

Alberto Rovighi (Ministero della Difesa, Stato Maggiore dell'Esercito, Ufficio Storico) l 24cm x 17.5cm l light blue paper covered hardback with cloth hinges l 1253pp l 52 maps l Istituto Poligrafico Dello Stato. l 1988 l Italian Text.

This volume covers the Italian front and includes the Italian Offensives, 1918 – the Battle of the Vittorio Veneto.

MAGGIORE ESERCITO: UFFICIO STORICO – L'ESERCITO ITALIANO NELLA GRANDE GUERRA 1915-18 VOLUME V TOMO 2 BIS – DOCUMENTI. (*The General Army's Historical Office - The Italian Army in the Great War 1915-1918 Volume V Book 2 Second Part Operations in 1918 – The Events from July to November - Documents.*)

Alberto Rovighi (Ministero della Difesa, Stato Maggiore dell'Esercito, Ufficio Storico) l 24cm x 17.5cm l light blue paper covered hardback with cloth hinges 1534pp l 669 appendices l 24 diagrams l Istituto Poligrafico Dello Stato. l 1988 l Italian Text.

MAGGIORE ESERCITO: UFFICIO STORICO – L'ESERCITO ITALIANO NELLA GRANDE GUERRA 1915-18 VOLUME V TOMO 2 TER - TAVOLE, CARTE, PANORAMI E

SCHIZZI. (*The General Army's Historical Office - The Italian Army in the Great War 1915-1918 Volume V Book 2 Thrid Part Operations in 1918 – The Events from July to November - Tables, Maps, Panoramas and Sketches.*)

> Anonymous (Ministero della Difesa, Stato Maggiore dell'Esercito, Ufficio Storico) | 24cm x 17.5cm | light blue paper covered hardback with cloth hinges | 47 maps | Istituto Poligrafico Dello Stato. | 1988 | Italian Text.

MAGGIORE ESERCITO: UFFICIO STORICO – L'ESERCITO ITALIANO NELLA GRANDE GUERRA 1915-18 VOLUME IV TOMO 1 LE ISTRUZIONI TATTICHE 1914-1915-1916. (*The General Army's Historical Office - The Italian Army in the Great War 1915-1918 Volume IV Book 1 Tactical Instructions 1914-1915-1916.*)

> Anonymous (Ministero della Guerra, Comando del Corpo di Stato Maggiore, Ufficio Storico) | 24cm x 17.5cm | light blue paper covered hardback with cloth hinges | v + 365pp | 74 diagrams | 3 tables | Istituto Poligrafico Dello Stato. | 1932 | Italian Text.
>
> A printing error on the cover and title page gives the title of this volume as "**L'Esercito Italiano nella Grande Guerra 1915-1918 Volume IV tomo 1**". The title should read "**L'Esercito Italiano nella Grande Guerra 1915-1918 Volume VI tomo 1**". There was an Errata slip issued with this volume highlighting this error.

MAGGIORE ESERCITO: UFFICIO STORICO – L'ESERCITO ITALIANO NELLA GRANDE GUERRA 1915-18 VOLUME VI TOMO 2 LE ISTRUZIONI TATTICHE 1917-1918. (*The General Army's Historical Office - The Italian Army in the Great War 1915-1918 Volume VI Book 2 Tactical Instructions 1917-1918.*)

> Anonymous (Ministero della Difesa, Stato Maggiore dell'Esercito, Ufficio Storico) | 24cm x 17.5cm | light blue paper covered hardback with cloth hinges | 529pp | 113 appendices | 34 diagrams | Istituto Poligrafico Dello Stato. | 1980 | Italian Text.

MAGGIORE ESERCITO: UFFICIO STORICO – L'ESERCITO ITALIANO NELLA GRANDE GUERRA 1915-18 VOLUME VII TOMO 1 LE OPERAZIONI FUORI DEL TERRITORIO NAZIONALE – IL CORPO DI SPEDIZIONE ITALIANO IN ESTREMO ORIENTE – NARRAZIONE. (*The General Army's Historical Office - The Italian Army in the Great War 1915-1918 Volume VII Book 1 The Operations Outside of Italy - the Italian Expedition Corps to the Far East – Narration.*)

> Anonymous (Ministero della Guerra, Comando del Corpo di Stato Maggiore, Ufficio Storico) | 24cm x 17.5cm | light blue paper covered hardback with cloth hinges | 259pp | 12 maps | 79 photographs | 10 tables | Istituto Poligrafico Dello Stato. | 1934 | Italian Text.

MAGGIORE ESERCITO: UFFICIO STORICO – L'ESERCITO ITALIANO NELLA GRANDE GUERRA 1915-18 VOLUME VII TOMO 2 LE OPERAZIONI FUORI DEL TERRITORIO NAZIONALE - SOLDATI D'ITALIA IN TERRA DI FRANCIA – NARRAZIONE. (*The General Army's Historical Office - The Italian Army in the Great War 1915-1918 Volume VII Book 2 The Operations Outside of Italy – Italian Soldiers in France – Narration.*)

> Anonymous (Ministero della Difesa, Stato Maggiore dell'Esercito, Ufficio Storico) | 24cm x 17.5cm | light blue paper covered hardback with cloth hinges | xvi + 419pp | Istituto Poligrafico Dello Stato. | 1951 | Italian Text.

MAGGIORE ESERCITO: UFFICIO STORICO – L'ESERCITO ITALIANO NELLA GRANDE GUERRA 1915-18 VOLUME VII TOMO 2 BIS – DOCUMENTI. (*The General Army's Historical Office - The Italian Army in the Great War 1915-1918 Volume VII Book 2 Second Part The Operations Outside of Italy – Italian Soldiers in France - Documents.*)

> Anonymous (Ministero della Difesa, Stato Maggiore dell'Esercito, Ufficio Storico) | 24cm x 17.5cm | light blue paper covered hardback with cloth hinges | xvi + 426pp | 243 appendices | 6 maps | 2 diagrams | Istituto Poligrafico Dello Stato. | 1980 | Italian Text.

MAGGIORE ESERCITO: UFFICIO STORICO – L'ESERCITO ITALIANO NELLA GRANDE GUERRA 1915-18 VOLUME VII TOMO 2 TER - TAVOLE, CARTE, PANORAMI E SCHIZZI. (*The General Army's Historical Office - The Italian Army in the Great War 1915-1918 Volume VII Book 2 Thrid Part The Operations Outside of Italy – Italian Soldiers in France - Tables, Maps, Panoramas and Sketches.*)

> Anonymous (Ministero della Difesa, Stato Maggiore dell'Esercito, Ufficio Storico) | 24cm x 17.5cm | light blue paper covered hardback with cloth hinges | 38 maps | Istituto Poligrafico Dello Stato. | 1980 | Italian Text.

MAGGIORE ESERCITO: UFFICIO STORICO – L'ESERCITO ITALIANO NELLA GRANDE GUERRA 1915-18 VOLUME VII TOMO 3 LE OPERAZIONI FUORI DEL TERRITORIO NAZIONALE - ALBANIA – MACEDONIA - MEDIO ORIENTE –

NARRAZIONE. (*The General Army's Historical Office - The Italian Army in the Great War 1915-1918 Volume VII Book 3 The Operations Outside of Italy --- Albania - Macedonia – Middle East – Narration.*)

> Anonymous (Ministero della Difesa, Stato Maggiore dell'Esercito, Ufficio Storico) | 24cm x 17.5cm | light blue paper covered hardback with cloth hinges | 396pp | 2 diagrams | Istituto Poligrafico Dello Stato. | 1983 | Italian Text.
> The Balkans.

MAGGIORE ESERCITO: UFFICIO STORICO – L'ESERCITO ITALIANO NELLA GRANDE GUERRA 1915-18 VOLUME VII TOMO 3 BIS – DOCUMENTI. (*The General Army's Historical Office - The Italian Army in the Great War 1915-1918 Volume VII Book 3 Second Part The Operations Outside of Italy --- Albania - Macedonia – Middle East - Documents.*)

> Anonymous (Ministero della Difesa, Stato Maggiore dell'Esercito, Ufficio Storico) | 24cm x 17.5cm | light blue paper covered hardback with cloth hinges | 371pp | 78 appendices | 1 diagrams | Istituto Poligrafico Dello Stato. | 1983 | Italian Text.

MAGGIORE ESERCITO: UFFICIO STORICO – L'ESERCITO ITALIANO NELLA GRANDE GUERRA 1915-18 VOLUME VII TOMO 3 TER - TAVOLE, CARTE, PANORAMI E SCHIZZI. (*The General Army's Historical Office - The Italian Army in the Great War 1915-1918 Volume VII Book 3 Thrid Part The Operations Outside of Italy --- Albania - Macedonia – Middle East -Tables, Maps, Panoramas and Sketches.*)

> Anonymous (Ministero della Difesa, Stato Maggiore dell'Esercito, Ufficio Storico) | 24cm x 17.5cm | light blue paper covered hardback with cloth hinges | 27 maps | Istituto Poligrafico Dello Stato. | 1983 | Italian Text.

Military Monographs:

STATO MAGGIORE DELL'ESERCITO - UFFICIO STORICO - GLI ALLEATI ITALIA DURANTE LA PRIMA GUERRA MONDIALE [1917-1918]. (*The Army's General Staff - Historical Office – The Allies in Italy during the First World War [1917 – 1918].*)

> Mariano Gabriele (Ministero della Difesa, Stato Maggiore dell'Esercito, Ufficio Storico) | 24.8cm x 17.2cm | green cloth hardback | gilt | black and white illustrated dust jacket | 537pp | 3 maps | 59 photographs | Ufficio Storico, Stato Maggiore Esercito. | 2008 | Italian Text.

STATO MAGGIORE DELL'ESERCITO - UFFICIO STORICO - Alle origini dello Stato sovietico. Missioni militari e Corps di spedizione italiani in Russia [1917-1921]. (*The Army's General Staff - Historical Office – The Origins of the Soviet State. The Italian Military Missions and Expeditionary Corps in Russia. [1917 – 1921].*)

> Francesco Randazzo (Ministero della Difesa, Stato Maggiore dell'Esercito, Ufficio Storico) | 24cm x 17cm | coloured illustrated paper covered softback | 302pp | 4 appendices | 8 maps | 55 photographs | Ufficio Storico, Stato Maggiore Esercito. | 2008 | Italian Text.

Order of Battle[34];

MAGGIORE ESERCITO: UFFICIO STORICO – LE GRANDI UNITA NELLA GUERRA ITALO-AUSTRIACA 1915-1918 VOLUME PRIMA. (*The General Army's Historical Office - Major Formations in the Italian-Austrian War 1915-1918 Volume One.*)

> *Maggiore* Enrico Pizzi (Ministero della Guerra, Comando del Corpo di Stato Maggiore, Ufficio Storico) | 24cm x 17.5cm | yellow paper covered hardback | 320pp | 72 photographs | Ministero della Guerra. | 1926 | Italian Text.

MAGGIORE ESERCITO: UFFICIO STORICO – LE GRANDI UNITA NELLA GUERRA ITALO-AUSTRIACA 1915-1918 VOLUME SECONDA. (*The General Army's Historical Office - Major Formations in the Italian-Austrian War 1915-1918 Volume Two.*)

---

[34] The titles of these two sets (for the Order of Battle and the Unit Summaries) were abbreviated on the spines, for example: "**Maggiore Esercito: Ufficio Storico – Le grandi unita nella guerra italo-austriaca 1915-1918 Volume Seconda**" was shown as "**Le grandi unita Volume II**" and "**Maggiore Esercito: Ufficio Storico – Riassunti storici dei Corpi e comandi nella guerra 1915-1918, Brigate di fanteria Volume Secondo Brigate di fanteria: Brescia,....**" as "**Brigate di fanteria Volume II.**"

Maggiore Enrico Pizzi (Ministero della Guerra, Comando del Corpo di Stato Maggiore, Ufficio Storico) | 24cm x 17.5cm | yellow paper covered hardback | 625pp | 29 photographs | Ministero della Guerra. | 1926 | Italian Text.

Unit Summaries:

MAGGIORE ESERCITO: UFFICIO STORICO – RIASSUNTI STORICI DEI CORPI E COMANDI NELLA GUERRA 1915-1918, BRIGATE DI FANTERIA VOLUME PRIMO - BRIGATE DI FANTERIA: GRANATIERI, RE, PIEMONTE, AOSTA, CUNEO, REGINA, CASALE, PINEROLO, SAVONA, ACQUI. (*The General Army's Historical Office - Historical Summaries of Units in the War 1915-1918: Infantry Brigades First Volume - Brigate di fanteria: Granatieri, Re, Piemonte, Aosta, Cuneo, Regina, Casale, Pinerolo, Savona, Acqui.*)
     Anonymous (Ministero della Guerra, Comando del Corpo di Stato Maggiore, Ufficio Storico) | 24cm x 17.5cm | yellow paper covered hardback | 241pp | 13 photographs | Ministero della Guerra. | 1924 | Italian Text.

MAGGIORE ESERCITO: UFFICIO STORICO – RIASSUNTI STORICI DEI CORPI E COMANDI NELLA GUERRA 1915-1918, BRIGATE DI FANTERIA VOLUME SECONDO BRIGATE DI FANTERIA: BRESCIA, CRMONA, COMO, GERGAM, PAVIA, PISA, SIENA, LIVORNO, PISTOIA, BOLOGNA, MODENA, FORLI. (*The General Army's Historical Office - Historical Summaries of Units in the War 1915-1918: Infantry Brigades Second Volume - Brigate di fanteria: Brescia, Crmona, Como, Gergam, Pavia, Pisa, Siena, Livorno, Pistoia, Bologna, Modena, Forli.*)
     Anonymous (Ministero della Guerra, Comando del Corpo di Stato Maggiore, Ufficio Storico) | 24cm x 17.5cm | yellow paper covered hardback | 295pp | 11 photographs | Ministero della Guerra. | 1925 | Italian Text.

MAGGIORE ESERCITO: UFFICIO STORICO – RIASSUNTI STORICI DEI CORPI E COMANDI NELLA GUERRA 1915-1918, BRIGATE DI FANTERIA VOLUME TREZO - BRIGATE DI FANTERIA: REGGIO, FERRARA, PARMA, ALPI, UMBRIA, MARCHE, ABRUZZI, CALABRIA, SICILIA, CAGLIRI, VALTELLINA, PALERMO, ANCONA, PUGLIE. (*The General Army's Historical Office - Historical Summaries of Units in the War 1915-1918: Infantry Brigades Thrid Volume - Brigate di fanteria: Reggio, Ferrara, Parma, Alpi, Umbria, Marche, Abruzzi, Calabria, Sicilia, Cagliri, Valtellina, Palermo, Ancona, Puglie.*)
     Anonymous (Ministero della Guerra, Comando del Corpo di Stato Maggiore, Ufficio Storico) | 24cm x 17.5cm | yellow paper covered hardback | 271pp | 11 photographs | Ministero della Guerra. | 1926 | Italian Text.

MAGGIORE ESERCITO: UFFICIO STORICO – RIASSUNTI STORICI DEI CORPI E COMANDI NELLA GUERRA 1915-1918, BRIGATE DI FANTERIA VOLUME QUARTO - BRIGATE DI FANTERIA: LOMBARDIA, NAPOLI, TOSCANA, ROMA, TORINO, VENEZIA, FRIULI, SALERNO, BASILICATA, MESSINA, SASSARI, LIGURIA, AREZZO, AVELLINO. (*The General Army's Historical Office - Historical Summaries of Units in the War 1915-1918: Infantry Brigades Fourth Volume - Brigate di fanteria: Lombardia, Napoli, Toscana, Roma, Torino, Venezia, Friuli, Salerno, Basilicata, Messina, Sassari, Liguria, Arezzo, Avellino.*)
     Anonymous (Ministero della Guerra, Comando del Corpo di Stato Maggiore, Ufficio Storico) | 24cm x 17.5cm | yellow paper covered hardback | 336pp | 15 photographs | Ministero della Guerra. | 1926 | Italian Text.

MAGGIORE ESERCITO: UFFICIO STORICO – RIASSUNTI STORICI DEI CORPI E COMANDI NELLA GUERRA 1915-1918, BRIGATE DI FANTERIA VOLUME QUINTO - BRIGATE DI FANTERIA: UDINE, GENOVA, PIACENZA, MANTOVA, TREVISO, PADOVA, EMILIA, MACERATA, CHIETI, SPEZIA, FIRENZE, PERUGIA, LAZIO, BENEVEUTO, CAMPANIA, BALETTA. (*The General Army's Historical Office - Historical Summaries of Units in the War 1915-1918: Infantry Brigades Fifth Volume - Brigate di fanteria: Udine, Genova, Piacenza, Mantova, Treviso, Padova, Emilia, Macerata, Chieti, Spezia, Firenze, Perugia, Lazio, Beneveuto, Campania, Baletta.*)
     Anonymous (Ministero della Guerra, Comando del Corpo di Stato Maggiore, Ufficio Storico) | 24cm x 17.5cm | yellow paper covered hardback | 353pp | 13 photographs | Ministero della Guerra. | 1927 | Italian Text.

MAGGIORE ESERCITO: UFFICIO STORICO – RIASSUNTI STORICI DEI CORPI E COMANDI NELLA GUERRA 1915-1918, BRIGATE DI FANTERIA VOLUME SESTO - BRIGATE DI FANTERIA: BARI, CATANZARO, TARANTO, CATANIA, CALTANISETTA,

TRAPANI, NOVARA, ALESSANDRIA, MILANO, IVREA, LUCCA, SESIA, TANARO, LAMBRO, TARO E 165° REGGIMENTO FANTERIA. (*The General Army's Historical Office - Historical Summaries of Units in the War 1915-1918: Infantry Brigades Sixth Volume - Brigate di fanteria: Bari, Catanzaro, Taranto, Catania, Caltanisetta, Trapani, Novara, Alessandria, Milano, Ivrea, Lucca, Sesia, Tanaro, Lambro, Taro e 165° reggimento fanteria.*)

Anonymous (Ministero della Guerra, Comando del Corpo di Stato Maggiore, Ufficio Storico) ǀ 24cm x 17.5cm ǀ yellow paper covered hardback ǀ 340pp ǀ 16 photographs ǀ Ministero della Guerra. ǀ 1928 ǀ Italian Text.

MAGGIORE ESERCITO: UFFICIO STORICO – RIASSUNTI STORICI DEI CORPI E COMANDI NELLA GUERRA 1915-1918, BRIGATE DI FANTERIA VOLUME SETTIMO - BRIGATE DI FANTERIA: BISAGNO, PESCARA, ARNO, TEVERE, VOLTURNO, SELE, IONIO, ETNA, ROVIGO, CAMPOBASSO, LARIO, PICENO, GROSSETO, PESARO, TERAMO, COSENZA, SIRACUSS. (*The General Army's Historical Office - Historical Summaries of Units in the War 1915-1918: Infantry Brigades Seventh Volume - Brigate di fanteria: Bisagno, Pescara, Arno, Tevere, Volturno, Sele, Ionio, Etna, Rovigo, Campobasso, Lario, Piceno, Grosseto, Pesaro, Teramo, Cosenza, Siracuss.*)

Anonymous (Ministero della Guerra, Comando del Corpo di Stato Maggiore, Ufficio Storico) ǀ 24cm x 17.5cm ǀ yellow paper covered hardback ǀ 323pp ǀ 17 photographs ǀ Ministero della Guerra. ǀ 1928 ǀ Italian Text.

MAGGIORE ESERCITO: UFFICIO STORICO – RIASSUNTI STORICI DEI CORPI E COMANDI NELLA GUERRA 1915-1918, BRIGATE DI FANTERIA OTTAVO VOLUME - BRIGATE DI FANTERIA: GIRGENTI, PALLANZA, MASSA, CARRARA, PORTO, MAURIZIO, VENTO, TORTONA, MURGE, ELBA, GAETA, LECCE, CASERTA, AQUILA, POTENZA, BELLUNO, VICENZA, FOGGIA E 313° REGGIMENTO FANTERIA. (*The General Army's Historical Office - Historical Summaries of Units in the War 1915-1918: Infantry Brigades Volume VIII Brigate di fanteria: Girgenti, Pallanza, Massa, Carrara, Porto, Maurizio, Vento, Tortona, Murge, Elba, Gaeta, Lecce, Caserta, Aquila, Potenza, Belluno, Vicenza, Foggia e 313° reggimento fanteria.*)

Anonymous (Ministero della Guerra, Comando del Corpo di Stato Maggiore, Ufficio Storico) ǀ 24cm x 17.5cm ǀ yellow paper covered hardback ǀ 290pp ǀ 17 photographs ǀ Ministero della Guerra. ǀ 1929 ǀ Italian Text.

MAGGIORE ESERCITO: UFFICIO STORICO – RIASSUNTI STORICI DEI CORPI E COMANDI NELLA GUERRA 1915-1918, BERSAGLIERI VOLUME NONO. (*The General Army's Historical Office - Historical Summaries of Units in the War 1915-1918 Ninth Volume Bersaglieri.*)

Anonymous (Ministero della Guerra, Comando del Corpo di Stato Maggiore, Ufficio Storico) ǀ 24cm x 17.5cm ǀ yellow paper covered hardback ǀ 638pp ǀ ? photographs ǀ 20 tables ǀ Ministero della Guerra. ǀ 1929 ǀ Italian Text.

MAGGIORE ESERCITO: UFFICIO STORICO – RIASSUNTI STORICI DEI CORPI E COMANDI NELLA GUERRA 1915-1918, ALPINI VOLUME DECIMO TOMO PRIMA - DIVISIONI, RAGGRUPPAMENTI, GRUPPI. (*The General Army's Historical Office - Historical Summaries of Units in the War 1915-1918: Infantry Brigades Tenth Volume Book One Alpini – Divisioni, raggruppamenti, gruppi.*)

Anonymous (Ministero della Guerra, Comando del Corpo di Stato Maggiore, Ufficio Storico) ǀ 24cm x 17.5cm ǀ yellow paper covered hardback ǀ 218pp ǀ 16 photographs ǀ Ministero della Guerra. ǀ 1930 ǀ Italian Text.

MAGGIORE ESERCITO: UFFICIO STORICO – RIASSUNTI STORICI DEI CORPI E COMANDI NELLA GUERRA 1915-1918, ALPINI VOLUME DECIMO TOMO SECONDA - REGIMENTI, BATTAGLIONI. (*The General Army's Historical Office - Historical Summaries of Units in the War 1915-1918: Infantry Brigades Tenth Volume Book Two Alpini – Regimenti, Battaglioni.*)

Anonymous (Ministero della Guerra, Comando del Corpo di Stato Maggiore, Ufficio Storico) ǀ 24cm x 17.5cm ǀ yellow paper covered hardback ǀ 1169pp ǀ 126 photographs ǀ Ministero della Guerra. ǀ 1931 ǀ Italian Text.

STATO MAGGIORE DELL'ESERCITO - UFFICIO STORICO – I REPARTI D'ASSALTO ITALIANI NELLA GRANDE GUERRA (1915-1918). (*The Army's General Staff - Historical Office - The Italian Assault Units in the Great War (1915-1918).*)

Anonymous (Ministero della Difesa, Stato Maggiore dell'Esercito, Ufficio Storico) | 29.5cm x 21cm | green cloth hardback | Gilt | colour illustrated Dust Jacket | 1022pp | 106 photographs | 35 tables | 37 sketches | Ministero della Guerra. | 2007 | Italian Text.
ISBN: 88-87940-69-X

Aviation Operations;

Aeronautica Militare - Ufficio Storico: L'aeronautica italiana nella 1a Guerra Mondiale. (*Military Aviation [Italian Air Force] - Historical Office: Italian Aeronautics in 1st World War.*)
> Giancarlo Montinaro and Marina Salvetti (Ministero della Aeronautica Militare - Ufficio Storico) | 29.5cm x 21cm | Air Force blue cloth hardback | Gilt | colour illustrated Dust Jacket | 588pp | x photographs | x tables | x sketches | Ministero della Aeronautica Militare. | 2007 | Italian Text.

Aeronautica Militare - Ufficio Storico: Ali sulle trincee - Ricognizione tattica ed osservazione aerea nell'aviazione italiana durante la Grande Guerra.. (*Military Aviation [Italian Air Force] - Historical Office: Wings of Trenches - Air Reconnaissance and Observation Tactics Italian Aviation during the Great War.*)
> Basilio Di Martino (Ministero della Aeronautica Militare - Ufficio Storico) | 29.5cm x 21cm | Air Force blue cloth hardback | Gilt | colour illustrated Dust Jacket | 309pp | x photographs | x tables | x sketches | Ministero della Aeronautica Militare. | 1999 | Italian Text.

Aeronautica Militare - Ufficio Storico: I Dirigibili italiani nella Grande Guerra. (*Military Aviation [Italian Air Force] - Historical Office: Italians Dirigibles in the Great War.*)
> Basilio Di Martino (Ministero della Aeronautica Militare - Ufficio Storico) | 29.5cm x 21cm | Air Force blue cloth hardback | Gilt | colour illustrated Dust Jacket | 392pp | x photographs | x tables | x sketches | Ministero della Aeronautica Militare. | 2005 | Italian Text.

Aviation Unit and Personnel Summaries:

Aeronautica Militare - Ufficio Storico: I Reparti dell'aviazione italiana nella Grande Guerra. (*Military Aviation [Italian Air Force] - Historical Office: The Italian Aviation Units in the Great War.*)
> Roberto Gentilli and Paolo Varriale (Ministero della Aeronautica Militare - Ufficio Storico) | 29.5cm x 21cm | Air Force blue cloth hardback | Gilt | colour illustrated Dust Jacket | 493pp | x photographs | x tables | x sketches | Ministero della Aeronautica Militare. | 1999 | Italian Text.

Aeronautica Militare - Ufficio Storico: Gli Assi dell'aviazione italiana nella Grande Guerra. (*Military Aviation [Italian Air Force] - Historical Office: The Italian Aviation Aces in Great War.*)
> Roberto Gentilli, Antonio Iozzi and Paolo Varriale (Ministero della Aeronautica Militare - Ufficio Storico) | 29.5cm x 21cm | Air Force blue cloth hardback | Gilt | colour illustrated Dust Jacket | 520pp | x photographs | 71 tables | x sketches | Ministero della Aeronautica Militare. | 2002 | Italian Text.

Aeronautica Militare - Ufficio Storico: Aviatori della Grande Guerra. (*Military Aviation [Italian Air Force] - Historical Office: Airmen of the Great War.*)
> Paolo Varriale (Ministero della Aeronautica Militare - Ufficio Storico) | 29.5cm x 21cm | Air Force blue cloth hardback | Gilt | colour illustrated Dust Jacket | 190pp | x photographs | x tables | x sketches | Ministero della Aeronautica Militare. | 2009 | Italian Text.

Photographs;

STATO MAGGIORE DELL'ESERCITO - UFFICIO STORICO - L'ESERCITO ITALIANO NELLA 1A GUERRA MONDIALE IMMAGINI. (*The Army's General Staff - Historical Office - The Italian Army in World War 1 - Images.*)
> *Colonnello* Oreste Bovio and *Capitano* Nicola della Volpe | 28cm x 22cm | white paper covered hardback with black and white illustration | lviii + 136pp | 232 photographs | 4 panaramas photographs | Typografia Regionale. | 1978 | Italian, English, French, German and Spanish Text.

This volume is multi lingal with all text – the introduction and the photographs captions - repeated in five languages.

MAGGIORE ESERCITO: UFFICIO STORICO – LE CARTOLINE DELLE BRIGATE E DEI REGGIMENTI DI FANTERIA NELLA GUERRA DEL 1915-18. (*The General Army's Historical Office - The Postcards of the Infantry Brigades and Regiments in the War of 1915-18.*)

Luigi Amedeo de Biase | 31cm x 22cm | yellow paper covered hardback | 484pp | 385 photographs | Ministero della Guerra. | 1993 | Italian Text.

Logistics Activities:

STATO MAGGIORE DELL'ESERCITO - UFFICIO STORICO - LA LOGISTICA DELL'ESERCITO ITALIANO (1831-1981) VOLUME II DALLA NASCITA DELL'ESERCITO ITALIANO ALLA PRIMA GUERRA MONDIALE (1861-1918). (*The Army's General Staff - Historical Office - The Logistics of the Italian Army (1831-1981) Volume II From the Birth of the Italian Army to the First World War (1861-1918).*)

Ferruccio Botti | 24cm x 17.5cm | white paper covered hardback | 963pp | 28 photographs | 19 graphs | Ministero della Guerra. | 1991 | Italian Text.

Only the second volume of this set, "**Stato Maggiore dell'Esercito - Ufficio Storico - La Logistica dell'Esercito Italiano (1831-1981) Volume II dalla Nascita dell'Esercito Italiano alla Prima Guerra Mondiale (1861-1918)**", covers the Great War period 1914-1918. The first volume of this set covers the pre Great War period 1831 to 1861, and the later volumes cover the post Great War period (the third volume covers 1919 to 1940.)

Munitions and Supply Activities:

STATO MAGGIORE DELL'ESERCITO - UFFICIO STORICO - L'INDUSTRIA ITALIANA NELLA GRANDE GUERRA. (*The Army's General Staff - Historical Office - Italian Industry in the Great War.*)

Massimo Mazzetti | 24cm x 17.5cm | white paper covered hardback | 254pp | ? photographs | Ministero della Guerra. | 1979 | Italian Text.

Military Uniforms:

STATO MAGGIORE DELL'ESERCITO - UFFICIO STORICO - L' UNIFORME GRIGIO-VERDE [1909 – 1918]. (*The Army's General Staff - Historical Office – The Grey-Green Uniform [1909 – 1918].*)

Andrea Viotti | 29.5cm x 21cm | red cloth covered hardback | 205pp | 50 photographs | colour illustrated dust jacket | 25 colour illustrations | 50 Black and white illustrations (of which 1 partially coloured) | Ministero della Guerra. | 1984 | Italian Text.

Miscellaneous:

L'IMPERIAL REGIO ESERCITO AUSTRO-UNGARICO SUL FRONTE ITALIANO (1915–1918). Dai documenti del Servizio informazioni dell'Esercito italiano. (*The Imperial Royal Austro-Hungarian Army on the Italian Front (1915–1918). From the Documents of the Italian Army Information Service.*)

Filippo Cappellano | 24 cm x 17.1cm | cream and olive coloured illustrated card softback | 518pp | 60 colour photographs | 10 black and white photographs | 29 colour illustrations (including 4 coloured maps) | 59 Black and white illustrations (including 4 maps and 1 graph) | 13 tables | Museo Storico Italiano della Guerra; Stato Maggiore dell'Esercito - Ufficio Storico. (Edizioni Osiride.) | 2003 | Italian Text.

This Italian official history "**L'Imperial regio Esercito austro-ungarico sul fronte italiano 1915–1918**" covers in detail the military forces of the primary Italian adversary during the Great War, and is regarded as a supplement to the principal Italian official military history "**L'Esercito italiano nella Grande Guerra 1915-18**".

Japanese Official Histories

The Japanese official histories for the Japanese Navy were written by the 海軍軍令部 (Kaigun Gunreibu - *Naval General Staff Historical Office*) and for the Japanese Army by the 参謀本部編纂 (Rikugun Sanbō Honbu - *Army General Staff Historical Office.*) They were published and issued internally within the respective services as confidential documents and for restrictive use only.[35]

Naval Operations;

大正三・四年 海軍戦史 巻 1. (Taishō san-yonen kaigun senshi: Kan 1. – *The Wartime History of the Navy in the Third and Fourth Year of the Taisho Era. [1914-1915]: Volumes 1.*)
> Anonymous - 海軍軍令部 (Kaigun Gunreibu - *Naval General Staff*). l 20cm x 27cm l ?pp l 海軍軍令部 (Kaigun Gunreibu- *Naval General Staff.*) l c1918-1921 l Japanese Text. l Japanese Kanji pictograms; Japanese Kana (Hiragana /Katakana) syllables and romaji (Latin) script.
> Alternative Transliteration: Taishō 3-4-nen Kaigun senshi.

大正三・四年 海軍戦史 巻 2. (Taishō san-yonen kaigun senshi: Kan 2. – *The Wartime History of the Navy in the Third and Fourth Year of the Taisho Era. [1914-1915]: Volumes 2.*)
> Anonymous - 海軍軍令部 (Kaigun Gunreibu - *Naval General Staff*). l 20cm x 27cm l ?pp l 海軍軍令部 (Kaigun Gunreibu- *Naval General Staff.*) l c1918-1921 l Japanese Text. l Japanese Kanji pictograms; Japanese Kana (Hiragana /Katakana) syllables and romaji (Latin) script.
> Alternative Transliteration: Taishō 3-4-nen Kaigun senshi.

大正三・四年 海軍戦史 巻 3. (Taishō san-yonen kaigun senshi: Kan 3. – *The Wartime History of the Navy in the Third and Fourth Year of the Taisho Era. [1914-1915]: Volumes 3.*)
> Anonymous - 海軍軍令部 (Kaigun Gunreibu - *Naval General Staff*). l 20cm x 27cm l ?pp l 海軍軍令部 (Kaigun Gunreibu- *Naval General Staff.*) l c1918-1921 l Japanese Text. l Japanese Kanji pictograms; Japanese Kana (Hiragana /Katakana) syllables and romaji (Latin) script.
> Alternative Transliteration: Taishō 3-4-nen Kaigun senshi.

大正三・四年 海軍戦史 巻 4. (Taishō san-yonen kaigun senshi: Kan 4. – *The Wartime History of the Navy in the Third and Fourth Year of the Taisho Era. [1914-1915]: Volumes 4.*)
> Anonymous - 海軍軍令部 (Kaigun Gunreibu - *Naval General Staff*). l 20cm x 27cm l ?pp l 海軍軍令部 (Kaigun Gunreibu- *Naval General Staff.*) l c1918-1921 l Japanese Text. l Japanese Kanji pictograms; Japanese Kana (Hiragana /Katakana) syllables and romaji (Latin) script.
> Alternative Transliteration: Taishō 3-4-nen Kaigun senshi.

大正三・四年 海軍戦史 巻 5. (Taishō san-yonen kaigun senshi: Kan 5. – *The Wartime History of the Navy in the Third and Fourth Year of the Taisho Era. [1914-1915]: Volumes 5.*)
> Anonymous - 海軍軍令部 (Kaigun Gunreibu - *Naval General Staff*). l 20cm x 27cm l ?pp l 海軍軍令部 (Kaigun Gunreibu- *Naval General Staff.*) l c1918-1921 l Japanese Text. l Japanese Kanji pictograms; Japanese Kana (Hiragana /Katakana) syllables and romaji (Latin) script.
> Alternative Transliteration: Taishō 3-4-nen Kaigun senshi.

大正三・四年 海軍戦史 巻 6. (Taishō san-yonen kaigun senshi: Kan 6. – *The Wartime History of the Navy in the Third and Fourth Year of the Taisho Era. [1914-1915]: Volumes 6.*)
> Anonymous - 海軍軍令部 (Kaigun Gunreibu - *Naval General Staff*). l 20cm x 27cm l ?pp l 海軍軍令部 (Kaigun Gunreibu- *Naval General Staff.*) l c1918-1921 l Japanese Text. l Japanese Kanji pictograms; Japanese Kana (Hiragana /Katakana) syllables and romaji (Latin) script.
> Alternative Transliteration: Taishō 3-4-nen Kaigun senshi.

---

[35] Please note that Japanese script is normally read vertically starting from the top righthand side of the page. It is shown here horizontally and from the left for convenience.

大正三・四年 海軍戰史 巻 7. (Taishō san-yonen kaigun senshi: Kan 7. – *The Wartime History of the Navy in the Third and Fourth Year of the Taisho Era. [1914-1915]: Volumes 7.*)

Anonymous - 海軍軍令部 (Kaigun Gunreibu - *Naval General Staff*). | 20cm x 27cm | ?pp | 海軍軍令部 (Kaigun Gunreibu- *Naval General Staff.*) | c1918-1921 | Japanese Text. | Japanese Kanji pictograms; Japanese Kana (Hiragana /Katakana) syllables and romaji (Latin) script.
Alternative Transliteration: Taishō 3-4-nen Kaigun senshi.

大正三・四年 海軍戰史 巻 8. (Taishō san-yonen kaigun senshi: Kan 8. – *The Wartime History of the Navy in the Third and Fourth Year of the Taisho Era. [1914-1915]: Volumes 8.*)

Anonymous - 海軍軍令部 (Kaigun Gunreibu - *Naval General Staff*). | 20cm x 27cm | ?pp | 海軍軍令部 (Kaigun Gunreibu- *Naval General Staff.*) | c1918-1921 | Japanese Text. | Japanese Kanji pictograms; Japanese Kana (Hiragana /Katakana) syllables and romaji (Latin) script.
Alternative Transliteration: Taishō 3-4-nen Kaigun senshi.

大正三・四年 海軍戰史 巻 9 大正三・四 年 戰役海軍衛生史. (Taishō san-yonen kaigun senshi. Kan 9. Taishō san-yonen sen'eki kaigun eiseishi. – *The Wartime History of the Navy in the Third and Fourth Year of the Taisho Era. [1914-1915]: Volumes 9 The Naval Medical Activities in the Third and Fourth Years of the Taisho Era. [1914-1915].*)

Anonymous - 海軍軍令部(Kaigun Gunreibu - *Naval General Staff.*) | 20cm x 27cm | ?pp | 海軍軍令部 (Kaigun Gunreibu- *Naval General Staff.*) | c1918-1921 | Japanese Text. | Japanese Kanji pictograms; Japanese Kana (Hiragana /Katakana) syllables and romaji (Latin) script.
Alternative Transliteration: Taishō 3-4-nen Kaigun eiseishi.

大正三・四年 海軍戰史 巻 10 大正三・四 年 戰役海軍衛生史. (Taishō san-yonen kaigun senshi. Kan 10. Taishō san-yonen sen'eki kaigun eiseishi. – *The Wartime History of the Navy in the Third and Fourth Year of the Taisho Era. [1914-1915]: Volumes 10 The Naval Medical Activities in the Third and Fourth Years of the Taisho Era. [1914-1915].*)

Anonymous - 海軍軍令部(Kaigun Gunreibu - *Naval General Staff.*) | 20cm x 27cm | ?pp | 海軍軍令部 (Kaigun Gunreibu- *Naval General Staff.*) | c1918-1921 | Japanese Text. | Japanese Kanji pictograms; Japanese Kana (Hiragana /Katakana) syllables and romaji (Latin) script.
Alternative Transliteration: Taishō 3-4-nen Kaigun eiseishi.

大正三・四年 海軍戰史 巻 11 大正三・四 年 戰役海軍衛生史. (Taishō san-yonen kaigun senshi. Kan 11. Taishō san-yonen sen'eki kaigun eiseishi. – *The Wartime History of the Navy in the Third and Fourth Year of the Taisho Era. [1914-1915]: Volumes 11 The Naval Medical Activities in the Third and Fourth Years of the Taisho Era. [1914-1915].*)

Anonymous - 海軍軍令部(Kaigun Gunreibu - *Naval General Staff.*) | 20cm x 27cm | ?pp | 海軍軍令部 (Kaigun Gunreibu- *Naval General Staff.*) | c1918-1921 | Japanese Text. | Japanese Kanji pictograms; Japanese Kana (Hiragana /Katakana) syllables and romaji (Latin) script.
Alternative Transliteration: Taishō 3-4-nen Kaigun eiseishi.

大正三・四年 海軍戰史 巻 12 大正三・四 年 戰役海軍衛生史. (Taishō san-yonen kaigun senshi. Kan 12. Taishō san-yonen sen'eki kaigun eiseishi. – *The Wartime History of the Navy in the Third and Fourth Year of the Taisho Era. [1914-1915]: Volumes 12 The Naval Medical Activities in the Third and Fourth Years of the Taisho Era. [1914-1915].*)

Anonymous - 海軍軍令部(Kaigun Gunreibu - *Naval General Staff.*) | 20cm x 27cm | ?pp | 海軍軍令部 (Kaigun Gunreibu- *Naval General Staff.*) | c1918-1921 | Japanese Text. | Japanese Kanji pictograms; Japanese Kana (Hiragana /Katakana) syllables and romaji (Latin) script.
Alternative Transliteration: Taishō 3-4-nen Kaigun eiseishi.

大正三・四年 海軍戰史 巻 13 大正三・四 年戰役海軍經理 計理 士. (Taishō san-yonen kaigun senshi. Kan 13. Taishō san-yonen sen'eki kaigun keirishi. - *The Wartime History of the Navy in the Third and Fourth Year of the Taisho Era. [1914-1915]: Volume 13The History of the Naval High Command in the Third and Fourth Years of the Taisho Era. [1914-1915].*)

Anonymous - 海軍軍令部(Kaigun Gunreibu - *Naval General Staff.*) | 20cm x 27cm | ?pp | 海軍軍令部 (Kaigun Gunreibu- *Naval General Staff.*) | c1918-1921 | Japanese Text. |

Japanese Kanji pictograms; Japanese Kana (Hiragana /Katakana) syllables and romaji (Latin) script.
Alternative Transliteration: Taishō 3-4-nen Kaigun keirishi.

大正三・四年 海軍戰史 卷 14 大正三・四 年戰役海軍經理 計理 士. (Taishō san-yonen kaigun senshi. Kan 14. Taishō san-yonen sen'eki kaigun keirishi. - *The Wartime History of the Navy in the Third and Fourth Year of the Taisho Era. [1914-1915]: Volume 14 The History of the Naval High Command in the Third and Fourth Years of the Taisho Era. [1914-1915].*)

Anonymous - 海軍軍令部(Kaigun Gunreibu - *Naval General Staff.*) Ι 20cm x 27cm Ι ?pp Ι 海軍軍令部 (Kaigun Gunreibu- *Naval General Staff.*) Ι c1918-1921 Ι Japanese Text. Ι Japanese Kanji pictograms; Japanese Kana (Hiragana /Katakana) syllables and romaji (Latin) script.
Alternative Transliteration: Taishō 3-4-nen Kaigun keirishi.

大正三・四年 海軍戰史 卷 15 大正三・四 年戰役海軍經理 計理 士. (Taishō san-yonen kaigun senshi. Kan 15. Taishō san-yonen sen'eki kaigun keirishi. - *The Wartime History of the Navy in the Third and Fourth Year of the Taisho Era. [1914-1915]: Volume 15 The History of the Naval High Command in the Third and Fourth Years of the Taisho Era. [1914-1915].*)

Anonymous - 海軍軍令部(Kaigun Gunreibu - *Naval General Staff.*) Ι 20cm x 27cm Ι ?pp Ι 海軍軍令部 (Kaigun Gunreibu- *Naval General Staff.*) Ι c1918-1921 Ι Japanese Text. Ι Japanese Kanji pictograms; Japanese Kana (Hiragana /Katakana) syllables and romaji (Latin) script.
Alternative Transliteration: Taishō 3-4-nen Kaigun keirishi.

大正三・四年 海軍戰史 卷 16 大正三・四 年 戰役艦船機關 士. (Taishō san-yonen kaigun senshi. Kan 16. Taishō san-yonen sen'eki kansen kikanshi. – *The Wartime History of the Navy in the Third and Fourth Year of the Taisho Era. [1914-1915]: Volumes 16 The History of Naval Engineering in the Third and Fourth Years of the Taisho Era. [1914-1915].*)

Anonymous - 海軍軍令部 (Kaigun Gunreibu - *Naval General Staff.*) Ι 20cm x 27cm Ι ?pp Ι 海軍軍令部 (Kaigun Gunreibu- *Naval General Staff.*) Ι c1918-1921 Ι Japanese Text. Ι Japanese Kanji pictograms; Japanese Kana (Hiragana /Katakana) syllables and romaji (Latin) script.
Alternative Transliteration: Taishō 3-4-nen Kaigun kikanshi.

大正三・四年 海軍戰史 卷 17 大正三・四 年 戰役艦船機關 士. (Taishō san-yonen kaigun senshi. Kan 17. Taishō san-yonen sen'eki kansen kikanshi. – *The Wartime History of the Navy in the Third and Fourth Year of the Taisho Era. [1914-1915]: Volumes 17 The History of Naval Engineering in the Third and Fourth Years of the Taisho Era. [1914-1915].*)

Anonymous - 海軍軍令部 (Kaigun Gunreibu - *Naval General Staff.*) Ι 20cm x 27cm Ι ?pp Ι 海軍軍令部 (Kaigun Gunreibu- *Naval General Staff.*) Ι c1918-1921 Ι Japanese Text. Ι Japanese Kanji pictograms; Japanese Kana (Hiragana /Katakana) syllables and romaji (Latin) script.
Alternative Transliteration: Taishō 3-4-nen Kaigun kikanshi.

大正三・四年 海軍戰史 卷 18 大正三・四 年 戰役艦船機關 士. (Taishō san-yonen kaigun senshi. Kan 18. Taishō san-yonen sen'eki kansen kikanshi. – *The Wartime History of the Navy in the Third and Fourth Year of the Taisho Era. [1914-1915]: Volumes 18 The History of Naval Engineering in the Third and Fourth Years of the Taisho Era. [1914-1915].*)

Anonymous - 海軍軍令部 (Kaigun Gunreibu - *Naval General Staff.*) Ι 20cm x 27cm Ι ?pp Ι 海軍軍令部 (Kaigun Gunreibu- *Naval General Staff.*) Ι c1918-1921 Ι Japanese Text. Ι Japanese Kanji pictograms; Japanese Kana (Hiragana /Katakana) syllables and romaji (Latin) script.
Alternative Transliteration: Taishō 3-4-nen Kaigun kikanshi.

大正三・四年 海軍戰史 卷 19 大正三・四 年 戰役艦船機關 士. (Taishō san-yonen kaigun senshi. Kan 19. Taishō san-yonen sen'eki kansen kikanshi. – *The Wartime History of the Navy in the Third and Fourth Year of the Taisho Era. [1914-1915]: Volumes 19 The History of Naval Engineering in the Third and Fourth Years of the Taisho Era. [1914-1915].*)

Anonymous - 海軍軍令部 (Kaigun Gunreibu - *Naval General Staff.*) Ι 20cm x 27cm Ι ?pp Ι 海軍軍令部 (Kaigun Gunreibu- *Naval General Staff.*) Ι c1918-1921 Ι Japanese Text. Ι Japanese Kanji pictograms; Japanese Kana (Hiragana /Katakana) syllables and romaji (Latin) script.
Alternative Transliteration: Taishō 3-4-nen Kaigun kikanshi.

大正三・四年 海軍戰史 巻 20 大正三・四 年 海軍戰史總目次. (Taishō san-yonen kaigun senshi. Kan 20. Taishō san-yonen, kaigun senshi sōmokuji. - *The Wartime History of the Navy in the Third and Fourth Years of the Taisho Era. [1914-1915]: Volume 20 The Index of Naval History in the Third and Fourth Year of the Taisho Era. [1914-1915].*)

Anonymous - 海軍軍令部 (Kaigun Gunreibu - *Naval General Staff.*) | 20cm x 27cm | ?pp | 海軍軍令部 (Kaigun Gunreibu- *Naval General Staff.*) | c1918-1921 | Japanese Text. | Japanese Kanji pictograms; Japanese Kana (Hiragana /Katakana) syllables and romaji (Latin) script.

Alternative Transliteration: Taishō 3-4-nen Kaigun senshi sōmokuji.

The set 大正三・四年 海軍戰史 (Taishō san-yonen kaigun senshi) records naval battles between 1914-15 in the South Pacific Area.

大正四年 乃至九年 海軍戰史 巻 1 (Taishō yonen naishi kunen kaigun senshi. Kan 1. – *The History of the Navy between the Fourth and Ninth Years of the Taisho Era. [1915-1923] Volume 1.*)

Anonymous - 海軍軍令部 (Kaigun Gunreibu - *Naval General Staff.*) | 20cm x 27cm | ?pp | 海軍軍令部 (Kaigun Gunreibu- *Naval General Staff.*) | c1923-1924 | Japanese Text. | Japanese Kanji pictograms; Japanese Kana (Hiragana /Katakana) syllables and romaji (Latin) script.

Alternative Transliteration: Taishō 4-nen naishi 9-nen Kaigun senshi.

大正四年 乃至九年 海軍戰史 巻 2 (Taishō yonen naishi kunen kaigun senshi. Kan 2. – *The History of the Navy between the Fourth and Ninth Years of the Taisho Era. [1915-1923] Volume 2.*)

Anonymous - 海軍軍令部 (Kaigun Gunreibu - *Naval General Staff.*) | 20cm x 27cm | ?pp | 海軍軍令部 (Kaigun Gunreibu- *Naval General Staff.*) | c1923-1924 | Japanese Text. | Japanese Kanji pictograms; Japanese Kana (Hiragana /Katakana) syllables and romaji (Latin) script.

Alternative Transliteration: Taishō 4-nen naishi 9-nen Kaigun senshi.

大正四年 乃至九年 海軍戰史 巻 3 (Taishō yonen naishi kunen kaigun senshi. Kan 3. – *The History of the Navy between the Fourth and Ninth Years of the Taisho Era. [1915-1923] Volume 3.*)

Anonymous - 海軍軍令部 (Kaigun Gunreibu - *Naval General Staff.*) | 20cm x 27cm | ?pp | 海軍軍令部 (Kaigun Gunreibu- *Naval General Staff.*) | c1923-1924 | Japanese Text. | Japanese Kanji pictograms; Japanese Kana (Hiragana /Katakana) syllables and romaji (Latin) script.

Alternative Transliteration: Taishō 4-nen naishi 9-nen Kaigun senshi.

大正四年 乃至九年 海軍戰史 巻 4 (Taishō yonen naishi kunen kaigun senshi. Kan 4. – *The History of the Navy between the Fourth and Ninth Years of the Taisho Era. [1915-1923] Volume 4.*)

Anonymous - 海軍軍令部 (Kaigun Gunreibu - *Naval General Staff.*) | 20cm x 27cm | ?pp | 海軍軍令部 (Kaigun Gunreibu- *Naval General Staff.*) | c1923-1924 | Japanese Text. | Japanese Kanji pictograms; Japanese Kana (Hiragana /Katakana) syllables and romaji (Latin) script.

Alternative Transliteration: Taishō 4-nen naishi 9-nen Kaigun senshi.

大正四年乃至九年 海軍戰史 巻 5 大正四年乃至九年 戰役艦船機關 士. (Taishō yonen naishi kunen kaigun senshi. Kan 5. Taishō yonen naishi kunen sen'eki kansen kikanshi. - *The History of the Navy between the Fourth and Ninth Year of the Taisho Era. [1915-1923] Volume 5. The History of Naval Engineering between the Fourth and Ninth Years of the Taisho Era. [1915-1923].*)

Anonymous - 海軍軍令部(Kaigun Gunreibu - *Naval General Staff.*) | 20cm x 27cm | ?pp | 海軍軍令部 (Kaigun Gunreibu- *Naval General Staff.*) | c1923-1924 | Japanese Text. | Japanese Kanji pictograms; Japanese Kana (Hiragana /Katakana) syllables and romaji (Latin) script.

Alternative Transliteration: Taishō 4-nen naishi 9-nen Kaigun seneki kansen kikanshi.

大正四年乃至九年 海軍戰史 巻 6 大正四年乃至九年 戰役艦船機關 士. (Taishō yonen naishi kunen kaigun senshi. Kan 6. Taishō yonen naishi kunen sen'eki kansen kikanshi. - *The History of the Navy between the Fourth and Ninth Year of the Taisho Era. [1915-1923] Volume 6. The History of Naval Engineering between the Fourth and Ninth Years of the Taisho Era. [1915-1923].)*

> Anonymous - 海軍軍令部(Kaigun Gunreibu - *Naval General Staff.*) | 20cm x 27cm | ?pp | 海軍軍令部 (Kaigun Gunreibu- *Naval General Staff.*) | c1923-1924 | Japanese Text. | Japanese Kanji pictograms; Japanese Kana (Hiragana /Katakana) syllables and romaji (Latin) script.
> Alternative Transliteration: Taishō 4-nen naishi 9-nen Kaigun seneki kansen kikanshi.

大正四年乃至九年 海軍戰史 巻 7 大正四年乃至九年 戰役艦船機關 士. (Taishō yonen naishi kunen kaigun senshi. Kan 7. Taishō yonen naishi kunen sen'eki kansen kikanshi. - *The History of the Navy between the Fourth and Ninth Year of the Taisho Era. [1915-1923] Volume 7. The History of Naval Engineering between the Fourth and Ninth Years of the Taisho Era. [1915-1923].)*

> Anonymous - 海軍軍令部(Kaigun Gunreibu - *Naval General Staff.*) | 20cm x 27cm | ?pp | 海軍軍令部 (Kaigun Gunreibu- *Naval General Staff.*) | c1923-1924 | Japanese Text. | Japanese Kanji pictograms; Japanese Kana (Hiragana /Katakana) syllables and romaji (Latin) script.
> Alternative Transliteration: Taishō 4-nen naishi 9-nen Kaigun seneki kansen kikanshi.

大正四年乃至九年 海軍戰史 巻 8 大正四年乃至九年 戰役海軍計理 経理 士. (Taishō yonen naishi kunen kaigun senshi. Kan 8. Taishō yonen naishi kunen sen'eki kaigun keirishi. - *The History of the Navy between the Fourth and Ninth Years of the Taisho Era. [1915-1923] Volume 8. The History of the Naval High Command between the Fourth and Ninth Year of the Taisho Era. [1915-1923].)*

> Anonymous - 海軍軍令部(Kaigun Gunreibu - *Naval General Staff.*) | 20cm x 27cm | ?pp | 海軍軍令部 (Kaigun Gunreibu- *Naval General Staff.*) | c1923-1924 | Japanese Kanji pictograms; Japanese Kana (Hiragana /Katakana) syllables and romaji (Latin) script.
> Alternative Transliteration: Taishō 4-nen naishi 9-nen Kaigun sen'eki kaigun keirishi.

大正四年乃至九年 海軍戰史 巻 9 大正四年乃至九年 戰役海軍計理 経理 士. (Taishō yonen naishi kunen kaigun senshi. Kan 9. Taishō yonen naishi kunen sen'eki kaigun keirishi. - *The History of the Navy between the Fourth and Ninth Years of the Taisho Era. [1915-1923] Volume 9. The History of the Naval High Command between the Fourth and Ninth Year of the Taisho Era. [1915-1923].)*

> Anonymous - 海軍軍令部(Kaigun Gunreibu - *Naval General Staff.*) | 20cm x 27cm | ?pp | 海軍軍令部 (Kaigun Gunreibu- *Naval General Staff.*) | c1923-1924 | Japanese Kanji pictograms; Japanese Kana (Hiragana /Katakana) syllables and romaji (Latin) script.
> Alternative Transliteration: Taishō 4-nen naishi 9-nen Kaigun sen'eki kaigun keirishi.
>
> This set **大正四年乃至九年 海軍戰史 (Taishō yonen naishi kunen kaigun senshi.)** records naval operations between 1915-23 including the convoy escort duties provided by the Japanese Navy in the Mediterranean.

Military Operations;

大正三年 日独戰史 上巻 (Taishō sannen Nichi-Doku senshi: jōkan. –*History of Japanese-German War during the Third Year of the Taisho Era. [1914]: Volume 1.* **)**

> Anonymous - 参謀本部編纂 (Rikugun. Sanbō Honbu - *Army General Staff.*) | 20cm x 27cm | 56pp | 東京偕行社 (Tōkyō Kaikōsha.) | 1916 | Japanese Text. | Japanese Kanji pictograms; Japanese Kana (Hiragana /Katakana) syllables and romaji (Latin) script.
> Alternative Transliteration: Taishō 3-nen Nichidoku senshi: jōkan.

大正三年 日独戰史 下巻 (Taishō sannen Nichi-Doku senshi: gekan. - *History of Japanese-German War during the Third Year of the Taisho Era. [1914]: Volume 2.* **)**

> Anonymous - 参謀本部編纂 (Rikugun. Sanbō Honbu - *Army General Staff.*) | 20cm x 27cm | 77pp | 東京偕行社 (Tōkyō Kaikōsha.) | 1916 | Japanese Text. | Japanese Kanji pictograms; Japanese Kana (Hiragana /Katakana) syllables and romaji (Latin) script.
> Alternative Transliteration: Taishō 3-nen Nichidoku senshi: gekan.

大正三年 日独戰史 附圖 (Taishō sannen Nichi-Doku senshi: Fuzu. - *History of Japanese-German War during the Third Year of the Taisho Era. [1914]: Volume 2 Maps.* **)**

Anonymous - 参謀本部編纂 (Rikugun. Sanbō Honbu - *Army General Staff.*) | 20cm x 27cm | 6pp | 36 Maps | 東京偕行社 (Tōkyō Kaikōsha.) | 1916 | Japanese Text. | Japanese Kanji pictograms; Japanese Kana (Hiragana /Katakana) syllables and romaji (Latin) script.
Alternative Transliteration: Taishō 3-nen Nichidoku senshi: Fuzu.

大正三年 日独戦史 写真帖 (Taishō sannen Nichi-Doku senshi: Shashin chō - *History of Japanese-German War during the Third Year of the Taisho Era. [1914]: Volume 3 Photographs Ablum.* **)**

Anonymous - 参謀本部編纂 (Rikugun. Sanbō Honbu - *Army General Staff.*) | 20cm x 27cm | 8pp | ? Photographs | 東京偕行社 (Tōkyō Kaikōsha.) | 1916 | Japanese Text. | Japanese Kanji pictograms; Japanese Kana (Hiragana /Katakana) syllables and romaji (Latin) script.
Alternative Transliteration: Taishō 3-nen Nichidoku senshi: Shashinchō.

This set **大正三年 日独戦史 (Taishō sannen Nichi-Doku senshi)** records army operations related to the besieging and capture of Tsingtao in 1914.

欧洲戦争實記 青島陥落紀念 第二世界大戰寫眞画報 第 8號増刊 (Ōshū sensō jikki: Chintao kanraku kinen. Daini Sekai taisen shashin gahō, dai 8-gō zōkan. - *Report of the European War, Remembrance of the Capture of Qingdao [Tsingtao], Photograph Collection of the Second Period of the Great World War, Special Edition Number 8.***),**

Anonymous - 参謀本部編纂 (Rikugun. Sanbō Honbu - *Army General Staff.*) | 26cm x 22cm | ? pp | 博文館 (Hakubunkan.) | 1924 | Japanese Text. | Japanese Kanji pictograms; Japanese Kana (Hiragana /Katakana) syllables and romaji (Latin) script.

大正三年 戰役所見集 (Taishō sannen, Seneki Shoken Shu. - *Collection of Reports and Observations on the War in the Third Year of Taisho [1914].***)**

Anonymous - 参謀本部編纂 (Rikugun. Sanbō Honbu - *Army General Staff.*) | 26cm x 22cm | ? pp | 博文館 (Hakubunkan.) | 1915 | Japanese Text. | Japanese Kanji pictograms; Japanese Kana (Hiragana /Katakana) syllables and romaji (Latin) script.
Alternative Transliteration: Taishō 3-nen Seneki Shoken Shu.

Medical Activities;

大正三年 年戰役衛生士 (Taishō sannen, Sen'eki Eiseishi. - *Record of the Army Medical Activities in the War in the Third Year of Taisho [1914].***)**

Anonymous - 戦争の部 (Rikugunsho - *Ministry of War.*) | 26cm x 22cm | ?pp | 博文館 (Hakubunkan.) | 1917 | Japanese Text. | Japanese Kanji pictograms; Japanese Kana (Hiragana /Katakana) syllables and romaji (Latin) script.
Alternative Transliteration: Taishō 3-nen Sen'eki Eiseishi.

Montenegrin (Yugoslavian) Official Histories

The Montenegrin official history was written in Yugoslavia (Montenegro becoming one of the member constituents of Yugoslavia in 1919) by the Voino-istoriski insttitut (*Army History Institute*).

Military Operations;

ОПЕРАЦИЈЕ ЦРНОГОРСКЕ ВОЈКСЕ У ПРВОМ СВЕТСКОМ РАТУ. (Operacije crnogorske vojske u prvom svetskom ratu. – *Montenegrin Army Operations in the First World War.***)**
> V[elimir] Terzió [Dragić Vujošević, I. Jovanović and Uroš Kostić] (Voino-istoriski insttitut). | 24cm x 22cm | 535pp | Vojno izdavački zavod Vojno Delo. | 1954 | Serbian Text. | Montenegrin Cyrillic script.

New Zealand Official Histories

The New Zealand primary official histories' were written under the authority of the New Zealand Defence Department's Historical War Record Office.

The Historical War Record Office was originally set up to gather information for the British official history. However the suggestion was put forward that an independent single volume New Zealand official history could and should be written for the military. The New Zealand government turned this idea down but then accepted the idea for a popular history for the consumption of the general public in New Zealand. This then was produced as the "Official History of New Zealand's Effort in the Great War" and thereby makes it somewhat different to most official histories from around the world where the histories were to be used in part by the militaries for education.

The general medical history was requested by the New Zealand Medical Corps to cover their work in the Great War so as to bring them in line with the coverage of the medical units from Britain and Australia.

General;

Official History of New Zealand's Effort in the Great War: Volume I The New Zealanders at Gallipoli.

Major Fred [Frederick L.] Waite | 22.5cm x 14cm | brown cloth covered hardback | white dust jacket with colour illustration | xx + 330pp | 6 appendices | 9 maps | 133 photographs | 7 diagrams | Whitcombe and Tombs Ltd. | 1921 | English Text.

The title of this volume was abbreviated on the spine and is shown as "...**Vol I Gallipoli.**"

This volume has been republished by the Naval and Military Press in 2003 in both soft and hard back editions.

The Victoria University of Wellington - New Zealand Electronic Text Centre has reproduced this volume "**Volume I The New Zealanders at Gallipoli**" on one of their world wide web pages: *http://www.nzetc.org/tm/scholarly/tei-WaiNewZ.html.*

A limited number of the "Official History of New Zealand's Effort in the Great War" were produced as deluxe copies bound in full green morocco leather and presented to key personalities. One such presentation copy of "**Volume I The New Zealanders at Gallipoli**" was presented to General Sir Alexander Godley who commanded the Australia and NZ Division of the ANZAC at Gallipoli and then rose to command the ANZAC in France until the end of the Great War.

Official History of New Zealand's Effort in the Great War: Volume II The New Zealanders in France.

Colonel H. [Hugh] Stewart | 22.5cm x 14cm | khaki cloth covered hardback | white dust jacket with colour illustration | xv + 634pp | 22 maps | 144 photographs | Whitcombe and Tombs Ltd. | 1921 | English Text.

The title of this volume was abbreviated on the spine and is shown as "...**Vol II France.**"

This volume has been republished by the Naval and Military Press in 2002 in both soft and hard back editions.

The Victoria University of Wellington - New Zealand Electronic Text Centre has reproduced this volume "**Volume II The New Zealanders in France**" on one of their world wide web pages: *http://www.nzetc.org/tm/scholarly/tei-WH1-Fran.html.*

Official History of New Zealand's Effort in the Great War: Volume III The New Zealanders in Sinai and Palestine.

Lieutenant-Colonel C. [Charles] Guy Powles (from material compiled by *Major Reverend* A.H. Wilkie) | 22.5cm x 14cm | green cloth covered hardback | white dust jacket with colour illustration | xv + 284pp | 3 appendices | 18 maps | 148 photographs | Whitcombe and Tombs Ltd. | 1922 | English Text.

The title of this volume was abbreviated on the spine and is shown as "...**Vol III Sinai and Palestine.**"

This volume has been republished by the Naval and Military Press in 2003 in both soft and hard back editions.

The Victoria University of Wellington - New Zealand Electronic Text Centre has reproduced this volume "**Volume III The New Zealanders in Sinai and Palestine**" on one of their world wide web pages: *http://www.nzetc.org/tm/scholarly/tei-WH1-Sina.html.*

Originally *Major* A.H. [Alexander Herbert] Wilkie was assigned to write the third volume of New Zealand's Official History and proceded to research and draft a manuscript. However once his manuscript had been reviewed, it was decided that his style of writing was "too dry" for public consumption. *Lieutenant Colonel* C. Guy Powles was therefore called in to redraft the manuscript in a more civilian friendly style whilst making use of Wilkie's original researches.

Official History of New Zealand's Effort in the Great War: Volume IV The War Effort of New Zealand.

Lieutenant H.T.B. [Henry Thomas Bertie] Drew (Editor) | 22.5cm x 14cm | yellow cloth covered hardback | white dust jacket with colour illustration | xxiv + 69pp | 1 appendix | 2 maps | 69 photographs | 1 diagram | Whitcombe and Tombs Ltd. | 1923 | English Text.

The Victoria University of Wellington - New Zealand Electronic Text Centre has reproduced this volume "**Volume IV The War Effort of New Zealand**" on one of their world wide web pages: *http://www.nzetc.org/tm/scholarly/tei-WH1-Effo.html.*

Medical Activities;

NEW ZEALAND MEDICAL SERVICES IN THE GREAT WAR - 1914-1919, BASED ON OFFICIAL DOCUMENTS.

Lieutenant-Colonel A.D. [Andrew Dillon] Carbery | 24cm x 14cm | yellow cloth covered hardback | dust jacket | xix + 567pp | 3 maps | 14 photographs | Whitcombe and Tombs Ltd. | 1924 | English Text.

The Naval and Military Press Ltd., republished this volume in 2004 in paperback format. There has been an increase in the number of pages: xxiv + 586pp.

The Victoria University of Wellington - New Zealand Electronic Text Centre has reproduced this volume "**New Zealand Medical Services in the Great War - 1914-1919**" on one of their world wide web pages: *http://www.nzetc.org/tm/scholarly/tei-WH1-Medi.html.*

This volume was not envisage in the original series of "Official History of New Zealand's Effort in the Great War" and was written as a separate entity. It grew out of the material collecting of the New Zealand Records Section, New Zealand Expeditionary Force Headquarters, London, in early 1919. The writing of this volume was then formalised by the committee under the Director General of the Medical Services, Sir Donald McGavin, Royal New Zealand Medical Corps.

Norwegian Official Histories

The Norwegian official history was written under the authority of the Marinens Admiralstab (The [Norwegian] Admiralty Staff).

Naval Operations;

Marinen. Nøytralitetsvernet 1914-1918, samt nøytralitetsvernets avvikling 1918-1919. (*The Navy. Neutrality Protection 1914-1918, also the Phasing Out of Neutrality Protection 1918-1919*)
> Anonymous - Marinens Admiralstab | 22cm x 15cm | light brown paper softback | 115pp | 22 tables | Industritrykkeriet A/S. | 1940 | Norwegian Text.

Polish Official Histories

Initially the Polish official histories were written by members of the Wojskowe Biuro Historyczne (*War History Bureau*) which had been formed in 1923. It was created as a sub department within the existing Instytutu Historyczno-Wojskowego I Sekcji Historyczno-Operacyjnej Oddziału III Naczelnego Dowództwa Wojska Polskiego (*Institute of Military History and the Operation Historical Section of the Polish Army High Command Department III*), which had itself only been formed on 17 September 1919.

In more recent years the Naczelna Dyrekcja Archiwów Państwowych (*The Head Office of State Archives*) has started to write histories, one of which relates to the Great War.

During the Great War 1914-1918, Poland as an independent state did not exist, with the northern region being part of Prussia (and as such was part of the German Empire), the central region being part of the Russian Empire and the southern region part of the Hapsburg Empire. Ethnic Poles fought in the respective armies of the above empires based on the recruitment area where they lived. Their military experience is therefore covered in the official histories of those countries. However, on the formation of Poland as an independent state, the new Polish Army quickly organised a high command and within it an historical section for archiving. The new section started to write a series of historical studies based mainly on the warfare that had occurred on Polish soil – the initial studies covered the Great War and the Polish-Soviet War (February 1919 – March 1921) periods. This work came to an end with the start of the Second World War.

The studies initially were published in book format, but due to financial restrictions a number of the shorter studies were published as articles by the Wojskowego Instytutu Naukowo-Wydawniczego (The Military Scientific Publishing Institute) in their military journal Belloną. After the Second World War during the Communist era, very little study work relating to the Great War was published. However since the collapse of the communist government of Poland in 1990, the Polish state archives have started to write a number of works on Polish freedom. As such, they have produced a study about the resistance movement in southern Poland, who during the Great War had fought against the Hapsburgs for a reunited and independent state.

Military Operations;

Studia z wojny światowej 1914-1918 roku Tom I: Kampania jesienna w Prusach Wschodnich sierpień - wrzesień 1914 roku. (*World War Studies Volume I: Studies from the World War Volume I: The Autumn Military Campaign inEastern Prussia August – September 1914.*)
Bolesława Zawadzkiego ǀ 25cm x ?cm ǀ white paper covered softback ǀ 317pp ǀ Wojskowego Instytutu Naukowo-Wydawniczego. ǀ 1924 ǀ Polish Text.

Studia z wojny światowej 1914-1918 roku Tom II: Bitwa konna pod Jarosławicami 21 sierpnia 1914 roku. (*World War Studies Volume II: The Cavalry Battle waged near Jarostawice 21 August 1914.*)
Jerzego Grobickiego ǀ 25cm x ?cm ǀ white paper covered softback ǀ 204pp ǀ 14 sketches ǀ 7 tables ǀ Instytutu Historyczno-Wojskowego. ǀ 1930 ǀ Polish Text.

Studia z wojny światowej 1914-1918 roku Tom III: Bitwa pod Komarówem 26 sierpień - 2 wrzesień 1914 roku. (*World War Studies Volume III: The Battle on Komarów 26 August – 2 September 1914.*)
Edwarda Izdebskiego ǀ 25cm x ?cm ǀ white paper covered softback ǀ 436pp + viii ǀ 12 tables ǀ Instytutu Historyczno-Wojskowego. ǀ 1931 ǀ Polish Text.

Studia z wojny światowej 1914-1918 roku Tom IV: Bitwa pod Lwówem. (*World War Studies Volume IV: The Battles of Lwow.*)
Tadeusza Pawlika ǀ 25cm x ?cm ǀ white paper covered softback ǀ xi + 341pp + xvii ǀ 20 tables ǀ Instytutu Historyczno-Wojskowego. ǀ 1932 ǀ Polish Text.
Reprinted 2007 ISBN: 978-83-924731-0-7.
The Polish city of Lwów was part of the Hapsburg Empire in 1914 and was known as Lemberg. It is now part of the Ukriane and is known as Lviv.

Studia z wojny światowej 1914-1918 roku Tom V: Monthyon: bój spotkaniowy niemieckiego IV korpusu rezerwowego z francuską grupą generała de Lamaze 5 września 1914 roku. (*World War Studies Volume V: Monthyon: The Combat Struggle Fought by the German IV Reserve Corps against the French Army Group Commanded by General de Lamaze on 5th September 1914.*)

Karola Riedla | 25cm x ?cm | white paper covered softback | 143pp | 13 tables | Instytutu Historyczno-Wojskowego. | 1939 | Polish Text.

The subject of this study, General de Lamaze, was in September 1914 commanding a temporary unit that formed a reserve for the French VII Army Corps made up of French colonial troops. This unit was used in action at Monthyon near Meaux in France. The action was part of the Battle on the Ourcq which was part of the Battle of the Marne. It involved the French and German Armies - the German IV Reserve Corps being raised in Prussian Saxony and the Thuringian states. It did not involve troops raised in Poland.

Studia z wojny światowej 1914-1918 roku Tom ?: Działania osłonowe w Małopolsce Wschodniej w sierpniu 1914 roku. (*World War Studies Volume ?: Protective Operations in Eastern Małopolsce August 1914.*)

Tadeusza Pawlika | 25cm x ?cm | white paper covered softback | xi + 341pp + xvii | 20 tables | Wojskowe Biuro Historyczne. | 1930 | Polish Text.

Studia z wojny światowej 1914-1918 roku Tom ?: Bitwa pod Włocławiem 10-13 listopada 1914 roku. (*World War Studies Volume ?: Battle on the Włocławiem 10 -13 November 1914.*)

Tadeusza Różyckiego | 25cm x ?cm | paper covered softback | ?pp | ? tables | Bellona S.A. | 1934 | Polish Text.

Studia z wojny światowej 1914-1918 roku Tom VII: Bitwa zimowa na Mazurach (6-21 lutego 1915 roku.) (*World War Studies Volume VII: The Winter Battle Waged in Masuria 6th – 21st February 1915.*)

Leona Mitkiewicza. | 25cm x ?cm | white paper covered softback | 129pp | 14 maps | Bellona S.A. | 1936 | Polish Text.

Służby wywiadowczo-informacyjne Austro-Węgier wobec radykalnego ruchu niepodległościowego w Królestwie Polskim 1914-1918. (*Intelligence and Information Services of Austria-Hungary towards the Polish Radical Independence Movement 1914-1918.*)

Jerzy Gaul | 24cm x ?cm | paper covered softback with photographs | 534pp | Naczelna Dyrekcja Archiwów Państwowych - Wydział Wydawnictw. | 2006 | Polish Text.
ISBN 978-83-89115-55-3

Portuguese Official Histories

The Portuguese official history was written by a senior member of the Estado-Maior do Exército (*General staff of the Army*) and the Conselho Superior do Exército Superior. (*The Army's General Council* .)

Military Operations;

Portugal na Grande Guerra Volume I. (*Portugal in the Great War. Volume I.*)
> *General* Luis Augusto Ferreira Martins[36] | 30cm x 23.5cm | illustrated orange-brown cloth covered hardback | gilt | 320pp | 5 maps | 202 photographs | 35 illustrations | 2 tables | Editorial Ática. | 1934 | Portuguese Text.

Portugal na Grande Guerra Volume II. (*Portugal in the Great War. Volume II.*)
> *General* Luis Augusto Ferreira Martins | 30cm x 23.5cm | illustrated orange-brown cloth covered hardback | gilt | 352 + xciv | 190 appendices + 4 notes | 13 maps | 197 photographs | 9 illustrations | 8 tables | Editorial Ática. | 1935 | Portuguese Text.
> General history: including the operations on the Western Front; operations in Africa and naval operations.

A cooperação anglo-portuguesa na Grande Guerra de 1914-1918. (*The Anglo-Portuguese Cooperation in the Great War of 1914-1918.*)
> *General* Luis Augusto Ferreira Martins | 22.5cm x 16cm | paper softback | 91pp | 6 photographs | Serviço de Informação e Imprensa da Embaixda Britânica. | 1942 | Portuguese Text.

---

[36] General Luis Augusto Ferreira Martins was the second in command of the Portuguese Expeditionary Corp to France 1916 - 1918. (*Sub-chefe do Estado Maior do Corpo Expedicionário Português em França.*)

Romanian Official Histories

The Romanian official history was written by members of the Ministerul Apărării Naționale; Marele Stat Major. Serviciul "Istoric" (*Romanian Ministry of Defence; Chief of General Staff. Historical Division*).

Military Operations;

ROMÂNIA ÎN RĂZBOI MONDIAL 1916-1919, VOLUMUL I. CAPITOLUL I – VIII. (*Romania in the World War 1916-1919, Volume I. Chapters I – VIII.*)
> Anonymous (Ministerul Apărării Naționale; Marele Stat Major. Serviciul "Istoric") | 24cm x 18.5cm | Green paper covered softback | 672pp | 42 annexes | Monitorul Oficial și Imprimeriile Statului: Imprimeria Națională. | 1934 | Romanian Text.

ROMÂNIA ÎN RĂZBOI MONDIAL 1916-1919, VOLUMUL I DOCUMENTE-ANEXE. (*Romania in the World War 1916-1919, Volume I. Documents.*)
> Anonymous (Ministerul Apărării Naționale; Marele Stat Major. Serviciul "Istoric") | 24cm x 18.5cm | Green paper covered softback | 737pp | Monitorul Oficial și Imprimeriile Statului: Imprimeria Națională. | 1934 | Romanian Text.

ROMÂNIA ÎN RĂZBOI MONDIAL 1916-1919, VOLUMUL II. CAPITOLUL IX – XIX. (*Romania in the World War 1916-1919, Volume II. Chapters IX – XIX.*)
> Anonymous (Ministerul Apărării Naționale; Marele Stat Major. Serviciul "Istoric") | 24cm x 18.5cm | Green paper covered softback | 885pp | 12 annexes | Monitorul Oficial și Imprimeriile Statului: Imprimeria Națională. | 1936 | Romanian Text.

ROMÂNIA ÎN RĂZBOI MONDIAL 1916-1919, VOLUMUL II. Documente-anexe. (*Romania in the World War 1916-1919, Volume II. Documents.*)
> Anonymous (Ministerul Apărării Naționale; Marele Stat Major. Serviciul "Istoric") | 24cm x 18.5cm | Green paper covered softback | 328pp | Monitorul Oficial și Imprimeriile Statului: Imprimeria Națională. | 1936 | Romanian Text.

ROMÂNIA ÎN RĂZBOI MONDIAL 1916-1919, VOLUMUL III, PARTEA 1. Capitolul XX – XXIV. (*Romania in the World War 1916-1919, Volume III, Part 1. Chapters XX – XXIV.*)
> Anonymous (Ministerul Apărării Naționale; Marele Stat Major. Serviciul "Istoric") | 24cm x 18.5cm | Green paper covered softback | 1032pp | 20 annexes | Monitorul Oficial și Imprimeriile Statului: Imprimeria Națională. | 1940 | Romanian Text.

ROMÂNIA ÎN RĂZBOI MONDIAL 1916-1919, VOLUMUL III, PARTEA 1. DOCUMENTE-ANEXE. (*Romania in the World War 1916-1919, Volume III, Part 1 Documents.*)
> Anonymous (Ministerul Apărării Naționale; Marele Stat Major. Serviciul "Istoric") | 24cm x 18.5cm | Green paper covered softback | 498pp | Monitorul Oficial și Imprimeriile Statului: Imprimeria Națională. | 1940 | Romanian Text.

ROMÂNIA ÎN RĂZBOI MONDIAL 1916-1919, VOLUMUL III, PARTEA 2. CAPITOLUL XXV – XXX. (*Romania in the World War 1916-1919, Volume III, Part 2. Chapters XXV – XXX.*)
> Anonymous (Ministerul Apărării Naționale; Marele Stat Major. Serviciul "Istoric") | 24cm x 18.5cm | Green paper covered softback | 906pp | 10 annexes | Monitorul Oficial și Imprimeriile Statului: Imprimeria Națională. | 1941 | Romanian Text.

ROMÂNIA ÎN RĂZBOI MONDIAL 1916-1919, VOLUMUL III, PARTEA 2. DOCUMENTE-ANEXE. (*Romania in the World War 1916-1919, Volume III, Part 2 Documents.*)
> Anonymous (Ministerul Apărării Naționale; Marele Stat Major. Serviciul "Istoric") | 24cm x 18.5cm | Green paper covered softback | ?pp | Monitorul Oficial și Imprimeriile Statului: Imprimeria Națională. | 1941 | Romanian Text.

ROMÂNIA ÎN RĂZBOI MONDIAL 1916-1919, VOLUMUL IV. (*Romania in the World War 1916-1919, Volume IV.*)
> Anonymous (Ministerul Apărării Naționale; Marele Stat Major. Serviciul "Istoric") | 24cm x 18.5cm | Green paper covered softback | ?pp | ? annexes | Monitorul Oficial și Imprimeriile Statului: Imprimeria Națională. | 1946 | Romanian Text.
>
> This set was edited and republished in c1966. The date of republishing occured during the period of the Cummunist Govenment (*Republica Populară Romînă* (People's Republic of Romania 1947-1965) followed by *Republica Socialistă România* (Socialist Republic of Romania 1965-1989).) All references to former King Ferdinand I (d.1927) and the Kingdom of Romania were removed.

Russian Official Histories

Due to the turmoil caused by the Russian Revolution of 1917 there has been no structured coverage of the Russian part in the Great War by a single official Russian body. There have been a number of political groups claiming to officially represent Russia since the start of the Great War with the result that each have produced their own official histories. Even within those main groups, there have been secondary groups writing officially, thereby creating a lot of confusion about by whose authority they were written and if they are official or not! Listed below are what are believed to be official histories.

The Russian official histories can therefore be divided up into those written by the authority of the following three groups:

i   the Russian Imperial Government during the pre revolution period (mainly relating to diplomatic histories).

ii the Russian Émigré Government in exile representing the deposed Imperial Government, after the revolution.

iii the Russian Soviet Government being the acting power within Russia after the revolution up to the start of glasnost.

However the history of the Russian official histories has not yet ended. Since the collapse of the Russian Soviet Government in 1990, it has been stated in Moscow that the present Russian Democratic Government is preparing an official history to be ready for release on the hundredth anniversary of the start of the Great War in 2014. [37]

Statistics;

РОССИЯ В МИРОВОЙ ВОЙНЕ 1914-1918 ГОДА (В ЦИФРАХ). (Rossiâ v Mirovoj Vojne 1914-1918 gg. (v cifrah) - *Russia in the World War 1914-1918 (In Figures).***)**

> Гозвоениздат (Gosvoenizdat – *Anonymous* - Soviet Government.) | ? | 103pp | СССР Центральное Статистическое Управление Отдел Военной Статистики (SSSR Central'noe Statističeskoe Upravlenie Otdel Voennoj Statistiki. - *The USSR Central Statistical Office Department of Military Statistics*) | 1925 | Russian Text. | Russian Cyrillic script.

МИРОВАЯ ВОЙНА В ЦИФРАХ. (Mirovaâ Vojna v Cifrah - *The World War in Figures.***)**

> Гозвоениздат (Gosvoenizdat – *Anonymous* - Soviet Government.) | Cream coloured paper covered card hardback | 128pp | Военгиз (Voengiz - *The State Military Publishing House*) | 1934 | Russian Text. | Russian Cyrillic script.

ВОЕННЫЕ УСИЛИЯ РОССИИ В МИРОВОЙ ВОЙНЕ. ТОМ I. (Voennye usiliâ Rossii v Mirovoj Vojne. Tom I - *Russia's Military Effort in the World War Volume I.***)**

> *Генералъ* Н.Н.[Николай Николаевич] Головин. (*Lieutenant-General N.N. [Nikolai Nikolaevich] Golovine* - Russian Émigré Government in exile.) | 26cm x 17cm | White paper covered softback | 210pp + x | Товарищество Объединенных Издателей (Tovarišestvo Ob'edinennyh Izdatelej) | 1939 | Russian Text. | Russian Cyrillic script.

ВОЕННЫЕ УСИЛИЯ РОССИИ В МИРОВОЙ ВОЙНЕ. ТОМ II. (Voennye usiliâ Rossii v Mirovoj Vojne. Tom II - *Russia's Military Effort in the World War Volume II.***)**

> *Генералъ* Н.Н.[Николай Николаевич] Головин. (*Lieutenant-General N.N. [Nikolai Nikolaevich] Golovine* - Russian Émigré Government in exile.) | 26cm x 17cm | White paper covered softback | 242pp + iv | Товарищество Объединенных Издателей (Tovarišestvo Ob''edinennyh Izdatelej) | 1939 | Russian Text. | Russian Cyrillic script.

These volumes **"ВОЕННЫЕ УСИЛИЯ РОССИИ В МИРОВОЙ ВОЙНЕ"** were originally published in Paris.

In 2001 they were republished in Moscow by Кучково as a single volume. The reprint is a blue covered hardback with Gilt titles on front cover and spine. The number of pages has been decreased to 440pp.

Naval Operations;

---

[37] As stated by *Professor* Norman Stone in his 'World War One – A Short History' published by Allen Lane in 2007.

ПОДГОТОВКА РОССИИ К МИРОВОЙ ВОЙНЕ НА МОРЕ. (Podgotovka Rossii k Mirovoj Vojne na more - *The Preparation of Russia for the World War at Sea*.)

М.А. Петров (M.A. Petrov - Soviet Government.) | ? | 260pp | Воениздат - (Voenizdat - *Ministry of Defense, USSR*) | 1926 | Russian Text. | Russian Cyrillic script.

ФЛОТ В ПЕРВОЙ МИРОВОЙ ВОЙНЕ: В ДВУХ ТОМАХ. ТОМ I: ДЕЙСТВИЯ РУССКОГО ФЛОТА. (Flot v Pervoi Mirovoi Voine. V Dvukh Tomakh. Tom I. Deystviya Russkogo Flota. - *The Fleet in the First World War: In Two Parts. Volume I. Operations of the Fleet.*)

Н.Б. Павловича ([*Rear Admiral Professor*] N.B. Pavlovich - Soviet Government.) | green cloth HB | 648pp | Воениздат - (Voenizdat - *Ministry of Defense, USSR*) | 1964 | Russian Text. | Russian Cyrillic script.

This volume was translated into English by the Smithsonian Institute as *The Fleet in the First World War. Volume 1: Operations of the Russian Fleet.* It was published by Amerind Publishing in 1979.

ФЛОТ В ПЕРВОЙ МИРОВОЙ ВОЙНЕ: В ДВУХ ТОМАХ. ТОМ II: ДЕЙСТВИЯ ФЛОТОВ НА СЕВЕРНОМ СРЕДИЗЕМНОМОРСКОМ И ОКЕАНСКИХ ТЕАТРАХ. (Flot v Pervoi Mirovoi Voine. V Dvukh Tomakh. Tom II Deystviya Flotov Na Severnom Sredizemnomorskom I Okeanskih Teatrah. - *The Fleet in the First World War: In Two Parts. Volume II. Fleet Operations in the Northern Mediterranean and Ocean Theatres*.)

Владимир А. Белли (Vladimir A Belli - Soviet Government.) | green cloth HB | 364pp | Воениздат - (Voenizdat - *Ministry of Defense, USSR*) | 1964 | Russian Text. | Russian Cyrillic script.

ПОДВОДНЫЕ ЛОДКИ В ОПЕРАЦИЯХ РУССКОГО ФЛОТА НА БАЛТИЙСКОМ МОРЕ В 1914-1915 ГГ. (Podvodnye lodki v operacijakh Russkogo flota na Baltijjskom more v 1914-1915 gg. - *Submarines Operations of the Russian fleet in the Baltic Sea 1914-1915.*)

А.В. Томашевич ([*Kapitan 1 Ranga*] A.V. Tomashevich - Soviet Government.) | grey cloth covered hardback | 23cm x ?cm | beige paper covered softback | 281 +1pp | Военмориздат (Voenmorizdat - Naval Ministry, USSR) | 1939 | Russian Text. | Russian Cyrillic script.

Military Operations;

РОССИЯ В МИРОВОЙ ВОЙНЕ 1914-1915 ГГ. (Rossiâ v Mirovoj Vojne 1914-1915 gg. - *Russia in the World War 1914-1915.*)

Генерал Юрий Н. Данилов (*General* Yuri N.[Nikolaevich] Danilov - Russian Émigré Government in exile.) | 22cm x ?cm | ? hardback | 396 + 4pp | 8 folding maps | "Слово" - Slovo-Verlagsges | 1924 | Russian Text. | Russian Cyrillic script.

This volume was translated into German and French. The German version was published by Verlag der Frommannsche Buchhandlung (Walter Biedermann) in 1925 under the title **"Russland im Weltkriege, 1914-1915"** and the French version was published by Éditions Payot under the title **"La Russie dans la guerre mondiale (1914-1917)"** in 1927.

ИЗ ИСТОРИИ КАМПАНИИ 1914 Г. НА РУССКОМ ФРОНТЕ. ПЛАН ВОЙНЫ. (Iz Istorii Kampanii 1914 g. na Russkom Fronte. Plan Vojny - *The History of the 1914 Campaign on the Russian front. The War Plans.*)

Генера́лъ Н.Н. Головин. (*Lieutenant-General* N.N.[Nikolai Nikolaevich] Golovine - Russian Émigré Government in exile.) | 25cm x ?cm | paper covered softback | viii + 280pp | 1 appendix | 36 maps | 8 diagram| 5 graphs | 25 tables | Издательство «Родник», Париж. (Izdatel'stvo "Rodnik", Pariž - *Publishing House "Spring", Paris*). | 1936 | Russian Text. | Russian Cyrillic script.

This volume can be viewed on the Internet Archive world wide web as a 'pdf file':
http://www.archive.org/stream/izistoriikampani00golo#page/n3/mode/2up

ИЗ ИСТОРИИ КАМПАНИИ 1914 Г. НА РУССКОМ ФРОНТЕ. НАЧАЛО ВОЙНЫ И ОПЕРАЦИИ В ВОСТОЧНОЙ ПРУССИИ. (Iz Istorii Kampanii 1914 g. na Russkom Fronte. Načalo vojny i operacii v Vostočnoj Prussii. - *The History of the 1914 Campaign on the Russian front. The Beginning of the War and the Operation in East Prussia.*)

Генера́лъ Н.Н. Головин. (*Lieutenant-General* N.N.[Nikolai Nikolaevich] Golovine - Russian Émigré Government in exile.) | 25cm x ?cm | paper covered softback | v + 436pp | ? appendix | ? maps | ? diagram| ? tables | Издательство «Пламя», Прага. (Izdatel'stvo "Plamâ", Praga - *Publishing House "Flame", Prague*.) | 1926 | Russian Text. | Russian Cyrillic script.

This volume was translated into English by A.G.S. [Arthur Godfrey Stephens] Muntz. The Command and General Staff School Press, Fort Leavenworth under the title **The Russian Campaign of 1914: the Beginning of the War and Operations in East Prussia** and was published by The Command and General Staff School Press, in 1933. This translation has now been republished in CD ROM format.

ИЗ ИСТОРИИ КАМПАНИИ 1914 Г. НА РУССКОМ ФРОНТЕ. ГАЛИЦИЙСКАЯ БИТВА (ПЕРВЫЙ ПЕРИОД - ДО 1 СЕНТЯБРЯ НОВ. СТ). (Iz Istorii Kampanii 1914 g. na Russkom Fronte. Galicijskaâ Bitva (Pervyj Period - do 1 sentâbrâ novogo stilâ). - *The History of the 1914 Campaign on the Russian front. – The Galicia Battles* (*The First Period -until 1 September, New Style*).)

Генера́лъ Н.Н. Головин. (*Lieutenant-General* N.N.[Nikolai Nikolaevich] Golovine - Russian Émigré Government in exile.) | 25cm x ?cm | paper covered softback | 559pp | ? appendix | ? maps | ? diagram| ? tables | Издательство «Родник»,. Париж. (Izdatel'stvo "Rodnik", Pariž - *Publishing House "Spring", Paris*). | 1930 | Russian Text. | Russian Cyrillic script.

ИЗ ИСТОРИИ КАМПАНИИ 1914 Г. НА РУССКОМ ФРОНТЕ. ДНИ ПЕРЕЛОМА ГАЛИЦИЙСКОЙ БИТВЫ. [1-3 СЕНТЯБРЯ НОВОГО СТИЛЯ]. (Iz Istorii Kampanii 1914 goda na Russkom Fronte. Dni pereloma Galicijskoj bitvy. [1-3 sentâbrâ novogo stilâ] - *The History of the 1914 Campaign on the Russian front. The Days of Crisis during the Galician Battles* (*1-3 September, New Style*).)

Генера́лъ Н.Н. Головин. (*Lieutenant-General* N.N.[Nikolai Nikolaevich] Golovine - Russian Émigré Government in exile.) | 25cm x ?cm | paper covered softback | 195pp | ? appendix | ? maps | ? diagram| ? tables | Издательство «Родник», Париж. (Izdatel'stvo "Rodnik", Pariž - *Publishing House "Spring", Paris*). | 1940 | Russian Text. | Russian Cyrillic script.

The Russian Army in the World War.

Lieutenant-General Nicholas N.[Nikolai Nikolaevich] Golovine (Translated by A.G.S. [Arthur Godfrey Stephens] Muntz) (Russian Émigré Government in exile.) | 30.5cm x 24.7cm | Black cloth covered hardback | Yellow duct jacket | xix + 287pp | Yale University Press, Carnegie Endowment for International Peace. | 1931 | English Text.

МАНЕВРЕННЫЙ ПЕРИОД ПЕРВОЙ МИРОВОЙ ИМПЕРИАЛИСТИĆЕСКОЙ ВОЙНЫ 1914 Г. ТОМ I. (Manevrennyj period pervoj mirovoj imperialističeskoj vojny 1914 g Tom I. - *The Period of Manoeuvre during the Imperialist First World Wars 1914, Volume I.*)

Александр Константиновič Коленковский (Aleksandr Konstantinovič Kolenkovskij - Soviet Government.) | ? | Воениздат - (Voenizdat - *Ministry of Defense, USSR*) | 1940 | Russian Text. | Russian Cyrillic script.

МАНЕВРЕННЫЙ ПЕРИОД ПЕРВОЙ МИРОВОЙ ИМПЕРИАЛИСТИĆЕСКОЙ ВОЙНЫ 1914 Г. ТОМ II. (Manevrennyj period pervoj mirovoj imperialističeskoj vojny 1914 g. Tom II. - *The Period of Manoeuvre during the Imperialist First World Wars 1914, Volume II.*)

Александр Константиновič Коленковский (Aleksandr Konstantinovič Kolenkovskij - Soviet Government.) | ? | Воениздат - (Voenizdat - *Ministry of Defense, USSR*) | 1940 | Russian Text. | Russian Cyrillic script.

ПЕРВАЯ МИРОВАЯ ВОЙНА 1914-1918 ГГ. (БОЕВЫЕ ДЕЙСТВИЯ НА СУШЕ И НА МОРЕ). (Pervaâ Mirovaâ Vojna 1914-1918 gg. (Boevye dejstviâ na suše i na more). - *The First World War 1914-1918.* (*Military Operations on Land and at Sea*).)

Н.А. Таленский (N.A. Talenskii - Soviet Government.) | ? | 124pp | ? maps | Госполитиздат (Gospolitizdat) | 1944 | Russian Text. | Russian Cyrillic script.

ЦАРСКАЯ АРМИЯ В ФЕВРАЛЬСКОМ ПЕВОЛЮЦИЯ. (Carskaâ Armiâ v Fevral'skom Pevolûciâ - *The Tsarist Army in the February Revolution*.)

Е.И. Мартынов (E.I.[Evgenii Ivanovich] Martynov - Soviet Government.) | ? | 212pp | Военнаиа типографииа Управлениииа делами Наркомвоенмор и РВС (Voennaia tipografiia Upravleniia delami Narkomvoenmor i RVS) | 1927 | Russian Text. | Russian Cyrillic script.

Aviation Activities;

ИСТОРИЙА ВОЗДУЦХОПЛАВАНИЙА И АВИАЦИИ В СССР: ПЕРИОД ПЕРВОЙ МИРОВОЙ ВОЙНЫ 1914-1918 ГГ. (Istorija vozduchoplavanija i aviacii v SSSR: Period Pervoj Mirovoj Vojny 1914-1918 gg. - *History of aeronautics and aviation in USSR: The First World War Period 1914-1918.*)

Пётр Дмитриевич Дуж (Petr Dmitrievich Duz' - Soviet Government.) | ? | 27cm x ?cm | iv + 298pp | 1960 | Гос. науц-тецхн. Изд – Оборонгиз (*Gos. nauč-techn. Izd – Oborongiz*) | Russian Text. | Russian Cyrillic script.

This volume was revised and republished in 1986 under the title "**ИСТОРИЙА ВОЗДУЦХОПЛАВАНИЙА И АВИАЦИИ В РОССИИ: ИЙУЛЬ 1914 Г. - ОКТЙАБРЬ 1917 Г. (Istorija vozduchoplavanija i aviacii v Rossii: ijul' 1914 g. – oktjabr' 1917 g.** - *History of Aeronautics and Aviation in Russia: July 1914 – October 1918.*)" by Издательство Машиностроение (*Izdatel'stvo Mašinostroenie*). It had an increase in the number of pages to 333pp. It had an increase in the number of pages to 364pp.

ИСТОРИЙА ВОЗДУЦХОПЛАВАНИЙА И АВИАЦИИ В СССР: ПЕРИОД ПЕРВОЙ МИРОВОЙ ВОЙНЫ 1914-1918 ГГ. ТОМ II. (Istorija vozduchoplavanija i aviacii v SSSR: Period Pervoj Mirovoj Vojny 1914-1918 gg. Tom II - *History of aeronautics and aviation in USSR: The First World War Period 1914-1918, Volume II.*)

Пётр Дмитриевич Дуж (Petr Dmitrievich Duz' - Soviet Government.) | ? | 27cm x ?cm | 276pp | 1963 | Гос. науц-тецхн. Изд – Оборонгиз (*Gos. nauč-techn. Izd – Oborongiz*) | Russian Text. | Russian Cyrillic script.

This volume was revised and republished in 1989 under the title "**ИСТОРИЙА ВОЗДУЦХОПЛАВАНИЙА И АВИАЦИИ В РОССИИ: ИЙУЛЬ 1914 Г. - ОКТЙАБРЬ 1917 Г. ТОМ II. (Istorija vozduchoplavanija i aviacii v Rossii: ijul' 1914 g. – oktjabr' 1917 g. Tom II** - *History of aeronautics and aviation in Russia: July 1914 – October 1918, Volume II.*)" by Издательство Машиностроение (*Izdatel'stvo Mašinostroenie*). It had an increase in the number of pages to 333pp. ISBN 5-217-00590-4.

Munitions and Supply:

БОЕВОЕ СНАБЖЕНИЕ РУССКОЙ АРМИИ В МИРОВУЮ ВОЙНУ. ТОМ I. (Boevoe Snabženie Russkoj Armii v Mirovuû Vojnu. Tom I. - *The War Supplies of the Russian Army during the World War. Volume I.*)

А.А. Маниковский (A.A.[Aleksei Alekseevich] Manikovskii - Soviet Government.) | Госиздат (Gosizdat – *The State Publishing House*) | 244pp | 1930 | Russian Text. | Russian Cyrillic script.

БОЕВОЕ СНАБЖЕНИЕ РУССКОЙ АРМИИ В МИРОВУЮ ВОЙНУ. ТОМ II. (Boevoe Snabženie Russkoj Armii v Mirovuû Vojnu. Tom II. - *The War Supplies of the Russian Army during World War. Volume II.*)

А.А. Маниковский (A.A.[Aleksei Alekseevich] Manikovskii - Soviet Government.) | Госиздат (Gosizdat – *The State Publishing House*) | 363pp | 1930 | Russian Text. | Russian Cyrillic script.

Serbian (Yugoslavian) Official Histories

The Serbian official histories were written in Yugoslavia (Serbia becoming one of the constituent members of Yugoslavia in 1919) by members of the Ministarstvo Odbrane (*Yugoslavian National Defence Ministry*).

Military Operations;

ВЕЛИКИ РАТ СРБИЈЕ ЗА ОСЛОБОЂЕЊЕ И УЈЕДИЊЕЊЕ СРБА, ХРВАТА И СЛОВЕНАЦА. КЊИГЕ ПРВА 1914 ГОДИНА. ЛРВИ ПЕРИОД ОПЕРАЦИЈА – ЦЕРСКА БИТКА. (Veliki rat Srbije za oslobođenje i ujedinenje Srba, Hrvata i Slovenaca. Knjige I. 1914 Godina. Prv period operacija. Cerska bitka. - *Serbia's Great War for the Liberation and Unification of the Serbs, Croats and Slovenians. First Book. 1914. First Operational Period. The Cerska Fight.*)
> Anonymous (Издање Главног Ђенералштаба - Iedalje Glavnog Đeneralštaba - *The General Staff*). I 24cm x 15.5cm I Green paper covered softback I xiii + 340pp I 22 appendices I Штампарска Радионица Мин.[истарство] Војске И Морнарице (Štamparska radionica Ministarstvo vojske i mornarice.) I 1924 I Serbian Text. I Serbo-Croatian Cyrillic
> This volume covers the period of August 1914.

ВЕЛИКИ РАТ СРБИЈЕ ЗА ОСЛОБОЂЕЊЕ И УЈЕДИЊЕЊЕ СРБА, ХРВАТА И СЛОВЕНАЦА. КЊИГЕ ПРВА 1914 ГОДИНА. ЛРВИ ПЕРИОД ОПЕРАЦИЈА – ЦЕРСКА БИТКА. (Veliki rat Srbije za oslobođenje i ujedinenje Srba, Hrvata i Slovenaca. Knjige I. 1914 Godina. Prv period operacija. Cerska bitka. - *Serbia's Great War for the Liberation and Unification of the Serbs, Croats and Slovenians. First Book. 1914. First Operational Period. The Cerska Fight.*) [Map Case]
> Anonymous (Издање Главног Ђенералштаба - Iedalje Glavnog Đeneralštaba - *The General Staff*). I 24cm x 15.5cm I paper envelope I 9 large folding maps. I Штампарска Радионица Мин.[истарство] Војске И Морнарице (Štamparska radionica Ministarstvo vojske i mornarice.) I 1924 I Serbian Text. I Serbo-Croatian Cyrillic

ВЕЛИКИ РАТ СРБИЈЕ ЗА ОСЛОБОЂЕЊЕ И УЈЕДИЊЕЊЕ СРБА, ХРВАТА И СЛОВЕНАЦА. КЊИГЕ ДРУГА 1914 ГОДИНА. ДРУГИ ПЕРИОД ОПЕРАЦИЈА –БИТКА НА ДРИНИ I., II. И III. ДЕО. (Veliki rat Srbije za oslobođenje i ujedinenje Srba, Hrvata i Slovenaca. Knjige II. 1914 godina. Drugi period operacija. Bitka na Drini. I II i III deo. - *Serbia's Great War for the Liberation and Unification of the Serbs, Croats and Slovenians. Second Book. 1914. Second Operational Period. The Fight Across the Drina. Parts I, II and III.*)
> Anonymous (Glavni đeneralštab - Ministarstvo vojske i mornarice). I 24cm x 15.5cm I Green paper covered softback I iv + 438pp I Štamparska radionica Ministarstvo vojske i mornarice Štamparija Ujedinjenje. I 1925 I Serbian Text. I Serbo-Croatian Cyrillic
> This volume covers the period of August 1914.

ВЕЛИКИ РАТ СРБИЈЕ ЗА ОСЛОБОЂЕЊЕ И УЈЕДИЊЕЊЕ СРБА, ХРВАТА И СЛОВЕНАЦА. КЊИГЕ ДРУГА 1914 ГОДИНА. ДРУГИ ПЕРИОД ОПЕРАЦИЈА –БИТКА НА ДРИНИ I., II. И III. ДЕО. (Veliki rat Srbije za oslobođenje i ujedinenje Srba, Hrvata i Slovenaca. Knjige II. 1914 godina. Drugi period operacija. Bitka na Drini. I II i III deo. - *Serbia's Great War for the Liberation and Unification of the Serbs, Croats and Slovenians. Second Book. 1914. Second Operational Period. The Fight Across the Drina. Parts I, II and III.*) [Map Case]
> Anonymous (Glavni đeneralštab - Ministarstvo vojske i mornarice). I 24cm x 15.5cm I paper envelope I 4 large folding maps. I Štamparska radionica Ministarstvo vojske i mornarice Štamparija Ujedinjenje. I 1925 I Serbian Text. I Serbo-Croatian Cyrillic

ВЕЛИКИ РАТ СРБИЈЕ ЗА ОСЛОБОЂЕЊЕ И УЈЕДИЊЕЊЕ СРБА, ХРВАТА И СЛОВЕНАЦА. КЊИГЕ ТРЕЋА 1914 ГОДИНА. ДРУГИ ПЕРИОД ОПЕРАЦИЈА –БИТКА НА ДРИНИ IV., V. И VI. ДЕО. (Veliki rat Srbije za oslobođenje i ujedinenje Srba, Hrvata i Slovenaca. Knjige treća. 1914 godina. Drugi period operacija. Bitka na Drini. IV V i VI deo. - *Serbia's Great War for the Salvation and Unification of the Serbs, Croats and Slovenians. Third Book. 1914. Second Operational Period. The Fight Across the Drina. Parts IV, V and VI.*)
> Anonymous (Glavni đeneralštab - Ministarstvo vojske i mornarice). I 24cm x 15.5cm I Green paper covered softback I viii + 410pp + i I Štamparska radionica Ministarstvo vojske i mornarice Štamparija Ujedinjenje. I 1925 I Serbian Text. I Serbo-Croatian Cyrillic
> This volume covers the period of October through to November 1914.

ВЕЛИКИ РАТ СРБИЈЕ ЗА ОСЛОБОЂЕЊЕ И УЈЕДИЊЕЊЕ СРБА, ХРВАТА И СЛОВЕНАЦА. КЊИГЕ ТРЕЋА 1914 ГОДИНА. ДРУГИ ПЕРИОД ОПЕРАЦИЈА –БИТКА НА ДРИНИ IV., V. И VI. ДЕО. (Veliki rat Srbije za oslobođenje i ujedinenje Srba, Hrvata i Slovenaca. Knjige treća. 1914 godina. Drugi period operacija. Bitka na Drini. IV V i VI deo. - *Serbia's Great War for the Salvation and Unification of the Serbs, Croats and Slovenians. Third Book. 1914. Second Operational Period. The Fight Across the Drina. Parts IV, V and VI.*) [Map Case]

Anonymous (Glavni đeneralštab - Ministarstvo vojske i mornarice). I 24cm x 15.5cm I paper envelope I 2 large folding maps. I Štamparska radionica Ministarstvo vojske i mornarice Štamparija Ujedinjenje. I 1925 I Serbian Text. I Serbo-Croatian Cyrillic

ВЕЛИКИ РАТ СРБИЈЕ ЗА ОСЛОБОЂЕЊЕ И УЈЕДИЊЕЊЕ СРБА, ХРВАТА И СЛОВЕНАЦА. КЊИГЕ ЧЕТВРТА 1914 ГОДИНА. ТРЕЋИ ПЕРИОД ОПЕРАЦИЈА. КОЛУБАРСКА БИТКА. I. ФАЗА – УВОДНА. (Veliki rat Srbije za oslobođenje i ujedinenje Srba, Hrvata i Slovenaca. Knjige četvrta. 1914 godina. Treći period operacija. Kolubarska bitka. I. faza - Uvodna. - *Serbia's Great War for the Liberation and Unification of the Serbs, Croats and Slovenians. Fourth Book. 1914. Thrid Operational Period. The Kolubarska Fight. First Phase - PRÉLIMINARIES.*)

Anonymous (Glavni đeneralštab - Ministarstvo vojske i mornarice). I 24cm x 15.5cm I Green paper covered softback I iv + 312pp I Štamparska radionica Ministarstvo vojske i mornarice Štamparija Ujedinjenje. I 1925 I Serbian Text. I Serbo-Croatian Cyrillic
This volume covers the period of November 1914.

ВЕЛИКИ РАТ СРБИЈЕ ЗА ОСЛОБОЂЕЊЕ И УЈЕДИЊЕЊЕ СРБА, ХРВАТА И СЛОВЕНАЦА. КЊИГЕ ЧЕТВРТА 1914 ГОДИНА. ТРЕЋИ ПЕРИОД ОПЕРАЦИЈА. КОЛУБАРСКА БИТКА. I. ФАЗА – УВОДНА. (Veliki rat Srbije za oslobođenje i ujedinenje Srba, Hrvata i Slovenaca. Knjige četvrta. 1914 godina. Treći period operacija. Kolubarska bitka. I. faza - Uvodna. - *Serbia's Great War for the Liberation and Unification of the Serbs, Croats and Slovenians. Fourth Book. 1914. Thrid Operational Period. The Kolubarska Fight. First Phase - PRÉLIMINARIES.*) [Map Case]

Anonymous (Glavni đeneralštab - Ministarstvo vojske i mornarice). I 24cm x 15.5cm I paper envelope I 1 large folding map. I Štamparska radionica Ministarstvo vojske i mornarice Štamparija Ujedinjenje. I 1925 I Serbian Text. I Serbo-Croatian Cyrillic

ВЕЛИКИ РАТ СРБИЈЕ ЗА ОСЛОБОЂЕЊЕ И УЈЕДИЊЕЊЕ СРБА, ХРВАТА И СЛОВЕНАЦА. КЊИГЕ ПЕТА 1914 ГОДИНА. ТРЕЋИ ПЕРИОД ОПЕРАЦИЈА. КОЛУБАРСКА БИТКА. II. ФАЗА – ОДБРАНБЕНА. (Veliki rat Srbije za oslobođenje i ujedinenje Srba, Hrvata i Slovenaca. Knjige peta. 1914 godina. Treći period operacija. Kolubarska bitka. II. faza - Odbranbena. - *Serbia's Great War for the Liberation and Unification of the Serbs, Croats and Slovenians. Fifth Book. 1914. Thrid Operational Period. The Kolubarska Fight. Second Phase – Defences.*)

Anonymous (Glavni đeneralštab - Ministarstvo vojske i mornarice). I 24cm x 15.5cm I Green paper covered softback I vii + 416pp I Štamparska radionica Ministarstvo vojske i mornarice Štamparija Ujedinjenje. I 1925 I Serbian Text. I Serbo-Croatian Cyrillic
This volume covers the period of November 1914.

ВЕЛИКИ РАТ СРБИЈЕ ЗА ОСЛОБОЂЕЊЕ И УЈЕДИЊЕЊЕ СРБА, ХРВАТА И СЛОВЕНАЦА. КЊИГЕ ПЕТА 1914 ГОДИНА. ТРЕЋИ ПЕРИОД ОПЕРАЦИЈА. КОЛУБАРСКА БИТКА. II. ФАЗА – ОДБРАНБЕНА. (Veliki rat Srbije za oslobođenje i ujedinenje Srba, Hrvata i Slovenaca. Knjige peta. 1914 godina. Treći period operacija. Kolubarska bitka. II. faza - Odbranbena. - *Serbia's Great War for the Liberation and Unification of the Serbs, Croats and Slovenians. Fifth Book. 1914. Thrid Operational Period. The Kolubarska Fight. Second Phase – Defences.*) [Map Case]

Anonymous (Glavni đeneralštab - Ministarstvo vojske i mornarice). I 24cm x 15.5cm I paper envelope I 1 large folding map. I Štamparska radionica Ministarstvo vojske i mornarice Štamparija Ujedinjenje. I 1925 I Serbian Text. I Serbo-Croatian Cyrillic

ВЕЛИКИ РАТ СРБИЈЕ ЗА ОСЛОБОЂЕЊЕ И УЈЕДИЊЕЊЕ СРБА, ХРВАТА И СЛОВЕНАЦА. КЊИГЕ ШЕСТА 1914 ГОДИНА. ТРЕЋИ ПЕРИОД ОПЕРАЦИЈА. КОЛУБАРСКА БИТКА. III. ФАЗА – НАПАДНА. (Veliki rat Srbije za oslobođenje i ujedinenje Srba, Hrvata i Slovenaca. Knjige šesta. 1914 godina. Treći period operacija. Kolubarska bitka. III. faza - Napadna. - *Serbia's Great War for the Liberation and Unification of* *the Serbs, Croats and Slovenians. Sixth Book. In the Year 1914. Thrid Operational Period. The Kolubarska Fight. Third Phase – Attacked.)*

> Anonymous (Glavni đeneralštab - Ministarstvo vojske i mornarice). I 24cm x 15.5cm I Green paper covered softback I iv + 360pp I Štamparska radionica Ministarstvo vojske i mornarice Štamparija Ujedinjenje. I 1925 I Serbian Text. I Serbo-Croatian Cyrillic
> This volume covers the period of December 1914.

ВЕЛИКИ РАТ СРБИЈЕ ЗА ОСЛОБОЂЕЊЕ И УЈЕДИЊЕЊЕ СРБА, ХРВАТА И СЛОВЕНАЦА. КЊИГЕ ШЕСТА 1914 ГОДИНА. ТРЕЋИ ПЕРИОД ОПЕРАЦИЈА. КОЛУБАРСКА БИТКА. III. ФАЗА – НАПАДНА. (Veliki rat Srbije za oslobođenje i ujedinenje Srba, Hrvata i Slovenaca. Knjige šesta. 1914 godina. Treći period operacija. Kolubarska bitka. III. faza - Napadna. - Serbia's Great War for the Liberation and Unification of the Serbs, Croats and Slovenians. Sixth Book. In the Year 1914. Thrid Operational Period. The Kolubarska Fight. Third Phase – Attacked.) [Map Case]

> Anonymous (Glavni đeneralštab - Ministarstvo vojske i mornarice). I 24cm x 15.5cm I paper envelope I 1 large folding map. I Štamparska radionica Ministarstvo vojske i mornarice Štamparija Ujedinjenje. I 1925 I Serbian Text. I Serbo-Croatian Cyrillic

ВЕЛИКИ РАТ СРБИЈЕ ЗА ОСЛОБОЂЕЊЕ И УЈЕДИЊЕЊЕ СРБА, ХРВАТА И СЛОВЕНАЦА. КЊИГЕ СЕДМА 1914 ГОДИНА. ТРЕЋИ ПЕРИОД ОПЕРАЦИЈА. КОЛУБАРСКА БИТКА. IV. ФАЗА – ЕКСПЛОАТАЦИЈА ПОБЕДЕ. (Veliki rat Srbije za oslobođenje i ujedinenje Srba, Hrvata i Slovenaca. Knjige sedma. 1914 godina. Treći period operacija. Kolubarska bitka. IV. faza – Eksploatacija Pobede - Serbia's Great War for the Liberation and Unification of the Serbs, Croats and Slovenians. Seventh Book. 1914. Thrid Operational Period. The Kolubarska Fight. Fourth Phase – Exploitation and Conquest.)

> Anonymous (Glavni đeneralštab - Ministarstvo vojske i mornarice). I 24cm x 15.5cm I Green paper covered softback I 398pp + iv I Štamparska radionica Ministarstvo vojske i mornarice Štamparija Ujedinjenje. I 1926 I Serbian Text. I Serbo-Croatian Cyrillic
> This volume covers the period of December 1914.
> No large format maps issued with this volume.

ВЕЛИКИ РАТ СРБИЈЕ ЗА ОСЛОБОЂЕЊЕ И УЈЕДИЊЕЊЕ СРБА, ХРВАТА И СЛОВЕНАЦА. КЊИГЕ VIII 1915 ГОДИНА. ПРВИ ПЕРИОД. ВОЈНО-ПОЛИТИЧКЕ ПРИПРЕМЕ. (Veliki rat Srbije za oslobođenje i ujedinenje Srba, Hrvata i Slovenaca. knjige VIII. 1915 godina. Prvi period. Vojno-političke pripreme. - Serbia's Great War for the Liberation and Unification of the Serbs, Croats and Slovenians. Book VIII. 1915 First Period. Preliminary Military Related Politics.)

> Anonymous (Glavni đeneralštab - Ministarstvo vojske i mornarice). I 24cm x 15.5cm I Green paper covered softback I 353pp + iii I Štamparska radionica Ministarstvo vojske i mornarice Štamparija Ujedinjenje. I 1926 I Serbian Text. I Serbo-Croatian Cyrillic
> Book number shown in Roman numerals.
> This volume covers the period of January - July 1915.
> No large format maps issued with this volume.

ВЕЛИКИ РАТ СРБИЈЕ ЗА ОСЛОБОЂЕЊЕ И УЈЕДИЊЕЊЕ СРБА, ХРВАТА И СЛОВЕНАЦА. КЊИГЕ IX 1915 ГОДИНА. ДРУГИ ПЕРИОД. АУСТРО-НЕМАЧКА ОФАНЗИВА ДО СТУПАЊА БУГАРСКЕ У АКЦИЈУ. (Veliki rat Srbije za oslobođenje i ujedinenje Srba, Hrvata i Slovenaca. knjige IX. 1915 godina. Druga period. Austro-nemačka ofanziva do stupanja Bugarske u akciju. - Serbia's Great War for the Liberation and Unification of the Serbs, Croats and Slovenians. Book IX. 1915 Second Period. Austro-German Offensive before the Bulgarian Action.)

> Anonymous (Glavni đeneralštab - Ministarstvo vojske i mornarice). I 24cm x 15.5cm I Green paper covered softback I iii + 258pp + iii I Štamparska radionica Ministarstvo vojske i mornarice Štamparija Ujedinjenje. I 1926 I Serbian Text. I Serbo-Croatian Cyrillic
> Book number shown in Roman numerals.
> This volume covers the period of August – 13 October 1915.

ВЕЛИКИ РАТ СРБИЈЕ ЗА ОСЛОБОЂЕЊЕ И УЈЕДИЊЕЊЕ СРБА, ХРВАТА И СЛОВЕНАЦА. КЊИГЕ IX 1915 ГОДИНА. ДРУГИ ПЕРИОД. АУСТРО-НЕМАЧКА ОФАНЗИВА ДО СТУПАЊА БУГАРСКЕ У АКЦИЈУ. (Veliki rat Srbije za oslobođenje i ujedinenje Srba, Hrvata i Slovenaca. knjige IX. 1915 godina. Druga period. Austro-nemačka ofanziva do stupanja Bugarske u akciju. - Serbia's Great War for the Liberation and Unification of the Serbs, Croats and Slovenians. Book IX. 1915 Second Period. Austro-German Offensive before the Bulgarian Action.) [Map Case]

Anonymous (Glavni đeneralštab - Ministarstvo vojske i mornarice). | 24cm x 15.5cm | paper envelope | 2 large folding maps. | Štamparska radionica Ministarstvo vojske i mornarice Štamparija Ujedinjenje. | 1926 | Serbian Text. | Serbo-Croatian Cyrillic

ВЕЛИКИ РАТ СРБИЈЕ ЗА ОСЛОБОЂЕЊЕ И УЈЕДИЊЕЊЕ СРБА, ХРВАТА И СЛОВЕНАЦА. КЊИГЕ X 1915. ТРЕЋИ ПЕРИОД. УДРУЖЕНА АУСТРО-НЕМАЧКА-БУГАРСКА ОФАНЗИВА ПРОТИВ СРБИЈЕ ОД 14. ДО 29. ОКТОБАР 1915. (Veliki rat Srbije za oslobođenje i ujedinenje Srba, Hrvata i Slovenaca. knjige X. 1915. Treći period. Udružena austro-nemačka-bugarska ofanziva protiv Srbije od 14 do 29 oktobar 1915. - *Serbia's Great War for the Liberation and Unification of the Serbs, Croats and Slovenians. Book X. 1915 Thrid Period. Combined Austro - Germany - Bulgaria Offensive against Serbia 14-29 October 1915.*)

Anonymous (Glavni đeneralštab - Ministarstvo vojske i mornarice). | 24cm x 15.5cm | Green paper covered softback | 371pp + i | Štamparska radionica Ministarstvo vojske i mornarice Štamparija Ujedinjenje. | 1926 | Serbian Text. | Serbo-Croatian Cyrillic

Book number shown in Roman numerals. The word "година" (*year*) not shown after the year date in the title.

This volume covers the period of 14-29 October 1915.

ВЕЛИКИ РАТ СРБИЈЕ ЗА ОСЛОБОЂЕЊЕ И УЈЕДИЊЕЊЕ СРБА, ХРВАТА И СЛОВЕНАЦА. КЊИГЕ X 1915. ТРЕЋИ ПЕРИОД. УДРУЖЕНА АУСТРО-НЕМАЧКА-БУГАРСКА ОФАНЗИВА ПРОТИВ СРБИЈЕ ОД 14. ДО 29. ОКТОБАР 1915. (Veliki rat Srbije za oslobođenje i ujedinenje Srba, Hrvata i Slovenaca. knjige X. 1915. Treći period. Udružena austro-nemačka-bugarska ofanziva protiv Srbije od 14 do 29 oktobar 1915. - *Serbia's Great War for the Liberation and Unification of the Serbs, Croats and Slovenians. Book X. 1915 Thrid Period. Combined Austro - Germany - Bulgaria Offensive against Serbia 14-29 October 1915.*) [Map Case]

Anonymous (Glavni đeneralštab - Ministarstvo vojske i mornarice). | 24cm x 15.5cm | paper envelope | 3 large folding maps. | Štamparska radionica Ministarstvo vojske i mornarice Štamparija Ujedinjenje. | 1926 | Serbian Text. | Serbo-Croatian Cyrillic

ВЕЛИКИ РАТ СРБИЈЕ ЗА ОСЛОБОЂЕЊЕ И УЈЕДИЊЕЊЕ СРБА, ХРВАТА И СЛОВЕНАЦА. ЈЕДАНАЕСТА КЊИГЕ 1915 ГОДИНА. ТРЕЋИ ПЕРИОД. ОПШТЕ ОДСТУПАЊЕ СРПСКЕ ВОЈСКЕ. ПРВА ФАЗА. ОДСТУПАЊЕ ГЛАВНЕ СНАГЕ НА ЗАПАДНУ И ЈУЖНУ МОРАВУ. (Veliki rat Srbije za oslobođenje i ujedinenje Srba, Hrvata i Slovenaca. Jedanaesta knjige. 1915 godina. Treći period. Opšte Odstupanje srpske vojske. Prva faza. Odstupanje Glavne Shage na Zapadnu i Južnu Moravu - *Serbia's Great War for the Liberation and Unification of the Serbs, Croats and Slovenians. Eleventh Book. 1915 Thrid Period. The General Withdrawal of the Serbian Army. First Phase. Main Withdrawal through the Južnu Moravu.*)

Anonymous (Glavni đeneralštab - Ministarstvo vojske i mornarice). | 24cm x 15.5cm | Green paper covered softback | vii + 371pp | Štamparska radionica Ministarstvo vojske i mornarice Štamparija Ujedinjenje. | 1927 | Serbian Text. | Serbo-Croatian Cyrillic

This volume covers the period of 29 October – November 1915.

ВЕЛИКИ РАТ СРБИЈЕ ЗА ОСЛОБОЂЕЊЕ И УЈЕДИЊЕЊЕ СРБА, ХРВАТА И СЛОВЕНАЦА. ЈЕДАНАЕСТА КЊИГЕ 1915 ГОДИНА. ТРЕЋИ ПЕРИОД. ОПШТЕ ОДСТУПАЊЕ СРПСКЕ ВОЈСКЕ. ПРВА ФАЗА. ОДСТУПАЊЕ ГЛАВНЕ СНАГЕ НА ЗАПАДНУ И ЈУЖНУ МОРАВУ. (Veliki rat Srbije za oslobođenje i ujedinenje Srba, Hrvata i Slovenaca. Jedanaesta knjige. 1915 godina. Treći period. Opšte Odstupanje srpske vojske. Prva faza. Odstupanje Glavne Shage na Zapadnu i Južnu Moravu - *Serbia's Great War for the Liberation and Unification of the Serbs, Croats and Slovenians. Eleventh Book. 1915 Thrid Period. The General Withdrawal of the Serbian Army. First Phase. Main Withdrawal through the Južnu Moravu.*) [Map Case]

Anonymous (Glavni đeneralštab - Ministarstvo vojske i mornarice). | 24cm x 15.5cm | paper envelope | 1 large folding map. | Štamparska radionica Ministarstvo vojske i mornarice Štamparija Ujedinjenje. | 1927 | Serbian Text. | Serbo-Croatian Cyrillic

ВЕЛИКИ РАТ СРБИЈЕ ЗА ОСЛОБОЂЕЊЕ И УЈЕДИЊЕЊЕ СРБА, ХРВАТА И СЛОВЕНАЦА. ДВАНАЕСТА КЊИГЕ 1915 ГОДИНА. ТРЕЋИ ПЕРИОД. ОПШТЕ ОДСТУПАЊЕ СРПСКЕ ВОЈСКЕ. ДРУГА ФАЗА. ОДСТУПАЊЕ ГЛАВНЕ СНАГЕ НА КОСОВО ПОЉЕ. (Veliki rat Srbije za oslobođenje i ujedinenje Srba, Hrvata i Slovenaca. Dvanaesta knjige. 1915 godina. Treći period. Opšte odstupanje srpske vojske. Druga faza - Odstupanje glavne snage na Kosovo polje. - *Serbia's Great War for the Liberation and Unification* *of the Serbs, Croats and Slovenians. Twelfth Book. 1915 Thrid Period. The General Withdrawal of the Serbian Armies. Second Phase. Main Withdrawal through the Kosovo Valley.*)

Anonymous (Glavni đeneralštab - Ministarstvo vojske i mornarice). | 24cm x 15.5cm | Green paper covered softback | v + 354pp | Štamparska radionica Ministarstvo vojske i mornarice Štamparija Ujedinjenje. | 1927 | Serbian Text. | Serbo-Croatian Cyrillic

This volume covers the period of mid November 1915.

ВЕЛИКИ РАТ СРБИЈЕ ЗА ОСЛОБОЂЕЊЕ И УЈЕДИЊЕЊЕ СРБА, ХРВАТА И СЛОВЕНАЦА. ДВАНАЕСТА КЊИГЕ 1915 ГОДИНА. ТРЕЋИ ПЕРИОД. ОПШТЕ ОДСТУПАЊЕ СРПСКЕ ВОЈСКЕ. ДРУГА ФАЗА. ОДСТУПАЊЕ ГЛАВНЕ СНАГЕ НА КОСОВО ПОЉЕ. (Veliki rat Srbije za oslobođenje i ujedinenje Srba, Hrvata i Slovenaca. Dvanaesta knjige. 1915 godina. Treći period. Opšte odstupanje srpske vojske. Druga faza - Odstupanje glavne snage na Kosovo polje. - *Serbia's Great War for the Liberation and Unification of the Serbs, Croats and Slovenians. Twelfth Book. 1915 Thrid Period. The General Withdrawal of the Serbian Armies. Second Phase. Main Withdrawal through the Kosovo Valley.*) [Map Case]

Anonymous (Glavni đeneralštab - Ministarstvo vojske i mornarice). | 24cm x 15.5cm | paper envelope | 1 large folding map. | Štamparska radionica Ministarstvo vojske i mornarice Štamparija Ujedinjenje. | 1927 | Serbian Text. | Serbo-Croatian Cyrillic

ВЕЛИКИ РАТ СРБИЈЕ ЗА ОСЛОБОЂЕЊЕ И УЈЕДИЊЕЊЕ СРБА, ХРВАТА И СЛОВЕНАЦА. КЊИГЕ ТРИНАЕСТА 1915 ГОДИНА. ТРЕЋИ ПЕРИОД. ОПШТЕ ОДСТУПАЊЕ СРПСКЕ ВОЈСКЕ. III. ФАЗА. ОДСТУПАЊЕ НА ЈАДРАНСКО ПРИМОРЈЕ. (Veliki rat Srbije za oslobođenje i ujedinenje Srba, Hrvata i Slovenaca. Knjige trinaesta. 1915 godina. Treći period. Opšte Odstupanje srpske vojske. III. faza. Odstupanje na Jadransko Primorje. – *Serbia's Great War for the Liberation and Unification of the Serbs, Croats and Slovenians. Thirteenth Book. 1915 Thrid Period. The General Withdrawal of the Serbian Armies. Thrid Phase. Main Withdrawal to the Adriatic Coast.*)

Anonymous (Glavni đeneralštab - Ministarstvo vojske i mornarice). | 24cm x 15.5cm | Blue paper covered softback | viii + 424pp + i | Štamparska radionica Ministarstvo vojske i mornarice Štamparija Ujedinjenje. | 1927 | Serbian Text. | Serbo-Croatian Cyrillic

This volume covers the period of late November – December 1915.

ВЕЛИКИ РАТ СРБИЈЕ ЗА ОСЛОБОЂЕЊЕ И УЈЕДИЊЕЊЕ СРБА, ХРВАТА И СЛОВЕНАЦА. КЊИГЕ ТРИНАЕСТА 1915 ГОДИНА. ТРЕЋИ ПЕРИОД. ОПШТЕ ОДСТУПАЊЕ СРПСКЕ ВОЈСКЕ. III. ФАЗА. ОДСТУПАЊЕ НА ЈАДРАНСКО ПРИМОРЈЕ. (Veliki rat Srbije za oslobođenje i ujedinenje Srba, Hrvata i Slovenaca. Knjige trinaesta. 1915 godina. Treći period. Opšte Odstupanje srpske vojske. III. faza. Odstupanje na Jadransko Primorje.– *Serbia's Great War for the Liberation and Unification of the Serbs, Croats and Slovenians. Thirteenth Book. 1915 Thrid Period. The General Withdrawal of the Serbian Armies. III Phase. Main Withdrawal to the Adriatic Coast.*) [Map Case]

Anonymous (Glavni đeneralštab - Ministarstvo vojske i mornarice). | 24cm x 15.5cm | paper envelope | 1 large folding map. | Štamparska radionica Ministarstvo vojske i mornarice Štamparija Ujedinjenje. | 1927 | Serbian Text. | Serbo-Croatian Cyrillic

ВЕЛИКИ РАТ СРБИЈЕ ЗА ОСЛОБОЂЕЊЕ И УЈЕДИЊЕЊЕ СРБА, ХРВАТА И СЛОВЕНАЦА. КЊИГЕ УЕРНАЕСТА 1916 ГОДИНА. ТРЕЋИ ПЕРИОД. ОПШТЕ ОДСТУПАЊЕ СРПСКЕ ВОЈСКЕ. IV. ФАЗА. ПРЕБАЦИВАЊЕ ИЗ АЛБАНИЈЕ НА ОСТРВО КРФ. (Veliki rat Srbije za oslobođenje i ujedinenje Srba, Hrvata i Slovenaca. Uernaesta knjige XIV. 1916 godina. Treći period. Opšte odstupanje srpske vojske. IV faza - Prebacivanje iz Albanije na ostrvo Krf. - *Serbia's Great War for the Liberation and Unification of the Serbs, Croats and Slovenians. Fourteenth Book. Thrid Period in the Year 1915. The General Withdrawal of the Serbian armies. IV Phase - Transportation from Albania across to the Island of Corfu.*)

Anonymous (Glavni đeneralštab - Ministarstvo vojske i mornarice). | 24cm x 15.5cm | Brown paper covered softback | vi + 354pp + i | Štamparska radionica Ministarstvo vojske i mornarice Štamparija Ujedinjenje. | 1928 | Serbian Text. | Serbo-Croatian Cyrillic

This volume covers the period of December 1915 - January 1916.

ВЕЛИКИ РАТ СРБИЈЕ ЗА ОСЛОБОЂЕЊЕ И УЈЕДИЊЕЊЕ СРБА, ХРВАТА И СЛОВЕНАЦА. КЊИГЕ УЕРНАЕСТА 1916 ГОДИНА. ТРЕЋИ ПЕРИОД. ОПШТЕ ОДСТУПАЊЕ СРПСКЕ ВОЈСКЕ. IV. ФАЗА. ПРЕБАЦИВАЊЕ ИЗ АЛБАНИЈЕ НА ОСТРВО КРФ. (Veliki rat Srbije za oslobođenje i ujedinenje Srba, Hrvata i Slovenaca. Uernaesta knjige XIV. 1916 godina. Treći period. Opšte odstupanje srpske vojske. IV faza - Prebacivanje iz Albanije na ostrvo Krf. - *Serbia's Great War for the Liberation and Unification of* *the Serbs, Croats and Slovenians. Fourteenth Book. Thrid Period in the Year 1915. The General Withdrawal of the Serbian armies. IV Phase - Transportation from Albania across to the Island of Corfu.*) [Map Case]

Anonymous (Glavni đeneralštab - Ministarstvo vojske i mornarice). | 24cm x 15.5cm | paper envelope | 1 large folding map. | Štamparska radionica Ministarstvo vojske i mornarice Štamparija Ujedinjenje. | 1928 | Serbian Text. | Serbo-Croatian Cyrillic

ВЕЛИКИ РАТ СРБИЈЕ ЗА ОСЛОБОЂЕЊЕ И УЈЕДИЊЕЊЕ СРБА, ХРВАТА И СЛОВЕНАЦА. КЊИГЕ XV 1916 ГОДИНА. РЕОРГАНИЗАЦИЈА СРПСКЕ ВОЈСКЕ НА КРФУ И ПРЕБАЦИВАЊЕ У СОЛУН И ОКОЛИНУ. (Veliki rat Srbije za oslobođenje i ujedinenje Srba, Hrvata i Slovenaca. knjige XV. 1916 godina. Reorganizacija srpske vojske na Krfu I prebacivanje u Solun I okolinu. - *Serbia's Great War for the Liberation and Unification of the Serbs, Croats and Slovenians. Book XV. 1916. Reorganisation of the Serbian Army Reorganisation of the Serbian Army in Corfu followed by Transportation to Solonika and the Surrounding Countryside.*)

Anonymous (Glavni đeneralštab - Ministarstvo vojske i mornarice). | 24cm x 15.5cm | Blue paper covered softback | xi + 468pp | Štamparska radionica Ministarstvo vojske i mornarice Štamparija Ujedinjenje. | 1929 | Serbian Text. | Serbo-Croatian Cyrillic

This volume covers the period of April – mid June 1916.

No large format maps issued with this volume.

ВЕЛИКИ РАТ СРБИЈЕ ЗА ОСЛОБОЂЕЊЕ И УЈЕДИЊЕЊЕ СРБА, ХРВАТА И СЛОВЕНАЦА. КЊИГЕ ШЕСНАЕСТА. ИЗЛАЗАК НА СОЛУНСКИ ФРОНТ И ПОУЕТАК ОПЕРАЦИЈА СРПСКЕ ВОЈСКЕ (ОД 17.-VI. ДО 16.-VIII.). (Veliki rat Srbije za oslobođenje i ujedinenje Srba, Hrvata i Slovenaca. Šesnaesta knjige. Izlazak na solunski front I početak operacija sepske vojske (od 17.-VI. do 16.-VIII.). - *Serbia's Great War for the Liberation and Unification of the Serbs, Croats and Slovenians. Sixteenth Book. Passage to the Solonika Front and the Beginning of Serbian Army Operations (17 June - 16 August).*)

Anonymous (Glavni đeneralštab - Ministarstvo vojske i mornarice). | 24cm x 15.5cm | Blue paper covered softback | xiii + 384pp + iii | Štamparska radionica Ministarstvo vojske i mornarice Štamparija Ujedinjenje. | 1929 | Serbian Text. | Serbo-Croatian Cyrillic

This volume covers the period of mid June - mid August 1916.

No year was given in the title of this volume!

ВЕЛИКИ РАТ СРБИЈЕ ЗА ОСЛОБОЂЕЊЕ И УЈЕДИЊЕЊЕ СРБА, ХРВАТА И СЛОВЕНАЦА. КЊИГЕ ШЕСНАЕСТА. ИЗЛАЗАК НА СОЛУНСКИ ФРОНТ И ПОУЕТАК ОПЕРАЦИЈА СРПСКЕ ВОЈСКЕ (ОД 17.-VI. ДО 16.-VIII.). (Veliki rat Srbije za oslobođenje i ujedinenje Srba, Hrvata i Slovenaca. Šesnaesta knjige. Izlazak na solunski front I početak operacija sepske vojske (od 17.-VI. do 16.-VIII.). - *Serbia's Great War for the Liberation and Unification of the Serbs, Croats and Slovenians. Sixteenth Book. Passage to the Solonika Front and the Beginning of Serbian Army Operations (17 June - 16 August).*) [Map Case]

Anonymous (Glavni đeneralštab - Ministarstvo vojske i mornarice). | 24cm x 15.5cm | paper envelope | 1 large folding map. | Štamparska radionica Ministarstvo vojske i mornarice Štamparija Ujedinjenje. | 1929 | Serbian Text. | Serbo-Croatian Cyrillic

ВЕЛИКИ РАТ СРБИЈЕ ЗА ОСЛОБОЂЕЊЕ И УЈЕДИЊЕЊЕ СРБА, ХРВАТА И СЛОВЕНАЦА. КЊИГЕ СЕДАМНАЕСТА 1916 ГОДИНА. ПРИПРЕМЕ ЗА ОФАНЗИВУ НА СОЛУНСКОМ ФРОНТУ ОД 17.АВГУСТ – 14.СЕПТЕМБАР. ЗАУСТАВЉАЊЕ БУГАРСКЕ ОФАНЗИВЕ Н ОФАНЗИВА СРПСКИХ ТРУПА. ПРВИ ПЕРИОД. ГОРНИУЕВСКА БИТКА. (Veliki rat Srbije za oslobođenje i ujedinenje Srba, Hrvata i Slovenaca. Knjige Sedamnaesta. 1916 godina. Pripreme za ofanzivu na solunskom frontu od 17 avgust – 14 septembar. Zaustavljanje bugarske ofanzive n ofanziva srpskih trupa. Prvi period. Gorniuevska bitka. - *Serbia's Great War for the Liberation and Unification of the Serbs, Croats and Slovenians. Seventeenth Book. The Preparations of the Offensive from the Solun Front between 17 August – 14 September. The Delay of the Bulgarian Offensive and the Serbian Offensive, First Period. The Gorniver Affair.*)

Anonymous (Glavni đeneralštab - Ministarstvo vojske i mornarice). | 24cm x 15.5cm | Pink paper covered softback | 568pp + vii | Štamparska radionica Ministarstvo vojske i mornarice Štamparija Ujedinjenje. | 1929 | Serbian Text. | Serbo-Croatian Cyrillic

This volume covers the period of August - September 1916.

ВЕЛИКИ РАТ СРБИЈЕ ЗА ОСЛОБОЂЕЊЕ И УЈЕДИЊЕЊЕ СРБА, ХРВАТА И СЛОВЕНАЦА. КЊИГЕ СЕДАМНАЕСТА 1916 ГОДИНА. ПРИПРЕМЕ ЗА ОФАНЗИВУ НА СОЛУНСКОМ ФРОНТУ ОД 17.АВГУСТ – 14.СЕПТЕМБАР. ЗАУСТАВЉАЊЕ

БУГАРСКЕ ОФАНЗИВЕ Н ОФАНЗИВА СРПСКИХ ТРУПА. ПРВИ ПЕРИОД. ГОРНИУЕВСКА БИТКА. (Veliki rat Srbije za oslobođenje i ujedinjenje Srba, Hrvata i Slovenaca. Knjige Sedamnaesta. 1916 godina. Pripreme za ofanzivu na solunskom frontu od 17 avgust – 14 septembar. Zaustavljanje bugarske ofanzive n ofanziva srpskih trupa. Prvi period. Gorniuevska bitka. - *Serbia's Great War for the Liberation and Unification of the Serbs, Croats and Slovenians. Seventeenth Book. The Preparations of the Offensive from the Solun Front between 17 August – 14 September. The Delay of the Bulgarian Offensive and the Serbian Offensive, First Period. The Gorniver Affair.*) [Map Case]

> Anonymous (Glavni đeneralštab - Ministarstvo vojske i mornarice). I 24cm x 15.5cm I paper envelope I 3 large folding maps. I Štamparska radionica Ministarstvo vojske i mornarice Štamparija Ujedinjenje. I 1929 I Serbian Text. I Serbo-Croatian Cyrillic

ВЕЛИКИ РАТ СРБИЈЕ ЗА ОСЛОБОЂЕЊЕ И УЈЕДИЊЕЊЕ СРБА, ХРВАТА И СЛОВЕНАЦА. КЊИГЕ ОСАМНАЕСТА 1916 ГОДИНА. ОФАНЗИВА СРПСКЕ ВОЈСКЕ НА СОЛУНСКОМ ФРОНТУ. ДРУГА ПЕРИОД. ЗАУЗЕЋЕ КАЈМАКУАЛАНА, СТАРКОВОГ ГРОБА И СОВИУКИХ ПОЛОЖАЈА. (Veliki rat Srbije za oslobođenje i ujedinenje Srba, Hrvata i Slovenaca. Knjige Osamnaesta. 1916 godina. Ofanziva srpske vojske na solunskom frontu. Druga period. Zauzede Kajmakualana, Starkovog Groba i Soviukih Položaja. - *Serbia's Great War for the Liberation and Unification of the Serbs, Croats and Slovenians. Eighteenth Book. The Serbian Offensive on the Solun Front during 1916. Second Period. Occupation of Kajmakualana, Starkovog Groba and the Soviuk Position.*)

> Anonymous (Glavni đeneralštab - Ministarstvo vojske i mornarice). I 24cm x 15.5cm I Green paper covered softback I 624pp + xi I Štamparska radionica Ministarstvo vojske i mornarice Štamparija Ujedinjenje. I 1930 I Serbian Text. I Serbo-Croatian Cyrillic

This volume covers the period of September 1916.

ВЕЛИКИ РАТ СРБИЈЕ ЗА ОСЛОБОЂЕЊЕ И УЈЕДИЊЕЊЕ СРБА, ХРВАТА И СЛОВЕНАЦА. КЊИГЕ ОСАМНАЕСТА 1916 ГОДИНА. ОФАНЗИВА СРПСКЕ ВОЈСКЕ НА СОЛУНСКОМ ФРОНТУ. ДРУГА ПЕРИОД. ЗАУЗЕЋЕ КАЈМАКУАЛАНА, СТАРКОВОГ ГРОБА И СОВИУКИХ ПОЛОЖАЈА. (Veliki rat Srbije za oslobođenje i ujedinenje Srba, Hrvata i Slovenaca. Knjige Osamnaesta. 1916 godina. Ofanziva srpske vojske na solunskom frontu. Druga period. Zauzede Kajmakualana, Starkovog Groba i Soviukih Položaja. - *Serbia's Great War for the Liberation and Unification of the Serbs, Croats and Slovenians. Eighteenth Book. The Serbian Offensive on the Solun Front during 1916. Second Period. Occupation of Kajmakualana, Starkovog Groba and the Soviuk Position.*) [Map Case]

> Anonymous (Glavni đeneralštab - Ministarstvo vojske i mornarice). I 24cm x 15.5cm I paper envelope I 1 large folding map. I Štamparska radionica Ministarstvo vojske i mornarice Štamparija Ujedinjenje. I 1930 I Serbian Text. I Serbo-Croatian Cyrillic

ВЕЛИКИ РАТ СРБИЈЕ ЗА ОСЛОБОЂЕЊЕ И УЈЕДИЊЕЊЕ СРБА, ХРВАТА И СЛОВЕНАЦА. 1914-1918 Г. КЊИГЕ ДЕВЕТНАЕСТА 1916 ГОДИНА. ОФАНЗИВА СРПСКЕ ВОЈСКЕ НА СОЛУНСКОМ ФРОНТУ 1916 Г. ТРЕЋИ ПЕРИОД. ОПЕРАЦИЈЕ НА ЦРНОЈ РЕЦИ И ЗАУЗЕЋЕ БИТОЉА. I ДЕО ЗАУЗЕЋЕ ТЕПАВАЧКИХ ПОЛОЖАЈА. (Veliki rat Srbije za oslobođenje i ujedinenje Srba, Hrvata i Slovenaca. 1914-1918 g. Knjige Devetnaesta. 1916 godina. Ofanziva srpske vojske na solunskom frontu 1916 godina. Treći period. Operacije na Crnoj Reci i Zauzeće Bitolja. I Deo Zauzeće Tepavačkih Položaja. - *Serbia's Great War for the Liberation and Unification of the Serbs, Croats and Slovenians. Ninteenth Book. 1916. The Serbian Offensive on the Solun Front during 1916. Thrid Period. Operation across Crnoj Reci and Zauzeće Bitolja. I Part War Operation on the River Crna Reka and the Occupation of the Town of Bitola. And Part Occupation of Tepava Position.*)

> Anonymous (Glavni đeneralštab - Ministarstvo vojske i mornarice). I 24cm x 15.5cm I Green paper covered softback I 745pp + ix I Štamparska radionica Ministarstvo vojske i mornarice Štamparija Ujedinjenje. I 1930 I Serbian Text. I Serbo-Croatian Cyrillic

There seems to have been a printing error in the title on both the cover and the title page of this volume with the part number and the description (I ДЕО ЗАУЗЕЋЕ ТЕПАВАЧКИХ ПОЛОЖАЈА) missing. On the copy reviewed, this oversight has been amended by glueing a correction slip of paper with the missing information to the titlepage only. It is therefore assumed that this correction was issued as part of an erratum sheet, distributed with a later volume.

This volume covers the period of 4 – 25 October 1916.

ВЕЛИКИ РАТ СРБИЈЕ ЗА ОСЛОБОЂЕЊЕ И УЈЕДИЊЕЊЕ СРБА, ХРВАТА И СЛОВЕНАЦА. 1914-1918 Г. КЊИГЕ ДЕВЕТНАЕСТА 1916 ГОДИНА. ОФАНЗИВА

СРПСКЕ ВОЈСКЕ НА СОЛУНСКОМ ФРОНТУ 1916 Г. ТРЕЋИ ПЕРИОД. ОПЕРАЦИЈЕ НА ЦРНОЈ РЕЦИ И ЗАУЗЕЋЕ БИТОЉА. I ДЕО ЗАУЗЕЋЕ ТЕПАВАЧКИХ ПОЛОЖАЈА. (Veliki rat Srbije za oslobođenje i ujedinenje Srba, Hrvata i Slovenaca. 1914-1918 g. Knjige Devetnaesta. 1916 godina. Ofanziva srpske vojske na solunskom frontu 1916 godina. Treći period. Operacije na Crnoj Reci i Zauzeće Bitolja. I Deo Zauzeće Tepavačkih Položaja. - Serbia's Great War for the Liberation and Unification of the Serbs, Croats and Slovenians 1914-1918. Ninteenth Book. 1916. The Serbian Offensive on the Solun Front during 1916. Thrid Period. Operation across Crnoj Reci and Zauzeće Bitolja. I Part War Operation on the River Crna Reka and the Occupation of the Town of Bitola. And Part Occupation of Tepava Position.) [Map Case]

> Anonymous (Glavni đeneralštab - Ministarstvo vojske i mornarice). | 24cm x 15.5cm | paper envelope | 1 large folding map. | Štamparska radionica Ministarstvo vojske i mornarice Štamparija Ujedinjenje. | 1930 | Serbian Text. | Serbo-Croatian Cyrillic

ВЕЛИКИ РАТ СРБИЈЕ ЗА ОСЛОБОЂЕЊЕ И УЈЕДИЊЕЊЕ СРБА, ХРВАТА И СЛОВЕНАЦА. 1914-1918 Г. КЊИГЕ ДВАДЕСЕТА. 1916 ГОДИНА. ОФАНЗИВА СРПСКЕ ВОЈСКЕ НА СОЛУНСКОМ ФРОНТУ. ТРЕЋИ ПЕРИОД. ОПЕРАЦИЈЕ НА ЦРНОЈ РЕЦИ И ЗАУЗЕЋЕ БИТОЉА. II ДЕО ОСВОЈЕЊЕ КОТА 1212 И 1378 И ПАД БИТОЉА. (Veliki rat Srbije za oslobođenje i ujedinenje Srba, Hrvata i Slovenaca. 1914-1918. Knjige Dvadeset. 1916 godina. Ofanziva srpske vojske na solunskom frontu. Ofanziva srpske vojske na solunskom frontu 1916 godina. Treći period. Operacije na Crnoj Reci i Zauzeće Bitolja. II Deo Osvojenje Kota 1212 i 1378 i Pad Bitolja. – Serbia's Great War for the Liberation and Unification of the Serbs, Croats and Slovenians 1914-1918. Twentieth Book. 1914-1918. The Serbian Offensive on the Solun Front during 1916. The Serbian Offensive on the Solun Thrid Period. Front during. War Operation Across the River Crnoj Reci and the Occupation of the Town Of Bitola. Second Phase of the Capture of Hill 1212 and 1378 and the Fall of Bitolja.)

> Anonymous (Glavni đeneralštab - Ministarstvo vojske i mornarice). | 24cm x 15.5cm | Green paper covered softback | 624pp + xi | Štamparska radionica Ministarstvo vojske i mornarice Štamparija Ujedinjenje. | 1930 | Serbian Text. | Serbo-Croatian Cyrillic
> This volume covers the period of 26 October - 19 December 1916.

ВЕЛИКИ РАТ СРБИЈЕ ЗА ОСЛОБОЂЕЊЕ И УЈЕДИЊЕЊЕ СРБА, ХРВАТА И СЛОВЕНАЦА. 1914-1918 Г. КЊИГЕ ДВАДЕСЕТА. 1916 ГОДИНА. ОФАНЗИВА СРПСКЕ ВОЈСКЕ НА СОЛУНСКОМ ФРОНТУ. ТРЕЋИ ПЕРИОД. ОПЕРАЦИЈЕ НА ЦРНОЈ РЕЦИ И ЗАУЗЕЋЕ БИТОЉА. II ДЕО ОСВОЈЕЊЕ КОТА 1212 И 1378 И ПАД БИТОЉА. (Veliki rat Srbije za oslobođenje i ujedinenje Srba, Hrvata i Slovenaca. 1914-1918. Knjige Dvadeset. 1916 godina. Ofanziva srpske vojske na solunskom frontu. Ofanziva srpske vojske na solunskom frontu 1916 godina. Treći period. Operacije na Crnoj Reci i Zauzeće Bitolja. II Deo Osvojenje Kota 1212 i 1378 i Pad Bitolja. – Serbia's Great War for the Liberation and Unification of the Serbs, Croats and Slovenians1914-1918. Twentieth Book. 1916. The Serbian Offensive on the Solun Front during 1916. The Serbian Offensive on the Solun Thrid Period. Front during. War Operation Across the River Crnoj Reci and the Occupation of the Town Of Bitola. Second Phase of the Capture of Hill 1212 and 1378 and the Fall of Bitolja.) [Map Case]

> Anonymous (Glavni đeneralštab - Ministarstvo vojske i mornarice). | 24cm x 15.5cm | paper envelope | 1 large folding map. | Štamparska radionica Ministarstvo vojske i mornarice Štamparija Ujedinjenje. | 1930 | Serbian Text. | Serbo-Croatian Cyrillic

ВЕЛИКИ РАТ СРБИЈЕ ЗА ОСЛОБОЂЕЊЕ И УЈЕДИЊЕЊЕ СРБА, ХРВАТА И СЛОВЕНАЦА 1914 – 1918Г. КЊИГЕ ДВАДЕСЕТ ПРВА. 1916 И 1917. ГОДИНА. РОВОВСКА ВОЈНА СРПСКЕ ВОЈСКЕ НА СОЛУНСКОМ ФРОНТУ. I ПЕРИОД. РОВОВСКЕ ВОЈНЕ. (Veliki rat Srbije za oslobođenje i ujedinenje Srba, Hrvata i Slovenaca 1914 – 1918. Knjige Dvadeset Prva. 1916 i 1917 godina. Rovovska vojna srpske vojske na solunskom frontu. I period. Rovovske Vojne. - Serbia's Great War for the Liberation and Unification of the Serbs, Croats and Slovenians 1914 – 1918. Twenty First Book. 1916 and 1917. Serbian Army's Trench Warfare on the Solun Front. The First Period of Trench Warfare.)

> Anonymous (Glavni đeneralštab - Ministarstvo vojske i mornarice). | 24cm x 15.5cm | Green paper covered softback | xxvii + 793pp + ii | Štamparska radionica Ministarstvo vojske i mornarice Štamparija Ujedinjenje. | 1931 | Serbian Text. | Serbo-Croatian Cyrillic
> This volume covers the period of 20 December 1916 – 31 March 1917.

ВЕЛИКИ РАТ СРБИЈЕ ЗА ОСЛОБОЂЕЊЕ И УЈЕДИЊЕЊЕ СРБА, ХРВАТА И СЛОВЕНАЦА 1914 – 1918Г. КЊИГЕ ДВАДЕСЕТ ПРВА. 1916 И 1917. ГОДИНА. РОВОВСКА ВОЈНА СРПСКЕ ВОЈСКЕ НА СОЛУНСКОМ ФРОНТУ. I ПЕРИОД. РОВОВСКЕ ВОЈНЕ. (Veliki rat Srbije za oslobođenje i ujedinenje Srba, Hrvata i Slovenaca

1914 – 1918. Knjige Dvadeset Prva. 1916 i 1917 godina. Rovovska vojna srpske vojske na solunskom frontu. I period. Rovovske Vojne. - *Serbia's Great War for the Liberation and Unification of the Serbs, Croats and Slovenians 1914 – 1918. Twenty First Book. 1916 and 1917. Serbian Army's Trench Warfare on the Solun Front. The First Period of Trench Warfare.*) [Map Case]

> Anonymous (Glavni đeneralštab - Ministarstvo vojske i mornarice). | 24cm x 15.5cm | paper envelope | 1 large folding map. | Štamparska radionica Ministarstvo vojske i mornarice Štamparija Ujedinjenje. | 1931 | Serbian Text. | Serbo-Croatian Cyrillic

ВЕЛИКИ РАТ СРБИЈЕ ЗА ОСЛОБОЂЕЊЕ И УЈЕДИЊЕЊЕ СРБА, ХРВАТА И СЛОВЕНАЦА 1914 – 1918Г. КЊИГЕ ДВАДЕСЕТ ДРУГА. 1917 ГОДИНА. РОВОВСКА ВОЈНА СРПСКЕ ВОЈСКЕ НА СОЛУНСКОМ ФРОНТУ. I ПЕРИОД. РОВОВСКЕ ВОЈНЕ. НАСТАВАК. (Veliki rat Srbije za oslobođenje i ujedinjenje Srba, Hrvata i Slovenaca 1914 – 1918. Knjige Dvadeset Druga. 1917 godina. Rovovska vojna srpske vojske na solunskom frontu. I period. Rovovske Vojne. Nastavak. - *Serbia's Great War for the Liberation and Unification of the Serbs, Croats and Slovenians 1914 – 1918. Twenty Second Book. 1917. Serbian Army's Trench Warfare on the Solun Front. Continuation of the First Period of Trench Warfare.*)

> Anonymous (Glavni đeneralštab - Ministarstvo vojske i mornarice). | 24cm x 15.5cm | Green paper covered softback | xx + 794pp + ii | Štamparska radionica Ministarstvo vojske i mornarice Štamparija Ujedinjenje. | 1932 | Serbian Text. | Serbo-Croatian Cyrillic
> This volume covers the period of 1 April – 23 May 1917.

ВЕЛИКИ РАТ СРБИЈЕ ЗА ОСЛОБОЂЕЊЕ И УЈЕДИЊЕЊЕ СРБА, ХРВАТА И СЛОВЕНАЦА 1914 – 1918Г. КЊИГЕ ДВАДЕСЕТ ДРУГА. 1917 ГОДИНА. РОВОВСКА ВОЈНА СРПСКЕ ВОЈСКЕ НА СОЛУНСКОМ ФРОНТУ. I ПЕРИОД. РОВОВСКЕ ВОЈНЕ. НАСТАВАК. (Veliki rat Srbije za oslobođenje i ujedinjenje Srba, Hrvata i Slovenaca 1914 – 1918. Knjige Dvadeset Druga. 1917 godina. Rovovska vojna srpske vojske na solunskom frontu. I period. Rovovske Vojne. Nastavak. - *Serbia's Great War for the Liberation and Unification of the Serbs, Croats and Slovenians 1914 – 1918. Twenty Second Book. 1917. Serbian Army's Trench Warfare on the Solun Front. Continuation of the First Period of Trench Warfare.*)
[Map Case]

> Anonymous (Glavni đeneralštab - Ministarstvo vojske i mornarice). | 24cm x 15.5cm | paper envelope | 3 large folding maps. | Štamparska radionica Ministarstvo vojske i mornarice Štamparija Ujedinjenje. | 1932 | Serbian Text. | Serbo-Croatian Cyrillic

ВЕЛИКИ РАТ СРБИЈЕ ЗА ОСЛОБОЂЕЊЕ И УЈЕДИЊЕЊЕ СРБА, ХРВАТА И СЛОВЕНАЦА 1914 – 1918Г. КЊИГЕ ДВАДЕСЕТ ТРЕЋА. 1917 ГОДИНА. РОВОВСКА ВОЈНА СРПСКЕ ВОЈСКЕ НА СОЛУНСКОМ ФРОНТУ. II ПЕРИОД. РОВОВСКЕ ВОЈНЕ. ДЕФАНЗИВА СРПСКЕ ВОЈСКЕ. (Veliki rat Srbije za oslobođenje i ujedinjenje Srba, Hrvata i Slovenaca 1914 – 1918. Knjige Dvadeset Treći. 1917 godina. Rovovska vojna srpske vojske na solunskom frontu. II period. Rovovske Vojne. Defanziva Srpske Vojske - *Serbia's Great War for the Liberation and Unification of the Serbs, Croats and Slovenians 1914 – 1918. Twenty Third Book. 1917. Serbian Army's Trench Warfare on the Solun Front. The Second Period of Trench Warfare. The Serbian Army's Defense.*)

> Anonymous (Glavni đeneralštab - Ministarstvo vojske i mornarice). | 24cm x 15.5cm | Green paper covered softback | xxxvii + 813pp + i | 7 tables | Štamparska radionica Ministarstvo vojske i mornarice Štamparija Ujedinjenje. | 1933 | Serbian Text. | Serbo-Croatian Cyrillic
> This volume covers the period of 24 May – 29 August 1917.
> No large format maps issued with this volume and therefore no map case issued.

ВЕЛИКИ РАТ СРБИЈЕ ЗА ОСЛОБОЂЕЊЕ И УЈЕДИЊЕЊЕ СРБА, ХРВАТА И СЛОВЕНАЦА 1914 – 1918Г. КЊИГЕ ДВАДЕСЕТ УЕТВРТА 1917 ГОДИНА. РОВОВСКА ВОЈНА СРПСКЕ ВОЈСКЕ НА СОЛУНСКОМ ФРОНТУ. II ПЕРИОД. РОВОВСКЕ ВОЈНЕ. ДЕФАНЗИВА СРПСКЕ ВОЈСКЕ. НАСТАВАК. (Veliki rat Srbije za oslobođenje i ujedinjenje Srba, Hrvata i Slovenaca 1914 – 1918. Knjige Dvadeset Uetvrta. 1917 godina. Rovovska vojna srpske vojske na solunskom frontu. II period. Rovovske Vojne. Defanziva Srpske Vojske. Nastavak. - *Serbia's Great War for the Liberation and Unification of the Serbs, Croats and Slovenians 1914 – 1918. Twenty Fourth Book. 1917. Serbian Army's Trench Warfare on the Solun Front. The Second Period of Trench Warfare. Continuation of the Serbian Army's Defense.*)

> Anonymous (Glavni đeneralštab - Ministarstvo vojske i mornarice). | 24cm x 15.5cm | Green paper covered softback | xxxiii + 708pp + i | 1 table | Štamparska radionica Ministarstvo vojske i mornarice Štamparija Ujedinjenje. | 1933 | Serbian Text. | Serbo-Croatian Cyrillic

This volume covers the period of 30 August – 31 December 1917.

ВЕЛИКИ РАТ СРБИЈЕ ЗА ОСЛОБОЂЕЊЕ И УЈЕДИЊЕЊЕ СРБА, ХРВАТА И СЛОВЕНАЦА 1914 – 1918Г. КЊИГЕ ДВАДЕСЕТ УЕТВРТА 1917 ГОДИНА. РОВОВСКА ВОЈНА СРПСКЕ ВОЈСКЕ НА СОЛУНСКОМ ФРОНТУ. II ПЕРИОД. РОВОВСКЕ ВОЈНЕ. ДЕФАНЗИВА СРПСКЕ ВОЈСКЕ. НАСТАВАК. (Veliki rat Srbije za oslobođenje i ujedinenje Srba, Hrvata i Slovenaca 1914 – 1918. Knjige Dvadeset Uetvrta. 1917 godina. Rovovska vojna srpske vojske na solunskom frontu. II period. Rovovske Vojne. Defanziva Srpske Vojske. Nastavak. - *Serbia's Great War for the Liberation and Unification of the Serbs, Croats and Slovenians 1914 – 1918. Twenty Fourth Book. 1917. Serbian Army's Trench Warfare on the Solun Front. The Second Period of Trench Warfare. Continuation of the Serbian Army's Defense.*) [Map Case]

Anonymous (Glavni đeneralštab - Ministarstvo vojske i mornarice). I 24cm x 15.5cm I paper envelope I 2 large folding maps. I Štamparska radionica Ministarstvo vojske i mornarice Štamparija Ujedinjenje. I 1933 I Serbian Text. I Serbo-Croatian Cyrillic

ВЕЛИКИ РАТ СРБИЈЕ ЗА ОСЛОБОЂЕЊЕ И УЈЕДИЊЕЊЕ СРБА, ХРВАТА И СЛОВЕНАЦА 1914 – 1918Г. КЊИГЕ ДВАДЕСЕТ ПЕТА 1918 ГОДИНА. РОВОВСКА ВОЈНА СРПСКЕ ВОЈСКЕ НА СОЛУНСКОМ ФРОНТУ. II ПЕРИОД. РОВОВСКЕ ВОЈНЕ. ДЕФАНЗИВА СРПСКЕ ВОЈСКЕ. НАСТАВАК. (Veliki rat Srbije za oslobođenje i ujedinenje Srba, Hrvata i Slovenaca 1914 – 1918. Knjige Dvadeset Peta. 1918 godina. Rovovska vojna srpske vojske na solunskom frontu. II period. Rovovske Vojne. Defanziva Srpske Vojske. Nastavak. - *Serbia's Great War for the Liberation and Unification of the Serbs, Croats and Slovenians 1914 – 1918. Twenty Fifth Book. 1918. Serbian Army's Trench Warfare on the Solun Front. The Second Period of Trench Warfare. Continuation of the Serbian Army's Defense.*)

Anonymous (Glavni đeneralštab - Ministarstvo vojske i mornarice). I 24cm x 15.5cm I Green paper covered softback I xxxiv + 673pp + i I Štamparska radionica Ministarstvo vojske i mornarice Štamparija Ujedinjenje. I 1934 I Serbian Text. I Serbo-Croatian Cyrillic
This volume covers the period of 1 January – 13 June 1918.

ВЕЛИКИ РАТ СРБИЈЕ ЗА ОСЛОБОЂЕЊЕ И УЈЕДИЊЕЊЕ СРБА, ХРВАТА И СЛОВЕНАЦА 1914 – 1918Г. КЊИГЕ ДВАДЕСЕТ ПЕТА 1918 ГОДИНА. РОВОВСКА ВОЈНА СРПСКЕ ВОЈСКЕ НА СОЛУНСКОМ ФРОНТУ. II ПЕРИОД. РОВОВСКЕ ВОЈНЕ. ДЕФАНЗИВА СРПСКЕ ВОЈСКЕ. НАСТАВАК. (Veliki rat Srbije za oslobođenje i ujedinenje Srba, Hrvata i Slovenaca 1914 – 1918. Knjige Dvadeset Peta. 1918 godina. Rovovska vojna srpske vojske na solunskom frontu. II period. Rovovske Vojne. Defanziva Srpske Vojske. Nastavak. - *Serbia's Great War for the Liberation and Unification of the Serbs, Croats and Slovenians 1914 – 1918. Twenty Fifth Book. 1918. Serbian Army's Trench Warfare on the Solun Front. The Second Period of Trench Warfare. Continuation of the Serbian Army's Defense.*) [Map Case]

Anonymous (Glavni đeneralštab - Ministarstvo vojske i mornarice). I 24cm x 15.5cm I paper envelope I 1 large folding map. I Štamparska radionica Ministarstvo vojske i mornarice Štamparija Ujedinjenje. I 1934 I Serbian Text. I Serbo-Croatian Cyrillic

ВЕЛИКИ РАТ СРБИЈЕ ЗА ОСЛОБОЂЕЊЕ И УЈЕДИЊЕЊЕ СРБА, ХРВАТА И СЛОВЕНАЦА 1914 – 1918Г. КЊИГЕ ДВАДЕСЕТ ШЕСТА 1918 ГОДИНА. РОВОВСКА ВОЈНА СРПСКЕ ВОЈСКЕ НА СОЛУНСКОМ ФРОНТУ. III ПЕРИОД. РОВОВСКЕ ВОЈНЕ. ДЕФАНЗИВА СРПСКЕ ВОЈСКЕ. ПРИПРЕМЕ ЗА ОФАНЗИВУ. (Veliki rat Srbije za oslobođenje i ujedinenje Srba, Hrvata i Slovenaca 1914 – 1918. Knjige Dvadeset Šesta. 1918 godina. Rovovska vojna srpske vojske na solunskom frontu. III period. Rovovske Vojne. Defanziva Srpske Vojske. Pripreme za Ofanzivu. - *Serbia's Great War for the Liberation and Unification of the Serbs, Croats and Slovenians 1914 – 1918. Twenty Sixth Book. 1918. Serbian Army's Trench Warfare on the Solun Front. The Second Period of Trench Warfare. Continuation of the Serbian Army's Defense. PRÉLIMINARIES for the Offensive.*)

Anonymous (Glavni đeneralštab - Ministarstvo vojske i mornarice). I 24cm x 15.5cm I Green paper covered softback I xx + 665pp + i I 6 tables I Štamparska radionica Ministarstvo vojske i mornarice Štamparija Ujedinjenje. I 1935 I Serbian Text. I Serbo-Croatian Cyrillic
This volume covers the period of 30 August - 13 September 1918.

ВЕЛИКИ РАТ СРБИЈЕ ЗА ОСЛОБОЂЕЊЕ И УЈЕДИЊЕЊЕ СРБА, ХРВАТА И СЛОВЕНАЦА 1914 – 1918Г. КЊИГЕ ДВАДЕСЕТ ШЕСТА 1918 ГОДИНА. РОВОВСКА ВОЈНА СРПСКЕ ВОЈСКЕ НА СОЛУНСКОМ ФРОНТУ. III ПЕРИОД. РОВОВСКЕ ВОЈНЕ. ДЕФАНЗИВА СРПСКЕ ВОЈСКЕ. ПРИПРЕМЕ ЗА ОФАНЗИВУ. (Veliki rat Srbije za oslobođenje i ujedinenje Srba, Hrvata i Slovenaca 1914 – 1918. Knjige Dvadeset Šesta. 1918 godina. Rovovska vojna srpske vojske na solunskom frontu. III period. Rovovske Vojne. Defanziva Srpske Vojske. Pripreme za Ofanzivu. - *Serbia's Great War for the Liberation and Unification of the Serbs, Croats and Slovenians 1914 – 1918. Twenty Sixth Book. 1918. Serbian Army's Trench Warfare on the Solun Front. The Second Period of Trench Warfare. Continuation of the Serbian Army's Defense. PRÉLIMINARIES for the Offensive.*) [Map Case]

    Anonymous (Glavni đeneralštab - Ministarstvo vojske i mornarice). | 24cm x 15.5cm | paper envelope | 1 large folding map. | Štamparska radionica Ministarstvo vojske i mornarice Štamparija Ujedinjenje. | 1935 | Serbian Text. | Serbo-Croatian Cyrillic

ВЕЛИКИ РАТ СРБИЈЕ ЗА ОСЛОБОЂЕЊЕ И УЈЕДИЊЕЊЕ СРБА, ХРВАТА И СЛОВЕНАЦА 1914 – 1918Г. КЊИГЕ ДВАДЕСЕТ СЕДМА 1918 ГОДИНА. ОФАНЗИВА ПРВИ ПЕРИОД: ДОБРОПОЉСКА БИТКА. Пробој непријате Фронтп и избијање српске воске на реку вардар. **(Veliki rat Srbije za oslobođenje i ujedinenje Srba, Hrvata i Slovenaca 1914 – 1918. Knjige Dvadeset Sedma. 1918 godina. Ofanziva. Prvi period: Dobropojska Bitka. Proboj neprijate Frontp i izbijanje srpske voske na reku vardar.** - *Serbia's Great War for the Liberation and Unification of the Serbs, Croats and Slovenians 1914 – 1918. Twenty Seventh Book. 1918. The First Offensive Period: The Battle of Dobropolje. The Break-Through the Hostile Front and the Advance of the Serbian Army to the River Vardar.*)

    Anonymous (Glavni đeneralštab - Ministarstvo vojske i mornarice). | 24cm x 15.5cm | Green paper covered softback | vi + 767pp + i | 3 tables | Štamparska radionica Ministarstvo vojske i mornarice Štamparija Ujedinjenje. | 1936| Serbian Text. | Serbo-Croatian Cyrillic
This volume covers the period of 14 – 21 September 1918.

ВЕЛИКИ РАТ СРБИЈЕ ЗА ОСЛОБОЂЕЊЕ И УЈЕДИЊЕЊЕ СРБА, ХРВАТА И СЛОВЕНАЦА 1914 – 1918Г. КЊИГЕ ДВАДЕСЕТ СЕДМА 1918 ГОДИНА. ОФАНЗИВА ПРВИ ПЕРИОД: ДОБРОПОЉСКА БИТКА. Пробој непријате Фронтп и избијање српске воске на реку вардар. **(Veliki rat Srbije za oslobođenje i ujedinenje Srba, Hrvata i Slovenaca 1914 – 1918. Knjige Dvadeset Sedma. 1918 godina. Ofanziva. Prvi period: Dobropojska Bitka. Proboj neprijate Frontp i izbijanje srpske voske na reku vardar.** - *Serbia's Great War for the Liberation and Unification of the Serbs, Croats and Slovenians 1914 – 1918. Twenty Seventh Book. 1918. The First Offensive Period: The Battle of Dobropolje. The Break-Through the Hostile Front and the Advance of the Serbian Army to the River Vardar.*) [Map Case]

    Anonymous (Glavni đeneralštab - Ministarstvo vojske i mornarice). | 24cm x 15.5cm | paper envelope | 3 large folding maps. | Štamparska radionica Ministarstvo vojske i mornarice Štamparija Ujedinjenje. | 1936 | Serbian Text. | Serbo-Croatian Cyrillic

ВЕЛИКИ РАТ СРБИЈЕ ЗА ОСЛОБОЂЕЊЕ И УЈЕДИЊЕЊЕ СРБА, ХРВАТА И СЛОВЕНАЦА 1914 – 1918Г. КЊИГЕ ДВАДЕСЕТ ССМА 1918 ГОДИНА. ОФАНЗИВА ДРУГИ ПЕРИОД: ГОНЕЊЕ – ПРВИ ФАЗА – Маневар српских армија у сливу Брегалнице заузеђе Царевот села, Овуег Поља и Скопља. **-** Капитулација Бугарске. **(Veliki rat Srbije za oslobođenje i ujedinenje Srba, Hrvata i Slovenaca 1914 – 1918. Knjige Dvadeset Ssma. 1918 godina. Ofanziva. Drugi period. Gonelje - Prvi faza. Manevar srpskih armija u slivu Bregalnice Zauzeće Carevot sela, Ovueg Poja i Skopja. - Kapitulacija Bugarske.** - *Serbia's Great War for the Liberation and Unification of the Serbs, Croats and Slovenians 1914 – 1918. Twenty Eighth Book. 1918. The Second Offensive Period. The First Pursuit Phase. Manoeuvre of the Serbian army to the Mouth of the River Bregalnica Conquest of the village Carevot, the field Ovueg, and the city Skopje. The Bulgarian Capitulation.*)

    Anonymous (Glavni đeneralštab - Ministarstvo vojske i mornarice). | 24cm x 15.5cm | Green paper covered softback | viii + 659pp + i | Štamparska radionica Ministarstvo vojske i mornarice Štamparija Ujedinjenje. | 1937 | Serbian Text. | Serbo-Croatian Cyrillic
This volume covers the period of 22 - 30 September 1918.

ВЕЛИКИ РАТ СРБИЈЕ ЗА ОСЛОБОЂЕЊЕ И УЈЕДИЊЕЊЕ СРБА, ХРВАТА И СЛОВЕНАЦА 1914 – 1918Г. КЊИГЕ ДВАДЕСЕТ ССМА 1918 ГОДИНА. ОФАНЗИВА ДРУГИ ПЕРИОД: ГОНЕЊЕ – ПРВИ ФАЗА – Маневар српских армија у сливу Брегалнице заузеђе Царевот села, Овуег Поља и Скопља. - Капитулација Бугарске. **(Veliki rat Srbije za oslobođenje i ujedinenje Srba, Hrvata i Slovenaca 1914 – 1918. Knjige Dvadeset Ssma. 1918 godina. Ofanziva. Drugi period Gonelje - Prvi faza. Manevar srpskih armija u slivu Bregalnice Zauzeće Carevot sela, Ovueg Poja i Skopja. - Kapitulacija Bugarske.** - *Serbia's Great War for the Liberation and Unification of the Serbs, Croats and Slovenians 1914 – 1918. Twenty Eighth Book. 1918. The Second Offensive Period. The First Pursuit Phase. Manoeuvre of the Serbian army to the Mouth of the River Bregalnica Conquest of the village Carevot, the field Ovueg, and the city Skopje. The Bulgarian Capitulation.*) [Map Case]

Anonymous (Glavni đeneralštab - Ministarstvo vojske i mornarice). I 24cm x 15.5cm I paper envelope I 1 large folding map. I Štamparska radionica Ministarstvo vojske i mornarice Štamparija Ujedinjenje. I 1937 I Serbian Text. I Serbo-Croatian Cyrillic

ВЕЛИКИ РАТ СРБИЈЕ ЗА ОСЛОБОЂЕЊЕ И УЈЕДИЊЕЊЕ СРБА, ХРВАТА И СЛОВЕНАЦА 1914 – 1918Г. КЊИГЕ ДВАДЕСЕТ ДЕВЕТА 1918 ГОДИНА. ОФАНЗИВА ДРУГИ ПЕРИОД: ГОНЕЊЕ – ДРУГИ ФАЗА – Надирање I армије ка Нишу и заузеће Ниша. Пребацивање II армије од Царевог села ка Куманову и Велесу. (Veliki rat Srbije za oslobođenje i ujedinenje Srba, Hrvata i Slovenaca 1914 – 1918. Knjige Dvadeset Deveta. 1918 godina. Ofanziva. Drugi period. Gonelje - Drugi faza. Nadiranje I armije ka Nišu i Zauzeće Niša. Prebacivanje II armije od Carevog sela ka Kumanovu i Velesu. - *Serbia's Great War for the Liberation and Unification of the Serbs, Croats and Slovenians 1914 – 1918. Twenty Ninth Book. 1918. The Second Offensive Period. The Second Pursuit Phase. The First Army's Advance and Capture of Nish. The Second Army's Advance toward Carevo Selo, Kumanovo and Veles.)*

Anonymous (Glavni đeneralštab - Ministarstvo vojske i mornarice). I 24cm x 15.5cm I Green paper covered softback I x + 611pp + iii I Štamparska radionica Ministarstvo vojske i mornarice Štamparija Ujedinjenje. I 1937 I Serbian Text. I Serbo-Croatian Cyrillic.

This volume covers the period of 1 - 13 October 1918.

ВЕЛИКИ РАТ СРБИЈЕ ЗА ОСЛОБОЂЕЊЕ И УЈЕДИЊЕЊЕ СРБА, ХРВАТА И СЛОВЕНАЦА 1914 – 1918Г. КЊИГЕ ДВАДЕСЕТ ДЕВЕТА 1918 ГОДИНА. ОФАНЗИВА ДРУГИ ПЕРИОД: ГОНЕЊЕ – ДРУГИ ФАЗА – Надирање I армије ка Нишу и заузеће Ниша. Пребацивање II армије од Царевог села ка Куманову и Велесу. (Veliki rat Srbije za oslobođenje i ujedinenje Srba, Hrvata i Slovenaca 1914 – 1918. Knjige Dvadeset Deveta. 1918 godina. Ofanziva. Drugi period. Gonelje - Drugi faza. Nadiranje I armije ka Nišu i zauzeće Niša. Prebacivanje II armije od Carevog sela ka Kumanovu i Velesu. - *Serbia's Great War for the Liberation and Unification of the Serbs, Croats and Slovenians 1914 – 1918. Twenty Ninth Book. 1918. The Second Offensive Period. The Second Pursuit Phase. The First Army's Advance and Capture of Nish. The Second Army's Advance toward Carevo Selo, Kumanovo and Veles.)* [Map Case]

Anonymous (Glavni đeneralštab - Ministarstvo vojske i mornarice). I 24cm x 15.5cm I paper envelope I 2 large folding maps. I Štamparska radionica Ministarstvo vojske i mornarice Štamparija Ujedinjenje. I 1937 I Serbian Text. I Serbo-Croatian Cyrillic

ВЕЛИКИ РАТ СРБИЈЕ ЗА ОСЛОБОЂЕЊЕ И УЈЕДИЊЕЊЕ СРБА, ХРВАТА И СЛОВЕНАЦА 1914 – 1918Г. КЊИГЕ ТРИДЕСЕТА 1918 ГОДИНА. ОФАНЗИВА ДРУГИ ПЕРИОД: ГОНЕЊЕ – ДРУГИ ФАЗА – Надирање I армије на север и излазак на Дунав и Саву. Пребацивање II армије од Велеса на Косово и њено избијање на Дрину. (Veliki rat Srbije za oslobođenje i ujedinenje Srba, Hrvata i Slovenaca 1914 – 1918. Knjige Trideseta. 1918 godina. Ofanziva. Drugi period. Gonelje - Drugi faza. Nadiranje I armije na Sever i izlazak na Dunav i Savu. Prebacivanje II armije od Velesa na Kosovo i njeno izbijanje na Drinu. - *Serbia's Great War for the Liberation and Unification of the Serbs, Croats and Slovenians 1914 – 1918. Thirtieth Book. 1918. The Second Offensive Period. The Second Pursuit Phase. The First Army's Advance Northwards until reaching the River Danube and the River Savu. The Second Army's Advance through Veles and Kosovo then the break-through to the River Drina.)*

Anonymous (Glavni đeneralštab - Ministarstvo vojske i mornarice). I 24cm x 15.5cm I Green paper covered softback I xii + 698pp + i I Štamparska radionica Ministarstvo vojske i mornarice Štamparija Ujedinjenje. I 1937 I Serbian Text. I Serbo-Croatian Cyrillic.

This volume covers the period of 14 October – 2 November 1918.

ВЕЛИКИ РАТ СРБИЈЕ ЗА ОСЛОБОЂЕЊЕ И УЈЕДИЊЕЊЕ СРБА, ХРВАТА И СЛОВЕНАЦА 1914 – 1918Г. КЊИГЕ ТРИДЕСЕТА 1918 ГОДИНА. ОФАНЗИВА ДРУГИ ПЕРИОД: ГОНЕЊЕ – ДРУГИ ФАЗА – Надирање I армије на север и излазак на Дунав и Саву. Пребацивање II армије од Велеса на Косово и њено избијање на Дрину. (Veliki rat Srbije za oslobođenje i ujedinenje Srba, Hrvata i Slovenaca 1914 – 1918. Knjige Trideseta. 1918 godina. Ofanziva. Drugi period. Gonelje - Drugi faza. Nadiranje I armije na sever i izlazak na Dunav i Savu. Prebacivanje II armije od Velesa na Kosovo i njeno izbijanje na Drinu. - *Serbia's Great War for the Liberation and Unification of the Serbs, Croats and Slovenians 1914 – 1918. Thirtieth Book. 1918. The Second Offensive Period. The Second Pursuit Phase. The First Army's Advance Northwards until reaching the River Danube and the River Savu. The Second Army's Advance through Veles and Kosovo then the break-through to the River Drina.)* [Map Case]

Anonymous (Glavni đeneralštab - Ministarstvo vojske i mornarice). | 24cm x 15.5cm | paper envelope | 1 large folding map. | Štamparska radionica Ministarstvo vojske i mornarice Štamparija Ujedinjenje. | 1937 | Serbian Text. | Serbo-Croatian Cyrillic

ВЕЛИКИ РАТ СРБИЈЕ 1914 – 1918. (Veliki Rat Srbije 1914 – 1918. - *Serbia's Great War 1914 – 1918.*)

Mihailo Vojvodić and Dragoljub Živojinović (Editors). | 23cm x 15.5cm | Blue Paper Softback | xxii + 530pp | Srpska knjievna zadruga. | 1970 | Serbian Text. | Serbo-Croatian Cyrillic

South African Official Histories

The South African Primary official histories were written by members of the South African Army's General Staff. In 1915 whilst the Great War was in its early days, *Lieutenant General* Jan-Christian Smuts, Minister of Defence, decided to initiate an official history program for the South African armed forces. His first choice for an Official Historian was *Brigadier General* J.J. Collyer, however Collyer was committed to active service with the South African Army in East Africa.

Smuts therefore asked three civilian historian/writers, namely *Professor* Leo Fouché, John Buchan and Hugh Wyndham, all of whom were engaged in the South African Army General Staff, to start work on various aspects of the histories. Fouché was asked to research and write a history of the rebellion, Buchan on the South African involvement on the European Western Front and Wyndham on the conquest of German South West Africa. Although the first two studies were completed and published, Wyndham's work was not completed due to the lack of the German records which at that time were still being sorted in Windhoek. Wyndham's history was left incomplete and therefore not published.

By the early nineteen-twenty's the South African Army's General Staff realised that there was not a full history that covered all the campaigns of the South African Army, especially those in Africa. Therefore the decision was taken to commission J.G.W. Leipoldt to write a general history covering all aspects of South Africa's military involvement in the Great War. Leipoldt wrote "**The Union of South Africa and the Great War 1914 – 1918**" drawing extensively on the earlier works and researches of Fouché, Wyndham, Buchan and Collyer.

Collyer meanwhile started to collect information concerning the African campaigns during the war with the intention of writing the official history as originally requested by Smuts. However he had to wait until the mid nineteen-thirties before he found the time to write his two volume history "**The Campaign in German South West Africa 1914 – 1915**" and "**The South Africans with General Smuts in German East Africa 1916.**"

Military Operations;

Union of South Africa: Report on the Outbreak of the Rebellion and the Policy of the Government with Regards to Its Suppression.
Anonymous [*Professor* Leo Fouché] | 33cm x 21cm | Blue Paper Softback | ii + 79pp | 1 appendix | 1 map | The Government Printing and Stationery Office. | 1915 | English Text.
This volume "**Report on the Outbreak of the Rebellion…**" was regarded as very sensitive and was therefore published as a H.M. Union of South Africa's Government's Blue Paper.

THE SOUTH AFRICAN FORCES IN FRANCE.
]*Lieutentenant-Colonel*] John Buchan | 22.5cm x 15cm | black cloth covered hardback | dust jacket | 404pp | 7 appendices | 22 maps | 17 photographs | 1 coloured illustration | Thomas Nelson and Sons Ltd. | 1920 | English Text.
This volume can be viewed on the Internet Archive world wide web:
http://www.archive.org/stream/historyofsouthaf00buchrich

THE UNION OF SOUTH AFRICA AND THE GREAT WAR 1914 – 1918.
[*Major*] J.G.W. [Johan] Leipoldt, [*Lieutentenant Colonel*] H. [Hugh] Wyndham et al. | 27cm x 20.5cm | red cloth covered hardback | dust jacket | 230pp | 2 appendices | 27 maps | 20 photographs | 1 black and white illustration | 3 tables | The Goverment Printing and Stationary Office. | 1924 | English Text.

THE CAMPAIGN IN GERMAN SOUTH WEST AFRICA 1914 – 1915.
Brigadier-General J.J. [John Johnston] Collyer | 21cm x 15.5cm | red cloth covered hardback | dust jacket | viii + 180pp | 16 maps | The Goverment Printing and Stationary Office. | 1937 | English Text.
This volume was also produced with a green cloth covered hardback, the significance of which is unknown. It is possible that this green covered variant was for military training use since the price on the upper cover of the red covered versions was replaced by the word "Official". Therefore it is assumed that the red cover version was for sale on to the general public.

THE SOUTH AFRICANS WITH GENERAL SMUTS IN GERMAN EAST AFRICA 1916.
Brigadier-General J.J. [John Johnston] Collyer | 21cm x 15.5cm | red cloth covered hardback | dust jacket | xxi + 299pp | 22 maps | The Goverment Printing and Stationary Office. | 1939 | English Text.
This volume was also produced with a green cloth covered hardback variant.

Swedish Official Histories

The Swedish official histories were written under the authority of the Kungliga Sjöfartsdepartementet (The Royal [Swedish] Shipping Department).

Naval Operations;

FLOTTANS NEUTRALITETSVAKT: REDOGÖRELSE FÖR FLOTTANS VERKSAMHET FÖR NEUTRALITETENS UPPRÄTTHÅLLANDE SAMT SJÖFARTENS OCH FISKETS TRYGGANDE M. M. UNDER VÄRLDSKRIGET 1914-18, INNEFATTANDE JÄMVÄL REDOGÖRELSER FÖR VISSA ÅTGÄRDER AV KUSTARTILLERIET OCH LOTSVERKET. (*Guarding the Naval Neutrality: Report of the Fleet Activities for the Enforcement of Neutrality including the Protection of the National Marchant Marine and Fisheries, during World War 1914-18; Also Statements Relating to Certain Swedish Coastal Artillery Defence Measures.*)

Erik Öberg and Axel Elis Biörklund assisted by Å. Hammarskjöld - Kungliga Sjöfartsdepartementet I 24cm x 16.5cm I Blue paper softback I 115pp I 10 appendices I 1 map I 9 tables I Kungliga boktryckeriet, P.A. Norstedt and söner I 1919 I Swedish Text.

On 3 August 1914, the Swedish government declared their neutrality and took steps to protect their neutrality by mobilising their Navy and Army. This volume covers the Swedish mobilisation and covers the following: an overview of the Swedish fleet activities after its mobilisation; the actions of the warring nations' navies in the vicinity of the Swedish coast; the reaction of Swedish navy towards the warring nations; The Swedish measures taken for the protection of their maritime transport and fisheries; the help given to coastal communities; the protection of the Swedish population at home and of Swedish refugees abroad; and finally how Swedish neutrality affected their navy.

Naval/Military Joint Operations;

ÅLANDSUPPGÖRELSEN. REDOGÖRELSE ÖVER DEN UNDER FEBRUARI MÅNAD ÅR 1918 UNDER SVENSK FÖRMEDLING ÖVERENSKOMNA UTRYMNINGEN AV ÅLAND FRÅN FINSKA OCH RYSKA TRUPPER JÄMTE TILLHÖRANDE AKTSTYCKEN. (*The Åland Settlement. Report of February 1918 on the Swedish Intermediation for the Agreed Evacuation of the Åland Islands by Finnish and Russian Troops, together with the Related Actions.*)

Carl Harald Åkermark - Kungliga Sjöfartsdepartementet I 24cm x 16.5cm I Blue paper softback I 39pp I 53 appendices I Kungliga boktryckeriet, P.A. Norstedt and söner I 1918 I Swedish Text.

This volume covers the actions of Sweden with respect to the Åland Islands which during the period covered was a Finnish possession. It is broken down into the following: The Swedish army's peacekeeping expedition to the islands in response to the islanders request, to remove the Russian garrison along with both "White" and "Red" Finnish troops, followed by the replacement of the Swedish Army by German troops. Finally this volume concludes with the Åland Islands Agreement of 20 October 1921 signed between the Danish, Estonian, Finnish, French, German, Italian, Latvian, Polish, Swedish and British governments for the demilitarizing and neutralisation of the Åland Islands and sovereignty of the islands being given to the Swedes.

Turkish Official Histories

All the Turkish official histories were written by members of the Genelkurmay Askeri Tarih ve Stratejik Etut (ATASE - *General Staff Military History and Strategy Institute*) or its predecessors. Even as the Kurtuluş Savaşı (the *Turkish War of Independence* between 19 May 1919 and 29 October 1923) was being fought, officers in the Genelkurmay (*General Staff*) started to records the events officially of the Turkish part in the Great War. Indeed it was intended to write a formal official history broken down into seven volumes, the first of which was published in 1922.[38] It is not clear now many volumes of this set were produced, but it is quite possible that at least three of them appeared as part of the "Büyük Harpte" (*The Great War*) set. The first volume was translated into English and is filed in the Public Records Office, London. However up to the early nineteen-sixty's with the exception of this proposed set, the other histories were written in a rather ad hoc manner with no real framework to them. The ones written before 1928 were written in Ottoman Turkish (Osmanli Turki) a form of Persian Arabic script. Some of these older works have since been revised and updated – some of the pre 1928 volumes have been transliterated into modern Turkish script using the extended Latin alphabet.

Since the nineteen-sixty's the Genelkurmay Askeri Tarih ve Stratejik Etut have produced a much more structured series of histories, covering Turkish military history, beginning with warfare in the Byzantine period through to the Korean War. The Great War is covered in Seri No: 3 (*Series Number 3*) comprising all aspects of the Turkish Armed Services and of the operations that they were involved during the war.

During the period of production of Seri No: 3, the Genelkurmay Askeri Tarih ve Stratejik Etut produced a more general history set with regard to the Turkish army that included coverage of the Great War period. They have also produced a number of monographs on individual Great War campaigns and operations. The Genelkurmay Askeri Tarih ve Stratejik Etut is still very active releasing monographs every year up to the present as well as revising and republishing older works.

There have been a couple of interesting developments with the Turkish official histories. Firstly the Genelkurmay Askeri Tarih ve Stratejik Etut has started to summarise some of the sub sets within the Seri No: 3 for the benefit of the more general non military reader. The Second is that the summary for the Dardanelles/Gallipoli campaign has now been translated into English for the benefit of a much larger International readership.

Post 1960 Publications.

General History of the Turkish Army:

T.C. GENELKURMAY HARP TARİHİ BAŞKANLIĞI RESMÎ YAYINLARI. SERİ NO: 2 - TÜRK SİLAHLİ KUVVETLERI TARİHİ III ncü CİLT 6 ncı KİSİM (1908-1920) 1 nci KİTAP. (*T.C. General Staff Military History Directorate Official Publication: Series No: 2 - History of the Turkish Armed Forces, 3rd Volume, 6th Part, (1908-1920) 1st Book.*)

---

[38] The first volume is entitled in English by the Public Records Office, London as **"A Short History of Turkish Operations in the Great War"** (PRO Ref.: AIR 1/2317/223/21/108). It is assumed that this was the original title for the planned set, since it has also been stated that the individual volumes were going to be as follows:

    Volume 1   The Dardanelles Campaign (Constantinople, 1922)
    Volume 2   Caucasus and Persian Campaign
    Volume 3   Campaign in Iraq and Persia
    Volume 4   Campaign in Palestine and Syria
    Volume 5   Campaign in Hejaz, Yemen and Asir
    Volume 6   Campaigns on other fronts (Galicia, Roumania and Macedonia)
    Volume 7   Miscellaneous and Supplementary Events (Thrace, Smyrna, Tripoli, Benghazi, and Naval Events).

I have not found if any of the other volumes of the planned set were ever published, however it is possible the volume **"Büyük Harpte İran Cephesi"** is possibly Volume 3 of this set.
There is another translated volume stored in the P.R.O., London is **"The Turco-British Campaign in Mesopotamia and Our Mistakes"** by *Staff Bimbashi* Muhammad Amin (PRO Ref.: CAB 44/32) and is dated 1920 although it is believed that this volume was not part of the above planned set.

Genel Kurmay Başkanı (General) Selahattin Karatamn (Retired). | 24.5cm x 17.2cm | White Paper Softback | xi + 534p + iip | 10 appendices | 16 maps | 5 photographs | 2 black and white illustrations | 8 colour illustrations | 21 tables | 23 organisation charts | Genelkurmay Basimevi (*The Turkish General Staff.*) | 1971 | Modern Turkish Text.

This volume is generally referred to as "**Türk Silahli Kuvvetlerı Tarihi III ncü Cilt 6 ncı Kisim (1908-1920) 1 nci Kitap**". It is part of a general history of the Turkish Army, with only this volume covering the period of the Great War. It also covers the Italo-Turkish War 1911-12 the First Balkan War of 1912 and the Second Balkan War of 1913. It was produced under the authority of the Genelkurmay Basimevi.

General History of the Turkish Army in the Great War:

KARA KUVVETLERI KOMUTANLIĞI YAYINLARI - BİRİNCİ CİHAN HARBİNDE TÜRK HARBİ, 1914 yılı harekatleri, BİRİNCİ CİLT. (*Land Forces Command Publications -The Turkish War during the First World War, Operations in 1914 First Volume.***)**

> *Genel Kurmay Başkanı (General)* Fahri Belen (Retired). | 24.5cm x 17.2cm | White Paper Softback | 200pp | 14 appendices | 26 maps | 4 organisation charts | Genelkurmay Basimevi (*The Turkish General Staff.*) | 1964 | Modern Turkish Text.
> This volume is generally referred to as "**Birinci Cihan Harbinde Türk Harbi, 1914 yılı harekatleri, Birinci Cilt**".

KARA KUVVETLERI KOMUTANLIĞI YAYINLARI - BİRİNCİ CİHAN HARBİNDE TÜRK HARBİ, 1915 yılı harekatleri, İKİNCİ CİLT. (*Land Forces Command Publications -The Turkish War during the First World War, Operations in 1915, Second Volume.***)**

> *Genel Kurmay Başkanı (General)* Fahri Belen (Retired). | 24.5cm x 17.2cm | White Paper Softback | iv + 258pp | 59 maps | 1 photographs | 2 tables | 11 organisation charts | Genelkurmay Basimevi (*The Turkish General Staff.*) | 1964 | Modern Turkish Text.
> This volume is generally referred to as "**Birinci Cihan Harbinde Türk Harbi, 1915 yılı harekatleri, İkinci Cilt**".

BİRİNCİ CİHAN HARBİNDE TÜRK HARBİ, 1916 YILI HAREKATLERİ, III ncu Cilt. (*The Turkish War during the First World War, Operations in 1916, 3rd Volume.***)**

> *Genel Kurmay Başkanı (General)* Fahri Belen (Retired). | 24.5cm x 17.2cm | White Paper Softback | xxi + 229pp | 59 maps | 23 organisation charts | Genelkurmay Basimevi (*The Turkish General Staff.*) | 1963 | Modern Turkish Text.

BİRİNCİ CİHAN HARBİNDE TÜRK HARBİ, 1917 YILI HAREKATLERİ, IV ncü Cilt. (*The Turkish War during the First World War, Operations in 1917, 4th Volume.***)**

> *Genel Kurmay Başkanı (General)* Fahri Belen (Retired). | 24.5cm x 17.2cm | White Paper Softback | 208pp | 44 maps | 13 organisation charts | Genelkurmay Basimevi (*The Turkish General Staff.*) | 1966 | Modern Turkish Text.

BİRİNCİ CİHAN HARBİNDE TÜRK HARBİ, 1918 YILI HAREKATLERİ, V nci Cilt. (*The Turkish War during the First World War, Operations in 1918, 5th Volume.***)**

> *Genel Kurmay Başkanı (General)* Fahri Belen (Retired). | 24.5cm x 17.2cm | White Paper Softback | xvi + 251pp | 44 maps | 1 table | 14 organisation charts | Genelkurmay Basimevi (*The Turkish General Staff.*) | 1967 | Modern Turkish Text.
> This five volume set "**Birinci Cihan Harbinde Türk Harbi**" is a general history of the Turkish Army in the Great War. It was produced under the authority of the Genelkurmay Basimevi.

Turkish Operations during the Great War:

Mobilisation;

GENELKURMAY HARP TARİHİ BAŞKANLIĞI RESMÎ YAYINLARI SERİ NO: 3 - BİRİNCİ DÜNYA HARBİNDE TÜRK HARBİ, I NCİ CİLT, OSMANLI İMPARATORLUĞU'NUM SİYASÎ VE ASKERÎ HAZIRLIKLARI VE HARBE GİRİŞİ. (*General Staff Military History Directorate Official Publication: Series No: 3 - The Turkish Battles in the First World War, 1ST Volume, The Political and Military Preparations of the Ottoman Empire and its Entry into the War.***)**

Tuğgeneral (*Brigadier*) Cemal Akbay (Retired). | 24.5cm x 17.2cm | white paper softback | viii + 295pp | 13 appendices | 7 maps | 8 photographs | 15 tables | 4 organisation charts | Genelkurmay Basimevi (*The Turkish General Staff.*) | 1970 | Modern Turkish Text.

This volume is generally referred to as "**Birinci Dünya Harbinde Türk Harbi, I nci Cilt, Osmanlı İmparatorluğu'num Siyasî ve Askerî Hazırlıkları ve Harbe Girişi**". It was revised and republished in 1991.

It appears that the earlier volumes published in this series '**Birinci Dünya Harbinde Türk Harbi**' were bound both as softbacks and hardbacks. The hardback editions had black cloth covering with silver text. At what date this option of hard covers ceased is unclear but it was probably before 2000.

Caucasus:

T.C. GENELKURMAY ASKERİ TARİH VE STRATEJİK ETÜD BAŞKANLIĞI ASKERİ TARİH YAYINLARI SERİ NO: 3 - BİRİNCİ DÜNYA HARBİNDE TÜRK HARBİ, KAFKAS CEPHESİ. 3 NCU ORDU HAREKÂTI. CİLT II, BİRİNCİ KİTAP. (*T.C. General Staff Directorate of Military History and Strategical Studies Military History Publication: Series No: 3 - The Turkish Battles in the First World War, The Caucasian Front, Thrid Army Operations. Volume II, First Book.*)

Albay (*Colonel*) Hakki Altinbilek (Retired) and *Albay* (*Colonel*) Naci Kir (Retired). | 24.5cm x 17.2cm | White Paper Softback | 879pp | 1 appendix | 75 maps | 1 table | 17 organisation charts | Genelkurmay Basimevi (*The Turkish General Staff.*) | 1993 | Modern Turkish Text.

This volume is generally referred to as "**Birinci Dünya Harbinde Türk Harbi, Cilt II, Birinci Kitap, Kafkas Cephesi. 3 ncu Ordu Harekâti**".

T.C. GENELKURMAY ASKERİ TARİH VE STRATEJİK ETÜD BAŞKANLIĞI ASKERİ TARİH YAYINLARI SERİ NO: 3 - BİRİNCİ DÜNYA HARBİNDE TÜRK HARBİ, KAFKAS CEPHESİ. 3 NCÜ ORDU HAREKÂTI. CİLT II, İKİNCİ KİTAP. (*T.C. General Staff Directorate of Military History and Strategical Studies Military History Publication: Series No: 3 - The Turkish Battles in the First World War, The Caucasian Front, 3rd Army Operations. Volume II, Second Book.*)

Albay (*Colonel*) Hakki Altinbilek (Retired) and *Albay* (*Colonel*) Naci Kir (Retired). | 24.5cm x 17.2cm | White Paper Softback | 888pp | 3 appendices | 73 maps | 17 organisation charts | 6 tables | Genelkurmay Basimevi (*The Turkish General Staff.*) | 1993 | Modern Turkish Text.

This volume is generally referred to as "**Birinci Dünya Harbinde Türk Harbi, Cilt II, 1 nci Kitap, Kafkas Cephesi. 3 ncü Ordu Harekâtı**".

T.C. GENELKURMAY ASKERİ TARİH VE STRATEJİK ETÜD BAŞKANLIĞI ASKERİ TARİH YAYINLARI SERİ NO: 3 - BİRİNCİ DÜNYA HARBİNDE TÜRK HARBİ, II NCİ CİLT, 2 NCİ KİSİM, KAFKAS CEPHESİ 2 NCİ ORDU HAREKÂTI. (*T.C. General Staff Directorate of Military History and Strategical Studies Military History Publication: Series No: 3 - The Turkish Battles in the First World War, Volume II, 2nd Book, The Caucasian Front, 2nd Army Operations, 1916-1918.*)

Albay (*Colonel*) Fikri Güleç (Retired). | 24.5cm x 17.2cm | White Paper Softback | viii + 352pp | 34 maps | 7 organisation charts | Genelkurmay Basimevi (*The Turkish General Staff.*) | 1978 | Modern Turkish Text.

This volume is generally referred to as "**Birinci Dünya Harbinde Türk Harbi, II nci Cilt, 2 nci Kisim, Kafkas Cephesi 2 nci Ordu Harekâti**". It was revised and republished in 1996.

Iraq and Iran:

T.C. GENELKURMAY ASKERİ TARİH VE STRATEJİK ETÜT BAŞKANLIĞI ASKERİ TARİH YAYINLARI SERİ NO: 3 - BİRİNCİ DÜNYA HARBİNDE TÜRK HARBİ, III nvü Cilt, IRAK-İRAN CEPHESI, 1914-1918, 1 nci Kisim. (*T.C. General Staff Directorate of Military History and Strategical Studies Military History Publication: Series No: 3 - The Turkish Battles in the First World War, IIIrd Volume, Iraq-Iran Front, 1914-1918, 1st Book.*)

Tuğgeneral (*Brigadier*) Nezhi Firat (Retired) and *Albay* (*Colonel*) Behzat Balkiç (Retired). | 24.5cm x 17.2cm | White Paper Softback | xxv + 840pp | 13 appendices | 66 maps | 29 photographs | 15 organisation charts | Genelkurmay Basimevi (*The Turkish General Staff.*) | 1979 | Modern Turkish Text.

This volume is generally referred to as "**Birinci Dünya Harbinde Türk Harbi, III nvü Cilt, Irak-İran Cephesı, 1914-1918, 1 nci Kisim**". It covers the campaign till the fall of Kut-al-Amara.

T.C. GENELKURMAY BAŞKANLIĞI ANKARA - BİRİNCİ DÜNYA HARBİ'NDE TÜRK HARBİ, IRAK-İRAN CEPHESI, 1914-1918, 3'ünvü Cilt, 2'nci Kisim. (*TC General Staff Directorate, Ankara - The Turkish Battles in the First World War, Iraq-Iran Front, 1914-1918, 3rd Volume, 2nd Book.*)

> *Albay* (*Colonel*) Özden Çalhan (Retired). | 24.5cm x 17.2cm | White Paper Softback | xix + 835pp | 16 appendices | 64 maps | 10 photographs | 11 organisation charts | Genelkurmay Basimevi (*The Turkish General Staff.*) | 2002 | Modern Turkish Text.
>
> This volume is generally referred to as "**Birinci Dünya Harbi'nde Türk Harbi, Irak-İran Cephesı, 1914-1918, 3'ünvü Cilt, 2'nci Kisim**". It covers the campaign after the fall of Kut-al-Amara.It was issued with an Corrigenda sheet.

Sinai, Paleatine and Syria:

T.C. GENELKURMAY ASKERİ TARİH VE STRATEJİK ETÜT BAŞKANLIĞI ASKERİ TARİH YAYINLARI SERİ NO: 3 - BİRİNCİ DÜNYA HARBİNDE TÜRK HARBİ, IV ncü Cilt, 1 nci Kisim, SİNA-FİLİSTİN CEPHESİ, Harbin Başlangicindan İkinci Gazze Muharebeleri Sonuna Kadar. (*T.C. General Staff Directorate of Military History and Strategical Studies Military History Publication: Series No: 3 - The Turkish Battles in the First World War, IVth Volume, 1st Book, Sinai-Paleatine Front from the Beginning of the War through to the end of the Second Battle of Gaza.*)

> *Genel Kurmay Başkanı* (*General*) Yahya Okçn (Retired) and *Albay* (*Colonel*) Hilmi Üstünsoy (Retired). | 24.5cm x 17.2cm | White Paper Softback | xxvii + 825pp | 7 appendices | 55 maps | 24 photographs | 3 tables | 10 organisation charts | Genelkurmay Basimevi (*The Turkish General Staff.*) | 1979 | Modern Turkish Text.
>
> This volume is generally referred to as "**Birinci Dünya Harbinde Türk Harbi, IV ncü Cilt, 1 nci Kisim, Sina-Filistin Cephesi, Harbin Başlangicindan İkinci Gazze Muharebeleri Sonuna Kadar**".

T.C. GENELKURMAY BAŞKANLIĞI ANKARA - BİRİNCİ DÜNYA HARBİNDE TÜRK HARBİ, IV Cilt, 2 nci Kisim SİNA-FİLİSTİN CEPHESİ, İkinci Gazze Muharebeleri Sonundan Mondros Mütarekesi'ne Kadar Yapılan Harekât, 21 Nisan 1917 – 30 Ekim 1918. (*T.C. General Staff Directorate, Ankara - The Turkish Battles in the First World War, IVth Volume, 2nd Book, Sinai-Paleatine Front Operations from the Second Battle of Gaza through to the Mudros Armistice, 21 November 1917 – 30 October 1918.*)

> *Tuğgeneral* (*Brigadier*) Merhum Önalp (Retired) and *Albay* (*Colonel*) Hilmi Üstünsoy (Retired). | 24.5cm x 17.2cm | White Paper Softback | xvi + 823pp | 4 appendices | 69 maps | 23 photographs | 4 organisation charts | Genelkurmay Basimevi (*The Turkish General Staff.*) | 1986 | Modern Turkish Text.
>
> This volume is generally referred to as "**Birinci Dünya Harbinde Türk Harbi, IV Cilt, 2 nci Kisim Sina-Filistin Cephesi, İkinci Gazze Muharebeleri Sonundan Mondros Mütarekesi'ne Kadar Yapılan Harekât, 21 Nisan 1917 – 30 Ekim 1918**".

Gallipoli:

TC GENELKURMAY BAŞKANLIĞI - BİRİNCİ DÜNYA HARBİNDE TÜRK HARBİ, V NCİ CİLT, ÇANAKKALE CEPHESİ HAREKÂTI, 1 NCİ KİTAP, HAZİRAN 1914 - 25 NISAN 1915. (*TC General Staff Directorate - The Turkish Battles in the First World War, Vth Volume, Operations on the Dardanelles/Gallipoli Front, 1st Book, June 1914 - 25 April 1915.*)

> *Albay* (*Colonel*) Muhterem Saral (Retired) and *Albay* (*Colonel*) Alpaslan Orhon (Retired). | 24.5cm x 17.2cm | White Paper Softback | xiv + 391pp | 7 appendices | 19 maps | 6 photographs | 15 tables | 13 organisation charts | Genelkurmay Basimevi (*The Turkish General Staff.*) | 1993 | Modern Turkish Text.
>
> This volume is generally referred to as "**Birinci Dünya Harbinde Türk Harbi, V nci Cilt, Çanakkale Cephesi Harekâtı, 1 nci Kitap, Haziran 1914 - 25 Nisan 1915**". It covers the Dardanelle naval operations and the military preparations on the Gallipoli peninsula.

T.C. GENELKURMAY HARP TARİHİ BAŞKANLIĞI HARP TARİHİ YAYINLARI. SERİ NO: 3 - BİRİNCİ DÜNYA HARBİNDE TÜRK HARBİ, V NCİ CİLT, ÇANAKKALE

CEPHESİ, 2 NCİ KİTAP, AMFİBİ HAREKÂTI. (*T.C. General Staff Military History Directorate Official Publication - The Turkish Battles in the First World War, V[th] Volume, Dardanelles/Gallipoli Front, 2rd Book, Amphibious Operations.*)

    Genel Kurmay Başkanı (*General*) Remzi Yiğitgüden (Retired), *Albay* (*Colonel*) Muhterem Saral (Retired) and *Albay* (*Colonel*) Reşat Halli (Retired). | 24.5cm x 17.2cm | White Paper Softback | xiv + 440pp | 3 appendices | 48 maps | 40 photographs | 13 organisation charts | Genelkurmay Basimevi (*The Turkish General Staff.*) | 1978 | Modern Turkish Text.

    This volume is generally referred to as "**Birinci Dünya Harbinde Türk Harbi, V nci Cilt, Çanakkale Cephesi, 2 nci Kitap, Amfibi Harekâtı**". It covers the allies' landings on the Gallipoli peninsula through to June 1915.

T.C. GENELKURMAY ASKERİ TARİH VE STRATEJİK ETÜT BAŞKANLIĞI ASKERİ TARİH YAYINLARI SERİ NO: 3 - TÜRK SİLAHLI KUVVETLERİ TARİHİ OSMANLI DEVRİ BİRİNCİ DÜNYA HARBİNDE TÜRK HARBİ, V nci Cilt, 3 ncu Kitap, ÇANAKKALE CEPHESİ, HAREKÂTI (HAZİRAN 1915 – OCAK 1916). (*T.C. General Staff Directorate of Military History and Strategical Studies Military History Publication: Series No: 3 - History of the Turkish Armed Forces Ottoman Period - The Turkish Battles in the First World War, V[th] Volume, 3rd Book, Operations on the Dardanelles/Gallipoli Front (June 1915 – January 1916).*)

    Albay (*Colonel*) İrfan Tekşüt (Retired) and *Albay* (*Colonel*) Necati Ökse (Retired). | 24.5cm x 17.2cm | White Paper Softback | 626pp | 16 appendices | 60 maps | 3 sketches | 11 tables | 16 organisation charts | Genelkurmay Basimevi (*The Turkish General Staff.*) | 1980 | Modern Turkish Text.

    This volume is generally referred to as "**Birinci Dünya Harbinde Türk Harbi, V nci Cilt, 3 ncu Kitap, Çanakkale Cephesi, Harekâtı (Haziran 1915 – Ocak 1916)**". It covers the period from June 1915 through to allies' evacuations from the Gallipoli peninsula through to June 1915.

Arabia:

T.C. GENELKURMAY ASKERİ TARİH VE STRATEJİK ETÜT BAŞKANLIĞI ASKERİ TARİH YAYINLARI SERİ NO: 3 - BİRİNCİ DÜNYA HARBİNDE TÜRK HARBİ, VI ncı CİLT, HİCAZ, ASİR, YEMEN CEPHELERİ VE LIBYA HAREKÂTI 1914 - 1918. (*T.C. General Staff Directorate of Military History and Strategical Studies Military History Publication: Series No: 3 - The Turkish Battles in the First World War, VIth Volume, Operations in Hejaz, Arabia, Yemen and Libya, 1914 - 1918.*)

    Albay (*Colonel*) Şükrü Erkal (Retired). | 24.5cm x 17.2cm | White Paper Softback | xxx + 944pp | 27 appendices | 91 maps | 37 photographs | 14 organisation charts | Genelkurmay Basimevi (*The Turkish General Staff.*) | 1978 | Modern Turkish Text.

    This volume is generally referred to as "**Birinci Dünya Harbinde Türk Harbi, VI ncı Cilt, Hicaz, Asir, Yeman Cepheleri Ve Libya Harekâtı 1914 - 1918**". It covers the Arab Revolt with the activities of Faisal bin al-Hussein bin Ali al-Hashemi and Colonel T.E. Lawence mentioned.

Europe:

T.C. Genelkurmay Başkanliği Harp Tarihi Dairesi Resmî Yayinlari. Seri No: 3 - BİRİNCİ DÜNYA HARBİ TÜRK HARBİ, VII nci Cilt, AVRUPA CEPHELERİ, 1 nci Kisim, (Galaçya Cephesi). (*T.C. General Staff Directorate Official History Publication: Series No: 3 - The Turkish Battles in the First World War, VIIth Volume, European Fronts, 1st Book, (Galician Campaign).*)

    Albay (*Colonel*) Cihat Akçakayalioğlu (Retired). | 24.5cm x 17.2cm | White Paper Softback | v + 116pp | 21 maps | 5 photographs | 2 organisation charts | Genelkurmay Basimevi (*The Turkish General Staff.*) | 1967 | Modern Turkish Text.

    This volume is generally referred to as "**Birinci Dünya Harbi Türk Harbi, VII nci Cilt, Avrupa Cepheleri, 1 nci Kisim, (Galaçya Cephesi)**".

T.C. Genelkurmay Başkanliği Harp Tarihi Dairesi Resmî Yayinlari. Seri No: 3 - BİRİNCİ DÜNYA HARBİ TÜRK HARBİ, VII nci Cilt, AVRUPA CEPHELERİ, 2 nci Kisim, (Romanya Cephesi). (*T.C. General Staff Directorate Official History Publication: Series No: 3 - The Turkish Battles in the First World War, VIIth Volume, European Fronts, 2nd Book, (Romanian Campaign).*)

    Albay (*Colonel*) Fazıl Karlidağ (Retired) and *Albay* (*Colonel*) Kâni Ciner (Retired) | 24.5cm x 17.2cm | White Paper Softback | vii + 172pp | 3 appendices | 40 maps | 6 photographs | 4 tables I 2 organisation charts I Genelkurmay Basimevi (*The Turkish General Staff.*) I 1967 I Modern Turkish Text.

This volume is generally referred to as "**Birinci Dünya Harbi Türk Harbi, VII nci Cilt, Avrupa Cepheleri, 2 nci Kisim, (Romanya Cephesi)**".

T.C. Genelkurmay Başkanliği Harp Tarihi Dairesi Resmî Yayinlari. Seri No: 3 - BİRİNCİ DÜNYA HARBİ TÜRK HARBİ, VII nci Cilt, AVRUPA CEPHELERİ, 3nci Kisim, (Makedonya Cephesi). (*T.C. General Staff Directorate Official History Publication: Series No: 3 - The Turkish Battles in the First World War, VIIth Volume, European Fronts, 3rd Book, (Macedonian Campaign).*)

Albay (*Colonel*) Fikri Güleç (Retired). I 24.5cm x 17.2cm I White Paper Softback I v + 85pp I 40 maps I 1 photograph I 4 tables I 2 organisation charts I Genelkurmay Basimevi (*The Turkish General Staff.*) I 1967 I Modern Turkish Text.

This volume is generally referred to as "**Birinci Dünya Harbi Türk Harbi, VII nci Cilt, Avrupa Cepheleri, 3nci Kisim, (Makedonya Cephesi)**".

Naval Operations;

T.C. GENELKURMAY HARP TARİHİ BAŞKANLIĞI RESMÎ YAYINLARI. SERİ NO: 3 - BİRİNCİ DÜNYA HARBİ TÜRK HARBİ, VIII nci Cilt, TÜRK DENIZ HAREKÂTI. (*T.C. General Staff Directorate Official History Publication: Series No: 3 - The Turkish Battles in the First World War, VIIIth Volume, Turkish Naval Operations.*)

Albay (*Colonel*) Saim Besbelli (Retired). I 24.5cm x 17.2cm I White Paper Softback I xxvi + 664pp I 47 appendices I 57 maps I 47 photographs I 7 organisation charts I 5 illustrations I Genelkurmay Basimevi Başkanlığı (*The Turkish General Staff.*) I 1976 I Modern Turkish Text.

This volume is generally referred to as "**Birinci Dünya Harbi Türk Harbi, VIII nci Cilt, Türk Denız Harekâtı**". Note one illustration is listed as a photograph.

Aviation Activities:

T.C. GENELKURMAY HARP TARİHİ BAŞKANLIĞI RESMÎ YAYINLARI. SERİ NO: 3 - BİRİNCİ DÜNYA HARBİ, IX ncu Cilt, TÜRK HAVA HAREKÂTI. (*T.C. General Staff Directorate Official History Publication: Series No: 3 - The First World War, IXth Volume, Turkish Aviation Operations.*)

Albay (*Colonel*) İhsan Göymen. I 24.5cm x 17.2cm I White Paper Softback I xii + 258pp + 3 I 18 appendices I 51 maps I 2 organisation charts I Genelkurmay Basimevi (*The Turkish General Staff.*) I 1969 I Modern Turkish Text.

This volume is generally referred to as "**Birinci Dünya Harbi, IX ncu Cilt, Türk Hava Harekâtı**".

Logistics Activities:

T.C. GENELKURMAY BAŞKANLIĞI ANKARA - BİRİNCİ DÜNYA HARBİ, İDARİ FAALİYETLER VE LOJİSTİK, "X ncu Cilt". (*T.C. General Staff Directorate, Ankara - The First World War, Administrative Support Activities and Logistics, "Xth Volume".*)

Tuğgeneral (*Brigadier*) Necmi Koral (Retired), *Albay* (*Colonel*) Remzi Önal (Retired), *Albay* (*Colonel*) Rauf Atakan (Retired), Albay (*Colonel*) Nusret Baycan (Retired) and *Albay* (*Colonel*) Selahattin Kizilirmak (Retired) I 24.5cm x 17.2cm I White Paper Softback I xiv + 791pp I 47 tables I 23 maps I 12 organisation charts I Genelkurmay Basimevi (*The Turkish General Staff.*) I 1985 I Modern Turkish Text.

This volume is generally referred to as "**Birinci Dünya Harbi, İdari Faaliyetler ve Lojistik, X ncu Cilt**".

Azerbaijan and Dagestan:

TC GENELKURMAY BAŞKANLIĞI ANKARA - BİRİNCİ DÜNYA SAVAŞI'NDA OSMANLI ORDUSUN'UN AZERBAYCAN VE DAĞISTAN HAREKÂTI, AZERBAYCAN VE DAĞISTAN'IN BAĞIMSIZLIĞINI KAZANMASI 1918. (*TC General Staff Directorate,*

Ankara - Ottoman Army Operations in the First World War in Azerbaijan and Dagestan. The Independence of Azerbaijan and Dağıstan in 1918.)

> Nâsir Yüceer. | 24.5cm x 17.2cm | White Paper Softback | xi + 201 + 20pp | 5 appendices | 10 maps | 3 organisation charts | 7 photographs | Genelkurmay Basimevi (*The Turkish General Staff.*) | 1996 | Modern Turkish Text.
>
> The Republic of Dagestan is now part of the Russian Federation and has borders with Azerbaijan and Georgia.
>
> This volume is generally referred to as "**Birinci Dünya Savaşı'nda Osmanlı Ordusun'un Azerbaycan ve Dağıstan Harekâtı, Azerbaycan ve Dağıstan'ın Bağımsızlığını Kazanması 1918**". It was republished in 2002 under the slightly revised title **Birinci Dünya Harbi'nde Osmanlı Ordusunun Azerbaycan ve Dağıstan Harekâtı, Azerbaycan ve Dağıstan'ın Bağımsızlığını Kazanması 1918** (ISBN No: 9754090750) which translates into English the same as the original title.

Armistice and Aftermath:

T.C. GENKUR. BŞK. HARB TARIHI DAIRESI RESMI YAYINLARI SERI NO: 1 - TÜRK İSTİKLAL HARBİ I, MONDROS MÜTAREKESI VE TATBIKATI. (*T.C. General Staff Directorate Official History Publication: Series No: 1 - Turkish War of Independence, The Mudros Armistice and Operations.*)

> *Albay (Colonel)* Tevfik Biyilioğlu (Retired)| 24.5cm x 17.2cm | White Paper Softback | xiv + 233pp | 22 appendices | 8 maps | 10 organisation charts | Genelkurmay Basimevi (*The Turkish General Staff.*) | 1962 | Modern Turkish Text.
>
> This volume is generally referred to as "**Türk İstiklal Harbi I, Mondros Mütarekesı ve Tatbikatı**". The third edition of this volume was published in 1999.

Summaries:

TC GENELKURMAY BAŞKANLIĞI ANKARA - BİRİNCİ DÜNYA HARBİNDE TÜRK HARBİ, V nci CİLT, ÇANAKKALE CEPHESİ HAREKÂTI, 1 nci, 2 nci, VE 3 ncu KİTAPLARIN ÖZETLENMİS TARİHİ, HAZİRAN 1914 - 9 OCAK 1916. (*TC General Staff Directorate, Ankara - The Turkish Battles in the First World War, Volume 5, Operations on the Dardanelles/Gallipoli Front, A Historical Summary of Books 1, 2 and 3, June 1914 to January 1916*)

> *Albay (Colonel)* Şükrü Erkal. | 24.5cm x 17.2cm | White Paper Softback | xiv + 380pp | 1 appendix | 1 chronology | 75 maps | 29 photographs | 1 illustration | 3 tables | 14 organisation charts | Genelkurmay Basimevi (*The Turkish General Staff.*) | 1997 | Modern Turkish Text.
>
> This volume is generally referred to as "**Birinci Dünya Harbinde Türk Harbi, V nci Cilt, Çanakkale Cephesi Harekâtı, 1 nci, 2 nci, VE 3 ncu Kitaplarin Özetlenmis Tarihi, Haziran 1914 - 9 Ocak 1916**". It was revised and republished in 2002 in order to give a greater coverage of the air operations during the Dardanelles and Gallipoli campaigns and is based on chapter III subchapter D part 2 in the "**Birinci Dünya Harbi, IX ncu Cilt, Türk Hava Harekâtı**".

THE TURKISH GENERAL STAFF, ANKARA - A BRIEF HISTORY OF THE ÇANAKKALE CAMPAIGN IN THE FIRST WORLD WAR (JUNE 1914 – JANUARY 1916).

> *Albay (Colonel)* Şükrü Erkal, translated by Serdar Demirtaş | 24.5cm x 17.2cm | Yellow Paper Softback | xiv + 306pp | 1 appendix | 1 chronology | 75 maps | 29 photographs | 1 illustration | 3 tables | 14 organisation charts | The Turkish General Staff Printing House. | 2004 | English Text.
>
> ISBN 975-409-307-5.
>
> Written under the authority of "The Turkish General Staff Directorate of Military History and Strategic Studies and Directorate of Inspection Publications".
>
> The Çanakkale Campaign is the Turkish name for both the Dardanelles and the Gallipoli Campaigns.
>
> This volume is generally referred to as "**A Brief History of the Çanakkale Campaign in the First World War (June 1914 – January 1916)**". It is the above revised volume "**Birinci Dünya Harbinde Türk Harbi, V nci Cilt, Çanakkale Cephesi Harekâtı, 1 nci, 2**

nci, Ve 3 ncu Kitaplarin Özetlenmis Tarihi, Haziran 1914 - 9 Ocak 1916." translated into English.

T.C. GENELKURMAY ASKERİ TARİH VE STRATEJİK ETÜT BAŞKANLIĞI YAYINLARI - BİRİNCİ DÜNYA HARBİ TÜRK HARBİ, AVRUPA CEPHELERİ (ÖZET). (*T.C. General Staff Directorate of Military History and Strategical Studies Publication - The Turkish Battles in the First World War, The European Fronts (Summary).*)

Albay (*Colonel*) Gülhan Barlars (Retired). | 24.5cm x 17.2cm | White Paper Softback | 251pp | 8 appendices | 73 maps | 25 photographs | 10 organisation charts | Genelkurmay Basimevi (*The Turkish General Staff.*) | 1996 | Modern Turkish Text.

This volume is generally referred to as "**Birinci Dünya Harbi Türk Harbi, Avrupa Cepheleri (Özet)**".

TC GENELKURMAY BAŞKANLIĞI ANKARA - BIRINCI DÜNYA SAVAŞI'NDA KAFKAS CEPHESI'NDEKI MUHAREBELER. (*TC General Staff Directorate, Ankara - The First World War, The Battles of the Caucasian Front.*)

Yayına Hazırlayan and Alev Keskin | 24.5cm x 17.2cm | Illustrated Paper Softback | 100 + 2pp | ? maps | ? organisation charts | Genelkurmay Basimevi (*The Turkish General Staff.*) | 2007 | Modern Turkish Text.

ISBN No: 9754093830.

This volume is generally referred to as "**Birinci Dünya Savaşı'nda Kafkas Cephesı'ndekı Muharebeler**".

Armenian Deportation and Massacre:

TC GENELKURMAY BAŞKANLIĞI - BİRİNCİ DÜNYA HARBİNDE, ERZURUM VE CEVRESİNDE ERMENİ HREKATETLERİ (1914–1918). (*TC General Staff Directorate - The First World War, Armenian Operations in Erzurum and the Surrounding Area; (1914-1918).*)

Muammer Demirel. | 24.5cm x 17.2cm | White Paper Softback | xi + 159pp | 3 tables | Genelkurmay Basimevi (*The Turkish General Staff.*) | 1996 | Modern Turkish Text.

TC GENELKURMAY BAŞKANLIĞI - BİRİNCİ DÜNYA SAVAŞINDA ERMENİLERİN TÜRKLERE YAPTIĞI KATLİAM FOTOĞRAFLARI. (*TC General Staff Directorate - The First World War, The Turkish Photographs of the Armenian Massacre.*)

Arş. Ş. Md. Lüğü. | 24.5cm x 17.2cm | White Paper Softback | ?pp |? photographs | Genelkurmay Basimevi (*The Turkish General Staff.*) | 2000 | Modern Turkish Text.

This volume is generally referred to as "**Birinci Dünya Savaşında Ermenilerin Türklere Yaptığı Katliam Fotoğrafları**".

Chronologies:

TC GENELKURMAY BAŞKANLIĞI ANKARA - BİRİNCİ DÜNYA SAVAŞI KRONOLOJİSİ. (*TC General Staff Directorate, Ankara - Chronology of the First World War.*)

Dr. Kemal Ari. | 24.5cm x 17.2cm | White Paper Softback | xxv + 412pp | Genelkurmay Basimevi (*The Turkish General Staff.*) | 1997 | Modern Turkish Text.

This volume is generally referred to as "**Birinci Dünya Savaşi Kronolojisi**".

General Aviation Official History:

HAVA KUVVETLERI BASIM VE NEŞRIYAT MÜD - HAVACİLİK TARİHİ TÜRKLER,
I. (*Air Force and Printing Publications Directorate - Turkish Aviation History, Volume 1.*)

Yavuz Kansu Sermet Şenöz. | 27cm x 20cm | White Paper Softback | 445pp | ? appendices | ? maps | ? photographs | ? organisation charts | Genelkurmay Basimevi (*The Turkish General Staff.*) | 1971 | Modern Turkish Text.

This volume is generally referred to as "**Havacilik Tarihi Türkler, I**". It is part of a general history of the Turkish Air Force, with only volume 1 covering the period of the Great War.

Pre 1960 Publications.

Earlier Formal Official History:

بويوق چهرپطه يرهك جهپحهثى بيريكّجِير جيلط (**Büyük Harpte İran Cephesi, Birinci Cilt.** - *The Iranian Front during the Great War, First Volume.*)[39]

    Erkan (*General*) Mehmet Kenan *Paşa* ǀ 42cm x 29.7cm ǀ Brown Paper Softback ǀ ?pp ǀ ? maps ǀ Askeri Mecmua ǀ 1344 (1928) ǀ Ottoman Turkish Text.
    This volume is generally referred to as "**Büyük Harpte İran Cephesi, Birinci Cilt**".

بويوق چهرپطه يرهك جهپحهثى يقيكّجير جيلط (**Büyük Harpte İran Cephesi, İkinci Cilt.** - *The Iranian Front during the Great War, Second Volume.*)

    Erkan (*General*) Mehmet Kenan *Paşa* ǀ 42cm x 29.7cm ǀ Brown Paper Softback ǀ 638pp ǀ ? maps ǀ Askeri Mecmua ǀ 1344 (1928) ǀ Ottoman Turkish Text.
    This volume is generally referred to as "**Büyük Harpte İran Cephesi, İkinci Cilt**".

BÜYÜK HARPTE İRAN CEPHESI, III CILT. (*The Iranian Front during the Great War, III Volume.*)

    Yarbay (*Lieutenant General*) E. Aysan ǀ 42cm x 29.7cm ǀ White Paper Softback ǀ ?pp ǀ ? maps ǀ Askeri Mecmua ǀ 1938 ǀ Modern Turkish Text.
    This volume is generally referred to as "**Büyük Harpte İran Cephesi, III Cilt**". It was produced as a special supplement to the first two volumes of this set.

Aviation Activities Monographs:

TÜRK HAVACİLİK TARİHİ, BIRİNCİ KİTAP, 1912-1914. (*Turkish Aviation History, Book One, 1912-1914.*)

    Anonymous. ǀ 21cm x 17cm ǀ White Paper Softback ǀ ?pp ǀ ? appendices ǀ ? maps ǀ ? photographs ǀ ? organisation charts ǀ Genelkurmay Basimevi (*The Turkish General Staff.*) ǀ 1950 ǀ Modern Turkish Text.

TÜRK HAVACİLİK TARİHİ, IKİNCİ KİTAP, BIRİNCİ CİLT, 1914-1916. (*Turkish Aviation History, Book Two, Volume One, 1914-1916.*)

    Anonymous. ǀ 21cm x 17cm ǀ White Paper Softback ǀ ?pp ǀ ? appendices ǀ ? maps ǀ ? photographs ǀ ? organisation charts ǀ Genelkurmay Basimevi (*The Turkish General Staff.*) ǀ 1951 ǀ Modern Turkish Text.

TÜRK HAVACİLİK TARİHİ, IKİNCİ KİTAP, IKİNCİ CİLT, 1917-1918. (*Turkish Aviation History, Book Two, Volume Two, 1917-1918.*)

    Anonymous. ǀ 21cm x 17cm ǀ White Paper Softback ǀ ?pp ǀ ? appendices ǀ ? maps ǀ ? photographs ǀ ? organisation charts ǀ Genelkurmay Basimevi (*The Turkish General Staff.*) ǀ 1952 ǀ Modern Turkish Text.

Transportation Activities:

BÜYÜK HARPTE DEMİRYOLLARİNİN ASKERI ROLLERİ VE YARİNA HAZİRLANİSLARİ. (*The Military Role of the Railways in the Great War and Their Preparations for the Future.*)

    Anonymous. ǀ 24.5cm x 17.2cm ǀ White Paper Softback ǀ ?pp ǀ ? appendices ǀ ? maps ǀ ? photographs ǀ ? organisation charts ǀ Genelkurmay Basimevi (*The Turkish General Staff.*) ǀ 1939 ǀ Modern Turkish Text.

Veterinary Activities:

HARP TARIHI ENCÜMENI - BÜYÜK HARB'İN BAYTARÎ TARİHİNİN METHAL - MERKEZ CİLDİNİN NETAYİC-İ İLMİYE FASLI. (*War History Commission - An Introduction to the Veterinary History during the Great War - Volume of the Netayic-i İlmiye Faslı Centre.*)

---

[39] Turkish Ottoman script is read from the right. I have not been able to review either of the two volumes "**Büyük Harpte İran Cephesi**" in their original format. The tiles found were listed in Latin script and have been transliterated back into Turkish Ottoman script. These Transliterations have not been checked, and therefore these Turkish Ottoman titles should be regarded as a guide only.

Anonymous (*Harp Tarihi Encümeni*). | 24.5cm x 17.2cm | White Paper Softback | ?pp | ? appendices | ? maps | ? photographs | Askeri Matbaa (The Military Printing House) | 1931 | Modern Turkish Text.

This volume is generally referred to as "**Büyük Harb'in Baytarî Tarihinin Methal**".

Part Two

Major Events Cross Referenced to the Related Official Histories

The events have been taken from the British Official History's 'Principal Events 1914-1918' 'Chronology of the War' Volume 1 to 3 and 'The Official Names of The Battles and Other Engagements Fought by the Military Forces of the British Empire during The Great War, 1914-1919 and The Third Afghan War, 1919'. For completeness I have added a small number of other events not listed in the above books. The official titles for battles have been used, but I have added the commonly accepted names in brackets. In the interest of space saving, the following abbreviations have been used:

AmOH .... American Official History
AuOH .... Australian Official History
AHOH .... Austro-Hungarian Official History
BgOH .... Belgium Official History
BrOH .... British Official History
BuOH .... Bulgarian Official History
CaOH .... Canadian Official History
CzOH .... Czechoslovakian Official History
EOH .... Éire (The Republic of Ireland) Official History
FrOH .... French Official History
GmOH .... German Official History
GrOH .... Greek Official History
HOH .... Hungarian Official History
IOH .... Italian Official History
JOH .... Japanese Official History
MOH .... Montenegrin Official History
NZOH .... New Zealand Official History
NwOH .... Norwegian Official History
PlOH .... Polish Official Histories
PgOH .... Portuguese Official Histories
RoOH .... Romanian Official History
RuOH .... Russian Official History
SeOH .... Serbian Official History
SAOH .... South African Official History
SwOH .... Swedish Official History
TOH .... Turkish Official Histories.

1914

29 July ....The bombardment of Belgrade. (Balkan Front)

AHOH: Österreich-Ungarns Letzter Krieg 1914-1918, Band I.

HOH: 1. A világháború 1914-1918. Különös tekintettel Magyarországra és a Magyar csapatok szereplésére Szerkeszti és kiadja a M. Kir. Hadtörténelmi Levéltár, köt 2.

2. A világháború 1914-1918. Különös tekintettel Magyarországra és a Magyar csapatok szereplésére Szerkeszti és kiadja a M. Kir. Hadtörténelmi Levéltár, köt 4.

SeOH: 1. Veliki rat Srbije za oslobođenje i ujedinenje Srba, Hrvata i Slovenaca. Knjige I. 1914 Godina. Prv period operacija. Cerska bitka.

2. Veliki rat Srbije za oslobođenje i ujedinenje Srba, Hrvata i Slovenaca. Knjige II. 1914 godina. Drugi period operacija. Bitka na Drini. I II i III deo.

2 August ....The bombardment of Libau. (Baltic Sea).

GmOH: Der Krieg zur See 1914-1918, Band 2, Der Krieg in der Ostsee, Teil 1, Von Kriegbeginn bis Mitte März 1915.

RuOH: ..Flot v Pervoi Mirovoi Voine. V Dvukh Tomakh. Tom I Deystviya Russkogo Flota.

4 August ....The bombardment of Philippeville and Bona. (Mediterranean Sea).

GmOH: Der Krieg zur See 1914-1918, Band 5, Der Krieg in den türkischen Gewässern, Teil 1, Die Mittelmeer-Division.

4 August ....Two German airships fly over Brussels by night – first hostile act in the air. (Western Front).

GmOH: Der Weltkrieg 1914 bis 1918, Die Militarischen Operationen zu Lande, Band 9, Die Operationen des Jahres 1915 – Die Ereignisse im Westen und auf dem Balkan vom Sommer bis Jahresschluß; Die Entwicklung der Luftstreitkrafte bis Ende 1915.

4 August – 16 September ....The Attack on Liége. (Western Front).

BgOH: 1. La Belgique et la Guerre, Tome II, L'Invasion allemande.

2. La Belgique et la Guerre, Tome III: Les Opérations Militaires.

GmOH: 1. Der Weltkrieg 1914 bis 1918, Die Militarischen Operationen zu Lande, Band 1, Die Grenzschlachten im Westen.

4 August – 25 September ....The defence of Namur. (Western Front).

BgOH: 1. La Belgique et la Guerre, Tome II, L'Invasion allemande.

2. La Belgique et la Guerre, Tome III: Les Opérations Militaires.

GmOH: 1. Der Weltkrieg 1914 bis 1918, Die Militarischen Operationen zu Lande, Band 1, Die Grenzschlachten im Westen.

6 August – 5 September ....The Battle of the Frontiers. (Western Front).

BgOH: 1. La Belgique et la Guerre, Tome II, L'Invasion allemande.

2. La Belgique et la Guerre, Tome III: Les Opérations Militaires.

FrOH: Les Armées Françaises dans la Grande Guerre, Tome I, La guerre de mouvement - opérations antérieurs au 14 novembre 1914, Volume 1, Les préliminaries - la bataille des frontières.

GmOH: 1. Der Weltkrieg 1914 bis 1918, Die Militarischen Operationen zu Lande, Band 1, Die Grenzschlachten im Westen.
2. Die Schlacht in Lothringen und in den Vogesen 1914 - Die Feuertaufe der Bayerischen Armee. Herausgegeben vom Bayerischen Kriegsarchiv.
3. Die Bayern im Großen Kriege 1914-1918.

6 August ....H.M.S. Amphion sunk by a mine in the North Sea. . (British Home Waters).

BrOH: Official History of the War, Naval Operations, Volume I To the Battle of the Falklands December 1914.

6 August ....The Action between H.M.S. Bristol and S.M.S. Karlsruhe. (Atlantic Ocean).

BrOH: 1. Official History of the War, Naval Operations, Volume I To the Battle of the Falklands December 1914.
2. Official History of the War, Seaborne Trade, Volume I, Cruiser Period.

GmOH: Der Krieg zur See 1914-1918, Band 3, Der Kreuzerkrieg in den ausländischen Gewässern, Teil 2, Die Tätigkeit der Kleinen Kreuzer "Emden", "Königberg" und "Karlsruhe" mit e Anhang: "Die Kriegsfahrt des Kleinen Kreuzers Geier".

6 August ....The Action between H.M.S. Gloucester and S.M.S. Goeben & Breslau. (Mediterranean Sea).

BrOH: Official History of the War, Naval Operations, Volume I To the Battle of the Falklands December 1914.

GmOH: Der Krieg zur See 1914-1918, Band 5, Der Krieg in den türkischen Gewässern, Teil 1, Die Mittelmeer-Division.

7 August 1914..................................The fall of the City of Liége. (Western Front).

BgOH: 1. La Belgique et la Guerre, Tome II, L'Invasion allemande.
2. La Belgique et la Guerre, Tome III: Les Opérations Militaires.

GmOH: Der Weltkrieg 1914 bis 1918, Die Militarischen Operationen zu Lande, Band 1, Die Grenzschlachten im Westen.

7-24 August ....The Battle of Alsace. (Western Front).

FrOH: Les Armées Françaises dans la Grande Guerre, Tome I, La guerre de mouvement - opérations antérieurs au 14 novembre 1914, Volume 1, Les préliminaries - la bataille des frontières.

GmOH: 1. Der Weltkrieg 1914 bis 1918, Die Militarischen Operationen zu Lande, Band 1, Die Grenzschlachten im Westen.
2. Die Schlacht in Lothringen und in den Vogesen 1914 - Die Feuertaufe der Bayerischen Armee. Herausgegeben vom Bayerischen Kriegsarchiv.
3. Die Bayern im Großen Kriege 1914-1918.

8 August..The capture of Lome. (Togoland).

BrOH: Official History of the War, Military Operations, Togoland and the Cameroons.

FrOH: Les Armées Françaises dans la Grande Guerre, Tome IX, Volume 2, Les campagnes coloniales: Cameroun – Togoland. – Opérations contre les Senoussis.

8 August ....The bombardment of Dar es Salaam. (Indian Ocean).

GmOH: 1. Der Krieg zur See 1914-1918, Band 3, Der Kreuzerkrieg in den ausländischen Gewässern, Teil 2, Die Tätigkeit der Kleinen Kreuzer "Emden", "Königberg" und "Karlsruhe" mit e Anhang: "Die Kriegsfahrt des Kleinen Kreuzers Geier".

2. Der Krieg zur See 1914-1918, Band 6, Die Kämpfe der Kaiserlichen Marine in den deutschen Kolonien, Teil 2, Deutsch-Ostafrika.

8 August ....H.M.S. Birmingham sinks S.M.S. U15 (North Sea).

BrOH: Official History of the War, Naval Operations, Volume I To the Battle of the Falklands December 1914.

GmOH: Der Krieg zur See 1914-1918, Band 1, Der Krieg in der Nordsee, Teil 1, Von Kriegbeginn bis Anfang September 1914.

13-25 August ....The First Austrian Invasion of Serbia. (Balkan Front).

AHOH:.Österreich-Ungarns Letzter Krieg 1914-1918, Band I.

GrOH: 1. Ho Hellenikos Stratos kata ton Proton Pankosmion Polemon 1914-1918 Tomos 1 - H Hellas kai ho Polemos eis ta Balkania.

2. Epitomh Istopia Ths Eummetochhs Tou Ellhnikou Stratou Ston Prpsto Pagkosmio Polemo 1914-1918. / A Concise History of the Participation of the Hellenic Army in The First World War 1914-1918.

HOH: 1. A világháború 1914-1918. Különös tekintettel Magyarországra és a Magyar csapatok szereplésére Szerkeszti és kiadja a M. Kir. Hadtörténelmi Levéltár, köt 2.

2. A világháború 1914-1918. Különös tekintettel Magyarországra és a Magyar csapatok szereplésére Szerkeszti és kiadja a M. Kir. Hadtörténelmi Levéltár, köt 4.

SeOH: Veliki rat Srbije za oslobođenje i ujedinenje Srba, Hrvata i Slovenaca. Knjige I. 1914 Godina. Prv period operacija. Cerska bitka.

13-15 August ....Four R.F.C. squadrons fly from Dover to France. (Western Front).

BrOH: Official History of the War, War in the Air, Volume I.

14 August - 12 September.................The Battle of the Frontiers – The Battle of Lorraine. (Western Front).

FrOH: Les Armées Françaises dans la Grande Guerre, Tome I, La guerre de mouvement - opérations antérieurs au 14 novembre 1914, Volume 1, Les préliminaries - la bataille des frontières.

GmOH: 1. Der Weltkrieg 1914 bis 1918, Die Militarischen Operationen zu Lande, Band 1, Die Grenzschlachten im Westen.

2. Die Schlacht in Lothringen und in den Vogesen 1914 - Die Feuertaufe der Bayerischen Armee. Herausgegeben vom Bayerischen Kriegsarchiv.

3. Die Bayern im Großen Kriege 1914-1918.

14-20 August ....The Battle of the Frontiers – The Battle of Lorraine – Battle of Morhange. (Western Front).

FrOH: Les Armées Françaises dans la Grande Guerre, Tome I, La guerre de mouvement - opérations antérieurs au 14 novembre 1914, Volume 1, Les préliminaries - la bataille des frontières.

GmOH: 1. Der Weltkrieg 1914 bis 1918, Die Militarischen Operationen zu Lande, Band 1, Die Grenzschlachten im Westen.

2. Die Schlacht in Lothringen und in den Vogesen 1914 - Die Feuertaufe der Bayerischen Armee. Herausgegeben vom Bayerischen Kriegsarchiv.

3. Die Bayern im Großen Kriege 1914-1918.

14-20 August ....The Battle of the Frontiers – The Battle of Lorraine – Battle of Sarrebourg. (Western Front).

FrOH: Les Armées Françaises dans la Grande Guerre, Tome I, La guerre de mouvement - opérations antérieurs au 14 novembre 1914, Volume 1, Les préliminaries - la bataille des frontières.

GmOH: 1. Der Weltkrieg 1914 bis 1918, Die Militarischen Operationen zu Lande, Band 1, Die Grenzschlachten im Westen.

2. Die Schlacht in Lothringen und in den Vogesen 1914 - Die Feuertaufe der Bayerischen Armee. Herausgegeben vom Bayerischen Kriegsarchiv.

3. Die Bayern im Großen Kriege 1914-1918.

14-30 August ....Operation of the New Zealand Expeditionary Force - the occupation of Samoa. (Pacific Ocean)

GmOH: Der Krieg zur See 1914-1918, Band 6, Die Kämpfe der Kaiserlichen Marine in den deutschen Kolonien, Teil 1, Tsingtau.

15 August..The capture of Taveta. (East Africa).

BgOH: Les Campagnes Coloniales Belges 1914-1918. Volume I. Introduction, les Operations au Cameroun, les Operations en Rhodésie, la Période Défensive à la Frontière Orientale.

BrOH: Official History of the War, Military Operations, East Africa, Volume I, August 1914-September 1916.

GmOH: Der Krieg zur See 1914-1918, Band 6, Die Kämpfe der Kaiserlichen Marine in den deutschen Kolonien, Teil 2, Deutsch-Ostafrika.

SAOH: .The Union of South Africa and the Great War 1914 – 1918.

16 August ....S.M.S. Zenta sunk by British squadron. (Adriatic Sea).

BrOH: Official History of the War, Naval Operations, Volume I To the Battle of the Falklands December 1914.

AHOH: Österreich-Ungarns Seekrieg 1914-1918, Lieferung I.

16-17 August 1914............................The capture of the last fort of Liége. (Western Front).

BgOH: 1. La Belgique et la Guerre, Tome II, L'Invasion allemande.

2. La Belgique et la Guerre, Tome III: Les Opérations Militaires.

GmOH: Der Weltkrieg 1914 bis 1918, Die Militarischen Operationen zu Lande, Band 1, Die Grenzschlachten im Westen.

17 August .... The First Austrian Invasion of Serbia - The Battle of the Tser and the Jadar. (Balkan Front).
AHOH:.Österreich-Ungarns Letzter Krieg 1914-1918, Band I.
GrOH: 1. Ho Hellenikos Stratos kata ton Proton Pankosmion Polemon 1914-1918 Tomos 1 - H Hellas kai ho Polemos eis ta Balkania.
2. Epitomh Istopia Ths Eummetochhs Tou Ellhnikou Stratou Ston Prpsto Pagkosmio Polemo 1914-1918. / A Concise History of the Participation of the Hellenic Army in The First World War 1914-1918.
HOH: 1. A világháború 1914-1918. Különös tekintettel Magyarországra és a Magyar csapatok szereplésére Szerkeszti és kiadja a M. Kir. Hadtörténelmi Levéltár, köt 2.
2. A világháború 1914-1918. Különös tekintettel Magyarországra és a Magyar csapatok szereplésére Szerkeszti és kiadja a M. Kir. Hadtörténelmi Levéltár, köt 4.
SeOH: Veliki rat Srbije za oslobođenje i ujedinenje Srba, Hrvata i Slovenaca. Knjige I. 1914 Godina. Prv period operacija. Cerska bitka.

18-19 August .... The Battle of the Gette. (the Battle of Tirlemont). (Belgium - Western Front).
BgOH: 1. La Belgique et la Guerre, Tome II, L'Invasion allemande.
2. La Belgique et la Guerre, Tome III: Les Opérations Militaires.
GmOH: Der Weltkrieg 1914 bis 1918, Die Militarischen Operationen zu Lande, Band 1, Die Grenzschlachten im Westen.

19-20 August .... The Battle of Gawaiten-Gumbinnen. (North Poland - Eastern Front).
GmOH: Der Weltkrieg 1914 bis 1918, Die Militarischen Operationen zu Lande, Band 5, Der Herbst - Feldzug im Osten bis zum Rückzug im Westem bis zum Stellumgskrieg.
PlOH: Studia z wojny światowej 1914-1918 roku Tom I: Kampania jesienna w Prusach Wschodnich sierpień - wrzesień 1914 roku.
RuOH: 1. The Russian Army in the World War.
2. The Russian Campaign of 1914. The Beginning of the World and Operations in East Prussia.
3. From the History of the 1914 Campaign.
4. A Strategic Outline of the War 1914 –1915.
5. A Strategic Outline of the War 1914 -1918.

21 August.. The Battle of the Jarostawice. (Poland - Eastern Front).
PlOH: 1. Studia z wojny światowej 1914-1918 roku Tom I: Kampania jesienna w Prusach Wschodnich sierpień - wrzesień 1914 roku.
2. Studia z wojny światowej 1914-1918 roku Tom II: Bitwa konna pod Jarosławicami 21 sierpnia 1914 roku.

3. Studia z wojny światowej 1914-1918 roku Tom ?: Działania osłonowe w Małopolsce Wschodniej w sierpniu 1914 roku.

21-24 August ....The Battle of the Frontiers – The Battle of Belgium - Battle of the Charleroi. (Western Front).
                    BgOH: 1. La Belgique et la Guerre, Tome II, L'Invasion allemande.
                    2. La Belgique et la Guerre, Tome III: Les Opérations Militaires.
                    FrOH: Les Armées Françaises dans la Grande Guerre, Tome I, La guerre de mouvement - opérations antérieurs au 14 novembre 1914, Volume 1, Les préliminaries - la bataille des frontières.
                    GmOH: 1. Der Weltkrieg 1914 bis 1918, Die Militarischen Operationen zu Lande, Band 1, Die Grenzschlachten im Westen.
                    2. Die Schlacht in Lothringen und in den Vogesen 1914 - Die Feuertaufe der Bayerischen Armee. Herausgegeben vom Bayerischen Kriegsarchiv.
                    3. Die Bayern im Großen Kriege 1914-1918.

22-24 August ....The Battle of the Frontiers – The Battle of Belgium - Battle of the Ardennes. (Western Front).
                    BgOH: 1. La Belgique et la Guerre, Tome II, L'Invasion allemande.
                      2. La Belgique et la Guerre, Tome III: Les Opérations Militaires.
                    FrOH: Les Armées Françaises dans la Grande Guerre, Tome I, La guerre de mouvement - opérations antérieurs au 14 novembre 1914, Volume 1, Les préliminaries - la bataille des frontières.
                    GmOH: 1. Der Weltkrieg 1914 bis 1918, Die Militarischen Operationen zu Lande, Band 1, Die Grenzschlachten im Westen.
                    2. Die Schlacht in Lothringen und in den Vogesen 1914 - Die Feuertaufe der Bayerischen Armee. Herausgegeben vom Bayerischen Kriegsarchiv.
                    3. Die Bayern im Großen Kriege 1914-1918.

23 August..The German airship Z8 shot down over Alsace. (Western Front).
                    GmOH: Der Weltkrieg 1914 bis 1918, Die Militarischen Operationen zu Lande, Band 9, Die Operationen des Jahres 1915 – Die Ereignisse im Westen und auf dem Balkan vom Sommer bis Jahresschluß; Die Entwicklung der Luftstreitkrafte bis Ende 1915.

23-24 August ....The Battle of the Frontiers – The Battle of Mons. (Western Front).
                    BrOH: Official History of the War, Military Operations, France and Belgium 1914 Volume I, Mons, The Retreat to the Seine, The Marne and The Aisne, August-October 1914.
                    GmOH: Der Weltkrieg 1914 bis 1918, Die Militarischen Operationen zu Lande, Band 1, Die Grenzschlachten im Westen.

23-31 August ....The Battle of Krasnik. (Southern Poland - Eastern Front)
                    AHOH: Österreich-Ungarns Letzter Krieg 1914-1918, Band I.
                    HOH: 1. A világháború 1914-1918. Különös tekintettel Magyarországra és a Magyar csapatok szereplésére

Szerkeszti és kiadja a M. Kir. Hadtörténelmi Levéltár, köt 2.

2. A világháború 1914-1918. Különös tekintettel Magyarországra és a Magyar csapatok szereplésére Szerkeszti és kiadja a M. Kir. Hadtörténelmi Levéltár, köt 4.

PlOH: 1. Studia z wojny światowej 1914-1918 roku Tom I: Kampania jesienna w Prusach Wschodnich sierpień - wrzesień 1914 roku.

2. Studia z wojny światowej 1914-1918 roku Tom ?: Działania osłonowe w Małopolsce Wschodniej w sierpniu 1914 roku.

RuOH: 1. The Russian Army in the World War.

2. From the History of the 1914 Campaign.

3. A Strategic Outline of the War 1914 –1915.

4. A Strategic Outline of the War 1914 -1918.

23-31 August ....The Battle of Tannenberg. (East Prussia - Eastern Front).

GmOH: Der Weltkrieg 1914 bis 1918, Die Militarischen Operationen zu Lande, Band 5, Der Herbst - Feldzug im Osten bis zum Rückzug im Westem bis zum Stellumgskrieg.

PlOH: Studia z wojny światowej 1914-1918 roku Tom I: Kampania jesienna w Prusach Wschodnich sierpień - wrzesień 1914 roku.

RuOH: 1. The Russian Army in the World War.

2. The Russian Campaign of 1914. The Beginning of the World and Operations in East Prussia.

3. From the History of the 1914 Campaign.

4. A Strategic Outline of the War 1914 –1915.

5. A Strategic Outline of the War 1914 -1918.

25-27 August ....The Battle of the Malines. (Belgium - Western Front).

BgOH: 1. La Belgique et la Guerre, Tome II, L'Invasion allemande.

2. La Belgique et la Guerre, Tome III: Les Opérations Militaires.

GmOH: Der Weltkrieg 1914 bis 1918, Die Militarischen Operationen zu Lande, Band 1 Die Grenzschlachten im Westen.

25-28 August ....The Battle of the Frontiers – The Battle of the Meuse. (Western Front).

BgOH: 1. La Belgique et la Guerre, Tome II, L'Invasion allemande.

2. La Belgique et la Guerre, Tome III: Les Opérations Militaires.

FrOH: Les Armées Françaises dans la Grande Guerre, Tome I, La guerre de mouvement - opérations antérieurs au 14 novembre 1914, Volume 1, Les préliminaries - la bataille des frontières.

GmOH: 1. Der Weltkrieg 1914 bis 1918, Die Militarischen Operationen zu Lande, Band 1, Die Grenzschlachten im Westen.

2. Die Schlacht in Lothringen und in den Vogesen 1914 - Die Feuertaufe der Bayerischen Armee. Herausgegeben vom Bayerischen Kriegsarchiv.

3. Die Bayern im Großen Kriege 1914-1918.

25 August – 3 September ....The Battle of the Frontiers – The Battle of Lorraine – Battle of Mortagne. (Western Front).

> FrOH: Les Armées Françaises dans la Grande Guerre, Tome I, La guerre de mouvement - opérations antérieurs au 14 novembre 1914, Volume 1, Les préliminaries - la bataille des frontières.
>
> GmOH: 1. Der Weltkrieg 1914 bis 1918, Die Militarischen Operationen zu Lande, Band 1, Die Grenzschlachten im Westen.
> 2. Die Schlacht in Lothringen und in den Vogesen 1914 - Die Feuertaufe der Bayerischen Armee. Herausgegeben vom Bayerischen Kriegsarchiv.
> 3. Die Bayern im Großen Kriege 1914-1918.

25-29 [29-30?] August ....The Battle of the Frontiers - The Battle of Guise. (Western Front).

> FrOH: Les Armées Françaises dans la Grande Guerre, Tome I, La guerre de mouvement - opérations antérieurs au 14 novembre 1914, Volume 1, Les préliminaries - la bataille des frontières.
>
> GmOH: 1. Der Weltkrieg 1914 bis 1918, Die Militarischen Operationen zu Lande, Band 1, Die Grenzschlachten im Westen.
> 2. Die Schlacht in Lothringen und in den Vogesen 1914 - Die Feuertaufe der Bayerischen Armee. Herausgegeben vom Bayerischen Kriegsarchiv.
> 3. Die Bayern im Großen Kriege 1914-1918.

26 August ....S.M.S. Magdeburg sunk by Russians squadron. German Naval Code Book captured. (Baltic Sea).

> GmOH: Der Krieg zur See 1914-1918, Band 2, Der Krieg in der Ostsee, Teil 1, Von Kriegbeginn bis Mitte März 1915.
>
> RuOH:..Flot v Pervoi Mirovoi Voine. V Dvukh Tomakh. Tom I Deystviya Russkogo Flota.

26 August ....The action between H.M.S. Highflyer and S.M.S. Kaiser Wilhelm der Grosse. (Atlantic Ocean).

> BrOH: Official History of the War, Naval Operations, Volume I To the Battle of the Falklands December 1914.
>
> GmOH: Der Krieg zur See 1914-1918, Band 3, Der Kreuzerkrieg in den ausländischen Gewässern, Teil 3, Die deutschen Hilfskreuzer.

26 August..The Battle of the Frontiers - the Battle of Le Cateau. (Western Front).

> BrOH: Official History of the War, Military Operations, France and Belgium 1914, Volume I, Mons, The Retreat to the Seine, The Marne and The Aisne, August-October 1914.
>
> GmOH: Der Weltkrieg 1914 bis 1918, Die Militarischen Operationen zu Lande, Band 1, Die Grenzschlachten im Westen.

26 August..The German Forces in Togoland capitulates.

> BrOH: Official History of the War, Military Operations, Togoland and the Cameroons.
>
> FrOH: Les Armées Françaises dans la Grande Guerre, Tome IX, Volume 2, Les campagnes colonials, Cameroun – Togoland. – Opérations contre les Senoussis.

26 August – 2 September ....The Battle of Zamosc-Komarów. (Southern Poland - Eastern Front).

> AHOH: Österreich-Ungarns Letzter Krieg 1914-1918, Band I.

HOH: 1. A világháború 1914-1918. Különös tekintettel Magyarországra és a Magyar csapatok szereplésére Szerkeszti és kiadja a M. Kir. Hadtörténelmi Levéltár, köt 2.

2. A világháború 1914-1918. Különös tekintettel Magyarországra és a Magyar csapatok szereplésére Szerkeszti és kiadja a M. Kir. Hadtörténelmi Levéltár, köt 4.

PlOH: 1. Studia z wojny światowej 1914-1918 roku Tom I: Kampania jesienna w Prusach Wschodnich sierpień - wrzesień 1914 roku.

2. Studia z wojny światowej 1914-1918 roku Tom III: Bitwa pod Komarówem 26 sierpień - 2 wrzesień 1914 roku.

3. Studia z wojny światowej 1914-1918 roku Tom ?: Działania osłonowe w Małopolsce Wschodniej w sierpniu 1914 roku.

RuOH: 1. The Russian Army in the World War.

2. From the History of the 1914 Campaign.

3. A Strategic Outline of the War 1914 – 1915.

4. A Strategic Outline of the War 1914 - 1918.

26-30 August .... The First Battle of Lemberg. (South Poland – Eastern Front).

AHOH: Österreich-Ungarns Letzter Krieg 1914-1918, Band I.

HOH: 1. A világháború 1914-1918. Különös tekintettel Magyarországra és a Magyar csapatok szereplésére Szerkeszti és kiadja a M. Kir. Hadtörténelmi Levéltár, köt 2.

2. A világháború 1914-1918. Különös tekintettel Magyarországra és a Magyar csapatok szereplésére Szerkeszti és kiadja a M. Kir. Hadtörténelmi Levéltár, köt 4.

PlOH: 1. Studia z wojny światowej 1914-1918 roku Tom I: Kampania jesienna w Prusach Wschodnich sierpień - wrzesień 1914 roku.

2. Studia z wojny światowej 1914-1918 roku Tom IV: Bitwa pod Lwówem.

RuOH: 1. The Russian Army in the World War.

2. From the History of the 1914 Campaign.

3. A Strategic Outline of the War 1914 – 1915.

4. A Strategic Outline of the War 1914 - 1918.

27 August .... The first attack on Mora. (Cameroons).

BgOH: Les campagnes coloniales Belges 1914-1918. Volume I. Introduction, les operations au Cameroun, les operations en Rhodésie, la période défensive à la Frontière Orientale.

BrOH: Official History of the War, Military Operations, Togoland and the Cameroons.

FrOH: Les Armées Françaises dans la Grande Guerre, Tome IX, Volume 2, Les campagnes coloniales: Cameroun – Togoland. – Opérations contre les Senoussis.

27 August .... The Imperial Japanese Navy blockades Kiaochow. - the Siege of Tsingtau. (China).

GmOH: Der Krieg zur See 1914-1918 Band 6 Die Kämpfe der Kaiserlichen Marine in den deutschen Kolonien. Teil 1 Tsingtau - Teil 2 Deutsch-Ostafrika.

JOH: Taishō san-yonen kaigun senshi: Kan 1-8.

28 August ....The action off Heligoland. (North Sea).
                        BrOH: Official History of the War, Naval Operations, Volume I To the Battle of the Falklands December 1914.
                        GmOH: Der Krieg zur See 1914-1918, Band 1, Der Krieg in der Nordsee, Teil 1, Von Kriegbeginn bis Anfang September 1914.

29 August...The German airship Z5 shot down over Mlawa, Northern Poland.
                        GmOH: Der Weltkrieg 1914 bis 1918, Die Militarischen Operationen zu Lande, Band 9, Die Operationen des Jahres 1915 – Die Ereignisse im Westen und auf dem Balkan vom Sommer bis Jahresschluß; Die Entwicklung der Luftstreitkrafte bis Ende 1915.

30 August...The First Attack on Garua. (Cameroons).
                        BgOH: Les campagnes coloniales Belges 1914-1918. Volume I. Introduction, les operations au Cameroun, les operations en Rhodésie, la période défensive à la Frontière Orientale.
                        BrOH: Official History of the War, Military Operations, Togoland and the Cameroons.
                        FrOH: Les Armées Françaises dans la Grande Guerre, Tome IX, Volume 2, Les campagnes coloniales: Cameroun – Togoland. – Opérations contre les Senoussis.

30 August...The German aircraft raid on Paris.
                        GmOH: Der Weltkrieg 1914 bis 1918, Die Militarischen Operationen zu Lande, Band 9, Die Operationen des Jahres 1915 – Die Ereignisse im Westen und auf dem Balkan vom Sommer bis Jahresschluß; Die Entwicklung der Luftstreitkrafte bis Ende 1915.

2 September – 7 November................Operation in Shantung - the Siege of Tsingtau. (China).
                        GmOH: Der Krieg zur See 1914-1918 Band 6 Die Kämpfe der Kaiserlichen Marine in den deutschen Kolonien. Teil 1 Tsingtau - Teil 2 Deutsch-Ostafrika.
                        JOH: 1. Taishō san-yonen kaigun senshi: Kan 1-8.
                                        2. Taishō sannen Nichi-Doku senshi: jōkan.
                                        3. Taishō sannen Nichi-Doku senshi: gekan.

2 September ....Allied Force landing at Lungkow - the Siege of Tsingtau. (China).
                        GmOH: Der Krieg zur See 1914-1918 Band 6 Die Kämpfe der Kaiserlichen Marine in den deutschen Kolonien. Teil 1 Tsingtau - Teil 2 Deutsch-Ostafrika.
                        JOH: 1. Taishō san-yonen kaigun senshi: Kan 1-8.
                                        2. Taishō sannen Nichi-Doku senshi: jōkan.
                                        3. Taishō sannen Nichi-Doku senshi: gekan.

3 September .....................................H.M.S. Speedy sunk by a mine in the North Sea. (British Home Waters).
                        BrOH: Official History of the War, Naval Operations, Volume I To the Battle of the Falklands December 1914.

4-12 September.................................The Battle of the Frontiers – the Battle of Lorraine – Battle of Grand Couronne. (Western Front).
                        FrOH: Les Armées Françaises dans la Grande Guerre, Tome I, La guerre de mouvement - opérations antérieurs au 14 novembre 1914, Volume 1, Les préliminaries - la bataille des frontières.

GmOH: 1. Der Weltkrieg 1914 bis 1918, Die Militarischen Operationen zu Lande, Band 1, Die Grenzschlachten im Westen.
2. Die Schlacht in Lothringen und in den Vogesen 1914 - Die Feuertaufe der Bayerischen Armee. Herausgegeben vom Bayerischen Kriegsarchiv.
3. Die Bayern im Großen Kriege 1914-1918.

5 September ....H.M.S. Pathfinder sunk by a submarine in the North Sea. (British Home Waters).

BrOH: Official History of the War, Naval Operations, Volume I To the Battle of the Falklands December 1914.

GmOH: Der Krieg zur See 1914-1918, Band 1, Der Krieg in der Nordsee, Teil 1, Von Kriegbeginn bis Anfang September 1914.

5-10 September ....The Battle of the Ourcq[1]. (Western Front).

FrOH: Les Armées Françaises dans la Grande Guerre, Tome I, La guerre de mouvement - opérations antérieurs au 14 novembre 1914, Volume 2, La manoeuvre en retraite et les préliminaries de la bataille de la Marne.

GmOH: 1. Der Weltkrieg 1914 bis 1918, Die Militarischen Operationen zu Lande, Band 3, Der Marne – Feldzug. Von der Sambre zur Marne.
2. Die Bayern im Großen Kriege 1914-1918.

PlOH: Studia z wojny światowej 1914-1918 roku Tom V: Monthyon: bój spotkaniowy niemieckiego IV korpusu rezerwowego z francuską grupą generała de Lamaze 5 września 1914 roku.

5-15 September ....The Battle of the Masurian Lakes. (Eastern Prussia - Eastern Front).

GmOH: Der Weltkrieg 1914 bis 1918, Die Militarischen Operationen zu Lande, Band 5, Der Herbst - Feldzug im Osten bis zum Rückzug im Westem bis zum Stellumgskrieg.

PlOH: Studia z wojny światowej 1914-1918 roku Tom I: Kampania jesienna w Prusach Wschodnich sierpień - wrzesień 1914 roku.

RuOH: 1. The Russian Army in the World War.
2. The Russian Campaign of 1914. The Beginning of the World and Operations in East Prussia.
3. From the History of the 1914 Campaign.
4. A Strategic Outline of the War 1914 –1915.
5. A Strategic Outline of the War 1914 -1918.

5-9 September ....The defence of Abercorn. (Rhodesia - East Africa).

BgOH: Les Campagnes Coloniales Belges 1914-1918. Volume I. Introduction, les Operations au Cameroun, les Operations en Rhodésie, la Période Défensive à la Frontière Orientale.

BrOH: Official History of the War, Military Operations, East Africa, Volume I, August 1914-September 1916.

GmOH: Der Krieg zur See 1914-1918, Band 6, Die Kämpfe der Kaiserlichen Marine in den deutschen Kolonien, Teil 2, Deutsch-Ostafrika.

SAOH: .The Union of South Africa and the Great War 1914 – 1918.

---

[1] **Officially the Battle of the Ourcq is included in the Battle of the Marne in spite of the dates as shown!**

6-13 September..................................The Battle of the Marne. (Western Front).
> BrOH: Official History of the War, Military Operations, France and Belgium 1914, Volume I, Mons, The Retreat to the Seine, The Marne and The Aisne, August-October 1914.
>
> FrOH: 1. Les Armées Françaises dans la Grande Guerre, Tome I, La guerre de mouvement - opérations antérieurs au 14 novembre 1914, Volume 3*, La bataille de la Marne.
> 2. Les Armées Françaises dans la Grande Guerre, Tome I, La guerre de mouvement - opérations antérieurs au 14 novembre 1914, Volume 3**, La bataille de la Marne.
>
> GmOH: 1. Der Weltkrieg 1914 bis 1918, Die Militarischen Operationen zu Lande, Band 3, Der Marne – Feldzug. Von der Sambre zur Marne.
> 2. Die Bayern im Großen Kriege 1914-1918.

6-10 September..................................The Battle of the Marne - the Battle of the Two Morins.
> FrOH: 1. Les Armées Françaises dans la Grande Guerre, Tome I, La guerre de mouvement - opérations antérieurs au 14 novembre 1914, Volume 3*, La bataille de la Marne.
> 2. Les Armées Françaises dans la Grande Guerre, Tome I, La guerre de mouvement - opérations antérieurs au 14 novembre 1914, Volume 3**, La bataille de la Marne.
>
> GmOH: 1. Der Weltkrieg 1914 bis 1918, Die Militarischen Operationen zu Lande, Band 3, Der Marne – Feldzug. Von der Sambre zur Marne.
> 2. Die Bayern im Großen Kriege 1914-1918.

6-10 September..................................The Battle of the Marne - the Battle of the Marshes of Saint-Gond. (Western Front).
> FrOH: 1. Les Armées Françaises dans la Grande Guerre, Tome I, La guerre de mouvement - opérations antérieurs au 14 novembre 1914, Volume 3*, La bataille de la Marne.
> 2. Les Armées Françaises dans la Grande Guerre, Tome I, La guerre de mouvement - opérations antérieurs au 14 novembre 1914, Volume 3**, La bataille de la Marne.
>
> GmOH: 1 Der Weltkrieg 1914 bis 1918, Die Militarischen Operationen zu Lande, Band 3, Der Marne – Feldzug. Von der Sambre zur Marne.
> 2. Die Bayern im Großen Kriege 1914-1918.

6-11 September..................................The Battle of the Marne - the Battle of Vitry. (Western Front).
> FrOH: 1. Les Armées Françaises dans la Grande Guerre, Tome I, La guerre de mouvement - opérations antérieurs au 14 novembre 1914, Volume 3*, La bataille de la Marne.
> 2. Les Armées Françaises dans la Grande Guerre, Tome I, La guerre de mouvement - opérations antérieurs au 14 novembre 1914, Volume 3**, La bataille de la Marne.
>
> GmOH: 1. Der Weltkrieg 1914 bis 1918, Die Militarischen Operationen zu Lande, Band 3, Der Marne – Feldzug. Von der Sambre zur Marne.
> 2. Die Bayern im Großen Kriege 1914-1918.

6-11 September..................................The Battle of the Marne - the Battle of Revigny.
> FrOH: 1. Les Armées Françaises dans la Grande Guerre, Tome I, La guerre de mouvement - opérations antérieurs au 14 novembre 1914, Volume 3*, La bataille de la Marne.

2. Les Armées Françaises dans la Grande Guerre, Tome I, La guerre de mouvement - opérations antérieurs au 14 novembre 1914, Volume 3**, La bataille de la Marne.

GmOH: 1. Der Weltkrieg 1914 bis 1918, Die Militarischen Operationen zu Lande, Band 3, Der Marne – Feldzug. Von der Sambre zur Marne.

2. Die Bayern im Großen Kriege 1914-1918.

6 September ....The affair of Tsavo. (East Africa).

BgOH: Les Campagnes Coloniales Belges 1914-1918. Volume I. Introduction, les Operations au Cameroun, les Operations en Rhodésie, la Période Défensive à la Frontière Orientale.

BrOH: Official History of the War, Military Operations, East Africa, Volume I, August 1914-September 1916.

GmOH: Der Krieg zur See 1914-1918, Band 6, Die Kämpfe der Kaiserlichen Marine in den deutschen Kolonien, Teil 2, Deutsch-Ostafrika.

SAOH: The Union of South Africa and the Great War 1914 – 1918.

7 September ....Naval Operations against Duala, Cameroons begin. (Atlantic Ocean).

BgOH: Les Campagnes Coloniales Belges 1914-1918. Volume I. Introduction, les Operations au Cameroun, les Operations en Rhodésie, la Période Défensive à la Frontière Orientale.

BrOH: 1. Official History of the War, Military Operations, Togoland and the Cameroons.

2. Official History of the War, Official History of the War, Naval Operations, Volume I To the Battle of the Falklands December 1914.

FrOH: Les Armées Françaises dans la Grande Guerre, Tome IX, Volume 2, Les campagnes coloniales: Cameroun – Togoland. – Opérations contre les Senoussis.

7-9 September ....The Battle of the Tarnavka. (South Poland - Eastern Front).

AHOH: Österreich-Ungarns Letzter Krieg 1914-1918, Band I.

HOH: 1. A világháború 1914-1918. Különös tekintettel Magyarországra és a Magyar csapatok szereplésére Szerkeszti és kiadja a M. Kir. Hadtörténelmi Levéltár, köt 3.

2. A világháború 1914-1918. Különös tekintettel Magyarországra és a Magyar csapatok szereplésére Szerkeszti és kiadja a M. Kir. Hadtörténelmi Levéltár, köt 5.

PlOH: Studia z wojny światowej 1914-1918 roku Tom I: Kampania jesienna w Prusach Wschodnich sierpień - wrzesień 1914 roku.

RuOH: 1. The Russian Army in the World War.

2. The Russian Campaign of 1914. The Beginning of the World and Operations in East Prussia.

3. From the History of the 1914 Campaign.

4. A Strategic Outline of the War 1914 –1915.

5. A Strategic Outline of the War 1914 -1918.

8-11 September ....The Second Battle of Lemberg. (South Poland - Eastern Front).

AHOH: Österreich-Ungarns Letzter Krieg 1914-1918, Band I.

HOH: 1. A világháború 1914-1918. Különös tekintettel Magyarországra és a Magyar csapatok szereplésére

Szerkeszti és kiadja a M. Kir. Hadtörténelmi Levéltár, köt 3.

2. A világháború 1914-1918. Különös tekintettel Magyarországra és a Magyar csapatok szereplésére Szerkeszti és kiadja a M. Kir. Hadtörténelmi Levéltár, köt 5.

PlOH: 1. Studia z wojny światowej 1914-1918 roku Tom I: Kampania jesienna w Prusach Wschodnich sierpień - wrzesień 1914 roku.

2. Studia z wojny światowej 1914-1918 roku Tom IV: Bitwa pod Lwówem.

RuOH: 1. The Russian Army in the World War.

2. The Russian Campaign of 1914. The Beginning of the World and Operations in East Prussia.

3. From the History of the 1914 Campaign.

4. A Strategic Outline of the War 1914 –1915.

5. A Strategic Outline of the War 1914 -1918.

8 September – 15 November..............The Second Austrian Invasion of Serbia. (Serbia - Balkan Front).

AHOH: Österreich-Ungarns Letzter Krieg 1914-1918, Band I.

GrOH: 1. Ho Hellenikos Stratos kata ton Proton Pankosmion Polemon 1914-1918 Tomos 1 - H Hellas kai ho Polemos eis ta Balkania.

2. Epitomh Istopia Ths Eummetochhs Tou Ellhnikou Stratou Ston Prpsto Pagkosmio Polemo 1914-1918. / A Concise History of the Participation of the Hellenic Army in The First World War 1914-1918.

HOH: 1. A világháború 1914-1918. Különös tekintettel Magyarországra és a Magyar csapatok szereplésére Szerkeszti és kiadja a M. Kir. Hadtörténelmi Levéltár, köt 3.

2. A világháború 1914-1918. Különös tekintettel Magyarországra és a Magyar csapatok szereplésére Szerkeszti és kiadja a M. Kir. Hadtörténelmi Levéltár, köt 5.

SeOH: 1. Veliki rat Srbije za oslobođenje i ujedinenje Srba, Hrvata i Slovenaca. Knjige II. 1914 godina. Drugi period operacija. Bitka na Drini. I II i III deo.

2. Veliki rat Srbije za oslobođenje i ujedinenje Srba, Hrvata i Slovenaca. Knjige treća. 1914 godina. Drugi period operacija. Bitka na Drini. IV V i VI deo.

3. Veliki rat Srbije za oslobođenje i ujedinenje Srba, Hrvata i Slovenaca. Knjige četvrta. 1914 godina. Treći period operacija. Kolubarska bitka. I. faza - Uvodna.

4. Veliki rat Srbije za oslobođenje i ujedinenje Srba, Hrvata i Slovenaca. Knjige peta. 1914 godina. Treći period operacija. Kolubarska bitka. II. faza - Odbranbena.

8-17 September..................................The Battle of the Drina. (Serbia – Balkan Front).

AHOH: Österreich-Ungarns Letzter Krieg 1914-1918, Band I.

GrOH: 1. Ho Hellenikos Stratos kata ton Proton Pankosmion Polemon 1914-1918 Tomos 1 - H Hellas kai ho Polemos eis ta Balkania.

2. Epitomh Istopia Ths Eummetochhs Tou Ellhnikou Stratou Ston Prpsto Pagkosmio Polemo 1914-1918. / A Concise History of the Participation of the Hellenic Army in The First World War 1914-1918.

HOH: 1. A világháború 1914-1918. Különös tekintettel Magyarországra és a Magyar csapatok szereplésére

Szerkeszti és kiadja a M. Kir. Hadtörténelmi Levéltár, köt 3.

2. A világháború 1914-1918. Különös tekintettel Magyarországra és a Magyar csapatok szereplésére Szerkeszti és kiadja a M. Kir. Hadtörténelmi Levéltár, köt 5.

SeOH: Veliki rat Srbije za oslobođenje i ujedinenje Srba, Hrvata i Slovenaca. Knjige II. 1914 godina. Drugi period operacija. Bitka na Drini. I II i III deo.

AHOH: Österreich-Ungarns Letzter Krieg 1914-1918, Band I.

GrOH: 1. Ho Hellenikos Stratos kata ton Proton Pankosmion Polemon 1914-1918 Tomos 1 - H Hellas kai ho Polemos eis ta Balkania.

2. Epitomh Istopia Ths Eummetochhs Tou Ellhnikou Stratou Ston Prpsto Pagkosmio Polemo 1914-1918. / A Concise History of the Participation of the Hellenic Army in The First World War 1914-1918.

HOH: 1. A világháború 1914-1918. Különös tekintettel Magyarországra és a Magyar csapatok szereplésére Szerkeszti és kiadja a M. Kir. Hadtörténelmi Levéltár, köt 3.

2. A világháború 1914-1918. Különös tekintettel Magyarországra és a Magyar csapatok szereplésére Szerkeszti és kiadja a M. Kir. Hadtörténelmi Levéltár, köt 5.

SeOH: 1. Veliki rat Srbije za oslobođenje i ujedinenje Srba, Hrvata i Slovenaca. Knjige II. 1914 godina. Drugi period operacija. Bitka na Drini. I II i III deo.

2. Veliki rat Srbije za oslobođenje i ujedinenje Srba, Hrvata i Slovenaca. Knjige treća. 1914 godina. Drugi period operacija. Bitka na Drini. IV V i VI deo.

GmOH: Der Krieg zur See 1914-1918, Band 6, Die Kämpfe der Kaiserlichen Marine in den deutschen Kolonien, Teil 1, Tsingtau - Teil 2, Deutsch-Ostafrika.

SAOH: .The Union of South Africa and the Great War 1914 – 1918.

AuOH: Official History of Australia in the War of 1914-1918, Volume IX, Royal Australian Navy.

BrOH: 1. Official History of the War, Naval Operations, Volume I To the Battle of the Falklands December 1914.

2. Official History of the War, Seaborne Trade, Volume I, Cruiser Period.

3. Official History of the War, The Merchant Navy, Volume I.

GmOH: Der Krieg zur See 1914-1918, Band 3, Der Kreuzerkrieg in den ausländischen Gewässern, Teil 2, Die Tätigkeit der Kleinen Kreuzer "Emden", "Königberg" und "Karlsruhe" mit e Anhang: "Die Kriegsfahrt des Kleinen Kreuzers Geier".

AuOH: Official History of Australia in the War of 1914-1918, Volume X, Southern Pacific.

11 September – 6 November..............Operation of the Australian Naval and Military Expeditionary Force - the affair of Herbertshöhe. (Pacific Ocean).
AuOH: Official History of Australia in the War of 1914-1918, Volume X, Southern Pacific.

12-21 September................................The First Battle of the Aisne. (Western Front).
BrOH: Official History of the War, Military Operations, France and Belgium 1914, Volume I, Mons, The Retreat to the Seine, The Marne and The Aisne, August-October 1914.
FrOH: Les Armées Françaises dans la Grande Guerre, Tome I, Volume 4, La bataille de l'Aisne, la course à la mer, La bataille des Flandre, les opérations sur le front stabilise.
GmOH: 1. Der Weltkrieg 1914 bis 1918, Band 5, Der Herbst - Feldzug im Osten bis zum Rückzug im Westem bis zum Stellumgskrieg.
2. Der Wettlauf um die Flanke in Nordfrankreich 1914. Herausgegeben vom Bayerischen Kriegsarchiv.
3. Die Bayern im Großen Kriege 1914-1918.

14 September....................................Action between H.M.S. Carmania & S.M.S. Cap Trafalgar. (Atlantic Ocean).
BrOH: Official History of the War, Naval Operations, Volume I To the Battle of the Falklands December 1914.
GmOH: Der Krieg zur See 1914-1918, Band 3, Der Kreuzerkrieg in den ausländischen Gewässern, Teil 3, Die deutschen Hilfskreuzer.

15 September – 28 December ....South African Rebellion. (South Africa).
SAOH: .The Union of South Africa and the Great War 1914 – 1918.

15 September....................................South African Rebellion breaks out. (South Africa).
SAOH: .The Union of South Africa and the Great War 1914 – 1918.

17 September....................................German New Guinea & surrounding colonies capitulate to the Australian Expeditionary Force. (Pacific Ocean).
AuOH: Official History of Australia in the War of 1914-1918, Volume X, Southern Pacific.

18 September....................................Allied Force landing at Laoshan Bay - the Siege of Tsingtau. (China).
GmOH: Der Krieg zur See 1914-1918 Band 6 Die Kämpfe der Kaiserlichen Marine in den deutschen Kolonien. Teil 1 Tsingtau - Teil 2 Deutsch-Ostafrika.
JOH: 1. Taishō san-yonen kaigun senshi: Kan 1-8.
2. Taishō sannen Nichi-Doku senshi: jōkan.
3. Taishō sannen Nichi-Doku senshi: gekan.

19 September....................................Cattaro bombarded by French squadron. (Mediterranean Sea).
FrOH: La Guerre des Croiseurs.

19 September....................................South African Forces capture Lüderitzbucht. (South West Africa [Namibia]).
SAOH: 1. The Union of South Africa and the Great War 1914 – 1918.

2. The Campaign in German South West Africa 1914 – 1915.

20 September .....................................H.M.S. Pegasus sunk by S.M.S. Königsberg. (Indian Ocean).

BrOH: Official History of the War, Naval Operations, Volume I To the Battle of the Falklands December 1914.

GmOH: Der Krieg zur See 1914-1918, Band 3, Der Kreuzerkrieg in den ausländischen Gewässern, Teil 2, Die Tätigkeit der Kleinen Kreuzer "Emden", "Königberg" und "Karlsruhe" mit e Anhang: "Die Kriegsfahrt des Kleinen Kreuzers Geier".

22 September .....................................H.M.S. Aboukir, H.M.S. Cressy & H.M.S. Hogue sunk by S.M.S. U. 9 in the North Sea. (British Home Waters).

BrOH: Official History of the War, Naval Operations, Volume I To the Battle of the Falklands December 1914.

GmOH: Der Krieg zur See 1914-1918, Band 1, Der Krieg in der Nordsee, Teil 2, Von Anfang September bis November 1914.

22 September ....Madras bombarded by S.M.S. Emden. (Indian Ocean).

AuOH: Official History of Australia in the War of 1914-1918, Volume IX, Royal Australian Navy.

BrOH: Official History of the War, Naval Operations, Volume I To the Battle of the Falklands December 1914.

GmOH: Der Krieg zur See 1914-1918, Band 3, Der Kreuzerkrieg in den ausländischen Gewässern, Teil 2, Die Tätigkeit der Kleinen Kreuzer "Emden", "Königberg" und "Karlsruhe" mit e Anhang: "Die Kriegsfahrt des Kleinen Kreuzers Geier".

22 September ....Papeete, Tahiti bombarded by von Spee's squadron. (Pacific Ocean).

GmOH: Der Krieg zur See 1914-1918, Band 3, Der Kreuzerkrieg in den ausländischen Gewässern, Teil 1, Das Kreuzergeschwader.

BrOH: Official History of the War, Naval Operations, Volume I To the Battle of the Falklands December 1914.

22 September ....The first British air raid on Germany – the airship sheds at Düsseldorf and Cologne.

BrOH: Official History of the War, War in the Air, Volume I.

GmOH: 1. Der Weltkrieg 1914 bis 1918, Die Militarischen Operationen zu Lande, Band 9, Die Operationen des Jahres 1915 – Die Ereignisse im Westen und auf dem Balkan vom Sommer bis Jahresschluß; Die Entwicklung der Luftstreitkrafte bis Ende 1915.

2. Die Deutschen Luftstreitkräfte von ihrer Entstehung bis zum Ende des Weltkrieges 1918. Kriegsgeschichtliche Einzelschriften der Luftwaffe. Siebenter Band: Die Deutschen Luftstreitkräfte von ihrer Entstehung bis zum Ende des Weltkrieges 1918. Sonderband: Der Militärische Heimatlutschutz im Weltkriege 1914 bis 1918.

3. Die Deutschen Luftstreitkräfte von ihrer Entstehung bis zum Ende des Weltkrieges 1918. Kriegsgeschichtliche Einzelschriften der Luftwaffe. Fünfter Band: Die deutschen Luftstreitkräfte von ihrer Entstehung bis zum Ende des Weltkrieges 1918. Technischer Sonderband II: Die technische Entwicklung der Flakwaffe bis zum Ende des Weltkrieges.

22 September ....The first use of wireless telegraphy from a R.F.C. aircraft directing an artillery shoot. (Western Front).

        BrOH: Official History of the War, War in the Air, Volume I.

22-26 September ....The First Battle of the Picardy. (Western Front).

        FrOH: Les Armées Françaises dans la Grande Guerre, Tome I, Volume 4, La bataille de l'Aisne, la course à la mer, La bataille des Flandre, les opérations sur le front stabilise.

        GmOH: 1. Der Weltkrieg 1914 bis 1918, Band 5, Der Herbst - Feldzug im Osten bis zum Rückzug im Westem bis zum Stellumgskrieg.

                2. Der Wettlauf um die Flanke in Nordfrankreich 1914. Herausgegeben vom Bayerischen Kriegsarchiv.

                3. Die Bayern im Großen Kriege 1914-1918.

24 September – 9 October.................The First Siege of Przemysl. (South Poland - Eastern Front).

        AHOH: Österreich-Ungarns Letzter Krieg 1914-1918, Band I.

        HOH: 1. A világháború 1914-1918. Különös tekintettel Magyarországra és a Magyar csapatok szereplésére Szerkeszti és kiadja a M. Kir. Hadtörténelmi Levéltár, köt 3.

                2. A világháború 1914-1918. Különös tekintettel Magyarországra és a Magyar csapatok szereplésére Szerkeszti és kiadja a M. Kir. Hadtörténelmi Levéltár, köt 5.

        PlOH: Studia z wojny światowej 1914-1918 roku Tom I: Kampania jesienna w Prusach Wschodnich sierpień - wrzesień 1914 roku.

        RuOH: 1. The Russian Army in the World War.

                2. The Russian Campaign of 1914. The Beginning of the World and Operations in East Prussia.

                3. From the History of the 1914 Campaign.

                4. A Strategic Outline of the War 1914 –1915.

                5. A Strategic Outline of the War 1914 -1918.

26 September ....The capture of Duala. (Cameroons).

        BgOH: Les Campagnes Coloniales Belges 1914-1918. Volume I. Introduction, les Operations au Cameroun, les Operations en Rhodésie, la Période Défensive à la Frontière Orientale.

        BrOH: Official History of the War, Military Operations, Togoland and the Cameroons.

        FrOH: Les Armées Françaises dans la Grande Guerre, Tome IX, Volume 2, Les campagnes coloniales: Cameroun – Togoland. – Opérations contre les Senoussis.

27-29 September ....The Battle of the Niemen. (East Prussia - Eastern Front).

        GmOH: Der Weltkrieg 1914 bis 1918, Die Militarischen Operationen zu Lande, Band 5, Der Herbst - Feldzug im Osten bis zum Rückzug im Westem bis zum Stellumgskrieg.

        PlOH: Studia z wojny światowej 1914-1918 roku Tom I: Kampania jesienna w Prusach Wschodnich sierpień - wrzesień 1914 roku.

        RuOH: 1. The Russian Army in the World War.

                2. The Russian Campaign of 1914. The Beginning of the World and Operations in East Prussia.

                3. From the History of the 1914 Campaign.

Ende des Weltkrieges 1918. Sonderband: Der Militärische Heimatlutschutz im Weltkriege 1914 bis 1918.

3. Die Deutschen Luftstreitkräfte von ihrer Entstehung bis zum Ende des Weltkrieges 1918. Kriegsgeschichtliche Einzelschriften der Luftwaffe. Fünfter Band: Die deutschen Luftstreitkräfte von ihrer Entstehung bis zum Ende des Weltkrieges 1918. Technischer Sonderband II: Die technische Entwicklung der Flakwaffe bis zum Ende des Weltkrieges.

9-19 October ....The First Battle of Warsaw. (Eastern Front).

GmOH: Der Weltkrieg 1914 bis 1918, Die Militarischen Operationen zu Lande, Band 5, Der Herbst - Feldzug im Osten bis zum Rückzug im Westem bis zum Stellumgskrieg.

RuOH: 1. The Russian Army in the World War.

2. The Russian Campaign of 1914. The Beginning of the World and Operations in East Prussia.

3. From the History of the 1914 Campaign.

4. A Strategic Outline of the War 1914–1915.

5. A Strategic Outline of the War 1914 -1918.

9-27 October ....The Battle of Ivangorod. (Northern Poland - Eastern Front).

GmOH: Der Weltkrieg 1914 bis 1918, Die Militarischen Operationen zu Lande, Band 5, Der Herbst - Feldzug im Osten bis zum Rückzug im Westem bis zum Stellumgskrieg.

RuOH: 1. The Russian Army in the World War.

2. The Russian Campaign of 1914. The Beginning of the World and Operations in East Prussia.

3. From the History of the 1914 Campaign.

4. A Strategic Outline of the War 1914–1915.

5. A Strategic Outline of the War 1914 -1918.

10 October ....The Battle of La Bassée. (Western Front).

BrOH: Official History of the War, Military Operations, France and Belgium 1914, Volume II, Antwerp, La Bassée, Armentières, Messines and Ypres, October-November 1914.

GmOH: Der Weltkrieg 1914 bis 1918, Die Militarischen Operationen zu Lande, Band 6, Der Herbst - Feldzug der Abschluß der Operationen im Westem und Osten.

11 October ....The Russian cruiser Pallada sunk by a submarine. (Baltic Sea).

GmOH: Der Krieg zur See 1914-1918, Band 2, Der Krieg in der Ostsee, Teil 1, Von Kriegbeginn bis Mitte März 1915.

RuOH:..Flot v Pervoi Mirovoi Voine. V Dvukh Tomakh. Tom I Deystviya Russkogo Flota.

11 October ....S.M.S. Komet sunk by H.M.A.S. Nusa. (Pacific Ocean).

AuOH:..Official History of Australia in the War of 1914-1918, Volume IX, Royal Australian Navy.

12 October – 2 November ....The First Battle of Messines, 1914. (Western Front).

BrOH: Official History of the War, Military Operations, France and Belgium 1914, Volume II, Antwerp, La Bassée, Armentières, Messines and Ypres: October-November 1914.

GmOH: 1. Der Weltkrieg 1914 bis 1918, Die Militarischen Operationen zu Lande, Band 6, Der Herbst - Feldzug der Abschluß der Operationen im Westem und Osten.
2. Die Bayern im Großen Kriege 1914-1918.

13 October – 13 November ....The First Battle of Flanders. (Western Front).
BgOH: 1. La Belgique et la Guerre, Tome II, L'Invasion allemande.
2. La Belgique et la Guerre, Tome III: Les Opérations Militaires.
BrOH: Official History of the War, Military Operations, France and Belgium 1914, Volume II, Antwerp, La Bassée, Armentières, Messines and Ypres: October-November 1914.
FrOH: Les Armées Françaises dans la Grande Guerre, Tome I, Volume 4, La bataille de l'Aisne, la course à la mer, La bataille des Flandre, les opérations sur le front stabilise.
GmOH: 1. Der Weltkrieg 1914 bis 1918, Die Militarischen Operationen zu Lande, Band 6, Der Herbst - Feldzug der Abschluß der Operationen im Westem und Osten.
2. Der Wettlauf um die Flanke in Nordfrankreich 1914. Herausgegeben vom Bayerischen Kriegsarchiv.
3. Die Bayern im Großen Kriege 1914-1918.

13 October – 2 November ....The First Battle of Flanders – the Battle of Armentières. (Western Front).
BrOH: Official History of the War, Military Operations, France and Belgium 1914, Volume II, Antwerp, La Bassée, Armentières, Messines and Ypres: October-November 1914.
GmOH: 1. Der Weltkrieg 1914 bis 1918, Die Militarischen Operationen zu Lande, Band 6, Der Herbst - Feldzug der Abschluß der Operationen im Westem und Osten.
2. Die Bayern im Großen Kriege 1914-1918.

13 October – 10 November ....The First Battle of Flanders - the First Battle of Yser. (Western Front).
BgOH: 1. La Belgique et la Guerre, Tome II, L'Invasion allemande.
2. La Belgique et la Guerre, Tome III: Les Opérations Militaires.
FrOH: Les Armées Françaises dans la Grande Guerre, Tome I, Volume 4, La bataille de l'Aisne, la course à la mer, La bataille des Flandre, les opérations sur le front stabilise.
GmOH: 1. Der Weltkrieg 1914 bis 1918, Die Militarischen Operationen zu Lande, Band 6, Der Herbst - Feldzug der Abschluß der Operationen im Westem und Osten.
2. Der Wettlauf um die Flanke in Nordfrankreich 1914. Herausgegeben vom Bayerischen Kriegsarchiv.
3. Die Bayern im Großen Kriege 1914-1918.

13 October – 2 November ....The Battle of Chyrow. (South Poland - Eastern Front).
AHOH: Österreich-Ungarns Letzter Krieg 1914-1918, Band I.
HOH: A világháború 1914-1918. Különös tekintettel Magyarországra és a Magyar csapatok szereplésére Szerkeszti és kiadja a M. Kir. Hadtörténelmi Levéltár, köt 6.
RuOH: 1. The Russian Army in the World War.
2. The Russian Campaign of 1914. The Beginning of the World and Operations in East Prussia.

3. From the History of the 1914 Campaign.
4. A Strategic Outline of the War 1914 –1915.
5. A Strategic Outline of the War 1914 -1918.

14 October ....The capture of Yabasi. (Cameroons)
> BgOH: Les Campagnes Coloniales Belges 1914-1918. Volume I. Introduction, les Operations au Cameroun, les Operations en Rhodésie, la Période Défensive à la Frontière Orientale.
> BrOH: Official History of the War, Military Operations, Togoland and the Cameroons.
> FrOH: Les Armées Françaises dans la Grande Guerre, Tome IX, Volume 2, Les campagnes coloniales: Cameroun – Togoland. – Opérations contre les Senoussis.

15 October ....H.M.S. Hawke sunk by a submarine in the North Sea. (British Home Waters).
> BrOH: Official History of the War, Naval Operations, Volume I To the Battle of the Falklands December 1914.
> GmOH: Der Krieg zur See 1914-1918, Band 1, Der Krieg in der Nordsee, Teil 1, Von Kriegbeginn bis Anfang September 1914.

15 October –13 November ....The First Battle of Flanders - the First Battle of Ypres. (Western Front).
> BrOH: Official History of the War, Military Operations, France and Belgium 1914, Volume II, Antwerp, La Bassée, Armentières, Messines and Ypres: October-November 1914.
> GmOH: 1. Der Weltkrieg 1914 bis 1918, Die Militarischen Operationen zu Lande, Band 6, Der Herbst - Feldzug der Abschluß der Operationen im Westem und Osten.
> 2. Der Wettlauf um die Flanke in Nordfrankreich 1914. Herausgegeben vom Bayerischen Kriegsarchiv.
> 3. Die Bayern im Großen Kriege 1914-1918.

16 October –10 November ....The Battle of the Yser. (Western Front).
> BgOH: 1. La Belgique et la Guerre, Tome II, L'Invasion allemande.
> 2. La Belgique et la Guerre, Tome III: Les Opérations Militaires.
> FrOH: Les Armées Françaises dans la Grande Guerre, Tome I, Volume 4, La bataille de l'Aisne, la course à la mer, La bataille des Flandre, les opérations sur le front stabilise.
> GmOH: 1. Der Weltkrieg 1914 bis 1918, Die Militarischen Operationen zu Lande, Band 6, Der Herbst - Feldzug der Abschluß der Operationen im Westem und Osten.
> 2. Der Wettlauf um die Flanke in Nordfrankreich 1914. Herausgegeben vom Bayerischen Kriegsarchiv.
> 3. Die Bayern im Großen Kriege 1914-1918.

17 October ....Action between H.M.S. Undaunted & destroyers and four German destroyers in the North Sea. (British Home Waters).
> BrOH: Official History of the War, Naval Operations, Volume I To the Battle of the Falklands December 1914.
> GmOH: Der Krieg zur See 1914-1918, Band 1, Der Krieg in der Nordsee, Teil 1, Von Kriegbeginn bis Anfang September 1914.

18 October ....Japanese cruiser Takachiho sunk by a German destroyer S.M.S. S.90. the Siege of Tsingtau. (China Sea).

GmOH:Der Krieg zur See 1914-1918 Band 6 Die Kämpfe der Kaiserlichen Marine in den deutschen Kolonien. Teil 1 Tsingtau - Teil 2 Deutsch-Ostafrika.

JOH: 1. Taishō san-yonen kaigun senshi: Kan 1-8.

20 October ....S.S. Glitra sunk by a German submarine – the first merchant vessel to be sunk by a German submarine. (North Sea).

BrOH: 1. Official History of the War, Naval Operations, Volume I To the Battle of the Falklands December 1914.
2. Official History of the War, Seaborne Trade, Volume II, Submarine Campaign, Part I.
3. Official History of the War, Merchant Navy, Volume I.

GmOH: Der Krieg zur See 1914-1918, Band 4, Der Handelskrieg mit U-Booten, Teil 1, Vorgeschichte.

21-24 October ....The First Battle of Flanders - the First Battle of Ypres – the Battle of Langemarck. (Western Front).

BrOH: Official History of the War, Military Operations, France and Belgium 1914, Volume II, Antwerp, La Bassée, Armentières, Messines and Ypres: October-November 1914.

FrOH: Les Armées Françaises dans la Grande Guerre, Tome I, Volume 4, La bataille de l'Aisne, la course à la mer, La bataille des Flandre, les opérations sur le front stabilise.

GmOH: 1. Der Weltkrieg 1914 bis 1918, Die Militarischen Operationen zu Lande, Band 6, Der Herbst - Feldzug der Abschluß der Operationen im Westem und Osten.
2. Der Wettlauf um die Flanke in Nordfrankreich 1914. Herausgegeben vom Bayerischen Kriegsarchiv.
3. Die Bayern im Großen Kriege 1914-1918.

26 October ....The capture of Edea. (Cameroons).

BgOH: Les Campagnes Coloniales Belges 1914-1918. Volume I. Introduction, les Operations au Cameroun, les Operations en Rhodésie, la Période Défensive à la Frontière Orientale.

BrOH: Official History of the War, Military Operations, Togoland and the Cameroons.

FrOH: Les Armées Françaises dans la Grande Guerre, Tome IX, Volume 2, Les campagnes coloniales: Cameroun – Togoland. – Opérations contre les Senoussis.

27 October ....H.M.S. Audacious sunk by a submarine. (Irish Sea).

BrOH: Official History of the War, Naval Operations, Volume I To the Battle of the Falklands December 1914.

GmOH: Der Krieg zur See 1914-1918, Band 4, Der Handelskrieg mit U-Booten, Teil 1, Vorgeschichte.

28 October ....S.M.S. Emden raids Penang Roads and sinks the Russian cruiser Zhemchug. (Indian Ocean).

AuOH: Official History of Australia in the War of 1914-1918, Volume IX, Royal Australian Navy.

BrOH: 1. Official History of the War, Naval Operations, Volume I To the Battle of the Falklands December 1914.
2. Official History of the War, Seaborne Trade, Volume I, Cruiser Period.

3. Official History of the War, The Merchant Navy, Volume I.

GmOH: Der Krieg zur See 1914-1918, Band 3, Der Kreuzerkrieg in den ausländischen Gewässern, Teil 2, Die Tätigkeit der Kleinen Kreuzer "Emden", "Könighberg" und "Karlsruhe" mit e Anhang: "Die Kriegsfahrt des Kleinen Kreuzers Geier".

29 October ....Odessa, Sevastopol and Theodosia bombarded by Turkish warships. (Black Sea).

GmOH: Der Krieg zur See 1914-1918, Band 5, Der Krieg in den türkischen Gewässern, Teil 1, Die Mittelmeer-Division.

TOH: Birinci Dünya Harbi, VIIInci Cilt, Türk Deniz Harekati.

RuOH:..Flot v Pervoi Mirovoi Voine. V Dvukh Tomakh. Tom I Deystviya Russkogo Flota.

29-31 October ....The First Battle of Flanders - the First Battle of Ypres – the Battle of Gheluvelt. (Western Front).

BrOH: Official History of the War, Military Operations, France and Belgium 1914, Volume II, Antwerp, La Bassée, Armentières, Messines and Ypres: October-November

GmOH: 1. Der Weltkrieg 1914 bis 1918, Die Militarischen Operationen zu Lande, Band 6, Der Herbst - Feldzug der Abschluß der Operationen im Westem und Osten.
2. Der Wettlauf um die Flanke in Nordfrankreich 1914. Herausgegeben vom Bayerischen Kriegsarchiv.
3. Die Bayern im Großen Kriege 1914-1918.

31 October ....H.M.S. Hermes sunk by a submarine. (Straits of Dover).

BrOH: Official History of the War, Naval Operations, Volume I To the Battle of the Falklands December 1914.

GmOH: Der Krieg zur See 1914-1918, Band 4, Der Handelskrieg mit U-Booten, Teil 1, Vorgeschichte.

31 October - 6 November...................Allied Force attack on Tsingtau - the Siege of Tsingtau. (China).

GmOH: Der Krieg zur See 1914-1918 Band 6 Die Kämpfe der Kaiserlichen Marine in den deutschen Kolonien. Teil 1 Tsingtau - Teil 2 Deutsch-Ostafrika.

JOH: 1. Taishō sannen Nichi-Doku senshi: jōkan.
2. Taishō sannen Nichi-Doku senshi: gekan.

1 November ....The action off Coronel. (Pacific Ocean).

BrOH: ..1. Official History of the War, Naval Operations, Volume I To the Battle of the Falklands December 1914.
2. Official History of the War, Seaborne Trade, Volume I, Cruiser Period.

GmOH: Der Krieg zur See 1914-1918, Band 3, Der Kreuzerkrieg in den ausländischen Gewässern, Teil 1, Das Kreuzergeschwader.

2 November ....S.M.S. Kaiserin Elizabeth sunk in Tsingtau harbour. (Pacific Ocean).

BrOH: Official History of the War, Naval Operations, Volume I To the Battle of the Falklands December 1914.

GmOH: Der Krieg zur See 1914-1918, Band 3, Der Kreuzerkrieg in den ausländischen Gewässern, Teil 1, Das Kreuzergeschwader.

2-5 November ....The Battle of Tanga. (East Africa).

BgOH: Les Campagnes Coloniales Belges 1914-1918. Volume I. Introduction, les Operations au Cameroun, les Operations en Rhodésie, la Période Défensive à la Frontière Orientale.

BrOH: Official History of the War, Military Operations, East Africa, Volume I, August 1914-September 1916.

GmOH: Der Krieg zur See 1914-1918, Band 6, Die Kämpfe der Kaiserlichen Marine in den deutschen Kolonien, Teil 2, Deutsch-Ostafrika.

SAOH: The Union of South Africa and the Great War 1914 – 1918.

3 November ....German naval raid on the British Coast. (British Home Waters).

BrOH: Official History of the War, Naval Operations, Volume I To the Battle of the Falklands December 1914.

GmOH: Der Krieg zur See 1914-1918, Band 1, Der Krieg in der Nordsee, Teil 2, Von Anfang September bis November 1914.

3 November ....Allied squadrons bombard the Turkish Forts. (Dardanelles).

BrOH: ..Official History of the War, Naval Operations, Volume I To the Battle of the Falklands December 1914.

3 November ....The affair of Longido. (East Africa).

BgOH: Les Campagnes Coloniales Belges 1914-1918. Volume I. Introduction, les Operations au Cameroun, les Operations en Rhodésie, la Période Défensive à la Frontière Orientale.

BrOH: Official History of the War, Military Operations, East Africa, Volume I, August 1914-September 1916.

GmOH: Der Krieg zur See 1914-1918, Band 6, Die Kämpfe der Kaiserlichen Marine in den deutschen Kolonien, Teil 2, Deutsch-Ostafrika.

SAOH: The Union of South Africa and the Great War 1914 – 1918.

4 November ....S.M.S. Karlsruhe sinks due to an internal explosion. (Atlantic Ocean).

BrOH: ..1. Official History of the War, Naval Operations, Volume I To the Battle of the Falklands December 1914.
2. Official History of the War, Seaborne Trade, Volume I, Cruiser Period.

GmOH: Der Krieg zur See 1914-1918, Band 3, Der Kreuzerkrieg in den ausländischen Gewässern, Teil 2, Die Tätigkeit der Kleinen Kreuzer "Emden", "Königberg" und "Karlsruhe" mit e Anhang: "Die Kriegsfahrt des Kleinen Kreuzers Geier".

4 November ....S.M.S. Yorck sunk by a mine. (North Sea).

GmOH: Der Krieg zur See 1914-1918, Band 1, Der Krieg in der Nordsee, Teil 2, Von Anfang September bis November 1914.

6-8 November ....The Battle of Goritten. (East Prussia - Eastern Front).

GmOH: Der Weltkrieg 1914 bis 1918, Die Militarischen Operationen zu Lande, Band 6, Der Herbst - Feldzug der Abschluß der Operationen im Westem und Osten.

RuOH: 1. The Russian Army in the World War.
2. The Russian Campaign of 1914. The Beginning of the World and Operations in East Prussia.

3. From the History of the 1914 Campaign.
4. A Strategic Outline of the War 1914–1915.
5. A Strategic Outline of the War 1914 -1918.

7 November ....Tsingtau capitulates to the Japanese. (China).
GmOH: Der Krieg zur See 1914-1918, Band 6, Die Kämpfe der Kaiserlichen Marine in den deutschen Kolonien, Teil 1, Tsingtau.

9 November ......................................S.M.S. Emden sunk by H.M.A.S. Sydney. (Indian Ocean).
AuOH: Official History of Australia in the War of 1914-1918, Volume IX, Royal Australian Navy.
BrOH: 1. Official History of the War, Naval Operations, Volume I To the Battle of the Falklands December 1914.
2. Official History of the War, Seaborne Trade, Volume I, Cruiser Period.
3. Official History of the War, The Merchant Navy, Volume I.
GmOH: Der Krieg zur See 1914-1918, Band 3, Der Kreuzerkrieg in den ausländischen Gewässern, Teil 2, Die Tätigkeit der Kleinen Kreuzer "Emden", "Königberg" und "Karlsruhe" mit e Anhang: "Die Kriegsfahrt des Kleinen Kreuzers Geier".

10 November – 22 March 1915 ....The second siege of Przemysl. (South Poland - Eastern Front).
AHOH: Österreich-Ungarns Letzter Krieg 1914-1918, Band I.
HOH: 1. A világháború 1914-1918. Különös tekintettel Magyarországra és a Magyar csapatok szereplésére Szerkeszti és kiadja a M. Kir. Hadtörténelmi Levéltár, köt 7.
2. A világháború 1914-1918. Különös tekintettel Magyarországra és a Magyar csapatok szereplésére Szerkeszti és kiadja a M. Kir. Hadtörténelmi Levéltár, köt 8.
RuOH: 1. The Russian Army in the World War.
2. The Russian Campaign of 1914. The Beginning of the World and Operations in East Prussia.
3. From the History of the 1914 Campaign.
4. A Strategic Outline of the War 1914–1915.
5. A Strategic Outline of the War 1914 -1918.

10-13 November ....The Battle of Kutno. (North Poland - Eastern Front).
GmOH: Der Weltkrieg 1914 bis 1918, Die Militarischen Operationen zu Lande, Band 6, Der Herbst - Feldzug der Abschluß der Operationen im Westem und Osten.
PlOH: Studia z wojny światowej 1914-1918 roku Tom ?: Bitwa pod Włocławiem 10-13 listopada 1914 roku
RuOH: 1. The Russian Army in the World War.
2. The Russian Campaign of 1914. The Beginning of the World and Operations in East Prussia.
3. From the History of the 1914 Campaign.
4. A Strategic Outline of the War 1914–1915.
5. A Strategic Outline of the War 1914 -1918.

10 November ....The action of Sheikh Saïd. (Arabia).
BrOH: Official History of the War, Military Operations, Egypt and Palestine, Volume I, From the Outbreak of War with Germany to June 1917.
TOH: 1. Büyük Harbin Sevkülceyşi.

2. Birinci Cihan Harbinde Türk Harbi, 1914 Yili Harekatleri, Inci Cilt.
3. Birinci Dünya Harbinde Türk Harbi VInci Cilt, Hicaz, Asir, Yeman Cepheleri ve Libya Harekati 1914-1918.
4. Büyük Harpte Misir Seferi.

11 November .....................................H.M.S. Niger sunk by a submarine. (Straits of Dover).
　　　　　　BrOH: 　Official History of the War, Naval Operations, Volume I To the Battle of the Falklands December 1914.
　　　　　　GmOH: Der Krieg zur See 1914-1918, Band 4, Der Handelskrieg mit U-Booten, Teil 1, Vorgeschichte.

11 November ....The First Battle of Flanders - the First Battle of Ypres – the Battle of Nonne Bosschen. (Western Front).
　　　　　　BrOH: 　Official History of the War, Military Operations, France and Belgium 1914, Volume II, Antwerp, La Bassée, Armentières, Messines and Ypres: October-November 1914.
　　　　　　FrOH: 　Les Armées Françaises dans la Grande Guerre, Tome I, Volume 4, La bataille de l'Aisne, la course à la mer, La bataille des Flandre, les opérations sur le front stabilise.
　　　　　　GmOH: 1. Der Weltkrieg 1914 bis 1918, Die Militarischen Operationen zu Lande, Band 6, Der Herbst - Feldzug der Abschluß der Operationen im Westem und Osten.
2. Der Wettlauf um die Flanke in Nordfrankreich 1914. Herausgegeben vom Bayerischen Kriegsarchiv.
3. Die Bayern im Großen Kriege 1914-1918.

13 November ....The Turkish battleship Messoudieh sunk by H.M.S. B11. (Dardanelles).
　　　　　　BrOH: 　Official History of the War, Naval Operations, Volume I To the Battle of the Falklands December 1914.

13-16 November ....The Battle of the Romintener Hiede. (Eastern Prussia - Eastern Front).
　　　　　　GmOH: Der Weltkrieg 1914 bis 1918, Die Militarischen Operationen zu Lande, Band 6, Der Herbst - Feldzug der Abschluß der Operationen im Westem und Osten.
　　　　　　RuOH: 1. The Russian Army in the World War.
2. The Russian Campaign of 1914. The Beginning of the World and Operations in East Prussia.
3. From the History of the 1914 Campaign.
4. A Strategic Outline of the War 1914 –1915.
5. A Strategic Outline of the War 1914 -1918.

14 November ....The S.M.S. Cormoran interned at Guam. (Pacific Ocean).
　　　　　　BrOH: 　Official History of the War, Naval Operations, Volume I To the Battle of the Falklands December 1914.
　　　　　　GmOH: Der Krieg zur See 1914-1918, Band 3, Der Kreuzerkrieg in den ausländischen Gewässern, Teil 3, Die deutschen Hilfskreuzer.

14-15 November ....The Battle of Wloclawek. (Central Poalnd - Eastern Front).
　　　　　　GmOH: Der Weltkrieg 1914 bis 1918, Die Militarischen Operationen zu Lande, Band 6, Der Herbst - Feldzug der Abschluß der Operationen im Westem und Osten.
　　　　　　RuOH: 1. The Russian Army in the World War.
2. The Russian Campaign of 1914. The Beginning of the World and Operations in East Prussia.
3. From the History of the 1914 Campaign.
4. A Strategic Outline of the War 1914 –1915.

5. A Strategic Outline of the War 1914 -1918.

15 November – 2 December ....The Battle of Cracow. (South Poland – Eastern Front).
AHOH: Österreich-Ungarns Letzter Krieg 1914-1918, Band I.
HOH: 1. A világháború 1914-1918. Különös tekintettel Magyarországra és a Magyar csapatok szereplésére Szerkeszti és kiadja a M. Kir. Hadtörténelmi Levéltár, köt 7.
       2. A világháború 1914-1918. Különös tekintettel Magyarországra és a Magyar csapatok szereplésére Szerkeszti és kiadja a M. Kir. Hadtörténelmi Levéltár, köt 8.
RuOH: 1. The Russian Army in the World War.
       2. The Russian Campaign of 1914. The Beginning of the World and Operations in East Prussia.
       3. From the History of the 1914 Campaign.
       4. A Strategic Outline of the War 1914 –1915.
       5. A Strategic Outline of the War 1914 -1918.

16 November – 17 December ....The Second Battle of Warsaw. (Eastern Front).
GmOH: Der Weltkrieg 1914 bis 1918, Die Militarischen Operationen zu Lande, Band 6, Der Herbst - Feldzug der Abschluß der Operationen im Western und Osten.
RuOH: 1. The Russian Army in the World War.
       2. The Russian Campaign of 1914. The Beginning of the World and Operations in East Prussia.
       3. From the History of the 1914 Campaign.
       4. A Strategic Outline of the War 1914 –1915.
       5. A Strategic Outline of the War 1914 -1918.

16 November – 15 December ....The Second Battle of Warsaw - the Battle of Lødz. (South Poland - Eastern Front) [Russian/German].
GmOH: Der Weltkrieg 1914 bis 1918, Die Militarischen Operationen zu Lande, Band 6, Der Herbst - Feldzug der Abschluß der Operationen im Western und Osten.
RuOH: 1. The Russian Army in the World War.
       2. The Russian Campaign of 1914. The Beginning of the World and Operations in East Prussia.
       3. From the History of the 1914 Campaign.
       4. A Strategic Outline of the War 1914 –1915.
       5. A Strategic Outline of the War 1914 -1918.

17 November ....The second bombardment of Libau. (Baltic Sea).
GmOH: Der Krieg zur See 1914-1918, Band 2, Der Krieg in der Ostsee, Teil 1, Von Kriegbeginn bis Mitte März 1915.
RuOH:..Flot v Pervoi Mirovoi Voine. V Dvukh Tomakh. Tom I Deystviya Russkogo Flota.

17 November ...................................S.M.S. Friedrich Carl Sunk by Mine. (North Sea).
BrOH: Official History of the War, Naval Operations, Volume I To the Battle of the Falklands December 1914.
GmOH: Der Krieg zur See 1914-1918, Band 1, Der Krieg in der Nordsee, Teil 2, Von Anfang September bis November 1914.

17 November ....The bombardment of Trebizond. (Black Sea).
GmOH: Der Krieg zur See 1914-1918, Band 5, Der Krieg in den türkischen Gewässern, Teil 1, Die Mittelmeer-Division.
TOH: Birinci Dünya Harbi, VIIInci Cilt, Türk Deniz Harekati.

RuOH:..Flot v Pervoi Mirovoi Voine. V Dvukh Tomakh. Tom I Deystviya Russkogo Flota.

18 November ....The action between Russian and Turkish Fleets. (Black Sea).
GmOH: Der Krieg zur See 1914-1918, Band 5, Der Krieg in den türkischen Gewässern, Teil 1, Die Mittelmeer-Division.
TOH: Birinci Dünya Harbi, VIIInci Cilt, Türk Deniz Harekati.
RuOH:..Flot v Pervoi Mirovoi Voine. V Dvukh Tomakh. Tom I Deystviya Russkogo Flota.

21 November ....The British air raid by the R.N.A.S. on airship sheds at Friedrichshaven, Germany.
BrOH: 1. Official History of the War, Naval Operations, Volume I To the Battle of the Falklands December 1914.
2. Official History of the War, War in the Air, Volume I.
GmOH: 1. Der Weltkrieg 1914 bis 1918, Die Militarischen Operationen zu Lande, Band 5, Der Herbst - Feldzug im Osten bis zum Rückzug im Westem bis zum Stellumgskrieg; Die Entwicklung der Luftstreitkrafte bis Ende 1915.
2. Die Deutschen Luftstreitkräfte von ihrer Entstehung bis zum Ende des Weltkrieges 1918. Kriegsgeschichtliche Einzelschriften der Luftwaffe. Siebenter Band: Die Deutschen Luftstreitkräfte von ihrer Entstehung bis zum Ende des Weltkrieges 1918. Sonderband: Der Militärische Heimatlutschutz im Weltkriege 1914 bis 1918.
3. Die Deutschen Luftstreitkräfte von ihrer Entstehung bis zum Ende des Weltkrieges 1918. Kriegsgeschichtliche Einzelschriften der Luftwaffe. Fünfter Band: Die deutschen Luftstreitkräfte von ihrer Entstehung bis zum Ende des Weltkrieges 1918. Technischer Sonderband II: Die technische Entwicklung der Flakwaffe bis zum Ende des Weltkrieges.

26 November .....................................H.M.S. Bulwark sinks due to internal explosion. (Sheerness Harbour).
BrOH: Official History of the War, Naval Operations, Volume I To the Battle of the Falklands December 1914.

30 November – 17 December ....The Second Battle of Warsaw - the Battle of Lowicz-Sanniki. (Eastern Front).
GmOH: Der Weltkrieg 1914 bis 1918, Die Militarischen Operationen zu Lande, Band 6, Der Herbst - Feldzug der Abschluß der Operationen im Westem und Osten.
RuOH: 1. The Russian Army in the World War.
2. The Russian Campaign of 1914. The Beginning of the World and Operations in East Prussia.
3. From the History of the 1914 Campaign.
4. A Strategic Outline of the War 1914 –1915.
5. A Strategic Outline of the War 1914 -1918.

1-17 December.....................................The Battle of Limanova-Lapanow. (South Poland - Eastern Front).
AHOH: Österreich-Ungarns Letzter Krieg 1914-1918, Band I.
HOH: A világháború 1914-1918. Különös tekintettel Magyarországra és a Magyar csapatok szereplésére Szerkeszti és kiadja a M. Kir. Hadtörténelmi Levéltár, köt 8.
RuOH: 1. The Russian Army in the World War.
2. The Russian Campaign of 1914. The Beginning of the World and Operations in East Prussia.

3. From the History of the 1914 Campaign.
4. A Strategic Outline of the War 1914 –1915.
5. A Strategic Outline of the War 1914 -1918.

3-6 December....................................The Battle of the Kolubara. (Balkan Front).
AHOH: Österreich-Ungarns Letzter Krieg 1914-1918, Band I.
GrOH: 1. Ho Hellenikos Stratos kata ton Proton Pankosmion Polemon 1914-1918 Tomos 1 - H Hellas kai ho Polemos eis ta Balkania.
2. Epitomh Istopia Ths Eummetochhs Tou Ellhnikou Stratou Ston Prpsto Pagkosmio Polemo 1914-1918. / A Concise History of the Participation of the Hellenic Army in The First World War 1914-1918.
HOH: A világháború 1914-1918. Különös tekintettel Magyarországra és a Magyar csapatok szereplésére Szerkeszti és kiadja a M. Kir. Hadtörténelmi Levéltár, köt 8.
SeOH: 1. Veliki rat Srbije za oslobođenje i ujedinenje Srba, Hrvata i Slovenaca. Knjige šesta. 1914 godina. Treći period operacija. Kolubarska bitka. III. faza - Napadna.
2. Veliki rat Srbije za oslobođenje i ujedinenje Srba, Hrvata i Slovenaca. Knjige sedma. 1914 godina. Treći period operacija. Kolubarska bitka. IV. faza – Eksploatacija Pobede

4-8 December....................................The first action of Qurna. (Mesopotamia).
BrOH: Official History of the War, Military Operations, Campaign in Mesopotamia, Volume I.
TOH: 1. Büyük Harbin Sevkülceyşi.
2. Birinci Cihan Harbinde Türk Harbi, 1914 Yili Harekatleri, Inci Cilt.
3. Birinci Dünya Harbinde Türk Harbi, IIInvi Cilt, Irak-Iran Cephesi, 1914-1918, 1nci Kisim.
4. Büyük Harpte Misir Seferi.

8 December....................................The Battle of the Falklands. (South Atlantic Ocean)
BrOH: 1. Official History of the War, Naval Operations, Volume I To the Battle of the Falklands December 1914.
2. Official History of the War, Seaborne Trade, Volume I, Cruiser Period.
GmOH: Der Krieg zur See 1914-1918, Band 3, Der Kreuzerkrieg in den ausländischen Gewässern, Teil 1, Das Kreuzergeschwader.

10 December....................................The bombardment of Batum. (Black Sea)
GmOH: Der Krieg zur See 1914-1918, Band 5, Der Krieg in den türkischen Gewässern, Teil 1, Die Mittelmeer-Division.
TOH: Birinci Dünya Harbi, VIIInci Cilt, Türk Deniz Harekati.
RuOH:..Flot v Pervoi Mirovoi Voine. V Dvukh Tomakh. Tom I Deystviya Russkogo Flota.

13 November ....................................H.M.S. B11 sinks the Turkish battleship Messudiyeh (Mediterranean).
BrOH: Official History of the War, Naval Operations, Volume I To the Battle of the Falklands December 1914.
TOH: Birinci Dünya Harbi, VIIInci Cilt, Türk Deniz Harekati.
RuOH:..Flot v Pervoi Mirovoi Voine. V Dvukh Tomakh. Tom I Deystviya Russkogo Flota.

16 December......................................The bombardment of Scarborough and Hartlepool in the North Sea. (North Sea).

> BrOH: Official History of the War, Naval Operations, Volume I To the Battle of the Falklands December 1914.
>
> GmOH: Der Krieg zur See 1914-1918, Band 1, Der Krieg in der Nordsee, Teil 3, Von Anfang November 1914 bis Anfang Februar 1915.

16 December......................................The Battle of the Rawka-Bzura. (Central Poland - Eastern Front).

> GmOH: Der Weltkrieg 1914 bis 1918, Die Militarischen Operationen zu Lande, Band 6, Der Herbst - Feldzug der Abschluß der Operationen im Westem und Osten.
>
> RuOH: 1. The Russian Army in the World War.
> 2. The Russian Campaign of 1914. The Beginning of the World and Operations in East Prussia.
> 3. From the History of the 1914 Campaign.
> 4. A Strategic Outline of the War 1914 –1915.
> 5. A Strategic Outline of the War 1914 -1918.

17-26 December................................The Kars Offensive. (Caucasus).

> TOH: 1. Büyük Harbin Sevkülceyşi.
> 2. Birinci Cihan Harbinde Türk Harbi, 1914 Yili Harekatleri, Inci Cilt.
> 3. Birinci Dünya Harbinde, Erzurum ve Cevresinde Ermeni Hrekatetleri. (1914–1918).
> 4. Birinci Dünya Harbinde Türk Harbi Kafkas Cephesi 3ncu Ordu Harekati, Cilt II, Birinci Kitap.
>
> RuOH: 1. The Russian Army in the World War.
> 2. From the History of the 1914 Campaign.
> 3. A Strategic Outline of the War 1914 –1915.
> 4. A Strategic Outline of the War 1914 -1918.

20 December - 17 March. (1915).......The Winter Offensive – the First Battle of Champagne. (Western Front).

> FrOH: Les Armées Françaises dans la Grande Guerre, Tome II, La stabilisation au front - Les attaques locales - 14 novembre 1914 – 1 mai 1915.
>
> GmOH: 1. Der Weltkrieg 1914 bis 1918, Die Militarischen Operationen zu Lande, Band 6, Der Herbst - Feldzug der Abschluß der Operationen im Westem und Osten.
> 2. Die Bayern im Großen Kriege 1914-1918.

21 December......................................The capture of Jasin. (East Africa).

> BgOH: Les Campagnes Coloniales Belges 1914-1918. Volume I. Introduction, les Operations au Cameroun, les Operations en Rhodésie, la Période Défensive à la Frontière Orientale.
>
> BrOH: Official History of the War, Military Operations, East Africa, Volume I, August 1914-September 1916.
>
> GmOH: Der Krieg zur See 1914-1918, Band 6, Die Kämpfe der Kaiserlichen Marine in den deutschen Kolonien, Teil 2, Deutsch-Ostafrika.
>
> SAOH: The Union of South Africa and the Great War 1914 – 1918.

21 December......................................The first German air raid on Britain, an aircraft drops bombs on the Port of Dover – the first bomb to fall onto British soil.

> BrOH: Official History of the War, War in the Air, Volume I.
>
> GmOH: Der Weltkrieg 1914 bis 1918, Die Militarischen Operationen zu Lande, Band 9, Die Operationen des

Jahres 1915 – Die Ereignisse im Westen und auf dem Balkan vom Sommer bis Jahresschluß; Die Entwicklung der Luftstreitkrafte bis Ende 1915.

23 December...................................The second German air raid on Britain, aircraft drops bombs on the Port of Dover that fell into the Sea.

BrOH: Official History of the War, War in the Air, Volume I.

GmOH: Der Weltkrieg 1914 bis 1918, Die Militarischen Operationen zu Lande, Band 9, Die Operationen des Jahres 1915 – Die Ereignisse im Westen und auf dem Balkan vom Sommer bis Jahresschluß; Die Entwicklung der Luftstreitkrafte bis Ende 1915.

25 December...................................The British seaplane raid on Germany – the airship sheds at Cuxhaven. (German Coast - North Sea).

BrOH: 1. Official History of the War, Naval Operations, Volume I To the Battle of the Falklands December 1914.

2. Official History of the War, War in the Air, Volume I.

GmOH: Der Weltkrieg 1914 bis 1918, Die Militarischen Operationen zu Lande, Band 9, Die Operationen des Jahres 1915 – Die Ereignisse im Westen und auf dem Balkan vom Sommer bis Jahresschluß; Die Entwicklung der Luftstreitkrafte bis Ende 1915.

26 December – 2 January (1915) ....The Battle of Sarikamish. (East Front – Russo-Turkish border).

TOH: 1. Büyük Harbin Sevkülceyşi.

2. Birinci Cihan Harbinde Türk Harbi, 1914 Yili Harekatleri, Inci Cilt.

3. Birinci Dünya Harbinde, Erzurum ve Cevresinde Ermeni Hrekatetleri. (1914–1918).

4. Birinci Dünya Harbinde Türk Harbi Kafkas Cephesi 3ncu Ordu Harekati, Cilt II, Birinci Kitap.

RuOH: 1. The Russian Army in the World War.

2. From the History of the 1914 Campaign.

3. A Strategic Outline of the War 1914 –1915.

4. A Strategic Outline of the War 1914 -1918.

28 December...................................South African Rebellion ends.

SAOH: .The Union of South Africa and the Great War 1914 – 1918.

1915

1 January..H.M.S. Formidable sunk by a submarine. (English Channel).

> BrOH: Official History of the War, Naval Operations, Volume II.
> GmOH: 1. Der Krieg zur See 1914-1918, Band 1, Der Krieg in der Nordsee, Teil 3, Von Anfang November 1914 bis Anfang Februar 1915.
> 2. Der Krieg zur See 1914-1918, Band 4, Der Handelskrieg mit U-Booten, Teil 1, Vorgeschichte.

8-14 January ....The Winter Actions – the action of Crouy. (The Battle of Soissons). (Western Front).

> FrOH: Les Armées Françaises dans la Grande Guerre, Tome II, La stabilisation au front - Les attaques locales - 14 novembre 1914 – 1 mai 1915.
> GmOH: Der Weltkrieg 1914 bis 1918, Die Militarischen Operationen zu Lande, Band 7, Die Operationen des Jahres 1915. Die Ereignisse Winter und Frühjahr.

10-11 January ....The defence of Muscat. (Arabia).

> BrOH: Official History of the War, Military Operations, Egypt and Palestine, Volume I, From the Outbreak of War with Germany to June 1917.
> TOH: 1. Büyük Harbin Sevkülceyşi.
> 2. Birinci Cihan Harbinde Türk Harbi, 1915 Yili Harekatleri, IInci Cilt.
> 3. Birinci Dünya Harbinde Türk Harbi VInci Cilt, Hicaz, Asir, Yeman Cepheleri ve Libya Harekati 1914-1918.
> 4. Büyük Harpte Misir Seferi.

11 January...South African Rebellion last rebels captured.

> SAOH: The Union of South Africa and the Great War 1914 – 1918.

12 January...The capture of Mafia Island. (East Africa).

> BgOH: Les Campagnes Coloniales Belges 1914-1918. Volume I. Introduction, les Operations au Cameroun, les Operations en Rhodésie, la Période Défensive à la Frontière Orientale.
> BrOH: Official History of the War, Military Operations, East Africa, Volume I, August 1914-September 1916.
> GmOH: Der Krieg zur See 1914-1918, Band 6, Die Kämpfe der Kaiserlichen Marine in den deutschen Kolonien, Teil 2, Deutsch-Ostafrika.
> SAOH: The Union of South Africa and the Great War 1914 – 1918.

14 January...The capture of Swakopmund. (South West Africa [Namibia]).

> SAOH: 1. The Union of South Africa and the Great War 1914 – 1918.
> 2. The Campaign in German South West Africa 1914 – 1915.

18-19 January ....The affair of Jasin. (East Africa).

> BgOH: Les Campagnes Coloniales Belges 1914-1918. Volume I. Introduction, les Operations au Cameroun, les Operations en Rhodésie, la Période Défensive à la Frontière Orientale.
> BrOH: Official History of the War, Military Operations, East Africa, Volume I, August 1914-September 1916.

GmOH: Der Krieg zur See 1914-1918, Band 6, Die Kämpfe der Kaiserlichen Marine in den deutschen Kolonien, Teil 2, Deutsch-Ostafrika.

SAOH: The Union of South Africa and the Great War 1914 – 1918.

19 January .... The first German airship raid on Britain, the East Coast of England.

BrOH: Official History of the War, War in the Air, Volume I.

GmOH: Der Weltkrieg 1914 bis 1918, Die Militarischen Operationen zu Lande, Band 9, Die Operationen des Jahres 1915 – Die Ereignisse im Westen und auf dem Balkan vom Sommer bis Jahresschluß; Die Entwicklung der Luftstreitkrafte bis Ende 1915.

23-24 January .... The defence of Upington. (South West Africa [Namibia]).

SAOH: 1. The Union of South Africa and the Great War 1914 – 1918.

2. The Campaign in German South West Africa 1914 – 1915.

24 January .... The action of the Dogger Bank – S.M.S. Blücher sunk. (British Home Waters).

BrOH: Official History of the War, Naval Operations, Volume I To the Battle of the Falklands December 1914.

GmOH: Der Krieg zur See 1914-1918, Band 1, Der Krieg in der Nordsee, Teil 3, Von Anfang November 1914 bis Anfang Februar 1915.

24 January .... The German airship PL19 shot down over Libau, Poland.

GmOH: Der Weltkrieg 1914 bis 1918, Die Militarischen Operationen zu Lande, Band 9, Die Operationen des Jahres 1915 – Die Ereignisse im Westen und auf dem Balkan vom Sommer bis Jahresschluß; Die Entwicklung der Luftstreitkrafte bis Ende 1915

28 January .... SV William P Frye [American Vessel] sunk by S.M.S. Prinz Eitel Friedrich. (Atlantic Ocean).

BrOH: Official History of the War, Seaborne Trade, Volume I, Cruiser Period.

GmOH: Der Krieg zur See 1914-1918, Band 3, Der Kreuzerkrieg in den ausländischen Gewässern, Teil 3, Die deutschen Hilfskreuzer.

29 January .... The bombardment of Walney Island Battery, Barrow in Furness.

BrOH: Official History of the War, Naval Operations, Volume I To the Battle of the Falklands December 1914.

GmOH: Der Krieg zur See 1914-1918, Band 1, Der Krieg in der Nordsee, Teil 3, Von Anfang November 1914 bis Anfang Februar 1915.

29 January - 3 February .... The Battle of the Beskid Pass. (Eastern Front).

TOH: 1. Büyük Harbin Sevkülceyşi.

2. Birinci Cihan Harbinde Türk Harbi, 1915 Yili Harekatleri, Ilinci Cilt.

3. Birinci Dünya Harbinde, Erzurum ve Cevresinde Ermeni Hrekatetleri. (1914–1918).

4. Birinci Dünya Harbinde Türk Harbi Kafkas Cephesi 3ncu Ordu Harekati, Cilt II, Birinci Kitap.

RuOH: 1. The Russian Army in the World War.

2. A Strategic Outline of the War 1914 –1915.
3. A Strategic Outline of the War 1914 -1918.

31 January - 2 February ....The Battle of Humin. (Eastern Front).
        TOH: 1. Büyük Harbin Sevkülceyşi.
               2. Birinci Cihan Harbinde Türk Harbi, 1915 Yili Harekatleri, Iinci Cilt.
               3. Birinci Dünya Harbinde, Erzurum ve Cevresinde Ermeni Hrekatetleri. (1914–1918).
               4. Birinci Dünya Harbinde Türk Harbi Kafkas Cephesi 3ncu Ordu Harekati, Cilt II, Birinci Kitap.
        RuOH: 1. The Russian Army in the World War.
               2. A Strategic Outline of the War 1914 –1915.
               3. A Strategic Outline of the War 1914 -1918.

3-4 February ....The attack on the Suez Canal. (Egypt and Sinai).
        AuOH: Official History of Australia in the War of 1914-1918, Volume VII, Sinai and Palestine.
        BrOH: Official History of the War, Military Operations, Egypt and Palestine, Volume I, From the Outbreak of War with Germany to June 1917.
        NZOH: Official History of New Zealand's Effort in the Great War, Volume III, Sinai and Palestine.
        TOH: 1. Büyük Harbin Sevkülceyşi.
               2. Birinci Cihan Harbinde Türk Harbi, 1915 Yili Harekatleri, Iinci Cilt.
               3. Birinci Dünya Harbinde Türk Harbi, 1nci Kisim, Sina-Filistin Cephesi Harbin Başlangicindan 1kinci Gazze Muharebeleri Sonuna Kadar.
               4. Büyük Harpte Misir Seferi.

4-22 February ....The Winter Battle in Masuria. (Eastern Front).
        GmOH: Der Weltkrieg 1914 bis 1918, Die Militarischen Operationen zu Lande, Band 7, Die Operationen des Jahres 1915. Die Ereignisse Winter und Frühjahr.
        PlOH: Studia z wojny światowej 1914-1918 roku Tom VII: Bitwa zimowa na Mazurach
        RuOH: 1. The Russian Army in the World War.
               2. A Strategic Outline of the War 1914 –1915.
               3. A Strategic Outline of the War 1914 -1918.

16 February......................................The capture of Oyem. (West Africa - Cameroons).
        BgOH: Les Campagnes Coloniales Belges 1914-1918. Volume I. Introduction, les Operations au Cameroun, les Operations en Rhodésie, la Période Défensive à la Frontière Orientale.
        BrOH: Official History of the War, Military Operations, Togoland and the Cameroons.
        FrOH: Les Armées Françaises dans la Grande Guerre, Tome IX, Volume 2, Les campagnes coloniales: Cameroun – Togoland. – Opérations contre les Senoussis.

17 February......................................The Winter Actions – the first action of Vauquois. (Western Front).
        FrOH: Les Armées Françaises dans la Grande Guerre, Tome II, La stabilisation au front - Les attaques locales - 14 novembre 1914 – 1 mai 1915.
        GmOH: Der Weltkrieg 1914 bis 1918, Die Militarischen Operationen zu Lande, Band 7, Die Operationen des Jahres 1915. Die Ereignisse Winter und Frühjahr.

17 February..The German airship L3 destroyed over Fanö and the German Airship L4 destroyed over Blaavands Huk, Denmark.

        GmOH: Der Weltkrieg 1914 bis 1918, Die Militarischen Operationen zu Lande, Band 9, Die Operationen des Jahres 1915 – Die Ereignisse im Westen und auf dem Balkan vom Sommer bis Jahresschluß; Die Entwicklung der Luftstreitkrafte bis Ende 1915.

17-21 February..................................The Winter Actions – the first action of Les Eparges. (Western Front).

        FrOH: Les Armées Françaises dans la Grande Guerre, Tome II, La stabilisation au front - Les attaques locales - 14 novembre 1914 – 1 mai 1915.

        GmOH: Der Weltkrieg 1914 bis 1918, Die Militarischen Operationen zu Lande, Band 7, Die Operationen des Jahres 1915. Die Ereignisse Winter und Frühjahr.

18 February ....German submarine blockade of Great Britain begins. (British Home Waters).

        BrOH: Official History of the War, Naval Operations, Volume II.

        GmOH: Der Krieg zur See 1914-1918, Band 4, Der Handelskrieg mit U-Booten, Teil 2, Februar bis September 1915.

19 February......................................S.S. Belridge – first neutral ship [Norwegian Vessel] - attacked without warning. (British Home Waters).

        BrOH: 1. Official History of the War, Naval Operations, Volume II.

        2. Official History of the War, Seaborne Trade, Volume II, Submarine Campaign, Part I.

        3. Official History of the War, The Merchant Navy, Volume I.

        GmOH: Der Krieg zur See 1914-1918, Band 4, Der Handelskrieg mit U-Booten, Teil 2, Februar bis September 1915.

19 February – 18 March....................The Dardanelles/Gallipoli Campaign - The naval attack on the Dardanelles Forts.

        BrOH: Official History of the War, Naval Operations, Volume II.

        TOH: 1. Birinci Cihan Harbinde Türk Harbi, 1915 Yili Harekatleri, IIinci Cilt.

        2. Birinci Dünya Harbinde Türk Harbi, Vnvi Cilt, Çanakkale Cephesi Harekati, 1nci Kitap.

        3. Birinci Dünya Harbinde Türk Harbi, V nci Cilt, Çanakkale Cephesi Harekâtı, 1 nci, 2 nci, Ve 3 ncu Kitaplarin Özetlenmis Tarihi, Haziran 1914 - 9 Ocak 1916 / A Brief History of the Çanakkale Campaign in the First World War (June 1914 – January 1916).

        4. Birinci Dünya Harbinde Türk Harbi, V nci Cilt, Çanakkale Cephesi Harekâtı, 1 nci, 2 nci, Ve 3 ncu Kitaplarin Özetlenmis Tarihi, Haziran 1914 - 9 Ocak 1916 / A Brief History of the Çanakkale Campaign in the First World War (June 1914 – January 1916).

22-27 February.................................The First Battle of Przasnysz. (Eastern Front).

        GmOH: Der Weltkrieg 1914 bis 1918, Die Militarischen Operationen zu Lande, Band 7, Die Operationen des Jahres 1915. Die Ereignisse Winter und Frühjahr.

        RuOH: 1. The Russian Army in the World War.

        2. A Strategic Outline of the War 1914 –1915.

        3. A Strategic Outline of the War 1914 -1918.

28 February – 6 March........................The Winter Actions – the second action of Vauquois. (Western Front).

FrOH: Les Armées Françaises dans la Grande Guerre, Tome II, La stabilisation au front - Les attaques locales - 14 novembre 1914 – 1 mai 1915.

GmOH: Der Weltkrieg 1914 bis 1918, Die Militarischen Operationen zu Lande, Band 7, Die Operationen des Jahres 1915. Die Ereignisse Winter und Frühjahr.

1 March...The British blockade of East Africa begins. (Indian Ocean).

BrOH: 1. Official History of the War, Naval Operations, Volume II.
2. Official History of the War – The Blockade of the Central Empires 1914-1918
3. Official History of the War, Military Operations, East Africa, Volume I, August 1914-September 1916.

GmOH: Der Krieg zur See 1914-1918, Band 6, Die Kämpfe der Kaiserlichen Marine in den deutschen Kolonien, Teil 2, Deutsch-Ostafrika.

SAOH: The Union of South Africa and the Great War 1914 – 1918.

1 March...The bombardment of Antivari. (Adriatic Sea).

AHOH: Österreich-Ungarns Seekrieg 1914-1918, Lieferung I.

HOH: A világháború 1914-1918. Különös tekintettel Magyarországra és a Magyar csapatok szereplésére Szerkeszti és kiadja a M. Kir. Hadtörténelmi Levéltár, köt 8.

3 March - 21 April ....The First Battle of the Woëvre. (Western Front).

FrOH: Les Armées Françaises dans la Grande Guerre, Tome II, La stabilisation au front - Les attaques locales - 14 novembre 1914 – 1 mai 1915.

GmOH: 1. Der Weltkrieg 1914 bis 1918, Die Militarischen Operationen zu Lande, Band 7, Die Operationen des Jahres 1915. Die Ereignisse Winter und Frühjahr.
2. Die Bayern im Großen Kriege 1914-1918.

4 March...S.M.S. U.8 sunk with the aid of "Indicatornets". (British Home Waters).

BrOH: Official History of the War, Naval Operations, Volume II.

GmOH: Der Krieg zur See 1914-1918, Band 4, Der Handelskrieg mit U-Booten, Teil 2, Februar bis September 1915.

5-16 March ....The Battle of Stolniki. (Eastern Front).

GmOH: Der Weltkrieg 1914 bis 1918, Die Militarischen Operationen zu Lande, Band 7, Die Operationen des Jahres 1915. Die Ereignisse Winter und Frühjahr.

RuOH: 1. The Russian Army in the World War.
2. A Strategic Outline of the War 1914 –1915.
3. A Strategic Outline of the War 1914 -1918.

10-13 March ....The Battle of Neuve Chapelle. (Western Front).

BrOH: Official History of the War, Military Operations, France and Belgium 1915 Volume I, Winter 1914-15, Neuve Chappelle, Ypres, December 1914-May.

GmOH: 1. Der Weltkrieg 1914 bis 1918, Die Militarischen Operationen zu Lande, Band 7, Die Operationen des Jahres 1915. Die Ereignisse Winter und Frühjahr.
2. Die Bayern im Großen Kriege 1914-1918.

13 March...S.S. Hanna – neutral ship [SwedishVessel] - sunk without warning. (British Home Waters).

> BrOH: 1. Official History of the War, Naval Operations, Volume II.
> 2. Official History of the War, Seaborne Trade, Volume II, Submarine Campaign, Part I.
> 3. Official History of the War, The Merchant Navy, Volume I.
>
> GmOH: Der Krieg zur See 1914-1918, Band 4, Der Handelskrieg mit U-Booten, Teil 2, Februar bis September 1915.
>
> SwOH: Flottans neutralitetsvakt: redogörelse för flottans verksamhet för neutralitetens upprätthållande samt sjöfartens och fiskets tryggande m. m. under världskriget 1914-18, innefattande jämväl redogörelser för vissa åtgärder av kustartilleriet och lotsverket.

14 March...S.M.S. Dresden sunk. (Pacific Ocean).

> BrOH: Official History of the War, Naval Operations, Volume II.
>
> GmOH: Der Krieg zur See 1914-1918, Band 3, Der Kreuzerkrieg in den ausländischen Gewässern, Teil 1, Das Kreuzergeschwader.

15 March...S.S. Blonde attacked by an aircraft. (North Sea).

> BrOH: 1. Official History of the War, Naval Operations, Volume II.
> 2. Official History of the War, Seaborne Trade, Volume II, Submarine Campaign, Part I.
> 3. Official History of the War, The Merchant Navy, Volume I.
>
> GmOH: 1. Der Krieg zur See 1914-1918, Band 4, Der Handelskrieg mit U-Booten, Teil 2, Februar bis September 1915.
> 2. Der Weltkrieg 1914 bis 1918, Die Militarischen Operationen zu Lande, Band 9, Die Operationen des Jahres 1915 – Die Ereignisse im Westen und auf dem Balkan vom Sommer bis Jahresschluß; Die Entwicklung der Luftstreitkrafte bis Ende 1915.

18-27 March ....The Winter Actions – the second action of Les Eparges. (Western Front).

> FrOH: Les Armées Françaises dans la Grande Guerre, Tome II, La stabilisation au front - Les attaques locales - 14 novembre 1914 – 1 mai 1915.
>
> GmOH: Der Weltkrieg 1914 bis 1918, Die Militarischen Operationen zu Lande, Band 7, Die Operationen des Jahres 1915. Die Ereignisse Winter und Frühjahr.

20 March...The capture of Aus. (South West Africa [Namibia]).

> SAOH: 1. The Union of South Africa and the Great War 1914 – 1918.
> 2. The Campaign in German South West Africa 1914 – 1915.

21 March...The first Airship raid on Paris.

> GmOH: Der Weltkrieg 1914 bis 1918, Die Militarischen Operationen zu Lande, Band IX, Die Operationen des Jahres 1915 – Die Ereignisse im Westen und auf dem

Balkan vom Sommer bis Jahresschluß. (Die Entwicklung der Luftstreitkrafte bis Ende 1915.)

25 March .... S.S. Medea – first neutral ship [DutchVessel] - sunk by a submarine after visit and search. (British Home Waters).

BrOH: 1. Official History of the War, Naval Operations, Volume II.
2. Official History of the War, Seaborne Trade, Volume II, Submarine Campaign, Part I.
3. Official History of the War, The Merchant Navy, Volume I.
GmOH: Der Krieg zur See 1914-1918, Band 4, Der Handelskrieg mit U-Booten, Teil 2, Februar bis September 1915.

28 March .... S.S. Falaba – first passenger ship - sunk by a submarine. (British Home Waters).

BrOH: 1. Official History of the War, Naval Operations, Volume II.
2. Official History of the War, Seaborne Trade, Volume II, Submarine Campaign, Part I.
3. Official History of the War, The Merchant Navy, Volume I.
GmOH: Der Krieg zur See 1914-1918, Band 4, Der Handelskrieg mit U-Booten, Teil 2, Februar bis September 1915.

30 March .... The actions of Jakalswater. (South West Africa [Namibia]).

SAOH: 1. The Union of South Africa and the Great War 1914 – 1918.
2. The Campaign in German South West Africa 1914 – 1915.

2-13 April .... The Battle of Laborcrzatal???? Gorlice-Tarnow?????. (Eastern Front).

AHOH: Österreich-Ungarns Letzter Krieg 1914-1918, Band II.
GmOH: Der Weltkrieg 1914 bis 1918, Die Militarischen Operationen zu Lande, Band 7, Die Operationen des Jahres 1915. Die Ereignisse Winter und Frühjahr.
HOH: A világháború 1914-1918. Különös tekintettel Magyarországra és a Magyar csapatok szereplésére Szerkeszti és kiadja a M. Kir. Hadtörténelmi Levéltár, köt 8.
RuOH: 1. The Russian Army in the World War.
2. A Strategic Outline of the War 1914 –1915.
3. A Strategic Outline of the War 1914 -1918.

5-12 April .... The Spring Action – the third action of Les Eparges. (Western Front).

FrOH: Les Armées Françaises dans la Grande Guerre, Tome II, La stabilisation au front - Les attaques locales - 14 novembre 1914 – 1 mai 1915.
GmOH: Der Weltkrieg 1914 bis 1918, Die Militarischen Operationen zu Lande, Band 7, Die Operationen des Jahres 1915. Die Ereignisse Winter und Frühjahr.

12-14 April .... The British Basra Operations - the Battle of Shaiba. (Mesopotamia).

BrOH: Official History of the War, Military Operations, Campaign in Mesopotamia, Volume I.
TOH: 1. Büyük Harbin Sevkülceyşi.
2. Birinci Cihan Harbinde Türk Harbi, 1915 Yili Harekatleri, Iinci Cilt.

                                    3. Birinci Dünya Harbinde Türk Harbi, IIInvi Cilt, Irak-Iran Cephesi, 1914-1918, 1nci Kisim.

                                    4. Büyük Harpte Misir Seferi.

17 April .... S.S. La Rosarina – first merchant ship to beating off a submarine after a visit and search. (British Home Waters).

        BrOH: 1. Official History of the War, Naval Operations, Volume II.

                 2. Official History of the War, Seaborne Trade, Volume II, Submarine Campaign, Part I.

                 3. Official History of the War, The Merchant Navy, Volume I.

        GmOH: Der Krieg zur See 1914-1918, Band 4, Der Handelskrieg mit U-Booten, Teil 2, Februar bis September 1915.

17-22 April .... The attack on Hill 60. (Western Front).

        BrOH: Official History of the War, Military Operations, France and Belgium 1915, Volume I, Winter 1914-15, Neuve Chappelle, Ypres, December 1914-May.

        GmOH: Der Weltkrieg 1914 bis 1918, Die Militarischen Operationen zu Lande, Band 7, Die Operationen des Jahres 1915. Die Ereignisse Winter und Frühjahr.

18 April – 10 June .... The Allied Operation against Garua. (West Africa - Cameroons).

        BgOH: Les Campagnes Coloniales Belges 1914-1918. Volume I. Introduction, les Operations au Cameroun, les Operations en Rhodésie, la Période Défensive à la Frontière Orientale.

        BrOH: Official History of the War, Military Operations, Togoland and the Cameroons.

        FrOH: Les Armées Françaises dans la Grande Guerre, Tome IX, Volume 2, Les campagnes coloniales: Cameroun – Togoland. – Opérations contre les Senoussis.

22 April – 25 May .... The Second Battle of Ypres.

        BrOH: Official History of the War, Military Operations, France and Belgium 1915, Volume I, Winter 1914-15, Neuve Chappelle, Ypres, December 1914-May.

        COH: 1. Official History of the Canadian Forces in the Great War 1914 – 1919, Volume I.

                 2. Canadian Expeditionary Force 1914 - 1919. The Official History of the Canadian Army in the First World War.

                 3. The Western Front 1914.

        FrOH: Les Armées Françaises dans la Grande Guerre, Tome III, Les offensives de 1915 - L'hiver de 1915–1916 - 1 mai 1915–21 février 1916

        GmOH: Der Weltkrieg 1914 bis 1918, Die Militarischen Operationen zu Lande, Band 7, Die Operationen des Jahres 1915. Die Ereignisse Winter und Frühjahr.

22 April .... The Gas Attack at Ypres.

        FrOH: Les Armées Françaises dans la Grande Guerre: Tome II La stabilisation au front - Les attaques locales - 14 novembre 1914 – 1 mai 1915.

        GmOH: Der Weltkrieg 1914 bis 1918, Die Militarischen Operationen zu Lande, Band 7, Die Operationen des Jahres 1915. Die Ereignisse Winter und Frühjahr.

22-23 April ....The Second Battle of Ypres – the Battle of Gravenstafel Ridge.

BrOH: Official History of the War, Military Operations, France and Belgium 1915, Volume I, Winter 1914-15, Neuve Chappelle, Ypres, December 1914-May.

COH: 1. Official History of the Canadian Forces in the Great War 1914 – 1919, Volume I.
2. Canadian Expeditionary Force 1914 - 1919. The Official History of the Canadian Army in the First World War.
3. The Western Front 1914.

FrOH: Les Armées Françaises dans la Grande Guerre: Tome II La stabilisation au front - Les attaques locales - 14 novembre 1914 – 1 mai 1915.

GmOH: Der Weltkrieg 1914 bis 1918, Die Militarischen Operationen zu Lande, Band 7, Die Operationen des Jahres 1915. Die Ereignisse Winter und Frühjahr.

23 April – 29 February 1916 ....The British blockade of the Cameroons. (West Africa).

BgOH: Les Campagnes Coloniales Belges 1914-1918. Volume I. Introduction, les Operations au Cameroun, les Operations en Rhodésie, la Période Défensive à la Frontière Orientale.

BrOH: 1. Official History of the War, Naval Operations, Volume II.
2. Official History of the War – The Blockade of the Central Empires 1914-1918
3. Official History of the War, Military Operations, Togoland and the Cameroons.

FrOH: Les Armées Françaises dans la Grande Guerre, Tome IX, Volume 2, Les campagnes coloniales: Cameroun – Togoland. – Opérations contre les Senoussis.

24 April – 4 May................................The Second Battle of Ypres – the Battle of St. Julien.

BrOH: Official History of the War, Military Operations, France and Belgium 1915, Volume I, Winter 1914-15, Neuve Chappelle, Ypres, December 1914-May.

COH: 1. Official History of the Canadian Forces in the Great War 1914 – 1919, Volume I.
2. Canadian Expeditionary Force 1914 - 1919. The Official History of the Canadian Army in the First World War.
3. The Western Front 1914.

FrOH: Les Armées Françaises dans la Grande Guerre: Tome II La stabilisation au front - Les attaques locales - 14 novembre 1914 – 1 mai 1915.

GmOH: Der Weltkrieg 1914 bis 1918, Die Militarischen Operationen zu Lande, Band 7, Die Operationen des Jahres 1915. Die Ereignisse Winter und Frühjahr.

24 April 1915–13 September 1922[1] ...The Armenian Massacres / The Great Calamity[2]

---

[1] The dates of the Armenian Massacres/Great Calamity are based on the dates given by the Armenian National Institute. The first date is when 250 Armenian intellectuals and community leaders were arrested in Constantinople and later executed and is generally seen as the starting point, although anti Armenians events including executions had taken place beforehand. The last date records the last of the massacres by the Turkish Army.

[2] Armenian Massacres is the Turkish name and The Great Calamity is the Armenian name given to the 1916-1922 mass murders of the Armenians by the Turks. It is also known as the Armenian Genocide or Holocaust.

TOH: 1. Birinci Dünya Harbinde, Erzurum Ve Cevresinde Ermeni Hrekatetleri 1914–1918.
2. Birinci Dünya Savaşında ermenilerin Türklere Yaptığı Katliam Fotoğrafları.

AuOH: 1. Official History of Australia in the War of 1914-1918, Volume I, The Story of Anzac Part I.
2. Official History of Australia in the War of 1914-1918, Volume II, The Story of Anzac Part II.
BrOH: 1. Official History of the War, Military Operations, Gallipoli, Volume I, Inception of the Campaign to May 1915.
2. Official History of the War, Military Operations, Gallipoli, Volume II, May 1915 to the Evacuation.
FrOH: Les Armées Françaises dans la Grande Guerre: Tome VIII La campagne d'Orient. Volume 1 La campagne d'Orient jusqu'a l'intervention de la Roumanie - février 1915-aöut 1916.
GmOH: Der Weltkrieg 1914 bis 1918, Die Militarischen Operationen zu Lande, Band 7, Die Operationen des Jahres 1915. Die Ereignisse Winter und Frühjahr.
NZOH: Official History of New Zealand's Effort in the Great War, Volume I Gallipoli.
TOH: 1. Birinci Cihan Harbinde Türk Harbi, 1915 Yili Harekatleri, IIinci Cilt.
2. Birinci Dünya Harbinde Türk Harbi, Vncu Cilt, Çanakkale Cephesi, 2nci Kitap, Amfibi Harekat.
3. Turk Silahe Kuvvetleri Tarihi Osmanlı Birinci Dünya Harbinde Türk Harbi, Vncu Cilt, Çanakkale Cephesi Harekati, 3ncu Kitap, Haziran 1915 – Ocak 1916.
4. Birinci Dünya Harbinde Türk Harbi, V nci Cilt, Çanakkale Cephesi Harekâtı, 1 nci, 2 nci, Ve 3 ncu Kitaplarin Özetlenmis Tarihi, Haziran 1914 - 9 Ocak 1916 / A Brief History of the Çanakkale Campaign in the First World War (June 1914 – January 1916).

BrOH: Official History of the War, Military Operations, Gallipoli, Volume I, Inception of the Campaign to May 1915.
GmOH: Der Weltkrieg 1914 bis 1918, Die Militarischen Operationen zu Lande, Band 7, Die Operationen des Jahres 1915. Die Ereignisse Winter und Frühjahr.
TOH: 1. Birinci Cihan Harbinde Türk Harbi, 1915 Yili Harekatleri, IIinci Cilt.
2. Birinci Dünya Harbinde Türk Harbi, Vncu Cilt, Çanakkale Cephesi, 2nci Kitap, Amfibi Harekat.
3. Birinci Dünya Harbinde Türk Harbi, V nci Cilt, Çanakkale Cephesi Harekâtı, 1 nci, 2 nci, Ve 3 ncu Kitaplarin Özetlenmis Tarihi, Haziran 1914 - 9 Ocak 1916 / A Brief History of the Çanakkale Campaign in the First World War (June 1914 – January 1916).

SAOH: .1. The Union of South Africa and the Great War 1914 – 1918.

2. The Campaign in German South West Africa 1914 – 1915.

25-26 April ....The Dardanelles/Gallipoli Campaign - the Battles of ANZAC - the landings at ANZAC.

      AuOH: Official History of Australia in the War of 1914-1918, Volume I, The Story of Anzac Part I.

      BrOH: Official History of the War, Military Operations, Gallipoli, Volume I, Inception of the Campaign to May 1915.

      GmOH: Der Weltkrieg 1914 bis 1918, Die Militarischen Operationen zu Lande, Band 7, Die Operationen des Jahres 1915. Die Ereignisse Winter und Frühjahr.

      NZOH: Official History of New Zealand's Effort in the Great War, Volume I Gallipoli.

      TOH: 1. Birinci Cihan Harbinde Türk Harbi, 1915 Yili Harekatleri, IIinci Cilt.

      2. Birinci Dünya Harbinde Türk Harbi, Vncu Cilt, Çanakkale Cephesi, 2nci Kitap, Amfibi Harekat.

      3. Birinci Dünya Harbinde Türk Harbi, V nci Cilt, Çanakkale Cephesi Harekâtı, 1 nci, 2 nci, Ve 3 ncu Kitaplarin Özetlenmis Tarihi, Haziran 1914 - 9 Ocak 1916 / A Brief History of the Çanakkale Campaign in the First World War (June 1914 – January 1916).

28 April...The Dardanelles/Gallipoli Campaign - the Battles of Helles - the First Battle of Krithia.

      BrOH: Official History of the War, Military Operations, Gallipoli, Volume I, Inception of the Campaign to May 1915.

      GmOH: Der Weltkrieg 1914 bis 1918, Die Militarischen Operationen zu Lande, Band 7, Die Operationen des Jahres 1915. Die Ereignisse Winter und Frühjahr.

      TOH: 1. Birinci Cihan Harbinde Türk Harbi, 1915 Yili Harekatleri, IIinci Cilt.

      2. Birinci Dünya Harbinde Türk Harbi, Vncu Cilt, Çanakkale Cephesi, 2nci Kitap, Amfibi Harekat.

      3. Birinci Dünya Harbinde Türk Harbi, V nci Cilt, Çanakkale Cephesi Harekâtı, 1 nci, 2 nci, Ve 3 ncu Kitaplarin Özetlenmis Tarihi, Haziran 1914 - 9 Ocak 1916 / A Brief History of the Çanakkale Campaign in the First World War (June 1914 – January 1916).

1 May...S.S. Gulflight – first American ship - sunk by a submarine without warning. (British Home Waters).

      BrOH: 1. Official History of the War, Naval Operations, Volume II.

      2. Official History of the War, Seaborne Trade, Volume II, Submarine Campaign, Part I.

      3. Official History of the War, The Merchant Navy, Volume I.

      GmOH: Der Krieg zur See 1914-1918, Band 4, Der Handelskrieg mit U-Booten, Teil 2, Februar bis September 1915.

1 May...The Battle of Dilman. (Eastern Front).

      TOH: Birinci Dünya Harbinde Türk Harbi, Cilt II, Birinci Kitap, Kafkas Cephesi. 3ncu Ordu Harekati

      RuOH: 1. The Russian Army in the World War.

      2. A Strategic Outline of the War 1914 –1915.

3. A Strategic Outline of the War 1914 -1918.

1 May...The action of Eski-Hissarlik. (Mesopotamia).
> BrOH: Official History of the War, Military Operations, Campaign in Mesopotamia, Volume I.
> TOH: 1. Büyük Harbin Sevkülceyşi.
> 2. Birinci Cihan Harbinde Türk Harbi, 1915 Yili Harekatleri, Iinci Cilt.
> 3. Birinci Dünya Harbinde Türk Harbi, IIInvi Cilt, Irak-Iran Cephesi, 1914-1918, 1nci Kisim.
> 4. Büyük Harpte Misir Seferi.

1-5 May ....The Spring Offensive in Galicia. (Galicia - Eastern Front).
> AHOH:.Österreich-Ungarns Letzter Krieg 1914-1918, Band II.
> HOH: A világháború 1914-1918. Különös tekintettel Magyarországra és a Magyar csapatok szereplésére Szerkeszti és kiadja a M. Kir. Hadtörténelmi Levéltár, köt 9.
> RuOH: 1. The Russian Army in the World War.
> 2. A Strategic Outline of the War 1914 –1915.
> 3. A Strategic Outline of the War 1914 -1918.

6-8 May ....The Dardanelles/Gallipoli Campaign - the Battles of Helles - the Second Battle of Krithia.
> BrOH: 1. Official History of the War, Military Operations, Gallipoli, Volume I, Inception of the Campaign to May 1915.
> 2. Official History of the War, Military Operations, Gallipoli, Volume II, May 1915 to the Evacuation.
> FrOH: Les Armées Françaises dans la Grande Guerre: Tome VIII La campagne d'Orient. Volume 1 La campagne d'Orient jusqu'a l'intervention de la Roumanie - février 1915-aöut 1916.
> GmOH: Der Weltkrieg 1914 bis 1918, Die Militarischen Operationen zu Lande, Band 7, Die Operationen des Jahres 1915. Die Ereignisse Winter und Frühjahr.
> TOH: 1. Birinci Cihan Harbinde Türk Harbi, 1915 Yili Harekatleri, Iinci Cilt.
> 2. Birinci Dünya Harbinde Türk Harbi, Vncu Cilt, Çanakkale Cephesi, 2nci Kitap, Amfibi Harekat.
> 3. Birinci Dünya Harbinde Türk Harbi, V nci Cilt, Çanakkale Cephesi Harekâtı, 1 nci, 2 nci, Ve 3 ncu Kitaplarin Özetlenmis Tarihi, Haziran 1914 - 9 Ocak 1916 / A Brief History of the Çanakkale Campaign in the First World War (June 1914 – January 1916).

7 May...S.S. Lusitania sunk by S.M.S. U.20. (British Home Waters).
> BrOH: 1. Official History of the War, Naval Operations, Volume II.
> 2. Official History of the War, Seaborne Trade, Volume II, Submarine Campaign, Part I.
> 3. Official History of the War, The Merchant Navy, Volume I.
> GmOH: Der Krieg zur See 1914-1918, Band 4, Der Handelskrieg mit U-Booten, Teil 2, Februar bis September 1915.

8-13 May ....The Second Battle of Ypres – the Battle of Frezenberg Ridge.

BrOH: Official History of the War, Military Operations, France and Belgium 1915, Volume I, Winter 1914-15, Neuve Chappelle, Ypres, December 1914-May.

COH: 1. Official History of the Canadian Forces in the Great War 1914 – 1919, Volume I.
2. Canadian Expeditionary Force 1914 - 1919. The Official History of the Canadian Army in the First World War.
3. The Western Front 1914.

GmOH: Der Weltkrieg 1914 bis 1918, Die Militarischen Operationen zu Lande, Band 7, Die Operationen des Jahres 1915. Die Ereignisse Winter und Frühjahr.

8-14 May ....The Battle of Sanok and Rzeszow. (Eastern Front).

AHOH: Österreich-Ungarns Letzter Krieg 1914-1918, Band II.

HOH: A világháború 1914-1918. Különös tekintettel Magyarországra és a Magyar csapatok szereplésére Szerkeszti és kiadja a M. Kir. Hadtörténelmi Levéltár, köt 9.

RuOH: 1. The Russian Army in the World War.
2. A Strategic Outline of the War 1914 –1915.
3. A Strategic Outline of the War 1914 -1918.

9 May..The Allied Spring Offensive – the Battle of Aubers Ridge.

BrOH: Official History of the War, Military Operations, France and Belgium 1915, Volume II, Battles of Aubers Ridge, Festubert and Loos.

GmOH: 1. Der Weltkrieg 1914 bis 1918, Die Militarischen Operationen zu Lande, Band 7, Die Operationen des Jahres 1915. Die Ereignisse Winter und Frühjahr.
2. Die Bayern im Großen Kriege 1914-1918.

9 May - 18 June ....The Allied Spring Offensive – the Second Battle of Artois.

FrOH: Les Armées Françaises dans la Grande Guerre, Tome III, Les offensives de 1915 - L'hiver de 1915–1916 - 1 mai 1915–21 février 1916.

GmOH: 1. Der Weltkrieg 1914 bis 1918, Die Militarischen Operationen zu Lande, Band 7, Die Operationen des Jahres 1915. Die Ereignisse Winter und Frühjahr.
2. Die Bayern im Großen Kriege 1914-1918.

13 May...The Dardanelles/Gallipoli Campaign - H.M.S. Goliath sunk.

BrOH: Official History of the War, Naval Operations, Volume II.

GmOH: Der Krieg zur See 1914-1918, Band 5, Der Krieg in den türkischen Gewässern, Teil 2, Der Kampf un die Meerengen.

TOH: Birinci Dünya Harbi, VIIInci Cilt, Türk Deniz Harekati.
3. Birinci Dünya Harbinde Türk Harbi, V nci Cilt, Çanakkale Cephesi Harekâtı, 1 nci, 2 nci, Ve 3 ncu Kitaplarin Özetlenmis Tarihi, Haziran 1914 - 9 Ocak 1916 / A Brief History of the Çanakkale Campaign in the First World War (June 1914 – January 1916).

13 May...The capture of Windhuk. (South West Africa [Namibia]).

SAOH: 1. The Union of South Africa and the Great War 1914 – 1918.
2. The Campaign in German South West Africa 1914 – 1915.

15–25 May ....The Allied Spring Offensive – the Battle of Festubert..

        BrOH: Official History of the War, Military Operations, France and Belgium 1915, Volume II, Battles of Aubers Ridge, Festubert and Loos.

        GmOH: 1. Der Weltkrieg 1914 bis 1918, Die Militarischen Operationen zu Lande, Band 7, Die Operationen des Jahres 1915. Die Ereignisse Winter und Frühjahr.
              2. Die Bayern im Großen Kriege 1914-1918.

16-23 May ....The Battle of San. (Eastern Front).

        AHOH: Österreich-Ungarns Letzter Krieg 1914-1918, Band II.

        HOH: A világháború 1914-1918. Különös tekintettel Magyarországra és a Magyar csapatok szereplésére Szerkeszti és kiadja a M. Kir. Hadtörténelmi Levéltár, köt 9.

        RuOH: 1. The Russian Army in the World War.
              2. A Strategic Outline of the War 1914 –1915.
              3. A Strategic Outline of the War 1914 -1918.

18 May – 3 June ....The Battle of Stryj and Drohobycz. (Eastern Front).

        GmOH: Der Weltkrieg 1914 bis 1918, Die Militarischen Operationen zu Lande, Band 7, Die Operationen des Jahres 1915. Die Ereignisse Winter und Frühjahr.

        RuOH: 1. The Russian Army in the World War.
              2. A Strategic Outline of the War 1914 –1915.
              3. A Strategic Outline of the War 1914 -1918.

19-21 May ....The Dardanelles/Gallipoli Campaign - the Battles of ANZAC - the defence of ANZAC.

        AuOH: 1. Official History of Australia in the War of 1914-1918, Volume I, The Story of Anzac Part I.
              2. Official History of Australia in the War of 1914-1918, Volume II, The Story of Anzac Part II.

        BrOH: Official History of the War, Military Operations, Gallipoli, Volume II, May 1915 to the Evacuation.

        GmOH: Der Weltkrieg 1914 bis 1918, Die Militarischen Operationen zu Lande, Band 7, Die Operationen des Jahres 1915. Die Ereignisse Winter und Frühjahr.

        NZOH: Official History of New Zealand's Effort in the Great War, Volume I Gallipoli.

        TOH: 1. Birinci Cihan Harbinde Türk Harbi, 1915 Yili Harekatleri, IIinci Cilt.
              2. Birinci Dünya Harbinde Türk Harbi, Vncu Cilt, Çanakkale Cephesi, 2nci Kitap, Amfibi Harekat.
              3. Birinci Dünya Harbinde Türk Harbi, V nci Cilt, Çanakkale Cephesi Harekâtı, 1 nci, 2 nci, Ve 3 ncu Kitaplarin Özetlenmis Tarihi, Haziran 1914 - 9 Ocak 1916 / A Brief History of the Çanakkale Campaign in the First World War (June 1914 – January 1916).

24-25 May ....The Second Battle of Ypres – the Battle of Bellewaerde Ridge.

        BrOH: Official History of the War, Military Operations, France and Belgium 1915, Volume II, Battles of Aubers Ridge, Festubert and Loos.

        COH: 1. Official History of the Canadian Forces in the Great War 1914 – 1919, Volume I.
              2. Canadian Expeditionary Force 1914 - 1919. The Official History of the Canadian Army in the First World War.

3. The Western Front 1914.

GmOH: 1. Der Weltkrieg 1914 bis 1918, Die Militarischen Operationen zu Lande, Band 7, Die Operationen des Jahres 1915. Die Ereignisse Winter und Frühjahr.
2. Die Bayern im Großen Kriege 1914-1918.

24 May – 11 June .... The Battle of Przemysl. (Eastern Front).

AHOH:.Österreich-Ungarns Letzter Krieg 1914-1918, Band II.

HOH: A világháború 1914-1918. Különös tekintettel Magyarországra és a Magyar csapatok szereplésére Szerkeszti és kiadja a M. Kir. Hadtörténelmi Levéltár, köt 9.

RuOH: 1. The Russian Army in the World War.
2. A Strategic Outline of the War 1914 –1915.
3. A Strategic Outline of the War 1914 -1918.

25 May .... The Dardanelles/Gallipoli Campaign - H.M.S. Triumph sunk by S.M.S. U21.

BrOH: Official History of the War, Naval Operations, Volume II.

GmOH: Der Krieg zur See 1914-1918, Band 5, Der Krieg in den türkischen Gewässern, Teil 2, Der Kampf un die Meerengen.

TOH: 1. Birinci Dünya Harbi, VIIInci Cilt, Türk Deniz Harekati.
2. Birinci Dünya Harbinde Türk Harbi, V nci Cilt, Çanakkale Cephesi Harekâtı, 1 nci, 2 nci, Ve 3 ncu Kitaplarin Özetlenmis Tarihi, Haziran 1914 - 9 Ocak 1916 / A Brief History of the Çanakkale Campaign in the First World War (June 1914 – January 1916).

27 May .... H.M.S. Princess Irene sunk by an internal explosion. (British Home Water).

BrOH: Official History of the War, Naval Operations, Volume II.

27 May .... The Dardanelles/Gallipoli Campaign - H.M.S. Majestic sunk by S.M.S. U21.

BrOH: Official History of the War, Naval Operations, Volume II.

GmOH: Der Krieg zur See 1914-1918, Band 5, Der Krieg in den türkischen Gewässern, Teil 2, Der Kampf un die Meerengen.

TOH: 1. Birinci Dünya Harbi, VIIInci Cilt, Türk Deniz Harekati.
2. Birinci Dünya Harbinde Türk Harbi, V nci Cilt, Çanakkale Cephesi Harekâtı, 1 nci, 2 nci, Ve 3 ncu Kitaplarin Özetlenmis Tarihi, Haziran 1914 - 9 Ocak 1916 / A Brief History of the Çanakkale Campaign in the First World War (June 1914 – January 1916).

30 May .... The affair of Sphinxhaven. (Rhodesia - East Africa).

BgOH: Les Campagnes Coloniales Belges 1914-1918. Volume I. Introduction, les Operations au Cameroun, les Operations en Rhodésie, la Période Défensive à la Frontière Orientale.

BrOH: Official History of the War, Military Operations, East Africa, Volume I, August 1914-September 1916.

GmOH: Der Krieg zur See 1914-1918, Band 6, Die Kämpfe der Kaiserlichen Marine in den deutschen Kolonien, Teil 2, Deutsch-Ostafrika.

SAOH: The Union of South Africa and the Great War 1914 – 1918.

31 May .... The first airship raid on London. (Britain).

> GmOH: Der Weltkrieg 1914 bis 1918, Die Militarischen Operationen zu Lande, Band 9, Die Operationen des Jahres 1915 – Die Ereignisse im Westen und auf dem Balkan vom Sommer bis Jahresschluß; Die Entwicklung der Luftstreitkrafte bis Ende 1915.

31 May – 3 June .... The second action of Qurna. (Mesopotamia).

> BrOH: Official History of the War, Military Operations, Campaign in Mesopotamia, Volume I.
>
> TOH: 1. Büyük Harbin Sevkülceyşi.
> 2. Birinci Cihan Harbinde Türk Harbi, 1915 Yili Harekatleri, IIinci Cilt.
> 3. Birinci Dünya Harbinde Türk Harbi, IIInvi Cilt, Irak-Iran Cephesi, 1914-1918, 1nci Kisim.
> 4. Büyük Harpte Misir Seferi.

31 May – 10June .... The Allied Operation against Garua – The Siege of Garua. (Cameroons).

> BgOH: Les Campagnes Coloniales Belges 1914-1918. Volume I. Introduction, les Operations au Cameroun, les Operations en Rhodésie, la Période Défensive à la Frontière Orientale.
>
> BrOH: Official History of the War, Military Operations, Togoland and the Cameroons.
>
> FrOH: Les Armées Françaises dans la Grande Guerre, Tome IX, Volume 2, Les campagnes coloniales: Cameroun – Togoland. – Opérations contre les Senoussis.

4 June .... The Dardanelles/Gallipoli Campaign - the Battles of Helles - the Third Battle of Krithia.

> BrOH: Official History of the War, Military Operations, Gallipoli, Volume II, May 1915 to the Evacuation.
>
> FrOH: Les Armées Françaises dans la Grande Guerre: Tome VIII La campagne d'Orient. Volume 1 La campagne d'Orient jusqu'a l'intervention de la Roumanie - février 1915-aòut 1916.
>
> GmOH: Der Weltkrieg 1914 bis 1918, Die Militarischen Operationen zu Lande, Band 7, Die Operationen des Jahres 1915. Die Ereignisse Winter und Frühjahr.
>
> TOH: 1. Birinci Cihan Harbinde Türk Harbi, 1915 Yili Harekatleri, IIinci Cilt.
> 2. Turk Silahe Kuvvetleri Tarihi Osmanlı Birinci Dünya Harbinde Türk Harbi, Vncu Cilt, Çanakkale Cephesi Harekati, 3ncu Kitap, Haziran 1915 – Ocak 1916.
> 3. Birinci Dünya Harbinde Türk Harbi, V nci Cilt, Çanakkale Cephesi Harekâtı, 1 nci, 2 nci, Ve 3 ncu Kitaplarin Özetlenmis Tarihi, Haziran 1914 - 9 Ocak 1916 / A Brief History of the Çanakkale Campaign in the First World War (June 1914 – January 1916).

7 June .... The first German airship LZ37 shot down and destroyed by an aircraft – Lt Warneford RNAS. (Western Front).

> BrOH: 1. Official History of the War, Naval Operations, Volume III.
> 2. Official History of the War, War in the Air, Volume II.
>
> GmOH: Der Weltkrieg 1914 bis 1918, Die Militarischen Operationen zu Lande, Band 9, Die Operationen des Jahres 1915 – Die Ereignisse im Westen und auf dem

Balkan vom Sommer bis Jahresschluß; Die Entwicklung der Luftstreitkrafte bis Ende 1915.

6-22 June ....The Battle of Zydaczow. (Eastern Front).

AHOH:.Österreich-Ungarns Letzter Krieg 1914-1918, Band II.

GmOH: Der Weltkrieg 1914 bis 1918, Die Militarischen Operationen zu Lande, Band 8, Die Operationen des Jahres 1915 - Die Ereignisse im Westen im Frühjahr im Sommer und Osten vom Frühjahr bis zum Jahresschluß.

HOH: A világháború 1914-1918. Különös tekintettel Magyarországra és a Magyar csapatok szereplésére Szerkeszti és kiadja a M. Kir. Hadtörténelmi Levéltár, köt 9.

RuOH: 1. The Russian Army in the World War.
2. A Strategic Outline of the War 1914 –1915.
3. A Strategic Outline of the War 1914 -1918.

12-15 June...The Battle of Mosciuska and Lubaczow. (Eastern Front).

AHOH: Österreich-Ungarns Letzter Krieg 1914-1918, Band II.

GmOH: Der Weltkrieg 1914 bis 1918, Die Militarischen Operationen zu Lande, Band 8, Die Operationen des Jahres 1915 - Die Ereignisse im Westen im Frühjahr im Sommer und Osten vom Frühjahr bis zum Jahresschluß.

HOH: A világháború 1914-1918. Különös tekintettel Magyarországra és a Magyar csapatok szereplésére Szerkeszti és kiadja a M. Kir. Hadtörténelmi Levéltár, köt 9.

RuOH: 1. The Russian Army in the World War.
2. A Strategic Outline of the War 1914 –1915.
3. A Strategic Outline of the War 1914 -1918.

14-15 June...The attack on Perim. (Arabia).

BrOH: ..Official History of the War, Military Operations, Egypt and Palestine, Volume I, From the Outbreak of War with Germany to June.

TOH: 1. Büyük Harbin Sevkülceyşi.
2. Birinci Cihan Harbinde Türk Harbi, 1915 Yili Harekatleri, IIinci Cilt.
3. Birinci Dünya Harbinde Türk Harbi VInci Cilt, Hicaz, Asir, Yeman Cepheleri ve Libya Harekati 1914-1918.
4..Büyük Harpte Misir Seferi.

17-22 June...The Thrid Battle of Lemberg. (Eastern Front).

AHOH: Österreich-Ungarns Letzter Krieg 1914-1918, Band II.

HOH: A világháború 1914-1918. Különös tekintettel Magyarországra és a Magyar csapatok szereplésére Szerkeszti és kiadja a M. Kir. Hadtörténelmi Levéltár, köt 9.

PlOH: Studia z wojny światowej 1914-1918 roku Tom IV: Bitwa pod Lwówem.

RuOH: 1. The Russian Army in the World War.
2. A Strategic Outline of the War 1914 –1915.
3. A Strategic Outline of the War 1914 -1918.

19 June – 1 July ....Advance and captured of Otavifontein. (South West Africa [Namibia]).

SAOH: 1. The Union of South Africa and the Great War 1914 – 1918.
2. The Campaign in German South West Africa 1914 – 1915.

27-29 June...The Battle of the Gnila Lipa. (Eastern Front).

AHOH: Österreich-Ungarns Letzter Krieg 1914-1918, Band II.

HOH: A világháború 1914-1918. Különös tekintettel Magyarországra és a Magyar csapatok szereplésére Szerkeszti és kiadja a M. Kir. Hadtörténelmi Levéltár, köt 9.

RuOH: 1. The Russian Army in the World War.
2. A Strategic Outline of the War 1914 –1915.
3. A Strategic Outline of the War 1914 -1918.

28 June...Ngaundere captured. (Cameroons).

BgOH: Les Campagnes Coloniales Belges 1914-1918. Volume I. Introduction, les Operations au Cameroun, les Operations en Rhodésie, la Période Défensive à la Frontière Orientale.

BrOH: Official History of the War, Military Operations, Togoland and the Cameroons.

FrOH: Les Armées Françaises dans la Grande Guerre, Tome IX, Volume 2, Les campagnes coloniales: Cameroun – Togoland. – Opérations contre les Senoussis.

28 June – 2 July ....The Dardanelles/Gallipoli Campaign - the action of Gully Ravine.

AuOH: Official History of Australia in the War of 1914-1918, Volume II, The Story of Anzac Part II.

BrOH: Official History of the War, Military Operations, Gallipoli, Volume II, May 1915 to the Evacuation.

GmOH: Der Weltkrieg 1914 bis 1918, Die Militarischen Operationen zu Lande, Band 8, Die Operationen des Jahres 1915 - Die Ereignisse im Westen im Frühjahr im Sommer und Osten vom Frühjahr bis zum Jahresschluß.

NZOH: Official History of New Zealand's Effort in the Great War, Volume I Gallipoli.

TOH: 1. Birinci Cihan Harbinde Türk Harbi, 1915 Yili Harekatleri, IIinci Cilt.
2. Turk Silahe Kuvvetleri Tarihi Osmanlı Birinci Dünya Harbinde Türk Harbi, Vncu Cilt, Çanakkale Cephesi Harekati, 3ncu Kitap, Haziran 1915 – Ocak 1916.
3. Birinci Dünya Harbinde Türk Harbi, V nci Cilt, Çanakkale Cephesi Harekâtı, 1 nci, 2 nci, Ve 3 ncu Kitaplarin Özetlenmis Tarihi, Haziran 1914 - 9 Ocak 1916 / A Brief History of the Çanakkale Campaign in the First World War (June 1914 – January 1916).

29 June – 7 July ....The First Battle of the Isonzo. (Italian Front).

AHOH:.Österreich-Ungarns Letzter Krieg 1914-1918, Band II.

HOH: A világháború 1914-1918. Különös tekintettel Magyarországra és a Magyar csapatok szereplésére Szerkeszti és kiadja a M. Kir. Hadtörténelmi Levéltár, köt 9.

IOH: Maggiore Esercito, Ufficio Storico, L'Esercito italiano nella grande guerra 1915-18, Volume II, Le Operazioni Del 1915.

1 July ....The capture of Otavifontein. (South West Africa [Namibia]).

SAOH: 1. The Union of South Africa and the Great War 1914 – 1918.
2. The Campaign in German South West Africa 1914 – 1915.

247

1-19 July .... The Second Battle of Krasnik. (Eastern Front).
                                                 AHOH: Österreich-Ungarns Letzter Krieg 1914-1918, Band II.
                                                 HOH: A világháború 1914-1918. Különös tekintettel Magyarországra és a Magyar csapatok szereplésére Szerkeszti és kiadja a M. Kir. Hadtörténelmi Levéltár, köt 9.
                                                 RuOH: 1. The Russian Army in the World War.
                                                         2. A Strategic Outline of the War 1914 –1915.
                                                          3. A Strategic Outline of the War 1914 -1918.

2 July .... The action of Gottland. (Baltic Sea).
                                                 GmOH: Der Krieg zur See, 1914-1918, Band 2, Der Krieg in der Ostsee, Teil 2, Das Kriegsjahr 1915.
                                                 RuOH:..Flot v Pervoi Mirovoi Voine. V Dvukh Tomakh. Tom I Deystviya Russkogo Flota.

4-5 July .... The action of Lahej. (Arabia).
                                                 BrOH: Official History of the War, Military Operations, Egypt and Palestine, Volume I, From the Outbreak of War with Germany to June.
                                                 TOH: 1. Büyük Harbin Sevkülceyşi.
                                                          2. Birinci Cihan Harbinde Türk Harbi, 1915 Yili Harekatleri, IIinci Cilt.
                                                          3. Birinci Dünya Harbinde Türk Harbi VInci Cilt, Hicaz, Asir, Yeman Cepheleri ve Libya Harekati 1914-1918.
                                                           4. Büyük Harpte Misir Seferi.

5 July .... The first action for Nasiriya. (Mesopotamia).
                                                 BrOH: Official History of the War, Military Operations, Campaign in Mesopotamia, Volume I.
                                                 TOH: 1. Büyük Harbin Sevkülceyşi.
                                                          2. Birinci Cihan Harbinde Türk Harbi, 1915 Yili Harekatleri, IIinci Cilt.
                                                         3. Birinci Dünya Harbinde Türk Harbi, IIInvi Cilt, Irak-Iran Cephesi, 1914-1918, 1nci Kisim.
                                                           4. Büyük Harpte Misir Seferi.

7 July .... The Italian cruiser Amalfi sunk. (Adriatic Sea).
                                                 IOH: Ufficio Storico della R. Marina, La Marina Italiana nella Grande Guerra, Volume II, L'Itervento Dell'Italia a Fianco Dell'Intesa e La Lotta in Adriatico.

9 July .... German South West Africa capitulates (South West Africa [Namibia]).
                                                 SAOH: 1. The Union of South Africa and the Great War 1914 – 1918.
                                                         2. The Campaign in German South West Africa 1914 – 1915.

11 July .... S.M.S. Königsberg destroyed in the Rufiji River. (East Africa).
                                                 BrOH: 1. Official History of the War, Naval Operations, Volume III.
                                                        2. Official History of the War, Military Operations, East Africa, Volume I, August 1914-September 1916.
                                                 GmOH: 1. Der Krieg zur See 1914-1918, Band 3, Der Kreuzerkrieg in den ausländischen Gewässern, Teil 2, Die Tätigkeit der Kleinen Kreuzer "Emden", "Königberg" und "Karlsruhe" Mit e Anhang: "Die Kriegsfahrt des Kleinen Kreuzers Geier".

2. Der Krieg zur See 1914-1918, Band 6, Die Kämpfe der Kaiserlichen Marine in den deutschen Kolonien, Teil 2, Deutsch-Ostafrika.

SAOH: The Union of South Africa and the Great War 1914 – 1918.

13-14 July ....The second action for Nasiriya. (Mesopotamia).

BrOH: Official History of the War, Military Operations, Campaign in Mesopotamia, Volume I.

TOH: 1. Büyük Harbin Sevkülceyşi.
2. Birinci Cihan Harbinde Türk Harbi, 1915 Yili Harekatleri, IIinci Cilt.
3. Birinci Dünya Harbinde Türk Harbi, IIInvi Cilt, Irak-Iran Cephesi, 1914-1918, 1nci Kisim.
4. Büyük Harpte Misir Seferi.

13-26 July ....The Austro-German offensives. (Eastern Front).

AHOH: Österreich-Ungarns Letzter Krieg 1914-1918, Band II.

GmOH: 1. Der Weltkrieg 1914 bis 1918, Die Militarischen Operationen zu Lande, Band 8, Die Operationen des Jahres 1915 - Die Ereignisse im Westen im Frühjahr im Sommer und Osten vom Frühjahr bis zum Jahresschluß.
2. Die Bayern im Großen Kriege 1914-1918.

HOH: A világháború 1914-1918. Különös tekintettel Magyarországra és a Magyar csapatok szereplésére Szerkeszti és kiadja a M. Kir. Hadtörténelmi Levéltár, köt 10.

RuOH: 1. The Russian Army in the World War.
2. A Strategic Outline of the War 1914 –1915.
3. A Strategic Outline of the War 1914 -1918.

13-26 July ....The Austro-German offensives – the Battle of the Narew and Bobr. (Eastern Front).

AHOH: Österreich-Ungarns Letzter Krieg 1914-1918, Band II.

GmOH: 1. Der Weltkrieg 1914 bis 1918, Die Militarischen Operationen zu Lande, Band 8, Die Operationen des Jahres 1915 - Die Ereignisse im Westen im Frühjahr im Sommer und Osten vom Frühjahr bis zum Jahresschluß.
2. Die Bayern im Großen Kriege 1914-1918.

HOH: A világháború 1914-1918. Különös tekintettel Magyarországra és a Magyar csapatok szereplésére Szerkeszti és kiadja a M. Kir. Hadtörténelmi Levéltár, köt 10.

RuOH: 1. The Russian Army in the World War.
2. A Strategic Outline of the War 1914 –1915.
3. A Strategic Outline of the War 1914 -1918.

13-17 July ....The Austro-German offensives – the Second Battle of Przasnysz. (Eastern Front).

GmOH: 1. Der Weltkrieg 1914 bis 1918, Die Militarischen Operationen zu Lande, Band 8, Die Operationen des Jahres 1915 - Die Ereignisse im Westen im Frühjahr im Sommer und Osten vom Frühjahr bis zum Jahresschluß.
2. Die Bayern im Großen Kriege 1914-1918.

RuOH: 1. The Russian Army in the World War.
2. A Strategic Outline of the War 1914 –1915.
3. A Strategic Outline of the War 1914 -1918.

13-18 July ....The Austro-German offensives – the Battle of Maslomencze and Grabowiec. (Eastern Front).

    AHOH:.Österreich-Ungarns Letzter Krieg 1914-1918, Band II.

    GmOH: 1. Der Weltkrieg 1914 bis 1918, Die Militarischen Operationen zu Lande, Band 8, Die Operationen des Jahres 1915 - Die Ereignisse im Westen im Frühjahr im Sommer und Osten vom Frühjahr bis zum Jahresschluß.

    2. Die Bayern im Großen Kriege 1914-1918.

    HOH: A világháború 1914-1918. Különös tekintettel Magyarországra és a Magyar csapatok szereplésére Szerkeszti és kiadja a M. Kir. Hadtörténelmi Levéltár, köt 10.

    RuUOH: 1. The Russian Army in the World War.

    2. A Strategic Outline of the War 1914 –1915.

    3. A Strategic Outline of the War 1914 -1918.

14-25 July ....The Battle of Schaulen. (Eastern Front).

    AHOH:.Österreich-Ungarns Letzter Krieg 1914-1918, Band II.

    GmOH: 1. Der Weltkrieg 1914 bis 1918, Die Militarischen Operationen zu Lande, Band 8, Die Operationen des Jahres 1915 - Die Ereignisse im Westen im Frühjahr im Sommer und Osten vom Frühjahr bis zum Jahresschluß.

    2. Die Bayern im Großen Kriege 1914-1918.

    HOH: A világháború 1914-1918. Különös tekintettel Magyarországra és a Magyar csapatok szereplésére Szerkeszti és kiadja a M. Kir. Hadtörténelmi Levéltár, köt 10.

    RuOH: 1. The Russian Army in the World War.

    2. A Strategic Outline of the War 1914 –1915.

    3. A Strategic Outline of the War 1914 -1918.

16-18 July ....The Battle of Krasnostav. (Eastern Front).

    AHOH:.Österreich-Ungarns Letzter Krieg 1914-1918, Band II.

    GmOH: 1. Der Weltkrieg 1914 bis 1918, Die Militarischen Operationen zu Lande, Band 8, Die Operationen des Jahres 1915 - Die Ereignisse im Westen im Frühjahr im Sommer und Osten vom Frühjahr bis zum Jahresschluß.

    2. Die Bayern im Großen Kriege 1914-1918.

    HOH: A világháború 1914-1918. Különös tekintettel Magyarországra és a Magyar csapatok szereplésére Szerkeszti és kiadja a M. Kir. Hadtörténelmi Levéltár, köt 10.

    RuOH: 1. The Russian Army in the World War.

    2. A Strategic Outline of the War 1914 –1915.

    3. A Strategic Outline of the War 1914 -1918.

17 July ....The Battle of Sienno. (Eastern Front).

    AHOH:.Österreich-Ungarns Letzter Krieg 1914-1918, Band II.

    HOH: A világháború 1914-1918. Különös tekintettel Magyarországra és a Magyar csapatok szereplésére Szerkeszti és kiadja a M. Kir. Hadtörténelmi Levéltár, köt 10.

    RuOH: 1. The Russian Army in the World War.

    2. A Strategic Outline of the War 1914 –1915.

    3. A Strategic Outline of the War 1914 -1918.

18 July ....The Italian cruiser Giuseppe Garibaldi sunk. (Adriatic Sea).

IOH: Ufficio Storico della R. Marina, La Marina Italiana nella Grande Guerra, Volume II, L'Itervento Dell'Italia a Fianco Dell'Intesa e La Lotta in Adriatico.

18 July – 10 August ....The Second Battle of the Isonzo. (Italian Front).

AHOH:.Österreich-Ungarns Letzter Krieg 1914-1918, Band II.

HOH: A világháború 1914-1918. Különös tekintettel Magyarországra és a Magyar csapatok szereplésére Szerkeszti és kiadja a M. Kir. Hadtörténelmi Levéltár, köt 10.

IOH: Maggiore Esercito, Ufficio Storico, L'Esercito italiano nella grande guerra 1915-18, Volume II, Le Operazioni Del 1915.

19-30 July ....The Battle of Hruhieszow and Wojslawice. (Eastern Front).

AHOH:.Österreich-Ungarns Letzter Krieg 1914-1918, Band II.

GmOH: 1. Der Weltkrieg 1914 bis 1918, Die Militarischen Operationen zu Lande, Band 8, Die Operationen des Jahres 1915 - Die Ereignisse im Westen im Frühjahr im Sommer und Osten vom Frühjahr bis zum Jahresschluß.
2. Die Bayern im Großen Kriege 1914-1918.

HOH: A világháború 1914-1918. Különös tekintettel Magyarországra és a Magyar csapatok szereplésére Szerkeszti és kiadja a M. Kir. Hadtörténelmi Levéltár, köt 10.

RuOH: 1. The Russian Army in the World War.
2. A Strategic Outline of the War 1914 –1915.
3. A Strategic Outline of the War 1914 -1918.

20 July ....The affair of Sheikh 'Othman. (Aden).

BrOH: Official History of the War, Military Operations, Campaign in Mesopotamia, Volume I.

TOH: 1. Büyük Harbin Sevkülceyşi.
2. Birinci Cihan Harbinde Türk Harbi, 1915 Yili Harekatleri, IInci Cilt.
3. Birinci Dünya Harbinde Türk Harbi, IIInvi Cilt, Irak-Iran Cephesi, 1914-1918, 1nci Kisim.
4. Büyük Harpte Misir Seferi.

20 July – 22 August ....The Allied Summer Actions – the Action of the Lingekopf. (Western Front).

FrOH: Les Armées Françaises dans la Grande Guerre, Tome III, Les offensives de 1915 - L'hiver de 1915–1916 - 1 mai 1915–21 février 1916.

GmOH: 1. Der Weltkrieg 1914 bis 1918, Die Militarischen Operationen zu Lande, Band 8, Die Operationen des Jahres 1915 - Die Ereignisse im Westen im Frühjahr im Sommer und Osten vom Frühjahr bis zum Jahresschluß.
2. Die Bayern im Großen Kriege 1914-1918.

20-21 July ....The Second Battle of Ivangorod. (Eastern Front).

AHOH: Österreich-Ungarns Letzter Krieg 1914-1918, Band II.

GmOH: 1. Der Weltkrieg 1914 bis 1918, Die Militarischen Operationen zu Lande, Band 8, Die Operationen des Jahres 1915 - Die Ereignisse im Westen im Frühjahr im Sommer und Osten vom Frühjahr bis zum Jahresschluß.
2. Die Bayern im Großen Kriege 1914-1918.

HOH: A világháború 1914-1918. Különös tekintettel Magyarországra és a Magyar csapatok szereplésére

Szerkeszti és kiadja a M. Kir. Hadtörténelmi Levéltár, köt 10.

RuOH: 1. The Russian Army in the World War.
2. A Strategic Outline of the War 1914 –1915.
3. A Strategic Outline of the War 1914 -1918.

BrOH: Official History of the War, Military Operations, Campaign in Mesopotamia, Volume I.
TOH: 1. Büyük Harbin Sevkülceyşi.
2. Birinci Cihan Harbinde Türk Harbi, 1915 Yili Harekatleri, IInci Cilt.
3. Birinci Dünya Harbinde Türk Harbi, IIInvi Cilt, Irak-Iran Cephesi, 1914-1918, 1nci Kisim.
4. Büyük Harpte Misir Seferi.

BgOH: Les Campagnes Coloniales Belges 1914-1918. Volume I. Introduction, les Operations au Cameroun, les Operations en Rhodésie, la Période Défensive à la Frontière Orientale.
BrOH: Official History of the War, Military Operations, East Africa, Volume I, August 1914-September 1916.
GmOH: Der Krieg zur See 1914-1918, Band 6, Die Kämpfe der Kaiserlichen Marine in den deutschen Kolonien, Teil 2, Deutsch-Ostafrika.
SAOH: The Union of South Africa and the Great War 1914 – 1918.

AHOH:.Österreich-Ungarns Letzter Krieg 1914-1918, Band II.
GmOH: 1. Der Weltkrieg 1914 bis 1918, Die Militarischen Operationen zu Lande, Band 8, Die Operationen des Jahres 1915 - Die Ereignisse im Westen im Frühjahr im Sommer und Osten vom Frühjahr bis zum Jahresschluß.
2. Die Bayern im Großen Kriege 1914-1918.
HOH: A világháború 1914-1918. Különös tekintettel Magyarországra és a Magyar csapatok szereplésére Szerkeszti és kiadja a M. Kir. Hadtörténelmi Levéltár, köt 10.
RuOH: 1. The Russian Army in the World War.
2. A Strategic Outline of the War 1914 –1915.
3. A Strategic Outline of the War 1914 -1918.

BrOH: Official History of the War, Military Operations, Campaign in Mesopotamia, Volume I.
TOH: 1. Büyük Harbin Sevkülceyşi.
2. Birinci Cihan Harbinde Türk Harbi, 1915 Yili Harekatleri, IInci Cilt.
3. Birinci Dünya Harbinde Türk Harbi, IIInvi Cilt, Irak-Iran Cephesi, 1914-1918, 1nci Kisim.
4. Büyük Harpte Misir Seferi.

IOH: Ufficio Storico della R. Marina, La Marina Italiana nella Grande Guerra, Volume II, L'Itervento Dell'Italia a Fianco Dell'Intesa e La Lotta in Adriatico.

29-30 July ....The Battle of Biskupice. (Eastern Front).
    AHOH:.Österreich-Ungarns Letzter Krieg 1914-1918, Band II.
    GmOH: 1. Der Weltkrieg 1914 bis 1918, Die Militarischen Operationen zu Lande, Band 8, Die Operationen des Jahres 1915 - Die Ereignisse im Westen im Frühjahr im Sommer und Osten vom Frühjahr bis zum Jahresschluß.
    2. Die Bayern im Großen Kriege 1914-1918.
    HOH: A világháború 1914-1918. Különös tekintettel Magyarországra és a Magyar csapatok szereplésére Szerkeszti és kiadja a M. Kir. Hadtörténelmi Levéltár, köt 10.
    RuOH: 1. The Russian Army in the World War.
    2. A Strategic Outline of the War 1914 –1915.
    3. A Strategic Outline of the War 1914 -1918.

30 July – 7 August ....The Battle of Kupischki. (Eastern Front).
    AHOH: Österreich-Ungarns Letzter Krieg 1914-1918, Band II.
    GmOH: 1. Der Weltkrieg 1914 bis 1918, Die Militarischen Operationen zu Lande, Band 8, Die Operationen des Jahres 1915 - Die Ereignisse im Westen im Frühjahr im Sommer und Osten vom Frühjahr bis zum Jahresschluß.
    2. Die Bayern im Großen Kriege 1914-1918.
    HOH: A világháború 1914-1918. Különös tekintettel Magyarországra és a Magyar csapatok szereplésére Szerkeszti és kiadja a M. Kir. Hadtörténelmi Levéltár, köt 10.
    RuOH: 1. The Russian Army in the World War.
    2. A Strategic Outline of the War 1914 –1915.
    3. A Strategic Outline of the War 1914 -1918.

31 July ....The Battle of Strelcze. (Eastern Front).
    AHOH: Österreich-Ungarns Letzter Krieg 1914-1918, Band II.
    GmOH: 1. Der Weltkrieg 1914 bis 1918, Die Militarischen Operationen zu Lande, Band 8, Die Operationen des Jahres 1915 - Die Ereignisse im Westen im Frühjahr im Sommer und Osten vom Frühjahr bis zum Jahresschluß.
    2. Die Bayern im Großen Kriege 1914-1918.
    HOH: A világháború 1914-1918. Különös tekintettel Magyarországra és a Magyar csapatok szereplésére Szerkeszti és kiadja a M. Kir. Hadtörténelmi Levéltár, köt 10.
    RuOH: 1. The Russian Army in the World War.
    2. A Strategic Outline of the War 1914 –1915.
    3. A Strategic Outline of the War 1914 -1918.

1 August..Constantinople harbour raided by a British submarine.
    BrOH: Official History of the War, Naval Operations, Volume II.
    GmOH: Der Krieg zur See 1914-1918, Band 5, Der Krieg in den türkischen Gewässern, Teil 2, Der Kampf un die Meerengen.

1-3 August ....The Battle of Cholm. (Eastern Front).
    AHOH: Österreich-Ungarns Letzter Krieg 1914-1918, Band II.
    GmOH: 1. Der Weltkrieg 1914 bis 1918, Die Militarischen Operationen zu Lande, Band 8, Die Operationen des Jahres 1915 - Die Ereignisse im Westen im Frühjahr im Sommer und Osten vom Frühjahr bis zum Jahresschluß.
    2. Die Bayern im Großen Kriege 1914-1918.

HOH: A világháború 1914-1918. Különös tekintettel Magyarországra és a Magyar csapatok szereplésére Szerkeszti és kiadja a M. Kir. Hadtörténelmi Levéltár, köt 10.

RuOH: 1. The Russian Army in the World War.
2. A Strategic Outline of the War 1914 –1915.
3. A Strategic Outline of the War 1914 -1918.

BrOH: Official History of the War, Military Operations, Gallipoli, Volume II, May 1915 to the Evacuation.

GmOH: Der Weltkrieg 1914 bis 1918, Die Militarischen Operationen zu Lande, Band 8, Die Operationen des Jahres 1915 - Die Ereignisse im Westen im Frühjahr im Sommer und Osten vom Frühjahr bis zum Jahresschluß.

TOH: 1. Birinci Cihan Harbinde Türk Harbi, 1915 Yili Harekatleri, IIinci Cilt.
2. Turk Silahe Kuvvetleri Tarihi Osmanlı Birinci Dünya Harbinde Türk Harbi, Vncu Cilt, Çanakkale Cephesi Harekati, 3ncu Kitap, Haziran 1915 – Ocak 1916.
3. Birinci Dünya Harbinde Türk Harbi, V nci Cilt, Çanakkale Cephesi Harekâtı, 1 nci, 2 nci, Ve 3 ncu Kitaplarin Özetlenmis Tarihi, Haziran 1914 - 9 Ocak 1916 / A Brief History of the Çanakkale Campaign in the First World War (June 1914 – January 1916).

BrOH: Official History of the War, Military Operations, Gallipoli, Volume II, May 1915 to the Evacuation.

GmOH: Der Weltkrieg 1914 bis 1918, Die Militarischen Operationen zu Lande, Band 8, Die Operationen des Jahres 1915 - Die Ereignisse im Westen im Frühjahr im Sommer und Osten vom Frühjahr bis zum Jahresschluß.

TOH: 1. Birinci Cihan Harbinde Türk Harbi, 1915 Yili Harekatleri, IIinci Cilt.
2. Turk Silahe Kuvvetleri Tarihi Osmanlı Birinci Dünya Harbinde Türk Harbi, Vncu Cilt, Çanakkale Cephesi Harekati, 3ncu Kitap, Haziran 1915 – Ocak 1916.
3. Birinci Dünya Harbinde Türk Harbi, V nci Cilt, Çanakkale Cephesi Harekâtı, 1 nci, 2 nci, Ve 3 ncu Kitaplarin Özetlenmis Tarihi, Haziran 1914 - 9 Ocak 1916 / A Brief History of the Çanakkale Campaign in the First World War (June 1914 – January 1916).

AHOH: Österreich-Ungarns Letzter Krieg 1914-1918, Band II.

GmOH: 1. Der Weltkrieg 1914 bis 1918, Die Militarischen Operationen zu Lande, Band 8, Die Operationen des Jahres 1915 - Die Ereignisse im Westen im Frühjahr im Sommer und Osten vom Frühjahr bis zum Jahresschluß.
2. Die Bayern im Großen Kriege 1914-1918.

HOH: A világháború 1914-1918. Különös tekintettel Magyarországra és a Magyar csapatok szereplésére Szerkeszti és kiadja a M. Kir. Hadtörténelmi Levéltár, köt 10.

RuOH: 1. The Russian Army in the World War.
2. A Strategic Outline of the War 1914 –1915.

3. A Strategic Outline of the War 1914 -1918.

7-12 August ....The Battle of Ucherka. (Eastern Front).
AHOH: Österreich-Ungarns Letzter Krieg 1914-1918, Band II.
GmOH: 1. Der Weltkrieg 1914 bis 1918, Die Militarischen Operationen zu Lande, Band 8, Die Operationen des Jahres 1915 - Die Ereignisse im Westen im Frühjahr im Sommer und Osten vom Frühjahr bis zum Jahresschluß.
2. Die Bayern im Großen Kriege 1914-1918.
HOH: A világháború 1914-1918. Különös tekintettel Magyarországra és a Magyar csapatok szereplésére Szerkeszti és kiadja a M. Kir. Hadtörténelmi Levéltár, köt 10.
RuOH: 1. The Russian Army in the World War.
2. A Strategic Outline of the War 1914 –1915.
3. A Strategic Outline of the War 1914 -1918.

8 August...Turkish battleship Barbarousse-Hairedine sunk by H.M.S. E11. (Black Sea).
BrOH: Official History of the War, Naval Operations, Volume III.
TOH: Birinci Dünya Harbi, VIIInci Cilt, Türk Deniz Harekati.
RuOH:..Flot v Pervoi Mirovoi Voine. V Dvukh Tomakh. Tom I Deystviya Russkogo Flota.

8 August...Bushire occupied. (Persia).
BrOH: Official History of the War, Military Operations, Operations in Persia 1915-1919.
TOH: 1. Büyük Harbin Sevkülceyşi.
2. Birinci Cihan Harbinde Türk Harbi, 1916 Yili Harekatleri, IIIncu Cilt.
3. Birinci Dünya Harbinde Türk Harbi VInci Cilt, Hicaz, Asir, Yeman Cepheleri ve Libya Harekati 1914-1918.
4. Büyük Harpte Misir Seferi.

8-10 August ....The Battle of Ostrov. (Eastern Front).
AHOH: Österreich-Ungarns Letzter Krieg 1914-1918, Band II.
GmOH: 1. Der Weltkrieg 1914 bis 1918, Die Militarischen Operationen zu Lande, Band 7, Die Operationen des Jahres 1915. Die Ereignisse Winter und Frühjahr.
2. Die Bayern im Großen Kriege 1914-1918.
HOH: A világháború 1914-1918. Különös tekintettel Magyarországra és a Magyar csapatok szereplésére Szerkeszti és kiadja a M. Kir. Hadtörténelmi Levéltár, köt 10.
RuOH: 1. The Russian Army in the World War.
2. A Strategic Outline of the War 1914 –1915.
3. A Strategic Outline of the War 1914 -1918.

8-18 August ....The Siege of Kowno. (Eastern Front).
AHOH: Österreich-Ungarns Letzter Krieg 1914-1918, Band II.
GmOH: 1. Der Weltkrieg 1914 bis 1918, Die Militarischen Operationen zu Lande, Band 8, Die Operationen des Jahres 1915 - Die Ereignisse im Westen im Frühjahr im Sommer und Osten vom Frühjahr bis zum Jahresschluß.
2. Die Bayern im Großen Kriege 1914-1918.
HOH: A világháború 1914-1918. Különös tekintettel Magyarországra és a Magyar csapatok szereplésére

Szerkeszti és kiadja a M. Kir. Hadtörténelmi Levéltár, köt 10.

RuOH: 1. The Russian Army in the World War.
2. A Strategic Outline of the War 1914 –1915.
3. A Strategic Outline of the War 1914 -1918.

8-21 August .... The attack on Riga.

GmOH: Der Weltkrieg 1914 bis 1918, Die Militarischen Operationen zu Lande, Band 8, Die Operationen des Jahres 1915 - Die Ereignisse im Westen im Frühjahr im Sommer und Osten vom Frühjahr bis zum Jahresschluß.

RuOH: 1. The Russian Army in the World War.
2. A Strategic Outline of the War 1914 –1915.
3. A Strategic Outline of the War 1914 -1918.

10 August.. The German airship L12 damaged by British aircraft over Ostend.

BrOH: Official History of the War, War in the Air, Volume III.

GmOH: Der Weltkrieg 1914 bis 1918, Die Militarischen Operationen zu Lande, Band 9, Die Operationen des Jahres 1915 – Die Ereignisse im Westen und auf dem Balkan vom Sommer bis Jahresschluß; Die Entwicklung der Luftstreitkrafte bis Ende 1915.

10 August .... First enemy ship sunk by torpedo lunched from British seaplane. (Dardanelles Sea).

BrOH: Official History of the War, Naval Operations, Volume III.

GmOH: Der Krieg zur See 1914-1918, Band 5, Der Krieg in den türkischen Gewässern, Teil 2, Der Kampf un die Meerengen.

11-12 August .... The Battle of Tschishew-Sambrow. (Eastern Front).

AHOH: Österreich-Ungarns Letzter Krieg 1914-1918, Band II.

GmOH: 1. Der Weltkrieg 1914 bis 1918, Die Militarischen Operationen zu Lande, Band 7, Die Operationen des Jahres 1915. Die Ereignisse Winter und Frühjahr.
2. Die Bayern im Großen Kriege 1914-1918.

HOH: A világháború 1914-1918. Különös tekintettel Magyarországra és a Magyar csapatok szereplésére Szerkeszti és kiadja a M. Kir. Hadtörténelmi Levéltár, köt 10.

RuOH: 1. The Russian Army in the World War.
2. A Strategic Outline of the War 1914 –1915.
3. A Strategic Outline of the War 1914 -1918.

12-16 August .... Destruction of Dilbar. (Persia).

BrOH: Official History of the War, Military Operations, Operations in Persia 1915-1919.

TOH: 1. Büyük Harbin Sevkülceyşi.
2. Birinci Cihan Harbinde Türk Harbi, 1916 Yili Harekatleri, IIIncu Cilt.
3. Birinci Dünya Harbinde Türk Harbi VInci Cilt, Hicaz, Asir, Yeman Cepheleri ve Libya Harekati 1914-1918.
4. Büyük Harpte Misir Seferi.

12-19 August .... The Battle of Schimanzy-Ponedeli. (Eastern Front).

AHOH: Österreich-Ungarns Letzter Krieg 1914-1918, Band II.

GmOH: 1. Der Weltkrieg 1914 bis 1918, Die Militarischen Operationen zu Lande, Band 8, Die Operationen des

Jahres 1915 - Die Ereignisse im Westen im Frühjahr im Sommer und Osten vom Frühjahr bis zum Jahresschluß.

2. Die Bayern im Großen Kriege 1914-1918.

HOH: A világháború 1914-1918. Különös tekintettel Magyarországra és a Magyar csapatok szereplésére Szerkeszti és kiadja a M. Kir. Hadtörténelmi Levéltár, köt 10.

RuOH: 1. The Russian Army in the World War.

2. A Strategic Outline of the War 1914 –1915.

3. A Strategic Outline of the War 1914 -1918.

13 August..H.M.T.S. Royal Edward sunk by a submarine. (Mediterranean Sea).

BrOH: Official History of the War, Naval Operations, Volume III.

GmOH: Der Krieg zur See 1914-1918, Band 5, Der Krieg in den türkischen Gewässern, Teil 2, Der Kampf un die Meerengen.

13-17 August ....The Battle of Wlodawa. (Eastern Front).

AHOH: Österreich-Ungarns Letzter Krieg 1914-1918, Band II.

GmOH: 1. Der Weltkrieg 1914 bis 1918, Die Militarischen Operationen zu Lande, Band 8, Die Operationen des Jahres 1915 - Die Ereignisse im Westen im Frühjahr im Sommer und Osten vom Frühjahr bis zum Jahresschluß.

2. Die Bayern im Großen Kriege 1914-1918.

HOH: A világháború 1914-1918. Különös tekintettel Magyarországra és a Magyar csapatok szereplésére Szerkeszti és kiadja a M. Kir. Hadtörténelmi Levéltár, köt 10.

RuOH: 1. The Russian Army in the World War.

2. A Strategic Outline of the War 1914 –1915.

3. A Strategic Outline of the War 1914 -1918.

16 August..Lowca and Harrington shelled by a German submarine in the North Sea. (British Home Waters).

BrOH: Official History of the War, Naval Operations, Volume III.

GmOH: 1. Der Krieg zur See 1914-1918, Band 1, Der Krieg in der Nordsee, Teil 3, Von Anfang November 1914 bis Anfang Februar 1915.

2. Der Krieg zur See 1914-1918, Band 4, Der Handelskrieg mit U-Booten, Teil 2, Februar bis September 1915.

19 August..S.S. Arabic sunk by German Submarine. (British Home Waters).

BrOH: 1. Official History of the War, Naval Operations, Volume III.

2. Official History of the War, Seaborne Trade, Volume II, Submarine Campaign, Part I.

3. Official History of the War, The Merchant Navy, Volume I.

GmOH: Der Krieg zur See 1914-1918, Band 4, Der Handelskrieg mit U-Booten, Teil 2, Februar bis September 1915.

19 August..S.M.S. U.27 sunk by H.M.S. Baralong. (British Home Waters).

BrOH: Official History of the War, Naval Operations, Volume III.

GmOH: Der Krieg zur See 1914-1918, Band 4, Der Handelskrieg mit U-Booten, Teil 2, Februar bis September 1915.

19 August...S.M.S. Moltke torpedoed by H.M.S. E1. (Baltic Sea).
                                 BrOH: Official History of the War, Naval Operations, Volume III.
                                 GmOH: Der Krieg zur See 1914-1918, Band 2, Der Krieg in der Ostsee, Teil 2, Das Kriegsjahr 1915.
                                 RuOH:..Flot v Pervoi Mirovoi Voine. V Dvukh Tomakh. Tom I Deystviya Russkogo Flota.

19 August...H.M.S. E13 attacked by German battleships. (Baltic Sea).
                                 BrOH: Official History of the War, Naval Operations, Volume III.
                                 GmOH: Der Krieg zur See 1914-1918, Band 2, Der Krieg in der Ostsee, Teil 2, Das Kriegsjahr 1915.
                                 RuOH:..Flot v Pervoi Mirovoi Voine. V Dvukh Tomakh. Tom I Deystviya Russkogo Flota.

19 August – 8 September...................The Battle of the Niemen. (Eastern Front).
                                 AHOH:.Österreich-Ungarns Letzter Krieg 1914-1918, Band II.
                                 GmOH: 1. Der Weltkrieg 1914 bis 1918, Die Militarischen Operationen zu Lande, Band 8, Die Operationen des Jahres 1915 - Die Ereignisse im Westen im Frühjahr im Sommer und Osten vom Frühjahr bis zum Jahresschluß.
                                 2. Die Bayern im Großen Kriege 1914-1918.
                                 HOH: A világháború 1914-1918. Különös tekintettel Magyarországra és a Magyar csapatok szereplésére Szerkeszti és kiadja a M. Kir. Hadtörténelmi Levéltár, köt 10.
                                 RuOH: 1. The Russian Army in the World War.
                                 2. A Strategic Outline of the War 1914 –1915.
                                 3. A Strategic Outline of the War 1914 -1918.

19-25 August ....The Battle of Bielst. (Eastern Front).
                                 AHOH: Österreich-Ungarns Letzter Krieg 1914-1918, Band II.
                                 GmOH: 1. Der Weltkrieg 1914 bis 1918, Die Militarischen Operationen zu Lande, Band 8, Die Operationen des Jahres 1915 - Die Ereignisse im Westen im Frühjahr im Sommer und Osten vom Frühjahr bis zum Jahresschluß.
                                   2. Die Bayern im Großen Kriege 1914-1918.
                                 HOH: A világháború 1914-1918. Különös tekintettel Magyarországra és a Magyar csapatok szereplésére Szerkeszti és kiadja a M. Kir. Hadtörténelmi Levéltár, köt 10.
                                 RuOH: 1. The Russian Army in the World War.
                                 2. A Strategic Outline of the War 1914 –1915.
                                 3. A Strategic Outline of the War 1914 -1918.

19-24 August ....The Battle of the Pulwa-Nursec. (Eastern Front).
                                 AHOH: Österreich-Ungarns Letzter Krieg 1914-1918, Band II.
                                 GmOH: 1. Der Weltkrieg 1914 bis 1918, Die Militarischen Operationen zu Lande, Band 7, Die Operationen des Jahres 1915 - Die Ereignisse im Westen im Frühjahr im Sommer und Osten vom Frühjahr bis zum Jahresschluß.
                                   2. Die Bayern im Großen Kriege 1914-1918.
                                 HOH: A világháború 1914-1918. Különös tekintettel Magyarországra és a Magyar csapatok szereplésére Szerkeszti és kiadja a M. Kir. Hadtörténelmi Levéltár, köt 10.
                                 RuOH: 1. The Russian Army in the World War.

2. A Strategic Outline of the War 1914 –1915.
3. A Strategic Outline of the War 1914 -1918.

20 August..The Battle for Novo-Georgievsk. (Eastern Front).
AHOH: Österreich-Ungarns Letzter Krieg 1914-1918, Band II.
GmOH: 1. Der Weltkrieg 1914 bis 1918, Die Militarischen Operationen zu Lande, Band 8, Die Operationen des Jahres 1915. Die Ereignisse Winter und Frühjahr.
2. Die Bayern im Großen Kriege 1914-1918.
HOH: A világháború 1914-1918. Különös tekintettel Magyarországra és a Magyar csapatok szereplésére Szerkeszti és kiadja a M. Kir. Hadtörténelmi Levéltár, köt 10.
RuOH: 1. The Russian Army in the World War.
2. A Strategic Outline of the War 1914 –1915.
3. A Strategic Outline of the War 1914 -1918.

20 August..The Battle for Osovets. (Eastern Front).
AHOH: Österreich-Ungarns Letzter Krieg 1914-1918, Band II.
GmOH: 1. Der Weltkrieg 1914 bis 1918, Die Militarischen Operationen zu Lande, Band 8, Die Operationen des Jahres 1915 - Die Ereignisse im Westen im Frühjahr im Sommer und Osten vom Frühjahr bis zum Jahresschluß.
2. Die Bayern im Großen Kriege 1914-1918.
HOH: A világháború 1914-1918. Különös tekintettel Magyarországra és a Magyar csapatok szereplésére Szerkeszti és kiadja a M. Kir. Hadtörténelmi Levéltár, köt 10.
RuOH: 1. The Russian Army in the World War.
2. A Strategic Outline of the War 1914 –1915.
3. A Strategic Outline of the War 1914 -1918.

21 August..German submarine fired on crew in lifeboats of S.S. Ruel. (British Home Waters).
BrOH: 1. Official History of the War, Naval Operations, Volume III.
2. Official History of the War, Seaborne Trade, Volume II, Submarine Campaign, Part I.
3. Official History of the War, The Merchant Navy, Volume I.
GmOH: Der Krieg zur See 1914-1918, Band 4, Der Handelskrieg mit U-Booten, Teil 2, Februar bis September 1915.

21 August..The Dardanelles/Gallipoli Campaign - the Battles of Suvla - the Battle of Scimitar Hill..
BrOH: Official History of the War, Military Operations, Gallipoli, Volume II, May 1915 to the Evacuation.
GmOH: Der Weltkrieg 1914 bis 1918, Die Militarischen Operationen zu Lande, Band 8, Die Operationen des Jahres 1915 - Die Ereignisse im Westen im Frühjahr im Sommer und Osten vom Frühjahr bis zum Jahresschluß.
TOH: 1. Birinci Cihan Harbinde Türk Harbi, 1915 Yili Harekatleri, IInci Cilt.
2. Turk Silahe Kuvvetleri Tarihi Osmanlı Birinci Dünya Harbinde Türk Harbi, Vncu Cilt, Çanakkale Cephesi Harekati, 3ncu Kitap, Haziran 1915 – Ocak 1916.
3. Birinci Dünya Harbinde Türk Harbi, V nci Cilt, Çanakkale Cephesi Harekâtı, 1 nci, 2 nci, Ve 3 ncu Kitaplarin Özetlenmis Tarihi, Haziran 1914 - 9 Ocak 1916

/ A Brief History of the Çanakkale Campaign in the First World War (June 1914 – January 1916).

25-26 August ....The Battle for Brest-Litovsk. (Eastern Front).

        AHOH: Österreich-Ungarns Letzter Krieg 1914-1918, Band II.

        GmOH: 1. Der Weltkrieg 1914 bis 1918, Die Militarischen Operationen zu Lande, Band 8, Die Operationen des Jahres 1915 - Die Ereignisse im Westen im Frühjahr im Sommer und Osten vom Frühjahr bis zum Jahresschluß.
2. Die Bayern im Großen Kriege 1914-1918.

        HOH: A világháború 1914-1918. Különös tekintettel Magyarországra és a Magyar csapatok szereplésére Szerkeszti és kiadja a M. Kir. Hadtörténelmi Levéltár, köt 10.

        RuOH: 1. The Russian Army in the World War.
2. A Strategic Outline of the War 1914 –1915.
3. A Strategic Outline of the War 1914 -1918.

27 August...The Battle of the Zlota-Lipa. (Eastern Front).

        AHOH: Österreich-Ungarns Letzter Krieg 1914-1918, Band II.

        GmOH: 1. Der Weltkrieg 1914 bis 1918, Die Militarischen Operationen zu Lande, Band 8, Die Operationen des Jahres 1915 - Die Ereignisse im Westen im Frühjahr im Sommer und Osten vom Frühjahr bis zum Jahresschluß.
2. Die Bayern im Großen Kriege 1914-1918.

        HOH: A világháború 1914-1918. Különös tekintettel Magyarországra és a Magyar csapatok szereplésére Szerkeszti és kiadja a M. Kir. Hadtörténelmi Levéltár, köt 10.

        RuOH: 1. The Russian Army in the World War.
2. A Strategic Outline of the War 1914 –1915.
3. A Strategic Outline of the War 1914 -1918.

31 August – 1 September...................The Battle of Horodec. (Eastern Front).

        AHOH: Österreich-Ungarns Letzter Krieg 1914-1918, Band II.

        GmOH: 1. Der Weltkrieg 1914 bis 1918, Die Militarischen Operationen zu Lande, Band 8, Die Operationen des Jahres 1915 - Die Ereignisse im Westen im Frühjahr im Sommer und Osten vom Frühjahr bis zum Jahresschluß.
2. Die Bayern im Großen Kriege 1914-1918.

        HOH: A világháború 1914-1918. Különös tekintettel Magyarországra és a Magyar csapatok szereplésére Szerkeszti és kiadja a M. Kir. Hadtörténelmi Levéltár, köt 10.

        RuOH: 1. The Russian Army in the World War.
2. A Strategic Outline of the War 1914 –1915.
3. A Strategic Outline of the War 1914 -1918.

1 September ....Ruad Island Occupied. (Mediterranean Sea).

        FrOH: Les Armées Françaises dans la Grande Guerre, Tome VIII, La campagne d'Orient, Volume 1, La campagne d'Orient jusqu'a l'intervention de la Roumanie - février 1915-aôut 1916.

2-3 September...................................The Battle of Grodno. (Eastern Front).

        AHOH: Österreich-Ungarns Letzter Krieg 1914-1918, Band II.

        GmOH: 1. Der Weltkrieg 1914 bis 1918, Die Militarischen Operationen zu Lande, Band 8, Die Operationen des

Jahres 1915 - Die Ereignisse im Westen im Frühjahr im Sommer und Osten vom Frühjahr bis zum Jahresschluß.

2. Die Bayern im Großen Kriege 1914-1918.

HOH: A világháború 1914-1918. Különös tekintettel Magyarországra és a Magyar csapatok szereplésére Szerkeszti és kiadja a M. Kir. Hadtörténelmi Levéltár, köt 10.

RuOH: 1. The Russian Army in the World War.

2. A Strategic Outline of the War 1914 –1915.

3. A Strategic Outline of the War 1914 -1918.

4-6 September....................................The Battle of Drohiczyn-Chomst. (Eastern Front).

AHOH: Österreich-Ungarns Letzter Krieg 1914-1918, Band II.

GmOH: 1. Der Weltkrieg 1914 bis 1918, Die Militarischen Operationen zu Lande, Band 8, Die Operationen des Jahres 1915 - Die Ereignisse im Westen im Frühjahr im Sommer und Osten vom Frühjahr bis zum Jahresschluß.

2. Die Bayern im Großen Kriege 1914-1918.

HOH: A világháború 1914-1918. Különös tekintettel Magyarországra és a Magyar csapatok szereplésére Szerkeszti és kiadja a M. Kir. Hadtörténelmi Levéltár, köt 10.

RuOH: 1. The Russian Army in the World War.

2. A Strategic Outline of the War 1914 –1915.

3. A Strategic Outline of the War 1914 -1918.

5 September ....The first action of Hafiz Kor. (NW Frontier of India).

BrOH: Official History of the War, Military Operations, Operations in Persia 1915-1919.

TOH: Birinci Cihan Harbinde Türk Harbi, 1915 Yili Harekatleri, IIinci Cilt.

6-7 September....................................The Battle of Wolkowyszk. (Eastern Front).

AHOH: Österreich-Ungarns Letzter Krieg 1914-1918, Band II.

GmOH: 1. Der Weltkrieg 1914 bis 1918, Die Militarischen Operationen zu Lande, Band 8, Die Operationen des Jahres 1915 - Die Ereignisse im Westen im Frühjahr im Sommer und Osten vom Frühjahr bis zum Jahresschluß.

2. Die Bayern im Großen Kriege 1914-1918.

HOH: A világháború 1914-1918. Különös tekintettel Magyarországra és a Magyar csapatok szereplésére Szerkeszti és kiadja a M. Kir. Hadtörténelmi Levéltár, köt 10.

RuOH: 1. The Russian Army in the World War.

2. A Strategic Outline of the War 1914 –1915.

3. A Strategic Outline of the War 1914 -1918.

6-16 September..................................The Battle of Tarnopol. (Eastern Front).

AHOH: Österreich-Ungarns Letzter Krieg 1914-1918, Band II.

GmOH: 1. Der Weltkrieg 1914 bis 1918, Die Militarischen Operationen zu Lande, Band 8, Die Operationen des Jahres 1915 - Die Ereignisse im Westen im Frühjahr im Sommer und Osten vom Frühjahr bis zum Jahresschluß.

2. Die Bayern im Großen Kriege 1914-1918.

HOH: A világháború 1914-1918. Különös tekintettel Magyarországra és a Magyar csapatok szereplésére Szerkeszti és kiadja a M. Kir. Hadtörténelmi Levéltár, köt 10.

RuOH: 1. The Russian Army in the World War.

2. A Strategic Outline of the War 1914 –1915.
3. A Strategic Outline of the War 1914 -1918.

8-9 September...................................The second attack on Mora. (Cameroons).
                     BgOH: Les Campagnes Coloniales Belges 1914-1918. Volume I. Introduction, les Operations au Cameroun, les Operations en Rhodésie, la Période Défensive à la Frontière Orientale.
                     BrOH: Official History of the War, Military Operations, Togoland and the Cameroons.
                     FrOH: Les Armées Françaises dans la Grande Guerre, Tome IX, Volume 2, Les campagnes coloniales: Cameroun – Togoland. – Opérations contre les Senoussis.

8-12 September.................................The Battle of the Zelwianka and the Niemen. (Eastern Front).
                     AHOH: Österreich-Ungarns Letzter Krieg 1914-1918, Band II.
                     GmOH: 1. Der Weltkrieg 1914 bis 1918, Die Militarischen Operationen zu Lande, Band 8, Die Operationen des Jahres 1915 - Die Ereignisse im Westen im Frühjahr im Sommer und Osten vom Frühjahr bis zum Jahresschluß.
                             2. Die Bayern im Großen Kriege 1914-1918.
                     HOH: A világháború 1914-1918. Különös tekintettel Magyarországra és a Magyar csapatok szereplésére Szerkeszti és kiadja a M. Kir. Hadtörténelmi Levéltár, köt 10.
                     RuOH: 1. The Russian Army in the World War.
                             2. A Strategic Outline of the War 1914 –1915.
                             3. A Strategic Outline of the War 1914 -1918.

9 September – 1 November...............The Battle of Dvinsk. (Eastern Front).
                     AHOH: Österreich-Ungarns Letzter Krieg 1914-1918, Band II.
                       GmOH: 1. Der Weltkrieg 1914 bis 1918, Die Militarischen Operationen zu Lande, Band 8, Die Operationen des Jahres 1915 - Die Ereignisse im Westen im Frühjahr im Sommer und Osten vom Frühjahr bis zum Jahresschluß.
                             2. Die Bayern im Großen Kriege 1914-1918.
                     HOH: A világháború 1914-1918. Különös tekintettel Magyarországra és a Magyar csapatok szereplésére Szerkeszti és kiadja a M. Kir. Hadtörténelmi Levéltár, köt 10.
                     RuOH: 1. The Russian Army in the World War.
                             2. A Strategic Outline of the War 1914 –1915.
                             3. A Strategic Outline of the War 1914 -1918.

9 September – 2 October...................The Battle of Vilna. (Eastern Front).
                     AHOH: Österreich-Ungarns Letzter Krieg 1914-1918, Band II.
                       GmOH: 1. Der Weltkrieg 1914 bis 1918, Die Militarischen Operationen zu Lande, Band 8, Die Operationen des Jahres 1915 - Die Ereignisse im Westen im Frühjahr im Sommer und Osten vom Frühjahr bis zum Jahresschluß.
                             2. Die Bayern im Großen Kriege 1914-1918.
                     HOH: A világháború 1914-1918. Különös tekintettel Magyarországra és a Magyar csapatok szereplésére Szerkeszti és kiadja a M. Kir. Hadtörténelmi Levéltár, köt 10.
                     RuOH: 1. The Russian Army in the World War.
                             2. A Strategic Outline of the War 1914 –1915.
                             3. A Strategic Outline of the War 1914 -1918.

12-17 September ....The Battle of the Szczara and Jelnia. (Eastern Front).

        AHOH: Österreich-Ungarns Letzter Krieg 1914-1918, Band II.

        GmOH: 1. Der Weltkrieg 1914 bis 1918, Die Militarischen Operationen zu Lande, Band 8, Die Operationen des Jahres 1915 - Die Ereignisse im Westen im Frühjahr im Sommer und Osten vom Frühjahr bis zum Jahresschluß..

        2. Die Bayern im Großen Kriege 1914-1918.

        HOH: A világháború 1914-1918. Különös tekintettel Magyarországra és a Magyar csapatok szereplésére Szerkeszti és kiadja a M. Kir. Hadtörténelmi Levéltár, köt 10.

        RuOH: 1. The Russian Army in the World War.

        2. A Strategic Outline of the War 1914 –1915.

        3. A Strategic Outline of the War 1914 -1918.

12-18 September ....The Battle of Slonim. (Eastern Front).

        AHOH: Österreich-Ungarns Letzter Krieg 1914-1918, Band II.

        GmOH: 1. Der Weltkrieg 1914 bis 1918, Die Militarischen Operationen zu Lande, Band 8, Die Operationen des Jahres 1915 - Die Ereignisse im Westen im Frühjahr im Sommer und Osten vom Frühjahr bis zum Jahresschluß.

        2. Die Bayern im Großen Kriege 1914-1918.

        HOH: A világháború 1914-1918. Különös tekintettel Magyarországra és a Magyar csapatok szereplésére Szerkeszti és kiadja a M. Kir. Hadtörténelmi Levéltár, köt 10.

        RuOH: 1. The Russian Army in the World War.

        2. A Strategic Outline of the War 1914 –1915.

        3. A Strategic Outline of the War 1914 -1918.

16 September ....The Battle for Pinsk. (Eastern Front).

        AHOH: Österreich-Ungarns Letzter Krieg 1914-1918, Band II.

        GmOH: 1. Der Weltkrieg 1914 bis 1918, Die Militarischen Operationen zu Lande, Band 7, Die Operationen des Jahres 1915. Die Ereignisse Winter und Frühjahr.

        2. Die Bayern im Großen Kriege 1914-1918.

        HOH: A világháború 1914-1918. Különös tekintettel Magyarországra és a Magyar csapatok szereplésére Szerkeszti és kiadja a M. Kir. Hadtörténelmi Levéltár, köt 10.

        RuOH: 1. The Russian Army in the World War.

        2. A Strategic Outline of the War 1914 –1915.

        3. A Strategic Outline of the War 1914 -1918.

25 September - 8 October ....The Allied Autumn Offensives - the Battle of Loos. (Western Front).

        BrOH: Official History of the War, Military Operations, France and Belgium 1915 Volume II, Battles of Aubers Ridge, Festubert and Loos.

        GmOH: 1. Der Weltkrieg 1914 bis 1918, Die Militarischen Operationen zu Lande, Band 7, Die Operationen des Jahres 1915. Die Ereignisse Winter und Frühjahr.

        2. Die Bayern im Großen Kriege 1914-1918.

25 September – 6 November..............The Allied Autumn Offensives - the Second Battle of Champagne. (Western Front).

        FrOH: Les Armées Françaises dans la Grande Guerre, Tome III, Les offensives de 1915 - L'hiver de 1915–1916 - 1 mai 1915–21 février 1916.

GmOH: Der Weltkrieg 1914 bis 1918, Die Militarischen Operationen zu Lande, Band 7, Die Operationen des Jahres 1915. Die Ereignisse Winter und Frühjahr.

25 September - 15 October ....The Allied Autumn Offensives - the Third Battle of Artois. (Western Front).

FrOH: Les Armées Françaises dans la Grande Guerre, Tome III, Les offensives de 1915 - L'hiver de 1915–1916 - 1 mai 1915–21 février 1916.

GmOH: 1. Der Weltkrieg 1914 bis 1918, Die Militarischen Operationen zu Lande, Band 7, Die Operationen des Jahres 1915. Die Ereignisse Winter und Frühjahr.
2. Die Bayern im Großen Kriege 1914-1918.

27 September ....The Italian warship Benedetto Brin sinks due to internal explosion. (Adriatic Sea).

IOH: Ufficio Storico della R. Marina, La Marina Italiana nella Grande Guerra, Volume II, L'Itervento Dell'Italia a Fianco Dell'Intesa e La Lotta in Adriatico.

28 September ....The British advance up the Tigris- the Battle of Kut, 1915. (Mesopotamia).

BrOH: Official History of the War, Military Operations, Campaign in Mesopotamia, Volume I.

TOH: 1. Büyük Harbin Sevkülceyşi.
2. Birinci Cihan Harbinde Türk Harbi, 1915 Yili Harekatleri, IIinci Cilt.
3. Birinci Dünya Harbinde Türk Harbi, IIInvi Cilt, Irak-Iran Cephesi, 1914-1918, 1nci Kisim.
4.. Büyük Harpte Misir Seferi.

28 September - 1 October ....The Battle of Kormin and the Putilovka. (Eastern Front).

AHOH: Österreich-Ungarns Letzter Krieg 1914-1918, Band II.

GmOH: 1. Der Weltkrieg 1914 bis 1918, Die Militarischen Operationen zu Lande, Band 8, Die Operationen des Jahres 1915 - Die Ereignisse im Westen im Frühjahr im Sommer und Osten vom Frühjahr bis zum Jahresschluß.
2. Die Bayern im Großen Kriege 1914-1918.

HOH: A világháború 1914-1918. Különös tekintettel Magyarországra és a Magyar csapatok szereplésére Szerkeszti és kiadja a M. Kir. Hadtörténelmi Levéltár, köt 10.

RuOH: 1. The Russian Army in the World War.
2. A Strategic Outline of the War 1914 –1915.
3. A Strategic Outline of the War 1914 -1918.

1 October – 1 April 1916 ....The Germans obtained air superiority due to the Fokker aircraft. (Western Front).

BrOH: ..Official History of the War, War in the Air, Volume III.

GmOH: Der Weltkrieg 1914 bis 1918, Die Militarischen Operationen zu Lande, Band 9, Die Operationen des Jahres 1915 – Die Ereignisse im Westen und auf dem Balkan vom Sommer bis Jahresschluß; Die Entwicklung der Luftstreitkrafte bis Ende 1915.

3 October ....S.S. Livonia – first German ship - sunk by a submarine without warning. (Baltic Sea).

BrOH: Official History of the War, Naval Operations, Volume III.

GmOH: Der Krieg zur See 1914-1918, Band 2, Der Krieg in der Ostsee, Teil 2, Das Kriegsjahr 1915.

RuOH: ..Flot v Pervoi Mirovoi Voine. V Dvukh Tomakh. Tom I Deystviya Russkogo Flota.

5 October ....Landings at Salonika. (Balkan Front).

BrOH: Official History of the War, Military Operations, Macedonia, Volume I: From the Outbreak of War to the Spring of 1917.

GrOH: 1. Ho Hellenikos Stratos kata ton Proton Pankosmion Polemon 1914-1918 Tomos 1 - H Hellas kai ho Polemos eis ta Balkania.

2. Epitomh Istopia Ths Eummetochhs Tou Ellhnikou Stratou Ston Prpsto Pagkosmio Polemo 1914-1918. / A Concise History of the Participation of the Hellenic Army in The First World War 1914-1918.

FrOH: Les Armées Françaises dans la Grande Guerre, Tome VIII, La campagne d'Orient, Volume 2, La campagne d'Orient depuis l'intervention de la Roumanie en aöut 1916 jusqu'en avril 1918.

6 October ....The second Austro-German-Bulgarian invasion of Serbia. (Balkan Front).

AHOH: Österreich-Ungarns Letzter Krieg 1914-1918, Band III.

BrOH: Official History of the War, Military Operations, Macedonia, Volume I: From the Outbreak of War to the Spring of 1917.

BuOH: 1. Bŭlgarskata armija vŭ svĕtovnata vojna 1915-1918 g. Томŭ I.

2. Bŭlgarskata armija vŭ svĕtovnata vojna 1915-1918 g. Томŭ II.

3. Bŭlgarskata armija vŭ svĕtovnata vojna 1915-1918 g. Томŭ III.

FrOH: Les Armées Françaises dans la Grande Guerre: Tome VIII La campagne d'Orient. Volume 1 La campagne d'Orient jusqu'a l'intervention de la Roumanie - février 1915-aöut 1916.

GmOH: Der Weltkrieg 1914 bis 1918, Die Militarischen Operationen zu Lande, Band 9, Die Operationen des Jahres 1915 – Die Ereignisse im Westen und auf dem Balkan vom Sommer bis Jahresschluß.

GrOH: 1. Ho Hellenikos Stratos kata ton Proton Pankosmion Polemon 1914-1918 Tomos 1 - H Hellas kai ho Polemos eis ta Balkania.

2. Epitomh Istopia Ths Eummetochhs Tou Ellhnikou Stratou Ston Prpsto Pagkosmio Polemo 1914-1918. / A Concise History of the Participation of the Hellenic Army in The First World War 1914-1918.

SeOH: Veliki rat Srbije za oslobođenje i ujedinenje Srba, Hrvata i Slovenaca. knjige IX. 1915 godina. Druga period. Austro-nemačka ofanziva do stupanja Bugarske u akciju.

9 October ....The second action of Hafiz Kor. (NW Frontier of India.

BrOH: Official History of the War, Military Operations, Operations in Persia 1915-1919.

TOH: Birinci Cihan Harbinde Türk Harbi, 1915 Yili Harekatleri, IIinci Cilt.

13 October ....The German airship raid on the East Coast of England and London causing approximately 200 casualties.

GmOH: Der Weltkrieg 1914 bis 1918, Die Militarischen Operationen zu Lande, Band 8, Die Operationen des Jahres 1915 - Die Ereignisse im Westen im Frühjahr im Sommer und Osten vom Frühjahr bis zum Jahresschluß.

14 October ....The first action of Strumitsa Station. (Balkan Front).

AHOH: Österreich-Ungarns Letzter Krieg 1914-1918, Band III.

BuOH: 1. Bŭlgarskata armija vŭ svĕtovnata vojna 1915-1918 g. Tomŭ II.
2. Bŭlgarskata armija vŭ svĕtovnata vojna 1915-1918 g. Tomŭ III.

FrOH: Les Armées Françaises dans la Grande Guerre, Tome VIII, La campagne d'Orient, Volume 2, La campagne d'Orient depuis l'intervention de la Roumanie en aôut 1916 jusqu'en avril 1918.

GmOH: Der Weltkrieg 1914 bis 1918, Die Militarischen Operationen zu Lande, Band 9, Die Operationen des Jahres 1915 – Die Ereignisse im Westen und auf dem Balkan vom Sommer bis Jahresschluß.

GrOH: 1. Ho Hellenikos Stratos kata ton Proton Pankosmion Polemon 1914-1918 Tomos 1 - H Hellas kai ho Polemos eis ta Balkania.
2. Epitomh Istopia Ths Eummetochhs Tou Ellhnikou Stratou Ston Prpsto Pagkosmio Polemo 1914-1918. / A Concise History of the Participation of the Hellenic Army in The First World War 1914-1918.

18 October – 3 November ....The Thrid Battle of the Isonzo. (Italian Front).

AHOH: Österreich-Ungarns Letzter Krieg 1914-1918, Band II.

IOH: Maggiore Esercito, Ufficio Storico, L'Esercito italiano nella grande guerra 1915-18, Volume II, Le Operazioni Del 1915.

21 October ....The second action of Strumitsa Station. (Balkan).

AHOH: Österreich-Ungarns Letzter Krieg 1914-1918, Band II.

BrOH: Official History of the War, Military Operations, Macedonia, Volume I: From the Outbreak of War to the Spring of 1917.

BuOH: Bŭlgarskata armija vŭ svĕtovnata vojna 1915-1918 g. Tomŭ IV.

FrOH: Les Armées Françaises dans la Grande Guerre: Tome VIII La campagne d'Orient. Volume 1 La campagne d'Orient jusqu'a l'intervention de la Roumanie - février 1915-aôut 1916.

GmOH: Der Weltkrieg 1914 bis 1918, Die Militarischen Operationen zu Lande, Band 9, Die Operationen des Jahres 1915 – Die Ereignisse im Westen und auf dem Balkan vom Sommer bis Jahresschluß.

MOH: Operacije crnogorske vojske u prvom svetskom ratu.

SeOH: Veliki rat Srbije za oslobođenje i ujedinenje Srba, Hrvata i Slovenaca. knjige X. 1915. Treći period. Udružena austro-nemačka-bugarska ofanziva protiv Srbije od 14 do 29 oktobar 1915.

21 October ....The Dardanelles/Gallipoli Campaign - Bombardment of Dede Agach.

BrOH: Official History of the War, Naval Operations, Volume II.

GmOH: 1. Der Krieg zur See 1914-1918, Band 5, Der Krieg in den türkischen Gewässern, Teil 2, Der Kampf un die Meerengen.

2. Der Weltkrieg 1914 bis 1918, Die Militarischen Operationen zu Lande, Band 8, Die Operationen des Jahres 1915 - Die Ereignisse im Westen im Frühjahr im Sommer und Osten vom Frühjahr bis zum Jahresschluß.

TOH: 1. Birinci Cihan Harbinde Türk Harbi, 1915 Yili Harekatleri, IIinci Cilt.

2. Birinci Dünya Harbinde Türk Harbi, Vnvi Cilt, Çanakkale Cephesi Harekati, 1nci Kitap.

3. Birinci Dünya Harbi, VIIInci Cilt, Türk Deniz Harekati.

4. Birinci Dünya Harbinde Türk Harbi, V nci Cilt, Çanakkale Cephesi Harekâtı, 1 nci, 2 nci, Ve 3 ncu Kitaplarin Özetlenmis Tarihi, Haziran 1914 - 9 Ocak 1916 / A Brief History of the Çanakkale Campaign in the First World War (June 1914 – January 1916).

23 October ....S.M.S. Prinz Adalbert sunk by H.M.S. E.8. (Baltic Sea).

BrOH: Official History of the War, Naval Operations, Volume III.

GmOH: Der Krieg zur See 1914-1918, Band 2, Der Krieg in der Ostsee, Teil 2, Das Kriegsjahr 1915.

RuOH:..Flot v Pervoi Mirovoi Voine. V Dvukh Tomakh. Tom I Deystviya Russkogo Flota.

27 October ....The first action of Krivolak. (Balkan Front).

AHOH: Österreich-Ungarns Letzter Krieg 1914-1918, Band III.

BrOH: Official History of the War, Military Operations, Macedonia, Volume I: From the Outbreak of War to the Spring of 1917.

BuOH: Bŭlgarskata armija vŭ svĕtovnata vojna 1915-1918 g. Томŭ IV.

FrOH: Les Armées Françaises dans la Grande Guerre: Tome VIII La campagne d'Orient. Volume 1 La campagne d'Orient jusqu'a l'intervention de la Roumanie - février 1915-aöut 1916.

GmOH: Der Weltkrieg 1914 bis 1918, Die Militarischen Operationen zu Lande, Band 9, Die Operationen des Jahres 1915 – Die Ereignisse im Westen und auf dem Balkan vom Sommer bis Jahresschluß.

GrOH: 1. Ho Hellenikos Stratos kata ton Proton Pankosmion Polemon 1914-1918 Tomos 1 - H Hellas kai ho Polemos eis ta Balkania.

2. Epitomh Istopia Ths Eummetochhs Tou Ellhnikou Stratou Ston Prpsto Pagkosmio Polemo 1914-1918. / A Concise History of the Participation of the Hellenic Army in The First World War 1914-1918.

SeOH: Veliki rat Srbije za oslobođenje i ujedinenje Srba, Hrvata i Slovenaca. knjige X. 1915. Treći period. Udružena austro-nemačka-bugarska ofanziva protiv Srbije od 14 do 29 oktobar 1915.

28 October ....H.M.S. Argyll wrecked. (British Home Waters).

BrOH: Official History of the War, Naval Operations, Volume III.

30 October ....The second action of Krivolak. (Balkan Front).

AHOH: Österreich-Ungarns Letzter Krieg 1914-1918, Band III.

BrOH: Official History of the War, Military Operations, Macedonia, Volume I: From the Outbreak of War to the Spring of 1917.

BuOH: Bŭlgarskata armija vŭ světovnata vojna 1915-1918 g. Tomŭ IV.

FrOH: Les Armées Françaises dans la Grande Guerre: Tome VIII La campagne d'Orient. Volume 1 La campagne d'Orient jusqu'a l'intervention de la Roumanie - février 1915-aöut 1916.

GmOH: Der Weltkrieg 1914 bis 1918, Die Militarischen Operationen zu Lande, Band 9, Die Operationen des Jahres 1915 – Die Ereignisse im Westen und auf dem Balkan vom Sommer bis Jahresschluß.

GrOH: 1. Ho Hellenikos Stratos kata ton Proton Pankosmion Polemon 1914-1918 Tomos 1 - H Hellas kai ho Polemos eis ta Balkania.
2. Epitomh Istopia Ths Eummetochhs Tou Ellhnikou Stratou Ston Prpsto Pagkosmio Polemo 1914-1918. / A Concise History of the Participation of the Hellenic Army in The First World War 1914-1918.

SeOH: Veliki rat Srbije za oslobođenje i ujedinenje Srba, Hrvata i Slovenaca. Jedanaesta knjige. 1915 godina. Treći period. Opšte Odstupanje srpske vojske. Prva faza. Odstupanje Glavne Shage na Zapadnu i Južnu Moravu.

30 October – 4 November..................The third attack on Mora. (Cameroons).

BgOH: Les Campagnes Coloniales Belges 1914-1918. Volume I. Introduction, les Operations au Cameroun, les Operations en Rhodésie, la Période Défensive à la Frontière Orientale.

BrOH: Official History of the War, Military Operations, Togoland and the Cameroons.

FrOH: Les Armées Françaises dans la Grande Guerre, Tome IX, Volume 2, Les campagnes coloniales: Cameroun – Togoland. – Opérations contre les Senoussis.

30 October – 5 November..................The Battle of Siemikowce. (Eastern Front).

AHOH: Österreich-Ungarns Letzter Krieg 1914-1918, Band II.

GmOH: 1. Der Weltkrieg 1914 bis 1918, Die Militarischen Operationen zu Lande, Band 7, Die Operationen des Jahres 1915. Die Ereignisse Winter und Frühjahr.
2. Die Bayern im Großen Kriege 1914-1918.

RuOH: 1. The Russian Army in the World War.
2. A Strategic Outline of the War 1914 –1915.
3. A Strategic Outline of the War 1914 -1918.

2 November ....The attacked on Babuna Pass. (Balkan Front).

AHOH: Österreich-Ungarns Letzter Krieg 1914-1918, Band III.

BrOH: Official History of the War, Military Operations, Macedonia, Volume I: From the Outbreak of War to the Spring of 1917.

BuOH: Bŭlgarskata armija vŭ světovnata vojna 1915-1918 g. Tomŭ V.

FrOH: Les Armées Françaises dans la Grande Guerre: Tome VIII La campagne d'Orient. Volume 1 La campagne d'Orient jusqu'a l'intervention de la Roumanie - février 1915-aöut 1916.

GmOH:Der Weltkrieg 1914 bis 1918, Die Militarischen Operationen zu Lande, Band 9, Die Operationen des

Jahres 1915 – Die Ereignisse im Westen und auf dem Balkan vom Sommer bis Jahresschluß.

GrOH: 1. Ho Hellenikos Stratos kata ton Proton Pankosmion Polemon 1914-1918 Tomos 1 - H Hellas kai ho Polemos eis ta Balkania.

2. Epitomh Istopia Ths Eummetochhs Tou Ellhnikou Stratou Ston Prpsto Pagkosmio Polemo 1914-1918. / A Concise History of the Participation of the Hellenic Army in The First World War 1914-1918.

SeOH: Veliki rat Srbije za oslobođenje i ujedinenje Srba, Hrvata i Slovenaca. Jedanaesta knjige. 1915 godina. Treći period. Opšte Odstupanje srpske vojske. Prva faza. Odstupanje Glavne Shage na Zapadnu i Južnu Moravu.

3-5 November ....The third action of Krivolak. (Balkan Front).

AHOH: Österreich-Ungarns Letzter Krieg 1914-1918, Band III.

BrOH: Official History of the War, Military Operations, Macedonia, Volume I: From the Outbreak of War to the Spring of 1917.

BuOH: 1. Bǔlgarskata armija vǔ světovnata vojna 1915-1918 g. Tomǔ V.

FrOH: Les Armées Françaises dans la Grande Guerre: Tome VIII La campagne d'Orient. Volume 1 La campagne d'Orient jusqu'a l'intervention de la Roumanie - février 1915-aöut 1916.

GmOH: Der Weltkrieg 1914 bis 1918, Die Militarischen Operationen zu Lande, Band 9, Die Operationen des Jahres 1915 – Die Ereignisse im Westen und auf dem Balkan vom Sommer bis Jahresschluß.

GrOH: 1. Ho Hellenikos Stratos kata ton Proton Pankosmion Polemon 1914-1918 Tomos 1 - H Hellas kai ho Polemos eis ta Balkania.

2. Epitomh Istopia Ths Eummetochhs Tou Ellhnikou Stratou Ston Prpsto Pagkosmio Polemo 1914-1918. / A Concise History of the Participation of the Hellenic Army in The First World War 1914-1918.

SeOH: Veliki rat Srbije za oslobođenje i ujedinenje Srba, Hrvata i Slovenaca. Jedanaesta knjige. 1915 godina. Treći period. Opšte Odstupanje srpske vojske. Prva faza. Odstupanje Glavne Shage na Zapadnu i Južnu Moravu.

4-6 November ....The capture of Banyo. (Cameroons).

BgOH: Les Campagnes Coloniales Belges 1914-1918. Volume I. Introduction, les Operations au Cameroun, les Operations en Rhodésie, la Période Défensive à la Frontière Orientale.

BrOH: Official History of the War, Military Operations, Togoland and the Cameroons.

FrOH: Les Armées Françaises dans la Grande Guerre, Tome IX, Volume 2, Les campagnes coloniales: Cameroun – Togoland. – Opérations contre les Senoussis.

5 November ....The German airship LZ39 shot down over Grodno, Poland. (Eastern Front).

GmOH: Der Weltkrieg 1914 bis 1918, Die Militarischen Operationen zu Lande, Band 9, Die Operationen des Jahres 1915 – Die Ereignisse im Westen und auf dem Balkan vom Sommer bis Jahresschluß; Die Entwicklung der Luftstreitkrafte bis Ende 1915.

5-8 November ....The Battle of Kachanik. (Balkan Front).

AHOH: Österreich-Ungarns Letzter Krieg 1914-1918, Band III.

BrOH: Official History of the War, Military Operations, Macedonia, Volume I: From the Outbreak of War to the Spring of 1917.

BuOH: Bŭlgarskata armija vŭ světovnata vojna 1915-1918 g. Tomŭ V.

FrOH: Les Armées Françaises dans la Grande Guerre: Tome VIII La campagne d'Orient. Volume 1 La campagne d'Orient jusqu'a l'intervention de la Roumanie - février 1915-aöut 1916.

GmOH: Der Weltkrieg 1914 bis 1918, Die Militarischen Operationen zu Lande, Band 9, Die Operationen des Jahres 1915 – Die Ereignisse im Westen und auf dem Balkan vom Sommer bis Jahresschluß.

GrOH: 1. Ho Hellenikos Stratos kata ton Proton Pankosmion Polemon 1914-1918 Tomos 1 - H Hellas kai ho Polemos eis ta Balkania.
2. Epitomh Istopia Ths Eummetochhs Tou Ellhnikou Stratou Ston Prpsto Pagkosmio Polemo 1914-1918. / A Concise History of the Participation of the Hellenic Army in The First World War 1914-1918.

SeOH: Veliki rat Srbije za oslobođenje i ujedinenje Srba, Hrvata i Slovenaca. Jedanaesta knjige. 1915 godina. Treći period. Opšte Odstupanje srpske vojske. Prva faza. Odstupanje Glavne Shage na Zapadnu i Južnu Moravu.

6 November ....The Egyptian cruiser Abbas sunk by a submarine. (Mediterranean Sea).

GmOH: Der Krieg zur See 1914-1918, Band 4, Der Handelskrieg mit U-Booten, Teil 2, Februar bis September 1915.

7 November ......................................S.M.S. Undine sunk by H.M.S. E.19. (Baltic Sea).

BrOH: Official History of the War, Naval Operations, Volume III.

GmOH: Der Krieg zur See 1914-1918, Band 2, Der Krieg in der Ostsee, Teil 2, Das Kriegsjahr 1915.

RuOH:..Flot v Pervoi Mirovoi Voine. V Dvukh Tomakh. Tom I Deystviya Russkogo Flota.

10 November – 10 December ....The Fourth Battle of the Isonzo. (Italian Front).

AHOH:.Österreich-Ungarns Letzter Krieg 1914-1918, Band II.

IOH: Maggiore Esercito, Ufficio Storico, L'Esercito italiano nella grande guerra 1915-18, Volume II, Le Operazioni Del 1915.

13 November ....The Battle of Czartorysk. (Eastern Front).

AHOH: Österreich-Ungarns Letzter Krieg 1914-1918, Band II.

GmOH: 1. Der Weltkrieg 1914 bis 1918, Die Militarischen Operationen zu Lande, Band 7, Die Operationen des Jahres 1915. Die Ereignisse Winter und Frühjahr.
2. Die Bayern im Großen Kriege 1914-1918.

RuOH: 1. The Russian Army in the World War.
2. A Strategic Outline of the War 1914 –1915.
3. A Strategic Outline of the War 1914 -1918.

17 November ....................................H.M.H.S. Anglia sunk by a mine. (British Home Waters).

BrOH: 1. Official History of the War, Naval Operations, Volume III.

2. Official History of the War, Seaborne Trade, Volume II, Submarine Campaign, Part I.

3. Official History of the War, The Merchant Navy, Volume II.

22-24 November ....The British advance on Baghdad, 1915 - the Battle of Ctesiphon. (Mesopotamia).

        BrOH: Official History of the War, Military Operations, Campaign in Mesopotamia, Volume I.

        TOH: 1. Büyük Harbin Sevkülceyşi.

             2. Birinci Cihan Harbinde Türk Harbi, 1915 Yili Harekatleri, IIinci Cilt.

             3. Birinci Dünya Harbinde Türk Harbi, IIInvi Cilt, Irak-Iran Cephesi, 1914-1918, 1nci Kisim.

             4. Büyük Harpte Misir Seferi.

3 November - 3 December ....The British retreat to Kut. (Mesopotamia).

        BrOH: Official History of the War, Military Operations, Campaign in Mesopotamia, Volume I.

        TOH: 1. Büyük Harbin Sevkülceyşi.

             2. Birinci Cihan Harbinde Türk Harbi, 1915 Yili Harekatleri, IIinci Cilt.

             3. Birinci Dünya Harbinde Türk Harbi, IIInvi Cilt, Irak-Iran Cephesi, 1914-1918, 1nci Kisim.

             4. Büyük Harpte Misir Seferi.

5-6 December.....................................The action of Demir Kapu. (Balkan Front).

        AHOH: Österreich-Ungarns Letzter Krieg 1914-1918, Band III.

        BrOH: Official History of the War, Military Operations, Macedonia, Volume I: From the Outbreak of War to the Spring of 1917.

        BuOH: Bŭlgarskata armija vŭ svĕtovnata vojna 1915-1918 g. Tомŭ V.

        FrOH: Les Armées Françaises dans la Grande Guerre: Tome VIII La campagne d'Orient. Volume 1 La campagne d'Orient jusqu'a l'intervention de la Roumanie - février 1915-aöut 1916.

        GmOH: Der Weltkrieg 1914 bis 1918, Die Militarischen Operationen zu Lande, Band 9, Die Operationen des Jahres 1915 – Die Ereignisse im Westen und auf dem Balkan vom Sommer bis Jahresschluß.

        GrOH: 1. Ho Hellenikos Stratos kata ton Proton Pankosmion Polemon 1914-1918 Tomos 1 - H Hellas kai ho Polemos eis ta Balkania.

             2. Epitomh Istopia Ths Eummetochhs Tou Ellhnikou Stratou Ston Prpsto Pagkosmio Polemo 1914-1918. / A Concise History of the Participation of the Hellenic Army in The First World War 1914-1918.

        SeOH: Veliki rat Srbije za oslobođenje i ujedinenje Srba, Hrvata i Slovenaca. Knjige trinaesta. 1915 godina. Treći period. Opšte Odstupanje srpske vojske. III. faza. Odstupanje na Jadransko Primorje.

6 December.......................................Durazzo bombarded. (Adriatic Sea).

        IOH: Ufficio Storico della R. Marina, La Marina Italiana nella Grande Guerra, Volume II, L'Itervento Dell'Italia a Fianco Dell'Intesa e La Lotta in Adriatico.

7-8 December....................................The action of Kosturino. (Balkan Front).

AHOH: Österreich-Ungarns Letzter Krieg 1914-1918, Band III.

BrOH: Official History of the War, Military Operations, Macedonia, Volume I: From the Outbreak of War to the Spring of 1917.

BuOH: Bŭlgarskata armija vŭ svĕtovnata vojna 1915-1918 g. Tomŭ V.

FrOH: Les Armées Françaises dans la Grande Guerre: Tome VIII La campagne d'Orient. Volume 1 La campagne d'Orient jusqu'a l'intervention de la Roumanie - février 1915-aöut 1916.

GmOH: Der Weltkrieg 1914 bis 1918, Die Militarischen Operationen zu Lande, Band 9, Die Operationen des Jahres 1915 – Die Ereignisse im Westen und auf dem Balkan vom Sommer bis Jahresschluß.

GrOH: 1. Ho Hellenikos Stratos kata ton Proton Pankosmion Polemon 1914-1918 Tomos 1 - H Hellas kai ho Polemos eis ta Balkania.
2. Epitomh Istopia Ths Eummetochhs Tou Ellhnikou Stratou Ston Prpsto Pagkosmio Polemo 1914-1918. / A Concise History of the Participation of the Hellenic Army in The First World War 1914-1918.

SeOH: Veliki rat Srbije za oslobođenje i ujedinenje Srba, Hrvata i Slovenaca. Knjige trinaesta. 1915 godina. Treći period. Opšte Odstupanje srpske vojske. III. faza. Odstupanje na Jadransko Primorje.

7 December – 29 April. (1916) .... The siege of Kut. (Mesopotamia).

BrOH: Official History of the War, Military Operations, Campaign in Mesopotamia, Volume I.

TOH: 1. Büyük Harbin Sevkülceyşi.
2. Birinci Cihan Harbinde Türk Harbi, 1915 Yili Harekatleri, IIinci Cilt.
3. Birinci Dünya Harbinde Türk Harbi, IIInvi Cilt, Irak-Iran Cephesi, 1914-1918, 1nci Kisim.
4. Büyük Harpte Misir Seferi.

11-13 December .... The affair of the Wadi Senab. (West Egypt/Sudan).

BrOH: Official History of the War, Military Operations, Egypt and Palestine, Volume I, From the Outbreak of War with Germany to June 1917.

TOH: 1. Büyük Harbin Sevkülceyşi.
2. Birinci Dünya Harbinde Türk Harbi, IIInvi Cilt, Irak-Iran Cephesi, 1914-1918, 1nci Kisim.

17 December .... S.M.S. Bremen sunk by a submarine. (Baltic Sea).

BrOH: Official History of the War, Naval Operations, Volume III.

GmOH: Der Krieg zur See 1914-1918, Band 2, Der Krieg in der Ostsee, Teil 2, Das Kriegsjahr 1915.

RuOH: ...Flot v Pervoi Mirovoi Voine. V Dvukh Tomakh. Tom I Deystviya Russkogo Flota.

19 December – 8 January (1916) .... The Dardanelles/Gallipoli Campaign - the Evacuation of the Galilipoli Peninsula. (Dardanelles).

AuOH: Official History of Australia in the War of 1914-1918, Volume II, The Story of Anzac Part II.

BrOH: 1. Official History of the War, Naval Operations, Volume III.

2. Official History of the War, Military Operations, Gallipoli, Volume II, May 1915 to the Evacuation.

FrOH: Les Armées Françaises dans la Grande Guerre: Tome VIII La campagne d'Orient. Volume 1 La campagne d'Orient jusqu'a l'intervention de la Roumanie - février 1915-aôut 1916.

GmOH: Der Weltkrieg 1914 bis 1918, Die Militarischen Operationen zu Lande, Band 7, Die Operationen des Jahres 1915. Die Ereignisse Winter und Frühjahr.

NZOH: Official History of New Zealand's Effort in the Great War, Volume I Gallipoli.

TOH: 1. Birinci Cihan Harbinde Türk Harbi, 1915 Yili Harekatleri, IIinci Cilt.

2. Birinci Cihan Harbinde Türk Harbi, 1916 Yili Harekatleri, IIIncu Cilt.

3. Turk Silahe Kuvvetleri Tarihi Osmanlı Birinci Dünya Harbinde Türk Harbi, Vncu Cilt, Çanakkale Cephesi Harekati, 3ncu Kitap, Haziran 1915 – Ocak 1916.

4. Birinci Dünya Harbinde Türk Harbi, V nci Cilt, Çanakkale Cephesi Harekâtı, 1 nci, 2 nci, Ve 3 ncu Kitaplarin Özetlenmis Tarihi, Haziran 1914 - 9 Ocak 1916 / A Brief History of the Çanakkale Campaign in the First World War (June 1914 – January 1916).

19-20 December ....The Dardanelles/Gallipoli Campaign - the Evacuation of the Galilipoli Peninsula - the Evacuation of Suvla & Anzac.

AuOH: Official History of Australia in the War of 1914-1918, Volume II, The Story of Anzac Part II.

BrOH: 1. Official History of the War, Naval Operations, Volume III.

2. Official History of the War, Military Operations, Gallipoli, Volume II, May 1915 to the Evacuation.

GmOH: Der Weltkrieg 1914 bis 1918, Die Militarischen Operationen zu Lande, Band 7, Die Operationen des Jahres 1915. Die Ereignisse Winter und Frühjahr.

NZOH: Official History of New Zealand's Effort in the Great War, Volume I Gallipoli.

TOH: 1. Birinci Cihan Harbinde Türk Harbi, 1915 Yili Harekatleri, IIinci Cilt.

2. Turk Silahe Kuvvetleri Tarihi Osmanlı Birinci Dünya Harbinde Türk Harbi, Vncu Cilt, Çanakkale Cephesi Harekati, 3ncu Kitap, Haziran 1915 – Ocak 1916.

3. Birinci Dünya Harbinde Türk Harbi, V nci Cilt, Çanakkale Cephesi Harekâtı, 1 nci, 2 nci, Ve 3 ncu Kitaplarin Özetlenmis Tarihi, Haziran 1914 - 9 Ocak 1916 / A Brief History of the Çanakkale Campaign in the First World War (June 1914 – January 1916).

20 December.....................................Durazzo occupied by the Italians. (Adriatic Sea).

IOH: Ufficio Storico della R. Marina, La Marina Italiana nella Grande Guerra, Volume II, L'Itervento Dell'Italia a Fianco Dell'Intesa e La Lotta in Adriatico.

23 December – 9 February. (1916) ....The British naval operations on Lake Tanganyika. (East Africa).

BgOH: Les Campagnes Coloniales Belges 1914-1918. Volume I. Introduction, les Operations au Cameroun, les Operations en Rhodésie, la Période Défensive à la Frontière Orientale.

BrOH: 1. Official History of the War, Naval Operations, Volume III.
2. Official History of the War, Military Operations, East Africa, Volume I, August 1914-September 1916.

GmOH: 1. Der Krieg zur See 1914-1918, Band 3, Der Kreuzerkrieg in den ausländischen Gewässern, Teil 2, Die Tätigkeit der Kleinen Kreuzer "Emden", "Königberg" und "Karlsruhe" mit e Anhang: "Die Kriegsfahrt des Kleinen Kreuzers Geier".
2. Der Krieg zur See 1914-1918, Band 6, Die Kämpfe der Kaiserlichen Marine in den deutschen Kolonien, Teil 2, Deutsch-Ostafrika.
3. Deutsche Tat im Weltkrieg 1914/18 - Geschichten der Kämpfe deutscher Truppen, Band 12. Tufani - Sturm über Deutsch-Ostafrika.

25 December .... The affair of the Wadi Majid. (West Egypt/Sudan).

BrOH: Official History of the War, Military Operations, Egypt and Palestine, Volume I, From the Outbreak of War with Germany to June 1917.

TOH: 1. Büyük Harbin Sevkülceyşi.
2. Birinci Cihan Harbinde Türk Harbi, 1915 Yili Harekatleri, IIinci Cilt.

25 December .... The siege of Kut – the Turkish Christmas Eve attack on Kut. (Mesopotamia).

BrOH: Official History of the War, Military Operations, Campaign in Mesopotamia, Volume I.

TOH: 1. Büyük Harbin Sevkülceyşi.
2. Birinci Cihan Harbinde Türk Harbi, 1915 Yili Harekatleri, IIinci Cilt.
3. Birinci Dünya Harbinde Türk Harbi, IIInvi Cilt, Irak-Iran Cephesi, 1914-1918, 1nci Kisim.
4. Büyük Harpte Misir Seferi.

26 December – 4 March (1916) .... S.M.S. Möwe's (Moewe's) first cruise. (Atlantic Ocean).

BrOH: 1. Official History of the War, Naval Operations, Volume III.
2. Official History of the War, Seaborne Trade, Volume I, Cruiser Period.
3. Official History of the War – The Merchant Navy, Volume II.

GmOH: 1. Der Krieg zur See 1914-1918, Band 3, Der Kreuzerkrieg in den ausländischen Gewässern, Teil 3, Die deutschen Hilfskreuzer.

26 December .... The British naval operations on Lake Tanganyika - S.M.S. Kingani captured by H.M.S. Mimi & H.M.S. Toutou. (East Africa).

BgOH: Les Campagnes Coloniales Belges 1914-1918. Volume I. Introduction, les Operations au Cameroun, les Operations en Rhodésie, la Période Défensive à la Frontière Orientale.

BrOH: 1. Official History of the War, Naval Operations, Volume III.
2. Official History of the War, Military Operations, East Africa, Volume I, August 1914-September 1916.

GmOH: 1. Der Krieg zur See 1914-1918, Band 3, Der Kreuzerkrieg in den ausländischen Gewässern, Teil 2, Die Tätigkeit der Kleinen Kreuzer "Emden", "Königberg" und

"Karlsruhe" mit e Anhang: "Die Kriegsfahrt des Kleinen Kreuzers Geier".

2. Der Krieg zur See 1914-1918, Band 6, Die Kämpfe der Kaiserlichen Marine in den deutschen Kolonien, Teil 2, Deutsch-Ostafrika.

3. Deutsche Tat im Weltkrieg 1914/18 - Geschichten der Kämpfe deutscher Truppen, Band 12. Tufani - Sturm über Deutsch-Ostafrika.

29 December......................................Durazzo raided by the Austrian. (Adriatic Sea).

IOH: Ufficio Storico della R. Marina, La Marina Italiana nella Grande Guerra, Volume II, L'Itervento Dell'Italia a Fianco Dell'Intesa e La Lotta in Adriatico.

30 December......................................H.M.S. Natal sinks due to an internal explosion. (British Home Waters).

BrOH: Official History of the War, Naval Operations, Volume III.

1916

1 January..The capture of Yaunde. (West Africa/Cameroons).

BgOH: Les Campagnes Coloniales Belges 1914-1918. Volume I. Introduction, les Operations au Cameroun, les Operations en Rhodésie, la Période Défensive à la Frontière Orientale.

BrOH: Official History of the War, Military Operations, Togoland and the Cameroons.

FrOH: Les Armées Françaises dans la Grande Guerre, Tome IX, Volume 2, Les campagnes coloniales: Cameroun – Togoland. – Opérations contre les Senoussis.

4-21 January ....The siege of Kut – the first attempt to relieve Kut. (Mesopotamia).

BrOH: Official History of the War, Military Operations, Campaign in Mesopotamia, Volume I.

TOH: 1. Büyük Harbin Sevkülceyşi.
2. Birinci Cihan Harbinde Türk Harbi, 1916 Yili Harekatleri, IIIncu Cilt.
3. Birinci Dünya Harbinde Türk Harbi, IIInvi Cilt, Irak-Iran Cephesi, 1914-1918, 1nci Kisim.
4. Büyük Harpte Misir Seferi.

6 January..H.M.S. King Edward VII sunk by a mine. (British Home Waters).

BrOH: Official History of the War, Naval Operations, Volume III.

6-8 January ....The siege of Kut – the first attempt to relieve Kut – the action of Sheikh Sa'ad. (Mesopotamia).

BrOH: Official History of the War, Military Operations, Campaign in Mesopotamia, Volume I.

TOH: 1. Büyük Harbin Sevkülceyşi.
2. Birinci Cihan Harbinde Türk Harbi, 1916 Yili Harekatleri, IIIncu Cilt.
3. Birinci Dünya Harbinde Türk Harbi, IIInvi Cilt, Irak-Iran Cephesi, 1914-1918, 1nci Kisim.
4. Büyük Harpte Misir Seferi.

7-8 January ....The Dardanelles/Gallipoli Campaign - The evacuation of the Galilipoli Peninsula - the evacuation of Cape Helles.

BrOH: 1. Official History of the War, Naval Operations, Volume III.
2. Official History of the War, Military Operations, Gallipoli, Volume II, May 1915 to the Evacuation.

FrOH: Les Armées Françaises dans la Grande Guerre: Tome VIII La campagne d'Orient. Volume 1 La campagne d'Orient jusqu'a l'intervention de la Roumanie - février 1915-aöut 1916.

GmOH: Der Weltkrieg 1914 bis 1918, Die Militarischen Operationen zu Lande, Band 7, Die Operationen des Jahres 1915. Die Ereignisse Winter und Frühjahr.

TOH: 1. Birinci Cihan Harbinde Türk Harbi, 1916 Yili Harekatleri, IIIncu Cilt.
2. Turk Silahe Kuvvetleri Tarihi Osmanlı Birinci Dünya Harbinde Türk Harbi, Vncu Cilt, Çanakkale Cephesi Harekati, 3ncu Kitap, Haziran 1915 – Ocak 1916.
3. Birinci Dünya Harbinde Türk Harbi, V nci Cilt, Çanakkale Cephesi Harekâtı, 1 nci, 2 nci, Ve 3 ncu Kitaplarin Özetlenmis Tarihi, Haziran 1914 - 9 Ocak 1916

/ A Brief History of the Çanakkale Campaign in the First World War (June 1914 – January 1916).

SeOH: Veliki rat Srbije za oslobođenje i ujedinenje Srba, Hrvata i Slovenaca. Uernaesta knjige XIV. 1916 godina. Treći period. Opšte odstupanje srpske vojske. IV faza - Prebacivanje iz Albanije na ostrvo Krf.

23 January...The action at Hazalin against the Senussi Rebels. (Egypt).

BrOH: Official History of the War, Military Operations, Egypt and Palestine, Volume I, From the Outbreak of War with Germany to June 1917.

FrOH: Les Armées Françaises dans la Grande Guerre, Tome IX, Volume 2, Les campagnes coloniales: Cameroun – Togoland. – Opérations contre les Senoussis.

NZOH: Official History of New Zealand's Effort in the Great War, Volume III, Sinai and Palestine.

SAOH: The Union of South Africa and the Great War 1914 – 1918.

TOH: 1. Büyük Harbin Sevkülceyşi.
2. Birinci Cihan Harbinde Türk Harbi, 1916 Yili Harekatleri, IIIncu Cilt.

25 January...The capture of San Giovanni di Medua, Albania. (Balkan Front).

AHOH:.Österreich-Ungarns Letzter Krieg 1914-1918, Band IV.

BrOH: Official History of the War, Military Operations, Macedonia, Volume I: From the Outbreak of War to the Spring of 1917.

BuOH: Bŭlgarskata armija vŭ světovnata vojna 1915-1918 g. Томŭ V.

FrOH: Les Armées Françaises dans la Grande Guerre: Tome VIII La campagne d'Orient. Volume 1 La campagne d'Orient jusqu'a l'intervention de la Roumanie - février 1915-aöut 1916.

GmOH: Der Weltkrieg 1914 bis 1918, Die Militarischen Operationen zu Lande, Band 9, Die Operationen des Jahres 1915 – Die Ereignisse im Westen und auf dem Balkan vom Sommer bis Jahresschluß.

GrOH: 1. Ho Hellenikos Stratos kata ton Proton Pankosmion Polemon 1914-1918 Tomos 1 - H Hellas kai ho Polemos eis ta Balkania.
2. Epitomh Istopia Ths Eummetochhs Tou Ellhnikou Stratou Ston Prpsto Pagkosmio Polemo 1914-1918. / A Concise History of the Participation of the Hellenic Army in The First World War 1914-1918.

MOH: Operacije crnogorske vojske u prvom svetskom ratu.

SeOH: Veliki rat Srbije za oslobođenje i ujedinenje Srba, Hrvata i Slovenaca. Uernaesta knjige XIV. 1916 godina. Treći period. Opšte odstupanje srpske vojske. IV faza - Prebacivanje iz Albanije na ostrvo Krf.

29 January...The last German airship raid on Paris.

GmOH: Der Weltkrieg 1914 bis 1918, Die Militarischen Operationen zu Lande, Band 10, Die Operationen des Jahres 1916 bis zum Wechsel in der Obersten Heeresleitung; Der Krieg zur Air.

31 January...The German airship raid on the East Coast and the Midlands of England causing 183 casualties.

BrOH: Official History of the War, War in the Air, Volume II.

GmOH: Der Weltkrieg 1914 bis 1918, Die Militarischen Operationen zu Lande, Band 10, Die Operationen des

Jahres 1916 bis zum Wechsel in der Obersten Heeresleitung; Der Krieg zur Air.

2 February...The German airship L19 founder in the North Sea.
        BrOH: Official History of the War, War in the Air, Volume II.
        GmOH: Der Weltkrieg 1914 bis 1918, Die Militarischen Operationen zu Lande, Band 10, Die Operationen des Jahres 1916 bis zum Wechsel in der Obersten Heeresleitung; Der Krieg zur Air.

8 February...The French cruiser Admiral Charner sunk by a submarine. (Mediterranean Sea).
        FrOH: Précis d'histoire de la guerre navale, 1914-1918.

9 February...The British Naval Operations on Lake Tanganyika - S.M.S. Hedwig von Wissman sunk by H.M.S. Mimi & H.M.S. Toutou. (East Africa).
        BgOH: Les Campagnes Coloniales Belges 1914-1918. Volume I. Introduction, les Operations au Cameroun, les Operations en Rhodésie, la Période Défensive à la Frontière Orientale.
        BrOH: 1. Official History of the War, Naval Operations, Volume III.
              2. Official History of the War, Military Operations, East Africa, Volume I, August 1914-September 1916.
        GmOH: 1. Der Krieg zur See 1914-1918, Band 3, Der Kreuzerkrieg in den ausländischen Gewässern, Teil 2, Die Tätigkeit der Kleinen Kreuzer "Emden", "Königberg" und "Karlsruhe" mit e Anhang: "Die Kriegsfahrt des Kleinen Kreuzers Geier".
              2. Der Krieg zur See 1914-1918, Band 6, Die Kämpfe der Kaiserlichen Marine in den deutschen Kolonien, Teil 2, Deutsch-Ostafrika.
              3. Deutsche Tat im Weltkrieg 1914/18 - Geschichten der Kämpfe deutscher Truppen, Band 12. Tufani - Sturm über Deutsch-Ostafrika.

11 February.......................................H.M.S. Arethusa sunk by a mine. (British Home Waters).
        BrOH: Official History of the War, Naval Operations, Volume III.

15 February – 17 March.....................The Fifth Battle of the Isonzo. (Italian Front).
        AHOH: Österreich-Ungarns Letzter Krieg 1914-1918, Band III.
        IOH: Maggiore Esercito, Ufficio Storico, L'Esercito italiano nella grande guerra 1915-18, Volume III, Tomo 1, Le Operazioni Del 1916 - Gli Avvenimenti.

17 February.......................................Chios in the Ægean occupied by British Forces. (Mediterranean Sea).
        BrOH: Official History of the War, Military Operations, Macedonia, Volume I: From the Outbreak of War to the Spring of 1917.
        GrOH: 1. Ho Hellenikos Stratos kata ton Proton Pankosmion Polemon 1914-1918 Tomos 1 - H Hellas kai ho Polemos eis ta Balkania.
              2. Epitomh Istopia Ths Eummetochhs Tou Ellhnikou Stratou Ston Prpsto Pagkosmio Polemo 1914-1918. / A Concise History of the Participation of the Hellenic Army in The First World War 1914-1918.

18 February......................................The capture of Mora – the conquest of the Cameroons completed. (West Africa/Cameroon).

BgOH: Les Campagnes Coloniales Belges 1914-1918. Volume I. Introduction, les Operations au Cameroun, les Operations en Rhodésie, la Période Défensive à la Frontière Orientale.

BrOH: Official History of the War, Military Operations, Togoland and the Cameroons.

FrOH: Les Armées Françaises dans la Grande Guerre, Tome IX, Volume 2, Les campagnes coloniales: Cameroun – Togoland. – Opérations contre les Senoussis.

21 February......................................The German airship LZ77 shot down over Revigny, France. (Western Front).

GmOH: Der Weltkrieg 1914 bis 1918, Die Militarischen Operationen zu Lande, Band 10, Die Operationen des Jahres 1916 bis zum Wechsel in der Obersten Heeresleitung; Der Krieg zur Air.

21 February –18 December...............The Battle of Verdun. (Western Front).

FrOH: 1. Les Armées Françaises dans la Grande Guerre, Tome IV, Verdun et la Somme, Volume 1, Les projets offensifs pour 1916 et la Bataille de Verdun - 21 février–1 mai 1916.

2. Les Armées Françaises dans la Grande Guerre, Tome IV, Verdun et la Somme, Volume 2, La Bataille de Verdun et les offensifs des Alliés - 1 mai–3 septembre 1916.

3. Les Armées Françaises dans la Grande Guerre, Tome IV, Verdun et la Somme, Volume 3, Bataille de la Somme. (fin) - Offensives Françaises à Verdun – 3 septembre-fin décembre 1916.

GmOH: 1. Der Weltkrieg 1914 bis 1918, Die Militarischen Operationen zu Lande, Band 10, Die Operationen des Jahres 1916 bis zum Wechsel in der Obersten Heeresleitung.

2. Der Weltkrieg 1914 bis 1918, Die Militarischen Operationen zu Lande, Band 11, Die Kriegführung im Herbst 1916 und im Winter 1916/17.

3. Die Bayern im Großen Kriege 1914-1918.

21 February - 31 August ....The Battle of Verdun – the Defensive Battle of Verdun. (Western Front).

FrOH: 1. Les Armées Françaises dans la Grande Guerre, Tome IV, Verdun et la Somme, Volume 1, Les projets offensifs pour 1916 et la Bataille de Verdun - 21 février–1 mai 1916.

2. Les Armées Françaises dans la Grande Guerre, Tome IV, Verdun et la Somme, Volume 2, La Bataille de Verdun et les offensifs des Alliés - 1 mai–3 septembre 1916.

GmOH: 1. Der Weltkrieg 1914 bis 1918, Die Militarischen Operationen zu Lande, Band 10, Die Operationen des Jahres 1916 bis zum Wechsel in der Obersten Heeresleitung.

2. Die Bayern im Großen Kriege 1914-1918.

25 February......................................The Battle of Verdun – the Defensive Battle of Verdun – the capture of the Fort de Douaumont by the Germans. (Western Front).

FrOH: Les Armées Françaises dans la Grande Guerre, Tome IV, Verdun et la Somme, Volume 1, Les projets offensifs pour 1916 et la Bataille de Verdun - 21 février–1 mai 1916.

GmOH: 1. Der Weltkrieg 1914 bis 1918, Die Militarischen Operationen zu Lande, Band 10, Die Operationen des Jahres 1916 bis zum Wechsel in der Obersten Heeresleitung.

2. Die Bayern im Großen Kriege 1914-1918.

26 February .... The action of Agagiya. against the Senussi Rebels. (West Egypt/Sudan).

BrOH: Official History of the War, Military Operations, Egypt and Palestine, Volume I, From the Outbreak of War with Germany to June 1917.

FrOH: Les Armées Françaises dans la Grande Guerre, Tome IX, Volume 2, Les campagnes coloniales: Cameroun – Togoland. – Opérations contre les Senoussis.

NZOH: Official History of New Zealand's Effort in the Great War, Volume III, Sinai and Palestine.

SAOH: The Union of South Africa and the Great War 1914 – 1918.

TOH: 1. Büyük Harbin Sevkülceyşi.

2. Birinci Cihan Harbinde Türk Harbi, 1916 Yili Harekatleri, IIIncu Cilt.

27 February .... Durazzo (Durrës) captured by Austrian Forces. (Balkan Front).

AHOH: 1. Österreich-Ungarns Seekrieg 1914-1918, Lieferung III.

2. Österreich-Ungarns Letzter Krieg 1914-1918, Band IV.

BuOH: Bŭlgarskata armija vŭ světovnata vojna 1915-1918 g. Tomŭ V.

GrOH: 1. Ho Hellenikos Stratos kata ton Proton Pankosmion Polemon 1914-1918 Tomos 1 - H Hellas kai ho Polemos eis ta Balkania.

2. Epitomh Istopia Ths Eummetochhs Tou Ellhnikou Stratou Ston Prpsto Pagkosmio Polemo 1914-1918. / A Concise History of the Participation of the Hellenic Army in The First World War 1914-1918.

IOH: Maggiore Esercito: Ufficio Storico – L'Esercito italiano nella grande guerra 1915-18 Volume VII Tomo 3 Le Operazioni Fuori del Territorio Nazionale - Albania – Macedonia - Medio Oriente.

MOH: Operacije crnogorske vojske u prvom svetskom ratu.

SeOH: Veliki rat Srbije za oslobođenje i ujedinenje Srba, Hrvata i Slovenaca. Uernaesta knjige XIV. 1916 godina. Treći period. Opšte odstupanje srpske vojske. IV faza - Prebacivanje iz Albanije na ostrvo Krf.

28 February .... The nucleus of the first British bombing squadron to attack German industrial centres formed. (Western Front).

BrOH: Official History of the War, War in the Air, Volume III.

GmOH: 1. Der Weltkrieg 1914 bis 1918, Die Militarischen Operationen zu Lande, Band 10, Die Operationen des Jahres 1916 bis zum Wechsel in der Obersten Heeresleitung; Der Krieg zur Air.

2. Die Deutschen Luftstreitkräfte von ihrer Entstehung bis zum Ende des Weltkrieges 1918. Kriegsgeschichtliche Einzelschriften der Luftwaffe. Siebenter Band: Die Deutschen Luftstreitkräfte von ihrer Entstehung bis zum

Ende des Weltkrieges 1918. Sonderband: Der Militärische Heimatlutschutz im Weltkriege 1914 bis 1918.

29 February ....The Action between S.M.S. Greif and H.M.S. Alcantara - Both sunk. (British Home Waters).

        BrOH: 1. Official History of the War, Naval Operations, Volume III.

                2. Official History of the War, Seaborne Trade, Volume I, Cruiser Period.

                3. Official History of the War – The Merchant Navy, Volume II.

        GmOH: 1. Der Krieg zur See 1914-1918, Band 3, Der Kreuzerkrieg in den ausländischen Gewässern, Teil 3, Die deutschen Hilfskreuzer.

4 March..S.M.S. Möwe's (Moewe's) first cruise finishes. (Atlantic Ocean).

        BrOH: 1. Official History of the War, Naval Operations, Volume III.

                2. Official History of the War, Seaborne Trade, Volume I, Cruiser Period.

                3. Official History of the War – The Merchant Navy, Volume II.

        GmOH: 1. Der Krieg zur See 1914-1918, Band 3, Der Kreuzerkrieg in den ausländischen Gewässern, Teil 3, Die deutschen Hilfskreuzer.

5 March..The British Offensive towards Kilimanjaro. (East Africa).

        BgOH: Les Campagnes Coloniales Belges 1914-1918. Volume I. Introduction, les Operations au Cameroun, les Operations en Rhodésie, la Période Défensive à la Frontière Orientale.

        BrOH: Official History of the War, Military Operations, East Africa, Volume I, August 1914-September 1916.

        GmOH: Der Krieg zur See 1914-1918, Band 6, Die Kämpfe der Kaiserlichen Marine in den deutschen Kolonien, Teil 2, Deutsch-Ostafrika.

        SAOH: 1. The Union of South Africa and the Great War 1914 – 1918.

                2. The South Africans with General Smuts in German East Africa 1916.

8 March..The Siege of Kut – the second attempt to relieve Kut – the attack on the Dujaila Redoubt. (Mesopotamia).

        BrOH: Official History of the War, Military Operations, Campaign in Mesopotamia, Volume I.

        TOH: 1. Büyük Harbin Sevkülceyşi.

                2. Birinci Cihan Harbinde Türk Harbi, 1916 Yili Harekatleri, IIIncu Cilt.

                3. Birinci Dünya Harbinde Türk Harbi, IIInvi Cilt, Irak-Iran Cephesi, 1914-1918, 1nci Kisim.

                4. Büyük Harpte Misir Seferi.

11-12 March ....The action of Latema Nek. (East Africa).

        BgOH: Les Campagnes Coloniales Belges 1914-1918. Volume I. Introduction, les Operations au Cameroun, les Operations en Rhodésie, la Période Défensive à la Frontière Orientale.

        BrOH: Official History of the War, Military Operations, East Africa, Volume I, August 1914-September 1916.

GmOH: 1. Der Krieg zur See 1914-1918, Band 6, Die Kämpfe der Kaiserlichen Marine in den deutschen Kolonien, Teil 2, Deutsch-Ostafrika.

SAOH: The Union of South Africa and the Great War 1914 – 1918.
2. The South Africans with General Smuts in German East Africa 1916.

12 March..The capture of Karind. (West Persia).

BrOH: Official History of the War, Military Operations, Operations in Persia 1915-1919.

TOH: 1. Büyük Harbin Sevkülceyşi.
2. Birinci Cihan Harbinde Türk Harbi, 1916 Yili Harekatleri, IIIncu Cilt.
3. Birinci Dünya Harbinde Türk Harbi VInci Cilt, Hicaz, Asir, Yeman Cepheleri ve Libya Harekati 1914-1918.
4. Büyük Harpte Misir Seferi.

RuOH: 1. The Russian Army in the World War.
2. A Strategic Outline of the War 1914 -1918.

13 March..The capture of New Moshi. (East Africa).

BgOH: Les Campagnes Coloniales Belges 1914-1918. Volume I. Introduction, les Operations au Cameroun, les Operations en Rhodésie, la Période Défensive à la Frontière Orientale.

BrOH: Official History of the War, Military Operations, East Africa, Volume I, August 1914-September 1916.

GmOH: Der Krieg zur See 1914-1918, Band 6, Die Kämpfe der Kaiserlichen Marine in den deutschen Kolonien, Teil 2, Deutsch-Ostafrika.

SAOH: 1. The Union of South Africa and the Great War 1914 – 1918.
2. The South Africans with General Smuts in German East Africa 1916.

14 March..The capture of Sollum. (West Egypt/Sudan).

BrOH: Official History of the War, Military Operations, Egypt and Palestine, Volume I, From the Outbreak of War with Germany to June 1917.

TOH: 1. Büyük Harbin Sevkülceyşi.
2. Birinci Cihan Harbinde Türk Harbi, 1916 Yili Harekatleri, IIIncu Cilt.

18 March – 30 April...........................The Battle of Lake Naroch. (Eastern Front) [Russian/German].

AHOH: Österreich-Ungarns Letzter Krieg 1914-1918 Band IV.

GmOH: Der Weltkrieg 1914 bis 1918, Die Militarischen Operationen zu Lande, Band 10, Die Operationen des Jahres 1916 bis zum Wechsel in der Obersten Heeresleitung.

RuOH: 1. The Russian Army in the World War.
2. A Strategic Outline of the War 1914 -1918.

18-27 March ....The Battle of Postawy. (Eastern Front).

AHOH: Österreich-Ungarns Letzter Krieg 1914-1918 Band IV.

GmOH: Der Weltkrieg 1914 bis 1918, Die Militarischen Operationen zu Lande, Band 10, Die Operationen des Jahres 1916 bis zum Wechsel in der Obersten Heeresleitung.

RuOH: 1. The Russian Army in the World War.

2. A Strategic Outline of the War 1914 -1918.

19-26 March .... The Battle of Jacobstadt. (Eastern Front).
                     AHOH: Österreich-Ungarns Letzter Krieg 1914-1918 Band IV.
                     GmOH: Der Weltkrieg 1914 bis 1918, Die Militarischen Operationen zu Lande, Band 10, Die Operationen des Jahres 1916 bis zum Wechsel in der Obersten Heeresleitung.
                     RuOH: 1. The Russian Army in the World War.
                                 2. A Strategic Outline of the War 1914 -1918.

21 March .... The action of Kahe. (East Africa).
                     BgOH: Les Campagnes Coloniales Belges 1914-1918. Volume I. Introduction, les Operations au Cameroun, les Operations en Rhodésie, la Période Défensive à la Frontière Orientale.
                     BrOH: Official History of the War, Military Operations, East Africa, Volume I, August 1914-September 1916.
                     GmOH: 1. Der Krieg zur See 1914-1918, Band 6, Die Kämpfe der Kaiserlichen Marine in den deutschen Kolonien, Teil 2, Deutsch-Ostafrika.
                     SAOH: The Union of South Africa and the Great War 1914 – 1918.
                                   2. The South Africans with General Smuts in German East Africa 1916.

24 March .... S.S. Sussex torpedoed by a submarine. (British Home Waters).
                     BrOH: Official History of the War, Naval Operations, Volume II.

30 March .... The Russian Hospital Ship Portugal sunk by a submarine. (Black Sea).
                     BrOH: Official History of the War, The Merchant Navy, Volume III.
                     RuOH: ..Flot v Pervoi Mirovoi Voine. V Dvukh Tomakh. Tom I Deystviya Russkogo Flota.

31 March .... The German airship raid on the East Coast of England causing 112 casualties - the German Airship L15 shot down over the mouth of the Thames.
                     BrOH: Official History of the War, War in the Air, Volume II.
                     GmOH: Der Weltkrieg 1914 bis 1918, Die Militarischen Operationen zu Lande, Band 10, Die Operationen des Jahres 1916 bis zum Wechsel in der Obersten Heeresleitung; Der Krieg zur Air.

1 April .... The Siege of Kut – the third attempt to relieve Kut. (Mesopotamia).
                     BrOH: Official History of the War, Military Operations, Campaign in Mesopotamia, Volume I.
                     TOH: 1. Büyük Harbin Sevkülceyşi.
                              2. Birinci Cihan Harbinde Türk Harbi, 1916 Yili Harekatleri, IIIncu Cilt.
                              3. Birinci Dünya Harbinde Türk Harbi, IIInvi Cilt, Irak-Iran Cephesi, 1914-1918, 1nci Kisim.
                              4. Büyük Harpte Misir Seferi.

5 April .... The Siege of Kut – the third attempt to relieve Kut – the action of Falahiya. (Mesopotamia).
                     BrOH: Official History of the War, Military Operations, Campaign in Mesopotamia, Volume I.
                     TOH: 1. Büyük Harbin Sevkülceyşi.

2. Birinci Cihan Harbinde Türk Harbi, 1916 Yili Harekatleri, IIIncu Cilt.

3. Birinci Dünya Harbinde Türk Harbi, IIInvi Cilt, Irak-Iran Cephesi, 1914-1918, 1nci Kisim.

4. Büyük Harpte Misir Seferi.

TOH: 1. Büyük Harbin Sevkülceyşi.

2. Birinci Cihan Harbinde Türk Harbi, 1916 Yili Harekatleri, IIIncu Cilt.

3. Birinci Dünya Harbinde, Erzurum ve Cevresinde Ermeni Hrekatetleri (1914–1918).

4. Birinci Dünya Harbinde Türk Harbi Kafkas Cephesi 3ncu Ordu Harekati, Cilt II, Birinci Kitap.

5. Birinci Dünya Harbinde Türk Harbi Kafkas Cephesi 3ncu Ordu Harekati, Cilt II, Ikinci Kitap.

6. Birinci Dünya Harbinde Türk Harbi, Iinci Cilt, 2nci Kisim, Kafkas Cephesi 2nci Ordu Harekati.

7. Birinci Dünya Savaşı'nda Osmanlı Ordusun'un Azerbaycan ve Dağıstan Harekati, Azerbaycan ve Dağıstan'in Bağımsızlığını Kazanması 1918.

8. Büyük Harpte Misir Seferi.

RuOH: 1. The Russian Army in the World War.

2. A Strategic Outline of the War 1914 -1918.

TOH: 1. Büyük Harbin Sevkülceyşi.

2. Birinci Cihan Harbinde Türk Harbi, 1916 Yili Harekatleri, IIIncu Cilt.

3. Birinci Dünya Harbinde, Erzurum ve Cevresinde Ermeni Hrekatetleri (1914–1918).

4. Birinci Dünya Harbinde Türk Harbi Kafkas Cephesi 3ncu Ordu Harekati, Cilt II, Birinci Kitap.

5. Birinci Dünya Harbinde Türk Harbi Kafkas Cephesi 3ncu Ordu Harekati, Cilt II, Ikinci Kitap.

6. Birinci Dünya Harbinde Türk Harbi, Iinci Cilt, 2nci Kisim, Kafkas Cephesi 2nci Ordu Harekati.

7. Birinci Dünya Savaşı'nda Osmanlı Ordusun'un Azerbaycan ve Dağıstan Harekati, Azerbaycan ve Dağıstan'in Bağımsızlığını Kazanması 1918.

8. Büyük Harpte Misir Seferi.

RuOH: 1. The Russian Army in the World War.

2. A Strategic Outline of the War 1914 -1918.

TOH: 1. Büyük Harbin Sevkülceyşi.

2. Birinci Cihan Harbinde Türk Harbi, 1916 Yili Harekatleri, IIIncu Cilt.

3. Birinci Dünya Harbinde, Erzurum ve Cevresinde Ermeni Hrekatetleri (1914–1918).

4. Birinci Dünya Harbinde Türk Harbi Kafkas Cephesi 3ncu Ordu Harekati, Cilt II, Birinci Kitap.

5. Birinci Dünya Harbinde Türk Harbi Kafkas Cephesi 3ncu Ordu Harekati, Cilt II, Ikinci Kitap.

6. Birinci Dünya Harbinde Türk Harbi, Iinci Cilt, 2nci Kisim, Kafkas Cephesi 2nci Ordu Harekati.

7. Birinci Dünya Savaşı'nda Osmanlı Ordusun'un Azerbaycan ve Dağıstan Harekati, Azerbaycan ve Dağıstan'in Bağımsızlığını Kazanması 1918.

8. Büyük Harpte Misir Seferi.
RuOH: 1. The Russian Army in the World War.
2. A Strategic Outline of the War 1914 -1918.

9 April...Constantinople and Adrianople bombed by R.N.A.S. aircraft. (Turkey).
BrOH: 1. Official History of the War, Naval Operations, Volume II.
2. Official History of the War, War in the Air, Volume II.
TOH: 1. Birinci Dünya Harbi, IXncu Cilt, Türk Hava Harekati.

2. Türk Havacilik Tarihi 1914-1916 (Ikinci Kitap).

17 April...The attack on Trebizond – the capture of Trebizond. (Eastern Front).
TOH: 1. Büyük Harbin Sevkülceyşi.
2. Birinci Cihan Harbinde Türk Harbi, 1916 Yili Harekatleri, IIIncu Cilt.
3. Birinci Dünya Harbinde, Erzurum ve Cevresinde Ermeni Hrekatetleri (1914–1918).
4. Birinci Dünya Harbinde Türk Harbi Kafkas Cephesi 3ncu Ordu Harekati, Cilt II, Birinci Kitap.
5. Birinci Dünya Harbinde Türk Harbi Kafkas Cephesi 3ncu Ordu Harekati, Cilt II, Ikinci Kitap.
6. Birinci Dünya Harbinde Türk Harbi, Iinci Cilt, 2nci Kisim, Kafkas Cephesi 2nci Ordu Harekati.
7. Birinci Dünya Savaşı'nda Osmanlı Ordusun'un Azerbaycan ve Dağıstan Harekati, Azerbaycan ve Dağıstan'in Bağımsızlığını Kazanması 1918.
8. Büyük Harpte Misir Seferi.
RuOH: 1. The Russian Army in the World War.
2. A Strategic Outline of the War 1914 -1918.

17-18 April ....The Siege of Kut – the third attempt to relieve Kut – the action of Bait Aissa. (Mesopotamia).
BrOH: Official History of the War, Military Operations, Campaign in Mesopotamia, Volume I.
TOH: 1. Büyük Harbin Sevkülceyşi.
2. Birinci Cihan Harbinde Türk Harbi, 1916 Yili Harekatleri, IIIncu Cilt.
3. Birinci Dünya Harbinde Türk Harbi, IIInvi Cilt, Irak-Iran Cephesi, 1914-1918, 1nci Kisim.
4. Büyük Harpte Misir Seferi.

17-19 April ....The capture of Kondoa Irangi. (East Africa).
BgOH: Les Campagnes Coloniales Belges 1914-1918. Volume I. Introduction, les Operations au Cameroun, les Operations en Rhodésie, la Période Défensive à la Frontière Orientale.
BrOH: Official History of the War, Military Operations, East Africa, Volume I, August 1914-September 1916.
GmOH: 1. Der Krieg zur See 1914-1918, Band 6, Die Kämpfe der Kaiserlichen Marine in den deutschen Kolonien, Teil 2, Deutsch-Ostafrika.
SAOH: The Union of South Africa and the Great War 1914 – 1918.
2. The South Africans with General Smuts in German East Africa 1916.

22 April...The German Transport Aud sinks herself after capture whilst trying to land arms on the Coast of Ireland. (British Home Waters).

BrOH: Official History of the War, Naval Operations, Volume III.

EOH: Irish Rebellion, 1916: Royal Commission on the Rebellion in Ireland. Report, Minutes of Evidence and Appendix of Documents.

TOH: 1. Büyük Harbin Sevkülceyşi.

2. Birinci Cihan Harbinde Türk Harbi, 1916 Yili Harekatleri, IIIncu Cilt.

3. Birinci Dünya Harbinde, Erzurum ve Cevresinde Ermeni Hrekatetleri (1914–1918).

4. Birinci Dünya Harbinde Türk Harbi Kafkas Cephesi 3ncu Ordu Harekati, Cilt II, Birinci Kitap.

5. Birinci Dünya Harbinde Türk Harbi Kafkas Cephesi 3ncu Ordu Harekati, Cilt II, Ikinci Kitap.

6. Birinci Dünya Harbinde Türk Harbi, Iinci Cilt, 2nci Kisim, Kafkas Cephesi 2nci Ordu Harekati.

7. Birinci Dünya Savaşı'nda Osmanlı Ordusun'un Azerbaycan ve Dağıstan Harekati, Azerbaycan ve Dağıstan'in Bağımsızlığını Kazanması 1918.

8. Büyük Harpte Misir Seferi.

RuOH: 1. The Russian Army in the World War.

2. A Strategic Outline of the War 1914 -1918.

BrOH: Official History of the War, Naval Operations, Volume III.

EOH: Irish Rebellion, 1916: Royal Commission on the Rebellion in Ireland. Report, Minutes of Evidence and Appendix of Documents.

BrOH: Official History of the War, Military Operations, Campaign in Mesopotamia, Volume I.

TOH: 1. Büyük Harbin Sevkülceyşi.

2. Birinci Cihan Harbinde Türk Harbi, 1916 Yili Harekatleri, IIIncu Cilt.

3. Birinci Dünya Harbinde Türk Harbi, IIInvi Cilt, Irak-Iran Cephesi, 1914-1918, 1nci Kisim.

4. Büyük Harpte Misir Seferi.

BrOH: Official History of the War, Military Operations, Campaign in Mesopotamia, Volume I.

TOH: 1. Büyük Harbin Sevkülceyşi.

2. Birinci Cihan Harbinde Türk Harbi, 1916 Yili Harekatleri, IIIncu Cilt.

3. Birinci Dünya Harbinde Türk Harbi, IIInvi Cilt, Irak-Iran Cephesi, 1914-1918, 1nci Kisim.

4. Büyük Harpte Misir Seferi.

BrOH: Official History of the War, Naval Operations, Volume III.

GmOH: Der Krieg zur See 1914-1918, Band 1, Der Krieg in der Nordsee, Teil 5, Von Januar bis Juni 1916.

27 April...H.M.S. Russell sunk by a mine. (Mediterranean Sea)
                                  BrOH: Official History of the War, Naval Operations, Volume III.

29 April...The Siege of Kut – the capitulation of Kut. (Mesopotamia).
                                  BrOH: Official History of the War, Military Operations, Campaign in Mesopotamia, Volume I.
                                  TOH: 1. Büyük Harbin Sevkülceyşi.
                                              2. Birinci Cihan Harbinde Türk Harbi, 1916 Yili Harekatleri, IIIncu Cilt.
                                              3. Birinci Dünya Harbinde Türk Harbi, IIInvi Cilt, Irak-Iran Cephesi, 1914-1918, 1nci Kisim.
                                            4. Büyük Harpte Misir Seferi.

1 May...The Collapse of the Irish Rebellion. (Ireland) .
                                  BrOH: Official History of the War, Naval Operations, Volume III.
                                  EOH: Irish Rebellion, 1916: Royal Commission on the Rebellion in Ireland. Report, Minutes of Evidence and Appendix of Documents.

3 May...The German airship L20 wrecked at Stavanger. (North Sea).
                                  GmOH: Der Weltkrieg 1914 bis 1918, Die Militarischen Operationen zu Lande, Band 10, Die Operationen des Jahres 1916 bis zum Wechsel in der Obersten Heeresleitung; Der Krieg zur Air.

4 May...The German airship L7 destroyed off the Slesvig Coast. (North Sea).
                                  GmOH: Der Weltkrieg 1914 bis 1918, Die Militarischen Operationen zu Lande, Band 10, Die Operationen des Jahres 1916 bis zum Wechsel in der Obersten Heeresleitung; Der Krieg zur Air.

5 May...The German airship LZ85 shot down over Salonika. (Balkan Front Front).
                                  BrOH: Official History of the War, War in the Air, Volume III.
                                  GmOH: Der Weltkrieg 1914 bis 1918, Die Militarischen Operationen zu Lande, Band 10, Die Operationen des Jahres 1916 bis zum Wechsel in der Obersten Heeresleitung; Der Krieg zur Air.
                                  GrOH: 1. Ho Hellenikos Stratos kata ton Proton Pankosmion Polemon 1914-1918 Tomos 1 - H Hellas kai ho Polemos eis ta Balkania.
                                            2. Epitomh Istopia Ths Eummetochhs Tou Ellhnikou Stratou Ston Prpsto Pagkosmio Polemo 1914-1918. / A Concise History of the Participation of the Hellenic Army in The First World War 1914-1918.
                                  SeOH: Veliki rat Srbije za oslobođenje i ujedinenje Srba, Hrvata i Slovenaca. knjige XV. 1916 godina. Reorganizacija srpske vojske na Krfu I prebacivanje u Solun I okolinu.

7 May...The capture of Qasr-i-Shirin. (West Persia).
                                  BrOH: Official History of the War, Military Operations, Operations in Persia 1915-1919.
                                  TOH: 1. Büyük Harbin Sevkülceyşi.
                                              2. Birinci Cihan Harbinde Türk Harbi, 1916 Yili Harekatleri, IIIncu Cilt.
                                              3. Birinci Dünya Harbinde Türk Harbi VInci Cilt, Hicaz, Asir, Yeman Cepheleri ve Libya Harekati 1914-1918.

4. Büyük Harpte Misir Seferi.

RuOH: 1. The Russian Army in the World War.

2. A Strategic Outline of the War 1914 -1918.

11 May...The capture of Kwash. (East Persia).

BrOH: Official History of the War, Military Operations, Operations in Persia 1915-1919.

TOH: 1. Büyük Harbin Sevkülceyşi.

2. Birinci Cihan Harbinde Türk Harbi, 1916 Yili Harekatleri, IIIncu Cilt.

3. Birinci Dünya Harbinde Türk Harbi VInci Cilt, Hicaz, Asir, Yeman Cepheleri ve Libya Harekati 1914-1918.

4. Büyük Harpte Misir Seferi.

14 May – 3 June...............................The Austrian Trentino Offensive. (Italian Front).

AHOH: Österreich-Ungarns Letzter Krieg 1914-1918, Band III.

IOH: Maggiore Esercito, Ufficio Storico, L'Esercito italiano nella grande guerra 1915-18, Volume III, Tomo 2, Le Operazioni Del 1916 - Gli Avvenimenti Dal Maggio Al Luglio.

15 May...The capture of Khanaqin & Rowanduz. (West Persia).

BrOH: Official History of the War, Military Operations, Operations in Persia 1915-1919.

TOH: 1. Büyük Harbin Sevkülceyşi.

2. Birinci Cihan Harbinde Türk Harbi, 1916 Yili Harekatleri, IIIncu Cilt.

3. Birinci Dünya Harbinde Türk Harbi VInci Cilt, Hicaz, Asir, Yeman Cepheleri ve Libya Harekati 1914-1918.

4. Büyük Harpte Misir Seferi.

RuOH: 1. The Russian Army in the World War.

2. A Strategic Outline of the War 1914 -1918.

22 May...The affair of Beringiya. (Darfur). (West Egypt/Sudan).

BrOH: Official History of the War, Military Operations, Egypt and Palestine, Volume I, From the Outbreak of War with Germany to June 1917.

TOH: 1. Büyük Harbin Sevkülceyşi.

2. Birinci Cihan Harbinde Türk Harbi, 1916 Yili Harekatleri, IIIncu Cilt.

23 May...The capture of El Fasher. (Darfur). (West Egypt/Sudan).

BrOH: Official History of the War, Military Operations, Egypt and Palestine, Volume I, From the Outbreak of War with Germany to June 1917.

TOH: 1. Büyük Harbin Sevkülceyşi.

2. Birinci Cihan Harbinde Türk Harbi, 1916 Yili Harekatleri, IIIncu Cilt.

25 May...The British advance from Northern Rhodesia. (East Africa).

BgOH: Les campagnes coloniales Belges 1914-1918. Volume II. la campagne de Tabora 1916.

BrOH: Official History of the War, Military Operations, East Africa, Volume I, August 1914-September 1916.

GmOH: Der Krieg zur See 1914-1918, Band 6, Die Kämpfe der Kaiserlichen Marine in den deutschen Kolonien, Teil 2, Deutsch-Ostafrika.

SAOH: 1. The Union of South Africa and the Great War 1914 – 1918.

                                        2. The South Africans with General Smuts in German
                                        East Africa 1916.

27 May...The capture of Neu Langenburg. (East Africa).
                              BgOH: Les campagnes coloniales Belges 1914-1918. Volume II.
                                        la campagne de Tabora 1916.
                              BrOH: Official History of the War, Military Operations, East
                                        Africa, Volume I, August 1914-September 1916.
                              GmOH:Der Krieg zur See 1914-1918, Band 6, Die Kämpfe der
                                        Kaiserlichen Marine in den deutschen Kolonien, Teil 2,
                                        Deutsch-Ostafrika.
                              SAOH: 1. The Union of South Africa and the Great War 1914 –
                                        1918.
                                        2. The South Africans with General Smuts in German
                                        East Africa 1916.

31 May -1 June ....The Battle of Jutland – losses on both side. (North Sea).
                              AuOH: Official History of Australia in the War of 1914-1918,
                                        Volume IX, Royal Australian Navy.
                              BrOH: Official History of the War, Naval Operations, Volume
                                        III.
                              COH: The Naval Service of Canada, It's Official History,
                                        Volume I, Origins and Early Years.
                              GmOH: Der Krieg zur See 1914-1918, Band 1, Der Krieg in der
                                        Nordsee, Teil 5, Von Januar bis Juni 1916.

2-13 June ....The Battle of Mount Sorrel. (Western Front).
                              BrOH: Official History of the War, Military Operations, France
                                        and Belgium 1916, Volume I, Sir Douglas Haig's
                                        Command to the 1st July, Battle of the Somme.
                              GmOH: Der Weltkrieg 1914 bis 1918, Die Militarischen
                                        Operationen zu Lande, Band 10, Die Operationen des
                                        Jahres 1916 bis zum Wechsel in der Obersten
                                        Heeresleitung.

4-16 June ....Italian local attacks on the Trentino Front. (Italian Front).
                              AHOH: Österreich-Ungarns Letzter Krieg 1914-1918, Band IV.
                              IOH: Maggiore Esercito, Ufficio Storico, L'Esercito italiano
                                        nella grande guerra 1915-18, Volume III, Tomo 2, Le
                                        Operazioni Del 1916 - Gli Avvenimenti Dal Maggio Al
                                        Luglio.

4 June – 10 August.............................The Brusilov's Offensive. (Eastern Front).
                              AHOH:.1. Österreich-Ungarns Letzter Krieg 1914-1918, Band IV.
                                        2. Österreich-Ungarns Letzter Krieg 1914-1918, Band V.
                              GmOH: 1. Der Weltkrieg 1914 bis 1918, Die Militarischen
                                        Operationen zu Lande, Band 10, Die Operationen des
                                        Jahres 1916 bis zum Wechsel in der Obersten
                                        Heeresleitung.
                                        2. Der Weltkrieg 1914 bis 1918, Die Militarischen
                                        Operationen zu Lande, Band 11, Die Kriegführung im
                                        Herbst 1916 und im Winter 1916/17.
                              RuOH: 1. The Russian Army in the World War.
                                        2. A Strategic Outline of the War 1914 -1918.
                              TOH: 1. Birinci Dünya Harbinde Türk Harbi, VIInci Cilt, 1nci
                                        Kisim, Avrupa Cepheleri, Galaçya Cephesi.
                                        2. Birinci Dünya Harbinde Türk Harbi, Avrupa Cepheleri
                                        (Özet).

4-10 June ....The Brusilov's Offensive – the Battle of Wosuszka-Sereth. (Eastern Front).

        AHOH: Österreich-Ungarns Letzter Krieg 1914-1918, Band IV.

        RuOH: 1. The Russian Army in the World War.

               2. A Strategic Outline of the War 1914 -1918.

5 June..H.M.S. Hampshire sunk by a mine. (British Home Waters).

        BrOH: Official History of the War, Naval Operations, Volume IV.

5 June – 22 September ....The Arab Revolt in the Hejaz begins. (Arabia).

        AuOH: Official History of Australia in the War of 1914-1918, Volume VII, Sinai and Palestine.

        BrOH: Official History of the War, Military Operations, Egypt and Palestine, Volume I, From the Outbreak of War with Germany to June 1917.

        NZOH: Official History of New Zealand's Effort in the Great War, Volume III, Sinai and Palestine.

        TOH: 1. Büyük Harbin Sevkülceyşi.

               2. Birinci Cihan Harbinde Türk Harbi, 1914 Yili Harekatleri, Inci Cilt.

               3. Birinci Dünya Harbinde Türk Harbi VInci Cilt, Hicaz, Asir, Yeman Cepheleri ve Libya Harekati 1914-1918.

               4. Büyük Harpte Misir Seferi.

5 June – 24 August.............................The Turkish Offensive. (West Persia.).

        BrOH: Official History of the War, Military Operations, Operations in Persia 1915-1919.

        TOH: 1. Büyük Harbin Sevkülceyşi.

               2. Birinci Cihan Harbinde Türk Harbi, 1916 Yili Harekatleri, IIIncu Cilt.

               3. Birinci Dünya Harbinde Türk Harbi VInci Cilt, Hicaz, Asir, Yeman Cepheleri ve Libya Harekati 1914-1918.

               4. Büyük Harpte Misir Seferi.

        RuOH: 1. The Russian Army in the World War.

               2. A Strategic Outline of the War 1914 -1918.

6 June..The Arab Revolt in the Hejaz – the Arab attack on Medina. (Arabia).

        AuOH: Official History of Australia in the War of 1914-1918, Volume VII, Sinai and Palestine.

        BrOH: Official History of the War, Military Operations, Egypt and Palestine, Volume I, From the Outbreak of War with Germany to June 1917.

        NZOH: Official History of New Zealand's Effort in the Great War, Volume III, Sinai and Palestine.

        TOH: 1. Büyük Harbin Sevkülceyşi.

               2. Birinci Cihan Harbinde Türk Harbi, 1914 Yili Harekatleri, Inci Cilt.

               3. Birinci Dünya Harbinde Türk Harbi VInci Cilt, Hicaz, Asir, Yeman Cepheleri ve Libya Harekati 1914-1918.

               4. Büyük Harpte Misir Seferi.

7 June..The Battle of Verdun – the Defensive Battle of Verdun – the capture of Fort de Vaux by the Germans. (Western Front).

        FrOH: Les Armées Françaises dans la Grande Guerre, Tome IV, Verdun et la Somme, Volume 2, La Bataille de Verdun et les offensifs des Alliés - 1 mai–3 septembre 1916.

        GmOH: 1. Der Weltkrieg 1914 bis 1918, Die Militarischen Operationen zu Lande, Band 10, Die Operationen des

Jahres 1916 bis zum Wechsel in der Obersten Heeresleitung.

2. Die Bayern im Großen Kriege 1914-1918.

8 June...The capture of Bismarckburg. (East Africa)].

BrOH: Official History of the War, Military Operations, East Africa, Volume I, August 1914-September 1916.

GmOH: Der Krieg zur See 1914-1918, Band 6, Die Kämpfe der Kaiserlichen Marine in den deutschen Kolonien, Teil 2, Deutsch-Ostafrika.

SAOH: 1. The Union of South Africa and the Great War 1914 – 1918.

2. The South Africans with General Smuts in German East Africa 1916.

9 June...The action of Mkaramo. (East Africa).

BgOH: Les campagnes coloniales Belges 1914-1918. Volume II. la campagne de Tabora 1916.

BrOH: Official History of the War, Military Operations, East Africa, Volume I, August 1914-September 1916.

GmOH: Der Krieg zur See 1914-1918, Band 6, Die Kämpfe der Kaiserlichen Marine in den deutschen Kolonien, Teil 2, Deutsch-Ostafrika.

SAOH: 1. The Union of South Africa and the Great War 1914 – 1918.

2. The South Africans with General Smuts in German East Africa 1916.

9 June...The Arab Revolt in the Hejaz – the capture of Jidda. (Arabia).

AuOH: Official History of Australia in the War of 1914-1918, Volume VII, Sinai and Palestine.

BrOH: Official History of the War, Military Operations, Egypt and Palestine, Volume I, From the Outbreak of War with Germany to June 1917.

NZOH: Official History of New Zealand's Effort in the Great War, Volume III, Sinai and Palestine.

TOH: 1. Büyük Harbin Sevkülceyşi.

2. Birinci Cihan Harbinde Türk Harbi, 1914 Yili Harekatleri, Inci Cilt.

3. Birinci Dünya Harbinde Türk Harbi VInci Cilt, Hicaz, Asir, Yeman Cepheleri ve Libya Harekati 1914-1918.

4. Büyük Harpte Misir Seferi.

9-10 June ....The German attack on Kondoa Irangi. (East Africa).

BgOH: Les campagnes coloniales Belges 1914-1918. Volume II. la campagne de Tabora 1916.

BrOH: Official History of the War, Military Operations, East Africa, Volume I, August 1914-September 1916.

GmOH: Der Krieg zur See 1914-1918, Band 6, Die Kämpfe der Kaiserlichen Marine in den deutschen Kolonien, Teil 2, Deutsch-Ostafrika.

SAOH: 1. The Union of South Africa and the Great War 1914 – 1918.

2. The South Africans with General Smuts in German East Africa 1916.

10 June...The Arab Revolt in the Hejaz – the surrender of Mecca to the Sherif. (Arabia).

AuOH: Official History of Australia in the War of 1914-1918, Volume VII, Sinai and Palestine.

BrOH: Official History of the War, Military Operations, Egypt and Palestine, Volume I, From the Outbreak of War with Germany to June 1917.

NZOH: Official History of New Zealand's Effort in the Great War, Volume III, Sinai and Palestine.

TOH: 1. Büyük Harbin Sevkülceyşi.
2. Birinci Cihan Harbinde Türk Harbi, 1914 Yili Harekatleri, Inci Cilt.
3. Birinci Dünya Harbinde Türk Harbi VInci Cilt, Hicaz, Asir, Yemen Cepheleri ve Libya Harekati 1914-1918.
4. Büyük Harpte Misir Seferi.

AHOH:.Österreich-Ungarns Letzter Krieg 1914-1918, Band VI, Part I.

GmOH: Der Weltkrieg 1914 bis 1918, Die Militarischen Operationen zu Lande, Band 10, Die Operationen des Jahres 1916 bis zum Wechsel in der Obersten Heeresleitung.

RuOH: 1. The Russian Army in the World War.
2. A Strategic Outline of the War 1914 -1918.

TOH: 1. Birinci Dünya Harbinde Türk Harbi, VIInci Cilt, 1nci Kisim, Avrupa Cepheleri, Galaçya Cephesi.
2. Birinci Dünya Harbinde Türk Harbi, Avrupa Cepheleri (Özet).

BrOH: Official History of the War, Military Operations, Operations in Persia 1915-1919.

TOH: 1. Büyük Harbin Sevkülceyşi.
2. Birinci Cihan Harbinde Türk Harbi, 1916 Yili Harekatleri, IIIncu Cilt.
3. Birinci Dünya Harbinde Türk Harbi VInci Cilt, Hicaz, Asir, Yemen Cepheleri ve Libya Harekati 1914-1918.
4. Büyük Harpte Misir Seferi.

AHOH:.1. Österreich-Ungarns Letzter Krieg 1914-1918, Band IV.
2. Österreich-Ungarns Letzter Krieg 1914-1918, Band V.

IOH: Maggiore Esercito, Ufficio Storico, L'Esercito italiano nella grande guerra 1915-18, Volume III, Tomo 2, Le Operazioni Del 1916 - Gli Avvenimenti Dal Maggio Al Luglio.

BrOH: Official History of the War, War in the Air, Volume II.

GmOH: Der Weltkrieg 1914 bis 1918, Die Militarischen Operationen zu Lande, Band 10, Die Operationen des Jahres 1916 bis zum Wechsel in der Obersten Heeresleitung.

BgOH: Les campagnes coloniales Belges 1914-1918. Volume II. la campagne de Tabora 1916.

BrOH: Official History of the War, Military Operations, East Africa, Volume I, August 1914-September 1916.

GmOH: Der Krieg zur See 1914-1918, Band 6, Die Kämpfe der Kaiserlichen Marine in den deutschen Kolonien, Teil 2, Deutsch-Ostafrika.

SAOH: 1. The Union of South Africa and the Great War 1914 – 1918.

2. The South Africans with General Smuts in German East Africa 1916.

20 June...The capture of Qasr-i-Shirin. (West Persia).

BrOH: Official History of the War, Military Operations, Operations in Persia 1915-1919.

TOH: 1. Büyük Harbin Sevkülceyşi.

2. Birinci Cihan Harbinde Türk Harbi, 1916 Yili Harekatleri, IIIncu Cilt.

3. Birinci Dünya Harbinde Türk Harbi VInci Cilt, Hicaz, Asir, Yeman Cepheleri ve Libya Harekati 1914-1918.

4. Büyük Harpte Misir Seferi.

RuOH: 1. The Russian Army in the World War.

2. A Strategic Outline of the War 1914 -1918.

23 June...The Battle of Verdun – the Defensive Battle of Verdun – the capture of the Ouvrage de Thiaumont by the Germans. (Western Front).

FrOH: Les Armées Françaises dans la Grande Guerre, Tome IV, Verdun et la Somme, Volume 2, La Bataille de Verdun et les offensifs des Alliés - 1 mai–3 septembre 1916.

GmOH: 1. Der Weltkrieg 1914 bis 1918, Die Militarischen Operationen zu Lande, Band 10, Die Operationen des Jahres 1916 bis zum Wechsel in der Obersten Heeresleitung.

2. Die Bayern im Großen Kriege 1914-1918.

30 June...The Battle of Verdun – the Defensive Battle of Verdun – the recapture of the Ouvrage de Thiaumont by the French. (Western Front).

FrOH: Les Armées Françaises dans la Grande Guerre, Tome IV, Verdun et la Somme, Volume 2, La Bataille de Verdun et les offensifs des Alliés - 1 mai–3 septembre 1916.

GmOH: 1. Der Weltkrieg 1914 bis 1918, Die Militarischen Operationen zu Lande, Band 10, Die Operationen des Jahres 1916 bis zum Wechsel in der Obersten Heeresleitung.

2. Die Bayern im Großen Kriege 1914-1918.

1 July –18 November.........................The Allied Summer Offensive – the Battle of the Somme. (Western Front).

AuOH: Official History of Australia in the War of 1914-1918, Volume III, France 1916.

BrOH: 1. Official History of the War, Military Operations, France and Belgium 1916, Volume I, Sir Douglas Haig's Command to the 1st July, Battle of the Somme.

2. Official History of the War, Military Operations, France and Belgium 1916 Volume II, 2nd July 1916 to the End of the Battles of the Somme.

COH: 1. Canadian Expeditionary Force 1914 - 1919. The Official History of the Canadian Army in the First World War.

2. The Western Front 1914.

FrOH: 1. Les Armées Françaises dans la Grande Guerre, Tome IV, Verdun et la Somme, Volume 2, La Bataille de

Verdun et les offensifs des Alliés - 1 mai–3 septembre 1916.

2. Les Armées Françaises dans la Grande Guerre, Tome IV, Verdun et la Somme, Volume 3, Bataille de la Somme. (fin) - Offensives Françaises à Verdun – 3 septembre-fin décembre 1916.

GmOH: 1. Der Weltkrieg 1914 bis 1918, Die Militarischen Operationen zu Lande, Band 10, Die Operationen des Jahres 1916 bis zum Wechsel in der Obersten Heeresleitung.

2. Der Weltkrieg 1914 bis 1918, Die Militarischen Operationen zu Lande, Band 11, Die Kriegführung im Herbst 1916 und im Winter 1916/17.

3. Die Bayern im Großen Kriege 1914-1918.

NZOH: Official History of New Zealand's Effort in the Great War, Volume II, France.

SAOH: 1. The South African Forces in France.

2. The Union of South Africa and the Great War 1914 – 1918.

1-13 July .... The Allied Summer Offensive – the Battle of the Somme – the Battle of Albert, 1916. (Western Front).

AuOH: Official History of Australia in the War of 1914-1918, Volume III, France 1916.

BrOH: 1. Official History of the War, Military Operations, France and Belgium 1916, Volume I, Sir Douglas Haig's Command to the 1st July, Battle of the Somme.

2. Official History of the War, Military Operations, France and Belgium 1916 Volume II, 2nd July 1916 to the End of the Battles of the Somme.

COH: 1. Canadian Expeditionary Force 1914 - 1919. The Official History of the Canadian Army in the First World War.

2. The Western Front 1914.

GmOH: 1. Der Weltkrieg 1914 bis 1918, Die Militarischen Operationen zu Lande, Band 10, Die Operationen des Jahres 1916 bis zum Wechsel in der Obersten Heeresleitung.

2. Die Bayern im Großen Kriege 1914-1918.

NZOH: Official History of New Zealand's Effort in the Great War, Volume II, France.

SAOH: 1. The South African Forces in France.

2. The Union of South Africa and the Great War 1914 – 1918.

1 July .... The capture of Kirmanshah. (West Persia).

BrOH: Official History of the War, Military Operations, Operations in Persia 1915-1919.

TOH: 1. Büyük Harbin Sevkülceyşi.

2. Birinci Cihan Harbinde Türk Harbi, 1916 Yili Harekatleri, IIIncu Cilt.

3. Birinci Dünya Harbinde Türk Harbi VInci Cilt, Hicaz, Asir, Yeman Cepheleri ve Libya Harekati 1914-1918.

4. Büyük Harpte Misir Seferi.

RuOH: 1. The Russian Army in the World War.

2. A Strategic Outline of the War 1914 -1918.

2-9 July .... The Brusilov's Offensive – the Battle of Baranovichi. (Eastern Front).

AHOH: Österreich-Ungarns Letzter Krieg 1914-1918, Band VI, Part II.

GmOH: Der Weltkrieg 1914 bis 1918, Die Militarischen Operationen zu Lande, Band 10, Die Operationen des Jahres 1916 bis zum Wechsel in der Obersten Heeresleitung.

RuOH: 1. The Russian Army in the World War.
2. A Strategic Outline of the War 1914 -1918.

TOH: 1. Birinci Dünya Harbinde Türk Harbi, VIInci Cilt, 1nci Kisim, Avrupa Cepheleri, Galaçya Cephesi.
2. Birinci Dünya Harbinde Türk Harbi, Avrupa Cepheleri (Özet).

7 July ....The capture of Tanga. (East Africa).

BgOH: Les campagnes coloniales Belges 1914-1918. Volume II. la campagne de Tabora 1916.

BrOH: Official History of the War, Military Operations, East Africa, Volume I, August 1914-September 1916.

GmOH: Der Krieg zur See 1914-1918, Band 6, Die Kämpfe der Kaiserlichen Marine in den deutschen Kolonien, Teil 2, Deutsch-Ostafrika.

SAOH: 1. The Union of South Africa and the Great War 1914 – 1918.
2. The South Africans with General Smuts in German East Africa 1916.

10 July ....German submarine S.S. Deutschland arrived at Norfolk, Virginia, USA. (Atlantic Ocean).

GmOH: Der Krieg zur See 1914-1918, Band 4, Der Handelskrieg Mit U-Booten, Teil 4, Februar bis Dezember 1917.

10 July ....Russian Hospital Ship Vpered sunk by a submarine. (Black Sea).

RuOH:..Flot v Pervoi Mirovoi Voine. V Dvukh Tomakh. Tom I Deystviya Russkogo Flota.

11 July ....Seaham, Durham shelled by a submarine. (British Home Waters).

BrOH: Official History of the War, Naval Operations, Volume IV.

GmOH: 1. Der Krieg zur See 1914-1918, Band 1, Der Krieg in der Nordsee, Teil 6, Von Juni 1916 bis Frühjahr 1917.
2. Der Krieg zur See 1914-1918, Band 4, Der Handelskrieg Mit U-Booten, Teil 4, Februar bis Dezember 1917.

10 July – 9 August ....The Brusilov's Offensive – the Battle of Baranovichi-Gorodichi. (Eastern Front).

AHOH: Österreich-Ungarns Letzter Krieg 1914-1918, Band VI, Part II.

GmOH: Der Weltkrieg 1914 bis 1918, Die Militarischen Operationen zu Lande, Band 10, Die Operationen des Jahres 1916 bis zum Wechsel in der Obersten Heeresleitung.

RuOH: 1. The Russian Army in the World War.
2. A Strategic Outline of the War 1914 -1918.

TOH: 1. Birinci Dünya Harbinde Türk Harbi, VIInci Cilt, 1nci Kisim, Avrupa Cepheleri, Galaçya Cephesi.
2. Birinci Dünya Harbinde Türk Harbi, Avrupa Cepheleri (Özet).

14 July ....The capture of Mwanza. (East Africa).

BgOH: Les campagnes coloniales Belges 1914-1918. Volume II. la campagne de Tabora 1916.

BrOH: Official History of the War, Military Operations, East Africa, Volume I, August 1914-September 1916.

GmOH: Der Krieg zur See 1914-1918, Band 6, Die Kämpfe der Kaiserlichen Marine in den deutschen Kolonien, Teil 2, Deutsch-Ostafrika.

SAOH: 1. The Union of South Africa and the Great War 1914 – 1918.

2. The South Africans with General Smuts in German East Africa 1916.

14-17 July ....The Allied Summer Offensive – the Battle of the Somme – the Battle of Bazentin Ridge. (Western Front).

AuOH:..Official History of Australia in the War of 1914-1918, Volume III, France 1916.

BrOH: Official History of the War, Military Operations, France and Belgium 1916 Volume II, 2nd July 1916 to the End of the Battles of the Somme.

COH: 1. Canadian Expeditionary Force 1914 - 1919. The Official History of the Canadian Army in the First World War.

2. The Western Front 1914.

GmOH: 1. Der Weltkrieg 1914 bis 1918, Die Militarischen Operationen zu Lande, Band 10, Die Operationen des Jahres 1916 bis zum Wechsel in der Obersten Heeresleitung.

2. Die Bayern im Großen Kriege 1914-1918.

NZOH: Official History of New Zealand's Effort in the Great War, Volume II, France.

SAOH: 1. The South African Forces in France.

2. The Union of South Africa and the Great War 1914 – 1918.

15 July – 3 September........................The Allied Summer Offensive – the Battle of the Somme – the Battle of Delville Wood. (Western Front).

AuOH: Official History of Australia in the War of 1914-1918, Volume III, France 1916.

BrOH: Official History of the War, Military Operations, France and Belgium 1916 Volume II, 2nd July 1916 to the End of the Battles of the Somme.

COH: 1. Canadian Expeditionary Force 1914 - 1919. The Official History of the Canadian Army in the First World War.

2. The Western Front 1914.

GmOH: 1. Der Weltkrieg 1914 bis 1918, Die Militarischen Operationen zu Lande, Band 10, Die Operationen des Jahres 1916 bis zum Wechsel in der Obersten Heeresleitung.

2. Die Bayern im Großen Kriege 1914-1918.

NZOH: Official History of New Zealand's Effort in the Great War, Volume II, France.

SAOH: 1. The South African Forces in France.

2. The Union of South Africa and the Great War 1914 – 1918.

16-23 July ....The Brusilov's Offensive – the Battle of Kekkau. (Eastern Front).

AHOH: Österreich-Ungarns Letzter Krieg 1914-1918, Band VI, Part II.

GmOH: Der Weltkrieg 1914 bis 1918, Die Militarischen Operationen zu Lande, Band 10, Die Operationen des Jahres 1916 bis zum Wechsel in der Obersten Heeresleitung.

RuOH: 1. The Russian Army in the World War.
2. A Strategic Outline of the War 1914 -1918.

TOH: 1. Birinci Dünya Harbinde Türk Harbi, VIInci Cilt, 1nci Kisim, Avrupa Cepheleri, Galaçya Cephesi.
2. Birinci Dünya Harbinde Türk Harbi, Avrupa Cepheleri (Özet).

AuOH:..Official History of Australia in the War of 1914-1918, Volume VII, Sinai and Palestine.

BrOH: Official History of the War, Military Operations, Egypt and Palestine, Volume I, From the Outbreak of War with Germany to June 1917.

NZOH: Official History of New Zealand's Effort in the Great War, Volume III, Sinai and Palestine.

TOH: 1. Büyük Harbin Sevkülceyşi.
2. Birinci Cihan Harbinde Türk Harbi, 1916 Yili Harekatleri, IIIncu Cilt.
3. Birinci Dünya Harbinde Türk Harbi, 1nci Kisim, Sina-Filistin Cephesi Harbin Başlangicindan 1kinci Gazze Muharebeleri Sonuna Kadar.
4. Büyük Harpte Misir Seferi.

AuOH: Official History of Australia in the War of 1914-1918, Volume III, France 1916.

BrOH: Official History of the War, Military Operations, France and Belgium 1916 Volume II, 2nd July 1916 to the End of the Battles of the Somme.

COH: 1. Canadian Expeditionary Force 1914 - 1919. The Official History of the Canadian Army in the First World War.
2. The Western Front 1914.

GmOH: 1. Der Weltkrieg 1914 bis 1918, Die Militarischen Operationen zu Lande, Band 10, Die Operationen des Jahres 1916 bis zum Wechsel in der Obersten Heeresleitung.
2. Die Bayern im Großen Kriege 1914-1918.

NZOH: Official History of New Zealand's Effort in the Great War, Volume II, France.

SAOH: 1. The South African Forces in France.
2. The Union of South Africa and the Great War 1914 – 1918.

BrOH: Official History of the War, The Merchant Navy, Volume I.

AuOH: Official History of Australia in the War of 1914-1918, Volume VII, Sinai and Palestine.

BrOH: Official History of the War, Military Operations, Egypt and Palestine, Volume I, From the Outbreak of War with Germany to June 1917.

NZOH: Official History of New Zealand's Effort in the Great War, Volume III, Sinai and Palestine.

TOH: 1. Büyük Harbin Sevkülceyşi.

2. Birinci Cihan Harbinde Türk Harbi, 1914 Yili Harekatleri, II inci Cilt.

3. Birinci Dünya Harbinde Türk Harbi, IIInvi Cilt, Irak-Iran Cephesi, 1914-1918, 1nci Kisim.

4. Birinci Dünya Harbinde Türk Harbi, 1nci Kisim, Sina-Filistin Cephesi Harbin Başlangicindan 1kinci Gazze Muharebeleri Sonuna Kadar.

5. Birinci Dünya Harbinde Türk Harbi VInci Cilt, Hicaz, Asir, Yeman Cepheleri ve Libya Harekati 1914-1918.

6. Büyük Harpte Misir Seferi.

28 July - 17 August .... The Brusilov's Offensive – the Battle of Kowel. (Eastern Front).

AHOH: Österreich-Ungarns Letzter Krieg 1914-1918, Band VI, Part II.

GmOH: Der Weltkrieg 1914 bis 1918, Die Militarischen Operationen zu Lande, Band 10, Die Operationen des Jahres 1916 bis zum Wechsel in der Obersten Heeresleitung.

RuOH: 1. The Russian Army in the World War.

2. A Strategic Outline of the War 1914 -1918.

TOH: 1. Birinci Dünya Harbinde Türk Harbi, VIInci Cilt, 1nci Kisim, Avrupa Cepheleri, Galaçya Cephesi.

2. Birinci Dünya Harbinde Türk Harbi, Avrupa Cepheleri (Özet).

28 July .... The Brusilov's Offensive – the Battle of Chocimjiercz. (Eastern Front).

AHOH: Österreich-Ungarns Letzter Krieg 1914-1918, Band VI, Part II.

GmOH: Der Weltkrieg 1914 bis 1918, Die Militarischen Operationen zu Lande, Band 10, Die Operationen des Jahres 1916 bis zum Wechsel in der Obersten Heeresleitung.

RuOH: 1. The Russian Army in the World War.

2. A Strategic Outline of the War 1914 -1918.

TOH: 1. Birinci Dünya Harbinde Türk Harbi, VIInci Cilt, 1nci Kisim, Avrupa Cepheleri, Galaçya Cephesi.

2. Birinci Dünya Harbinde Türk Harbi, Avrupa Cepheleri (Özet).

30 July .... First aerial operations carried out by the combined British and French Air Services. (Western Front).

BrOH: Official History of the War, War in the Air, Volume III.

31 July .... The capture of Kilmatinde. (East Africa).

BgOH: Les campagnes coloniales Belges 1914-1918. Volume II. la campagne de Tabora 1916.

BrOH: Official History of the War, Military Operations, East Africa, Volume I, August 1914-September 1916.

GmOH: Der Krieg zur See 1914-1918, Band 6, Die Kämpfe der Kaiserlichen Marine in den deutschen Kolonien, Teil 2, Deutsch-Ostafrika.

SAOH: 1. The Union of South Africa and the Great War 1914 – 1918.

         2. The South Africans with General Smuts in German East Africa 1916.

2 August..The Italian dreadnought Leonardo da Vinci sunk by an internal explosion. (Adriatic Sea).

        IOH: Ufficio Storico della R. Marina, La Marina Italiana nella Grande Guerra, Volume III, Sviluppi Della Guerra Adriatico dal Salvataggio Dell'Esercito Serbo Sino alla Fine Dell'Anno 1916.

2-21 August ....The Battle of Doiran. (Balkan Front).

        AHOH: Österreich-Ungarns Letzter Krieg 1914-1918, Band V.

        BrOH: Official History of the War, Military Operations, Macedonia, Volume I: From the Outbreak of War to the Spring of 1917.

        BuOH: 1. Bŭlgarskata armija vŭ světovnata vojna 1915-1918 g. Tomŭ VI.

                2. Bŭlgarskata armija vŭ světovnata vojna 1915-1918 g. Tomŭ VII.

        FrOH: Les Armées Françaises dans la Grande Guerre: Tome VIII La campagne d'Orient. Volume 1 La campagne d'Orient jusqu'a l'intervention de la Roumanie - février 1915-aöut 1916.

        GrOH: 1. Ho Hellenikos Stratos kata ton Proton Pankosmion Polemon 1914-1918 Tomos 1 - H Hellas kai ho Polemos eis ta Balkania.

                2. Epitomh Istopia Ths Eummetochhs Tou Ellhnikou Stratou Ston Prpsto Pagkosmio Polemo 1914-1918. / A Concise History of the Participation of the Hellenic Army in The First World War 1914-1918.

        SeOH: 1. Veliki rat Srbije za oslobođenje i ujedinenje Srba, Hrvata i Slovenaca. Šesnaesta knjige. Izlazak na solunski front I početak operacija sepske vojske (od 17.-VI. do 16.-VIII.).

                2. Veliki rat Srbije za oslobođenje i ujedinenje Srba, Hrvata i Slovenaca. knjige Sedamnaesta. 1916 godina. Pripreme za ofanzivu na solunskom frontu od 17 avgust – 14 septembar. Zaustavljanje bugarske ofanzive n ofanziva srpskih trupa. Prvi period. Gorniuevska bitka.

3 August..The capture of Ujiji. (East Africa).

        BgOH: Les campagnes coloniales Belges 1914-1918. Volume II. la campagne de Tabora 1916.

        BrOH: Official History of the War, Military Operations, East Africa, Volume I, August 1914-September 1916.

        GmOH: Der Krieg zur See 1914-1918, Band 6, Die Kämpfe der Kaiserlichen Marine in den deutschen Kolonien, Teil 2, Deutsch-Ostafrika.

        SAOH: 1. The Union of South Africa and the Great War 1914 – 1918.

                2. The South Africans with General Smuts in German East Africa 1916.

3 August..*Commander* Ernest Dunning: First aircraft to land a deck of a ship. (British Home Water).

        BrOH: 1. Official History of the War, Naval Operations, Volume V.

                2. Official History of the War, War in the Air, Volume VI.

4-5 August ....The defence of the Suez Canal - the Battle of Rumani. (Egypt).

AuOH: Official History of Australia in the War of 1914-1918, Volume VII, Sinai and Palestine.

BrOH: Official History of the War, Military Operations, Egypt and Palestine, Volume I, From the Outbreak of War with Germany to June 1917.

NZOH: Official History of New Zealand's Effort in the Great War, Volume III, Sinai and Palestine.

TOH: 1. Büyük Harbin Sevkülceyşi.
2. Birinci Cihan Harbinde Türk Harbi, 1916 Yili Harekatleri, IIIncu Cilt.
3. Birinci Dünya Harbinde Türk Harbi, IIInvi Cilt, Irak-Iran Cephesi, 1914-1918, 1nci Kisim.
4. Birinci Dünya Harbinde Türk Harbi, 1nci Kisim, Sina-Filistin Cephesi Harbin Başlangicindan 1kinci Gazze Muharebeleri Sonuna Kadar.
5. Birinci Dünya Harbinde Türk Harbi VInci Cilt, Hicaz, Asir, Yeman Cepheleri ve Libya Harekati 1914-1918.
6. Büyük Harpte Misir Seferi.

6–17 August......................................The Sixth Battle of the Isonzo. (Italian Front).

AHOH: Österreich-Ungarns Letzter Krieg 1914-1918, Band V.

IOH: Maggiore Esercito, Ufficio Storico, L'Esercito italiano nella grande guerra 1915-18, Volume III, Tomo 3, Le Operazioni Del 1916 - Gli Avvenimenti Dal Agusto Al Dicembre.

7 August..The Brusilov's Offensive – the Battle of Tlumacz. (Eastern Front).

AHOH: Österreich-Ungarns Letzter Krieg 1914-1918, Band V.

GmOH: Der Weltkrieg 1914 bis 1918, Die Militarischen Operationen zu Lande, Band 10, Die Operationen des Jahres 1916 bis zum Wechsel in der Obersten Heeresleitung.

RuOH: 1. The Russian Army in the World War.
2. A Strategic Outline of the War 1914 -1918.

TOH: 1. Birinci Dünya Harbinde Türk Harbi, VIInci Cilt, 1nci Kisim, Avrupa Cepheleri, Galaçya Cephesi.
2. Birinci Dünya Harbinde Türk Harbi, Avrupa Cepheleri (Özet).

7-10 August ....The Brusilov's Offensive – the Battle of Zalozce. (Eastern Front).

AHOH: Österreich-Ungarns Letzter Krieg 1914-1918, Band V.

GmOH: Der Weltkrieg 1914 bis 1918, Die Militarischen Operationen zu Lande, Band 10, Die Operationen des Jahres 1916 bis zum Wechsel in der Obersten Heeresleitung.

RuOH: 1. The Russian Army in the World War.
2. A Strategic Outline of the War 1914 -1918.

TOH: 1. Birinci Dünya Harbinde Türk Harbi, VIInci Cilt, 1nci Kisim, Avrupa Cepheleri, Galaçya Cephesi.
2. Birinci Dünya Harbinde Türk Harbi, Avrupa Cepheleri (Özet).

8 August..*Commander* Ernest Dunning: Second attempted but unsuccessful landing on board a ship resulting in the fatality of Dunning . (British Home Water).

BrOH: 1. Official History of the War, Naval Operations, Volume V.
2. Official History of the War, War in the Air, Volume VI.

10 August..The capture of Hamadan. (West Persia).
           BrOH: Official History of the War, Military Operations, Operations in Persia 1915-1919.
           TOH: 1. Büyük Harbin Sevkülceyşi.
                 2. Birinci Cihan Harbinde Türk Harbi, 1916 Yili Harekatleri, IIIncu Cilt.
                 3. Birinci Dünya Harbinde Türk Harbi VInci Cilt, Hicaz, Asir, Yeman Cepheleri ve Libya Harekati 1914-1918.
                 4. Büyük Harpte Misir Seferi.
           RuOH: 1. The Russian Army in the World War.
                 2. A Strategic Outline of the War 1914 -1918.

11 August..The capture of Mpwapwa. (East Africa).
           BgOH: Les campagnes coloniales Belges 1914-1918. Volume II. la campagne de Tabora 1916.
           BrOH: Official History of the War, Military Operations, East Africa, Volume I, August 1914-September 1916.
           GmOH: Der Krieg zur See 1914-1918, Band 6, Die Kämpfe der Kaiserlichen Marine in den deutschen Kolonien, Teil 2, Deutsch-Ostafrika.
           SAOH: 1. The Union of South Africa and the Great War 1914 – 1918.
                 2. The South Africans with General Smuts in German East Africa 1916.

15 August..The capture of Bagamoyo. (East Africa).
           BgOH: Les campagnes coloniales Belges 1914-1918. Volume II. la campagne de Tabora 1916.
           BrOH: Official History of the War, Military Operations, East Africa, Volume I, August 1914-September 1916.
           GmOH: Der Krieg zur See 1914-1918, Band 6, Die Kämpfe der Kaiserlichen Marine in den deutschen Kolonien, Teil 2, Deutsch-Ostafrika.
           SAOH: 1. The Union of South Africa and the Great War 1914 – 1918.
                 2. The South Africans with General Smuts in German East Africa 1916.

17-19 August ....The Battle of Doiran – the Bulgarian Counter-Offensive. (Balkan Front).
           AHOH: Österreich-Ungarns Letzter Krieg 1914-1918, Band V.
           BrOH: Official History of the War, Military Operations, Macedonia, Volume I: From the Outbreak of War to the Spring of 1917.
           BuOH: Bŭlgarskata armija vŭ světovnata vojna 1915-1918 g. Tomŭ VII.
           FrOH: Les Armées Françaises dans la Grande Guerre: Tome VIII La campagne d'Orient. Volume 1 La campagne d'Orient jusqu'a l'intervention de la Roumanie - février 1915-aöut 1916.
           GrOH: 1. Ho Hellenikos Stratos kata ton Proton Pankosmion Polemon 1914-1918 Tomos 1 - H Hellas kai ho Polemos eis ta Balkania.
                 2. Epitomh Istopia Ths Eummetochhs Tou Ellhnikou Stratou Ston Prpsto Pagkosmio Polemo 1914-1918. / A Concise History of the Participation of the Hellenic Army in The First World War 1914-1918.
           SeOH: Veliki rat Srbije za oslobođenje i ujedinenje Srba, Hrvata i Slovenaca. knjige Sedamnaesta. 1916 godina. Pripreme za ofanzivu na solunskom frontu od 17 avgust – 14 septembar.

Zaustavljanje bugarske ofanzive n ofanziva srpskih trupa. Prvi period. Gorniuevska bitka.

19 August..H.M.S. Falmouth and H.M.S. Nottingham sunk by a submarine. (North Sea).

        BrOH: Official History of the War, Naval Operations, Volume IV.

        GmOH: 1. Der Krieg zur See 1914-1918, Band 4, Der Handelskrieg Mit U-Booten, Teil 3, Oktober 1915 bis Januar 1917.

        2. Der Krieg zur See 1914-1918, Band 1, Der Krieg in der Nordsee, Teil 6, Von Juni 1916 bis Frühjahr 1917.

19 August..The Battle of Doiran – the Bulgarian Counter-Offensive – the Battle of Florina. (Balkan Front).

        AHOH: Österreich-Ungarns Letzter Krieg 1914-1918, Band V.

        BrOH: Official History of the War, Military Operations, Macedonia, Volume I: From the Outbreak of War to the Spring of 1917.

        BuOH: Bŭlgarskata armija vŭ svĕtovnata vojna 1915-1918 g. Tomŭ VII.

        FrOH: Les Armées Françaises dans la Grande Guerre: Tome VIII La campagne d'Orient. Volume 1 La campagne d'Orient jusqu'a l'intervention de la Roumanie - février 1915-aöut 1916.

        GrOH: 1. Ho Hellenikos Stratos kata ton Proton Pankosmion Polemon 1914-1918 Tomos 1 - H Hellas kai ho Polemos eis ta Balkania.

        2. Epitomh Istopia Ths Eummetochhs Tou Ellhnikou Stratou Ston Prpsto Pagkosmio Polemo 1914-1918. / A Concise History of the Participation of the Hellenic Army in The First World War 1914-1918.

        SeOH: Veliki rat Srbije za oslobođenje i ujedinenje Srba, Hrvata i Slovenaca. knjige Sedamnaesta. 1916 godina. Pripreme za ofanzivu na solunskom frontu od 17 avgust – 14 septembar. Zaustavljanje bugarske ofanzive n ofanziva srpskih trupa. Prvi period. Gorniuevska bitka.

22 August..The capture of Kilosa. (East Africa).

        BgOH: Les campagnes coloniales Belges 1914-1918. Volume II. la campagne de Tabora 1916.

        BrOH: Official History of the War, Military Operations, East Africa, Volume I, August 1914-September 1916.

        GmOH: Der Krieg zur See 1914-1918, Band 6, Die Kämpfe der Kaiserlichen Marine in den deutschen Kolonien, Teil 2, Deutsch-Ostafrika.

        SAOH: 1. The Union of South Africa and the Great War 1914 – 1918.

        2. The South Africans with General Smuts in German East Africa 1916.

23 August..The German submarine S.S. Deutschland returns to Germany. (Atlantic Ocean).

        GmOH: Der Krieg zur See 1914-1918, Band 4, Der Handelskrieg Mit U-Booten, Teil 4, Februar bis Dezember 1917.

23 August..The Turkish Offensive into West Persia – the Battle Of Rayat. (Eastern Front).

BrOH: Official History of the War, Military Operations, Operations in Persia 1915-1919.

TOH: 1. Büyük Harbin Sevkülceyşi.

2. Birinci Cihan Harbinde Türk Harbi, 1916 Yili Harekatleri, IIIncu Cilt.

3. Birinci Dünya Harbinde Türk Harbi VInci Cilt, Hicaz, Asir, Yeman Cepheleri ve Libya Harekati 1914-1918.

4. Büyük Harpte Misir Seferi.

RuOH: 1. The Russian Army in the World War.

2. A Strategic Outline of the War 1914 -1918.

26 August...The capture of Morogoro. (East Africa).

BgOH: Les campagnes coloniales Belges 1914-1918. Volume II. la campagne de Tabora 1916.

BrOH: Official History of the War, Military Operations, East Africa, Volume I, August 1914-September 1916.

GmOH: Der Krieg zur See 1914-1918, Band 6, Die Kämpfe der Kaiserlichen Marine in den deutschen Kolonien, Teil 2, Deutsch-Ostafrika.

SAOH: 1. The Union of South Africa and the Great War 1914 – 1918.

2. The South Africans with General Smuts in German East Africa 1916.

28 August...The Rumanian invasion of Transylvania. (Eastern Front).

AHOH: Österreich-Ungarns Letzter Krieg 1914-1918, Band V.

BuOH: Bŭlgarskata armija vŭ svĕtovnata vojna 1915-1918 g. Томŭ VIII.

RoOH: România în război mondial 1916-1919, Volumul I.

TOH: 1. Birinci Dünya Harbinde Türk Harbi, VIInci Cilt, 2nci Kisim, Avrupa Cepheleri, Romanya Cephesi.

2. Birinci Dünya Harbinde Türk Harbi, Avrupa Cepheleri (Özet).

29 August...The capture of Iringa. (East Africa).

BgOH: Les campagnes coloniales Belges 1914-1918. Volume II. la campagne de Tabora 1916.

BrOH: Official History of the War, Military Operations, East Africa, Volume I, August 1914-September 1916.

GmOH: 1. Der Krieg zur See 1914-1918, Band 6, Die Kämpfe der Kaiserlichen Marine in den deutschen Kolonien, Teil 2, Deutsch-Ostafrika.

2. Deutsche Tat im Weltkrieg 1914/18 - Geschichten der Kämpfe deutscher Truppen, Band 12. Tufani - Sturm über Deutsch-Ostafrika.

SAOH: 1. The Union of South Africa and the Great War 1914 – 1918.

2. The South Africans with General Smuts in German East Africa 1916.

31 August...The Brusilov's Offensive – the Battle of Zborow. (Eastern Front).

AHOH: Österreich-Ungarns Letzter Krieg 1914-1918, Band V.

GmOH: Der Weltkrieg 1914 bis 1918, Die Militarischen Operationen zu Lande, Band 10, Die Operationen des Jahres 1916 bis zum Wechsel in der Obersten Heeresleitung.

RuOH: 1. The Russian Army in the World War.

2. A Strategic Outline of the War 1914 -1918.

TOH: 1. Birinci Dünya Harbinde Türk Harbi, VIInci Cilt, 1nci Kisim, Avrupa Cepheleri, Galaçya Cephesi.
2. Birinci Dünya Harbinde Türk Harbi, Avrupa Cepheleri (Özet).

1-30 September ....The Battle of the Carpathians. (Eastern Front).

AHOH: Österreich-Ungarns Letzter Krieg 1914-1918, Band V.

GmOH: Der Weltkrieg 1914 bis 1918, Die Militarischen Operationen zu Lande, Band 10, Die Operationen des Jahres 1916 bis zum Wechsel in der Obersten Heeresleitung.

RuOH: 1. The Russian Army in the World War.
2. A Strategic Outline of the War 1914 -1918.

TOH: 1. Birinci Dünya Harbinde Türk Harbi, VIInci Cilt, 1nci Kisim, Avrupa Cepheleri, Galaçya Cephesi.
2. Birinci Dünya Harbinde Türk Harbi, Avrupa Cepheleri (Özet).

1-8 September ....The Battle of the Carpathians - the First Battle of the Narajowka and the Zlota-Lipa. (Eastern Front).

AHOH: Österreich-Ungarns Letzter Krieg 1914-1918, Band V.

GmOH: Der Weltkrieg 1914 bis 1918, Die Militarischen Operationen zu Lande, Band 10, Die Operationen des Jahres 1916 bis zum Wechsel in der Obersten Heeresleitung.

RuOH: 1. The Russian Army in the World War.
2. A Strategic Outline of the War 1914 -1918.

TOH: 1. Birinci Dünya Harbinde Türk Harbi, VIInci Cilt, 1nci Kisim, Avrupa Cepheleri, Galaçya Cephesi.
2. Birinci Dünya Harbinde Türk Harbi, Avrupa Cepheleri (Özet).

2-3 September ....German ships seized in Piræus Harbour. (Mediterranean Sea).

BrOH: ..Official History of the War, Naval Operations, Volume IV.

GrOH: 1. Ho Hellenikos Stratos kata ton Proton Pankosmion Polemon 1914-1918 Tomos 1 - H Hellas kai ho Polemos eis ta Balkania.
2. Epitomh Istopia Ths Eummetochhs Tou Ellhnikou Stratou Ston Prpsto Pagkosmio Polemo 1914-1918. / A Concise History of the Participation of the Hellenic Army in The First World War 1914-1918.

3-6 September ....The Allied Summer Offensive – the Battle of the Somme – the Battle of Guillemont. (Western Front).

AuOH: Official History of Australia in the War of 1914-1918, Volume III, France 1916.

BrOH: Official History of the War, Military Operations, France and Belgium 1916 Volume II, 2nd July 1916 to the End of the Battles of the Somme.

COH: 1. Canadian Expeditionary Force 1914 - 1919. The Official History of the Canadian Army in the First World War.
2. The Western Front 1914.

GmOH: Der Weltkrieg 1914 bis 1918, Die Militarischen Operationen zu Lande, Band 11, Die Kriegführung im Herbst 1916 und im Winter 1916/17.

NZOH: Official History of New Zealand's Effort in the Great War, Volume II, France.

SAOH: 1. The South African Forces in France.
2. The Union of South Africa and the Great War 1914 – 1918.

3-6 September.....................................The Allied Summer Offensive – the Battle of the Somme – the Battle of Ginchy. (Western Front).

AuOH: Official History of Australia in the War of 1914-1918, Volume III, France 1916.

BrOH: Official History of the War, Military Operations, France and Belgium 1916 Volume II, 2nd July 1916 to the End of the Battles of the Somme.

COH: 1. Canadian Expeditionary Force 1914 - 1919. The Official History of the Canadian Army in the First World War.
2. The Western Front 1914.

GmOH: Der Weltkrieg 1914 bis 1918, Die Militarischen Operationen zu Lande, Band 11, Die Kriegführung im Herbst 1916 und im Winter 1916/17.

NZOH: Official History of New Zealand's Effort in the Great War, Volume II, France.

SAOH: 1. The South African Forces in France.
2. The Union of South Africa and the Great War 1914 – 1918.

4 September.....................................The capture of Dar es Salaam. (East Africa).

BgOH: Les Campagnes Coloniales Belges 1914-1918. Volume II. La Campagne de Tabora 1916.

BrOH: Official History of the War, Military Operations, East Africa, Volume I, August 1914-September 1916.

GmOH: Der Krieg zur See 1914-1918, Band 6, Die Kämpfe der Kaiserlichen Marine in den deutschen Kolonien, Teil 2, Deutsch-Ostafrika.

SAOH: 1. The Union of South Africa and the Great War 1914 – 1918.
2. The South Africans with General Smuts in German East Africa 1916.

7 September.....................................The affair & capture of Kisaki. (East Africa).

BgOH: Les campagnes coloniales Belges 1914-1918. Volume II. la campagne de Tabora 1916.

BrOH: Official History of the War, Military Operations, East Africa, Volume I, August 1914-September 1916.

GmOH: Der Krieg zur See 1914-1918, Band 6, Die Kämpfe der Kaiserlichen Marine in den deutschen Kolonien, Teil 2, Deutsch-Ostafrika.

AOH: 1. The Union of South Africa and the Great War 1914 – 1918.
2. The South Africans with General Smuts in German East Africa 1916.

11 September.....................................The German airship SL77 shot down over Cuffley by an aircraft. (Britain).

BrOH: Official History of the War, War in the Air, Volume II.

GmOH: Der Weltkrieg 1914 bis 1918, Die Militarischen Operationen zu Lande, Band 11, Die Kriegführung im Herbst 1916 und im Winter 1916/17; Der Krieg zur Air.

13-14 September.............................The Action of Machukovo. (Balkan Front).

AHOH: Österreich-Ungarns Letzter Krieg 1914-1918, Band V.

BrOH: Official History of the War, Military Operations, Macedonia, Volume I: From the Outbreak of War to the Spring of 1917.

BuOH: Bŭlgarskata armija vŭ světovnata vojna 1915-1918 g. Tomŭ IX.

FrOH: Les Armées Françaises dans la Grande Guerre: Tome VIII La campagne d'Orient. Volume 2 La campagne d'Orient depuis l'intervention de la Roumanie en aöut 1916 jusqu'en avril 1918.

GrOH: 1. Ho Hellenikos Stratos kata ton Proton Pankosmion Polemon 1914-1918 Tomos 1 - H Hellas kai ho Polemos eis ta Balkania.
2. Epitomh Istopia Ths Eummetochhs Tou Ellhnikou Stratou Ston Prpsto Pagkosmio Polemo 1914-1918. / A Concise History of the Participation of the Hellenic Army in The First World War 1914-1918.

SeOH: Veliki rat Srbije za oslobođenje i ujedinenje Srba, Hrvata i Slovenaca. knjige Osamnaesta. 1916 godina. Ofanziva srpske vojske na solunskom frontu. Druga period. Zauzede Kajmakualana, Starkovog Groba i Soviukih Položaja.

14 September – 3 October.................The Battle of Kaimakchalan-Florina. (Balkan Front).

AHOH: Österreich-Ungarns Letzter Krieg 1914-1918, Band V.

BrOH: Official History of the War, Military Operations, Macedonia, Volume I: From the Outbreak of War to the Spring of 1917.

BuOH: Bŭlgarskata armija vŭ světovnata vojna 1915-1918 g. Tomŭ IX.

FrOH: Les Armées Françaises dans la Grande Guerre: Tome VIII La campagne d'Orient. Volume 2 La campagne d'Orient depuis l'intervention de la Roumanie en aöut 1916 jusqu'en avril 1918.

GrOH: 1. Ho Hellenikos Stratos kata ton Proton Pankosmion Polemon 1914-1918 Tomos 1 - H Hellas kai ho Polemos eis ta Balkania.
2. Epitomh Istopia Ths Eummetochhs Tou Ellhnikou Stratou Ston Prpsto Pagkosmio Polemo 1914-1918. / A Concise History of the Participation of the Hellenic Army in The First World War 1914-1918.

SeOH: Veliki rat Srbije za oslobođenje i ujedinenje Srba, Hrvata i Slovenaca. knjige Osamnaesta. 1916 godina. Ofanziva srpske vojske na solunskom frontu. Druga period. Zauzede Kajmakualana, Starkovog Groba i Soviukih Položaja.

14–18 September ....The Seventh Battle of the Isonzo. (Italian Front).

AHOH: Österreich-Ungarns Letzter Krieg 1914-1918, Band V.

IOH: Maggiore Esercito, Ufficio Storico, L'Esercito italiano nella grande guerra 1915-18, Volume III, Tomo 3, Le Operazioni Del 1916 - Gli Avvenimenti Dal Agusto Al Dicembre.

15–22 September ....The Allied Summer Offensive – the Battle of the Somme – the Battle of Flers-Courcerlette. (Western Front).

AuOH: Official History of Australia in the War of 1914-1918, Volume III, France 1916.

BrOH: Official History of the War, Military Operations, France and Belgium 1916 Volume II, 2nd July 1916 to the End of the Battles of the Somme.

COH: 1. Canadian Expeditionary Force 1914 - 1919. The Official History of the Canadian Army in the First World War.

2. The Western Front 1914.

GmOH: Der Weltkrieg 1914 bis 1918, Die Militarischen Operationen zu Lande, Band 11, Die Kriegführung im Herbst 1916 und im Winter 1916/17.

NZOH: Official History of New Zealand's Effort in the Great War, Volume II, France.

SAOH: 1. The South African Forces in France.

2. The Union of South Africa and the Great War 1914 – 1918.

15 September ....The Allied Summer Offensive – the Battle of the Somme – the Battle of Flers-Courcerlette – the first aerial co-operation with tanks. (Western Front).

AuOH: Official History of Australia in the War of 1914-1918, Volume III, France 1916.

BrOH: Official History of the War, Military Operations, France and Belgium 1916 Volume II, 2nd July 1916 to the End of the Battles of the Somme.

COH: 1. Canadian Expeditionary Force 1914 - 1919. The Official History of the Canadian Army in the First World War.

2. The Western Front 1914.

GmOH: Der Weltkrieg 1914 bis 1918, Die Militarischen Operationen zu Lande, Band 11, Die Kriegführung im Herbst 1916 und im Winter 1916/17.

NZOH: Official History of New Zealand's Effort in the Great War, Volume II, France.

SAOH: 1. The South African Forces in France.

2. The Union of South Africa and the Great War 1914 – 1918.

16 September ....The capture of Lindi. (East Africa).

BgOH: Les campagnes coloniales Belges 1914-1918. Volume II. La campagne de Tabora 1916.

BrOH: Official History of the War, Military Operations, East Africa, Volume I, August 1914-September 1916.

GmOH: Der Krieg zur See 1914-1918, Band 6, Die Kämpfe der Kaiserlichen Marine in den deutschen Kolonien, Teil 2, Deutsch-Ostafrika.

SAOH: 1. The Union of South Africa and the Great War 1914 – 1918.

2. The South Africans with General Smuts in German East Africa 1916.

19 September ....The capture of Tabora. (East Africa).

BgOH: Les campagnes coloniales Belges 1914-1918. Volume II. La campagne de Tabora 1916.

BrOH: Official History of the War, Military Operations, East Africa, Volume I, August 1914-September 1916.

GmOH: Der Krieg zur See 1914-1918, Band 6, Die Kämpfe der Kaiserlichen Marine in den deutschen Kolonien, Teil 2, Deutsch-Ostafrika.

SAOH: 1. The Union of South Africa and the Great War 1914 – 1918.

2. The South Africans with General Smuts in German East Africa 1916.

22 September ....The Arab Revolt in the Hejaz – the Capture of Taif. (Arabia).

AuOH:..Official History of Australia in the War of 1914-1918, Volume VII, Sinai and Palestine.

BrOH: Official History of the War, Military Operations, Egypt and Palestine, Volume I, From the Outbreak of War with Germany to June 1917.

NZOH:.Official History of New Zealand's Effort in the Great War, Volume III, Sinai and Palestine.

TOH: 1. Büyük Harbin Sevkülceyşi.
2. Birinci Cihan Harbinde Türk Harbi, 1916 Yili Harekatleri, IIIncu Cilt.
3. Birinci Dünya Harbinde Türk Harbi VInci Cilt, Hicaz, Asir, Yeman Cepheleri ve Libya Harekati 1914-1918.
4. Büyük Harpte Misir Seferi.

23-24 September ....The German airship raid on the East Coast of England and London causing approximately 170 casualties - the German airship L32 destroyed by an aircraft over Billericay - the German airship L33 shot down by gunfire. (Britain).

BrOH: Official History of the War, War in the Air, Volume II.

GmOH: Der Weltkrieg 1914 bis 1918, Die Militarischen Operationen zu Lande, Band 11, Die Kriegführung im Herbst 1916 und im Winter 1916/17; Der Krieg zur Air.

24 September ....The Krupp Works, Essen bombed by French aircraft. (Germany).

GmOH: 1. Der Weltkrieg 1914 bis 1918, Die Militarischen Operationen zu Lande, Band 10, Die Operationen des Jahres 1916 bis zum Wechsel in der Obersten Heeresleitung; Der Krieg zur Air.
2. Die Deutschen Luftstreitkräfte von ihrer Entstehung bis zum Ende des Weltkrieges 1918. Kriegsgeschichtliche Einzelschriften der Luftwaffe. Siebenter Band: Die Deutschen Luftstreitkräfte von ihrer Entstehung bis zum Ende des Weltkrieges 1918. Sonderband: Der Militärische Heimatlutschutz im Weltkriege 1914 bis 1918.

25-28 September ....The Allied Summer Offensive – the Battle of the Somme – the Battle of Morval. (Western Front).

AuOH: Official History of Australia in the War of 1914-1918, Volume III, France 1916.

BrOH: Official History of the War, Military Operations, France and Belgium 1916 Volume II, 2nd July 1916 to the End of the Battles of the Somme.

COH: 1. Canadian Expeditionary Force 1914 - 1919. The Official History of the Canadian Army in the First World War.
2. The Western Front 1914.

GmOH: Der Weltkrieg 1914 bis 1918, Die Militarischen Operationen zu Lande, Band 11, Die Kriegführung im Herbst 1916 und im Winter 1916/17.

NZOH: Official History of New Zealand's Effort in the Great War, Volume II, France.

SAOH: 1. The South African Forces in France.
2. The Union of South Africa and the Great War 1914 – 1918.

26-28 September .... The Allied Summer Offensive – the Battle of the Somme – the Battle of Thiepval Ridge. (Western Front).

AuOH: Official History of Australia in the War of 1914-1918, Volume III, France 1916.

BrOH: Official History of the War, Military Operations, France and Belgium 1916 Volume II, 2nd July 1916 to the End of the Battles of the Somme.

COH: 1. Canadian Expeditionary Force 1914 - 1919. The Official History of the Canadian Army in the First World War.
2. The Western Front 1914.

GmOH: Der Weltkrieg 1914 bis 1918, Die Militarischen Operationen zu Lande, Band 11, Die Kriegführung im Herbst 1916 und im Winter 1916/17.

NZOH: Official History of New Zealand's Effort in the Great War, Volume II, France.

SAOH: 1. The South African Forces in France.
2. The Union of South Africa and the Great War 1914 – 1918.

26-29 September .... The Battle of the Carpathians - the Battle of Sibiu. (Eastern Front).

AHOH: Österreich-Ungarns Letzter Krieg 1914-1918, Band V.

GmOH: Der Weltkrieg 1914 bis 1918, Die Militarischen Operationen zu Lande, Band 11, Die Kriegführung im Herbst 1916 und im Winter 1916/17.

RuOH: 1. The Russian Army in the World War.
2. A Strategic Outline of the War 1914 -1918.

26-19 September .... The Battle of the Carpathians - the Second Battle of the Narajowka and the Zlota-Lipa. (Eastern Front).

AHOH: Österreich-Ungarns Letzter Krieg 1914-1918, Band V.

GmOH: Der Weltkrieg 1914 bis 1918, Die Militarischen Operationen zu Lande, Band 11, Die Kriegführung im Herbst 1916 und im Winter 1916/17.

RuOH: 1. The Russian Army in the World War.
2. A Strategic Outline of the War 1914 -1918.

30 September – 2 October .... The Battle of Brzezany. (Eastern Front).

AHOH: Österreich-Ungarns Letzter Krieg 1914-1918, Band V.

GmOH: Der Weltkrieg 1914 bis 1918, Die Militarischen Operationen zu Lande, Band 11, Die Kriegführung im Herbst 1916 und im Winter 1916/17.

RuOH: 1. The Russian Army in the World War.
2. A Strategic Outline of the War 1914 -1918.

30 September – 4 October .... The action of the Karajaköi Bala. (Balkan Front).

AHOH: Österreich-Ungarns Letzter Krieg 1914-1918, Band V.

BrOH: Official History of the War, Military Operations, Macedonia, Volume I: From the Outbreak of War to the Spring of 1917.

BuOH: Bŭlgarskata armija vŭ svĕtovnata vojna 1915-1918 g. Томŭ IX.

FrOH: Les Armées Françaises dans la Grande Guerre: Tome VIII La campagne d'Orient. Volume 2 La campagne d'Orient depuis l'intervention de la Roumanie en aöut 1916 jusqu'en avril 1918.

GrOH: 1. Ho Hellenikos Stratos kata ton Proton Pankosmion Polemon 1914-1918 Tomos 1 - H Hellas kai ho Polemos eis ta Balkania.

2. Epitomh Istopia Ths Eummetochhs Tou Ellhnikou Stratou Ston Prpsto Pagkosmio Polemo 1914-1918. / A Concise History of the Participation of the Hellenic Army in The First World War 1914-1918.

SeOH: Veliki rat Srbije za oslobođenje i ujedinenje Srba, Hrvata i Slovenaca. knjige Osamnaesta. 1916 godina. Ofanziva srpske vojske na solunskom frontu. Druga period. Zauzede Kajmakualana, Starkovog Groba i Soviukih Položaja.

1-2 October ....The German airship L31 destroyed by an aircraft near to Potter Bar. (Britain).

BrOH: Official History of the War, War in the Air, Volume II.

GmOH: Der Weltkrieg 1914 bis 1918, Die Militarischen Operationen zu Lande, Band 11, Die Kriegführung im Herbst 1916 und im Winter 1916/17; Der Krieg zur Air.

1-18 October ....The Allied Summer Offensive – the Battle of the Somme – the Battle of Transloy Ridges. (Western Front).

AuOH: Official History of Australia in the War of 1914-1918, Volume III, France 1916.

BrOH: Official History of the War, Military Operations, France and Belgium 1916 Volume II, 2nd July 1916 to the End of the Battles of the Somme.

COH: 1. Canadian Expeditionary Force 1914 - 1919. The Official History of the Canadian Army in the First World War.
2. The Western Front 1914.

GmOH: Der Weltkrieg 1914 bis 1918, Die Militarischen Operationen zu Lande, Band 11, Die Kriegführung im Herbst 1916 und im Winter 1916/17.

NZOH: Official History of New Zealand's Effort in the Great War, Volume II, France.

SAOH: 1. The South African Forces in France.
2. The Union of South Africa and the Great War 1914 – 1918.

1 October – 11 November ....The Allied Summer Offensive – the Battle of the Somme – the Battle of Ancre Heights. (Western Front).

AuOH: Official History of Australia in the War of 1914-1918, Volume III, France 1916.

BrOH: Official History of the War, Military Operations, France and Belgium 1916 Volume II, 2nd July 1916 to the End of the Battles of the Somme.

COH: 1. Canadian Expeditionary Force 1914 - 1919. The Official History of the Canadian Army in the First World War.
2. The Western Front 1914.

GmOH: Der Weltkrieg 1914 bis 1918, Die Militarischen Operationen zu Lande, Band 11, Die Kriegführung im Herbst 1916 und im Winter 1916/17.

NZOH: Official History of New Zealand's Effort in the Great War, Volume II, France.

SAOH: 1. The South African Forces in France.
2. The Union of South Africa and the Great War 1914 – 1918.

5-6 October ....The Third Battle of the Narajowka and the Zlota-Lipa. (Eastern Front).

AHOH: Österreich-Ungarns Letzter Krieg 1914-1918, Band V.

GmOH: Der Weltkrieg 1914 bis 1918, Die Militarischen Operationen zu Lande, Band 11, Die Kriegführung im Herbst 1916 und im Winter 1916/17.

RuOH: 1. The Russian Army in the World War.
2. A Strategic Outline of the War 1914 -1918.

5 October - 11 December ....The Battle of the Cerna and Monastir. (Balkan Front).

AHOH: Österreich-Ungarns Letzter Krieg 1914-1918, Band V.

BrOH: Official History of the War, Military Operations, Macedonia, Volume I: From the Outbreak of War to the Spring of 1917.

BuOH: Bŭlgarskata armija vŭ světovnata vojna 1915-1918 g. Томŭ IX.

FrOH: Les Armées Françaises dans la Grande Guerre: Tome VIII La campagne d'Orient. Volume 2 La campagne d'Orient depuis l'intervention de la Roumanie en aöut 1916 jusqu'en avril 1918.

GrOH: 1. Ho Hellenikos Stratos kata ton Proton Pankosmion Polemon 1914-1918 Tomos 1 - H Hellas kai ho Polemos eis ta Balkania.
2. Epitomh Istopia Ths Eummetochhs Tou Ellhnikou Stratou Ston Prpsto Pagkosmio Polemo 1914-1918. / A Concise History of the Participation of the Hellenic Army in The First World War 1914-1918.

SeOH: Veliki rat Srbije za oslobođenje i ujedinenje Srba, Hrvata i Slovenaca. 1914-1918 g. Knjige Devetnaesta. 1916 godina. Ofanziva srpske vojske na solunskom frontu 1916 godina. Treći period. Operacije na Crnoj Reci i Zauzeće Bitolja. I Deo Zauzeħe Tepavačkih Položaja.

8 October ....S.M.S. U.53 captures and sinks five ships outside Newport, Rhode Island. (Atlantic Ocean).

BrOH: 1. Official History of the War, Seaborne Trade, Volume III, Submarine Campaign Part II.
2. Official History of the War, The Merchant Navy, Volume III.

GmOH: Der Krieg zur See 1914-1918, Band 4, Der Handelskrieg Mit U-Booten, Teil 3, Oktober 1915 bis Januar 1917.

7-9 October ....The Battle of Brasov. (Eastern Front).

AHOH: Österreich-Ungarns Letzter Krieg 1914-1918, Band V.

GmOH: Der Weltkrieg 1914 bis 1918, Die Militarischen Operationen zu Lande, Band 11, Die Kriegführung im Herbst 1916 und im Winter 1916/17.

RuOH: 1. The Russian Army in the World War.
2. A Strategic Outline of the War 1914 -1918.

9-12 October ....The Eighth Battle of the Isonzo. (Italian Front).

AHOH:.Österreich-Ungarns Letzter Krieg 1914-1918, Band V.

IOH: Maggiore Esercito, Ufficio Storico, L'Esercito italiano nella grande guerra 1915-18, Volume III, Tomo 3, Le Operazioni Del 1916 - Gli Avvenimenti Dal Agusto Al Dicembre.

15-22 October ....The Battle of the Lower Narajowka. (Eastern Front).

AHOH: Österreich-Ungarns Letzter Krieg 1914-1918, Band V.

GmOH: Der Weltkrieg 1914 bis 1918, Die Militarischen Operationen zu Lande, Band 11, Die Kriegführung im Herbst 1916 und im Winter 1916/17.

RuOH: 1. The Russian Army in the World War.

2. A Strategic Outline of the War 1914 -1918.

17-22 October ....The affairs in the Dakhla Oasis. (West Egypt/Sudan).

BrOH: Official History of the War, Military Operations, Egypt and Palestine, Volume I, From the Outbreak of War with Germany to June 1917.

TOH: 1. Büyük Harbin Sevkülceyşi.

2. Birinci Cihan Harbinde Türk Harbi, 1914 Yili Harekatleri, II inci Cilt.

3. Birinci Dünya Harbinde Türk Harbi, 1nci Kisim, Sina-Filistin Cephesi Harbin Başlangicindan 1kinci Gazze Muharebeleri Sonuna Kadar.

4. Büyük Harpte Misir Seferi.

19-21 October ....The Battle of the Topraisar-Cobadinu. (Eastern Front).

AHOH: Österreich-Ungarns Letzter Krieg 1914-1918, Band V.

GmOH: Der Weltkrieg 1914 bis 1918, Die Militarischen Operationen zu Lande, Band 11, Die Kriegführung im Herbst 1916 und im Winter 1916/17.

RuOH: 1. The Russian Army in the World War.

2. A Strategic Outline of the War 1914 -1918.

20 October ....The Russian dreadnought Imperatritza Mariya sunk by an internal explosion. (Black Sea) [Russian].

RuOH:..Flot v Pervoi Mirovoi Voine. V Dvukh Tomakh. Tom I Deystviya Russkogo Flota.

22 October ....The captured of Constanza. (Eastern Front).

AHOH: Österreich-Ungarns Letzter Krieg 1914-1918, Band V.

GmOH: Der Weltkrieg 1914 bis 1918, Die Militarischen Operationen zu Lande, Band 11, Die Kriegführung im Herbst 1916 und im Winter 1916/17.

RuOH: 1. The Russian Army in the World War.

2. A Strategic Outline of the War 1914 -1918.

24 October - 18 December ....The Battle of Verdun – the First Offensive Battle of Verdun. (Western Front).

FrOH: Les Armées Françaises dans la Grande Guerre, Tome IV, Verdun et la Somme, Volume 3, Bataille de la Somme. (fin) - Offensives Françaises à Verdun – 3 septembre-fin décembre 1916.

GmOH: 1. Der Weltkrieg 1914 bis 1918, Die Militarischen Operationen zu Lande, Band 11, Die Kriegführung im Herbst 1916 und im Winter 1916/17.

2. Die Bayern im Großen Kriege 1914-1918.

24 October ....The Battle of Verdun – the First Offensive Battle of Verdun – the recapture of the Fort de Douaumont by the French. (Western Front).

FrOH: Les Armées Françaises dans la Grande Guerre, Tome IV, Verdun et la Somme, Volume 3, Bataille de la Somme. (fin) - Offensives Françaises à Verdun – 3 septembre-fin décembre 1916.

GmOH: 1. Der Weltkrieg 1914 bis 1918, Die Militarischen Operationen zu Lande, Band 11, Die Kriegführung im Herbst 1916 und im Winter 1916/17.
2. Die Bayern im Großen Kriege 1914-1918.

26-27 October ....The German destroyer's raid in Dover Straits. (British Home Waters).
BrOH: Official History of the War, Naval Operations, Volume IV.
GmOH: Der Krieg zur See 1914-1918, Band 1, Der Krieg in der Nordsee, Teil 6, Von Juni 1916 bis Frühjahr 1917.

28 October ....The British Hospital Ship Galeka sunk by a mine. (British Home Waters).
BrOH: 1. Official History of the War, Naval Operations, Volume IV.
2. Official History of the War, The Merchant Navy, Volume III.

28 October ....*Hauptmann* Oswald Boelcke killed in action. (Western Front).
BrOH: Official History of the War, War in the Air, Volume II.
GmOH: Der Weltkrieg 1914 bis 1918, Die Militarischen Operationen zu Lande, Band 11, Die Kriegführung im Herbst 1916 und im Winter 1916/17.

31 October – 4 November.................The Ninth Battle of the Isonzo. (Italian Front).
AHOH: Österreich-Ungarns Letzter Krieg 1914-1918, Band V.
IOH: Maggiore Esercito, Ufficio Storico, L'Esercito italiano nella grande guerra 1915-18, Volume III, Tomo 3, Le Operazioni Del 1916 - Gli Avvenimenti Dal Agusto Al Dicembre.

1 November ....The Battle of Verdun – the First Offensive Battle of Verdun – the recapture of the Fort de Vaux by the French. (Western Front).
FrOH: Les Armées Françaises dans la Grande Guerre, Tome IV, Verdun et la Somme, Volume 3, Bataille de la Somme. (fin) - Offensives Françaises à Verdun – 3 septembre-fin décembre 1916.
GmOH: 1. Der Weltkrieg 1914 bis 1918, Die Militarischen Operationen zu Lande, Band 11, Die Kriegführung im Herbst 1916 und im Winter 1916/17.
2. Die Bayern im Großen Kriege 1914-1918.

6 November ....The affairs of Gyuba. (Darfur). (West Egypt/Sudan).
BrOH: Official History of the War, Military Operations, Egypt and Palestine, Volume I, From the Outbreak of War with Germany to June 1917.
TOH: 1. Büyük Harbin Sevkülceyşi.
2. Birinci Cihan Harbinde Türk Harbi, 1914 Yili Harekatleri, II inci Cilt.
3. Birinci Dünya Harbinde Türk Harbi VInci Cilt, Hicaz, Asir, Yeman Cepheleri ve Libya Harekati 1914-1918.
4. Büyük Harpte Misir Seferi.

10-11 November ....The Battle of Czurduk. (Eastern Front).
AHOH: Österreich-Ungarns Letzter Krieg 1914-1918, Band V.
GmOH: Der Weltkrieg 1914 bis 1918, Die Militarischen Operationen zu Lande, Band 11, Die Kriegführung im Herbst 1916 und im Winter 1916/17.
RuOH: 1. The Russian Army in the World War.

2. A Strategic Outline of the War 1914 -1918.

12 November ....The capture of Shiraz. (Persia).
BrOH: Official History of the War, Military Operations, Operations in Persia 1915-1919.
TOH: 1. Büyük Harbin Sevkülceyşi.
2. Birinci Cihan Harbinde Türk Harbi, 1916 Yili Harekatleri, IIIncu Cilt.
3. Birinci Dünya Harbinde Türk Harbi VInci Cilt, Hicaz, Asir, Yeman Cepheleri ve Libya Harekati 1914-1918.
4. Büyük Harpte Misir Seferi.

15 November ....The third affair of Hafiz Kor. (NW Frontier India).
BrOH: Official History of the War, Military Operations, Operations in Persia 1915-1919.
TOH: 1. Büyük Harbin Sevkülceyşi.
2. Birinci Cihan Harbinde Türk Harbi, 1916 Yili Harekatleri, IIIncu Cilt.
3. Birinci Dünya Harbinde Türk Harbi VInci Cilt, Hicaz, Asir, Yeman Cepheleri ve Libya Harekati 1914-1918.
4. Büyük Harpte Misir Seferi.

15 November - 21 December ....The British advance into the Sinai. (Palestine) [British/Turkish].
AuOH: Official History of Australia in the War of 1914-1918, Volume VII, Sinai and Palestine.
BrOH: Official History of the War, Military Operations, Egypt and Palestine, Volume I, From the Outbreak of War with Germany to June 1917.
NZOH: Official History of New Zealand's Effort in the Great War, Volume III, Sinai and Palestine.
TOH: 1. Büyük Harbin Sevkülceyşi.
2. Birinci Cihan Harbinde Türk Harbi, 1914 Yili Harekatleri, II inci Cilt.
3. Birinci Dünya Harbinde Türk Harbi VInci Cilt, Hicaz, Asir, Yeman Cepheleri ve Libya Harekati 1914-1918.
4. Büyük Harpte Misir Seferi.

16-17 November ....The Battle of Târga-Jiu. (Eastern Front).
AHOH: Österreich-Ungarns Letzter Krieg 1914-1918, Band V.
GmOH: Der Weltkrieg 1914 bis 1918, Die Militarischen Operationen zu Lande, Band 11, Die Kriegführung im Herbst 1916 und im Winter 1916/17.
RuOH: 1. The Russian Army in the World War.
2. A Strategic Outline of the War 1914 -1918.

21 November ....The British Hospital Ship Britannic sunk by a mine. (Ægean Sea, Mediterranean Sea).
BrOH: 1. Official History of the War, Naval Operations, Volume IV.
2. Official History of the War, The Merchant Navy, Volume III.

22 November .... S.M.S. Seeadler leaves Germany. (Atlantic Ocean).
BrOH: Official History of the War, Naval Operations, Volume IV.
GmOH: Der Krieg zur See 1914-1918, Band 3, Der Kreuzerkrieg in den ausländischen Gewässern, Teil 3, Die deutschen Hilfskreuzer.

23 November ....The British Hospital Ship Britannic sunk by a mine. (Ægean Sea, Mediterranean Sea).

> BrOH: 1. Official History of the War, Naval Operations, Volume IV.
> 2. Official History of the War, The Merchant Navy, Volume III.

25 November ....The German Air Force established as separate branch of the German Army. (Germany).

> GmOH: Der Weltkrieg 1914 bis 1918, Die Militarischen Operationen zu Lande, Band 11, Die Kriegführung im Herbst 1916 und im Winter 1916/17; Der Krieg zur Air.

26 November ....Lowestoft raided for a second time by German battlecruiser squadron. (British Home Waters).

> BrOH: Official History of the War, Naval Operations, Volume IV.
> GmOH: Der Krieg zur See 1914-1918, Band 1, Der Krieg in der Nordsee, Teil 6, Von Juni 1916 bis Frühjahr 1917.

26 November ....The French dreadnought Suffren sunk by a submarine. (Atlantic Ocean).

> FrOH: Précis d'histoire de la guerre navale, 1914-1918.
> GmOH: Der Krieg zur See 1914-1918, Band 4, Der Handelskrieg Mit U-Booten, Teil 3, Oktober 1915 bis Januar 1917.

26 November – 22 March. (1917)......S.M.S. Möwe's (Moewe's) second cruise. (Atlantic Ocean).

> BrOH: Official History of the War, Naval Operations, Volume IV.
> GmOH: Der Krieg zur See 1914-1918, Band 3, Der Kreuzerkrieg in den ausländischen Gewässern, Teil 3, Die deutschen Hilfskreuzer.

27-28 November ....The German airship raid on the East Coast of England - the German airship L34 destroyed by an aircraft off Hartlepool - the German airship L21 destroyed by an aircraft off Yarmouth. (Britain).

> BrOH: Official History of the War, War in the Air, Volume III.
> GmOH: Der Weltkrieg 1914 bis 1918, Die Militarischen Operationen zu Lande, Band 11, Die Kriegführung im Herbst 1916 und im Winter 1916/17; Der Krieg zur Air.

28 November ....The German daylight aircraft raid (single aircraft) on London. (Britain).

> BrOH: Official History of the War, War in the Air, Volume III.
> GmOH: Der Weltkrieg 1914 bis 1918, Die Militarischen Operationen zu Lande, Band 11, Die Kriegführung im Herbst 1916 und im Winter 1916/17; Der Krieg zur Air.

30 November – 1 December ....The attack on Piræus Harbour. (Mediterranean Sea).

> BrOH: Official History of the War, Naval Operations, Volume IV.
> GrOH: 1. Ho Hellenikos Stratos kata ton Proton Pankosmion Polemon 1914-1918 Tomos 1 - H Hellas kai ho Polemos eis ta Balkania.
> 2. Epitomh Istopia Ths Eummetochhs Tou Ellhnikou Stratou Ston Prpsto Pagkosmio Polemo 1914-1918. / A Concise History of the Participation of the Hellenic Army in The First World War 1914-1918.

1 December.......................................S.M.S. Wolff leaves Germany. (Atlantic Ocean).

BrOH: Official History of the War, Naval Operations, Volume IV.

GmOH: Der Krieg zur See 1914-1918, Band 3, Der Kreuzerkrieg in den ausländischen Gewässern, Teil 3, Die deutschen Hilfskreuzer.

1 December ....Fighting between the Greek Army loyal to the Greek Government under Prime Minister Lambros and Allied Naval and Marine Landing Parties in Athens

BrOH: Official History of the War, Naval Operations, Volume IV.

GrOH: 1. Ho Hellenikos Stratos kata ton Proton Pankosmion Polemon 1914-1918 Tomos 1 - H Hellas kai ho Polemos eis ta Balkania.
2. Epitomh Istopia Ths Eummetochhs Tou Ellhnikou Stratou Ston Prpsto Pagkosmio Polemo 1914-1918. / A Concise History of the Participation of the Hellenic Army in The First World War 1914-1918.

3 December ....Funchal, Madeira bombarded by a submarine. (Atlantic Ocean).

FrOH: Précis d'histoire de la guerre navale, 1914-1918.

GmOH: Der Krieg zur See 1914-1918, Band 4, Der Handelskrieg Mit U-Booten, Teil 3, Oktober 1915 bis Januar 1917.

PgOH: Portugal na Grande Guerra II.

1-5 December ....The Battle of the Arges. (Eastern Front).

AHOH: Österreich-Ungarns Letzter Krieg 1914-1918, Band V.

BuOH: Bŭlgarskata armija vŭ svĕtovnata vojna 1915-1918 g. Tomŭ VIII.

GmOH: Der Weltkrieg 1914 bis 1918, Die Militarischen Operationen zu Lande, Band 11, Die Kriegführung im Herbst 1916 und im Winter 1916/17.

RoOH: România în război mondial 1916-1919, Volumul II.

RuOH: 1. The Russian Army in the World War.
2. A Strategic Outline of the War 1914 -1918.

TOH: 1. Birinci Dünya Harbinde Türk Harbi, VIInci Cilt, 2nci Kisim, Avrupa Cepheleri, Romanya Cephesi.
2. Birinci Dünya Harbinde Türk Harbi, Avrupa Cepheleri (Özet).

7 December ....The affair of Jabir. (Aden).

AuOH: Official History of Australia in the War of 1914-1918, Volume VII, Sinai and Palestine.

BrOH: Official History of the War, Military Operations, Campaign in Mesopotamia, Volume I.

NZOH: Official History of New Zealand's Effort in the Great War, Volume III, Sinai and Palestine.

TOH: 1. Büyük Harbin Sevkülceyşi.
2. Birinci Cihan Harbinde Türk Harbi, 1916 Yili Harekatleri, IIIncu Cilt.
3. Birinci Dünya Harbinde Türk Harbi VInci Cilt, Hicaz, Asir, Yeman Cepheleri ve Libya Harekati 1914-1918.
4. Büyük Harpte Misir Seferi.

11 December ....The Italian dreadnought Regina Margherita sunk by a mine. (Mediterranean Sea).

IOH: Ufficio Storico della R. Marina, La Marina Italiana nella Grande Guerra, Volume III, Sviluppi Della Guerra

Adriatico dal Salvataggio Dell'Esercito Serbo Sino alla Fine Dell'Anno 1916.

21-27 December..................................The Battle of Rimnicul-Sarat. (Eastern Front).
        AHOH: Österreich-Ungarns Letzter Krieg 1914-1918, Band V.
        BuOH: Bŭlgarskata armija vŭ svĕtovnata vojna 1915-1918 g. Tomŭ VIII.
        GmOH: Der Weltkrieg 1914 bis 1918, Die Militarischen Operationen zu Lande, Band 11, Die Kriegführung im Herbst 1916 und im Winter 1916/17.
        RoOH: România în război mondial 1916-1919, Volumul III Partea 1.
        RuOH: 1. The Russian Army in the World War.
              2. A Strategic Outline of the War 1914 -1918.
        TOH: 1. Birinci Dünya Harbinde Türk Harbi, VIInci Cilt, 2nci Kisim, Avrupa Cepheleri, Romanya Cephesi.
              2. Birinci Dünya Harbinde Türk Harbi, Avrupa Cepheleri (Özet).

26 December – 7 January. (1917) ......The Austro-German Offensive towards Trotuş. (Eastern Front).
        AHOH: Österreich-Ungarns Letzter Krieg 1914-1918, Band V.
        BuOH: Bŭlgarskata armija vŭ svĕtovnata vojna 1915-1918 g. Tomŭ IX.
        GmOH: Der Weltkrieg 1914 bis 1918, Die Militarischen Operationen zu Lande, Band 11, Die Kriegführung im Herbst 1916 und im Winter 1916/17.
        RoOH: România în război mondial 1916-1919, Volumul III Partea 1.
        RuOH: 1. The Russian Army in the World War.
               2. A Strategic Outline of the War 1914 -1918.
        TOH: 1. Birinci Dünya Harbinde Türk Harbi, VIInci Cilt, 2nci Kisim, Avrupa Cepheleri, Romanya Cephesi.
              2. Birinci Dünya Harbinde Türk Harbi, Avrupa Cepheleri (Özet).

27 December.....................................The French dreadnought Gaulois sunk by a submarine. (Mediterranean Sea).
        AHOH: Österreich-Ungarns Seekrieg 1914-1918, Lieferung IV.
        FrOH: Précis d'histoire de la guerre navale, 1914-1918.
        GmOH: Der Krieg zur See 1914-1918, Band 4, Der Handelskrieg Mit U-Booten , Teil 4, Februar bis Dezember 1917.

1917

3 January..The action of Beho-Beho. (East Africa).

BgOH: Les campagnes coloniales Belges 1914-1918. Volume II. la campagne de Tabora 1916.

GmOH: Der Krieg zur See 1914-1918, Band 6, Die Kämpfe der Kaiserlichen Marine in den deutschen Kolonien, Teil 2, Deutsch-Ostafrika.

SAOH: The Union of South Africa and the Great War 1914 – 1918.

4 January..The Russian dreadnought Peresvyet sunk by a mine. (Mediterranean Sea).

RuOH:..Flot v Pervoi Mirovoi Voine. V Dvukh Tomakh. Tom II Deystviya Flotov Na Severnom Sredizemnomorskom I Okeanskih Teatrah.

4-8 January ....The Battle of the Putna. (Eastern Front).

AHOH: Österreich-Ungarns Letzter Krieg 1914-1918, Band VI.

BuOH: Bŭlgarskata armija vŭ světovnata vojna 1915-1918 g. Томŭ IX.

GmOH: Der Weltkrieg 1914 bis 1918, Die Militarischen Operationen zu Lande, Band 11, Die Kriegführung im Herbst 1916 und im Winter 1916/17.

RoOH: România în război mondial 1916-1919, Volumul III Partea 2.

RuOH: 1. The Russian Army in the World War.
2. A Strategic Outline of the War 1914 -1918.

TOH: 1. Birinci Dünya Harbinde Türk Harbi, VIInci Cilt, 3nci Kisim, Avrupa Cepheleri, Makedonya Cephesi, Romanya Cephesi.
2. Birinci Dünya Harbinde Türk Harbi, Avrupa Cepheleri (Özet).

5 January – 3 February......................The Battle of the Aa. (Eastern Front).

AHOH: Österreich-Ungarns Letzter Krieg 1914-1918, Band VI.

BuOH: Bŭlgarskata armija vŭ světovnata vojna 1915-1918 g. Томŭ IX.

GmOH: Der Weltkrieg 1914 bis 1918, Die Militarischen Operationen zu Lande, Band 11, Die Kriegführung im Herbst 1916 und im Winter 1916/17.

RoOH: România în război mondial 1916-1919, Volumul IV.

RuOH: 1. The Russian Army in the World War.
2. A Strategic Outline of the War 1914 -1918.

TOH: 1. Birinci Dünya Harbinde Türk Harbi, VIInci Cilt, 3nci Kisim, Avrupa Cepheleri, Makedonya Cephesi, Romanya Cephesi.
2. Birinci Dünya Harbinde Türk Harbi, Avrupa Cepheleri (Özet).

5 January..The capture of Brăila. (Eastern Front).

AHOH: Österreich-Ungarns Letzter Krieg 1914-1918, Band VI.

BuOH: Bŭlgarskata armija vŭ světovnata vojna 1915-1918 g. Томŭ IX.

GmOH: Der Weltkrieg 1914 bis 1918, Die Militarischen Operationen zu Lande, Band 11, Die Kriegführung im Herbst 1916 und im Winter 1916/17.

RoOH: România în război mondial 1916-1919, Volumul IV.

RuOH: 1. The Russian Army in the World War.
2. A Strategic Outline of the War 1914 -1918.

TOH: 1. Birinci Dünya Harbinde Türk Harbi, VIInci Cilt, 3nci Kisim, Avrupa Cepheleri, Makedonya Cephesi, Romanya Cephesi.

2. Birinci Dünya Harbinde Türk Harbi, Avrupa Cepheleri (Özet).

9 January..H.M.S. Cornwallis sunk by a mine. (Mediterranean Sea).

BrOH: Official History of the War, Naval Operations, Volume IV.

9 January..The action of Rafah. (Mesopotamia).

AuOH: Official History of Australia in the War of 1914-1918, Volume VII, Sinai and Palestine.

BrOH: Official History of the War, Military Operations, Campaign in Mesopotamia, Volume I.

NZOH: Official History of New Zealand's Effort in the Great War, Volume III, Sinai and Palestine.

TOH: 1. Büyük Harbin Sevkülceyşi.

2. Birinci Cihan Harbinde Türk Harbi, 1917 Yili Harekatleri, IVncu Cilt.

3. Birinci Dünya Harbinde Türk Harbi VInci Cilt, Hicaz, Asir, Yeman Cepheleri ve Libya Harekati 1914-1918.

4. Büyük Harpte Misir Seferi.

9 January – 24 February.....................The British Operations to capture Kut, 1917 - the Battle of Kut, 1917. (Mesopotamia).

AuOH: Official History of Australia in the War of 1914-1918, Volume VII, Sinai and Palestine.

BrOH: Official History of the War, Military Operations, Campaign in Mesopotamia, Volume I.

NZOH: Official History of New Zealand's Effort in the Great War, Volume III, Sinai and Palestine.

TOH: 1. Büyük Harbin Sevkülceyşi.

2. Birinci Cihan Harbinde Türk Harbi, 1917 Yili Harekatleri, IVncu Cilt.

3. Birinci Dünya Harbinde Türk Harbi VInci Cilt, Hicaz, Asir, Yeman Cepheleri ve Libya Harekati 1914-1918.

4. Büyük Harpte Misir Seferi.

14 January..The Japanese battlecruiser Tsukuba sunk by an internal explosion. (Pacific Ocean).

JOH: Taishō yonen naishi kunen kaigun senshi. Kan 1.

23 January..The destroyer raid on Southwold and Wangford, Suffolk. (British Home Waters).

BrOH: Official History of the War, Naval Operations, Volume IV.

GmOH: Der Krieg zur See 1914-1918, Band 1, Der Krieg in der Nordsee, Teil 6, Von Juni 1916 bis Frühjahr 1917.

24 January..The action between the Harwich Flotilla and the 6th Torpedo-Boat Flotilla – H.M.S. Simoom sunk. (British Home Waters).

BrOH: Official History of the War, Naval Operations, Volume IV.

GmOH: Der Krieg zur See 1914-1918, Band 1, Der Krieg in der Nordsee, Teil 6, Von Juni 1916 bis Frühjahr 1917.

24 January..The Arab Forces capture Wejh. (Arabia).

BrOH: Official History of the War, Military Operations, Egypt and Palestine, Volume I, From the Outbreak of War with Germany to June 1917.

TOH: 1. Büyük Harbin Sevkülceyşi.
2. Birinci Cihan Harbinde Türk Harbi, 1917 Yili Harekatleri, IVncu Cilt.
3. Birinci Dünya Harbinde Türk Harbi, IIInvi Cilt, Irak-Iran Cephesi, 1914-1918, 1nci Kisim.
4. Birinci Dünya Harbinde Türk Harbi, 1nci Kisim, Sina-Filistin Cephesi Harbin Başlangicindan 1kinci Gazze Muharebeleri Sonuna Kadar.
5. Birinci Dünya Harbinde Türk Harbi VInci Cilt, Hicaz, Asir, Yeman Cepheleri ve Libya Harekati 1914-1918.
6. Büyük Harpte Misir Seferi.

1 February ....German unrestricted submarine warfare begins. (British Home Waters).

BrOH: 1. Official History of the War, Naval Operations, Volume IV.
2. Official History of the War, Seaborne Trade, Volume III, Submarine Campaign, Part II.
3. Official History of the War, The Merchant Navy, Volume III.

GmOH: Der Krieg zur See 1914-1918, Band 4, Der Handelskrieg Mit U-Booten, Teil 4, Februar bis Dezember 1917.

3 - 5 February ....The affairs in the Siwa Oasis. (West Egypt/Sudan).

BrOH: Official History of the War, Military Operations, Egypt and Palestine, Volume I, From the Outbreak of War with Germany to June 1917.

TOH: 1. Büyük Harbin Sevkülceyşi.
2. Birinci Cihan Harbinde Türk Harbi, 1917 Yili Harekatleri, IVncu Cilt.
3. Birinci Dünya Harbinde Türk Harbi, IIInvi Cilt, Irak-Iran Cephesi, 1914-1918, 1nci Kisim.
4. Birinci Dünya Harbinde Türk Harbi, 1nci Kisim, Sina-Filistin Cephesi Harbin Başlangicindan 1kinci Gazze Muharebeleri Sonuna Kadar.
5. Birinci Dünya Harbinde Türk Harbi VInci Cilt, Hicaz, Asir, Yeman Cepheleri ve Libya Harekati 1914-1918.
6. Büyük Harpte Misir Seferi.

7 February ....The first British experimental Coal Convoy to France sailed. (British Home Waters).

BrOH: 1. Official History of the War, Naval Operations, Volume IV.
2. Official History of the War – The Merchant Navy, Volume III.

21 February ....The Ålanders asking Sweden for protection from Finnish and Russian Troops. (Baltic Sea).

SwOH: Ålandsuppgörelsen. Redogörelse över den under februari månad år 1918 under svensk förmedling överenskomna utrymningen av Åland från finska och ryska trupper jämte tillhörande aktstycken.

24 February ....The Swedish Expeditionary Force land on Åland islands and remove Finnish and Russian Troops by peaceful agreement. (Baltic Sea).

SwOH: Ålandsuppgörelsen. Redogörelse över den under februari månad år 1918 under svensk förmedling överenskomna utrymningen av Åland från finska och ryska trupper jåmte tillhörande aktstycken.

25 February.......................................S.S. Laconia sunk by a submarine. (British Home Waters).
> BrOH: 1. Official History of the War, Seaborne Trade, Volume III, Submarine Campaign, Part II.
> 2. Official History of the War, The Merchant Navy, Volume III.
> GmOH: Der Krieg zur See 1914-1918, Band 4, Der Handelskrieg Mit U-Booten, Teil 4, Februar bis Dezember 1917.

25 February.......................................The destroyer raid on Margate and Broadstairs, Kent. (British Home Waters).
> BrOH: Official History of the War, Naval Operations, Volume IV.
> GmOH: Der Krieg zur See 1914-1918, Band 1, Der Krieg in der Nordsee, Teil 6, Von Juni 1916 bis Frühjahr 1917.

25 February-11 March ....The pursuit of the Turkish Forces from Kut to Baghdad. (Mesopotamia).
> BrOH: Official History of the War, Military Operations, Campaign in Mesopotamia, Volume I.
> TOH: 1. Büyük Harbin Sevkülceyşi.
> 2. Birinci Cihan Harbinde Türk Harbi, 1917 Yili Harekatleri, IVncu Cilt.
> 3. Birinci Dünya Harbinde Türk Harbi, IIInvi Cilt, Irak-Iran Cephesi, 1914-1918, 1nci Kisim.
> 4. Birinci Dünya Harbinde Türk Harbi, 1nci Kisim, Sina-Filistin Cephesi Harbin Başlangicindan 1kinci Gazze Muharebeleri Sonuna Kadar.
> 5. Birinci Dünya Harbinde Türk Harbi VInci Cilt, Hicaz, Asir, Yeman Cepheleri ve Libya Harekati 1914-1918.
> 6. Büyük Harpte Misir Seferi.

1 March...The British Hospital Ship Glenart Castle damaged by a mine. (British Home Waters).
> BrOH: 1. Official History of the War, Naval Operations, Volume IV.
> 2. Official History of the War, The Merchant Navy, Volume III.

7 March...The replacement of the Swedish Expeditionary Force by a German Swedish Expeditionary Force on Åland islands. (Baltic Sea).
> SwOH: Ålandsuppgörelsen. Redogörelse över den under februari månad år 1918 under svensk förmedling överenskomna utrymningen av Åland från finska och ryska trupper jåmte tillhörande aktstycken.

11 March..Baghdad occupied. (Mesopotamia).
> BrOH: Official History of the War, Military Operations, Campaign in Mesopotamia, Volume I.
> TOH: 1. Büyük Harbin Sevkülceyşi.
> 2. Birinci Cihan Harbinde Türk Harbi, 1917 Yili Harekatleri, IVncu Cilt.
> 3. Birinci Dünya Harbinde Türk Harbi, IIInvi Cilt, Irak-Iran Cephesi, 1914-1918, 1nci Kisim.
> 4. Birinci Dünya Harbinde Türk Harbi, 1nci Kisim, Sina-Filistin Cephesi Harbin Başlangicindan 1kinci Gazze Muharebeleri Sonuna Kadar.

5. Birinci Dünya Harbinde Türk Harbi VInci Cilt, Hicaz, Asir, Yeman Cepheleri ve Libya Harekati 1914-1918.
6. Büyük Harpte Misir Seferi.

11-26 March ....The Allied Offensive to free Monastir. (Balkan Front).
AHOH: Österreich-Ungarns Letzter Krieg 1914-1918, Band VI.
BrOH: Official History of the War, Military Operations, Macedonia, Volume I: From the Outbreak of War to the Spring of 1917.
BuOH: Bŭlgarskata armija vŭ svĕtovnata vojna 1915-1918 g. Tомŭ VIII.
FrOH: Les Armées Françaises dans la Grande Guerre: Tome VIII La campagne d'Orient. Volume 2 La campagne d'Orient depuis l'intervention de la Roumanie en aöut 1916 jusqu'en avril 1918.
GmOH: Der Weltkrieg 1914 bis 1918, Die Militarischen Operationen zu Lande, Band 11, Die Kriegführung im Herbst 1916 und im Winter 1916/17.
GrOH: 1. Ho Hellenikos Stratos kata ton Proton Pankosmion Polemon 1914-1918 Tomos 1 - H Hellas kai ho Polemos eis ta Balkania.
2. Epitomh Istopia Ths Eummetochhs Tou Ellhnikou Stratou Ston Prpsto Pagkosmio Polemo 1914-1918. / A Concise History of the Participation of the Hellenic Army in The First World War 1914-1918.
MOH: Operacije crnogorske vojske u prvom svetskom ratu.
SeOH: Veliki rat Srbije za oslobođenje i ujedinenje Srba, Hrvata i Slovenaca 1914 – 1918. Knjige Dvadeset Prva. 1916 i 1917 godina. Rovovska vojna srpske vojske na solunskom frontu. I period. Rovovske Vojne.
TOH: 1. Birinci Dünya Harbinde Türk Harbi, VIInci Cilt, 3nci Kisim, Avrupa Cepheleri, Makedonya Cephesi, Romanya Cephesi.
2. Birinci Dünya Harbinde Türk Harbi, Avrupa Cepheleri (Özet).

11-19 March ....The Allied Offensive to free Monastir – the Battle of Lake Prespa. (Balkan Front).
AHOH: Österreich-Ungarns Letzter Krieg 1914-1918, Band VI.
BrOH: Official History of the War, Military Operations, Macedonia, Volume I: From the Outbreak of War to the Spring of 1917.
BuOH: Bŭlgarskata armija vŭ svĕtovnata vojna 1915-1918 g. Tомŭ VIII.
FrOH: Les Armées Françaises dans la Grande Guerre: Tome VIII La campagne d'Orient. Volume 2 La campagne d'Orient depuis l'intervention de la Roumanie en aöut 1916 jusqu'en avril 1918.
GmOH: Der Weltkrieg 1914 bis 1918, Die Militarischen Operationen zu Lande, Band 11, Die Kriegführung im Herbst 1916 und im Winter 1916/17.
GrOH: 1. Ho Hellenikos Stratos kata ton Proton Pankosmion Polemon 1914-1918 Tomos 1 - H Hellas kai ho Polemos eis ta Balkania.
2. Epitomh Istopia Ths Eummetochhs Tou Ellhnikou Stratou Ston Prpsto Pagkosmio Polemo 1914-1918. / A Concise History of the Participation of the Hellenic Army in The First World War 1914-1918.
MOH: Operacije crnogorske vojske u prvom svetskom ratu.

SeOH: Veliki rat Srbije za oslobođenje i ujedinenje Srba, Hrvata i Slovenaca 1914 – 1918. Knjige Dvadeset Prva. 1916 i 1917 godina. Rovovska vojna srpske vojske na solunskom frontu. I period. Rovovske Vojne.

TOH: 1. Birinci Dünya Harbinde Türk Harbi, VIInci Cilt, 3nci Kisim, Avrupa Cepheleri, Makedonya Cephesi, Romanya Cephesi.
2. Birinci Dünya Harbinde Türk Harbi, Avrupa Cepheleri (Özet).

12 March...The Russian Revolution begins. (Eastern Front).

RuOH: Carskaâ Armiâ v Fevral'skom Pevolûciâ

13-23 March ....The Allied Offensive to free Monastir – the Battle of Hill 1248. (Balkan Front).

AHOH: Österreich-Ungarns Letzter Krieg 1914-1918, Band VI.

BrOH: Official History of the War, Military Operations, Macedonia, Volume I: From the Outbreak of War to the Spring of 1917.

BuOH: Bǔlgarskata armija vǔ světovnata vojna 1915-1918 g. Tomǔ VIII.

FrOH: Les Armées Françaises dans la Grande Guerre: Tome VIII La campagne d'Orient. Volume 2 La campagne d'Orient depuis l'intervention de la Roumanie en aöut 1916 jusqu'en avril 1918.

GmOH: Der Weltkrieg 1914 bis 1918, Die Militarischen Operationen zu Lande, Band 11, Die Kriegführung im Herbst 1916 und im Winter 1916/17.

GrOH: 1. Ho Hellenikos Stratos kata ton Proton Pankosmion Polemon 1914-1918 Tomos 1 - H Hellas kai ho Polemos eis ta Balkania.
2. Epitomh Istopia Ths Eummetochhs Tou Ellhnikou Stratou Ston Prpsto Pagkosmio Polemo 1914-1918. / A Concise History of the Participation of the Hellenic Army in The First World War 1914-1918.

MOH: Operacije crnogorske vojske u prvom svetskom ratu.

SeOH: Veliki rat Srbije za oslobođenje i ujedinenje Srba, Hrvata i Slovenaca 1914 – 1918. Knjige Dvadeset Prva. 1916 i 1917 godina. Rovovska vojna srpske vojske na solunskom frontu. I period. Rovovske Vojne.

TOH: 1. Birinci Dünya Harbinde Türk Harbi, VIInci Cilt, 3nci Kisim, Avrupa Cepheleri, Makedonya Cephesi, Romanya Cephesi.
2. Birinci Dünya Harbinde Türk Harbi, Avrupa Cepheleri (Özet).

14 March – 5 April. (17 March).........The German retreat to the Hindenburg Line. (Western Front).

AuOH: Official History of Australia in the War of 1914-1918, Volume IV, France 1917.

BrOH: Official History of the War, Military Operations, France and Belgium 1917, Volume I, The German Retreat to the Hindenburg Line and the Battles of Arras.

COH: Canadian Expeditionary Force 1914 - 1919. The Official History of the Canadian Army in the First World War.

FrOH: Les Armées Françaises dans la Grande Guerre, Tome V, L'offensives d'avril 1917, les opérations à objectifs limités – 1 novembre 1916-1 novembre 1917, Volume 1, L'offensives d'avril 1917.

GmOH: Der Weltkrieg 1914 bis 1918, Die Militarischen Operationen zu Lande, Band 11, Die Kriegführung im Herbst 1916 und im Winter 1916/17.

NZOH: Official History of New Zealand's Effort in the Great War, Volume II, France.

SAOH: 1. The South African Forces in France.
2. The Union of South Africa and the Great War 1914 – 1918.

16 March..S.M.S. Leopard sunk by H.M.S. Achilles. (British Home Waters).

BrOH: Official History of the War, Naval Operations, Volume IV.

GmOH: Der Krieg zur See 1914-1918, Band 1, Der Krieg in der Nordsee, Teil 6, Von Juni 1916 bis Frühjahr 1917.

16 March..Mutiny breaks out in the Russian Fleet. (Baltic Sea).

RuOH: Flot v Pervoi Mirovoi Voine. V Dvukh Tomakh. Tom I Deystviya Russkogo Flota.

17 March..The German airship L39 destroyed by an aircraft over Compiègne. (France).

GmOH: Der Weltkrieg 1914 bis 1918, Die Militarischen Operationen zu Lande, Band 12, Die Kriegführung im Frühjahr 1917; Der Krieg zur Air.

18 March..The destroyer raid on Ramsgate and Broadstairs, Kent. . (British Home Waters).

BrOH: Official History of the War, Naval Operations, Volume IV.

GmOH: Der Krieg zur See 1914-1918, Band 1, Der Krieg in der Nordsee, Teil 6, Von Juni 1916 bis Frühjahr 1917.

19 March..The French dreadnought Danton sunk by a submarine. (Mediterranean Sea).

AHOH: Österreich-Ungarns Seekrieg 1914-1918, Lieferung IV.

GmOH: Der Krieg zur See 1914-1918, Band 4, Der Handelskrieg Mit U-Booten , Teil 5 Januar bis November 1918.

21 March..The British Hospital Ship Asturias damaged by a submarine. (British Home Waters).

BrOH: 1. Official History of the War, Naval Operations, Volume IV.
2. Official History of the War, The Merchant Navy, Volume III.

GmOH: Der Krieg zur See 1914-1918, Band 1, Der Krieg in der Nordsee, Teil 6, Von Juni 1916 bis Frühjahr 1917.

24 March 1917 – 12 March. (1918) ...The First British Offensive into Palestine. (Palestine).

AuOH: Official History of Australia in the War of 1914-1918, Volume VII, Sinai and Palestine.

BrOH: Official History of the War, Military Operations, Egypt and Palestine, Volume I, From the Outbreak of War with Germany to June 1917.

NZOH: Official History of New Zealand's Effort in the Great War, Volume III, Sinai and Palestine.

TOH: 1. Büyük Harbin Sevkülceyşi.
2. Birinci Cihan Harbinde Türk Harbi, 1917 Yili Harekatleri, IVncu Cilt

COH: 1. Canadian Expeditionary Force 1914 - 1919. The Official History of the Canadian Army in the First World War.
2. The Western Front 1914.

GmOH: Der Weltkrieg 1914 bis 1918, Die Militarischen Operationen zu Lande, Band 12, Die Kriegführung im Frühjahr 1917.

9-14 April ....The Battle of Arras – the Battle of Vimy Ridge. (Western Front).

AuOH: Official History of Australia in the War of 1914-1918, Volume IV, France 1917.

BrOH: Official History of the War, Military Operations, France and Belgium 1917, Volume I, The German Retreat to the Hindenburg Line and the Battles of Arras.

GmOH: Der Weltkrieg 1914 bis 1918, Die Militarischen Operationen zu Lande, Band 12, Die Kriegführung im Frühjahr 1917.

9-14 April ....The Battle of Arras – the First Battle of the Scarpe, 1917. (Western Front).

AuOH: Official History of Australia in the War of 1914-1918, Volume IV, France 1917.

BrOH: Official History of the War, Military Operations, France and Belgium 1917, Volume I, The German Retreat to the Hindenburg Line and the Battles of Arras.

COH: 1. Canadian Expeditionary Force 1914 - 1919. The Official History of the Canadian Army in the First World War.
2. The Western Front 1914.

GmOH: Der Weltkrieg 1914 bis 1918, Die Militarischen Operationen zu Lande, Band 12, Die Kriegführung im Frühjahr 1917.

10 April..The British Hospital Ship Salta by a mine. (British Home Waters).

BrOH: 1.Official History of the War, Naval Operations, Volume IV.
2. Official History of the War, The Merchant Navy, Volume III.

11 April..The first British Scandinavian convoy – second experimental convoy agreed. (British Home Waters).

BrOH: 1. Official History of the War, Naval Operations, Volume IV.
2. Official History of the War – The Merchant Navy, Volume III.

NwOH: Marinen. Nøytralitetsvernet 1914-1918, samt nøytralitetsvernets avvikling 1918-1919.

17 April..The British Ambulance Ships Lanfranc and Donegal Sunk damaged by a submarine. (British Home Waters).

BrOH: Official History of the War, Naval Operations, Volume IV.

GmOH: Der Krieg zur See 1914-1918, Band 1, Der Krieg in der Nordsee, Teil 6, Von Juni 1916 bis Frühjahr 1917.

17-19 April ....The First British Offensive into Palestine – the Second Battle of Gaza. (Palestine).

AuOH: Official History of Australia in the War of 1914-1918, Volume VII, Sinai and Palestine.

BrOH: Official History of the War, Military Operations, Egypt and Palestine, Volume I, From the Outbreak of War with Germany to June 1917.

NZOH: Official History of New Zealand's Effort in the Great War, Volume III, Sinai and Palestine.

TOH: 1. Büyük Harbin Sevkülceyşi.
2. Birinci Cihan Harbinde Türk Harbi, 1917 Yili Harekatleri, IVncu Cilt
3. Birinci Dünya Harbinde Türk Harbi VInci Cilt, Hicaz, Asir, Yeman Cepheleri ve Libya Harekati 1914-1918.
4. Büyük Harpte Misir Seferi.

20 April...The German Destroyers raid in Dover Straits. (British Home Waters).

BrOH: Official History of the War, Naval Operations, Volume IV.

GmOH: Der Krieg zur See 1914-1918, Band 1, Der Krieg in der Nordsee, Teil 6, Von Juni 1916 bis Frühjahr 1917.

23-24 April ....The Battle of Arras – the Second Battle of the Scarpe, 1917. (Western Front).

AuOH: Official History of Australia in the War of 1914-1918, Volume IV, France 1917.

BrOH: Official History of the War, Military Operations, France and Belgium 1917, Volume I, The German Retreat to the Hindenburg Line and the Battles of Arras.

COH: 1. Canadian Expeditionary Force 1914 - 1919. The Official History of the Canadian Army in the First World War.
2. The Western Front 1914.

GmOH: Der Weltkrieg 1914 bis 1918, Die Militarischen Operationen zu Lande, Band 12, Die Kriegführung im Frühjahr 1917.

24-25 April ....The Battle of Doiran, 1917. (First Phase). (Balkan Front).

AHOH: Österreich-Ungarns Letzter Krieg 1914-1918, Band VI.

BrOH: Official History of the War, Military Operations, Macedonia, Volume I: From the Outbreak of War to the Spring of 1917.

BuOH: Bŭlgarskata armija vŭ světovnata vojna 1915-1918 g. Tomŭ VIII.

FrOH: Les Armées Françaises dans la Grande Guerre: Tome VIII La campagne d'Orient. Volume 2 La campagne d'Orient depuis l'intervention de la Roumanie en aöut 1916 jusqu'en avril 1918.

GmOH: Der Weltkrieg 1914 bis 1918, Die Militarischen Operationen zu Lande, Band 11, Die Kriegführung im Herbst 1916 und im Winter 1916/17.

GrOH: 1. Ho Hellenikos Stratos kata ton Proton Pankosmion Polemon 1914-1918 Tomos 1 - H Hellas kai ho Polemos eis ta Balkania.
2. Epitomh Istopia Ths Eummetochhs Tou Ellhnikou Stratou Ston Prpsto Pagkosmio Polemo 1914-1918. / A Concise History of the Participation of the Hellenic Army in The First World War 1914-1918.

MOH: Operacije crnogorske vojske u prvom svetskom ratu.

SeOH: Veliki rat Srbije za oslobođenje i ujedinenje Srba, Hrvata i Slovenaca 1914 – 1918. Knjige Dvadeset Prva. 1916 i 1917 godina. Rovovska vojna srpske vojske na solunskom frontu. I period. Rovovske Vojne.

TOH: 1. Birinci Dünya Harbinde Türk Harbi, VIInci Cilt, 3nci Kisim, Avrupa Cepheleri, Makedonya Cephesi, Romanya Cephesi.

2. Birinci Dünya Harbinde Türk Harbi, Avrupa Cepheleri (Özet).

26-27 April .... The Destroyer raid on Ramsgate, Kent. (British Home Waters).

BrOH: Official History of the War, Naval Operations, Volume IV.

GmOH: Der Krieg zur See 1914-1918, Band 1, Der Krieg in der Nordsee, Teil 6, Von Juni 1916 bis Frühjahr 1917.

28-29 April .... The Battle of Arras – the Battle Arleux. (Western Front).

AuOH: Official History of Australia in the War of 1914-1918, Volume IV, France 1917.

BrOH: Official History of the War, Military Operations, France and Belgium 1917, Volume I, The German Retreat to the Hindenburg Line and the Battles of Arras.

COH: 1. Canadian Expeditionary Force 1914 - 1919. The Official History of the Canadian Army in the First World War.

2. The Western Front 1914.

GmOH: Der Weltkrieg 1914 bis 1918, Die Militarischen Operationen zu Lande, Band 12, Die Kriegführung im Frühjahr 1917.

1 May .... The British adopt the Convoy system. (High Seas).

BrOH: 1. Official History of the War, Naval Operations, Volume IV.

2. Official History of the War – The Merchant Navy, Volume III.

3-4 May .... The Battle of Arras – the Third Battle of the Scarpe, 1917. (Western Front).

AuOH: Official History of Australia in the War of 1914-1918, Volume IV, France 1917.

BrOH: Official History of the War, Military Operations, France and Belgium 1917, Volume I, The German Retreat to the Hindenburg Line and the Battles of Arras.

COH: 1. Canadian Expeditionary Force 1914 - 1919. The Official History of the Canadian Army in the First World War.

2. The Western Front 1914.

GmOH: Der Weltkrieg 1914 bis 1918, Die Militarischen Operationen zu Lande, Band 12, Die Kriegführung im Frühjahr 1917.

3-17 May .... The Battle of Arras – The Battle of Bullecourt. (Western Front).

AuOH: Official History of Australia in the War of 1914-1918, Volume IV, France 1917.

BrOH: Official History of the War, Military Operations, France and Belgium 1917, Volume I, The German Retreat to the Hindenburg Line and the Battles of Arras.

COH: 1. Canadian Expeditionary Force 1914 - 1919. The Official History of the Canadian Army in the First World War.

2. The Western Front 1914.

GmOH: Der Weltkrieg 1914 bis 1918, Die Militarischen Operationen zu Lande, Band 12, Die Kriegführung im Frühjahr 1917.

5-22 May ....The Battle of Vardar. (Balkan Front).
AHOH: Österreich-Ungarns Letzter Krieg 1914-1918, Band VI.
BrOH: Official History of the War – Military Operations, Macedonia, Volume II:, From the Spring of 1917 to the End of the War.
FrOH: Les Armées Françaises dans la Grande Guerre: Tome VIII La campagne d'Orient. Volume 2 La campagne d'Orient depuis l'intervention de la Roumanie en aöut 1916 jusqu'en avril 1918.
GmOH: Der Weltkrieg 1914 bis 1918, Die Militarischen Operationen zu Lande, Band 13, Die Kriegführung im Sommer und Herbst 1917.
GrOH: 1. Ho Hellenikos Stratos kata ton Proton Pankosmion Polemon 1914-1918 Tomos 1 - H Hellas kai ho Polemos eis ta Balkania.
2. Epitomh Istopia Ths Eummetochhs Tou Ellhnikou Stratou Ston Prpsto Pagkosmio Polemo 1914-1918. / A Concise History of the Participation of the Hellenic Army in The First World War 1914-1918.
MOH: Operacije crnogorske vojske u prvom svetskom ratu.
SeOH: 1. Veliki rat Srbije za oslobođenje i ujedinenje Srba, Hrvata i Slovenaca 1914 – 1918. Knjige Dvadeset Druga. 1917 godina. Rovovska vojna srpske vojske na solunskom frontu. I period. Rovovske Vojne. Nastavak.
2. Veliki rat Srbije za oslobođenje i ujedinenje Srba, Hrvata i Slovenaca 1914 – 1918. Knjige Dvadeset Treći. 1917 godina. Rovovska vojna srpske vojske na solunskom frontu. II period. Rovovske Vojne. Defanziva Srpske Vojske
TOH: 1. Birinci Dünya Harbinde Türk Harbi, VIInci Cilt, 3nci Kisim, Avrupa Cepheleri, Makedonya Cephesi, Romanya Cephesi.
2. Birinci Dünya Harbinde Türk Harbi, Avrupa Cepheleri (Özet).

7 May..The German night aircraft raid (single aircraft) on London. (Britain).
BrOH: Official History of the War, War in the Air, Volume V.
GmOH: Der Weltkrieg 1914 bis 1918, Die Militarischen Operationen zu Lande, Band 13, Die Kriegführung im Sommer und Herbst 1917; Der Krieg zur Air.

7 May..*Captain* Albert Ball killed in action. (Western Front).
BrOH: Official History of the War, War in the Air, Volume III.
GmOH: Der Weltkrieg 1914 bis 1918, Die Militarischen Operationen zu Lande, Band 13, Die Kriegführung im Sommer und Herbst 1917.

8-9 May ....The Battle of Doiran, 1917. (Second Phase). (Balkan Front).
AHOH: Österreich-Ungarns Letzter Krieg 1914-1918, Band VI.
BrOH: Official History of the War – Military Operations, Macedonia, Volume II:, From the Spring of 1917 to the End of the War.
FrOH: Les Armées Françaises dans la Grande Guerre: Tome VIII La campagne d'Orient. Volume 2 La campagne d'Orient

depuis l'intervention de la Roumanie en aöut 1916 jusqu'en avril 1918.

GmOH: Der Weltkrieg 1914 bis 1918, Die Militarischen Operationen zu Lande, Band 13, Die Kriegführung im Sommer und Herbst 1917.

GrOH: 1. Ho Hellenikos Stratos kata ton Proton Pankosmion Polemon 1914-1918 Tomos 1 - H Hellas kai ho Polemos eis ta Balkania.
2. Epitomh Istopia Ths Eummetochhs Tou Ellhnikou Stratou Ston Prpsto Pagkosmio Polemo 1914-1918. / A Concise History of the Participation of the Hellenic Army in The First World War 1914-1918.

MOH: Operacije crnogorske vojske u prvom svetskom ratu.

SeOH: Veliki rat Srbije za oslobođenje i ujedinenje Srba, Hrvata i Slovenaca 1914 – 1918. Knjige Dvadeset Druga. 1917 godina. Rovovska vojna srpske vojske na solunskom frontu. I period. Rovovske Vojne. Nastavak.

TOH: 1. Birinci Dünya Harbinde Türk Harbi, VIInci Cilt, 3nci Kisim, Avrupa Cepheleri, Makedonya Cephesi, Romanya Cephesi.
2. Birinci Dünya Harbinde Türk Harbi, Avrupa Cepheleri (Özet).

9-19 May .... The Battle of the Cerna Bend. (Balkan Front).

AHOH: Österreich-Ungarns Letzter Krieg 1914-1918, Band VI.

BrOH: Official History of the War – Military Operations, Macedonia, Volume II:, From the Spring of 1917 to the End of the War.

FrOH: Les Armées Françaises dans la Grande Guerre: Tome VIII La campagne d'Orient. Volume 2 La campagne d'Orient depuis l'intervention de la Roumanie en aöut 1916 jusqu'en avril 1918.

GmOH: Der Weltkrieg 1914 bis 1918, Die Militarischen Operationen zu Lande, Band 13, Die Kriegführung im Sommer und Herbst 1917.

GrOH: 1. Ho Hellenikos Stratos kata ton Proton Pankosmion Polemon 1914-1918 Tomos 1 - H Hellas kai ho Polemos eis ta Balkania.
2. Epitomh Istopia Ths Eummetochhs Tou Ellhnikou Stratou Ston Prpsto Pagkosmio Polemo 1914-1918. / A Concise History of the Participation of the Hellenic Army in The First World War 1914-1918.

MOH: Operacije crnogorske vojske u prvom svetskom ratu.

SeOH: Veliki rat Srbije za oslobođenje i ujedinenje Srba, Hrvata i Slovenaca 1914 – 1918. Knjige Dvadeset Druga. 1917 godina. Rovovska vojna srpske vojske na solunskom frontu. I period. Rovovske Vojne. Nastavak.

TOH: 1. Birinci Dünya Harbinde Türk Harbi, VIInci Cilt, 3nci Kisim, Avrupa Cepheleri, Makedonya Cephesi, Romanya Cephesi.
2. Birinci Dünya Harbinde Türk Harbi, Avrupa Cepheleri (Özet).

10 May .... First Convoy from Gibraltar to United Kingdom. (Atlantic Ocean).

BrOH: 1. Official History of the War, Naval Operations, Volume IV.
2. Official History of the War, Seaborne Trade, Volume III, Submarine Campaign, Part II.

3. Official History of the War, The Merchant Navy, Volume III.

10 May...The action of Kharkhwasta. (NW Frontier India).
                  BrOH: Official History of the War, Military Operations, Operations in Persia 1915-1919.
                  TOH: 1. Büyük Harbin Sevkülceyşi.
                  2. Birinci Cihan Harbinde Türk Harbi, 1917 Yili Harekatleri, IVncu Cilt.
                  3. Birinci Dünya Harbinde Türk Harbi VInci Cilt, Hicaz, Asir, Yeman Cepheleri ve Libya Harekati 1914-1918.
                  4. Büyük Harpte Misir Seferi.

12 May – 8 June................................The Tenth Battle of the Isonzo. (Italian Front).
                  AHOH: Österreich-Ungarns Letzter Krieg 1914-1918, Band VI.
                  IOH: Maggiore Esercito, Ufficio Storico, L'Esercito italiano nella grande guerra 1915-18, Volume IV, Tomo 2, Le Operazioni Del 1917 - Gli Avvenimenti Dal Giugno Al Settembre.

14 May...The German airship L22 destroyed. (British Home Waters).
                  BrOH: Official History of the War, War in the Air, Volume II.
                  GmOH: Der Weltkrieg 1914 bis 1918, Die Militarischen Operationen zu Lande, Band 12, Die Kriegführung im Frühjahr 1917; Der Krieg zur Air.

15 May...The Austrian raid in the Straits of Otranto – 14 British drifters sunk. (Adriatic Sea).
                  AHOH: Österreich-Ungarns Seekrieg 1914-1918, Lieferung IV.
                  BrOH: Official History of the War, Naval Operations, Volume IV.

24 May...First Convoy from Newport News to United Kingdom. (Atlantic Ocean).
                  BrOH: 1. Official History of the War, Naval Operations, Volume V.
                  2. Official History of the War, Seaborne Trade, Volume III, Submarine Campaign, Part II.
                  3. Official History of the War, The Merchant Navy, Volume III.

25 May...The German aircraft raid on the East Coast of England. (Kent) causing approximately 290 casualties.
                  BrOH: Official History of the War, War in the Air, Volume V.
                  GmOH: Der Weltkrieg 1914 bis 1918, Die Militarischen Operationen zu Lande, Band 13, Die Kriegführung im Sommer und Herbst 1917; Der Krieg zur Air.

26 May...The British Hospital Ship Dover Castle sunk by a submarine. (Mediterranean Sea).
                  AHOH: Österreich-Ungarns Seekrieg 1914-1918, Lieferung IV.
                  BrOH: 1. Official History of the War, Naval Operations, Volume IV.
                  2. Official History of the War, The Merchant Navy, Volume III.
                  GmOH: Der Krieg zur See 1914-1918, Band 4, Der Handelskrieg Mit U-Booten, Teil 5, Januar bis November 1918.

5 June...The German aircraft raid on Sheerness Naval Yard. (Britain).
                  BrOH: Official History of the War, War in the Air, Volume V.

GmOH: Der Weltkrieg 1914 bis 1918, Die Militarischen Operationen zu Lande, Band 13, Die Kriegführung im Sommer und Herbst 1917; Der Krieg zur Air.

7 June – 10 November .... The Flanders Offensive. (Western Front) [British & French/ German].

AuOH: Official History of Australia in the War of 1914-1918, Volume IV, France 1917.

BrOH: Official History of the War, Military Operations, France and Belgium 1917, Volume II, 7th June - 10th November: Messines and Third Ypres.

COH: 1. Canadian Expeditionary Force 1914 - 1919. The Official History of the Canadian Army in the First World War.
2. The Western Front 1914.

FrOH: Les Armées Françaises dans la Grande Guerre, Tome V, L'offensives d'avril 1917, les opérations à objectifs limités – 1 novembre 1916-1 novembre 1917, Volume 2, Les opérations à objectifs limités.

GmOH: Der Weltkrieg 1914 bis 1918, Die Militarischen Operationen zu Lande, Band 13, Die Kriegführung im Sommer und Herbst 1917.

NZOH: Official History of New Zealand's Effort in the Great War, Volume II, France.

7-14 June .... The Flanders Offensive - the Battle of Messines. (Western Front).

AuOH: Official History of Australia in the War of 1914-1918, Volume IV, France 1917.

BrOH: Official History of the War, Military Operations, France and Belgium 1917, Volume II, 7th June - 10th November: Messines and Third Ypres.

COH: 1. Canadian Expeditionary Force 1914 - 1919. The Official History of the Canadian Army in the First World War.
2. The Western Front 1914.

GmOH: Der Weltkrieg 1914 bis 1918, Die Militarischen Operationen zu Lande, Band 13, Die Kriegführung im Sommer und Herbst 1917.

NZOH: Official History of New Zealand's Effort in the Great War, Volume II, France.

12 June... Corinth and Larissa Occupied. (Mediterranean Sea).

GrOH: 1. Ho Hellenikos Stratos kata ton Proton Pankosmion Polemon 1914-1918 Tomos 1 - H Hellas kai ho Polemos eis ta Balkania.
2. Epitomh Istopia Ths Eummetochhs Tou Ellhnikou Stratou Ston Prpsto Pagkosmio Polemo 1914-1918. / A Concise History of the Participation of the Hellenic Army in The First World War 1914-1918.

13 June... The German aircraft raid on London causing approximately 590 casualties.

BrOH: Official History of the War, War in the Air, Volume IV.

GmOH: Der Weltkrieg 1914 bis 1918, Die Militarischen Operationen zu Lande, Band 13, Die Kriegführung im Sommer und Herbst 1917; Der Krieg zur Air.

14 June... Admiralty approves merchant convoys [British].

BrOH: 1. Official History of the War, Naval Operations, Volume V.

2. Official History of the War, Seaborne Trade, Volume III, Submarine Campaign, Part II.

3. Official History of the War, The Merchant Navy, Volume III.

14 June...The airship L43 destroyed in the North Sea. (British Home Waters).

BrOH: Official History of the War, War in the Air, Volume IV.

GmOH: Der Weltkrieg 1914 bis 1918, Die Militarischen Operationen zu Lande, Band 13, Die Kriegführung im Sommer und Herbst 1917; Der Krieg zur Air.

17 June...The airship L48 destroyed by an aircraft over Theberton, Suffolk. (Britian).

BrOH: Official History of the War, War in the Air, Volume IV.

GmOH: Der Weltkrieg 1914 bis 1918, Die Militarischen Operationen zu Lande, Band 13, Die Kriegführung im Sommer und Herbst 1917; Der Krieg zur Air.

21 June...Mutiny breaks out in Russian Fleet. (Black Sea).

RuOH:..Flot v Pervoi Mirovoi Voine. V Dvukh Tomakh. Tom I Deystviya Russkogo Flota.

24 June...The actions in the Shahur Valley. (NW Frontier India).

BrOH: Official History of the War, Military Operations, Operations in Persia 1915-1919.

TOH: 1. Büyük Harbin Sevkülceyşi.

2. Birinci Cihan Harbinde Türk Harbi, 1917 Yili Harekatleri, IVncu Cilt.

3. Birinci Dünya Harbinde Türk Harbi VInci Cilt, Hicaz, Asir, Yeman Cepheleri ve Libya Harekati 1914-1918.

4. Büyük Harpte Misir Seferi.

27 June...The French cruiser Kléber sunk by a submarine. (British Home Waters).

GmOH: Der Krieg zur See 1914-1918, Band 4, Der Handelskrieg Mit U-Booten, Teil 4, Februar bis Dezember 1917.

29 June – 28 July ....The Russian Summer Offensive - the Brusilov Offensive. (Eastern Front).

AHOH: Österreich-Ungarns Letzter Krieg 1914-1918, Band VI.

GmOH: Der Weltkrieg 1914 bis 1918, Die Militarischen Operationen zu Lande, Band 13, Die Kriegführung im Sommer und Herbst 1917.

RuOH: 1. The Russian Army in the World War.

2. A Strategic Outline of the War 1914 -1918.

30 June...The Russian Summer Offensive – the Battle of Brzezany. (Eastern Front).

AHOH: Österreich-Ungarns Letzter Krieg 1914-1918, Band VI.

GmOH: Der Weltkrieg 1914 bis 1918, Die Militarischen Operationen zu Lande, Band 13, Die Kriegführung im Sommer und Herbst 1917.

RuOH: 1. The Russian Army in the World War.

2. A Strategic Outline of the War 1914 -1918.

30 June...The Russian Summer Offensive – the Battle of Koniuchy. (Eastern Front).

AHOH: Österreich-Ungarns Letzter Krieg 1914-1918, Band VI.

GmOH: Der Weltkrieg 1914 bis 1918, Die Militarischen Operationen zu Lande, Band 13, Die Kriegführung im Sommer und Herbst 1917.

RuOH: 1. The Russian Army in the World War.
2. A Strategic Outline of the War 1914 -1918.

30 June – 6 July ....The Russian Summer Offensive – the Battle of Zborov. (Eastern Front).

AHOH: Österreich-Ungarns Letzter Krieg 1914-1918, Band VI.

GmOH: Der Weltkrieg 1914 bis 1918, Die Militarischen Operationen zu Lande, Band 13, Die Kriegführung im Sommer und Herbst 1917.

RuOH: 1. The Russian Army in the World War.
2. A Strategic Outline of the War 1914 -1918.

1-2 July ....The Russian Summer Offensive – the Battle of Zloczow. (Eastern Front).

AHOH: Österreich-Ungarns Letzter Krieg 1914-1918, Band VI.

CzOH: 1. První československý odboj. Česká Legíe 1914-1920.
2. O samostatny československý stát 1914-1918.

GmOH: Der Weltkrieg 1914 bis 1918, Die Militarischen Operationen zu Lande, Band 13, Die Kriegführung im Sommer und Herbst 1917.

RuOH: 1. The Russian Army in the World War.
2. A Strategic Outline of the War 1914 -1918.

2 July ....The first merchant convoy sails from Hampton Roads. (Atlantic Ocean).

AmOH: U.S. Office of Naval Records and Library, Monographs, Publication No. 1, German Submarine Activities on the Atlantic Coast of the United States and Canada

BrOH: 1. Official History of the War, Naval Operations, Volume V.
2. Official History of the War, Seaborne Trade, Volume III, Submarine Campaign, Part II.
3. Official History of the War, The Merchant Navy, Volume III.

GmOH: Der Krieg zur See 1914-1918, Band 4, Der Handelskrieg Mit U-Booten, Teil 4, Februar bis Dezember 1917.

3 July ....The affair of Aba-el-Lissan. (Arabia).

AuOH: Official History of Australia in the War of 1914-1918, Volume VII, Sinai and Palestine.

BrOH: Official History of the War, Military Operations, Egypt and Palestine, Volume II, From June 1917 to the End of the War.

NZOH: Official History of New Zealand's Effort in the Great War, Volume III, Sinai and Palestine.

TOH: 1. Büyük Harbin Sevkülceyşi.
2. Birinci Cihan Harbinde Türk Harbi, 1917 Yili Harekatleri, IVncu Cilt.
3. Birinci Dünya Harbinde Türk Harbi VInci Cilt, Hicaz, Asir, Yeman Cepheleri ve Libya Harekati 1914-1918.
4. Büyük Harpte Misir Seferi.

4 July ....Ponta Delgada shelled by a submarine. (Atlantic Ocean).

FrOH: Précis d'histoire de la guerre navale, 1914-1918.

GmOH: Der Krieg zur See 1914-1918, Band 4, Der Handelskrieg Mit U-Booten, Teil 4, Februar bis Dezember 1917.

PgOH: Portugal na Grande Guerra II.

4 July ....The concerted attack by a submarines on United States' Transports defeated. (Atlantic Ocean).

> AmOH: U.S. Office of Naval Records and Library, Monographs, Publication No. 1, German Submarine Activities on the Atlantic Coast of the United States and Canada.
> BrOH: 1. Official History of the War, Naval Operations, Volume V.
> 2. Official History of the War, Seaborne Trade, Volume III, Submarine Campaign, Part II.
> 3. Official History of the War, The Merchant Navy, Volume III.
> GmOH: Der Krieg zur See 1914-1918, Band 4, Der Handelskrieg Mit U-Booten, Teil 4, Februar bis Dezember 1917.

6 July ....The Arab Forces capture Aqaba. (Arabia).

> AuOH: Official History of Australia in the War of 1914-1918, Volume VII, Sinai and Palestine.
> BrOH: Official History of the War, Military Operations, Egypt and Palestine, Volume II, From June 1917 to the End of the War.
> NZOH: Official History of New Zealand's Effort in the Great War, Volume III, Sinai and Palestine.
> TOH: 1. Büyük Harbin Sevkülceyşi.
> 2. Birinci Cihan Harbinde Türk Harbi, 1917 Yili Harekatleri, IVncu Cilt.
> 3. Birinci Dünya Harbinde Türk Harbi VInci Cilt, Hicaz, Asir, Yeman Cepheleri ve Libya Harekati 1914-1918.
> 4. Büyük Harpte Misir Seferi.

7 July ....The German aircraft raid on Margate and London, approximately 250 casualties – last daylight raid on London. (Britain).

> BrOH: Official History of the War, War in the Air, Volume IV.
> GmOH: Der Weltkrieg 1914 bis 1918, Die Militarischen Operationen zu Lande, Band 13, Die Kriegführung im Sommer und Herbst 1917; Der Krieg zur Air.

9 July ....H.M.S. Vanguard sunk by an internal explosion. (British Home Waters).

> BrOH: Official History of the War, Naval Operations, Volume V.

18-28 July ....The Russian Summer Offensive – the Battle of East Galicia. (Galicia - Eastern Front).

> AHOH: Österreich-Ungarns Letzter Krieg 1914-1918, Band VI.
> GmOH: Der Weltkrieg 1914 bis 1918, Die Militarischen Operationen zu Lande, Band 13, Die Kriegführung im Sommer und Herbst 1917.
> RuOH: 1. The Russian Army in the World War.
> 2. A Strategic Outline of the War 1914 -1918.

18-25 July ....The Russian Summer Offensive – the Battle of Dvinsk. (Eastern Front).

> AHOH: Österreich-Ungarns Letzter Krieg 1914-1918, Band VI.
> GmOH: Der Weltkrieg 1914 bis 1918, Die Militarischen Operationen zu Lande, Band 13, Die Kriegführung im Sommer und Herbst 1917.
> RuOH: 1. The Russian Army in the World War.
> 2. A Strategic Outline of the War 1914 -1918.

19 July ....The action of Narungombe. (East Africa).

BgOH: Les campagnes coloniales Belges 1914-1918. Volume III. la campagne de Mahenge 1917.

GmOH: Der Krieg zur See 1914-1918, Band 6, Die Kämpfe der Kaiserlichen Marine in den deutschen Kolonien, Teil 2, Deutsch-Ostafrika.

SAOH: The Union of South Africa and the Great War 1914 – 1918.

19-27 July ....The Russian Summer Offensive – the Battle of Smorgon-Krevo. (Eastern Front).

AHOH: Österreich-Ungarns Letzter Krieg 1914-1918, Band VI.

GmOH: Der Weltkrieg 1914 bis 1918, Die Militarischen Operationen zu Lande, Band 13, Die Kriegführung im Sommer und Herbst 1917.

RuOH: 1. The Russian Army in the World War.
2. A Strategic Outline of the War 1914 -1918.

22 July – 1 August ....The Rumanian Offensive – the Battle of Marasesti first phase. (Eastern Front).

AHOH: Österreich-Ungarns Letzter Krieg 1914-1918, Band VI.

GmOH: Der Weltkrieg 1914 bis 1918, Die Militarischen Operationen zu Lande, Band 13, Die Kriegführung im Sommer und Herbst 1917.

RoOH: România în război mondial 1916-1919, Volumul IV.

26 July ....The formation of thw first German fighter group: Jagdgeschwader 1. (Western Front).

BrOH: Official History of the War, War in the Air, Volume V.

GmOH: Der Weltkrieg 1914 bis 1918, Die Militarischen Operationen zu Lande, Band 13, Die Kriegführung im Sommer und Herbst 1917; Der Krieg zur Air.

31 July -9 October..............................The Flanders Offensive - the Third Battle of Ypres [1]. (Western Front).

AuOH: Official History of Australia in the War of 1914-1918, Volume IV, France 1917.

BrOH: Official History of the War, Military Operations, France and Belgium 1917, Volume II, 7th June - 10th November: Messines and Third Ypres.

COH: 1. Canadian Expeditionary Force 1914 - 1919. The Official History of the Canadian Army in the First World War.
2. The Western Front 1914.

FrOH: Les Armées Françaises dans la Grande Guerre, Tome V, L'offensives d'avril 1917, les opérations à objectifs limités – 1 novembre 1916-1 novembre 1917, Volume 2, Les opérations à objectifs limités.

GmOH: Der Weltkrieg 1914 bis 1918, Die Militarischen Operationen zu Lande, Band 13, Die Kriegführung im Sommer und Herbst 1917.

NZOH: Official History of New Zealand's Effort in the Great War, Volume II, France.

31 July –2August ....The Flanders Offensive - the Third Battle of Ypres - the Battle of Pilckem Ridge. (Western Front).

AuOH: Official History of Australia in the War of 1914-1918, Volume IV, France 1917.

---

[1] **Known to the French as The Second Battle of Flanders**

BrOH: Official History of the War, Military Operations, France and Belgium 1917, Volume II, 7th June - 10th November: Messines and Third Ypres.

COH: 1. Canadian Expeditionary Force 1914 - 1919. The Official History of the Canadian Army in the First World War.

2. The Western Front 1914.

GmOH: Der Weltkrieg 1914 bis 1918, Die Militarischen Operationen zu Lande, Band 13, Die Kriegführung im Sommer und Herbst 1917.

NZOH: Official History of New Zealand's Effort in the Great War, Volume II, France.

2 August..S.M.S. Seeadler wrecked on Mopelia Island. (Pacific Ocean).

GmOH: Der Krieg zur See 1914-1918, Band 3, Der Kreuzerkrieg in den ausländischen Gewässern, Teil 3, Die deutschen Hilfskreuzer.

3 August..Mutiny breaks out in German Fleet. (German Home Waters).

GmOH: Der Krieg zur See 1914-1918, Band 1, Der Krieg in der Nordsee, Teil 7, Von Sommer 1917 bis zum Kriegsende 1918.

6 August – 3 September.....................The Rumanian Offensive – the Battle of Marasesti second phase. (Eastern Front).

AHOH: Österreich-Ungarns Letzter Krieg 1914-1918, Band VI.

GmOH: Der Weltkrieg 1914 bis 1918, Die Militarischen Operationen zu Lande, Band 13, Die Kriegführung im Sommer und Herbst 1917.

RoOH: România în război mondial 1916-1919, Volumul IV.

16-18 August ....The Flanders Offensive - the Third Battle of Ypres - the Battle of Langemarck, 1917. (Western Front).

AuOH: Official History of Australia in the War of 1914-1918, Volume IV, France 1917.

BrOH: Official History of the War, Military Operations, France and Belgium 1917, Volume II, 7th June - 10th November: Messines and Third Ypres.

COH: 1. Canadian Expeditionary Force 1914 - 1919. The Official History of the Canadian Army in the First World War.

2. The Western Front 1914.

GmOH: Der Weltkrieg 1914 bis 1918, Die Militarischen Operationen zu Lande, Band 13, Die Kriegführung im Sommer und Herbst 1917.

NZOH: Official History of New Zealand's Effort in the Great War, Volume II, France.

15-25 August ....The Battle of Hill 70. (Western Front).

AuOH: Official History of Australia in the War of 1914-1918, Volume IV, France 1917.

BrOH: Official History of the War, Military Operations, France and Belgium 1917, Volume II, 7th June - 10th November: Messines and Third Ypres.

COH: 1. Canadian Expeditionary Force 1914 - 1919. The Official History of the Canadian Army in the First World War.

2. The Western Front 1914.

GmOH: Der Weltkrieg 1914 bis 1918, Die Militarischen Operationen zu Lande, Band 13, Die Kriegführung im Sommer und Herbst 1917.

NZOH: Official History of New Zealand's Effort in the Great War, Volume II, France.

17 August – 12 September ....The Eleventh Battle of the Isonzo. (Italian Front).

AHOH: Österreich-Ungarns Letzter Krieg 1914-1918, Band VI.

IOH: Maggiore Esercito, Ufficio Storico, L'Esercito italiano nella grande guerra 1915-18, Volume IV, Tomo 2, Le Operazioni Del 1917, Gli Avvenimenti Dal Giugno Al Settembre.

20 August – 15 December...................Pétain's Limited Offensives – the Second Offensive Battle of Verdun. (Western Front).

FrOH: Les Armées Françaises dans la Grande Guerre, Tome V, L'offensives d'avril 1917, les opérations à objectifs limités – 1 novembre 1916-1 novembre 1917, Volume 2, Les opérations à objectifs limités.

GmOH: Der Weltkrieg 1914 bis 1918, Die Militarischen Operationen zu Lande, Band 13, Die Kriegführung im Sommer und Herbst 1917.

21 August..The airship L23 destroyed in the North Sea. (British Home Waters).

BrOH: Official History of the War, War in the Air, Volume V.

GmOH: Der Weltkrieg 1914 bis 1918, Die Militarischen Operationen zu Lande, Band 13, Die Kriegführung im Sommer und Herbst 1917; Der Krieg zur Air.

22 August..The last daylight raid by German aircraft on Kent Coast. (Britain).

BrOH: Official History of the War, War in the Air, Volume V.

GmOH: Der Weltkrieg 1914 bis 1918, Die Militarischen Operationen zu Lande, Band 13, Die Kriegführung im Sommer und Herbst 1917; Der Krieg zur Air.

1-5 September....................................The Battle of Riga. (Eastern Front).

GmOH: Der Weltkrieg 1914 bis 1918, Die Militarischen Operationen zu Lande, Band 13, Die Kriegführung im Sommer und Herbst 1917.

RuOH: 1. The Russian Army in the World War.
2. A Strategic Outline of the War 1914 -1918.

2-3 September....................................The first severe German aircraft raid by moonlight on Kent, approximately 250 casualties. (Britain).

BrOH: Official History of the War, War in the Air, Volume V.

GmOH: Der Weltkrieg 1914 bis 1918, Die Militarischen Operationen zu Lande, Band 13, Die Kriegführung im Sommer und Herbst 1917; Der Krieg zur Air.

3-4 September....................................The severe German aircraft raid by moonlight on Kent, approximately 230 casualties. (Britain).

BrOH: Official History of the War, War in the Air, Volume V.

GmOH: Der Weltkrieg 1914 bis 1918, Die Militarischen Operationen zu Lande, Band 13, Die Kriegführung im Sommer und Herbst 1917; Der Krieg zur Air.

4 September ....The submarine raid on Scarborough, Yorkshire. (British Home Waters).

BrOH: Official History of the War, Naval Operations, Volume V.

GmOH: 1. Der Krieg zur See 1914-1918, Band 1, Der Krieg in der Nordsee, Teil 7, Von Sommer 1917 bis zum Kriegsende 1918.

2. Der Krieg zur See 1914-1918, Band 4, Der Handelskrieg Mit U-Booten , Teil 4, Februar bis Dezember 1917.

4-5 September .... The first mass German aircraft raid by moonlight on London,. (Britain).

BrOH: Official History of the War, War in the Air, Volume V.

GmOH: Der Weltkrieg 1914 bis 1918, Die Militarischen Operationen zu Lande, Band 13, Die Kriegführung im Sommer und Herbst 1917; Der Krieg zur Air.

11 September .... *Capitaine* Georges Guynemer killed in action. (Western Front).

GmOH: Der Weltkrieg 1914 bis 1918, Die Militarischen Operationen zu Lande, Band 13, Die Kriegführung im Sommer und Herbst 1917.

21-22 September .... The capture of Jacobstadt. (Eastern Front).

GmOH: Der Weltkrieg 1914 bis 1918, Die Militarischen Operationen zu Lande, Band 13, Die Kriegführung im Sommer und Herbst 1917.

RuOH: 1. The Russian Army in the World War.

2. A Strategic Outline of the War 1914 -1918.

20-25 September .... The Flanders Offensive - the Third Battle of Ypres - the Battle of Menin Road Ridge. (Western Front).

AuOH: Official History of Australia in the War of 1914-1918, Volume IV, France 1917.

BrOH: Official History of the War, Military Operations, France and Belgium 1917, Volume II, 7th June - 10th November: Messines and Third Ypres.

COH: 1. Canadian Expeditionary Force 1914 - 1919. The Official History of the Canadian Army in the First World War.

2. The Western Front 1914.

GmOH: Der Weltkrieg 1914 bis 1918, Die Militarischen Operationen zu Lande, Band 13, Die Kriegführung im Sommer und Herbst 1917.

NZOH: Official History of New Zealand's Effort in the Great War, Volume II, France.

26 September – 3 October .... The Flanders Offensive - the Third Battle of Ypres - the Battle of Polygon Wood. (Western Front).

AuOH: Official History of Australia in the War of 1914-1918, Volume IV, France 1917.

BrOH: Official History of the War, Military Operations, France and Belgium 1917, Volume II, 7th June - 10th November: Messines and Third Ypres.

COH: 1. Canadian Expeditionary Force 1914 - 1919. The Official History of the Canadian Army in the First World War.

2. The Western Front 1914.

GmOH: Der Weltkrieg 1914 bis 1918, Die Militarischen Operationen zu Lande, Band 13, Die Kriegführung im Sommer und Herbst 1917.

NZOH: Official History of New Zealand's Effort in the Great War, Volume II, France.

2 October ....H.M.S. Drake sunk by a submarine. (British Home Waters).

        BrOH: Official History of the War, Naval Operations, Volume V.

        GmOH: 1. Der Krieg zur See 1914-1918, Band 1, Der Krieg in der Nordsee, Teil 7, Von Sommer 1917 bis zum Kriegsende 1918.

        2. Der Krieg zur See 1914-1918, Band 4, Der Handelskrieg Mit U-Booten , Teil 4, Februar bis Dezember 1917.

4 October ....The Flanders Offensive - the Third Battle of Ypres - the Battle of Broodseinde. (Western Front).

        AuOH: Official History of Australia in the War of 1914-1918, Volume IV, France 1917.

        BrOH: Official History of the War, Military Operations, France and Belgium 1917, Volume II, 7th June - 10th November: Messines and Third Ypres.

        COH: 1. Canadian Expeditionary Force 1914 - 1919. The Official History of the Canadian Army in the First World War.

        2. The Western Front 1914.

        GmOH: Der Weltkrieg 1914 bis 1918, Die Militarischen Operationen zu Lande, Band 13, Die Kriegführung im Sommer und Herbst 1917.

        NZOH: Official History of New Zealand's Effort in the Great War, Volume II, France.

9 October ....The Flanders Offensive - the Third Battle of Ypres - the Battle of Poelchappelle. (Western Front).

        AuOH: Official History of Australia in the War of 1914-1918, Volume IV, France 1917.

        BrOH: Official History of the War, Military Operations, France and Belgium 1917, Volume II, 7th June - 10th November: Messines and Third Ypres.

        COH: 1. Canadian Expeditionary Force 1914 - 1919. The Official History of the Canadian Army in the First World War.

        2. The Western Front 1914.

        GmOH: Der Weltkrieg 1914 bis 1918, Die Militarischen Operationen zu Lande, Band 13, Die Kriegführung im Sommer und Herbst 1917.

        NZOH: Official History of New Zealand's Effort in the Great War, Volume II, France.

10 October ....The British Hospital Ship Goorkha damaged by a mine. (Mediterranean Sea).

        BrOH: Official History of the War, The Merchant Navy, Volume III.

11-20 October ....The German Operations against the Baltic Islands. (Baltic Sea).

        GmOH: 1. Der Weltkrieg 1914 bis 1918, Die Militarischen Operationen zu Lande, Band 13, Die Kriegführung im Sommer und Herbst 1917.

        2. Der Krieg zur See 1914-1918, Band 2, Der Krieg in der Ostsee, Teil 3, Von Anfang 1916 bis zum Kriegsende.

        RuOH: 1. The Russian Army in the World War.

        2. A Strategic Outline of the War 1914 -1918.

        3. Flot v Pervoi Mirovoi Voine. V Dvukh Tomakh. Tom I Deystviya Russkogo Flota.

11-16 October ....The German Operations against the Baltic Islands – the capture of Ösel Island. (Baltic Sea).

GmOH: 1. Der Weltkrieg 1914 bis 1918, Die Militarischen Operationen zu Lande, Band 13, Die Kriegführung im Sommer und Herbst 1917.

2. Der Krieg zur See 1914-1918, Band 2, Der Krieg in der Ostsee, Teil 3, Von Anfang 1916 bis zum Kriegsende.

RuOH: 1. The Russian Army in the World War.

2. A Strategic Outline of the War 1914 -1918.

3. Flot v Pervoi Mirovoi Voine. V Dvukh Tomakh. Tom I Deystviya Russkogo Flota.

12 October ....The Flanders Offensive - the Third Battle of Ypres - the First Battle of Passchendaele. (Western Front).

AuOH: Official History of Australia in the War of 1914-1918, Volume IV, France 1917.

BrOH: Official History of the War, Military Operations, France and Belgium 1917, Volume II, 7th June - 10th November: Messines and Third Ypres.

COH: 1. Canadian Expeditionary Force 1914 - 1919. The Official History of the Canadian Army in the First World War.

2. The Western Front 1914.

GmOH: Der Weltkrieg 1914 bis 1918, Die Militarischen Operationen zu Lande, Band 13, Die Kriegführung im Sommer und Herbst 1917.

NZOH: Official History of New Zealand's Effort in the Great War, Volume II, France.

16 October ....The German Operations against the Baltic Islands – the Naval action in Gulf of Riga - the Russian dreadnought Slava sunk. (Baltic Sea).

GmOH: 1. Der Weltkrieg 1914 bis 1918, Die Militarischen Operationen zu Lande, Band 13, Die Kriegführung im Sommer und Herbst 1917.

2. Der Krieg zur See 1914-1918, Band 2, Der Krieg in der Ostsee, Teil 3, Von Anfang 1916 bis zum Kriegsende.

RuOH: 1. The Russian Army in the World War.

2. A Strategic Outline of the War 1914 -1918.

3. Flot v Pervoi Mirovoi Voine. V Dvukh Tomakh. Tom I Deystviya Russkogo Flota.

16-19 October ....The action of Nyangao. (East Africa).

BgOH: Les campagnes coloniales Belges 1914-1918. Volume III. la campagne de Mahenge 1917.

GmOH: Der Krieg zur See 1914-1918, Band 6, Die Kämpfe der Kaiserlichen Marine in den deutschen Kolonien, Teil 2, Deutsch-Ostafrika.

SAOH: The Union of South Africa and the Great War 1914 – 1918.

17 October ....German cruisers raid on British Scandinavian Convoy, H.M.S. Strongbow and H.M.S. Mary Rose sunk. (British Home Waters).

BrOH: 1. Official History of the War, Naval Operations, Volume V.

2. Official History of the War, The Merchant Navy, Volume III.

GmOH: Der Krieg zur See 1914-1918, Band 1, Der Krieg in der Nordsee, Teil 7, Von Sommer 1917 bis zum Kriegsende 1918.

NwOH: Marinen. Nøytralitetsvernet 1914-1918, samt nøytralitetsvernets avvikling 1918-1919.

17-18 October ....The German Operations against the Baltic Islands – the capture of Dagö Island. (Baltic Sea).

GmOH: 1. Der Weltkrieg 1914 bis 1918, Die Militarischen Operationen zu Lande, Band 13, Die Kriegführung im Sommer und Herbst 1917.
2. Der Krieg zur See 1914-1918, Band 2, Der Krieg in der Ostsee, Teil 3, Von Anfang 1916 bis zum Kriegsende.

RuOH: 1. The Russian Army in the World War.
2. A Strategic Outline of the War 1914 -1918.
3. Flot v Pervoi Mirovoi Voine. V Dvukh Tomakh. Tom I Deystviya Russkogo Flota.

19 October ....The last mass German airship raid on London by a squadron of eleven airships – eight of the airships driven across to France by the weather conditions. (Britain).

BrOH: Official History of the War, War in the Air, Volume V.

GmOH: Der Weltkrieg 1914 bis 1918, Die Militarischen Operationen zu Lande, Band 13, Die Kriegführung im Sommer und Herbst 1917; Der Krieg zur Air.

20 October ....Three of the German airships from the London raid shot down over France – L44 at St. Clément, L45 at Laragne and L49 at Bourbonne-les-Bains.

GmOH: Der Weltkrieg 1914 bis 1918, Die Militarischen Operationen zu Lande, Band 13, Die Kriegführung im Sommer und Herbst 1917; Der Krieg zur Air.

21 October ....The Turkish attack on Petra. (Arabia).

AuOH: Official History of Australia in the War of 1914-1918, Volume VII, Sinai and Palestine.

BrOH: Official History of the War, Military Operations, Egypt and Palestine, Volume II, From June 1917 to the End of the War.

NZOH: Official History of New Zealand's Effort in the Great War, Volume III, Sinai and Palestine.

TOH: 1. Büyük Harbin Sevkülceyşi.
2. Birinci Cihan Harbinde Türk Harbi, 1917 Yili Harekatleri, IVncu Cilt.
3. Birinci Dünya Harbinde Türk Harbi VInci Cilt, Hicaz, Asir, Yeman Cepheleri ve Libya Harekati 1914-1918.
4. Büyük Harpte Misir Seferi.

21 October ....The German airship L50 from the London raid shot down in to the Mediterranean Sea. (Mediterranean Sea).

GmOH: Der Weltkrieg 1914 bis 1918, Die Militarischen Operationen zu Lande, Band 13, Die Kriegführung im Sommer und Herbst 1917; Der Krieg zur Air.

23 October - 1 November..................Pétain's Limited Offensives – the Battle of La Malmaison. (Western Front).

FrOH: Les Armées Françaises dans la Grande Guerre, Tome V, L'offensives d'avril 1917, les opérations à objectifs limités – 1 novembre 1916-1 novembre 1917, Volume 2, Les opérations à objectifs limités.

GmOH: Der Weltkrieg 1914 bis 1918, Die Militarischen Operationen zu Lande, Band 13, Die Kriegführung im Sommer und Herbst 1917.

24 October – 18 November ....The Austro-German Offensive in the Julian Alps - the Twelfth Battle of the Isonzo (The Battle of Caporetto). (Italian Front).

AHOH: Österreich-Ungarns Letzter Krieg 1914-1918, Band VI.
GmOH: 1. Der Weltkrieg 1914 bis 1918, Die Militarischen Operationen zu Lande, Band 13, Die Kriegführung im Sommer und Herbst 1917.
2. Die Bayern im Großen Kriege 1914-1918.
IOH: Maggiore Esercito, Ufficio Storico, L'Esercito italiano nella grande guerra 1915-18, Volume IV, Tomo 3. Le Operazioni Del 1917 - Gli Avvenimenti Dal Ottobre Al Dicembre.

26 October– 10 November ....The Flanders Offensive - the Third Battle of Ypres - the Second Battle of Passchendaele. (Western Front).

AuOH: Official History of Australia in the War of 1914-1918, Volume IV, France 1917.
BrOH: Official History of the War, Military Operations, France and Belgium 1917, Volume II, 7th June - 10th November: Messines and Third Ypres.
COH: 1. Canadian Expeditionary Force 1914 - 1919. The Official History of the Canadian Army in the First World War.
2. The Western Front 1914.
GmOH: Der Weltkrieg 1914 bis 1918, Die Militarischen Operationen zu Lande, Band 13, Die Kriegführung im Sommer und Herbst 1917.
NZOH: Official History of New Zealand's Effort in the Great War, Volume II, France.

27 October – 7 November ....The Second British Offensive into Palestine - the Third Battle of Gaza. (Palestine).

AuOH: Official History of Australia in the War of 1914-1918, Volume VII, Sinai and Palestine.
BrOH: Official History of the War, Military Operations, Egypt and Palestine, Volume II, From June 1917 to the End of the War.
NZOH: Official History of New Zealand's Effort in the Great War, Volume III, Sinai and Palestine.
TOH: 1. Büyük Harbin Sevkülceyşi.
2. Birinci Cihan Harbinde Türk Harbi, 1917 Yili Harekatleri, IVncu Cilt.
3. Birinci Dünya Harbinde Türk Harbi VInci Cilt, Hicaz, Asir, Yeman Cepheleri ve Libya Harekati 1914-1918.
4. Büyük Harpte Misir Seferi.

2 November ....The British Naval Light Forces raid the Kattegat. (British Home Waters).

BrOH: Official History of the War, Naval Operations, Volume V.

16 November ....Jaffa occupied by British Forces. (Palestine).

AuOH: Official History of Australia in the War of 1914-1918, Volume VII, Sinai and Palestine.
BrOH: Official History of the War, Military Operations, Egypt and Palestine, Volume II, From June 1917 to the End of the War.

NZOH: Official History of New Zealand's Effort in the Great War, Volume III, Sinai and Palestine.

TOH: 1. Büyük Harbin Sevkülceyşi.

2. Birinci Cihan Harbinde Türk Harbi, 1917 Yili Harekatleri, IVncu Cilt.

3. Birinci Dünya Harbinde Türk Harbi VInci Cilt, Hicaz, Asir, Yeman Cepheleri ve Libya Harekati 1914-1918.

4. Büyük Harpte Misir Seferi.

17 November .... The light cruiser action off Heligoland. (British Home Waters).

BrOH: ..Official History of the War, Naval Operations, Volume V.

GmOH: Der Krieg zur See 1914-1918, Band 1, Der Krieg in der Nordsee, Teil 7, Von Sommer 1917 bis zum Kriegsende 1918.

17-24 November .... The British Operation for Jerusalem – the Battle of Nebi Samwil. (Palestine).

AuOH: Official History of Australia in the War of 1914-1918, Volume VII, Sinai and Palestine.

BrOH: Official History of the War, Military Operations, Egypt and Palestine, Volume II, From June 1917 to the End of the War.

NZOH: Official History of New Zealand's Effort in the Great War, Volume III, Sinai and Palestine.

TOH: 1. Büyük Harbin Sevkülceyşi.

2. Birinci Cihan Harbinde Türk Harbi, 1917 Yili Harekatleri, IVncu Cilt.

3. Birinci Dünya Harbinde Türk Harbi VInci Cilt, Hicaz, Asir, Yeman Cepheleri ve Libya Harekati 1914-1918.

4. Büyük Harpte Misir Seferi.

20 November – 3 December .... The Battle of Cambrai, 1917. (Western Front).

AmOH: United States Army in the World War 1917–1919, Volume 4, Operations, Cambrai/ Somme/ Lys/ Chateau Thierry.

AuOH: Official History of Australia in the War of 1914-1918, Volume IV, France 1917.

BrOH: Official History of the War, Military Operations, France and Belgium 1917, Volume III, The Battle of Cambrai.

COH: 1. Canadian Expeditionary Force 1914 - 1919. The Official History of the Canadian Army in the First World War.

2. The Western Front 1914.

GmOH: Der Weltkrieg 1914 bis 1918, Die Militarischen Operationen zu Lande, Band 13, Die Kriegführung im Sommer und Herbst 1917.

NZOH: Official History of New Zealand's Effort in the Great War, Volume II, France.

21 November .... The German airship L59 leaves from Yambol for East Africa. (Balkan Front).

GmOH: 1. Der Krieg zur See 1914-1918, Band 6, Die Kämpfe der Kaiserlichen Marine in den deutschen Kolonien, Teil 2, Deutsch-Ostafrika.

2. Deutsche Tat im Weltkrieg 1914/18 - Geschichten der Kämpfe deutscher Truppen, Band 12. Tufani - Sturm über Deutsch-Ostafrika.

23 November ....The German airship L59 reaches East Africa, but turns back without landing. (East African).

           GmOH: Der Krieg zur See 1914-1918, Band 6, Die Kämpfe der Kaiserlichen Marine in den deutschen Kolonien, Teil 2, Deutsch-Ostafrika.

25 November – 1 December ....The German Operations in Portuguese East Africa. (East Africa).

           GmOH: Der Krieg zur See 1914-1918, Band 6, Die Kämpfe der Kaiserlichen Marine in den deutschen Kolonien, Teil 2, Deutsch-Ostafrika.

           PgOH: 1. Portugal na Grande Guerra.

                 2. A cooperação anglo-portuguesa na Grande Guerra de 1914-1918.

           SAOH: The Union of South Africa and the Great War 1914 – 1918.

25 November ....The German airship L59 returns to Yambol from flight to East Africa – a record flight up to that date. (Balkan Front).

           GmOH: 1. Der Krieg zur See 1914-1918, Band 6, Die Kämpfe der Kaiserlichen Marine in den deutschen Kolonien, Teil 2, Deutsch-Ostafrika.

                 2. Deutsche Tat im Weltkrieg 1914/18 - Geschichten der Kämpfe deutscher Truppen, Band 12. Tufani - Sturm über Deutsch-Ostafrika.

28 November ....The surrender of Tafel Force. (East Africa).

           GmOH: Der Krieg zur See 1914-1918, Band 6, Die Kämpfe der Kaiserlichen Marine in den deutschen Kolonien, Teil 2, Deutsch-Ostafrika.

           PgOH: 1. Portugal na Grande Guerra.

                 2. A cooperação anglo-portuguesa na Grande Guerra de 1914-1918.

           SAOH: The Union of South Africa and the Great War 1914 – 1918.

7-9 December....................................The British Operation for Jerusalem - the capture of Jerusalem. (Palestine).

           AuOH: Official History of Australia in the War of 1914-1918, Volume VII, Sinai and Palestine.

           BrOH: Official History of the War, Military Operations, Egypt and Palestine, Volume II, From June 1917 to the End of the War.

           NZOH: Official History of New Zealand's Effort in the Great War, Volume III, Sinai and Palestine.

           TOH: 1. Büyük Harbin Sevkülceyşi.

                 2. Birinci Cihan Harbinde Türk Harbi, 1917 Yili Harekatleri, IVncu Cilt.

                 3. Birinci Dünya Harbinde Türk Harbi VInci Cilt, Hicaz, Asir, Yeman Cepheleri ve Libya Harekati 1914-1918.

                 4. Büyük Harpte Misir Seferi.

9-10 December...................................The Italian naval raid on Trieste Harbour, S.M.S. Wien sunk. (Adriatic Sea).

           AHOH: Österreich-Ungarns Seekrieg 1914-1918, Lieferung IV.

           IOH: Ufficio Storico della R. Marina, La Marina Italiana nella Grande Guerra, Volume VIII, La Vittoria Mutilata in Adriatico.

12 December.....................................The German destroyer raid on British Scandinavian convoy, H.M.S. Partridge sunk. (British Home Waters) [British].

        BrOH: 1. Official History of the War, Naval Operations, Volume V.

                  2. Official History of the War – The Merchant Navy

        GmOH: Der Krieg zur See 1914-1918, Band 1, Der Krieg in der Nordsee, Teil 7, Von Sommer 1917 bis zum Kriegsende 1918.

        NwOH: Marinen. Nøytralitetsvernet 1914-1918, samt nøytralitetsvernets avvikling 1918-1919.

12 December.....................................Funchal, Madeira bombarded by a submarine. (Atlantic Ocean).

        FrOH: Précis d'histoire de la guerre navale, 1914-1918.

        GmOH: Der Krieg zur See 1914-1918, Band 4, Der Handelskrieg Mit U-Booten, Teil 4, Februar bis Dezember 1917.

        PgOH: Portugal na Grande Guerra II.

14 December.....................................The French cruiser Château Renault sunk by a submarine. (Mediterranean Sea).

        AHOH: Österreich-Ungarns Seekrieg 1914-1918, Lieferung IV.

        GmOH: Der Krieg zur See 1914-1918, Band 4, Der Handelskrieg Mit U-Booten, Teil 5 Januar bis November 1918.

21-22 December..............................The British Operation for Jerusalem – the Battle of Jaffa. (Palestine).

        AuOH: Official History of Australia in the War of 1914-1918, Volume VII, Sinai and Palestine.

        BrOH: Official History of the War, Military Operations, Egypt and Palestine, Volume II, From June 1917 to the End of the War.

        NZOH: Official History of New Zealand's Effort in the Great War, Volume III, Sinai and Palestine.

        TOH: 1. Büyük Harbin Sevkülceyşi.

                  2. Birinci Cihan Harbinde Türk Harbi, 1917 Yili Harekatleri, IVncu Cilt.

                  3. Birinci Dünya Harbinde Türk Harbi VInci Cilt, Hicaz, Asir, Yeman Cepheleri ve Libya Harekati 1914-1918.

                  4. Büyük Harpte Misir Seferi.

26-30 December..............................The British Operation for Jerusalem - the defence of Jerusalem. (Palestine).

        AuOH: Official History of Australia in the War of 1914-1918, Volume VII, Sinai and Palestine.

        BrOH: Official History of the War, Military Operations, Egypt and Palestine, Volume II, From June 1917 to the End of the War.

        NZOH: Official History of New Zealand's Effort in the Great War, Volume III, Sinai and Palestine.

        TOH: 1. Büyük Harbin Sevkülceyşi.

                  2. Birinci Cihan Harbinde Türk Harbi, 1917 Yili Harekatleri, IVncu Cilt.

                  3. Birinci Dünya Harbinde Türk Harbi VInci Cilt, Hicaz, Asir, Yeman Cepheleri ve Libya Harekati 1914-1918.

                  4. Büyük Harpte Misir Seferi.

1918

4 January...The British Hospital Ship Rewa sunk by a submarine. (British Home Waters).
  BrOH: Official History of the War, The Merchant Navy, Volume III.

8 January...The capture of Qsar-i-Shirin. (West Persia).
  BrOH: Official History of the War, Military Operations, Operations in Persia 1915-1919.
  TOH: 1. Büyük Harbin Sevkülceyşi.
        2. Birinci Cihan Harbinde Türk Harbi, 1918 Yili Harekatleri, Vnci Cilt.
        3. Birinci Dünya Harbinde Türk Harbi VInci Cilt, Hicaz, Asir, Yeman Cepheleri ve Libya Harekati 1914-1918.
        4. Büyük Harpte Misir Seferi.
  RuOH: 1. The Russian Army in the World War.
        2. A Strategic Outline of the War 1914 -1918.

8-28 January ....The Arab actions for Et Tafile. (Arabia).
  AuOH: Official History of Australia in the War of 1914-1918, Volume VII, Sinai and Palestine.
  BrOH: Official History of the War, Military Operations, Egypt and Palestine, Volume II, From June 1917 to the End of the War.
  NZOH: Official History of New Zealand's Effort in the Great War, Volume III, Sinai and Palestine.
  TOH: 1. Büyük Harbin Sevkülceyşi.
        2. Birinci Cihan Harbinde Türk Harbi, 1917 Yili Harekatleri, IVncu Cilt.
        3. Birinci Dünya Harbinde Türk Harbi VInci Cilt, Hicaz, Asir, Yeman Cepheleri ve Libya Harekati 1914-1918.
        4. Büyük Harpte Misir Seferi.

14 January.......................................The destroyer raid on Yarmouth, Norfolk. (British Home Waters).
  BrOH: Official History of the War, Naval Operations, Volume V.
  GmOH: Der Krieg zur See 1914-1918, Band 1, Der Krieg in der Nordsee, Teil 7, Von Sommer 1917 bis zum Kriegsende 1918.

18 January - 8 May ....The German advance into Russia. (Eastern Front).
  GmOH: Der Weltkrieg 1914 bis 1918, Die Militarischen Operationen zu Lande, Band 14, Die Kriegführung an der Westfront im Jahre 1918.
  RuOH: 1. The Russian Army in the World War.
        2. A Strategic Outline of the War 1914 -1918.

20 January.......................................The Naval Action - H.M.S. Raglan and S.M.S. Breslau sunk, S.M.S. Goeben damaged by a mine and beached. (Mediterranean Sea).
  BrOH: Official History of the War, Naval Operations, Volume V.
  GmOH: Der Krieg zur See 1914-1918, Band 5, Der Krieg in den türkischen Gewässern, Teil 1, Die Mittelmeer-Division.

27 January.......................................S.M.S. Goeben refloated. (Mediterranean Sea).
  GmOH: Der Krieg zur See 1914-1918, Band 5, Der Krieg in den türkischen Gewässern, Teil 1, Die Mittelmeer-Division.

27 January.......................................The Turkish Dead Sea Flotilla seized by Arab Camelry at El Mezraa. (Dead Sea).

AuOH: Official History of Australia in the War of 1914-1918, Volume VII, Sinai and Palestine.

BrOH: Official History of the War, Military Operations, Egypt and Palestine, Volume II, From June 1917 to the End of the War.

NZOH: Official History of New Zealand's Effort in the Great War, Volume III, Sinai and Palestine.

TOH: 1. Büyük Harbin Sevkülceyşi.

2. Birinci Cihan Harbinde Türk Harbi, 1917 Yili Harekatleri, IVncu Cilt.

3. Birinci Dünya Harbinde Türk Harbi VInci Cilt, Hicaz, Asir, Yeman Cepheleri ve Libya Harekati 1914-1918.

4. Büyük Harpte Misir Seferi.

5 February..The U.S. Troop Ship S.S. Tuscania sunk by a submarine. (British Home Waters).

BrOH: 1. Official History of the War, Naval Operations, Volume V.

2. Official History of the War, The Merchant Navy, Volume III.

GmOH: Der Krieg zur See 1914-1918, Band 4, Der Handelskrieg Mit U-Booten, Teil 5, Januar bis November 1918.

15-16 February.................................The German destroyers raid in the Dover Straits. (British Home Waters).

BrOH: Official History of the War, Naval Operations, Volume V.

GmOH: Der Krieg zur See 1914-1918, Band 1, Der Krieg in der Nordsee, Teil 7, Von Sommer 1917 bis zum Kriegsende 1918.

16 February......................................Dover, Kent bombarded by a submarine. (British Home Waters).

BrOH: Official History of the War, Naval Operations, Volume V.

GmOH: 1. Der Krieg zur See 1914-1918, Band 1, Der Krieg in der Nordsee, Teil 7, Von Sommer 1917 bis zum Kriegsende 1918.

2. Der Krieg zur See 1914-1918, Band 4, Der Handelskrieg Mit U-Booten, Teil 5, Januar bis November 1918.

24 February...................................... S.M.S. Wolff returns to Germany. (Atlantic Ocean).

BrOH: Official History of the War, Naval Operations, Volume V.

GmOH: Der Krieg zur See 1914-1918, Band 3, Der Kreuzerkrieg in den ausländischen Gewässern, Teil 3, Die deutschen Hilfskreuzer.

24 February......................................The recapture of Trebizond. (Eastern Front).

GmOH: Der Weltkrieg 1914 bis 1918, Die Militarischen Operationen zu Lande, Band 14, Die Kriegführung an der Westfront im Jahre 1918.

RuOH: 1. The Russian Army in the World War.

2. A Strategic Outline of the War 1914 -1918.

25 February......................................The capture of Reval and Pernau. (Eastern Front).

GmOH: Der Weltkrieg 1914 bis 1918, Die Militarischen Operationen zu Lande, Band 14, Die Kriegführung an der Westfront im Jahre 1918.

RuOH: 1. The Russian Army in the World War.

2. A Strategic Outline of the War 1914 -1918.

26 February......................................The British Hospital Ship Glenart Castle sunk by a submarine. (British Home Waters).

> BrOH: Official History of the War, The Merchant Navy, Volume III.

1-3 March ....The German advance into Russia – the capture of Kiev. (Eastern Front).

> GmOH: Der Weltkrieg 1914 bis 1918, Die Militarischen Operationen zu Lande, Band 14, Die Kriegführung an der Westfront im Jahre 1918.
>
> RuOH: 1. The Russian Army in the World War.
> 2. A Strategic Outline of the War 1914 -1918.

2 March...The German operations against the Baltic Islands – the capture of Aaland Islands. (Baltic Sea).

> GmOH: 1. Der Weltkrieg 1914 bis 1918, Die Militarischen Operationen zu Lande, Band 14, Die Kriegführung an der Westfront im Jahre 1918.
> 2. Der Krieg zur See 1914-1918, Band 2, Der Krieg in der Ostsee, Teil 3, Von Anfang 1916 bis zum Kriegsende.
>
> RuOH: 1. The Russian Army in the World War.
> 2. A Strategic Outline of the War 1914 -1918.
> 3. Flot v Pervoi Mirovoi Voine. V Dvukh Tomakh. Tom I Deystviya Russkogo Flota.

3 March...The capture of Meshed. (North East Persia).

> BrOH: Official History of the War, Military Operations, Operations in Persia 1915-1919.
>
> TOH: 1. Büyük Harbin Sevkülceyşi.
> 2. Birinci Cihan Harbinde Türk Harbi, 1918 Yili Harekatleri, Vnci Cilt.
> 3. Birinci Dünya Harbinde Türk Harbi VInci Cilt, Hicaz, Asir, Yeman Cepheleri ve Libya Harekati 1914-1918.
> 4. Büyük Harpte Misir Seferi.

7-8 March .... The first German aircraft raid on London on a moonless night. (Britain).

> BrOH: Official History of the War, War in the Air, Volume V.
>
> GmOH: Der Weltkrieg 1914 bis 1918, Die Militarischen Operationen zu Lande, Band 14, Die Kriegführung an der Westfront im Jahre 1918; Der Krieg zur Air.

8-13 March ....The German advance into Russia – The Battle of Bakhmach (Eastern Front).

> CzOH: 1. První československý odboj. Česká Legíe 1914-1920.
> 2. O samostatny československý stát 1914-1918.
>
> GmOH: Der Weltkrieg 1914 bis 1918, Die Militarischen Operationen zu Lande, Band 14, Die Kriegführung an der Westfront im Jahre 1918.
>
> RuOH: 1. The Russian Army in the World War.
> 2. A Strategic Outline of the War 1914 -1918.

10 March..The British Hospital Ship Guildford Castle torpedoed by a submarine. (British Home Waters).

> BrOH: Official History of the War, The Merchant Navy, Volume III.

13 March..The German advance into Russia – the capture of Odessa. (Eastern Front).

BrOH: 1. Official History of the War, Military Operations, France and Belgium 1918, Volume I, The German March Offensive and its Preliminaries.
2. Official History of the War, Military Operations, France and Belgium 1918, Volume II, March - April: Continuation of the German Offensive.

COH: 1. Canadian Expeditionary Force 1914 - 1919.
2. The Official History of the Canadian Army in the First World War. The Western Front 1914.

FrOH: Les Armées Françaises dans la Grande Guerre, Tome VI L'hiver 1917–1918 - L'offensives allemande - 1 novembre 1917–18 julliet 1918, Volume 1, La preparation de la campagne de 1918, l'offensives allemande de l'Oise à la mer du nord.

GmOH: Der Weltkrieg 1914 bis 1918, Die Militarischen Operationen zu Lande, Band 14, Die Kriegführung an der Westfront im Jahre 1918.

NZOH: Official History of New Zealand's Effort in the Great War, Volume II, France.

21 March - 9 April ....The German Spring Offensive in Picardy – the First Battle of the Somme, 1918. (The Second Battle of Picardy). (Western Front).

AuOH: Official History of Australia in the War of 1914-1918, Volume V, France 1918, Part I.

BrOH: 1. Official History of the War, Military Operations, France and Belgium 1918, Volume I, The German March Offensive and its Preliminaries.
2. Official History of the War, Military Operations, France and Belgium 1918, Volume II, March - April: Continuation of the German Offensive.

COH: 1. Canadian Expeditionary Force 1914 - 1919.
2. The Official History of the Canadian Army in the First World War. The Western Front 1914.

FrOH: Les Armées Françaises dans la Grande Guerre, Tome VI L'hiver 1917–1918 - L'offensives allemande - 1 novembre 1917–18 julliet 1918, Volume 1, La preparation de la campagne de 1918, l'offensives allemande de l'Oise à la mer du nord.

GmOH: Der Weltkrieg 1914 bis 1918, Die Militarischen Operationen zu Lande, Band 14, Die Kriegführung an der Westfront im Jahre 1918.

NZOH: Official History of New Zealand's Effort in the Great War, Volume II, France.

21 March - 9 April ....The German Spring Offensive in Picardy - the First Battle of the Somme, 1918. (The Second Battle of Picardy) - the First Battle of Noyon. (Western Front).

AuOH: Official History of Australia in the War of 1914-1918, Volume V, France 1918, Part I.

BrOH: 1. Official History of the War, Military Operations, France and Belgium 1918, Volume I, The German March Offensive and its Preliminaries.
2. Official History of the War, Military Operations, France and Belgium 1918, Volume II, March - April: Continuation of the German Offensive.

COH: 1. Canadian Expeditionary Force 1914 - 1919.
2. The Official History of the Canadian Army in the First World War. The Western Front 1914.

FrOH: Les Armées Françaises dans la Grande Guerre, Tome VI L'hiver 1917–1918 - L'offensives allemande - 1 novembre 1917–18 julliet 1918, Volume 1, La preparation de la campagne de 1918, l'offensives allemande de l'Oise à la mer du nord.

GmOH: Der Weltkrieg 1914 bis 1918, Die Militarischen Operationen zu Lande, Band 14, Die Kriegführung an der Westfront im Jahre 1918.

NZOH: Official History of New Zealand's Effort in the Great War, Volume II, France.

24-25 March ....The German Spring Offensive in Picardy - the First Battle of the Somme, 1918. (The Second Battle of Picardy) - the Battle of Bapaume. (Western Front).

AuOH: Official History of Australia in the War of 1914-1918, Volume V, France 1918, Part I.

BrOH: 1. Official History of the War, Military Operations, France and Belgium 1918, Volume I, The German March Offensive and its Preliminaries.
2. Official History of the War, Military Operations, France and Belgium 1918, Volume II, March - April: Continuation of the German Offensive.

COH: 1. Canadian Expeditionary Force 1914 - 1919.
2. The Official History of the Canadian Army in the First World War. The Western Front 1914.

FrOH: Les Armées Françaises dans la Grande Guerre, Tome VI L'hiver 1917–1918 - L'offensives allemande - 1 novembre 1917–18 julliet 1918, Volume 1, La preparation de la campagne de 1918, l'offensives allemande de l'Oise à la mer du nord.

GmOH: Der Weltkrieg 1914 bis 1918, Die Militarischen Operationen zu Lande, Band 14, Die Kriegführung an der Westfront im Jahre 1918.

NZOH: Official History of New Zealand's Effort in the Great War, Volume II, France.

25 March...The German airship raid on Naples. (Italian).

GmOH: Der Weltkrieg 1914 bis 1918, Die Militarischen Operationen zu Lande, Band 14, Die Kriegführung an der Westfront im Jahre 1918; Der Krieg zur Air.

26-27 March ....The German Spring Offensive in Picardy - the First Battle of the Somme, 1918. (The Second Battle of Picardy) - the Battle of Rosières. (Western Front).

AuOH: Official History of Australia in the War of 1914-1918, Volume V, France 1918, Part I.

BrOH: Official History of the War, Military Operations, France and Belgium 1918, Volume II, March - April: Continuation of the German Offensive.

COH: 1. Canadian Expeditionary Force 1914 - 1919.
2. The Official History of the Canadian Army in the First World War. The Western Front 1914.

FrOH: Les Armées Françaises dans la Grande Guerre, Tome VI L'hiver 1917–1918 - L'offensives allemande - 1 novembre 1917–18 julliet 1918, Volume 1, La preparation de la campagne de 1918, l'offensives allemande de l'Oise à la mer du nord.

GmOH: Der Weltkrieg 1914 bis 1918, Die Militarischen Operationen zu Lande, Band 14, Die Kriegführung an der Westfront im Jahre 1918.

NZOH: Official History of New Zealand's Effort in the Great War, Volume II, France.

28 March...The German Spring Offensive in Picardy - the First Battle of the Somme, 1918. (The Second Battle of Picardy) - the First Battle of Arras, 1918. (Western Front).

AuOH: Official History of Australia in the War of 1914-1918, Volume V, France 1918, Part I.

BrOH: Official History of the War, Military Operations, France and Belgium 1918, Volume II, March - April: Continuation of the German Offensive.

COH: 1. Canadian Expeditionary Force 1914 - 1919.
2. The Official History of the Canadian Army in the First World War. The Western Front 1914.

FrOH: Les Armées Françaises dans la Grande Guerre, Tome VI L'hiver 1917–1918 - L'offensives allemande - 1 novembre 1917–18 julliet 1918, Volume 1, La preparation de la campagne de 1918, l'offensives allemande de l'Oise à la mer du nord.

GmOH: Der Weltkrieg 1914 bis 1918, Die Militarischen Operationen zu Lande, Band 14, Die Kriegführung an der Westfront im Jahre 1918.

NZOH: Official History of New Zealand's Effort in the Great War, Volume II, France.

1 April..The Royal Flying Corps and the Royal Naval Air Service amalgamate to form the Royal Air Force.

BrOH: Official History of the War, War in the Air, Volume IV.

3-4 April ....The German operations against the Baltic Islands – the capture of Hangö. (Baltic Sea).

GmOH: 1. Der Weltkrieg 1914 bis 1918, Die Militarischen Operationen zu Lande, Band 14, Die Kriegführung an der Westfront im Jahre 1918.
2. Der Krieg zur See 1914-1918, Band 1, Der Krieg in der Ostsee, Teil 3, Von Anfang 1916 bis zum Kriegsende.

RuOH:..Flot v Pervoi Mirovoi Voine. V Dvukh Tomakh. Tom I Deystviya Russkogo Flota.

4 April..British submarines destroyed at Helsingfors to avoid capture. (Baltic Sea).

BrOH: Official History of the War, Naval Operations, Volume V.

4 April..The German Spring Offensive in Picardy - the First Battle of the Somme, 1918. (The Second Battle of Picardy) - the Battle of the Avre. (Western Front).

AuOH: Official History of Australia in the War of 1914-1918, Volume V, France 1918, Part I.

BrOH: Official History of the War, Military Operations, France and Belgium 1918, Volume II, March - April: Continuation of the German Offensive.

COH: 1. Canadian Expeditionary Force 1914 - 1919.
2. The Official History of the Canadian Army in the First World War. The Western Front 1914.

FrOH: Les Armées Françaises dans la Grande Guerre, Tome VI L'hiver 1917–1918 - L'offensives allemande - 1 novembre 1917–18 julliet 1918, Volume 1, La preparation de la campagne de 1918, l'offensives allemande de l'Oise à la mer du nord.

GmOH: Der Weltkrieg 1914 bis 1918, Die Militarischen Operationen zu Lande, Band 14, Die Kriegführung an der Westfront im Jahre 1918.

NZOH: Official History of New Zealand's Effort in the Great War, Volume II, France.

5 April...Landings at Vladivostok. (Pacific Ocean) [British & Japanese/ Russian].

BrOH: Official History of the War, Naval Operations, Volume V.

5 April...The German Spring Offensive in Picardy - the First Battle of the Somme, 1918. (The Second Battle of Picardy) - the Battle of the Ancre, 1918. (Western Front).

AuOH: Official History of Australia in the War of 1914-1918, Volume V, France 1918, Part I.

BrOH: Official History of the War, Military Operations, France and Belgium 1918, Volume II, March - April: Continuation of the German Offensive.

COH: 1. Canadian Expeditionary Force 1914 - 1919.
2. The Official History of the Canadian Army in the First World War. The Western Front 1914.

FrOH: Les Armées Françaises dans la Grande Guerre, Tome VI L'hiver 1917–1918 - L'offensives allemande - 1 novembre 1917–18 julliet 1918, Volume 1, La preparation de la campagne de 1918, l'offensives allemande de l'Oise à la mer du nord.

GmOH: Der Weltkrieg 1914 bis 1918, Die Militarischen Operationen zu Lande, Band 14, Die Kriegführung an der Westfront im Jahre 1918.

NZOH: Official History of New Zealand's Effort in the Great War, Volume II, France.

9-30 April ....The German Spring Offensive in Flanders – the Battle of the Lys. (Western Front).

AuOH: Official History of Australia in the War of 1914-1918, Volume V, France 1918, Part I.

BrOH: Official History of the War, Military Operations, France and Belgium 1918, Volume II, March - April: Continuation of the German Offensive.

COH: 1. Canadian Expeditionary Force 1914 - 1919.
2. The Official History of the Canadian Army in the First World War. The Western Front 1914.

FrOH: Les Armées Françaises dans la Grande Guerre, Tome VI L'hiver 1917–1918 - L'offensives allemande - 1 novembre 1917–18 julliet 1918, Volume 1, La preparation de la campagne de 1918, l'offensives allemande de l'Oise à la mer du nord.

GmOH: Der Weltkrieg 1914 bis 1918, Die Militarischen Operationen zu Lande, Band 14, Die Kriegführung an der Westfront im Jahre 1918.

NZOH: Official History of New Zealand's Effort in the Great War, Volume II, France.

PgOH: 1. Portugal na Grande Guerra.
2. A cooperação anglo-portuguesa na Grande Guerra de 1914-1918.

9-11 April ....The German Spring Offensive in Flanders – the Battle of the Lys – the Battle of Estaires. (Western Front).

AuOH: Official History of Australia in the War of 1914-1918, Volume V, France 1918, Part I.

BrOH: Official History of the War, Military Operations, France and Belgium 1918, Volume II, March - April: Continuation of the German Offensive.

COH: 1. Canadian Expeditionary Force 1914 - 1919.
2. The Official History of the Canadian Army in the First World War. The Western Front 1914.

FrOH: Les Armées Françaises dans la Grande Guerre, Tome VI L'hiver 1917–1918 - L'offensives allemande - 1 novembre 1917–18 julliet 1918, Volume 1, La preparation de la campagne de 1918, l'offensives allemande de l'Oise à la mer du nord.

GmOH: Der Weltkrieg 1914 bis 1918, Die Militarischen Operationen zu Lande, Band 14, Die Kriegführung an der Westfront im Jahre 1918.

NZOH: Official History of New Zealand's Effort in the Great War, Volume II, France.

PgOH: 1. Portugal na Grande Guerra.
2. A cooperação anglo-portuguesa na Grande Guerra de 1914-1918.

10 April..Monrovia, Liberia bombarbed by a submarine. (Atlantic Ocean).

FrOH: Précis d'histoire de la guerre navale, 1914-1918.

GmOH: Der Krieg zur See 1914-1918 Band 4 Der Handelskrieg Mit U-Booten. Teil 5 Januar bis November 1918.

10-11 April ....The German Spring Offensive in Flanders – the Battle of the Lys – the Battle of Messines, 1918. (Western Front).

AuOH: Official History of Australia in the War of 1914-1918, Volume V, France 1918, Part I.

BrOH: Official History of the War, Military Operations, France and Belgium 1918, Volume II, March - April: Continuation of the German Offensive.

COH: 1. Canadian Expeditionary Force 1914 - 1919.
2. The Official History of the Canadian Army in the First World War. The Western Front 1914.

FrOH: Les Armées Françaises dans la Grande Guerre, Tome VI L'hiver 1917–1918 - L'offensives allemande - 1 novembre 1917–18 julliet 1918, Volume 1, La preparation de la campagne de 1918, l'offensives allemande de l'Oise à la mer du nord.

GmOH: Der Weltkrieg 1914 bis 1918, Die Militarischen Operationen zu Lande, Band 14, Die Kriegführung an der Westfront im Jahre 1918.

NZOH: Official History of New Zealand's Effort in the Great War, Volume II, France.

PgOH: 1. Portugal na Grande Guerra.
2. A cooperação anglo-portuguesa na Grande Guerra de 1914-1918.

12-15 April ....The German Spring Offensive in Flanders – the Battle of the Lys – the Battle of Hazebrouck. (Western Front).

AuOH: Official History of Australia in the War of 1914-1918, Volume V, France 1918, Part I.

BrOH: Official History of the War, Military Operations, France and Belgium 1918, Volume II, March - April: Continuation of the German Offensive.

COH: 1. Canadian Expeditionary Force 1914 - 1919.
2. The Official History of the Canadian Army in the First World War. The Western Front 1914.

FrOH: Les Armées Françaises dans la Grande Guerre, Tome VI L'hiver 1917–1918 - L'offensives allemande - 1 novembre 1917–18 julliet 1918, Volume 1, La preparation de la campagne de 1918, l'offensives allemande de l'Oise à la mer du nord.

GmOH: Der Weltkrieg 1914 bis 1918, Die Militarischen Operationen zu Lande, Band 14, Die Kriegführung an der Westfront im Jahre 1918.

NZOH: Official History of New Zealand's Effort in the Great War, Volume II, France.

PgOH: 1. Portugal na Grande Guerra.
2. A cooperação anglo-portuguesa na Grande Guerra de 1914-1918.

12 April...The last successful German airship raid over England – 27 casualties. (Britain).

BrOH: ..Official History of the War, War in the Air, Volume V.

GmOH: Der Weltkrieg 1914 bis 1918, Die Militarischen Operationen zu Lande, Band 14, Die Kriegführung an der Westfront im Jahre 1918; Der Krieg zur Air.

13 April...Helsingfors captured. (Baltic Sea).

GmOH: 1. Der Weltkrieg 1914 bis 1918, Die Militarischen Operationen zu Lande, Band 14, Die Kriegführung an der Westfront im Jahre 1918.
2. Der Krieg zur See 1914-1918, Band 2, Der Krieg in der Ostsee, Teil 3, Von Anfang 1916 bis zum Kriegsende.

RuOH: ..Flot v Pervoi Mirovoi Voine. V Dvukh Tomakh. Tom I Deystviya Russkogo Flota.

13-15 April ....The German Spring Offensive in Flanders – the Battle of the Lys – the Battle of Bailleul. (Western Front).

AuOH: Official History of Australia in the War of 1914-1918, Volume V, France 1918, Part I.

BrOH: Official History of the War, Military Operations, France and Belgium 1918, Volume II, March - April: Continuation of the German Offensive.

COH: 1. Canadian Expeditionary Force 1914 - 1919.
2. The Official History of the Canadian Army in the First World War. The Western Front 1914.

FrOH: Les Armées Françaises dans la Grande Guerre, Tome VI L'hiver 1917–1918 - L'offensives allemande - 1 novembre 1917–18 julliet 1918, Volume 1, La preparation de la campagne de 1918, l'offensives allemande de l'Oise à la mer du nord.

GmOH: Der Weltkrieg 1914 bis 1918, Die Militarischen Operationen zu Lande, Band 14, Die Kriegführung an der Westfront im Jahre 1918.

NZOH: Official History of New Zealand's Effort in the Great War, Volume II, France.

PgOH: 1. Portugal na Grande Guerra.
2. A cooperação anglo-portuguesa na Grande Guerra de 1914-1918.

15 April..The British Naval Light Forces' raid the Kattegat. (British Home Waters).

BrOH: Official History of the War, Naval Operations, Volume V.

GmOH: Band 1 Der Krieg in der Nordsee, Band 2, Der Krieg in der Ostsee, Teil 3, Von Anfang 1916 bis zum Kriegsende.

15 April..Batum captured. (Eastern Front).

GmOH: Der Weltkrieg 1914 bis 1918, Die Militarischen Operationen zu Lande, Band 14, Die Kriegführung an der Westfront im Jahre 1918.

RuOH: 1. The Russian Army in the World War.
2. A Strategic Outline of the War 1914 -1918.

17-19 April ....The German Spring Offensive in Flanders – the Battle of the Lys – the First Battle of Kemmel Ridge. (Western Front).

AuOH: Official History of Australia in the War of 1914-1918, Volume V, France 1918, Part I.

BrOH: Official History of the War, Military Operations, France and Belgium 1918, Volume II, March - April: Continuation of the German Offensive.

COH: 1. Canadian Expeditionary Force 1914 - 1919.
2. The Official History of the Canadian Army in the First World War. The Western Front 1914.

FrOH: Les Armées Françaises dans la Grande Guerre, Tome VI L'hiver 1917–1918 - L'offensives allemande - 1 novembre 1917–18 julliet 1918, Volume 1, La preparation de la campagne de 1918, l'offensives allemande de l'Oise à la mer du nord.

GmOH: Der Weltkrieg 1914 bis 1918, Die Militarischen Operationen zu Lande, Band 14, Die Kriegführung an der Westfront im Jahre 1918.

NZOH: Official History of New Zealand's Effort in the Great War, Volume II, France.

PgOH: 1. Portugal na Grande Guerra.
2. A cooperação anglo-portuguesa na Grande Guerra de 1914-1918.

18 April..The German Spring Offensive in Flanders – the Battle of the Lys – the Battle of Béthume. (Western Front).

AuOH: Official History of Australia in the War of 1914-1918, Volume V, France 1918, Part I.

BrOH: Official History of the War, Military Operations, France and Belgium 1918, Volume II, March - April: Continuation of the German Offensive.

COH: 1. Canadian Expeditionary Force 1914 - 1919.
2. The Official History of the Canadian Army in the First World War. The Western Front 1914.

FrOH: Les Armées Françaises dans la Grande Guerre, Tome VI L'hiver 1917–1918 - L'offensives allemande - 1 novembre 1917–18 julliet 1918, Volume 1, La preparation de la campagne de 1918, l'offensives allemande de l'Oise à la mer du nord.

GmOH: Der Weltkrieg 1914 bis 1918, Die Militarischen Operationen zu Lande, Band 14, Die Kriegführung an der Westfront im Jahre 1918.

NZOH: Official History of New Zealand's Effort in the Great War, Volume II, France.

PgOH: 1. Portugal na Grande Guerra.

2. A cooperação anglo-portuguesa na Grande Guerra de 1914-1918.

21 April...*Rittmeister* Manfred Freherr von Richthofen. (Leading German Ace) killed in action. (Western Front).
> BrOH: Official History of the War, War in the Air, Volume IV.
> GmOH: Der Weltkrieg 1914 bis 1918, Die Militarischen Operationen zu Lande, Band 14, Die Kriegführung an der Westfront im Jahre 1918.

22-23 April ....The blocking raid on Ostend and Zeebrugge. (British Home Waters).
> BrOH: Official History of the War, Naval Operations, Volume V.
> GmOH: Der Weltkrieg 1914 bis 1918, Die Militarischen Operationen zu Lande, Band 14, Die Kriegführung an der Westfront im Jahre 1918.

25-26 April ....The German Spring Offensive in Flanders – the Battle of the Lys – the Second Battle of Kemmel Ridge. (Western Front).
> AuOH: Official History of Australia in the War of 1914-1918, Volume V, France 1918, Part I.
> BrOH: Official History of the War, Military Operations, France and Belgium 1918, Volume II, March - April: Continuation of the German Offensive.
> COH: 1. Canadian Expeditionary Force 1914 - 1919.
> 2. The Official History of the Canadian Army in the First World War. The Western Front 1914.
> FrOH: Les Armées Françaises dans la Grande Guerre, Tome VI L'hiver 1917–1918 - L'offensives allemande - 1 novembre 1917–18 julliet 1918, Volume 1, La preparation de la campagne de 1918, l'offensives allemande de l'Oise à la mer du nord.
> GmOH: Der Weltkrieg 1914 bis 1918, Die Militarischen Operationen zu Lande, Band 14, Die Kriegführung an der Westfront im Jahre 1918.
> NZOH: Official History of New Zealand's Effort in the Great War, Volume II, France.
> PgOH: 1. Portugal na Grande Guerra.
> 2. A cooperação anglo-portuguesa na Grande Guerra de 1914-1918.

29 April...The German Spring Offensive in Flanders – the Battle of the Lys – the Battle of the Scherpenberg. (Western Front).
> AuOH: Official History of Australia in the War of 1914-1918, Volume V, France 1918, Part I.
> BrOH: Official History of the War, Military Operations, France and Belgium 1918, Volume II, March - April: Continuation of the German Offensive.
> COH: 1. Canadian Expeditionary Force 1914 - 1919.
> 2. The Official History of the Canadian Army in the First World War. The Western Front 1914.
> FrOH: Les Armées Françaises dans la Grande Guerre, Tome VI L'hiver 1917–1918 - L'offensives allemande - 1 novembre 1917–18 julliet 1918, Volume 1, La preparation de la campagne de 1918, l'offensives allemande de l'Oise à la mer du nord.
> GmOH: Der Weltkrieg 1914 bis 1918, Die Militarischen Operationen zu Lande, Band 14, Die Kriegführung an der Westfront im Jahre 1918.

NZOH: Official History of New Zealand's Effort in the Great War, Volume II, France.

PgOH: 1. Portugal na Grande Guerra.

2. A cooperação anglo-portuguesa na Grande Guerra de 1914-1918.

30 April -1 May .... The German advance into Russia – the capture of Sevastopol. (Eastern Front).

GmOH: Der Weltkrieg 1914 bis 1918, Die Militarischen Operationen zu Lande, Band 14, Die Kriegführung an der Westfront im Jahre 1918.

RuOH: 1. The Russian Army in the World War.

2. A Strategic Outline of the War 1914 -1918.

30 April .... The German operations against the Baltic Islands – the capture of Viborg. (Baltic Sea).

GmOH: 1. Der Weltkrieg 1914 bis 1918, Die Militarischen Operationen zu Lande, Band 14, Die Kriegführung an der Westfront im Jahre 1918.

2. Der Krieg zur See 1914-1918, Band 2, Der Krieg in der Ostsee, Teil 3, Von Anfang 1916 bis zum Kriegsende.

RuOH:..Flot v Pervoi Mirovoi Voine. V Dvukh Tomakh. Tom I Deystviya Russkogo Flota.

1 May .... Sevastopol captured. (Black Sea).

GmOH: Der Weltkrieg 1914 bis 1918, Die Militarischen Operationen zu Lande, Band 14, Die Kriegführung an der Westfront im Jahre 1918.

TOH: Birinci Dünya Harbi, VIIInci Cilt, Türk Deniz Harekati.

RuOH: 1. The Russian Army in the World War.

2. A Strategic Outline of the War 1914 -1918.

3. Flot v Pervoi Mirovoi Voine. V Dvukh Tomakh. Tom I Deystviya Russkogo Flota.

9-10 May .... The blocking raid on Ostend – H.M.S. Vindictive sunk. (British Home Waters).

BrOH: Official History of the War, Naval Operations, Volume V.

GmOH: Der Weltkrieg 1914 bis 1918, Die Militarischen Operationen zu Lande, Band 14, Die Kriegführung an der Westfront im Jahre 1918.

14 May .... The raid on Pola Harbour. (Adriatic Sea).

AHOH: Österreich-Ungarns Seekrieg 1914-1918, Lieferung V.

IOH: Ufficio Storico della R. Marina, La Marina Italiana nella Grande Guerra, Volume VIII, La Vittoria Mutilata in Adriatico.

15 May .... The submarine raid on St. Kilda. (British Home Waters).

GmOH: 1. Der Krieg zur See 1914-1918, Band 1, Der Krieg in der Nordsee, Teil 7, Von Sommer 1917 bis zum Kriegsende 1918.

2. Der Krieg zur See 1914-1918, Band 4, Der Handelskrieg Mit U-Booten, Teil 5, Januar bis November 1918.

18 May .... The first retaliatory air raid on Germany – Cologne bombed by day. (Germany).

BrOH: Official History of the War, War in the Air, Volume VI.

GmOH: 1. Der Weltkrieg 1914 bis 1918, Die Militarischen Operationen zu Lande, Band 14, Die Kriegführung an der Westfront im Jahre 1918; Der Krieg zur Air; Der Krieg zur Air.

2. Die Deutschen Luftstreitkräfte von ihrer Entstehung bis zum Ende des Weltkrieges 1918. Kriegsgeschichtliche Einzelschriften der Luftwaffe. Siebenter Band: Die Deutschen Luftstreitkräfte von ihrer Entstehung bis zum Ende des Weltkrieges 1918. Sonderband: Der Militärische Heimatlutschutz im Weltkriege 1914 bis 1918.

3. Die Deutschen Luftstreitkräfte von ihrer Entstehung bis zum Ende des Weltkrieges 1918. Kriegsgeschichtliche Einzelschriften der Luftwaffe. Fünfter Band: Die deutschen Luftstreitkräfte von ihrer Entstehung bis zum Ende des Weltkrieges 1918. Technischer Sonderband II: Die technische Entwicklung der Flakwaffe bis zum Ende des Weltkrieges.

19 May..The last successful German aircraft raid on England – 226 casualties.
        BrOH: Official History of the War, War in the Air, Volume V.
        GmOH: Der Weltkrieg 1914 bis 1918, Die Militarischen Operationen zu Lande, Band 14, Die Kriegführung an der Westfront im Jahre 1918; Der Krieg zur Air.

19 May..The German aircraft raid on the British Base Camp at Etaples. (Western Front).
        BrOH: Official History of the War, War in the Air, Volume V.
        GmOH: Der Weltkrieg 1914 bis 1918, Die Militarischen Operationen zu Lande, Band 14, Die Kriegführung an der Westfront im Jahre 1918; Der Krieg zur Air.

27 May – 5 June................................The German Spring Offensive in Champagne - the Battle of the Aisne, 1918. (Western Front).
        AmOH: United States Army in the World War 1917–1919, Volume 4, Operations, Cambrai/ Somme/ Lys/ Chateau Thierry.
        AuOH: Official History of Australia in the War of 1914-1918, Volume V, France 1918, Part I.
        BrOH: Official History of the War, Military Operations, France and Belgium 1918, Volume III, May-July, The German Diversion Offensives and the First Allied Counter-Offensive. France and Belgium 1918.
        COH: 1. Canadian Expeditionary Force 1914 - 1919.
        2. The Official History of the Canadian Army in the First World War. The Western Front 1914.
        FrOH: Les Armées Françaises dans la Grande Guerre, Tome VI, L'hiver 1917–1918 - L'offensives allemande - 1 novembre 1917–18 julliet 1918, Volume 2, L'offensives allemande contre les armée Françaises
        GmOH: Der Weltkrieg 1914 bis 1918, Die Militarischen Operationen zu Lande, Band 14, Die Kriegführung an der Westfront im Jahre 1918.
        NZOH: Official History of New Zealand's Effort in the Great War, Volume II, France.

27 May..*Captain* Robert Little (Leading Australian Ace) killed in action. (Western Front).
        AuOH: Official History of Australia in the War of 1914-1918, Volume VIII, Australian Flying Corp.

BroH: Official History of the War, War in the Air, VolumeIV.

GmOH: Der Weltkrieg 1914 bis 1918, Die Militarischen Operationen zu Lande, Band 14, Die Kriegführung an der Westfront im Jahre 1918.

4 June..The landings at Pechenga. (White Sea).

No known official history coverage for this operation.

5-14 June ....The German Spring Offensive in Champagne - the Battle of the Matz. (Western Front).

AuOH: Official History of Australia in the War of 1914-1918, Volume V, France 1918, Part I.

BrOH: Official History of the War, Military Operations, France and Belgium 1918, Volume III, May-July, The German Diversion Offensives and the First Allied Counter-Offensive. France and Belgium 1918.

COH: 1. Canadian Expeditionary Force 1914 - 1919.
2. The Official History of the Canadian Army in the First World War. The Western Front 1914.

FrOH: Les Armées Françaises dans la Grande Guerre, Tome VI, L'hiver 1917–1918 - L'offensives allemande - 1 novembre 1917–18 julliet 1918, Volume 2, L'offensives allemande contre les armée Françaises

GmOH: Der Weltkrieg 1914 bis 1918, Die Militarischen Operationen zu Lande, Band 14, Die Kriegführung an der Westfront im Jahre 1918.

NZOH: Official History of New Zealand's Effort in the Great War, Volume II, France.

5 June..The Independent Air Force constituted [British].

BrOH: Official History of the War, War in the Air, Volume IV.

6 June..The Dutch Hospital Ship Koningen Regentes sunk. (British Home Waters).

BrOH: Official History of the War, The Merchant Navy, Volume III.

7 June..Kem captured. (White Sea).

No known official history coverage for this operation.

8 June..The landings at Poti. (Black Sea).

RuOH:...Flot v Pervoi Mirovoi Voine. V Dvukh Tomakh. Tom I Deystviya Russkogo Flota.

10 June..The naval action off Premuda Island – S.M.S. Szent Istvan sunk by Italian motor launch MAS-15. (Adriatic Sea).

AHOH: Österreich-Ungarns Seekrieg 1914-1918, Lieferung V.

IOH: Ufficio Storico della R. Marina, La Marina Italiana nella Grande Guerra, Volume VIII, La Vittoria Mutilata in Adriatico.

15-24 June..The Austrian Summer Offensive, 1918. (Italian Front).

AHOH: Österreich-Ungarns Letzter Krieg 1914-1918, Band VII.

BrOH: Official History of the War, Military Operations, Italy, 1915-1919.

IOH: Maggiore Esercito, Ufficio Storico, L'Esercito italiano nella grande guerra 1915-18, Volume V, Tomo 1, Le Operazioni Del 1918 - Gli Avvenimenti Dal Gennaio Al Maggio.

15-24 June...The Austrian Summer Offensive, 1918 - the Battle of the Piave. (Italian Front).

> AHOH: Österreich-Ungarns Letzter Krieg 1914-1918, Band VII.
> BrOH: Official History of the War, Military Operations, Italy, 1915-1919.
> IOH: Maggiore Esercito, Ufficio Storico, L'Esercito italiano nella grande guerra 1915-18, Volume V, Tomo 1, Le Operazioni Del 1918 - Gli Avvenimenti Dal Gennaio Al Maggio.

18 June...The Russian battleship Svobodnaya sunk to prevent capture. (Black Sea).

> RuOH:..Flot v Pervoi Mirovoi Voine. V Dvukh Tomakh. Tom I Deystviya Russkogo Flota.

19 June 1918.....................................*Maggiore* Francesco Baracca. (Leading Italian Ace) killed in action. (Italian Front).

> AHOH: Österreich-Ungarns Letzter Krieg 1914-1918, Band VII.
> IOH: Maggiore Esercito, Ufficio Storico, L'Esercito italiano nella grande guerra 1915-18, Volume V, Tomo 1, Le Operazioni Del 1918 - Gli Avvenimenti Dal Gennaio Al Maggio.

23 June...The British Expeditionary Force lands at Murmansk. (Artic - North Russia.).

> No known official history coverage for this operation.

27 June...British Hospital Ship Llandovery Castle sunk by a submarine. (British Home Waters).

> BrOH: Official History of the War, The Merchant Navy, Volume III.

29-30 June...The British Expeditionary Force seize Murmansk-Soroki. (Artic – North Russia).

> No known official history coverage for this operation.

3 July ....The affair of Nyamakura. (East Africa).

> GmOH: Der Krieg zur See 1914-1918, Band 6, Die Kämpfe der Kaiserlichen Marine in den deutschen Kolonien, Teil 2, Deutsch-Ostafrika.
> PgOH: 1. Portugal na Grande Guerra.
> 2. A cooperação anglo-portuguesa na Grande Guerra de 1914-1918.

9 July ....*Major* Edward McCudden. (Leading British Ace) killed in flying accident. (Western Front).

> BrOH: Official History of the War, War in the Air, Volume IV.

12 July ....The Japanese battleship Kawachi sunk by an internal explosion. (Pacific Ocean).

> JOH: Taishō yonen naishi kunen kaigun senshi. Kan 4.

15-18 July ....The German Spring Offensive in Champagne - the Fourth Battle of Champagne. (Western Front).

> AuOH: Official History of Australia in the War of 1914-1918, Volume V, France 1918, Part I.
> BrOH: Official History of the War, Military Operations, France and Belgium 1918, Volume III, May-July, The German

Diversion Offensives and the First Allied Counter-Offensive. France and Belgium 1918.

COH: 1. Canadian Expeditionary Force 1914 - 1919.
2. The Official History of the Canadian Army in the First World War. The Western Front 1914.

FrOH: Les Armées Françaises dans la Grande Guerre, Tome VI, L'hiver 1917–1918 - L'offensives allemande - 1 novembre 1917–18 julliet 1918, Volume 2, L'offensives allemande contre les armée Françaises

GmOH: Der Weltkrieg 1914 bis 1918, Die Militarischen Operationen zu Lande, Band 14, Die Kriegführung an der Westfront im Jahre 1918.

NZOH: Official History of New Zealand's Effort in the Great War, Volume II, France.

15-18 July ....The German Spring Offensive in Champagne - the Fourth Battle of Champagne – the Battle of the Montagne de Reims. (Western Front).

AuOH: Official History of Australia in the War of 1914-1918, Volume V, France 1918, Part I.

BrOH: Official History of the War, Military Operations, France and Belgium 1918, Volume III, May-July, The German Diversion Offensives and the First Allied Counter-Offensive. France and Belgium 1918.

COH: 1. Canadian Expeditionary Force 1914 - 1919.
2. The Official History of the Canadian Army in the First World War. The Western Front 1914.

FrOH: Les Armées Françaises dans la Grande Guerre, Tome VI, L'hiver 1917–1918 - L'offensives allemande - 1 novembre 1917–18 julliet 1918, Volume 2, L'offensives allemande contre les armée Françaises

GmOH: Der Weltkrieg 1914 bis 1918, Die Militarischen Operationen zu Lande, Band 14, Die Kriegführung an der Westfront im Jahre 1918.

NZOH: Official History of New Zealand's Effort in the Great War, Volume II, France.

15-18 July ....The German Spring Offensive in Champagne - the Fourth Battle of Champagne - the Battle of Prosnes-Massiges. (Western Front).

AmOH: United States Army in the World War 1917–1919, Volume 4, Operations, Cambrai/ Somme/ Lys/ Chateau Thierry.

AuOH: Official History of Australia in the War of 1914-1918, Volume V, France 1918, Part I.

BrOH: Official History of the War, Military Operations, France and Belgium 1918, Volume III, May-July, The German Diversion Offensives and the First Allied Counter-Offensive. France and Belgium 1918.

COH: 1. Canadian Expeditionary Force 1914 - 1919.
2. The Official History of the Canadian Army in the First World War. The Western Front 1914.

FrOH: Les Armées Françaises dans la Grande Guerre, Tome VI, L'hiver 1917–1918 - L'offensives allemande - 1 novembre 1917–18 julliet 1918, Volume 2, L'offensives allemande contre les armée Françaises

GmOH: Der Weltkrieg 1914 bis 1918, Die Militarischen Operationen zu Lande, Band 14, Die Kriegführung an der Westfront im Jahre 1918.

NZOH: Official History of New Zealand's Effort in the Great War, Volume II, France.

18 July –7 August ....The Allied Counter-Offensive in Champagne - the Second Battle of the Marne. (Western Front).

AmOH: United States Army in the World War 1917–1919, Volume 4, Operations, Cambrai/ Somme/ Lys/ Chateau Thierry.

AuOH: Official History of Australia in the War of 1914-1918, Volume V, France 1918, Part I.

BrOH: Official History of the War, Military Operations, France and Belgium 1918, Volume III, May-July, The German Diversion Offensives and the First Allied Counter-Offensive. France and Belgium 1918.

COH: 1. Canadian Expeditionary Force 1914 - 1919.
2. The Official History of the Canadian Army in the First World War. The Western Front 1914.

FrOH: Les Armées Françaises dans la Grande Guerre, Tome VI, L'hiver 1917–1918 - L'offensives allemande - 1 novembre 1917–18 julliet 1918, Volume 2, L'offensives allemande contre les armée Françaises

GmOH: Der Weltkrieg 1914 bis 1918, Die Militarischen Operationen zu Lande, Band 14, Die Kriegführung an der Westfront im Jahre 1918.

NZOH: Official History of New Zealand's Effort in the Great War, Volume II, France.

19 July ....Royal Navy aircraft raid lunched from aircraft carrier H.M.S. Furious on the airship sheds at Tondern – airships Z54 and Z60 destroyed. (Germany).

BrOH: 1. Official History of the War, Naval Operations, Volume V.
2. Official History of the War, War in the Air, Volume V.

GmOH: Der Weltkrieg 1914 bis 1918, Die Militarischen Operationen zu Lande, Band 14, Die Kriegführung an der Westfront im Jahre 1918; Der Krieg zur Air.

19 July ....U.S.S. San Diego sunk by a mine. (Fire Island, Atlantic Ocean).

AmOH: U.S. Office of Naval Records and Library – Monographs, Publication No. 1 - German Submarine Activities on the Atlantic Coast of the United States and Canada.

20 July -7 August.............................The Allied Counter-Offensive in Champagne - the Second Battle of the Marne - the Battle of Tardenois. (Western Front).

AmOH: United States Army in the World War 1917–1919, Volume 4, Operations, Cambrai/ Somme/ Lys/ Chateau Thierry.

AuOH: Official History of Australia in the War of 1914-1918, Volume V, France 1918, Part I.

BrOH: Official History of the War, Military Operations, France and Belgium 1918, Volume III, May-July, The German Diversion Offensives and the First Allied Counter-Offensive. France and Belgium 1918.

COH: 1. Canadian Expeditionary Force 1914 - 1919.
2. The Official History of the Canadian Army in the First World War. The Western Front 1914.

FrOH: Les Armées Françaises dans la Grande Guerre, Tome VI, L'hiver 1917–1918 - L'offensives allemande - 1 novembre 1917–18 julliet 1918, Volume 2, L'offensives allemande contre les armée Françaises

GmOH: Der Weltkrieg 1914 bis 1918, Die Militarischen Operationen zu Lande, Band 14, Die Kriegführung an der Westfront im Jahre 1918.

NZOH: Official History of New Zealand's Effort in the Great War, Volume II, France.

20 July ....The unsuccessful last German aircraft raid on England. (Britain).

BrOH: Official History of the War, War in the Air, Volume V.

GmOH: Der Weltkrieg 1914 bis 1918, Die Militarischen Operationen zu Lande, Band 14, Die Kriegführung an der Westfront im Jahre 1918; Der Krieg zur Air.

23 July -2 August...............................The Allied Counter-Offensive in Champagne - the Second Battle of the Marne - the Battle of the Soissonais and of the Ourcq. (Western Front).

AmOH: United States Army in the World War 1917–1919, Volume 4, Operations, Cambrai/ Somme/ Lys/ Chateau Thierry.

AuOH: Official History of Australia in the War of 1914-1918, Volume V, France 1918, Part I.

BrOH: Official History of the War, Military Operations, France and Belgium 1918, Volume III, May-July, The German Diversion Offensives and the First Allied Counter-Offensive. France and Belgium 1918.

COH: 1. Canadian Expeditionary Force 1914 - 1919.
2. The Official History of the Canadian Army in the First World War. The Western Front 1914.

FrOH: Les Armées Françaises dans la Grande Guerre, Tome VI, L'hiver 1917–1918 - L'offensives allemande - 1 novembre 1917–18 julliet 1918, Volume 2, L'offensives allemande contre les armée Françaises

GmOH: Der Weltkrieg 1914 bis 1918, Die Militarischen Operationen zu Lande, Band 14, Die Kriegführung an der Westfront im Jahre 1918.

NZOH: Official History of New Zealand's Effort in the Great War, Volume II, France.

26 July 1918.....................................*Major* Edward (Mick) Mannock killed in action. (Western Front).

BrOH: Official History of the War, War in the Air, Volume IV.

GmOH: Der Weltkrieg 1914 bis 1918, Die Militarischen Operationen zu Lande, Band 14, Die Kriegführung an der Westfront im Jahre 1918.

30 July 1918.....................................*Oberleutnant* Frank Linke-Crawford (Leading Austrian -Hungarian Ace) killed in action. (Italian Front).

AHOH: Österreich-Ungarns Letzter Krieg 1914-1918, Band VII.

IOH: Maggiore Esercito, Ufficio Storico, L'Esercito italiano nella grande guerra 1915-18, Volume V, Tomo 2 Le Operazioni Del 1918 - Gli Avvenimenti Dal Giugno Al Novembre.

31 July 1918.....................................*Captain* George McElroy (Leading Irish Ace) killed in action. (Western Front).

BrOH: Official History of the War, War in the Air, Volume IV.

GmOH: Der Weltkrieg 1914 bis 1918, Die Militarischen Operationen zu Lande, Band 14, Die Kriegführung an der Westfront im Jahre 1918.

1 August...The British Expeditionary Force attack Archangel. (North Russia).

No known official history coverage for this operation.

2 August..The British Expeditionary Force capture Archangel. (North Russia).
No known official history coverage for this operation.

3 August..British Ambulance Transport Warida sunk by a submarine. (British Home Waters).
BrOH: ..Official History of the War, The Merchant Navy, Volume III.

3 August..The landings at Vladivostok. (Pacific Ocean).
No known official history coverage for this operation.

4 August..The British Force arrives at Baku. (Caucasus).
TOH: Birinci Dünya Savaşi'nda Osmanli Ordusun'un Azerbaycan ve Dağistan Harekâti, Azerbaycan ve Dağistan'in Bağimsizliğini Kazanmasi 1918.

5 August..The unsuccessful last German airship raid over England – the German airship L70 destroyed. (Britain).
GmOH: Der Weltkrieg 1914 bis 1918, Die Militarischen Operationen zu Lande, Band 14, Die Kriegführung an der Westfront im Jahre 1918; Der Krieg zur Air.

7 August..The French cruiser Dupetit Thouars sunk by a submarine. (Atlantic Ocean).
FrOH: 1. Histoire de la guerre sous-marine allemande - 1914-1918.
2. La Guerre des Croiseurs.
GmOH: Der Krieg zur See 1914-1918, Band 4, Der Handelskrieg Mit U-Booten, Teil 5, Januar bis November 1918.

8 August –11 November ....The Allied Offensive in Picardy. (Western Front).
AmOH: United States Army in the World War 1917 – 1919, Volume 7, Operations, Somme.
AuOH: Official History of Australia in the War of 1914-1918, Volume V, France 1918, Part I.
BrOH: Official History of the War, Military Operations, Volume IV, 8th August - 26th September, The Franco-British Offensive. France and Belgium 1918.
COH: 1. Canadian Expeditionary Force 1914 - 1919.
2. The Official History of the Canadian Army in the First World War. The Western Front 1914.
FrOH: Les Armées Françaises dans la Grande Guerre, Tome VII, La campagne offensives de 1918 et la marche au Rhin - 18 julliet 1918-28 juin 1919, Tome VII, La campagne offensives de 1918 et la marche au Rhin - 18 julliet 1918-28 juin 1919, Volume 1, 18 julliet 1918-25 septembre 1918.
GmOH: 1.Der Weltkrieg 1914 bis 1918, Die Militarischen Operationen zu Lande, Band 14, Die Kriegführung an der Westfront im Jahre 1918.
2. Der Weltkrieg 1914 bis 1918, Die Militarischen Operationen zu Lande, Band 14, Die Kriegführung an der Westfront im Jahre 1918; Der Krieg zur Air; Der Krieg zur Air.
3. Die Deutschen Luftstreitkräfte von ihrer Entstehung bis zum Ende des Weltkrieges 1918. Kriegsgeschichtliche Einzelschriften der Luftwaffe. Sechster Band: Die Deutschen Luftstreitkräfte von ihrer Entstehung bis zum

Ende des Weltkrieges 1918. Sonderband: Die Luftstreitkräfte in der Abwehreschlacht zwischen Somme und Oise vom 8 bis 12 August 1918.

NZOH: Official History of New Zealand's Effort in the Great War, Volume II, France.

8-11 August .... The Allied Offensive in Picardy – the Battle of Amiens. (Western Front).

AmOH: United States Army in the World War 1917 – 1919, Volume 7, Operations, Somme.

AuOH: Official History of Australia in the War of 1914-1918, Volume V, France 1918, Part I.

BrOH: Official History of the War, Military Operations, Volume IV, 8th August - 26th September, The Franco-British Offensive. France and Belgium 1918.

COH: 1. Canadian Expeditionary Force 1914 - 1919.
2. The Official History of the Canadian Army in the First World War. The Western Front 1914.

FrOH: Les Armées Françaises dans la Grande Guerre, Tome VII, La campagne offensives de 1918 et la marche au Rhin - 18 juillet 1918-28 juin 1919, Tome VII, La campagne offensives de 1918 et la marche au Rhin - 18 juillet 1918-28 juin 1919, Volume 1, 18 juillet 1918-25 septembre 1918.

GmOH: 1. Der Weltkrieg 1914 bis 1918, Die Militarischen Operationen zu Lande, Band 14, Die Kriegführung an der Westfront im Jahre 1918.
2. Der Weltkrieg 1914 bis 1918, Die Militarischen Operationen zu Lande, Band 14, Die Kriegführung an der Westfront im Jahre 1918; Der Krieg zur Air; Der Krieg zur Air.
3. Die Deutschen Luftstreitkräfte von ihrer Entstehung bis zum Ende des Weltkrieges 1918. Kriegsgeschichtliche Einzelschriften der Luftwaffe. Sechster Band: Die Deutschen Luftstreitkräfte von ihrer Entstehung bis zum Ende des Weltkrieges 1918. Sonderband: Die Luftstreitkräfte in der Abwehreschlacht zwischen Somme und Oise vom 8 bis 12 August 1918.

NZOH: Official History of New Zealand's Effort in the Great War, Volume II, France.

8 August – 3 September .... The Allied Offensive in Picardy – the Second Battle of the Somme, 1918. (The Third Battle of Picardy). (Western Front).

AmOH: United States Army in the World War 1917 – 1919, Volume 7, Operations, Somme.

AuOH: Official History of Australia in the War of 1914-1918, Volume V, France 1918, Part I.

BrOH: Official History of the War, Military Operations, Volume IV, 8th August - 26th September, The Franco-British Offensive. France and Belgium 1918.

COH: 1. Canadian Expeditionary Force 1914 - 1919.
2. The Official History of the Canadian Army in the First World War. The Western Front 1914.

FrOH: Les Armées Françaises dans la Grande Guerre, Tome VII, La campagne offensives de 1918 et la marche au Rhin - 18 juillet 1918-28 juin 1919, Tome VII, La campagne offensives de 1918 et la marche au Rhin - 18 juillet 1918-28 juin 1919, Volume 1, 18 juillet 1918-25 septembre 1918.

GmOH: 1. Der Weltkrieg 1914 bis 1918, Die Militarischen Operationen zu Lande, Band 14, Die Kriegführung an der Westfront im Jahre 1918.

2. Der Weltkrieg 1914 bis 1918, Die Militarischen Operationen zu Lande, Band 14, Die Kriegführung an der Westfront im Jahre 1918; Der Krieg zur Air; Der Krieg zur Air.

3. Die Deutschen Luftstreitkräfte von ihrer Entstehung bis zum Ende des Weltkrieges 1918. Kriegsgeschichtliche Einzelschriften der Luftwaffe. Sechster Band: Die Deutschen Luftstreitkräfte von ihrer Entstehung bis zum Ende des Weltkrieges 1918. Sonderband: Die Luftstreitkräfte in der Abwehreschlacht zwischen Somme und Oise vom 8 bis 12 August 1918.

NZOH: Official History of New Zealand's Effort in the Great War, Volume II, France.

8-15 August .... The Allied Offensive in Picardy – the Second Battle of the Somme, 1918. (The Third Battle of Picardy) - the Battle of Montdidier. (Western Front).

AmOH: United States Army in the World War 1917 – 1919, Volume 7, Operations, Somme.

AuOH: Official History of Australia in the War of 1914-1918, Volume V, France 1918, Part I.

BrOH: Official History of the War, Military Operations, Volume IV, 8th August - 26th September, The Franco-British Offensive. France and Belgium 1918.

COH: 1. Canadian Expeditionary Force 1914 - 1919.

2. The Official History of the Canadian Army in the First World War. The Western Front 1914.

FrOH: Les Armées Françaises dans la Grande Guerre, Tome VII, La campagne offensives de 1918 et la marche au Rhin - 18 julliet 1918-28 juin 1919, Tome VII, La campagne offensives de 1918 et la marche au Rhin - 18 julliet 1918- 28 juin 1919, Volume 1, 18 julliet 1918-25 septembre 1918.

GmOH: 1. Der Weltkrieg 1914 bis 1918, Die Militarischen Operationen zu Lande, Band 14, Die Kriegführung an der Westfront im Jahre 1918.

2. Der Weltkrieg 1914 bis 1918, Die Militarischen Operationen zu Lande, Band 14, Die Kriegführung an der Westfront im Jahre 1918; Der Krieg zur Air; Der Krieg zur Air.

3. Die Deutschen Luftstreitkräfte von ihrer Entstehung bis zum Ende des Weltkrieges 1918. Kriegsgeschichtliche Einzelschriften der Luftwaffe. Sechster Band: Die Deutschen Luftstreitkräfte von ihrer Entstehung bis zum Ende des Weltkrieges 1918. Sonderband: Die Luftstreitkräfte in der Abwehreschlacht zwischen Somme und Oise vom 8 bis 12 August 1918.

NZOH: Official History of New Zealand's Effort in the Great War, Volume II, France.

11 August.. The German airship L53 destroyed off Frisian Coast. (North Sea).

GmOH: Der Weltkrieg 1914 bis 1918, Die Militarischen Operationen zu Lande, Band 14, Die Kriegführung an der Westfront im Jahre 1918; Der Krieg zur Air.

17-28 August ....The Allied Offensive in Picardy – the Second Battle of the Somme, 1918. (the Third Battle of Picardy) - the Second Battle of Noyon. (Western Front).

> AmOH: United States Army in the World War 1917 – 1919, Volume 7, Operations, Somme.
>
> AuOH: Official History of Australia in the War of 1914-1918, Volume V, France 1918, Part I.
>
> BrOH: Official History of the War, Military Operations, Volume IV, 8th August - 26th September, The Franco-British Offensive. France and Belgium 1918.
>
> COH: 1. Canadian Expeditionary Force 1914 - 1919.
> 2. The Official History of the Canadian Army in the First World War. The Western Front 1914.
>
> FrOH: Les Armées Françaises dans la Grande Guerre, Tome VII, La campagne offensives de 1918 et la marche au Rhin - 18 julliet 1918-28 juin 1919, Tome VII, La campagne offensives de 1918 et la marche au Rhin - 18 julliet 1918-28 juin 1919, Volume 1, 18 julliet 1918-25 septembre 1918.
>
> GmOH: Der Weltkrieg 1914 bis 1918, Die Militarischen Operationen zu Lande, Band 14, Die Kriegführung an der Westfront im Jahre 1918.
>
> NZOH: Official History of New Zealand's Effort in the Great War, Volume II, France.

18 August – 6 September ....The Allied Offensive in Flanders. (Western Front).

> AmOH: United States Army in the World War 1917 – 1919, Volume 6, Operations, Oise-Aisne/ Ypres-Lys/ Vittorio Veneto.
>
> AuOH: Official History of Australia in the War of 1914-1918, Volume V, France 1918, Part I.
>
> BrOH: Official History of the War, Military Operations, Volume IV, 8th August - 26th September, The Franco-British Offensive. France and Belgium 1918.
>
> COH: 1. Canadian Expeditionary Force 1914 - 1919.
> 2. The Official History of the Canadian Army in the First World War. The Western Front 1914.
>
> FrOH: Les Armées Françaises dans la Grande Guerre, Tome VII, La campagne offensives de 1918 et la marche au Rhin - 18 julliet 1918-28 juin 1919, Tome VII, La campagne offensives de 1918 et la marche au Rhin - 18 julliet 1918-28 juin 1919, Volume 1, 18 julliet 1918-25 septembre 1918.
>
> GmOH: Der Weltkrieg 1914 bis 1918, Die Militarischen Operationen zu Lande, Band 14, Die Kriegführung an der Westfront im Jahre 1918.
>
> NZOH: Official History of New Zealand's Effort in the Great War, Volume II, France.

21-23 August ....The Allied Offensive in Picardy – the Second Battle of the Somme, 1918. (the Third Battle of Picardy) - the Battle of Albert, 1918. (Western Front).

> AmOH: United States Army in the World War 1917 – 1919, Volume 7, Operations, Somme.
>
> AuOH: Official History of Australia in the War of 1914-1918, Volume V, France 1918, Part I.
>
> BrOH: Official History of the War, Military Operations, Volume IV, 8th August - 26th September, The Franco-British Offensive. France and Belgium 1918.

COH: 1. Canadian Expeditionary Force 1914 - 1919.
2. The Official History of the Canadian Army in the First World War. The Western Front 1914.
FrOH: Les Armées Françaises dans la Grande Guerre, Tome VII, La campagne offensives de 1918 et la marche au Rhin - 18 julliet 1918-28 juin 1919, Tome VII, La campagne offensives de 1918 et la marche au Rhin - 18 julliet 1918-28 juin 1919, Volume 1, 18 julliet 1918-25 septembre 1918.
GmOH: Der Weltkrieg 1914 bis 1918, Die Militarischen Operationen zu Lande, Band 14, Die Kriegführung an der Westfront im Jahre 1918.
NZOH: Official History of New Zealand's Effort in the Great War, Volume II, France.

31 August – 3 September...................The Allied Offensive in Picardy – the Second Battle of the Somme, 1918. (the Third Battle of Picardy) - the Second Battle of Bapume. (Western Front).
AmOH: United States Army in the World War 1917 – 1919, Volume 7, Operations, Somme.
AuOH: Official History of Australia in the War of 1914-1918, Volume V, France 1918, Part I.
BrOH: Official History of the War, Military Operations, Volume IV, 8th August - 26th September, The Franco-British Offensive. France and Belgium 1918.
COH: 1. Canadian Expeditionary Force 1914 - 1919.
2. The Official History of the Canadian Army in the First World War. The Western Front 1914.
FrOH: Les Armées Françaises dans la Grande Guerre, Tome VII, La campagne offensives de 1918 et la marche au Rhin - 18 julliet 1918-28 juin 1919, Tome VII, La campagne offensives de 1918 et la marche au Rhin - 18 julliet 1918-28 juin 1919, Volume 1, 18 julliet 1918-25 septembre 1918.
GmOH: Der Weltkrieg 1914 bis 1918, Die Militarischen Operationen zu Lande, Band 14, Die Kriegführung an der Westfront im Jahre 1918.
NZOH: Official History of New Zealand's Effort in the Great War, Volume II, France.

26 August – 3 September...................The Allied Offensive against the Hindenburg Line – the Second Battle of Arras, 1918. (Western Front).
AmOH: United States Army in the World War 1917 – 1919, Volume 7, Operations, Somme.
AuOH: Official History of Australia in the War of 1914-1918, Volume V, France 1918, Part I.
BrOH: Official History of the War, Military Operations, Volume IV, 8th August - 26th September, The Franco-British Offensive. France and Belgium 1918.
COH: 1. Canadian Expeditionary Force 1914 - 1919.
2. The Official History of the Canadian Army in the First World War. The Western Front 1914.
FrOH: Les Armées Françaises dans la Grande Guerre, Tome VII, La campagne offensives de 1918 et la marche au Rhin - 18 julliet 1918-28 juin 1919, Tome VII, La campagne offensives de 1918 et la marche au Rhin - 18 julliet 1918-28 juin 1919, Volume 1, 18 julliet 1918-25 septembre 1918.

GmOH: Der Weltkrieg 1914 bis 1918, Die Militarischen Operationen zu Lande, Band 14, Die Kriegführung an der Westfront im Jahre 1918.

NZOH: Official History of New Zealand's Effort in the Great War, Volume II, France.

26-30 August .... The Allied Offensive against the Hindenburg Line – the Second Battle of Arras, 1918 – the Battle of the Scarpe, 1918. (Western Front).

AmOH: United States Army in the World War 1917 – 1919, Volume 7, Operations, Somme.

AuOH: Official History of Australia in the War of 1914-1918, Volume V, France 1918, Part I.

BrOH: Official History of the War, Military Operations, Volume IV, 8th August - 26th September, The Franco-British Offensive. France and Belgium 1918.

COH: 1. Canadian Expeditionary Force 1914 - 1919.
2. The Official History of the Canadian Army in the First World War. The Western Front 1914.

FrOH: Les Armées Françaises dans la Grande Guerre, Tome VII, La campagne offensives de 1918 et la marche au Rhin - 18 julliet 1918-28 juin 1919, Tome VII, La campagne offensives de 1918 et la marche au Rhin - 18 julliet 1918-28 juin 1919, Volume 1, 18 julliet 1918-25 septembre 1918.

GmOH: Der Weltkrieg 1914 bis 1918, Die Militarischen Operationen zu Lande, Band 14, Die Kriegführung an der Westfront im Jahre 1918.

NZOH: Official History of New Zealand's Effort in the Great War, Volume II, France.

26 August – 15 September .... The defence of Baku. (Caucasus).

TOH: Birinci Dünya Savaşı'nda Osmanlı Ordusun'un Azerbaycan Ve Dağıstan Harekâtı, Azerbaycan Ve Dağıstan'ın Bağımsızlığını Kazanması 1918.

2-3 September .... The Allied Offensive against the Hindenburg Line – the Second Battle of Arras, 1918 – the Battle of the Drocourt – Quéant Line. (Western Front).

AmOH: United States Army in the World War 1917 – 1919, Volume 7, Operations, Somme.

AuOH: Official History of Australia in the War of 1914-1918, Volume V, France 1918, Part I.

BrOH: Official History of the War, Military Operations, Volume IV, 8th August - 26th September, The Franco-British Offensive. France and Belgium 1918.

COH: 1. Canadian Expeditionary Force 1914 - 1919.
2. The Official History of the Canadian Army in the First World War. The Western Front 1914.

FrOH: Les Armées Françaises dans la Grande Guerre, Tome VII, La campagne offensives de 1918 et la marche au Rhin - 18 julliet 1918-28 juin 1919, Tome VII, La campagne offensives de 1918 et la marche au Rhin - 18 julliet 1918-28 juin 1919, Volume 1, 18 julliet 1918-25 septembre 1918.

GmOH: Der Weltkrieg 1914 bis 1918, Die Militarischen Operationen zu Lande, Band 14, Die Kriegführung an der Westfront im Jahre 1918.

NZOH: Official History of New Zealand's Effort in the Great War, Volume II, France.

5-10 September.................................Kazan Operation - Czechoslovak Legion against Red Russians. (Eastern Front).

CzOH: 1. První československý odboj. Česká Legíe 1914-1920.
2. O samostatny československý stát 1914-1918.

10-20 September...............................The Allied Offensive in Champagne – the Battle of Savy-Dallon. (Western Front).

AmOH: United States Army in the World War 1917 – 1919, Volume 7, Operations, Somme.

AuOH: Official History of Australia in the War of 1914-1918, Volume V, France 1918, Part I.

BrOH: Official History of the War, Military Operations, Volume IV, 8th August - 26th September, The Franco-British Offensive. France and Belgium 1918.

COH: 1. Canadian Expeditionary Force 1914 - 1919.
2. The Official History of the Canadian Army in the First World War. The Western Front 1914.

FrOH: Les Armées Françaises dans la Grande Guerre, Tome VII, La campagne offensives de 1918 et la marche au Rhin - 18 julliet 1918-28 juin 1919, Tome VII, La campagne offensives de 1918 et la marche au Rhin - 18 julliet 1918-28 juin 1919, Volume 1, 18 julliet 1918-25 septembre 1918.

GmOH: Der Weltkrieg 1914 bis 1918, Die Militarischen Operationen zu Lande, Band 14, Die Kriegführung an der Westfront im Jahre 1918.

NZOH: Official History of New Zealand's Effort in the Great War, Volume II, France.

12-13 September................................The American Autumn Offensive – the Battle of St. Mihiel. (Western Front).

AmOH: United States Army in the World War 1917 – 1919, Volume 8, Operations, St. Mihiel.

FrOH: Les Armées Françaises dans la Grande Guerre, Tome VII, La campagne offensives de 1918 et la marche au Rhin - 18 julliet 1918-28 juin 1919, Tome VII, La campagne offensives de 1918 et la marche au Rhin - 18 julliet 1918-28 juin 1919, Volume 1, 18 julliet 1918-25 septembre 1918.

GmOH: Der Weltkrieg 1914 bis 1918, Die Militarischen Operationen zu Lande, Band 14, Die Kriegführung an der Westfront im Jahre 1918.

12 September - 9 October ....The Allied Offensive against the Hindenburg Line – the Battles of the Hindenburg Line. (Western Front).

AmOH: United States Army in the World War 1917 – 1919, Volume 7, Operations, Somme.

AuOH: Official History of Australia in the War of 1914-1918, Volume V, France 1918, Part I.

BrOH: Official History of the War, Military Operations, Volume IV, 8th August - 26th September, The Franco-British Offensive. France and Belgium 1918.

COH: 1. Canadian Expeditionary Force 1914 - 1919.
2. The Official History of the Canadian Army in the First World War. The Western Front 1914.

FrOH: Les Armées Françaises dans la Grande Guerre, Tome VII, La campagne offensives de 1918 et la marche au Rhin - 18 julliet 1918-28 juin 1919, Tome VII, La campagne offensives de 1918 et la marche au Rhin - 18 julliet 1918-28 juin 1919, Volume 1, 18 julliet 1918-25 septembre 1918.

GmOH: Der Weltkrieg 1914 bis 1918, Die Militarischen Operationen zu Lande, Band 14, Die Kriegführung an der Westfront im Jahre 1918.

NZOH: Official History of New Zealand's Effort in the Great War, Volume II, France.

12 September ....The Allied Offensive against the Hindenburg Line – the Battles of the Hindenburg Line – the Battle of Havrincourt. (Western Front).

AmOH: United States Army in the World War 1917 – 1919, Volume 7, Operations, Somme.

AuOH: Official History of Australia in the War of 1914-1918, Volume V, France 1918, Part I.

BrOH: Official History of the War, Military Operations, Volume IV, 8th August - 26th September, The Franco-British Offensive. France and Belgium 1918.

COH: 1. Canadian Expeditionary Force 1914 - 1919.
2. The Official History of the Canadian Army in the First World War. The Western Front 1914.

FrOH: Les Armées Françaises dans la Grande Guerre, Tome VII, La campagne offensives de 1918 et la marche au Rhin - 18 julliet 1918-28 juin 1919, Tome VII, La campagne offensives de 1918 et la marche au Rhin - 18 julliet 1918-28 juin 1919, Volume 1, 18 julliet 1918-25 septembre 1918.

GmOH: Der Weltkrieg 1914 bis 1918, Die Militarischen Operationen zu Lande, Band 14, Die Kriegführung an der Westfront im Jahre 1918.

NZOH: Official History of New Zealand's Effort in the Great War, Volume II, France.

14-15 September ....The Allied Offensive in Champagne – the Battle of Vauxaillon. (Western Front).

AmOH: United States Army in the World War 1917 – 1919, Volume 7, Operations, Somme.

AuOH: Official History of Australia in the War of 1914-1918, Volume V, France 1918, Part I.

BrOH: Official History of the War, Military Operations, Volume IV, 8th August - 26th September, The Franco-British Offensive. France and Belgium 1918.

COH: 1. Canadian Expeditionary Force 1914 - 1919.
2. The Official History of the Canadian Army in the First World War. The Western Front 1914.

FrOH: Les Armées Françaises dans la Grande Guerre, Tome VII, La campagne offensives de 1918 et la marche au Rhin - 18 julliet 1918-28 juin 1919, Tome VII, La campagne offensives de 1918 et la marche au Rhin - 18 julliet 1918-28 juin 1919, Volume 1, 18 julliet 1918-25 septembre 1918.

GmOH: Der Weltkrieg 1914 bis 1918, Die Militarischen Operationen zu Lande, Band 14, Die Kriegführung an der Westfront im Jahre 1918.

NZOH: Official History of New Zealand's Effort in the Great War, Volume II, France.

14-15 September ....The capture of Baku. (Caucasus).
TOH: Birinci Dünya Savaşi'nda Osmanli Ordusun'un Azerbaycan ve Dağistan Harekâti, Azerbaycan ve Dağistan'in Bağimsizliğini Kazanmasi 1918.

15-16 September ....The Battle of the Dobropolje. (Battle of the Moglenitza). (Balkan Front).
AHOH: Österreich-Ungarns Letzter Krieg 1914-1918, Band VII.
BrOH: Official History of the War – Military Operations, Macedonia, Volume II:, From the Spring of 1917 to the End of the War.
FrOH: Les Armées Françaises dans la Grande Guerre: Tome VIII La campagne d'Orient. Volume 2 La campagne d'Orient depuis l'intervention de la Roumanie en aöut 1916 jusqu'en avril 1918.
GmOH: Der Weltkrieg 1914 bis 1918, Die Militarischen Operationen zu Lande, Band 14, Die Kriegführung an der Westfront im Jahre 1918.
GrOH: 1. Ho Hellenikos Stratos kata ton Proton Pankosmion Polemon 1914-1918 Tomos 2 H Summetochh ths Hellados eis ton Polemon 1918.
2. Epitomh Istopia Ths Eummetochhs Tou Ellhnikou Stratou Ston Prpsto Pagkosmio Polemo 1914-1918. / A Concise History of the Participation of the Hellenic Army in The First World War 1914-1918.
MOH: Operacije crnogorske vojske u prvom svetskom ratu.
SeOH: Veliki rat Srbije za oslobođenje i ujedinenje Srba, Hrvata i Slovenaca 1914 – 1918. Knjige Dvadeset Sedma. 1918 godina. Ofanziva. Prvi period: Dobropojska Bitka. Proboj neprijate Frontp i izbijanje srpske voske na reku vardar.
TOH: 1. Birinci Dünya Harbinde Türk Harbi, VIInci Cilt, 3nci Kisim, Avrupa Cepheleri, Makedonya Cephesi, Romanya Cephesi.
2. Birinci Dünya Harbinde Türk Harbi, Avrupa Cepheleri (Özet).

16 September ......................................H.M.S. Glatton sunk. (British Home Waters).
BrOH: ..Official History of the War, Naval Operations, Volume V.

16 September ....The last German aircraft raid on Paris. (France).
GmOH: Der Weltkrieg 1914 bis 1918, Die Militarischen Operationen zu Lande, Band 14, Die Kriegführung an der Westfront im Jahre 1918; Der Krieg zur Air.

18-24 September ....The Battle of Monastir-Doiran. (Balkan Front).
AHOH: Österreich-Ungarns Letzter Krieg 1914-1918, Band VII.
BrOH: Official History of the War – Military Operations, Macedonia, Volume II:, From the Spring of 1917 to the End of the War.
FrOH: Les Armées Françaises dans la Grande Guerre: Tome VIII La campagne d'Orient. Volume 2 La campagne d'Orient depuis l'intervention de la Roumanie en aöut 1916 jusqu'en avril 1918.
GmOH: Der Weltkrieg 1914 bis 1918, Die Militarischen Operationen zu Lande, Band 14, Die Kriegführung an der Westfront im Jahre 1918.

GrOH: 1. Ho Hellenikos Stratos kata ton Proton Pankosmion Polemon 1914-1918 Tomos 2 H Summetochh ths Hellados eis ton Polemon 1918.
2. Epitomh Istopia Ths Eummetochhs Tou Ellhnikou Stratou Ston Prpsto Pagkosmio Polemo 1914-1918. / A Concise History of the Participation of the Hellenic Army in The First World War 1914-1918.

MOH: Operacije crnogorske vojske u prvom svetskom ratu.

SeOH: 1. Veliki rat Srbije za oslobođenje i ujedinenje Srba, Hrvata i Slovenaca 1914 – 1918. Knjige Dvadeset Sedma. 1918 godina. Ofanziva. Prvi period: Dobropojska Bitka. Proboj neprijate Frontp i izbijanje srpske voske na reku vardar.
2. Veliki rat Srbije za oslobođenje i ujedinenje Srba, Hrvata i Slovenaca 1914 – 1918. Knjige Dvadeset Ssma. 1918 godina. Ofanziva. Drugi period. Gonelje - Prvi faza. Manevar srpskih armija u slivu Bregalnice Zauzeće Carevot sela, Ovueg Poja i Skopja. - Kapitulacija Bugarske.

TOH: 1. Birinci Dünya Harbinde Türk Harbi, VIInci Cilt, 3nci Kisim, Avrupa Cepheleri, Makedonya Cephesi, Romanya Cephesi.
2. Birinci Dünya Harbinde Türk Harbi, Avrupa Cepheleri (Özet).

18 September ....The Allied Offensive against the Hindenburg Line – the Battles of the Hindenburg Line – the Battle of Epéhy. (Western Front).

AmOH: United States Army in the World War 1917 – 1919, Volume 7, Operations, Somme.

AuOH: Official History of Australia in the War of 1914-1918, Volume V, France 1918, Part I.

BrOH: Official History of the War, Military Operations, Volume IV, 8th August - 26th September, The Franco-British Offensive. France and Belgium 1918.

COH: 1. Canadian Expeditionary Force 1914 - 1919.
2. The Official History of the Canadian Army in the First World War. The Western Front 1914.

FrOH: Les Armées Françaises dans la Grande Guerre, Tome VII, La campagne offensives de 1918 et la marche au Rhin - 18 julliet 1918-28 juin 1919, Tome VII, La campagne offensives de 1918 et la marche au Rhin - 18 julliet 1918-28 juin 1919, Volume 1, 18 julliet 1918-25 septembre 1918.

GmOH: Der Weltkrieg 1914 bis 1918, Die Militarischen Operationen zu Lande, Band 14, Die Kriegführung an der Westfront im Jahre 1918.

NZOH: Official History of New Zealand's Effort in the Great War, Volume II, France.

18-19 September ....The Battle of Doiran, 1918. (Balkan Front).

AHOH: Österreich-Ungarns Letzter Krieg 1914-1918, Band VII.

BrOH: Official History of the War – Military Operations, Macedonia, Volume II:, From the Spring of 1917 to the End of the War.

FrOH: Les Armées Françaises dans la Grande Guerre: Tome VIII La campagne d'Orient. Volume 2 La campagne d'Orient depuis l'intervention de la Roumanie en aöut 1916 jusqu'en avril 1918.

GmOH: Der Weltkrieg 1914 bis 1918, Die Militarischen Operationen zu Lande, Band 14, Die Kriegführung an der Westfront im Jahre 1918.

GrOH: 1. Ho Hellenikos Stratos kata ton Proton Pankosmion Polemon 1914-1918 Tomos 2 H Summetochh ths Hellados eis ton Polemon 1918.

2. Epitomh Istopia Ths Eummetochhs Tou Ellhnikou Stratou Ston Prpsto Pagkosmio Polemo 1914-1918. / A Concise History of the Participation of the Hellenic Army in The First World War 1914-1918.

MOH: Operacije crnogorske vojske u prvom svetskom ratu.

SeOH: Veliki rat Srbije za oslobođenje i ujedinenje Srba, Hrvata i Slovenaca 1914 – 1918. Knjige Dvadeset Sedma. 1918 godina. Ofanziva. Prvi period: Dobropojska Bitka. Proboj neprijate Frontp i izbijanje srpske voske na reku vardar.

TOH: 1. Birinci Dünya Harbinde Türk Harbi, VIInci Cilt, 3nci Kisim, Avrupa Cepheleri, Makedonya Cephesi, Romanya Cephesi.

2. Birinci Dünya Harbinde Türk Harbi, Avrupa Cepheleri (Özet).

19-25 September ....The Final British Offensives in Palestine. (Palestine).

AuOH: Official History of Australia in the War of 1914-1918, Volume VII, Sinai and Palestine.

BrOH: Official History of the War, Military Operations, Egypt and Palestine, Volume II, From June 1917 to the End of the War.

FrOH: Les Armées Françaises dans la Grande Guerre, Tome IX, Les fronts secondaires, Volume 1, Théâtre d'opérations de Levant [Ëgypte – Palestine -Syria – Hodjaz] – La propagande allemande au Maroc.

NZOH: Official History of New Zealand's Effort in the Great War, Volume III, Sinai and Palestine.

TOH: 1. Büyük Harbin Sevkülceyşi.

2. Birinci Cihan Harbinde Türk Harbi, 1918 Yili Harekatleri, Vnci Cilt.

3. Birinci Dünya Harbinde Türk Harbi VInci Cilt, Hicaz, Asir, Yeman Cepheleri ve Libya Harekati 1914-1918.

4. Büyük Harpte Misir Seferi.

19-25 September ....The Final British Offensives in Palestine – the Battle of Megiddo. (Palestine).

AuOH: Official History of Australia in the War of 1914-1918, Volume VII, Sinai and Palestine.

BrOH: Official History of the War, Military Operations, Egypt and Palestine, Volume II, From June 1917 to the End of the War.

FrOH: Les Armées Françaises dans la Grande Guerre, Tome IX, Les fronts secondaires, Volume 1, Théâtre d'opérations de Levant [Ëgypte – Palestine -Syria – Hodjaz] – La propagande allemande au Maroc.

NZOH: Official History of New Zealand's Effort in the Great War, Volume III, Sinai and Palestine.

TOH: 1. Büyük Harbin Sevkülceyşi.

2. Birinci Cihan Harbinde Türk Harbi, 1918 Yili Harekatleri, Vnci Cilt.

3. Birinci Dünya Harbinde Türk Harbi VInci Cilt, Hicaz, Asir, Yeman Cepheleri ve Libya Harekati 1914-1918.

4. Büyük Harpte Misir Seferi.

19-25 September ....The Final British Offensives in Palestine – the Battle of Megiddo - the Battle of Sharon. (Palestine).

AuOH: Official History of Australia in the War of 1914-1918, Volume VII, Sinai and Palestine.

BrOH: Official History of the War, Military Operations, Egypt and Palestine, Volume II, From June 1917 to the End of the War.

FrOH: Les Armées Françaises dans la Grande Guerre, Tome IX, Les fronts secondaires, Volume 1, Théâtre d'opérations de Levant [Égypte – Palestine -Syria – Hodjaz] – La propagande allemande au Maroc.

NZOH: Official History of New Zealand's Effort in the Great War, Volume III, Sinai and Palestine.

TOH: 1. Büyük Harbin Sevkülceyşi.
2. Birinci Cihan Harbinde Türk Harbi, 1918 Yili Harekatleri, Vnci Cilt.
3. Birinci Dünya Harbinde Türk Harbi VInci Cilt, Hicaz, Asir, Yeman Cepheleri ve Libya Harekati 1914-1918.
4. Büyük Harpte Misir Seferi.

19-25 September ....The Final British Offensives in Palestine – the Battle of Megiddo - the Battle of Nablus. (Palestine).

AuOH: Official History of Australia in the War of 1914-1918, Volume VII, Sinai and Palestine.

BrOH: Official History of the War, Military Operations, Egypt and Palestine, Volume II, From June 1917 to the End of the War.

FrOH: Les Armées Françaises dans la Grande Guerre, Tome IX, Les fronts secondaires, Volume 1, Théâtre d'opérations de Levant [Égypte – Palestine -Syria – Hodjaz] – La propagande allemande au Maroc.

NZOH: Official History of New Zealand's Effort in the Great War, Volume III, Sinai and Palestine.

TOH: 1. Büyük Harbin Sevkülceyşi.
2. Birinci Cihan Harbinde Türk Harbi, 1918 Yili Harekatleri, Vnci Cilt.
3. Birinci Dünya Harbinde Türk Harbi VInci Cilt, Hicaz, Asir, Yeman Cepheleri ve Libya Harekati 1914-1918.
4. Büyük Harpte Misir Seferi.

23 September ....The Final British Offensives in Palestine – Haifa and Acre captured. (Palestine).

AuOH: Official History of Australia in the War of 1914-1918, Volume VII, Sinai and Palestine.

BrOH: Official History of the War, Military Operations, Egypt and Palestine, Volume II, From June 1917 to the End of the War.

FrOH: Les Armées Françaises dans la Grande Guerre, Tome IX, Les fronts secondaires, Volume 1, Théâtre d'opérations de Levant [Égypte – Palestine -Syria – Hodjaz] – La propagande allemande au Maroc.

NZOH: Official History of New Zealand's Effort in the Great War, Volume III, Sinai and Palestine.

TOH: 1. Büyük Harbin Sevkülceyşi.
2. Birinci Cihan Harbinde Türk Harbi, 1918 Yili Harekatleri, Vnci Cilt.
3. Birinci Dünya Harbinde Türk Harbi VInci Cilt, Hicaz, Asir, Yeman Cepheleri ve Libya Harekati 1914-1918.
4. Büyük Harpte Misir Seferi.

26 September - 15 October ....The Allied Offensive in Champagne – the Battle of Champagne and Argonne. (Western Front).

> AmOH: United States Army in the World War 1917–1919, Volume 9, Operations, Meuse-Argonne.
>
> AuOH: Official History of Australia in the War of 1914-1918, Volume VI, France 1918, Part II.
>
> BrOH: Official History of the War, Military Operations, Volume V, 26th September - 11th November, The Advance to Victory.
>
> COH: 1. Canadian Expeditionary Force 1914 - 1919.
> 2. The Official History of the Canadian Army in the First World War. The Western Front 1914.
>
> FrOH: Les Armées Françaises dans la Grande Guerre, Tome VII, La campagne offensives de 1918 et la marche au Rhin - 18 julliet 1918-28 juin 1919, Tome VII, La campagne offensives de 1918 et la marche au Rhin - 18 julliet 1918-28 juin 1919, Volume 2 26 septembre 1918-28 juin 1919.
>
> GmOH: Der Weltkrieg 1914 bis 1918, Die Militarischen Operationen zu Lande, Band 14, Die Kriegführung an der Westfront im Jahre 1918.
>
> NZOH: Official History of New Zealand's Effort in the Great War, Volume II, France.

26 September - 15 October ....The Allied Offensive in Champagne – the Battle of Champagne and Argonne. (Western Front).

> AmOH: United States Army in the World War 1917–1919, Volume 9, Operations, Meuse-Argonne.
>
> AuOH: Official History of Australia in the War of 1914-1918, Volume VI, France 1918, Part II.
>
> BrOH: Official History of the War, Military Operations, Volume V, 26th September - 11th November, The Advance to Victory.
>
> COH: 1. Canadian Expeditionary Force 1914 - 1919.
> 2. The Official History of the Canadian Army in the First World War. The Western Front 1914.
>
> FrOH: Les Armées Françaises dans la Grande Guerre, Tome VII, La campagne offensives de 1918 et la marche au Rhin - 18 julliet 1918-28 juin 1919, Tome VII, La campagne offensives de 1918 et la marche au Rhin - 18 julliet 1918-28 juin 1919, Volume 2 26 septembre 1918-28 juin 1919.
>
> GmOH: Der Weltkrieg 1914 bis 1918, Die Militarischen Operationen zu Lande, Band 14, Die Kriegführung an der Westfront im Jahre 1918.
>
> NZOH: Official History of New Zealand's Effort in the Great War, Volume II, France.

26 September - 31 October ....The British Pursuit through Syria. (Palestine).

> AuOH: Official History of Australia in the War of 1914-1918, Volume VII, Sinai and Palestine.
>
> BrOH: Official History of the War, Military Operations, Egypt and Palestine, Volume II, From June 1917 to the End of the War.
>
> FrOH: Les Armées Françaises dans la Grande Guerre, Tome IX, Les fronts secondaires, Volume 1, Théâtre d'opérations de Levant [Ëgypte – Palestine -Syria – Hodjaz] – La propagande allemande au Maroc.
>
> NZOH: Official History of New Zealand's Effort in the Great War, Volume III, Sinai and Palestine.
>
> TOH: 1. Büyük Harbin Sevkülceyşi.

2. Birinci Cihan Harbinde Türk Harbi, 1918 Yili Harekatleri, Vnci Cilt.
3. Birinci Dünya Harbinde Türk Harbi VInci Cilt, Hicaz, Asir, Yeman Cepheleri ve Libya Harekati 1914-1918.
4. Büyük Harpte Misir Seferi.

27 September - 1 October ....The Allied Offensive against the Hindenburg Line – the Battles of the Hindenburg Line – the Battle of the Canal du Nord. (Western Front).

AmOH: United States Army in the World War 1917 – 1919, Volume 7, Operations, Somme.

AuOH: Official History of Australia in the War of 1914-1918, Volume VI, France 1918, Part II.

BrOH: Official History of the War, Military Operations, Volume V, 26th September - 11th November, The Advance to Victory.

COH: 1. Canadian Expeditionary Force 1914 - 1919.
2. The Official History of the Canadian Army in the First World War. The Western Front 1914.

FrOH: Les Armées Françaises dans la Grande Guerre, Tome VII, La campagne offensives de 1918 et la marche au Rhin - 18 julliet 1918-28 juin 1919, Tome VII, La campagne offensives de 1918 et la marche au Rhin - 18 julliet 1918-28 juin 1919, Volume 2 26 septembre 1918-28 juin 1919.

GmOH: Der Weltkrieg 1914 bis 1918, Die Militarischen Operationen zu Lande, Band 14, Die Kriegführung an der Westfront im Jahre 1918.

NZOH: Official History of New Zealand's Effort in the Great War, Volume II, France.

28 September - 11 November ....The Allied Offensive in Flanders – the Battle of Belgium. (Western Front).

AmOH: United States Army in the World War 1917 – 1919, Volume 6, Operations, Oise-Aisne/ Ypres-Lys/ Vittorio Veneto.

AuOH: Official History of Australia in the War of 1914-1918, Volume VI, France 1918, Part II.

BrOH: Official History of the War, Military Operations, Volume V, 26th September - 11th November, The Advance to Victory.

COH: 1. Canadian Expeditionary Force 1914 - 1919.
2. The Official History of the Canadian Army in the First World War. The Western Front 1914.

FrOH: Les Armées Françaises dans la Grande Guerre, Tome VII, La campagne offensives de 1918 et la marche au Rhin - 18 julliet 1918-28 juin 1919, Tome VII, La campagne offensives de 1918 et la marche au Rhin - 18 julliet 1918-28 juin 1919, Volume 2 26 septembre 1918-28 juin 1919.

GmOH: Der Weltkrieg 1914 bis 1918, Die Militarischen Operationen zu Lande, Band 14, Die Kriegführung an der Westfront im Jahre 1918.

NZOH: Official History of New Zealand's Effort in the Great War, Volume II, France.

28 September - 2 October ....The Allied Offensive in Flanders – the Battle of Belgium - the Battle of Ypres, 1918. (Western Front).

AmOH: United States Army in the World War 1917 – 1919, Volume 6, Operations, Oise-Aisne/ Ypres-Lys/ Vittorio Veneto.

AuOH: Official History of Australia in the War of 1914-1918, Volume VI, France 1918, Part II.

BrOH: Official History of the War, Military Operations, Volume V, 26th September - 11th November, The Advance to Victory.

COH: 1. Canadian Expeditionary Force 1914 - 1919.
2. The Official History of the Canadian Army in the First World War. The Western Front 1914.

FrOH: Les Armées Françaises dans la Grande Guerre, Tome VII, La campagne offensives de 1918 et la marche au Rhin - 18 julliet 1918-28 juin 1919, Tome VII, La campagne offensives de 1918 et la marche au Rhin - 18 julliet 1918-28 juin 1919, Volume 2 26 septembre 1918-28 juin 1919.

GmOH: Der Weltkrieg 1914 bis 1918, Die Militarischen Operationen zu Lande, Band 14, Die Kriegführung an der Westfront im Jahre 1918.

NZOH: Official History of New Zealand's Effort in the Great War, Volume II, France.

AmOH: United States Army in the World War 1917 – 1919, Volume 6, Operations, Oise-Aisne/ Ypres-Lys/ Vittorio Veneto.

AuOH: Official History of Australia in the War of 1914-1918, Volume VI, France 1918, Part II.

BrOH: Official History of the War, Military Operations, Volume V, 26th September - 11th November, The Advance to Victory.

COH: 1. Canadian Expeditionary Force 1914 - 1919.
2. The Official History of the Canadian Army in the First World War. The Western Front 1914.

FrOH: Les Armées Françaises dans la Grande Guerre, Tome VII, La campagne offensives de 1918 et la marche au Rhin - 18 julliet 1918-28 juin 1919, Tome VII, La campagne offensives de 1918 et la marche au Rhin - 18 julliet 1918-28 juin 1919, Volume 2 26 septembre 1918-28 juin 1919.

GmOH: Der Weltkrieg 1914 bis 1918, Die Militarischen Operationen zu Lande, Band 14, Die Kriegführung an der Westfront im Jahre 1918.

NZOH: Official History of New Zealand's Effort in the Great War, Volume II, France.

AmOH: United States Army in the World War 1917 – 1919, Volume 7, Operations, Somme.

AuOH: Official History of Australia in the War of 1914-1918, Volume VI, France 1918, Part II.

BrOH: Official History of the War, Military Operations, Volume V, 26th September - 11th November, The Advance to Victory.

COH: 1. Canadian Expeditionary Force 1914 - 1919.
2. The Official History of the Canadian Army in the First World War. The Western Front 1914.

FrOH: Les Armées Françaises dans la Grande Guerre, Tome VII, La campagne offensives de 1918 et la marche au Rhin - 18 julliet 1918-28 juin 1919, Tome VII, La campagne

offensives de 1918 et la marche au Rhin - 18 julliet 1918-
28 juin 1919, Volume 2 26 septembre 1918-28 juin 1919.

GmOH: Der Weltkrieg 1914 bis 1918, Die Militarischen
Operationen zu Lande, Band 14, Die Kriegführung an der
Westfront im Jahre 1918.

NZOH: Official History of New Zealand's Effort in the Great
War, Volume II, France.

29 September ....*Second Lieutenant* Frank Luke (Leading American Ace to be killed)
killed in action. (Western Front).

AmOH: The United States Air Service in World War I, Volume 1,
The Final Report and A Tactical History.

GmOH: Der Weltkrieg 1914 bis 1918, Die Militarischen
Operationen zu Lande, Band 14, Die Kriegführung an der
Westfront im Jahre 1918.

30 September ....The Hostilities against the Bulgaria cease. (12 noon local time). (Balkan
Front).

AHOH: Österreich-Ungarns Letzter Krieg 1914-1918, Band VII.

BrOH: Official History of the War – Military Operations,
Macedonia, Volume II:, From the Spring of 1917 to the
End of the War.

FrOH: Les Armées Françaises dans la Grande Guerre: Tome VIII
La campagne d'Orient. Volume 2 La campagne d'Orient
depuis l'intervention de la Roumanie en aöut 1916
jusqu'en avril 1918.

GmOH: Der Weltkrieg 1914 bis 1918, Die Militarischen
Operationen zu Lande, Band 14, Die Kriegführung an der
Westfront im Jahre 1918.

GrOH: 1. Ho Hellenikos Stratos kata ton Proton Pankosmion
Polemon 1914-1918 Tomos 2 H Summetochh ths
Hellados eis ton Polemon 1918.
2. Epitomh Istopia Ths Eummetochhs Tou Ellhnikou
Stratou Ston Prpsto Pagkosmio Polemo 1914-1918. / A
Concise History of the Participation of the Hellenic Army
in The First World War 1914-1918.

MOH: Operacije crnogorske vojske u prvom svetskom ratu.

SeOH: Veliki rat Srbije za oslobođenje i ujedinenje Srba, Hrvata i
Slovenaca 1914 – 1918. Knjige Dvadeset Ssma. 1918
godina. Ofanziva. Drugi period. Gonelje - Prvi faza.
Manevar srpskih armija u slivu Bregalnice Zauzeće
Carevot sela, Ovueg Poja i Skopja. - Kapitulacija Bugarske.

TOH: 1. Birinci Dünya Harbinde Türk Harbi, VIInci Cilt, 3nci
Kisim, Avrupa Cepheleri, Makedonya Cephesi, Romanya
Cephesi.
2. Birinci Dünya Harbinde Türk Harbi, Avrupa Cepheleri
(Özet).

30 September - 4 October ....The Allied Offensive in Champagne – the Battle of Champagne and
Argonne – the Battle of St. Thierry. (Western Front).

AmOH: United States Army in the World War 1917–1919,
Volume 9, Operations, Meuse-Argonne.

AuOH: Official History of Australia in the War of 1914-1918,
Volume VI, France 1918, Part II.

BrOH: Official History of the War, Military Operations, Volume
V, 26th September - 11th November, The Advance to
Victory.

COH: 1. Canadian Expeditionary Force 1914 - 1919.

2. The Official History of the Canadian Army in the First World War. The Western Front 1914.

FrOH: Les Armées Françaises dans la Grande Guerre, Tome VII, La campagne offensives de 1918 et la marche au Rhin - 18 julliet 1918-28 juin 1919, Tome VII, La campagne offensives de 1918 et la marche au Rhin - 18 julliet 1918-28 juin 1919, Volume 2 26 septembre 1918-28 juin 1919.

GmOH: Der Weltkrieg 1914 bis 1918, Die Militarischen Operationen zu Lande, Band 14, Die Kriegführung an der Westfront im Jahre 1918.

NZOH: Official History of New Zealand's Effort in the Great War, Volume II, France.

1 October ....Net barrage placed across the Otranto Straits. (Adriatic Sea).

AHOH: Österreich-Ungarns Seekrieg 1914-1918, Lieferung IV.

IOH: Ufficio Storico della R. Marina, La Marina Italiana nella Grande Guerra, Volume VIII, La Vittoria Mutilata in Adriatico.

2 October ....Durazzo bombarded. (Adriatic Sea).

AHOH: Österreich-Ungarns Seekrieg 1914-1918, Lieferung IV.

IOH: Ufficio Storico della R. Marina, La Marina Italiana nella Grande Guerra, Volume VIII, La Vittoria Mutilata in Adriatico.

3-5 October ....The Allied Offensive against the Hindenburg Line – the Battles of the Hindenburg Line – the Battle of the Beaurevoir Line. (Western Front).

AmOH: United States Army in the World War 1917–1919, Volume 7, Operations:- Somme.

AuOH: Official History of Australia in the War of 1914-1918, Volume VI, France 1918, Part II.

BrOH: Official History of the War, Military Operations, Volume V, 26th September - 11th November, The Advance to Victory.

COH: 1. Canadian Expeditionary Force 1914 - 1919.
2. The Official History of the Canadian Army in the First World War. The Western Front 1914.

FrOH: Les Armées Françaises dans la Grande Guerre, Tome VII, La campagne offensives de 1918 et la marche au Rhin - 18 julliet 1918-28 juin 1919, Tome VII, La campagne offensives de 1918 et la marche au Rhin - 18 julliet 1918-28 juin 1919, Volume 2 26 septembre 1918-28 juin 1919.

GmOH: Der Weltkrieg 1914 bis 1918, Die Militarischen Operationen zu Lande, Band 14, Die Kriegführung an der Westfront im Jahre 1918.

NZOH: Official History of New Zealand's Effort in the Great War, Volume II, France.

7 October ....Beirut occupied. (Palestine).

AuOH: Official History of Australia in the War of 1914-1918, Volume VII, Sinai and Palestine.

BrOH: Official History of the War, Military Operations, Egypt and Palestine, Volume II, From June 1917 to the End of the War.

FrOH: Les Armées Françaises dans la Grande Guerre, Tome IX, Les fronts secondaires, Volume 1, Théâtre d'opérations de Levant [Ëgypte – Palestine -Syria – Hodjaz] – La propagande allemande au Maroc.

NZOH: Official History of New Zealand's Effort in the Great War, Volume III, Sinai and Palestine.

TOH: 1. Büyük Harbin Sevkülceyşi.

2. Birinci Cihan Harbinde Türk Harbi, 1918 Yili Harekatleri, Vnci Cilt.

3. Birinci Dünya Harbinde Türk Harbi VInci Cilt, Hicaz, Asir, Yeman Cepheleri ve Libya Harekati 1914-1918.

4. Büyük Harpte Misir Seferi.

8-9 October ....The Allied Offensive against the Hindenburg Line – the Battles of the Hindenburg Line – the Battle of Cambrai, 1918. (Western Front).

AmOH: United States Army in the World War 1917–1919, Volume 7, Operations:- Somme.

AuOH: Official History of Australia in the War of 1914-1918, Volume VI, France 1918, Part II.

BrOH: Official History of the War, Military Operations, Volume V, 26th September - 11th November, The Advance to Victory.

COH: 1. Canadian Expeditionary Force 1914 - 1919.

2. The Official History of the Canadian Army in the First World War. The Western Front 1914.

FrOH: Les Armées Françaises dans la Grande Guerre, Tome VII, La campagne offensives de 1918 et la marche au Rhin - 18 julliet 1918-28 juin 1919, Tome VII, La campagne offensives de 1918 et la marche au Rhin - 18 julliet 1918-28 juin 1919, Volume 2 26 septembre 1918-28 juin 1919.

GmOH: Der Weltkrieg 1914 bis 1918, Die Militarischen Operationen zu Lande, Band 14, Die Kriegführung an der Westfront im Jahre 1918.

NZOH: Official History of New Zealand's Effort in the Great War, Volume II, France.

9-12 October ....The Allied Offensive in Flanders – the Battle of Belgium - the Battle of Roulers. (Western Front).

AmOH: United States Army in the World War 1917 – 1919, Volume 6, Operations, Oise-Aisne/ Ypres-Lys/ Vittorio Veneto.

AuOH: Official History of Australia in the War of 1914-1918, Volume VI, France 1918, Part II.

BrOH: Official History of the War, Military Operations, Volume V, 26th September - 11th November, The Advance to Victory.

COH: 1. Canadian Expeditionary Force 1914 - 1919.

2. The Official History of the Canadian Army in the First World War. The Western Front 1914.

FrOH: Les Armées Françaises dans la Grande Guerre, Tome VII, La campagne offensives de 1918 et la marche au Rhin - 18 julliet 1918-28 juin 1919, Tome VII, La campagne offensives de 1918 et la marche au Rhin - 18 julliet 1918-28 juin 1919, Volume 2 26 septembre 1918-28 juin 1919.

GmOH: Der Weltkrieg 1914 bis 1918, Die Militarischen Operationen zu Lande, Band 14, Die Kriegführung an der Westfront im Jahre 1918.

NZOH: Official History of New Zealand's Effort in the Great War, Volume II, France.

10 October ....The Irish Mail Boat Leinster sunk by a submarine. (British Home Waters).

BrOH: 1. Official History of the War, Seaborne Trade, Volume III, Submarine Campaign Part II.
2. Official History of the War, The Merchant Navy, Volume II.

GmOH: Der Krieg zur See 1914-1918, Band 4, Der Handelskrieg Mit U-Booten, Teil 5, Januar bis November 1918.

13 October ....Tripoli occupied. (Palestine).

AuOH: Official History of Australia in the War of 1914-1918, Volume VII, Sinai and Palestine.

BrOH: Official History of the War, Military Operations, Egypt and Palestine, Volume II, From June 1917 to the End of the War.

FrOH: Les Armées Françaises dans la Grande Guerre, Tome IX, Les fronts secondaires, Volume 1, Théâtre d'opérations de Levant [Ëgypte – Palestine -Syria – Hodjaz] – La propaganda allemande au Maroc.

NZOH: Official History of New Zealand's Effort in the Great War, Volume III, Sinai and Palestine.

TOH: 1. Büyük Harbin Sevkülceyşi.
2. Birinci Cihan Harbinde Türk Harbi, 1918 Yili Harekatleri, Vnci Cilt.
3. Birinci Dünya Harbinde Türk Harbi VInci Cilt, Hicaz, Asir, Yeman Cepheleri ve Libya Harekati 1914-1918.
4. Büyük Harpte Misir Seferi.

14 October ....Durazzo recaptured. (Adriatic Sea).

AHOH: 1. Österreich-Ungarns Seekrieg 1914-1918, Lieferung IV.
2. Österreich-Ungarns Letzter Krieg 1914-1918, Band VII.

IOH: 1. Ufficio Storico della R. Marina, La Marina Italiana nella Grande Guerra, Volume VIII, La Vittoria Mutilata in Adriatico.
2. Maggiore Esercito, Ufficio Storico, L'Esercito italiano nella grande guerra 1915-18, Volume V, Tomo 2 Le Operazioni Del 1918 - Gli Avvenimenti Dal Giugno Al Novembre.

14-19 October ....The Allied Offensive in Flanders – the Battle of Belgium - the Battle of Courtrai. (Western Front).

AmOH: United States Army in the World War 1917 – 1919, Volume 6, Operations, Oise-Aisne/ Ypres-Lys/ Vittorio Veneto.

AuOH: Official History of Australia in the War of 1914-1918, Volume VI, France 1918, Part II.

BrOH: Official History of the War, Military Operations, Volume V, 26th September - 11th November, The Advance to Victory.

COH: 1. Canadian Expeditionary Force 1914 - 1919.
2. The Official History of the Canadian Army in the First World War. The Western Front 1914.

FrOH: Les Armées Françaises dans la Grande Guerre, Tome VII, La campagne offensives de 1918 et la marche au Rhin - 18 julliet 1918-28 juin 1919, Tome VII, La campagne offensives de 1918 et la marche au Rhin - 18 juin 1918-28 juin 1919, Volume 2 26 septembre 1918-28 juin 1919.

GmOH: Der Weltkrieg 1914 bis 1918, Die Militarischen Operationen zu Lande, Band 14, Die Kriegführung an der Westfront im Jahre 1918.

NZOH: Official History of New Zealand's Effort in the Great War, Volume II, France.

14-30 October ....The Allied Offensive in Flanders – the Battle of Belgium - the Battle of Thourout-Thielt. (Western Front).

AmOH: United States Army in the World War 1917 – 1919, Volume 6, Operations, Oise-Aisne/ Ypres-Lys/ Vittorio Veneto.

AuOH: Official History of Australia in the War of 1914-1918, Volume VI, France 1918, Part II.

BrOH: Official History of the War, Military Operations, Volume V, 26th September - 11th November, The Advance to Victory.

COH: 1. Canadian Expeditionary Force 1914 - 1919.
2. The Official History of the Canadian Army in the First World War. The Western Front 1914.

FrOH: Les Armées Françaises dans la Grande Guerre, Tome VII, La campagne offensives de 1918 et la marche au Rhin - 18 julliet 1918-28 juin 1919, Tome VII, La campagne offensives de 1918 et la marche au Rhin - 18 julliet 1918-28 juin 1919, Volume 2 26 septembre 1918-28 juin 1919.

GmOH: Der Weltkrieg 1914 bis 1918, Die Militarischen Operationen zu Lande, Band 14, Die Kriegführung an der Westfront im Jahre 1918.

NZOH: Official History of New Zealand's Effort in the Great War, Volume II, France.

15-20 October ....The Final French Offensives – the Battles of the Oise. (Western Front).

AmOH: United States Army in the World War 1917 – 1919, Volume 7, Operations:- Somme.

AuOH: Official History of Australia in the War of 1914-1918, Volume VI, France 1918, Part II.

BrOH: Official History of the War, Military Operations, Volume V, 26th September - 11th November, The Advance to Victory.

COH: 1. Canadian Expeditionary Force 1914 - 1919.
2. The Official History of the Canadian Army in the First World War. The Western Front 1914.

FrOH: Les Armées Françaises dans la Grande Guerre, Tome VII, La campagne offensives de 1918 et la marche au Rhin - 18 julliet 1918-28 juin 1919, Tome VII, La campagne offensives de 1918 et la marche au Rhin - 18 julliet 1918-28 juin 1919, Volume 2 26 septembre 1918-28 juin 1919.

GmOH: Der Weltkrieg 1914 bis 1918, Die Militarischen Operationen zu Lande, Band 14, Die Kriegführung an der Westfront im Jahre 1918.

NZOH: Official History of New Zealand's Effort in the Great War, Volume II, France.

15-20 October ....The Final French Offensives – the Battle of Mont d'Origny. (Western Front).

AmOH: United States Army in the World War 1917 – 1919, Volume 7, Operations:- Somme.

AuOH: Official History of Australia in the War of 1914-1918, Volume VI, France 1918, Part II.

BrOH: Official History of the War, Military Operations, Volume V, 26th September - 11th November, The Advance to Victory.

COH: 1. Canadian Expeditionary Force 1914 - 1919.

2. The Official History of the Canadian Army in the First World War. The Western Front 1914.

FrOH: Les Armées Françaises dans la Grande Guerre, Tome VII, La campagne offensives de 1918 et la marche au Rhin - 18 julliet 1918-28 juin 1919, Tome VII, La campagne offensives de 1918 et la marche au Rhin - 18 julliet 1918-28 juin 1919, Volume 2 26 septembre 1918-28 juin 1919.

GmOH: Der Weltkrieg 1914 bis 1918, Die Militarischen Operationen zu Lande, Band 14, Die Kriegführung an der Westfront im Jahre 1918.

NZOH: Official History of New Zealand's Effort in the Great War, Volume II, France.

17 October .... Ostend recaptured. (Western Front).

AmOH: United States Army in the World War 1917 – 1919, Volume 6, Operations, Oise-Aisne/ Ypres-Lys/ Vittorio Veneto.

AuOH: Official History of Australia in the War of 1914-1918, Volume VI, France 1918, Part II.

BgOH: La Belgique et la Guerre, Tome III: Les Opérations Militaires.

BrOH: Official History of the War, Military Operations, Volume V, 26th September - 11th November, The Advance to Victory.

COH: 1. Canadian Expeditionary Force 1914 - 1919.
2. The Official History of the Canadian Army in the First World War. The Western Front 1914.

FrOH: Les Armées Françaises dans la Grande Guerre, Tome VII, La campagne offensives de 1918 et la marche au Rhin - 18 julliet 1918-28 juin 1919, Tome VII, La campagne offensives de 1918 et la marche au Rhin - 18 julliet 1918-28 juin 1919, Volume 2 26 septembre 1918-28 juin 1919.

GmOH: Der Weltkrieg 1914 bis 1918, Die Militarischen Operationen zu Lande, Band 14, Die Kriegführung an der Westfront im Jahre 1918.

NZOH: Official History of New Zealand's Effort in the Great War, Volume II, France.

17 October .... The Allied Offensive in Artois. (Western Front).

AmOH: United States Army in the World War 1917 – 1919, Volume 6, Operations, Oise-Aisne/ Ypres-Lys/ Vittorio Veneto.

AuOH: Official History of Australia in the War of 1914-1918, Volume VI, France 1918, Part II.

BrOH: Official History of the War, Military Operations, Volume V, 26th September - 11th November, The Advance to Victory.

COH: 1. Canadian Expeditionary Force 1914 - 1919.
2. The Official History of the Canadian Army in the First World War. The Western Front 1914.

FrOH: Les Armées Françaises dans la Grande Guerre, Tome VII, La campagne offensives de 1918 et la marche au Rhin - 18 julliet 1918-28 juin 1919, Tome VII, La campagne offensives de 1918 et la marche au Rhin - 18 julliet 1918-28 juin 1919, Volume 2 26 septembre 1918-28 juin 1919.

GmOH: Der Weltkrieg 1914 bis 1918, Die Militarischen Operationen zu Lande, Band 14, Die Kriegführung an der Westfront im Jahre 1918.

NZOH: Official History of New Zealand's Effort in the Great War, Volume II, France.

17-25 October .... The Allied Offensive in Picardy – the Battle of the Selle. (Western Front).

AmOH: United States Army in the World War 1917 – 1919, Volume 7, Operations:- Somme.

AuOH: Official History of Australia in the War of 1914-1918, Volume VI, France 1918, Part II.

BrOH: Official History of the War, Military Operations, Volume V, 26th September - 11th November, The Advance to Victory.

COH: 1. Canadian Expeditionary Force 1914 - 1919.
2. The Official History of the Canadian Army in the First World War. The Western Front 1914.

FrOH: Les Armées Françaises dans la Grande Guerre, Tome VII, La campagne offensives de 1918 et la marche au Rhin - 18 julliet 1918-28 juin 1919, Tome VII, La campagne offensives de 1918 et la marche au Rhin - 18 julliet 1918-28 juin 1919, Volume 2 26 septembre 1918-28 juin 1919.

GmOH: Der Weltkrieg 1914 bis 1918, Die Militarischen Operationen zu Lande, Band 14, Die Kriegführung an der Westfront im Jahre 1918.

NZOH: Official History of New Zealand's Effort in the Great War, Volume II, France.

19 October .... Zeebrugge and Bruges recaptured. (Western Front).

AmOH: United States Army in the World War 1917 – 1919, Volume 6, Operations, Oise-Aisne/ Ypres-Lys/ Vittorio Veneto.

AuOH: Official History of Australia in the War of 1914-1918, Volume VI, France 1918, Part II.

BgOH: La Belgique et la Guerre, Tome III: Les Opérations Militaires.

BrOH: Official History of the War, Military Operations, Volume V, 26th September - 11th November, The Advance to Victory.

COH: 1. Canadian Expeditionary Force 1914 - 1919.
2. The Official History of the Canadian Army in the First World War. The Western Front 1914.

FrOH: Les Armées Françaises dans la Grande Guerre, Tome VII, La campagne offensives de 1918 et la marche au Rhin - 18 julliet 1918-28 juin 1919, Tome VII, La campagne offensives de 1918 et la marche au Rhin - 18 julliet 1918-28 juin 1919, Volume 2 26 septembre 1918-28 juin 1919.

GmOH: Der Weltkrieg 1914 bis 1918, Die Militarischen Operationen zu Lande, Band 14, Die Kriegführung an der Westfront im Jahre 1918.

NZOH: Official History of New Zealand's Effort in the Great War, Volume II, France.

20 October .... Belgian coast completely recaptured. (Western Front).

AmOH: United States Army in the World War 1917 – 1919, Volume 6, Operations, Oise-Aisne/ Ypres-Lys/ Vittorio Veneto.

AuOH: Official History of Australia in the War of 1914-1918, Volume VI, France 1918, Part II.

BgOH: La Belgique et la Guerre, Tome III: Les Opérations Militaires.

BrOH: Official History of the War, Military Operations, Volume V, 26th September - 11th November, The Advance to Victory.

COH: 1. Canadian Expeditionary Force 1914 - 1919.
2. The Official History of the Canadian Army in the First World War. The Western Front 1914.

FrOH: Les Armées Françaises dans la Grande Guerre, Tome VII, La campagne offensives de 1918 et la marche au Rhin - 18 julliet 1918-28 juin 1919, Tome VII, La campagne offensives de 1918 et la marche au Rhin - 18 julliet 1918-28 juin 1919, Volume 2 26 septembre 1918-28 juin 1919.

GmOH: Der Weltkrieg 1914 bis 1918, Die Militarischen Operationen zu Lande, Band 14, Die Kriegführung an der Westfront im Jahre 1918.

NZOH: Official History of New Zealand's Effort in the Great War, Volume II, France.

20-30 October .... The Final French Offensives – the Battle of the Serre. (Western Front).

AmOH: United States Army in the World War 1917 – 1919, Volume 7, Operations:- Somme.

AuOH: Official History of Australia in the War of 1914-1918, Volume VI, France 1918, Part II.

BrOH: Official History of the War, Military Operations, Volume V, 26th September - 11th November, The Advance to Victory.

COH: 1. Canadian Expeditionary Force 1914 - 1919.
2. The Official History of the Canadian Army in the First World War. The Western Front 1914.

FrOH: Les Armées Françaises dans la Grande Guerre, Tome VII, La campagne offensives de 1918 et la marche au Rhin - 18 julliet 1918-28 juin 1919, Tome VII, La campagne offensives de 1918 et la marche au Rhin - 18 julliet 1918-28 juin 1919, Volume 2 26 septembre 1918-28 juin 1919.

GmOH: Der Weltkrieg 1914 bis 1918, Die Militarischen Operationen zu Lande, Band 14, Die Kriegführung an der Westfront im Jahre 1918.

NZOH: Official History of New Zealand's Effort in the Great War, Volume II, France.

22 October .... The Affair of Imad. (Aden).

AuOH: Official History of Australia in the War of 1914-1918, Volume VII, Sinai and Palestine.

BrOH: Official History of the War, Military Operations, Egypt and Palestine, Volume II, From June 1917 to the End of the War.

FrOH: Les Armées Françaises dans la Grande Guerre, Tome IX, Les fronts secondaires, Volume 1, Théâtre d'opérations de Levant [Ëgypte – Palestine -Syria – Hodjaz] – La propagande allemande au Maroc.

NZOH: Official History of New Zealand's Effort in the Great War, Volume III, Sinai and Palestine.

TOH: 1. Büyük Harbin Sevkülceyşi.
2. Birinci Cihan Harbinde Türk Harbi, 1918 Yili Harekatleri, Vnci Cilt.
3. Birinci Dünya Harbinde Türk Harbi VInci Cilt, Hicaz, Asir, Yeman Cepheleri ve Libya Harekati 1914-1918.
4. Büyük Harpte Misir Seferi.

24 October - 4 November .... The Italian Offensives, 1918. (Italian Front).

AHOH: Österreich-Ungarns Letzter Krieg 1914-1918, Band VII.

AmOH: United States Army in the World War 1917 – 1919, Volume 6, Operations, Oise-Aisne/ Ypres-Lys/ Vittorio Veneto.

BrOH: Official History of the War, Military Operations, Italy, 1915-1919.

IOH: Maggiore Esercito, Ufficio Storico, L'Esercito italiano nella grande guerra 1915-18, Volume V, Tomo 2 Le Operazioni Del 1918 - Gli Avvenimenti Dal Giugno Al Novembre.

24 October - 4 November...................The Italian Offensives, 1918 – the Battle of the Vittorio Veneto. (Italian Front).

AHOH: Österreich-Ungarns Letzter Krieg 1914-1918, Band VII.

AmOH: United States Army in the World War 1917 – 1919, Volume 6, Operations, Oise-Aisne/ Ypres-Lys/ Vittorio Veneto.

BrOH: Official History of the War, Military Operations, Italy, 1915-1919.

IOH: Maggiore Esercito, Ufficio Storico, L'Esercito italiano nella grande guerra 1915-18, Volume V, Tomo 2 Le Operazioni Del 1918 - Gli Avvenimenti Dal Giugno Al Novembre.

28-30 October ....The British advance on Mosul, 1918 – the Battle of the Sharqat. (Balkan Front).

AHOH: Österreich-Ungarns Letzter Krieg 1914-1918, Band VII.

BrOH: Official History of the War – Military Operations, Macedonia, Volume II:, From the Spring of 1917 to the End of the War.

FrOH: Les Armées Françaises dans la Grande Guerre: Tome VIII La campagne d'Orient. Volume 2 La campagne d'Orient depuis l'intervention de la Roumanie en aöut 1916 jusqu'en avril 1918.

GmOH: Der Weltkrieg 1914 bis 1918, Die Militarischen Operationen zu Lande, Band 14, Die Kriegführung an der Westfront im Jahre 1918.

GrOH: 1. Ho Hellenikos Stratos kata ton Proton Pankosmion Polemon 1914-1918 Tomos 2 H Summetochh ths Hellados eis ton Polemon 1918.
2. Epitomh Istopia Ths Eummetochhs Tou Ellhnikou Stratou Ston Prpsto Pagkosmio Polemo 1914-1918. / A Concise History of the Participation of the Hellenic Army in The First World War 1914-1918.

MOH: Operacije crnogorske vojske u prvom svetskom ratu.

SeOH: 1. Veliki rat Srbije za oslobođenje i ujedinenje Srba, Hrvata i Slovenaca 1914 – 1918. Knjige Dvadeset Deveta. 1918 godina. Ofanziva. Drugi period. Gonelje - Drugi faza. Nadiranje I armije ka Nišu i Zauzeće Niša. Prebacivanje II armije od Carevog sela ka Kumanovu i Velesu.
2. Veliki rat Srbije za oslobođenje i ujedinenje Srba, Hrvata i Slovenaca 1914 – 1918. Knjige Trideseta. 1918 godina. Ofanziva. Drugi period. Gonelje - Drugi faza. Nadiranje I armije na Sever i izlazak na Dunav i Savu. Prebacivanje II armije od Velesa na Kosovo i njeno izbijanje na Drinu.

TOH: 1. Birinci Dünya Harbinde Türk Harbi, VIInci Cilt, 3nci Kisim, Avrupa Cepheleri, Makedonya Cephesi, Romanya Cephesi.

2. Birinci Dünya Harbinde Türk Harbi, Avrupa Cepheleri (Özet).

29 October ....SanGiovanni di Medua recaptured. (Adriatic Sea).

AHOH: 1. Österreich-Ungarns Seekrieg 1914-1918, Lieferung IV.
2. Österreich-Ungarns Letzter Krieg 1914-1918, Band VII.

IOH: 1. Ufficio Storico della R. Marina, La Marina Italiana nella Grande Guerra, Volume VIII, La Vittoria Mutilata in Adriatico.
2. Maggiore Esercito, Ufficio Storico, L'Esercito italiano nella grande guerra 1915-18, Volume V, Tomo 2 Le Operazioni Del 1918 - Gli Avvenimenti Dal Giugno Al Novembre.

31 October ....The Hostilities against the Turkey cease. (12am local time). (Palestine Front).

AuOH: Official History of Australia in the War of 1914-1918, Volume VII, Sinai and Palestine.

BrOH: Official History of the War, Military Operations, Egypt and Palestine, Volume II, From June 1917 to the End of the War.

FrOH: Les Armées Françaises dans la Grande Guerre, Tome IX, Les fronts secondaires, Volume 1, Théâtre d'opérations de Levant [Ëgypte – Palestine -Syria – Hodjaz] – La propagande allemande au Maroc.

NZOH: Official History of New Zealand's Effort in the Great War, Volume III, Sinai and Palestine.

TOH: 1. Büyük Harbin Sevkülceyşi.
2. Birinci Cihan Harbinde Türk Harbi, 1918 Yili Harekatleri, Vnci Cilt.
3. Birinci Dünya Harbinde Türk Harbi VInci Cilt, Hicaz, Asir, Yeman Cepheleri ve Libya Harekati 1914-1918.
4. Büyük Harpte Misir Seferi.

31 October-4 November ....The Allied Offensive in Flanders – the Battle of Belgium - the Battle of the Lys and the Escaut. (Western Front).

AmOH: United States Army in the World War 1917 – 1919, Volume 6, Operations, Oise-Aisne/ Ypres-Lys/ Vittorio Veneto.

AuOH: Official History of Australia in the War of 1914-1918, Volume VI, France 1918, Part II.

BrOH: Official History of the War, Military Operations, Volume V, 26th September - 11th November, The Advance to Victory.

COH: 1. Canadian Expeditionary Force 1914 - 1919.
2. The Official History of the Canadian Army in the First World War. The Western Front 1914.

FrOH: Les Armées Françaises dans la Grande Guerre, Tome VII, La campagne offensives de 1918 et la marche au Rhin - 18 julliet 1918-28 juin 1919, Tome VII, La campagne offensives de 1918 et la marche au Rhin - 18 julliet 1918-28 juin 1919, Volume 2 26 septembre 1918-28 juin 1919.

GmOH: Der Weltkrieg 1914 bis 1918, Die Militarischen Operationen zu Lande, Band 14, Die Kriegführung an der Westfront im Jahre 1918.

NZOH: Official History of New Zealand's Effort in the Great War, Volume II, France.

1 November .... S.M.S. Viribus Unitis sunk (Croatian former Austrian battleship) by an underwater limpet mine on the bottom of its hull placed by two Italian divers on a manned torpedo, from the Italian motor torpedo launch MAS 95,. (Adriatic Sea).

        AHOH: Österreich-Ungarns Seekrieg 1914-1918, Lieferung IV.

        IOH: Ufficio Storico della R. Marina, La Marina Italiana nella Grande Guerra, Volume VIII, La Vittoria Mutilata in Adriatico.

1 November .... The attack on Fife, Rhodesia. (East Africa).

        BgOH: Les Campagnes Coloniales Belges 1914-1918. Volume I. Introduction, les Operations au Cameroun, les Operations en Rhodésie, la Période Défensive à la Frontière Orientale.

        GmOH: Der Krieg zur See 1914-1918, Band 6, Die Kämpfe der Kaiserlichen Marine in den deutschen Kolonien, Teil 2, Deutsch-Ostafrika.

        PgOH: 1. Portugal na Grande Guerra.
               2. A cooperação anglo-portuguesa na Grande Guerra de 1914-1918.

        SAOH: The Union of South Africa and the Great War 1914 – 1918.

1 November .... The capture of Kasama, Rhodesia. (East Africa).

        BgOH: Les Campagnes Coloniales Belges 1914-1918. Volume I. Introduction, les Operations au Cameroun, les Operations en Rhodésie, la Période Défensive à la Frontière Orientale.

        GmOH: Der Krieg zur See 1914-1918, Band 6, Die Kämpfe der Kaiserlichen Marine in den deutschen Kolonien, Teil 2, Deutsch-Ostafrika.

        PgOH: 1. Portugal na Grande Guerra.
               2. A cooperação anglo-portuguesa na Grande Guerra de 1914-1918.

        SAOH: The Union of South Africa and the Great War 1914 – 1918.

1-2 November .... The Allied Offensive in Picardy – the Battle of Valenciennes. (Western Front).

        AmOH: United States Army in the World War 1917 – 1919, Volume 7, Operations:- Somme.

        AuOH: Official History of Australia in the War of 1914-1918, Volume VI, France 1918, Part II.

        BgOH: La Belgique et la Guerre, Tome III: Les Opérations Militaires.

        BrOH: Official History of the War, Military Operations, Volume V, 26th September - 11th November, The Advance to Victory.

        COH: 1. Canadian Expeditionary Force 1914 - 1919.
              2. The Official History of the Canadian Army in the First World War. The Western Front 1914.

        FrOH: Les Armées Françaises dans la Grande Guerre, Tome VII, La campagne offensives de 1918 et la marche au Rhin - 18 julliet 1918-28 juin 1919, Tome VII, La campagne offensives de 1918 et la marche au Rhin - 18 julliet 1918-28 juin 1919, Volume 2 26 septembre 1918-28 juin 1919.

GmOH: Der Weltkrieg 1914 bis 1918, Die Militärischen Operationen zu Lande, Band 14, Die Kriegführung an der Westfront im Jahre 1918.

NZOH: Official History of New Zealand's Effort in the Great War, Volume II, France.

1-5 November ....The Final French Offensives – the Battle of le Chesne and Buzancy. (Western Front).

AmOH: United States Army in the World War 1917 – 1919, Volume 7, Operations:- Somme.

AuOH: Official History of Australia in the War of 1914-1918, Volume VI, France 1918, Part II.

BgOH: La Belgique et la Guerre, Tome III: Les Opérations Militaires.

BrOH: Official History of the War, Military Operations, Volume V, 26th September - 11th November, The Advance to Victory.

COH: 1. Canadian Expeditionary Force 1914 - 1919.
2. The Official History of the Canadian Army in the First World War. The Western Front 1914.

FrOH: Les Armées Françaises dans la Grande Guerre, Tome VII, La campagne offensives de 1918 et la marche au Rhin - 18 julliet 1918-28 juin 1919, Tome VII, La campagne offensives de 1918 et la marche au Rhin - 18 julliet 1918-28 juin 1919, Volume 2 26 septembre 1918-28 juin 1919.

GmOH: Der Weltkrieg 1914 bis 1918, Die Militärischen Operationen zu Lande, Band 14, Die Kriegführung an der Westfront im Jahre 1918.

NZOH: Official History of New Zealand's Effort in the Great War, Volume II, France.

2 November ....S.S. Surada and S.S. Murcia sunk by a submarine – last British merchant ships to be sunk. (Mediterranean Sea).

AHOH: Österreich-Ungarns Seekrieg 1914-1918, Lieferung IV.

BrOH: 1. Official History of the War, Seaborne Trade, Volume III, Submarine Campaign Part II.
2. Official History of the War, The Merchant Navy, Volume III.

GmOH: Der Krieg zur See 1914-1918, Band 4, Der Handelskrieg Mit U-Booten , Teil 5, Januar bis November 1918.

3 November ....Mutiny breaks out in the German Fleet. (German Home Waters).

GmOH: Der Krieg zur See 1914-1918, Band 1, Der Krieg in der Nordsee, Teil 7, Von Sommer 1917 bis zum Kriegsende 1918.

3 November ....Trieste occupied. (Adriatic Sea).

AHOH: 1. Österreich-Ungarns Seekrieg 1914-1918, Lieferung IV.
2. Österreich-Ungarns Letzter Krieg 1914-1918, Band VII.

IOH: 1. Ufficio Storico della R. Marina, La Marina Italiana nella Grande Guerra, Volume VIII, La Vittoria Mutilata in Adriatico.
2. Maggiore Esercito, Ufficio Storico, L'Esercito italiano nella grande guerra 1915-18, Volume V, Tomo 2 Le Operazioni Del 1918 - Gli Avvenimenti Dal Giugno Al Novembre.

4 November ....Antivari occupied. (Adriatic Sea).

AHOH: 1. Österreich-Ungarns Seekrieg 1914-1918, Lieferung IV.
2. Österreich-Ungarns Letzter Krieg 1914-1918, Band VII.

IOH: 1. Ufficio Storico della R. Marina, La Marina Italiana nella Grande Guerra, Volume VIII, La Vittoria Mutilata in Adriatico.
2. Maggiore Esercito, Ufficio Storico, L'Esercito italiano nella grande guerra 1915-18, Volume V, Tomo 2 Le Operazioni Del 1918 - Gli Avvenimenti Dal Giugno Al Novembre.

4 November ....The Hostilities on the Italian Front cease. (12am Central European Time). (Italian Front).

AmOH: United States Army in the World War 1917 – 1919, Volume 6, Operations, Oise-Aisne/ Ypres-Lys/ Vittorio Veneto.

AHOH: Österreich-Ungarns Letzter Krieg 1914-1918, Band VII.

BrOH: Official History of the War, Military Operations, Italy, 1915-1919.

IOH: Maggiore Esercito, Ufficio Storico, L'Esercito italiano nella grande guerra 1915-18, Volume V, Tomo 2 Le Operazioni Del 1918 - Gli Avvenimenti Dal Giugno Al Novembre.

4 November ....The Allied Offensive in Picardy – the Battles of the Sambre. (Western Front).

AmOH: United States Army in the World War 1917 – 1919, Volume 7, Operations:- Somme.

AuOH: Official History of Australia in the War of 1914-1918, Volume VI, France 1918, Part II.

BgOH: La Belgique et la Guerre, Tome III: Les Opérations Militaires.

BrOH: Official History of the War, Military Operations, Volume V, 26th September - 11th November, The Advance to Victory.

COH: 1. Canadian Expeditionary Force 1914 - 1919.
2. The Official History of the Canadian Army in the First World War. The Western Front 1914.

FrOH: Les Armées Françaises dans la Grande Guerre, Tome VII, La campagne offensives de 1918 et la marche au Rhin - 18 julliet 1918-28 juin 1919, Tome VII, La campagne offensives de 1918 et la marche au Rhin - 18 julliet 1918-28 juin 1919, Volume 2 26 septembre 1918-28 juin 1919.

GmOH: Der Weltkrieg 1914 bis 1918, Die Militarischen Operationen zu Lande, Band 14, Die Kriegführung an der Westfront im Jahre 1918.

NZOH: Official History of New Zealand's Effort in the Great War, Volume II, France.

4-5 November ....The Final French Offensives – the Second Battle of Guise. (Western Front).

AmOH: United States Army in the World War 1917 – 1919, Volume 7, Operations:- Somme.

AuOH: Official History of Australia in the War of 1914-1918, Volume VI, France 1918, Part II.

BgOH: La Belgique et la Guerre, Tome III: Les Opérations Militaires.

BrOH: Official History of the War, Military Operations, Volume V, 26th September - 11th November, The Advance to Victory.
COH: 1. Canadian Expeditionary Force 1914 - 1919.
2. The Official History of the Canadian Army in the First World War. The Western Front 1914.
FrOH: Les Armées Françaises dans la Grande Guerre, Tome VII, La campagne offensives de 1918 et la marche au Rhin - 18 julliet 1918-28 juin 1919, Tome VII, La campagne offensives de 1918 et la marche au Rhin - 18 julliet 1918-28 juin 1919, Volume 2 26 septembre 1918-28 juin 1919.
GmOH: Der Weltkrieg 1914 bis 1918, Die Militarischen Operationen zu Lande, Band 14, Die Kriegführung an der Westfront im Jahre 1918.
NZOH: Official History of New Zealand's Effort in the Great War, Volume II, France.

5 November .... Fiume occupied. (Adriatic Sea).
IOH: Ufficio Storico della R. Marina, La Marina Italiana nella Grande Guerra, Volume VIII, La Vittoria Mutilata in Adriatico.

5 November .... H.M.S. Campania Sunk. (British Home Waters) [British].
BrOH: Official History of the War, Naval Operations, Volume V.

6-11 November .... The Final French Offensives – the Battle of Thiérache. (Western Front).
AmOH: United States Army in the World War 1917 – 1919, Volume 7, Operations:- Somme.
AuOH: Official History of Australia in the War of 1914-1918, Volume VI, France 1918, Part II.
BgOH: La Belgique et la Guerre, Tome III: Les Opérations Militaires.
BrOH: Official History of the War, Military Operations, Volume V, 26th September - 11th November, The Advance to Victory.
COH: 1. Canadian Expeditionary Force 1914 - 1919.
2. The Official History of the Canadian Army in the First World War. The Western Front 1914.
FrOH: Les Armées Françaises dans la Grande Guerre, Tome VII, La campagne offensives de 1918 et la marche au Rhin - 18 julliet 1918-28 juin 1919, Tome VII, La campagne offensives de 1918 et la marche au Rhin - 18 julliet 1918-28 juin 1919, Volume 2 26 septembre 1918-28 juin 1919.
GmOH: Der Weltkrieg 1914 bis 1918, Die Militarischen Operationen zu Lande, Band 14, Die Kriegführung an der Westfront im Jahre 1918.
NZOH: Official History of New Zealand's Effort in the Great War, Volume II, France.

8-11 November .... The Final French Offensives – the Battle of Mézières. (Western Front).
AmOH: United States Army in the World War 1917 – 1919, Volume 7, Operations:- Somme.
AuOH: Official History of Australia in the War of 1914-1918, Volume VI, France 1918, Part II.
BgOH: La Belgique et la Guerre, Tome III: Les Opérations Militaires.
BrOH: Official History of the War, Military Operations, Volume V, 26th September - 11th November, The Advance to Victory.

COH: 1. Canadian Expeditionary Force 1914 - 1919.
2. The Official History of the Canadian Army in the First World War. The Western Front 1914.

FrOH: Les Armées Françaises dans la Grande Guerre, Tome VII, La campagne offensives de 1918 et la marche au Rhin - 18 julliet 1918-28 juin 1919, Tome VII, La campagne offensives de 1918 et la marche au Rhin - 18 julliet 1918-28 juin 1919, Volume 2 26 septembre 1918-28 juin 1919.

GmOH: Der Weltkrieg 1914 bis 1918, Die Militarischen Operationen zu Lande, Band 14, Die Kriegführung an der Westfront im Jahre 1918.

NZOH: Official History of New Zealand's Effort in the Great War, Volume II, France.

7 November .....................................S.S. Sarpedon attacked by a submarine – last attack on a British merchant ships. (Mediterranean Sea) [British/German].

AHOH: Österreich-Ungarns Seekrieg 1914-1918, Lieferung IV.

BrOH: 1. Official History of the War, Seaborne Trade, Volume III, Submarine Campaign Part II.
2. Official History of the War, The Merchant Navy, Volume III.

GmOH: Der Krieg zur See 1914-1918, Band 4, Der Handelskrieg Mit U-Booten , Teil 5, Januar bis November 1918.

9 November .....................................H.M.S. Britannia sunk by a submarine. (Atlantic Ocean).

BrOH: 1. Official History of the War, Seaborne Trade, Volume III, Submarine Campaign Part II.
2. Official History of the War, The Merchant Navy, Volume III.

GmOH: Der Krieg zur See 1914-1918, Band 4, Der Handelskrieg Mit U-Booten , Teil 5, Januar bis November 1918.

9 November ....Alexandretta occupied. (Mediterranean Sea).

AuOH: Official History of Australia in the War of 1914-1918, Volume VII, Sinai and Palestine.

BrOH: Official History of the War, Military Operations, Egypt and Palestine, Volume II, From June 1917 to the End of the War.

FrOH: Les Armées Françaises dans la Grande Guerre, Tome IX, Les fronts secondaires, Volume 1, Théâtre d'opérations de Levant [Ëgypte – Palestine -Syria – Hodjaz] – La propagande allemande au Maroc.

NZOH: Official History of New Zealand's Effort in the Great War, Volume III, Sinai and Palestine.

TOH: Türk İstiklal Harbi I, Mondros Mütarekesi Ve Tatbikati.

11 November ....The Hostilities on the Western Front cease. (11 a.m. local European time). (Western Front).

AmOH: United States Army in the World War 1917–1919, Volume 10, The Armistice.

AuOH: Official History of Australia in the War of 1914-1918, Volume VI, France 1918, Part II.

BgOH: La Belgique et la Guerre, Tome III, Les Opérations Militaires.

BrOH: Official History of the War, Military Operations, Volume V, 26th September - 11th November, The Advance to Victory.

COH: 1. Canadian Expeditionary Force 1914 - 1919.

2. The Official History of the Canadian Army in the First World War. The Western Front 1914.

FrOH: Les Armées Françaises dans la Grande Guerre, Tome VII, La campagne offensives de 1918 et la marche au Rhin - 18 julliet 1918-28 juin 1919, Tome VII, La campagne offensives de 1918 et la marche au Rhin - 18 julliet 1918-28 juin 1919, Volume 1, 18 julliet 1918-25 septembre 1918.

GmOH: Der Weltkrieg 1914 bis 1918, Die Militarischen Operationen zu Lande, Band 14, Die Kriegführung an der Westfront im Jahre 1918.

NZOH: Official History of New Zealand's Effort in the Great War, Volume II, France.

14 November ....The Hostilities in East Africa cease. (East African).

GmOH: Der Krieg zur See 1914-1918, Band 6, Die Kämpfe der Kaiserlichen Marine in den deutschen Kolonien, Teil 2, Deutsch-Ostafrika.

PgOH: 1. Portugal na Grande Guerra.

2. A cooperação anglo-portuguesa na Grande Guerra de 1914-1918.

SAOH: .The Union of South Africa and the Great War 1914 – 1918.

14 November ....................................H.M.S. Cochrane wrecked. (British Home Waters).

BrOH: ..Official History of the War, Naval Operations, Volume V.

17 November ....Baku reoccupied. (Caucasus).

TOH: Birinci Dünya Savaşı'nda Osmanli Ordusun'un Azerbaycan ve Dağistan Harekâti, Azerbaycan ve Dağistan'in Bağimsizliğini Kazanmasi 1918.

20 November ....First contingent of submarines surrender at Harwich. (British Home Waters) [British/German].

BrOH: Official History of the War, Naval Operations, Volume V.

GmOH: 1. Der Krieg zur See 1914-1918, Band 1, Der Krieg in der Nordsee, Teil 7, Von Sommer 1917 bis zum Kriegsende 1918.

2. Der Krieg zur See 1914-1918, Band 4, Der Handelskrieg Mit U-Booten, Teil 5, Januar bis November 1918.

21 November ....The German High Sea Fleet arrives at Rosyth on route for internment at Scapa Flow. (British Home Waters).

BrOH: Official History of the War, Naval Operations, Volume V.

GmOH: Der Krieg zur See 1914-1918, Band 1, Der Krieg in der Nordsee, Teil 7, Von Sommer 1917 bis zum Kriegsende 1918.

21 November - 2 October 1930..........French Troops arrive at Constantinople. (Turkey).

BrOH: Official History of the War, The Occupation of Constantinople 1918-1923.

FrOH: Les Armées Françaises dans la Grande Guerre, Tome VIII, La campagne d'Orient, Volume 3, La campagne d'Orient d'avril 1918 à décembre 1918.

TOH: 1. Büyük Harbin Sevkülceyşi.

2. Birinci Cihan Harbinde Türk Harbi, 1918 Yili Harekatleri, Vnci Cilt.

26 November ....The Allied Fleet arrives at Sevastopol and takes over Russian Black Sea
Fleet from the Germans. (Black Sea).
                BrOH: Official History of the War, Naval Operations, Volume V.
                RuOH:..Flot v Pervoi Mirovoi Voine. V Dvukh Tomakh. Tom I
                         Deystviya Russkogo Flota.

1 December 1918-30 June 1930.........The occupation of the Rhineland.
                AmOH: United States Army in the World War 1917 – 1919,
                         Volume 11, The Occupation of Germany.
                BrOH: Official History of the War, The Occupation of the
                         Rhineland 1918-1929.
                FrOH: Les Armées Françaises dans la Grande Guerre, Tome VII,
                         La campagne offensives de 1918 et la marche au Rhin - 18
                         julliet 1918-28 juin 1919, Volume 2 26 septembre 1918-28
                         juin 1919

4 December......................................H.M.S. Cassandra sunk by a mine. (Baltic Sea).
                BrOH: Official History of the War, Naval Operations, Volume V.
                RuOH:..Flot v Pervoi Mirovoi Voine. V Dvukh Tomakh. Tom I
                         Deystviya Russkogo Flota.

8 December......................................Naval action. (Caspian Sea).
                BrOH: Official History of the War, Naval Operations, Volume V.
                RuOH:..Flot v Pervoi Mirovoi Voine. V Dvukh Tomakh. Tom I
                         Deystviya Russkogo Flota.

11 December....................................Odessa Occupied by Petyura's Force. (Black Sea).
                RuOH:..Flot v Pervoi Mirovoi Voine. V Dvukh Tomakh. Tom I
                         Deystviya Russkogo Flota.

13 December....................................Hodeida captured. (Arabia).
                  AuOH: Official History of Australia in the War of 1914-1918,
                         Volume VII, Sinai and Palestine.
                BrOH: Official History of the War, Military Operations, Egypt
                         and Palestine, Volume II, From June 1917 to the End of
                         the War.
                NZOH: Official History of New Zealand's Effort in the Great
                         War, Volume III, Sinai and Palestine.
                TOH: 1. Büyük Harbin Sevkülceyşi.
                         2. Birinci Cihan Harbinde Türk Harbi, 1918 Yili
                         Harekatleri, Vnci Cilt.
                         3. Birinci Dünya Harbinde Türk Harbi VInci Cilt, Hicaz,
                         Asir, Yeman Cepheleri ve Libya Harekati 1914-1918.
                         4. Büyük Harpte Misir Seferi.

27 December....................................Batum occupied. (Black Sea).
                RuOH:..Flot v Pervoi Mirovoi Voine. V Dvukh Tomakh. **Tom I**
                         Deystviya Russkogo Flota.

Appendix One

Secondary Official Histories Bibliography

American Secondary Official Histories

Naval Staff Papers;

THE DARDANELLE EXPEDITION.
> *Captain* William Dilworth Puleston, USN | 26cm x 18.5cm | grey paper softback | 154pp | 68 maps | United States Naval Institute/Government Printing Office | 1926 | English Text.
> This volume was republished in 2007 by Kessinger Publishing.

Army Staff Paper;

FINAL REPORT OF GENERAL JOHN J. PERSHING.
> *General* John J.(Joseph) Pershing | 24.75cm x 18.5cm | grey paper softback | 96pp | 16 maps | Government Printing Office | 1919 | English Text.

U. S. Army Chemical Corps Historical Studies;

U. S. ARMY CHEMICAL CORPS HISTORICAL STUDIES - GAS WARFARE IN WORLD WAR I - GAS WARFARE AT BELLEAU WOOD, JUNE 1918. [Study] No. 1.
> Rexmond C.(Canning) Cochrane *Ph.D.* (U. S. Army Chemical Corps Historical Office) | 26.7cm x 19cm | grey paper softback | 85pp | Government Printing Office | 1957 | English Text.
> This volume can be viewed on the Indiana University Digital Archive world wide web as a pdf file:
> *http://bl-libg-doghill.ads.iu.edu/gpd-web/historical/acchs/acchs1.pdf*

U. S. ARMY CHEMICAL CORPS HISTORICAL STUDIES - GAS WARFARE IN WORLD WAR I - THE 78th DIVISION AT THE KRIEMHILDE STELLUNG, OCTOBER 1918. Study No. 2.
> Rexmond C.(Canning) Cochrane *Ph.D.* (U. S. Army Chemical Corps Historical Office) | 26.7cm x 19cm | grey paper softback | 107pp | Government Printing Office | 1957 | English Text.
> This volume can be viewed on the Indiana University Digital Archive world wide web as a pdf file:
> *http://bl-libg-doghill.ads.iu.edu/gpd-web/historical/acchs/acchs2.pdf*

U. S. ARMY CHEMICAL CORPS HISTORICAL STUDIES - GAS WARFARE IN WORLD WAR I - THE 1st DIVISION IN THE MEUSE-ARGONNE, 1-12 OCTOBER 1918. [Study] No. 3.
> Rexmond C.(Canning) Cochrane *Ph.D.* (U. S. Army Chemical Corps Historical Office) | 26.7cm x 19cm | grey paper softback | 75pp | Government Printing Office | 1957 | English Text.
> This volume can be viewed on the Indiana University Digital Archive world wide web as a pdf file:
> *http://bl-libg-doghill.ads.iu.edu/gpd-web/historical/acchs/acchs3.pdf*

U. S. ARMY CHEMICAL CORPS HISTORICAL STUDIES - GAS WARFARE IN WORLD WAR I: THE 26th DIVISION IN THE AISNE-MARNE CAMPAIGN, JULY 1918. Study No. 4.
> Rexmond C.(Canning) Cochrane *Ph.D.* (U. S. Army Chemical Corps Historical Office) | 26.7cm x 19cm | grey paper softback | 91pp | Government Printing Office | 1957 | English Text.
> This volume can be viewed on the Indiana University Digital Archive world wide web as a pdf file:
> *http://bl-libg-doghill.ads.iu.edu/gpd-web/historical/acchs/acchs4.pdf*

U. S. ARMY CHEMICAL CORPS HISTORICAL STUDIES - GAS WARFARE IN WORLD WAR I - THE USE OF GAS AT SAINT MIHIEL (90th DIVISION IN SEPTEMBER 1918). Study No. 5.
> Rexmond C.(Canning) Cochrane *Ph.D.* (U. S. Army Chemical Corps Historical Office) | 26.7cm x 19cm | grey paper softback | 90pp | Government Printing Office | 1957 | English Text.
> This volume can be viewed on the Indiana University Digital Archive world wide web as a pdf file:

U. S. ARMY CHEMICAL CORPS HISTORICAL STUDIES - GAS WARFARE IN WORLD WAR I - THE 89th DIVISION COMES INTO THE LINE, AUGUST 1918. Study No. 6.

Rexmond C.(Canning) Cochrane *Ph.D.* (U. S. Army Chemical Corps Historical Office) | 26.7cm x 19cm | grey paper softback | 72pp | Government Printing Office | 1958 | English Text.

This volume can be viewed on the Indiana University Digital Archive world wide web as a pdf file:

U. S. ARMY CHEMICAL CORPS HISTORICAL STUDIES - GAS WARFARE IN WORLD WAR I - THE 5th DIVISION CAPTURES FRAPELLE, AUGUST 1918. Study No. 7.

Rexmond C.(Canning) Cochrane *Ph.D.* (U. S. Army Chemical Corps Historical Office) | 26.7cm x 19cm | grey paper softback | 54pp | Government Printing Office | 1958 | English Text.

This volume can be viewed on the Indiana University Digital Archive world wide web as a pdf file:

U. S. ARMY CHEMICAL CORPS HISTORICAL STUDIES - GAS WARFARE IN WORLD WAR I - THE 33rd DIVISION ALONG THE MEUSE, OCTOBER 1918. Study No. 8.

Rexmond C.(Canning) Cochrane *Ph.D.* (U. S. Army Chemical Corps Historical Office) | 26.7cm x 19cm | grey paper softback | 102pp | Government Printing Office | 1958 | English Text.

This volume can be viewed on the Indiana University Digital Archive world wide web as a pdf file:

U. S. ARMY CHEMICAL CORPS HISTORICAL STUDIES - GAS WARFARE IN WORLD WAR I - THE 1st DIVISION AT ANSAUVILLE, JANUARY - APRIL 1918. Study No. 9.

Rexmond C.(Canning) Cochrane *Ph.D.* (U. S. Army Chemical Corps Historical Office) | 26.7cm x 19cm | grey paper softback | 62pp | Government Printing Office | 1958 | English Text.

This volume can be viewed on the Indiana University Digital Archive world wide web as a pdf file:

U. S. ARMY CHEMICAL CORPS HISTORICAL STUDIES - GAS WARFARE IN WORLD WAR I - THE USE OF GAS IN THE MEUSE-ARGONNE CAMPAIGN, SEPTEMBER-NOVEMBER 1918. [Study] No. 10.

Rexmond C.(Canning) Cochrane *Ph.D.* (U. S. Army Chemical Corps Historical Office) | 26.7cm x 19cm | grey paper softback | 96pp | Government Printing Office | 1958 | English Text.

This volume can be viewed on the Indiana University Digital Archive world wide web as a pdf file:

U. S. ARMY CHEMICAL CORPS HISTORICAL STUDIES - GAS WARFARE IN WORLD WAR I - THE 1st DIVISION AT CANTIGNY, MAY 1918. Study Number 11.

Rexmond C.(Canning) Cochrane *Ph.D.* (U. S. Army Chemical Corps Historical Office) | 26.7cm x 19cm | grey paper softback | 91pp | Government Printing Office | 1959 | English Text.

This volume can be viewed on the Indiana University Digital Archive world wide web as a pdf file:

U. S. ARMY CHEMICAL CORPS HISTORICAL STUDIES - GAS WARFARE IN WORLD WAR I - THE 32nd DIVISION ADVANCES TO FISMES, AUGUST 1918. Study No. 12.

Rexmond C.(Canning) Cochrane *Ph.D.* (U. S. Army Chemical Corps Historical Office) | 26.7cm x 19cm | grey paper softback | 77pp | Government Printing Office | 1959 | English Text.

This volume can be viewed on the Indiana University Digital Archive world wide web as a pdf file:

U. S. ARMY CHEMICAL CORPS HISTORICAL STUDIES - GAS WARFARE IN WORLD WAR I - THE END OF THE AISNE-MARNE CAMPAIGN, AUGUST 1918. Study No. 13.

Rexmond C.(Canning) Cochrane *Ph.D.* (U. S. Army Chemical Corps Historical Office) | 26.7cm x 19cm | grey paper softback | 57pp | Government Printing Office | 1960 | English Text.

This volume can be viewed on the Indiana University Digital Archive world wide web as a pdf file:

http://bl-libg-doghill.ads.iu.edu/gpd-web/historical/acchs/acchs13.pdf

U. S. ARMY CHEMICAL CORPS HISTORICAL STUDIES - GAS WARFARE IN WORLD WAR I - THE 3rd DIVISION AT CHATEAU THIERRY, JULY 1918. Study No. 14.

Rexmond C.(Canning) Cochrane *Ph.D.* (U. S. Army Chemical Corps Historical Office) | 26.7cm x 19cm | grey paper softback | 113pp | Government Printing Office | 1959 | English Text.

This volume can be viewed on the Indiana University Digital Archive world wide web as a pdf file:

http://bl-libg-doghill.ads.iu.edu/gpd-web/historical/acchs/acchs14.pdf

U. S. ARMY CHEMICAL CORPS HISTORICAL STUDIES - GAS WARFARE IN WORLD WAR I - THE 29th DIVISION IN THE CÔTES DE MEUSE, OCTOBER 1918. Study No. 15.

Rexmond C.(Canning) Cochrane *Ph.D.* (U. S. Army Chemical Corps Historical Office) | 26.7cm x 19cm | grey paper softback | 91pp | Government Printing Office | 1959 | English Text.

This volume can be viewed on the Indiana University Digital Archive world wide web as a pdf file:

http://bl-libg-doghill.ads.iu.edu/gpd-web/historical/acchs/acchs15.pdf

U. S. ARMY CHEMICAL CORPS HISTORICAL STUDIES - GAS WARFARE IN WORLD WAR I - THE 92nd DIVISION IN THE MARBACHE SECTOR, OCTOBER 1918. Study No. 16.

Rexmond C.(Canning) Cochrane *Ph.D.* (U. S. Army Chemical Corps Historical Office) | 26.7cm x 19cm | grey paper softback | 89pp | Government Printing Office | 1959 | English Text.

This volume can be viewed on the Indiana University Digital Archive world wide web as a pdf file:

http://bl-libg-doghill.ads.iu.edu/gpd-web/historical/acchs/acchs16.pdf

U. S. ARMY CHEMICAL CORPS HISTORICAL STUDIES - GAS WARFARE IN WORLD WAR I - THE 42nd DIVISION BEFORE LANDRES-et-St GEORGES, OCTOBER 1918. Study No. 17.

Rexmond C.(Canning) Cochrane *Ph.D.* (U. S. Army Chemical Corps Historical Office) | 26.7cm x 19cm | grey paper softback | 94pp | Government Printing Office | 1960 | English Text.

This volume can be viewed on the Indiana University Digital Archive world wide web as a pdf file:

http://bl-libg-doghill.ads.iu.edu/gpd-web/historical/acchs/acchs17.pdf

U. S. ARMY CHEMICAL CORPS HISTORICAL STUDIES - GAS WARFARE IN WORLD WAR I - THE 89th DIVISION IN THE BOIS de BANTHEVILLE, OCTOBER 1918. Study No. 18.

Rexmond C.(Canning) Cochrane *Ph.D.* (U. S. Army Chemical Corps Historical Office) | 26.7cm x 19cm | grey paper softback | 96pp | Government Printing Office | 1960 | English Text.

This volume can be viewed on the Indiana University Digital Archive world wide web as a pdf file:

http://bl-libg-doghill.ads.iu.edu/gpd-web/historical/acchs/acchs18.pdf

U.S. ARMY CHEMICAL CORPS HISTORICAL STUDIES - GAS WARFARE IN WORLD WAR I - THE 79th DIVISION AT MONTFAUCON, OCTOBER 1918. Study No. 19.

Rexmond C.(Canning) Cochrane *Ph.D.* (U. S. Army Chemical Corps Historical Office) | 26.7cm x 19cm | grey paper softback | 101pp | Government Printing Office | 1960 | English Text.

This volume can be viewed on the Indiana University Digital Archive world wide web as a pdf file:

http://bl-libg-doghill.ads.iu.edu/gpd-web/historical/acchs/acchs19.pdf

U. S. ARMY CHEMICAL CORPS HISTORICAL STUDIES - GAS WARFARE IN WORLD WAR I - THE 26th DIVISION EAST OF THE MEUSE, OCTOBER 1918. Study No. 20.

Rexmond C.(Canning) Cochrane *Ph.D.* (U. S. Army Chemical Corps Historical Office) | 26.7cm x 19cm | grey paper softback | 82pp | Government Printing Office | 1960 | English Text.

This volume can be viewed on the Indiana University Digital Archive world wide web as a pdf file:

http://bl-libg-doghill.ads.iu.edu/gpd-web/historical/acchs/acchs20.pdf

Each volume of this set has a foreword with the following statement: "This study is not presented as a definitive and official history, but is reproduced for current reference use within the Military Establishment pending the publication of an approved history". However since it was written under the authority of the U. S. Army Chemical Corps then it must be considered as a semi official history.

Fort Leavenworth Command Papers;

Leavenworth Papers No. 4; The Dynamics of Doctrine: The Changes in German Tactical Doctrine During the First World War.

Captain Timothy T. Lupfer | 24.75cm x 19.7cm | white paper softback | 73pp | 4 maps | 3 sketches | Combat Studies Institute - U.S. Army Command and General Staff College | 1981 | English Text.

This volume has been translated into German and published under the title '**Die Dynamik der Kriegslehre: der Wandel der taktischen Grundsätze des deutschen Heeres im Ersten Weltkrieg**' by E.S. Mitler in 1988.

Leavenworth Papers No. 10; Chemical Warfare in World War 1: The American Experience, 1917 – 1918.

Major(P) Charles E. Heller, U.S.A.R. | 24.75cm x 19.7cm | white paper softback | 109pp | Combat Studies Institute - U.S. Army Command and General Staff College | 1984 | English Text.

There are at present twenty two Leavenworth Papers covering various aspects in different wars. Only the above two (No. 4 and No. 10) cover the Great War period.

Air;

IDEAS and WEAPONS: EXPLOITATION OF THE AERIAL WEAPON BY THE UNITED STATES DURING WORLD WAR I: A STUDY IN THE RELATIONSHIP OF TECHNOLOGICAL ADVANCE, MILITARY DOCTRINE, AND THE DEVELOPMENT OF WEAPONS.

[Professor] I.B. (Irving Brinton) Holley Jr. - The Office of Air Force History. | 30.5cm x 24.75cm | light blue cloth hardback | xiv + 222 pp | 3 schematic diagrams | 12 tables | Yale University Press/Government Printing Office | 1953 | English Text.

This study "**Ideas and Weapons**" is part of a series known as "The United States Air Force Special Studies" that covers all United State's Air Force history. It was republished in 1971, 1983 and again 1997 for public readership.

AMERICA'S FIRST EAGLES: The Official History of the U. S. Air Service, 1917-1918.

[Lieutenant] Lucien H. Thayer | 24.75cm x 19.7cm | blue cloth hardback | Illustrated dust jacket | 359pp | 157 photographs | 7 maps | 69 sketches | R. James Publishing & Champlin Fighter Museum Press | ISBN: 0912138246 | 1983 | English Text.

The title of this volume "**America's First Eagles: The Official History of the U. S. Air Service, 1917-1918**" states that it is an "Official History" and as such is listed here.

Photographic;

U.S. Official Pictures *of the* World War SHOWING AMERICA'S PARTICIPATION Selected from the Official Files of the War Department, With Unofficial Introductory Photographs .

Captain William E. Moore *U.S.A.* and *Captain* James C. Russell *U.S.A.* - Pictorial Bureau | 24.75cm x 30.5cm | green cloth hardback | Illustrated cover | 576pp | 991 photograph | 1 table | 6 maps | Government Printing Office | 1920 | English Text.

The United States Navy in the World War: Official Pictures Selected from the files of the Navy Department, the War Department and the United States Marine Corps, With supplemental photographs from unofficial sources.

[*Captain*] James C. Russell and [*Captain*] William E. Moore - Pictorial Bureau I 24.75cm x 30.5cm I green cloth hardback I Illustrated cover I 320pp I 680 photograph I 1 table I 4 sketches I Government Printing Office I 1921 I English Text.

Austro-Hungarian Secondary Official Histories

Naval;

𝕭𝖎𝖑𝖉𝖉𝖔𝖐𝖚𝖒𝖊𝖓𝖙𝖊 𝖆𝖚𝖋 Ö𝖘𝖙𝖊𝖗𝖗𝖊𝖎𝖈𝖍−𝖀𝖓𝖌𝖆𝖗𝖓𝖋 𝕾𝖊𝖊𝖐𝖗𝖎𝖊𝖌 1914−1918. 𝕭𝖆𝖓𝖉 𝕵.
(Bilddokumente aus Österreich-Ungarns Seekrieg 1914-1918. Band II. - *Pictures and Documentation of the Austro-Hungary's Sea War 1914-1918. Volume I.*);
    Nikolaus von Martiny I 23cm x 15.5cm I Blue cloth hardback I xix + 182pp I 122 photograph I Leykam Verlag. I 1939 I German Text. I Fraktur Script.
𝕭𝖎𝖑𝖉𝖉𝖔𝖐𝖚𝖒𝖊𝖓𝖙𝖊 𝖆𝖚𝖋 Ö𝖘𝖙𝖊𝖗𝖗𝖊𝖎𝖈𝖍−𝖀𝖓𝖌𝖆𝖗𝖓𝖋 𝕾𝖊𝖊𝖐𝖗𝖎𝖊𝖌 1914−1918. 𝕭𝖆𝖓𝖉 𝕵𝕵.
(Bilddokumente aus Österreich-Ungarns Seekrieg 1914-1918. Band II. - *Pictures and Documentation of the Austro-Hungary's Sea War 1914-1918. Volume II.*);
    Nikolaus von Martiny I 23cm x 15.5cm I Blue cloth hardback I 214pp I 109 photograph I 8 maps I 2 appendices I Leykam Verlag. I 1939 I German Text. I Fraktur Script.
    Both volumes republished in 1973 by Akademische Druck und Verlagsantalt.
    Although Austrian publishing houses had ceased using Fraktur Script at the end of the Great War, it appears that after the Anschluß they reintroduced it to bring their publications into line with German publishing.
    The two volumes '**Bilddokumente aus Österreich-Ungarns Seekrieg 1914-1918**' are unofficial, but based on official archive documents and photographs.

Belgian Secondary Official Histories

Army Staff Papers[1];

LA GUERRE DE 1914. L'ACTION DE L'ARMEE BELGE POUR LA DEFENSE DU PAYS ET LE RESPECT DE SA NEUTRALITE (RAPPORT DU COMMANDEMENT DE L'ARMEE) PERIODE DU 31 JUILLET AU 31 DECEMBRE 1914. (*The War of 1914. The Action of the Belgian Army for the Defense of the Country with Respect to its Neutrality (Report of the Army Command) for the Period 31st July to 31st December, 1914*).

Anonymous (*King* Albert I) | 23cm x 18.5cm | grey blue cloth hardback | 97pp | 11 maps | Chapelot | 1915 | French Text.

Although the author's name does not appear on the title page, the title makes the statement that this volume is the Rapport du Commandement de L'Armee – the Report of the Commander-in-Chief - which was *King* Albert I. However it is much more likely that *Lieutenant-General* Chevalier de Selliers de Moranville who was the Belgian Army's Chief of the General Staff compiled this report.

Translated into English and published in London in 1915 by W. H. & L. Collingridge under the title '**The War of 1914, Military Operations of Belgium in Defence of the Country and to Uphold Her Neutrality. Report compiled by the Commander-in-Chief of the Belgian Army (For the period July 31st to December 31st, 1914)**'.

---

[1] A series of official articles under the general heading 'Les Opérations de l'Armée Belge au cours de la Guerre 1914-1918' (Belgian Army Operations during the Course of the 1914-1918 War) relating to military operations were published by the Service Historique des Forces Armée in the Belgian Army's magazine 'Bulletin Belge des Sciences Militaires' between 1920 and 1932. I have not listed these articles in this bibliography, as they were not published as books.

British Secondary Official Histories

General;

THE OFFICIAL NAMES OF THE BATTLES AND OTHER ENGAGEMENTS FOUGHT BY THE MILITARY FORCES OF THE BRITISH EMPIRE DURING THE GREAT WAR, 1914-1919 AND THE THIRD AFGHAN WAR, 1919. [Cmd. 1138].

Anonymous (The Nomenclature Committee) | 33.4cm x 21cm | white paper softback | 63pp | His Majesty's Stationery Office. | 1922 | English Text.
Republished in 1992 by The Naval & Military Press.

Chronology;

CHRONOLOGY OF THE WAR VOL. 1 1914. 1915.

Major General Lord Edward Gleichen | 24.75cm x 19.7cm | orange cloth hardback | 211pp | 2 appendices | Constable and Co. Ltd. | 1918 | English Text.

CHRONOLOGY OF THE WAR VOLUME 2 1916-17

Major General Lord Edward Gleichen | 24.75cm x 19.7cm | orange cloth hardback | 330pp | 2 appendices | 4 tables | Constable and Co. Ltd. | 1919 | English Text.

CHRONOLOGY OF THE WAR VOLUME 3 1918-19

Major General Lord Edward Gleichen | 24.75cm x 19.7cm | orange cloth hardback | 258pp | 2 appendices + section of Statistics | 35 tables | Constable and Co. Ltd. | 1920 | English Text.
This Volume '**Chronology of the War Volume 3 1918-19**' has a Corrigenda to the first two volumes of this set located on page 258.
This set '**Chronology of the War**' was issued under the Auspices of the Ministry of Information.
The set has been republished by Greenhill Books in 1988.

Naval;

ROYAL NAVAL AIR SERVICE NO. 1 AEROPLANE WING OPERATION.

Anonymous (Admiralty. Intelligence Division) | 33.4cm x 21.4cm | blue paper softback | 79pp | His Majesty's Stationery Office. | 1916 | English Text.

THE TWO CRUISES OF THE RAIDER "MÖWE" [I.D.1171].

Anonymous (Admiralty. Intelligence Division) | 33.4cm x 21.4cm | blue paper softback | 51pp | His Majesty's Stationery Office. | 1918 | English Text.

GRAF VON SPEE'S SQUADRON. [I.D.1173].

Anonymous (Admiralty. Intelligence Division) | 33.4cm x 21.4cm | blue paper softback | 51pp | 5 maps | His Majesty's Stationery Office. | 1918 | English Text.

THE CRUISE OF THE RAIDER "WOLF" [I.D.1192].

Anonymous (Admiralty. Intelligence Division) | 33.4cm x 21.4cm | blue paper softback | 32pp | 3 photograph | 1 painting | His Majesty's Stationery Office. | 1918 | English Text.

GERMAN NAVAL WARFARE, 1914-1919 [C.B.0693].

Anonymous (Admiralty. Intelligence Division) | 33.4cm x 21.4cm | blue paper softback | ?pp | His Majesty's Stationery Office. | ND. c1919 | English Text.

GERMAN NAVY (SUBMARINES) [C.B.1182S.].

Anonymous (Admiralty. Intelligence Division) | 33.4cm x 21.4cm | blue paper softback | ?pp | His Majesty's Stationery Office. | 1918 | English Text.

LOSSES OF ENEMY SUBMARINES WITH SUMMARY OF CASES, FINAL RETURN [C.B.1292G].

Anonymous (Admiralty. Intelligence Division) | 33.4cm x 21.4cm | blue paper softback | ?pp | His Majesty's Stationery Office. | 1919 | English Text.

GERMAN ORDERS FOR RUTHLESS SUBMARINE WARFARE [C.B.1360].

Anonymous (Admiralty. Intelligence Division) | 33.4cm x 21.4cm | blue paper softback | ?pp | His Majesty's Stationery Office. | 1917 | English Text.

ACTION OFF THE FALKLAND ISLANDS 8 DECEMBER 1914: REPORT OF VICE-ADMIRAL SIR F.C.D. STURDEE.

Vice-Admiral Sir F.C.D.(Frederick Charles Doveton) Sturdee | 33.4cm x 21.4cm | blue paper softback | ?pp | ? maps | His Majesty's Stationery Office. | 1915 | English Text.

SEAPLANE OPERATIONS AGAINST CUXHAVEN 25 DECEMBER 1914: REPORT.
Anonymous (Admiralty. Training and Staff Duties Division.) | 33.4cm x 21.4cm | blue paper softback | ?pp | ? maps | His Majesty's Stationery Office. | 1915 | English Text.

ACTION OFF JUTLAND 31 MAY - 1 JUNE 1916: NARRATIVE. [C.B.1256/O.U.6169].
Anonymous (Admiralty. Training and Staff Duties Division.) | 33.4cm x 21.4cm | blue paper softback | ?pp | ? maps | His Majesty's Stationery Office. | 1916 | English Text.

GERMAN DESTROYERS: THE THIRD FLOTILLA AND THE ACTION OF 21 APRIL. [C.B.1313 OXO].
Anonymous (Admiralty. Training and Staff Duties Division.) | 33.4cm x 21.4cm | blue paper softback | ?pp | ? maps | His Majesty's Stationery Office. | 1917 | English Text.

THE GERMAN CRUISER SQUADRON IN THE PACIFIC, 1914. [O.U.6029].
Anonymous (Admiralty. Training and Staff Duties Division.) | 33.4cm x 21.4cm | blue paper softback | ?pp | ? maps | His Majesty's Stationery Office. | 1919 | English Text.

OPERATIONS LEADING UP TO THE BATTLE OF CORONEL, NOVEMBER 1914 [O.U.6031].
Anonymous (Admiralty. Training and Staff Duties Division.) | 33.4cm x 21.4cm | blue paper softback | ?pp | ? maps | His Majesty's Stationery Office. | 1919 | English Text.

OPERATION LEADING UP TO THE BATTLE OF THE FALKLAND ISLANDS, NOVEMBER 1914. [O.U.6038].
Anonymous (Admiralty. Training and Staff Duties Division.) | 33.4cm x 21.4cm | blue paper softback | ?pp | ? maps | His Majesty's Stationery Office. | 1919 | English Text.

NAVAL OPERATIONS IN THE CAMEROONS, 1914. [O.U.6039].
Anonymous (Admiralty. Training and Staff Duties Division.) | 33.4cm x 21.4cm | blue paper softback | ?pp | ? maps | His Majesty's Stationery Office. | 1919 | English Text.

OPERATIONS IN THE MEDITERRANEAN, 4 - 10 AUGUST 1914. [O.U.6040]
Anonymous (Admiralty. Training and Staff Duties Division.) | 33.4cm x 21.4cm | blue paper softback | ?pp | ? maps | His Majesty's Stationery Office. | 1919 | English Text.

THE ECONOMIC BLOCKADE, 1914-1919. [C.B.1554].
Anonymous (Admiralty. Training and Staff Duties Division.) | 33.4cm x 21.4cm | blue paper softback | ?pp | ? maps | His Majesty's Stationery Office. | 1920 | English Text.

HISTORY OF BRITISH MINESWEEPING IN THE WAR. [C.B.1553/B.R.315].
Captain Lionel L. Preston | 33.4cm x 21.4cm | blue paper softback | ?pp | ? maps | His Majesty's Stationery Office. | 1920 | English Text.

THE HISTORY OF BRITISH MINE FIELDS. VOLUME I. [C.B. ?].
Captain Lockhart Lieth | 33.4cm x 21.4cm | blue paper softback | ?pp | ? maps | His Majesty's Stationery Office. | 1920 | English Text.

THE HISTORY OF BRITISH MINE FIELDS. VOLUME II. [C.B. ?].
Captain Lockhart Lieth | 33.4cm x 21.4cm | blue paper softback | ?pp | ? maps | His Majesty's Stationery Office. | 1920 | English Text.

THE TENTH CRUISER SQUADRON DURING THE COMMAND OF ADMIRAL DE CHAIR [C.B.935/O.U.5473].
Anonymous (Admiralty. Training and Staff Duties Division.) | 33.4cm x 21.4cm | blue paper softback | ?pp | ? maps | His Majesty's Stationery Office. | 1921 | English Text.

THE EASTERN SQUADRONS, 1914 [C.B.917 (C)/O.U.5413C].
Anonymous (Admiralty. Training and Staff Duties Division.) | 33.4cm x 21.4cm | blue paper softback | ?pp | ? maps | His Majesty's Stationery Office. | 1922 | English Text.

GRAND FLEET GUNNERY AND TORPEDO MEMORANDA ON NAVAL ACTIONS, 1914-1918. [CB925/OU5444].
Anonymous (Admiralty. Gunnery Division.) | 24.3cm x 15.4cm | green paper softback | 66pp | His Majesty's Stationery Office. | 1922 | English Text.

MINING OPERATIONS BY GERMAN SUBMARINES AROUND THE BRITISH ISLES 1915-1918 [O.U.6333]
Anonymous (Admiralty. Training and Staff Duties Division.) | 24.3cm x 15.4cm | paper softback | ?pp | His Majesty's Stationery Office. | 1939 | English Text.

OPERATIONS OFF THE EAST COAST OF GREAT BRITAIN, 1914-1918. [C.B. ?].
> Anonymous (Admiralty. Staff Studies Division.) | 33.4cm x 21.4cm | blue paper softback | 27pp | 4 maps | His Majesty's Stationery Office. | 1940 | English Text.

REVIEW OF GERMAN CRUISER WARFARE 1914-1918 [O.U.6337 (40)].
> Anonymous | 33.4cm x 21.4cm | green paper softback | 34pp | 15 maps | 1 appendix | 16 tables | His Majesty's Stationery Office. | 1940 | English Text.
> There were other Naval Intelligence Blue Papers written, but only the ones known about are listed.

SUBMARINE V. SUBMARINE. – TECHNICAL HISTORY NO. 1 [C,B.01515(1)].
> Anonymous (Admiralty. Technical History Section.) | 33.4cm x 21.4cm | blue paper softback | ?pp | ? maps | His Majesty's Stationery Office. | 1919 | English Text.

NAVAL MEDICAL TRANSPORT DURING THE WAR. – TECHNICAL HISTORY NO. 3 [C.B.01515(3)].
> Anonymous (Admiralty. Technical History Section.) | 33.4cm x 21.4cm | blue paper softback | ?pp | ? maps | His Majesty's Stationery Office. | 1919 | English Text.

AIRCRAFT V. SUBMARINE. SUBMARINE CAMPAIGN, 1918 – TECHNICAL HISTORY NO. 4 [C.B. 01515(4)].
> Anonymous (Admiralty. Technical History Section.) | 33.4cm x 21.4cm | blue paper softback | ?pp | ? maps | His Majesty's Stationery Office. | 1919 | English Text.

THE ANTI-SUBMARINE DIVISION OF THE NAVAL STAFF, DECEMBER 1916-NOVEMBER 1918 – TECHNICAL HISTORY NO. 7 [C.B. 01515(7)].
> Anonymous (Admiralty. Technical History Section.) | 33.4cm x 21.4cm | blue paper softback | ?pp | ? maps | His Majesty's Stationery Office. | 1919 | English Text.

SCANDINAVIAN AND EAST COAST CONVOY SYSTEM, 1917-1918 – TECHNICAL HISTORY NO. 8 [C.B.01515(8)].
> Anonymous (Admiralty. Technical History Section.) | 33.4cm x 21.4cm | blue paper softback | ?pp | ? maps | His Majesty's Stationery Office. | 1919 | English Text.

DEFENSIVE ARMING OF MERCHANT SHIPS – TECHNICAL HISTORY NO. 13 [C.B.01515(13)].
> Anonymous (Admiralty. Technical History Section.) | 33.4cm x 21.4cm | blue paper softback | ?pp | ? maps | His Majesty's Stationery Office. | 1919 | English Text.

THE ATLANTIC CONVOY SYSTEM, 1917-1918 – TECHNICAL HISTORY NO. 14 [C.B.01515(14)].
> Anonymous (Admiralty. Technical History Section.) | 33.4cm x 21.4cm | blue paper softback | ?pp | ? maps | His Majesty's Stationery Office. | 1919 | English Text.

CONVOY STATISTICS AND DIAGRAMS – TECHNICAL HISTORY NO. 15 [C.B.01515(15)].
> Anonymous (Admiralty. Technical History Section.) | 33.4cm x 21.4cm | blue paper softback | ?pp | ? maps | His Majesty's Stationery Office. | 1920 | English Text.

THE DEVELOPMENT OF THE GYRO-COMPASS PRIOR TO AND DURING THE WAR TECHNICAL HISTORY NO. 20 [C.B. 01515(20)].
> Anonymous (Admiralty. Technical History Section.) | 33.4cm x 21.4cm | blue paper softback | ?pp | ? maps | His Majesty's Stationery Office. | 1920 | English Text.

SUBMARINE ADMINISTRATION, TRAINING, AND CONSTRUCTION. – TECHNICAL HISTORY NO. 21 [C.B.01515(21)].
> Anonymous (Admiralty. Technical History Section.) | 33.4cm x 21.4cm | blue paper softback | ?pp | ? maps | His Majesty's Stationery Office. | 1920 | English Text.

FIRE CONTROL IN H.M. SHIPS. – TECHNICAL HISTORY NO. 23 [C.B. 01515(23)].
> Anonymous (Admiralty. Technical History Section.) | 33.4cm x 21.4cm | blue paper softback | ?pp | ? maps | His Majesty's Stationery Office. | 1920 | English Text.

STORAGE AND HANDLING OF EXPLOSIVES IN WARSHIPS. – TECHNICAL HISTORY NO. 24 [C.B. 01515(24)].
> Anonymous (Admiralty. Technical History Section.) | 33.4cm x 21.4cm | blue paper softback | ?pp | ? maps | His Majesty's Stationery Office. | 1920 | English Text.

GUINS AND GUN MOUNTINGS. – TECHNICAL HISTORY NO. 28 [C.B.01515(28)].
> Anonymous (Admiralty. Technical History Section.) | 33.4cm x 21.4cm | blue paper softback | ?pp | ? maps | His Majesty's Stationery Office. | 1920 | English Text.

AMMUNITION FOR NAVAL GUNS. – TECHNICAL HISTORY NO. 29 [C.B.01515(29)].

Anonymous (Admiralty. Technical History Section.) | 33.4cm x 21.4cm | blue paper softback | ?pp | ? maps | His Majesty's Stationery Office. | 1920 | English Text.

CONTROL OF MERCANTILE MOVEMENTS. PART I TEXT – TECHNICAL HISTORY NO. 30 [C.B.01515(30)].

Anonymous (Admiralty. Technical History Section.) | 33.4cm x 21.4cm | blue paper softback | ?pp | ? maps | His Majesty's Stationery Office. | 1920 | English Text.

CONTROL OF MERCANTILE MOVEMENTS. PART II APPENDICES – TECHNICAL HISTORY NO. 31 [C.B.01515(31)].

Anonymous (Admiralty. Technical History Section.) | 33.4cm x 21.4cm | blue paper softback | ?pp | ? maps | His Majesty's Stationery Office. | 1920 | English Text.

CONTROL OF MERCANTILE MOVEMENTS. PART III PLANS – TECHNICAL HISTORY NO. 32 [C.B.01515(32)].

Anonymous (Admiralty. Technical History Section.) | 33.4cm x 21.4cm | blue paper softback | ?pp | ? maps | His Majesty's Stationery Office. | 1920 | English Text.

INCEPTION AND DEVELOPMENT OF THE NORTHERN BASE (SCAPA FLOW). CONVOYS – TECHNICAL HISTORY NO. 37 [C.B.01515(37)].

Anonymous (Admiralty. Technical History Section.) | 33.4cm x 21.4cm | blue paper softback | ?pp | ? maps | His Majesty's Stationery Office. | 1920 | English Text.

MISCELLANEOUS CONVOYS – TECHNICAL HISTORY NO. 39 [C.B.01515(39)].

Anonymous (Admiralty. Technical History Section.) | 33.4cm x 21.4cm | blue paper softback | ?pp | ? maps | His Majesty's Stationery Office. | 1920 | English Text.

ANTI-SUBMARINE DEVELOPMENT AND EXPERIMENTS PRIOR TO DECEMBER 1916. – TECHNICAL HISTORY NO. 40 [C.B.01515(40)].

Anonymous (Admiralty. Technical History Section.) | 33.4cm x 21.4cm | blue paper softback | ?pp | ? maps | His Majesty's Stationery Office. | 1920 | English Text.

ADMIRALTY AIRSHIP SHEDS. – TECHNICAL HISTORY NO. 43 [C.B.01515(43)].

Anonymous (Admiralty. Technical History Section.) | 33.4cm x 21.4cm | blue paper softback | ?pp | ? maps | His Majesty's Stationery Office. | 1920 | English Text.

DEVELOPMENT OF THE PARAVANE – TECHNICAL HISTORY NO. 51 [C.B.01515(51)].

Anonymous (Admiralty. Technical History Section.) | 33.4cm x 21.4cm | blue paper softback | ?pp | ? maps | His Majesty's Stationery Office. | 1920 | English Text.

CORONEL. - MONOGRAPH NO. 1 [C.B.917/O.U.5413].

Anonymous (Admiralty. Training and Staff Duties Division.) | 33.4cm x 21.4cm | blue paper softback | ?pp | ? maps | His Majesty's Stationery Office. | 1919 | English Text.
This monograph was superseded by monograph no. 27.

GERMAN CRUISER SQUADRON IN THE PACIFIC. - MONOGRAPH NO. 2 [C.B.917/O.U.5413].

Anonymous (Admiralty. Training and Staff Duties Division.) | 33.4cm x 21.4cm | blue paper softback | ?pp | ? maps | His Majesty's Stationery Office. | 1920 | English Text.

FALKLANDS. - MONOGRAPH NO. 3 [C.B.917/O.U.5413].

Anonymous (Admiralty. Training and Staff Duties Division.) | 33.4cm x 21.4cm | blue paper softback | ?pp | ? maps | His Majesty's Stationery Office. | 1919 | English Text.
This monograph was superseded by monograph no. 27.

GOEBEN AND BRESLAU. - MONOGRAPH NO. 4 [C.B.917/O.U.5413].

Anonymous (Admiralty. Training and Staff Duties Division.) | 33.4cm x 21.4cm | blue paper softback | ?pp | ? maps | His Majesty's Stationery Office. | 1919 | English Text.
It would appears that the first four monographs were group together and issued with the same C.B./O.U. numbers.
This monograph was superseded by monograph no. 21.

CAMEROONS, 1914. - MONOGRAPH NO. 5 [C.B.917A/O.U.5413A].

Anonymous (Admiralty. Training and Staff Duties Division.) | 33.4cm x 21.4cm | blue paper softback | ?pp | ? maps | His Majesty's Stationery Office. | 1919 | English Text.

PASSAGE OF THE BRITISH EXPEDITIONARY FORCE, AUG. 1914. - MONOGRAPH NO. 6 [C.B. ?].

Anonymous (Admiralty. Training and Staff Duties Division.) | 33.4cm x 21.4cm | blue paper softback | ?pp | ? maps | His Majesty's Stationery Office. | 1919 | English Text.

THE PATROL FLOTILLAS AT THE COMMENCEMENT OF THE WAR. - MONOGRAPH NO. 7 [C.B. ?].

Anonymous (Admiralty. Training and Staff Duties Division.) | 33.4cm x 21.4cm | blue paper softback | ?pp | ? maps | His Majesty's Stationery Office. | 1919 | English Text.

NAVAL OPERATIONS CONNECTED WITH THE RAID ON THE NORTH-EAST COAST, DECEMBER 16TH 1914. - MONOGRAPH NO. 8 [C.B.1552].

Anonymous (Admiralty. Training and Staff Duties Division.) | 33.4cm x 21.4cm | blue paper softback | 38pp | 3 maps | 4 appendices | His Majesty's Stationery Office. | 1920 | English Text.

This monograph was was revised and included in monograph no. 28.

A HISTORY OF THE WHITE SEA STATION, 1914-1919. - MONOGRAPH NO. 9 [C.B.1555A /O.U.6244A].

Anonymous (Admiralty. Training and Staff Duties Division.) | 33.4cm x 21.4cm | blue paper softback | 77pp | 5 photograph | 1 map | His Majesty's Stationery Office. | 1921 | English Text.

EAST AFRICA TO JULY 1915. - MONOGRAPH NO. 10 [C.B.917A/O.U.5413A].

Anonymous (Admiralty. Training and Staff Duties Division.) | 33.4cm x 21.4cm | blue paper softback | ?pp | ? maps | His Majesty's Stationery Office. | 1921 | English Text.

THE BATTLE OF HELIGOLAND BIGHT, AUGUST 28TH 1914. - MONOGRAPH NO. 11 [C.B. ?].

Anonymous (Admiralty. Training and Staff Duties Division.) | 33.4cm x 21.4cm | blue paper softback | ?pp | ? maps | His Majesty's Stationery Office. | 1921 | English Text.

THE ACTION OF DOGGER BANK, JAN. 24TH 1915. - MONOGRAPH NO. 12 [C.B.1585/O.U.6181].

Anonymous (Admiralty. Training and Staff Duties Division.) | 33.4cm x 21.4cm | blue paper softback | ?pp | ? maps | His Majesty's Stationery Office. | 1921 | English Text.

SUMMARY OF THE OPERATIONS OF THE GRAND FLEET, AUGUST 1914 TO NOVEMBER 1916. - MONOGRAPH NO. 13 [C.B. ?].

Anonymous (Admiralty. Training and Staff Duties Division.) | 33.4cm x 21.4cm | blue paper softback | ?pp | ? maps | His Majesty's Stationery Office. | 1921 | English Text.

THE FIRST AUSTRALIAN CONVOY, 1914 – MONOGRAPH NO. 14 [C.B. ?].

Anonymous (Admiralty. Training and Staff Duties Division.) | 33.4cm x 21.4cm | blue paper softback | ?pp | ? maps | His Majesty's Stationery Office. | 1921 | English Text.

NAVAL OPERATIONS IN MESOPOTAMIA AND THE PERSIAN GULF - MONOGRAPH NO. 15 [C.B.917B(1)/O.U.5413B].

Anonymous (Admiralty. Training and Staff Duties Division.) | 33.4cm x 21.4cm | blue paper softback | ?pp | ? maps | His Majesty's Stationery Office. | 1921 | English Text.

THE CHINA SQUADRON, 1914 – MONOGRAPH NO. 16 [C.B. ?].

Anonymous (Admiralty. Training and Staff Duties Division.) | 33.4cm x 21.4cm | blue paper softback | ?pp |? maps | His Majesty's Stationery Office. | 1922 | English Text.

THE EAST INDIES SQUADRON, 1914 – MONOGRAPH NO. 17 [C.B. ?].

Anonymous (Admiralty. Training and Staff Duties Division.) | 33.4cm x 21.4cm | blue paper softback | ?pp |? maps | His Majesty's Stationery Office. | 1922 | English Text.

THE DOVER COMMAND, VOLUME I. - MONOGRAPH NO. 18 [C.B. 917D/O.U.5413D].

Anonymous (Admiralty. Training and Staff Duties Division.) | 33.4cm x 21.4cm | blue paper softback | ?pp |? maps | His Majesty's Stationery Office. | 1922 | English Text.

There was not a volume II produced.

TENTH CRUISER SQUADRON VOLUME I - MONOGRAPH NO. 19 [C.B.917E/ O.U.5413E].

Anonymous (Admiralty. Training and Staff Duties Division.) | 33.4cm x 21.4cm | blue paper softback | ?pp | ? maps | His Majesty's Stationery Office. | 1922 | English Text.

There was not a volume II produced. This monograph covered the period August 1914 to February 1916.

THE CAPE OF GOOD HOPE STATION, 1914 – MONOGRAPH NO. 20 [C.B. ?].

Anonymous (Admiralty. Training and Staff Duties Division.) | 33.4cm x 21.4cm | blue paper softback | ?pp |? maps | His Majesty's Stationery Office. | 1922 | English Text.

THE MEDITERRANEAN, 1914-1915 - MONOGRAPH NO. 21 [C.B.917F/ O.U.5413F].

Anonymous (Admiralty. Training and Staff Duties Division.) | 33.4cm x 21.4cm | blue paper softback | ?pp | ? maps | His Majesty's Stationery Office. | 1923 | English Text.

THE ATLANTIC OCEAN: 1914-1915, INCLUDING THE BATTLES OF CORONEL AND THE FALKLAND ISLANDS. - MONOGRAPH NO. 22 [C.B. 917(G)/O.U.5413G].

Anonymous (Admiralty. Training and Staff Duties Division.) | 33.4cm x 21.4cm | blue paper softback | ?pp | ? maps | His Majesty's Stationery Office. | 1923 | English Text.

HOME WATERS, PART I: FROM THE OUTBREAK OF WAR TO 27 AUGUST 1914. - MONOGRAPH NO. 23 [C.B.917H /O.U.5528].

Anonymous (Admiralty. Training and Staff Duties Division.) | 33.4cm x 21.4cm | blue paper softback | ?pp | ? maps | His Majesty's Stationery Office. | 1924 | English Text.

HOME WATERS, PART II: SEPTEMBER-OCTOBER 1914. - MONOGRAPH NO. 24 [C.B.917I/O.U.5528A].

Anonymous (Admiralty. Training and Staff Duties Division.) | 33.4cm x 21.4cm | blue paper softback | ?pp | ? maps | His Majesty's Stationery Office. | 1924 | English Text.
Short title: Atlantic i.

THE BALTIC, 1914 - MONOGRAPH NO. 25 [C.B.917E/O.U.5413E].

Anonymous (Admiralty. Training and Staff Duties Division.) | 33.4cm x 21.4cm | blue paper softback | ?pp | ? maps | His Majesty's Stationery Office. | 1924 | English Text.

THE ATLANTIC OCEAN: FROM THE BATTLE OF THE FALKLANDS TO MAY 1915 - MONOGRAPH NO. 26 [C.B. ?].

Anonymous (Admiralty. Training and Staff Duties Division.) | 33.4cm x 21.4cm | blue paper softback | ?pp | ? maps | His Majesty's Stationery Office. | 1924 | English Text.
Short title: Atlantic ii.

THE BATTLES OF CORONEL AND THE FALKLAND ISLANDS - MONOGRAPH NO. 27 [C.B. ?].

Anonymous (Admiralty. Training and Staff Duties Division.) | 33.4cm x 21.4cm | blue paper softback | ?pp | ? maps | His Majesty's Stationery Office. | 1924 | English Text.

HOME WATERS, PART III : FROM NOVEMBER 1914 TO THE END OF JANUARY 1915. - MONOGRAPH NO. 28 [C.B.917J/O.U.5528B].

Anonymous (Admiralty. Training and Staff Duties Division.) | 33.4cm x 21.4cm | blue paper softback | ?pp | ? maps | His Majesty's Stationery Office. | 1925 | English Text.

HOME WATERS, PART IV : FROM FEBRUARY TO JULY 1915. - MONOGRAPH NO. 29 [O.U.5528C].

Anonymous (Admiralty. Training and Staff Duties Division.) | 33.4cm x 21.4cm | blue paper softback | ?pp | ? maps | His Majesty's Stationery Office. | 1925 | English Text.

HOME WATERS, PART V : FROM JULY TO OCTOBER 1915. - MONOGRAPH NO. 30 [C.B.917L/O.U.5528D].

Anonymous (Admiralty. Training and Staff Duties Division.) | 33.4cm x 21.4cm | blue paper softback | ?pp | ? maps | His Majesty's Stationery Office. | 1926 | English Text.

HOME WATERS, PART VI : FROM OCTOBER 1915 TO MAY 1916. - MONOGRAPH NO. 31 [C.B.917M/O.U.5528E].

Anonymous (Admiralty. Training and Staff Duties Division.) | 33.4cm x 21.4cm | blue paper softback | ?pp | ? maps | His Majesty's Stationery Office. | 1926 | English Text.

LOWESTOFT RAID, 24TH-25TH APRIL 1916. - MONOGRAPH NO. 32 [C.B.917N/ O.U.5413H].

Anonymous (Admiralty. Training and Staff Duties Division.) | 33.4cm x 21.4cm | blue paper softback | ?pp | ? maps | His Majesty's Stationery Office. | 1927 | English Text.

HOME WATERS, PART VII : FROM JUNE 1916 TO NOVEMBER 1916. - MONOGRAPH NO. 33 [C.B.917B/O.U.5528F].

Anonymous (Admiralty. Training and Staff Duties Division.) | 33.4cm x 21.4cm | blue paper softback | ?pp | ? maps | His Majesty's Stationery Office. | 1927 | English Text.

HOME WATERS, PART VIII : DECEMBER 1916 TO APRIL 1917. - MONOGRAPH NO. 34 [C.B. ?].

Anonymous (Admiralty. Training and Staff Duties Division.) | 33.4cm x 21.4cm | blue paper softback | ?pp | ? maps | His Majesty's Stationery Office. | 1927 | English Text.

HOME WATERS, PART IX : MAY 1917 -JULY, 1917. - MONOGRAPH NO. 35 [C.B. ?].

Anonymous (Admiralty. Training and Staff Duties Division.) | 33.4cm x 21.4cm | blue paper softback | ?pp | ? maps | His Majesty's Stationery Office. | 1928 | English Text.

ORGANISATION OF THE ARCHANGEL RIVER FLOTILLA 1919 [C.B.918/O.U.5443].

Anonymous (Admiralty. Training and Staff Duties Division.) | 33.4cm x 21.4cm | blue paper softback | ?pp | ? maps | His Majesty's Stationery Office. | 1920 | English Text.
This monograph was not given a sequence number.

MEDITERRANEAN STAFF PAPERS RELATING TO NAVAL OPERATIONS FROM AUGUST 1917 TO DECEMBER 1918 [C.B. ?].

Anonymous (Admiralty. Training and Staff Duties Division.) (Admiralty. Training and Staff Duties Division.) | 33.4cm x 21.4cm | blue paper softback | v + 135pp | 5 photograph | ? maps | His Majesty's Stationery Office. | 1920 | English Text.

This monograph was not given a sequence number.

NAVAL STAFF APPRECIATION OF JUTLAND [C.B. 938]

Anonymous (*Captain* A.C.(Alfred Charles) Dewar, R.N. and *Captain* K.G.B.(Kenneth Gilbert Balmain) Dewar, R.N.) | 33.4cm x 21.4cm | blue paper softback | ?pp | ? maps | His Majesty's Stationery Office. | 1922 | English Text.

This monograph was not given a sequence number.

The Naval Staff's monograph '**Naval Staff Appreciation of Jutland**' was written in 1921-1922 under the authority of *Admiral* David Beatty. However it caused a great deal of concern amongst senior Naval Officers at the Admiralty, who then at the time of completion prevented the release of the monograph. The controversy surrounding this book lasted a number of years until the then First Sea Lord *Admiral* Madden took it upon himself to order the pulping of all the copies of the book. Few if any copies have survived.

THE NAVAL STAFF OF THE ADMIRALTY. ITS WORK AND DEVELOPMENT. [B.R.1875].

Anonymous (Admiralty. Training and Staff Duties Division.) | 33.4cm x 21.4cm | blue paper softback | v + 135pp | 5 photograph | ? maps | His Majesty's Stationery Office. | 1929 | English Text.

This monograph was not given a sequence number.

There were other Naval Staff College Text Books written, but only the ones known about are listed.

OFFICIAL RECORD OF THE BATTLE OF JUTLAND.

Captain J.E.P. [John Ernest Troyes] Harper, R.N. et al. | 25cm x 16cm | blue cloth hardback | 121pp | 4 tables | 10 appendices (see note below) | His Majesty's Stationery Office. | 1920 | English Text.

This volume "**Official Record of the Battle of Jutland**" was only published as proof copies. It was issued to a limited number of proof readers within the Admiralty, and is commonly known as "**Harper's Record**". Only a few copies have survived; however the original draft manuscript and some of the returned proof copies have survived and can be found in the Harper papers located in the British Museum (MSS. 54477-54480). See also the note for the "**Reproduction of the Record of the Battle of Jutland**" below.

REPRODUCTION OF THE RECORD OF THE BATTLE OF JUTLAND. [Cmd. 2870].

Captain J.E.P.[John Ernest Troyes] Harper, R.N. et al. | 25cm x 16cm | blue cloth hardback | 121pp | 4 tables | 10 appendices (see note below) | His Majesty's Stationery Office. | 1927 | English Text.

Officially to quote the Explanatory Note 5 (page iv.) from this monograph:

"During the preparation of the work information was accumulating from German sources, and it became evident that an account based solely upon British official evidence would be incorrect, and its publication therefore unjustifiable. This new information showed that substantial corrections were necessary in the diagrams.

It was therefore decided to expend the chronological Record into a more connected Narrative that would present the course of the Action as seen from both sides.

Objections were put forward by the Publishers [Longmans, Green & Co.] of Sir Julian Corbett's work, however to the issue of a Narrative closely in advance of *Sir* Julian Corbett's volume containing his account of the Battle. It was decided therefore to place the record prepared by Captain Harper and his associates, and all the material in the possession of the Admiralty, at *Sir* Julian Corbett's disposal, to be published or used as he saw fit…"

However in the words of Captain A.C. Dewar in his hand written introduction to his copy of this monograph:

"Between 1919-1926 there was much talk & writing about Harper's Report not having been published & that the truth & the great secret would be found in Harper's Report I suggested to D.T.S.D. Director Training and Staff Duties (Captain Noel Laurence), to which my Section (Historical Section) was attached that Harper's Record should be published without the correction of a single word as finally submitted for printing by Captain Harper."

There is however another version of the events to the delay in the publication of this monograph. Almost from the moment that the Battle of Jutland finished, a controversy began within the British Admiralty over the handling of the British forces during the battle. There was a good deal of animosity between *Admiral* John *Viscount* Jellicoe (Commander-in-Chief of the Grand Fleet during the battle) and *Admiral* David *Earl* Beatty (commander of the Battlecrusier Fleet during the battle) along with their respective supporters. The "**Official Record of the Battle of Jutland**", was written during the period 1919-1920 at the request of the then First Sea Lord of the Admiralty *Admiral Sir* Rosslyn Wemyss. *Captain* John Harper was selected to write the report which was to be the Admiralty official account of the battle. By the time it had been completed, Wemyss had been replaced as the First Sea Lord by Beatty, who insisted on revisions, to which Jellicoe immediately objected. Due to this disagreement, Harper refused to revise his monograph with the result that all the proof copies were ordered to be destroyed and a new monograph was to be prepared, but using different and more sympathetic authors to Beatty, namely the Dewar brothers. This replacement monograph was issued as the "**Naval Staff Appreciation of Jutland [C.B. 0938]**".

However not all the copies of the original monograph were destroyed (for example as well as the copies in Harper's possession, Beatty still had his own copy which is to be found today in the National Maritime Museum, Greenwich) and when *Admiral Sir* Charles Madden (Jellicoe's brother-in-law) took over the office of First Sea Lord from Beatty in 1927, he ordered its publication. However, there is still some speculation that the "**Official Record of the Battle of Jutland**" had its text revised for the new monograph.

The author's name was incorrectly printed on the covers and title page as J.E.P. Harper instead of his correct name J.E.T. Harper.

On the title page of this volume it is stated under the author's name 'by direction of the Admiralty', however it is then stated in the Explanatory Note 3 (page iii.) by the Admiralty that 'this [volume] is not regarded as an official report'.

Although all the appendices are shown at the rear of this volume; the last three were left blank since they had been published in "**Battle of Jutland 30th May To 1st June 1916 Official Despatches with Appendices [Cmd. 1068]**" of 1920, there being a reference regarding this under the appendices titles. The eighteen coloured diagrams that were prepared for the "**Official Record of the Battle of Jutland**" were not issued with this volume although there was a note stating that copies of them could be viewed at the Admiralty.

NARRATIVE OF THE BATTLE OF JUTLAND.

Anonymous (*Captain* A.C.(Alfred Charles) Dewar, R.N. and *Captain* K.G.B.(Kenneth Gilbert Balmain) Dewar, R.N.) l 25cm x 16cm l blue cloth hardback l iv + 121pp l 45 maps l 2 tables l 7 appendices l His Majesty's Stationery Office. l 1924 l English Text.

Like "**The Record of the Battle of Jutland**" above, the monograph "**Naval Staff Appreciation of Jutland [C.B. 0938]** " caused a similar stir amongst the senior naval officers at the Admiralty at the time of its completion. With its strong bais towards Beatty, its release was prevented and in its place a censored version was produced and renamed the "**Narrative of The Battle of Jutland**". It was printed and dated 1924; however it was not released for public consumption until 1925.

Print run of 1500 copies.

THE LOSS OF H.M.S. HAMPSHIRE ON 5TH JUNE 1916. [Cmd. 2710].

Anonymous (Admiralty) l 25cm x 16cm l blue cloth hardback l 28pp l His Majesty's Stationery Office. l 1926 l English Text.

OFFICIAL RECORD OF THE SURRENDER OF THE GERMAN FLEET, THE TRIUMPH OF THE ROYAL NAVY.

[*Major*] Perceval Gibbon (R.M.) l 33.4cm x 21.4cm l white paper softback l 48pp l ? photograph l Hodder & Stoughton Limited. l 1919 l English Text.

This photograph album was published by the authority of the Admiralty.

HISTORICAL RESEARCH MEMORANDUM NO. 1: SURFACE AND AIR ANTI-SUBMARINE ESCORT OF SHIPPING IN CONVOY, AND ANTI-SUBMARINE TRANSIT AREA PATROLS IN TWO WORLD WARS.

Anonymous (Admiralty Historical Section) | 33.4cm x 21.4cm | blue paper softback | ?pp | His Majesty's Stationery Office. | 1953 | English Text.

This memorandum is a general history of the anti-submarine work with regard to convoys with the first part covering the Great War.

NOTES ON THE CONVOY SYSTEM OF NAVAL WARFARE, THIRTEENTH TO TWENTIETH CENTURIES. PART 2: FIRST WORLD WAR, 1914-18.

Anonymous (Admiralty Historical Section) | 33.4cm x 21.4cm | blue paper softback | ?pp | His Majesty's Stationery Office. | 1960 | English Text.

These notes are a general history of convoys with only part 2 covering the Great War.

Military;

Military History for the Staff College: A Brief Summary of the Campaigns, With Questions and Answers.

Captain E.W.[Eric William] Sheppard *OBE., MC.* | 24.8cm x 19.7cm | red cloth hardback | xi + 122pp | 9 folding maps | 1 appendix | Gale & Polden, Ltd. | 1932 | English Text.

This text book 'Military History for the Staff College: A Brief Summary of the Campaigns, With Questions and Answers' covered campaigns of previous wars as well as the Great War. This volume was revised to the new Staff College Regulations and republished in 1937. An Addenda was released in accordance to the revised 1939 syllabus two years later.

A BRIEF RECORD OF THE ADVANCE OF THE EGYPTIAN EXPEDITIONARY FORCE UNDER THE COMMAND OF GENERAL SIR EDMUND H.H. ALLENBY G.C.B., G.C.M.G. - JULY 1917 TO OCTOBER 1918. – Compiled from Official Sources.

Lieutenant-Colonel H. Pirie-Gordon (Editor) et al. | 28.4cm x 22cm | karki paper broads/ karki cloth covered spine hardback | vi + 113 + 112pp | 1 photograph | 56 maps | His Majesty's Stationery Office. | 1919 | English Text.

This volume **"A Brief Record of the Advance of the Egyptian Expeditionary Force"** was the Second Edition. The first edition was published in "The Palestine News."

An abbreviated title was printed on the front cover: 'A Brief Record of the Advance of the Egyptian Expeditionary Force July 1917 to October 1918 Compiled from Official Sources' in title case.

It has often been noted that the two sections covering the Arab Movement and their desert revolt in this volume were attributed, although not acknowledged, by *Colonel* T.E. Lawrence. It would appears that Lawrence's contributions were extracted from his official reports and can be found in the descriptions of the "Sherifian Co-operation in September." and the "Story of the Arab Movement" located opposite the plates 48-52.

OPERATIONS OF I.E.F. [Indian Expeditionary Force] "D" IN MESOPOTAMIA 1914-1917

Anonymous (General Head Quarters I.E.F. "D".) | 17.3cm x 10.8cm | white paper softback | 11pp | 1 folding map | General Head Quarters I.E.F.. | 1917 | English Text.

CRITICAL STUDY OF THE CAMPAIGN IN MESOPOTAMIA UP TO APRIL 1917.

Anonymous (Quetta Army Staff College) | 24cm x 21.4cm | white paper softback | ii + 361pp | 19 photograph plates | His Majesty's Stationery Office. | 1925 | English Text.

This is the report written by members of the Army Staff College, Quetta, India, October-November 1923.

CRITICAL STUDY OF THE CAMPAIGN IN MESOPOTAMIA UP TO APRIL 1917. [map folder]

Anonymous (Quetta Army Staff College) | 24cm x 21.4cm | white paper softback | 26 maps | His Majesty's Stationery Office. | 1925 | English Text.

REPORT OF THE COMMITTEE ON THE LESSONS OF THE GREAT WAR. (War Office).

Anonymous (*Major General* A.E. McNamara - Kirke Committee) | 33.4cm x 21.4cm | white paper softback | 128pp | His Majesty's Stationery Office. | 1932 | English Text.

This is the report written up by the 'Kirke Committee' commonly known as the 'Kirke Report.' It was republished as a British Army Review Special Edition – April 2001.

There were probably other Army Staff Papers written, but only the ones known about are listed.

CORRESPONDENCE RELATING TO THE MILITARY OPERATIONS IN THE TOGOLAND. [Cd.7872].

Anonymous | 33.4cm x 21.4cm | white paper softback | 49pp | 1 map | 6 tables | His Majesty's Stationery Office. | 1915 | English Text.

CORRESPONDENCE RELATING TO THE OCCUPATION OF THE GERMAN SAMOA BY AN EXPEDITIONARY FORCE FROM NEW ZEALAND. [Cd.7972].

Anonymous | 33.4cm x 21.4cm | white paper softback | 14pp | His Majesty's Stationery Office. | 1915 | English Text.

CORRESPONDENCE RESPECTING MILITARY OPERATIONS AGAINST GERMAN POSSESSIONS IN THE WESTERN PACIFIC. [Cd.7975].

Anonymous | 33.4cm x 21.4cm | white paper softback | 26pp | His Majesty's Stationery Office. | 1915 | English Text.

CORRESPONDENCE RELATIVE TO THE ALLEGED ILL-TREATMENT OF GERMAN SUBJECTS CAPTURED IN THE CAMEROONS. [Cd. .] Revised.

Anonymous | 33.4cm x 21.4cm | white paper softback | 47pp | His Majesty's Stationery Office. | 19159 | English Text.

The command paper number was left blank for this paper.

MESOPOTAMIA COMMISSION. REPORT OF THE Commission Appointed by Act of Parliament to Enquire into the Operations of War IN MESOPOTAMIA TOGETHER WITH A Separate Report BY COMMANDER J. WEDGWOOD, D.S.O., M.P., AND Appendices. [Cd. 8610].

Anonymous | 33.4cm x 21.4cm | white paper softback | 188pp | 1 map | 1 graph | 3 appendices | His Majesty's Stationery Office. | 1917 | English Text.

DARDANELLES COMMISSION. FIRST REPORT. [Cd. 8490].

Anonymous | 33.4cm x 21.4cm | white paper softback | 60pp | His Majesty's Stationery Office. | 1917 | English Text.

DARDANELLES COMMISSION. SUPPLEMENT TO FIRST REPORT. [Cd. 8502].

Anonymous | 33.4cm x 21.4cm | white paper softback | 3pp | His Majesty's Stationery Office. | 1917 | English Text.

THE FINAL REPORT OF THE DARDANELLES COMMISSION. [Cmd. 371].

Anonymous | 33.4cm x 21.4cm | white paper softback | 186pp | 2 large format maps | 2 appendices | 10 tables | His Majesty's Stationery Office. | 1919 | English Text.

Air Activities;

OFFICIAL HISTORY OF THE AIR SERVICES DURING THE WAR [Air Council Précis 149]

H. McAnally | 21.5cm x 14cm | grey blue paper softback | ?pp | His Majesty's Stationery Office. | 1918 | English Text.

A SHORT HISTORY OF THE ROYAL AIR FORCE. [FS Publication 136]

Anonymous (Air Ministry, Air Historical Branch) | 21.5cm x 14cm | grey blue paper softback | 276pp | His Majesty's Stationery Office. | 1920 | English Text.

This volume "**A Short History of the Royal Air Force**" was written as a text book for the R.A.F. College, Cranfield. It has been revised periodically and republished, since it was originally published to bring the text up to date. Known republishing dates are 1927; 1936; 1984 and 1994.

The Imperial War Museum Department of Printed Books in association with the Battery Press republished the 1936 third revised and enlarged edition (iv + 502 pp) of this volume in 1996 as a hardback under the title "**The Royal Air Force in the Great War**". The Battery Press referred to it in their review as "an abridgment of the 7 volume British Official History of the R.F.C./R.A.F. entitled – "**The War in the Air**". This is not the case since the original edition of "**A Short History of the Royal Air Force**" was published in 1920 two years before the first volume of "**The War in the Air**". The Battery Press edition has been given the ISBN: 0-89839-251-9.

SHORT HISTORY OF THE ROYAL NAVAL AIR SERVICE.

J. C. Nerney (Air Ministry, Air Historical Branch) I 21.5cm x 14cm I grey blue paper softback I ?pp I His Majesty's Stationery Office. I nd I English Text.

DEVELOPMENT AND OPERATIONS OF THE R.N.A.S. IN HOME WATERS. PART I, FLEET CO-OPERATION.

J. C. Nerney (Air Ministry, Air Historical Branch) I 21.5cm x 14cm I grey blue paper softback I ?pp I His Majesty's Stationery Office. I ND. c1919 I English Text.

DEVELOPMENT AND OPERATIONS OF THE R.N.A.S. IN HOME WATERS. PART II, SUBMARINE CAMPAIGN. JANUARY 1917 – APRIL 1918

J. C. Nerney (Air Ministry, Air Historical Branch) I 21.5cm x 14cm I grey blue paper softback I ?pp I His Majesty's Stationery Office. I ND. c1919 I English Text.

DEVELOPMENT AND OPERATIONS OF THE R.N.A.S. IN HOME WATERS. PART III, BELGIUM COAST OPERATIONS. 1917.

J. C. Nerney (Air Ministry, Air Historical Branch) I 21.5cm x 14cm I grey blue paper softback I ?pp I His Majesty's Stationery Office. I ND. c1919 I English Text.

THE R.A.F. IN THE BOMBER OFFENSIVE AGAINST GERMANY VOLUME 1: PRE-WAR EVOLUTION OF BOMBER COMMAND, 1917-1939

Anonymous (Air Ministry, Air Historical Branch) I 21.5cm x 14cm I grey blue paper softback I ?pp I His Majesty's Stationery Office. I ND. c1950 I English Text.

This monograph "**The R.A.F. in the Bomber Offensive against Germany**" is the first part of a set that is a general history of bomber offensive operations with the first part of this volume covering the Great War period.

PHOTOGRAPHIC RECONNAISSANCE VOLUME 1, 1914-APR. 1941

Anonymous (Air Ministry, Air Historical Branch) I 21.5cm x 14cm I grey blue paper softback I ?pp I His Majesty's Stationery Office. I ND. c1950 I English Text.

This monograph "**Photographic Reconnaissance**" is the first part of a set that is a general history of the use of aerial photographic reconnaissance with the first part of this volume covering the Great War period.

AIR ATTACKS ON OSTEND-ZEEBRUGGE-BRUGES DISTRICTS.

Captain M.F.[Murray Fraser] Sueter (Historical Branch) I 21.5cm x 14cm I grey blue paper softback I ?pp I His Majesty's Stationery Office. I 1915 I English Text.

HISTORY OF ANTI-SUBMARINE CAMPAIGN, 1914-1917.

J. C. Nerney (Air Ministry, Air Historical Branch) I 21.5cm x 14cm I grey blue paper softback I ?pp I His Majesty's Stationery Office. I ND. c1919 I English Text.

REVIEW OF AIRCRAFT ANTI-SUBMARINE CAMPAIGN, 1918.

Lieutenant Colonel L.H. Strain (Air Ministry, Air Historical Branch) I 21.5cm x 14cm I grey blue paper softback I ?pp I His Majesty's Stationery Office. I ND. c1919 I English Text.

BALLOON DEFENCES, 1914-1945

Anonymous (Air Ministry, Air Historical Branch) I 21.5cm x 14cm I grey blue paper softback I ?pp I His Majesty's Stationery Office. I ND. c1950 I English Text.

BALLOON DEFENCES, APPENDICES AND MAPS

Anonymous (Air Ministry, Air Historical Branch) I 21.5cm x 14cm I grey blue paper softback I ?pp I His Majesty's Stationery Office. I ND. c1950 I English Text.

This monograph "**Balloon Defences**" is a general history of the use of balloons in air defence with the first part covering the Great War.

Statistics;

STATISTICAL REVIEW OF THE WAR AGAINST MERCHANT SHIPPING.

Anonymous (Naval Director of Statistics) I 33.4cm x 21.4cm I blue paper softback I 37pp I 4 large format maps I His Majesty's Stationery Office. I 1918 I English Text.

STATISTICAL ABSTRACT OF INFORMATION REGARDING THE ARMIES AT HOME AND ABROAD, 1914-1920.

Anonymous (War Office Committee) | 33.4cm x 21.4cm | white paper softback | 876pp | His Majesty's Stationery Office. | 1920 | English Text.

MEMORANDUM UPON THE TABULATION OF MEDICAL AND SURGICAL STATISTICS OF THE WAR.

Anonymous (Medical Research Committee) | 33.4cm x 21.4cm | white paper softback | 33pp | His Majesty's Stationery Office. | 1918 | English Text.

Despatches;

I. NAVAL AND MILITARY DESPATCHES, RELATING TO OPERATIONS IN THE WAR. SEPTEMBER, OCTOBER AND NOVEMBER 1914.

Anonymous | 24cm x 15cm | blue paper softback | 89pp | 1 map | His Majesty's Stationery Office. | 1915 | English Text.
Reprinted 1920.

II. NAVAL AND MILITARY DESPATCHES, RELATING TO OPERATIONS IN THE WAR. PART II. NOVEMBER 1914. - JUNE 1915.

Anonymous | 24cm x 15cm | blue paper softback | 204pp | 1 map | His Majesty's Stationery Office. | 1915 | English Text.

III. NAVAL AND MILITARY DESPATCHES, RELATING TO OPERATIONS IN THE WAR. PART III. JULY 1915 - OCTOBER 1915.

Anonymous | 24cm x 15cm | blue paper softback | 79pp | 2 tables | His Majesty's Stationery Office. | 1916 | English Text.
The first three Despatches were numbered with consecutive numbers i.e. 1-89, 90-293 and 294-372.

IV. NAVAL AND MILITARY DESPATCHES, RELATING TO OPERATIONS IN THE WAR. PART IV. DESPATCH, DATED 11th DECEMBER 1915 FROM GENERAL SIR IAN HAMILTON G.C.B., DESCRIBING THE OPERATIONS IN THE GALLIPOLI PENINSULA, INCLUDING THE LANDING AT SUVLA BAY.

General Sir Ian Hamilton *G.C.B.* | 24cm x 15cm | blue paper softback | 48pp | 2 tables | His Majesty's Stationery Office. | 1916 | English Text.

V. NAVAL AND MILITARY DESPATCHES, RELATING TO OPERATIONS IN THE WAR. PART V. (PUBLISHED IN THE "LONDON GAZETTE," JANUARY TO APRIL 1916.)

Anonymous | 24cm x 15cm | blue paper softback | 196pp | 1 table | His Majesty's Stationery Office. | 1916 | English Text.

VI. NAVAL AND MILITARY DESPATCHES, RELATING TO OPERATIONS IN THE WAR. PART VI. (PUBLISHED IN THE "LONDON GAZETTE," MAY TO DECEMBER 1916.)

Anonymous | 24cm x 15cm | blue paper softback | 255pp | His Majesty's Stationery Office. | 1917 | English Text.

VII. NAVAL AND MILITARY DESPATCHES, RELATING TO OPERATIONS IN THE WAR. PART VII. (PUBLISHED IN THE "LONDON GAZETTE," DECEMBER 1916, TO JULY 1917.)

Anonymous | 24cm x 15cm | blue paper softback | 171pp | His Majesty's Stationery Office. | 1918 | English Text.

VIII. NAVAL AND MILITARY DESPATCHES, RELATING TO OPERATIONS IN THE WAR. PART VIII. (PUBLISHED IN THE "LONDON GAZETTE," JULY 1917, TO JUNE 1918.)

Anonymous | 24cm x 15cm | blue paper softback | 217pp | His Majesty's Stationery Office. | 1919 | English Text.

IX. NAVAL AND MILITARY DESPATCHES, RELATING TO OPERATIONS IN THE WAR. PART IX. (PUBLISHED IN THE "LONDON GAZETTE," JULY 1918, TO DECEMBER 1918.)

Anonymous | 24cm x 15cm | blue paper softback | 156pp | His Majesty's Stationery Office. | 1919 | English Text.

X. NAVAL AND MILITARY DESPATCHES, RELATING TO OPERATIONS IN THE WAR. PART X. (PUBLISHED IN THE "LONDON GAZETTE," JANUARY 1919, TO JANUARY 1920.)

Anonymous | 24cm x 15cm | blue paper softback | 297pp | 2 tables | His Majesty's Stationery Office. | 1920 | English Text.

BATTLE OF JUTLAND 30th May to 1st June 1916 OFFICIAL DESPATCHES WITH APPENDICES (Cmd. 1068).
    Captain A.C.(Alfred Charles) Dewar, R.N. | 24.8cm x 16cm | blue cloth hardback | iv + 603pp | 37 maps | His Majesty's Stationery Office. | 1920 | English Text.
BATTLE OF JUTLAND 30th May to 1st June 1916 OFFICIAL DESPATCHES WITH APPENDICES (Cmd. 1068). [Map box].
    Captain A.C.(Alfred Charles) Dewar, R.N. | 24.8cm x 16cm | blue cloth hardback | 19 large format maps | His Majesty's Stationery Office. | 1920 | English Text.

Photographic;

THE BATTLE OF THE SOMME.
    Anonymous [H [Hugh] Noel Williams] | 27.8cm x 21.7cm | blue cloth hardback | 392pp | 587 photographs | 1 map | 1 plan | 7 sketches | Hutchinson and Co.| English Text.
    This book '**The Battle of the Somme**' has no title page. The title is shown only on the spine. It contains photography taken at the front during the battle and has no indication who published it or who authorised it. However since all British photography was strictly prohibited by the High Command with the exception of that by official cameramen, then it can be assumed that this book was produced with official authority. A number of the photographs were stills taken from the cinematic film taken during and just after the battle. It is listed in the WorldCat web site as "**Sir Douglas Haig's great push: the battle of the Somme: a popular, pictorial and authoritative work on one of the great battles in history: illustrated by about 700 wonderful official photographs & cinematograph films and other authentic pictures**" :
    http://www.worldcat.org/search?q=THE+BATTLE+OF+THE+SOMME+H+Noel+Williams&qt=notfound_page&search=Search .

Prisoners of War;

GERMAN PRISONERS IN GREAT BRITAIN.
    Anonymous (Royal Flying Corp Photographic Section) | 27cm x 20.5cm | Khaki paper hardback | 62pp | 108 photograph | Tillotson and Son Ltd. | c1919 | English Text.
    In 1916, members of the Royal Flying Corps Photographic Section took a number of black and white photographs of German prisoners of war depicting life in six of the largest prison camps in Great Britain: Donington Hall, Alexandra Palace, Dorchester, Handforth, Lofthouse Park and Eastcote. These photographs were to be displayed at the Württemberg Kriegsausstellung (*Württemberg War Exhibition*). After requests from the prisoners themselves, an album was produced entitled "**Deutsche Gefangene in England**" which was then sold to the prisoners. In 1918 the British authorities decided to use the album as a propaganda tool. "**Deutsche Gefangene in England**" was reproduced and was aimed at the war weary, but still fighting German soldiers on the Western Front. By mid 1918, with the failure of the German Spring Offensives and the decline in moral within the German Army, this volume was used to induce German soldiers to give up fighting and to surrender. Batches of them were rolled up, tied with tape, and then dropped by Royal Air Force aeroplanes over the German trenches and other places where German soldiers tended to congregate. It would appears that this ploy, in part, had the desired effect as shown by the large number of German soldiers who did surrender from early August 1918 to the end of the war.[2]
    After the war (probably in 1919) this book, with the photograph descriptions translated into English, was sold to the British public under the title "**German Prisoners in Great Britain**".

---

[2] During the period when the "**Deutsche Gefangene in England**" albums were being dropped over the German lines, a R.A.F. crew was shot down and captured. They were tried by a German military court marshal and found guilty of war crimes. The two members of the aircrew were then sentenced to long prison terms with hard labour. However they were released soon after the armistice came into effect.

It was also translated into Spanish and published under the title "**Los prisoneros Alemanes en la Gran Bretaña**".

Munitions;

Technical Records of Explosives Supply, 1915-1918, No. 1. RECOVERY OF SULPHURIC AND NITRIC ACIDS FROM ACIDS USED IN THE MANUFACTURE OF EXPLOSIVES: DENITRATION AND ABSORBTION.

W[William] MacNab | 30.5cm x 24.8cm | grey paper covered hardback | viii +56pp | ? photograph | ? tables | ? diagrams | ? graphs | His Majesty's Stationery Office. | 1920 | English Text.

Print run of 500 copies.

Technical Records of Explosives Supply, 1915-1918, No. 2. MANUFACTURE OF TRINITRSTOLUNE (TNT) AND ITS INTERMEDIATE PRODUCTS.

W[William] MacNab | 30.5cm x 24.8cm | grey paper covered hardback | viii + 116pp | ? photograph | ? tables | ? diagrams | ? graphs | His Majesty's Stationery Office. | 1920 | English Text.

Print run of 500 copies.

Technical Records of Explosives Supply, 1915-1918, No. 3. SULPHURIC ACID CONCENTRATION.

W[William] MacNab | 30.5cm x 24.8cm | grey paper covered hardback | vi + 91pp | ? photograph | ? tables | ? diagrams | ? graphs | His Majesty's Stationery Office. | 1921 | English Text.

Print run of 500 copies.

Technical Records of Explosives Supply, 1915-1918, No. 4. THE THEORY AND PRACTICE OF ACID MIXING.

W[William] MacNab | 30.5cm x 24.8cm | grey paper covered hardback | vi + 93pp | ? photograph | ? tables | ? diagrams | ? graphs | His Majesty's Stationery Office. | 1921 | English Text.

Print run of 500 copies.

Technical Records of Explosives Supply, 1915-1918, No. 5. MANUFACTURE OF SULPHURIC ACID BY CONTACT PROCESS.

W[William] MacNab | 30.5cm x 24.8cm | grey paper covered hardback | vi +128pp | ? photograph | ? tables | ? diagrams | ? graphs | His Majesty's Stationery Office. | 1921 | English Text.

Print run of 500 copies.

Technical Records of Explosives Supply, 1915-1918, No. 6. SYNTHETIC PHENOL AND PICRIC ACID.

W[William] MacNab | 30.5cm x 24.8cm | grey paper covered hardback | vi + 97pp | ? photograph | ? tables | ? diagrams | ? graphs | His Majesty's Stationery Office. | 1921 | English Text.

Print run of 500 copies.

Technical Records of Explosives Supply, 1915-1918, No. 7. MANUFACTURE OF NITRIC ACID FROM NITRE AND SULPHURIC ACID.

W[William] MacNab | 30.5cm x 24.8cm | grey paper covered hardback | vi + 86pp | ? photograph | ? tables | ? diagrams | ? graphs | His Majesty's Stationery Office. | 1921 | English Text.

Print run of 500 copies.

Technical Records of Explosives Supply, 1915-1918, No. 8. SOLVENT SUPPLY.

W[William] MacNab | 30.5cm x 24.8cm | grey paper covered hardback | iv + 22pp | ? photograph | ? tables | ? diagrams | ? graphs | His Majesty's Stationery Office. | 1921 | English Text.

Print run of 500 copies.

Technical Records of Explosives Supply, 1915-1918, No. 9. HEAT TRANSMISSION.

W[William] MacNab | 30.5cm x 24.8cm | grey paper covered hardback | iv + 48pp | ? photograph | ? tables | ? diagrams | ? graphs | His Majesty's Stationery Office. | 1921 | English Text.

Print run of 500 copies.

This set, Technical Records of Explosives Supply, was authorised by the Ministry of Munitions and the Department of Scientific and Industrial Research.

Canadian Secondary Official Histories

General;

Canada in Flanders: The Official Story of the Canadian Expeditionary Force, Volume 1.
> *Sir* Max[William Maxwell] Aitkin *M.P.* | 19cm x 12.5cm | dark red cloth hardback | xix + 252 + 5pp | 5 Appendices |? photograph | ? maps | Hodder and Stoughton. | 1916 | English Text.

Canada in Flanders: The Official Story of the Canadian Expeditionary Force, Volume 2.
> *Lord* Beaverbrook (William Maxwell Aitken, Lord Beaverbrook). | 19cm x 12.5cm | dark red cloth hardback | xx + 258 + 1pp | ? photograph | 8 maps | Hodder and Stoughton. | 1917 | English Text.

Canada in Flanders: The Official Story of the Canadian Expeditionary Force, Volume 3.
> Charles G.D.[George Douglas] Roberts. | 19cm x 12.5cm | dark red cloth hardback | xiv + 144pp | ? photograph | ? maps | Hodder and Stoughton. | 1918 | English Text.

Military Monographs;

The Western Front 1914.[3]
> Anonymous (Canadian Historical Section, General Staff, Army Headquarters; Directorate of Military Training, Army Headquarters.) | 19.5cm x 14. 5cm | Yellow Paper Softback | vi + 192pp | 18 maps | Edmond Cloutier, Queen's Printer. | 1957 | English Text.
> It appears that a French language version of this volume was not published.

Canada and the Battle of Vimy Ridge. 9-12 April 1917.
> Brereton Greenhous and Stephen J. Harris (Department of National Defence) | 30.4cm x 23.4cm | Brown Cloth Hardback | Gilt | Paper Dust Jacket | ii + 149pp | 2 maps | 124 photographs | Ministry of Supplies and Services Canada. | 1992 | English Text.
> ISBN: 0 660936542
> The title shown on the spine is abrevated to "**The Battle of Vimy Ridge.**"
> This volume can be viewed on the Canadian Forces' world wide web as a 'pdf files':
> *http://www.cmp-cpm.forces.gc.ca/dhh-dhp/his/docs/Vimy_e.pdf*

Le Canada et la Bataille de Vimy, 9-12 avril 1917. (version in French of the above.)
> Brereton Greenhous and Steve Harris - Department of National Defence | 30.4cm x 23.4cm | Brown Cloth Hardback | Gilt | Paper Dust Jacket | ii + 149pp | 2 maps | 124 photographs | Editions Art Global. | 1992 | French Text.
> ISBN: 0-660-93654-2

---

[3] This book "The Western Front 1914" is one of a group of Canadian Official Histories known as the "Yellow Books" and were produced by various members of the Directorate of History covering the whole of Canadian military history for officers studying for promotional examinations in lieu of a full official history.

French Secondary Official Histories

Educational Text Books;

COURS D'HISTOIRE TOME III LA GUERRE MONDIALE 1914 – 1918. (History Course, Book III - The World War 1914 - 1918).

    Anonymous (Ecoles Militaires) I 25cm x 17cm I yellow paper softback I 426pp I Imprimerie Nationale. I 1921 I French Text.

COURS D'HISTOIRE TOME III LA GUERRE MONDIALE 1914 – 1918. CARTES ET CROQUIS. (History Course, Book III - The World War 1914 – 1918. Maps and Sketches).

    Anonymous (Ecoles Militaires) I 25cm x 17cm I yellow paper softback I vii pp I 82 maps and sketches I Imprimerie Nationale. I 1921 I French Text.

    The '**Cours d'Histoire**' set were the standard textbooks for French officer students covering French military history with Tome III being the only part devoted to the Great War.

Photographic;

"LA GUERRE" - DOCUMENTS DE LA SECTION PHOTOGRAPHIQUE DE L'ARMÉE (MINISTÈRE DE LA GUERRE). [1re SÉRIE.] FASCICULE I LA VIE DU SOLDAT. (*"The War" - The Army Photographic Section's Documents. (Ministry of War). [1st Series.] Section I The Life of the Soldier.*)

    Victor-Eugène Ardouin-Dumazet (Section Photographique de l'Armée Françaisese) I 28.2cm x 35.3cm I white illustrated paper softback I 28pp I ? photograph I Librarie Armand Colin. I 1915 I French, English, German, Portuguese and Italian Text.

"LA GUERRE" - DOCUMENTS DE LA SECTION PHOTOGRAPHIQUE DE L'ARMÉE (MINISTÈRE DE LA GUERRE). [1re SÉRIE.] FASCICULE II ABRIS ET TRANCHEES. (*"The War" - The Army Photographic Section's Documents. (Ministry of War). [1st Series.] Section II Shelters and Trenches.*)

    Victor-Eugène Ardouin-Dumazet (Section Photographique de l'Armée Françaisese) I 28.2cm x 35.3cm I white illustrated paper softback I 28pp I ? photograph I Librarie Armand Colin. I 1915 I French, English, German, Portuguese and Italian Text.

"LA GUERRE" - DOCUMENTS DE LA SECTION PHOTOGRAPHIQUE DE L'ARMÉE (MINISTÈRE DE LA GUERRE). [1re SÉRIE.] FASCICULE III LES ALLIES A SALONIQUE. (*"The War" - The Army Photographic Section's Documents. (Ministry of War). [1st Series.] Section III The Allies in Salonika.*)

    Victor-Eugène Ardouin-Dumazet (Section Photographique de l'Armée Françaisese) I 28.2cm x 35.3cm I white illustrated paper softback I 28pp I ? photograph I Librarie Armand Colin. I 1916 I French, English, German, Portuguese and Italian Text.

"LA GUERRE" - DOCUMENTS DE LA SECTION PHOTOGRAPHIQUE DE L'ARMÉE (MINISTÈRE DE LA GUERRE). [1re SÉRIE.] FASCICULE FASCICULE IV DANS LA FORET D'ARGONNE. (*"The War" - The Army Photographic Section's Documents. (Ministry of War). [1st Series.] Section IV The Argonne Forest.*)

    Victor-Eugène Ardouin-Dumazet (Section Photographique de l'Armée Françaisese) I 28.2cm x 35.3cm I white illustrated paper softback I 28pp I ? photograph I Librarie Armand Colin. I 1916 I French, English, German, Portuguese and Italian Text.

"LA GUERRE" - DOCUMENTS DE LA SECTION PHOTOGRAPHIQUE DE L'ARMÉE (MINISTÈRE DE LA GUERRE). [1re SÉRIE.] FASCICULE V BATAILLE DE CHAMPAGNE. (*"The War" - The Army Photographic Section's Documents. (Ministry of War). [1st Series.] Section V The Battle of Champagne.*)

    Victor-Eugène Ardouin-Dumazet (Section Photographique de l'Armée Françaisese) I 28.2cm x 35.3cm I white illustrated paper softback I 28pp I ? photograph I Librarie Armand Colin. I 1916 I French, English, German, Portuguese and Italian Text.

"LA GUERRE" - DOCUMENTS DE LA SECTION PHOTOGRAPHIQUE DE L'ARMÉE (MINISTÈRE DE LA GUERRE). [1re SÉRIE.] FASCICULE VI RIEMS, SOISSONS, ARRAS. (*"The War" - The Army Photographic Section's Documents. (Ministry of War). [1st Series.] Section VI Rhiems, Soissons, Arras.*)

    Victor-Eugène Ardouin-Dumazet (Section Photographique de l'Armée Françaisese) I 28.2cm x 35.3cm I white illustrated paper softback I 28pp I 59 photograph I Librarie Armand Colin. I 1916 I French, English, German, Portuguese and Italian Text.

"LA GUERRE" - DOCUMENTS DE LA SECTION PHOTOGRAPHIQUE DE L'ARMÉE (MINISTÈRE DE LA GUERRE). [1ʳᵉ SÉRIE.] FASCICULE VII EN ALSACE RECONQUISE. (*"The War" - The Army Photographic Section's Documents. (Ministry of War). [1ˢᵗ Series.] Section VII In Recovered Alsace.*)

> Victor-Eugène Ardouin-Dumazet (Section Photographique de l'Armée Françaisese) | 28.2cm x 35.3cm | white illustrated paper softback | 28pp | 63 photograph | Librarie Armand Colin. | 1916 | French, English, German, Portuguese and Italian Text.

"LA GUERRE" - DOCUMENTS DE LA SECTION PHOTOGRAPHIQUE DE L'ARMÉE (MINISTÈRE DE LA GUERRE). [1ʳᵉ SÉRIE.] FASCICULE VIII ARMES ET MUNITIONS. (*"The War" - The Army Photographic Section's Documents. (Ministry of War). [1ˢᵗ Series.] Section VIII Arms and Munitions.*)

> Victor-Eugène Ardouin-Dumazet (Section Photographique de l'Armée Françaisese) | 28.2cm x 35.3cm | white illustrated paper softback | 28pp | 74 photograph | Librarie Armand Colin. | 1916 | French, English, German, Portuguese and Italian Text.

"LA GUERRE" - DOCUMENTS DE LA SECTION PHOTOGRAPHIQUE DE L'ARMÉE (MINISTÈRE DE LA GUERRE). [1ʳᵉ SÉRIE.] FASCICULE IX EN ARTOIS. (*"The War" - The Army Photographic Section's Documents. (Ministry of War). [1ˢᵗ Series.] Section IX In Artois.*)

> Victor-Eugène Ardouin-Dumazet (Section Photographique de l'Armée Françaisese) | 28.2cm x 35.3cm | white illustrated paper softback | 28pp | 58 photograph | Librarie Armand Colin. | 1916 | French, English, German, Portuguese and Italian Text.

"LA GUERRE" - DOCUMENTS DE LA SECTION PHOTOGRAPHIQUE DE L'ARMÉE (MINISTÈRE DE LA GUERRE). [1ʳᵉ SÉRIE.] FASCICULE X AVIONS ET AUTOS. (*"The War" - The Army Photographic Section's Documents. (Ministry of War). [1ˢᵗ Series.] Section X Aircrafts and Vehicles.*)

> Victor-Eugène Ardouin-Dumazet (Section Photographique de l'Armée Françaisese) | 28.2cm x 35.3cm | white illustrated paper softback | 28pp | 45 photograph | Librarie Armand Colin. | 1916 | French, English, German, Portuguese and Italian Text.

"LA GUERRE" - DOCUMENTS DE LA SECTION PHOTOGRAPHIQUE DE L'ARMÉE (MINISTÈRE DE LA GUERRE). [2ᵉ SERIE.] FASCICULE XI PRISONNIERS ET TROPHEES. (*"The War" - The Army Photographic Section's Documents. (Ministry of War). [2ⁿᵈ Series.] Section XI Prisoners and Trophies.*)

> Victor-Eugène Ardouin-Dumazet (Section Photographique de l'Armée Françaisese) | 28.2cm x 35.3cm | white illustrated paper softback | 28pp | 52 photograph | Librarie Armand Colin. | 1916 | French, English, German, Portuguese and Italian Text.

"LA GUERRE" - DOCUMENTS DE LA SECTION PHOTOGRAPHIQUE DE L'ARMÉE (MINISTÈRE DE LA GUERRE). [2ᵉ SERIE.] FASCICULE XII DE L'YSER A LA MER DU NORD. (*"The War" - The Army Photographic Section's Documents. (Ministry of War). [2ⁿᵈ Series.] Section XII Between the Yser and the North Sea.*)

> Victor-Eugène Ardouin-Dumazet (Section Photographique de l'Armée Françaisese) | 28.2cm x 35.3cm | white illustrated paper softback | 28pp | 56 photograph | Librarie Armand Colin. | 1916 | French, English, German, Portuguese and Italian Text.

"LA GUERRE" - DOCUMENTS DE LA SECTION PHOTOGRAPHIQUE DE L'ARMÉE (MINISTÈRE DE LA GUERRE). [2ᵉ SERIE.] FASCICULE XIII VERDUN. (*"The War" - The Army Photographic Section's Documents. (Ministry of War). [2ⁿᵈ Series.] Section XIII Verdun.*)

> Victor-Eugène Ardouin-Dumazet (Section Photographique de l'Armée Françaisese) | 28.2cm x 35.3cm | white illustrated paper softback | 24pp | 56 photograph | Librarie Armand Colin. | 1916 | French, English, German, Portuguese and Italian Text.

"LA GUERRE" - DOCUMENTS DE LA SECTION PHOTOGRAPHIQUE DE L'ARMÉE (MINISTÈRE DE LA GUERRE). [2ᵉ SERIE.] FASCICULE XIV LES ETAPES DU BLESSE. (*"The War" - The Army Photographic Section's Documents. (Ministry of War). [2ⁿᵈ Series.] Section XIV The Stages of the Wounded.*)

> Victor-Eugène Ardouin-Dumazet (Section Photographique de l'Armée Françaisese) | 28.2cm x 35.3cm | white illustrated paper softback | 28pp | 61 photograph | Librarie Armand Colin. | 1916 | French, English, German, Portuguese and Italian Text.

"LA GUERRE" - DOCUMENTS DE LA SECTION PHOTOGRAPHIQUE DE L'ARMÉE (MINISTÈRE DE LA GUERRE). [2ᵉ SERIE.] FASCICULE XV LA MARINE DE GUERRE. (*"The War" - The Army Photographic Section's Documents. (Ministry of War). [2ⁿᵈ Series.] Section XV The War at Sea.*)

Victor-Eugène Ardouin-Dumazet (Section Photographique de l'Armée Françaisese) | 28.2cm x 35.3cm | white illustrated paper softback | 28pp | 53 photograph | Librarie Armand Colin. | 1916 | French, English, German, Portuguese and Italian Text.

"LA GUERRE" - DOCUMENTS DE LA SECTION PHOTOGRAPHIQUE DE L'ARMÉE (MINISTÈRE DE LA GUERRE). [2ᵉ SERIE.] FASCICULE XVI EN ORIENT. (*"The War" - The Army Photographic Section's Documents. (Ministry of War). [2ⁿᵈ Series.] Section XVI In the Near East.*)

Victor-Eugène Ardouin-Dumazet (Section Photographique de l'Armée Françaisese) | 28.2cm x 35.3cm | white illustrated paper softback | 28pp | 60 photograph | Librarie Armand Colin. | 1916 | French, English, German, Portuguese and Italian Text.

"LA GUERRE" - DOCUMENTS DE LA SECTION PHOTOGRAPHIQUE DE L'ARMÉE (MINISTÈRE DE LA GUERRE). [2ᵉ SERIE.] FASCICULE XVII EQUIPEMENT ET RAVITAILLEMENT. (*"The War" - The Army Photographic Section's Documents. (Ministry of War). [2ⁿᵈ Series.] Section XVII Equipment and Provisioning.*)

Victor-Eugène Ardouin-Dumazet (Section Photographique de l'Armée Françaisese) | 28.2cm x 35.3cm | white illustrated paper softback | 28pp | 54 photograph | Librarie Armand Colin. | 1917 | French, English, German, Portuguese and Italian Text.

"LA GUERRE" - DOCUMENTS DE LA SECTION PHOTOGRAPHIQUE DE L'ARMÉE (MINISTÈRE DE LA GUERRE). [2ᵉ SERIE.] FASCICULE XVIII L'ARMEE COLONIALE. (*"The War" - The Army Photographic Section's Documents. (Ministry of War). [2ⁿᵈ Series.] Section XVIII The Colonial Army.*)

Victor-Eugène Ardouin-Dumazet (Section Photographique de l'Armée Françaisese) | 28.2cm x 35.3cm | white illustrated paper softback | 28pp | 67 photograph | Librarie Armand Colin. | 1918 | French, English, German, Portuguese and Italian Text.

"LA GUERRE" - DOCUMENTS DE LA SECTION PHOTOGRAPHIQUE DE L'ARMÉE (MINISTÈRE DE LA GUERRE). [2ᴱ SERIE.] FASCICULE XIX L'OFFENSIVE DE LA SOMME. (*"The War" - The Army Photographic Section's Documents. (Ministry of War). [2ⁿᵈ Series.] Section XIX The Somme Offensive.*)

Victor-Eugène Ardouin-Dumazet (Section Photographique de l'Armée Françaisese) | 28.2cm x 35.3cm | white illustrated paper softback | 28pp | 50 photograph | Librarie Armand Colin. | 1919 | French, English, German, Portuguese and Italian Text.

"LA GUERRE" - DOCUMENTS DE LA SECTION PHOTOGRAPHIQUE DE L'ARMÉE (MINISTÈRE DE LA GUERRE). [2ᵉ SERIE.] FASCICULE XX LA MARNE. (*"The War" - The Army Photographic Section's Documents. (Ministry of War). [2ⁿᵈ Series.] Section XX The Marne.*)

Victor-Eugène Ardouin-Dumazet (Section Photographique de l'Armée Françaisese) | 28.2cm x 35.3cm | white illustrated paper softback | 28pp | 50 photograph | Librarie Armand Colin. | 1920 | French, English, German, Portuguese and Italian Text.

These periodicals **"La Guerre" - Documents de la Section Photographique de L'Armee (Ministere de la Guerre)** were produced officially during the war for popular consumption. They were issued in two series and each series had consecutive page numbers (namely pages 1-280). All the issues were produced to the same format with a two page introduction, followed by 24 plates, and finishing with two pages of notes. Each plate had from one to five photographs with each photograph having a description in French at the bottom of each plate. The notes consisted of the photograph descriptions translated into English, German, Portuguese and Italian.

LA MARCHE SUR TRIESTE - DOCUMENTS DE LA SECTION PHOTOGRAPHIQUE DE L'ARMÉE. (*The March on Trieste - The Army Photographic Section's Documents.*)

Anonymous – Section Photographique de l'Armée Françaisese | 28.2cm x 35.3cm | Beige decorrated paper softback | 40pp | ? photographs | 1 maps | Edité par le Flambeau. | c1916 | French Text.

LA BATAILLE DE CHAMPAGNE - DOCUMENTS DE LA SECTION PHOTOGRAPHIQUE DE L'ARMÉE. (*The Battle of Champagne - The Army Photographic Section's Documents.*)

Anonymous – Section Photographique de l'Armée Françaisese | 28.2cm x 35.3cm | Beige decorrated paper softback | 36pp | 68 photograph (1 panarama) | 1 maps | Edité par le Flambeau. | c1916 | French, English and Spanish Text.

This volume "**La Bataille de Champagne - Documents de la Section Photographique de l'Armée**" produced to the same format as "**La Guerre**" with a two page introduction followed by 32 plates and finishing with two pages of notes. Each plate had from one to four photographs with each photograph having a description in French. The notes consisted of the photograph descriptions translated into English and Spanish.

LA DÉFENSE DE VERDUN - DOCUMENTS DE LA SECTION PHOTOGRAPHIQUE DE L'ARMÉE. (*The Defense of Verdun - The Army Photographic Section's Documents.*)

Anonymous – Section Photographique de l'Armée Françaisese | 28.2cm x 35.3cm | Beige decorated paper softback | 36pp | 83 photograph | 1 panarama sketch | Edité par le Pays de France. | c1916 | French, English, Russian and Italian Text.

Like the above volume "**La Bataille de Champagne - Documents de la Section Photographique de l'Armée**", this volume "**La Defense de Verdun - Documents de la Section Photographique de L'Armée**" was produced to the same format as "**La Guerre**" however without the two page introduction, instead a title page followed by a page of notes, then the 32 plates, and finishing with two more pages of notes. Each plate had from one to six photographs with each photograph having a description in French. The notes consisted of the photograph descriptions translated into English, Russian and Italian.

1916 - DOCUMENTS DE LA SECTION PHOTOGRAPHIQUE DE L'ARMÉE FRANÇAISE. (*1916 - The French Army Photographic Section's Documents.*)

Anonymous – Section Photographique de l'Armée Françaisese | 15.5cm x 24.5cm | Beige paper softback | 56pp | 50 photographs | ? | c1917 | French, Portugese, Italian, Spanish and English Text.

Unlike the "**La Guerre**" this volume "**1916 - Documents de la Section Photographique de L'Armée Françaisese**" consisted of just 50 plates without an introduction or any notes. Each plate has a single photograph and has the description repeated in the five languages below each photograph.

1917 Nº 1 [LE SOURIRE DE LA FRANCE] - DOCUMENTS DE LA SECTION PHOTOGRAPHIQUE DE L'ARMÉE FRANÇAISE. (*1917 Nº 1 [The Smile of France] - The French Army Photographic Section's Documents.*)

Jean Richepin – Section Photographique de l'Armée Françaises | 28.2cm x 35.3cm | Beige decorated paper softback | 48pp | ? photograph | Emile Paul Libraire. | c1918 | French, English, Italian, Portuguese, Spanish, and German Text.

Like the periodicals "**La Guerre**" - Documents de la Section Photographique de L'Armee (Ministere de la Guerre) this volume was produced officially during the war for popular consumption. It was produced to the same format with a two page introduction followed by 46 plates. Each plate had from one to seven photographs with each photograph having descriptions in French, English, Italian, Portuguese, Spanish, and German. The title on the cover of this volume is shown as "**1917 Nº 1 - Documents de la Section Photographique de L'Armée Française**", however the introduction has a sub title shown - "**Le sourire de la France.**"

1917 Nº 2 [LA GUERRE AU SEUIL DE 1917] - DOCUMENTS DE LA SECTION PHOTOGRAPHIQUE DE L'ARMÉE FRANÇAISE. (*1917 Nº 2 [The War at the Front 1917] - The French Army Photographic Section's Documents.*)

Jean Richepin – Section Photographique de l'Armée Françaises | 28.2cm x 35.3cm | Beige decorated paper softback | 48pp | ? photograph | Emile Paul Libraire. | c1918 | French, English, Italian, Portuguese, Spanish, and German Text.

Like the periodicals "**La Guerre**" - Documents de la Section Photographique de L'Armee (Ministere de la Guerre) this volume was produced officially during the war for popular consumption. It was produced to the same format with a two page introduction followed by 46 plates. Each plate had from one to seven photographs with each photograph having descriptions in French, English, Italian, Portuguese, Spanish, and German. The title on the cover of this volume is shown as "**1917 Nº 2 - Documents de la Section Photographique de L'Armée Française**," however the introduction has a sub title shown - "**La guerre au seuil de 1917.**"

1917 Nº 3 [LEUR ARMÉE] - DOCUMENTS DE LA SECTION PHOTOGRAPHIQUE DE L'ARMÉE FRANÇAISE. (*1917 Nº 3 [Their Army] - The French Army Photographic Section's Documents.*)

Jean Richepin – Section Photographique de l'Armée Françaises | 28.2cm x 35.3cm | Beige decorated paper softback | 48pp | 163 photograph | Emile Paul Libraire. | c1918 | French, English, Italian, Portuguese, Spanish, and German Text.

Like the periodicals **"La Guerre" - Documents de la Section Photographique de L'Armee (Ministere de la Guerre)** this volume was produced officially during the war for popular consumption. It was produced to the same format with a two page introduction followed by 46 plates. Each plate had from one to seven photographs with each photograph having descriptions in French, English, Italian, Portuguese, Spanish, and German. The title on the cover of this volume is shown as **"1917 Nº 3 - Documents de la Section Photographique de L'Armée Française",** however the introduction has a sub title shown - **"Leur armée."**

1917 Nº 4 [LE BON SOLDAT DE FRANCE] - DOCUMENTS DE LA SECTION PHOTOGRAPHIQUE DE L'ARMÉE FRANÇAISE. (*1917 Nº 4 [The Good Soldier of France] - The French Army Photographic Section's Documents.*)

Jean Richepin – Section Photographique de l'Armée Françaises | 28.2cm x 35.3cm | Beige decorated paper softback | 48pp | ? photograph | Emile Paul Libraire. | c1918 | French, English, Italian, Portuguese, Spanish, and German Text.

Like the periodicals **"La Guerre" - Documents de la Section Photographique de L'Armee (Ministere de la Guerre)** this volume was produced officially during the war for popular consumption. It was produced to the same format with a two page introduction followed by 46 plates. Each plate had from one to seven photographs with each photograph having descriptions in French, English, Italian, Portuguese, Spanish, and German. The title on the cover of this volume is shown as **"1917 Nº 4 - Documents de la Section Photographique de L'Armée Française",** however the introduction has a sub title shown - **"Le bon soldat de France."**

1917 Nº 5 [LE MONDE AVEC LA FRANCE POUR LA LIBERTÉ] - DOCUMENTS DE LA SECTION PHOTOGRAPHIQUE DE L'ARMÉE FRANÇAISE. (*1917 Nº 5 [The World with France for Liberty] - The French Army Photographic Section's Documents.*)

Jean Richepin – Section Photographique de l'Armée Françaises | 28.2cm x 35.3cm | Beige decorated paper softback | 48pp | 155 photograph | Emile Paul Libraire. | c1918 | French, English, Italian, Portuguese, Spanish, and German Text.

Like the periodicals **"La Guerre" - Documents de la Section Photographique de L'Armee (Ministere de la Guerre)** this volume was produced officially during the war for popular consumption. It was produced to the same format with a one page introduction followed by 46 plates. Each plate had from one to six photographs with each photograph having descriptions in French, English, Italian, Portuguese, Spanish, and German. The title on the cover of this volume is shown as **"1917 Nº 5 - Documents de la Section Photographique de L'Armée Française",** however the introduction has a sub title shown - **"Le monde avec la France pour la liberté."**

1917 Nº 6 [La France d'aujourd'hui] - DOCUMENTS DE LA SECTION PHOTOGRAPHIQUE DE L'ARMÉE FRANÇAISE. (*1917 Nº 6 [France of Today] - The French Army Photographic Section's Documents.*)

Jean Richepin – Section Photographique de l'Armée Françaises | 28.2cm x 35.3cm | Beige decorated paper softback | 48pp | ? photograph | Emile Paul Libraire. | c1918 | French, English, Italian, Portuguese, Spanish, and German Text.

Like the periodicals **"La Guerre" - Documents de la Section Photographique de L'Armee (Ministere de la Guerre)** this volume was produced officially during the war for popular consumption. It was produced to the same format with a one page introduction followed by 46 plates. Each plate had from one to six photographs with each photograph having descriptions in French, English, Italian, Portuguese, Spanish, and German. The title on the cover of this volume is shown as **"1917 Nº 6 - Documents de la Section Photographique de L'Armée Française",** however the introduction has a sub title shown - **"La France d'aujourd'hui. "**

1917 Nº 7 [DU LANGUAGE DE LA RENOMMÉE ET DE LA PHOTOGRAPHIE] - DOCUMENTS DE LA SECTION PHOTOGRAPHIQUE DE L'ARMÉE FRANÇAISE. (*1917 Nº 7 [The Language of the Renown and the Photography] - The French Army Photographic Section's Documents.*)

Jean Richepin – Section Photographique de l'Armée Françaises | 28.2cm x 35.3cm | Beige decorated paper softback | 48pp | ? photograph | Emile Paul Libraire. | c1918 | French, English, Italian, Portuguese, Spanish, and German Text.

Like the periodicals **"La Guerre" - Documents de la Section Photographique de L'Armee (Ministere de la Guerre)** this volume was produced officially during the war for popular consumption. It was produced to the same format with a one page introduction followed by 46 plates. Each plate had from one to six photographs with each photograph having descriptions in French, English, Italian, Portuguese, Spanish, and German. The title on the cover of this volume is shown as "**1917 N° 7 - Documents de la Section Photographique de L'Armée Française**," however the introduction has a sub title shown - "**Du language de la renommée et de la photographie.** "

1917 N° 8 [LA VICTOIRE PROCHAINE DU DROIT] - DOCUMENTS DE LA SECTION PHOTOGRAPHIQUE DE L'ARMÉE FRANÇAISE. (*1917 N° 8 [The Righteous Forthcoming Victory] - The French Army Photographic Section's Documents.*)

Jean Richepin – Section Photographique de l'Armée Françaises | 28.2cm x 35.3cm | Beige decorated paper softback | 48pp | ? photograph | Emile Paul Libraire. | c1918 | French, English, Italian, Portuguese, Spanish, and German Text.

Like the periodicals **"La Guerre" - Documents de la Section Photographique de L'Armee (Ministere de la Guerre)** this volume was produced officially during the war for popular consumption. It was produced to the same format with a one page introduction followed by 46 plates. Each plate had from one to six photographs with each photograph having descriptions in French, English, Italian, Portuguese, Spanish, and German. The title on the cover of this volume is shown as "**1917 N° 8 - Documents de la Section Photographique de L'Armée Française**," however the introduction has a sub title shown - "**La victoire prochaine du droit.** "

1917 N° 9 [L'HOMMAGE DE L'ITALIE] - DOCUMENTS DE LA SECTION PHOTOGRAPHIQUE DE L'ARMÉE FRANÇAISE. (*1917 N° 9 [Hommage to Italy] - The French Army Photographic Section's Documents.*)

Jean Richepin – Section Photographique de l'Armée Françaises | 28.2cm x 35.3cm | Beige decorated paper softback | 48pp | ? photograph | Emile Paul Libraire. | c1918 | French, English, Italian, Portuguese, Spanish, and German Text.

Like the periodicals **"La Guerre" - Documents de la Section Photographique de L'Armee (Ministere de la Guerre)** this volume was produced officially during the war for popular consumption. It was produced to the same format with a one page introduction followed by 46 plates. Each plate had from one to six photographs with each photograph having descriptions in French, English, Italian, Portuguese, Spanish, and German. The title on the cover of this volume is shown as "**1917 N° 9 - Documents de la Section Photographique de L'Armée Française**," however the introduction has a sub title shown - "**L'hommage de l'Italie**". R.A. Gallenga-Stuart (Membre del Parlament italien).

1917 N° 10 [?] - DOCUMENTS DE LA SECTION PHOTOGRAPHIQUE DE L'ARMÉE FRANÇAISE. (*1917 N° 10 [?] - The French Army Photographic Section's Documents.*)

Jean Richepin – Section Photographique de l'Armée Françaises | 28.2cm x 35.3cm | Beige decorated paper softback | 48pp | ? photograph | Emile Paul Libraire. | c1918 | French, English, Italian, Portuguese, Spanish, and German Text.

It has been assumed that there was a "**1917 N° 10 - Documents de la Section Photographique de L'Armée Française**" produced.

1917 N° 11 [LE SANG N'EST PAS DE L'EAU] - DOCUMENTS DE LA SECTION PHOTOGRAPHIQUE DE L'ARMÉE FRANÇAISE. (*1917 N° 11 [The Blood is not Water] - The French Army Photographic Section's Documents.*)

Jean Richepin – Section Photographique de l'Armée Françaises | 28.2cm x 35.3cm | Beige decorated paper softback | 48pp | 173 photograph | Emile Paul Libraire. | c1918 | French, English, Italian, Portuguese, Spanish, and German Text.

Like the periodicals **"La Guerre" - Documents de la Section Photographique de L'Armee (Ministere de la Guerre)** this volume was produced officially during the war for popular consumption. It was produced to the same format with a one page introduction followed by 46 plates. Each plate had from one to ten photographs with each photograph having descriptions in French, English, Italian, Portuguese, Spanish, and German. The title on the cover of this volume is shown as "**1917 N° 11 - Documents de la Section Photographique de L'Armée Française**," however the introduction has a sub title shown - "**Le sang n'est pas de l'eau.** "

LA FRANCE ET SES ALLIÉS - DOCUMENTS DE LA SECTION PHOTOGRAPHIQUE DE L'ARMÉE FRANÇAISE. L'EFFORT AMÉRICAIN. (*France and her Allies - The French Army Photographic Section's Documents. The American Effort* .)

André Tardieu – Section Photographique de l'Armée Françaises I 24.5cm x 32cm I Beige decorated paper softback I 120pp I ? photograph I Emile Paul Libraire. I c1918 I French, English, Italian, Portuguese, Spanish, and German Text.

DOCUMENTS DE LA SECTION PHOTOGRAPHIQUE DE L'ARMÉE FRANÇAISE. * (*The French Army Photographic Section's Documents. **)

Anonymous – Section Photographique de l'Armée Françaisese I 24.5cm x 32cm I Green card softback I Gilt I 24pp I 24 photographs I A. Serment I c1917 I French Text.

DOCUMENTS DE LA SECTION PHOTOGRAPHIQUE DE L'ARMÉE FRANÇAISE. ** (*The French Army Photographic Section's Documents. ***)

Anonymous – Section Photographique de l'Armée Françaisese I 24.5cm x 32cm I Green card softback I Gilt I 24pp I 24 photographs I A. Serment I c1917 I French Text.

DOCUMENTS DE LA SECTION PHOTOGRAPHIQUE DE L'ARMÉE FRANÇAISE. *** (*The French Army Photographic Section's Documents. ****)

Anonymous – Section Photographique de l'Armée Françaisese I 24.5cm x 32cm I Green card softback I Gilt I 21pp I 21 photographs I A. Serment I c1917 I French Text.

This series "**Documents de la Section Photographique de l'Armée Française**" consists of bound portfolios of photographs (12.5cm x 17.5cm gelatin silver prints) mounted on green paper.

LES AMERICAINS EN FRANCE - DOCUMENTS DE LA SECTION PHOTOGRAPHIQUE DE L'ARMÉE FRANÇAISES (MINISTÈRE DE LA GUERRE). (*The Americans in France - The French Army Photographic Section's Documents. (Ministry of War).*)

Gilbert Chinard – Section Photographique de l'Armée Françaises I 34cm x 46cm I Green card softback I 29pp I 29 photograph I A. Serment . I c1918 I French Text.

This volume "**Les Americains en France**" in similar to the three volumes above and consists of a bound portfolio of photographs (16.5cm x 22.5cm gelatin silver prints) mounted on green paper.

German Secondary Official Histories

Naval Staff Papers;

𝕭𝖆𝖓𝖉 1. 𝕯𝖎𝖊 𝕰𝖓𝖗𝖜𝖎𝖈𝖐𝖑𝖚𝖓𝖌 𝖉𝖊𝖗 𝕺𝖕𝖊𝖗𝖆𝖙𝖎𝖔𝖓𝖊𝖓 𝖎𝖓 𝖉𝖊𝖗 𝕹𝖔𝖗𝖉𝖘𝖊𝖊 𝖇𝖎𝖘 𝖟𝖚𝖗 𝕾𝖈𝖍𝖑𝖆𝖈𝖍𝖙. (Band 1. Die Enrwicklung der Operationen in der Nordsee bis zur Schlacht. - *Volume 1. The Development of Operations in the North Sea to the Battle of Jutland.*)

Otto Groos | ?cm x ?cm | white paper softback? | ?pp | ? photograph | ? maps | ? | 1928 | German Text. | Fraktur Script.

𝕭𝖆𝖓𝖉 2. 𝕯𝖎𝖊 𝖀𝖓𝖙𝖊𝖗𝖓𝖊𝖍𝖒𝖚𝖓𝖌 𝖉𝖊𝖗 𝖉𝖊𝖚𝖙𝖘𝖈𝖍𝖊𝖓 𝕳𝖔𝖈𝖍𝖘𝖊𝖊𝖋𝖑𝖔𝖙𝖙𝖊 𝖆𝖒 19 𝕬𝖚𝖌𝖚𝖘𝖙 1916. 𝖀-𝕭𝖔𝖔𝖙𝖘𝖛𝖊𝖗𝖜𝖊𝖓𝖉𝖚𝖓𝖌, 𝕬𝖚𝖋𝖐𝖆𝖗𝖚𝖓𝖌 𝖚𝖓𝖉 𝕾𝖎𝖈𝖍𝖊𝖗𝖚𝖓𝖌 𝖉𝖊𝖗 𝕱𝖑𝖔𝖙𝖙𝖊 𝖉𝖚𝖗𝖈𝖍 𝕷𝖚𝖋𝖙𝖋𝖆𝖍𝖗𝖟𝖊𝖚𝖌𝖊, 𝕳𝖆𝖓𝖉𝖍𝖆𝖇𝖚𝖓𝖌 𝖉𝖊𝖗 𝕱𝖚𝖓𝖐𝖊𝖓𝖙𝖊𝖑𝖊𝖌𝖗𝖗𝖆𝖕𝖍𝖎𝖊. (Band 2. Die Unternehmung der deutschen Hochseeflotte am 19 August 1916. U-Bootsverwendung, Aufkarung und Sicherung der Flotte durch Luftfahrzeuge, Handhabung der Funkentelegrraphie. - *Volume 2. The Actions of the German High Sea Fleet on 19th August 1916. Employment of Submarines, Communications and Safety of the Fleet by Aircraft and Use of Radiotelegraphy.*)

Arno Spindler | ?cm x ?cm | white paper softback? | ?pp | ? photograph | ? maps | ? | 1928 | German Text. | Fraktur Script.

𝕭𝖆𝖓𝖉 3. 𝕯𝖆𝖘 𝖎𝖓𝖙𝖊𝖗𝖓𝖆𝖙𝖎𝖔𝖓𝖆𝖑𝖊 𝕾𝖊𝖊𝖐𝖗𝖎𝖊𝖌𝖘𝖗𝖊𝖈𝖍𝖙 𝖚𝖓𝖉 𝖉𝖎𝖊 𝖉𝖊𝖚𝖙𝖘𝖈𝖍𝖊 𝖀𝖇𝖊𝖗𝖘𝖊𝖊𝖛𝖊𝖗𝖘𝖔𝖗𝖌𝖚𝖓𝖌 𝖎𝖒 𝖂𝖊𝖑𝖙𝖐𝖗𝖎𝖊𝖌𝖊. (Band 3. Das internationale Seekriegsrecht und die deutsche Uberseeversorgung im Weltkriege. – *Volume 3. International Naval Law and German Overseas Supplies in the World War.*)

Georg Schramm | ?cm x ?cm | white paper softback? | ?pp | ? photograph | ? maps | ? | 1928 | German Text. | Fraktur Script.

𝕭𝖆𝖓𝖉 4. 𝕰𝖎𝖓𝖎𝖌𝖊 𝕷𝖊𝖍𝖗𝖊𝖓 𝖉𝖊𝖗 𝕿𝖆𝖐𝖙𝖎𝖐 𝖚𝖓𝖉 𝖂𝖆𝖋𝖋𝖊𝖓𝖛𝖊𝖗𝖜𝖊𝖓𝖉𝖚𝖓𝖌 𝖎𝖓 𝖉𝖊𝖗 𝕾𝖈𝖍𝖑𝖆𝖈𝖍𝖙 𝖛𝖔𝖗 𝖉𝖊𝖒 𝕾𝖐𝖆𝖌𝖊𝖗𝖗𝖆𝖐. (Band 4. Einige Lehren der Taktik und Waffenverwendung in der Schlacht vor dem Skagerrak. – *Volume 4. Some of the Lesson in Tactics and Employment of Weapons in the Battle of Jutland.*)

Otto Groos | ?cm x ?cm | white paper softback? | ?pp | ? photograph | ? maps | ? | 1928 | German Text. | Fraktur Script.

𝕭𝖆𝖓𝖉 5. 𝕲𝖊𝖘𝖈𝖍𝖜𝖎𝖓𝖉𝖎𝖌𝖐𝖊𝖎𝖙. (Band 5. Geschwindigkeit. – *Volume 5. Speed.*)

Hermann von Fischel | ?cm x ?cm | white paper softback? | ?pp | ? photograph | ? maps | ? | 1929 | German Text. | Fraktur Script.

𝕭𝖆𝖓𝖉 6. 𝕾𝖕𝖊𝖗𝖗𝖆𝖓𝖌𝖗𝖎𝖋𝖋𝖊. (Band 6. Sperrangriffe. – *Volume 6. Attacking by Blockade.*)

Konrad Zander | ?cm x ?cm | white paper softback? | ?pp | ? photograph | ? maps | ? | 1929 | German Text. | Fraktur Script.

𝕭𝖆𝖓𝖉 7. 𝕯𝖎𝖊 𝕷𝖚𝖋𝖙𝖘𝖈𝖍𝖎𝖋𝖋𝖊 𝖎𝖒 𝕯𝖎𝖊𝖓𝖘𝖙 𝖉𝖊𝖗 𝕸𝖆𝖗𝖎𝖓𝖊 1912–1918. (Band 7. Die Luftschiffe im Dienst der Marine 1912-1918. – *Volume 7. Airships in Naval Service 1912-1918.*)

Horst Freiherr Treusch von Buttlar-Brandenfels | ?cm x ?cm | white paper softback? | ?pp | ? photograph | ? maps | ? | 1929 | German Text. | Fraktur Script.

𝕭𝖆𝖓𝖉 8. 𝕯𝖎𝖊 𝕶𝖗𝖎𝖊𝖌𝖒𝖆̈𝖘𝖘𝖎𝖌𝖊 𝕳𝖊𝖗𝖗𝖎𝖈𝖍𝖙𝖚𝖓𝖌 𝖊𝖎𝖓𝖊𝖘 𝖀𝖓𝖙𝖊𝖗𝖘𝖊𝖊𝖇𝖔𝖔𝖙𝖘𝖘𝖙𝖚̈𝖙𝖟𝖕𝖚𝖓𝖐𝖙𝖊𝖘 𝖆𝖚𝖋 𝖉𝖊𝖗 𝕰𝖒𝖘 𝖚𝖓𝖉 𝖉𝖎𝖊 𝖎𝖒 𝕶𝖗𝖎𝖊𝖌𝖘𝖇𝖊𝖙𝖗𝖎𝖊𝖇 𝖉𝖊𝖗 III. 𝖀𝖓𝖙𝖊𝖗𝖘𝖊𝖊𝖇𝖔𝖔𝖙𝖘𝖋𝖑𝖔𝖙𝖙𝖎𝖑𝖑𝖊 𝖌𝖊𝖜𝖔𝖓𝖓𝖊𝖓𝖊𝖓 𝕰𝖗𝖋𝖆𝖍𝖗𝖚𝖓𝖌𝖊𝖓. (Band 8. Die Kriegmässige Herrichtung eines Unterseebootsstützpunktes auf der Ems und die im Kriegsbetrieb der III. Unterseebootsflottille gewonnenen Erfahrungen. – *Volume 8. Setting up a Submarine Base in the Ems under Wartime Conditions and the Experiences Gained in the 3rd Submarine Flotilla during the War.*)

Albert Gayer | ?cm x ?cm | white paper softback? | ?pp | ? photograph | ? maps | ? | 1930 | German Text. | Fraktur Script.

𝕭𝖆𝖓𝖉 9. 𝕯𝖊𝖗 𝕺𝖗𝖌𝖆𝖓𝖎𝖘𝖒𝖚𝖘 𝖉𝖊𝖗 𝕶𝖆𝖎𝖘𝖊𝖗𝖑𝖎𝖈𝖍𝖊𝖓 𝕸𝖆𝖗𝖎𝖓𝖊 𝖚𝖓𝖉 𝖉𝖊𝖗 𝖂𝖊𝖑𝖙𝖐𝖗𝖎𝖊𝖌. (Band 9. Der Organismus der Kaiserlichen Marine und der Weltkrieg. – *Volume 9. The Organisation of the Imperial Navy and the World War.*)

Adolf von Trotha | ?cm x ?cm | white paper softback? | ?pp | ? photograph | ? maps | ? | 1930 | German Text. | Fraktur Script.

Band 10. Der Artillerieoffizier eines Grosskampfschiffes im Kriege 1914-1918. (Band 10. Der Artillerieoffizier eines Grosskampfschiffes im Kriege 1914-1918. – *Volume 10. The Gunnery Officer on a Large Battleship during the War 1914-1918.*)

> Erich Mahrholz | ?cm x ?cm | white paper softback? | ?pp | ? photograph | ? maps | ? | 1930 | German Text. | Fraktur Script.

Band 11. Die Verwendung der Torpedowaffe in dem Schlachtkreuzergefecht auf der Doggerbank und in der Skagerrakschlacht. (Band 11. Die Verwendung der Torpedowaffe in dem Schlachtkreuzergefecht auf der Doggerbank und in der Skagerrakschlacht. – *Volume 11. The Employment of the Torpedo Weapon during the Action of the Battlecruisers on the Doggerbank and in the Battle of Jutland.*)

> Theodor Krancke | ?cm x ?cm | white paper softback? | ?pp | ? photograph | ? maps | ? | 1930 | German Text. | Fraktur Script.

Band 12. Kriegserfahrungen über Versalzungen von Kriegschiffmaschinenanlagen. (Band 12. Kriegserfahrungen über Versalzungen von Kriegschiffmaschinenanlagen. - *Volume 12. Wartime Experience of Salt Damage to Warships' Engine rooms.*)

> Willy Zieb | ?cm x ?cm | white paper softback? | ?pp | ? photograph | ? maps | ? | 1937 | German Text. | Fraktur Script.

Band 13. Der Einfluss der Funkaufklärung auf die Seekriegsführung in der Nordsee 1914-1918. (Band 13. Der Einfluss der Funkaufklärung auf die Seekriegsführung in der Nordsee 1914-1918. – *Volume 13. The Influence of Radio-Reconnaissance on the Naval Events in the North Sea 1914-1918.*)

> Gustav Kleikamp | ?cm x ?cm | white paper softback? | ?pp | ? photograph | ? maps | ? | 1934 | German Text. | Fraktur Script.

Band 14. Mine und Seestrategie. Verwendung der Mine nach den Erfahrungen des Weltkrieges. (Band 14. Mine und Seestrategie. Verwendung der Mine nach den Erfahrungen des Weltkrieges. – *Volume 14. The Mine and Naval Strategy. Employment of the Mine after the Experience of the World War.*)

> Winfried Hagen | ?cm x ?cm | white paper softback? | ?pp | ? photograph | ? maps | ? | 1935 | German Text. | Fraktur Script.

Band 15. Der Kramf der Marine gegan Versailles 1919-1935. (Band 15. Der Kramf der Marine gegan Versailles 1919-1935. – *Volume 15. The Fight of the Navy against Versailles.*)

> Adalbert Schüssler | ?cm x ?cm | white paper softback? | ?pp | ? photograph | ? maps | ? | 1937 | German Text. | Fraktur Script.

Army Staff Papers (Pre War Planning);

Dienstschriften des Chefs des Generalstabes des Armee Generalfeldmarschalls Graf von Schlieffen. Band 1 Die Taktisch – Strategischen Aufgaben auf den Jahren 1891-1905. (Dienstschriften des Chefs des Generalstabes des Armee Generalfeldmarschalls Graf von Schlieffen. Band 1 Die Taktisch – Strategischen Aufgaben aus den Jahren 1891-1905. - *Official Writings of the Chief of the General Staff of the Army Field Marshal Graf von Schlieffen. Volume 1 The Tactical – Strategical Problems of the Years 1891-1905.*)

> *Generalfeldmarschall* Alfred *Graf* von Schlieffen | 24cm x 17cm | red cloth hardback | xv + 143pp | 6 large format maps | 40 sketch maps | 1 appendix | Verlag Ernst Siegfried Mittler und Sohn. | 1937 | German Text. | Fraktur Script.

Dienstschriften des Chefs des Generalstabes des Armee Generalfeldmarschalls Graf von Schlieffen. Band 2 Die Großen Generalstabsreisen - Ost - auf den Jahren 1891-1905. (Dienstschriften des Chefs des Generalstabes des Armee Generalfeldmarschalls Graf von Schlieffen. Band 2 Die Großen Generalstabsreisen – Ost – aus den Jahren 1891-1905. - *Official Writings of the Chief of the General Staff of the Army Field Marshal Graf von Schlieffen. Volume 2 The Great General Staff Rides – East - in the Years 1891-1905.*)

Generalfeldmarschall Alfred *Graf* von Schlieffen | 24cm x 17cm | red cloth hardback | xv + 315pp | 15 large format maps | 37 sketch maps | Verlag Ernst Siegfried Mittler und Sohn. | 1938 | German Text. | Fraktur Script.

It was intended to publish three volumes in this series; the "**Dienstschriften des Chefs des Generalstabes des Armee Generalfeldmarschalls Graf von Schlieffen.**" - the third covering von Schlieffen's General Staff Rides in the West. Although this third book had been started at the outbreak of the Second World War, the draft and the archives relating to it were destroyed in an Allied bombing raid and so never completed nor published.

Miltärwiſſenſchaftliche Rundſchau Herausgegeben vom Reichſkriegſminiſterium – SONDERHEFT Schlieffenſ Vermächtniſ (Miltärwissenschaftliche Rundschau Herausgegeben vom Reichskriegsministerium - SONDERHEFT Schlieffens Vermächtnis – *Military Scientific Review Published by the Reich War Ministry – Special Edition Schlieffen's Legacy.*)

Generalleutnant außer Dienst von Joellner | 24cm x 17cm | red paper softback | 56pp | 4 maps | 2 photographs | Verlag Ernst Siegfried Mittler und Sohn. | 1938 | German Text. | Fraktur Script.

Army Staff Papers;

Studien zur Kriegſgeſchichte und Taktik – Begegnungſgefechte. (Studien zur Kriegsgeschichte und Taktik – Begegnungsgefechte. - *Studies of War History and Tactics – Combat Encounters.*)

Anonymous | 24cm x 17cm | red cloth hardback | xv + 214pp | 24 large format maps | 25 sketch maps | 6 panarama photographs | 21 tables | 33 appendices | Verlag Ernst Siegfried Mittler und Sohn. | 1939 | German Text. | Fraktur Script.

Kriegſberichte auſ dem Großen Hauptquartier. Band 1 Erinnerungen auſ den Tagen der Kapitulation und Übergabe der Feſtung Maubeuge – Unſer Sieg bei Soiſſonſ – Daſ Gefecht von Hurtebiſ am 25–26 Januar – Die Kämpfe im Oberelſaß Mitte und Ende Januar. (Kriegsberichte aus dem Großen Hauptquartier. Band 1 Erinnerungen aus den Tagen der Kapitulation und Übergabe der Festung Maubeuge – Unser Sieg bei Soissons – Das Gefecht von Hurtebis am 25-26 Januar – Die Kämpfe im Oberelsaß Mitte und Ende Januar. - *Reports from General Headquarters. Volume 1 Memories from the Days of the Capitulation and Surrender of the Fortress of Maubeuge – Our Victory near Soissons – The Battle of Hurtebis from the 25th to 26th January – The Battle in the Upper Alsace in the Middle to the End of January.*)

Anonymous | 24cm x 17cm | white paper softback | illustrated cover | 26pp | 1 map | Deutsche Verlagsanstalt. | 1915 | German Text. | Fraktur Script.

Kriegſberichte auſ dem Großen Hauptquartier. Band 2 Die Kämpfe im Argonner Wald. (Kriegsberichte aus dem Großen Hauptquartier. Band 2 Die Kämpfe im Argonner Wald. - *Reports from General Headquarters. Volume 2 The Fighting in the Argonne Forest.*)

Anonymous | 24cm x 17cm | white paper softback | illustrated cover | 18pp | 1 map | Deutsche Verlagsanstalt. | 1915 | German Text. | Fraktur Script.

Kriegſberichte auſ dem Großen Hauptquartier. Band 3 Die Ereigniſſe auf dem öſtlichen Kriegſſchauplatz ſeit Mitte September. – Die neutägige Winterſchlacht in Maſuren. – Die Kämpfe bei Wirballen am 10 Februar 1915. (Kriegsberichte aus dem Großen Hauptquartier. Band 3 Die Ereignisse auf dem östlichen Kriegsschauplatz seit Mitte September. – Die neutägige Winterschlacht in Masuren. – Die Kämpfe bei Wirballen am 10 Februar 1915. - *Reports from General Headquarters. Volume 3 The Events on the Eastern Front of the War since the Middle of September. – The Nine Days Winter Battle in Masuren. – The Battles in Wirballen on the 10th February 1915.*)

Anonymous | 24cm x 17cm | white paper softback | illustrated cover | 56pp | 9 maps | Deutsche Verlagsanstalt. | 1915 | German Text. | Fraktur Script.

𝔎𝔯𝔦𝔢𝔤𝔰𝔟𝔢𝔯𝔦𝔠𝔥𝔱𝔢 auf dem Großen Hauptquartier. Band 4 Die deutschen Truppen in den Karpathen. – Die Kämpfe bei Münster. (Kriegsberichte aus dem Großen Hauptquartier. Band 4 Die deutschen Truppen in den Karpathen. - Die Kämpfe bei Münster. - *Reports from General Headquarters. Volume 4 The German Troops in the Carpathian. – The Battles in Münster.*)

    Anonymous | 24cm x 17cm | white paper softback | illustrated cover | ?pp | 2 maps | Deutsche Verlagsanstalt. | 1915 | German Text. | Fraktur Script.

𝔎𝔯𝔦𝔢𝔤𝔰𝔟𝔢𝔯𝔦𝔠𝔥𝔱𝔢 auf dem Großen Hauptquartier. Band 5 Auf den Kämpfen im Osten. (Kriegsberichte aus dem Großen Hauptquartier. Band 5 Aus den Kämpfen im Osten. - *Reports from General Headquarters. Volume 5 From the Fights in the East.*)

    Anonymous | 24cm x 17cm | white paper softback | illustrated cover | 67pp | 8 maps | Deutsche Verlagsanstalt. | 1915 | German Text. | Fraktur Script.

𝔎𝔯𝔦𝔢𝔤𝔰𝔟𝔢𝔯𝔦𝔠𝔥𝔱𝔢 auf dem Großen Hauptquartier. Band 6 Die Kämpfe im zwischen Maas und Mosel. (Kriegsberichte aus dem Großen Hauptquartier. Band 6 Die Kämpfe im zwischen Maas und Mosel. - *Reports from General Headquarters. Volume 6 The Battles between the Maas and the Moselle.*)

    Anonymous | 24cm x 17cm | white paper softback | illustrated cover | 17pp | 1 map | Deutsche Verlagsanstalt. | 1915 | German Text. | Fraktur Script.

𝔎𝔯𝔦𝔢𝔤𝔰𝔟𝔢𝔯𝔦𝔠𝔥𝔱𝔢 auf dem Großen Hauptquartier. Band 7 Die Durchbruchsschlacht in Galizien bis zur Einnahme von Przemysl. (Kriegsberichte aus dem Großen Hauptquartier. Band 7 Die Durchbruchsschlacht in Galizien bis zur Einnahme von Przemysl. - *Reports from General Headquarters. Volume 7 The Break-Through Battle in Galicia until the Capture of Przemysl.*)

    Anonymous | 24cm x 17cm | white paper softback | illustrated cover | ?pp | 1 map | Deutsche Verlagsanstalt. | 1915 | German Text. | Fraktur Script.

𝔎𝔯𝔦𝔢𝔤𝔰𝔟𝔢𝔯𝔦𝔠𝔥𝔱𝔢 auf dem Großen Hauptquartier. Band 8 Die Kämpfe im Galizien – Der Kampf um Grodek – Die Einnahme von Limberg. (Kriegsberichte aus dem Großen Hauptquartier. Band 8 Die Kämpfe im Galizien – Der Kampf um Grodek – Die Einnahme von Limberg. - *Reports from General Headquarters. Volume 8 The Fights in Galicia – the Fight for Grodek – the Capture of Limberg.*)

    Anonymous | 24cm x 17cm | white paper softback | illustrated cover | ?pp | 2 maps | Deutsche Verlagsanstalt. | 1915 | German Text. | Fraktur Script.

𝔎𝔯𝔦𝔢𝔤𝔰𝔟𝔢𝔯𝔦𝔠𝔥𝔱𝔢 auf dem Großen Hauptquartier. Band 9 Die Kämpfe bei Ypern – Die Kämpfe bei Les Eparges – Der Kampf um Ban de Sapt. (Kriegsberichte aus dem Großen Hauptquartier. Band 9 Die Kämpfe bei Ypern – Die Kämpfe bei Les Eparges – Der Kampf um Ban de Sapt. - *Reports from General Headquarters. Volume 9 The Fighting for Ypres – the Fighting for Les Eparges – the Fighting for the Ban de Sapt.*)

    Anonymous | 24cm x 17cm | white paper softback | illustrated cover | ?pp | 3 maps | Deutsche Verlagsanstalt. | 1915 | German Text. | Fraktur Script.

𝔎𝔯𝔦𝔢𝔤𝔰𝔟𝔢𝔯𝔦𝔠𝔥𝔱𝔢 auf dem Großen Hauptquartier. Band 10 Neues von Feldmarschall Hindenburg. (Kriegsberichte aus dem Großen Hauptquartier. Band 10 Neues von Feldmarschall Hindenburg. - *Reports from General Headquarters. Volume 10 News from Field Marshal Hindenburg.*)

    Anonymous | 24cm x 17cm | white paper softback | illustrated cover | 23pp | 1 map | Deutsche Verlagsanstalt. | 1915 | German Text. | Fraktur Script.

𝔎𝔯𝔦𝔢𝔤𝔰𝔟𝔢𝔯𝔦𝔠𝔥𝔱𝔢 auf dem Großen Hauptquartier. Band 11 Die Argonnenkämpfe vom 20 Juni und vom 13/14 Juli 1915. (Kriegsberichte aus dem Großen Hauptquartier. Band 11 Die Argonnenkämpfe vom 20 Juni und vom 13/14 Juli 1915. - *Reports from General Headquarters. Volume 11 The Fighting in the Argonne from 20th June and from 13th/14th July 1915.*)

    Anonymous | 24cm x 17cm | white paper softback | illustrated cover | ?pp | 4 maps | Deutsche Verlagsanstalt. | 1915 | German Text. | Fraktur Script.

𝔎𝔯𝔦𝔢𝔤𝔰𝔟𝔢𝔯𝔦𝔠𝔥𝔱𝔢 auf dem Großen Hauptquartier. Band 12 Die Schlacht von La Bassée und Arras im Mai 1915 – Lorettoschlacht. (Kriegsberichte aus dem Großen Hauptquartier. Band 12 Die Schlacht von La Bassée und Arras im Mai 1915 -

Lorettoschlacht. - *Reports from General Headquarters. Volume 12 The Battle between La Bassée and Arras in May 1915 - The Battle of Notre Dame de Lorette.*)

> Anonymous | 24cm x 17cm | white paper softback | illustrated cover | ?pp | 4 maps | Deutsche Verlagsanstalt. | 1915 | German Text. | Fraktur Script.

𝕶𝖗𝖎𝖊𝖌𝖘𝖇𝖊𝖗𝖎𝖈𝖍𝖙𝖊 𝖆𝖚𝖋 𝖉𝖊𝖒 𝕲𝖗𝖔𝖘𝖊𝖓 𝕳𝖆𝖚𝖕𝖙𝖖𝖚𝖆𝖗𝖙𝖎𝖊𝖗. 𝕭𝖆𝖓𝖉 13 𝕯𝖎𝖊 𝕶ämpfe in Serbien und Östlich von Wilna. (Kriegsberichte aus dem Großen Hauptquartier. Band 13 Die Kämpfe in Serbien und Östlich von Wilna. - *Reports from General Headquarters. Volume 13 The Fighting in Serbia and to the East of Wilna.*)

> Anonymous | 24cm x 17cm | white paper softback | illustrated cover | 26pp | 3 maps | Deutsche Verlagsanstalt. | 1916 | German Text. | Fraktur Script.

𝕶𝖗𝖎𝖊𝖌𝖘𝖇𝖊𝖗𝖎𝖈𝖍𝖙𝖊 𝖆𝖚𝖋 𝖉𝖊𝖒 𝕲𝖗𝖔𝖘𝖊𝖓 𝕳𝖆𝖚𝖕𝖙𝖖𝖚𝖆𝖗𝖙𝖎𝖊𝖗. 𝕭𝖆𝖓𝖉 14 𝕯𝖊𝖗 𝕯𝖚𝖗𝖈𝖍𝖇𝖗𝖚𝖈𝖍 𝖇𝖊𝖎 Praznysz – Unser Kaiser bei der Armeeabteilung Woyrsch – Wie Kowno erobert wurde. (Kriegsberichte aus dem Großen Hauptquartier. Band 14 Der Durchbruch bei Praznysz – Unser Kaiser bei der Armeeabteilung Woyrsch – Wie Kowno erobert wurde. - *Reports from General Headquarters. Volume 14 The Break-Through at Praznysz – The Kaiser's Visit to Woyrsch's Army Division – The Conquest of Kowno.*)

> Anonymous | 24cm x 17cm | white paper softback | illustrated cover | 18pp | 2 maps | Deutsche Verlagsanstalt. | 1916 | German Text. | Fraktur Script.

𝕶𝖗𝖎𝖊𝖌𝖘𝖇𝖊𝖗𝖎𝖈𝖍𝖙𝖊 𝖆𝖚𝖋 𝖉𝖊𝖒 𝕲𝖗𝖔𝖘𝖊𝖓 𝕳𝖆𝖚𝖕𝖙𝖖𝖚𝖆𝖗𝖙𝖎𝖊𝖗. 𝕭𝖆𝖓𝖉 15 𝕾𝖈𝖍𝖚𝖑𝖙𝖊𝖗 𝖆𝖓 Schulter mit unseren Verbündeten. (Kriegsberichte aus dem Großen Hauptquartier. Band 15 Schulter an Schulter mit unseren Verbündeten. - *Reports from General Headquarters. Volume 15 Shoulder to Shoulder with our Allies.*)

> Anonymous | 24cm x 17cm | white paper softback | illustrated cover | ?pp | 1 map | Deutsche Verlagsanstalt. | 1916 | German Text. | Fraktur Script.

𝕶𝖗𝖎𝖊𝖌𝖘𝖇𝖊𝖗𝖎𝖈𝖍𝖙𝖊 𝖆𝖚𝖋 𝖉𝖊𝖒 𝕲𝖗𝖔𝖘𝖊𝖓 𝕳𝖆𝖚𝖕𝖙𝖖𝖚𝖆𝖗𝖙𝖎𝖊𝖗. 𝕭𝖆𝖓𝖉 16 𝕬𝖚𝖋 𝖉𝖊𝖓 𝕾𝖕𝖚𝖗𝖊𝖓 der Bug–Armee. (Kriegsberichte aus dem Großen Hauptquartier. Band 16 Auf den Spuren der Bug-Armee. - *Reports from General Headquarters. Volume 16 In the Tracks of the Army of the Bug.*)

> Anonymous | 24cm x 17cm | white paper softback | illustrated cover | ?pp | 1 map | Deutsche Verlagsanstalt. | 1916 | German Text. | Fraktur Script.

𝕶𝖗𝖎𝖊𝖌𝖘𝖇𝖊𝖗𝖎𝖈𝖍𝖙𝖊 𝖆𝖚𝖋 𝖉𝖊𝖒 𝕲𝖗𝖔𝖘𝖊𝖓 𝕳𝖆𝖚𝖕𝖙𝖖𝖚𝖆𝖗𝖙𝖎𝖊𝖗. 𝕭𝖆𝖓𝖉 17 𝕯𝖎𝖊 𝕱𝖗ühlingskämpfe 1916. (Kriegsberichte aus dem Großen Hauptquartier. Band 17 Die Frühlingskämpfe 1916. - *Reports from General Headquarters. Volume 17 The Spring Fighting of 1916.*)

> Anonymous | 24cm x 17cm | white paper softback | illustrated cover | 23pp | 2 maps | Deutsche Verlagsanstalt. | 1916 | German Text. | Fraktur Script.

𝕶𝖗𝖎𝖊𝖌𝖘𝖇𝖊𝖗𝖎𝖈𝖍𝖙𝖊 𝖆𝖚𝖋 𝖉𝖊𝖒 𝕲𝖗𝖔𝖘𝖊𝖓 𝕳𝖆𝖚𝖕𝖙𝖖𝖚𝖆𝖗𝖙𝖎𝖊𝖗. 𝕭𝖆𝖓𝖉 18 1916. 𝕯𝖎𝖊 russische Märzoffensive – Der Krieg zu Lande in den Monaten Mai und Juni – Siegesglaube. (Kriegsberichte aus dem Großen Hauptquartier. Band 18 1916. Die russische Märzoffensive – Der Krieg zu Lande in den Monaten Mai und Juni – Siegesglaube. - *Reports from General Headquarters. Volume 18 1916 The Russian March Offensive – The Land Warfare in the Months of May and June – Faith in Victory.*)

> Anonymous | 24cm x 17cm | white paper softback | illustrated cover | 24pp | 2 maps | Deutsche Verlagsanstalt. | 1916 | German Text. | Fraktur Script.

𝕶𝖗𝖎𝖊𝖌𝖘𝖇𝖊𝖗𝖎𝖈𝖍𝖙𝖊 𝖆𝖚𝖋 𝖉𝖊𝖒 𝕲𝖗𝖔𝖘𝖊𝖓 𝕳𝖆𝖚𝖕𝖙𝖖𝖚𝖆𝖗𝖙𝖎𝖊𝖗. 𝕭𝖆𝖓𝖉 19 𝕯𝖎𝖊 𝕾𝖈𝖍𝖑𝖆𝖈𝖍𝖙 𝖆𝖓 der Somme im Monat Juli. (Kriegsberichte aus dem Großen Hauptquartier. Band 19 Die Schlacht an der Somme im Monat Juli. - *Reports from General Headquarters. Volume 19 The Battle of the Somme in the Month of July.*)

> Anonymous | 24cm x 17cm | white paper softback | illustrated cover | 110pp | 19 maps | Deutsche Verlagsanstalt. | 1916 | German Text. | Fraktur Script.

𝕶𝖗𝖎𝖊𝖌𝖘𝖇𝖊𝖗𝖎𝖈𝖍𝖙𝖊 𝖆𝖚𝖋 𝖉𝖊𝖒 𝕲𝖗𝖔𝖘𝖊𝖓 𝕳𝖆𝖚𝖕𝖙𝖖𝖚𝖆𝖗𝖙𝖎𝖊𝖗. 𝕭𝖆𝖓𝖉 20 𝕯𝖎𝖊 𝖗𝖚𝖘𝖘𝖎𝖘𝖈𝖍𝖊 Sommeroffensive 1916. (Kriegsberichte aus dem Großen Hauptquartier. Band 20 Die russische Sommeroffensive 1916. - *Reports from General Headquarters. Volume 20 The Russian Summer Offensive, 1916.*)

> Anonymous | 24cm x 17cm | white paper softback | illustrated cover | 56pp | 7 maps | Deutsche Verlagsanstalt. | 1916 | German Text. | Fraktur Script.

𝕶𝖗𝖎𝖊𝖌𝖋𝖇𝖊𝖗𝖎𝖈𝖍𝖙𝖊 𝖆𝖚𝖋 𝖉𝖊𝖒 𝖊𝖗𝖔𝖋𝖊𝖓 𝕳𝖆𝖚𝖕𝖙𝖖𝖚𝖆𝖗𝖙𝖎𝖊𝖗. 𝕭𝖆𝖓𝖉 21 𝕯𝖎𝖊 𝕾𝖈𝖍𝖑𝖆𝖈𝖍𝖙 𝖛𝖔𝖗 𝕭𝖊𝖗𝖉𝖚𝖓 — 𝕯𝖎𝖊 𝕾𝖈𝖍𝖑𝖆𝖈𝖍𝖙 𝖆𝖓 𝖉𝖊𝖗 𝕾𝖔𝖒𝖒𝖊. (Kriegsberichte aus dem Großen Hauptquartier. Band 21 Die Schlacht vor Verdun - Die Schlacht an der Somme. - *Reports from General Headquarters. Volume 21 The Battle of Verdun – The Battle of the Somme.*)

Anonymous | 24cm x 17cm | white paper softback | illustrated cover | ?pp | 2 maps | Deutsche Verlagsanstalt. | 1916 | German Text. | Fraktur Script.

𝕶𝖗𝖎𝖊𝖌𝖋𝖇𝖊𝖗𝖎𝖈𝖍𝖙𝖊 𝖆𝖚𝖋 𝖉𝖊𝖒 𝔾𝖗𝖔𝖋𝖊𝖓 𝕳𝖆𝖚𝖕𝖙𝖖𝖚𝖆𝖗𝖙𝖎𝖊𝖗. 𝕭𝖆𝖓𝖉 22 𝕯𝖊𝖗 𝕯𝖔𝖇𝖗𝖚𝖉𝖋𝖈𝖍𝖆-𝖋𝖊𝖑𝖉𝖟𝖚𝖌. (Kriegsberichte aus dem Großen Hauptquartier. Band 22 Der Dobrudscha-Feldzug. - *Reports from General Headquarters. Volume 22 The Dobrudscha Campaign.*)

Anonymous | 24cm x 17cm | white paper softback | illustrated cover | ?pp | 1 map | Deutsche Verlagsanstalt. | 1916 | German Text. | Fraktur Script.

𝕶𝖗𝖎𝖊𝖌𝖋𝖇𝖊𝖗𝖎𝖈𝖍𝖙𝖊 𝖆𝖚𝖋 𝖉𝖊𝖒 𝔾𝖗𝖔𝖋𝖊𝖓 𝕳𝖆𝖚𝖕𝖙𝖖𝖚𝖆𝖗𝖙𝖎𝖊𝖗. 𝕭𝖆𝖓𝖉 23 𝕬𝖚𝖋 𝖉𝖊𝖓 𝕶𝖆𝖒𝖕𝖋𝖊𝖓 𝖉𝖊𝖗 𝖉𝖊𝖚𝖙𝖋𝖈𝖍𝖊𝖓 𝕶𝖆𝖗𝖕𝖆𝖙𝖍𝖊𝖓𝖙𝖗𝖚𝖕𝖕𝖊𝖓 (1916) — 𝕯𝖎𝖊 𝕺𝖋𝖙𝖋𝖗𝖔𝖓𝖙 𝖎𝖒 𝕹𝖔𝖛𝖊𝖒𝖇𝖊𝖗 1916. (Kriegsberichte aus dem Großen Hauptquartier. Band 23 Aus den Kämpfen der deutschen Karpathentruppen (1916) – Die Ostfront im November 1916. - *Reports from General Headquarters. Volume 23 The Fighting of the German Troops in the Carpathians [1916] – The Eastern Front in November 1916.*)

Anonymous | 24cm x 17cm | white paper softback | illustrated cover | ?pp | 1 map | Deutsche Verlagsanstalt. | 1916 | German Text. | Fraktur Script.

𝕶𝖗𝖎𝖊𝖌𝖋𝖇𝖊𝖗𝖎𝖈𝖍𝖙𝖊 𝖆𝖚𝖋 𝖉𝖊𝖒 𝔾𝖗𝖔𝖋𝖊𝖓 𝕳𝖆𝖚𝖕𝖙𝖖𝖚𝖆𝖗𝖙𝖎𝖊𝖗. 𝕭𝖆𝖓𝖉 24 𝕯𝖎𝖊 𝕺𝖕𝖊𝖗𝖆𝖙𝖎𝖔𝖓𝖊𝖓 𝖉𝖊𝖋 𝕬𝖑𝖕𝖊𝖓𝖐𝖔𝖗𝖕𝖋 𝖛𝖔𝖒 𝕽𝖔𝖙𝖊𝖓-𝕿𝖚𝖗𝖒-𝕻𝖆𝖋𝖋 𝖇𝖎𝖋 𝕿𝖎𝖙𝖚 — 𝕯𝖎𝖊 𝕰𝖗𝖔𝖇𝖊𝖗𝖚𝖓𝖌 𝖛𝖔𝖓 𝕿𝖚𝖙𝖗𝖆𝖐𝖆𝖓. (Kriegsberichte aus dem Großen Hauptquartier. Band 24 Die Operationen des Alpenkorps vom Roten-Turm-Pass bis Titu – Die Eroberung von Tutrakan. - *Reports from General Headquarters. Volume 24 The Operations of the Alpine Corps from the Roten-Turm Pass to Titu - The Capture of Tutrakan.*)

Anonymous | 24cm x 17cm | white paper softback | illustrated cover | 24pp | 2 map | Deutsche Verlagsanstalt. | 1917 | German Text. | Fraktur Script.

𝕶𝖗𝖎𝖊𝖌𝖋𝖇𝖊𝖗𝖎𝖈𝖍𝖙𝖊 𝖆𝖚𝖋 𝖉𝖊𝖒 𝔾𝖗𝖔𝖋𝖊𝖓 𝕳𝖆𝖚𝖕𝖙𝖖𝖚𝖆𝖗𝖙𝖎𝖊𝖗. 𝕭𝖆𝖓𝖉 25 𝕯𝖊𝖗 𝕰𝖎𝖓𝖇𝖗𝖚𝖈𝖍 𝖎𝖓 𝖉𝖎𝖊 𝖂𝖆𝖑𝖆𝖈𝖍𝖊𝖎 — 𝕯𝖊𝖗 𝖁𝖔𝖗𝖒𝖆𝖗𝖋𝖈𝖍 𝖉𝖊𝖗 𝕯𝖔𝖓𝖆𝖚-𝕬𝖗𝖒𝖊𝖊 𝖛𝖔𝖓 𝕭𝖚𝖎𝖐𝖆𝖗𝖊𝖋𝖙 𝖆𝖚𝖋 𝕭𝖗𝖆𝖎𝖑𝖆. (Kriegsberichte aus dem Großen Hauptquartier. Band 25 Der Einbruch in die Walachei – Der Vormarsch der Donau-Armee von Buikarest auf Braila. - *Reports from General Headquarters. Volume 25 The Break-Through into the Walachei – The Advance of the Danube Army to Bucharest and on to Braila.*)

Anonymous | 24cm x 17cm | white paper softback | illustrated cover | ?pp | 2 maps | Deutsche Verlagsanstalt. | 1917 | German Text. | Fraktur Script.

𝕶𝖗𝖎𝖊𝖌𝖋𝖇𝖊𝖗𝖎𝖈𝖍𝖙𝖊 𝖆𝖚𝖋 𝖉𝖊𝖒 𝔾𝖗𝖔𝖋𝖊𝖓 𝕳𝖆𝖚𝖕𝖙𝖖𝖚𝖆𝖗𝖙𝖎𝖊𝖗. 𝕭𝖆𝖓𝖉 26 𝕯𝖎𝖊 𝕶𝖆𝖒𝖕𝖋𝖊 𝖆𝖓 𝖉𝖊𝖗 𝕬𝖓𝖈𝖗𝖊. (Kriegsberichte aus dem Großen Hauptquartier. Band 26 Die Kämpfe an der Ancre. - *Reports from General Headquarters. Volume 26 The Fighting on the Ancre.*)

Anonymous | 24cm x 17cm | white paper softback | illustrated cover | ?pp | 3 maps | Deutsche Verlagsanstalt. | 1917 | German Text. | Fraktur Script.

𝕶𝖗𝖎𝖊𝖌𝖋𝖇𝖊𝖗𝖎𝖈𝖍𝖙𝖊 𝖆𝖚𝖋 𝖉𝖊𝖒 𝔾𝖗𝖔𝖋𝖊𝖓 𝕳𝖆𝖚𝖕𝖙𝖖𝖚𝖆𝖗𝖙𝖎𝖊𝖗. 𝕭𝖆𝖓𝖉 27 𝕯𝖎𝖊 𝕶𝖆𝖒𝖕𝖋𝖊 𝖉𝖊𝖋 𝕶𝖔𝖗𝖕𝖋 𝕸𝖔𝖗𝖌𝖊𝖓 𝖛𝖔𝖓 𝕮𝖆𝖒𝖕𝖔𝖑𝖚𝖓𝖌 𝖇𝖎𝖋 𝖋𝖔𝖈𝖋𝖆𝖓𝖎 — 𝕿𝖊𝖎𝖑𝖓𝖆𝖍𝖒𝖊 𝖉𝖊𝖗 9 𝕬𝖗𝖒𝖊𝖊 𝖆𝖓 𝖉𝖊𝖗 𝕾𝖈𝖍𝖑𝖆𝖈𝖍𝖙 𝖆𝖒 𝕬𝖗𝖌𝖊𝖋 — 1-5 𝕯𝖊𝖟𝖊𝖒𝖇𝖊𝖗 1916 𝖚𝖓𝖉 𝖎𝖍𝖗𝖊 𝖋𝖙𝖗𝖆𝖙𝖊𝖌𝖎𝖋𝖋𝖈𝖍𝖊 𝕭𝖊𝖉𝖊𝖚𝖙𝖚𝖓𝖌. (Kriegsberichte aus dem Großen Hauptquartier. Band 27 Die Kämpfe des Korps Morgen von Campolung bis Focsani – Teilnahme der 9 Armee an der Schlacht am Arges - 1-5 Dezember 1916 und ihre strategissche Bedeutung. – *Reports from General Headquarters. Volume 27 The Fighting of the Morgen Corps from Campolung to Focsani – Participation of the 9th Army at the Battle on the Arges - 1st-5th December 1916 and its Strategic Meaning.*)

Anonymous | 24cm x 17cm | white paper softback | illustrated cover | 23pp | 5 maps | Deutsche Verlagsanstalt. | 1917 | German Text. | Fraktur Script.

𝕶𝖗𝖎𝖊𝖌𝖋𝖇𝖊𝖗𝖎𝖈𝖍𝖙𝖊 𝖆𝖚𝖋 𝖉𝖊𝖒 𝔾𝖗𝖔𝖋𝖊𝖓 𝕳𝖆𝖚𝖕𝖙𝖖𝖚𝖆𝖗𝖙𝖎𝖊𝖗. 𝕭𝖆𝖓𝖉 28 𝕬𝖗𝖗𝖆𝖋 1917. (Kriegsberichte aus dem Großen Hauptquartier. Band 28 Arras 1917. - *Reports from General Headquarters. Volume 28 Arras 1917.*).

Anonymous | 24cm x 17cm | white paper softback | illustrated cover | ?pp | 1 map | Deutsche Verlagsanstalt. | 1917 | German Text. | Fraktur Script.

𝕶𝖗𝖎𝖊𝖌𝖘𝖇𝖊𝖗𝖎𝖈𝖍𝖙𝖊 𝖆𝖚𝖋 𝖉𝖊𝖒 𝕲𝖗𝖔ß𝖊𝖓 𝕳𝖆𝖚𝖕𝖙𝖖𝖚𝖆𝖗𝖙𝖎𝖊𝖗. 𝕭𝖆𝖓𝖉 29 𝕯𝖎𝖊 𝖟𝖜ö𝖋𝖙𝖊 𝕴𝖘𝖔𝖓𝖟𝖔𝖘𝖈𝖍𝖑𝖆𝖈𝖍𝖙. (Kriegsberichte aus dem Großen Hauptquartier. Band 29 Die zwölfte Isonzoschlacht. - *Reports from General Headquarters. Volume 29 The Twelfth Battle of the Isonzo.*)

Anonymous | 24cm x 17cm | white paper softback | illustrated cover | ?pp | 2 maps | Deutsche Verlagsanstalt. | 1917 | German Text. | Fraktur Script.

𝕶𝖗𝖎𝖊𝖌𝖘𝖇𝖊𝖗𝖎𝖈𝖍𝖙𝖊 𝖆𝖚𝖋 𝖉𝖊𝖒 𝕲𝖗𝔬ß𝖊𝖓 𝕳𝖆𝖚𝖕𝖙𝖖𝖚𝖆𝖗𝖙𝖎𝖊𝖗. 𝕭𝖆𝖓𝖉 30 𝕬𝖚𝖋 𝖉𝖊𝖓 𝕶ä𝖒𝖕𝖋𝖊𝖓 𝖚𝖓 𝕽𝖎𝖌𝖆 – 𝕯𝖎𝖊 𝕭𝖊𝖘𝖎𝖙𝖟𝖓𝖆𝖍𝖒𝖊 𝖛𝖔𝖓 𝕺𝖊𝖘𝖊𝖑. (Kriegsberichte aus dem Großen Hauptquartier. Band 30 Aus den Kämpfen un Riga – Die Besitznahme von Oesel. - *Reports from General Headquarters. Volume 30 About the Fighting for Riga – The Capture of Oesel.*)

Anonymous | 24cm x 17cm | white paper softback | illustrated cover | ?pp | 3 maps | Deutsche Verlagsanstalt. | 1918 | German Text. | Fraktur Script.

𝕶𝖗𝖎𝖊𝖌𝖘𝖇𝖊𝖗𝖎𝖈𝖍𝖙𝖊 𝖆𝖚𝖋 𝖉𝖊𝖒 𝕲𝖗𝔬ß𝖊𝖓 𝕳𝖆𝖚𝖕𝖙𝖖𝖚𝖆𝖗𝖙𝖎𝖊𝖗. 𝕭𝖆𝖓𝖉 31 𝕯𝖎𝖊 𝕾𝖈𝖍𝖑𝖆𝖈𝖍𝖙 𝖛𝖔𝖓 𝕬𝖗𝖒𝖊𝖓𝖙𝖎è𝖗𝖊𝖘 – 𝕯𝖎𝖊 𝕰𝖗𝖔𝖇𝖊𝖗𝖚𝖓𝖌 𝖉𝖊𝖘 𝕶𝖊𝖒𝖒𝖊𝖑. (Kriegsberichte aus dem Großen Hauptquartier. Band 31 Die Schlacht von Armentières – Die Eroberung des Kemmel. - *Reports from General Headquarters. Volume 31 The Battle of Armentières – The Capture of Mont Kemmel.*)

Anonymous | 24cm x 17cm | white paper softback | illustrated cover | ?pp | 3 maps | Deutsche Verlagsanstalt. | 1918 | German Text. | Fraktur Script.

𝕶𝖗𝖎𝖊𝖌𝖘𝖇𝖊𝖗𝖎𝖈𝖍𝖙𝖊 𝖆𝖚𝖋 𝖉𝖊𝖒 𝕲𝖗𝔬ß𝖊𝖓 𝕳𝖆𝖚𝖕𝖙𝖖𝖚𝖆𝖗𝖙𝖎𝖊𝖗. 𝕭𝖆𝖓𝖉 32 𝕯𝖎𝖊 𝕾𝖈𝖍𝖑𝖆𝖈𝖍𝖙 𝖟𝖜𝖎𝖘𝖈𝖍𝖊𝖓 𝕾𝖔𝖎𝖘𝖘𝖔𝖓𝖘 𝖚𝖓𝖉 𝕽𝖊𝖎𝖒𝖘 – 27 𝕸𝖆𝖎 𝖇𝖎𝖘 6 𝕵𝖚𝖓𝖎 1918. (Kriegsberichte aus dem Großen Hauptquartier. Band 32 Die Schlacht zwischen Soissons und Reims - 27 Mai bis 6 Juni 1918. - *Reports from General Headquarters. Volume 32 The Battle between Soissons and Reims - 27 May to 6th June 1918.*)

Anonymous | 24cm x 17cm | white paper softback | illustrated cover | ?pp | 3 maps | Deutsche Verlagsanstalt. | 1918 | German Text. | Fraktur Script.

𝕯𝖊𝖗 𝕲𝖗𝔬ß𝖊 𝕶𝖗𝖎𝖊𝖌 𝖎𝖓 𝕰𝖎𝖓𝖟𝖊𝖑𝖉𝖆𝖗𝖘𝖙𝖊𝖑𝖑𝖚𝖓𝖌𝖊𝖓. 𝖀𝖓𝖙𝖊𝖗 𝕭𝖊𝖓𝖚𝖙𝖟𝖚𝖓𝖌 𝖆𝖒𝖙𝖑𝖎𝖈𝖍𝖊𝖗 𝕼𝖚𝖊𝖑𝖑𝖊𝖓 𝖍𝖊𝖗𝖆𝖚𝖋𝖌𝖊𝖌𝖊𝖇𝖊𝖓 𝖎𝖒 𝕬𝖚𝖋𝖙𝖗𝖆𝖌𝖊 𝖉𝖊𝖘 𝕲𝖗𝔬ß𝖊𝖓 𝕲𝖊𝖓𝖊𝖗𝖆𝖑𝖘𝖙𝖆𝖇𝖊𝖘. 𝕳𝖊𝖋𝖙 1 𝕷ü𝖙𝖙𝖎𝖘𝖈𝖍 – 𝕹𝖆𝖒𝖚𝖗. (Der Große Krieg in Einzeldarstellungen. Unter Benutzung amtlicher Quellen herausgegeben im Auftrage des Großen Generalstabes. Heft 1 Lüttisch - Namur. - *Individual Studies of the Great War. With Utilization of Official Sources Published on Behalf of the Great General Staff Booklet 1 Liége – Namur.*)

Rolf von Bieberstein | 24cm x 17cm | white paper softback | illustrated cover | 96pp | 1 large format maps | 4 maps | Verlag von Gerhard Stalling. | 1918 | German Text. | Fraktur Script.

𝕯𝖊𝖗 𝕲𝖗𝔬ß𝖊 𝕶𝖗𝖎𝖊𝖌 𝖎𝖓 𝕰𝖎𝖓𝖟𝖊𝖑𝖉𝖆𝖗𝖘𝖙𝖊𝖑𝖑𝖚𝖓𝖌𝖊𝖓. 𝖀𝖓𝖙𝖊𝖗 𝕭𝖊𝖓𝖚𝖙𝖟𝖚𝖓𝖌 𝖆𝖒𝖙𝖑𝖎𝖈𝖍𝖊𝖗 𝕼𝖚𝖊𝖑𝖑𝖊𝖓 𝖍𝖊𝖗𝖆𝖚𝖋𝖌𝖊𝖌𝖊𝖇𝖊𝖓 𝖎𝖒 𝕬𝖚𝖋𝖙𝖗𝖆𝖌𝖊 𝖉𝖊𝖘 𝕲𝖗𝔬ß𝖊𝖓 𝕲𝖊𝖓𝖊𝖗𝖆𝖑𝖘𝖙𝖆𝖇𝖊𝖘. 𝕳𝖊𝖋𝖙 2 𝕯𝖎𝖊 𝕾𝖈𝖍𝖑𝖆𝖈𝖍𝖙 𝖎𝖓 𝕷𝖔𝖙𝖍𝖗𝖎𝖓𝖌𝖊𝖓. (Der Große Krieg in Einzeldarstellungen. Unter Benutzung amtlicher Quellen herausgegeben im Auftrage des Großen Generalstabes. Heft 2 Die Schlacht bei Lothringen. - *Individual Studies of the Great War. With Utilization of Official Sources Published on Behalf of the Great General Staff Booklet 2 The Battle in Lorriane.*)

Anonymous | 24cm x 17cm | white paper softback | illustrated cover | ?pp | ? maps | Verlag von Gerhard Stalling. | 1919 | German Text. | Fraktur Script

𝕯𝖊𝖗 𝕲𝖗𝔬ß𝖊 𝕶𝖗𝖎𝖊𝖌 𝖎𝖓 𝕰𝖎𝖓𝖟𝖊𝖑𝖉𝖆𝖗𝖘𝖙𝖊𝖑𝖑𝖚𝖓𝖌𝖊𝖓. 𝖀𝖓𝖙𝖊𝖗 𝕭𝖊𝖓𝖚𝖙𝖟𝖚𝖓𝖌 𝖆𝖒𝖙𝖑𝖎𝖈𝖍𝖊𝖗 𝕼𝖚𝖊𝖑𝖑𝖊𝖓 𝖍𝖊𝖗𝖆𝖚𝖋𝖌𝖊𝖌𝖊𝖇𝖊𝖓 𝖎𝖒 𝕬𝖚𝖋𝖙𝖗𝖆𝖌𝖊 𝖉𝖊𝖘 𝕲𝖗𝔬ß𝖊𝖓 𝕲𝖊𝖓𝖊𝖗𝖆𝖑𝖘𝖙𝖆𝖇𝖊𝖘. 𝕳𝖊𝖋𝖙 3 𝕯𝖎𝖊 𝕾𝖈𝖍𝖑𝖆𝖈𝖍𝖙 𝖇𝖊𝖎 𝕷𝖔𝖓𝖌𝖜𝖞. (Der Große Krieg in Einzeldarstellungen. Unter Benutzung amtlicher Quellen herausgegeben im Auftrage des Großen Generalstabes. Heft 3 Die Schlacht bei Longwy. - *Individual Studies of the Great War. With Utilization of Official Sources Published on Behalf of the Great General Staff Booklet 3 The Battle of Longwy.*)

Erhard von Mutius | 24cm x 17cm | white paper softback | illustrated cover | 79pp | 15 maps | Verlag von Gerhard Stalling. | 1919 | German Text. | Fraktur Script

Der Große Krieg in Einzeldarstellungen. Unter Benutzung amtlicher Quellen herausgegeben im Auftrage des Großen Generalstabes. Heft 4 Die Schlacht bei Sedan. (Der Große Krieg in Einzeldarstellungen. Unter Benutzung amtlicher Quellen herausgegeben im Auftrage des Großen Generalstabes. Heft 4 Die Schlacht bei Sedan. - *Individual Studies of the Great War. With Utilization of Official Sources Published on Behalf of the Great General Staff Booklet 4 The Battle of Sedan.*)

Anonymous l 24cm x 17cm l white paper l illustrated cover l ?pp l ? maps l Verlag von Gerhard Stalling. l 1919 l German Text. l Fraktur Script.

Der Große Krieg in Einzeldarstellungen. Unter Benutzung amtlicher Quellen herausgegeben im Auftrage des Großen Generalstabes. Heft 5 Die Schlacht bei Mons. (Der Große Krieg in Einzeldarstellungen. Unter Benutzung amtlicher Quellen herausgegeben im Auftrage des Großen Generalstabes. Heft 5 Die Schlacht bei Mons. - *Individual Studies of the Great War. With Utilization of Official Sources Published on Behalf of the Great General Staff Booklet 5 The Battle of Mons.*)

Freiherr Raimund von Gleichen-Russwurm & Ernst Zurborn l 24cm x 17cm l white paper softback l illustrated cover l 68pp l ? maps l Verlag von Gerhard Stalling. l 1919 l German Text. l Fraktur Script.

Der Große Krieg in Einzeldarstellungen. Unter Benutzung amtlicher Quellen herausgegeben im Auftrage des Großen Generalstabes. Heft 6 Die Schlacht bei St. Quentin. (Der Große Krieg in Einzeldarstellungen. Unter Benutzung amtlicher Quellen herausgegeben im Auftrage des Großen Generalstabes. Heft 6 Die Schlacht bei St. Quentin. - *Individual Studies of the Great War. With Utilization of Official Sources Published on Behalf of the Great General Staff Booklet 6 The Battle of St. Quentin.*)

Anonymous l 24cm x 17cm l white paper softback l illustrated cover l ?pp l ? maps l Verlag von Gerhard Stalling. l 1919 l German Text. l Fraktur Script.

Der Große Krieg in Einzeldarstellungen. Unter Benutzung amtlicher Quellen herausgegeben im Auftrage des Großen Generalstabes. Heft 7 Die Schlacht am Ourcq. (Der Große Krieg in Einzeldarstellungen. Unter Benutzung amtlicher Quellen herausgegeben im Auftrage des Großen Generalstabes. Heft 7 Die Schlacht am Ourcq. - *Individual Studies of the Great War. With Utilization of Official Sources Published on Behalf of the Great General Staff Booklet 7 The Battle on the Ourcq.*)

Anonymous l 24cm x 17cm l white paper softback l illustrated cover l ?pp l ? maps l Verlag von Gerhard Stalling. l 1919 l German Text. l Fraktur Script.

Der Große Krieg in Einzeldarstellungen. Unter Benutzung amtlicher Quellen herausgegeben im Auftrage des Großen Generalstabes. Heft 8 Antwerpen — Maubeuge. (Der Große Krieg in Einzeldarstellungen. Unter Benutzung amtlicher Quellen herausgegeben im Auftrage des Großen Generalstabes. Heft 8 Antwerpen - Maubeuge. - *Individual Studies of the Great War. With Utilization of Official Sources Published on Behalf of the Great General Staff Booklet 8 Antwerp - Maubeuge.*)

Anonymous l 24cm x 17cm l white paper softback l illustrated cover l ?pp l ? maps l Verlag von Gerhard Stalling. l 1919 l German Text. l Fraktur Script.

Der Große Krieg in Einzeldarstellungen. Unter Benutzung amtlicher Quellen herausgegeben im Auftrage des Großen Generalstabes. Heft 9 Die Tätigkeit der Kavallerie in Belgien und Nordfrontreich während der Herbstmonate 1914. (Der Große Krieg in Einzeldarstellungen. Unter Benutzung amtlicher Quellen herausgegeben im Auftrage des Großen Generalstabes. Heft 9 Die Tätigkeit der Kavallerie in Belgien und Nordfrontreich während der Herbstmonate 1914. - *Individual Studies of the Great War. With Utilization of Official Sources Published on Behalf of the Great General Staff Booklet 9 The Activity of the Cavalry in Belgium and the Kingdom's North Front during the autumn months 1914.*)

Anonymous l 24cm x 17cm l white paper softback l illustrated cover l ?pp l ? maps l Verlag von Gerhard Stalling. l 1919 l German Text. l Fraktur Script.

Der Große Krieg in Einzeldarstellungen. Unter Benutzung amtlicher Quellen herausgegeben im Auftrage des Großen Generalstabes. Heft 10 Die Schlacht an der Yser und bei Ypern in Herbst 1914. (Der Große Krieg in Einzeldarstellungen. Unter Benutzung amtlicher Quellen herausgegeben im Auftrage des Großen Generalstabes. Heft 10 Die Schlacht an der Yser und bei Ypern in Herbst 1914. - *Individual Studies of the Great War. With Utilization of Official Sources Published on Behalf of the Great General Staff Booklet 10 The Battle on the Yser and Ypres in the Autumn of 1914.*)

Otto Schwink | 24cm x 17cm | white paper softback | illustrated cover | 97pp | 8 maps | Verlag von Gerhard Stalling. | 1918 | German Text. | Fraktur Script.

Der Große Krieg in Einzeldarstellungen. Unter Benutzung amtlicher Quellen herausgegeben im Auftrage des Großen Generalstabes. Heft 11 Kämpfe in der Champagne – Winter 1914 bis Herbst 1915. (Der Große Krieg in Einzeldarstellungen. Unter Benutzung amtlicher Quellen herausgegeben im Auftrage des Großen Generalstabes. Heft 11 Kämpfe in der Champagne – Winter 1914 bis Herbst 1915. - *Individual Studies of the Great War. With Utilization of Official Sources Published on Behalf of the Great General Staff Booklet 11 The Fighting in Champagne – Winter 1914 until Autumn 1915.*)

Arndt von Kirchbach | 24cm x 17cm | white paper softback | illustrated cover | 121pp | 10 maps | Verlag von Gerhard Stalling. | 1919 | German Text. | Fraktur Script.

Der Große Krieg in Einzeldarstellungen. Unter Benutzung amtlicher Quellen herausgegeben im Auftrage des Großen Generalstabes. Heft 12 Kämpfe im Artois und in Flandern – Mai 1915 bis Herbst 1915. (Der Große Krieg in Einzeldarstellungen. Unter Benutzung amtlicher Quellen herausgegeben im Auftrage des Großen Generalstabes. Heft 12 Kämpfe im Artois und in Flandern – Mai 1915 bis Herbst 1915. - *Individual Studies of the Great War. With Utilization of Official Sources Published on Behalf of the Great General Staff Booklet 12 The Fighting in Artois and in Flanders – May 1915 to the Autumn 1915.*)

Anonymous | 24cm x 17cm | white paper softback | illustrated cover | ?pp | ? maps | Verlag von Gerhard Stalling. | c1919 | German Text. | Fraktur Script.

Der Große Krieg in Einzeldarstellungen. Unter Benutzung amtlicher Quellen herausgegeben im Auftrage des Großen Generalstabes. Heft 13 Vogesenkämpfe. (Der Große Krieg in Einzeldarstellungen. Unter Benutzung amtlicher Quellen herausgegeben im Auftrage des Großen Generalstabes. Heft 13 Vogesenkämpfe. - *Individual Studies of the Great War. With Utilization of Official Sources Published on Behalf of the Great General Staff Booklet 13 The Fighting in Vosges.*)

Anonymous | 24cm x 17cm | white paper softback | illustrated cover | ?pp | ? maps | Verlag von Gerhard Stalling. | c1919 | German Text. | Fraktur Script.

Der Große Krieg in Einzeldarstellungen. Unter Benutzung amtlicher Quellen herausgegeben im Auftrage des Großen Generalstabes. Heft 14 Gefechte an der Aisne (Soissons, Bailly, Craonne, Bille au Bois). (Der Große Krieg in Einzeldarstellungen. Unter Benutzung amtlicher Quellen herausgegeben im Auftrage des Großen Generalstabes. Heft 14 Gefechte an der Aisne (Soissons, Bailly, Craonne, Bille au Bois). - *Individual Studies of the Great War. With Utilization of Official Sources Published on Behalf of the Great General Staff Booklet 14 Engagements on the Aisne (Soissons, Bailly, Craonne, Bille au Bois).*)

Anonymous | 24cm x 17cm | white paper softback | illustrated cover | ?pp | ? maps | Verlag von Gerhard Stalling. | c1919 | German Text. | Fraktur Script.

Der Große Krieg in Einzeldarstellungen. Unter Benutzung amtlicher Quellen herausgegeben im Auftrage des Großen Generalstabes. Heft 15 Verdun. (Der Große Krieg in Einzeldarstellungen. Unter Benutzung amtlicher Quellen herausgegeben im Auftrage des Großen Generalstabes. Heft 15 Verdun. - *Individual Studies of the Great War. With Utilization of Official Sources Published on Behalf of the Great General Staff Booklet 15 Verdun.*)

Anonymous | 24cm x 17cm | white paper softback | illustrated cover | ?pp | ? maps | Verlag von Gerhard Stalling. | c1919 | German Text. | Fraktur Script.

Der Große Krieg in Einzeldarstellungen. Unter Benutzung amtlicher Quellen herausgegeben im Auftrage des Großen Generalstabes. Heft 16 Somme. (Der Große Krieg in Einzeldarstellungen. Unter Benutzung amtlicher Quellen herausgegeben im

Auftrage des Großen Generalstabes. Heft 16 Somme. - *Individual Studies of the Great War. With Utilization of Official Sources Published on Behalf of the Great General Staff Booklet 16 Somme.*)

      Anonymous I 24cm x 17cm I white paper softback I illustrated cover I ?pp I ? maps I Verlag von Gerhard Stalling. I c1919 I German Text. I Fraktur Script.

Der Große Krieg in Einzeldarstellungen. Unter Benutzung amtlicher Quellen heraufgegeben im Auftrage des Großen Generalstabes. Heft 17 Tannenberg und Schlacht an den Masurischen Seen. (Der Große Krieg in Einzeldarstellungen. Unter Benutzung amtlicher Quellen herausgegeben im Auftrage des Großen Generalstabes. Heft 17 Tannenberg und Schlacht an den Masurischen Seen. - *Individual Studies of the Great War. With Utilization of Official Sources Published on Behalf of the Great General Staff Booklet 17 Tannenberg and the Battle of the Masurischen Lakes.*)

      Anonymous I 24cm x 17cm I white paper softback I illustrated cover I ?pp I ? maps I Verlag von Gerhard Stalling. I c1919 I German Text. I Fraktur Script.

Der Große Krieg in Einzeldarstellungen. Unter Benutzung amtlicher Quellen heraufgegeben im Auftrage des Großen Generalstabes. Heft 18 Kämpfe in Polen September und October 1914. (Der Große Krieg in Einzeldarstellungen. Unter Benutzung amtlicher Quellen herausgegeben im Auftrage des Großen Generalstabes. Heft 18 Kämpfe in Polen September und October 1914. - *Individual Studies of the Great War. With Utilization of Official Sources Published on Behalf of the Great General Staff Booklet 18 The Fighting in Poland September and October 1914.*)

      Anonymous I 24cm x 17cm I white paper softback I illustrated cover I ?pp I ? maps I Verlag von Gerhard Stalling. I c1919 I German Text. I Fraktur Script.

Der Große Krieg in Einzeldarstellungen. Unter Benutzung amtlicher Quellen heraufgegeben im Auftrage des Großen Generalstabes. Heft 19 Die Schlacht bei Lodz. (Der Große Krieg in Einzeldarstellungen. Unter Benutzung amtlicher Quellen herausgegeben im Auftrage des Großen Generalstabes. Heft 19 Die Schlacht bei Lodz. - *Individual Studies of the Great War. With Utilization of Official Sources Published on Behalf of the Great General Staff Booklet 19 The Battle of Lodz.*)

      Karl von Wulffen I 24cm x 17cm I white paper softback I illustrated cover I 110pp I 8 maps I Verlag von Gerhard Stalling. I 1918 I German Text. I Fraktur Script.

Der Große Krieg in Einzeldarstellungen. Unter Benutzung amtlicher Quellen heraufgegeben im Auftrage des Großen Generalstabes. Heft 20 Die Winterschlacht in Masuren. (Der Große Krieg in Einzeldarstellungen. Unter Benutzung amtlicher Quellen herausgegeben im Auftrage des Großen Generalstabes. Heft 20 Die Winterschlacht in Masuren. - *Individual Studies of the Great War. With Utilization of Official Sources Published on Behalf of the Great General Staff Booklet 20 The Winter Battle of Masuren.*)

      Hans von Redern I 24cm x 17cm I white paper softback I illustrated cover I ?pp I ? maps I Verlag von Gerhard Stalling. I 1918 I German Text. I Fraktur Script.

Der Große Krieg in Einzeldarstellungen. Unter Benutzung amtlicher Quellen heraufgegeben im Auftrage des Großen Generalstabes. Heft 21 Gorlice-Tarnow. (Der Große Krieg in Einzeldarstellungen. Unter Benutzung amtlicher Quellen herausgegeben im Auftrage des Großen Generalstabes. Heft 21 Gorlice-Tarnow. - *Individual Studies of the Great War. With Utilization of Official Sources Published on Behalf of the Great General Staff Booklet 21 Gorlice-Tarnow.*)

      Freiherr von Rothkirch and Leonhard *Graf* von Trach I 24cm x 17cm I white paper softback I illustrated cover I 87pp I 8 maps I Verlag von Gerhard Stalling. I 1918 I German Text. I Fraktur Script.

Der Große Krieg in Einzeldarstellungen. Unter Benutzung amtlicher Quellen heraufgegeben im Auftrage des Großen Generalstabes. Heft 22 Kämpfe am San. (Der Große Krieg in Einzeldarstellungen. Unter Benutzung amtlicher Quellen herausgegeben im Auftrage des Großen Generalstabes. Heft 22 Kämpfe am San. - *Individual Studies of the Great War. With Utilization of Official Sources Published on Behalf of the Great General Staff Booklet 2 The Fighting on the San.*)

      Anonymous I 24cm x 17cm I white paper softback I illustrated cover I ?pp I ? maps I Verlag von Gerhard Stalling. I c1919 I German Text. I Fraktur Script.

Der Große Krieg in Einzeldarstellungen. Unter Benutzung amtlicher Quellen herausgegeben im Auftrage des Großen Generalstabes. Heft 23 Die Eroberung Kurlands. (Der Große Krieg in Einzeldarstellungen. Unter Benutzung amtlicher Quellen herausgegeben im Auftrage des Großen Generalstabes. Heft 23 Die Eroberung Kurlands. - *Individual Studies of the Great War. With Utilization of Official Sources Published on Behalf of the Great General Staff Booklet 23 The Conquest of Kurlands.*)
    Anonymous | 24cm x 17cm | white paper softback | illustrated cover | ?pp | ? maps | Verlag von Gerhard Stalling. | c1919 | German Text. | Fraktur Script.

Der Große Krieg in Einzeldarstellungen. Unter Benutzung amtlicher Quellen herausgegeben im Auftrage des Großen Generalstabes. Heft 24 Die Schlacht bei Grodek-Lemberg. (Der Große Krieg in Einzeldarstellungen. Unter Benutzung amtlicher Quellen herausgegeben im Auftrage des Großen Generalstabes. Heft 24 Die Schlacht bei Grodek-Lemberg. - *Individual Studies of the Great War. With Utilization of Official Sources Published on Behalf of the Great General Staff Booklet 24 The Battle of Grodek-Lemberg.*)
    Hermann Müller-Brandenburg | 24cm x 17cm | white paper softback | illustrated cover | 88pp | 8 maps | Verlag von Gerhard Stalling. | 1918 | German Text. | Fraktur Script.

Der Große Krieg in Einzeldarstellungen. Unter Benutzung amtlicher Quellen herausgegeben im Auftrage des Großen Generalstabes. Heft 25 Von Munkacz bis zur Zolta Lipa, Kämpfe der Armee Linsingen. (Der Große Krieg in Einzeldarstellungen. Unter Benutzung amtlicher Quellen herausgegeben im Auftrage des Großen Generalstabes. Heft 25 Von Munkacz bis zur Zolta Lipa, Kämpfe der Armee Linsingen. - *Individual Studies of the Great War. With Utilization of Official Sources Published on Behalf of the Great General Staff Booklet 25 From Munkacz to the Zolta Lipa, fights of the Linsingen's Army.*)
    Anonymous | 24cm x 17cm | white paper softback | illustrated cover | ?pp | ? maps | Verlag von Gerhard Stalling. | 1918 | German Text. | Fraktur Script.

Der Große Krieg in Einzeldarstellungen. Unter Benutzung amtlicher Quellen herausgegeben im Auftrage des Großen Generalstabes. Heft 26 Die Kämpfe der Bug-Armee. (Der Große Krieg in Einzeldarstellungen. Unter Benutzung amtlicher Quellen herausgegeben im Auftrage des Großen Generalstabes. Heft 26 Die Kämpfe der Bug-Armee. - *Individual Studies of the Great War. With Utilization of Official Sources Published on Behalf of the Great General Staff Booklet 26 The Fighting of the Army of the Bug.*)
    Pehlmann | 24cm x 17cm | white paper softback | illustrated cover | 63pp | 8 maps | Verlag von Gerhard Stalling. | 1918 | German Text. | Fraktur Script.

Der Große Krieg in Einzeldarstellungen. Unter Benutzung amtlicher Quellen herausgegeben im Auftrage des Großen Generalstabes. Heft 27 Schlacht am Narew - Juli-August 1915. (Der Große Krieg in Einzeldarstellungen. Unter Benutzung amtlicher Quellen herausgegeben im Auftrage des Großen Generalstabes. Heft 27 Schlacht am Narew - Juli-August 1915. - *Individual Studies of the Great War. With Utilization of Official Sources Published on Behalf of the Great General Staff Booklet 27 The Battle on the Narew – July-August 1915.*)
    Gustav Meyer | 24cm x 17cm | white paper softback | illustrated cover | ?pp | ? maps | Verlag von Gerhard Stalling. | 1919 | German Text. | Fraktur Script.

Der Große Krieg in Einzeldarstellungen. Unter Benutzung amtlicher Quellen herausgegeben im Auftrage des Großen Generalstabes. Heft 28 Nowo-Georgiewsk - Kowno. (Der Große Krieg in Einzeldarstellungen. Unter Benutzung amtlicher Quellen herausgegeben im Auftrage des Großen Generalstabes. Heft 28 Nowo-Georgiewsk - Kowno. - *Individual Studies of the Great War. With Utilization of Official Sources Published on Behalf of the Great General Staff Booklet 28 Nowo-Georgiewsk - Kowno.*)
    Gustav Meyer | 24cm x 17cm | white paper softback | illustrated cover | ?pp | ? maps | Verlag von Gerhard Stalling. | 1918 | German Text. | Fraktur Script.

Der Große Krieg in Einzeldarstellungen. Unter Benutzung amtlicher Quellen herausgegeben im Auftrage des Großen Generalstabes. Heft 29 Die Schlacht bei Smorgon-Wilna. (Der Große Krieg in Einzeldarstellungen. Unter Benutzung amtlicher Quellen herausgegeben im Auftrage des Großen Generalstabes. Heft 29 Die Schlacht bei

Smorgon-Wilna. - *Individual Studies of the Great War. With Utilization of Official Sources Published on Behalf of the Great General Staff Booklet 29 The Battle of Smorgon-Wilna.*)

    Anonymous I 24cm x 17cm I white paper softback I illustrated cover I ?pp I ? maps I Verlag von Gerhard Stalling. I 1918 I German Text. I Fraktur Script.

Der Große Krieg in Einzeldarstellungen. Unter Benutzung amtlicher Quellen herausgegeben im Auftrage des Großen Generalstabes. Heft 30 Der Übergang über die Donau. (Anfang Ottober 1915). (Der Große Krieg in Einzeldarstellungen. Unter Benutzung amtlicher Quellen herausgegeben im Auftrage des Großen Generalstabes. Heft 30 Der Übergang über die Donau. (Anfang Ottober 1915). - *Individual Studies of the Great War. With Utilization of Official Sources Published on Behalf of the Great General Staff Booklet 30 The Crossing Over the Donau. (Beginning of October 1915).*)

    Anonymous I 24cm x 17cm I white paper softback I illustrated cover I ?pp I ? maps I Verlag von Gerhard Stalling. I 1918 I German Text. I Fraktur Script.

Der Große Krieg in Einzeldarstellungen. Unter Benutzung amtlicher Quellen herausgegeben im Auftrage des Großen Generalstabes. Heft 31 Die russisch Frühjahrsoffensive 1916. (Der Große Krieg in Einzeldarstellungen. Unter Benutzung amtlicher Quellen herausgegeben im Auftrage des Großen Generalstabes. Heft 31 Die russisch Frühjahrsoffensive 1916. - *Individual Studies of the Great War. With Utilization of Official Sources Published on Behalf of the Great General Staff Booklet 31 The Russian Spring Offensive 1916.*)

    Anonymous I 24cm x 17cm I white paper softback I illustrated cover I ?pp I ? maps I Verlag von Gerhard Stalling. I 1918 I German Text. I Fraktur Script.

Der Große Krieg in Einzeldarstellungen. Unter Benutzung amtlicher Quellen herausgegeben im Auftrage des Großen Generalstabes. Heft 32 Die Kämpfe bei Baranowitschi (Sommer 1916). (Der Große Krieg in Einzeldarstellungen. Unter Benutzung amtlicher Quellen herausgegeben im Auftrage des Großen Generalstabes. Heft 32 Die Kämpfe bei Baranowitschi (Sommer 1916). – *Individual Studies of the Great War. With Utilization of Official Sources Published on Behalf of the Great General Staff Booklet 32 The Fighting for Baranowitschi (Summer 1916).*)

    Anonymous I 24cm x 17cm I white paper softback I illustrated cover I ?pp I ? maps I Verlag von Gerhard Stalling. I 1918 I German Text. I Fraktur Script.

Der Große Krieg in Einzeldarstellungen. Unter Benutzung amtlicher Quellen herausgegeben im Auftrage des Großen Generalstabes. Heft 33 Die Befreiung Siebenürgens und die Schlachten bei Targu Jiu und am Argesch. (Der Große Krieg in Einzeldarstellungen. Unter Benutzung amtlicher Quellen herausgegeben im Auftrage des Großen Generalstabes. Heft 33 Die Befreiung Siebenürgens und die Schlachten bei Targu Jiu und am Argesch. - *Individual Studies of the Great War. With Utilization of Official Sources Published on Behalf of the Great General Staff Booklet 33 The Liberation of Siebenürgens and the Battles near Targu Jiu and on the River Argesch.*)

    Walther Vogel I 24cm x 17cm I white paper softback I illustrated cover I 134pp I 8 maps I Verlag von Gerhard Stalling. I 1918 I German Text. I Fraktur

Der Große Krieg in Einzeldarstellungen. Unter Benutzung amtlicher Quellen herausgegeben im Auftrage des Großen Generalstabes. Heft 34 ? (Der Große Krieg in Einzeldarstellungen. Unter Benutzung amtlicher Quellen herausgegeben im Auftrage des Großen Generalstabes. Heft 34 ? - *Individual Studies of the Great War. With Utilization of Official Sources Published on Behalf of the Great General Staff Booklet 34 ?*)

    Anonymous I 24cm x 17cm I white paper softback I illustrated cover I ?pp I ? maps I Verlag von Gerhard Stalling. I 1918 I German Text. I Fraktur Script.

    Although I assume that it was published, I have not been able to trace Part 34 of this set "**Der Große Krieg in Einzeldarstellungen**".

Der Große Krieg in Einzeldarstellungen. Unter Benutzung amtlicher Quellen herausgegeben im Auftrage des Großen Generalstabes. Heft 35 Der Durchbruch bei Zloczow. (Der Große Krieg in Einzeldarstellungen. Unter Benutzung amtlicher Quellen herausgegeben im Auftrage des Großen Generalstabes. Heft 35 Der

Durchbruch bei Zloczow. - *Individual Studies of the Great War. With Utilization of Official Sources Published on Behalf of the Great General Staff Booklet 35 The breakthrough at Zloczow.*)
    Anonymous | 24cm x 17cm | white paper softback | illustrated cover | ?pp | ? maps | Verlag von Gerhard Stalling. | 1918 | German Text. | Fraktur Script.

𝕯𝖊𝖗 𝕲𝖗𝖔𝖘𝖊 𝕶𝖗𝖎𝖊𝖌 𝖎𝖓 𝕰𝖎𝖓𝖟𝖊𝖑𝖉𝖆𝖗𝖘𝖙𝖊𝖑𝖑𝖚𝖓𝖌𝖊𝖓. 𝖀𝖓𝖙𝖊𝖗 𝕭𝖊𝖓𝖚𝖙𝖟𝖚𝖓𝖌 𝖆𝖒𝖙𝖑𝖎𝖈𝖍𝖊𝖗 𝕼𝖚𝖊𝖑𝖑𝖊𝖓 𝖍𝖊𝖗𝖆𝖚𝖘𝖌𝖊𝖌𝖊𝖇𝖊𝖓 𝖎𝖒 𝕬𝖚𝖋𝖙𝖗𝖆𝖌𝖊 𝖉𝖊𝖘 𝕲𝖗𝖔𝖘𝖊𝖓 𝕲𝖊𝖓𝖊𝖗𝖆𝖑𝖘𝖙𝖆𝖇𝖊𝖘. 𝕳𝖊𝖋𝖙 36a 𝕽𝖎𝖌𝖆 𝖎𝖓 𝕯𝖊𝖚𝖙𝖘𝖈𝖍𝖊𝖗 𝕳𝖆𝖓𝖉. (Der Große Krieg in Einzeldarstellungen. Unter Benutzung amtlicher Quellen herausgegeben im Auftrage des Großen Generalstabes. Heft 36a Riga in Deutscher Hand. - *Individual Studies of the Great War. With Utilization of Official Sources Published on Behalf of the Great General Staff Booklet 36a Riga in German Hands.*)
    Anonymous | 24cm x 17cm | white paper softback | illustrated cover | ?pp | ? maps | Verlag von Gerhard Stalling. | c1919 | German Text. | Fraktur Script.

𝕯𝖊𝖗 𝕲𝖗𝖔𝖘𝖊 𝕶𝖗𝖎𝖊𝖌 𝖎𝖓 𝕰𝖎𝖓𝖟𝖊𝖑𝖉𝖆𝖗𝖘𝖙𝖊𝖑𝖑𝖚𝖓𝖌𝖊𝖓. 𝖀𝖓𝖙𝖊𝖗 𝕭𝖊𝖓𝖚𝖙𝖟𝖚𝖓𝖌 𝖆𝖒𝖙𝖑𝖎𝖈𝖍𝖊𝖗 𝕼𝖚𝖊𝖑𝖑𝖊𝖓 𝖍𝖊𝖗𝖆𝖚𝖘𝖌𝖊𝖌𝖊𝖇𝖊𝖓 𝖎𝖒 𝕬𝖚𝖋𝖙𝖗𝖆𝖌𝖊 𝖉𝖊𝖘 𝕲𝖗𝖔𝖘𝖊𝖓 𝕲𝖊𝖓𝖊𝖗𝖆𝖑𝖘𝖙𝖆𝖇𝖊𝖘. 𝕳𝖊𝖋𝖙 36b 𝕯𝖎𝖊 𝕰𝖗𝖘𝖙ü𝖗𝖒𝖚𝖓𝖌 𝖉𝖊𝖘 𝕭𝖗ü𝖈𝖐𝖊𝖓𝖐𝖔𝖕𝖋𝖊𝖘 𝖛𝖔𝖓 𝕵𝖆𝖈𝖔𝖇𝖘𝖙𝖆𝖉𝖙. (Der Große Krieg in Einzeldarstellungen. Unter Benutzung amtlicher Quellen herausgegeben im Auftrage des Großen Generalstabes. Heft 36b Die Erstürmung des Brückenkopfes von Jacobstadt. - *Individual Studies of the Great War. With Utilization of Official Sources Published on Behalf of the Great General Staff Booklet 36b The Storming of the Bridgeheads at Jacobstadt.*)
    Anonymous | 24cm x 17cm | white paper softback | illustrated cover | ?pp | ? maps | Verlag von Gerhard Stalling. | c1919 | German Text. | Fraktur Script.

𝕯𝖊𝖗 𝕲𝖗𝖔𝖘𝖊 𝕶𝖗𝖎𝖊𝖌 𝖎𝖓 𝕰𝖎𝖓𝖟𝖊𝖑𝖉𝖆𝖗𝖘𝖙𝖊𝖑𝖑𝖚𝖓𝖌𝖊𝖓. 𝖀𝖓𝖙𝖊𝖗 𝕭𝖊𝖓𝖚𝖙𝖟𝖚𝖓𝖌 𝖆𝖒𝖙𝖑𝖎𝖈𝖍𝖊𝖗 𝕼𝖚𝖊𝖑𝖑𝖊𝖓 𝖍𝖊𝖗𝖆𝖚𝖘𝖌𝖊𝖌𝖊𝖇𝖊𝖓 𝖎𝖒 𝕬𝖚𝖋𝖙𝖗𝖆𝖌𝖊 𝖉𝖊𝖘 𝕲𝖗𝖔𝖘𝖊𝖓 𝕲𝖊𝖓𝖊𝖗𝖆𝖑𝖘𝖙𝖆𝖇𝖊𝖘. 𝕳𝖊𝖋𝖙 36c 𝕯𝖊𝖚𝖙𝖘𝖈𝖍𝖑𝖆𝖓𝖉𝖘 𝕱𝖑𝖆𝖌𝖌𝖊 𝖆𝖚𝖋 𝖉𝖊𝖓 𝕴𝖓𝖘𝖊𝖑𝖓 𝖉𝖊𝖘 𝕽𝖎𝖌𝖆𝖊𝖗 𝕸𝖊𝖊𝖗𝖇𝖚𝖘𝖊𝖓𝖘. (Der Große Krieg in Einzeldarstellungen. Unter Benutzung amtlicher Quellen herausgegeben im Auftrage des Großen Generalstabes. Heft 36c Deutschlands Flagge auf den Inseln des Rigaer Meerbusens. - *Individual Studies of the Great War. With Utilization of Official Sources Published on Behalf of the Great General Staff Booklet 36c Raising the German Flag on the Island of Rigaer Meerbusens.*)
    Anonymous | 24cm x 17cm | white paper softback | illustrated cover | ?pp | ? maps | Verlag von Gerhard Stalling. | c1919 | German Text. | Fraktur Script.

𝕯𝖊𝖗 𝕲𝖗𝖔𝖘𝖊 𝕶𝖗𝖎𝖊𝖌 𝖎𝖓 𝕰𝖎𝖓𝖟𝖊𝖑𝖉𝖆𝖗𝖘𝖙𝖊𝖑𝖑𝖚𝖓𝖌𝖊𝖓. 𝖀𝖓𝖙𝖊𝖗 𝕭𝖊𝖓𝖚𝖙𝖟𝖚𝖓𝖌 𝖆𝖒𝖙𝖑𝖎𝖈𝖍𝖊𝖗 𝕼𝖚𝖊𝖑𝖑𝖊𝖓 𝖍𝖊𝖗𝖆𝖚𝖘𝖌𝖊𝖌𝖊𝖇𝖊𝖓 𝖎𝖒 𝕬𝖚𝖋𝖙𝖗𝖆𝖌𝖊 𝖉𝖊𝖘 𝕲𝖗𝖔𝖘𝖊𝖓 𝕲𝖊𝖓𝖊𝖗𝖆𝖑𝖘𝖙𝖆𝖇𝖊𝖘. 𝕳𝖊𝖋𝖙 37 𝕯𝖎𝖊 𝕶ä𝖒𝖕𝖋𝖊 𝖚𝖒 𝕯𝖎𝖓𝖆𝖓𝖙. (Der Große Krieg in Einzeldarstellungen. Unter Benutzung amtlicher Quellen herausgegeben im Auftrage des Großen Generalstabes. Heft 37 Die Kämpfe um Dinant. – *Individual Studies of the Great War. With Utilization of Official Sources Published on Behalf of the Great General Staff Booklet 37 The Fighting around Dinant.*)
    Anonymous | 24cm x 17cm | white paper softback | illustrated cover | ?pp | ? maps | Verlag von Gerhard Stalling. | 1918 | German Text. | Fraktur Script.

𝕯𝖊𝖗 𝕲𝖗𝖔𝖘𝖊 𝕶𝖗𝖎𝖊𝖌 𝖎𝖓 𝕰𝖎𝖓𝖟𝖊𝖑𝖉𝖆𝖗𝖘𝖙𝖊𝖑𝖑𝖚𝖓𝖌𝖊𝖓. 𝖀𝖓𝖙𝖊𝖗 𝕭𝖊𝖓𝖚𝖙𝖟𝖚𝖓𝖌 𝖆𝖒𝖙𝖑𝖎𝖈𝖍𝖊𝖗 𝕼𝖚𝖊𝖑𝖑𝖊𝖓 𝖍𝖊𝖗𝖆𝖚𝖘𝖌𝖊𝖌𝖊𝖇𝖊𝖓 𝖎𝖒 𝕬𝖚𝖋𝖙𝖗𝖆𝖌𝖊 𝖉𝖊𝖘 𝕲𝖗𝖔𝖘𝖊𝖓 𝕲𝖊𝖓𝖊𝖗𝖆𝖑𝖘𝖙𝖆𝖇𝖊𝖘. 𝕳𝖊𝖋𝖙 38 𝕯𝖎𝖊 𝕶ä𝖒𝖕𝖋𝖊 𝖇𝖊𝖎 𝕮𝖍𝖆𝖗𝖑𝖊𝖗𝖔𝖎. (Der Große Krieg in Einzeldarstellungen. Unter Benutzung amtlicher Quellen herausgegeben im Auftrage des Großen Generalstabes. Heft 38 Die Kämpfe bei Charleroi. – *Individual Studies of the Great War. With Utilization of Official Sources Published on Behalf of the Great General Staff Booklet 38 The Fighting at Charleroi.*)
    Anonymous | 24cm x 17cm | white paper softback | illustrated cover | ?pp | ? maps | Verlag von Gerhard Stalling. | 1918 | German Text. | Fraktur Script.

𝕯𝖊𝖗 𝕲𝖗𝖔𝖘𝖊 𝕶𝖗𝖎𝖊𝖌 𝖎𝖓 𝕰𝖎𝖓𝖟𝖊𝖑𝖉𝖆𝖗𝖘𝖙𝖊𝖑𝖑𝖚𝖓𝖌𝖊𝖓. 𝖀𝖓𝖙𝖊𝖗 𝕭𝖊𝖓𝖚𝖙𝖟𝖚𝖓𝖌 𝖆𝖒𝖙𝖑𝖎𝖈𝖍𝖊𝖗 𝕼𝖚𝖊𝖑𝖑𝖊𝖓 𝖍𝖊𝖗𝖆𝖚𝖘𝖌𝖊𝖌𝖊𝖇𝖊𝖓 𝖎𝖒 𝕬𝖚𝖋𝖙𝖗𝖆𝖌𝖊 𝖉𝖊𝖘 𝕲𝖗𝖔𝖘𝖊𝖓 𝕲𝖊𝖓𝖊𝖗𝖆𝖑𝖘𝖙𝖆𝖇𝖊𝖘. 𝕳𝖊𝖋𝖙 39 𝕯𝖎𝖊 𝕭𝖊𝖋𝖗𝖊𝖎𝖚𝖓𝖌 𝖛𝖔𝖓 𝕷𝖎𝖛𝖑𝖆𝖓𝖉 𝖚𝖓𝖉 𝕰𝖘𝖙𝖑𝖆𝖓𝖉 — 18 𝕱𝖊𝖇𝖗𝖚𝖆𝖗 𝖇𝖎𝖘 5 𝕸ä𝖗𝖟. (Der Große Krieg in Einzeldarstellungen. Unter Benutzung amtlicher Quellen herausgegeben im Auftrage des Großen Generalstabes. Heft 39 Die Befreiung von Livland und Estland - 18 Februar bis 5 März. - *Individual Studies of the Great War. With Utilization of Official Sources Published on Behalf of the Great General Staff Booklet 39 The Liberation of Lapland und Esthonia - 18th February to 5th March.*)

Hugo Kaupisch | 24cm x 17cm | white paper softback | illustrated cover | 88pp | ? maps | Verlag von Gerhard Stalling. | 1918 | German Text. | Fraktur Script.

Forechungen und Darstellungen auf dem Reichsarchiv Heft 1 Die Sendung des Oberstleutnants Hentsch am 8–10 September 1914. (Forechungen und Darstellungen aus dem Reichsarchiv Heft 1 Die Sendung des Oberstleutnants Hentsch am 8-10 September 1914. – *Researches and Descriptions from the Imperial Archives Booklet 1 The Mission of Oberstleutnants Hentsch from the 8th to 10th September 1914.*)

Wilhelm Müller-Loebnitz | 24cm x 17cm | white paper softback | illustrated cover | 68pp | 1 maps | 6 appendices. | Verlag Ernst Siegfried Mittler und Sohn. | 1922 | German Text. | Fraktur Script.

Forechungen und Darstellungen auf dem Reichsarchiv Heft 2 Deutsch Wirtschaftspropaganda im Weltkrieg. (Forechungen und Darstellungen aus dem Reichsarchiv Heft 2 Deutsch Wirtschaftspropaganda im Weltkrieg. - *Researches and Descriptions from the Imperial Archives Booklet 2 German Economic Propaganda in the World War.*)

Rudolf Wiehler | 24cm x 17cm | white paper softback | illustrated cover | ?pp | ? maps | Verlag Ernst Siegfried Mittler und Sohn. | ? | 1922 | German Text. | Fraktur Script.

Forechungen und Darstellungen auf dem Reichsarchiv Heft 3 Die Organisation des Deutschen Heeres im Weltkriege. Dargestellt auf Grund Kriegsakten. (Forechungen und Darstellungen aus dem Reichsarchiv Heft 3 Die Organisation des Deutschen Heeres im Weltkriege. Dargestellt auf Grund Kriegsakten. - *Researches and Descriptions from the Imperial Archives Booklet 3 The Organization of the German Army in the World War. Represented on the Basis of the War Acts.*)

Hermann Cron | 24cm x 17cm | white paper softback | illustrated cover | ?pp | ? maps | ? | Verlag Ernst Siegfried Mittler und Sohn. | 1922 | German Text. | Fraktur Script.

Erinnerungsblatter Deutsche Regimenter – Bayerischen Armee Einser Bilderbuch (Erinnerungsblatter Deutsche Regimenter - Bayerischen Armee Einser Bilderbuch - *German Regiments' Memories - First Bavarian Army's Picture Book*)

Herbert Knorr | ?cm x ?cm | brown leather hardback | gilt | ?pp | ? maps | ? | 1926 | German Text. | Fraktur Script.

Italian Secondary Official Histories

Naval Monographs;

UFFICIO DEL CAPO DI STATO MAGGIORE DELLA MARINA (UFFICIO STORICO) - CRONISTORIA DOCUMENTATA DELLA GUERRA MARITTIMA ITALO-AUSTRIACA 1915-1918 - LA PREPARAZIONE DEI MEZZI, FASCICOLO I⁰ - PREPARAZIONE ED IMPIEGO DEL PERSONALE. (*Office of the Chief of the General Staff of the Navy, (Historical Office) - Documented Chronicle of the Austro-Italian Naval War, 1915-1918 - The Preparation of the Means, Part I - Preparation and Use of Personnel.*)
> Anonymous - Ufficio del Capo di Stato Maggiore della Marina Ufficio Storico. I 30cm x 21cm I Light blue Paper Softback I 13pp I ? maps I ? tables I Tip. dell'Ufficio del Capo di Stato Maggiore. I c1919 I Italian Text.

UFFICIO DEL CAPO DI STATO MAGGIORE DELLA MARINA (UFFICIO STORICO) - CRONISTORIA DOCUMENTATA DELLA GUERRA MARITTIMA ITALO-AUSTRIACA 1915-1918 - LA PREPARAZIONE DEI MEZZI, FASCICOLO II⁰ - COSTRUZIONE E RIPARAZIONE DEL NAVIGLIO, APPRONTAMENTO ED IMPIEGO DELLE ARMI E MATERIALE VARIO DI GUERRA. (*Office of the Chief of the General Staff of the Navy, (Historical Office) - Documented Chronicle of the Austro-Italian Naval War, 1915-1918 - The Preparation of the Means, Part II - Construction and Repair of the Fleet, Development and Employment of Arms and War Material.*)
> Anonymous - Ufficio del Capo di Stato Maggiore della Marina Ufficio Storico. I 30cm x 21cm I Light blue Paper Softback I 27pp I ? maps I ? tables I Tip. dell'Ufficio del Capo di Stato Maggiore. I c1919 I Italian Text.
> An Errata sheet was inserted in this volume.

UFFICIO DEL CAPO DI STATO MAGGIORE DELLA MARINA (UFFICIO STORICO) - CRONISTORIA DOCUMENTATA DELLA GUERRA MARITTIMA ITALO-AUSTRIACA 1915-1918 - LA PREPARAZIONE DEI MEZZI, FASCICOLO III⁰ - SERVIZI LOGISTICI E SERVICI SANITARI DELLA R. MARINA DURANTE LA GUERRA. (*Office of the Chief of the General Staff of the Navy, (Historical Office) - Documented Chronicle of the Austro-Italian Naval War, 1915-1918 - The Preparation of the Means, Part III - The Logistical Services and Medical Services of The R.[Royal Italian] Navy During The War.*)
> Anonymous - Ufficio del Capo di Stato Maggiore della Marina Ufficio Storico. I 30cm x 21cm I Light blue Paper Softback I ?pp I ? maps I ? tables I Tip. dell'Ufficio del Capo di Stato Maggiore. I c1919 I Italian Text.

UFFICIO DEL CAPO DI STATO MAGGIORE DELLA MARINA (UFFICIO STORICO) - CRONISTORIA DOCUMENTATA DELLA GUERRA MARITTIMA ITALO-AUSTRIACA 1915-1918 - LA PREPARAZIONE DEI MEZZI, FASCICOLO IV⁰ - DIFESE COSTIERE E LORO SVILUPPO DURANTE LA GUERRA. (*Office of the Chief of the General Staff of the Navy, (Historical Office - Documented Chronicle of the Austro-Italian Naval War, 1915-1918 - The Preparation of the Means, Part IV – The Coastal Defenses and their Development during the War.*)
> Anonymous - Ufficio del Capo di Stato Maggiore della Marina Ufficio Storico. I 30cm x 21cm I Light blue Paper Softback I ?pp I ? maps I ? tables I Tip. dell'Ufficio del Capo di Stato Maggiore. I c1920 I Italian Text.

UFFICIO DEL CAPO DI STATO MAGGIORE DELLA MARINA (UFFICIO STORICO) - CRONISTORIA DOCUMENTATA DELLA GUERRA MARITTIMA ITALO-AUSTRIACA 1915-1918 - LA PREPARAZIONE DEI MEZZI, FASCICOLO V⁰ - SBARRAMENTO DEL CANALE D'OTRANTO. (*Office of the Chief of the General Staff of the Navy, (Historical Office) - Documented Chronicle of the Austro-Italian Naval War, 1915-1918 - The Preparation of the Means, Part V – The Barrier across the Straights of Otranto*)
> Anonymous - Ufficio del Capo di Stato Maggiore della Marina Ufficio Storico. I 30cm x 21cm I Light blue Paper Softback I 71pp I ? maps I ? tables I Tip. dell'Ufficio del Capo di Stato Maggiore. I c1920 I Italian Text.

UFFICIO DEL CAPO DI STATO MAGGIORE DELLA MARINA (UFFICIO STORICO) - CRONISTORIA DOCUMENTATA DELLA GUERRA MARITTIMA ITALO-AUSTRIACA 1915-1918 - LA PREPARAZIONE DEI MEZZI, FASCICOLO VI⁰ - MIGLIORAMENTI NAUTICI AI PORTI, CANALI NAVIGABILI, ALTRE OPERE DI PUBBLICA UTILITÀ COMPIUTE DALLA R. MARINA DURANTE LA GUERRA. (*Office of the Chief of the General Staff of the Navy, (Historical Office) - Documented Chronicle of the Austro-Italian Naval War,*

1915-1918 - The Preparation of the Means, Part VI - Improvements to Nautical and Waterways Ports and Other Works of Public Utilities completed by the R. Marine during the War. Documented Chronicle of the Italo-Austrian Naval War 1915 - 1918.)

Anonymous - Ufficio del Capo di Stato Maggiore della Marina Ufficio Storico. | 30cm x 21cm | Light blue Paper Softback | 47pp | ? maps | ? tables | Tip. dell'Ufficio del Capo di Stato Maggiore. | 1920 | Italian Text.

UFFICIO DEL CAPO DI STATO MAGGIORE DELLA MARINA (UFFICIO STORICO) - CRONISTORIA DOCUMENTATA DELLA GUERRA MARITTIMA ITALO-AUSTRIACA 1915-1918 - LA PREPARAZIONE DEI MEZZI, FASCICOLO VII° - L'AVIAZIONE MARITTIMA DURANTE LA GUERRA. (*Office of the Chief of the General Staff of the Navy, (Historical Office) - Documented Chronicle of the Austro-Italian Naval War, 1915-1918 -The Preparation of the Means, Part VII – Naval Aviation during the War.*)

Anonymous - Ufficio del Capo di Stato Maggiore della Marina Ufficio Storico. | 30cm x 21cm | Light blue Paper Softback | 326pp | ? maps | ? tables | Tip. dell'Ufficio del Capo di Stato Maggiore. | c1921 | Italian Text.
An Errata sheet was inserted in this volume.

UFFICIO DEL CAPO DI STATO MAGGIORE DELLA MARINA (UFFICIO STORICO) - CRONISTORIA DOCUMENTATA DELLA GUERRA MARITTIMA ITALO-AUSTRIACA 1915-1918 - LA PREPARAZIONE DEI MEZZI, FASCICOLO VIII° - COOPERAZIONE DELLA MARINA ALLE OPERAZIONI DELL'ESERCITO SUL FRONTE TERRESTRE. (*Office of the Chief of the General Staff of the Navy, (Historical Office) - Documented Chronicle of the Austro-Italian Naval War, 1915-1918 - The Preparation of the Means, Part VIII - Cooperation by the Navy on Army Operations on the Land Front.*)

Anonymous - Ufficio del Capo di Stato Maggiore della Marina Ufficio Storico. | 30cm x 21cm | Light blue Paper Softback | v + 279pp + lxi | ? maps | ? tables | Tip. dell'Ufficio del Capo di Stato Maggiore. | c1921 | Italian Text.

UFFICIO DEL CAPO DI STATO MAGGIORE DELLA MARINA UFFICIO STORICO - CHRONISTORIA DOCUMENTATA DELLA GUERRA MARITTIMA ITALO-AUSTRIACA 1915-1918. L'IMPIEGO DELLE FORZE NAVALI, FASCICOLO I^O CONCORSO DELLE FORZE NAVALI DEL BASSO ADRIATICO ALLE OPERAZIONI MILITARI NEI BALCANI. (*Office of the Chief of the General Naval Staff Historical Office -Documented Chronicle of the Austro-Italian Naval War, 1915-1918. The Employment of the Navy, Part I, Contribution of the Naval Forces of the Lower Adriatic to Military Operations in the Balkans.*)

Anonymous - Ufficio del capo di Stato Maggiore della Marina Ufficio Storico | 32cm x ?cm | softback | gilt | 82pp | 9 tables | Tip. dell'Ufficio del Capo di Stato Maggiore. | 1922 | Italian Text.

UFFICIO DEL CAPO DI STATO MAGGIORE DELLA MARINA UFFICIO STORICO - CHRONISTORIA DOCUMENTATA DELLA GUERRA MARITTIMA ITALO-AUSTRIACA 1915-1918. L'IMPIEGO DELLE FORZE NAVALI, FASCICOLO II° DATI STATISTICI SULL'IMPIEGO DEL NAVIGLIO DURANTE LA GUERRA. (*Office of the Chief of the General Naval Staff Historical Office - Documented Chronicle of the Austro-Italian Naval War, 1915-1918. The Employment of the Navy, Part II Statistical Data on the Use of the Fleet during the War.*)

Anonymous - Ufficio del capo di Stato Maggiore della Marina Ufficio Storico | 32cm x ?cm | softback | gilt | 31pp | 15 tables | Tip. dell'Ufficio del Capo di Stato Maggiore. | c1919 | Italian Text.

UFFICIO DEL CAPO DI STATO MAGGIORE DELLA MARINA UFFICIO STORICO - CHRONISTORIA DOCUMENTATA DELLA GUERRA MARITTIMA ITALO-AUSTRIACA 1915-1918. L'IMPIEGO DELLE FORZE NAVALI, FASCICOLO III° L'APERTURA DELLE OSTILITÀ IN MARE. (*Office of the Chief of the General Naval Staff Historical Office - Documented Chronicle of the Austro-Italian Naval War, 1915-1918. The Employment of the Navy, Part III Opening of Hostilities on the sea.*)

Anonymous - Ufficio del capo di Stato Maggiore della Marina Ufficio Storico | 32cm x ?cm | softback | gilt | 126pp | 9 tables | Tip. dell'Ufficio del Capo di Stato Maggiore. | c1919 | Italian Text.

UFFICIO DEL CAPO DI STATO MAGGIORE DELLA MARINA UFFICIO STORICO - CHRONISTORIA DOCUMENTATA DELLA GUERRA MARITTIMA ITALO-AUSTRIACA 1915-1918. L'IMPIEGO DELLE FORZE NAVALI, FASCICOLO IV° ALCUNE AZIONI NAVALI MINORI NEL BASSO ED ALTO ADRIATICO. (*Office of the Chief of the General*

Naval Staff Historical Office - Documented Chronicle of the Austro-Italian Naval War, 1915-1918. The Employment of the Navy, Part IV Some Minor Naval Operations in the Lower and Upper Adriatic.)

    Anonymous - Ufficio del capo di Stato Maggiore della Marina Ufficio Storico l 32cm x ?cm l softback l gilt l 61pp l 8 tables l Tip. dell'Ufficio del Capo di Stato Maggiore. l 1922 l Italian Text.

UFFICIO DEL CAPO DI STATO MAGGIORE DELLA MARINA UFFICIO STORICO - CHRONISTORIA DOCUMENTATA DELLA GUERRA MARITTIMA ITALO-AUSTRIACA 1915-1918. L'IMPIEGO DELLE FORZE NAVALI, FASCICOLO V^O AZIONE NAVALE DEL 29 DICEMBRE 1915 NEL BASSO ADRIATICO. (*Office of the Chief of the General Naval Staff Historical Office - Documented Chronicle of the Austro-Italian Naval War, 1915-1918. The Employment of the Navy, Part V The Naval Action of 29 December 1915 in the Lower Adriatic.*)

    Anonymous - Ufficio del capo di Stato Maggiore della Marina Ufficio Storico l 32cm x ?cm l softback l gilt l 45pp l 9 tables l Tip. dell'Ufficio del Capo di Stato Maggiore. l 1919 l Italian Text.

UFFICIO DEL CAPO DI STATO MAGGIORE DELLA MARINA UFFICIO STORICO - CHRONISTORIA DOCUMENTATA DELLA GUERRA MARITTIMA ITALO-AUSTRIACA 1915-1918. L'IMPIEGO DELLE FORZE NAVALI, FASCICOLO VI° AZIONE NAVALE DEL 15 MAGGIO 1917 NEL BASSO ADRIATICO. (*Office of the Chief of the General Naval Staff Historical Office - Documented Chronicle of the Austro-Italian Naval War, 1915-1918. The Employment of the Navy, Part VI The Naval Action of 15 May 1917 in the Lower Adriatic.*)

    Anonymous - Ufficio del capo di Stato Maggiore della Marina Ufficio Storico l 32cm x ?cm l softback l gilt l 72pp l 11 tables l Tip. dell'Ufficio del Capo di Stato Maggiore. l c1920 l Italian Text.

UFFICIO DEL CAPO DI STATO MAGGIORE DELLA MARINA UFFICIO STORICO - CHRONISTORIA DOCUMENTATA DELLA GUERRA MARITTIMA ITALO-AUSTRIACA 1915-1918. L'IMPIEGO DELLE FORZE NAVALI, FASCICOLO VII° IL BOMBARDAMENTO DI DURAZZO NEL 1918. (*Office of the Chief of the General Naval Staff Historical Office - Documented Chronicle of the Austro-Italian Naval War, 1915-1918. The Employment of the Navy, Part VII The Bombardment of Durazzo in 1918.*)

    Anonymous - Ufficio del capo di Stato Maggiore della Marina Ufficio Storico l 32cm x ?cm l softback l gilt l 54pp l 5 tables l Tip. dell'Ufficio del Capo di Stato Maggiore. l c1921 l Italian Text.

UFFICIO DEL CAPO DI STATO MAGGIORE DELLA MARINA UFFICIO STORICO - CHRONISTORIA DOCUMENTATA DELLA GUERRA MARITTIMA ITALO-AUSTRIACA 1915-1918. L'IMPIEGO DELLE FORZE NAVALI, FASCICOLO VIII° OCCUPAZIONE DELL'ISOLA DI PELAGOSA. (*Office of the Chief of the General Naval Staff Historical Office. Documented Chronicle of the Austro-Italian Naval War, 1915-1918. The Employment of the Navy, Part VIII Occupation of the Island of Pelagosa.*)

    Anonymous - Ufficio del capo di Stato Maggiore della Marina Ufficio Storico l 32cm x ?cm l softback l gilt l 83pp l 18 tables l Tip. dell'Ufficio del Capo di Stato Maggiore. l 1922 l Italian Text.

UFFICIO DEL CAPO DI STATO MAGGIORE DELLA MARINA UFFICIO STORICO - CHRONISTORIA DOCUMENTATA DELLA GUERRA MARITTIMA ITALO-AUSTRIACA 1915-1918. L'IMPIEGO DELLE FORZE NAVALI, FASCICOLO IX° LE GESTA DEI M.A.S. (*Office of the Chief of the General Naval Staff Historical Office - Documented Chronicle of the Austro-Italian Naval War, 1915-1918. The Employment of the Navy, Part IX The Exploits of the M. A. S's.*)

    Anonymous - Ufficio del capo di Stato Maggiore della Marina Ufficio Storico l 32cm x ?cm l softback l gilt l iv + 332pp l 18 tables l Tip. dell'Ufficio del Capo di Stato Maggiore. l c1922 l Italian Text.

UFFICIO DEL CAPO DI STATO MAGGIORE DELLA MARINA UFFICIO STORICO - CHRONISTORIA DOCUMENTATA DELLA GUERRA MARITTIMA ITALO-AUSTRIACA 1915-1918. L'IMPIEGO DELLE FORZE NAVALI, FASCICOLO X^O L'AZIONE DI PREMUDA. (*Office of the Chief of the General Naval Staff Historical Office - Documented Chronicle of the Austro-Italian Naval War, 1915-1918. The Employment of the Navy, Part X The Premuda Action.*)

Anonymous - Ufficio del capo di Stato Maggiore della Marina Ufficio Storico | 32cm x ?cm | softback | gilt | 76pp | 5 tables | Tip. dell'Ufficio del Capo di Stato Maggiore. | c1923 | Italian Text.

MINISTERO DELLA MARINA, UFFICIO DEL CAPO DI STATO MAGGIORE - UFFICIO STORICO - CRONISTORIA DOCUMENTATA DELLA GUERRA MARITTIMA ITALO-AUSTRIACA 1915-1918 - I NOMI DELLE NOSTRE NAVI DA GUERRA: MONOGRAFIE ILLUSTRATIVE. (*Ministry of the Navy, Office of the Chief of the General Staff, Historical Office. - Documented Chronicle of the Austro-Italian Naval War, 1915-1918 - The Names of our Warships: An Illustrated Monograph.*)

    Uldarigo Ceci. - Ufficio del capo di Stato Maggiore della Marina Ufficio Storico | 25cm x ?cm | softback | gilt | xxiii + 1418pp | ? photographs | Istituto poligrafico dello stato. | 1929 | Italian Text.

UFFICIO DEL CAPO DI STATO MAGGIORE, UFFICIO STORICO. UFFICIO DEL CAPO DI STATO MAGGIORE. UFFICIO STORICO. LE OCCUPAZIONI ADRIATICHE. (*Office of the Chief of the General [Naval] Staff, Historical Office. The Occupation of the Adriatic.*)

    Udalrigo Ceci - Ministero della Marina: Ufficio Storico | 30cm x 21cm | ? | 429pp | ? | Vallecchi Editore. | 1932 | Italian Text.

UFFICIO DEL CAPO DI STATO MAGGIORE, UFFICIO STORICO: I NOSTRI SOMMERGIBILI DURANTE LA GUERRA 1915-18. (*Office of the Chief of the General [Naval] Staff, Historical Office. Our Submarines During the War 1915-18.*)

    Anonymous - Ministero della Marina: Ufficio Storico | 30cm x 21cm | Light Grey Paper Softback | 333pp | 25 maps | 2 tables | Tip. dell'Ufficio del Capo di Stato Maggiore. | 1933 | Italian Text.

UFFICIO STORICO DELLA MARINA MILITARE. LA MARINA ITALIANA E L'ADRIATICO. IL POTERE MARITTIMO IN UN TEATRO RISTRETTO. (*Historical Office Of Navy. The Navy and the Adriatic. Martine Power in a Restricted Theatre.*)

    Riccardo Nassigh - Ministero della Marina: Ufficio Storico | 30cm x 21cm | Light Grey Paper Softback | 323pp | 25 maps | 2 tables | Tip. dell'Ufficio del Capo di Stato Maggiore. | 1998 | Italian Text.

Educational Text Books;

MINISTERO DELLA GUERRA COMANDO DEL CORPO DI STATO MAGGIORE – STORIA MILITARE PER I CORSI ALLIEVE UFFICIALI DE COMPLENTO. (*Ministry of War General Staff Corps Command - Military History to Complement the Officer Students' Courses.*)

    Anonymous - Ministero della Guerra Comando del Corpo di Stato Maggiore | 22.4cm x 16.2cm | yellow paper softback | 88pp | 1 large format map | Edizioni de "le Forze Armate" | 1938 | Italian Text.

LA GUERRA MONDIALE: LA CAMPAGNA DEL 1914 (*The World War: The 1914 Campaign.*)

    Colonnello di Fanteria Pietro Maravigna - Scuola di Guerra | 26.5cm x 21cm | yellow paper softback | xxvii + 406pp | ? | Editrice Schioppo | 1922 | Italian Text

GUERRA E VITTORIA (1915 - 1918). (*War and Victory (1915 - 1918).*)

    Colonnello di Fanteria Pietro Maravigna - Comando Supremo | 26.5cm x 21cm | yellow paper softback | iv + ?pp | 18 map | 10 coloured photographs | 10 tables | 455 illustions | Unione Tipografico Editrice Torinese | ? | Italian Text.

    This volume was enlarged and republished in 1927 (iv + 576pp) and again in 1936 (xii + 698pp).

Army Staff Papers;

STATO MAGGIORE DEL R. ESERCITO - UFFICIO STORICO – LA CONQUISTA DEL MONTE NERO. (*The General Staff of the Royal Army – Historical Office - The Conquest of Monte Nero.*)

Anonymous - Comando Supremo | 24.4cm x 16.7cm | grey paper softback | 114pp | 3 large format maps | 2 panorama photographs | Stabilimento Poligrafico per l'Amministrazione della Guerra | 1921 | Italian Text.

The mountain Monte Nero is located in present day Slovenia and has the Slovenian name of Krn.

REGIO ESERCITO ITALIANO – COMANDO SUPREMO - LA BATTAGLIA DEL PIAVE (15 - 23 GIUGNO 1918). (*The Royal Italian Army – Surpreme Command - The Battle of the Piave. (15-23 July 1918).*)

Anonymous - Comando Supremo | 24.4cm x 16.7cm | grey paper softback | 63pp | 10 large format colour maps | Tipografia Cuggiani. | 1920 | Italian Text.

This monograph "**La battaglia del Piave (15 - 23 Giugno 1918)**" was translated by Mary Prichard Agnetti into English and republished under the tile "**The battle of the Piave (June 15-23, 1918)**" and was published by Hodder and Stoughton in 1921.

REGIO ESERCITO ITALIANO – COMANDO SUPREMO - LA BATTAGLIA DALL'ASTICO AL MARE (15 GIUGNO - 6 LUGLIO 1918). (*The Royal Italian Army – Surpreme Command - The battle from Astico to the Sea (15 June - 6 July 1918).*)

Anonymous - Comando Supremo | 24.4cm x 16.7cm | grey paper softback | 19pp | 10 large format colour maps | Tipografia Bodoni. | 1918 | Italian Text.

REGIO ESERCITO ITALIANO – COMANDO SUPREMO - LA BATTAGLIA DI VITTORIO VENETO 24 OTTOBRE – 4 NOVEMBRE 1918 (*The Royal Italian Army – Surpreme Command - The Battle of Vittorio Veneto 24 October – 4 November 1918.*)

Anonymous - Comando Supremo | 30.7cm x 21cm | brown paper softback | 41pp | 3 large format maps | Stabilimento Poligrafico per l'Amministrazione della Guerra. | 1920 | Italian Text.

This monograph "**La battaglia di Vittorio Veneto 24 Ottobre – 4 Novembre 1918**" was translated into English and republished under the tile "**Royal Italian Army – Report by the Comando Supremo on The Battle of Vittorio Veneto (24th October – 4th November 1918.**)" It had light grey paper covers. The original Italian version did not have the name of the publisher nor the date of publication; however the translation had both and it is assumed that it was the same for both versions.

REGIO ESERCITO ITALIANO – COMANDO SUPREMO - IL II°CORPO D'ARMATA SULLA FRONTE FRANCESE, APRILE-NOVEMBRE 1918. (*The Royal Italian Army – Surpreme Command - The Second Army Corp on the French Front, April - November 1918.*)

Anonymous - Comando supremo | 24cm x 17.5cm | white paper covered hardback | 30pp | ? large format maps | Tipografia Cuggiani. | 1920 | Italian Text.

REGIO ESERCITO ITALIANO – COMANDO SUPREMO - AZIONE DELLE TRUPPE AUSILIARIE IN FRANCIA, APRILE-NOVEMBRE 1918. (*The Royal Italian Army – Surpreme Command - Action of the Auxiliary Troops in France, April - November 1918.*)

Anonymous - Comando supremo | 24cm x 17.5cm | white paper covered hardback | 8pp | ? photographs | Tipografia Cuggiani. | 1920 | Italian Text.

REGIO ESERCITO ITALIANO – COMANDO SUPREMO - IL CORPO DI SPEDIZIONE ITALIANO IN MACEDONIA. (*The Royal Italian Army – Surpreme Command - The Italian Expeditionary Corp in Macedonia.*)

Anonymous - Comando supremo | 24cm x 17.5cm | white paper covered hardback | 21pp | 1 large format map | Istituto ven. di Arti grafiche. | c1917 | Italian Text.

ARMISTIZIO DI VILLA GIUSTI: 3 NOVEMBRE 1918. (*The Villa Giusti Armistice: 3 November 1918.*)

Anonymous - Comando supremo. | 31cm x ?cm | white paper covered hardback | 15pp | 1 large format map | Sezione Tipo-Litografica del Comando Supremo. | 1918 | Italian Text.

It is believed that there was at least one more Staff Paper written by the Comando Supremo with reference to La dodicesima battaglia dell'Isonzo - La Battaglia di Caporetto (The Twelfth Battle of the Isonzo - The Battle of Caporetto [called Karfreit by the Austro- Germans but now has the Slovenian name of Kobarid]).

Military Monographs;

MINISTERO DELLA GUERRA - COMANDO DEL CORPO DI STATO MAGGIORE - UFFICIO STORICO - COLLANA DI MONOGRAFIE STORICHE SULLA GUERRA DEL 1915-1918 NO. I^O - COME SI GIUNSE A MONTE NERO. (*Ministry of War - The Head of the General Staff - Historical Office - Series of Historical Monographs on the War of 1915-1918 No. I - As We Arrived on Monte Nero.*)

Primo Capitano Pietro Barbier and Alberto Reiter | 24cm x ?cm | yellow paper softback | 116pp | ? map | ? tables | ? illustions | Tipografico Regionale. | 1932 | Italian Text.

MINISTERO DELLA GUERRA - COMANDO DEL CORPO DI STATO MAGGIORE - UFFICIO STORICO - COLLANA DI MONOGRAFIE STORICHE SULLA GUERRA DEL 1915-1918 NO. II° - LA CONQUISTA DI PLAVA. (*Ministry of War - The Head of the General Staff - Historical Office - Series of Historical Monographs on the War of 1915-1918 No. II - The Conquest of Plava.*)

Colonnello Gustavo Reisoli - Comando Supremo | 24cm x ?cm | yellow paper softback | 111pp | ? map | ? tables | ? illustions | Tipografico Regionale. | 1932 | Italian Text.

MINISTERO DELLA GUERRA - COMANDO DEL CORPO DI STATO MAGGIORE - UFFICIO STORICO - COLLANA DI MONOGRAFIE STORICHE SULLA GUERRA DEL 1915-1918 NO. III° - D'INVERNO IN TRINCEA. (*Ministry of War - The Head of the General Staff - Historical Office - Series of Historical Monographs on the War of 1915-1918 No. III - The Winter in Trenches.*)

Tenente Colonnello Ildebrando Fiocca - Comando Supremo | 24cm x ?cm | yellow paper softback | 103pp | ? map | ? tables | ? illustions | Tipografico Regionale. | 1933 | Italian Text.

MINISTERO DELLA GUERRA - COMANDO DEL CORPO DI STATO MAGGIORE - UFFICIO STORICO - COLLANA DI MONOGRAFIE STORICHE SULLA GUERRA DEL 1915-1918 NO. IV° - SABOTINO. (*Ministry of War - The Head of the General Staff - Historical Office - Series of Historical Monographs on the War of 1915-1918 No. IV - Sabotage.*)

Colonnello Efisio Marras - Comando Supremo | 24cm x ?cm | yellow paper softback | 100pp | ? map | ? tables | ? illustions | Tipografico Regionale. | 1933 | Italian Text.

MINISTERO DELLA GUERRA - COMANDO DEL CORPO DI STATO MAGGIORE - UFFICIO STORICO - COLLANA DI MONOGRAFIE STORICHE SULLA GUERRA DEL 1915-1918 NO. V^O - MONTE PASUBIO. (*Ministry of War - The Head of the General Staff - Historical Office - Series of Historical Monographs on the War of 1915-1918 No. V - Monte Pasubio.*)

Maggiore Amedeo Tosti - Comando Supremo | 24cm x ?cm | yellow paper softback | 93pp | ? map | ? tables | ? illustions | Tipografico Regionale. | 1933 | Italian Text.

MINISTERO DELLA GUERRA - COMANDO DEL CORPO DI STATO MAGGIORE - UFFICIO STORICO - COLLANA DI MONOGRAFIE STORICHE SULLA GUERRA DEL 1915-1918 NO. VI° - LA GUERRA SUL GHIACCIAIO. PARTE PRIMA, SULL'ADAMELLO DAL 1915 AL 1918; PARTE SECONDA, LA CONQUISTA DEL CORNO DI CAVENTO (15 GIUGNO 1917). (*Ministry of War - The Head of the General Staff - Historical Office - Series of Historical Monographs on the War of 1915-1918 No. VI - The War on the Glacier. Part One, on the Adamello from 1915 to 1918; Part Two, the Conquest of the Horn of Cavento (15 June 1917).*)

Tenente Colonnello Angelo Ravenni and *Tenente Colonnello* Emilio Battisti. - Comando Supremo | 24cm x ?cm | yellow paper softback | 105pp | ? map | ? tables | ? illustions | Tipografico Regionale. | 1933 | Italian Text.

First part, by tenente colonnello Angelo Ravenni, and second part by tenente colonnello Emilio Battisti.

MINISTERO DELLA GUERRA - COMANDO DEL CORPO DI STATO MAGGIORE - UFFICIO STORICO - COLLANA DI MONOGRAFIE STORICHE SULLA GUERRA DEL 1915-1918 NO. VII° - LA BRIGATA TEVERE DAL CARSO AL PIAVE (*Ministry of War - The Head of the General Staff - Historical Office - Series of Historical Monographs on the War of 1915-1918 No. VII - The Tevere Brigade from the Carso to the Piave.*)

Generale di Divisione Vincenzo Carbone. - Comando Supremo | 24cm x ?cm | yellow paper softback | 108pp | ? map | ? tables | ? illustions | Tipografico Regionale. | 1933 | Italian Text.

MINISTERO DELLA GUERRA - COMANDO DEL CORPO DI STATO MAGGIORE - UFFICIO STORICO - COLLANA DI MONOGRAFIE STORICHE SULLA GUERRA DEL 1915-1918 NO. VIII° - DAVANTI A S. MARTINO DEL CARSO COLLA BRIGATA PISA: L'ATTACCO AUSTRIACO DEL 29 GIUGNO 1916. (*Ministry of War - The Head of the General*

Staff - Historical Office - Series of Historical Monographs on the War of 1915-1918 No. VIII - In Front of S. Martino on the Carso with the Pisa Brigade: the Austrian Attack of 29 June 1916.)

Generale di Divisione Cesare Faccini. - Comando Supremo | 24cm x ?cm | yellow paper softback | 98pp | ? map | ? tables | ? illustions | Tipografico Regionale. | 1933 | Italian Text.

MINISTERO DELLA GUERRA - COMANDO DEL CORPO DI STATO MAGGIORE - UFFICIO STORICO - COLLANA DI MONOGRAFIE STORICHE SULLA GUERRA DEL 1915-1918 NO. IX° - COI LEGIONARI CECOSLOVACCHI AL FRONTE ITALIANO ED IN SLOVACCHIA (1918-1919). (*Ministry of War - The Head of the General Staff - Historical Office - Series of Historical Monographs on the War of 1915-1918 No. IX - With the Czechoslovakian Legionaries to Italian Front and in Slovakia (1918-1919).*)

Tenente Colonnello Giulio Cesare Gotti Porcinari - Comando Supremo | 24cm x ?cm | yellow paper softback | 136pp | ? map | ? tables | ? illustions | Tipografico Regionale. | 1933 | Italian Text.

MINISTERO DELLA GUERRA - COMANDO DEL CORPO DI STATO MAGGIORE - UFFICIO STORICO - COLLANA DI MONOGRAFIE STORICHE SULLA GUERRA DEL 1915-1918 NO. X^O - CON LA QUARTA ARMATA ALLA PRIMA DIFESA DEL GRAPPA (NOVEMBRE 1917). (*Ministry of War - The Head of the General Staff - Historical Office - Series of Historical Monographs on the War of 1915-1918 No. X - With the Fourth Army up to the First Defense of Grappa (November 1917).*)

Generale Alberto Baldini - Comando Supremo | 24cm x ?cm | yellow paper softback | 114pp | ? map | ? tables | ? illustions | Tipografico Regionale. | 1933 | Italian Text.

MINISTERO DELLA GUERRA - COMANDO DEL CORPO DI STATO MAGGIORE - UFFICIO STORICO - COLLANA DI MONOGRAFIE STORICHE SULLA GUERRA DEL 1915-1918 NO. XI° - LA BATTAGLIA D'ARRESTO SULL'ALTOPIANO D'ASIAGO (10 NOVEMBRE - 25 DICEMBRE 1917). (*Ministry of War - The Head of the General Staff - Historical Office - Series of Historical Monographs on the War of 1915-1918 No. XI - The Defensive Battle on the Asiago High Plateau (10 November -25 December 1917.*)

Generale Pompilio Schiarini - Comando Supremo | 24cm x ?cm | yellow paper softback | ?pp | ? map | ? tables | ? illustions | Tipografico Regionale. | 1934 | Italian Text.

MINISTERO DELLA GUERRA - COMANDO DEL CORPO DI STATO MAGGIORE - UFFICIO STORICO - COLLANA DI MONOGRAFIE STORICHE SULLA GUERRA DEL 1915-1918 NO. XII° - LA 65° DIVISIONE (15 LUGLIO - 31 OTTOBRE 1917). (*Ministry of War - The Head of the General Staff - Historical Office - Series of Historical Monographs on the War of 1915-1918 No. XII - The 65th Division (15July -31 October 1917).*)

Generale Carlo Geloso. - Comando Supremo | 24cm x ?cm | yellow paper softback | 159pp | ? map | ? tables | ? illustions | Tipografico Regionale. | 1934 | Italian Text.

MINISTERO DELLA GUERRA - COMANDO DEL CORPO DI STATO MAGGIORE - UFFICIO STORICO - COLLANA DI MONOGRAFIE STORICHE SULLA GUERRA DEL 1915-1918 NO. XIII° - CON L'82° FANTERIA SUL PIAVE. (*Ministry of War - The Head of the General Staff - Historical Office - Series of Historical Monographs on the War of 1915-1918 No. XIII - With the 82nd infantry on the Piave.*)

Tenente Colonnello Giulio Cesare Gotti Porcinari - Comando Supremo | 24cm x ?cm | yellow paper softback | 97pp | ? map | ? tables | ? illustions | Tipografico Regionale. | 1934 | Italian Text.

MINISTERO DELLA GUERRA - COMANDO DEL CORPO DI STATO MAGGIORE - UFFICIO STORICO - COLLANA DI MONOGRAFIE STORICHE SULLA GUERRA DEL 1915-1918 NO. XIV° - DAL PIEDE ALLA CIMA DEL COL DI LANA (GIUGNO 1915 - APRILE 1916). (*Ministry of War - The Head of the General Staff - Historical Office - Series of Historical Monographs on the War of 1915-1918 No. XIV - By Foot to the Top of the Col di Lana (June 1915-April 1916).*)

Generale Ottorino Mezzetti. - Comando Supremo | 24cm x ?cm | yellow paper softback | 143pp | ? map | ? tables | ? illustions | Tipografico Regionale. | 1934 | Italian Text.

MINISTERO DELLA GUERRA - COMANDO DEL CORPO DI STATO MAGGIORE - UFFICIO STORICO - COLLANA DI MONOGRAFIE STORICHE SULLA GUERRA DEL 1915-1918 NO. XV° - LA CONQUISTA DELLE ALPI DI FASSA. (*Ministry of War - The Head of the General Staff - Historical Office - Series of Historical Monographs on the War of 1915-1918 No. XV - The Conquest of the Alpi di Fassa.*)

Tenente Colonnello Giacomo Carboni - Comando Supremo | 24cm x ?cm | yellow paper softback | 103pp | ? map | ? tables | ? illustions | Tipografico Regionale. | 1935 | Italian Text.

MINISTERO DELLA GUERRA - COMANDO DEL CORPO DI STATO MAGGIORE - UFFICIO STORICO - COLLANA DI MONOGRAFIE STORICHE SULLA GUERRA DEL 1915-1918 NO. XVI° - LA SORTE DI UNA BANDIERA (BRIGATA REGGIO). (*Ministry of War - The Head of the General Staff - Historical Office - Series of Historical Monographs on the War of 1915-1918 No. XVI - The Fate of a Flag (Reggio Brigade).*)

Attilio Zincone - Comando Supremo | 24cm x ?cm | yellow paper softback | ?pp | ? map | ? tables | ? illustions | Tipografico Regionale. | 1935 | Italian Text.

MINISTERO DELLA GUERRA - COMANDO DEL CORPO DI STATO MAGGIORE - UFFICIO STORICO - COLLANA DI MONOGRAFIE STORICHE SULLA GUERRA DEL 1915-1918 NO. XVII° - DALLA BAINSIZZA AL PIAVE AL COMANDO DEL 14° GRUPPO CANNONI DA 105: DIARIO DI GUERRA DI UN COMBATTENTE. (*Ministry of War - The Head of the General Staff - Historical Office - Series of Historical Monographs on the War of 1915-1918 No. XVII - From the Bainsizza [Plateau] to the [River] Piave in command of the 14° group 105mm guns: The War Diary of a Combattant.*)

Colonnello Carlo Romano - Comando Supremo | 24cm x ?cm | yellow paper softback | 148pp | ? map | ? tables | ? illustions | Tipografico Regionale. | 1935 | Italian Text.

MINISTERO DELLA GUERRA - COMANDO DEL CORPO DI STATO MAGGIORE - UFFICIO STORICO - COLLANA DI MONOGRAFIE STORICHE SULLA GUERRA DEL 1915-1918 NO. XVIII° - I VIVI. DIARIO DI GUERRA. (*Ministry of War - The Head of the General Staff - Historical Office - Series of Historical Monographs on the War of 1915-1918 No. XVIII - Survival. War Diary.*)

Mercedes Astuto - Comando Supremo | 24cm x ?cm | yellow paper softback | ?pp | ? map | ? tables | ? illustions | Tipografico Regionale. | 1935 | Italian Text.

MINISTERO DELLA GUERRA - COMANDO DEL CORPO DI STATO MAGGIORE - UFFICIO STORICO - COLLANA DI MONOGRAFIE STORICHE SULLA GUERRA DEL 1915-1918 NO. XIX° - LA CONQUISTA DEL PASSO DELLA SENTINELLA. (*Ministry of War - The Head of the General Staff - Series of Historical Monographs on the War of 1915-1918 No. XIX - The Conquest of the Sentinella Pass.*)

Generale Aldo Cabiati - Comando Supremo | 24cm x ?cm | yellow paper softback | ?pp | ? map | ? tables | ? illustions | Tipografico Regionale. | 1938 | Italian Text.

MINISTERO DELLA GUERRA - COMANDO DEL CORPO DI STATO MAGGIORE - UFFICIO STORICO - COLLANA DI MONOGRAFIE STORICHE SULLA GUERRA DEL 1915-1918 NO. XX° - LA DIFESA DEL PASUBIO E DEL CORNO BATTISTI. (*Ministry of War - The Head of the General Staff - Historical Office - Series of Historical Monographs on the War of 1915-1918 No. XX - The Defence of Pasubio and Horn of Battisti.*)

Carlo Ferrario - Comando Supremo | 24cm x ?cm | yellow paper softback | ?pp | ? map | ? tables | ? illustions | Tipografico Regionale. | 1936 | Italian Text.

MAGGIORE ESERCITO: UFFICIO STORICO – LA STORIA DELL'ESERCITO ITALIANO (1861-1990). (*The Army's General Staff - Historical Office - The History of the Italian Army (1861-1990).*)

Oreste Bovio | 24cm x 17.5cm | white paper covered hardback | ?pp | ? photographs | Ministero della Guerra. | 1991 | Italian Text.
This volume "**La Storia dell'Esercito Italiano (1861-1990)**" is a general history of the Italian Army that covers in part the Great War period.

MAGGIORE ESERCITO: UFFICIO STORICO – LA CONQUISTA DELLE ALPI FASSIA. (*The conquest of the Alps at Fassia.*)

Giacomo Carboni | 24cm x 17.5cm | white paper covered hardback | ?pp | ? photographs | Ministero della Guerra. | 1935 | Italian Text..

MAGGIORE ESERCITO: UFFICIO STORICO – CON LA QUARTA ARMATA ALLA PRIMA DIFESA DEL GRAPPA (NOVEMBRE 1917). (*The Army's General Staff - Historical Office - The Forth Army's First Defence of Monte Grappa (November 1917).*)

Anonymous - Ministero della Guerra | 24cm x 17.5cm | white paper covered hardback | 114pp | 3 maps | Ministero della Guerra. | 1934 | Italian Text.

MAGGIORE ESERCITO: UFFICIO STORICO – DAL PIEDE ALLA CIMA DEL COL DI LANA. (*The Army's General Staff - Historical Office - From the Foot to the Summit of the Col di Lana.*)

Ottorino Mazzetti | 24cm x 17.5cm | white paper covered hardback | ?pp | ? photographs | Ministero della Guerra. | 1934 | Italian Text.

MAGGIORE ESERCITO: UFFICIO STORICO – LE TRUPPE ITALIANE IN ALBANIA (Anni 1914-20 e 1939). (*The Army's General Staff - Historical Office - Italian Troops in Albania (1914-20 and 1939).*)

Mario Montanari | 24cm x 17.5cm | white paper covered hardback | 443pp | ? photographs| Ministero della Guerra. | 1978 | Italian Text.

MAGGIORE ESERCITO: UFFICIO STORICO – IN RUSSIA TRA GUERRA E RIVOLUZIONE, LA MISSIONE MILITARE ITALIANA 1915-1918 (*The Army's General Staff - Historical Office - In Russia Between War and Revolution. The Italian Military Mission 1915-1918*)

Antonello Biagini. | 24cm x 17.5cm | white paper covered hardback | ?pp | Ministero della Guerra. | 1983 | Italian Text.

MAGGIORE ESERCITO: UFFICIO STORICO – L'ARMISTIZIO DI VILLA GIUSTI. (*The Army's General Staff - Historical Office - The Villa Giusti Armistice.*)

Adriano Alberti | 24cm x 17.5cm | white paper covered hardback | ?pp | Ministero della Guerra. | 1925 | Italian Text.

STATO MAGGIORE DELL'ESERCITO - UFFICIO STORICO – L'IMPORTANZA DELL'AZIONE MILITARE ITALIANA LE CAUSE MILITARI DI CAPORETTO. (*The Army's General Staff - Historical Office – The Importance of the Italian Military Action. The Military Causes of Caporetto.*)

[*General of Brigade*] Adriano Alberti (Andrea Ungari Editor) | 25cm x 18cm | red cloth hardback | Gilt | colour illustrated Dust Jacket | iv + 383pp | 1 map | 30 photographs | Ministero della Guerra. | 2004 | Italian Text.

This volume was written in draft form in 1923 by Adriano Alberti, but was left unpublished until 2004. It was given a new 63 page introduction by Andrea Ungari who also prepared the draft manuscript for publishing.

STATO MAGGIORE DELL'ESERCITO - UFFICIO STORICO – GLI ALLEATI IN ITALIA DURANTE LA PRIMA GUERRA MONDIALE (1917-1918). (*The Army's General Staff - Historical Office - The Allies in Italy during the First World War (1917-1918).*)

Mariano Gabriele | 24cm x 17cm | red cloth hardback | Gilt | colour illustrated Dust Jacket | 536pp | 62 photographs | Ministero della Guerra. | 2008 | Italian Text.
ISBN: 097-88-87940-90-9

Military Postal Services;

STATO MAGGIORE DELL'ESERCITO - UFFICIO STORICO – LA POSTA MILITARE ITALIANA NELLA PRIMA GUERRA MONDIALE. (*The Army's General Staff - Historical Office - The Italian Military Postal in the First World War.*)

Beniamino Cadioli and Aldo Cecchi | 24.5cm x 17cm | white paper covered hardback | 315pp | 32 photographs | 80 photograph | Istituto Poligrafico Dello Stato. | 1978 | Italian Text.

Propaganda Activities;

STATO MAGGIORE DELL'ESERCITO - UFFICIO STORICO - ESERCITO E PROPAGANDA NELLA GRANDE GUERRA: 1915-1918. (*The Army's General Staff - Historical Office - The Army and Propaganda in the Great War: 1915-1918.*)

Capitano Nicola della Volpe | 24cm x 17.5cm | 372pp | 278 colour photographs of illustrations | 91 black and white photographs of illustrations (including 20 stripes from cinema graphic film) | Ministero della Guerra. | 1989 | Italian Text.

Aviation Monographs;

UFFICIO STORICO STATO MAGGIORE AERONAUTICA - LA PRIMA ORGANIZZAZIONE DELL'AERONAUTICA MILITARE IN ITALIA DAL 1884 AL 1925.

(*The Army's General Staff - The Original Organisation of Military Aviation in Italy from 1884 to 1925.*)

   Alessandro Fraschetti | ?cm x ?cm | hardback | ?pp | Ufficio Storico Aeronautica Militare. | 1986 | Italian Text.

   This volume "**La Prima Organizzazione dell'Aeronautica Militare in Italia dal 1884 al 1925**" is a general history of early Italian military aviation which covers in part the Great War period.

UFFICIO STORICO STATO MAGGIORE AERONAUTICA - L'AVIAZIONE DA RICOGNIZIONE ITALIANA DURANTE LA GUERRA EUROPEA (MAGGIO 1915 – NOVEMBER 1918). (*The Army's General Staff - Italian Reconnaissance Aviation during the European War (May 1915 – November 1918).*)

   Manlio Molfese | 24cm x 17.5cm | hardback | 157pp | 48 photographs | 5 tables | Provveditorato Generale dello Stato Libreria. | 1925 | Italian Text.

UFFICIO STORICO STATO MAGGIORE AERONAUTICA - GLI AVIATORI ITALANI DEL BOMBARDIMENTO NELLA GUERRA 1915-1918. (*Office Historical of the Air Force's General Staff - Italian Aviation Bombers in the War 1915-1918.*)

   Domenico Ludovico | ?cm x ?cm | hardback | ?pp | Ufficio Storico Aeronautica Militare. | 1980 | Italian Text.

UFFICIO STORICO STATO MAGGIORE AERONAUTICA - PALLONI, DIRIGIBILI ED AERIE DEL REGIO ESERCITO (1884-1923). (*Office Historical of the Air Force's General Staff - Balloons, Dirigibles and Aircraft of the Royal Italian Army (1884-1923).*)

   Amadeo Chiusano | ?cm x ?cm | hardback | ?pp | Ufficio Storico Aeronautica Militare. | 1998 | Italian Text.

Miscellanious;

STATO MAGGIORE DELL'ESERCITO - UFFICIO STORICO – LO SPORT E LA GRANDE GUERRA. (*The Army's General Staff - Historical Office – Sport and the Great War.*)

   Sergio Giuntini | 25cm x 18cm | red cloth hardback | Gilt | colour illustrated Dust Jacket | 196pp | 1 map | 30 photographs | Ministero della Guerra. | 2000 | Italian Text.
   ISBN: 097-88-887940-04-6

Photographic;

LA GUERRA - VOLUME PRIMO. IN ALTA MONTAGNA. (*The War – First Volume. In the High Mountains.*)

   Anonymous - Commando Supremo | 32.5cm x 23.5cm | illustrated white paper softback | 65pp | 81 photographs | Fratelli Treves Editori. | 1916 | see note.

   The title on the front cover is shown as "**LA GUERRA - IN ALTA MONTAGNA DALLE RACCOLTE DEL REPARTO FOTOGRAFICO DEL COMANDO SUPREMO DEL R. ESERCITO. VOL. 1^O.** (*The War – In the High Mountains from the Collections of the Photographic Department of the Supreme Command of the Royal Army – Vol. 1.*)" and is often given instead of that shown on the title page.

LA GUERRA – VOLUME SECONDO. IL CARSO. (*The War – Second Volume. The Carso.*)

   Anonymous - Commando Supremo | 32.5cm x 23.5cm | illustrated white paper softback | 65pp | 1 map | 91 photographs | Fratelli Treves Editori. | 1916 | see note.

   The title on the front cover is shown as "**LA GUERRA - IL CARSO. DALLE RACCOLTE DEL REPARTO FOTOGRAFICO DEL COMANDO SUPREMO DEL R. ESERCITO. VOL. 2^O.** (*The War - The Carso from the Collections of the Photographic Department of the Supreme Command of the Royal Army. Vol. 2.*)" and is often given instead of that shown on the title page.

LA GUERRA VOLUME TERZO. LA BATTAGLIA TRA BRENTA ED ADRIGE. (*The War – Thrid Volume. The Battle between Brenta and Adrige.*)

   Anonymous - Commando Supremo | 32.5cm x 23.5cm | illustrated white paper softback | 65pp | 1 large format map | 97 photographs | Fratelli Treves Editori. | 1916 | see note.

   The title on the front cover is shown as "**LA GUERRA - LA BATTAGLIA TRA BRENTA ED ADRIGE DALLE RACCOLTE DEL REPARTO FOTOGRAFICO DEL COMANDO SUPREMO DEL R. ESERCITO. VOL. 3°.** (*The War – The Battle the Brenta and the Adrige from the Collections of the Photographic Department of the*

Supreme Command of the Royal Army. Vol. 3.)" and is often given instead of that shown on the title page.

LA GUERRA - VOLUME QUARTO. LA BATTAGLIA DI GORIZIA. (*The War – Fourth Volume. The Battle of Gorizia.***)**

Anonymous - Commando Supremo | 32.5cm x 23.5cm | illustrated white paper softback | 65pp | 1 map | 112 photographs | Fratelli Treves Editori. | 1916 | see note.

The title on the front cover is shown as "**LA GUERRA - LA BATTAGLIA DI GORIZIA DALLE RACCOLTE DEL REPARTO FOTOGRAFICO DEL COMANDO SUPREMO DEL R. ESERCITO. VOL. 4.** (*The War – The Battle of Gorizia from the Collections of the Photographic Department of the Supreme Command of the Royal Army. Vol. 4.*)" and is often given instead of that shown on the title page.

LA GUERRA –VOLUME QUINTO. L'ALTO ISONZO. (*The War – Fifth Volume. The High Isonzo.***)**

Anonymous - Commando Supremo | 32.5cm x 23.5cm | illustrated white paper softback | 65pp | 1 large format map | 83 photographs | Fratelli Treves Editori. | 1916 | see note.

The title on the front cover is shown as "**LA GUERRA - L'ALTO ISONZO DALLE RACCOLTE DEL REPARTO FOTOGRAFICO DEL COMANDO SUPREMO DEL R. ESERCITO. VOL. 5.** (*The War – The High Isonzo from the Collections of the Photographic Department of the Supreme Command of the Royal Army. Vol. 5.*)" and is often given instead of that shown on the title page.

LA GUERRA - VOLUME SESTO. L'AERONAUTICA. (*The War – Sixth Volume 6 Aeronautics.***)**

Anonymous - Commando Supremo | 32.5cm x 23.5cm | illustrated white paper softback | 63pp | 1 large format map | ? photographs | Fratelli Treves Editori. | 1917 | see note.

The title on the front cover is shown as "**LA GUERRA - L'AERONAUTICA DALLE RACCOLTE DEL REPARTO FOTOGRAFICO DEL COMANDO SUPREMO DEL R. ESERCITO. VOL. 6.** (*The War – Aeronautics from the Collections of the Photographic Department of the Supreme Command of the Royal Army. Vol. 6.*)" and is often given instead of that shown on the title page.

LA GUERRA –VOLUME SETTIMO. L'ALBANIA. (*The War – Seventh Volume. Albania.***)**

Anonymous - Commando Supremo | 32.5cm x 23.5cm | illustrated white paper softback | 65pp | 1 large format map | 117 photographs | Fratelli Treves Editori. | 1917 | see note.

The title on the front cover is shown as "**LA GUERRA - L'ALBANIA DALLE RACCOLTE DEL REPARTO FOTOGRAFICO DEL COMANDO SUPREMO DEL R. ESERCITO. VOL. 7.** (*The War – Albania from the Collections of the Photographic Department of the Supreme Command of the Royal Army. Vol. 7.*)" and is often given instead of that shown on the title page.

LA GUERRA – VOLUME OTTAVO. LA CARNIA. (*The War – Eighth Volume. Carnia.***)**

Anonymous - Commando Supremo | 32.5cm x 23.5cm | illustrated white paper softback | 65pp | ? photographs | Fratelli Treves Editori. | c1917 | see note.

The title on the front cover is shown as "**LA GUERRA - LA CARNIA DALLE RACCOLTE DEL REPARTO FOTOGRAFICO DEL COMANDO SUPREMO DEL R. ESERCITO. VOL. 8.** (*The War – Carnia from the Collections of the Photographic Department of the Supreme Command of the Royal Army. Vol. 8.*)" and is often given instead of that shown on the title page.

LA GUERRA –VOLUME NONO. ARMI E MUNIZIONI. (*The War - Ninth Volume. Arms and Ammunition.***)**

Anonymous - Commando Supremo | 32.5cm x 23.5cm | illustrated white paper softback | 60pp | ? photographs | Fratelli Treves Editori. | c1917 | see note.

The title on the front cover is shown as "**LA GUERRA - ARMI E MUNIZIONI DALLE RACCOLTE DEL REPARTO FOTOGRAFICO DEL COMANDO SUPREMO DEL R. ESERCITO. VOL. 9.** (*The War – Arms and Ammunition from the Collections of the Photographic Department of the Supreme Command of the Royal Army. Vol. 9.*)" and is often given instead of that shown on the title page.

LA GUERRA - VOLUME DECIMO. LA MACEDONIA. (*The War – Tenth Volume. Macedonia.***)**

Anonymous - Commando Supremo | 32.5cm x 23.5cm | illustrated white paper softback | 65pp | 1 large format map | 83 photographs | Fratelli Treves Editori. | 1917 | see note.

The title on the front cover is shown as "**LA GUERRA - LA MACEDONIA DALLE RACCOLTE DEL REPARTO FOTOGRAFICO DEL COMANDO SUPREMO DEL R. ESERCITO. VOL. 10.** (*The War – Macedonia from the Collections of the Photographic Department of the Supreme Command of the Royal Army. Vol. 10.*)" and is often given instead of that shown on the title page.

LA GUERRA - VOLUME UNDICESIMO. LA BATTAGLIA DA PIAVE AL MARE. (*The War – Eleventh Volume. The Battle from Piave to the Sea.*)

Anonymous - Commando Supremo | 32.5cm x 23.5cm | illustrated white paper softback | 63pp | 1 large format map | ? photographs | Fratelli Treves Editori. | 1917 | see note.

The title on the front cover is shown as "**LA GUERRA - LA BATTAGLIA DA PIAVE AL MARE DALLE RACCOLTE DEL REPARTO FOTOGRAFICO DEL COMANDO SUPREMO DEL R. ESERCITO. VOL. 11.** (*The War – The Battle from Piave to the Sea from the Collections of the Photographic Department of the Supreme Command of the Royal Army. Vol. 11.*)" and is often given instead of that shown on the title page.

LA GUERRA - VOLUME DODICESIMA. LA BATTAGLIA DALLA BAINSIZZA AL TIMAVO. (*The War - Twelveth Volume. The Battle from the Bainsizza to the Timavo.*)

Anonymous - Commando Supremo | 32.5cm x 23.5cm | illustrated white paper softback | 63pp | 1 large format map | ? photographs | Fratelli Treves Editori. | c1917 | see note.

The title on the front cover is shown as "**LA GUERRA - LA BATTAGLIA DALLA BAINSIZZA AL TIMAVO DALLE RACCOLTE DEL REPARTO FOTOGRAFICO DEL COMANDO SUPREMO DEL R. ESERCITO. VOL. 12.** (*The War – The Battle from the Bainsizza to the Timavo from the Collections of the Photographic Department of the Supreme Command of the Royal Army. Vol. 12.*)" and is often given instead of that shown on the title page.

LA GUERRA – VOLUME TREDICESIMO. DALLE RIVE DEL PIAVE AI PROPUGNACOLI ALPINI. (*The War – Thriteenth Volume. From the Shores of the Piave to the Heights of Propugnacoli.*)

Anonymous - Commando Supremo | 32.5cm x 23.5cm | illustrated white paper softback | 49pp | 1 large format map | 81 photographs | Fratelli Treves Editori. | 1918 | see note.

The title on the front cover is shown as "**LA GUERRA - DALLE RIVE DEL PIAVE AI PROPUGNACOLI ALPINI DALLE RACCOLTE DEL REPARTO FOTOGRAFICO DEL COMANDO SUPREMO DEL R. ESERCITO. VOL. 13.** (*The War – From the Shores of the Piave to the Heights of Propugnacoli from the Collections of the Photographic Department of the Supreme Command of the Royal Army. Vol. 13.*)" and is often given instead of that shown on the title page.

LA GUERRA - VOLUME QUATTORDICESIMO. LA BATTAGLIA DALL'ASTICO AL PIAVE. (*The War -Fourteenth Volume. The Battle from the Astico to the Piave.*)

Anonymous - Commando Supremo | 32.5cm x 23.5cm | illustrated white paper softback | 46pp | 1 large format map | ? photographs | Fratelli Treves Editori. | c1918 | see note.

The title on the front cover is shown as "**LA GUERRA - LA BATTAGLIA DALL'ASTICO AL PIAVE DALLE RACCOLTE DEL REPARTO FOTOGRAFICO DEL COMANDO SUPREMO DEL R. ESERCITO. VOL. 14.** (*The War – The Battle from the Astico to the Piave from the Collections of the Photographic Department of the Supreme Command of the Royal Army. Vol. 14.*)" and is often given instead of that shown on the title page.

LA GUERRA - VOLUME QUINDICESIMO. I SERVIZI LOGISTICI. (*The War – Fifteenth Volume. The Logistic Services.*)

Anonymous - Commando Supremo | 32.5cm x 23.5cm | illustrated white paper softback | 45pp | ? photographs | Fratelli Treves Editori. | c1918| see note.

The title on the front cover is shown as "**LA GUERRA - I SERVIZI LOGISTICI DALLE RACCOLTE DEL REPARTO FOTOGRAFICO DEL COMANDO SUPREMO DEL R. ESERCITO. VOL. 15.** (*The War – The Logistic Services from the Collections of the Photographic Department of the Supreme Command of the Royal Army. Vol. 15.*)" and is often given instead of that shown on the title page.

LA GUERRA - LA BATTAGLIA DI VITTORIO VENETO (IN DUE VOLUMI). VOLUME SEDICESSIMO. (*The War - The Battle of Vittorio Veneto (In Two Volumes). Sixtheenth Volume.*)

Anonymous - Commando Supremo | 32.5cm x 23.5cm | illustrated white paper softback | 53pp | 80 photographs | Fratelli Treves Editori. | 1919 | see note.

The title on the front cover is shown as "**LA GUERRA - LA BATTAGLIA DI VITTORIO VENETO [PARTE 1] DALLE RACCOLTE DEL REPARTO FOTOGRAFICO DEL COMANDO SUPREMO DEL R. ESERCITO. VOL. 16.** (*The War – The Battle of Vittorio Veneto [Part 1] from the Collections of the Photographic Department of the Supreme Command of the Royal Army. Vol. 16.*)" and is often given instead of that shown on the title page.

LA GUERRA - LA BATTAGLIA DI VITTORIO VENETO (IN DUE VOLUMI). VOLUME DICIASSETTESIMO. (*The War - The Battle of Vittorio Veneto (In Two Volumes). Seventheenth Volume.*)

Anonymous - Commando Supremo | 32.5cm x 23.5cm | illustrated white paper softback | 47pp | 1 large format map | 159 photographs | Fratelli Treves Editori. | 1919 | see note.

The title on the front cover is shown as "**LA GUERRA - LA BATTAGLIA DI VITTORIO VENETO [PARTE 2] DALLE RACCOLTE DEL REPARTO FOTOGRAFICO DEL COMANDO SUPREMO DEL R. ESERCITO. VOL. 17.** (*The War – The Battle of Vittorio Veneto [Part 2] from the Collections of the Photographic Department of the Supreme Command of the Royal Army. Vol. 17.*)" and is often given instead of that shown on the title page.

LA GUERRA - IL QUADRIENNIO DELLA MARINA. VOLUME DICIOTTESIMO. (*The War - The Four-Year Duration for the Navy. Eighteenth Volume.*)

Anonymous - Commando Supremo | 32.5cm x 23.5cm | illustrated white paper softback | 47pp | 1 large format map | ? photographs | Fratelli Treves Editori. | 1921 | see note.

The title on the front cover is shown as "**LA GUERRA - IL QUADRIENNIO DELLA MARINA DALLE RACCOLTE DEL REPARTO FOTOGRAFICO DEL COMANDO SUPREMO DEL R. ESERCITO. VOL. 18.** (*The War – The Four-Year Duration for the Navy from the Collections of the Photographic Department of the Supreme Command of the Royal Army. Vol. 18.*)" and is often given instead of that shown on the title page.

This series "**La Guerra dalle Raccolte del Reparto Fotografico del Comando Supremo del R. Esercito.**" was produced officially during the war for popular consumption. The volumes were grouped into three series although the series numbers did not appear in the titles but the volume groupings were shown in advertisements in the later volumes. It was published with Italian, French, English and Spanish descriptions to all the photographs, for propaganda reasons aimed at neutral states, but the volume titles and introductions were in Italian only. However, the volumes were also published in 'English' - the titles and introductions were in English and not Italian, but retaining the multi-language descriptions to the photographs. There were also cheaper versions produced for the serving soldiers within the Italian army at the same time as the public editions. These 'army editions' had brown paper covers instead of the glossy white paper covers of the 'public editions' and were split into two parts, thereby making twice as many 'volumes' as the 'public editions'.

From 1916 through to 1921 the individual volumes that had already been published were bound together in groups of three and sold as hardback books – the first three volumes being bound and published in 1916 with the rest being published chorologically. The first bound group was also produced as an English version, it was called "**The War in Italy**", and was published 1916.

PANORAMI DELLA GUERRA DALLE RACCOLTE DELLA SEZIONE FOTOGRAFICA DEL COMANDO SUPREMO DEL REGIO ESERCITO. ROMBON-PLEZZO. FASCICOLO I^O (*Panoramas of the War from the Collections of the Royal Army's Supreme Command Photographic Section. Rombon-Plezzo. Part I.*)

Anonymous - Commando Supremo | 33.8cm x 25.4cm | grey-green paper softback | gilt | 2pp | 1 map | 1 panorama photograph | Casa Editrice d'Arte Bestetti e Tumminelli | c1916 | Italian Text.

PANORAMI DELLA GUERRA DALLE RACCOLTE DELLA SEZIONE FOTOGRAFICA DEL COMANDO SUPREMO DEL REGIO ESERCITO. IL CARSO DA TRIESTE AL SABOTINO. FASCICOLO II° - III° (*Panoramas of the War from the Collections of the Royal Army's Supreme Command Photographic Section. The Carso from Trieste to Sabotino. Parts II and III.*)

Anonymous - Commando Supremo | 33.8cm x 25.4cm | grey-green paper softback | gilt | 2pp | 1 map | 1 panorama photograph | Casa Editrice d'Arte Bestetti e Tumminelli | c1916 | Italian Text.

PANORAMI DELLA GUERRA DALLE RACCOLTE DELLA SEZIONE FOTOGRAFICA DEL COMANDO SUPREMO DEL REGIO ESERCITO. LE ALPI CADORINE DA MONTE POMAGAGNON. FASCICOLO IV° (*Panoramas of the War from the Collections of the Royal Army's Supreme Command Photographic Section. The Alps from Monte Pomagagnon. Part IV.*)

Anonymous - Commando Supremo I 33.8cm x 25.4cm I grey-green paper softback I gilt I 2pp I 1 map I 1 panorama photograph I Casa Editrice d'Arte Bestetti e Tumminelli I c1916 I Italian Text.

PANORAMI DELLA GUERRA DALLE RACCOLTE DELLA SEZIONE FOTOGRAFICA DEL COMANDO SUPREMO DEL REGIO ESERCITO. LA VALLE DEL SEEBACH DAL CONFINSPITZEN. FASCICOLO V^O (*Panoramas of the War from the Collections of the Royal Army's Supreme Command Photographic Section. Valle del Seebach to Confinspitzen. Part V.*)

Anonymous - Commando Supremo I 33.8cm x 25.4cm I grey-green paper softback I gilt I 2pp I 1 map I 1 panorama photograph I Casa Editrice d'Arte Bestetti e Tumminelli I c1916 I Italian Text.

PANORAMI DELLA GUERRA DALLE RACCOLTE DELLA SEZIONE FOTOGRAFICA DEL COMANDO SUPREMO DEL REGIO ESERCITO. GORZIA VISTA DAL PODGORA. FASCICOLO VI° (*Panoramas of the War from the Collections of the Royal Army's Supreme Command Photographic Section. View of Gorzia from Podgora. Part VI.*)

Anonymous - Commando Supremo I 33.8cm x 25.4cm I grey-green paper softback I gilt I 2pp I 1 map I 1 panorama photograph I Casa Editrice d'Arte Bestetti e Tumminelli I c1917 I Italian Text.

PANORAMI DELLA GUERRA DALLE RACCOLTE DELLA SEZIONE FOTOGRAFICA DEL COMANDO SUPREMO DEL REGIO ESERCITO. IL TRENTINO L'ALPE DI VAL TRAVIGNOLO. FASCICOLO VII° (*Panoramas of the War from the Collections of the Royal Army's Supreme Command Photographic Section. The Trentino: l'Alpe of Val Travignolo. Part VII.*)

Anonymous - Commando Supremo I 33.8cm x 25.4cm I grey-green paper softback I gilt I 2pp I 1 map I 1 panorama photograph I Casa Editrice d'Arte Bestetti e Tumminelli I c1917 I Italian Text.

PANORAMI DELLA GUERRA DALLE RACCOLTE DELLA SEZIONE FOTOGRAFICA DEL COMANDO SUPREMO DEL REGIO ESERCITO. IL TRENTINO VAL SUGANA, M.^{TE} PASUBIO ALTIP.^{NI} DI LAVARONE E LUSERNA. FASCICOLO VIII° - IX° (*Panoramas of the War from the Collections of the Royal Army's Supreme Command Photographic Section. The Trentino: Val Sugana, Monte Pasubio, the Heights of Lavarone and Luserna. Parts VIII and IX.*)

Anonymous - Commando Supremo I 33.8cm x 25.4cm I grey-green paper softback I gilt I 2pp I 1 map I 2 panorama photograph I 1 photograph I Casa Editrice d'Arte Bestetti e Tumminelli I c1917 I Italian Text.

PANORAMI DELLA GUERRA DALLE RACCOLTE DELLA SEZIONE FOTOGRAFICA DEL COMANDO SUPREMO DEL REGIO ESERCITO. IL TRENTINO IL GARDA, LA VALLE DEL SARCA E LA VALLE LARGINA. FASCICOLO X^O (*Panoramas of the War from the Collections of the Royal Army's Supreme Command Photographic Section. The Trentino: [Lake] Garda, The Valle del Sarca and The Valle Largina. Part X.*)

Anonymous - Commando Supremo I 33.8cm x 25.4cm I grey-green paper softback I gilt I 2pp I 1 map I 1 panorama photograph I Casa Editrice d'Arte Bestetti e Tumminelli I c1917 I Italian Text.

PANORAMI DELLA GUERRA DALLE RACCOLTE DELLA SEZIONE FOTOGRAFICA DEL COMANDO SUPREMO DEL REGIO ESERCITO. IL TRENTINO LE ALPI DELLO STELVIO. FASCICOLO XI° (*Panoramas of the War from the Collections of the Royal Army's Supreme Command Photographic Section. The Trentino Stelvio Alps. Part XI.*)

Anonymous - Commando Supremo I 33.8cm x 25.4cm I grey-green paper softback I gilt I 2pp I 1 map I 1 panorama photograph I Casa Editrice d'Arte Bestetti e Tumminelli I c1918 I Italian Text.

PANORAMI DELLA GUERRA DALLE RACCOLTE DELLA SEZIONE FOTOGRAFICA DEL COMANDO SUPREMO DEL REGIO ESERCITO. LE ALPI CADORINE DA COL DI MEZZO. FASCICOLO XII° (*Panoramas of the War from the Collections of the Royal Army's Supreme Command Photographic Section. The Alps from the Col di Mezzo. Part XII.*)

Anonymous - Commando Supremo I 33.8cm x 25.4cm I grey-green paper softback I gilt I 2pp I 1 map I 1 panorama photograph I Casa Editrice d'Arte Bestetti e Tumminelli I c1918 I Italian Text.

PANORAMI DELLA GUERRA DALLE RACCOLTE DELLA SEZIONE FOTOGRAFICA DEL COMANDO SUPREMO DEL REGIO ESERCITO. TONALE. FASCICOLO XIII[O]
(Panoramas of the War from the Collections of the Royal Army's Supreme Command Photographic Section. Tonale. Part XIII.)

Anonymous - Commando Supremo | 33.8cm x 25.4cm | grey-green paper softback | gilt | 2pp | 1 map | 1 panorama photograph | Casa Editrice d'Arte Bestetti e Tumminelli | c1918 | Italian Text.

All thirteen parts of this series "**Panorami della Guerra dalle Raccolte della Sezione Fotografica del Comando Supremo del Regio Esercito**" were bound together in a single cloth covered hardback book and published in 1919.

New Zealand Secondary Official Histories

New Zealand Expeditionary Force record of personal services during the war of officers, nurses, and first-class warrant officers, and other facts relating to the N.Z.E.F.: unofficial but based on official records.

Lieutenant Colonel J.[John] Studholme (Compiler) | 24cm x 14cm | cloth hardback | 563pp | ? photographs | Govenment Printer,. | 1928 | English Text

This volume is listed within Hingham's under the title '**Some Records of the New Zealand Expeditionary Force - Unofficial, but based on official records**'.

THE SAMOA (N.Z.) EXPEDITIONARY FORCE 1914-1915: An account based on official records of the Seizure and Occupation by New Zealand of the German Islands of Western Samoa.

[*Sergeant*] Stephen John Smith | 24cm x 14cm | grey blue cloth hardback | 218pp | 135 photographs | Ferguson & Osborn Limitied | 1924 | English Text

This volume can be viewed on the Internet Archive world wide web:

http://www.nzetc.org/tm/scholarly/WH1-Samo-fig-WH1-SamoFCo.html

a product of the Victoria University of Wellington and is located on the New Zealand Electronic Text Centre.

Romanian Secondary Official Histories

The Romanian official history was written by members of the Ministartvo Odbrane ([Romanian] National Defence Ministry).

Military;

România în anii primulu război mondial tomo 1. (*Romania in the Years of the First World War Book 1.*)
> Anonymous I 24cm x ?cm I Editura Militara. I 1987 I Romanian Text.

România în anii primulu război mondial tomo 2. (*Romania in the Years of the First World War Book 2.*)
> Anonymous I 24cm x ?cm I Editura Militara. I 1987 I Romanian Text.

Russian Secondary Official Histories

Pre-War Planning;

ПОДГОТОВКА РОССИИ К ИМПЕРИАЛИСТИЧЕСКОЙ ВОЙНЕ: ПЛАНЫ ВОЙНЫ.
(**Podgotovka Rossii k imperialističeskoj vojne: Plany Vojny.** - *Russia's Preparation for the Imperialist War: War Plans.*)

[*Генера́л От Инфанте́рии*] А.М.[Андрей Медардович] Зайончковский (*General of the Infantry* A.M.[Andrej Medardovič] Zajončkovskij) - СССР Военнайа Академийа РККА Имени М. В. Фрунзе (SSSR Voennaja Akademija RKKA Imeni M. V. Frunze – *USSR M. V. Frunze's RKKA (Red Army) Military Academy*) | ? | 425pp | 15 maps | Гос. Военное Издат (Gos. Voennoe Izdat.) | 1926 | Russian Text. | Russian Cyrillic script.

ПОДГОТОВКА РОССИИ К МИРОВОЙ ВОЙНЕ В МЕЖДУНАРОДНОМ ОТНОШЕНИИ.
(**Podgotovka Rossii k Mirovoj vojne v meždunarodnom otnošenii** - *Preparation of Russia to the International World War.*)

[*Генера́л От Инфанте́рии*] А.М.[Андрей Медардович] Зайончковский (*General of the Infantry* A.M.[Andrej Medardovič] Zajončkovskij) - СССР Военнайа Академийа РККА Имени М. В. Фрунзе (SSSR Voennaja Akademija RKKA Imeni M. V. Frunze – *USSR M. V. Frunze's RKKA (Red Army) Military Academy*) | ? | ?pp | ? maps | Гос. Военное Издат (Gos. Voennoe Izdat.) | 1926 | Russian Text. | Russian Cyrillic script.

Military Operations;

АВСТРО-ВЕНГРИЯ В ГОДЫ МИРОВОЙ ВОЙНЫ. (**Avstro-Vengriâ v gody Mirovoj vojny** - *Austria-Hungary during the World War Years.*)

С. А. Котляревский. (*S. A. Kotlârevskij.*) | ? | ?pp | ? maps | Государственное издательство (Gosudarstvennoe izdatel'stvo) | 1922 | Russian Text. | Russian Cyrillic script.

ОПЕРАЦИИ НА ВОСТОЧНОЙ ГРАНИЦЕ ГЕРМАНИИ В 1914 Г. ЧАСТЬ 1. ВОСТОЧНО-ПРУССКАЙА ОПЕРАЦИЙА (**Operacii na vostočnoj granice Germanii v 1914 g. Čast' 1. Vostočno-prusskaja operacija.** - *The Operation on the Eastern German Border 1914. Part 1. The East Prussian Operation.*)

И.И.[Иоаким Иоакимович] Вацетис (I.I.[Ioakim Ioakimovič] Vacetis) - СССР Военнайа Академийа РККА Имени М. В. Фрунзе (SSSR Voennaja Akademija RKKA Imeni M. V. Frunze – *USSR M. V. Frunze's RKKA (Red Army) Military Academy*) | ? | vi + 339pp | 18 maps | Государственное издательство (Gosudarstvennoe izdatel'stvo) | 1929 | Russian Text. | Russian Cyrillic script.

БОЕВЫЕ ДЕЙСТВИЯ В ВОСТОЧНОЙ ПРУССИИ В ИЮЛЕ, АВГУСТЕ И НАЧАЛЕ СЕНТЯБРЯ 1914 Г. (**Boevye dejstviâ v Vostočnoj Prussii v iûle, avguste i načale sentâbrâ 1914 g** - *The Fighting in Eastern Prussia in July, August and early September 1914.*)

И.И.[Иоаким Иоакимович] Вацетис (I.I.[Ioakim Ioakimovič] Vacetis) - СССР Военнайа Академийа РККА Имени М. В. Фрунзе (SSSR Voennaja Akademija RKKA Imeni M. V. Frunze – *USSR M. V. Frunze's RKKA (Red Army) Military Academy*) | ? | 105pp | ? maps | Государственное издательство (Gosudarstvennoe izdatel'stvo) | 1923 | Russian Text. | Russian Cyrillic script.

МИРОВАЙА ВОЙНА. МАНЕВРЕННЫЙ ПЕРИОД 1914-1915 ГОДОВ НА РУССКОМ (ЕВРОПЕЙСКОМ) ТЕАТРЕ. С ПРИЛОЖ. АЛЬБОМА СЦХЕМ. (**Mirovaja vojna. Manevrennyj period 1914-1915 godov na russkom (evropejskom) teatre. S prilož. Al'boma schem.** – *The World War. The War of Movement during the 1914-1915 Period on Russian European Theatre of War.*)

[*Генера́л От Инфанте́рии*] А.М.[Андрей Медардович] Зайончковский (*General of the Infantry* A.M.[Andrej Medardovič] Zajončkovskij) - СССР Военнайа Академийа РККА Имени М. В. Фрунзе (SSSR Voennaja Akademija RKKA Imeni M. V. Frunze – *USSR M. V. Frunze's RKKA (Red Army) Military Academy*) | ? | 415pp | Государственное издательство (Gosudarstvennoe izdatel'stvo) | 1929 | Russian Text. | Russian Cyrillic script.

МИРОВАЙА ВОЙНА. МАНЕВРЕННЫЙ ПЕРИОД 1914-1915 ГОДОВ НА РУССКОМ (ЕВРОПЕЙСКОМ) ТЕАТРЕ. С ПРИЛОЖ. АЛЬБОМА СЦХЕМ. (Mirovaja vojna. Manevrennyj period 1914-1915 godov na russkom (evropejskom) teatre. S prilož. Al'boma schem. – *The World War. The War of Movement during the 1914-1915 Period on Russian European Theatre of War.*) [Map Case.]

[*Генера́л От Инфанте́рии*] А.М.[Андрей Медардович] Зайончковский (*General of the Infantry* А.М.[Andrej Medardovič] Zajončkovskij) - СССР Военнайа Академийа РККА Имени М. В. Фрунзе (SSSR Voennaja Akademija RKKA Imeni M. V. Frunze – *USSR M. V. Frunze's RKKA (Red Army) Military Academy*) | ? | ? maps | Государственное издательство (Gosudarstvennoe izdatel'stvo) | 1929 | Russian Text. | Russian Cyrillic script.

СТРАТЕГИЧЕСКИЙ ОЧЕРК ВОЙНЫ 1914—1918 ГГ. ЧАСТЬ I. ПЕРИОД ОТ ОБЪЯВЛЕНИЯ ВОЙНЫ ДО НАЧАЛА СЕНТЯБРЯ 1914 Г. ПЕРВОЕ ВТОРЖЕНИЕ РУССКИХ АРМИЙ В ВОСТ. ПРУССИЮ И ГАЛИЦИЙСКАЯ БИТВА. (Strategičeskij očerk vojny 1914—1918 gg. Časť I. Period ot ob''âvleniâ vojny do načala sentâbrâ 1914 g. Pervoe vtorženie russkih armij v Vost. Prussiû i Galicijskaâ bitva. - *Strategic Outline of the War 1914—1918 Part I. Period from Declarations of War to Early September 1914: The First Russian Army's Invasion into Eastern Prussia and Galician Bitva.*)

[*Генерал-Лейтенант*] Я.К.[Януарий Казимирович] Цихович (*Lieutenant General* Â. K.[Ânuarij Kazimirovič] Cihovič) Compiler - СССР Военнайа Академийа РККА Имени М. В. Фрунзе (SSSR Voennaja Akademija RKKA Imeni M. V. Frunze – *USSR M. V. Frunze's RKKA (Red Army) Military Academy*) | ? | ? maps | Государственное издательство (Gosudarstvennoe izdatel'stvo) | 1922 | Russian Text. | Russian Cyrillic script.

СТРАТЕГИЧЕСКИЙ ОЧЕРК ВОЙНЫ 1914—1918 ГГ. ЧАСТЬ II. ПЕРИОД С 1 (14) СЕНТЯБРЯ ПО 15 (28) НОЯБРЯ 1914 Г. АВГУСТОВСКОЕ СРАЖЕНИЕ, ВАРШАВСКО-ИВАНГОРОДСКАЯ, КРАКОВСКАЯ И ЛОДЗИНСКАЯ ОПЕРАЦИИ, ОПЕРАЦИИ В ГАЛИЦИИ И КАРПАТАХ, ХЫРОВСКОЕ СРАЖЕНИЕ. (Strategičeskij očerk vojny 1914—1918 gg. Časť II. Period s 1 (14) sentâbrâ 1914 g. po 15 (28) noâbrâ 1914 g. Avgustovskoe Sraženie, Varšavsko-Ivangorodskaâ, Krakovskaâ I Lodzinskaâ Operacii, Operacii V Galicii I Karpatah, Hyrovskoe Sraženie. - *Strategic Outline of the War 1914—1918 Part II. Period from 1 (14) September to 15 (28) November 1914. The August battles, The Warsaw-Ivangorod, Cracow and Łódź Operations, Operations in Galicia and the Carpathians, Hyrovskoe Battle.*)

[*Генерал-Лейтенант*] Г.К. Корольков (*Lieutenant General* G.K. Korol'kov) Compiler - СССР Военнайа Академийа РККА Имени М. В. Фрунзе (SSSR Voennaja Akademija RKKA Imeni M. V. Frunze – *USSR M. V. Frunze's RKKA (Red Army) Military Academy*) | ? | ? maps | Государственное издательство (Gosudarstvennoe izdatel'stvo) | 1923 | Russian Text. | Russian Cyrillic script.

СТРАТЕГИЧЕСКИЙ ОЧЕРК ВОЙНЫ 1914—1918 ГГ. ЧАСТЬ III. ПЕРИОД С 12 (25) НОЯБРЯ 1914 Г. ПО 15 (28) МАРТА 1915 Г. (Strategičeskij očerk vojny 1914—1918 gg. Časť III. Period s 12 (25) noâbrâ 1914 g. po 15 (28) marta 1915 g. - *Strategic Outline of the War 1914—1918 Part III. From 12 (25) November 1914 to 15 (28) March 1915.*)

[*Подполковник*] А.А. Незнамов. (*Lieutenant Colonel* A.A. Neznamov) Compiler - СССР Военнайа Академийа РККА Имени М. В. Фрунзе (SSSR Voennaja Akademija RKKA Imeni M. V. Frunze – *USSR M. V. Frunze's RKKA (Red Army) Military Academy*) | iv + 88pp | ? maps | Государственное издательство (Gosudarstvennoe izdatel'stvo) | 1922 | Russian Text. | Russian Cyrillic script.

СТРАТЕГИЧЕСКИЙ ОЧЕРК ВОЙНЫ 1914—1918 ГГ. ЧАСТЬ IV. (Strategičeskij očerk vojny 1914—1918 gg. Časť IV. - *Strategic Outline of the War 1914—1918 Part IV.*)

[*Подполковник*] А.А. Незнамов. (*Lieutenant Colonel* A.A. Neznamov) Compiler - СССР Военнайа Академийа РККА Имени М. В. Фрунзе (SSSR Voennaja Akademija RKKA Imeni M. V. Frunze – *USSR M. V. Frunze's RKKA (Red Army) Military Academy*) | ? | ? maps | Государственное издательство (Gosudarstvennoe izdatel'stvo) | 1922 | Russian Text. | Russian Cyrillic script.

СТРАТЕГИЧЕСКИЙ ОЧЕРК ВОЙНЫ 1914—1918 ГГ. ЧАСТЬ V. ПЕРИОД С ОКТЯБРЯ 1915 Г. ПО ОКТЯБРЯ 1916 г. ПОЗИЦИОННАЯ ВОЙНА И ПРОРЫВ АВСТРИЙЦЕВ ЮГО-ЗАПАДНЫМ ФРОНТОМ. (Strategičeskij očerk vojny 1914—1918 gg. Časť V. Period s oktâbrâ 1915 g. po oktâbrâ 1916 g Pozicionnaâ Vojna I Proryv Avstrijcev Ûgo-Zapadnym Frontom. - *Strategic Outline of the War 1914—1918 Part V. From October 1915 to October 1916. The Trench War and the Breakthrough on the Austro Southwest Front.*)

[*Генерал От Инфантерии*] В.Н.[Владислав Наполеонович] Клембовский. (*General of the Infantry* V.N.[Vladislav Napoleonovič] Klembovskij.) Compiler - СССР Военнайа Академийа РККА Имени М. В. Фрунзе (SSSR Voennaja Akademija RKKA Imeni M. V. Frunze – *USSR M. V. Frunze's RKKA (Red Army) Military Academy*) | ? | ? maps | Государственное издательство (Gosudarstvennoe izdatel'stvo) | 1920 | Russian Text. | Russian Cyrillic script.

СТРАТЕГИЧЕСКИЙ ОЧЕРК ВОЙНЫ 1914—1918 ГГ. ЧАСТЬ VI. ПЕРИОД ОТ ПРОРЫВА ЮГО-ЗАПАДНОГО ФРОНТА В МАЕ 1916 ДО КОНЦА ВОЙНЫ. (Strategičeskij očerk vojny 1914—1918 gg. Časть VI. Period Ot Proryva Ûgo-Zapadnogo Fronta V Mae 1916 Do Konca Vojny. - *Strategic Outline of the War 1914—1918 Part VI. Period from the Breakthrough on the South-West Front in May 1916 until the End of the War.***)**

[*Генерал От Инфантерии*] А.М.[Андрей Медардович] Зайончковский (*General of the Infantry* А.М.[Andrej Medardovič] Zajončkovskij) Compiler - СССР Военнайа Академийа РККА Имени М. В. Фрунзе (SSSR Voennaja Akademija RKKA Imeni M. V. Frunze – *USSR M. V. Frunze's RKKA (Red Army) Military Academy*) | 137pp | ? maps | Государственное издательство (Gosudarstvennoe izdatel'stvo) | 1923 | Russian Text. | Russian Cyrillic script.

СТРАТЕГИЧЕСКИЙ ОЧЕРК ВОЙНЫ 1914—1918 ГГ. ЧАСТЬ VII. КАМПАНИЯ 1917. Г. (Strategičeskij očerk vojny 1914—1918 gg. Časть VII. Kampaniâ 1917 G. - *Strategic Outline of the War 1914—1918 Part VII. Campaign of 1917.***)**

[*Генерал От Инфантерии*] А.М.[Андрей Медардович] Зайончковский (*General of the Infantry* А.М.[Andrej Medardovič] Zajončkovskij) Compiler - СССР Военнайа Академийа РККА Имени М. В. Фрунзе (SSSR Voennaja Akademija RKKA Imeni M. V. Frunze – *USSR M. V. Frunze's RKKA (Red Army) Military Academy*) | 188pp | ? maps | Государственное издательство (Gosudarstvennoe izdatel'stvo) | 1923 | Russian Text. | Russian Cyrillic script.

СТРАТЕГИЧЕСКИЙ ОЧЕРК ВОЙНЫ 1914—1918 ГГ. ЧАСТЬ VIII. РУМЫНСКИЙ ФРОНТ. (Strategičeskij očerk vojny 1914—1918 gg. Časть VIII. Rumynskij front. - *Strategic Outline of the War 1914—1918 Part VIII.The Romanian front.***)**

Ф. И. Васильев (F. I. Vasil'ev) Compiler - СССР Военнайа Академийа РККА Имени М. В. Фрунзе (SSSR Voennaja Akademija RKKA Imeni M. V. Frunze – *USSR M. V. Frunze's RKKA (Red Army) Military Academy*) | ? | ? maps | Государственное издательство (Gosudarstvennoe izdatel'stvo) | 1922 | Russian Text. | Russian Cyrillic script.
This set "**Стратегический Очерк Войны 1914—1918 гг**" was commissioned by the Комиссия по исследованию и использованию опыта мировой и гражданской войны. (Komissiâ po issledovaniû i ispolьzovaniû opyta mirovoj i graždanskoj vojny. - *The Commission on the Exploration using the Experiences of the World War and the Civil War.*)

ПОДГОТОВКА РОССИИ К МИРОВОЙ ВОЙНЕ В МЕЖДУНАРОДНОМ ОТНОШЕНИИ. (Podgotovka Rossii k mirovoj vojne v meždunarodnom otnošenii. - *Training Russia in the World War in the international.***)**

[*Генерал От Инфантерии*] А.М.[Андрей Медардович] Зайончковский (*General of the Infantry* А.М.[Andrej Medardovič] Zajončkovskij) - СССР Военнайа Академийа РККА Имени М. В. Фрунзе (SSSR Voennaja Akademija RKKA Imeni M. V. Frunze – *USSR M. V. Frunze's RKKA (Red Army) Military Academy*) | ? | ? maps | Государственное издательство (Gosudarstvennoe izdatel'stvo) | 1926 | Russian Text. | Russian Cyrillic script.

МИРОВАЯ ВОЙНА 1914—1918 ГГ. ТОМ 1. (Mirovaâ vojna 1914—1918 gg. Tom 1. - *World War 1914—1918. Volume 1.***)**

[*Генерал От Инфантерии*] А.М.[Андрей Медардович] Зайончковский (*General of the Infantry* А.М.[Andrej Medardovič] Zajončkovskij) - СССР Военнайа Академийа РККА Имени М. В. Фрунзе (SSSR Voennaja Akademija RKKA Imeni M. V. Frunze – *USSR M. V. Frunze's RKKA (Red Army) Military Academy*) | ? | 455pp | ? maps | Гос военное Изд-во Наркомата обороны Сойуза ССР (Gos. voennoe Izd-vo Narkomata oborony Sojuza SSR) | 1924/31 | Russian Text. | Russian Cyrillic script.

МИРОВАЯ ВОЙНА 1914—1918 ГГ. ТОМ 2. (Mirovaâ vojna 1914—1918 gg. Tom 2. - *World War 1914—1918. Volume 2.***)**

[*Генерал От Инфантерии*] А.М.[Андрей Медардович] Зайончковский (*General of the Infantry* А.М.[Andrej Medardovič] Zajončkovskij) - СССР Военнайа Академийа РККА

Имени М. В. Фрунзе (SSSR Voennaja Akademija RKKA Imeni M. V. Frunze – *USSR M. V. Frunze's RKKA (Red Army) Military Academy*) | ? | 455pp | ? maps | Гос военное Изд-во Наркомата обороны Сойуза ССР (Gos. voennoe Izd-vo Narkomata oborony Sojuza SSR) | 1938 | Russian Text. | Russian Cyrillic script.

МИРОВАЯ ВОЙНА 1914—1918 ГГ. ТОМ 3. (Mirovaâ vojna 1914—1918 gg. Tom 3. - *World War 1914—1918. Volume 3.*)

[Генерал От Инфантерии] А.М.[Андрей Медардович] Зайончковский (*General of the Infantry* А.М.[Andrej Medardovič] Zajončkovskij) - СССР Военнайа Академийа РККА Имени М. В. Фрунзе (SSSR Voennaja Akademija RKKA Imeni M. V. Frunze – *USSR M. V. Frunze's RKKA (Red Army) Military Academy*) | ? | 455pp | ? maps | Гос военное Изд-во Наркомата обороны Сойуза ССР (Gos. voennoe Izd-vo Narkomata oborony Sojuza SSR) | 1939 | Russian Text. | Russian Cyrillic script.

ПОДГОТОВКА РОССИИ К МИРОВОЙ ВОЙНЕ В МЕЖДУНАРОДНОМ ОТНОШЕНИИ (Podgotovka Rossii k mirovoj vojne v meždunarodnom otnošenii - *Russia's Preparations for the World War in International Relations.*)

[Генерал От Инфантерии] А.М.[Андрей Медардович] Зайончковский and М[Мицхаил] П Павлович (*General of the Infantry Professor* А.М.[Andrej Medardovič] Zajončkovskij and M.P.[Michail] Pavlovič) - Штаб РККА Управление по Исследованию и Использованию Опыта Вojн. (Štab RKKA Upravlenie po Issledovaniju i Ispol'zovaniju Opyta Vojn. - *RKKA (The Red Army) General Staff The Office for the Research on the Experience of War.*) | ? | 401pp | ? maps | Гос военное Изд-во Наркомата обороны Сойуза ССР (Gos. voennoe Izd-vo Narkomata oborony Sojuza SSR) | 1926 | Russian Text. | Russian Cyrillic script.

МИРОВАЙА ВОЙНА. 1914-1918 ГГ. КАМПАНИЙА 1914 ГОДА В БЕЛЬГИИ И ФРАНЦИИ. Т. И. (ОТ НАЧАЛА ВОЙНЫ ДО РАСПОЛОЖЕНИЙА СТОРОН НА МАРНЕ.) ТОМ I. (Mirovaja Vojna. 1914-1918 gg. Kampanija 1914 goda v Bel'gii i Francii.) Ot načala vojny do raspoloženija storon na Marne.) Tom I. – *The World War. 1914-1918. The Campaign in Belgium and France 1914. (From the Outbreak of War to the Battle of the Marne.) Volume I.*)

В.Ф.[Василий] Новицкий (V.F.[Vasilij] Novickij) - СССР Военнайа Академийа РККА Имени М. В. Фрунзе (SSSR Voennaja Akademija RKKA Imeni M. V. Frunze – *USSR M. V. Frunze's RKKA (Red Army) Military Academy*) | ? | xiv + 516pp | 19 folding maps | Государственное издательство (Gosudarstvennoe izdatel'stvo) | 1926 | Russian Text. | Russian Cyrillic script.

МИРОВАЙА ВОЙНА. 1914-1918 ГГ. КАМПАНИЙА 1914 ГОДА В БЕЛЬГИИ И ФРАНЦИИ. Т. И. (ОТ ЗАВЙАЗКИ СРАЖЕНИЙА НА Р. МАРНЕ ДО УСТАНОВЛЕНИЙА ПОЗИЦИОННОЙ ВОЙНЫ.) ТОМ II. (Mirovaja Vojna. 1914-1918 gg. Kampanija 1914 goda v Bel'gii i Francii. (Ot zavjazki sraženija na r. Marne do ustanovlenija pozicionnoj vojny.) Tom II. – *The World War. 1914-1918. The Campaign in Belgium and France 1914. (The Start of the Battle of the Marne until Positional War.) Volume II.*)

В.Ф.[Василий] Новицкий (V.F.[Vasilij] Novickij) - СССР Военнайа Академийа РККА Имени М. В. Фрунзе (SSSR Voennaja Akademija RKKA Imeni M. V. Frunze – *USSR M. V. Frunze's RKKA (Red Army) Military Academy*) | ? | viii + 424pp | 18 folding maps | Государственное издательство (Gosudarstvennoe izdatel'stvo) | 1928 | Russian Text. | Russian Cyrillic script.

РУССКАЯ АРТИЛЛЕРИЯ В МИРОВОЙ ВОЙНЕ 1914-1918 ГГ. ТОМ ПЕРВЫЙ. (Russkaâ artilleriâ v Mirovoj Vojne 1914-1918 gg. Tom pervyj - *The Russian Artillery in the World War 1914-1918. Volume One.*)

Е. Барсуков (*E. Barsukov* - Soviet Government.) | Государственное издательство (Gosudarstvennoe izdatel'stvo) | 1938 | Russian Text. | Russian Cyrillic script.

РУССКАЯ АРТИЛЛЕРИЯ В МИРОВОЙ ВОЙНЕ 1914-1918 ГГ. ТОМ ВТОРОЕ. (Russkaâ artilleriâ v Mirovoj Vojne 1914-1918 gg. Tom vtoroe. - *The Russian Artillery in the World War 1914-1918. Volume Two.*)

Е. Барсуков (*E. Barsukov* - Soviet Government.) | Государственное издательство (Gosudarstvennoe izdatel'stvo) | 1938 | Russian Text. | Russian Cyrillic script.

Strategic Studies:

СТРАТЕГИЧЕСКАЯ ОЧЕРК ВОЙНЫ 1914 - 1915 ГГ. (Strategičeskaâ Očerk Vojny 1914 - 1915 gg. - *A Strategic Outline of the War 1914 –1915.*)

В.М. Клембовский (*V.M. Klembovskii* - Soviet Government.) | ? | Выссхии военныи редактсионныи совет (Vysshii voennyi redaktsionnyi sovet) | 1920 | Russian Text. | Russian Cyrillic script.

КРАТКИЙ СТРАТЕГИЧЕСКИЙ ОЧЕРК ВОЙНЫ 1914-1918 ГГ. РУССКИЙ ФРОНТ. ЧАСТИ I. (Kratkij strategičeskij očerk vojny 1914-1918 gg. Russkij front. Časti I. - *Brief strategic description of war 1914-1918 yr. Russian Front. Parts I.*)

В Борисов. (V Borisov- Soviet Government.) | ? | Выссхии военныи редактсионныи совет (Vysshii voennyi redaktsionnyi sovet) | 1918 | Russian Text. | Russian Cyrillic script.

КРАТКИЙ СТРАТЕГИЧЕСКИЙ ОЧЕРК ВОЙНЫ 1914-1918 ГГ. РУССКИЙ ФРОНТ. ЧАСТИ II. (Kratkij strategičeskij očerk vojny 1914-1918 gg. Russkij front. Časti II. - *Brief strategic description of war 1914-1918 yr. Russian Front. Parts II.*)

В Борисов. (V Borisov- Soviet Government.) | ? | Выссхии военныи редактсионныи совет (Vysshii voennyi redaktsionnyi sovet) | 1919 | Russian Text. | Russian Cyrillic script.

СТРАТЕГИЧЕСНИЙ ОЧЕРК ВОЙНЫ 1914 - 1918 ГГ. (Strategičesnij Očerk Vojny 1914 - 1918 gg. - *A Strategic Outline of the War 1914 –1918.*)

Ж.К. Цыхович (*J.K. Tsikhovich* - Soviet Government.) | 240pp | Выссхии военныи редактсионныи совет (Vysshii voennyi redaktsionnyi sovet) | 1922 | Russian Text. | Russian Cyrillic script.

БРУСИЛОВСКИЙ ПРОРЫВ: ОПЕРАТИВНО - СТРАТЕГИЧЕСКИЙ ОЧЕРК. (Brusilovskij proryv: Operativno - strategičeskij očerk – *Brusilovs' Breakthrough. Operational and Strategic Study.*)

Л. В. Ветошников (L. V.Vetošnikov - Soviet Government.) | ? | 183pp | 5 maps | | Государственное Военное Издательство Наркомата Обороны Соûза ССР (Gosudarstvennoe Voennoe Izdatel'stvo Narkomata Oborony Soûza SSR - *State military publishing house of the people's commissariat of the defense of the USSR*) | 1940 | Russian Text. | Russian Cyrillic script.

Military Documentation:

РАСПАД АРМИИ В 1917 Г. СОБРАНИЕ ДОКУМЕНТОВ. (Raspad Armii v 1917 g. Sobranie dokumentov - *The Decomposition of the Army in 1917. A Collection of Documents.*)

Н.Е. Какурин, М.Н. Покровский и И.А. Яковлев (*N.E. [Nikolai Evgeńevič] Kakurin, M.N. [Mikhail Nikolaevich] Pokrovskii and I.A. Iakovlev* - Soviet Government.) | Государственное издательство (Gosudarstvennoe izdatel'stvo) | 1925 | Russian Text. | Russian Cyrillic script.

ПОРАЖЕНИЕ ГЕРМАНИИ В 1918 Г. СОБРАНИЕ МАТЕРИАЛОВ И ДОКУМЕНТОВ. (Poraženie Germanii v 1918 g. Sobranie materialov i dokumentov - *The Defeat of the Germans in 1918. A Collection of Material and Documents.*)

Гозвоениздат (Gosvoenizdat – *Anonymous* - Soviet Government.) | Государственное издательство (Gosudarstvennoe izdatel'stvo) | 1943 | Russian Text. | Russian Cyrillic script.

СБОРНИК ДОКУМЕНТОВ МИРОВОЙ ИМПЕРИАЛИСТИЧЕСКОЙ ВОЙНЫ НА РУССКОМ ФРОНТЕ (1914-1917 ГГ). (Sbornik dokumentov mirovoj imperialističeskoj vojny na russkom fronte (1914-1917 gg.) - *Collection of Imperialist World War Documents on the Russian Front (1914-1917).*)

Гозвоениздат (Gosvoenizdat – *Anonymous* - Soviet Government.) | Государственное издательство (Gosudarstvennoe izdatel'stvo) | 1941 | Russian Text. | Russian Cyrillic script.

ЦАРСКАЯ РОССИЯ И ВОЙНА. (Carskaâ Rossiâ i Vojna - *Tsarist Russia and the War.*)

М.Н. Покровский ([*Professor*] *M.N.[Mikhail Nikolaevich] Pokrovskii* - Soviet Government.) | Paper covered softback | i + 87pp | Государственное издательство

(Gosudarstvennoe izdatel'stvo) | 1924 | French Text /Russian Text. | Part Latin script, part Russian Cyrillic script.

ЦАРСКАЯ РОССИЯ В МИРОВОЙ ВОЙНЕ. ТОМ I. (Carskaâ Rossiâ v Mirovoj vojne - *Tsarist Russia in the World War I. Volume I.)*

Гозвоениздат (Gosvoenizdat– *Anonymous Central Archives, foreword by* М.Н. Покровского. *M.N.[Mikhail Nikolaevich] Pokrovskii.*) | Paper covered softback | xxiv + 302pp | Государственное издательство (Gosudarstvennoe izdatel'stvo - *State Publishing House*) | 1926 | Russian Text. | Russian Cyrillic script.

It appears that only the first volume of this proposed set was published.

War Economics:

ВОЕННАЙА ÉКОНОМИКА ГЕРМАНИИ 1914--1918 ГГ. ОПЫТ ТЕОРЕТИČЕСКОГО АНАЛИЗА ВОЕННОГО ЦХОЗЙАЙСТВА. (Voennaja Ékonomika Germanii 1914--1918 gg. Opyt teoretičeskogo analiza voennogo chozjajstva. – *The Germany War Economics 1914-1918. An Attempt at Theoretical Analysis of the Wartime Economy.)*

Е.Л. Цхмельницкайа (*E.L. [Elizaveta Leonidovna] Chmel'nickaja* - Soviet Government.) | ? | vii + 239pp | Государственное издательство (Gosudarstvennoe izdatel'stvo) | 1929 | Russian Text. | Russian Cyrillic script.

South African Secondary Official Histories

Government Reports on the Rebellion;

Union of South Africa: Report of the Select Parliamentary Committee on the Rebellion.
> *Sir* Patrick Duncan (chairman - Parliament of South Africa. House of Assembly. Select Committee on Rebellion.) | 25cm x 21cm | Blue Paper Softback | xxv + 369pp | Cape Times Limited. | 1915 | English Text.

Union of South Africa: Report of the Judicial Commission of Inquiry into the Causes of and Circumstances relating to the Recent Rebellion in South Africa.
> *Sir* Johannes Henricus Lange (chairman - Judicial Commission of Inquiry) | 33cm x 21cm | Blue Paper Softback | x + 147pp | 1 folding map | ? maps | Cape Times Limited. | 1916 | English Text.

Union of South Africa: Report of the Rebellion Losses Commission.
> Maurice S. [Smethurst] Evans (chairman - Rebellion Losses Commission) | 33cm x 21cm | Blue Paper Softback | i + 13pp | Cape Times Limited. | 1916 | English Text.

Turkish Secondary Official Histories

Earlier Naval Monographs:

Ordu ve donanmanın müşterek harekâtı (*Army and Navy's Joint Operations*)
 Kaymakam (*Lieutenant Colonel*) Bahattin | 24.5cm x 17.2cm | White Paper Softback | 46pp | Genelkurmay Başkanlığı (*The Turkish General Staff.*) | 1935 | Modern Turkish Text.
 The rank of *Kaymakam* (*Lieutenant Colonel*) has changed to *Yarbay*.

Büyük harbin Türk Deniz cephesi (*The Great War on the Turkish Naval Front*)
 Haydar Alpagut | 24.5cm x 17.2cm | White Paper Softback | iv + 79pp | 3 large format maps | Genelkurmay Başkanlığı (*The Turkish General Staff.*) | 1937 | Modern Turkish Text.
 Published under the authority of Genelkurmay Başkanlığı IX. Şube (*The Chief of the General Staff, Department IX.*)

1915'de Çanakkale'de Türk. (*The Turks at Gallipoli, 1915*)
 Anonymous (Milli Müdafaa Vekaleti) | 24.5cm x 17.2cm | White Paper Softback | 52pp | 3 maps | 3 photographs | 24 organisation charts | Genelkurmay Basimevi (*The Turkish General Staff.*) | 1957 | Modern Turkish Text.
 Part of the "Erkâniharbiyei Umumiye Riyaseti Harb Tarihi Dairesi Başkanlığı" set.

1914-1918 Çanakkale'de Türk bahriyesı. (*The Turks at Gallipoli 1914-1918.*)
 Albay (*Colonel*) Saim Besbelli (Retired). (Deniz Kuvvetleri Kumandanlığı). | 24cm x 17.2cm | White Paper Softback | 40pp | 3 maps | 3 photographs | 24 organisation charts | Basimevi (*The Turkish General Staff.*) | 1959 | Modern Turkish Text.

Earlier Military Monographs:

يلضيريم ٣٣٣١ ـ ٤٣٣١ (Yıldırım 1333-1334 – *Lightning 1917-1918.*)[4]
 Kaymakam (*Lieutenant Colonel*) Hüseyin Hüsnü Emir. | 27cm x 17.2cm | White Paper Softback | 365pp | 17 large format maps in pocket | 92 folded illustrations in rear pocket on 49 plates | Dersaadet: Matbaa-i Askeriye | 1337 (1921) | Ottoman Turkish Text.
 This volume was part of the "**Erkân-ı Harbiye-i Umumiye Tarih-i Harp Neşriyat-5 Hususiye külliyatı; 1**" set.
 The word Yıldırım was the name given to the Turkish army on the Palestine front during the 1917-1918 period.
 An English translation of this volume produced soon after the publication of the original Ottoman Turkish edition and probably used in the writing of the British and Australian official histories can be found reproduced on the Australian Light Horse Studies Centre world wide web site as a 'pdf file':
 http://alh-research.tripod.com/turk.htm
 This volume was transliterated into Modern Turkish and republished in 1955 and again in 2002 under the slightly revised title **YILDIRIM - 1917-1918** (ISBN 9754092141) both editions. The 2002 edition has the following pages: xii + 433pp. The author's name and rank has likewise been updated – the revised form being *Tümgeneral* (*Major General*) Hüseyin Hüsnü Emir Erkilet.

ىلضيريمين هقيبهطى ـ مهضمع٤٣٣١ مونضروس موتهرهقهرسينه قهضمهر (Yıldırımin Akibeti - 1334'dem Mondros Mütarekersine Kadar - *The Finish of Lightning - 1918 to the Mudros Armistice.*)
 Ahmed Mirliva Sedad. | 27cm x 17.2cm | White Paper Softback | 322pp | 18 maps + 5 large format maps in rear pocket | 2 illustrations | 9 organisation charts + 8 organisation charts in

---

[4] Turkish Ottoman script is read from the right. I have not been able to review either of the two volumes "**Yıldırım 1333-1334**" and "**Yıldırımin Akibeti - 1334'dem Mondros Mütarekersine Kadar**" in their original format. The tiles found were listed in Latin script and have been transliterated back into Turkish Ottoman script. These translitorations have not been checked, and therefore these Turkish Ottoman titles should be regarded as a guide only.

rear pocket I 1 table + 2 talbes in rear pocket I Genelkurmay Basimevi (*The Turkish General Staff*.) I 1343 (1927) I Ottoman Turkish Text.

Part of the "Erkân-i Harbiye-yi Umumiye Talim ve Terbiye Dairesi" set.

Büyük Harpte Misir Seferi. (*The Egyptian Campaign during the Great War.*)
Albay (*Colonel*) Mütekait Miralay Behçet. I 27cm x 17.2cm I White Paper Softback I 34pp I 1 folding maps I Genelkurmay Basimevi (*The Turkish General Staff*.) I 1930 I Modern Turkish Text.

This volume was a supplement to 76 Numaralı Askeri Mecmuaya.

Büyük Harpte Kafkas Cephesi Hatıraları. (*Caucasus Front during the Great War.*)
Albay (*Colonel*) Aziz Samih İlter (Büyük Erkânıharbiye Reisliği) I 29cm x 20cm I White Paper Softback I 114pp I ? appendices I ? maps I ? photographs I ? organisation charts I Büyük Erkânıharbiye Matbaası I 1934 I Modern Turkish Text.

This volume has been republished in 2007 by the Genelkurmay Basimevi under the revised title "**Birinci Dünya Savaşı Kafkas Cephesi Hatıraları. (*The First World War on the Caucasus Front*).**"

Büyük Harpte Makedonya Cephesi (*The Macedonian Campaign during the Great War.*)
Nureddin Fuad Alpkartal I 26cm x 19cm I Brown Paper Softback I 53pp I Genelkurmay Matbasi I 1938 I Modern Turkish Text.

Büyük Harpte Osmanlı imparatorluğunun nun 1916-1917 yilindaki vaziyeti ve Birüssebi-Gazze meydan muharebesi ve Yirminci kolordusu. (*The Situation of the Ottoman Empire during the Great War 1916-1917 - The Twentieth Army Corps and the Battles of Beersheba and Gaza.*)
Ali Fuat Cebesoy. I 26cm x 20cm I White Paper Softback I 80pp I ? appendices I ? maps I ? photographs I ? organisation charts I Genelkurmay Basimevi (*The Turkish General Staff*.) I 1938 I Modern Turkish Text.

Published under the authority of Genelkurmay Başkanlığı X. Şube (*The Chief of the General Staff, Department X.*)

Çanakkale Conkbayırı Savaşları, ATATÜRK'ün Yaptırdığı Görülmemiş Yiğitçe Süngü Hücumu. (*The Battles of Chunuk Bair and Sari Bair, Ataturk's Unprecedented Bold Bayonet Attack.*)
Cemil Conk (Harp Tarihi Dairesi Başkanlığı) I 24.5cm x 17.2cm I White Paper Softback I 94pp I ? appendices I ? maps I ? photographs I ? organisation charts I Erkânıharbiyei Umumiye Basımevi I 1959 I Modern Turkish Text.

Part of the Erkânıharbiyei Umumiye Riyaseti Harb Tarihi Dairesi yayınları. Hamâset serisi 2" set.

Later Military Monographs:

T.C. GENELKURMAY BAŞKANLIĞI ANKARA - KAFKAS CEPHESİ'NDE 10 NCU KOLORDUNUN BİRİNCİ DÜNYA SAVAŞI'NIN BAŞLANGICINDAN SARIKAMIŞ MUHAREBELERİNİN SONUNA KADAR OLAN HAREKÂTI. (*T.C. General Staff Directorate, Ankara - The 10th Army Corps' Sarikamis Battles on the Caucasian Front, until the end of the Operations during the First World War,.*)
Yarbay (*Lieutenant Colonel*) Selahattin (Retired). I 24.5cm x 17.2cm I Illustrated Paper Softback I xi + 212 + 25pp I 19 maps I 2 organisation charts I 6 tables I 1 photograph I Genelkurmay Basimevi (*The Turkish General Staff*.) I 2006 I Modern Turkish Text.

ISBN No: 9754093822

The city of Sarikamish is in the Caucasus Mountains and was the scene of the Armenian uprising.

SARİKAMİŞ HAREKÂTI (12 - 24 ARALIK 1914). (*Sarikamis Operations (12 - 24 December 1914*).)

Nikolski | 24.5cm x 17.2cm | White Paper Softback | ?pp | ? appendices | ? maps | ? photographs | ? organisation charts | Genelkurmay Basimevi (*The Turkish General Staff.*) | 1990 | Modern Turkish Text.

BİRİNCİ DÜNYA SAVAŞINDA MISIR SEFERİ ÇERÇEVESİNDE BİRİNCİ KANAL AKINI. (*The First World War: Egypt in the Framework of the First Assault on the [Suez] Canal*)

Albay (*Colonel*) Muzaffer | 24.5cm x 17.2cm | White Paper Softback | ?pp | ? appendices | ? maps | ? photographs | ? organisation charts | Genelkurmay Basimevi (*The Turkish General Staff.*) | 2006 | Modern Turkish Text.

BİRİNCİ DÜNYA SAVAŞINDA DOĞU CEPHESİNDE SAĞ KANAT HAREKÂTI. (*The First World War: the Right Wing Campaign of the Eastern Front*)

Albay (*Colonel*) Recep Balkan | 24.5cm x 17.2cm | White Paper Softback | ?pp | ? appendices | ? maps | ? photographs | ? organisation charts | Genelkurmay Basimevi (*The Turkish General Staff.*) | 2006 | Modern Turkish Text.

SELMAN-I PAK MUHAREBESİ BİRİNCİ DÜNYA HARBİNDE. (*The Battle of Ctesiphon during the First World War.*)

Mehmet Emin. | 24.5cm x 17.2cm | White Paper Softback | ?pp | ? appendices | ? maps | ? photographs | ? organisation charts | Genelkurmay Basimevi (*The Turkish General Staff.*) | 1964 | Modern Turkish Text.

This is possibly a republished earlier work – the original published with Mehmet Emin name written in the older style of *Binbaşı* (*Staff Major*) Muhammad Amin *Bey*.

Appendix Two

Official Diplomatic Histories Bibliography

Austro-Hungarian Official Histories

The Austria-Hungary official diplomatic histories were compiled during the war years by the Österreichisch-Ungarischen Ministeriums des Aeußern (*the Austro-Hungarian Ministry of Foreign Affairs*) followed by the Österreichisch Ministeriums des Aeußern (*the Austrian Ministry of Foreign Affairs*);

Österreichisch-ungarisches Rotbuch 1914. (*Austro-Hungarian Red Book 1914.*)
> Anonymous (Österreichisch-Ungarischen Ministeriums des Aeußern) | 22.5cm x 15.5cm | red paper softback | x + 144pp | Österreichischer Bundesverlag | 1915 | German text.
> This volumes relates to the general outbreak and declarations of the war.

Österreichisch-ungarisches Rotbuch 1915. (*Austro-Hungarian Red Book 1915.*)
> Anonymous (Österreichisch-Ungarischen Ministeriums des Aeußern) | 22.5cm x 15.5cm | red paper softback | x + 213pp | Österreichischer Bundesverlag | 1915 | German text.
> This volumes relates to the declaration of war with Italy.

Österreichisch-ungarisches Rotbuch 1916. (*Austro-Hungarian Red Book 1916.*)
> Anonymous (Österreichisch-Ungarischen Ministeriums des Aeußern) | 22.5cm x 15.5cm | red paper softback | vii + 68pp | Österreichischer Bundesverlag | 1916 | German text.
> This volumes relates to the declaration of war with Rumania.

Österreich-ungarns Außenpolitik von der Bosnischen Krise 1908 bis zum Kriegsausbruch 1914. Band I. (*Austria-Hungary foreign policy of the Bosnian crisis 1908 to the outbreak of war 1914. Volume I.*)
> Ludwig Bittner & Hans Übersberger (Österreichisch Ministeriums des Aeußern) | Hard Back | Österreichischer Bundesverlag | 1930 | German Text.

Österreich-ungarns Außenpolitik von der Bosnischen Krise 1908 bis zum Kriegsausbruch 1914. Band II. (*Austria-Hungary foreign policy of the Bosnian crisis 1908 to the outbreak of war 1914. Volume II.*)
> Ludwig Bittner & Hans Übersberger (Österreichisch Ministeriums des Aeußern) | Hard Back | Österreichischer Bundesverlag | 1930 | German Text.

Österreich-ungarns Außenpolitik von der Bosnischen Krise 1908 bis zum Kriegsausbruch 1914. Band III. (*Austria-Hungary foreign policy of the Bosnian crisis 1908 to the outbreak of war 1914. Volume III.*)
> Ludwig Bittner & Hans Übersberger (Österreichisch Ministeriums des Aeußern) | Hard Back | Österreichischer Bundesverlag | 1930 | German Text.

Österreich-ungarns Außenpolitik von der Bosnischen Krise 1908 bis zum Kriegsausbruch 1914. Band IV. (*Austria-Hungary foreign policy of the Bosnian crisis 1908 to the outbreak of war 1914. Volume IV.*)
> Ludwig Bittner & Hans Übersberger (Österreichisch Ministeriums des Aeußern) | Hard Back | Österreichischer Bundesverlag | 1930 | German Text.

Österreich-ungarns Außenpolitik von der Bosnischen Krise 1908 bis zum Kriegsausbruch 1914. Band V. (*Austria-Hungary foreign policy of the Bosnian crisis 1908 to the outbreak of war 1914. Volume V.*)
> Ludwig Bittner & Hans Übersberger (Österreichisch Ministeriums des Aeußern) | Hard Back | Österreichischer Bundesverlag | 1930 | German Text.

Österreich-ungarns Außenpolitik von der Bosnischen Krise 1908 bis zum Kriegsausbruch 1914. Band VI. (*Austria-Hungary foreign policy of the Bosnian crisis 1908 to the outbreak of war 1914. Volume VI.*)
> Ludwig Bittner & Hans Übersberger (Österreichisch Ministeriums des Aeußern) | Hard Back | Österreichischer Bundesverlag | 1930 | German Text.

Österreich-ungarns Außenpolitik von der Bosnischen Krise 1908 bis zum Kriegsausbruch 1914. Band VII. (*Austria-Hungary foreign policy of the Bosnian crisis 1908 to the outbreak of war 1914. Volume VII.*)
> Ludwig Bittner & Hans Übersberger (Österreichisch Ministeriums des Aeußern) | Hard Back | Österreichischer Bundesverlag | 1930 | German Text.

Österreich-ungarns Außenpolitik von der Bosnischen Krise 1908 bis zum Kriegsausbruch 1914. Band VIII. (*Austria-Hungary foreign policy of the Bosnian crisis 1908 to the outbreak of war 1914. Volume VIII.*)

Ludwig Bittner & Hans Übersberger (Österreichisch Ministeriums des Aeußern) I Hard Back I Österreichischer Bundesverlag I 1930 I German Text.

Österreich-ungarns Außenpolitik von der Bosnischen Krise 1908 bis zum Kriegsausbruch 1914. Register-Band. (*Austria-Hungary foreign policy of the Bosnian crisis 1908 to the outbreak of war 1914. Index.***)**

Ludwig Bittner & Hans Übersberger (Österreichisch Ministeriums des Aeußern) I Hard Back I Österreichischer Bundesverlag I 1930 I German Text.

Belgian Diplomatic Official Histories

The Belgian diplomatic official histories were compiled by members of the Ministère des Affaires Étrangères (*the [Belgian] Ministry of Foreign Affairs*).

Royaume de Belgique. Ministère des affaires étrangères. Correspondance Diplomatique Relative à la Guerre de 1914 - 24 juillet – 29 août. (*Kingdom of Belgium. Ministry of Foreign Affairs. Diplomatic Correspondence relating to the War of 1914 – 24 July - 29 August.*)

Anonymous (Ministère des Affaires Étrangères) | grey paper softback | 24.5cm x 15.5cm | vii + 56pp | Librairie Hachette et Cie | 1914 | French text.

This volume, '**Correspondance Diplomatique Relative à la Guerre de 1914**' is commonly known as the first Belgian Grey Book.

It was translated into German by the Swiss publisher K.J. Wyss of Berne who published it as a bilingual volume with the original French at the end of 1914. The title of this translation was "**Correspondance Diplomatique du Ministère des Affaires étrangères du royaume de Belgique relative à la guerre de 1914. 24 juillet-29 aout. Diplomatische Korrespondenz des Außenministeriums des Königreich Belgiens bezüglich des Krieges von 1914 zu dem Krieg von 1914. Livre gris belge. Belgisches Graubuch.**" The French text is shown on the odd pages and the German text on the opposite pages with each page number being shown twice (firstly for the French page and then the corresponding German page), causing an increase in the number of pages to xvi + 70pp totalling 138pp. It was also translated into Dutch "**Réimpression textuelle publiée par la Légation de Belgique à La Haye. Correspondance Diplomatique Relative à la Guerre de 1914 - 24 juillet – 29 août.**" It has a slightly larger format of 32cm x 21cm, but with a reduction in the number of pages to 27.

Royaume de Belgique. Ministère des affaires étrangères. Correspondance Diplomatique Relative à la Guerre de 1914-1915. (*Kingdom of Belgium. Ministry of Foreign Affairs. Diplomatic Correspondence relating to the War of 1914.*)

Anonymous (Ministère des Affaires Étrangères) | grey paper softback | 24.5cm x 15.5cm | vii + 136pp | Librairie Hachette et Cie | 1915 | French text.

This volume, "**Correspondance Diplomatique Relative à la Guerre de 1914-1915**", is commonly known as the second Belgian Grey Book.

It is in two parts, the first part covering the correspondence of the rupture of diplomatic relations between Belgium and Turkey (6 November) and the second part contains the Belgian Government's protests addressed to the German and Austro-Hungarian governments with regard to the violations of the laws of war and of The Hague conventions up to 1 May 1915.

Royaume de Belgique. Ministère de la Justice et des Affaires Etrangeres. Guerre de 1914-1916, Réponse au Livre Blanc Allemand du 10 Mai 1915. (*Kingdom of Belgium. Ministry of Justice and Foreign Affairs. 1914-1916 War, Response to the German White Book, 10 May 1915.*)

Anonymous (Ministère de la Justice et des Affaires Étrangères) | grey paper softback | 31.5m x 21.3cm | viii + 517pp | 1 map | Berger-Levrault, Libraires-Editeurs| 1916 | French text.

This volume was given the sub title in German of "**Die völkerrechtswidrige Führung des belgischen Volkskriegs.**" (*Contrary to International Behaviour during the Belgian People's War.*)

It was produced in two editions during 1916. They were produced for the diplomatic market with the first one having a print run of 50 copies and the second a print run of 25.

An analytical study of this volume was undertaken by Fernand Passelecq and was published by Librairie Militaire Berger-Levrault in 1916. It has 84 pages. There were also foreign language editions published, including ones in German and Dutch.

British Diplomatic Official Histories

The British diplomatic official histories were compiled by members of the office of the Historical Adviser to the Foreign Office.

Great Britain and the European Crisis – Correspondence, and Statements in Parliament, Together with an Introductory Narrative of Events.

> Anonymous (The [British] Foreign Office) | 23cm x 14.5cm | blue paper softback | xxvi + 102pp | His Majesty's Stationery Office. | 1914 | English Text.
>
> This H.M. Government Paper 'Great Britain and the European Crisis' was split into two parts along with an introduction. The introduction consisted of a general background, titled 'Introductory Narrative of Events', followed by a 'Table of Contents of Correspondence laid before Parliament' and a 'List of Principal Persons mentioned in the Correspondence, showing their official positions'. Part I consisted of a compilation of three previous governmental papers reproducing diplomatic documents mainly relating to the actions of H.M. Government and their representatives – **"Miscellaneous No. 6 (1914) [Cd. 7467]"**, **"Miscellaneous No. 8 (1914) [Cd. 7445]"** and **"Miscellaneous No. 10 (1914) [Cd. 7596]"**. Part II consisted of five 'Speeches in the House of Commons'

Miscellaneous No. 13 (1914) Correspondence Respecting Events Leading to the Rupture of Relation with Turkey. [Cd. 7628]

> Anonymous (The [British] Foreign Office) | 33.3cm x 21cm | white paper wraps | 7pp | His Majesty's Stationery Office. | 1914 | English Text.

Miscellaneous No. 10 (1915) Collected Diplomatic Documents relating to the outbreak of the European War. [Cd. 7860]

> Anonymous (The [British] Foreign Office) | 24.2cm x 15.5cm | blue paper softback | iii + 561pp | His Majesty's Stationery Office. | 1915 | English Text.
>
> All H.M. Government's papers have wraps. In the past, the thicker booklets had blue wraps, hence the name 'blue books'. However, on the thinner ones, the blue wraps were not used, using instead just plain white paper, but were still referred to as 'blue books'. Each country had a similar set up for their governmental papers, but often using different coloured wraps – white for the German, yellow for the French, orange for the Russian, etc., and are commonly referred to by their respective colours, for example **"Das Deutsche Weißbuch"** (The German White Book). There were a huge number of 'blue books' published over the course of time, however this particular one 'Miscellaneous No. 10 (1915)' has a direct historical bearing on the origins of the Great War. This book consisted of a compilation of all the warring states' governmental papers containing diplomatic documents pertaining to the outbreak of war (including H.M. Government's 'Great Britain and the European Crisis' and translations of the other government's non-English books into English – most of which had already been published individually as 'Miscellaneous' papers in 1914). This particular book is commonly known as 'The British Blue Book'.

British Documents on the Origins of the War Volume I The End of British Isolation.

> G.P. Gooch and Harold Temperley | 28cm x 19.5cm | Burgundy Red Cloth Hardback | Gilt | xxxii + 355pp | 1 appendix | His Majesty's Stationery Office. | 1927 | English Text.

British Documents on the Origins of the War Volume II Anglo-Japanese Alliance and the Franco-British Entente.

> G.P. Gooch and Harold Temperley | 28cm x 19.5cm | Burgundy Red Cloth Hardback | Gilt | xxxii + 430pp | 1 appendix | His Majesty's Stationery Office. | 1927 | English Text.

British Documents on the Origins of the War Volume III The Testing of the Entente 1904 – 6.

> G.P. Gooch and Harold Temperley | 28cm x 19.5cm | Burgundy Red Cloth Hardback | Gilt | xlii + 487 pp + 8pp of errata | 4 appendices | His Majesty's Stationery Office. | 1928 | English Text.

British Documents on the Origins of the War Volume IV The Anglo-Russia Rapprochement 1903 – 7.

> G.P. Gooch and Harold Temperley | 28cm x 19.5cm | Burgundy Red Cloth Hardback | Gilt | lii + 656pp | 4 appendices | His Majesty's Stationery Office. | 1929 | English Text.

British Documents on the Origins of the War Volume V The Near East Macedonian Problem 1903 – 9.

G.P. Gooch and Harold Temperley | 28cm x 19.5cm | Burgundy Red Cloth Hardback | Gilt | lxix + 886pp | 5 appendices | His Majesty's Stationery Office. | 1928 | English Text.

British Documents on the Origins of the War Volume VI Anglo-German Tension 1907 – 12.

G.P. Gooch and Harold Temperley | 28cm x 19.5cm | Burgundy Red Cloth Hardback | Gilt | lv + 867pp | 6 appendices | His Majesty's Stationery Office. | 1930 | English Text.

British Documents on the Origins of the War Volume VII The Agadir Crisis.

G.P. Gooch and Harold Temperley | 28cm x 19.5cm | Burgundy Red Cloth Hardback | Gilt | lxxii + 917pp | 7 appendices | His Majesty's Stationery Office. | 1932 | English Text.

British Documents on the Origins of the War Volume VIII Arbitration, Neutrality and Security.

G.P. Gooch and Harold Temperley | 28cm x 19.5cm | Burgundy Red Cloth Hardback | Gilt | lxiv + 797pp | 3 appendices | His Majesty's Stationery Office. | 1932 | English Text.

British Documents on the Origins of the War Volume IX Part I The Balkan Wars - The Prelude.

G.P. Gooch and Harold Temperley | 28cm x 19.5cm | Burgundy Red Cloth Hardback | Gilt | lxxvi + 873pp | 8 appendices | His Majesty's Stationery Office. | 1933 | English Text.

British Documents on the Origins of the War Volume IX Part II The Balkan Wars - The League and Turkey.

G.P. Gooch and Harold Temperley | 28cm x 19.5cm | Burgundy Red Cloth Hardback | Gilt | c + 1190pp | 7 appendices | His Majesty's Stationery Office. | 1934 | English Text.

British Documents on the Origins of the War Volume X Part I The Near and Middle East on the Eve of War.

G.P. Gooch and Harold Temperley | 28cm x 19.5cm | Burgundy Red Cloth Hardback | Gilt | lxx + 1009pp | 1 appendix | His Majesty's Stationery Office. | 1936 | English Text.

British Documents on the Origins of the War Volume X Part II The Last Years of Peace.

G.P. Gooch and Harold Temperley | 28cm x 19.5cm | Burgundy Red Cloth Hardback | Gilt | lx + 921pp | 3 appendices | 3 photographs | His Majesty's Stationery Office. | 1938 | English Text.

British Documents on the Origins of the War Volume XI The Outbreak of War.

G.P. Gooch and Harold Temperley | 28cm x 19.5cm | Burgundy Red Cloth Hardback | Gilt | xl + 389pp | 2 appendices | 1 photograph | His Majesty's Stationery Office. | 1926 | English Text.

The Outbreak of the War 1914 - 1918 - A Narrative Based Mainly on British Official Documents.

C. Oman | 33.3cm x 21cm | green paper softback | vi + 146pp | His Majesty's Stationery Office. | 1919 | English Text.

Conditions of an Armistice with Germany. Signed November 11th, 1918. [Cd. 9212]

Terms of the Armistices Concluded Between the Allied Governments and the Governments of Germany, Austria-Hungary and Turkey. [Army Cmd. 53]

Anonymous (The [British] Foreign Office) | 33.3cm x 21cm | white paper wraps | 27pp | His Majesty's Stationery Office. | 1919 | English Text.

Treaty of Peace Between the Allied and Associated Powers and Germany. (Treaty Series No. 4 (1919))

Anonymous (The [British] Foreign Office) | 33.3cm x 21cm | blue paper softback | vii + 213pp | 5 maps | His Majesty's Stationery Office. | 1919 | English Text.

Protocols & Correspondance Between the Supreme Council & the Conference of Ambassadors & the German Government & the German Peace Delegation Between Jan 10, 1920 & Jul 17,1920 Respecting the Execution of the Treaty of Versailles of Jun 28, 1919. (Misc.N.15)

Anonymous (The [British] Foreign Office) | 33.3cm x 21cm | white paper wraps | 178pp | His Majesty's Stationery Office. | 1921 | English Text.

Index to the Treaty of Peace Between the Allied and Associated Powers and Germany. (Treaty Series No. 1 (1920))

Anonymous (The [British] Foreign Office) | 33.3cm x 21cm | white paper wraps | 59pp | His Majesty's Stationery Office. | 1920 | English Text.

Treaty of Peace Between the Allied and Associated Powers and Austria. (Treaty Series No. 11 (1919))

Anonymous (The [British] Foreign Office) | 33.3cm x 21cm | blue paper softback | iii + 118pp | 1 map | His Majesty's Stationery Office. | 1919 | English Text.

Treaty of Peace Between the Allied and Associated Powers and Hungary. (Treaty Series No. 10 (1920))

Anonymous (The [British] Foreign Office) | 33.3cm x 21cm | blue paper softback | iv + 113pp | 1 map | His Majesty's Stationery Office. | 1920 | English Text.

Treaty of Peace Between the Allied and Associated Powers and Bulgaria. (Treaty Series No. 5 (1920))

Anonymous (The [British] Foreign Office) | 33.3cm x 21cm | blue paper softback | iv + 87pp | 1 map | His Majesty's Stationery Office. | 1920 | English Text.

Treaty of Peace Between the Allied and Associated Powers and Turkey. (Treaty Series No. 10 (1920))

Anonymous (The [British] Foreign Office) | 33.3cm x 21cm | blue paper softback | 100pp | 3 maps | His Majesty's Stationery Office. | 1920 | English Text.

Treaty of Peace with Turkey, and Other Instruments, Together with Agreements between Greece and Turkey Signed on January 30, 1923, and Subsidiary Documents Forming Part of the Turkish Peace Settlement. (Treaty Series No. 16 (1923))

Anonymous (The [British] Foreign Office) | 24.3cm x 24.3cm | blue paper softback | iv + 243pp | 1 map | His Majesty's Stationery Office. | 1923 | English Text.

French Diplomatic Official Histories

The French diplomatic official histories were compiled by members of the Ministère des Affaires Étrangères (*the [French] Ministry of Foreign Affairs*).

Ministère des Affaires Étrangères Documents Diplomatiques, 1914. La Guerre Européenne, I, Pièces Relatives aux Négociations qui ont Pécédé le a Déclaration de Guerre de l'Allemagne à la Russie (1ᵉʳ août 1914) et à la France (3 août 1914) Déclaration du 4 septembre 1914. (*The Ministry of Foreign Affairs Diplomatic Documents, 1914. The European War, I, Pieces Relative to the Negotiations that preceded the Declaration of War by Germany upon Russia (1ˢᵗ August 1914) and upon France (3ʳᵈ August 1914) as declared on 4ᵗʰ September 1914.*)
> Anonymous (Ministère des Affaires Étrangères.) I 15.5cm x 22.7cm I yellow paper softback I xx + 194pp I Librairie Hachette et Cie I 1914 I French text.
> This book, 'Ministère des Affaires Étrangères Documents Diplomatiques, 1914' is commonly known as the French Yellow Book.

Documents Diplomatiques Français 1871 - 1914. Première série: 1871-1900. Tome I: 10 mai 1871 - 30 juin 1875. (*French Diplomatic Documents 1871 - 1914. First Series: 1871-1900. Book I: 10 May 1871 - 30 June 1875.*)
> Anonymous (Commission de publication des documents relatifs aux origines de la guerre de 1914) I 27.5cm x 18.5cm I Yellow Paper Softback I xlvii + 496pp I Imprimerie Nationale, Alfred Coste Libraire éditeur I 1929 I French Text.

Documents Diplomatiques Français 1871 - 1914. Première série: 1871-1900. Tome II: 1ᵉʳ juillet 1875 - 31 décembre 1879. (*French Diplomatic Documents 1871 - 1914. First Series: 1871-1900. Book II: 1 July 1875 - 31 December 1879.*)
> Anonymous (Commission de publication des documents relatifs aux origines de la guerre de 1914) I 27.5cm x 18.5cm I Yellow Paper Softback I ? + ?pp I Imprimerie Nationale, Alfred Coste Libraire éditeur I 1930 I French Text.

Documents Diplomatiques Français 1871 - 1914. Première série: 1871-1900. Tome III: 2 janvier 1880 - 13 mai 1881. (*French Diplomatic Documents 1871 - 1914. First Series: 1871-1900. Book III: 2 January 1880 - 13 May 1881.*)
> Anonymous (Commission de publication des documents relatifs aux origines de la guerre de 1914) I 27.5cm x 18.5cm I Yellow Paper Softback I xxvi + 438pp I 1 Table I Imprimerie Nationale, Alfred Coste Libraire éditeur I 1931 I French Text.

Documents Diplomatiques Français 1871 - 1914. Première série: 1871-1900. Tome IV: 13 mai 1881 - 20 février 1883. (*French Diplomatic Documents 1871 - 1914. First Series: 1871-1900. Book IV: 13 May 1881 - 20 February 1883.*)
> Anonymous (Commission de publication des documents relatifs aux origines de la guerre de 1914) I 27.5cm x 18.5cm I Yellow Paper Softback I xxxvii + 614pp I Imprimerie Nationale, Alfred Coste Libraire éditeur I 1932 I French Text.

Documents Diplomatiques Français 1871 - 1914. Première série: 1871-1900. Tome V: 23 février 1883 - 9 avril 1885. (*French Diplomatic Documents 1871 - 1914. First Series: 1871-1900. Book V: 23 February 1883 - 9 April 1885.*)
> Anonymous (Commission de publication des documents relatifs aux origines de la guerre de 1914) I 27.5cm x 18.5cm I Yellow Paper Softback I ? + ?pp I Imprimerie Nationale, Alfred Coste Libraire éditeur I c1933 I French Text.

Documents Diplomatiques Français 1871 - 1914. Première série: 1871-1900. Tome VI: 8 avril 1885 - 30 décembre 1887. (*French Diplomatic Documents 1871 - 1914. First Series: 1871-1900. Book VI: 8 April 1885 - 30 December 1887.*)
> Anonymous (Commission de publication des documents relatifs aux origines de la guerre de 1914) I 27.5cm x 18.5cm I Yellow Paper Softback I xxxix + 694pp I Imprimerie Nationale, Alfred Coste Libraire éditeur I 1934 I French Text.

Documents Diplomatiques Français 1871 - 1914. Première série: 1871-1900. Tome VI bis: 4 mars 1885 - 29 décembre 1887. (*French Diplomatic Documents 1871 - 1914. First Series: 1871-1900. Book VI Supplement: 4 March 1885 - 29 December 1887.*)
> Anonymous (Commission de publication des documents relatifs aux origines de la guerre de 1914) I 27.5cm x 18.5cm I Yellow Paper Softback I ? + ?pp I Imprimerie Nationale, Alfred Coste Libraire éditeur I c1935 I French Text.

Documents Diplomatiques Français 1871 - 1914. Première série: 1871-1900. Tome VII: 1er janvier 1888 - 19 mars 1890. (*French Diplomatic Documents 1871 - 1914. First Series: 1871-1900. Book VII: 1 January 1888 - 19 March 1890.*)

Anonymous (Commission de publication des documents relatifs aux origines de la guerre de 1914) | 27.5cm x 18.5cm | Yellow Paper Softback | ? + ?pp | Imprimerie Nationale, Alfred Coste Libraire éditeur | c1936 | French Text.

Documents Diplomatiques Français 1871 - 1914. Première série: 1871-1900. Tome VIII: 20 mars 1890-28 août 1891. (*French Diplomatic Documents 1871 - 1914. First Series: 1871-1900. Book VIII: 20 March 1890-28 August 1891.*)

Anonymous (Commission de publication des documents relatifs aux origines de la guerre de 1914) | 27.5cm x 18.5cm | Yellow Paper Softback | ? + ?pp | Imprimerie Nationale, Alfred Coste Libraire éditeur | c1937 | French Text.

Documents Diplomatiques Français 1871 - 1914. Première série: 1871-1900. Tome IX: 23 août 1891-19 août 1892. (*French Diplomatic Documents 1871 - 1914. First Series: 1871-1900. Book IX: 23 August 1891-19 August 1892.*)

Commission de publication des documents relatifs aux origines de la guerre de 1914| 27.5cm x 18.5cm | Yellow Paper Softback | xl + 727pp | Imprimerie Nationale, Alfred Coste Libraire éditeur | 1939 | French Text.

Documents Diplomatiques Français 1871 - 1914. Première série: 1871-1900. Tome X: 21 août 1892-31 décembre 1893. (*French Diplomatic Documents 1871 - 1914. First Series: 1871-1900. Book X: 21 August 1892-31 December 1893.*)

Anonymous (Commission de publication des documents relatifs aux origines de la guerre de 1914) | 27.5cm x 18.5cm | Yellow Paper Softback | ? + ?pp | Imprimerie Nationale, Alfred Coste Libraire éditeur | c1948 | French Text.

Documents Diplomatiques Français 1871 - 1914. Première série: 1871-1900. Tome XI: 1er janvier 1894 - 7 mai 1895. (*French Diplomatic Documents 1871 - 1914. First Series: 1871-1900. Book XI: 1 January 1894 - 7 May 1895.*)

Anonymous (Commission de publication des documents relatifs aux origines de la guerre de 1914) | 27.5cm x 18.5cm | Yellow Paper Softback | ? + ?pp | Imprimerie Nationale, Alfred Coste Libraire éditeur | c1949 | French Text.

Documents Diplomatiques Français 1871 - 1914. Première série: 1871-1900. Tome XII: 8 mai 1895 - 14 octobre 1896. (*French Diplomatic Documents 1871 - 1914. First Series: 1871-1900. Book XII: 8 May 1895 - 14 October 1896.*)

Anonymous (Commission de publication des documents relatifs aux origines de la guerre de 1914) | 27.5cm x 18.5cm | Yellow Paper Softback | ? + ?pp | Imprimerie Nationale, Alfred Coste Libraire éditeur | c1950 | French Text.

Documents Diplomatiques Français 1871 - 1914. Première série: 1871-1900. Tome XIII: 16 octobre 1896 - 31 décembre 1897. (*French Diplomatic Documents 1871 - 1914. First Series 1871-1900. Book XIII: 16 October 1896 - 31 December 1897.*)

Anonymous (Commission de publication des documents relatifs aux origines de la guerre de 1914) | 27.5cm x 18.5cm | Yellow Paper Softback | xxxvi + 677pp | Imprimerie Nationale, Alfred Coste Libraire éditeur | 1953 | French Text.

Documents Diplomatiques Français 1871 - 1914. Première série: 1871-1900. Tome XIV: 6 janvier - 30 décembre 1898. (*French Diplomatic Documents 1871 - 1914. First Series: 1871-1900. Book XIV: 6 January - 30 December 1898.*)

Anonymous (Commission de publication des documents relatifs aux origines de la guerre de 1914) | 27.5cm x 18.5cm | Yellow Paper Softback | xl + 957pp | 1 Table | Imprimerie Nationale, Alfred Coste Libraire éditeur | 1957 | French Text.

Documents Diplomatiques Français 1871 - 1914. Première série: 1871-1900. Tome XV: 2 janvier - 14 novembre 1899. (*French Diplomatic Documents 1871 - 1914. First Series: 1871-1900. Book XV: 2 January - 14 November 1899.*)

Anonymous (Commission de publication des documents relatifs aux origines de la guerre de 1914) | 27.5cm x 18.5cm | Yellow Paper Softback | xxxv + 552pp | 1 Table | Imprimerie Nationale, Alfred Coste Libraire éditeur | 1959 | French Text.

Documents Diplomatiques Français 1871 - 1914. Première série : 1871-1900. Tome XVI: 18 novembre 1899 - 30 décembre 1900. (*French Diplomatic Documents 1871 - 1914. First Series: 1871-1900. Book XVI: 18 November 1899 - 30 December 1900.*)

Anonymous (Commission de publication des documents relatifs aux origines de la guerre de 1914) l 27.5cm x 18.5cm l Yellow Paper Softback l ? + ?pp l Imprimerie Nationale, Alfred Coste Libraire éditeur l c1960 l French Text.

Documents Diplomatiques Français 1871 - 1914. Deuxième série: 1901-1911. Tome I: 2 janvier - 31 décembre 1901. (*French Diplomatic Documents 1871 - 1914. Second Series: 1901-1911. Book I: 2 January - 31 December 1901.*)

Anonymous (Commission de publication des documents relatifs aux origines de la guerre de 1914) l 27.5cm x 18.5cm l Yellow Paper Softback l xx + 723pp l 1 Table l Imprimerie Nationale, Alfred Coste Libraire éditeur l 1930 l French Text.

Documents Diplomatiques Français 1871 - 1914. Deuxième série: 1901-1911. Tome II: 1ᵉʳ janvier - 31 décembre 1902. (*French Diplomatic Documents 1871 - 1914. Second Series: 1901-1911. Book II: 1 January - 31 December 1902.*)

Anonymous (Commission de publication des documents relatifs aux origines de la guerre de 1914) l 27.5cm x 18.5cm l Yellow Paper Softback l xxix + 726pp l 1 Table l Imprimerie Nationale, Alfred Coste Libraire éditeur l 1931 l French Text.

Documents Diplomatiques Français 1871 - 1914. Deuxième série: 1901-1911. Tome III: 3 janvier - 4 octobre 1903. (*French Diplomatic Documents 1871 - 1914. Second Series: 1901-1911. Book III: 3 January - 4 October 1903.*)

Anonymous (Commission de publication des documents relatifs aux origines de la guerre de 1914) l 27.5cm x 18.5cm l Yellow Paper Softback l xxviii + 640pp l 1 Table l Imprimerie Nationale, Alfred Coste Libraire éditeur l 1931 l French Text.

Documents Diplomatiques Français 1871 - 1914. Deuxième série: 1901-1911. Tome IV: 5 octobre 1903 - 8 avril 1904. (*French Diplomatic Documents 1871 - 1914. Second Series: 1901-1911. Book IV: 5 October 1903 - 8 April 1904.*)

Anonymous (Commission de publication des documents relatifs aux origines de la guerre de 1914) l 27.5cm x 18.5cm l Yellow Paper Softback l xxvii + 565pp l 1 Table l Imprimerie Nationale, Alfred Coste Libraire éditeur l 1932 l French Text.

Documents Diplomatiques Français 1871 - 1914. Deuxième série: 1901-1911. Tome V: 9 avril - 31 décembre 1904. (*French Diplomatic Documents 1871 - 1914. Second Series: 1901-1911. Book V: 9 April - 31 December 1904.*)

Anonymous (Commission de publication des documents relatifs aux origines de la guerre de 1914) l 27.5cm x 18.5cm l Yellow Paper Softback l xl + 655pp l 1 Table l Imprimerie Nationale, Alfred Coste Libraire éditeur l 1934 l French Text.

Documents Diplomatiques Français 1871 - 1914. Deuxième série: 1901-1911. Tome VI: 2 janvier - 6 juin 1905. (*French Diplomatic Documents 1871 - 1914. Second Series: 1901-1911. Book VI: 2 January - 6 June 1905.*)

Anonymous (Commission de publication des documents relatifs aux origines de la guerre de 1914) l 27.5cm x 18.5cm l Yellow Paper Softback l ? + ?pp l Imprimerie Nationale, Alfred Coste Libraire éditeur l c1935 l French Text.

Documents Diplomatiques Français 1871 - 1914. Deuxième série: 1901-1911. Tome VII: 7 juin - 28 septembre 1905. (*French Diplomatic Documents 1871 - 1914. Second Series: 1901-1911. Book VII: 7 June - 28 September 1905.*)

Anonymous (Commission de publication des documents relatifs aux origines de la guerre de 1914) l 27.5cm x 18.5cm l Yellow Paper Softback l ? + ?pp l Imprimerie Nationale, Alfred Coste Libraire éditeur l c1936 l French Text.

Documents Diplomatiques Français 1871 - 1914. Deuxième série: 1901-1911. Tome VIII: 29 septembre 1905 - 15 janvier 1906. (*French Diplomatic Documents 1871 - 1914. Second Series: 1901-1911. Book VIII: 29 September 1905 – 15 January 1906.*)

Anonymous (Commission de publication des documents relatifs aux origines de la guerre de 1914) l 27.5cm x 18.5cm l Yellow Paper Softback l ? + 590pp l 1 Table l Imprimerie Nationale, Alfred Coste Libraire éditeur l 1938 l French Text.

Documents Diplomatiques Français 1871 - 1914. Deuxième série: 1901-1911. Tome IX, Partie 1: 16 janvier - 1ᵉʳ mars 1906. (*French Diplomatic Documents 1871 - 1914. Second Series: 1901-1911. Book IX, Part 1: 16 January - 1 March 1906.*)

Anonymous (Commission de publication des documents relatifs aux origines de la guerre de 1914) l 27.5cm x 18.5cm l Yellow Paper Softback l ? + xxxpp l Imprimerie Nationale, Alfred Coste Libraire éditeur l c1939 l French Text.

Documents Diplomatiques Français 1871 - 1914. Deuxième série: 1901-1911. Tome IX, Partie 2: 2 mars - 7 avril 1906. (*French Diplomatic Documents 1871 - 1914. Second Series: 1901-1911. Book IX, Part 2: 2 March - 7 April 1906.*)

> Anonymous (Commission de publication des documents relatifs aux origines de la guerre de 1914) | 27.5cm x 18.5cm | Yellow Paper Softback | ? + ?pp | Imprimerie Nationale, Alfred Coste Libraire éditeur | c1948 | French Text.

Documents Diplomatiques Français 1871 - 1914. Deuxième série: 1901-1911. Tome X: 10 avril 1906 - 16 mai 1907. (*French Diplomatic Documents 1871 - 1914. Second Series: 1901-1911. Book X: 10 April 1906 – 16 May 1907.*)

> Anonymous (Commission de publication des documents relatifs aux origines de la guerre de 1914) | 27.5cm x 18.5cm | Yellow Paper Softback | ? + ?pp | Imprimerie Nationale, Alfred Coste Libraire éditeur | c1950 | French Text.

Documents Diplomatiques Français 1871 - 1914. Deuxième série: 1901-1911. Tome XI: 15 mai 1907 - 8 février 1909. (*French Diplomatic Documents 1871 - 1914. Second Series: 1901-1911. Book XI: 15 May 1907 – 8 February 1909.*)

> Anonymous (Commission de publication des documents relatifs aux origines de la guerre de 1914) | 27.5cm x 18.5cm | Yellow Paper Softback | ? + ?pp | Imprimerie Nationale, Alfred Coste Libraire éditeur | c1952 | French Text.

Documents Diplomatiques Français 1871 - 1914. Deuxième série: 1901-1911. Tome XII: 9 février 1909 - 26 octobre 1910. (*French Diplomatic Documents 1871 - 1914. Second Series: 1901-1911. Book XII: 9 February 1909 – 26 October 1910.*)

> Anonymous (Commission de publication des documents relatifs aux origines de la guerre de 1914) | 27.5cm x 18.5cm | Yellow Paper Softback | ? + ?pp | Imprimerie Nationale, Alfred Coste Libraire éditeur | c1953 | French Text.

Documents Diplomatiques Français 1871 - 1914. Deuxième série: 1901-1911. Tome XIII: 26 octobre 1910 - 30 juin 1911. (*French Diplomatic Documents 1871 - 1914. Second Series: 1901-1911. Book XIII: 26 October 1910 – 30 June 1911.*)

> Anonymous (Commission de publication des documents relatifs aux origines de la guerre de 1914) | 27.5cm x 18.5cm | Yellow Paper Softback | ? + ?pp | Imprimerie Nationale, Alfred Coste Libraire éditeur | c1954 | French Text.

Documents Diplomatiques Français 1871 - 1914. Deuxième série: 1901-1911. Tome XIV: 1ᵉʳ juillet - 4 novembre 1911. (*French Diplomatic Documents 1871 - 1914. Second Series: 1901-1911. Book XIV: 1 July – 4 November 1911.*)

> Commission de publication des documents relatifs aux origines de la guerre de 1914| 27.5cm x 18.5cm | Yellow Paper Softback | xl + 779pp | 1 map | 1 Table | 1 schematic | Imprimerie Nationale, Alfred Coste Libraire éditeur | 1955 | French Text.

Documents Diplomatiques Français 1871 - 1914. Troisième série: 1911-1914. Tome I: 4 novembre 1911-7 février 1912. (*French Diplomatic Documents 1871 - 1914. Thrid Series : 1911-1914. Book I: 4 November 1911 – 7 February 1912.*)

> Anonymous (Commission de publication des documents relatifs aux origines de la guerre de 1914) | 27.5cm x 18.5cm | Yellow Paper Softback | xxxi + 659pp | 1 Table | Imprimerie Nationale, Alfred Coste Libraire éditeur | 1929 | French Text.

Documents Diplomatiques Français 1871 - 1914. Troisième série: 1911-1914. Tome II: 8 février-10 mai 1912. (*French Diplomatic Documents 1871 - 1914. Thrid Series : 1911-1914. Book II: 8 February – 10 May 1912.*)

> Anonymous (Commission de publication des documents relatifs aux origines de la guerre de 1914) | 27.5cm x 18.5cm | Yellow Paper Softback | xxviii + 473pp | 1 Table | Imprimerie Nationale, Alfred Coste Libraire éditeur | 1931 | French Text.

Documents Diplomatiques Français 1871 - 1914. Troisième série: 1911-1914. Tome III: 11 mai-30 septembre 1912. (*French Diplomatic Documents 1871 - 1914. Thrid Series : 1911-1914. Book III: 11 May– 30 September 1912.*)

> Anonymous (Commission de publication des documents relatifs aux origines de la guerre de 1914) | 27.5cm x 18.5cm | Yellow Paper Softback | xxxv + 601pp | 1 Table | Imprimerie Nationale, Alfred Coste Libraire éditeur | 1931 | French Text.

Documents Diplomatiques Français 1871 - 1914. Troisième série: 1911-1914. Tome IV: 4 octobre -4 décembre 1912. (*French Diplomatic Documents 1871 - 1914. Thrid Series : 1911-1914. Book IV: 4 October– 4 December 1912.*)

Anonymous (Commission de publication des documents relatifs aux origines de la guerre de 1914) | 27.5cm x 18.5cm | Yellow Paper Softback | ? + 688pp | 1 Table | Imprimerie Nationale, Alfred Coste Libraire éditeur | 1932 | French Text.

Documents Diplomatiques Français 1871 - 1914. Troisième série: 1911-1914. Tome V: 5 décembre 1912-14 mars 1913. (*French Diplomatic Documents 1871 - 1914. Thrid Series : 1911-1914. Book V: 5 December 1912 – 14 May 1913.***)**

Anonymous (Commission de publication des documents relatifs aux origines de la guerre de 1914) | 27.5cm x 18.5cm | Yellow Paper Softback | xxxviii + 730pp | 1 Table | Imprimerie Nationale, Alfred Coste Libraire éditeur | 1933 | French Text.

Documents Diplomatiques Français 1871 - 1914. Troisième série: 1911-1914. Tome VI: 15 mars-30 mai 1913. (*French Diplomatic Documents 1871 - 1914. Thrid Series : 1911-1914. Book VI: 15 May – 30 May 1913.***)**

Anonymous (Commission de publication des documents relatifs aux origines de la guerre de 1914) | 27.5cm x 18.5cm | Yellow Paper Softback | ? + ?pp | Imprimerie Nationale, Alfred Coste Libraire éditeur | c1934 | French Text.

Documents Diplomatiques Français 1871 - 1914. Troisième série: 1911-1914. Tome VII: 31 mai-10 août 1913. (*French Diplomatic Documents 1871 - 1914. Thrid Series : 1911-1914. Book VII: 31 May– 10 August 1913.***)**

Anonymous (Commission de publication des documents relatifs aux origines de la guerre de 1914) | 27.5cm x 18.5cm | Yellow Paper Softback | ? + ?pp | Imprimerie Nationale, Alfred Coste Libraire éditeur | c1935| French Text.

Documents Diplomatiques Français 1871 - 1914. Troisième série: 1911-1914. Tome VIII: 11 août-31 décembre 1913. (*French Diplomatic Documents 1871 - 1914. Thrid Series : 1911-1914. Book VIII: 11 August – 30 December 1913.***)**

Anonymous (Commission de publication des documents relatifs aux origines de la guerre de 1914) | 27.5cm x 18.5cm | Yellow Paper Softback | ? + ?pp | Imprimerie Nationale, Alfred Coste Libraire éditeur | 19xx | French Text.

Documents Diplomatiques Français 1871 - 1914. Troisième série: 1911-1914. Tome IX: 1ᵉʳ janvier- 16 mars 1914. (*French Diplomatic Documents 1871 - 1914. Thrid Series : 1911-1914. Book IX: 1 January – 16 May 1914.***)**

Anonymous (Commission de publication des documents relatifs aux origines de la guerre de 1914) | 27.5cm x 18.5cm | Yellow Paper Softback | xli + 639pp | 1 Table | Imprimerie Nationale, Alfred Coste Libraire éditeur | 1936 | French Text.

Documents Diplomatiques Français 1871 - 1914. Troisième série: 1911-1914. Tome X: 17 mars-23 juillet 1914. (*French Diplomatic Documents 1871 - 1914. Thrid Series : 1911-1914. Book X: 17 May– 23 July 1914.***)**

Anonymous (Commission de publication des documents relatifs aux origines de la guerre de 1914) | 27.5cm x 18.5cm | Yellow Paper Softback | ? + 832pp | Imprimerie Nationale, Alfred Coste Libraire éditeur | 1936 | French Text.

Documents Diplomatiques Français 1871 - 1914. Troisième série: 1911-1914. Tome XI: 24 juillet-4 août 1914. (*French Diplomatic Documents 1871 - 1914. Thrid Series : 1911-1914. Book XI: 24 July– 4 August 1914.***)**

Anonymous (Commission de publication des documents relatifs aux origines de la guerre de 1914) | 27.5cm x 18.5cm | Yellow Paper Softback | ? + ?pp | Imprimerie Nationale, Alfred Coste Libraire éditeur | c1937 | French Text.

German Diplomatic Official Histories

The German Diplomatic official histories were compiled by members of the Auswärtigen Amte (*the [German] Foreign Office.*)

Das Deutſche Weißbuch über den Aufbruch des deutſch—ruſſiſch—franzöſiſchen Kriegſ. Aktenſtücke zum Kriegſaufbruch. Herauſgegeben vom Aufwärtigen Amte. (**Das Deutsche Weißbuch über den Ausbruch des deutsch-russisch-französischen Kriegs. Aktenstücke zum Kriegsausbruch. Herausgegeben vom Auswärtigen Amte.** - *The German White Book Relating to the Outbreak of the German-Russian-French war. Documents Relating to the Outbreak of War.*)

> Anonymous (Auswärtigen Amte) | 15.2cm x 22.5cm | White paper softback | 47pp | Nordische Verlagsanstalt. | 1914 | German Text. | Fraktur Script.
>
> The title shown on the cover is "**Das Deutsche Weißbuch über den Ausbruch des deutsch-russisch-französischen Kriegs**", however it has been stated in the British Government's translation that the title was "**Aktenstücke zum Kriegsausbruch. Herausgegeben vom Auswärtigen Amte**". This second title may have been the title shown on the title page; therefore I have given both titles here. This book is commonly known as the German White Book, and the German Government's 1914 English translation published by the Oxford University Press was so named.

Die deutſchen Dokumente zum Kriegſaufbruch 1914. Band 1: Vom Attentat in Sarajewo biſ zum Eintreffen der ſerbiſchen Antwortnote in Berlin nebſt einigen Dokumenten auf den vorhergehenden Wochen. (**Die deutschen Dokumente zum Kriegsausbruch 1914.Band 1: Vom Attentat in Sarajewo bis zum Eintreffen der serbischen Antwortnote in Berlin nebst einigen Dokumenten aus den vorhergehenden Wochen.** - *The German Documents on the Outbreak of War.Volume 1: From the Assassination Attempt in Sarajevo to Berlin's Reply to the Arrival of the Serbian Note, together with Some Documents from the Preceding Weeks.*)

> Karl Kautsky | ?cm x ?cm | White paper softback | ? + ?pp |. |. | 1919 | German Text. | Fraktur Script.

Die deutſchen Dokumente zum Kriegſaufbruch 1914. Band 2: Vom Eintreffen der ſerbiſchen Antwortnote in Berlin biſ zum Bekanntwerden der ruſſiſchen allgemeinen Mobilmachung. (**Die deutschen Dokumente zum Kriegsausbruch 1914. Band 2: Vom Eintreffen der serbischen Antwortnote in Berlin bis zum Bekanntwerden der russischen allgemeinen Mobilmachung.** - *The German Documents on the Outbreak of War. Volume 2: From Berlin's Reply to the Arrival of the Serbian Notes to the Russian General Mobilization becoming Known.*)

> Karl Kautsky | ?cm x ?cm | White paper softback | ? + ?pp |. |. | 1919 | German Text. | Fraktur Script.

Die deutſchen Dokumente zum Kriegſaufbruch 1914. Band 3: Vom Bekanntwerden der ruſſiſchen allgemeinen Mobilmachung biſ zur Kriegſerklärung an Frankreich. (**Die deutschen Dokumente zum Kriegsausbruch 1914. Band 3: Vom Bekanntwerden der russischen allgemeinen Mobilmachung bis zur Kriegserklärung an Frankreich.** - *The German Documents on the Outbreak of War. Volume 3: From the Russian General Mobilization becoming known to the Declaration of War on France.*)

> Karl Kautsky | ?cm x ?cm | White paper softback | ? + ?pp |. |. | 1919 | German Text. | Fraktur Script.

Die deutſchen Dokumente zum Kriegſaufbruch 1914. Die deutſchen Dokumente zum Kriegſaufbruch 1914. Band 4: Von der Kriegſerklärung an Frankreich biſ zur Kriegſerkl rung Öſterreich—Ungarnſ an Rußland nebſt Anhang. (**Die deutschen Dokumente zum Kriegsausbruch 1914. Band 4: Von der Kriegserklärung an Frankreich bis zur Kriegserkl rung Österreich-Ungarns an Rußland nebst Anhang.** - *The German Documents on the Outbreak of War. Volume 4: From the Declaration of*

War on France to the Declaration of War by Austro-Hungary on Russia, together with an Appendix.)

Karl Kautsky | ?cm x ?cm | White paper softback | ? + ?pp |. |. | 1919 | German Text. | Fraktur Script.

Die Große Politik der Europäischen Kabinette 1871–1914. Reihe 1: Die Bismarckzeit – 1871-1890. Band 1: Der Frankfurter Friede und seine Nachwirkungen 1871-1890. **(Die Große Politik der Europäischen Kabinette 1871-1914. Reihe 1: Die Bismarckzeit - 1871 – 1890. Band 1: Der Frankfurter Friede und seine Nachwirkungen 1871–1890. -** *The High Policy of the European Cabinets. File 1: The Times of Bismarck - 1871–1890. Volume 1: The Frankfurt Peace and its After Effect 1871– 1890.)*

A. Mendelssohn-Bartholdy, J. Lepsius and F. Thimme | ?cm x ?cm | White paper softback | ? + ?pp | ? | see note | German Text. | Fraktur Script.

Die Große Politik der Europäischen Kabinette 1871–1914. Reihe 1: Die Bismarckzeit – 1871-1890. Band 2: Der Berliner Kongreß und seine Vorgeschichte. **(Die Große Politik der Europäischen Kabinette 1871-1914. Reihe 1: Die Bismarckzeit - 1871–1890. Band 2: Der Berliner Kongreß und seine Vorgeschichte. -** *The High Policy of the European Cabinets. File 1: The Times of Bismarck - 1871 – 1890. Volume 2: The Birlin's Citizen Congress and its Prehistory.)*

A. Mendelssohn-Bartholdy, J. Lepsius and F. Thimme | ?cm x ?cm | White paper softback | ? + ?pp | ? | see note | German Text. | Fraktur Script.

Die Große Politik der Europäischen Kabinette 1871–1914. Reihe 1: Die Bismarckzeit – 1871-1890. Band 3: Das Bismarck'sche Bündnissystem. **(Die Große Politik der Europäischen Kabinette 1871-1914. Reihe 1: Die Bismarckzeit - 1871 – 1890. Band 3: Das Bismarck'sche Bündnissystem. -** *The High Policy of the European Cabinets. File 1: The Times of Bismarck - 1871–1890. Volume 3: Bismarck's Alliance System.)*

A. Mendelssohn-Bartholdy, J. Lepsius and F. Thimme | ?cm x ?cm | White paper softback | ? + ?pp | ? | see note | German Text. | Fraktur Script.

Die Große Politik der Europäischen Kabinette 1871–1914. Reihe 1: Die Bismarckzeit – 1871-1890. Band 4: Die Dreibundmächte und England. **(Die Große Politik der Europäischen Kabinette 1871-1914. Reihe 1: Die Bismarckzeit - 1871–1890. Band 4: Die Dreibundmächte und England. -** *The High Policy of the European Cabinets. File 1: The Times of Bismarck - 1871–1890. Volume 4: The Powers of the Three Federations and England.)*

A. Mendelssohn-Bartholdy, J. Lepsius and F. Thimme | ?cm x ?cm | White paper softback | ? + ?pp | ? | see note | German Text. | Fraktur Script.

Die Große Politik der Europäischen Kabinette 1871–1914. Reihe 1: Die Bismarckzeit – 1871-1890. Band 5: Neue Verwicklungen im Osten. **(Die Große Politik der Europäischen Kabinette 1871-1914. Reihe 1: Die Bismarckzeit - 1871–1890. Band 5: Neue Verwicklungen im Osten. -** *The High Policy of the European Cabinets. File 1: The Times of Bismarck - 1871–1890. Volume 5: The New Entanglement of the East.)*

A. Mendelssohn-Bartholdy, J. Lepsius and F. Thimme | ?cm x ?cm | White paper softback | ? + ?pp | ? | see note | German Text. | Fraktur Script.

Die Große Politik der Europäischen Kabinette 1871–1914. Reihe 1: Die Bismarckzeit – 1871-1890. Band 6: Kriegsgefahr in Ost und West. Ausklang der Bismarckzeit. **(Die Große Politik der Europäischen Kabinette 1871-1914. Reihe 1: Die Bismarckzeit - 1871–1890. Band 6: Kriegsgefahr in Ost und West. Ausklang der Bismarckzeit. —** *The High Policy of the European Cabinets. File 1: The Times of Bismarck - 1871–1890. Volume 6: The War Danger in the East and the West. The End of Bismarck's Period.)*

A. Mendelssohn-Bartholdy, J. Lepsius and F. Thimme | ?cm x ?cm | White paper softback | ? + ?pp | ? | see note | German Text. | Fraktur Script.

Die Große Politik der Europäischen Kabinette 1871–1914. Reihe 2: Der neue Kurs-1890-1899. Band 7: Die Anfänge des Neuen Kurses. **(Die Große Politik der Europäischen Kabinette 1871-1914. Reihe 2: Der neue Kurs-1890-1899. Band 7: Die**

Anfänge des Neuen Kurses. - *The High Policy of the European Cabinets. File 2: The New Course – 1890-1899.* **Volume 7: The Beginnings of the New Course.)**

A. Mendelssohn-Bartholdy, J. Lepsius and F. Thimme | ?cm x ?cm | White paper softback | ? + ?pp | ? | see note | German Text. | Fraktur Script.

Die Große Politik der Europäischen Kabinette 1871–1914. Reihe 2: Der neue Kurs–1890-1899. Die Große Politik der Europäischen Kabinette 1871–1914. Reihe 2: Der neue Kurs–1890-1899. Band 8: Die Anfänge des Neuen Kurses. Teil 1: Der Russische Draht. **(Die Große Politik der Europäischen Kabinette 1871-1914. Reihe 2: Der neue Kurs-1890-1899. Band 8: Die Anfänge des Neuen Kurses. Teil 1: Der Russische Draht.** - *The High Policy of the European Cabinets. File 2: The New Course – 1890-1899. Volume 8: The Beginnings of the New Course. Part 1: The Russian Wire.)*

A. Mendelssohn-Bartholdy, J. Lepsius and F. Thimme | ?cm x ?cm | White paper softback | ? + ?pp | ? | see note | German Text. | Fraktur Script.

Die Große Politik der Europäischen Kabinette 1871–1914. Reihe 2: Der neue Kurs–1890-1899. Die Große Politik der Europäischen Kabinette 1871–1914. Reihe 2: Der neue Kurs–1890-1899. Band 8: Die Anfänge des Neuen Kurses. Teil 2: Die Stellung Englands zwischen den Mächten. **(Die Große Politik der Europäischen Kabinette 1871-1914. Reihe 2: Der neue Kurs-1890-1899. Band 8: Die Anfänge des Neuen Kurses. Teil 2: Die Stellung Englands zwischen den Mächten.-** *The High Policy of the European Cabinets. File 2: The New Course – 1890-1899. Volume 8: The Beginnings of the New Course. Part 2: The Position of England between the Other Powers.)*

A. Mendelssohn-Bartholdy, J. Lepsius and F. Thimme | ?cm x ?cm | White paper softback | ? + ?pp | ? | see note | German Text. | Fraktur Script.

Die Große Politik der Europäischen Kabinette 1871–1914. Reihe 2: Der neue Kurs–1890-1899. Band 9: Der Nahe und Ferne Osten. **(Die Große Politik der Europäischen Kabinette 1871-1914. Reihe 2: Der neue Kurs-1890-1899. Band 9: Der Nahe und Ferne Osten.** - *The High Policy of the European Cabinets. File 2: The New Course – 1890-1899. Volume 9: The Near and Far East.)*

A. Mendelssohn-Bartholdy, J. Lepsius and F. Thimme | ?cm x ?cm | White paper softback | ? + ?pp | ? | see note | German Text. | Fraktur Script.

Die Große Politik der Europäischen Kabinette 1871–1914. Reihe 2: Band 10: Das türkische Problem. **(Die Große Politik der Europäischen Kabinette 1871-1914. Reihe 2: Der neue Kurs-1890-1899. Band 10: Das türkische Problem.** - *The High Policy of the European Cabinets. File 2: The New Course – 1890-1899. Volume 10: The Turkish Problem.)*

A. Mendelssohn-Bartholdy, J. Lepsius and F. Thimme | ?cm x ?cm | White paper softback | ? + ?pp | ? | see note | German Text. | Fraktur Script.

Die Große Politik der Europäischen Kabinette 1871–1914. Reihe 2: Der neue Kurs–1890-1899. Band 11: Die Krügerdepesche und das europäische Bündnissystem 1896. **(Die Große Politik der Europäischen Kabinette 1871-1914. Reihe 2: Der neue Kurs-1890-1899. Band 11: Die Krügerdepesche und das europäische Bündnissystem 1896.** - *The High Policy of the European Cabinets. File 2: The New Course – 1890-1899. Volume 11: The Kruger Telegram and the European Alliance System 1896.)*

A. Mendelssohn-Bartholdy, J. Lepsius and F. Thimme | ?cm x ?cm | White paper softback | ? + ?pp | ? | see note | German Text. | Fraktur Script.

Die Große Politik der Europäischen Kabinette 1871–1914. Reihe 2: Der neue Kurs–1890-1899. Band 12: Alte und neue Balkanhändel 1898–1899. Teil 1. **(Die Große Politik der Europäischen Kabinette 1871-1914. Reihe 2: Der neue Kurs-1890-1899. Band 12: Alte und neue Balkanhändel 1898-1899. Teil 1.** - *The High Policy of the European Cabinets. File 2: The New Course – 1890-1899. Volume 12: Old and New Balkans Business 1898-1899. Part 1.)*

A. Mendelssohn-Bartholdy, J. Lepsius and F. Thimme | ?cm x ?cm | White paper softback | ? + ?pp | ? | see note | German Text. | Fraktur Script.

Die Große Politik der Europäischen Kabinette 1871–1914. Reihe 2: Der neue Kurs–1890-1899. Band 12: Alte und neue Balkanhändel 1898–1899. Teil 2. (Die Große Politik der Europäischen Kabinette 1871-1914. Reihe 2: Der neue Kurs-1890-1899. Band 12: Alte und neue Balkanhändel 1898-1899. Teil 2. - *The High Policy of the European Cabinets. File 2: The New Course – 1890-1899. Volume 12: Old and New Balkans Business 1898-1899. Part 2.*)

    A. Mendelssohn-Bartholdy, J. Lepsius and F. Thimme | ?cm x ?cm | White paper softback | ? + ?pp | ? | see note | German Text. | Fraktur Script.

Die Große Politik der Europäischen Kabinette 1871–1914. Reihe 3: Die Politik der freien Hand – 1897-1904. Band 13: Die Europäischen Mächte untereinander 1897–1899. (Die Große Politik der Europäischen Kabinette 1871-1914. Reihe 3: Die Politik der freien Hand - 1897–1904. Band 13: Die Europäischen Mächte untereinander 1897-1899. - *The High Policy of the European Cabinets. File 3: The Free Hand Policy - 1897–1904. Volume 13: The European Powers Among Themselves 1897-1899.*)

    A. Mendelssohn-Bartholdy, J. Lepsius and F. Thimme | ?cm x ?cm | White paper softback | ? + ?pp | ? | see note | German Text. | Fraktur Script.

Die Große Politik der Europäischen Kabinette 1871–1914. Reihe 3: Die Politik der freien Hand – 1897-1904. Band 14: Weltpolitische Rivalitäten. Teil 1. (Die Große Politik der Europäischen Kabinette 1871-1914. Reihe 3: Die Politik der freien Hand - 1897 – 1904. Band 14: Weltpolitische Rivalitäten. . - *The High Policy of the European Cabinets. File 3: The Free Hand Policy - 1897 – 1904. Volume 14: World Policial Rivalries. Part 1.*)

    A. Mendelssohn-Bartholdy, J. Lepsius and F. Thimme | ?cm x ?cm | White paper softback | ? + ?pp | ? | see note | German Text. | Fraktur Script.

Die Große Politik der Europäischen Kabinette 1871–1914. Reihe 3: Die Politik der freien Hand – 1897-1904. Band 14: Weltpolitische Rivalitäten. Teil 2. (Die Große Politik der Europäischen Kabinette 1871-1914. Reihe 3: Die Politik der freien Hand - 1897 – 1904. Band 14: Weltpolitische Rivalitäten. Teil 2. - *The High Policy of the European Cabinets. File 3: The Free Hand Policy - 1897 – 1904. Volume 14: World Policial Rivalries. Part 2.*)

    A. Mendelssohn-Bartholdy, J. Lepsius and F. Thimme | ?cm x ?cm | White paper softback | ? + ?pp | ? | see note | German Text. | Fraktur Script.

Die Große Politik der Europäischen Kabinette 1871–1914. Reihe 3: Die Politik der freien Hand – 1897-1904. Band 15: Rings um die Erste Haager Friedenskonferenz. (Die Große Politik der Europäischen Kabinette 1871-1914. Reihe 3: Die Politik der freien Hand - 1897–1904. Band 15: Rings um die Erste Haager Friedenskonferenz. - *The High Policy of the European Cabinets. File 3: The Free Hand Policy - 1897–1904. Volume 15: Ring Around the First Hague Peace Conference.*)

    A. Mendelssohn-Bartholdy, J. Lepsius and F. Thimme | ?cm x ?cm | White paper softback | ? + ?pp | ? | see note | German Text. | Fraktur Script.

Die Große Politik der Europäischen Kabinette 1871–1914. Reihe 3: Die Politik der freien Hand – 1897-1904. Band 16: Die Chinawirren und die Mächte 1900–1902. (Die Große Politik der Europäischen Kabinette 1871-1914. Reihe 3: Die Politik der freien Hand - 1897–1904. Band 16: Die Chinawirren und die Mächte 1900-1902. - *The High Policy of the European Cabinets. File 3: The Free Hand Policy - 1897–1904. Volume 16: Confussion over China with Other Powers 1900-1902.*)

    A. Mendelssohn-Bartholdy, J. Lepsius and F. Thimme | ?cm x ?cm | White paper softback | ? + ?pp | ? | see note | German Text. | Fraktur Script.

Die Große Politik der Europäischen Kabinette 1871–1914. Reihe 3: Die Politik der freien Hand – 1897 – 1904. Band 17: Die Wendung im Deutsch–Englischen Verhältnis. (Die Große Politik der Europäischen Kabinette 1871-1914. Reihe 3: Die Politik der freien Hand - 1897 – 1904. Band 17: Die Wendung im Deutsch-

Englischen Verhältnis. - *The High Policy of the European Cabinets. File 3: The Free Hand Policy - 1897 – 1904. Volume 17: The Idiom in the German-English Relationship.*)
      A. Mendelssohn-Bartholdy, J. Lepsius and F. Thimme | ?cm x ?cm | White paper softback | ? + ?pp | ? | see note | German Text. | Fraktur Script.

Die Große Politik der Europäischen Kabinette 1871−1914. Reihe 3: Die Politik der freien Hand − 1897-1904. Band 18: Zweibund und Dreibund. Teil 1. (Die Große Politik der Europäischen Kabinette 1871-1914. Reihe 3: Die Politik der freien Hand - 1897–1904. Band 18: Zweibund und Dreibund. Teil 1. - *The High Policy of the European Cabinets. File 3: The Free Hand Policy - 1897–1904. Volume 18: The Two and Three Federation. Part 1.*)
      A. Mendelssohn-Bartholdy, J. Lepsius and F. Thimme | ?cm x ?cm | White paper softback | ? + ?pp | ? | see note | German Text. | Fraktur Script.

Die Große Politik der Europäischen Kabinette 1871−1914. Reihe 3: Die Politik der freien Hand − 1897-1904. Band 18: Zweibund und Dreibund. Teil 2. (Die Große Politik der Europäischen Kabinette 1871-1914. Reihe 3: Die Politik der freien Hand - 1897–1904. Band 18: Zweibund und Dreibund. Teil 2. - *The High Policy of the European Cabinets. File 3: The Free Hand Policy - 1897 – 1904. Volume 18: The Two and Three Federation. Part 2.*)
      A. Mendelssohn-Bartholdy, J. Lepsius and F. Thimme | ?cm x ?cm | White paper softback | ? + ?pp | ? | see note | German Text. | Fraktur Script.

Die Große Politik der Europäischen Kabinette 1871−1914. Reihe 4: Die Isolierung der Mittelmächte − 1904-1908. Band 19: Der Russisch−Japanische Krieg. Teil 1. (Die Große Politik der Europäischen Kabinette 1871-1914. Reihe 4: Die Isolierung der Mittelmächte - 1904–1908. Band 19: Der Russisch-Japanische Krieg. Teil 1. - *The High Policy of the European Cabinets. File 4: The Isolation of the Central Powers - 1904 – 1908. Volume 19: The Russo-Japanese War. Part 1.*)
      A. Mendelssohn-Bartholdy, J. Lepsius and F. Thimme | ?cm x ?cm | White paper softback | ? + ?pp | ? | see note | German Text. | Fraktur Script.

Die Große Politik der Europäischen Kabinette 1871−1914. Reihe 4: Die Isolierung der Mittelmächte − 1904-1908. Band 19: Der Russisch−Japanische Krieg. Teil 2. (Die Große Politik der Europäischen Kabinette 1871-1914. Reihe 4: Die Isolierung der Mittelmächte - 1904–1908. Band 19: Der Russisch-Japanische Krieg. Teil 2. - *The High Policy of the European Cabinets. File 4: The Isolation of the Central Powers - 1904 – 1908. Volume 19: The Russo-Japanese War. Part 2.*)
      A. Mendelssohn-Bartholdy, J. Lepsius and F. Thimme | ?cm x ?cm | White paper softback | ? + ?pp | ? | see note | German Text. | Fraktur Script.

Die Große Politik der Europäischen Kabinette 1871−1914. Reihe 4: Die Isolierung der Mittelmächte − 1904-1908. Band 20: Entente cordiale und erste Marokkokrise 1904-1905. Teil 1. (Die Große Politik der Europäischen Kabinette 1871-1914. Reihe 4: Die Isolierung der Mittelmächte - 1904–1908. Band 20: Entente cordiale und erste Marokkokrise 1904-1905. Teil 1. - *The High Policy of the European Cabinets. File 4: The Isolation of the Central Powers - 1904 – 1908. Volume 20: The Entente Cordiale and the First Moroccan Crisis 1904-1905. Part 1.*)
      A. Mendelssohn-Bartholdy, J. Lepsius and F. Thimme | ?cm x ?cm | White paper softback | ? + ?pp | ? | see note | German Text. | Fraktur Script.

Die Große Politik der Europäischen Kabinette 1871−1914. Reihe 4: Die Isolierung der Mittelmächte − 1904-1908. Band 20: Entente cordiale und erste Marokkokrise 1904-1905. Teil 2. (Die Große Politik der Europäischen Kabinette 1871-1914. Reihe 4: Die Isolierung der Mittelmächte - 1904–1908. Band 20: Entente cordiale und erste Marokkokrise 1904-1905. Teil 2. - *The High Policy of the European Cabinets. File 4: The Isolation of the Central Powers - 1904 – 1908. Volume 20: The Entente Cordiale and the First Moroccan Crisis 1904-1905. Part 2.*)
      A. Mendelssohn-Bartholdy, J. Lepsius and F. Thimme | ?cm x ?cm | White paper softback | ? + ?pp | ? | see note | German Text. | Fraktur Script.

Die Große Politik der Europäischen Kabinette 1871–1914. Reihe 4: Die Isolierung der Mittelmächte – 1904–1908. Band 21: Die Konferenz von Algeciras und ihre Auswirkung. Teil 1. (Die Große Politik der Europäischen Kabinette 1871-1914. Reihe 4: Die Isolierung der Mittelmächte - 1904–1908. Band 21: Die Konferenz von Algeciras und ihre Auswirkung. Teil 1. - *The High Policy of the European Cabinets. File 4: The Isolation of the Central Powers - 1904 – 1908. Volume 21: The Algerian Conference and its Effect. Part 1.*)

A. Mendelssohn-Bartholdy, J. Lepsius and F. Thimme | ?cm x ?cm | White paper softback | ? + ?pp | ? | see note | German Text. | Fraktur Script.

Die Große Politik der Europäischen Kabinette 1871–1914. Reihe 4: Die Isolierung der Mittelmächte – 1904–1908. Band 21: Die Konferenz von Algeciras und ihre Auswirkung. Teil 2. (Die Große Politik der Europäischen Kabinette 1871-1914. Reihe 4: Die Isolierung der Mittelmächte - 1904–1908. Band 21: Die Konferenz von Algeciras und ihre Auswirkung. Teil 2. - *The High Policy of the European Cabinets. File 4: The Isolation of the Central Powers - 1904 – 1908. Volume 21: The Algerian Conference and its Effect. Part 2.*)

A. Mendelssohn-Bartholdy, J. Lepsius and F. Thimme | ?cm x ?cm | White paper softback | ? + ?pp | ? | see note | German Text. | Fraktur Script.

Die Große Politik der Europäischen Kabinette 1871–1914. Reihe 4: Die Isolierung der Mittelmächte – 1904–1908. Band 22: Die Österreichisch-Russische Entente und der Balkan 1904–1907. (Die Große Politik der Europäischen Kabinette 1871-1914. Reihe 4: Die Isolierung der Mittelmächte - 1904–1908. Band 22: Die Österreichisch-Russische Entente und der Balkan 1904-1907. - *The High Policy of the European Cabinets. File 4: The Isolation of the Central Powers - 1904 – 1908. Volume 22: The Austro-Russian Entente and the Balkans 1904-1907.*)

A. Mendelssohn-Bartholdy, J. Lepsius and F. Thimme | ?cm x ?cm | White paper softback | ? + ?pp | ? | see note | German Text. | Fraktur Script.

Die Große Politik der Europäischen Kabinette 1871–1914. Reihe 4: Die Isolierung der Mittelmächte – 1904–1908. Band 23: Die Zweite Haager Friedenskonferenz. Nordsee– und Ostsee–Abkommen. Teil 1. (Die Große Politik der Europäischen Kabinette 1871-1914. Reihe 4: Die Isolierung der Mittelmächte - 1904–1908. Band 23: Die Zweite Haager Friedenskonferenz. Nordsee - und Ostsee-Abkommen. Teil 1. - *The High Policy of the European Cabinets. File 4: The Isolation of the Central Powers - 1904 – 1908. Volume 23: The Second Hague Peace Conference. The North Sea and the Baltic Sea Agreement. Part 1.*)

A. Mendelssohn-Bartholdy, J. Lepsius and F. Thimme | ?cm x ?cm | White paper softback | ? + ?pp | ? | see note | German Text. | Fraktur Script.

Die Große Politik der Europäischen Kabinette 1871–1914. Reihe 4: Die Isolierung der Mittelmächte – 1904–1908. Band 23: Die Zweite Haager Friedenskonferenz. Nordsee– und Ostsee–Abkommen. Teil 2. (Die Große Politik der Europäischen Kabinette 1871-1914. Reihe 4: Die Isolierung der Mittelmächte - 1904–1908. Band 23: Die Zweite Haager Friedenskonferenz. Nordsee - und Ostsee-Abkommen. Teil 2. - *The High Policy of the European Cabinets. File 4: The Isolation of the Central Powers - 1904 – 1908. Volume 23: The Second Hague Peace Conference. The North Sea and the Baltic Sea Agreement. Part 2.*)

A. Mendelssohn-Bartholdy, J. Lepsius and F. Thimme | ?cm x ?cm | White paper softback | ? + ?pp | ? | see note | German Text. | Fraktur Script.

Die Große Politik der Europäischen Kabinette 1871–1914. Reihe 4: Die Isolierung der Mittelmächte – 1904–1908. Band 24: Deutschland und die Westmächte 1907–1908. (Die Große Politik der Europäischen Kabinette 1871-1914. Reihe 4: Die Isolierung der Mittelmächte - 1904–1908. Band 24: Deutschland und die Westmächte 1907-1908. - *The High Policy of the European Cabinets. File 4: The Isolation of the Central Powers - 1904 – 1908. Volume 24: Germany and the Western Powers 1907-1908.*)

A. Mendelssohn-Bartholdy, J. Lepsius and F. Thimme | ?cm x ?cm | White paper softback | ? + ?pp | ? | see note | German Text. | Fraktur Script.

Die Große Politik der Europäischen Kabinette 1871–1914. Reihe 4: Die Isolierung der Mittelmächte – 1904–1908. Band 25: Die Englisch-Russische Entente und der Osten. Teil 1. (Die Große Politik der Europäischen Kabinette 1871-1914. Reihe 4: Die Isolierung der Mittelmächte - 1904–1908. Band 25: Die Englisch-Russische Entente und der Osten. Teil 1. - *The High Policy of the European Cabinets. File 4: The Isolation of the Central Powers - 1904 – 1908. Volume 25: The English-Russian Entente and the East. Part 1.*)

    A. Mendelssohn-Bartholdy, J. Lepsius and F. Thimme I ?cm x ?cm I White paper softback I ? + ?pp I ? I see note I German Text. I Fraktur Script.

Die Große Politik der Europäischen Kabinette 1871–1914. Reihe 4: Die Isolierung der Mittelmächte – 1904–1908. Band 25: Die Englisch-Russische Entente und der Osten. Teil 2. (Die Große Politik der Europäischen Kabinette 1871-1914. Reihe 4: Die Isolierung der Mittelmächte - 1904–1908. Band 25: Die Englisch-Russische Entente und der Osten. Teil 2. - *The High Policy of the European Cabinets. File 4: The Isolation of the Central Powers - 1904 – 1908. Volume 25: The English-Russian Entente and the East. Part 2.*)

    A. Mendelssohn-Bartholdy, J. Lepsius and F. Thimme I ?cm x ?cm I White paper softback I ? + ?pp I ? I see note I German Text. I Fraktur Script.

Die Große Politik der Europäischen Kabinette 1871–1914. Reihe 5: Weltpolitische Komplikationen – 1908–1911. Band 26: Die Bosnische Krise 1908–1909. Teil 1. (Die Große Politik der Europäischen Kabinette 1871-1914. Reihe 5: Weltpolitische Komplikationen - 1908–1911. Band 26: Die Bosnische Krise 1908-1909. Teil 1. - *The High Policy of the European Cabinets. File 5: World Political Complications - 1908–1911. Volume 26: The Bosnian Crisis 1908-1909. Part 1.*)

    A. Mendelssohn-Bartholdy, J. Lepsius and F. Thimme I ?cm x ?cm I White paper softback I ? + ?pp I ? I see note I German Text. I Fraktur Script.

Die Große Politik der Europäischen Kabinette 1871–1914. Reihe 5: Weltpolitische Komplikationen – 1908–1911. Band 26: Die Bosnische Krise 1908–1909. Teil 2. (Die Große Politik der Europäischen Kabinette 1871-1914. Reihe 5: Weltpolitische Komplikationen - 1908–1911. Band 26: Die Bosnische Krise 1908-1909. Teil 2. - *The High Policy of the European Cabinets. File 5: World Political Complications - 1908–1911. Volume 26: The Bosnian Crisis 1908-1909. Part 2.*)

    A. Mendelssohn-Bartholdy, J. Lepsius and F. Thimme I ?cm x ?cm I White paper softback I ? + ?pp I ? I see note I German Text. I Fraktur Script.

Die Große Politik der Europäischen Kabinette 1871–1914. Reihe 5: Weltpolitische Komplikationen – 1908–1911. Band 27: Zwischen den Balkankriegen 1909–1911. Teil 1. (Die Große Politik der Europäischen Kabinette 1871-1914. Reihe 5: Weltpolitische Komplikationen - 1908–1911. Band 27: Zwischen den Balkankriegen 1909-1911. Teil 1. - *The High Policy of the European Cabinets. File 5: World Political Complications - 1908–1911. Volume 27: Before the Balkans Wars 1909-1911. Part 1.*)

    A. Mendelssohn-Bartholdy, J. Lepsius and F. Thimme I ?cm x ?cm I White paper softback I ? + ?pp I ? I see note I German Text. I Fraktur Script.

Die Große Politik der Europäischen Kabinette 1871–1914. Reihe 5: Weltpolitische Komplikationen – 1908–1911. Band 27: Zwischen den Balkankriegen 1909–1911. Teil 2. (Die Große Politik der Europäischen Kabinette 1871-1914. Reihe 5: Weltpolitische Komplikationen - 1908–1911. Band 27: Zwischen den Balkankriegen 1909-1911. Teil 2. - *The High Policy of the European Cabinets. File 5: World Political Complications - 1908–1911. Volume 27: Before the Balkans Wars 1909-1911. Part 2.*)

    A. Mendelssohn-Bartholdy, J. Lepsius and F. Thimme I ?cm x ?cm I White paper softback I ? + ?pp I ? I see note I German Text. I Fraktur Script.

Die Große Politik der Europäischen Kabinette 1871–1914. Reihe 5: Weltpolitische Komplikationen – 1908–1911. Band 28: England und die Deutsche Flotte 1908–1911. (Die Große Politik der Europäischen Kabinette 1871-1914. Reihe 5: Weltpolitische Komplikationen - 1908–1911. Band 28: England und die Deutsche

Flotte 1908-1911. - *The High Policy of the European Cabinets. File 5: World Political Complications - 1908–1911. Volume 28: England and the German Fleet 1908-1911.*)

    A. Mendelssohn-Bartholdy, J. Lepsius and F. Thimme | ?cm x ?cm | White paper softback | ? + ?pp | ? | see note | German Text. | Fraktur Script.

Die Große Politik der Europäischen Kabinette 1871–1914. Reihe 5: Weltpolitische Komplikationen – 1908-1911. Band 29: Die Zweite Marokkokrise 1911. (Die Große Politik der Europäischen Kabinette 1871-1914. Reihe 5: Weltpolitische Komplikationen - 1908–1911. Band 29: Die Zweite Marokkokrise 1911. - *The High Policy of the European Cabinets. File 5: World Political Complications - 1908–1911. Volume 29: The Second Moroccan Crisis 1911.*)

    A. Mendelssohn-Bartholdy, J. Lepsius and F. Thimme | ?cm x ?cm | White paper softback | ? + ?pp | ? | see note | German Text. | Fraktur Script.

Die Große Politik der Europäischen Kabinette 1871–1914. Reihe 6: Weltpolitische Komplikationen – 1911-1914. Band 30: Der Italienisch – Türkische Krieg 1911–1912. Teil 1. (Die Große Politik der Europäischen Kabinette 1871-1914. Reihe 6: Weltpolitische Komplikationen - 1911 – 1914. Band 30: Der Italienisch-Türkische Krieg 1911-1912. Teil 1. - *The High Policy of the European Cabinets. File 6: World Political Complications - 1911- 1914. Volume 30: The Italian-Turkish War 1911-1912. Part 1.*)

    A. Mendelssohn-Bartholdy, J. Lepsius and F. Thimme | ?cm x ?cm | White paper softback | ? + ?pp | ? | see note | German Text. | Fraktur Script.

Die Große Politik der Europäischen Kabinette 1871–1914. Reihe 6: Weltpolitische Komplikationen – 1911-1914. Band 30: Der Italienisch – Türkische Krieg 1911–1912. Teil 2. (Die Große Politik der Europäischen Kabinette 1871-1914. Reihe 6: Weltpolitische Komplikationen - 1911 – 1914. Band 30: Der Italienisch-Türkische Krieg 1911-1912. Teil 2. - *The High Policy of the European Cabinets. File 6: World Political Complications - 1911- 1914. Volume 30: The Italian-Turkish War 1911-1912. Part 2.*)

    A. Mendelssohn-Bartholdy, J. Lepsius and F. Thimme | ?cm x ?cm | White paper softback | ? + ?pp | ? | see note | German Text. | Fraktur Script.

Die Große Politik der Europäischen Kabinette 1871–1914. Reihe 6: Weltpolitische Komplikationen – 1911-1914. Band 31: Das Scheitern der Haldane–Mission und ihre Rückwirkung auf die Tripel–Entente 1911–1912. (Die Große Politik der Europäischen Kabinette 1871-1914. Reihe 6: Weltpolitische Komplikationen - 1911–1914. Band 31: Das Scheitern der Haldane-Mission und ihre Rückwirkung auf die Tripel-Entente 1911-1912. - *The High Policy of the European Cabinets. File 6: World Political Complications - 1911-1914. Volume 31: The Failure of the Haldane Mission and the Reaction upon the Triple Entente 1911-1912.*)

    A. Mendelssohn-Bartholdy, J. Lepsius and F. Thimme | ?cm x ?cm | White paper softback | ? + ?pp | ? | see note | German Text. | Fraktur Script.

Die Große Politik der Europäischen Kabinette 1871–1914. Reihe 6: Weltpolitische Komplikationen – 1911-1914. Band 32: Die Mächte und Ostasien 1909–1914. (Die Große Politik der Europäischen Kabinette 1871-1914. Reihe 6: Weltpolitische Komplikationen - 1911–1914. Band 32: Die Mächte und Ostasien 1909-1914. - *The High Policy of the European Cabinets. File 6: World Political Complications - 1911-1914. Volume 32: The Powers and East Asia 1909-1914.*)

    A. Mendelssohn-Bartholdy, J. Lepsius and F. Thimme | ?cm x ?cm | White paper softback | ? + ?pp | ? | see note | German Text. | Fraktur Script.

Die Große Politik der Europäischen Kabinette 1871–1914. Reihe 6: Weltpolitische Komplikationen – 1911-1914. Band 33: Der Erste Balkankrieg 1912. (Die Große Politik der Europäischen Kabinette 1871-1914. Reihe 6: Weltpolitische Komplikationen - 1911 – 1914. Band 33: Der Erste Balkankrieg 1912. - *The High Policy of the European Cabinets. File 6: World Political Complications - 1911- 1914. Volume 33: The First Balkans Wars 1912.*)

    A. Mendelssohn-Bartholdy, J. Lepsius and F. Thimme | ?cm x ?cm | White paper softback | ? + ?pp | ? | see note | German Text. | Fraktur Script.

Die Große Politik der Europäischen Kabinette 1871–1914. Reihe 7: Europa vor der Katastrophe – 1912–1914. Band 34,: Die Londoner Botschafterreunion und der Zweite Balkankrieg 1912 bis 1913. Teil 1. (Die Große Politik der Europäischen Kabinette 1871-1914. Reihe 7: Europa vor der Katastrophe - 1912-1914. Band 34,: Die Londoner Botschafterreunion und der Zweite Balkankrieg 1912 bis 1913. Teil 1. - *The High Policy of the European Cabinets. File 7: Europe before the Catastrophe - 1912-1914. Volume 34: The Return of the London Ambassador and the Second Balkans Wars 1912 to 1913. Part 1.*)

    A. Mendelssohn-Bartholdy, J. Lepsius and F. Thimme | ?cm x ?cm | White paper softback | ? + ?pp | ? | see note | German Text. | Fraktur Script.

Die Große Politik der Europäischen Kabinette 1871–1914. Reihe 7: Europa vor der Katastrophe – 1912–1914. Band 34,: Die Londoner Botschafterreunion und der Zweite Balkankrieg 1912 bis 1913. Teil 2. (Die Große Politik der Europäischen Kabinette 1871-1914. Reihe 7: Europa vor der Katastrophe - 1912-1914. Band 34,: Die Londoner Botschafterreunion und der Zweite Balkankrieg 1912 bis 1913. Teil 2. - *The High Policy of the European Cabinets. File 7: Europe before the Catastrophe - 1912-1914. Volume 34: The Return of the London Ambassador and the Second Balkans Wars 1912 to 1913. Part 2.*)

    A. Mendelssohn-Bartholdy, J. Lepsius and F. Thimme | ?cm x ?cm | White paper softback | ? + ?pp | ? | see note | German Text. | Fraktur Script.

Die Große Politik der Europäischen Kabinette 1871–1914. Reihe 7: Europa vor der Katastrophe – 1912–1914. Band 35: Der Dritte Balkankrieg 1913. (Die Große Politik der Europäischen Kabinette 1871-1914. Reihe 7: Europa vor der Katastrophe - 1912-1914. Band 35: Der Dritte Balkankrieg 1913. - *The High Policy of the European Cabinets. File 7: Europe before the Catastrophe - 1912-1914. Volume 35: The Third Balkans Wars 1913.*)

    A. Mendelssohn-Bartholdy, J. Lepsius and F. Thimme | ?cm x ?cm | White paper softback | ? + ?pp | ? | see note | German Text. | Fraktur Script.

Die Große Politik der Europäischen Kabinette 1871–1914. Reihe 7: Europa vor der Katastrophe – 1912–1914. Band 36: Die Liquidierung der Balkankriege 1913–1914. Teil 1. (Die Große Politik der Europäischen Kabinette 1871-1914. Reihe 7: Europa vor der Katastrophe - 1912-1914. Band 36: Die Liquidierung der Balkankriege 1913-1914. Teil 1. - *The High Policy of the European Cabinets. File 7: Europe before the Catastrophe - 1912-1914. Volume 36: The End of the Balkans Wars 1912-1913. Part 1.*)

    A. Mendelssohn-Bartholdy, J. Lepsius and F. Thimme | ?cm x ?cm | White paper softback | ? + ?pp | ? | see note | German Text. | Fraktur Script.

Die Große Politik der Europäischen Kabinette 1871–1914. Reihe 7: Europa vor der Katastrophe – 1912–1914. Band 36: Die Liquidierung der Balkankriege 1913–1914. Teil 2. (Die Große Politik der Europäischen Kabinette 1871-1914. Reihe 7: Europa vor der Katastrophe - 1912-1914. Band 36: Die Liquidierung der Balkankriege 1913-1914. Teil 2. - *The High Policy of the European Cabinets. File 7: Europe before the Catastrophe - 1912-1914. Volume 36: The End of the Balkans Wars 1912-1913. Part 2.*)

    A. Mendelssohn-Bartholdy, J. Lepsius and F. Thimme | ?cm x ?cm | White paper softback | ? + ?pp | ? | see note | German Text. | Fraktur Script.

Die Große Politik der Europäischen Kabinette 1871–1914. Reihe 7: Europa vor der Katastrophe – 1912–1914. Band 37: Entspannung unter den Mächten 1912–1913. Teil 1. (Die Große Politik der Europäischen Kabinette 1871-1914. Reihe 7: Europa vor der Katastrophe - 1912-1914. Band 37: Entspannung unter den Mächten 1912-1913. Teil 1. - *The High Policy of the European Cabinets. File 7: Europe before the Catastrophe - 1912-1914. Volume 37: The Relaxation of Tension between the Powers 1912-1913. Part 1.*)

    A. Mendelssohn-Bartholdy, J. Lepsius and F. Thimme | ?cm x ?cm | White paper softback | ? + ?pp | ? | see note | German Text. | Fraktur Script.

Die Große Politik der Europäischen Kabinette 1871–1914. Reihe 7: Europa vor der Katastrophe – 1912–1914. Band 37: Entspannung unter den Mächten 1912–1913. Teil 2. (Die Große Politik der Europäischen Kabinette 1871-1914. Reihe 7: Europa vor der Katastrophe - 1912-1914. Band 37: Entspannung unter den Mächten 1912-1913. Teil 2. - *The High Policy of the European Cabinets. File 7: Europe before the Catastrophe - 1912-1914. Volume 37: The Relaxation of Tension between the Powers 1912-1913. Part 2.*)

    A. Mendelssohn-Bartholdy, J. Lepsius and F. Thimme | ?cm x ?cm | White paper softback | ? + ?pp | ? | see note | German Text. | Fraktur Script.

Die Große Politik der Europäischen Kabinette 1871–1914. Reihe 7: Europa vor der Katastrophe – 1912–1914. Band 38: Neue Gefahrenzonen im Orient 1913–1914. (Die Große Politik der Europäischen Kabinette 1871-1914. Reihe 7: Europa vor der Katastrophe - 1912-1914. Band 38: Neue Gefahrenzonen im Orient 1913-1914. - *The High Policy of the European Cabinets. File 7: Europe before the Catastrophe - 1912-1914. Volume 38: New Danger Areas in the Orient 1912-1913.*)

    A. Mendelssohn-Bartholdy, J. Lepsius and F. Thimme | ?cm x ?cm | White paper softback | ? + ?pp | ? | see note | German Text. | Fraktur Script.

Die Große Politik der Europäischen Kabinette 1871–1914. Reihe 7: Europa vor der Katastrophe – 1912–1914. Band 39: Das Nahen des Weltkrieges 1912–1914. (Die Große Politik der Europäischen Kabinette 1871-1914. Reihe 7: Europa vor der Katastrophe - 1912-1914. Band 39: Das Nahen des Weltkrieges 1912-1914. - *The High Policy of the European Cabinets. File 7: Europe before the Catastrophe - 1912-1914. Volume 39: The Approach of the World Wars 1912-1914.*)

    A. Mendelssohn-Bartholdy, J. Lepsius and F. Thimme | ?cm x ?cm | White paper softback | ? + ?pp | ? | see note | German Text. | Fraktur Script.

Die Große Politik der Europäischen Kabinette 1871–1914. Reihe 7: Europa vor der Katastrophe – 1912–1914. Band 40: Namenregister zu Band 26 bis 39. (Die Große Politik der Europäischen Kabinette 1871-1914. Reihe 7: Europa vor der Katastrophe - 1912-1914. Band 40: Namenregister zu Band 26 bis 39.- *The High Policy of the European Cabinets. File 7: Europe before the Catastrophe - 1912-1914. Volume 40: Index of Names to volumes 26 to 39.*)

    A. Mendelssohn-Bartholdy, J. Lepsius and F. Thimme | ?cm x ?cm | White paper softback | ? + ?pp | ? | see note | German Text. | Fraktur Script.

This series "**Die Große Politik der Europäischen Kabinette 1871-1914**" was published over the period 1922 to 1927.

Italian Diplomatic Official Histories

The Italian diplomatic official histories were written by members of the Ministero degli Affari Esteri (*The [Italian] Foreign Affairs Ministry*).

Atti Parliamentari. Legislatura XXIV – Sessione 1913-1915 Camera dei Deputati N. XXXII (Documenti). Documenti Diplomatici presentati Al Parlamento Italiano dal Ministero Degli Affari Esteri (Sonnino). Austria-Ungheria. Seduta del 20 maggio 1915. (*Acts of Parliament. Legislature XXIV – sessions 1913-1915. Chamber of Deputies N. XXXII (Documents). Diplomatic Documents submitted to the Italian Parliament by the Minister for Foreign Affairs (Sonnino). Austria-Hungary. Session of the 20th May 1915.*)

>Anonymous (Ministero degli Affari Esteri) | 27cm x 18cm | green paper softback | 46pp | Tipografia Editrice Nazionale. | 1915 | Italian Text.
>
>The book, 'Atti Parliamentari. Legislatura XXIV – Sessione 1913-1915', is commonly known as the Italian Green Book.

Ministero degli Affari Esteri - Commissione per la Pubblicazione dei Documenti Diplomatici, Documenti Diplomatici Italiani (Quinta serie): 1914-1918. Volume I. (*Ministry of Foreign Affairs - Commission for the Publication of Diplomatic Documents, Italian Diplomatic Documents (Fourth Series): 1914-1918. Volume I.*);

>Anonymous (Ministero degli Affari Esteri) | ?cm x ?cm | green paper softback | ? + ?pp | la libreria dello stato. | 1952 | Italian Text.

Ministero degli Affari Esteri - Commissione per la Pubblicazione dei Documenti Diplomatici, Documenti Diplomatici Italiani (Quinta serie): 1914-1918. Volume II. (*Ministry of Foreign Affairs - Commission for the Publication of Diplomatic Documents, Italian Diplomatic Documents (Fourth Series): 1914-1918. Volume II.*);

>Anonymous (Ministero degli Affari Esteri) | ?cm x ?cm | green paper softback | ? + ?pp | la libreria dello stato. | c1955 | Italian Text.

Ministero degli Affari Esteri - Commissione per la Pubblicazione dei Documenti Diplomatici, Documenti Diplomatici Italiani (Quinta serie): 1914-1918. Volume III. (*Ministry of Foreign Affairs - Commission for the Publication of Diplomatic Documents, Italian Diplomatic Documents (Fourth Series): 1914-1918. Volume III.*);

>Anonymous (Ministero degli Affari Esteri) | ?cm x ?cm | green paper softback | ? + ?pp | la libreria dello stato. | c1958 | Italian Text.

Ministero degli Affari Esteri - Commissione per la Pubblicazione dei Documenti Diplomatici, Documenti Diplomatici Italiani (Quinta serie): 1914-1918. Volume IV. (*Ministry of Foreign Affairs - Commission for the Publication of Diplomatic Documents, Italian Diplomatic Documents (Fourth Series): 1914-1918. Volume IV.*);

>Anonymous (Ministero degli Affari Esteri) | ?cm x ?cm | green paper softback | ? + ?pp | la libreria dello stato. | c1961 | Italian Text.

Ministero degli Affari Esteri - Commissione per la Pubblicazione dei Documenti Diplomatici, Documenti Diplomatici Italiani (Quinta serie): 1914-1918. Volume V. (*Ministry of Foreign Affairs - Commission for the Publication of Diplomatic Documents, Italian Diplomatic Documents (Fourth Series): 1914-1918. Volume V.*);

>Anonymous (Ministero degli Affari Esteri) | ?cm x ?cm | green paper softback | ? + ?pp | la libreria dello stato. | c1964 | Italian Text.

Ministero degli Affari Esteri - Commissione per la Pubblicazione dei Documenti Diplomatici, Documenti Diplomatici Italiani (Quinta serie): 1914-1918. Volume VI. (*Ministry of Foreign Affairs - Commission for the Publication of Diplomatic Documents, Italian Diplomatic Documents (Fourth Series): 1914-1918. VolumeVI.*);

>Anonymous (Ministero degli Affari Esteri) | ?cm x ?cm | green paper softback | ? + ?pp | la libreria dello stato. | c1967 | Italian Text.

Ministero degli Affari Esteri - Commissione per la Pubblicazione dei Documenti Diplomatici, Documenti Diplomatici Italiani (Quinta serie): 1914-1918. Volume VII. (*Ministry of Foreign Affairs - Commission for the Publication of Diplomatic Documents, Italian Diplomatic Documents (Fourth Series): 1914-1918. Volume VII.*);

>Anonymous (Ministero degli Affari Esteri) | ?cm x ?cm | green paper softback | ? + ?pp | la libreria dello stato. | c1970 | Italian Text.

Ministero degli Affari Esteri - Commissione per la Pubblicazione dei Documenti Diplomatici, Documenti Diplomatici Italiani (Quinta serie): 1914-1918. Volume VIII. (*Ministry of Foreign Affairs - Commission for the Publication of Diplomatic Documents, Italian Diplomatic Documents (Fourth Series): 1914-1918. Volume VIII.*);
> Anonymous (Ministero degli Affari Esteri) | ?cm x ?cm | green paper softback | ? + ?pp | la libreria dello stato. | c1974 | Italian Text.

Ministero degli Affari Esteri - Commissione per la Pubblicazione dei Documenti Diplomatici, Documenti Diplomatici Italiani (Quinta serie): 1914-1918. Volume IX. (*Ministry of Foreign Affairs - Commission for the Publication of Diplomatic Documents, Italian Diplomatic Documents (Fourth Series): 1914-1918. Volume IX.*);
> Anonymous (Ministero degli Affari Esteri) | ?cm x ?cm | green paper softback | ? + ?pp | la libreria dello stato. | c1977 | Italian Text.

Ministero degli Affari Esteri - Commissione per la Pubblicazione dei Documenti Diplomatici, Documenti Diplomatici Italiani (Quinta serie): 1914-1918. Volume X. (*Ministry of Foreign Affairs - Commission for the Publication of Diplomatic Documents, Italian Diplomatic Documents (Fourth Series): 1914-1918. Volume X.*);
> Anonymous (Ministero degli Affari Esteri) | ?cm x ?cm | green paper softback | ? + ?pp | la libreria dello stato. | c1981 | Italian Text.

Ministero degli Affari Esteri - Commissione per la Pubblicazione dei Documenti Diplomatici, Documenti Diplomatici Italiani (Quinta serie): 1914-1918. Volume XI Tomo 1. (*Ministry of Foreign Affairs - Commission for the Publication of Diplomatic Documents, Italian Diplomatic Documents (Fourth Series): 1914-1918. Volume XI Book 1.*);
> Anonymous (Ministero degli Affari Esteri) | ?cm x ?cm | green paper softback | ? + ?pp | la libreria dello stato. | 1986 | Italian Text.

Ministero degli Affari Esteri - Commissione per la Pubblicazione dei Documenti Diplomatici, Documenti Diplomatici Italiani (Quinta serie): 1914-1918. Volume XI Tomo 2. (*Ministry of Foreign Affairs - Commission for the Publication of Diplomatic Documents, Italian Diplomatic Documents (Fourth Series): 1914-1918. Volume XI Book 2.*);
> Anonymous (Ministero degli Affari Esteri) | ?cm x ?cm | green paper softback | ? + ?pp | la libreria dello stato. | 1986 | Italian Text.

Japanese Diplomatic Official Histories

The Japanese diplomatic official histories were produced by Japan's Foreign Affairs Office.

日本外交文書 大正3年 大正4年. (Nihon gaikō bunsho Taishō 3-nen, Taishō 4-nen. - *Japan's Foreign Policy Document, Third and Forth Year of the Taisho Era.* **[1914-15].)**
> Anonymous | ?cm x ?cm | ?pp | 外務省 (Gaimushō, Shōwa 41) | 1966 | Japanese Text. | Kanji/Hiragana /Katakana (Japanese) Script.

Romanian Politico-Diplomatic Official Histories

The Romanian diplomatic official history was written by members of the Romanian National Defence Ministry.

România în primulu război mondial. (*Romania in the First World War.*)
Anonymous | 24cm x ?cm | Editura Militara. | 1979 | Romanian Text.

Russian Diplomatic Official Histories

The Russian diplomatic official histories were written by the authority of three groups:

i the Russian Imperial Government during the pre revolution period

ii the Russian Émigré Government in exile representing the deposed Imperial Government, after the revolution

iii the Soviet Government being the acting power within Russia after the revolution.

Ministère des Affaires Étrangères, Recueil de Documents Diplomatiques. Négociations ayant précédé la guerre 10/23 Juillet – 24 Juillet/6 Août, 1914. (*The Ministry of Foreign Affairs Diplomatic Documents. Negotiations that preceded the War. 10th/23rd July –24th July/6th August 1914.*)

Anonymous ([The Russian] Ministère des Affaires Étrangères) | 23cm x 30.5cm | orange paper softback | 59pp | Imprimere de lÉtat. | 1914 | French text.

This book, the 'Ministère des Affaires Étrangères, Recueil de Documents Diplomatiques' is commonly known as the Russian Orange Book. In line with a lot of European countries of this period, the Russian diplomatic service used the French language and not their own - in this case Russian - as their official diplomatic language; hence this book was written and published in French. It was written on behalf of the Imperial Government, in power at the time of compiling.

МЕЖДУНАРОДНЫЕ ОТНОШЕНИЯ В ЭПОХУ ИМПЕРИАЛИЗМА: ДОКУМЕНТЫ ИЗ АРХИВОВ ЦАРСКОГО И ВРЕМЕННОГО ПРАВИТЕЛЬСТВ. 1878-1917 гг. ТОМ 1. (**Meždunarodnye otnošeniâ v èpohu imperializma: dokumenty iz arhivov carskogo i vremennogo pravitel'stv. 1878-1917 gg. Tom 1.** - *International Relations in the Imperial Era: Documents from Tsars' Archives and the Interim Government 1878-1917. Volume 1.*) [Third Series]

Гозвоениздат (*Gosvoenizdat – Anonymous* - Soviet Government.) | 1931 | Russian Text. | Russian Cyrillic script.

МЕЖДУНАРОДНЫЕ ОТНОШЕНИЯ В ЭПОХУ ИМПЕРИАЛИЗМА: ДОКУМЕНТЫ ИЗ АРХИВОВ ЦАРСКОГО И ВРЕМЕННОГО ПРАВИТЕЛЬСТВ. 1878-1917 гг. ТОМ 2. (**Meždunarodnye otnošeniâ v èpohu imperializma: dokumenty iz arhivov carskogo i vremennogo pravitel'stv. 1878-1917 gg. Tom 2.** - *International Relations in the Imperial Era: Documents from Tsars' Archives and the Interim Government 1878-1917. Volume 2.*) [Third Series]

Гозвоениздат (*Gosvoenizdat – Anonymous* - Soviet Government.) | c1931 | Russian Text. | Russian Cyrillic script.

МЕЖДУНАРОДНЫЕ ОТНОШЕНИЯ В ЭПОХУ ИМПЕРИАЛИЗМА: ДОКУМЕНТЫ ИЗ АРХИВОВ ЦАРСКОГО И ВРЕМЕННОГО ПРАВИТЕЛЬСТВ. 1878-1917 гг. ТОМ 3. (**Meždunarodnye otnošeniâ v èpohu imperializma: dokumenty iz arhivov carskogo i vremennogo pravitel'stv. 1878-1917 gg. Tom 3.** - *International Relations in the Imperial Era: Documents from Tsars' Archives and the Interim Government 1878-1917. Volume 3.*) [Third Series]

Гозвоениздат (*Gosvoenizdat – Anonymous* - Soviet Government.) | c1932 | Russian Text. | Russian Cyrillic script.

МЕЖДУНАРОДНЫЕ ОТНОШЕНИЯ В ЭПОХУ ИМПЕРИАЛИЗМА: ДОКУМЕНТЫ ИЗ АРХИВОВ ЦАРСКОГО И ВРЕМЕННОГО ПРАВИТЕЛЬСТВ. 1878-1917 гг. ТОМ 4. (**Meždunarodnye otnošeniâ v èpohu imperializma: dokumenty iz arhivov carskogo i vremennogo pravitel'stv. 1878-1917 gg. Tom 4.** - *International Relations in the Imperial Era: Documents from Tsars' Archives and the Interim Government 1878-1917. Volume 4.*) [Third Series]

Гозвоениздат (*Gosvoenizdat – Anonymous* - Soviet Government.) | c1933 | Russian Text. | Russian Cyrillic script.

МЕЖДУНАРОДНЫЕ ОТНОШЕНИЯ В ЭПОХУ ИМПЕРИАЛИЗМА: ДОКУМЕНТЫ ИЗ АРХИВОВ ЦАРСКОГО И ВРЕМЕННОГО ПРАВИТЕЛЬСТВ. 1878-1917 гг. ТОМ 5. (**Meždunarodnye otnošeniâ v èpohu imperializma: dokumenty iz arhivov carskogo i vremennogo pravitel'stv. 1878-1917 gg. Tom 5.** - *International Relations in the Imperial Era: Documents from Tsars' Archives and the Interim Government 1878-1917. Volume 5.*) [Third Series]

Гозвоениздат (*Gosvoenizdat – Anonymous* - Soviet Government.) | c1934 | Russian Text. | Russian Cyrillic script.

МЕЖДУНАРОДНЫЕ ОТНОШЕНИЯ В ЭПОХУ ИМПЕРИАЛИЗМА: ДОКУМЕНТЫ ИЗ АРХИВОВ ЦАРСКОГО И ВРЕМЕННОГО ПРАВИТЕЛЬСТВ. 1878-1917 гг. ТОМ 6. (**Meždunarodnye otnošeniâ v èpohu imperializma: dokumenty iz arhivov carskogo i vremennogo**

pravitel'stv. 1878-1917 gg. Tom 6. - *International Relations in the Imperial Era: Documents from Tsars' Archives and the Interim Government 1878-1917. Volume 6.*) [Third Series]

Гозвоениздат (*Gosvoenizdat – Anonymous* - Soviet Government.) | c1935 | Russian Text. | Russian Cyrillic script.

МЕЖДУНАРОДНЫЕ ОТНОШЕНИЯ В ЭПОХУ ИМПЕРИАЛИЗМА: ДОКУМЕНТЫ ИЗ АРХИВОВ ЦАРСКОГО И ВРЕМЕННОГО ПРАВИТЕЛЬСТВ. 1878-1917 гг. ТОМ 7. (**Meždunarodnye otnošeniâ v èpohu imperializma: dokumenty iz arhivov carskogo i vremennogo pravitel'stv. 1878-1917 gg. Tom 7.** - *International Relations in the Imperial Era: Documents from Tsars' Archives and the Interim Government 1878-1917. Volume 7.*) [Third Series]

Гозвоениздат (*Gosvoenizdat – Anonymous* - Soviet Government.) | c1936 | Russian Text. | Russian Cyrillic script.

МЕЖДУНАРОДНЫЕ ОТНОШЕНИЯ В ЭПОХУ ИМПЕРИАЛИЗМА: ДОКУМЕНТЫ ИЗ АРХИВОВ ЦАРСКОГО И ВРЕМЕННОГО ПРАВИТЕЛЬСТВ. 1878-1917 гг. ТОМ 8. (**Meždunarodnye otnošeniâ v èpohu imperializma: dokumenty iz arhivov carskogo i vremennogo pravitel'stv. 1878-1917 gg. Tom 8.** - *International Relations in the Imperial Era: Documents from Tsars' Archives and the Interim Government 1878-1917. Volume 8.*) [Third Series]

Гозвоениздат (*Gosvoenizdat – Anonymous* - Soviet Government.) | c1937 | Russian Text. | Russian Cyrillic script.

МЕЖДУНАРОДНЫЕ ОТНОШЕНИЯ В ЭПОХУ ИМПЕРИАЛИЗМА: ДОКУМЕНТЫ ИЗ АРХИВОВ ЦАРСКОГО И ВРЕМЕННОГО ПРАВИТЕЛЬСТВ. 1878-1917 гг. ТОМ 9. (**Meždunarodnye otnošeniâ v èpohu imperializma: dokumenty iz arhivov carskogo i vremennogo pravitel'stv. 1878-1917 gg. Tom 9.** - *International Relations in the Imperial Era: Documents from Tsars' Archives and the Interim Government 1878-1917. Volume 9.*) [Third Series]

Гозвоениздат (*Gosvoenizdat – Anonymous* - Soviet Government.) | c1938 | Russian Text. | Russian Cyrillic script.

МЕЖДУНАРОДНЫЕ ОТНОШЕНИЯ В ЭПОХУ ИМПЕРИАЛИЗМА: ДОКУМЕНТЫ ИЗ АРХИВОВ ЦАРСКОГО И ВРЕМЕННОГО ПРАВИТЕЛЬСТВ. 1878-1917 гг. ТОМ 10. (**Meždunarodnye otnošeniâ v èpohu imperializma: dokumenty iz arhivov carskogo i vremennogo pravitel'stv. 1878-1917 gg. Tom 10.** - *International Relations in the Imperial Era: Documents from Tsars' Archives and the Interim Government 1878-1917. Volume 10.*) [Third Series]

Гозвоениздат (*Gosvoenizdat – Anonymous* - Soviet Government.) | 1938 | Russian Text. | Russian Cyrillic script.

Higham's lists this set as "Soviet Official Histories".

ЦАРСКАЯ РОССИЯ В МИРОВОЙ ВОЙНЕ 1914-1918 ГГ. ТОМ I. (**Carskaâ Rossiâ v Mirovoj Vojne 1914-1918 gg. Tom I.** - *Tsarist Russia in the World War 1914-1918. Volume I.*)

М.Н. Покровского (*M.N. Pokrovskogo* - Soviet Government.) | 24.6cm x 17.6cm | Grey blue cloth covered spine paper covered boards hardback | xxiv + 302pp | 1926 | Центральная Статистическая Комиссия (Central'naâ Statističeskaâ Komissiâ - *Central Statistical Board*) | Russian Text. | Russian Cyrillic script.

М.Н. Покровского was the pseudonym of М.Н. Покровский ([*Professor*] *M.N.* [*Mikhail Nikolaevich*] *Pokrovskii.*).

The Центральная Статистическая Комиссия used the records found in the С.Ф.С.Р. Tсентральныи архив (S.F.S.R. Tsentral'nyi arkhiv – *The Soviet Russian Central Archives.*) to produce this volume.

A German translation of this volume was produced and published under the title: "**Das zaristische Russland im Weltkriege ("Царская Россия в мировой войне"): neue Dokumente aus den Russischen Staatsarchiven uber den Eintritt der Turkei, Bulgariens, Rumaniens und Italien in den Weltkrieg.** (*Tsarist Russia in the World War* ("**Царская Россия в мировой войне**") *New Documents from the Russian State Archives Regarding the Entry of the Turkey, Bulgaria, Rumania and Italy into the World War.*)" by the Deutsche Verlagsgesellschaft fur Politik und Geschichte in 1927.

I can find no record of a second volume "**Царская Россия в Мировой Войне 1914-1918 Гг. Том II.**" being produced or published.

Political;

The War and the Russian Government.

Paul P. Gronsky and Nicholas J. Astrov | black cloth hardback | yellow dust jacket | ? + ?pp | 1929 | English text.

Higham's lists these as "Émigré Histories of the World War (1914-1917)" Sponsored by the 'Russian Government in Exile'. These 'Émigré Histories' were published in America and most were either written in or translated into English, presumably for the American market.

The End of the Russian Empire.

M.T. Florinsky | black cloth hardback | yellow dust jacket | ? + ?pp | 1931 | English text.

Higham's lists this volume as "Émigré Histories of World War (1914-1917)".

Russian Local Government during the War and the Union of Zemstvos.

T.I. Polner, V.A. Obolensky & S.P. Turin | black cloth hardback | yellow dust jacket | ? + ?pp | 1930 | English text.

Higham's lists this volume as "Émigré Histories of World War (1914-1917)".

ПАДЕНИЕ ЦАРСКОГО РЕЖИМА. ТОМ 1. (PADENIE CARSKOGO REŽIMA. Том I. - *The Downfall of the Tsarist Regime. Volume I.)*

П.Е. Щеголёв (*P.E. Shchegolev* - Soviet Government.) | 1924 | Russian Text. | Russian Cyrillic script.

ПАДЕНИЕ ЦАРСКОГО РЕЖИМА. ТОМ II. (PADENIE CARSKOGO REŽIMA. Том II. - *The Downfall of the Tsarist Regime. Volume II.)*

П.Е. Щеголёв (*P.E. Shchegolev* - Soviet Government.) | Soviet Government. | c1925 | Russian Text. | Russian Cyrillic script.

ПАДЕНИЕ ЦАРСКОГО РЕЖИМА. ТОМ III. (PADENIE CARSKOGO REŽIMA. Том III. *- The Downfall of the Tsarist Regime. Volume III.)*

П.Е. Щеголёв (*P.E. Shchegolev* - Soviet Government.) | Soviet Government. | c1925 | Russian Text. | Russian Cyrillic script.

ПАДЕНИЕ ЦАРСКОГО РЕЖИМА. ТОМ IV. (PADENIE CARSKOGO REŽIMA. Том IV. - *The Downfall of the Tsarist Regime. Volume IV.)*

П.Е. Щеголёв (*P.E. Shchegolev* - Soviet Government.) | Soviet Government. | c1925 | Russian Text. | Russian Cyrillic script.

ПАДЕНИЕ ЦАРСКОГО РЕЖИМА. ТОМ V. (PADENIE CARSKOGO REŽIMA. Том V. - *The Downfall of the Tsarist Regime. Volume V.)*

П.Е. Щеголёв (*P.E. Shchegolev* - Soviet Government.) | Soviet Government. | c1926 | Russian Text. | Russian Cyrillic script.

ПАДЕНИЕ ЦАРСКОГО РЕЖИМА. ТОМ VI. (PADENIE CARSKOGO REŽIMA. Том VI. - *The Downfall of the Tsarist Regime. Volume VI.)*

П.Е. Щеголёв (*P.E. Shchegolev* - Soviet Government.) | Soviet Government. | c1926 | Russian Text. | Russian Cyrillic script.

ПАДЕНИЕ ЦАРСКОГО РЕЖИМА. ТОМ VII. (PADENIE CARSKOGO REŽIMA. Том VII. - *The Downfall of the Tsarist Regime. Volume VII.)*

П.Е. Щеголёв (*P.E. Shchegolev* - Soviet Government.) | Soviet Government. | 1927 | Russian Text. | Russian Cyrillic script.

Higham's lists this set as "Soviet Official Histories".

ОТНОШЕНИЯ С СОЮЗНИКАМИ ПО ВОЕННЫМ ВОПРОСАМ ВО ВРЕМЯ ВОЙНЫ 1914-1918 ГГ. (Otnošeniâ s Soûznikami po Voennym Voprosam vo Vremâ Vojny 1914-1918 gg. *- The Relations with the Allies on Military Questions during the War 1914-1918.)*

Н. Валентинов (*N. Valentinov* - Soviet Government.) | 1920 | Russian Text. | Russian Cyrillic script.

Higham's lists this volume as a "Soviet Official History".

ПОДГОТОВКА РОССИИ К МИРОВОЙ ВОЙНЕ В МЕЖДУНАРОДНЫХ ОТНОШЕНИЯХ. ТОМ I. (Podgotovka Rossii k Mirovoj Vojne v Meždunarodnyh Otnošeniâh. **Том I.** *- The Preparation of Russia for the World War in International Relations. Volume I.)*

А.М. Зайончковский (*A.M. Zajončkovskij* - Soviet Government.) | 1926 | Russian Text. | Russian Cyrillic script.

ПОДГОТОВКА РОССИИ К МИРОВОЙ ВОЙНЕ В МЕЖДУНАРОДНЫХ ОТНОШЕНИЯХ. ТОМ II. (Podgotovka Rossii k Mirovoj Vojne v Meždunarodnyh

Otnošeniâh. Том II. - *The Preparation of Russia for the World War in International Relations. Volume II.*)

A.M. Зайончковский (*A.M. Zajončkovskij* - Soviet Government.) | 1926 | Russian Text. | Russian Cyrillic script.

Higham's lists this set as "Soviet Official Histories".

БОРЬБА БОЛЬШЕВИСТСКОЙ ПАРТИИ ЗА АРМИЮ ВО ВРЕМЯ ПЕРВОЙ МИРОВОЙ ВОЙНЫ. (Bor'ba Bol'ševistskoj partii za Armiû vo vremâ Pervoj Mirovoj Vojny. - *The Struggle of the Bolshevik Party for the Army during the First World War.*)

С.Г. Капшуков (*S.G. Kapshukov* - Soviet Government.) | 1957 | Russian Text. | Russian Cyrillic script.

Higham's lists this volume as a "Soviet Official History".

РЕВОЛЮЦИОННОЕ ДВИЖЕНИЕ В РОССИЙСКОЙ АРМИИ В 1917 Г. (Revolûcionnoe dviženie v Rossijskoj Armii v 1917 g. - *The Revolutionary Movement in the Russian Army in 1917.*)

Х.И. Муратов (*Kh. I. Muratov* - Soviet Government). | 1958 | Russian Text. | Russian Cyrillic script.

Higham's lists this volume as a "Soviet Official History".

БОЛЬШЕВИКИ НА ЗАПАДНОМ ФРОНТЕ В 1917 Г. МЕМУАРЫ. (Bol'ševiki na Zapadnom fronte v 1917 g. Memuary. - *The Bolsheviks on the Western Front in 1917. Memoirs.*)

Н. Петров (N. Petrov - Soviet Government.) | 1959 | Russian Text. | Russian Cyrillic script.

Higham's lists this volume as a "Soviet Official History".

Spanish Politico-Diplomatic Official Histories

The Spanish diplomatic official history was written under the authority of the Ministerio de Asuntos Exteriores (Ministry of Foreign Affairs).

La neutralidad de Espana durante la Primera Guerra Mundial (1914-1918) (Biblioteca diplomatica espanola. Fuentes). (The Neutrality of Spain during the First World War (1914-1918) (Sources: Spanish Diplomatic Library).)
  Nuño Aguirre de Cárcer (Ministerio de Asuntos Exteriores) | 23cm x ?cm | ? | xxxix + 426pp | Ministerio de Asuntos Exteriores. | 1995 | Spanish text.
  ISBN: 8487661696

Appendix Three

Further Reading

Books:

Das Reichsarchiv
Karl Demeter, Bernard & Graefe, 1969

Genelkurmay Atase Başkanliği Yayin Kataloğu.
Anon, Genelkurmay Askerî Tarih ve Stratejik Etüt Başkanlığı Yayınları, 2009

Histories of the First and Second World Wars Sectional List No.60
Anonymous, H.M.S.O., 1965

Official Histories
Robin Higham, Kansas State University Library, 1970

Official Military Historical Offices and Sources, Volume I: Europe, Africa, the Middle East, and India
Robin Higham, Greenwood Press, 2000

Official Military Historical Offices and Sources, Volume II: The Western Hemisphere and the Pacific Rim
Robin Higham, Greenwood Press, 2000

Planning for War Against Russia and Serbia
Graydon A. Tunstall, Columbia Universty Press, 1993

Sir Walter Raleigh and the Air History
H.A. Jones, M.C., Eward Arnold & Co, 1922

The Dogma of the Battle of Annihilation
Jehuda L. Wallach, Greenwood Press, 1986

The First World War and British Military History
Brian Bond, Oxford University Press, 1991

The Last Word? Essays on Official History in the United States and British Commonwealth
Jeffrey Grey, Praeger Publishers, 2003

The Turkish Official Military Histories of the First World War: A Bibliographic Essay.
Edward J. Erickson, Middle Eastern Studies, Vol. 39, No. 3, 2003

Writing the Great War: Sir James Edmonds and the Official Histories 1915-1948.
Andrew Green, Frank Cass Publishers, 2003

Official History and Great War History Web Sites:

Bundesarchiv:
http://www.bundesarchiv.de/bestaende_findmittel/bestaendeuebersicht/body.html

Institut Deutsche Adelsforschung :
http://home.foni.net/~adelsforschung/schlacht00.htm

Collectif de Recherche International et de Débat sur la Guerre de 1914-1918 - CRID 14 18 (*The International Collective for Research and Debate on the First World War*):
http://www.crid1418.org/bibliographie/alphabetique/biblio_alpha.pdf

Genelkurmay Askerî Tarih ve Stratejik Etüt Başkanlığı Yayın Kataloğu ([*Turkish Army's*] *General Staff Directorate of Military History and Strategical Studies Military History Publications Catalogue*):
http://www.tsk.tr/9_YAYINLAR/9_5_Genelkurmay_ATASE_Baskanligi_Yayin_Katalogu/yayi n_katologu.pdf

Repubblica Italiana – Ministero della Difesa, Catalogo della Biblioteca (*Republic of Italy – the Ministry of Defence, library catalogue*):
http://catalogo.casd.difesa.it/Document.htm&numrec=031902568918430

International Library Catalogue Web Sites:

The University of Queensland - National Library Catalogues (for List of International Libraries):
http://www.library.uq.edu.au/natlibs/e-k.html

Bayerische Staatsbibliothek (Bavarian State Library) Online Catalogue:
http://www.bsb-muenchen.de/index.php?L=3

British Library Integrated Catalogue:
http://catalogue.bl.uk/F/?func=file&file_name=login-bl-list

Cambridge University Library (Newton Library Catalogues):
http://www.lib.cam.ac.uk/newton

Library of Congress Online Catalogue:
http://catalog.loc.gov

Copac National, Academic, & Specialist Library Catalogue:
http://copac.ac.uk

Bibliothèque nationale de France (National Library of France) Online Catalogue:
http://catalogue.bnf.fr/jsp/recherchemots_simple.jsp?nouvelleRecherche=O&nouveaute=O&ho st=catalogue

Deutsche Nationalbibliothek (German National Library) Online Catalogue:
http://www.d-nb.de/eng/index.htm

Hochschulbibliothekszentrum des Landes Nordrhein-Westfalen (*State of North Rhine-Westphalia High School Library Centre*):
http://digilink.digibib.net/wk/links.pl

Oxford University (including the Bodleian) Libuary Online Catalogue (OLIS):
http://library.ox.ac.uk/WebZ/html/geacscan.html?sessionid=01-56486-189101897:active=3:dbchoice=1:dbname=ADVANCE1

Sebina Open Library OPAC (Polo Biblioteca Nazionale di Napoli):
http://83.103.45.71/SebinaOpac/Opac?locale=en_GB

Stanford University Libuary Online Catalogue (SULAIR):
http://searchworks.stanford.edu

Universität Karlsruhe – Universitätsbibliothek – Karlsruher Virtueller Katalog (KVK) (*Karlsruhe University's Libuary Virtual Catalogue*):
http://www.ubka.uni-karlsruhe.de/hylib/en/kvk.html

World Catalogue:
http://www.worldcat.org/advancedsearch

Book Trade Search Engine Web Sites:

AbeBooks:
http://www.abebooks.com

Alibris:
http://www.alibris.com

Amazon:
http://www.amazon.com/books-used-books-textbooks/b?ie=UTF8&node=266239

Antikvariat:
http://www.antikvariat.net/get/search.cgi?post

Antiqbook:
http://www.antiqbook.co.uk

Livre Rare Book:
http://www.livre-rare-book.com/cgi-bin/libbcgi?I=2033649464&P=1580&G=1580&B =1&L=EN

Mare Magnum:
http://www.maremagnum.com/showPage.php?template=HOME&id=2

Nadirkitap:
http://www.nadirkitap.com/english.html

Nemira:
http://www.nemira.ro

Zentrales Verzeichnis Antiquarischer Bücher (zvab):
http://www.zvab.com/index.do

Choose Books (English version of the above Z.V.A.B.):
http://www.choosebooks.com/index.do

Post Script

I have tried to produce the definitive bibliography of Great War official histories, however I know that this has been an impossible task. In a work of such complexity, I know that there are bound to be errors and omissions, indeed as already noted, there are some histories still to be written. Therefore I would welcome any comments from readers stating corrections or new information, with a view to publishing a revised edition of this work in the future.

Please email any comments to:

ww1.official.histories.comments@googlemail.com

Lightning Source UK Ltd.
Milton Keynes UK
UKHW031833140819
347919UK00004B/162/P